S0-AZT-457

INTRODUCTION TO
Paralegalism

PERSPECTIVES, PROBLEMS, AND SKILLS

SEVENTH EDITION

DELMAR CENGAGE Learning

Options.

Over 300 products in every area of the law: textbooks, online courses, CD-ROMs, reference books, companion websites, and more – helping you succeed in the classroom and on the job.

Support.

We offer unparalleled, practical support: robust instructor and student supplements to ensure the best learning experience, custom publishing to meet your unique needs, and other benefits such as Delmar Cengage Learning's Student Achievement Award. And our sales representatives are always ready to provide you with dependable service.

Feedback.

As always, we want to hear from you! Your feedback is our best resource for improving the quality of our products. Contact your sales representative or write us at the address below if you have any comments about our materials or if you have a product proposal.

Accounting and Financials for the Law Office • Administrative Law • Alternative Dispute Resolution • Bankruptcy Business Organizations/Corporations • Careers and Employment • Civil Litigation and Procedure • CLA Exam Preparation • Computer Applications in the Law Office • Constitutional Law • Contract Law • Court Reporting Criminal Law and Procedure • Document Preparation • Elder Law • Employment Law • Environmental Law • Ethics Evidence Law • Family Law • Health Care Law • Immigration Law • Intellectual Property • Internships Interviewing and Investigation • Introduction to Law • Introduction to Paralegalism • Juvenile Law • Law Office Management • Law Office Procedures • Legal Nurse Consulting • Legal Research, Writing, and Analysis • Legal Terminology • Legal Transcription • Media and Entertainment Law • Medical Malpractice Law Product Liability • Real Estate Law • Reference Materials • Social Security • Sports Law • Torts and Personal Injury Law • Wills, Trusts, and Estate Administration • Workers' Compensation Law

DELMAR CENGAGE Learning
5 Maxwell Drive
Clifton Park, New York 12065-2919

For additional information, find us online at:
www.delmar.cengage.com

INTRODUCTION TO
PARALEGALISM

PERSPECTIVES, PROBLEMS, AND SKILLS

SEVENTH EDITION

William P. Statsky

DELMAR
CENGAGE Learning™

Australia • Brazil • Japan • Korea • Mexico • Singapore • Spain • United Kingdom • United States

Introduction to Paralegalism: Perspectives, Problems, and Skills, Seventh Edition
William P. Statsky

Vice President, Career and Professional Editorial: Dave Garza

Director of Learning Solutions: Sandy Clark

Acquisitions Editor: Shelley Esposito

Managing Editor: Larry Main

Senior Product Manager: Melissa Riveglia

Editorial Assistant: Lyss Zaza

Vice President, Career and Professional Marketing: Jennifer McAvey

Marketing Director: Debbie Yarnell

Marketing Manager: Erin Brennan

Marketing Coordinator: Jonathan Sheehan

Production Director: Wendy Troeger

Production Manager: Mark Bernard

Senior Content Project Manager: Betty L. Dickson

Senior Art Director: Joy Kocsis

Technology Project Manager: Ben Knapp

Production Technology Analyst: Thomas Stover

© 1974, 1982, 1986, 1992, 1997, 2003, 2009 Delmar, Cengage Learning

ALL RIGHTS RESERVED. No part of this work covered by the copyright herein may be reproduced, transmitted, stored, or used in any form or by any means graphic, electronic, or mechanical, including but not limited to photocopying, recording, scanning, digitizing, taping, Web distribution, information networks, or information storage and retrieval systems, except as permitted under Section 107 or 108 of the 1976 United States Copyright Act, without the prior written permission of the publisher.

For product information and technology assistance, contact us at
Professional & Career Group Customer Support, 1-800-648-7450

For permission to use material from this text or product,
submit all requests online at **cengage.com/permissions**
Further permissions questions can be emailed to
permissionrequest@cengage.com

Library of Congress Control Number: 2008921493

ISBN-13: 978-1-4354-0006-1

ISBN-10: 1-4354-0006-2

Delmar
5 Maxwell Drive
Clifton Park, NY 12065-2919
USA

Cengage Learning products are represented in Canada by Nelson Education, Ltd.

For your lifelong learning solutions, visit **delmar.cengage.com**

Visit our corporate website at **cengage.com**

Notice to the Reader

Publisher does not warrant or guarantee any of the products described herein or perform any independent analysis in connection with any of the product information contained herein. Publisher does not assume, and expressly disclaims, any obligation to obtain and include information other than that provided to it by the manufacturer. The reader is expressly warned to consider and adopt all safety precautions that might be indicated by the activities described herein and to avoid all potential hazards. By following the instructions contained herein, the reader willingly assumes all risks in connection with such instructions. The reader is notified that this text is an educational tool, not a practice book. Since the law in constant change, no rule or statement of law in this book should be relied upon for any service to any client. The reader should always refer to standard legal sources for the current rule or law. If legal advice or other expert assistance is required, the services of the appropriate professional should be sought. The publisher makes no representations or warranties of any kind, including but not limited to, the warranties of fitness for particular purpose or merchantability, nor are any such representations implied with respect to the material set forth herein, and the publisher takes no responsibility with respect to such material. The publisher shall not be liable for any special, consequential, or exemplary damages resulting, in whole or part, from the readers' use of, or reliance upon, this material.

Printed in the United States of America
1 2 3 4 5 6 7 12 11 10 09 08

For Patricia Farrell Statsky,
whose wisdom, light, and love
have sustained more than she knows

BY THE SAME AUTHOR

The California Paralegal: Essential Rules, Documents, and Resources. Clifton Park, N.Y.: Delmar Cengage Learning, 2008 (with S. Sandberg)

Case Analysis and Fundamentals of Legal Writing, 4th ed. St. Paul: West Group, 1995 (with J. Wernet)

Essentials of Paralegalism: Perspectives, problems, and Skills, 4th ed. Clifton Park, N.Y.: Delmar Cengage Learning, 2006

Essentials of Torts, 2d ed. Clifton Park, N.Y.: Delmar Cengage Learning, 2001

Family Law: The Essentials, 2d ed. Clifton Park, N.Y.: Delmar Cengage learning, 2004

Family Law, 5th ed. Clifton Park, N.Y.: Delmar Cengage Learning, 2002

The Florida Paralegal: Essential Rules, Documents, and Resources. Clifton Park, N.Y.: Delmar Cengage Learning, 2009 (with B. Diotalevi & P. Linquist)

Inmate Involvement in Prison Legal Services: Roles and Training Options for the Inmate as Paralegal. Chicago: American Bar Association, Commission on Correctional Facilities and Services, 1974

Legal Desk Reference. St. Paul: West Group, 1990 (with B. Hussey, M. Diamond, & R. Nakamura)

The Legal Paraprofessional as Advocate and Assistant: Training Concepts and Materials. New York: Center on Social Welfare Policy and Law, 1971 (with P. Lang)

Legal Research and Writing: Some Starting Points, 5th ed. Clifton Park, N.Y.: Delmar Cengage Learning, 1999

Legal Thesaurus/Dictionary: A Resource for the Writer and Computer Researcher. St. Paul: West Group, 1985

Legislative Analysis and Drafting, 2d ed. St. Paul: West Group, 1984

The New York Paralegal: Essential Rules, Documents, and Resources. Clifton Park, N.Y.: Delmar Cengage Learning, 2009 (with R. Sarachan)

The Ohio Paralegal: Essential Rules, Documents, and Resources. Clifton Park, N.Y.: Delmar Cengage Learning, 2008 (with K. Reed & B. Moore)

Paralegal Employment: Facts and Strategies for the 1990s, 2d ed. St. Paul: West Group, 1993

Paralegal Ethics and Regulation, 2d ed. St. Paul: West Group, 1993

The Pennsylvania Paralegal: Essential Rules, Documents, and Resources. Clifton Park, N.Y.: Delmar Cengage Learning, 2009 (with J. DeLeo & J. Geis)

The Texas Paralegal: Essential Rules, Documents, and Resources. Clifton Park, N.Y.: Delmar Cengage Learning, 2009 (with L. Crossett)

Torts: Personal Injury Litigation, 4th ed. Clifton Park, N.Y.: Delmar Cengage Learning, 2001

Rights of the Imprisoned: Cases, Materials, and Directions. Indianapolis, Ind.: Bobbs-Merrill Company, 1974 (with R. Singer)

What Have Paralegals Done? A Dictionary of Functions. Washington, D.C.: National Paralegal Institute, 1973

Contents in Brief

Contents

Preface

Six editions ago—in 1974—many were asking the question "What's a paralegal?" That day has long passed, although there is still a great deal of information that people need to have in order to appreciate the outstanding contribution paralegals have made in the delivery of legal services. This book seeks to provide that information and, at the same time, to introduce you to some of the fundamental skills needed to thrive in this still-developing career—a career whose members may one day outnumber attorneys in the traditional and untraditional law office.

It's a fascinating time to study law. So many aspects of our lives revolve around the making, interpretation, and application of laws. As integral members of the attorney's team, paralegals have a unique opportunity to view the legal system in operation as it wrestles with the legal issues of the day.

Back in the 1970s when the first edition of this book came out, Kathy Lowery, a Kansas City paralegal, was asked what impressed her most about the paralegal profession. She said that the two best things about the field were the two constants that were ever present: challenges and opportunities to "learn and grow." Well said about the 1970s and equally true as we continue into the twenty-first century.

CHANGES IN THE SEVENTH EDITION

In addition to the updated material in the book on employment, salaries, roles, ethics, and regulation, a number of particular changes in the seventh edition should be mentioned:

- At the end of each chapter, Review Questions allow the student to reinforce every major theme in the chapter.
- The last entry in the "Helpful Web Sites" feature at the end of many chapters consists of special Google searches that broaden the scope of additional material that is available online.
- The "How to Study" section before chapter 1 includes expanded abbreviations for note taking and new material on active studying and the use of mnemonics as a study aid.

- Chapter 1 introduces fourteen kinds of paralegal associations that exist in the country.
- Chapter 1 covers an emerging consensus on the use of the *paralegal* title.
- Chapter 1 adds coverage of the American rule and the English rule in the payment of legal fees and expands on the standards courts apply when awarding paralegal fees.
- Chapter 1 examines the realization rate that a law firm uses to assess profitability of attorneys and paralegals.
- Chapter 1 adds a section that cautions students to avoid engaging in the unauthorized practice of law when friends and relatives find out they are studying law.
- Chapters 1 and 2 include coverage of paralegals who have run for political office.
- Chapter 2 compares working in large versus smaller private offices.
- A major chart has been added to chapter 2 that lists the major employment settings (e.g., private law firm, corporate law department, government office) and states the likelihood that a paralegal will encounter specified working conditions in each setting.
- Chapter 2 adds a new specialty (gaming law) to the dictionary of functions.
- Chapter 2 covers doing due diligence on a prospective employer.
- A form has been added to chapter 3 to help keep track of networking contacts.
- Chapter 4 presents an overview of the tests used by courts to determine what constitutes the practice of law.
- Chapter 4 covers additional states that have established their own certification programs.
- Chapter 4 adds to the list of torts for which law office personnel can be sued and broadens the discussion of when negligence liability will be imposed.
- Chapter 5 provides further clarification of the relationship between confidentiality and the attorney-client privilege.

- Chapter 5 adds an example of a confidentiality agreement that some law offices ask paralegals to sign.
- Chapter 5 has a new chart on conflict of interest.
- For conflicts checks, chapter 5 contains a new career client list form to track client matters.
- A discussion of new ethical problems peculiar to the digital age (e.g., metadata) has been added to chapter 5.
- Chapter 6 has a new section on equity.
- Chapter 8 now contains an example of a timeline that can be used in interviewing and elsewhere in litigation.
- New material on evidence logs has been added to chapter 9.
- A section called "The Ethical Investigator" has been added to chapter 9.
- Chapter 10 adds paralegal roles to the charts on the overview of civil and criminal litigation.
- The section on complaints in chapter 10 has been moved to the beginning of the overview of pretrial roles for paralegals.
- Chapter 11 extensively revises the research technique of doing legal research by e-mail.
- Chapter 12 contains more extensive coverage of plain language laws.
- Chapter 13 includes materials on Wiki, podcasts, RSS (really simple syndication), and assessing the reliability of Internet sites.
- Chapter 14 includes a discussion of the consequences of outsourcing in law office administration.

ANCILLARY MATERIALS

Instructor's Manual

An Instructor's Manual and Test Bank by the author of the text accompany this edition and have been greatly expanded to incorporate changes in the text and to provide comprehensive teaching support. They include the following:

- Class ideas, such as lecture ideas and suggestions for using selected assignments
- A test bank of 645 questions, which includes a variety of questions in true/false, multiple-choice, and essay format

Student CD-ROM

The new accompanying CD-ROM provides additional material to help students master the important concepts in the course. This CD-ROM includes StudyWare with true/false questions, multiple-choice questions, case study questions, and crossword puzzles for each chapter.

Instructor's eResource CD-ROM

The new eResource component provides instructors with all the tools they need in one convenient CD-ROM. Instructors will find that this resource provides them with a turnkey solution to help them teach by making available PowerPoint® slides for each chapter, a computerized Test Bank, and an electronic version of the Instructor's Manual.

All of these instructor materials are also posted on our Web site in the "Online Resources" section.

WebTutor™

WebTutor on WebCT and BlackBoard

The WebTutor™ supplement to accompany *Introduction to Paralegalism* allows you, as the instructor, to take learning beyond the classroom. This Online Courseware is designed to complement the text and benefit students and instructors alike by helping you better manage your time, prepare for exams, organize your notes, and more. WebTutor™ allows you to extend your reach beyond the classroom.

Online Companion™

The Online Companion™ contains a Study Guide with review questions, short writing exercises, and additional enrichment materials. The Online Companion™ can be found at www.paralegal.delmar.cengage.com in the "Online Companion™" section of the Web site.

Web Page

Come visit our Web site at www.paralegal.delmar. cengage.com, where you will find valuable information such as hot links and sample materials to download, as well as other Delmar Cengage Learning products.

ACKNOWLEDGMENTS

It is difficult to name all the individuals who have provided guidance in the preparation of the seven editions of this book. Looking back over the years, a number of people have played important roles in my initiation and growth as a student of paralegal education. I owe a debt to Jean and Edgar Cahn, founders of the Legal Technician Program at Antioch School of Law, where I worked; Bill Fry, Director of the National Paralegal Institute and a valued colleague since our days together at Columbia Law School, where he was my dean in one of the first paralegal training programs in the country, the Program for Legal Service Assistants; Dan Oran, who helped me plan the first edition; Michael Manna; Ed Schwartz; Bill Mulkeen; and finally, Juanita Hill, Willie Nolden, and Linda Saunders, some of my early students who taught me so much.

I wish to thank the following people at Delmar Cengage Learning: Shelley Esposito, Acquisitions Editor; Melissa Riveglia, Senior Product Manager; Lyss Zaza, Editorial Assistant; Betty Dickson, Senior Content Project Manager; and Mark Bernard, Production Manager.

Finally, a word of thanks to the reviewers who made valuable suggestions for improving the text:

Hank Arnold
Aiken Technical College
Aiken, SC

Michele Bradford
Gadsden State Community College
Gadsden, AL

Mary Conwell
Edison College
Fort Myers, FL

Dora Dye
City College of San Francisco
San Francisco, CA

Patricia Johnson
Berkeley College
New York, NY

Orsolya Furi
Bridgewater State College
Bridgewater, MA

Brain McCully
Fresno City College
Fresno, CA

Timothy Hart
College of the Sequoias
Visalia, CA

Derek Thomson
Bryant and Stratton College
Rochester, NY

[The] expanded use of well-trained assistants, sometimes called "paralegals," has been an important development. Today there are . . . double the number of . . . schools for training paralegals [as the number of schools for training attorneys]. . . . The advent of the paralegal enables law offices to perform high quality legal services at a lower cost. Possibly we have only scratched the surface of this development.

Warren E. Burger, Chief Justice
of the United States Supreme Court, February 3, 1980

Paralegals are an absolutely essential component of quality legal services in the future.

James Fellers, President,
American Bar Association, April 4, 1975

The court also commends the firm of Stull, Stull & Brody for the extensive use of paralegals rather than attorneys for various tasks, reducing the cost of litigation.

U.S. District Court Judge Helen Berregan, Feinberg v. Hibernia Corp., 966 F. Supp. 442, 448 (E.D. La., 1997)

Employment of paralegals and legal assistants is projected to grow 22 percent between 2006 and 2016, much faster than the average for all occupations. Employers are trying to reduce costs and increase the availability and efficiency of legal services by hiring paralegals to perform tasks once done by lawyers. Paralegals are performing a wider variety of duties, making them more useful to businesses.

U.S. Department of Labor, Occupational Outlook Handbook (2008–2009 edition) (www.bls.gov/oco/ocos114.htm)

Please note that the Internet resources are of a time-sensitive nature and URL addresses may often change or be deleted.

How to Study Law in the Classroom and on the Job

[SECTION A]

CLASSROOM LEARNING

Education does not come naturally to most of us. It is a struggle. This is all the more true for someone entering a totally new realm of training such as legal education. Much of the material will seem foreign and difficult. There is a danger of becoming overwhelmed by the vast quantity of laws and legal material that confronts you. How do you study law? How do you learn law? What is the proper perspective that a student of law should have about the educational process? These are our concerns in this introduction to the process of studying law. In short, our theme is training to be trained—the art of effective learning.

The first step is to begin with a proper frame of mind. Too many students have false expectations of what legal education can accomplish. This can interfere with effective studying.

1. Your Legal Education Has Two Phases. Phase I Begins Now and Ends When You Complete This Training Program. Phase II Begins When This Training Program Ends and Is Not Completed until the Last Day of Your Employment as a Paralegal.

You have entered a career that will require you to be a perpetual student. The learning never ends. This is true not only because the boundary lines of law are vast, but also because the law is changing every day. No one knows all of the law. Phase I of your legal education is designed to provide you with the foundation that will enable you to become a good student in phase II.

2. Your Legal Education Has Two Dimensions: The Content of the Law (the rules) and the Practical Techniques of Using That Content in a Law Office (the skills).

Rules

There are two basic kinds of rules or laws:

Substantive Law: Those nonprocedural rules that govern rights and duties, e.g., the requirements for the sale of land and the elements of battery;

Procedural Law: Those rules that govern the mechanics of resolving a dispute in court or in an administrative agency, e.g., the number of days within which a party must respond to a claim stated in a complaint.

The law library contains millions of substantive and procedural laws written by courts (in volumes called *reporters*), by legislatures (in volumes called *statutory codes*), and by administrative agencies (in volumes called *administrative codes*). A great deal of the material in these volumes is also available on the Internet, as we will see. A substantial portion of your time in school will involve study of the substantive and procedural law of your state, and often of the federal government as well.

Skills

By far the most important dimension of your legal education will be the skills of using rules. Without the skills, the content of rules is close to worthless. Examples of legal skills include:

- How to analyze the facts of a client's case in order to identify legal issues (see chapter 7)
- How to interview a client (see chapter 8)
- How to investigate the facts of a case (see chapter 9)
- How to draft a complaint, the document that initiates a lawsuit (see chapter 10)
- How to digest or summarize data found in a case file (see chapter 10)
- How to do a cite check or perform other legal research in a law library (see chapter 11)
- How to write a search query for an online database (see chapter 13)

The overriding skill that, to one degree or another, is the basis for all others is the skill of legal analysis (see chapter 7). Some make the mistake of concluding that legal analysis is the exclusive domain of the attorney. Without an understanding of at least the fundamentals of legal analysis, however, paralegals cannot understand the legal system and cannot intelligently carry out many of the more demanding tasks they are assigned.

3. You Must Force Yourself to Suspend What You Already Know About the Law in Order to Be Able to Absorb (a) That Which Is New and (b) That Which Conflicts with Your Prior Knowledge and Experience.

Place yourself in the position of training students to drive a car. Your students undoubtedly already know something about driving. They have watched others drive and maybe have even had a lesson or two from friends. It would be ideal, however, if you could begin your instruction from point zero. There is a very real danger that the students have picked up bad habits from others. This may interfere with their capacity to listen to what you are saying. The danger is that they will block out anything you say that does not conform to previously learned habits and knowledge. If the habits or knowledge is defective, your job as a trainer is immensely more difficult.

The same is true in studying law. Everyone knows something about the law from government or civics courses as a teenager and from the various treatments of the law in the media. Some of you may have been involved in the law as a party or as a witness in court. Others may have worked, or currently work, in law offices. Will this prior knowledge and experience be a help or a hindrance to you in your future legal education? For some, it will be a help. For most of us, however, there is a danger of interference.

This is particularly so with respect to the portrayal of the law on TV and in the movies. Contrary to what some TV programs may lead you to believe, it is highly unlikely that a judge would say to a witness, "I wouldn't believe you if your tongue came notarized."[1] TV and movies can easily give viewers the impression that all attorneys are trial attorneys and that most legal problems are solved by dramatically tricking a hostile witness on the stand into finally telling the truth. Not so. The practice of law is not an endless series of confessions and concessions that are pried loose from opponents. Nor are most of the more recent TV programs much more realistic. Every attorney does not spend all day engaged in the kind of case that makes front page news. Recently a New Jersey paralegal left her job with a sole practitioner to take another paralegal position with a law firm that she thought was going to be like the one on the TV drama she faithfully watched every week. Three months later, she begged her old boss to take her back after discovering the huge gap between reality and the law office on that show. (See also the discussion in chapter 8 of the Academy Award–winning movie *Erin Brockovich* involving the legal assistant who helped win a multimillion-dollar tort case.)

Another potentially misleading portrayal of the law came in the O.J. Simpson criminal and civil trials, which captivated the nation from 1995 to 1997. Very few parties to litigation have teams of attorneys, investigators, and experts ready to do battle with each other. The vast majority of legal disputes are never litigated in court. Most are either settled or simply dropped by one or both parties. Of the small number that are litigated, most involve no more than two opposing attorneys and several witnesses. In short, it is rare for the legal system to become the spectacle—some would say the circus—that the occasional high-profile case leads us to believe is common in the practice of law. While excitement and drama can be part of the legal system, they are not everyday occurrences. What is dominant is painstaking and meticulous hard work. This reality is almost never portrayed in the media.

Therefore, it is strongly recommended that you place yourself in the position of a stranger to the material you will be covering in your courses, regardless of your background and exposure to the field. Cautiously treat everything as a new experience. Temporarily suspend what you already know. Resist the urge to pat yourself on the back by saying "I already knew that" or "I already know how to do that." For many students, such statements lead to relaxation. They do not work as hard once they have convinced themselves that there is nothing new to learn. No problem exists, of course, if these students are right. The danger, however, is that they are wrong or that they are only partially right. Students are not always the best judge of what they know and of what they can do. Do not become too comfortable. Adopt the following healthy attitude: "I've heard about that before or I've already done that, but maybe I can learn something new about it." Every new teacher, every new supervisor, every new setting is an opportunity to add a dimension to your prior knowledge and experience. Be open to these opportunities. No two people practice law exactly the same way. Your own growth as a student and as a paralegal will depend in large part on your capacity to listen for, explore, and absorb this diversity.

4. Be Sure That You Know the Goals and Context of Every Assignment.

Throughout your education, you will be given a variety of assignments: class exercises, text readings, drafting tasks, field projects, research assignments, etc. You should ask yourself the following questions about each one:

- What are the goals of this assignment? What am I supposed to learn from it?
- How does this assignment fit into what I have already learned? What is the context of the assignment?

Successfully completing an assignment depends in part on understanding its goals and how these goals relate to the overall context of the course.

Keeping an eye on the broader picture will also be important on the job. Each assignment should prompt you to ask yourself a series of questions: What is the goal of this assignment? Why am I being asked to perform the task in this way? Has it always been done this way? Are there more efficient ways? After you have performed the task a number of times, you may be able to propose a more effective *system* of handling the task.

5. Design a Study Plan.

Make current *lists* of everything that you must do. Update them regularly. Divide every list into long-term projects (what is due next week or at the end of the semester) and short-term projects (what is due tomorrow). Have a plan for each day. Establish the following norm for yourself: every day you will focus in some way on *all* of your assignments. Every day you will review your long-term and short-term lists. Priority, of course, will be given to the short-term tasks. Yet some time, however small, will also be devoted to the long-term tasks. For example, on a day that you will be mainly working on the short-term projects, try to set aside 5 percent of your time for a long-term project by doing some background reading or by preparing a very rough first draft of an outline. It is critical that you establish *momentum* toward the accomplishment of *all* your tasks. This is done by never letting anything sit on the back burner. Set yourself the goal of making at least *some* progress on everything every day. Without this goal, momentum may be difficult to achieve and sustain.

Once you have decided what tasks you will cover on a given study day, the next question is: In what *order* will you cover them? There are a number of ways in which you can classify the things you must do—for example: (1) easy tasks that will require a relatively short time to complete, (2) complex tasks requiring more time, and (3) tasks with time demands that will be unknown until you start them. At the beginning of your study time, spend a few seconds preparing an outline of the order in which you will cover the tasks that day and the approximate amount of time that you will set aside for each task. You may want to start with some of the easier tasks so that you can feel a sense of accomplishment relatively soon. Alternatively, you may want to devote early study time to the third kind of task listed above (3) so that you can obtain a clearer idea of the scope and difficulty of such assignments. The important point is that you establish a schedule. It does not have to be written in stone. Quite the contrary—it is healthy that you have enough flexibility to revise your day's schedule so that you can respond to unfolding realities as you study. Adaptation is not a sign of disorganization, but the total absence of an initial plan often is.

6. Add 50 Percent to the Time You Initially Think You Will Need to Study a Subject.

You are kidding yourself if you have not set aside a substantial amount of time to study law outside the classroom. The conscientious study of law takes time—lots of it. It is true that some students must work and take care of family responsibilities. You cannot devote time that you do not have. Yet the reality is that limited study time can lead to limited education.

Generally, people will find time for what they want to do. You may *wish* to do many things for which there will never be enough time. You will find the time, however, to do what you really *want* to do. Once you have decided that you want something badly enough, you will find the time to do it.

How much of each of your work hours is productive time? For most of us, the answer is about twenty minutes. The rest of the hour is spent worrying, relaxing, repeating ourselves, socializing, etc. One answer to the problem of limited time availability is to increase the amount of productive time that you derive out of each work hour. You may not be able to add any new hours to the clock, but you can add to your net productive time. How about moving up to thirty minutes an hour? Forty? You will be amazed at the time that you can "find" simply by making a conscious effort to remove some of the waste. When asked how a masterpiece was created, a great sculptor once responded: "You start with a block of stone and you cut away everything that is not art." In your study habits, start with a small block of time and work to cut away everything that is not productive.

In addition, look for ways to fit study time into your other activities. Always carry something to study in the event that time becomes available. For example, photocopy portions of a difficult chapter in a class textbook and bring it with you whenever you can. Such "pocket work" might be perfect for that unexpectedly long wait at the dentist's office.

There are no absolute rules on how much time you will need to study law. It depends on the complexity of the subject matter you must master. It is probably accurate to say that most of us need to study more than we do—as a rule of thumb, about 50 percent more. You should be constantly on the alert for ways to increase the time you have available or, more accurately, to increase the productive time that you can make available.

Resolving time management problems as a student will be good practice for you when you are confronted with similar (and more severe) time management problems as a working paralegal. Many law offices operate at a hectic pace. One of the hallmarks of a professional is a pronounced reverence for deadlines and the clock. Time is money. An ability to find and handle time effectively can also be one of the preconditions for achieving justice in a particular case.

Soon you will be gaining a reputation among other students, teachers, supervisors, and employers. You should make a concerted effort to make sure you acquire a reputation for hard work, punctuality, and conscientiousness about the time you devote to your work. In large measure, success follows from such a reputation. It is as important, if not more important, than raw ability or intelligence. Phrased another way, your legal skills are unlikely to put bread on the table if you are casual about the clock.

7. Create Your Own Study Area Free from Distractions.

It is essential that you find study areas that are quiet and free from distractions. Otherwise, concentration is obviously impossible. It may be that the worst places to study are at home or at the library unless you can find a corner that is cut off from noise and people who want to talk. If possible, study away from phones, TVs, iPods, and instant computer messaging. Do not make yourself too available. If you study in the corridor, at the first table at the entrance to the library, or at the kitchen table, you are inviting distraction. You need to be able to close yourself off for two to three hours at a time. It is important for you to interact with other people—but not while you are studying material that requires considerable concentration. You will be tempted to digress and to socialize. You are in the best position to know where these temptations are. You are also the most qualified person to know how to avoid the temptations.

8. Conduct a Self-Assessment of Your Prior Study Habits and Establish a Program to Reform the Weaknesses.

If you were to describe the way you study, would you be proud of the description? Here is a partial list of some of the main weaknesses of attitude or practice that students have about studying:

- They have done well in the past with only minimal study effort. Why change now?
- Others in the class do not appear to be studying very much. Why be different?
- They learn best by listening in class. Hence, instead of studying on their own, why not wait until someone explains it in person?
- They simply do not like to study; there are more important things to do in life.
- They can't concentrate.
- They study with lots of distractions, e.g., cell phones, radios, TVs, computers, iPODS.
- They get bored easily. "I can't stay motivated for long."
- They do not understand what they are supposed to study.
- They skim read.
- They do not stop to look up strange words or phrases.
- They study only at exam time—they cram for exams.
- They do not study at a consistent pace. They spend an hour (or less) here and there and have no organized, regular study times.
- They do not like to memorize.
- They do not take notes on what they are reading.

What other interferences with effective studying can you think of? Or, more important, which of the above items apply to you? How do you plead? In law, it is frequently said that you cannot solve a problem until you obtain the facts. What are the facts in the case of your study habits? Make your personal list of attitude problems, study patterns, or environmental interferences.

Place these items in some order. Next, establish a plan for yourself. Which item on the list are you going to try to correct tonight? What will the plan be for this week? For next week? For the coming month? What specific steps will you take to try to change some bad habits? Do not, however, be too hard on yourself. Be determined but realistic. The more serious problems are obviously going to take more time to correct. Improvement will come if you are serious about improvement. If one corrective method does not work, try another. If the fifth does not work, try a sixth. Discuss techniques of improvement with other students and with teachers. Prove to yourself that change is possible.

9. Engage in Active Studying.

Even without distractions, the mind often wanders away from what should be the focus of your study. "Daydreaming" during study time is not uncommon. If this occurs, do some active studying by forcing yourself to do something other than (or in addition to) reading. For example, write out definitions of key terms, create your own chart or graph that contains pieces or components of a topic you are studying, and create mnemonics to help you remember important concepts. (On mnemonics, see Section 16 below.)

10. Conduct a Self-Assessment on Grammar, Spelling, and Composition. Then Design a Program to Reform Weaknesses.

The legal profession lives by the written word. Talking is important for some activities, but writing is crucial in almost every area of law. You cannot function in this environment without a grasp of the basics of spelling, grammar, and composition. A major complaint made by employers today is that paralegals are consistently violating these basics. The problem is very serious. Here are eight steps that will help solve it:

Step One

Take responsibility for your training in grammar, spelling, and composition. Do not wait for someone to teach (or reteach) you these basics. Do not wait until someone points out your weaknesses. Make a personal commitment to train yourself. If English courses are available to you, great. It is essential, however, that you understand that a weekly class may not be enough.

Step Two

Raise your consciousness about the writing around you. When you are reading a newspaper, for example, try to be conscious of semicolons and paragraph structure in what you are reading. At least occasionally ask yourself why a certain punctuation mark was used by a writer. You are surrounded by writing. You read this writing for content. Begin a conscious effort to focus on the structure of the writing as well. This dual level of observation exists in other aspects of our lives. When people come out of the theater, for example, they often comment about how impressive the acting was. In addition to following the story or content of the play or movie, they were aware of its form and structure as well. These levels of consciousness (content and form) should also be developed for everything you read.

Step Three

Commit yourself to spending ten minutes a day, five or six days a week, on improving your grammar skills. For a total of about an hour a week, drill yourself on the fundamentals of our language. Go to any general search engine on the Internet such as:

> www.google.com
> www.yahoo.com

Type "English grammar" in the search box of the engine you use. Do some surfing to find grammar sites that not only give basic rules but also provide examples of the application of the rules and practice drills to allow you to test yourself on what you know. Avoid sites that charge fees or that are simply selling books. Here are some examples of sites you might find useful:

> www.edufind.com/english/grammar
> www.ccc.commnet.edu/grammar
> andromeda.rutgers.edu/~jlynch/Writing/c.html
> englishplus.com/grammar
> www.tnellen.com/cybereng/32.html

Sites such as these may provide links to comparable sites. Try several. Ask fellow students what sites they have found helpful.

How do you know what areas of grammar you should study? Begin at the beginning. Start with the most basic instruction offered on the site you choose. If you consistently give correct answers to the exercises on a particular area of writing, move on to another area on the site.

One way to test your progress is to try the exercises at different sites. Suppose, for example, that you are on a site studying the distinction between *that* clauses and *which* clauses. After you finish the that/which exercises at this site, go to another grammar site and find its section on that/which. Read the examples and do the exercises at this site. Are you reinforcing what you learned at the first site, or are the examples and exercises at the second site making you realize that you need more work understanding this area of grammar? Using more than one site in this way will help you assess how well you are grasping the material.

Step Four

Improve your spelling. Use a dictionary often. Begin making a list of words that you are spelling incorrectly. Work on these words. Ask other students, relatives, or friends to test you on them by reading the words to you one by one. Spell the words out loud or on paper. You can drill yourself into spelling perfection, or close to it, by this method. When you have the slightest doubt about the spelling of a word, check the dictionary. Add difficult words to your list. Again, the more often you take this approach now, the less often you will need to use the dictionary later.

Use the Internet as a resource. Type "spelling rules" in a search engine. You will be led to many sites that will provide guidance. Examples include:

www2.gsu.edu/~wwwesl/egw/susan.htm
www.spelling.hemscott.net

As we will see in chapter 13 on computers, many word processing programs have "spell checkers" that not only identify words you may have misspelled but also provide suggested corrections. Does this new technology mean that your spelling problems have been solved forever? Hardly. Spell checkers can catch many spelling blunders, but they can be very misleading. First of all, they cannot tell you how to spell many proper names such as the surnames of individuals (unless you add these names to the base of words being checked). An even more serious problem is that spell checkers do not alert you to improper word choices. Every word in the following sentence, for example, is incorrect, but a spell checker would tell you that the sentence has no spelling problems:

"Its to later too by diner."

Here is what should have been written:

"It's too late to buy dinner."

Since the first sentence has no misspellings, you are led—misled—to believe that you have written a flawless sentence.

Step Five

Enroll in English and writing courses. Find out if drop-in help labs or remedial centers are available to you. Check offerings at local schools like adult education programs in the public schools or at colleges. Call your local public library and ask what resources are available in the community.

Step Six

Find out which law courses in your curriculum require the most writing from students. If possible, take these courses—no matter how painful you find writing to be. In fact, the more painful it is, the more you need to place yourself in an environment where writing is demanded of you on a regular basis.

Step Seven

Simplify your writing. Cut down the length of your sentences. Often a long-winded sentence can be effectively rewritten into two shorter sentences. How can you tell if your sentences are too long? There are, of course, no absolute rules that will answer this question. Yet there is a general consensus that sentences on legal topics tend to be too long. (We will return to this topic in chapter 12.)

Several writing scholars have devised readability formulas that allow you to measure sentence length and readability. Among the most popular are the Gunning Fog Index, the Flesch Reading Ease Score, and the Flesch-Kincaid Grade Level Score. You can find them described on many Internet sites such as:

tech-head.com/fog.htm
en.wikipedia.org/wiki/Flesch-Kincaid_Readability_Test
www.nightscribe.com/Education/eschew_obfuscation.htm

Try a readability formula on your own writing. It will take only a few minutes to apply. Find out if the word processor you use (e.g., Word or WordPerfect) has a formula built into the program that is ready to use every time you write something.

Readability formulas are no more than rough guides. Use them to help raise your consciousness about your writing. As you review sentences you have written, you should be asking yourself self-editing questions such as "Would I have been clearer if I had made that sentence shorter?" The conscientious use of readability formulas will help you ask and answer such questions.

For an online manual on writing, including material on readability, see *A Plain English Handbook* of the Securities and Exchange Commission (www.sec.gov/pdf/handbook.pdf). Although this manual focuses on financial document filings, it contains many useful guidelines for any kind of writing.

Step Eight

Prepare a self-assessment of your weaknesses. Make a list of what you must correct. Then set a schedule for improvement. Set aside a small amount of time each day to work on your writing weaknesses. Be consistent about this time. Do not wait for the weekend or for next semester when you will have more time. The reality is that you will probably never have substantially more time than you have now. The problem is not so much the absence of time as it is an unwillingness to dig into the task. Progress will be slow and you will be on your own. Hence there is a danger that you will be constantly finding excuses to put it off.

11. Consider Forming a Student Study Group, but Be Cautious.

Students sometimes find it useful to form study groups. A healthy exchange with your colleagues can be very productive. One difficulty is finding students with whom you are compatible. Trial and error may be the only way to identify such students. A more serious concern is trying to define the purpose of the study group. It should not be used as a substitute for your own individual study. Course review, however, is an appropriate group task. Divide a course into parts, with each member of the group having responsibility for reviewing his or her assigned part with the rest of the group.

The group can be very valuable for mutual editing on writing assignments. Suppose, for example, that you are drafting complaints in a course. Print a copy of the complaint for each member of the group or send a copy to each member as an e-mail attachment. The group then collectively comments upon and edits the complaint according to the standards discussed in class and in the course materials. (Be sure to check with your teacher in advance if group editing on such assignments is allowed.) Similarly, you could try to obtain copies of old exams in the course and collectively examine answers prepared by group members. Ask your teacher for fact situations that could be the basis of legal analysis memos (see chapter 7) or other drafting assignments. Make up fact situations of your own. The student whose work is being scrutinized must be able to take constructive criticism. The criticism should be intense if it is to be worthwhile. Students should be asked to rewrite the draft after incorporating suggestions made. The rewrite should later be subjected to another round of mutual editing. Do not hesitate to subject your writing to the scrutiny of other students. You can learn a great deal from each other.

12. Use Your Legal Research Skills to Help You Understand Components of a Course That Are Giving You Difficulty.

The law library is more than the place to go to find law that governs the facts of a client's case. A great deal of the material in the law library consists of explanations/summaries/overviews of the same law that you will be covering in your courses. You need to learn how to gain access to this material through texts such as legal encyclopedias, legal treatises, and legal periodicals. (See Exhibit 11.18 in chapter 11 on doing background research in such materials.) They will be invaluable as outside reading to help resolve conceptual and practical difficulties you are having in class.

13. Organize Your Learning through Definitions or Definitional Questions.

Among the most sophisticated questions an attorney or paralegal can ask are these: What does that word or phrase mean? Should it be defined broadly or narrowly? To a very large extent, the practice of law is a probing for definitions of key words or phrases in the context of facts that have arisen. Can a five-year-old be liable for negligence? (What is *negligence?*) Can the government tax a church-run bingo game? (What is the *free exercise of religion?*) Can attorneys in a law firm strike and obtain the protection of the National Labor Relations Act? (What is a *covered employee* under the labor statute?) Can one spouse rape another? (What is the definition of *rape?*) Can a citizen slander the president of the United States? (What is a *defamatory statement?*) Etc.

For every course that you take, you will come across numerous technical words and phrases in class and in your readings. Begin compiling a list of these words and phrases for each class. Try to limit yourself to what you think are the major ones. When in doubt about whether to include something on your list, resolve the doubt by including it.

Then pursue definitions. Find definitions in class lectures, your textbook, a legal dictionary, or a legal encyclopedia. (For legal dictionaries on the Internet, type "legal dictionary" in any search engine such as *www.google.com.*) Ask your teacher for guidance in finding definitions.

For some words, you may have difficulty obtaining definitions. Do not give up your pursuit. Keep searching. Keep probing. Keep questioning. For some words, there may be more than one definition. Others may require definitions of the definitions.

Of course, you cannot master a course simply by knowing the definitions of all the key words and phrases involved. Yet these words and phrases are the *vocabulary* of the course and are the foundation and point of reference for learning the other aspects of the course. Begin with vocabulary.

Consider a system of three-by-five or two-by-three cards to help you learn the definitions. On one side of the card, place a single word or phrase. On the other side, write the definition with a brief page reference or citation to the source of the definition. Using the cards, test yourself periodically. If you are in a study group, ask other members to test you. Ask a relative to test you. Establish a plan of ongoing review.

14. Studying Ambiguity—Coping with Unanswered Questions.

Legal studies can be frustrating because there is so much uncertainty in the law. Legions of unanswered questions exist. Definitive answers to legal questions are not always easy to find, no matter how good your legal research techniques are. Every new fact situation presents the potential for a new law. Every law seems to have an exception. Furthermore, advocates frequently argue for exceptions to the exceptions. As indicated, when terms are defined, the definitions often need definitions. A law office is not always an easy environment in which to work because of this reality.

The study of law is in large measure an examination of ambiguity that is identified, dissected, and manipulated.

The most effective way to handle frustration with this state of affairs is to be realistic about what the law is and isn't. Do not expect definitive answers to all legal questions. Search for as much clarity as you can, but do not be surprised if the conclusion of your search is further questions. A time-honored answer to many legal questions is, "It depends!" Become familiar with the following equation, since you will see it used often:

> If "X" is present, then the conclusion is "A," but if "Y" is so, then the conclusion is "B," but if "Z" is....

The practice of law may sometimes appear to be an endless puzzle. Studying law, therefore, must engage you in similar thinking processes. Again, look for precision and clarity, but do not expect the puzzle to disappear.

15. Develop the Skill of Note Taking.

Note taking is an important skill. You will regularly be told to "write it down" or "put it in a memo." Effective note taking is often a precondition to being able to do any kind of writing in the law.

First, take notes on what you are reading for class preparation and for research assignments. Do not rely exclusively on your memory. After reading hundreds of pages (or more), you will not be able to remember what you have read at the end of the semester, or even at the end of the day. Copy what you think are the essential portions of the materials you are reading. Be sure to include definitions of important words and phrases as indicated in Guideline 13 above.

To be sure, note taking will add time to your studying. Yet you will discover that it was time well spent, particularly when you begin reviewing for an exam or writing your memorandum.

Second, take notes in class. You must develop the art of taking notes while simultaneously listening to what is being said. On the job, you may have to do this frequently—for example, when:

- Interviewing a client
- Interviewing a witness during field investigation
- Receiving instructions from a supervisor
- Talking with someone on the phone

If your supervisor asks you to attend a deposition or a trial, you may need to take detailed notes on the testimony of a particular witness. (A deposition, as you will learn in chapter 10, is a method of discovery by which parties and their prospective witnesses are questioned outside the courtroom before trial.) A good place to begin learning how to write and listen at the same time is during your classes.

Most students take poor class notes. This is due to a number of reasons:

- They may write slowly.
- They may not like to take notes; it's hard work.
- They may not know if what is being said is important enough to be noted until after it is said—when it is too late because the teacher has gone on to something else.
- They do not think it necessary to take notes on a discussion that the teacher is having with another student.
- They take notes only when they see other students taking notes.
- Some teachers ramble.

A student who uses these excuses for not taking comprehensive notes in class will eventually be using similar excuses on the job when precise note taking is required for a case. This is unfortunate. You must overcome whatever resistances you have acquired to the admittedly difficult task of note taking. Otherwise, you will pay the price in your schoolwork and on the job.

Develop your own shorthand system of abbreviations for note taking. Here are some commonly used abbreviations in the law (some of the terms have more than one abbreviation; pick the one that works best for you):

a	action	cv	civil	jt	judgment	s	sum
aa	administrative agency	cz	cause	jur	jurisdiction	S	statute
a/c	appellate court	d	danger/dangerous	juv	juvenile	$	suppose
aff	affirmed	dba	doing business as	k	contract	s/b	should be
aka	also known as	d/e	direct examination	l	liable, liability	sn/b	should not be
ans	answer	dept	department	ll	landlord	sc	supreme court
app	appeal	df	defendant	lit	litigation	s/f	statute of frauds
appnt	appellant	dist	district	max	maximum	s/j	summary judgment
appee	appellee	dmg	damages	mfr	manufacturer	sl	strict liability
ar	administrative regulation	dob	date of birth	mfg	manufacturing	s/l	statute of limitations
a/r	assumption of risk	dod	date of death	min	minimum	ss	state statute
assn	association	ee	employee	mkt	market	std	standard
atty	attorney	eg	example	>	more than; greater than	sub	substantial
b	business	egs	examples	<	less than; smaller than	subj	subject
b/c	because	eq	equity	mun	municipal	t	tort
b/k	breach of contract	eqbl	equitable	n/a	not applicable	t/c	trial court
b/p	burden of proof	er	employer	natl	national	tee	trustee
bfp	bona fide purchaser	est	estimate	negl	negligence	tp	third party
©	consideration	ev	evidence	#	number	vs	against; versus
¢	complaint	f	fact	O	owner	w	wife
ca	court of appeals	fed	federal	op	opinion	w/	with
c/a	cause of action	fs	federal statute	p/c	proximate cause	wd	wrongful death
c/c	counterclaim	gvt	government	p/f	prima facie	w/i	within
cc	child custody	h	husband	pg	page	w/o	without
c/e	cross-examination	hdc	holder in due course	pl	plaintiff	x	cross
cert	certiorari	indl	individual	®	reasonable	x/e	cross-examination
c/l	common law	indp	independent	re	real estate	?	question
con l	constitutional law	info	information	reg	regulation	+	plus
cr	criminal	ins	insurance	rep	representative	\	therefore
crc	criminal court	intl	international	rev	reverse	Δ	defendant
cs	child support	j	judge, justice	revd	reversed	π	plaintiff
ct	court	jj	judges, justices	rr	railroad		

If you are participating in class by talking with the teacher, it will obviously be difficult for you to take notes at the same time. After class, take a few moments to jot down some notes on what occurred during the discussion. Then ask someone else who was in class to review these notes for accuracy and completeness. Sometimes you will have to begin taking notes at the moment the person starts talking rather than wait until the end of what he or she is saying. Try different approaches to increasing the completeness of your notes.

Don't fill up entire sheets of paper with notes. Keep at least a three-inch right-hand margin that is blank while you take notes. Later, fill in this space with notes on things you missed in the lecture or that you better understood as the class progressed. Read the notes of fellow students. When their notes contain material you missed, copy it into the right-margin space.

Sometimes so much is happening and being said during a class that it is difficult to take notes. Things can sometimes get a bit chaotic. When this happens, at least write down what appear to be key nouns or verbs that the teacher uses. Leave additional space around these words so that you can come back later and fill in details and context that you may have missed initially.

Pay particular attention to definitions and lists. Every time the teacher defines something, be sure your notes record the definition—exactly. Sometimes teachers will redefine the same term with slight modifications. Take notes on the modifications because they will often help clarify what is being discussed. Also, be conscientious about lists. A teacher might begin a topic by saying that "there are three elements" to a particular rule, or that "we will be examining four major categories of examples of the kinds of cases that can arise." When you hear that a list is coming by such language, have your pen at the ready. Lists of this kind are very important in the law.

16. Studying Rules—the Role of Memory.

Memory plays a significant role in the law. Applicants for the bar, for example, are not allowed to take notes into the exam room. An advocate in court or at an administrative hearing may be able to refer to notes, but the notes are of little value if the advocate does not have a solid grasp of the case. Most of the courses you will be taking have a memory component. This is true even for open-book exams, since you will not have time to go through all the material while responding to the questions.

Students often make two mistakes with respect to the role of memory:

- They think that memorizing is beneath their dignity.
- They think that because they understand something, they know it sufficiently to be able to give it back in an examination.

Of course, you should not be memorizing what you do not understand. Rote memorization is close to worthless. This is not so for important material that you comprehend. Yet simply understanding something does not necessarily mean that you have a sufficient grasp of it for later use.

Many systems for memorizing material can be effective:

- Reading it over and over
- Copying important parts of it
- Having other students ask you questions about it
- Making summaries or outlines of it
- Tape-recording yourself reading difficult material from a textbook and playing the tape back while driving or doing house chores
- Creating your own mnemonics

Mnemonics are simply aids to memory that you create yourself. The most common mnemonics consist of a series of letters that represent items on a list. For example, suppose you are studying section § 100, an important statute in criminal law, which requires proof of the following three elements:

     Intent to steal
     Personal property
     Resulting financial harm

To help you remember these elements, you could assign the letter "I" to the first element, "P" to the second, and "R" to the third. You can then scramble these letters to make the word *RIP*:

     Resulting financial harm [R]
     Intent to steal [I]
     Personal property [P]

The word *RIP* can now be used to help you remember the elements of § 100. RIP is a real word. Easy-to-remember nonwords (e.g., GGET or ANAR) can also be useful mnemonics. You are in control of the letters to be assigned to items on the list. Since your goal is to come up with something that will help you recall the list, the only criterion is to come up with something memorable!

If you do not have a photographic mind, you must resort to such techniques. Try different systems. Ask other students for tips on how they memorize material.

You will have to find out from your teacher what material you will be expected to know for the course. You can also check with other students who have had this teacher in the past. It may not always be easy to find out how much a teacher expects you to know from memory. Teachers have been known to surprise students on examinations! Some teachers do not like to admit that they are asking their students to memorize material for their courses, yet they still give examinations that require considerable memorization.

17. Studying Skills—the Necessity of Feedback.

Memory is most important when you are studying the basic principles of substantive and procedural law. Memory plays a less significant role in learning the skills of interviewing, investigation, legal analysis, drafting, coordinating, digesting, and advocacy. These skills have their own vocabulary that you must know, but it is your judgmental rather than your memory faculties that are key to becoming competent in such skills.

They are developed primarily by practice drills or exercises. The learning comes from the feedback that you obtain while engaged in the skill exercises. What are the ways that a student obtains feedback?

- Evaluations on assignments and exams
- Role-playing exercises that are critiqued in class
- Comparisons between your work (particularly writing projects) and models that are provided by the teacher or that you find on your own in the library
- Critiques that you receive from students in study groups

Be constantly looking for feedback. Do not wait to be called on. Do not wait to see what feedback is planned for you at the end of the course. Take the initiative immediately. Seek conferences or e-mail contact with your teachers. Find out who is available to read your writing or to observe your performance in any of the other skills. Set up your own role-playing sessions with your fellow students. Seek critiques of your rewrites even if rewriting was not required. Look for opportunities to critique other students on the various skills. Ask other students for permission to read their graded examinations so that you can compare their papers with your own. Create your own hypotheticals for analysis in study groups. (A *hypothetical* is simply a set of facts invented for the purpose of discussion and analysis.) Do additional reading on the skills. Become actively involved in your own skills development.

18. The Value of Speed-Reading Courses in the Study of Law.

In the study of law, a great deal of reading is required. Should you, therefore, take a speed-reading course? No, unless the course helps you slow down the speed of your reading! This advice may be quite distasteful to advocates (and salespersons) of speed-reading courses. The reality, however, is that statutes, regulations, and court opinions cannot be speed-read. They must be carefully picked apart and read word for word, almost as if you were translating from one language into another. If you are troubled by how long it takes you to read, do not despair. Do not worry about having to read material over and over again. Keep reading. Keep rereading. The pace of your reading will pick up as you gain experience. Never strive, however, to be able to fly through the material. Strive for comprehensiveness. Strive for understanding. For most of us, this will come through the slow process of note taking and rereading. It is sometimes argued that comprehension is increased through speed. Be careful of this argument. Reading law calls for careful thinking about what you read—and taking notes on these thoughts. There may be no harm in rapidly reading legal material for the first time. At your second, third, and fourth reading, however, speed is rarely helpful.

[SECTION B]
ON-THE-JOB LEARNING: THE ART OF BEING SUPERVISED

A great deal of learning will occur when you are on the job. Some of it may come through formal in-house office training and by the study of office procedure manuals. Most of the learning, however, will come in day-to-day interaction with your supervisors as you are given assignments. The learning comes through being supervised. Here are some guidelines to assist you in this important dimension of your legal education.

1. Don't Play "King's Clothes" with the Instructions That You Receive.

Recall the story of the king's (or emperor's) clothes. The king was naked, but everybody kept saying what a beautiful wardrobe he had on. As new people arrived, they saw that he had no clothes, but they heard everyone talking as if he were fully dressed. The new people did not want to appear unintelligent, so they, too, began admiring the king's wardrobe. When paralegals are receiving instructions on an assignment, they play "king's clothes" when they pretend that they understand all the instructions but in fact do not. They do not want to appear to be uninformed. They do not want to give the impression that they are unsure of themselves. For obvious reasons, this is a serious mistake.

Whenever you are given an assignment in a new area—that is, an assignment on something that you have not done before—there should be a great deal that you do not understand. This is particularly true during your first few months on the job, when just about everything is new! Do not pretend to be something you are not. Constantly ask questions about new things. Do not be reluctant to ask for explanations. Learn how to ask for help. It will not be a sign of weakness. Quite the contrary. People who take steps to make sure that they fully understand all their instructions will soon gain a reputation for responsibility and conscientiousness.

2. Repeat the Instructions to Your Supervisor before You Leave the Room.

Once your supervisor has told you what he or she wants you to do, do not leave the room in silence or with the general observation "I'll get on that right away." Repeat the instructions back to the supervisor as you understand them. Make sure that you and your supervisor are on the same wavelength by explaining back what you think you were told to do. This will be an excellent opportunity for the supervisor to determine what you did or did not understand and to provide you with clarifications where needed.

Supervisors will not always be sure of what they want you to do. By trying to obtain clarity on the instructions, you are providing them with the opportunity to think through what they want done. In the middle of the session with you, the supervisor may change his or her mind on what is to be done.

3. Write Your Instructions Down.

Never go to your supervisor without pen and paper. Preferably, keep an instructions notebook, diary, or journal in which you record the following information:

- Notes on what you are asked to do
- Whether the tasks in the assignment are billable (i.e., whether a particular client will be asked to pay fees for the performance of those tasks)
- The date you received the assignment
- The date by which the supervisor expects you to complete all or part of the assignment; if an exact due date is not provided, an estimate of the amount of time the task should take (sometimes referred to as a *time budget*)
- The date you actually complete the assignment
- Comments made by supervisors or others on what you submit

The notes will serve as your memory bank. Whenever any questions arise about what you were supposed to do, you have something concrete to refer to.

Exhibit A contains an assignment checklist on which you can record this kind of data for every major assignment you receive.

4. Ask for a Due Date and a Statement of Priorities.

You need to know when an assignment is due. Ask for a due date *even if the supervisor tells you to "get to it when you can."* This phrase may mean "relatively soon" or "before the end of the month" to your supervisor, but not to you. If the supervisor says he or she does not know when it should be done, ask for an approximate due date. Tell the supervisor you want to place the assignment on

EXHIBIT A	Checklist for Major Assignments

Name of supervisor for the assignment:

What you have been asked to do:

Identification of the client or matter for which the task is being done:

Specific areas or tasks you have been told not to cover, if any:

Format supervisor expects, e.g., outline only, rough draft, final copy ready for supervisor's signature:

Date you are given the assignment:

Expected due date:

Time budget (an estimate of the amount of time the task should take):

Is the task billable to a client? If so, to what account?

Location of samples or models in the office to check as possible guides:

Possible resource people in the office you may want to contact for help:

Practice manuals or treatises in the library that might provide background or general guidance:

Dates you contacted supervisor or others for help before due date:

Date you completed the assignment:

Positive, negative, or neutral comments from supervisor or others on the quality of your work on the assignment:

Things you would do differently the next time you do an assignment of this kind:

---

your calendar so that it can be completed in a timely manner along with all your other assignments. Ask what priority the assignment has. Where does it fit in with your other assignments? If you have more than enough to fill the day, you need to know what takes priority. If you do not ask for a priority listing, the supervisor may assume you are under no time pressures.

5. If the Instructions Appear to Be Complicated, Ask Your Supervisor to Identify the Sequence of Tasks Involved.

As you receive instructions, you may sometimes feel overwhelmed by all that is being asked of you. Many supervisors do not give instructions in clear, logical patterns. They may talk in a rambling, stream-of-consciousness fashion. When confronted with this situation, simply say:

> OK, but can you break that down for me a little more so that I know what you want me to do first? I think I will be able to do the entire assignment, but it would help if I approach it one step at a time. Where do you want me to start?

6. As Often as Possible, Write Your Instructions and What You Do in the Form of Checklists.

A methodical mind is one that views a project in "doable" steps and that tackles one step at a time. You need to have a methodical mind in order to function in a busy law office. One of the best ways to develop such a mind is to think in terms of checklists. Attorneys love checklists. A great deal of the practice material published by bar associations, for example, consists of page after page of detailed checklists of things to do and/or to consider when completing a project for a client. Attorneys want to be thorough. An unwritten "rule" of law practice seems to be that you cannot be thorough without a checklist.

A checklist is simply a chronological sequencing of tasks that must be done in order to complete an assignment. Convert the instructions from your supervisor into checklists. In the process of actually carrying out instructions, you go through many steps—all of which could become part of a detailed checklist. The steps you went through to complete the task become a checklist of things to do in order to complete such a task in the future. To be sure, it can be time-consuming to draft checklists. Keep in mind, however, that:

- The checklists will be a benefit to you in organizing your own time and in assuring completeness.
- The checklists can be invaluable for other employees who are given similar assignments in the future.

You will not be able to draft checklists for everything that you do. Perhaps you will not be able to write more than one checklist a week. Perhaps you will have to use some of your own time to write checklists. Whatever time you can devote will be profitably spent so long as you are serious about writing and using the checklists. They may have to be rewritten or modified later. This should not deter you from the task, since most things that are worth doing require testing and reassessment.

Here is how one veteran paralegal describes the process:

> When you are doing a multistep task (thinking out each step as you move through it)... create a checklist that will help you do it faster next time. Don't just create the checklist; create a notebook to store it in so that when the job comes around again you can find it! This is trickier to do on a busy day than you may think, but well worth doing. Think of these checklists as expanding your professional options. In time, they may become resources for training you give to newer paralegals.[2]

Many how-to manuals found in law offices were created out of the checklists workers compiled on tasks they frequently performed.

7. Find Out What Manuals and Checklists Already Exist in Your Office.

It does not make sense to reinvent the wheel. If manuals and checklists on the topic of your assignment already exist in your office, you should find and use them. (Also check in computer databases where the office may store frequently used forms and instructions.) Unfortunately, the how-to-do-it information may be buried in the heads of the attorneys, paralegals, and secretaries of the office. No one has taken the time to write it all down. If this is not the case, you should find out where it is written down and try to adapt what you find to the assignment on which you are working.

8. Ask for a Model.

One of the best ways to make sure you know what a supervisor wants is to ask whether he or she knows of any models that you could use as a guide for what you are being asked to do. Such models may be found in closed case files, manuals, form books, and practice texts. They may also be available on the Internet. Many forms, for example, can be obtained on the major fee-based databases we will discuss in chapter 13: Westlaw (www.westlaw.com) and LexisNexis (www.lexis.com). Free forms are also available. In any general search engine (e.g., www.google.com), type the name of your state and the phrase "legal forms" (e.g., "New York" "legal forms"). You could also include the specific name of the form you are seeking (e.g., "New York" "legal form" "articles of incorporation"). Try to find sites that give actual examples of forms rather than sites that merely want you to purchase them.

Caution is needed whenever using models. Every new legal problem is potentially unique. What will work in one case may not work in another. A model is a guide, a starting point—and nothing more. Changes in the model will often be needed in order to adapt it to the particular facts of your assignment. Whenever you find a possible model your supervisor has not seen, bring it to his or her attention and ask whether it can be adapted and used. (See also Exhibit 10.4 in chapter 10 on how to avoid abusing forms.)

9. Do Some Independent Legal Research on the Instructions You Are Given.

Often you will be told what to do without being given more than a cursory explanation of why it needs to be done that way. Most instructions for legal tasks are based upon the requirements of the law. A complaint, for example, is served on an opposing party in a designated way because the law has imposed rules on how such service is to be made. You may be asked to serve a complaint in a certain way without being told what section of the state code (or of your court rules) requires it to be served in that way. It would be highly impractical to read all the law that is the foundation for an assigned task. It is not necessary to do so and you would not have time to do so.

What you can occasionally do, however, is focus on selected instructions for an assignment and do some background legal research to gain a greater appreciation for why the instructions were necessary. (See the checklist on doing background legal research in Exhibit 11.18 in chapter 11.) You will probably have to do such legal research on your own time unless the assignment you are given includes doing some legal research. Research can be time-consuming, but you will find it enormously educational. It can place a totally new perspective on the assignment and, indeed, on your entire job.

10. Get on the Office Mailing Lists for New Publications.

A law office frequently buys publications for its law library that are relevant to its practice. The publications often include legal treatises and legal periodicals. Before these publications are shelved in the library, they are often routed to the attorneys in the office so that they can become acquainted with current legal writing that will be available in the library. Each attorney usually keeps the publication for a few hours or a few days for review before passing it on to the next person on the mailing list. If the actual publication is not passed around in this manner, those on the mailing list might receive brief summaries of recent publications or photocopies of their tables of contents. Another option in some offices is the use of e-mail to inform attorneys of new publications.

Ask to be included in these mailing lists. The publications are often excellent self-education opportunities, particularly the articles in legal periodicals.

You can also subscribe to free Internet alerts on your area of practice. For example, Findlaw (www.findlaw.com) allows you to subscribe to newsletters that give summaries of recent cases in designated areas of law. One of the areas covered by the newsletters is family law (newsletters. findlaw.com/nl). If your office practices in this area, you should consider subscribing.

11. Ask Secretaries and Other Paralegals for Help.

Secretaries and paralegals who have worked in the office for a long period of time can be very helpful to you if you approach them properly. Everybody wants to feel important. Everybody wants to be respected. When someone asks for something in a way that gives the impression he or she is entitled to what is being sought, difficulties usually result. Think of how you would like to be approached if you were in the position of the secretary or paralegal. What behavior or attitude of another employee would irritate you? What would make you want to go out of your way to cooperate with and assist a new employee who needs your help? Your answers (and sensitivity) to questions such as these will go a long way toward enabling you to draw on the experience of others in the office.

12. Obtain Feedback on an Assignment before the Date It Is Due.

Unless the assignment you are given is a very simple one, do not wait until the date that it is due to communicate with your supervisor. If you are having trouble with the assignment, you will want to check with your supervisor as soon as possible and as often as necessary. It would be a mistake, however, to contact the supervisor only when trouble arises. Of course, you want to avoid wasting anyone's time, including your own. You should limit your contacts with a busy supervisor to essential matters. You could take the following approach with your supervisor:

> Everything seems to be going fine on the project you gave me. I expect to have it in to you on time. I'm wondering, however, if you could give me a few moments of your time. I want to bring you up to date on where I am so that you can let me know if I am on the right track.

Perhaps this contact could take place on the phone or during a brief office visit. Suppose that you have gone astray on the assignment without knowing it? It is obviously better to discover this before the date the assignment is due. The more communication you have with your supervisor, the more likely it is that you will catch such errors before a great deal of time is wasted.

13. Ask to Participate in Office and Community Training Programs.

Sometimes a law office conducts training sessions for its attorneys. Ask if you can be included. Bar associations and paralegal associations often conduct all-day seminars on legal topics relevant to your work. They are part of what is called continuing legal education (CLE). Seek permission to attend some of these sessions if they are held during work hours. If they are conducted after hours, invest some of your own time to attend. Also check into what is available on the Internet. Online CLE has become increasingly popular because you can take courses at any time and in any location where you have access to the Internet. To find out what is available, type "continuing legal education" (or "CLE") in the Web search boxes of national and local paralegal associations (see appendix B for addresses) and of bar associations in your area (see appendix C). Your employer may be willing to pay all or a part of the cost of such courses. Even if you must pay the entire cost, it will be a worthwhile long-term investment.

14. Ask to Be Evaluated Regularly.

When you first interview for a paralegal position, inquire about the policy of the office on evaluations. Are they conducted on a regular basis? Are they done in writing? Will you know in advance the specific criteria that will be used to evaluate your performance? If you are hired in an office that does not have a formal evaluation structure or procedure, you will need to take the initiative to let supervisors know that you consider evaluations to be important to your professional development. It may take a while for you to feel confident enough to make this known, but the importance of doing so cannot be overestimated.

For a number of reasons, many offices do not have formal evaluations:

- Evaluations can be time-consuming.
- Evaluators are reluctant to say anything negative, especially in writing.
- Most of us do not like to be evaluated: it's too threatening to our ego.

Go out of your way to let your supervisor know that you want to be evaluated and that you can handle criticism. If you are defensive when you are criticized, you will find that the evaluations of your performance will go on behind your back! Such a work environment is obviously very unhealthy. Consider this approach that a paralegal might take with a supervisor:

> I want to know what you think of my work. I want to know where you think I need improvement. That's the only way I'm going to learn. I also want to know when I'm doing things correctly, but I'm mainly interested in your suggestions on what I can do to increase my skills.

If you take this approach and mean it, the chances are good that you will receive some very constructive criticism and gain a reputation for professionalism.

15. Proceed One Step at a Time.

Perhaps the most important advice you can receive in studying law in school and on the job is to concentrate on what is immediately before you. Proceed one step at a time. What are your responsibilities in the next fifteen minutes? Block everything else out. Make *the now* as productive as you can. Your biggest enemy is worry about the future: worry about the exams ahead of you, worry about your family, worry about the state of the world, worry about finding employment, etc. Leave tomorrow alone! Worrying about it will only interfere with your ability to make the most of what you must do now. Your development in the law will come slowly, in stages. Map out these stages in very small time blocks—beginning with the time that is immediately ahead of you. If you must worry, limit your concern to how to make the next fifteen minutes a more valuable learning experience.

SUMMARY

Legal education is a lifelong endeavor; a competent paralegal never stops learning about the law and the skills of applying it. A number of important guidelines will help you become a good student in the classroom and on the job. Do not let the media blur your understanding of what the practice of law is actually like. To avoid studying in a vacuum, be sure that you know the goals of an assignment and how it fits into the other assignments. Organize your day around a study plan. Since the time demands on you will probably be greater than you anticipated, it is important that you design a system of studying. Assess your study habits, such as how you handle distractions or how you commit things to memory. Then promise yourself that you will do something about your weaknesses.

Increase your proficiency in the basics of writing. How many of the rules about the comma can you identify? Do you know when to use *that* rather than *which* in your sentences? How many of your paragraphs have topic sentences? Are there zero spelling errors on every page of your writing? You have entered a field where the written word is paramount. You must take personal responsibility—now—for the improvement of your grammar, spelling, and composition skills.

Use the law library to help you understand difficult areas of the law. But don't expect absolute clarity all the time. Seek out evaluations of your work. Become a skillful note taker. Get into the habit of looking for definitions.

These suggestions also apply once you are on the job. Don't pretend you understand what you don't. Repeat instructions back to your supervisor before you begin an assignment. Ask for due dates and priorities if you are given several things to do. Write down your instructions in your own notebook or journal. Become an avid user of checklists, including those you create on your own. Find out if an assignment has been done by others in the past. If so, seek their help. Try to find a model and adapt it as needed. Be prepared to do some independent research. Ask if you can be on internal office mailing lists for new publications. Find out what's available on the Internet to keep current in your area of the law. Participate in training programs at the law office and in the legal community. Ask to be evaluated regularly. Seek feedback before an assignment is due.

Review Questions

1. Why must a student of law be a perpetual student?
2. Distinguish between substantive and procedural law.
3. What are the two dimensions of your legal education?
4. How do you design a study plan?
5. How can you increase your available productive time?
6. What are some of the major interferences with effective studying?
7. What are some of the techniques of active studying?
8. What steps can you take on your own to increase your proficiency in grammar, spelling, and composition?
9. What danger do you need to be aware of when using computer spell checkers?
10. What are readability formulas and how can they assist you?
11. How can study groups help you?
12. How can legal research help you handle difficult aspects of any course?
13. What is meant by studying ambiguity in the law?
14. Why is note taking important in the practice and study of law?
15. What are some of the steps you can take to increase your powers of retention?
16. Where and how can you obtain feedback on your schoolwork?
17. What is meant by playing "king's clothes" with the assignments you receive on the job?
18. What are the major techniques of receiving instructions from your supervisor on assignments?
19. Why is it important to obtain a specific due date and a statement of priorities for assignments? What is a time budget?
20. How can you translate instructions into checklists?
21. How can you obtain help on an office assignment from (1) office manuals/checklists, (2) models, (3) independent legal research, and (4) secretaries and other paralegals?
22. How can you obtain feedback on an assignment from a busy supervisor?
23. Why are performance evaluations sometimes ineffective and what can you do to obtain meaningful ones on the job?

Helpful Web Sites: More on the Process of Effective Studying

Study Techniques
- www.how-to-study.com
- www.scs.tamu.edu/selfhelp/elibrary/basic_study_techniques.asp
- www.oberlin.edu/psych/studytech
- www.adprima.com/studyout.htm

Note Taking
- www.sas.calpoly.edu/asc/ssl/notetaking.systems.html
- www.csbsju.edu/academicadvising/help/lec-note.htm
- www.dartmouth.edu/~acskills/success/notes.html
- www.wcupa.edu/_academics/cae.tut/TCornell.htm
- www.academictips.org/acad/literature/notetaking.html

Online Flashcards for Paralegals
- www.flashcardexchange.com
  (type "paralegal" in the search box)

Taking Tests
- www.testtakingtips.com/test
- www.studygs.net/tsttak1.htm
- www.ctl.ua.edu/sss/college_survival_skills.htm

Google Searches (run the following searches for more sites)
- grammar help
- study skills
- memory skills
- note taking
- test taking
- supervision skills
- "being supervised"
- memory skills
- study groups

Endnotes

1. Lynda Richardson, *From the Bench, Judgment and Sass*, New York Times, March 27, 2001, at p. A25.
2. Deborah Bogen, *Paralegal Success* 79 (2000).

The Paralegal in the Legal System

Introduction to a New Career in Law

[SECTION A]

LAUNCHING YOUR CAREER

Welcome to the field! You probably fall into one or more of the following categories:

- You have never worked in a law office.
- You are or once were employed in a law office and now want to upgrade your skills.
- You want to explore the variety of careers in law for which a paralegal education can be a point of entry.

As you begin your legal education, you may have a large number of questions:

- What is a paralegal?
- Where do paralegals work?
- What are the functions of a paralegal?
- How do I obtain a job?
- What is the difference between an attorney and a paralegal?
- What is the difference between a paralegal and the clerical staff of a law office?
- What problems do some paralegals encounter on the job, and how can these problems be resolved?
- How is the paralegal field regulated? Who does the regulating and for what purposes?
- What are the ethical guidelines that govern paralegal conduct?
- What career options are available once a paralegal has obtained experience?

Some of these questions, particularly those involving regulation, do not have definitive answers. The paralegal field is still evolving, even though it has been a part of the legal system for about forty years. All of the boundary lines of paralegal responsibility, for example, have not yet been fully defined. Consequently, you are about to enter a career that you can help shape. To do so, you will need a comprehensive understanding of the opportunities that await you and the challenges that will require your participation. Our goal in this book is to provide you with this understanding.

It is an exciting time to be working in the law. So many aspects of our everyday lives have legal dimensions. The law plays a dominant role in a spectrum of issues that range from the status of the unborn to the termination of life support systems. Eighty million lawsuits are filed every year, about 152 a minute.[1] One study concludes that 52 percent of Americans have a legal problem; one out of three will need the advice of an attorney in the next twelve months.[2] Almost 90 percent of U.S. corporations are involved in some type of litigation.[3] The news media are preoccupied with laws that have been broken, laws that no longer make sense, and laws that need to be passed in order to create a more just society. Caught up in the whirlwind of these debates is the attorney. And paralegals are essential members of the attorney's team.

Once you have completed your paralegal education and gained experience on the job, you will find numerous career options open to you in and outside of traditional law offices, as we will see in chapter 2. Legal skills are valued in many different kinds of work. Peggy Marino would certainly agree. She decided to use her paralegal background to run for political office, winning a seat on the Board of Education in New Jersey. Peggy now serves on the financial and negotiations committees of the board. "She credits her experience as a legal assistant as having prepared her for those roles."[3a]

[SECTION B]
DO YOU KNOW WHAT TIME IT IS?

Perhaps you're wondering what working in the law will be like. One of the hallmarks of legal work is its diversity. In five years, if you meet the person sitting next to you now in class and compare notes on what your workdays are like as paralegals, you will probably be startled by the differences. Of course, there will also be similarities.

One way to gauge what working in a law office might be like is to answer a particular question. Stop what you are doing for a moment and answer this question:

Do you know what time it is?

Depending on when you are reading this book, you will probably look at your watch or the clock on the wall and answer 9:45 A.M., 1:30 P.M., 3:32 P.M., 11:28 P.M., etc. There are hundreds of possible answers. But if you answered in this manner, you've made your first mistake in the study and practice of law. Look at the question again. Read it slowly. You were *not* asked, *What time is it?* You were asked, *Do you know* what time it is? There are *only* two possible answers to this question: *yes* or *no*.

Welcome to the law! One of the singular characteristics of the field you are about to enter is its *precision* and *attention to detail*. Vast amounts of time can be wasted answering the wrong question.[4] In fact, attorneys will tell you that one of the most important skills in the law is the ability to identify and focus on the question—the issue—that needs to be resolved.

Developing this sensitivity begins with the skill of *listening*—listening very carefully. It also involves *thinking before responding*, noting distinctions, noting what is said and what is not said, being aware of differences in emphasis, and being aware that slight differences in the facts can lead to dramatically different conclusions. Even relatively minor variations in punctuation can sometimes have legal consequences. Compare, for example, the following two statements:

Johnson said the officer hid the evidence.

Johnson, said the officer, hid the evidence.

The hallmark of a professional is precision in language and the ability to identify what is different or unique about a particular person or situation. In this sense, highly competent paralegals are true professionals.

Another major characteristic of law is its focus on definitions. Attorneys are preoccupied with questions such as "What definition did the legislature intend?" and "What does that clause mean?" For example, when two airplanes struck the two towers of the World Trade Center on September 11, 2001, was the landlord of the towers entitled to one insurance payment of $3.5 billion or two payments totaling $7 billion? The answer turned on the definition of one word—"occurrence"—in the insurance contracts. Was there one attack, one "occurrence," or two? Another dramatic example of controversy generated by a definition occurred during a famous grand jury hearing that was videotaped and later played on national television. The witness giving testimony under oath was a graduate of the Yale Law School and a former constitutional law professor. In testimony that captivated the nation, he said that his answer to a particular question would depend on what the "definition of 'is' is" in the question. The attorney giving this testimony was President Bill Clinton.

In short, you have a great deal ahead of you in the study of law; it's going to be a fascinating adventure.

[SECTION C]
MAJOR PLAYERS: THE BIG FIVE

During this course, we will meet many organizations. Five in particular have had a dramatic influence on the development of paralegalism. These five (not necessarily listed in order of influence) are as follows:

- National Federation of Paralegal Associations (NFPA) www.paralegals.org
- National Association of Legal Assistants (NALA) www.nala.org
- American Bar Association Standing Committee on Paralegals (SCOP) www.abanet.org
- Your state bar association (see appendix C)
- Your local paralegal association (see appendix B)

These organizations will be covered in some detail throughout the remaining chapters of the book, but a brief word about each will be helpful at this point.

NATIONAL FEDERATION OF PARALEGAL ASSOCIATIONS (NFPA)

The NFPA is an association of over fifty state and local paralegal associations throughout the country—representing more than 11,000 paralegals. (See appendix B.) Individual paralegals can also be members, but most are connected to NFPA through their local paralegal association.

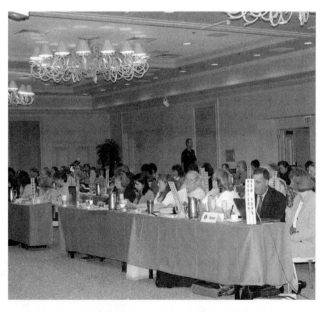

Annual convention of the National Federation of Paralegal Associations (NFPA). Reprinted with permission of the National Federation of Paralegal Associations.

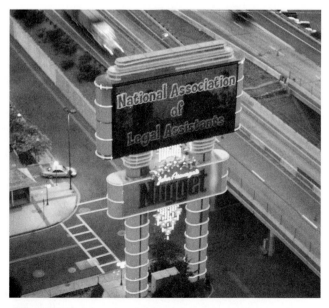

Annual convention of the National Association of Legal Assistants (NALA). Photo courtesy of NALA and Ken Frakes.

From its national headquarters in Washington State, NFPA promotes paralegalism through **continuing legal education (CLE)** programs and political action. As we will see in chapter 4, NFPA has a voluntary certification exam for *advanced* paralegals called PACE (Paralegal Advanced Certification Exam). NFPA opposes certification for *entry-level* paralegals, i.e., those with no paralegal experience. This is a major difference between NFPA and the other important national association of paralegals, the National Association of Legal Assistants (NALA), which has a certification exam for individuals with no paralegal experience.

continuing legal education (CLE) Training in the law (usually short term) that a person receives after completing his or her formal legal training.

NATIONAL ASSOCIATION OF LEGAL ASSISTANTS (NALA)

NALA is primarily an association of individual paralegals, although ninety state and local paralegal associations are affiliated with the organization. (See appendix B.) More than 18,000 paralegals in the country are represented by NALA. Most of them have passed NALA's voluntary certification exam for *entry-level* paralegals called the CLA (Certified Legal Assistant) exam. By *entry-level*, we mean that the exam can be taken without having paralegal job experience. NALA has a separate certification exam for advanced paralegals. From its national headquarters in Oklahoma, NALA is equally active in the continuing legal education and political arenas.

Over the years, NALA and the NFPA have carried on a lively debate on major issues such as whether there should be entry-level certification. As indicated, NALA offers such certification and NFPA does not. The two associations also differ on whether the terms *paralegal* and *legal assistant* are synonymous. NALA says they are; NFPA disagrees. Later we will examine this controversy as well as their disagreement over certification. Such debates over the years have contributed greatly to the vitality of the field. Both associations can be reached by their "snail" mail street addresses (see appendix B) and on the Internet (see Exhibit 1.1).

AMERICAN BAR ASSOCIATION (ABA)

The ABA is a voluntary association of attorneys; no attorney must be a member. Yet it is a powerful entity because of its resources, its prestige, and the large number of attorneys who have joined. The ABA has a Standing Committee on Paralegals (SCOP) that has had a significant impact on the growth of the field. The role of the ABA has included the publication of research on paralegals, the establishment of a voluntary program of approving paralegal schools, and the creation of an associate membership category for paralegals. The latter development was not initially welcomed by everyone, as we will see in chapter 4.

STATE BAR ASSOCIATION OF YOUR STATE

Most state bar associations have taken positions on paralegals. These positions take one of two forms: (1) guidelines on the proper use of paralegals by attorneys, and (2) ethical opinions that apply the state's ethical code to specific questions that have arisen concerning an attorney's use of paralegals. We will examine both kinds of positions in chapter 5. Some state bar associations have followed the lead of the ABA and allow paralegals to become associate or affiliate members.

YOUR LOCAL PARALEGAL ASSOCIATION

Paralegal associations fall into at least fourteen categories:

1. nationwide (e.g., NFPA and NALA)
2. statewide (e.g., Illinois Paralegal Association)
3. regionwide encompassing more than one state (e.g., Rocky Mountain Paralegal Association)
4. regionwide within a state (e.g., South Florida Paralegal Association)
5. countywide (e.g., Santa Clara County Paralegal Association)
6. citywide (e.g., San Francisco Paralegal Association)
7. theme specific (e.g., Houston Corporate Paralegal Association)
8. division of a bar association (e.g., Paralegal Division of the State Bar of Texas)
9. association of associations (e.g., Empire State Alliance of Paralegal Associations)
10. schoolwide (e.g., Fresno City College Paralegal Association)
11. association that is manager focused (e.g., International Paralegal Management Association)
12. association whose membership is limited to paralegals (e.g., Orange County Paralegal Association)

EXHIBIT 1.1 The Major National Paralegal Associations on the Internet: NFPA (www.paralegals.org) and NALA (www.nala.org)

13. association whose membership consists of paralegals, legal secretaries, and other nonattorneys (e.g., NALS the Association for Legal Professionals)
14. foreign (e.g., Canadian Paralegal Association)

In appendix B, you will find a list of every paralegal association in the country (other than those whose membership is limited to one school). Most paralegals in the country have joined a state, regional, county, city, or bar-affiliated paralegal association. (They are collectively referred to in this book as *local paralegal associations*.) A great many paralegals have found major career support and inspiration through active participation in their local paralegal association. If any of them have a student membership rate (see appendix B), you should consider joining now.

ASSIGNMENT 1.1

It is not too early to begin learning about and communicating with important associations.

(a) Go to the Internet addresses of NFPA, NALA, SCOP, your state bar association, and your local paralegal association. (If your local association does not have an Internet address, go to the closest paralegal association that has an Internet address.) On each of these sites:

   (i) What e-mail address is available to write for additional information about the organization?
   (ii) Quote any sentence on the site that pertains to paralegal careers. Following the quote, give the citation to the site. In your citation to an Internet page, include the name of the site, the date you visited the site, and the Internet address, e.g., National Association of Legal Assistants (visited May 2, 2008), www.nala.org.

(b) Type "*paralegal*" in the search boxes of Yahoo groups (groups.yahoo.com) and Google groups (groups.google.com). Make a list of the five largest groups from each search. Ask your professor which of these groups you should join. (Caution: while online groups can be very informative, they often subject members to spam.)

(c) Run the following searches in Google (www.google.com), Microsoft search (www.live.com), or Ask (www.ask.com):

   "paralegal blog"
   "paralegal listserv"

   Blogs are the equivalent of online journals; listservs are online mailing lists (both of which we will cover in greater detail later). Make a list of five blogs and five listservs. Select ones that are noncommercial and that appear to be the most informative. (By *noncommercial*, we mean sites that are not trying to sell you something.) Once you have your list, ask your professor which listservs you should join and which blogs you should regularly check. (Caution: spam can also be a problem when joining listservs.) Examples of outstanding paralegal blogs are indianaparalegals.blogspot.com; www.myparalegalspace.snappville.com, estrinlegaled.typepad.com, and paralegalgateway.typepad.com/my_weblog.

Although NFPA, NALA, SCOP, your state bar association, and your local paralegal association will dominate our discussion of paralegalism, we will also be referring to other important groups, such as the following:

- NALS the Association for Legal Professionals (NALS), formerly called the National Association of Legal Secretaries: NALS is a national association that contains many members with the titles *paralegal*, *legal assistant*, and *legal secretary*; membership is open to all "persons engaged in work of a legal nature." NALS has two major national certification examinations: PLS (Professional Legal Secretary) and PP (Professional Paralegal) (www.nals.org).
- International Paralegal Management Association (IPMA): an association of paralegal supervisors of other paralegals in large law offices (www.paralegalmanagement.org).
- American Association for Paralegal Education (AAfPE): an association of paralegal schools (www.aafpe.org).
- Association of Legal Administrators (ALA): an association of individuals (mostly non-attorneys) who administer or manage law offices (www.alanet.org/home.html).
- American Alliance of Paralegals, Inc. (AAPI): a recently formed national association of paralegals in which membership is available to individuals who meet specified educational or experience requirements. An AAPI member can be certified as an American Alliance Certified Paralegal (AACP) (www.aapipara.org).

[SECTION D]

JOB TITLES

For convenience, this book uses the title *paralegal*. Another common title is *legal assistant*. For years most people agreed that these titles were synonymous, just as the titles *attorney* and *lawyer* are synonymous. Yet the titles *paralegal* and *legal assistant* have been the source of confusion and debate. For example, in some state governments, legal assistant positions are attorney positions. In the federal government, most legal secretaries are now called legal assistants. More significantly, many private law offices have changed the title of their legal secretaries to *legal assistants* without significantly changing their job responsibility. Proponents of the change say that it reflects the broader role that many secretaries perform. Cynics, however, argue that the change is due to the fact that courts can give attorneys separate fees for the work of their legal assistants but not for that of their secretaries. We will be examining such fees later in the chapter.

The shift in title from *secretary* to *legal assistant* has not been universal; there are still many legal secretaries in offices throughout the country. Yet the shift has led to an emerging preference for the *paralegal* title. For example, many local associations have voted to change their name from legal assistant association to paralegal association. One of the largest paralegal organizations in the country, the Legal Assistant Division of the State Bar of Texas, recently changed its name to the Paralegal Division of the State Bar of Texas. As indicated, an extremely important committee of the American Bar Association is the Standing Committee on Paralegals. Its name only a few years ago was the Standing Committee on Legal Assistants.

The National Association of Legal Assistants (NALA), however, is adamant that "the terms legal assistant and paralegal are used interchangeably." This is also the view of the International Paralegal Management Association (IPMA), yet even IPMA has gone through a name change—it was once known as the Legal Assistant Management Association. The trend, however, is toward the paralegal title. NALA itself has acknowledged this trend. As we will see in chapter 4, if you take and pass NALA's certification exam, you have a choice of being called a certified legal assistant (CLA) or a certified paralegal (CP). The former title has been available since the 1970s; the latter was added as an option in 2004.

What will *your* title be upon employment? The answer will depend on the preference or practice of the office where you work. Whatever title the office decides to use will be your title. If you work for a small office of one or two attorneys, you may be given a choice. For most other offices, the choice is made by the office.

This is not to say that *paralegal* and *legal assistant* are the only titles in the field. Far from it. There is a great diversity of additional titles that have been used. Several reasons account for this diversity.

First, there are no national standards regulating the paralegal field. Every state is free to regulate or to refuse to regulate a particular occupation. Second, most states have not imposed the kind of regulation on paralegals that would lead to greater consistency on titles within a particular state. For example, most states have not imposed minimum educational requirements or licensing. Hence few restrictions exist on who can call themselves paralegals, legal assistants, or related titles. Although there are some major exceptions in states such as California, Florida, and Maine, for the most part, the field is unregulated.

traditional paralegal A paralegal who is an employee of an attorney.

independent contractor One who operates his or her own business and contracts to do work for others who do not control many of the administrative details of how the work is performed.

To begin sorting through the maze, we examine two broad categories of paralegals: those who are employees of attorneys (often called **traditional paralegals**) and those who are **independent contractors**. In general, independent contractors are self-employed individuals who control many of the administrative *details* of performing tasks; the *objectives* or end products of what they do are controlled by those who buy their services. We will be examining two kinds of paralegals who are independent contractors: those who sell their services to attorneys (a relatively small group) and those who sell their services to the public without attorney supervision (a larger and more controversial group).

Within these categories, you will find considerable diversity (and overlap) in the titles that are used:

1. EMPLOYEES OF ATTORNEYS

The vast majority (over 95 percent) are employees of attorneys. They may be called:

paralegal	lawyer's assistant
legal assistant	attorney assistant
professional legal assistant	lawyer's aide

legal service assistant

paralegal specialist

paralegal assistant

law specialist

legal analyst

legal technician

legal paraprofessional

They are all traditional paralegals because they are employees of attorneys. Most are full-time employees. Some, however, are temporary employees who work part-time or who work full-time for a limited period when a law firm needs temporary help, usually from paralegals with experience in a particular area of the law.

If a law firm has a relatively large number of paralegals, it might call its entry-level people:

paralegal I

legal assistant I

project case assistant

document clerk

document production specialist

project clerk

legal assistant clerk

paralegal clerk

case clerk

Large law firms may also have individuals who help recruit, train, and supervise all paralegals in the office. This supervisor might be called:

paralegal supervisor

legal assistant supervisor

supervising legal assistant

paralegal manager

manager of paralegal services

legal assistant manager

director of paralegal services

director of legal assistant services

director of legal assistants

director of practice support

paralegal coordinator

senior paralegal

legal assistant coordinator

case manager

paralegal administrator

legal assistant administrator

As indicated earlier, these individuals have their own association, the International Paralegal Management Association (IPMA). For more on entry-level and supervisory paralegals, see the discussion of career ladders later in the chapter.

All of the titles listed thus far are generic in that they do not tell you what the person's primary skills are or in what area of the law he or she specializes. Other employee job titles are more specific:

litigation assistant

litigation practice support specialist

corporate paralegal

corporate law analyst

family law paralegal

probate specialist

real estate paralegal

senior medical paralegal

health care/elder care paralegal

bankruptcy paralegal

water law paralegal

international trade paralegal

government relations paralegal

compliance paralegal

workers' compensation paralegal

Other examples include *judicial assistant*, who works for a federal, state, or local court system; *conflicts specialist* (also called *conflicts analyst* or *conflicts researcher*), who helps the office determine whether it should refrain from taking a case because of a conflict of interest with present or prior clients (see chapter 5); and *depo summarizer*, who summarizes pretrial testimony, particularly depositions (in which attorneys question potential witnesses outside the courtroom in preparation for trial). A *nurse paralegal* is a nurse who has become a paralegal, using his or her medical training to help personal injury **(PI)** attorneys locate and decipher medical records and performing other

PI Personal injury.

ASSIGNMENT 1.2

In appendix 2.A at the end of chapter 2, the Web sites of many large law firms are listed. Pick any ten law firms in your state or in neighboring states. Try to find paralegal and related positions on these sites. On the homepage of a site, click words such as *careers, employment, join us, people,* or any other words that invite the viewer to learn about personnel at the firm. On the sites that you select, what job titles or job descriptions do you find for individuals who are neither attorneys nor secretaries?

litigation tasks. Nurse paralegals are usually employees of law offices. When they function though their own independent businesses, they are often called *legal nurse consultant* (LNC) or, if certified, *legal nurse consultant certified* (LNCC). See the American Association of Legal Nurse Consultants (www.aalnc.org).

Some law firms divide their paralegals into two broad categories: litigation and transactional. Litigation paralegals work on cases in litigation, particularly in the pretrial stages of litigation. A **transactional paralegal** provides assistance to attorneys whose clients are engaged in a large variety of transactions that involve contracts, leases, mergers, incorporations, estate planning, patents, etc.

A few large law firms have positions called *specialist*, *analyst*, or *consultant*. These are nonattorneys who have a high degree of expertise in a particular area, e.g., immigration, pensions, medicine, accounting, or environmental regulation. Skilled paralegals are sometimes promoted into these positions.

Occasionally, when an office wants its paralegal to perform more than one job, hybrid titles are used. For example, an office might call an employee a *paralegal/investigator*, a *paralegal/librarian*, or a *paralegal/legal secretary*. In one of the online mailing lists (**listservs**) for paralegals, a person recently signed his e-mail message with the title *administrative assistant/paralegal*. In general, the smaller the law office, the more likely an employee will be asked to play multiple roles, even if he or she does not have a hybrid title. For example, an employee of an office with one attorney (a sole practitioner) could be the paralegal, the bookkeeper, the librarian, the investigator, the secretary, and the receptionist!

Perhaps the strangest—and thankfully the rarest—hybrid title you may see is *attorney/paralegal*. A California law firm placed an ad in a Los Angeles legal newspaper looking for an individual who would work under this title. What's going on? The legal job market fluctuates. Depending on the state of the economy, jobs for attorneys might be abundant or scarce. In lean times, parts of the country could be flooded with unemployed attorneys, many of whom are recent law school graduates. Occasionally, these attorneys apply for paralegal jobs. An article in the *American Bar Association Journal*, taking note of the plight of unemployed attorneys, was entitled *Post–Law School Job May Be as Paralegal*.[5] Some law firms are willing to hire a desperate attorney at a paralegal's salary because the firm can charge clients a higher billing rate for an attorney's time than for a paralegal's time. Most law firms, however, think it is unwise to hire an attorney for a paralegal's position. The two fields are separate employment categories, and the firms know that the attorneys are not interested in careers as paralegals. Yet there will continue to be attorneys available for paralegal positions and law firms willing to hire them, particularly when the firms need temporary legal help.

There is a small category of attorneys who *frequently* seek work as paralegals. An attorney who has been disbarred or suspended from the practice of law may try to continue working in a law office by taking a job as a paralegal until he or she can reapply for full admission. Such work is highly controversial because of the temptation to go beyond paralegal work and continue to practice law. Consequently, some states forbid disbarred or suspended attorneys from working as paralegals. In other states, however, it is allowed with restrictions, as we will see in chapter 5.

2. SELF-EMPLOYED INDIVIDUALS WORKING FOR ATTORNEYS

Independent contractors who sell their services to attorneys perform many different kinds of tasks. For example, they might draft an estate tax return for a probate attorney or digest (i.e., summarize) pretrial documents for a litigation attorney. Some work out of a home office or in office space that they rent. Others do their work in the law offices of the attorneys for whom they work. (See Exhibit 2.2 in chapter 2 for the Internet site of an independent paralegal and appendix J on setting up an independent business.) An independent contractor might work primarily for one law firm, although most work for different firms around town. Even though independent contractors are not employees, the attorneys who use their services are still obligated to supervise what they do. (In chapter 5, we will study the ethical problem that can arise because of the difficulty of supervising a nonemployee. In addition, we will cover the conflict-of-interest danger that can exist when an independent contractor works for more than one attorney.) There is no uniform title that these self-employed individuals use. Here are the most common:

independent paralegal	contract paralegal
freelance paralegal	legal technician
freelance legal assistant	

transactional paralegal One who provides paralegal services for an attorney who represents clients in transactions such as entering contracts, incorporating a business, closing a real estate sale, or planning an estate.

listserv A program that manages computer mailing lists automatically, including the receipt and distribution of messages from and to members of the list. (Listservs are discussed in chapter 13.)

independent paralegal An independent contractor (1) who sells his or her paralegal services to, and works under the supervision of, one or more attorneys; or (2) who sells his or her paralegal services directly to the public without attorney supervision. Note, however, that in some states, the *paralegal* and *legal assistant* titles are limited to those who work under attorney supervision (see the next section).

3. SELF-EMPLOYED INDIVIDUALS SERVING THE PUBLIC

Finally, we examine those independent contractors who sell their services directly to the public. They do not work for (and are not supervised by) attorneys. They may have special authorization to provide limited services, as when a statute allows them to assist clients in Social Security cases.

Here are the most common titles these independent contractors use:

independent paralegal	paralegal
contract paralegal	legal technician

To find out what titles they use in your area, check the Yellow Pages under entries such as *paralegal*, *legal*, *divorce*, and *bankruptcy*. In the main, independent paralegals have been unregulated. In most states, anyone can start advertising himself or herself as a paralegal.

Controversy over these paralegals has come from three main sources. First, a few of their disgruntled clients have filed complaints against them that have resulted in state prosecution for the **unauthorized practice of law (UPL)**. Second, the organized bar has instigated similar UPL charges on the ground that the public needs protection from independent paralegals, particularly those who lack formal training. The bar also complains that the public might be confused into thinking that anyone called a paralegal works for an attorney. An unstated reason for opposition from the bar is the unwelcome competition that independent paralegals give to some practicing attorneys. Third, a significant number of traditional paralegals resent the use of the paralegal title by independent contractors who work directly for the public. Most traditional paralegals have been through a rigorous training program and are subject to close attorney supervision on the job. These traditional paralegals resent anyone being able to use the paralegal title without similar training and supervision.

In most states, this formidable opposition from those three sources has *not* put independent paralegals out of business. In fact, their numbers are growing. Yet a few states have imposed increased regulation on them. In California, for example, independent contractors cannot call themselves paralegals or legal assistants unless they work under attorney supervision. If a California attorney is not responsible for their work, they must call themselves *legal document assistants (LDAs)*. If they provide landlord-tenant help, they must be called *unlawful detainer assistants (UDAs)*. In Arizona, nonattorneys who help citizens with legal documents are called *certified legal document preparers (CLDPs)*. At the federal level, even greater restrictions have been placed on individuals who provide bankruptcy assistance. In every state, they must be called *bankruptcy petition preparers (BPPs)*. Later, in chapters 4 and 5, we will more closely examine the controversy generated by these independent contractors.

> **unauthorized practice of law (UPL)** Conduct by a person who does not have a license to practice law or other special authorization needed for that conduct.

[SECTION E]

DEFINITIONS OF A PARALEGAL

Different definitions of a paralegal exist, although there is substantial similarity among them. Definitions have been written by:

- State legislatures and state courts
- State bar associations
- Local bar associations
- The American Bar Association
- The national paralegal associations: NFPA and NALA
- Local paralegal associations

By far the most important definitions are those written by state legislatures and courts. Not every state has definitions written by their legislature or courts, but the number of states that have them is steadily growing. If the legislature or courts in your state have not adopted a definition, your state or local bar association probably has. You need to find out as soon as possible whether the legislature, courts, or bar association in your state has adopted a definition. (See your state in appendix E, which collects many definitions from across the country.) The definitions proposed by the American Bar Association and by paralegal associations have been influential, but they are not controlling if the legislature, court, or bar association in your state uses its own definition.

Here is an example of a definition enacted by a state legislature—the Illinois State Legislature. This definition is typical of the definitions used in many states:

> "Paralegal" means a person who is qualified through education, training, or work experience and is employed by a lawyer, law office, governmental agency, or other entity to work under the

direction of an attorney in a capacity that involves the performance of substantive legal work that usually requires a sufficient knowledge of legal concepts and would be performed by the attorney in the absence of the paralegal. 5 Illinois Compiled Statutes Annotated § 70/1.35 (2001).

In these definitions, the term *paralegal* usually includes the term *legal assistant*. In addition, the definitions are usually interpreted to include independent contractors who sell their services to attorneys.

Here are the characteristics that are common to definitions in many states. A paralegal:

- Has special qualifications due to education, training, or on-the-job experience
- Works under attorney supervision
- Performs **substantive legal work** that the attorney would have to perform if the paralegal was not present (*substantive work* refers to nonclerical tasks that require legal experience or training and for which paralegal fees—see discussion below—can be awarded)

substantive legal work
Nonclerical tasks that require legal experience or training; tasks that justify an award of paralegal fees. (See also NFPA's definition of *substantive* in Exhibit 1.2.)

On the last point, suppose that the attorney could not delegate the task to a secretary because it was beyond the skill level of all the secretaries in the office. Hence the attorney would have to perform it. A paralegal task, therefore, was one that the attorney would have to perform because there was no one else who could perform it.

What about independent contractors who sell their services directly to the public? Some states specifically include them in their definition. For example, note the last clause in the following definition adopted by the Montana State Legislature:

> "Paralegal" or "legal assistant" means a person qualified through education, training, or work experience to perform substantive legal work that requires knowledge of legal concepts and that is customarily but not exclusively performed by a lawyer and who may be retained or employed by one or more lawyers, law offices, governmental agencies, or other entities *or who may be authorized by administrative, statutory, or court authority to perform this work*. Montana Code Annotated § 37-60-101 (12) (2000) (emphasis added).

The clause in italics at the end of the definition covers those paralegals who are not supervised by attorneys but who have special authority to provide limited legal assistance to the public (see chapter 4).

As we have seen, a few states such as California limit the title of *paralegal* (or *legal assistant*) to individuals who work under attorney supervision. Those who provide assistance directly to the public must call themselves something else in these states.

The American Bar Association and the national paralegal associations have recommended definitions of a paralegal. Some of these definitions have been adopted, with or without modification, by state legislatures, state courts, and state bar associations. (See Exhibit 1.2.)

EXHIBIT 1.2   Definitions Recommended by the American Bar Association and National Paralegal Associations

American Bar Association (ABA)
A legal assistant or paralegal is a person qualified by education, training, or work experience who is employed or retained by a lawyer, law office, corporation, governmental agency, or other entity and who performs specifically delegated substantive legal work for which a lawyer is responsible. (www.abaparalegals.org)

National paralegal associations that have adopted the definition of the American Bar Association:
National Association of Legal Assistants (NALA) (www.nala.org)
NALS the Association for Legal Professionals (www.nals.org)

National Federation of Paralegal Associations (NFPA)
A paralegal is a person qualified through education, training, or work experience to perform substantive legal work that requires knowledge of legal concepts and is customarily, but not exclusively, performed by a lawyer. This person may be retained or employed by a lawyer, law office, governmental agency, or other entity or may be authorized by administrative, statutory, or court authority to perform this work. *Substantive* shall mean work requiring recognition, evaluation, organization, analysis, and communication of relevant facts and legal concepts (www.paralegals.org).

American Alliance of Paralegals, Inc. (AAPI)
A paralegal is a person qualified by education, training, or work experience who performs specifically delegated substantive legal work for which a lawyer is ultimately responsible or who is authorized by administrative, statutory, or court authority to perform substantive legal work (www.aapipara.org/Positionstatements.htm).

[SECTION F]

PARALEGAL FEES

The most common kinds of fees that attorneys charge are hourly fees and contingent fees. Hourly fees (which can differ dramatically from attorney to attorney) are determined, in the main, by how much time is spent on a client's case. In general, hourly attorney fees are due regardless of whether the client wins or loses. (In chapters 8 and 14, we will examine variations on this kind of fee.) A **contingent fee** is dependent on obtaining a favorable outcome of the case. For example, in a personal injury (PI) case, the client may agree to pay one-third of whatever the attorney wins from a court judgment or settlement; no attorney fees are paid if the client recovers nothing. (Special costs such as filing fees and witness fees, however, are usually paid by the client in both hourly fee and contingent fee cases, regardless of the outcome.)

When a law office charges by the hour, clients pay for attorney time *and for paralegal time*. The work of a paralegal can be separately charged to the client. These charges are called **paralegal fees**. (Of course, paralegals themselves do not charge or receive these fees; the fees are paid to the law office that employs the paralegals.) In most cases, paralegal work is not considered part of **overhead**, which includes the cost of insurance, utilities, clerical staff, and other everyday needs of a business. With few exceptions, a client who hires a law firm is not separately charged for overhead such as for the secretary's time in typing a client letter or the portion of the electricity the firm uses when it helps the client. Paralegals are not clerical employees and, therefore, with relatively few exceptions, paralegals are not considered to be part of overhead.

We follow the **American rule** on the payment of fees. Under this rule, clients pay their own attorney fees and costs of litigation. Under the **English rule** (also called *loser pays*), the party who loses the litigation pays the winner's attorney fees and costs. There are, however, three important exceptions to the American rule. First, a special statute might authorize a court to order the loser to pay the winner's fees and costs. Second, the parties may have a prior contract between them that provides for such payment. Third, a court may order the payment because of bad faith committed by the loser in the litigation. (The process of forcing one party to pay another's attorney fees and litigation costs under these three exceptions is called **fee shifting**.)

Cases under the first exception on special statutes that order the loser to pay the winner's fees and costs are called **statutory fee cases**. Such statutes often involve antitrust law, environmental protection, and employment discrimination or other civil rights matters. The fees must be reasonable in light of the nature and complexity of the tasks for which the fees are sought. The method of calculating an award of attorney fees authorized by statute is called the **lodestar**. Under this method, the number of reasonable hours spent on the case is multiplied by a reasonable hourly rate. Other factors might also be considered above the lodestar in setting the fee, e.g., the quality of representation, any delay in receiving payment, and the risk at the outset of the litigation that the prevailing attorney will receive no fee.

Most of the special statutes include an award of the winner's *paralegal* fees along with or as part of the winner's attorney's fees. Paralegal fees in statutory fee cases can be substantial. Here, for example, are the total paralegal fees (calculated at $85 per hour) claimed by the winning side in a 1999 water distribution case:

Example of a Request for Paralegal Fees in a Large Statutory Fee Case			
Name of Paralegal	**Hrs.**	**Rate**	
Sonia Rosenberg	935	$85	$ 79,475
Ronald Horne	614.2	$85	$ 52,207
Michael Gershon	88.9	$85	$ 7,556.50
Total hours claimed	1,638.1		$139,238.50[6]

One of the main reasons paralegalism has blossomed as a new profession is the ability of a law firm to collect paralegal fees from its own clients in most cases and from a losing opponent in special statutory fee cases. Care is needed, however, in exercising the right to receive paralegal fees. Although paralegals are not clerical employees, they sometimes perform clerical functions in the office. This is not unusual, since attorneys themselves perform clerical functions on occasion,

---

contingent fee A fee that is paid only if the case is successfully resolved by litigation or settlement. (The fee is also referred to as a *contingency*.)

paralegal fee A fee that an attorney can collect for the nonclerical work of his or her paralegal on a client case.

overhead The operating expenses of a business (e.g., office rent, furniture, insurance, and clerical staff) for which customers or clients are not charged a separate fee.

American rule The winning party cannot recover attorney fees and costs of litigation from the losing party unless (1) a statute authorizes such payment, (2) a contract between the parties provides for such payment, or (3) the court finds that the losing party acted in bad faith in the litigation.

English rule The losing side in litigation must pay the winner's attorney fees and costs.

fee shifting The process of forcing one party to pay another's attorney fees and costs in litigation.

statutory fee case A case applying a special statute that gives a judge authority to order the losing party to pay the winning party's attorney and paralegal fees.

lodestar A method of calculating an award of attorney fees authorized by statute. The number of reasonable hours spent on the case is multiplied by a reasonable hourly rate. Other factors might also be considered above the lodestar in setting the fee, e.g., the quality of representation, any delay in receiving payment, and the risk at the outset of the litigation that the prevailing attorney will receive no fee.

particularly when the office is shorthanded, facing a deadline, or trying to respond to a crisis in a client's case. When a paralegal performs a purely clerical task, such as filing letters in an office folder or ordering supplies for the copy machine, paralegal fees should not be charged. There is nothing wrong or unethical about a paralegal filing letters or ordering supplies. A good team player does whatever is needed at the time. When, however, paralegals perform such tasks, their boss should not be trying to collect paralegal fees for them. Furthermore, it *is* unethical for an attorney to claim that a paralegal performed paralegal work when in fact the paralegal was performing clerical work. (See chapter 5 on ethics.)

So, too, an attorney should not charge attorney rates for performing tasks that should have been delegated to someone else in the office, such as a paralegal. One court phrased the problem this way: "Routine tasks, if performed by senior partners in large firms, should not be billed at their usual rates. A Michelangelo should not charge Sistine Chapel rates for painting a farmer's barn."[7] In short, the dollar value of a task is not enhanced simply because an attorney performs it.[8] The same is true of tasks that paralegals perform. Numerous court opinions have been written in which judges reduce or disallow statutory fees for attorneys performing paralegal tasks and for paralegals performing secretarial or clerical tasks.

It is quite remarkable that law firms are being challenged in court for improperly delegating tasks among attorneys, paralegals, and secretaries in fee-dispute cases. Part of the difficulty is that the line between paralegal tasks and clerical tasks is not always easy to draw once we get beyond tasks that are obviously clerical.

What is a paralegal task? This question must be answered to avoid litigation over the collectability of paralegal fees, particularly in statutory fee cases. Paralegals perform a wide variety of tasks. (See "Paralegal Specialties" in chapter 2.) Which ones qualify for paralegal fees? The definitions of a paralegal that we discussed earlier are not always helpful in answering this question. In describing what paralegals do, most of the definitions use vague phrases such as "substantive legal work." What is meant by substantive? We said earlier that it consists of tasks that require legal experience or training. This definition helps separate out tasks that clearly do not fall into this category (e.g., photocopying a document). Yet the definition does not resolve all doubt, particularly when a task has clerical and nonclerical components. In statutory fee cases, in which an attorney asks for paralegal fees, the opponent often argues against the award of these fees on the grounds that much of what the paralegal did was secretarial work. To resolve such controversies, judges need more guidance than the distinction between substantive work and clerical work.

This need has led some states to create task-specific definitions of a paralegal. For example, notice the detail in the following definition enacted by the Florida State Legislature:

> "[L]egal assistant" means a person, who under the supervision and direction of a licensed attorney engages in legal research, and case development or planning in relation to modifications or initial proceedings, services, processes, or applications; or who prepares or interprets legal documents or selects, compiles, and uses technical information from references such as digests, encyclopedias, or practice manuals and analyzes and follows procedural problems that involve independent decisions. Florida Statutes Annotated § 57.104 (2001).

Here is another attempt at a definition, this one found in an Iowa administrative regulation governing juvenile delinquency cases. To achieve the same objective of identifying what activities qualify for paralegal fees, a state might focus on the specific tasks that qualify. For example, in Iowa juvenile delinquency cases, the Iowa Administrative Code specifies that "paralegal time" means:

> [T]ime spent preparing pleadings and motions, reviewing transcripts, performing legal research, interviewing witnesses in person, and attending staffings in juvenile cases. In Class A felony cases in which only one attorney is appointed, paralegal time may include time spent in court assisting the appointed attorney. Paralegal time does not include typing, scheduling, answering the telephone, talking on the telephone except when interviewing witnesses, or other clerical activities or activities that duplicate work performed by the appointed attorney. Iowa Administrative Code § 493–7.1 (13B, 815).

Regardless of which definition is used in a particular state or how the state reaches its definition, paralegals must keep detailed time sheets covering precisely what they did. Their supervising attorney may need to enter these time sheets into evidence in order to justify the award of paralegal fees in statutory fee cases. Furthermore, courts want to be convinced that attorneys are not using paralegals as an excuse for obtaining higher fees. Here is an example of what one court requires attorneys to demonstrate in their petition for paralegal fees:

The services of a qualified legal assistant may be included in an attorney fee award, and to fit into this category, (1) the services performed by the nonlawyer personnel must be legal in nature; (2) the performance of these services must be supervised by an attorney; (3) the qualifications of the person performing the services must be specified in the request for fees in sufficient detail to demonstrate that the person is qualified by virtue of education, training, or work experience to perform substantive legal work; (4) the nature of the services performed must be specified in the request for fees in order to allow the reviewing court to determine that the services performed were legal rather than clerical; (5) as with attorney time, the amount of time expended must be set forth and must be reasonable; and (6) the amount charged must reflect reasonable community standards for charges by that category of personnel.[9]

Before we leave the topic of paralegal fees and the definition of a paralegal, there is one other issue we need to discuss. In a statutory fee case, assume the court is convinced that the tasks performed by the paralegal are genuinely paralegal tasks for which an award of paralegal fees is justified. The questions then become, How much should be awarded? How much is a paralegal's time worth? Two possibilities exist:

- Prevailing market rate for paralegals: the market rate is the amount, on average, that law firms in the community charge their own clients for paralegal time (e.g., $90 per hour).
- Actual cost to the law firm: actual cost is the amount that a law firm must pay to keep its paralegal (e.g., $30 per hour to cover the paralegal's salary, fringe benefits, office space, and other overhead costs related to maintaining any employee).

Of course, the winning side in a statutory fee case will argue that it should receive the market rate for paralegal time, while the losing side wants an actual-cost standard. In 1989, the United States Supreme Court in the landmark case of *Missouri v. Jenkins* resolved the issue in favor of using market rates.

The *Jenkins* case involved a Missouri desegregation suit under § 1988 of a Civil Rights Attorney's Fees Awards Act. (This was a special statute of Congress that allowed fee shifting in civil rights cases.) The lower court awarded the winning party $40 an hour for paralegal time, which was the market rate for paralegals in the 1980s in the Kansas City area. On appeal, the losing party argued that it should pay no more than $15 an hour, which was the actual cost to the law firm of having a paralegal in the office. In addition to paralegal fees, the case concerned the award of fees for **law clerks**, who are students still in law school or law school graduates who have not yet passed the bar. Like paralegals, law clerks are nonattorneys. As you can see from the opinion, the Supreme Court rejected an actual-cost standard for these employees.

> law clerk An attorney's employee who is in law school studying to become an attorney or who has graduated from law school and is waiting to pass the bar examination. (See glossary for other definitions of *law clerk*.)

Missouri v. Jenkins

United States Supreme Court
491 U.S. 274, 109 S. Ct. 2463, 105 L. Ed. 2d 229 (1989)

Justice BRENNAN delivered the opinion of the Court.

This is the attorney's fee aftermath of major school desegregation litigation in Kansas City, Missouri. [One of the issues we need to resolve is] should the fee award compensate the work of paralegals and law clerks by applying the market rate for their work.

This litigation began in 1977 as a suit by the Kansas City Missouri School District (KCMSD), the school board, and the children of two school board members, against the State of Missouri and other defendants. The plaintiffs alleged that the State, surrounding school districts, and various federal agencies had caused and perpetuated a system of racial segregation in the schools of the Kansas City metropolitan area. They sought various desegregation remedies. . . . After lengthy proceedings, including a trial that lasted 7½ months during 1983 and 1984, the District Court found the State of Missouri and KCMSD liable. . . .

The plaintiff class has been represented, since 1979, by Kansas City lawyer Arthur Benson and, since 1982, by the NAACP Legal Defense and Educational Fund, Inc. (LDF). Benson and the LDF requested attorney's fees under the Civil Rights Attorney's

Fees Awards Act of 1976, 42 U.S.C. § 1988.* Benson and his associates had devoted 10,875 attorney hours to the litigation, as well as 8,108 hours of paralegal and law clerk time. . . . [T]he District Court awarded Benson a total of approximately $1.7 million and the LDF $2.3 million. [On appeal, the defendant now argues] that the District Court erred in compensating the work of law clerks and paralegals (hereinafter collectively "paralegals") at the market rates for their services, rather than at their cost to the attorney. While Missouri agrees that compensation for the cost of these personnel should be included in the fee award, it suggests that an hourly rate of $15—which it argued below corresponded to their salaries, benefits, and overhead—would be appropriate, rather than the market rates of $35 to $50. . . .

---
*Section 1988 provides in relevant part: "In any action or proceeding to enforce a provision of . . . the Civil Rights Act of 1964 [42 U.S.C. § 2000d], the court, in its discretion, may allow the prevailing party, other than the United States, a reasonable attorney's fee as part of the costs."

(continues)

Missouri v. Jenkins—continued

[T]o bill paralegal work at market rates . . . makes economic sense. By encouraging the use of lower cost paralegals rather than attorneys wherever possible, permitting market-rate billing of paralegal hours "encourages cost-effective delivery of legal services and, by reducing the spiraling cost of civil rights litigation, furthers the policies underlying civil rights statutes." *Cameo Convalescent Center, Inc. v. Senn*, 738 F.2d 836, 846 (CA7 1984).**

Such separate billing appears to be the practice in most communities today.*** In the present case, Missouri

concedes that "the local market typically bills separately for paralegal services," Transcript of Oral Argument 14, and the District Court found that the requested hourly rates of $35 for law clerks, $40 for paralegals, and $59 for recent law graduates were the prevailing rates for such services in the Kansas City area. . . . Under these circumstances, the court's decision to award separate compensation at these rates was fully in accord with § 1988 [of the Civil Rights Attorney's Fees Awards Act].

**It has frequently been recognized in the lower courts that paralegals are capable of carrying out many tasks, under the supervision of an attorney, that might otherwise be performed by a lawyer and billed at a higher rate. Such work might include, for example, factual investigation, including locating and interviewing witnesses; assistance with depositions, interrogatories, and document production; compilation of statistical and financial data; checking legal citations; and drafting correspondence. Much such work lies in a gray area of tasks that might appropriately be performed either by an attorney or a paralegal. To the extent that fee applicants under § 1988 are not permitted to bill for the work of paralegals at market rates, it would not be surprising to see a greater amount of such work performed by attorneys themselves, thus increasing the overall cost of litigation.

Of course, purely clerical or secretarial tasks should not be billed at a paralegal rate, regardless of who performs them. What the court in *Johnson v. Georgia Highway Express, Inc.*, 488 F.2d 714, 717 (CA5 1974), said in regard to the work of attorneys is applicable by analogy to paralegals: "It is appropriate to distinguish between legal work, in the strict sense, and investigation, clerical work, compilation of facts and statistics and other work which can often be accomplished by non-lawyers but which a lawyer may do because he has no other help available. Such non-legal work may command a lesser rate. Its dollar value is not enhanced just because a lawyer does it."

***Amicus National Association of Legal Assistants reports that 77 percent of 1,800 legal assistants responding to a survey of the association's membership stated that their law firms charged clients for paralegal work on an hourly billing basis. Brief for National Association of Legal Assistants as Amicus Curiae 11.

ASSIGNMENT 1.3

1. Justice William Brennan in *Missouri v. Jenkins* says that using a market rate for paralegals will help reduce the "spiraling cost of civil rights litigation." How can forcing a losing party to pay more for paralegals reduce the cost of litigation?
2. Examine the full text of *Missouri v. Jenkins* to determine why Chief Justice William Rehnquist filed a dissenting opinion on paralegal fees. If you do not have access to a library to examine the opinion on the shelf, read it online at Findlaw (www.findlaw.com/casecode/supreme.html). In Citation Search, type 491 in the first box and 274 in the second box so that it reads 491 US 274. Then click "get it."

Keep in mind that *Missouri v. Jenkins* is a federal case involving one federal statute—the Civil Rights Attorney's Fees Awards Act. The following categories of cases are *not* required to adopt the conclusion of *Jenkins*:

- Federal cases interpreting other federal statutes
- State cases interpreting state statutes

It is quite possible for a *state* court to refuse to award paralegal fees or, if it awards paralegal fees, to calculate them at actual cost rather than at the prevailing market rate. A state court, for example, could deny paralegal fees on the ground that paralegal costs are part of overhead. Nevertheless, *Missouri v. Jenkins* has been quite persuasive. The vast majority of federal and state courts have adopted its reasoning for allowing paralegal fees at market rates in statutory fee cases. This is the reason why *Missouri v. Jenkins* is a landmark case. Indeed, the *Jenkins* holding was reinforced in 2008 when the Supreme Court held in the *Richlin* case that paralegal fees were recoverable at market rates under a different federal fee-shifting statute (the Equal Access to Justice Act). In *Richlin*, everyone agreed that attorneys were to be compensated at market rates under the Act and that other expenses such as those involved in preparing exhibits were recoverable at cost. "Surely," announced the Court, "paralegals are more analogous to attorneys" than to other litigation expenses of this kind. (*Richlin Sec. Service Co. v. Chertoff*, 2008 WL 2229175.)

SUMMARY OF RULES ON PARALEGAL FEES

In all cases:

contemporaneous Existing or occurring in the same period of time; pertaining to records that are prepared on events as the events are occurring or shortly thereafter.

1. Paralegals must keep detailed records (e.g., time sheets) on the tasks they perform and the time spent performing them. (**Contemporaneous** record keeping is preferred over time records that are assembled long after the task is performed.)
2. Attorneys in private law firms can charge their own clients a separate fee for the nonclerical work of their paralegals.

3. The amount of time a paralegal takes to perform a task must be reasonable in light of the nature and complexity of the task.
4. The amount of the fee itself must be reasonable.

In statutory fee cases:

a. The loser can be required to pay the attorney and paralegal fees of the winner.
b. The attorney may be required to demonstrate the paralegal's qualifications (e.g., education and experience) for the fees requested.
c. Attorney fees cannot be awarded when an attorney performs paralegal tasks.
d. Paralegal fees cannot be awarded when a paralegal performs clerical tasks.
e. The amount of the fee is based on the prevailing market rate that attorneys in the legal community charge their clients for paralegal tasks. (This market-rate rule applies *if* a court adopts the rationale of *Missouri v. Jenkins*, as most courts have.)

[SECTION G]

CAREER LADDERS IN LARGE LAW OFFICES

There is no career ladder for paralegals working in a small law office that consists of several attorneys, a secretary, and a paralegal. In an office with more than three paralegals, career ladders are more likely to exist. One of the more experienced paralegals, for example, might become the paralegal coordinator or manager, with duties such as:

- Recruiting and screening candidates for paralegal positions
- Orienting new paralegals to office procedures
- Training paralegals to operate software used in the office
- Training paralegals to perform certain substantive tasks, such as digesting (i.e., summarizing) pretrial testimony
- Coordinating assignments of paralegals among the different attorneys in the office to help ensure that paralegals are given assignments they are able to perform and that they complete them on time

Many law offices in the country have fifty or more paralegals. As indicated earlier, paralegal managers have formed their own association, the International Paralegal Management Association (www.paralegalmanagement.org).

The more paralegals in an office, the greater the likelihood that a career ladder exists for them in that office. The structure of the ladder might be fairly simple. For example, Paralegal I might be the entry-level position; Paralegal II, the intermediate position; and Paralegal III, the senior or supervisory position. Not all offices with career ladders, however, use the same titles, as we have seen. (The Web sites of some large firms refer to their career ladders. For a list of Web sites of the largest law firms in the country, see appendix 2.A at the end of chapter 2.) Here are the career titles recommended by the International Paralegal Management Association:

- Paralegal Clerk [Legal Assistant Clerk]
  Performs clerical tasks such as numbering documents, labeling folders, filing, and completing other tasks that do not require substantive knowledge or litigation skills; paralegal clerks may be supervised by paralegals.
- Paralegal [Legal Assistant]
  Performs factual research, document analysis, and cite checking; drafts pleadings; administers trusts and estates; and handles other substantive tasks that do not require a law degree.
- Senior Paralegal [Senior Legal Assistant]
  Supervises or trains other paralegals. May be a specialist in a particular area.
- Supervising Paralegal [Supervising Legal Assistant]
  Spends approximately half of his or her work time on cases as a paralegal and half of work time supervising other paralegals.
- Case Manager
  Coordinates or directs paralegals on large projects such as major litigation or corporate transaction.
- Paralegal Manager [Legal Assistant Manager, Paralegal Administrator, or Director of Paralegal Services]
  Recruits, interviews, and hires paralegals; helps train paralegals and monitors their assignments; and helps administer budget and billing requirements of all paralegals.[10]

The tendency of large law offices and departments is to design their own categories of titles and tiers for paralegals. Here, for example, is a seven-level career path of paralegals in the legal department of DuPont Corporation:

- Entry-level legal assistant (0–1 years of experience)
- Legal assistant (1–3 years of experience)
- Senior legal assistant, level one (4–7 years of experience)
- Senior legal assistant, level two (8–12 years of experience)
- Corporate legal assistant, level one (13+ years of experience)
- Corporate legal assistant, level two (20+ years of experience)
- Specialist (experience requirement depends on the specialty)[11]

[SECTION H]

PARALEGAL SALARIES

How much do paralegals make? Although some data are available to answer this question, there is no definitive answer because of the great variety of employment settings. Here are some relevant statistics for the years indicated:

- According to a 2008 survey by Robert Half Legal, a major legal staffing firm, the salary range for paralegals/case clerks with 0–2 years of experience was:
  - $29,000–37,250 in law firms with 75 or more attorneys
  - $28,750–36,000 in law firms with between 35 and 75 attorneys
  - $26,500–32,750 in law firms with between 10 and 35 attorneys
  - $24,250–30,750 in law firms with between 1 and 10 attorneys
  - $30,000–38,750 in corporate law offices[12]

- According to a 2006 survey by the National Federation of Paralegal Associations (NFPA):
  - The average current salary was a mean of $50,496 and a median of $49,000.
  - 25 percent earned $40,000 or below; 25 percent earned $60,000 or above.
  - One-third of paralegals received a bonus.
  - The average overall bonus was a mean of $2,994 and a median of $900.
  - The average overtime received was a mean of just over $5,000 and a median of $3,500.[13]

- According to a 2007 survey by International Paralegal Management Association (IPMA):
  - The median salary for paralegals was $53,500.
  - Annual bonuses were received by approximately 83 percent of paralegals working in law firms and 24 percent in corporate law departments.
  - The median annual bonus was $2,500.
  - The median overtime compensation was $4,177.
  - Total cash compensation nationally for paralegals was $59,973, up 9 percent from 2006.
  - Full-time paralegal managers of a paralegal program took home a median $102,000, plus an additional cash bonus of $8,500. Only 10 percent of paralegal managers received overtime compensation ($1,936). Total cash compensation in 2007 was $109,303, up 7.2 percent from the previous year.[14]

- According to 2006 data of the Bureau of Labor Statistics of the U.S. Department of Labor:
  - The median salary of paralegals was $43,040.
  - 25 percent of paralegals earned more than $54,700.
  - 10 percent of paralegals earned more than $67,500.
  - 25 percent of paralegals earned less than $33,900.
  - 10 percent of paralegals earned less than $27,500.[15]

- According to 2008 data by the National Association of Legal Assistants, the national average salary of paralegals was $50,953 with an average annual bonus of $3,808. On average, the paralegals surveyed had seventeen years of experience. Here is a further breakdown of average total compensation correlated with years of experience:
  - $38,960: 1–5 years of experience
  - $46,929: 6–10 years of experience
  - $51,580: 11–15 years of experience
  - $54,842: 16–20 years of experience
  - $53,473: 21–25 years of experience[16]

- According to 2006 data of the Bureau of Labor Statistics of the U.S. Department of Labor:
  - The median annual earnings of paralegals working for the federal government was $56,080.
  - The median annual earnings of paralegals working for a state government was $38,020; for those working for a local government, it was $42,170.[17]
- According to 2007 data reported by Salary.com:
  - The base salary range for the paralegal I position was $31,095 to $56,112.
  - The base salary range for the more advanced paralegal II position was $39,136 to $64,697.
  - The base salary range for the paralegal manager position was $56,477 to $116,338.[18]
- According to 2007 data reported by Legal Assistant Today (www.legalassistanttoday.com):
  - The national average salary for paralegals was $52,979 (a 3.7 percent increase over 2006)
  - Average salary of paralegals in law firms: $51,686
  - Average salary of paralegals in corporations: $61,764
  - Average salary of paralegals in government: $51,028
  - Highest full-time salary: $120,000
  - Lowest full-time salary: $18,000

Experienced paralegals do very well. If they have good résumés and have developed specialties that are in demand, they usually improve their financial picture significantly.

A number of other generalizations can be made about salaries across the country:

- Paralegals who work in the law departments of corporations, banks, insurance companies, and other businesses tend to make more than those who work in private law firms.
- Paralegals who work in large private law firms tend to make more than those who work in smaller private law firms.
- Paralegals who work in large metropolitan areas (over a million in population) tend to make more than those who work in rural areas.
- Paralegals who work in legal aid or legal service offices that are funded by government grants and charitable contributions to serve the poor tend to make less than most other paralegals.
- Paralegals who work for attorneys who understand the value of paralegals tend to make more than those working for attorneys who have a poor or weak understanding of what paralegals can do.
- Paralegals who work in an office where there is a career ladder for paralegals, plus periodic evaluations and salary reviews, tend to make more than those who work in offices without these options.
- Paralegals who are career oriented tend to make more than those less interested in a long-term commitment to paralegal work.

In addition to the payment of bonuses, other fringe benefits must be considered (e.g., vacation time, health insurance, and parking facilities). A comprehensive list of such benefits will be presented in chapter 2. (See Exhibit 2.14.)

One final point to keep in mind about salaries: once a person has gained training *and experience* as a paralegal, this background may be used to go into other law-related positions. For example, a corporate paralegal in a law firm might leave the firm to take a higher-paying position as a securities analyst for a corporation or an estates paralegal at a law firm might leave for a more lucrative position as a trust administrator at a bank. Perhaps the most dramatic example of a paralegal position being used as a stepping-stone for other jobs is the large number of former paralegals who have used their legal training and experience to run for political office, particularly at the city and county levels of government. An extensive list of these law-related jobs will be given at the end of chapter 2. (See Exhibit 2.17.)

[SECTION I]

FACTORS INFLUENCING THE GROWTH OF PARALEGALISM

In the late 1960s, most attorneys would draw a blank if you mentioned the words *paralegal* or *legal assistant*. According to Webster's *Ninth New Collegiate Dictionary*, the earliest recorded use of the word *paralegal* in English occurred in 1971. Today, the situation has changed radically. Most law offices either have paralegals or are seriously considering their employment. (A major exception to this trend is the one- or two-attorney office in which the only staff member is a secretary who often performs paralegal tasks.) Some surveys show that there is one paralegal for every four attorneys

EXHIBIT 1.3	Fastest-Growing Occupations 2004–2014		

| | Numbers Employed | | |
Occupation	2004	2014	Percent Increase (%)
Physician assistants	62,000	93,000	49.6
Dental hygienists	158,000	226,000	43.3
Forensic science technicians	10,000	13,000	36.4
Computer systems analysts	487,000	640,000	31.4
Paralegals/legal assistants	224,000	291,000	29.7

Source: U.S. Department of Labor, Bureau of Labor Statistics, Occupational Employment Projections to 2014 (November 2005) (www.bls.gov/opub/mlr/2007/11/art5full.pdf).

in law firms and one paralegal for every two attorneys in the law departments of corporations. It has been estimated that the number of paralegals may eventually exceed the number of attorneys in the practice of law. The U.S. Bureau of Labor Statistics has projected paralegal employment to grow 29.7 percent through the year 2014 (see Exhibit 1.3), making paralegals one of the fastest-growing occupations in the country.

What has caused this dramatic change? The following factors have been instrumental in bringing paralegalism to its present state of prominence:

1. The pressure of economics
2. The call for efficiency and delegation
3. The promotion by bar associations
4. The organization of paralegals

1. THE PRESSURE OF ECONOMICS

Perhaps the greatest incentive to employ paralegals has been arithmetic. Law firms simply add up what they earn without paralegals, add up what they could earn with paralegals, compare the two figures, and conclude that the employment of paralegals is profitable. There "can be little doubt that the principal motivation prompting law firms to hire legal assistants is the economic benefit enjoyed by the firm."[19] The key to increased profits is **leveraging**. Leverage, often expressed as a ratio, is the ability to make a profit from the income-generating work of others. The higher the ratio of paralegals to partners in the firm, the more profit to the partners or owners of the firm (assuming everyone is generating income from billable time). The same is true of associates in the firm. The higher the ratio of associates to partners, the greater the profit to the partners/owners.

In the best of all worlds, some of this increased profit will result in lower fees to the client. For example, Chief Justice Warren Burger felt that some attorneys charge "excessive fees for closing real-estate transactions for the purchase of a home. A greater part of that work can be handled by trained paralegals, and, in fact, many responsible law firms are doing just that to reduce costs for their clients."[20] If the state requires an attorney to be present at a closing, then, of course, the law would have to be changed to allow paralegals to do what Chief Justice Burger suggests. We will discuss such changes in chapter 4.

Exhibit 1.4 provides an example of the economic impact of using a paralegal. In the example, a client comes to a lawyer to form a corporation.[21] We will compare (a) the economics of an attorney and secretary working on the case, assuming a fee of $2,500; and (b) the economics of an attorney, secretary, *and* paralegal working on the same case, assuming a fee of $2,000. As you can see, with a paralegal added to the team, the firm's profit is increased about 16 percent in spite of the lower fee, and the attorney has more billable time to spend elsewhere. Some studies have claimed an even higher profit increase because of the effective use of paralegals.

The example assumes that the attorney's fee is $250 per hour and that the attorney billed the client $60 per hour for the paralegal's time. According to a recent survey:

- The average billing rate attorneys charged clients for paralegal time was:
  - $85 per hour in law firms with 2 to 5 attorneys
  - $90 per hour in law firms with 51 to 55 attorneys
  - $112 per hour in law firms with 96 to 100 attorneys

leveraging Making profit from the income-generating work of others.

EXHIBIT 1.4	The Profitability of Using Paralegals

TASK: TO FORM A CORPORATION

a. Attorney and Secretary

Function	Attorney Time	Secretary Time
1. Interviewing	1.0	1.0
2. Advising	1.0	0.0
3. Gathering information	1.0	0.0
4. Preparing papers	2.0	4.0
5. Executing and filing papers	1.0	1.0
	6.0	5.0

Assume that the attorney's hourly rate is $250 per hour and that the overhead cost of maintaining a secretary is $25 per hour.

Attorney (6 × $250)	$1,500
Secretary (5 × $25)	125
Total cost	$1,625

Fee	$2,500
Less cost	1,625
Gross profit	$ 875

b. Attorney, Secretary, *and* Paralegal

Function	Attorney Time	Paralegal Time	Secretary Time
1. Interviewing	0.5	0.5	0.0
2. Advising	1.0	0.0	0.0
3. Gathering information	0.0	1.0	0.0
4. Preparing papers	0.5	1.5	4.0
5. Executing and filing papers	0.5	0.5	1.0
	2.5	3.5	5.0

Assume a paralegal hourly rate of $60 per hour.

Attorney (2.5 × $250)	$625
Paralegal (3.5 × $60)	210
Secretary (5 × $25)	125
Total cost	$960

Fee	$2,000
Less cost	960
Gross profit	$1,040

COMPARISON

Fee:	a. Attorney and Secretary	$2,500
	b. Attorney, Secretary, and Paralegal	$2,000
Saving to client		$500
Increased profitability to attorney ($1,040 vs. $875)		$165

By using a paralegal on the case, the attorney's profit increases almost 19% over the profit realized without the paralegal, and the client can be charged a lower fee. Furthermore, the attorney has 3.5 hours that are now available to work on other cases, bringing in additional revenue of $875 (3.5 × the attorney's hourly rate of $250).

- On billable hours:
  - 50 percent of paralegals billed 36–40 hours per week.
  - 24 percent of paralegals billed 41–45 hours per week.
  - 4 percent of paralegals billed 26–30 hours per week.[22]

A study of thousands of paralegals at large law firms concluded that the average number of annual billable hours worked by all paralegal positions was 1,412.[23] (Later, in chapter 14, on law office management, we will further examine the implications of these statistics.) In many firms, paralegals are expected to turn in a minimum number of billable hours per week, month, or other designated period. This is known as a **billable hours quota** or billable hour goal.

When a law firm bills clients for paralegal time, the paralegal becomes a *profit center* in the firm. In such cases, paralegals are not simply part of the cost of doing business reflected in the firm's overhead. They generate revenue (and, therefore, profit) for the firm. To calculate the amount of profit, the **rule of three** is sometimes used as a general guideline. To be profitable, a paralegal must bill three times his or her salary. Of the total revenue brought in through paralegal billing, one-third is allocated to salary, one-third to overhead, and one-third to profit. Phrased another way, when the gross revenue generated through paralegal billing equals three times the paralegal's salary, the firm has achieved its minimum profit expectations.

billable hours quota A minimum number of hours expected from a timekeeper on client matters that can be charged (billed) to clients per week, month, year, or other time period.

rule of three A general guideline used by some law firms to identify budget expectations from hiring paralegals: gross revenue generated through paralegal billing should equal three times a paralegal's salary.

For example:

Paralegal's salary:	$32,000
Paralegal rate:	$80 per hour
Billings the firm hopes this paralegal will generate:	$96,000 ($32,000 × 3)
Rule-of-three allocation:	
—paralegal salary:	$32,000
—overhead for this paralegal:	$32,000
—profit to the law firm:	$32,000[24]

Some firms use a Rule of 3½, under which gross revenue generated through paralegal billing should equal three and a half times a paralegal's salary.

ASSIGNMENT 1.4

(a) In the example given in Exhibit 1.4, how many billable hours per year would this paralegal have to produce in order to generate $30,000 per year in profits for the firm? Is this number realistic? If not, what must be done?

(b) Assume that a paralegal seeks a salary of $25,000 a year and that the law firm would like to be able to pay this salary. Using the "rule of three," if this person is able to generate 1,400 billable hours per year, at what hourly rate must this paralegal's time be billed in order for the attorney and the paralegal to be happy?

Of course, the rule of three (or 3½) is not an absolute gauge for determining profit expectations from using paralegals. Other factors affect the profitability of paralegals to an office. A high turnover of paralegals in the office, for example, often means that the office will have substantially increased overhead costs in recruiting and orienting new paralegals. A recent survey concluded that "an 11%-to-25% annual attrition rate for paralegals is now the norm at a majority of law firms."[25] Another factor that can offset the rule of three is the extent to which attorneys have more billable time because of a paralegal's performance of nonbillable tasks. Some paralegals perform many tasks that cannot be billed to clients. Examples include recruiting new employees, helping to maintain the law library, organizing the office's closed case files, and doing most of the work on certain kinds of cases that an attorney would normally do for free (e.g., probating the estate of the attorney's brother-in-law). The more nonbillable tasks such as these that a paralegal performs, the less time he or she will have available to devote to billable tasks. This, however, does not mean that the paralegal is a drain on profits. A nonbillable task that a paralegal performs is often a task that the attorney, at least in part, does *not* have to perform. This, of course, enables the attorney to direct more of his or her efforts to fee-generating (i.e., billable) matters.

realization rate The hourly rate that a law office actually collects from the billable hours submitted by an attorney or paralegal.

Directly related to a paralegal's profitability is his or her **realization rate**. A law firm rarely collects 100 percent of every bill it sends to all its clients. Some clients simply refuse to pay, or they bargain down bills initially sent to them. The realization rate is the rate that a law office actually collects from the total amounts billed. If, for example, the office fails to collect 10 percent of all the bills sent out during a given period, its realization rate is 90 percent for that period. Attorneys and paralegals have realization rates based on the percentage of the amounts billed from their hours that were actually collected. Of course, a paralegal has no control over whether the office is able to collect every billable hour submitted. Yet many paralegals inquire about their current realization rate for their own information and possible use when discussing their value to the office, perhaps at bonus time.

2. THE CALL FOR EFFICIENCY AND DELEGATION

Attorneys are overtrained for many of the tasks that they once performed frequently in a traditional law firm. It eventually became clear that this was not the way to run an effcient office. The creation of the paralegal role was a major step toward reform. The results have been quite satisfactory, as evidenced by the following comments from attorneys who have hired paralegals:[26]

A competent legal assistant for several years has been effectively doing 25% to 35% of the actual work that I had been doing for many years prior to that time.

The results of our 3 attorney–3 paralegal system have been excellent. Our office's efficiency has been improved and our clients are receiving better service.

It has been our experience that clients now ask for the paralegal. Client calls to the attorneys have been reduced an estimated 75%.

In light of such comments, it is surprising that the legal profession took so long to recognize the need to create the position of paralegal. The following historical perspective presents an overview of how attorneys came to this conclusion.[27]

During the American colonial period, the general populace distrusted attorneys because many of them sided with King George III against the emerging independent nation. This is illustrated by the following 1770 census report sent back to the king about a county in New Hampshire:

> Your Royal Majesty, Grafton County consists of 1,212 square miles. It contains 6,489 souls most of whom are engaged in agriculture, but included in that number are 69 wheelwrights, 8 doctors, 29 blacksmiths, 87 preachers, and 90 students at a new college. There is not one lawyer, for which fact we take no personal credit but thank an Almighty and merciful God.[28]

Some colonies tolerated the existence of attorneys but established roadblocks to their practice. In 1641, for example, the Massachusetts Bay Colony prohibited freemen from hiring attorneys for a fee:

> "Every man that findeth himself unfit to plead his own cause in any court shall have libertie to employ any man against whom the court doth not except, to help him, Provided he gave him noe fee or reward for his pains."[29]

Furthermore, almost anyone could become an attorney without having to meet rigorous admission requirements.

Up until the nineteenth century, the attorney did not have assistants other than an occasional apprentice studying to be an attorney himself. The attorney basically worked alone. He carried "his office in his hat."[30] A very personal attachment and devotion to detail were considered to be part of the process of becoming an attorney and of operating a practice. In the early nineteenth century, George Wythe commented;

> It is only by drudgery that the exactness, accuracy and closeness of thought so necessary for a good lawyer are engendered.[31]

The same theme came from Abraham Lincoln in his famous *Notes for a Law Lecture*:

> If anyone . . . shall claim an exemption from the drudgery of the law, his case is a failure in advance.[32]

Attorneys would be somewhat reluctant to delegate tasks to someone working for them, according to this theory of legal education.

During this period, attorneys often placed a high premium on the personal relationship between attorney and client. As late as 1875, for example, Clarence Seward and his partners "would have none of the newfangled typewriters" because clients would "resent the lack of personal attention implied in typed letters."[33] The coming of the Industrial Revolution, however, brought the practice of law closer to industry and finance. Some law offices began to specialize. As attorneys assumed new responsibilities, the concern for organization and efficiency grew. To be sure, large numbers of attorneys continued to carry their law offices "in their hats" and to provide an essentially one-to-one service. Many law offices in the 1850s, however, took a different direction.

Machines created new jobs. The typewriter introduced the typist. Librarians, investigators, bookkeepers, office managers, accountants, tax and fiduciary specialists, and research assistants soon found their way into the large law office. Although nonattorneys were hired primarily to undertake clerical or administrative responsibilities, they were soon delegated more challenging roles. This can be seen in the following comments from a study of employees in a Midwestern law office:

> In addition, these women were given considerable responsibility in connection with their positions as secretary or head bookkeeper. The head bookkeeper acted as assistant secretary to the partner-secretary of certain charitable corporations the firm represented. In this capacity, she recorded minutes of director's meetings, issued proxy statements, [and] supervised the filing of tax returns for the organization.[34]

In this fashion, attorneys began delegating more and more nonclerical duties to their clerical staff. This was not always done in a planned manner. An employee might suddenly be performing dramatically new duties as emergencies arose on current cases and as new clients arrived in an already busy office. In such an environment, an attorney may not know what the employee is capable of doing until the employee does it. Despite its haphazard nature, the needs of the moment and OJT (on-the-job training) worked wonders for staff development.

By the 1960s, attorneys started to ask whether a new kind of employee should be created. Instead of expanding the duties of a secretary, why not give the expanded duties to a new category of employee—the paralegal? A number of studies were conducted to determine how receptive attorneys would be to this idea on a broad scale. The results were very encouraging. The conclusion soon became inevitable that attorneys can delegate many tasks to paralegals. Today, this theme has become a dominant principle of law office management. Many attorneys no longer ask, "Can I delegate?" Rather they ask, "Why *can't* this be delegated?" Or "How can the delegation be effectively managed?" It is a given that substantial delegation is a necessity.

This is not to say, however, that all attorneys immediately endorse the paralegal concept with enthusiasm. Some older attorneys are initially hesitant, as demonstrated by the following report on the hiring of legal assistants within the California Department of Health, Education, and Welfare (HEW):

> When the legal assistant program began in early 1977 in HEW, it was met with some skepticism, especially in offices in cities other than Sacramento. There was concern that the quality of the work might be diminished by legal assistants. However, team leaders and deputies are not only no longer skeptical, they are now enthusiastic supporters of the legal assistant program. The attorneys feel that the work product is at least as good, and more thorough, than that provided by attorneys, mainly because the legal assistants have developed an expertise in a narrow area of the law. . . . The legal assistants processed 152 cases in fiscal year 1977/78 and 175 cases in 1978/79. It was estimated that legal assistants are as efficient as attorneys in processing the preliminary phase of these cases. As a result, a legal assistant in this instance produces as many pleadings as a deputy attorney general would have produced in the same amount of time. For this reason the section has been able to provide a faster turnaround time for the client agencies.[35]

A call for more cost-effective methods of practicing law by the government came from the Council for Citizens against Government Waste (the "Grace Commission"), which recommended that the U.S. Department of Justice increase the ratio of paralegals to attorneys in order to achieve a savings of $13.4 million over three years. Soon thereafter, legislation was proposed in Congress to establish an Office of Paralegal Coordination and Activities in the Department of Justice to work toward the increased use of paralegals in the department.[36] Although Congress did not pass this proposal, the effort is typical of the momentum toward paralegal use throughout the practice of law.

3. THE PROMOTION BY BAR ASSOCIATIONS

The bar associations assumed a large role in the development of paralegals. This has given great visibility to the field. In 1968, the House of Delegates of the American Bar Association established a Special Committee on Lay Assistants for Lawyers (subsequently renamed the Standing Committee on Paralegals) and resolved:

> (1)   That the legal profession recognize that there are many tasks in serving client's needs which can be performed by a trained, non-lawyer assistant working under the direction and supervision of a lawyer; [and]
> (2)   That the profession encourage the training and employment of such assistants.[37]

Most of the state bar associations now have committees that cover the area of paralegal utilization. Many of these committees have established guidelines for the use of paralegals in a law office. (For developments in your state, see appendix E.) Some bar associations, including the American Bar Association, have allowed paralegals to become associate members of their association. The real impact on the growth of paralegalism, however, has come from those bar association committees that deal with legal economics and law office management. Such committees have sponsored numerous conferences for practicing attorneys. These conferences, plus articles in bar association journals, have extensively promoted paralegals.

Although the role of bar associations in the development of paralegalism has been and continues to be of critical importance, their involvement has not been without controversy. At one time, some argued that the organized bar had a conflict of interest in regulating paralegals in light of the profit motive attorneys have in using paralegals. (The concern was that occupation A could not have the best interests of occupation B in mind if occupation A had a profit objective in regulating occupation B). Today, however, this concern is rarely raised.

4. THE ORGANIZATION OF PARALEGALS

Paralegals have been organizing. There are approximately 200 paralegal organizations throughout the country. (See the list in appendix B.) This has greatly helped raise everyone's consciousness about the potential of paralegalism. We will be examining the work, impact, and value of these associations in the next several chapters. It is no longer true that attorneys are the sole organized voice speaking for paralegals and shaping the development of the field.

NOTE ON ROLES FOR NONATTORNEYS IN THE DELIVERY OF LEGAL SERVICES IN OTHER COUNTRIES

England

The English legal profession has two main branches, consisting of solicitors and barristers. The *solicitor* handles the day-to-day legal problems of the public but has only limited rights to represent clients in certain lower courts. The bulk of litigation in the higher courts is conducted by the *barrister*. When representation in such courts is needed, the solicitor arranges for the barrister to enter the case. Solicitors often employ one or more *legal executives*, who for many years had been considered the equivalent of the American paralegal. Legal executives undergo extensive training and take rigorous examinations at the Institute of Legal Executives (ILE). Over the years, their roles have been expanded to the extent that legal executives are now referred to as *lawyers*—"the third branch of the legal profession alongside solicitors and barristers." They do not, however, have independent practice rights; they must still operate under the supervision of solicitors (www.ilex .org.uk). Recently, the term *paralegal* has become common in England. English paralegals work under the supervision of barristers, solicitors, or legal executives. The ILE has created the Institute for Legal Executives Paralegal Programmes to conduct paralegal training. Paralegals are encouraged to take this training and to view it as an "opportunity to transfer to the Legal Executive route to become a qualified lawyer" (www.ilexpp.co.uk).

Canada

The Canadian Association of Paralegals says that the definition of a paralegal may vary slightly from province to province, but that "in most provinces paralegals (who may also be called law clerks, legal assistants, legal technicians, technical clerks, etc., depending on the province in which they work and on the designations in use by individual employers) are professionals who are qualified by virtue of education, training and experience to engage in substantive legal work including managerial or administrative duties, working independently but under the ultimate direction of a lawyer. The work performed by paralegals is generally of a nature that requires sufficient knowledge of legal concepts such that, in the absence of a paralegal, a lawyer would perform those duties. Paralegals are not permitted to represent themselves to the public as lawyers."[38] The government of Canada has an official description of paralegals and what it calls the "related occupations" of notaries public, trade mark agents, and independent paralegals: "Legal assistants and paralegals in law firms assist lawyers by preparing legal documents, maintaining records and files and conducting research. Notaries public prepare promissory notes, wills, mortgages and other legal documents. Trade mark agents research and prepare trade mark applications. Legal assistants, paralegals, notaries public and trade mark agents are employed by law firms and in legal departments throughout the public and private sectors. . . . Independent paralegals provide certain legal services to the public, as allowed by provincial legislation, and are usually self-employed."[39]

Japan

Attorneys (*bengoshi*) are not the only providers of legal services in Japan. A separate category of workers called *judicial scriveners* (*shiho shoshi*) has special authority to assist the public in preparing legal documents such as contracts and deeds. The granting of this authority is conditioned on the successful completion of an examination (en.wikipedia.org/wiki/Judicial_scrivener).

Cuba

In Cuba, legal assistants work with attorneys in law offices or collectives called *bufetes*. The assistants draft legal documents, interview clients, conduct legal research, file papers in court, negotiate for trial dates, etc.

Russia

Attorneys-at-law in Russia are organized in lawyers' colleges. Membership in the colleges is granted to three kinds of individuals: first, graduates from university law schools; second, individuals with legal training of six months or more, experience in judicial work, or at least one year as a judge, governmental attorney, investigator, or legal counsel; and third, persons without legal training but with at least three years' experience. There are also nonlawyer notaries who prepare contracts and wills for the public.

Finland

In Finland, only members of the Finnish Bar Association can use the title of advocate. Advocates, however, do not enjoy an exclusive right of audience in the courts. Litigants can plead their own case or retain a representative who does not have to be an advocate.

Germany

The main providers of legal services in Germany are the lawyer (*Rechtsanwalt*) and the notary (*Notar*). The notary drafts contracts, wills, and other legal documents. "A third type of individual providing legal services is the *Rechtsberater*, which means 'legal assistant.' " While *Rechtsberaters* often operate like American paralegals, they are "also permitted under German law to operate independently of attorney supervision. *Rechtsberaters* can open their own offices and provide legal services to the public in a limited range of areas. . . . This includes small claims matters, no-contest domestic matters, etc." A *Rechtsberater* must pass a licensing exam and maintain liability insurance.[40]

Egypt

In Egypt, there is a nonattorney who sells legal services directly to the public. He is called *ard haal-gy*, which roughly means someone who explains the situation. He sits outside the courts with his briefcase. Clients flock to the *ard haal-gy* for help with their court cases. He provides this help by drafting complaints, writs, and other legal documents that do not require the signature of an attorney. *Ard haal-gy* do not have formal liberal arts or legal training. But they are masters of the Egyptian language, largely because of their study of the Koran. Many are present or former sheiks who can recite up to a third of the Koran from memory. This gives them excellent skills in writing and speaking, which they use in drafting legal documents. They charge relatively modest fees, around $1.50 to $3.00 per case, and can earn up to $400 a month, a large sum considering their low overhead. Many *ard haal-gy* have their own assistants who help them handle cases. *Ard haal-gy* are probably practicing law illegally, but they are so entrenched by tradition and custom that no one challenges them.

Other Countries

Australia
Law clerk (legal executive, paralegal)
www.myfuture.edu.au
(In Search, type "paralegal"s)

Scotland
Paralegals
www.scottish-paralegal.org.uk

Sierra Leone
www.yale.edu/yjil/PDFs/vol_31/Maru.pdf

South Africa
www.paralegaladvice.org.za/docs/
chap15/06.html

Switzerland
Paralegals
www.swissparalegal.org

[SECTION J]

"OH, YOU'RE STUDYING LAW?"

"Can the landlord put my furniture out on the curb?" "What happens if I refuse to cosign the note?" Once your friends and relatives find out that you are studying law, you will probably start receiving legal questions such as these. Later, in chapters 4 and 5, we will examine legal advice in some detail. You need to be very careful to avoid giving such advice. You do not want to begin your legal career with a charge of engaging in the unauthorized practice of law. Politely refuse to answer all questions that seek to find out how the law applies to particular fact situations. Even if you know the answer, the proper response is "That's something an attorney would have to look into."

[SECTION K]

CONCLUSION

As we will learn in subsequent chapters, there have been some dramatic developments in paralegalism in recent years, beginning in 2000, when California inaugurated a major program of paralegal regulation. This has prompted many other states to consider their own version of regulation. Change is clearly in the air.

In a recent keynote address, Robert Stein, executive director of the American Bar Association, said that the four most important areas affecting the practice of law in the future were diversity, globalization, electronic contracts, and the growth of paralegals. "The paralegal profession," he said, "is undergoing a remarkable transformation as the value of a well trained paralegal is recognized by more and more law firms, corporations and governments as a means of providing cost effective services in an era of rising expenses and complex litigation."[41] These are some of the themes we will be exploring as you now begin the journey of becoming a "well trained paralegal."

ASSIGNMENT 1.5

Assume that you are going to speak before a group of high school seniors on career day at the high school. You will give a presentation on paralegals. Write out your presentation. Assume that your audience knows very little about the law and almost nothing about the practice of law. Be sure to avoid using any legal terms that you do not define. You want to give your audience enough information about the paralegal to help them decide whether to consider such a career for themselves.

Chapter Summary

The law has a wide-ranging impact on our society. Precision and attention to detail are critical attributes of anyone working in the law. Among the most important organizations in paralegalism are the National Federation of Paralegal Associations (NFPA), the National Association of Legal Assistants (NALA), the American Bar Association (ABA), your state bar association, and your local paralegal association. The titles *paralegal* and *legal assistant* are synonymous, although as more and more legal secretaries assume the title of legal assistant, many in the field prefer the title of paralegal. While some states have laws that restrict the use of specific titles, most states do not. Paralegals are either employees of attorneys (traditional paralegals) or independent contractors who sell their services to attorneys or who have authorization to sell limited services directly to the public.

Independent contractors who work without attorney supervision are sometimes charged with the unauthorized practice of law. They must call themselves bankruptcy petition preparers if they work in bankruptcy. In California, other independents must be called legal document assistants or unlawful detainer assistants. A few other states have similar restrictions and limit the use of the titles *paralegal* and *legal assistant* to those who work under attorney supervision.

Definitions of a paralegal have been written by legislatures, courts, bar associations, and paralegal associations. The most common characteristics of the definitions are that the paralegal has special qualifications due to education, training, or on-the-job experience; works under attorney supervision; and performs substantive (i.e., nonclerical) legal work that the attorney would have to perform if the paralegal was not present. The most important definitions are those written by the legislatures and courts.

In most states, attorneys can charge their clients paralegal fees in addition to fees for attorney time. In statutory fee cases, the losing side in litigation can be forced to pay the attorney fees of the winning side. These fees can include separate fees for paralegal tasks. Under the landmark civil rights case of *Missouri v. Jenkins* (which has been followed by many state courts and by many federal courts in non–civil right cases), paralegal fees are determined by market rate. The court must decide which paralegal tasks qualify for an award of paralegal fees in statutory fee cases. To make this decision, the court may need a more precise definition of a paralegal. This need has led to the creation of task-specific definitions of a paralegal. Paralegals must keep detailed time sheets that indicate what tasks they performed. Career ladders for paralegals exist mainly in law offices with four or more paralegals.

Paralegal salaries are influenced by a number of factors: experience, education, level of responsibility, kind of employer, geographic area, the employer's understanding of the paralegal's role, and the extent to which the paralegal is committed to the field as a career. One rough measure of paralegal profitability to a firm is the rule of three. This guideline states that gross revenue generated through paralegal billing should equal three times a paralegal's salary.

Bar associations and paralegal associations have promoted the value of paralegals extensively. The economic impact they have had on the practice of law is the major reason the paralegal field has flourished and grown so rapidly. In a properly leveraged firm, paralegals can be a "profit center" without any sacrifice in the quality of the service delivered by the firm. Also, a paralegal can help attorneys redirect some of their energies from nonbillable to billable tasks.

Key Terms

continuing legal education (CLE)	independent paralegal	overhead	law clerk
traditional paralegal	unauthorized practice of law (UPL)	American rule	contemporaneous
independent contractor		English rule	leveraging
PI	substantive legal work	fee shifting	billable hours quota
transactional paralegal	contingent fee	statutory fee case	rule of three
listserv	paralegal fee	lodestar	realization rate

Review Questions

1. Approximately how many Americans have legal problems?
2. What are the five major institutional players in the development of paralegalism?
3. What are some of the major differences between NFPA and NALA?
4. How have bar associations affected the development of paralegalism?
5. Name fourteen categories of paralegal associations.
6. Describe the debate over whether there is a difference between a paralegal and legal assistant.
7. What is the distinction between traditional paralegals and paralegals who are independent contractors?
8. What are some of the major titles that employers use for traditional paralegals?
9. Distinguish between a generic and a specific title of a paralegal.
10. What are nurse paralegals and legal nurse consultants?
11. What is a transactional paralegal?
12. What is a hybrid title? Give some examples.
13. What are some of the main titles used by self-employed paralegals (1) who do work for attorneys and (2) who sell their services directly to the public?
14. What are the three sources of opposition to those who sell their services directly to the public?
15. State two meanings of the title *independent paralegal*.
16. What is the unauthorized practice of law?
17. What six entities have written paralegal definitions? Which are the most important?
18. What three characteristics are common to most paralegal definitions?
19. What is substantive legal work?
20. Distinguish between an hourly fee and a contingent fee.
21. What is meant by paralegal fees?
22. What is overhead?
23. Distinguish between the American rule and the English rule.
24. What is fee shifting?
25. What is a statutory fee case?
26. What challenge is sometimes made against attorneys who fail to delegate tasks to paralegals?
27. What tasks qualify for paralegal fees in statutory fee cases? What tasks do not qualify?
28. What was decided in *Missouri v. Jenkins*? Why is this a landmark case?
29. What is a law clerk?
30. What are contemporaneous records?
31. What are the duties of a paralegal coordinator or manager?
32. What factors determine paralegal salaries?
33. Name four major factors that have been instrumental in the emergence of paralegalism to its present state of prominence.
34. What is meant by leveraging?
35. What is a billable hours quota?
36. What is the rule of three?
37. What is a realization rate?
38. What factors, other than paralegal fees, affect the profitability of using paralegals in an office?
39. Give examples of a paralegal's nonbillable tasks.
40. What kinds of bar committees cover paralegals?

Helpful Web Sites: More on the New Career in Law

Definitions of a Paralegal
- www.nala.org/terms.htm
- www.paralegals.org

Paralegal Fees
- www.paralegals.org/displaycommon. cfm?an=1&subarticlenbr=368
- www.caparalegal.org/fees.html

Overview of Paralegal Development and Roles
- www.nala.org/whatis.htm
- www.legalassistanttoday.com/profession

Occupational Outlook Handbook (Paralegals and Legal Assistants)
- www.bls.gov/oco
- www.bls.gov/oco/ocos114.htm

Occupational Information Network (Paralegals and Legal Assistants)
- www.onetcodeconnector.org/ccreport/23–2011.00

American Bar Association Guidelines for the Utilization of Paralegal Services
- www.abanet.org/legalservices/paralegals/downloads/ modelguidelines.pdf

Video on Paralegals
- www.acinet.org/acinet/videos_by_occupation.asp?id=27 (Under Paralegals and Legal Assistants, click view.)

Paralegals According to Wikipedia
- en.wikipedia.org/wiki/paralegal

Paralegal Salaries
- salary.com
- www.payscale.com
- hotjobs.yahoo.com/salary
- promotions.monster.com/salary
- www.infirmation.com/shared/insider/payscale.tcl

Lawyers in Other Countries
- www.worldlii.org/catalog/3016.html

Google Searches (run the following searches for more sites)

- paralegal career
- paralegal occupation
- (Name of your state) paralegal

- paralegal salary
- Missouri Jenkins paralegal
- "paralegal fees"

Endnotes

1. Gary Lockwood, *Seeking Cover in the Age of Litigation*, 9 Business Lawyer Today 10 (September/October 2001).

2. American Bar Association, *Findings of the Comprehensive Legal Needs Study* (1994).

3. Fulbright & Jaworski, *Litigation Trends Survey* (2005) (www.fulbright.com).

3a. Michael Acker, *Three Incumbents Run Unopposed in So. River*, Sentinel (ebs.gmnews.com/news/2006/0413/Schools/037.html) (visited June 5, 2007).

4. See Jane Cracroft, *Developing Effective Witnesses*, The Legal Investigator, 7 (August 1991).

5. H. Samborn, *Post-Law School Job May Be as Paralegal*, 81 American Bar Association Journal 14 (March 1995).

6. *Rural Water System No. 1 v. City of Sioux Center, Iowa*, 38 F. Supp. 2d 1057, 1061 (N.D. Iowa 1999).

7. *Ursic v. Bethlehem Mines*, 719 F.2d 670, 677 (3d Cir. 1983).

8. *Johnson v. Georgia Highway Express, Inc.*, 488 F.2d 714, 717 (5th Cir. 1974).

9. *North Coast Elec. Co. v. Selig*, 151 P.3d 211, 215 (Wash. App. Div. 1, 2007)

10. Ernst & Young, *Legal Assistant Managers and Legal Assistants* 388 (3d ed. 1989).

11. Arthur Greene & Therese Cannon, *Paralegals, Profitability, and the Future of Your Law Practice* 48 American Bar Association, 2003.

12. Robert Half Legal, *2008 Salary Guide* 13, 15 (2008) (www.roberthalflegal.com) (800–870–8367).

13. National Federation of Paralegal Associations, *2006 Compensation & Benefits Study Report* (September 2006) (www.paralegals.org/associations/2270/files/NFPA_Salary_Survey_Executive_Summary_06_v2.pdf).

14. International Paralegal Management Association, *2007 Annual Compensation Survey for Paralegals/Legal Assistants and Managers* (www.paralegalmanagement.org) (www.altmanweil.com) (www.altmanweil.com/ParalegalComp).

15. Bureau of Labor Statistics, *Occupational Employment Survey*; America's Career InfoNet, a component of CareerOneStop (www.acinet.org).

16. NALA, *2008 National Utilization and Compensation Survey Report*, tbl. 4.2 (2008).

17. Bureau of Labor Statistics, U.S. Department of Labor, *Occupational Outlook Handbook*, 2008–09 ed. (www.bls.gov/oco/ocos114.htm).

18. www.salary.com (type "paralegal" in the Job Title search box).

19. Subcommittee on Legal Assistants, New York State Bar Association, *The Expanding Role of Legal Assistants in New York State* 7 (1982).

20. *U.S. News & World Report*, February 22, 1982, at 32.

21. Adapted from Jespersen, *Paralegals: Help or Hindrance?*, The Houston Lawyer 114–16 (March/April 1977).

22. NALA, *2004 National Utilization and Compensation Survey Report*, tbls. 3.3 & 3.7 (2004).

23. Supra note 16.

24. Adapted from State Bar of Texas, *Attorneys Guide to Practicing with Legal Assistants*, VI(3)(1986).

25. How LAMA Data Can Help You Retain Your Paralegals, in *IOMA's Report on Compensation and Benefits for Law Offices* 1 (April 2001).

26. Legal Assistants Committee, Oregon State Bar, *Legal Assistant Survey* (1977).

27. The research for this part of the section on the historical background of paralegalism was conducted by the author and subsequently used with his permission in *Expansion of the Lawyering Process through a New Delivery System: The Emergence and State of Paraprofessionalism*, 71 Columbia Law Review 1153, 1169ff (1971).

28. Thomas Brown, *President's Page*, 19 Virginia Bar Association Journal 2 (Winter 1993).

29. Body of Liberties, cited in Ralph Warner, *Independent Paralegal's Handbook* 8 (1986).

30. Lee, *Large Law Offices*, 57 American Law Review 788 (1923).

31. Lewis, ed., George Wythe, in *Great American Lawyers: A History of the Legal Profession in America* 55 (1907).

32. John Nicolay & John Hay, eds., Notes for a Law Lecture, in *Complete Works of Abraham Lincoln* 142 (1894). See also Paul Frank, *Lincoln as a Lawyer* 3 (1961).

33. Robert Swaine, *The Cravath Firm and Its Predecessors: 1819–1947* 365, 449 (1984).

34. Emily Dodge, *Evolution of a City Law Office*, 1955 Wisconsin Law Review 180, 187.

35. Management Analysis Section, California Department of Justice, *Study of Paralegal Utilization in the California Attorney General's Office* 23 (December 1980).

36. H.R. 5107, 99th Cong., 2d Sess. (1986). A Bill to Increase Government Economy and Efficiency Regarding the Increased Use of Paralegals.

37. *Proceedings of the House of Delegates of the American Bar Association*, 54 A.B.A.J. 1017, 1021 (1968).

38. Canadian Association of Paralegals (www.caplegal.ca), *Questions* (http://www.caplegal.ca/?p=faq&l=en&m=11).

39. Human Resources and Skills Development Canada, *Paralegal and Related Occupations* (www.jobfutures.ca/noc/4211.shtml).

40. Robert Loomis, *Practicing Law in Germany*, 11 WSPA Findings and Conclusions 6 (Washington State Paralegal Association, January 1995).

41. Robert Stein, *Practice of Law in the New Century* (American Bar Association 1999).

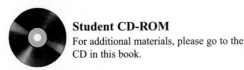

Student CD-ROM
For additional materials, please go to the CD in this book.

Online Companion™
For additional resources, please go to http://www.paralegal.delmar.cengage.com

Paralegal Employment

CHAPTER OUTLINE

[SECTION A]
THE JOB MARKET

The paralegal job market goes through cycles. (The same is true for attorneys.) There are periods when law offices are desperate for people to hire; at other times, offices are flooded with job applications. Don't be surprised if the job market on the day you begin your paralegal training program is not the same as the market on the day you graduate. Geography also plays an important role. In general, a large metropolitan area will present more employment prospects than rural areas simply because cities have more attorneys seeking paralegal help. In light of this reality, the safest course is to be prepared for competition when you begin to apply for employment. A central theme of this chapter, therefore, is the job-search strategy that will be needed in a market where there will be more applicants than available jobs.

It is important to make the distinction between jobs for entry-level paralegals and jobs for experienced paralegals. Almost always, your first job will be the toughest to obtain. A very large number of law offices are seeking paralegals with one, two, three, or more years of law office experience, often in a particular area of the law. Once you have proven your worth as a practicing paralegal, numerous opportunities open up to you, as we will see later in the chapter. Those looking for their first paralegal job may have a tougher time. Don't be discouraged, however, because there are many things you can do now to increase your chances of finding the job that is right for you.

Competition for paralegal jobs is likely to come from several sources:

- Other recent graduates from paralegal training programs
- Secretaries and clerks now working in law offices who want to be promoted into paralegal positions

- Paralegals with a year or more of experience who are seeking a job change
- People with no legal training or experience who walk into an office "cold" seeking a job
- People with no legal training or experience but who have connections (a friend of an important client or a relative of a partner)

How long will it take for you to find a paralegal job? Of course, no one can accurately answer this question. Many variables are involved, including your competence and the record you establish in paralegal school. According to a guideline used by one veteran legal recruiter (a guideline that applies to good nonlegal jobs as well), for every $10,000 in salary you hope to earn, you will need to set aside one month of search time. "So if you want $25,000 per year, your search should take about two and one-half months. But do not be disappointed if it takes longer."[1] Some graduates obtain jobs very quickly. Be prepared, however, for a competitive job market.

In this environment, the two keys to success are *information* about the employment scene and *techniques* to market yourself. With these objectives in mind, we turn now to the following themes:

- Places where paralegals work
- Paralegal specialties
- Effective job-finding strategies
- Alternative career options

[SECTION B]

WHERE PARALEGALS WORK

There are nine major locations where paralegals work. They are summarized in Exhibit 2.1, along with the approximate percentage of paralegals working in each location. Later, in Exhibit 2.3, you will find a chart that lists some of the major characteristics of work in these locations.

In general, the more attorneys in a law firm, the greater the likelihood that significant numbers of paralegals will be working there. Where do attorneys work? Appendix 2.A at the end of this chapter identifies a selected sample of some of the large employers of attorneys in the country.

1. PRIVATE LAW FIRMS

Almost 75 percent of paralegals work for **private law firms**. Although the need for paralegals may be just as great in the other categories, private law firms have been doing most of the hiring. A private law firm is simply one that generates its income primarily from the fees of individual clients. In 1996, there were 24 paralegals for every 100 attorneys in private law firms. Today the ratio is closer to 35 per 100 attorneys.[2]

private law firm A law firm that generates its income from the fees of individual clients.

Most private law firms are engaged in general practice, meaning that they handle a wide variety of legal problems presented by clients. Firms that specialize (sometimes called **boutique law firms**) are also common, particularly in areas of the law such as employment discrimination, bankruptcy, and immigration.

boutique law firm A firm that specializes in one area of the law.

EXHIBIT 2.1	Where Do Paralegals Work and in What Percentages?

1. Private law firms
   A. Small firm: 1–10 attorneys (28%)
   B. Medium firm: 11–50 attorneys (16%)
   C. Large firm: over 50 attorneys (30%)
2. Law departments of corporations, banks, insurance companies, and other businesses (8%)
3. Government
   A. Federal government (4%)
   B. State government (2%)
   C. Local government (1%)
4. Legal service/legal aid offices (civil law) (3%)

5. Special interest groups or associations (1%)
6. Criminal law offices
   A. Prosecution (1%)
   B. Defense (1%)
7. Freelance or independent paralegals (1%)
8. Service companies/consulting firms (1%)
9. Related fields (3%)
   A. Law librarian
   B. Paralegal teacher
   C. Paralegal supervisor/office administrator
   D. Elected official, etc.

Paralegals often wonder about the differences between working for a large private law firm versus a smaller one. Here are some comparisons:

Paralegals in large private law firms:

- Tend to specialize in one area of the law
- Are among the highest paid
- Often have more employee benefits
- Are likely to work with or under a paralegal supervisor or coordinator
- Are likely to have a variety of supervisors, e.g., a supervising attorney, a paralegal manager or coordinator, a legal administrator, and a managing partner
- Are likely to have the administrative aspects of their job spelled out in a firm-wide employment policy manual
- Have been politically active in forming paralegal associations and interacting with bar associations
- Are likely to have a career ladder within the office
- Are likely to have more in-office training and professional development opportunities
- Are likely to use more sophisticated computer equipment and software
- Are likely to have access to other support personnel within the office
- Are likely to be able to perform some of the same tasks as newly hired attorneys (occasionally leading to competition between experienced paralegals and newly hired attorneys as both seek to increase their billable hours)
- Have better opportunities when seeking other paralegal jobs

Paralegals in smaller private law firms:

- Have more variety in their work (they work in more than one area of the law)
- Have more client contact
- Tend to be given more responsibility early in their employment
- Are more likely to perform clerical/administrative tasks along with their paralegal duties
- Are more likely to be asked to perform personal errands for a supervisor
- Are more likely to work for an office with low or no malpractice liability insurance and are more likely to be asked to ignore or participate in unethical conduct by a supervisor (see chapter 5)

Of course, these observations do not apply to every large office and every small office. Paralegals in some small firms, for example, might experience many of the realities listed for large firms. Each law office tends to have its unique character. In chapter 3 and later chapters, we will examine in greater detail some of the realities outlined in the observations. And later in this chapter, we will extensively cover techniques for finding employment in any private law office.

2. LAW DEPARTMENTS OF CORPORATIONS, BANKS, INSURANCE COMPANIES, AND OTHER BUSINESSES

general counsel The chief attorney in a corporate law department. Also called corporate counsel.

Many large corporations and businesses in the country have their own in-house law department under the direction of an attorney who is often called the **general counsel** or the corporate counsel. The attorneys in this department have only one client—the corporation or business itself. Fees are not involved; the department is funded from the corporate treasury. Examples of businesses and other institutions that often have law departments include manufacturers, retailers, transportation companies, publishers, general insurance companies, real estate and title insurance companies, estate and trust departments of large banks, hospitals, and universities. In increasing numbers, paralegals are being hired in these settings. The average corporate law department employs five paralegals and seventeen staff attorneys. Paralegal salaries are relatively high because the employer (like the large private law office) can often afford to pay good wages.

For information about corporate law departments and employment, check:

- Association of Corporate Counsel (www.acc.com)
- Corporate Counsel (www.law.com/jsp/cc/index.jsp)
- Federation of Defense and Corporate Counsel (www.thefederation.org)
- American Bar Association, Business Law Section (www.abanet.org/buslaw/home.shtml)
- Paralegal jobs in corporations. Here is an example of a way to find a paralegal position in corporations (more of which will be covered later):
  - Go to the site of the Association of Corporate Counsel (www.acc.com)
  - Click "Career Development" and "Find a Job"
  - Click "Advanced Search"

- For "Locations," select your state
- Type "paralegal" or "legal assistant" in the search box
- Or click "Other" for "Job Level"

Paralegals who work for law departments are often members of national and local paralegal associations. There are, however several specialty associations devoted to the interests of in-house paralegals:

- Metroplex Association of Corporate Paralegals (www.macp.net)
- Cincinnati Paralegal Association, Corporate Specialty Section (www.cincinnatiparalegals .org/corporate.htm)
- San Francisco Paralegal Association, Corporate Practice Section (www.sfpa.com/a-ps.htm)

3. GOVERNMENT

The **civil service** departments of federal, state, and local governments have established standards and classifications for many different kinds of government paralegals. For every ten government attorneys, there are three paralegals. These paralegals work in four main areas of government:

- In the office of the chief government attorney (e.g., attorney general or city attorney) for an entire **jurisdiction** (e.g., state, county, or city)
- In the office of the chief attorney (often called the general counsel) for individual government agencies (e.g., the Department of Justice and Child Welfare Bureau)
- In the office of the chief attorney (again often called the general counsel) for units within an individual government agency (e.g., civil rights division or enforcement bureau)
- In the office of individual legislators, legislative committees, legislative counsel, or the legislative drafting office of the legislature

civil service Nonmilitary government employment, often obtained through merit and competitive exams.

jurisdiction The geographic area over which a particular court system or other government unit has authority. (See glossary for other meanings of jurisdiction.)

Federal Government

Thousands of paralegals work for the federal government in the capital (Washington, D.C.) and the main regional cities of the federal government (Atlanta, Boston, Chicago, Dallas, Denver, Kansas City, New York, Philadelphia, San Francisco, and Seattle). The most important job classification for this position is the **paralegal specialist**. The occupational code for this position is GS-950. (GS means *general schedule*, the main pay scale in the federal government.) The paralegal specialist performs "legal support functions which require discretion and independent judgment," according to the U.S. Office of Personnel Management (OPM), the federal agency in charge of hiring standards within the federal government. Here is OMP's overview of the duties performed by paralegal specialists in the federal government:

paralegal specialist The major civil service job classification for paralegals who work for the federal government and for some state governments.

Paralegal Specialist in the Federal Government (GS-950)

Duties may include the following:

- Interviewing and evaluating potential witnesses; preparing for hearings and court appearances by briefing attorneys on the issues and by assembling and arranging case files, documents, and exhibits
- Examining case files to determine sufficiency of evidence or documentation
- Initiating additional fact-finding by agency personnel; developing and justifying recommendations for agency action on legal issues
- Searching for legal precedents and preparing digests of points of law involved
- Drafting pleadings and litigation papers for review and approval of attorneys
- Analyzing legal issues involved in requests for agency records; analyzing subpoenaed documents for possible patterns and trends relevant to litigation
- Analyzing appellate records to isolate facts pertinent to distinct legal issues
- Attending court hearings to keep abreast of the status of agency cases in litigation
- Testifying in court concerning exhibits prepared[3]

Paralegal specialists are found throughout the federal government. Some federal agencies are large users of paralegals. For example:

Agency	Number of Attorneys	Number of Paralegals
Department of Justice	9,629	2,073
U.S. Air Force	1,392	960

Other agencies with larger numbers of paralegals include the Departments of Health and Human Services, Treasury, Transportation, and Interior. (For a list of federal agencies, see appendix D at the end of the book.) They are also extensively employed within the U.S. court system.

Some agencies have their own titles and system of recruiting employees. Here, for example, is a recent announcement on the Web site of the Central Intelligence Agency (CIA) for a "paralegal professional":

Paralegal in the CIA

The Central Intelligence Agency is seeking Paralegal professionals to provide case management, legal research, case-cite verification, blue book citations and general paralegal support to the Office of General Counsel. Paralegals support legal issues relating to foreign intelligence, counterintelligence activities, and both civil and criminal litigation. All applicants must successfully complete a thorough medical and psychological exam, a polygraph interview and an extensive background investigation. To be considered suitable for Agency employment, applicants must generally not have used illegal drugs within the last twelve months. The issue of illegal drug use prior to twelve months ago is carefully evaluated during the medical and security processing. (Salary: $43,365 to $81,747)

There are many other nonattorney positions in the federal government where legal skills are valued. Examples:

Civil rights analyst	Intelligence analyst
Claims examiner	Internal revenue agent
Clerk of court	Land law examiner
Contract specialist	Legal assistant
Contracts examiner	Legal clerk
Criminal investigator	Legal instruments examiner
Employee benefits specialist	Legal technician
Environmental protection specialist	Public utilities examiner
Equal employment opportunity specialist	Social services representative
Equal opportunity assistant	Tax examiner
Freedom of Information Act/Privacy Act specialist	Unemployment insurance specialist
	Wage and hour compliance specialist
Hearings and appeals officer	Workers' compensation claims
Import specialist	examiner

Here are some Internet sites that can provide extensive information about the federal government and about legal jobs within its various branches, departments, and offices:

- *United States Government Manual* (www.gpoaccess.gov/gmanual/index.html) provides descriptions and addresses of all agencies and courts of the federal government.
- United States Office of Personnel Management (OPM) (www.opm.gov) oversees standards of employment within the federal government.
- USAJobs (www.usajobs.gov) is the official job site of the federal government (in the search box, type "paralegal"); this site will send you e-mail messages on all available paralegal job openings (click "MYUSAJOBS" to register for this service).
- Fed World (www.fedworld.gov) (click "Find a Federal Government Job").
- Career OneStop (www.onestopcoach.org) provides extensive help in finding federal employment.
- Online guides. There are several online guides available:
  - In Google or any general search engine, type the following search, "how to get a job in the federal government"
  - At the site of the National Association of Legal Employers (www.nalp.org), type "federal employment" without the quotation marks; although the focus of the guide on "Federal Legal Employment" is the attorney, the guide has information that is useful for paralegal employment

State and Local Government

When looking for work in a state or local government, do not limit your search to paralegal or legal assistant positions. As in the federal government, legal jobs for nonattorneys in state and local government may be listed under a variety of titles such as *research assistant, legal analyst, administrative aide, administrative officer, executive assistant, examiner, assistant, investigator,* etc. Here are some steps to find out about such jobs:

- Go to the main personnel/civil service site for your state to inquire about current openings and the application process. For a list of these sites, see appendix 2B at the end of this chapter. See also the National Association of State Personnel Executives (www.naspe.net) (click "Links of Interest" and "State Personnel").
- Go to the Web site of your state, county, city, or other local unit of government. Links to these sites are often found on the main site of your state government. See also State and Local Government on the Net (www.statelocalgov.net). On the sites of local governments in your state, look for links to employment or type "employment" in the site's search feature.
- Go to the Web sites of every state court in your state. Such sites often have information on job openings. See the National Center for State Courts (www.ncsconline.org) (click "Court Web Sites").
- Go to the Web site of your representatives in the state legislature; send them an e-mail asking how to find out about employment opportunities in the state legislature. To find your representatives, go to the National Conference of State Legislatures (www.ncsl.org/public/leglinks.cfm) (click "Legislatures" and "Web Sites").
- In any major search engine (e.g., www.google.com, www.live.com, www.ask.com, or www.yahoo.com), run a search for "state government jobs" plus the name of your state (e.g., *Georgia state government jobs*).

4. LEGAL SERVICE/LEGAL AID OFFICES (CIVIL LAW)

Community or neighborhood legal service offices and legal aid offices exist throughout the country. They obtain most of their funds from the government, often in the form of yearly grants to provide legal services to **indigents**—those without funds to hire a private attorney. Here we are referring to **civil** (noncriminal) legal matters. Offices that handle criminal cases will be discussed later.

In addition to government funding, legal service/legal aid offices are also supported by **IOLTA programs** (Interest on Lawyers Trust Accounts). Attorneys often have client trust accounts containing client funds that earn interest. Under IOLTA programs, the interest is sent to a foundation or other entity to be used to help run law offices that serve indigents (www.iolta.org).

Legal service/legal aid offices make extensive use of paralegals with titles such as:

Paralegal	Immigration paralegal
Legal assistant	Information and referral specialist
Administrative hearing representative	Legislative advocate
Bankruptcy law specialist	Paralegal coordinator
Case advocate	Paralegal supervisor
Community law specialist	Public benefits paralegal
Disability law specialist	Social security specialist
Domestic relations specialist	Tribal court representative
Food stamp specialist	Veterans law advocate
Housing/tenant law specialist	

As we will see in chapter 4 some administrative agencies permit nonattorneys to represent citizens at hearings before those agencies. Legal service and legal aid offices take advantage of this authorization. Some of their paralegals undertake extensive agency representation. The distinction between attorneys and paralegals in such offices is less pronounced than in many other settings. Unfortunately, however, these paralegals are among the lowest paid because of the limited resources of the offices where they work.

Here are some examples of the duties of a public benefits paralegal in a legal service office:

- Interview clients for eligibility for free legal services.
- Investigate claims of discrimination.
- Represent clients at SSI (supplemental security income) hearings.
- Assist individuals who are representing themselves in an **uncontested** divorce.
- Help prepare (and sometimes distribute) leaflets on poverty law topics, e.g., eligibility for food stamps.

indigent A person who is without funds to hire a private attorney. Impoverished.

civil Pertaining to a private right or matter. Noncriminal; nonmilitary. (See the glossary for other meanings of civil.)

IOLTA program (Interest on Lawyers Trust Accounts) A program that helps fund legal services for the poor with funds that attorneys are required to turn over from interest earned in client trust accounts containing client funds.

uncontested Unchallenged; without opposition.

- Assist attorneys to prepare for an appeal of a denial of benefits.
- Assist the office to collect data needed for quarterly reports to a funding source.

Legal service or legal aid offices are not the only way the government helps provide legal services to indigents. Many cities and counties have "volunteer lawyer" organizations that recruit private attorneys to provide **pro bono** (i.e., free) legal services. These organizations often employ paralegals.

pro bono Concerning or involving legal services that are provided for the public good (pro bono publico) without fee or compensation. Sometimes also applied to services given at a reduced rate. Shortened to pro bono.

Here are sources of further information about programs that serve the poor and paralegal job opportunities within them:

- Legal service programs in your state
  - www.lsc.gov (click your state on the map) (LSC is the Legal Services Corporation, a federal agency that funds many legal services programs).
  - www.ptla.org/links/services.htm.
  - www.abanet.org/legalservices/probono/directory.html.
  - In any major search engine (e.g., www.google.com, www.live.com, www.ask.com, or www.yahoo.com), run a search for legal services plus the name of your state, e.g., *Ohio legal services*).
  - www.nlada.org (click "Member Services," then "Directory of Legal Aid and Defender Offices").
- Examples of legal service programs in the country
  - California: www.lawhelpcalifornia.org
  - Florida: www.floridalawhelp.org
  - Illinois: www.illinoislegalaid.org
  - New York: www.lawhelp.org/NY
  - Ohio: www.ohiolegalservices.org
  - Pennsylvania: www.palawhelp.org
  - Texas: www.texaslawhelp.org
- Job opportunities for paralegals and attorneys in legal service/legal aid offices
  - www.nlada.org (click "jobs" and your state on the map)
- Pro bono programs in your state
  - www.abanet.org/legalservices/probono/directory.html.
  - In any search engine, run a search for *pro bono* and your state (e.g., *pro bono Florida* or *pro bono law Florida*).

5. SPECIAL INTEREST GROUPS OR ASSOCIATIONS

special interest group An organization that serves a particular group or cause.

Many **special interest groups** exist in our society: unions, business associations, environmental protection groups, taxpayer associations, consumer protection groups, trade associations, citizen action groups, etc. Examples of such groups include:

- American Bankers Association www.aba.com
- National Foundation for Credit Counseling www.nfcc.org
- National Association of Home Builders www.nahb.com
- National Organization for Women www.now.org
- Parents, Families, and Friends of Lesbians and Gays www.pflag.org

test case Litigation brought to try to create a new legal principle or right.

Large groups may have their own offices, libraries, and legal staff, including paralegals. The legal work often involves monitoring legislation, lobbying, preparing studies, etc. Direct legal services to individual members of the groups are usually not provided. The legal work relates to the needs (or a cause) of the organization as a whole. Occasionally, however, the legal staff will litigate **test cases** of individual members that have a broad impact on the organization's membership.

prepaid legal services A plan by which a person pays premiums to cover future legal services. Also called legal plan and group legal services.

A different concept in the use of attorneys and paralegals by some special interest groups is **prepaid legal services**, also referred to as *legal plans* or *group legal services*. Members of unions, for example, pay a monthly fee to the organization for which they are entitled to designated legal services, such as preparation of a will or uncontested divorce representation. The members pay *before* the legal problems arise. Prepaid legal service systems are a form of legal insurance that operates in a manner similar to health insurance. Specified services are provided *if* the need for them arises. The prepaid legal service office will usually employ paralegals. Here are some sources of information about these services:

- American Bar Association, Group and Prepaid Legal Services (www.abanet.org/legalservices/prepaid/home.html)
- American Prepaid Legal Services Institute (www.aplsi.org)
- Hyatt Legal Plans (www.legalplans.com)

6. CRIMINAL LAW OFFICES

Criminal cases are brought by government attorneys called prosecutors, district attorneys, or attorneys general. Defendants are represented by private attorneys if they can afford the fees. If they are indigent, they might be represented by **public defenders**, who are attorneys appointed by the court and paid by the government to represent the poor in a criminal case. Public defenders are usually government employees. (To find out if this is so in your state, go to the Web site of your state or county government and type "public defender" in its search box.) Sometimes a court will appoint a private attorney to represent someone. A court-appointed private attorney in a criminal or civil case is often called **assigned counsel**.

The use of paralegals in the practice of criminal law is increasing, particularly due to the encouragement of organizations such as the National District Attorneys Association and the National Legal Aid & Defender Association. Sources of information on work in criminal justice include:

- National Legal Aid & Defender Association (NLADA) (www.nlada.org)
- National District Attorneys Association (www.ndaa.org)
- National Association of Attorneys General (www.naag.org)
- National Association of Criminal Defense Lawyers (www.criminaljustice.org)
- Criminal Defense Attorney Directory (www.criminal-attorneys-us.com)
- American Bar Association, Criminal Justice Section (www.abanet.org/crimjust/home.html)
- Web Cites for Federal Defenders (www.rashkind.com)
- Prosecutor Web sites (http://207.74.121.45/Prosecutor/proslist.htm)
- National Criminal Justice Reference Service (www.ncjrs.org) (type "paralegal" in the search box)

7. FREELANCE PARALEGALS

As we learned in chapter 1, many **freelance paralegals** are self-employed independent contractors who sell their services to attorneys. They are also called *independent paralegals*, *contract paralegals*, and *legal technicians*. Freelance paralegals perform their services in their own office or in the offices of the attorneys who hire them for special projects. Often they advertise in publications read by attorneys, such as legal newspapers and bar association journals. Such an ad might look something like this:

> Improve the quality and
> ****cost-effectiveness****
> of your practice with the help of:
> Lawyer's Assistant, Inc.

In addition, these paralegals will usually have a flyer or brochure that describes their services. Here is an excerpt from such a flyer:

> Our staff consists of individuals with formal paralegal training and an average of five years of experience in such areas as estates and trusts, litigation, real estate, tax, and corporate law. Whether you require a real estate paralegal for one day or four litigation paralegals for one month, we can provide you with reliable qualified paralegals to meet your specific needs.

Most freelance paralegals have Web sites. To find them in your state, run a search in Google, Yahoo, Ask, or other general search engine for "freelance paralegal" or "paralegal services" and the name of your state (e.g., *Michigan paralegal services*). For an example of a freelance paralegal service on the Internet, see Exhibit 2.2. The attorneys in a law firm may be convinced of the value of

public defender An attorney (usually a government employee) appointed by a court and paid by the government to represent an indigent person in a criminal case.

assigned counsel An attorney (usually in private practice) appointed by the court to represent an indigent person in a criminal or civil case.

freelance paralegal An independent contractor who sells his or her paralegal services to, and works under the supervision of, one or more attorneys.

EXHIBIT 2.2   Example of a Freelance Paralegal Service Site on the Internet (www.paralegalserv.com)

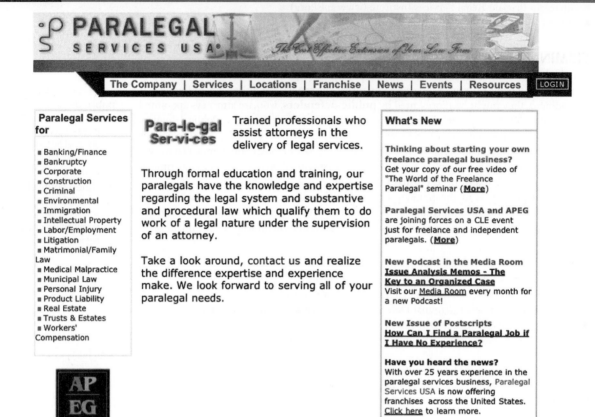

paralegals but not have enough business to justify hiring a full-time paralegal employee. A freelance paralegal is an alternative.

There are freelancers who operate entirely online and hence are sometimes called *virtual assistants*. The work they do for attorneys is transmitted primarily by e-mail or other electronic means. Although many of the services provided are clerical (e.g., typing transcripts of testimony and proofreading), more sustentative tasks are also offered (e.g., digesting discovery documents and performing legal research). Some virtual assistants have joined the International Virtual Assistants Association (www.ivaa.org).

outsourcing Paying an outside company or service to perform tasks usually performed by one's own employees.

As **outsourcing** of this kind has become increasingly common, ethical and management issues have been raised, particularly when the work is performed in distant countries such as India where English-speaking workers are available. We will examine these issues in later chapters.

For an overview on how to start a freelance business, see appendix J.

As indicated, there are also self-employed paralegals who sell their services directly to the public without attorney supervision. They, too, are sometimes called freelance paralegals, although the terms *legal technician* and *independent paralegal* are more common. In California, however, individuals selling law-related services directly to the public are not allowed to call themselves paralegals or legal assistants. The legally accepted title for them is *legal document assistant* (LDA) or, if they work with evictions, *unlawful detainer assistant* (UDA). The titles *paralegal* and *legal assistant* in California (and in a few other states) are limited to those who work under attorney supervision. Here are sources of information on this area of work:

- California Association of Legal Document Assistants (www.calda.org)
- Nolo (www.nolo.com) (type "independent paralegal" in the search box)

We will be examining freelance paralegals, LDAs, and other independent contractors in greater detail in chapter 4 and in appendices G and J.

8. SERVICE COMPANIES/CONSULTING FIRMS

Service companies and consulting firms sell special services to attorneys. Some individual free-lance paralegals also do so but usually on a less sophisticated level. Examples of services provided by established service companies and consulting firms include:

- Designing litigation graphics
- Selecting a computer system for a law office
- Designing and managing a computer-assisted document control system for a large case
- Managing a large employer's unemployment compensation claims and appeals
- Helping a law firm establish a marketing strategy
- Designing a filing or financial system for the office
- Incorporating a new company in all fifty states
- Conducting a trademark search
- Digesting discovery documents
- Undertaking a UCC (Uniform Commercial Code) search and filing in all fifty states

To accomplish such tasks, these service companies and consulting firms recruit highly specialized staffs of management experts, accountants, economists, former administrators, etc. More and more paralegals are joining these staffs as employees; many of them are paralegals with prior law office experience, particularly computer experience.

Here are some examples of service companies and consulting firms on the Internet:

- Deposums (digesting discovery documents) www.deposums.com/depositionsummaries.html
- First Advantage (litigation support services) www.fadv.com
- Blum Shapiro (forensic accounting) www.blumshapiro.com/litigation
- Law Marketing Portal (law firm marketing services) www.lawmarketing.com

A special category of consultant with medical training is the legal nurse consultant (LNC). This person is a nurse who provides a wide range of support services to attorneys in the medical aspects of medical malpractice, products liability, environment, and labor cases. For example, they have a large role in obtaining, summarizing, and interpreting medical records. Legal nurse consultants have formed their own association, the American Association of Legal Nurse Consultants (AALNC) www.aalnc.org. (As we saw in chapter 1, AALNC has its own certification program.) AALNC considers LNCs to be a specialty practice of the nursing profession rather than a special category of paralegals. Not everyone, however, agrees with this position. A growing number of legal nurses consider themselves to be full-fledged paralegals.

9. RELATED FIELDS

Experienced paralegals have also been using their training and experience in a number of non-practice legal fields. Many are becoming law librarians at firms. Paralegal schools often hire parale-gals to teach or co-teach courses and to work in administration. Law offices with large numbers of paralegals have hired paralegal administrators or supervisors to help recruit, train, and manage the paralegals. Some paralegals have become legal administrators or office managers with administrative responsibilities throughout the firm. Paralegals are also running for public office, often citing their legal background as a qualification for office. Former paralegals have won seats on state legislatures, city councils, and boards of supervisors. They have also been elected court clerk and probate judge (in states that do not require such judges to be attorneys). See appendix L for a photo of former paralegal and current probate judge, Arleen Keegan. It is clear that we have not seen the end of the development of new roles for paralegals within the law firm or in related areas of the law. At the end of the chapter, a more extensive list of such roles will be provided. (See Exhibit 2.17.)

ASSIGNMENT 2.1

Find want ads for any seven categories or subcategories of employment mentioned in Exhibit 2.1. Cut each ad out and tape it on a sheet of paper. Beneath the ad, state where it was published, the date, and the page of the publication. You can use general circulation newspapers, legal newspapers, magazines, newsletters, the Internet, etc.

10. SUMMARY

Exhibit 2.3 presents an overview of some of the major characteristics of the largest employment settings we began exploring in Exhibit 2.1 at the beginning of the chapter. We will be returning to most of the themes in Exhibit 2.3 in later chapters.

Exhibit 2.3   General Observations about Paralegal Work in Different Kinds of Law Offices

WHAT IS THE LIKELIHOOD OF A PARALEGAL:

Kind of Office	Being hired without experience	Having very good pay	Having very good benefits	Having variety in assignments	Having clerical tasks to perform	Having a tightly defined role	Having a career ladder	Having client contact	Having access to support staff	Having formal in-house training	Working with state-of-the-art equipment	Having an hourly billing requirement	Having overtime required by employer	Having work-life balance (diversity)
Large private law firm	Low	High	High	Low	Low	High	High	Low	High	High	High	High	High	High
Medium size private law firm	Moderate	Moderate	Moderate	Moderate	Low	Moderate	High	Low	High	Moderate	High	High	High	Moderate
Small private law firm	Moderate	Moderate	Moderate	High	High	Low	Low	High	Low	Low	Low	Moderate	Moderate	Low
Corporate law department	Moderate	High	High	Moderate	Low	High	High	High	High	High	High	N/A	Low	High
Federal government	High	High	High	Moderate	Low	High	Low	High	High	High	Moderate	N/A	Low	High
State government	High	Moderate	High	Moderate	Low	High	Moderate	High	High	High	Moderate	N/A	Low	High
Local government	High	Moderate	Moderate	Moderate	Low	High	Low	High	Moderate	Moderate	Moderate	N/A	Low	High
Legal service/legal aid (public) law office	High	Low	Low	High	High	Moderate	Low	High	Low	Moderate	Low	N/A	Low	Moderate
Special interest group or organization	Moderate	Moderate	Moderate	High	Moderate	Moderate	Low	Moderate	Moderate	Low	Moderate	Low	Low	High
Freelance (offering services to attorneys)	Low	Moderate	Low	Moderate	High	High	Low	Low	Low	Low	Low	N/A	N/A	Low

PARALEGAL SPECIALTIES: A DICTIONARY OF FUNCTIONS

We now examine forty-six areas of specialty work throughout the nine categories of paralegal employment just discussed. Paralegals often work in more than one of these specialties, and there is considerable overlap in the functions performed. The trend, however, is for paralegals to specialize, particularly in larger law offices. This follows the pattern of most attorneys.

For each specialty, you will find examples of duties performed by paralegals. For most of the specialties, comments from paralegals or their supervisors about the paralegal's work in the specialty are included. For the six specialties where most paralegals work (corporate law, estate law, family law, litigation, real estate law, and tort law), you will also find excerpts from want ads to give you an idea of what employers are looking for when hiring for those specialties. Law offices that practice these specialties are almost always busy. The economy has a lot to do with how busy some of the other specialties are. For example, intellectual property was "hot" during the dot.com boom era, whereas bankruptcy attorneys are very busy during recessions. For all of the specialties, you are given an Internet address where you will find more information about the kind of law involved in the specialty. Another way to find out what kind of law is practiced in a particular specialty is to go to the Internet site of a major law firm and click the sections called "Areas of Practice," "What We Do," "Services," or "About the Firm." In such sections, specialty areas of the law are listed and described. For the Internet addresses of many law firms in the country, see appendix 2.A at the end of this chapter. For a general overview of paralegal responsibilities in many areas of law, see also:

- www.lectlaw.com/files/pap01.htm
- www.lawcost.com/paras.htm
- www.CAPAralegal.org/duties.html
- www.paralegals.org (click "CLE" then "Paralegal Responsibilities")
- www.cobar.org/sectandcomms.cfm (click "Paralegal" then "Guidelines for the Utilization of Paralegals")

Note that there is a separate section on litigation (no. 32). This is not meant to suggest that the other forty-five areas of specialty do not involve litigation. In fact, between 60 and 70 percent of paralegals work in litigation. This is because the organizational skills of paralegals are highly valued in litigation, where numerous documents, facts, and potential witnesses are often involved. The section on litigation, therefore, potentially applies to all of the other specialty areas.

Paralegal Specialties

1. Administrative law
2. Admiralty law
3. Advertising law
4. Antitrust law
5. Banking law
6. Bankruptcy law
7. Civil rights law
8. Collections law
9. Communications law
10. Construction law
11. Contract law
12. Corporate law
13. Criminal law
14. Employee benefits law
15. Entertainment law
16. Environmental law
17. Estates, trusts, and probate law
18. Ethics and professional responsibility
19. Family law
20. Gaming law
21. Government contract law
22. Immigration law
23. Insurance law
24. Intellectual property law
25. International law
26. Judicial administration
27. Labor and employment law
28. Landlord and tenant law
29. Law librarianship
30. Law office administration
31. Legislation
32. Litigation (civil)
33. Military law
34. Municipal finance law
35. Oil and gas law
36. Parajudge (lay judge)
37. Pro bono work
38. Public sector
39. Real estate law
40. Social security law
41. Tax law
42. Tort law
43. Tribal law
44. Water law
45. Welfare law (public assistance)
46. Worker's compensation law

Note: Paralegal in the White House

ASSIGNMENT 2.2

From the list of forty-six specialties, pick one that interests you, at least preliminarily.

(a) Explain why you might want to work in this area of the law.

(b) Find two Internet sites that provide explanations of any aspect of the substantive or procedural law in this area. (Start by checking the Internet sites presented in the text for that specialty under the heading "More on This Area of the Law on the Net." If needed, check other sites as well.) What sites did you select? Quote at least two sentences from each site on any aspect of the law it covers.

(c) In appendix 2.A, at the end of the chapter, there are many Internet addresses of law firms. Find one firm that practices this specialty. Quote at least two sentences from this firm's site on what it does in this specialty.

(d) Find a want ad for this area of the law. (Check your local newspaper, available legal newspapers, the Internet, etc.)

1. Administrative Law

I.   Government Employment
     Many paralegals work for specific administrative agencies. (See also appendix 2.B for a list of paralegal functions in state agencies.) They might:

A.   Handle questions and complaints from citizens.
B.   Draft proposed regulations for the agency.
C.   Perform legal research.
D.   Provide litigation assistance in the agency and in court.
E.   Represent the government at administrative hearings where authorized.
F.   Manage the law office.
G.   Train and supervise other nonattorney personnel.

II. Representation of Citizens While Working in Nongovernment Offices
     Some administrative agencies authorize nonattorneys to represent citizens at hearings and other agency proceedings. For an example of a paralegal using this authorization while working in a private law office, see the summary of Formal Opinion 1988–103 in Appendix E in which a paralegal represents clients at a workers' compensation hearing. (See also *immigration law, pro bono work, public sector, social security law,* and *welfare law.*)

A.   Interview client.
B.   Conduct investigation.
C.   Perform legal research.
D.   Engage in informal advocacy at the agency.
E.   Represent the client at agency hearing.
F.   Draft documents for submission at hearing.
G.   Monitor activities of the agency, e.g., attend rulemaking hearings to take notes on matters relevant to particular clients.
H.   Prepare witnesses, reports, and exhibits designed to influence the drafting of regulations at the agency.

● *Comment on Paralegal Work in This Area:*
     We "have a great deal of autonomy and an opportunity to develop expertise in particular areas." We have our "own caseloads, interview clients and then represent those clients at administrative hearings." Georgia Ass'n of Legal Assistants, *Sallye Jenkins Sapp, Atlanta Legal Aid; Sharon Mahaffey Hill, Georgia Legal Services,* 10 Paragraph 5.

     When I got my first case at a hearing before the State Department of Mental Health, I was "scared to death!" But the attorneys in the office were very supportive. "They advised me to make a good record, noting objections for the transcript, in case of future appeal. Making the right objections was scary." Milano, *New Responsibilities Being Given to Paralegals,* 8 Legal Assistant Today 27, 28.

● *More on This Area of the Law on the Net:*
     ■ *findlaw.com/01topics/00administrative*
     ■ *www.abanet.org/adminlaw/home.html*
     ■ *www.law.fsu.edu/library/admin*
     ■ *www.law.cornell.edu/wex/index.php/ Administrative_law*
     ■ *en.wikipedia.org/wiki/Administrative_law*

2. Admiralty Law

     This area of the law, also referred to as *maritime law,* covers accidents, injuries, and death connected with vessels on navigable waters. Special legislation exists in this area, such as the Jones Act. (See also *international law, litigation,* and *tort law.*)

I.   Investigation
A.   Obtain the facts of the event involved.
B.   Arrange to board the vessel to photograph the scene of the accident.
C.   Collect facts relevant to the seaworthiness of the vessel.
D.   Take statements from witnesses.

II. Legal Research
A.   Research liability under the applicable statutes.
B.   Research special procedures to obtain compensation.

III. Subrogation
A.   Handle small cargo subrogation files.
B.   Prepare status reports for clients.

IV. Litigation
A.   Draft complaints and other pleadings.
B.   Respond to discovery requests.
C.   Monitor all maritime files needed to keep track of discovery deadlines.
D.   Coordinate projects by expert witnesses.
E.   Provide general trial assistance.

● *Comment on Paralegal Work in This Area:*
     Jimmie Muvern, CLA (Certified Legal Assistant), works for a sole practitioner in Baton Rouge, Louisiana, who specializes in maritime litigation: "If there is a doubt regarding the plaintiff's status as a Jones Act seaman, this issue is generally raised by a

motion for summary judgment filed well in advance of trial, and it is good practice for the legal assistant who may be gathering facts regarding the client's accident to also gather facts from the client and from other sources, which might assist the attorney in opposing summary judgment on the issue of the client's status as a Jones Act seaman." J. deGravelles & J. Muvern, *Who Is a Jones Act Seaman?* 12 Facts & Findings 34 (NALA).

- *More on This Area of the Law on the Net:*
  - *www.admiraltylawguide.com/index.html*
  - *findlaw.com/01topics/39admiralty*
  - *www.law.cornell.edu/wex/index.php/Admiralty*

3. Advertising Law

(See also *administrative law* and *intellectual property law*.)

I. Compliance Work

A. *Advertising:* Review advertising of company products to identify claims made in the advertising about the product. Collect data needed to support the accuracy of the claims pursuant to regulations of the Federal Trade Commission, state laws, and company guidelines.

B. *Labels:* Review labels of company products to ensure compliance with the regulations on deception of the Federal Trade Commission and other agencies. Monitor compliance with the Food & Drug Administration and company policy on:
   1. Product identity,
   2. Weight statement,
   3. Ingredient list,
   4. Name and address of manufacturer/distributor,
   5. Nutrition information.

C. *Product promotions:* Review promotions for company products (coupons, sweepstakes, bonus packs, etc.) to ensure compliance with Federal Trade Commission guidelines, state laws, and company policy.

II. Inquiries and Complaints

A. Keep up to date on government regulations on advertising.

B. Help company attorney respond to inquiries and complaints from the public, a competitor, the Federal Trade Commission, the Food & Drug Administration, the state's attorney general, etc.

- *Comment on Paralegal Work in This Area:*

  "On the surface, my job certainly does not fit the 'traditional' paralegal role. [Years ago, if] a fortune teller had ever read my coffee grounds, I might have learned that my paralegal career would include being part of the production of commercials and labels for household products I had grown up with." "My employer, the Procter & Gamble Company, is one of the largest consumer product companies in the United States." Its "Legal Division consists of forty attorneys and nine paralegals. Advertising law is challenging. It requires ingenuity, fast thinking and mastery of tight deadlines." Kothman, *Advertising Paralegal Finds Own Label*, National Paralegal Reporter 12 (NFPA).

- *More on This Area of the Law on the Net:*
  - *www.hg.org/advert.html*
  - *www.advertisinglaw.com*
  - *www.nadreview.org*

4. Antitrust Law

(See also *administrative law*, *corporate law*, *criminal law*, and *litigation*.)

I. Investigation/Analysis

A. Accumulate statistical and other technical data on a company or industry involved in litigation. Check Securities & Exchange Commission (SEC) filings, annual reports, advertising brochures, etc.

B. Prepare reports on economic data.

C. Obtain data from government bodies.

D. Find and interview potential witnesses.

II. Administrative Agency

A. Monitor the regulations and decisions of the Federal Trade Commission.

B. Prepare drafts of answers to requests for information from the Federal Trade Commission.

III. Litigation

A. Assist in drafting pleadings.

B. Request company witness files and other documents in preparation for deposition.

C. Schedule depositions.

D. Draft interrogatories.

E. Prepare special exhibits.

F. Organize, index, and digest voluminous records and lengthy documents.

G. Prepare trial notebook.

H. Attend trial and take notes on testimony of witnesses.

I. Cite check briefs of attorneys.

J. Provide general trial assistance.

- *Comment on Paralegal Work in This Area:*

  When Mitchell became a permanent employee at the firm, "he was given three days' worth of files to read in order to familiarize himself with the [antitrust] case. At this point in the case, the firm had already gone through discovery of 27,000 documents. Mitchell analyzed and summarized documents with the other ten paralegals hired to work on the case. With a major case such as this one, paralegals did not have a regular nine to five work day. Mitchell frequently worked seventy hours a week (for which he was paid overtime). In January, Mitchell and his team were sent across the country to take depositions for the case. His air transportation, accommodations, and meals were all 'first class,' but this was not a vacation; he worked around the clock." R. Berkey, *New Career Opportunities in the Legal Profession* 47 (Arco).

- *More on This Area of the Law on the Net:*
  - *www.findlaw.com/01topics/01antitrust*
  - *www.usdoj.gov/atr/index.html*
  - *www.abanet.org/antitrust*
  - *unclaw.com/chin/teaching/antitrust/links.htm*
  - *www.clubi.ie/competition/compframesite/index.htm*

5. Banking Law

Paralegals employed by banks often work in the bank trust department. They also work in the bank's legal department, where they become involved with litigation, real estate, bankruptcy, consumer affairs, and securities law. In addition to banks, paralegals work for savings and loan institutions and other commercial lenders. Finally, some paralegals are employed in law firms that specialize in banking law. The following overview of duties is limited to the paralegal working for the legal department of a bank. (See also *administrative law, corporate law, estates law,* and *municipal finance law.*)

I. Claims

Assist legal staff in assessing bank liability for various claims, such as negligence and collection abuse.

II. Compliance Analysis

Determine whether the bank is complying with the regulations and statutes that regulate the banking industry.

III. Monitoring

Keep track of the rulemaking and other activities of the various banking regulatory agencies and the bill-drafting activities of the legislative committees with jurisdiction over banks.

IV. Litigation

Assist attorneys litigating claims.

V. Miscellaneous

A. Draft and/or review loan applications and accompanying credit documents.

B. Perform document analysis on:
 1. Financial statements,
 2. Mortgages,
 3. Assignments, and
 4. Security agreements.

C. Conduct UCC (Uniform Commercial Code) searches.

D. Assemble closing documents.

E. Arrange for and attend loan closings.

F. Notarize documents.

G. Monitor recordation.

H. Act as liaison among the supervising attorney at the bank, the loan officer, and the customer.

I. Perform routine legal research and analysis for the Compliance Department.

● **Comment on Paralegal Work in This Area:**

Ruth Sendecki is the first paralegal at Merchants National Bank, one of the Midwest's largest bank holding companies. Most paralegals employed at banks today work in the trust department; Ruth, however, works with "general banking" at Merchants. Before this job, she worked at a bank, but not in a legal capacity. "You don't have to limit yourself to a law firm. You can combine being a paralegal with other interests." Her "primary responsibility is in the commercial loan department.... She also serves the mortgage loan, correspondent banking and the international banking departments." According to her supervisor at the bank, "She is readily accessible for the benefit of the attorney, the loan officer and the customer to facilitate completion of the arrangements for both sides." Furthermore, she "is expanding her knowledge base, and other departments are drawing on her knowledge." Kane, *A Banker with the Soul of a Legal Assistant,* 5 Legal Assistant Today 65.

● **More on This Area of the Law on the Net:**
 ■ *www.law.cornell.edu/wex/index.php/Banking*
 ■ *findlaw.com/01topics/02banking*

 ■ *www.occ.treas.gov*
 ■ *www.fdic.gov*

6. **Bankruptcy Law**

Paralegals in this area of law may be employed by a law firm that represents the debtor (e.g., an individual, a business); a creditor (e.g., a bank-mortgagee); or the trustee in bankruptcy. (A trustee in bankruptcy does not have to be an attorney. Some paralegals with bankruptcy experience have become trustees.) A few paralegals work directly for a bankruptcy judge as a clerk or deputy in Bankruptcy Court. (Someone who provides bankruptcy assistance as an independent contractor, rather than as an employee of an attorney, is called a *bankruptcy petition preparer,* a position we will examine in chapter 4.) The following overview assumes the paralegal works for a firm that represents the debtor. (See also *banking law, collections law, contract law,* and *litigation.*)

I. Interviewing/Data Collection

A. Help client fill out an extensive questionnaire on assets and liabilities. May visit client's place of business to determine the kinds of records kept there.

B. Help client assemble documents:
 1. Loan agreements
 2. Deeds of trust
 3. Security agreements
 4. Creditor lists
 5. Payables lists
 6. Employment contracts
 7. Financial statements
 8. Leases

II. Investigation

A. Confirm amounts of indebtedness.

B. Identify secured and unsecured claims of creditors.

C. Check UCC (Uniform Commercial Code) filings at the secretary of state's office and at the county clerk's office.

D. Check real property records in the clerk's office in the county where the property is located.

E. Verify taxes owed; identify tax liens.

F. Identify exempt property.

III. Asset Control

A. Open bankruptcy file.

B. Prepare inventories of assets and liabilities.

C. Arrange for valuation of assets.

IV. Creditor Contact

A. Answer inquiries of creditors on the status of the case.

B. Request documentation from creditors on claims.

V. Drafting

A. Original bankruptcy petition.

B. Schedule of liabilities.

C. Statement of affairs.

D. Status reports.

E. Final account.

VI. Coordination

A. Serve as liaison with trustee in bankruptcy.

B. Coordinate meeting of creditors.

C. Prepare calendar of filing and other deadlines.

● *Comment on Paralegal Work in This Area:*

"As a paralegal, you can play a major role in the representation of a Chapter 11 debtor. From prefiling activities through confirmation of the plan of reorganization, there are numerous duties which you can perform to assist in the successful reorganization of the debtor." Morzak, *Organizing Reorganization*, 5 Legal Assistant Today 33.

"Bankruptcy work is unusual in a number of ways—extremely short statutes of limitation, for example. . . . The field is one in which there's lots of opportunity for paralegals. The paralegal does everything except sign the papers. . . . Most attorneys do not like bankruptcy, but if you do all the legwork for them, you can make a lot of money for them." Johnson, *The Role of the Paralegal/Legal Assistant in Bankruptcy and Foreclosure*, AALA News 7 (Alaska Ass'n of Legal Assistants).

● *More on This Area of the Law on the Net:*
  ■ *www.abiworld.org*
  ■ *findlaw.com/01topics/03bankruptcy*
  ■ *www.hg.org/bankrpt.html*
  ■ *www.law.cornell.edu/wex/index.php/Bankruptcy*

7. Civil Rights Law

(See also *labor and employment law, pro bono work,* and *public sector.*)

I. Government Paralegal

A. Help identify and resolve discrimination complaints (based on sex, race, age, disability, etc.) made by government employees against the government.

B. Help government attorneys litigate discrimination complaints (based on sex, race, age, disability, etc.) brought by citizens against the government, against other citizens, or against companies.

II. Representation of Citizens While Working in Nongovernment Offices

Assist law firms representing citizens in their discrimination complaints filed against the government, other citizens, or companies:

A. In court.

B. In special agencies created to hear discrimination cases, such as the Equal Employment Opportunity Commission or the Human Rights Commission.

● *Comment on Paralegal Work in This Area:*

"One aspect that Matthews likes is that each case is a different story, a different set of facts. 'There is a lot of interaction with people in the courts and with the public. We do a great deal of civil rights litigation, everything from excessive police force to wrongful termination. Sometimes there are as many as 60 witnesses. The lawyers depend on me to separate the witnesses out and advise them which ones would do best in the courtroom. A lot of time the lawyer does not know the witness and has not seen the witness until the person is in the courtroom testifying.' For one case, Matthews reviewed more than 1,000 slides taken in a nightclub, looking for examples of unusual or rowdy behavior. The slides include everything from male strippers to people flashing. Autopsy and horrible injury photographs are also part of the job." *Broadening into the Paralegal Field*, 39 The Docket 7(NALS).

● *More on This Area of the Law on the Net:*
  ■ *www.law.cornell.edu/wex/index.php/Civil_rights*
  ■ *www.usdoj.gov/crt/crt-home.html*
  ■ *findlaw.com/01topics/36civil*
  ■ *www.aclu.org*

8. Collections Law[4]

(See also *banking law, bankruptcy law, contract law,* and *litigation.*)

I. Acceptance of Claims
A. Open file.
B. Prepare index of parties.
C. Prepare inventory of debts of debtor.

II. Investigation
A. Conduct asset check.
B. Verify address.
C. Verify filings at secretary of state's office and county clerk's office (e.g., UCC filings).
D. Contact credit bureau.
E. Verify information in probate court, registry of deeds, etc.

III. Litigation Assistant (Civil Court, Small Claims Court, etc.)
A. Draft pleadings.
B. Arrange for witnesses.
C. File documents in court.
D. Assist in settlement/negotiation of claim.
E. Assist in enforcement work, such as:
  1. Wage attachment (prejudgment attachment),
  2. Supplementary process,
  3. Execution, and
  4. Seizure of personal property.

● *Comment on Paralegal Work in This Area:*

"O.K.—So, [collections work] is not the nicest job in the world, but somebody has to do it, right? If the attorney you work for does not want to do it, there are plenty more in town who will. For a paralegal working in this area, there is always something new to learn. . . . It is sometimes difficult to see the results of your labor right away in this kind of work, as very few files are paid in full and closed in a short period of time. It is disheartening to go through many steps and possibly spend a great deal of time just trying to get someone served or to locate someone, and then end up with nothing. I will admit that collections can be very frustrating, but boring they are not!" Wexel, *Collections: Persistence Pay$ Off,* The Paraview (Metrolina Paralegal Ass'n).

"I currently have responsibility for some 400 collection cases. My days are spent on the phone talking to debtors, drafting the necessary pleadings, executing forms, and hopefully depositing the money collected. The exciting part of collection is executing on a judgment. We were successful in garnishing an insurance company's account for some $80,000 when they refused to pay a judgment that had been taken against them. We have also gone with the Sheriff to a beer distributorship two days before St. Patrick's Day to change the locks on the building housing gallons and gallons of green beer. The debtor suddenly found a large sum of money to pay us so that we would release the beer in time for St. Patrick's Day." R. Swoagerm, *Collections Paralegal,* The Citator 9 (Legal Assistants of Central Ohio).

● *More on This Area of the Law on the Net:*
  ▪ *www.nacm.org*
  ▪ *www.consumerlaw.org*

9. Communications Law
(See also *administrative law* and *entertainment law*.)

I. Government Paralegal

Assist attorneys at the Federal Communications Commission (FCC) in regulating the communications industry—for example, help with rulemaking, license applications, and hearings.

II. Representation of Citizens or Companies While Working in Nongovernment Offices
A. Draft application for licenses.
B. Prepare compliance reports.
C. Prepare exemption applications.
D. Prepare statistical analyses.
E. Monitor activities of the FCC.
F. Assist in litigation:
    1. Within the FCC and
    2. In court.

● *Comment on Paralegal Work in This Area:*

The current specialty of Carol Woods is the regulation of television and radio. "I am able to do work that is important and substantive, and am able to work independently. I have an awful lot of contact with clients, with paralegals at the client's office, and with government agencies. One of the liabilities of private practice for both attorneys and paralegals is that there is so much repetition and you can get bored. A lot of times as a paralegal you can't call the shots or know everything that goes into the planning of a project. However, when you can participate in all facets of a project, it's great!" A. Fins, *Opportunities in Paralegal Careers* 84 (Nat'l Textbook Co.).

● *More on This Area of the Law on the Net:*
  ▪ *www.fcc.gov*
  ▪ *findlaw.com/01topics/05communications*
  ▪ *www.law.cornell.edu/wex/index.php/Communications*

10. Construction Law
(See also *contract law*, *litigation*, and *tort law*.)

I. Claims Assistance
A. Work with engineering consultants in the preparation of claims.

II. Data Collection
A. Daily manpower hours.
B. Amount of materials used, e.g., concrete poured.
C. Change orders.

III. Document Preparation
A. Prepare graphs.
B. Prepare special studies—e.g., compare *planned* with *actual* progress on construction project.
C. Prepare documents for negotiation/settlement.
D. Help draft arbitration claim forms.

IV. Assist in Litigation
● *Comment on Paralegal Work in This Area:*

"Because of the complex factual issues that arise with construction disputes, legal assistants are critical in identifying, organizing, preparing, and analyzing the extensive relevant factual information. In many cases, whether a party wins or loses depends on how effectively facts are developed from documents, depositions, interviews, and site inspections. Thus, a successful construction litigation team will generally include a legal assistant skilled in organization and management of complex and voluminous facts. . . . Construction litigation also provides legal assistants with a very distinctive area for expertise and specialization." M. Gowen, *A Guide for Legal Assistants 229* (Practicing Law Institute).

● *More on This Area of the Law on the Net:*
  ▪ *findlaw.com/01topics/40construction*
  ▪ *www.constructionlaw.com*
  ▪ *www.constructionweblinks.com*

11. Contract Law
The law of contracts is involved in a number of different paralegal specialties. (See *advertising law, antitrust law, banking law, bankruptcy law, collections law, construction law, corporate law, employee benefits law, entertainment law, family law, government contract law, insurance law, intellectual property law, international law, labor and employment law, landlord and tenant law, municipal finance law, oil and gas law, real estate law,* and *tax law*.)

I.   Contract Review
A. Review contracts to determine compliance with terms.
B. Investigate facts involving alleged breach of contract.
C. Do legal research on the law of contracts in a particular specialty.

II. Litigation Assistance

III. Preparation of Contract Forms
A. Separation agreements
B. Employment contracts
C. Contracts for sale, etc.

● *Comment on Paralegal Work in This Area:*

"The . . . paralegal also assists two attorneys in drafting, reviewing, researching, revising and finalizing a variety of contracts, including Entertainment, Participant and Operational Agreements. Much of the . . . paralegal's time is spent studying existing contracts looking for provisions that may answer any inquiries or disputes. With hundreds of agreements presently active, researching, reviewing, amending, terminating, revising and executing contracts is an everyday activity for [the] . . . Legal Department." Miquel, *Walt Disney World Company's Legal Assistants: Their Role in the Show,* 16 Facts and Findings 29.

"Initially, my primary job was to review contracts, and act as Plan Administrator for the 401(k). I was also involved in the negotiation and development of a distributor agreement to market SPSS software to the Soviet Union. Most contract amendments were to software license agreements. The pace picked up when I was promoted to Manager of Human Services, while retaining all of my previous responsibilities." Illinois Paralegal Ass'n, *Spotlight on . . . Laurel Bauer,* 20 Outlook 21.

- *More on This Area of the Law on the Net:*
  - *www.law.cornell.edu/wex/index.php/Contracts*
  - *www.law.cornell.edu/wex/index.php/ Commercial_law*
  - *findlaw.com/01topics/07contracts*
  - *findlaw.com/01topics/04commercial*

12. Corporate Law

Paralegals involved in corporate law mainly work in one of two settings: law firms that represent corporations and law departments of corporations. (See also *banking law, employee benefits law, insurance law, labor and employment law, real estate law,* and *tax law.*)

I. Incorporation and General Corporate Work
A. Preincorporation.
  1. Check availability of proposed corporate name and, if available, reserve it.
  2. Draft preincorporation subscriptions and consent forms for initial board of directors where required by statute.
  3. Record articles of incorporation.
  4. Order corporate supplies.
B. Incorporation.
  1. Draft and file articles of incorporation with appropriate state agency for:
     a. Subchapter S corporation,
     b. Close corporation, or
     c. Nonprofit corporation.
  2. Draft minutes of initial meetings of incorporators and directors.
  3. Draft corporate bylaws.
  4. Obtain corporate seal, minutes book, and stock certificate book.
  5. Prepare necessary documents to open a corporate bank account.
C. Directors meetings.
  1. Prepare and send out waivers and notices of meetings.
  2. Draft minutes of directors meetings.
  3. Draft resolutions to be considered by directors:
     a. Sale of stock,
     b. Increase in capitalization,
     c. Stock split,
     d. Stock option,
     e. Pension plan,
     f. Dividend distribution, or
     g. Election of officers.
D. Shareholders meetings (annual and special)
  1. Draft sections of annual report relating to business activity, officers, and directors of company.
  2. Draft notice of meeting, proxy materials, and ballots.
  3. Prepare agenda and script of meeting.
  4. Draft oath, report of judge of elections, and other compliance documents when required.
  5. Maintain corporate minutes books and resolutions.
E. Draft and prepare documents:
  1. Shareholder agreement,
  2. Employment contract,
  3. Employee benefit plan,
  4. Stock option plan,
  5. Trust agreement,
  6. Tax return, and
  7. Closing papers on corporate acquisition.
  8. See also drafting tasks listed above for directors and shareholders meetings.

II. Public Sale of Securities
A. Compile information concerning officers and directors for use in Registration Statement.
B. Assist in research of blue sky requirements.
C. Closing:
  1. Prepare agenda,
  2. Obtain certificates from state agencies on good standing of company and certified corporate documents, and
  3. Prepare index and organize closing binders.

III. Research
A. Monitor pending legislation that may affect office clients.
B. Extract requested information from corporate records and documents.
C. Assemble financial data from records on file at SEC (Securities and Exchange Commission) and state securities regulatory agencies.

IV. General Assistance
A. Analyze government regulations to assure that the policies and practices of the corporation are in compliance.
B. Maintain tickler system (specifying, for example, dates of next corporate meeting, shareholder meeting, upcoming trial, appellate court appearance).
C. Monitor the daily law journal or legal newspaper to identify relevant cases on calendars of courts, current court decisions, articles, etc., and forward such data to appropriate office attorneys.
D. Act as file managers for certain clients: index, digest, and monitor documents in the file, prepare case profiles, etc.
E. Maintain corporate forms file.

V. Miscellaneous
A. Act as the corporate secretary
B. Prepare documents for qualification to do business in foreign jurisdictions.
C. Prepare filings with regulatory agencies.
D. Provide assistance in processing patent, copyright, and trademark applications.
E. Coordinate escrow transactions.
F. Work on certificates of occupancy.
G. Prepare documents needed to amend bylaws or Articles of Incorporation.
H. Prepare interrogatories.
I. Digest deposition testimony.
J. Perform cite checks.

- *Comment on Paralegal Work in This Area:*
  "When the majority of people describe a legal assistant or a paralegal, they often think of courtroom battles, million dollar lawsuits and mountains of depositions. For those of us in

the corporate area, these sights are replaced with board room battles, million dollar mergers and mountains of prospectuses. Some of us have NEVER seen the inside of a courtroom or have never touched a pleading. I guess it can be said that 'we don't do windows, we don't type, and we don't do litigation.' A corporate paralegal is never without a multitude of projects that offer excitement or anxiety. This isn't to say, however, that the corporate field is without its fair share of boredom. . . . The future is only limited by your imagination. Not every paralegal wants the drama of a landmark case. Some of us are quite content seeing a client's company written up in the *Wall Street Journal* for the first time!" D. Zupanovich, *The Forming of a Corporate Paralegal*, 2 California Paralegal 4.

"The company I work for is a major worldwide producer of chemicals. . . . I recently had to obtain some technical information about the computer system at a hotel in a foreign country in order to set up documents on a disk that would be compatible with the computer system in that country before one of the attorneys went there for contract negotiations." "One of the most thrilling experiences I have had since working for the company was that of working on the closing of a leveraged buyout of a portion of our business in Delaware. To experience first-hand the intensity of the negotiating table, the numerous last-minute changes to documents, the multitudinous shuffle of papers, and the late, grueling hours was both exhausting and exhilarating." Grove, *Scenes from a Corporate Law Department*, The Paraview 2 (Metrolina Paralegal Ass'n).

"Even 'dream jobs' have their moments of chaos. After only two months on the job [at Nestle Foods Corporation] Cheryl had to prepare for a Federal Trade Commission Second Request for Production of Documents relating to an acquisition. She suddenly was thrown into the job of obtaining and organizing over 6,000 documents from around the world, creating a document database and managing up to 10 temporary paralegals at a time. Of course, this preparation included weekends and evenings for a six-week period. Cheryl calls December the 'lost month.'" Scior, *Paralegal Profile: Corporate Paralegal*, Post Script 14 (Manhattan Paralegal Ass'n).

- *Quotes from Want Ads:*
  Law firm seeks paralegal for corporate work: "Ideal candidate is a self-starter with good communications skills and is willing to work overtime." "Ability to work independently is a must." Paralegal needed to assist corporate secretary: "Analytical, professional attitude essential. Knowledge of state and/or federal regulatory agencies required." "Ability to work under pressure." "All candidates must possess excellent writing and drafting skills." "Ideal candidate is a self-starter with good communication/research skills and is willing to work overtime." "Candidates having less than three years experience in general corporate legal assistance need not apply." Position requires "word processing experience and ability to manage multiple projects." Position requires "intelligent, highly motivated individual who can work with little supervision." "Great opportunity to learn all aspects of corporate business transactions." Position requires "career-minded paralegal with excellent organizational and communications skills, keen analytical ability and meticulous attention to detail." Position requires "an experienced paralegal with a strong blue-sky background,

particularly in public and private real estate syndication." Applicant must have "excellent academic credentials, be analytical, objective, and dedicated to performing thorough quality work and to displaying a professional attitude to do whatever it takes to get the job done and meet deadlines."

- *More on This Area of the Law on the Net:*
  - www.law.cornell.edu/wex/index.php/Corporations
  - www.sec.gov
  - www.acc.com
  - findlaw.com/01topics/08corp
  - findlaw.com/01topics/34securities

13. Criminal Law[5]
(See also *litigation* and *military law*.)

I. Paralegal Working for a Prosecutor
A. Log incoming cases.
B. Help office screen out cases that are inappropriate for arrest, cases that are eligible for diversion, etc.
C. Act as liaison with police department and other law enforcement agencies.
D. Prepare statistical caseload reports.
E. Interview citizens who are seeking the prosecution of alleged wrongdoers; prepare case files.
F. Help the Consumer Fraud Department resolve minor consumer complaints—for instance, contact the business involved to determine whether a settlement of the case is possible without prosecution.
G. Conduct field investigations as assigned.
H. Prepare documents for UIFSA cases (Uniform Interstate Family Support Act).
I. Monitor status of UIFSA cases.
J. Help office maintain its case calendar.
K. Act as liaison among the prosecutor, the victim, and witnesses while the case is being prepared for trial and during the trial.
L. Act as general litigation assistant during the trial and the appeal.

II. Paralegal Working for a Criminal Defense Attorney
A. Interview defendants to determine eligibility for free legal defense (if the paralegal works for a public defender).
B. Conduct comprehensive interview of defendant on matters relevant to the criminal charge(s).
C. Help the defendant gather information relevant to the determination of bail.
D. Help the defendant gather information relevant to eligibility for diversion programs.
E. Conduct field investigations; interview witnesses.
F. Help obtain discovery, particularly through police reports and search warrants.
G. Act as general litigation assistant during the trial and the appeal.

- *Comment on Paralegal Work in This Area:*
  "Ivy speaks with an obvious love for her current job in the State Attorney's office. In fact, she said she would not want to do anything else! She also said there is no such thing as a typical day in her office, which is one of the many aspects of

her job she enjoys. She not only helps interview witnesses and prepare them for trial, but she often must locate a witness, requiring some detective work! Ivy assisted in a case involving an elderly woman who was victimized after the death of her husband. The woman was especially vulnerable because of her illiteracy. Through the help of the State Attorney's office, the woman was able to recover her money and get assistance with housing and learning to read. Ivy . . . feels the experience to be very rewarding." Frazier, *Spotlight on Ivy Hart-Daniel*, JLA News 2 (Jacksonville Legal Assistants, Inc.).

"Kitty Polito says she and other lawyers at McClure, McClure & Kammen use the firm's sole paralegal not only to do investigations but 'to pick cases apart piece by piece.' Polito credits legal assistant Juliann Klapp with 'cracking the case' of a client who was accused by a codefendant of hitting the victim on the back of the head. At trial, the pathologist testified that the victim had been hit from left to right. Klapp passed a note to the attorneys pointing out that such a motion would have been a back-handed swing for their right-handed client. Thus it was more likely that the codefendant, who is left-handed, was the one who hit the victim. The defendant won." Brandt, *Paralegals' Acceptance and Utilization Increasing in Indy's Legal Community*, 1 The Indiana Lawyer 1.

- *More on This Area of the Law on the Net:*
  - *www.law.cornell.edu/wex/index.php/Criminal_law*
  - *findlaw.com/01topics/09criminal*
  - *www.fbi.gov*

14. Employee Benefits Law[6]

Employee benefits paralegals work in a number of different settings: in law firms, banks, large corporations, insurance companies, or accounting firms. The following overview of tasks covers a paralegal working for a law firm. (See also *contract law, corporate law, labor and employment law, social security law,* and *workers' compensation law.*)

I. Drafting of Employee Plans
A. Work closely with the attorney, the plan sponsor, the plan administrator, and the trustee in preparing and drafting qualified employee plans, such as:
    1. Stock bonus plans,
    2. Profit-sharing plans,
    3. Money purchase pensions,
    4. Trust agreements,
    5. Individual retirement account (IRA) plans,
    6. Annuity plans,
    7. HR-10 or Keogh plans,
    8. Employee stock ownership plans,
    9. Life and health insurance plans,
    10. Workers' compensation plans, and
    11. Social Security plans.

II. Document Preparation and Program Monitoring
A. Gather information.
B. Determine eligibility for participation and benefits.
C. Notify employees of participation.
D. Complete input forms for document assembly.
E. Assemble elections to participate.
F. Determine beneficiary designations.

G. Record elections to contribute.
H. Allocate annual contributions to the individual participant accounts.
I. Prepare annual account statements for participants.
J. Identify potential discrimination problems in the program.

III. Government Compliance Work Pertaining to:
A. Tax requirements for qualification, amendment, and termination of plan.
B. Department of Labor reporting and disclosure requirements.
C. Insurance requirements.
D. Welfare and Pension Plans Disclosure Act requirements.
E. ERISA (Employee Retirement Income Security Act) requirements.
F. Pension Benefit Guaranty Corporation requirements.

IV. Miscellaneous
A. Help draft summary plan descriptions for distribution to employees.
B. Help prepare and review annual reports of plans.
C. Continue education in current law of the field—for instance, study to become a Certified Employee Benefit Specialist (CEBS).

- *Comment on Paralegal Work in This Area:*
  "Michael Montchyk was looking to use his undergraduate degree in statistics. . . . He now works for attorneys specializing in employee benefits, where understanding numbers and familiarity with the law are key skills." Lehren, *Paralegal Work Enhancing Careers of Many*, Philadelphia Business Journal 9B.
  "This area is not for everybody. To succeed, you need considerable detail orientation, solid writing skills, self-motivation, the ability to keep up with a legal landscape that is never the same, and a knack for handling crisis situations, which arise when least expected." Germani, *Opportunities in Employee Benefits*, SJPA Reporter 7 (South Jersey Paralegal Ass'n).

- *More on This Area of the Law on the Net:*
  - *www.ifebp.org*
  - *www.benefitslink.com*
  - *www.pensionrights.org*
  - *www.weblocator.com/attorney/ca/law/b21.html*

15. Entertainment Law

(See also *contract law, corporate law* and *intellectual property law.*)

I. Types of Client Problem Areas
A. *Copyright and trademark law:* Apply for government protection for intellectual property, such as plays, films, video, music, Web sites, and novels.
B. *Contract law:* Help negotiate and draft contracts, and ensure their enforcement.
C. *Labor law:* Assist a client to comply with the contracts of unions or guilds.
D. *Corporate law:*
    1. Assist in formation of business organizations.
    2. Work on mergers.
    3. Maintain compliance with federal and state reporting laws and regulations.

E. *Tax law:* Planning and compliance.
   1. Report passive royalty income, talent advances, residuals, etc.
   2. Allocate expenditures to specific projects.
F. *Family law:* Assist with prenuptial agreements, divorces, child custody, etc.

II. Miscellaneous Tasks
A. Register copyrights.
B. Help a client affiliate with his or her guild.
C. Monitor remake and sequel rights to films.
D. Prepare documents to grant a license to use client's music.
E. Check title registrations with the Motion Picture Association of America.
F. Read scripts to determine whether clearances are needed for certain kinds of material and references.
G. Apply for permits and licenses.
H. Calculate costs of property rights.

● *Comment on Paralegal Work in This Area:*
   "I am a paralegal in the field of entertainment law, one of the fastest growing, and, to me, most exciting areas of the paralegal profession, and one whose duties are as varied as the practices of the lawyers for whom we work. . . . I started in a very large Century City firm whose entertainment practice covers everything from songwriters to financing of major motion pictures, and from major recording stars and producers to popular novelists. . . . My specialty (yes, a specialty within a specialty) is music. . . . My husband is also an entertainment paralegal who works for 20th Century Fox. . . . Never, ever a dull moment!" Birkner, *Entertainment Law: A Growing Industry for the Paralegal*, 2 California Paralegal Magazine 7.

● *More on This Area of the Law on the Net:*
   ■ *dir.yahoo.com/Government/law/entertainment*
   ■ *findlaw.com/01topics/12entertainsport*
   ■ *www.ascap.com*

16. Environmental Law[7]

(See also *legislation, litigation, oil and gas law, real estate law,* and *water law.*)

I. Research
A. Research questions pertaining to the environment, land use, water pollution, and the National Environmental Policy Act.
   1. Locate and study pertinent state and federal statutes, case law, regulations, and law review articles.
   2. Obtain nonlegal secondary materials (maps, articles, and books) useful for broadening the information base.
   3. Contact, when appropriate, government officials or other informants for information.
   4. Obtain and develop personality profiles of members of Congress, members of relevant bureaucracies, and other political figures.
   5. Help prepare memoranda of findings, including citations and supporting documents.
B. Develop research notebooks for future reference. When new topics arise in environmental law, prepare notebooks to facilitate future research.
C. Prepare bibliographies on environmental topics.

II. Drafting
A. Draft memoranda regarding new federal and state laws, regulations, or findings of research.
B. Draft memoranda discussing pertinent issues, problems, and solutions regarding public policy developments.
C. Draft narrative histories of legislation regarding political impulses, the impact of administrative and court rulings, and substantive and technical differences between drafts of legislation or results of amendments.
D. Draft and edit articles on coastal management programs and problems, conservation, water pollution, and the National Environmental Policy Act.
E. Edit environmental impact statements.
F. Assist in the preparation of briefs.
   1. Cite-check brief.
   2. Develop table of contents, table of authorities, and certificate of service.

III. Hearing Participation
A. Locate and schedule witnesses.
B. Gather pertinent research materials (local documents, maps, etc.).

IV. Litigation: Provide General Trial Assistance

● *Comment on Paralegal Work in This Area:*
   Erin Brockovich, "the feisty paralegal (played by Julia Roberts in the movie named after her), helped a California town's residents win $333 million from a utility that had leaked chromium into their water" (www.corpwatch.org/article.php?id=13004). "Bill Moyers TV special revealed how the public was kept in the dark about the dangers of toxic chemicals. Every powerful story about fighting for truth and justice has its heroes . . . like Erin Brockovich, the paralegal–turned–movie icon who fought against toxic polluters in California" (www.alternet.org/story/10600).
   Mary Peterson's firm has made a specialty of environmental and land use law. In a recent major hazardous waste case, "we will try to prove that the paint companies, dry cleaning stores and even the federal government, which used the property to build aircraft during the war," are responsible. "Some of the toxic waste dumped there was cited by federal agencies even back to 1935." Her job is to investigate the types of hazardous wastes and, with the help of the Freedom of Information Act, gather all available evidence. Then she studies it, duplicates, indexes, and writes summaries, which she distributes to the partners and associates. It's a case that has taken eight months so far and may go on for several years "because you don't know what you will uncover tomorrow. The toxins and pollutants could be different. There is no standard, just a constantly changing picture." Edwards, *The General Practice Paralegal*, 8 Legal Assistant Today 49.

● *More on This Area of the Law on the Net:*
   ■ *www.epa.gov*
   ■ *findlaw.com/01topics/13environmental*
   ■ *www.eli.org*

17. Estates, Trusts, and Probate Law

(See also *banking law, collections law, employee benefits law, family law,* and *social security law.*)

I. Estate Planning
A. Collect data (birth dates, fair market value of assets, current assets and liabilities, etc.).
B. Using computer-generated forms, prepare preliminary drafts of wills or trusts.
C. Perform investment analysis in order to provide attorney (who is the fiduciary of the estate) with information relevant to investment options.

II. Office Management
A. Maintain tickler system.
B. Maintain attorney's calendar.
C. Open, index, monitor, and keep current the office file on the client's trust and estate case.
D. Using computer programs, manage the accounting of trusts and estates administered by the office.
E. Act as office law librarian (keeping looseleaf texts up to date, etc.).
F. Train secretaries and other paralegals in the system used by the office to handle trusts, estates, and probate cases.
G. Selectively discard certain mail and underline significant parts of other mail.

III. Estate of Decedent
A. Assets phase.
  1. Collect assets (such as bank accounts, custody accounts, insurance proceeds, social security death benefits, safety deposit box contents, and apartment contents).
  2. Assist in the valuation of assets.
  3. Maintain records (for example, wills and trusts, vault inventories, powers of attorney, property settlements, fee cards, bill-payment letters).
  4. Record and file wills and trusts.
  5. Notify beneficiaries.
  6. Prepare profiles of wills and trusts for attorney review.
B. Accounting phase.
  1. Prepare preliminary drafts of federal and state death tax returns.
  2. Apply the income-principal rules to the estate.
  3. Organize data relevant to taxation of estates.
  4. Prepare accountings: final and accounts current (for example, set up a petition for a first and final accounting).
C. Termination-distribution phase.
  1. Apply for the transfer of securities into the names of the people entitled.
  2. Draw checks for the signature of executors.
  3. Monitor legacies to charitable clients.
  4. File and prepare tax waivers.
  5. Assist with the closing documents.
  6. Calculate distributable net income.
  7. Follow up on collection and delivery.

IV. Litigation
  1. Perform legal research.
  2. Conduct factual research (investigation), e.g., track down the names and addresses of all possible claimants and contact them.
  3. Prepare pleadings.
  4. Digest depositions (review, condense, point out inconsistencies, etc.).
  5. Prepare drafts of interrogatories.
  6. Prepare drafts of answers to interrogatories.
  7. Notarize documents.
  8. Act as court witness as to decedent's signature.
  9. Assist with litigation.

- ***Comment on Paralegal Work in This Area:***
  "What I like best about estate planning is that you work with people on a very individual basis. I don't think that in many other areas of law you get that one-on-one contact with the client. . . . You're working with people while they are thinking about the most important things in their lives—their families, their wealth and how to distribute it, and what they want to happen after they pass on. A lot of the clients contact me directly with their questions for the attorneys. Some of the widows especially are more comfortable calling me with their questions. They seem to think their questions might be 'stupid' and they're embarrassed to ask the attorneys directly. I can take their questions and see that the attorneys respond to them promptly." Bassett, *Top Gun Patricia Adams: Legal Assistant of the Year*, 6 Legal Assistant Today 70.

  "The position can be very stressful. But it is seldom boring. My typical day involves responding to many telephone inquiries from clients, dictating memos, or letters requesting additional information concerning life insurance policies, valuation of assets, or simply sending notice of an upcoming hearing 'to all persons entitled,' etc. I draft virtually all documents needed in the administration of an estate, beginning with the initial petition for probate. . . . The decedent may have had an interest in a closely-held business, or leave minor or handicapped children, or leave a spouse with no knowledge of the family assets; these all require additional attention. Every case is different. Probate paralegals to some extent must be 'snoopy,' because you do learn a great deal about people, both deceased and living. In most cases your client is facing a difficult time with trepidation and it is your role to provide confidence. The end results are very rewarding." Rose, *Still a Probate Paralegal*, 12 The Journal 5 (Sacramento Ass'n of Legal Assistants).

- ***Quotes from Want Ads:***
  Law firm seeks someone with "experience preparing the 706 estate tax return, asset funding including preparing property deeds, and drafting estate planning documents. Being a notary public is a plus." Bank has opening for "trust tax administrator, with emphasis on personal and trust planning." Paralegal must have "technical understanding of wills and estate plans and terminology. Must be self-starter." "This is a full-time position with extensive responsibility for both court-supervised and noncourt-supervised estates and trusts." Position requires a person who "enjoys writing and proofreading, and who has excellent grammatical skills." Job is "for individual who enjoys the complexity and detail of accounting and bookkeeping in a legal environment." "Applicants must be prepared to handle tax work."

- ***More on This Area of the Law on the Net:***
  - *www.actec.org*
  - *www.abanet.org/rppt/home.html*
  - *www.law.cornell.edu/wex/index.php/Estates_and_Trusts*
  - *findlaw.com/01topics/31probate*

18. Ethics and Professional Responsibility

Paralegals in this area work in two main settings: (1) in large law firms as a conflicts specialist (also called a conflicts analyst or conflicts researcher), helping the firm determine whether conflicts of interest exist between prospective clients and current or former clients; and (2) in state disciplinary agencies or boards that investigate complaints against attorneys for unethical behavior.

I. Law Firm
A. Research
   1. Identify all persons or companies with a personal or business relationship with the prospective client.
   2. Determine whether the firm has ever represented the prospective client and/or any of its related parties.
   3. Determine whether the firm has ever represented an opponent of the prospective client and/or any of its related parties.
B. *Reports:* Notify attorney of data indicating possible conflict of interest.
C. *Database work:* Update information in client database on current and past clients for purposes of future conflicts checks.

II. Disciplinary Agency
A. Screen incoming data on new ethical complaints against attorneys.
B. Help investigate complaints.
C. Provide general litigation assistance to disciplinary attorneys during the proceedings at the agency and in court.

● ***Comment on Paralegal Work in This Area:***
Jane Palmer "does all the research on every prospective client, identifying all the related parties." Her computerized database tells her if the firm has ever represented a party on either side, or been adverse to them. "The most valuable thing has been my experience with the firm, developing somewhat of a corporate memory. The job takes extreme attention to detail. You may not always have all the information you need, so you have to be a detective. Quick response is important; so is making sure to keep things confidential." Sacramento Ass'n of Legal Assistants, *New Responsibilities Given to Paralegals,* The Journal 5.

● ***More on This Area of the Law on the Net:***
  ■ *www.legalethics.com*
  ■ *www.abanet.org/cpr/home.html*
  ■ *findlaw.com/01topics/14ethics*

19. Family Law[8]

(See also *contract law, employee benefits law, estates law, litigation, pro bono work,* and *public sector.*)

I. Problem Areas Covered
A. Adoption
B. Divorce
C. Contracts (prenuptial agreement, separation agreement, surrogacy agreement, etc.)
D. Child Support
E. Child Custody
F. Annulment

II. Commencement of Action
A. Interview client to obtain initial information for pleadings.
B. Prepare initial pleadings, including petition, summons and waiver of service, affidavit as to children, and response.
C. Draft correspondence to be sent to clients, courts, and other attorneys.
D. Arrange for service of process.

III. Temporary Orders
A. Prepare motions for temporary orders, e.g., a temporary injunction.
B. Draft notice and request for hearings.
C. Assist in settlement negotiations.
D. Draft stipulations for temporary orders after negotiations.

IV. Financial Affidavits
A. Help clients gather and compile financial information.
B. Analyze income and expense information provided by client.
C. Work with accountants, financial advisors, brokers, and other financial experts retained by client.
D. Hire appraisers for real estate, business, and personal property.
E. Prepare financial affidavits.

V. Discovery
A. Prepare discovery requests.
B. Help clients organize documents and data to respond to discovery requests.
C. Help prepare responses to discovery requests.
D. Organize, index, and summarize materials obtained by discovery.

VI. Settlement Negotiations
A. Assist attorney in analysis of proposed settlements.
B. Research legal questions and assist in drafting memoranda and briefs.
C. Assist in drafting separation agreement.

VII. Hearings
A. Help prepare for hearings on final orders.
B. Assist in the preparation of trial exhibits and trial notebooks.
C. Arrange for expert witnesses and assist in preparing witnesses and clients for trial.
D. Prepare draft of decree.

VIII. Post-Decree
A. Prepare documents for transfers of assets.
B. Arrange to file and record all transfer documents.
C. Review bills for tax-deductible fees and help prepare opinion letter to client.
D. Draft pleadings for withdrawal from case.

IX. Special Projects
A. Develop forms for fact gathering from clients.
B. Maintain files on separation-agreement provisions, current case law, resource materials for clients, and experts in various fields (e.g., custody, evaluation, and business appraisals).

● ***Comment on Paralegal Work in This Area:***
Karen Dunn, a family law paralegal, "draws considerable satisfaction from a divorce case where the client was a woman in her sixties whose husband had left her, a situation which

created predictable distress, notably during discussion of financial aspects. She was able to tell me things she couldn't tell the attorney. I found out she had a thyroid condition, so she was able to get more money in the end. I worked with her on the financial affidavit and drafted temporary orders to provide child support and spousal maintenance until the decree was entered." Edwards, *The General Practice Paralegal*, 8 Legal Assistant Today 49.

"As the only paralegal in a one-attorney family law practice, my job responsibilities are numerous. I work for an attorney who believes her paralegal should handle nearly all the legal functions she does, with the exception of appearing in court on behalf of clients, taking depositions and giving legal advice. My skills are used to the maximum, as I gather and organize all case information, allowing the attorney to prepare for court and be more cost-effective. I am the liaison person between clients and the attorney. I am able to deal with the human, emotional aspects of our clients, and not just the technical aspects of the law. As each person is different, so is every case, which makes this job a continuing challenge." Lenihan, *Role of the Family Law Paralegal*, 10 Paragram 6 (Oregon Legal Assistants Ass'n).

- *Quotes from Want Ads:*
  Position is "excellent for a highly motivated person with excellent organizational skills and the ability to interface with clients." "Two swamped attorneys need reliable paralegal to work in fully computerized office. Must have excellent research and writing skills." Applicant must be "self-motivated, well-organized person who has initiative and can assume responsibility." Position requires "ability, experience, and attention to detail." "Looking for very professional applicants."

- *More on This Area of the Law on the Net:*
  - *findlaw.com/01topics/15family*
  - *www.divorcecentral.com*
  - *www.abanet.org/family/home.html*
  - *patriot.net/~crouch/fln.html*

20. Gaming Law

I. Applications
A. Obtain applications and related documents needed by a business to acquire licenses and permits needed to operate a gaming business:
  1. State gaming business license
  2. Local gaming business license
  3. Liquor license
  4. State sales/use tax permit
  5. Health permit
  6. Unemployment insurance registration
  7. Workers' compensation clearance
B. Help conduct due diligence and licensing history research.
C. Coordinate the obtaining of gaming bonds.
D. Arrange meetings for the execution of licensing applications, affidavits, and declarations.

II. Compliance
A. Research business license and land use compliance.
B. Maintain a tickler system for timely filings of compliance reports.
C. File board meeting agendas and related materials.

D. When a regulatory agency investigates the internal operations of a client, assist in providing information on finances, securities, product sales, political contributions, and personal data on senior management.

III. Collection and Judgments
A. Assist on out-of-state (including international) marker collection cases.
B. Prepare and file judgment renewals.

- *Comment on Paralegal Work in This Area:*
  "The commercial casino industry is one of the most heavily regulated industries in the nation." In this position the "work done for clients translates into a business operation that you can see, watch prosper, and grow. Whether it is assisting a client in the opening of the five-star restaurant . . . or the newest casino hotel resort . . . the result of your hard work manifests itself into things that are seen and realized." Lorraine Oehlschlaeger, *The Expanding Role of the Paralegal in the Gaming Industry* Career Chronicle 42 (National Association of Legal Assistants)

- *More on This Area of the Law on the Net:*
  - *www.findlaw.com/01topics/43gaming/index.html*
  - *www.megalaw.com/top/gaming.php*

21. Government Contract Law[9]

(See also *administrative law, construction law, contract law, litigation,* and *water law.*)

I. Calendar
A. Maintain calendar for court and appeal board appearances.
B. Record dates when briefs are due, etc.

II. Claims
A. Gather, review, summarize, and index client files.
B. Assist in drafting contract claims.
C. Conduct preliminary research on selected legal issues.

III. Appeals
A. Draft and answer interrogatories and requests for production of documents.
B. Summarize and index answers to discovery.
C. Assist in drafting appeal.
D. Prepare questions for witnesses and summarize their prior testimony.
E. Maintain documents during hearing.

IV. Posthearing Briefs
A. Summarize and index transcripts.
B. Assist with analysis of government's brief.
C. Conduct preliminary research on selected issues.
D. Assist in drafting the posthearing brief.

- *More on This Area of the Law on the Net:*
  - *www.law.cornell.edu/wex/index.php/Government_contracts*
  - *findlaw.com/01topics/18govcontracts*

22. Immigration Law

(See also *administrative law, family law, international law, labor and employment law,* and *public sector.*)

I. Problem Identification
A. Help individual who has difficulty in obtaining:
1. Visa,
2. Permanent residency based on occupation,
3. Nonimmigrant status, or
4. Citizenship status.
B. Help those faced with deportation proceedings.

II. Providing Information on:
A. Visas,
B. Permanent residency,
C. Nonimmigrant status,
D. Registration,
E. Citizenship, or
F. Deportation.

III. Investigation
Assist the individual in obtaining data and documentation on birth, travel, residency, etc.

IV. Referral
Refer individuals to foreign consulates, nationality organizations, government officials, etc., for assistance concerning their immigration status.

V. Applications/Forms
Assist the individual in filling out visa applications, permanent residency applications, etc.

VI. Monitor Consular Processing Procedure

● ***Comment on Paralegal Work in This Area:***
"This is not a specialty for the faint-hearted or the misanthrope. The immigration paralegal may deal with much more than the timely filing of paperwork. One distinguishing feature of immigration work is our knowledge of intensely personal aspects of the client's life. We know his criminal record, the success and failure of his personal life, how much money he makes, and his dreams and aspirations. . . . Some clients have a very laissez-faire attitude towards perjury, and may invite the paralegal to participate without a blush. In America, [said one client] you lie *to* your attorney. In my country, you cook up the lie *with* your attorney." Myers & Raman, *Sweet-Talking Clients and Intransigent Bureaucrats*, 15 National Paralegal Reporter 4 (NFPA).

● ***More on This Area of the Law on the Net:***
■ *www.wave.net/upg/immigration/resource.html*
■ *findlaw.com/01topics/20immigration*
■ *www.aila.org*

23. Insurance Law
The specialty of representing insurance companies that challenge claims brought against them (or their policy holders) is referred to as **insurance defense**. A paralegal in this field might work for a law firm hired by an insurance company or may work within an insurance company itself. The most common kind of insurance defense work involves personal injury (PI) claims that arise out of standard liability policies. The following overview covers the latter. (See also *corporate law, employee benefits law, litigation, social security law,* and *workers' compensation law.*)

I. Compliance
A. Analyze government regulations on the insurance industry to assure that insurance policies and other company products are in compliance.
B. Prepare applications for new insurance products to obtain approval from the state department of insurance.

II. Claims
A. Assist in processing disputed claims.
B. Provide trial assistance by coordinating activities of company attorneys with outside counsel.

III. Monitoring and Research
A. Monitor regulations of agencies and statutes of the legislatures that affect the insurance industry, particularly the committees of the legislature with jurisdiction over the industry.
B. Provide factual and legal research on inquiries that come into the office from agents and brokers.

IV. Outside Counsel
A. Act as liaison between the insurance company and the outside law firm hired by the company to litigate cases brought by or against the company.
B. Help with record keeping and oversight of the bills submitted by outside counsel.

● ***Comment on Paralegal Work in This Area:***
"Compliance is an insurance industry term which refers to keeping the company and its products in compliance with state and federal law, and procuring licenses for the company in states where it is not licensed. Compliance is a good field for paralegals because there is opportunity to work autonomously and also to advance within most companies." I am a "Senior Compliance Analyst" at a life insurance company. "I have met many paralegals who are compliance analysts, compliance specialists, and compliance managers." Maston, *Insurance*, The Citator 8 (Legal Assistants of Central Ohio).

● ***More on This Area of the Law on the Net:***
■ *www.law.cornell.edu/topics/insurance.html*
■ *findlaw.com/01topics/44insurance*

24. Intellectual Property Law
Paralegals in this area work on copyrights, patents, and trademarks. (See also *contract law* and *entertainment law.*)

I. Copyrights
A. Application
1. Help client apply for copyright registration for a novel, play, or other "original works of authorship" with the U.S. Copyright Office.
2. Help apply for protection in foreign countries.
3. Collect data for the application (e.g., the nature of the work, date completed, name of creator/author, name of the work, its owner).
4. Help identify the classification for the copyright.
5. Examine accuracy of certificate-of-copyright registration.
B. Marketing
1. Identify potential users/licensees of the copyright.
2. Help prepare contracts.

C. Infringement
  1. Conduct investigations to determine whether an infringement exists—e.g., compare the copyrighted work with the alleged infringing work.
  2. Provide general litigation assistance.

II. Patent
A. Application
  1. Help the inventor apply for a patent with the U.S. Patent and Trademark Office.
  2. Help describe the invention by using designs, diagrams, notebooks, etc.
  3. Check technical libraries to determine the current state of the art.
  4. Conduct a patent search.
  5. Determine filing fees.
  6. Apply for protection in foreign countries.
  7. Monitor the responses from government offices.
  8. Examine certificate of patent for accuracy.
B. Marketing the invention
  1. Help identify licensees. Solicit bids, conduct financial checks, study the market, etc.
  2. Help prepare contracts.
C. Infringement
  1. Conduct investigation on products that may have violated the patent.
  2. Provide general litigation assistance.

III. Trademarks
A. Registration
  1. Research trademark files or order search of trademark (or trade name) preliminary to an application before the U.S. Patent and Trademark Office.
  2. Examine indexes and directories.
  3. Conduct investigations to determine when the mark was first used, where, on what products, etc.
  4. Prepare foreign trademark applications.
  5. Respond to actions taken by government offices.
  6. Examine the certificate of trademark for accuracy.
  7. Maintain files for renewals.
B. Infringement
  1. Conduct investigations into who else used the mark, when, where, in what market, etc.
  2. Provide general litigation assistance.

- *Comment on Paralegal Work in This Area:*
  "With the right training, trademark paralegals can find richly rewarding experiences waiting for them, whether they remain in paralegal work or go on to build careers in some other facet of trademark law. Trademark work is very dynamic." Wilkinson, *The Case for a Career in Trademark Law,* 7 Legal Professional 29.
  "Paula Rein was a trademark paralegal before such a job title was even invented. Her career has spanned over 19 years, leading her to some of the biggest corporations and law firms in New York City. Her extensive knowledge of trademark administration has made her one of the most resourceful trademark paralegals in her occupation. In her current 'diversified position,' at a law firm that specializes in intellectual property, she works on the cases of clients in the food and service industries and professional associations. Paula thrives in her current position." Scior, *Paralegal Profile,* Postscript 13 (Manhattan Paralegal Ass'n).

- *More on This Area of the Law on the Net:*
  - *www.loc.gov/copyright*
  - *www.uspto.gov*
  - *www.aipla.org*
  - *findlaw.com/01topics/23intellectprop*

25. International Law
  Example: a paralegal working on a "dumping" case in international trade.

I. Investigation
A. Examine the normal behavior in the industry or market affected by the alleged dumping.
B. Do statistical research (cost and price data).
C. Prepare profiles of domestic competitors.

II. Preparation of Documents
A. Help prepare presentation before the Commerce Department.
B. Help prepare presentation before the Court of International Trade.

III. Accounting Research

IV. Coordination of data from:
A. Members of Congress,
B. Foreign embassies,
C. State Department, and
D. U.S. Special Trade Representative.

- *Comment on Paralegal Work in This Area:*
  Steven Stark works "40–50 hours a week, specializing in international legal assisting, a hot area, while the Japanese are busy buying up American properties. [Steve became the liaison for the firm's Tokyo branch office. He originally expected to stay at the firm only three years but found that] the longer you're here, the more they value you. New things still come up. You work with the constant tension of everyone being expected to perform at a very high level, at all times. This is a high-stakes game, with million and billion dollar deals. It's a peaked, emotional atmosphere, with long hours." Milano, *Career Profiles,* 8 Legal Assistant Today 35.

- *More on This Area of the Law on the Net:*
  - *www.abanet.org/intlaw/home.html*
  - *www.law.cornell.edu/topics/international.html*
  - *www.law.cornell.edu/topics/foreign_relations.html*
  - *findlaw.com/01topics/24international*

26. Judicial Administration
  Many courts have law clerks (attorneys who help judges decide cases and write opinions) and administrative clerks (attorneys and nonattorneys who help with the administrative aspects of the court). Recently the U.S. Supreme Court had an opening for an assistant clerk to help screen incoming cases. Some courts have positions that use the *paralegal* title (e.g., procedural motions paralegal in the U.S. Court of Appeals for the Ninth Circuit), although a more common title is *judicial*

assistant. Examples of tasks performed include determining whether the parties have been properly notified of trial dates, checking filings and proposed orders from attorneys to determine whether anything appears inappropriate or premature, obtaining additional information for a judge, etc. (To find openings for positions performing such tasks, go to the Web site of any court and look for employment links on the site.)

- *Comment on Paralegal Work in This Area:*

"The Shreveport City Court has employed me as its paralegal in the civil department for the past six years. The Baton Rouge City Court employs several paralegals." We handle many matters such as determining if the legal delays for pleading have expired "before initialing the pleading and passing it on to the clerk or judge for signature. The most important task is the handling of default judgments. I must certify that proper service has been made. Perhaps I could be called a "nitpicker" about these cases, but the judge acts on my certificate that everything is in order. It is always challenging to stay informed on our constantly changing procedural laws; I must keep a set of the Civil Procedure [laws] at my desk." Waterman, *The Court's Paralegal,* 3 NWLPA News 5 (Northwest Louisiana Paralegal Ass'n).

- *More on This Area of the Law on the Net:*
  - *www.law.cornell.edu/wex/index.php/ Judicial_administration*
  - *www.ncsconline.org*

27. Labor and Employment Law

(See also *civil rights law, contract law, employee benefits law,* and *workers' compensation law.*)

I. Investigation
   Look into:
A. Sexual harassment.
B. Wrongful discharge.
C. Violation of occupational safety and health laws.
D. Violation of labor laws on collective bargaining, union organization, arbitration, etc.
E. Violation of Civil Rights Act protecting against discrimination on the basis of race, national origin, sex, or physical handicap.
F. Violation of Age Discrimination in Employment Act.
G. Violation of Americans with Disabilities Act.

II. Compliance
    Assist companies in implementing policies on:
A. Drug and alcohol testing.
B. AIDS in the workplace.
C. Race, sex, disability, and age discrimination.

III. Litigation Assistance
A. Help handle labor disputes before the National Labor Relations Board, state labor board, civil service commission, human rights board, courts, etc.
B. Perform a variety of tasks:
   1. Maintain case files.
   2. Digest and index data in files.
   3. Arrange for depositions.
   4. Help draft petition and other pleadings.
   5. Maintain tickler system of due dates.
   6. Prepare exhibits.
   7. Prepare statistical data.
   8. Help prepare appeal.

- *Comment on Paralegal Work in This Area:*

"My experience in the labor and employment area has proven to be both diverse and unique. It is diverse because of the various labor-related issues accessible to me as a paralegal. It is unique because it is an area of specialty which involves very few paralegals in my part of the state." Batke, *Labor and Employment Paralegal,* The Citator 3 (Legal Assistants of Central Ohio).

"In the labor law area, I was responsible for doing background research, preparing witnesses and drafting arbitration briefs. I also assisted with the drafting of revised language during contract negotiations with unions." Diebold, *A Paralegal of Another Kind,* 16 Facts and Findings 38 (NALA).

- *More on This Area of the Law on the Net:*
  - *findlaw.com/01topics/27labor*
  - *www.abanet.org/labor/home.html*
  - *www.law.cornell.edu/wex/index.php/Labor*
  - *topics.law.cornell.edu/wex/table_labor*

28. Landlord and Tenant Law

Paralegals in real estate law firms occasionally become involved in commercial lease cases, such as a dispute over the interpretation of the lease of a supermarket at a large shopping mall. Such landlord-tenant cases, however, are not as common as the cases that arise between landlords and tenants who live in the apartments they rent. For example, a landlord of a small apartment seeks to evict a tenant for nonpayment of rent. Many of these cases are handled by publicly funded legal service or legal aid offices that do not charge fees. (See also *public sector, oil and gas law,* and *real estate law.*)

- *Comment on Paralegal Work in This Area:*

"The Legal Action Center is the largest non-governmental social service agency in the state. As a paralegal, Virginia Farley handles all eviction calls to the landlord-tenant unit. Three afternoons a week are designated intake times. She screens all eviction cases, determines whether the applicant is eligible for free assistance according to the Center's guidelines, recommends a plan once a case is accepted and assists in carrying out the plan under an attorney's supervision. [After arriving in the city], Farley made a commitment to work directly with the poor and started serving as a volunteer in five organizations until a job opened up for her at the Legal Action Center." Roche, *Paralegal Profile,* 4 Findings and Conclusions 5 (Washington Ass'n of Legal Assistants).

- *More on This Area of the Law on the Net:*
  - *www.law.cornell.edu/topics/landlord_tenant.html*
  - *www.hg.org/landlord.html*

29. Law Librarianship

There is a separate degree that a law librarian can obtain. This degree, however, is not a requirement to be a law librarian. A number of small or medium-sized law offices are hiring paralegals to perform library chores exclusively or in combination with paralegal duties on cases. (See also *law office administration* and *litigation*.)

I. Administration
A. Order books for law library.
B. File looseleaf material and pocket parts in appropriate volumes.
C. Pay bills of library vendors.
D. Test and recommend computer equipment, software, and services for the law library.
E. Prepare budget for library.

II. Cite Checking
A. Check the citations in briefs, speeches, articles, opinion letters, and other legal documents to determine the accuracy of quoted material.
B. Check the citations to determine the accuracy of citation format according to local court rules, the Uniform System of Citation (the Bluebook), or other citation guidelines.

III. Research
A. Perform factual research.
B. Perform legal research.

IV. Training
A. Train office staff in traditional legal research techniques.
B. Train office staff in computer research, e.g., Westlaw and LexisNexis.
C. Train office staff in cite checking.

- *Comment on Paralegal Work in This Area:*
  "I suppose my entry into the law librarianship profession might be considered unorthodox because I had no formal educational courses in librarianship. My experience was that of working first as a legal secretary and later evolving into a legal assistant. My job in a small general practice firm included taking care of the office library such as filing supplements and pocket parts (because no one else would do it!!); doing the bookkeeping and paying the bills." I did some legal research "as an extension of legal drafting." "In all my working years (and they are many) I had the greatest satisfaction from my work as a law librarian because each day I learned new things." Lewek, *The Legal Assistant as Law Librarian*, 17 Facts & Findings 28 (NALA).

- *More on This Area of the Law on the Net:*
  - *www.aallnet.org/index.asp*
  - *www.llrx.com*
  - *www.washlaw.edu/subject/law.libraries.html*

30. Law Office Administration

At the beginning of chapter 14, you will find a detailed job description of the legal administrator and of the paralegal manager. (See Exhibits 14.2 and 14.3.) Some experienced paralegals move into management positions at a law office. This might involve helping to administer the *entire* office, or *one component* of it, such as the administration of all the legal assistants in the office or the administration of the legal assistants and other support personnel working on a large case. As we saw in chapter 1, paralegals who supervise other paralegals in large offices have formed an association, the International Paralegal Management Association (IPMA). In many smaller

offices, paralegals perform office management duties along with paralegal duties. (See also *law librarianship* and *litigation*.)

- *Comment on Paralegal Work in This Area:*
  The partners at the firm decided to upgrade their legal assistant program and needed a nonlawyer to run it. They offered Linda Katz the new position. "The firm is segmented into practice areas, with legal assistants dispersed throughout the areas. They report to supervising attorneys for work assignments each day. I serve as administrative supervisor, assuring consistency in how legal assistants are treated and utilized, and what opportunities they have for benefits and advancement." Milano, *Career Profiles*, 8 Legal Assistant Today 35.

  "A good paralegal litigation manager [in a large document case] has both strong paralegal skills and strong management skills. Such a manager must be able to analyze the case's organizational needs, develop methods to cope with them effectively, and often must act as paralegal, office manager and computer expert—all in a day's work." Kaufman, *The Litigation Manager*, 6 Legal Professional 55.

- *More on This Area of the Law on the Net:*
  - *www.abanet.org/lpm/home.shtml*
  - *www.soholawoffice.com*
  - *www.ioma.com*
  - *www.paralegalmanagement.org*

31. Legislation

I. Monitoring
Keep track of all events, persons, and organizations involved in the passing of legislation relevant to the clients of the office.

II. Legislative History
Locate or compile the legislative history of a statute.

III. Helping Draft Proposed Legislation

IV. Lobbying
A. Prepare reports and studies on the subject of proposed legislation.
B. Arrange for and help prepare witnesses who will testify at legislative hearings.

- *Comment on Paralegal Work in This Area:*
  Margo Horner "is a legislative analyst for the Nat'l Federation of Independent Business (NFIB). With paralegal training and a master's degree in history, her job is research, creating legislative strategy, working with [legislators] and their staffs to produce legislation favorable to [NFIB]. Margo likes the frenetic tempo of her life." Smith, *Margo*, 1 Legal Assistant Today 14.

- *More on This Area of the Law on the Net:*
  - *www.law.cornell.edu/wex/index.php/Legislation*
  - *www.state.ak.us/local/akpages/ADMIN/apoc/lobstadx.htm*

32. Litigation (Civil)

Civil litigation involves court disputes in every area of the law other than a case where the government is charging (prosecuting) someone for the commission of a crime. Hence civil litigation can potentially involve *every* specialty other than criminal law.

I.   File Monitoring
A.   Index all files.
B.   Write case profile based on information in the files.
C.   Read attorney briefs to check accuracy of the information in the litigation file.
D.   Organize, index, and digest documents obtained through answers to interrogatories, depositions, and other discovery devices.
E.   Encode documents into a computer database.

II. Investigation
A.   Locate documents:
   1.   Medical records
   2.   Police records
   3.   Birth and death records
   4.   Marriage records
   5.   Adoption and custody records
   6.   Incorporation records, etc.
B.   Research records. For example:
   1.   Prepare a profit history report of a company.
   2.   Identify the corporate structure of a parent company and its subsidiaries.
   3.   Trace UCC (Uniform Commercial Code) filings.
   4.   Find out from court dockets if a particular merchant is being sued, has sued before, etc.
   5.   Identify the "real owner" of a building.
   6.   Check housing code agency to find out if a landlord has other building code violations against it on record.
C.   Gather facts (other than from documents). In a wide range of cases (such as real estate, corporate, divorce, and custody), the investigator substantiates facts, follows leads for possible evidence, etc.

III. Discovery
A.   Draft interrogatories.
B.   Draft answers to interrogatories.
C.   Draft deposition questions.
D.   Help prepare witnesses for deposition.
E.   Prepare witness books for deposition.
F.   Arrange time and place of deposition.
G.   Draft requests for admissions.
H.   Draft answers to requests for admissions.
I.   Draft requests for production of documents.
J.   Draft answers to production requests.
K.   Ensure that responses to discovery sent out by the office do not contain privileged material.
L.   Index and digest discovery data.
M.   Work with computer programmer in designing a system to manage discovery documents.

IV. Filings/Serving
   File and/or serve documents in court, at agencies, on parties, on attorneys, etc.

V.   General Assistance
A.   Arrange for clients and others to be interviewed.
B.   Coordinate ADR (alternative dispute resolution), e.g., help schedule arbitration or mediation.

C.   Arrange for expert witnesses to appear in court or at depositions.
D.   Reconstruct (from a large collection of disparate records and other evidence) what happened at a particular time and place.
E.   Assist clients in completing information questionnaire, especially in class-action cases.
F.   Help organize the trial notebook containing items the attorney will need during the trial, such as charts and tables to be used as exhibits at trial.
G.   Evaluate prospective jurors from jury book and during voir dire.
H.   Sit at counsel's table at trial to take notes and be available to assist trial attorney, e.g., locate documents the attorney needs for questioning a witness on the stand.
I.   Attend (and report on) hearings in related cases.
J.   Supervise document encodation on a computer project related to a case in litigation.
K.   Help prepare the notice of appeal.
L.   Order the trial transcript and locate testimony in the transcript needed by the attorney drafting the appellate brief.

VI. Legal Research
A.   Shepardize cited authority; perform other cite check duties.
B.   Write preliminary memos and briefs.
C.   Prepare bibliographies of source materials related to a case in litigation.

VII. Pleadings
   Write preliminary draft of pleadings using standard forms and/or adapting other pleadings written by attorneys on similar cases.

VIII. Expert Analysis
   Assist in obtaining expert opinions for attorneys on:
A.   Taxation.
B.   Accounting.
C.   Statistics.
D.   Economics (e.g., calculation of damages).

IX. Court Witness.
A.   Act as witness as to service of process.
B.   Act as witness as to data uncovered or photographed (e.g., the condition of an apartment building).

● ***Comment on Paralegal Work in This Area:***
   "There are boxes and boxes with an infinite number of documents to be indexed. There are depositions to be summarized. There are cases whose cites need checking. There are trips to the courthouse downtown. There is red-lining of documents to determine changes between two documents. There is Bates-stamping of documents. And there are the exciting trips to visit clients." Lasky, *Impressions of a New Paralegal*, 17 Reporter 5 (Los Angeles Paralegal Ass'n).
   "I organized. I tabbed and tagged, listed and labelled, hoisted and hole-punched, folded and filed, boxed and Bates-stamped, indexed and itemized, sorted and summarized." Klinkseick, *Aim High*, 16 On Point 4 (Nat'l Capital Area Paralegal Ass'n).
   "Initially, it was overwhelming with the number of files and the names to learn and things to remember, but with help, I learned skills and techniques and polished them day after

day as each new case brought with it new quirks and new challenges. I've attended depositions, shaft inspections, and pig farm operations. I've calculated medical expenses, reviewed medical records, and been baffled at how salesmen keep time records! But the ultimate of all experiences, I have to admit, are the trials. You prepare and prepare and hope that you haven't missed any of the details. Then before you know it, the jury has been selected and you're off! The trials keep your adrenaline flowing. They frazzle your patience. They show you your limitations. They elevate you when you win. They shake your confidence when you lose." Riske, *In the Limelight*, 7 Red River Review 4 (Red River Valley Legal Assistants, North Dakota).

"For almost six years now . . . , I've experienced the variety (and the drudgery) of preparing civil cases for trial. I've spent countless hours photocopying documents never read by any judge or jury, or worst of all, by anyone else. I've tracked down witnesses and encouraged them to talk only to find out that they know nothing about the case. In this business of endless paper where no two cases are alike, I've come to understand . . . that flexibility is essential and a sense of humor is invaluable in dealing with people, be they stressed out attorneys or reluctant witnesses." Vore, *A Litigation Recipe*, 16 On Point 4 (Nat'l Capital Area Paralegal Ass'n).

Rebecca McLaughlin tells of a particularly memorable event during her experience as a paralegal. "It was a few minutes after 12:00 noon on Friday, and presiding Judge Barbour always recesses court at precisely 12:30 on Fridays. The Government's star witness was on the stand and denied he had ever seen a certain letter. One of the trial attorneys motioned me to counsel table and asked if we had any proof that the witness had, in fact, seen this letter." Since there were well over 900 defense exhibits, almost 300 government exhibits, and well over forty file cabinets filled with supporting documents, Rebecca felt little hope for success [in finding out quickly]. "She hurried across the street to the office, found the witness' original copy of the letter with his handwritten notes in the margin, and returned to the courtroom with a BIG SMILE. The witness was impeached with his own document minutes before recess." "Later, Rebecca received a well-deserved standing ovation from the attorneys, and all the trial team members. It was the highlight of her career." Johnson, *MALA Spotlight: Rebecca McLaughlin*, 8 The Assistant 17 (Mississippi Ass'n of Legal Assistants).

- *Quotes from Want Ads:*
  "Excellent writing skills and attention to detail are absolute requirements." "Plaintiff's medical malpractice firm seeks non-smoker with word processing abilities." Position requires "extensive writing, document summarizing, and medical records research." Must have an ability "to work independently in handling cases from inception through trial preparation; familiarity with drafting law motions pleadings is essential." High-energy candidate "needs to be assertive and should have an excellent academic background." "Wanted: a sharp, take-charge litigation paralegal." "Knowledge of computerized litigation support is a plus; good communications and organizational skills are a must." "Candidate must be a multitasker with strong computer skills in Word, Excel, Summation, Concordance, Access, and document management databases." "Applicant must possess a thorough working knowledge of all phases of trial work."

"Successful candidate will be professional, prompt, pleasant and personable. No egomaniacs or job hoppers, please." "Overtime flexibility required." "Defense litigation paralegal needed. Must be a self-starter with the ability to accept unstructured responsibility." "Applicant must have a thorough knowledge of state and federal court procedures." Position requires an ability "to organize and manage documents in large multi-party litigation." "Applicants must possess strong supervisory, analytic, writing, and investigative skills, and an ability to perform under pressure." "Position requires good analytical and writing skills, and the ability to organize and control several projects simultaneously." "Deposition summarizer needed; work in your own home on your own computer." "Part-time proofreader for deposition summaries needed."

- *More on This Area of the Law on the Net:*
  - *www.abanet.org/litigation*
  - *www.atlanet.org*
  - *www.dri.org*

33. Military Law

In the U.S. Navy, a nonattorney who assists attorneys in the practice of law is called a **legalman**. (Click the "Legalman Link" at www.nrjag.org.) Depending upon the assignment, the legalman can work in a large variety of areas of the law—for example, admiralty law, contracts, and military justice. The following paralegal job functions in the military are not limited to legalmen or to any particular branch of the armed services.

I. Military Proceedings
A. Assist in processing the following proceedings:
   1. Special court-martial.
   2. General court-martial.
   3. Courts of inquiry.
   4. Line-of-duty investigations.
   5. Reclassification board proceedings.
B. Prepare orders designating membership of special and general courts-martial and courts of inquiry.
C. Assure that charges are properly prepared and that specifications are completed and accurate.
D. Make initial determination on jurisdiction of court, status of accused, and subject matter of offenses.
E. Examine completed records of investigations and other records requiring legal review to ensure that they are administratively correct.
F. Prepare court-martial sentencing orders.
G. Assure that records of court-martial are correct and complete before disposing of case.
H. Transmit bad-conduct discharge court-martial cases to appropriate officials.

II. Claims against the Government
A. Conduct examinations.
B. Process claims against the United States, e.g., under the Federal Tort Claims Act.
C. Manage claim funds.
D. Undertake research on FLITE (Federal Legal Information through Electronics).
E. Write briefs.

III. Administrative Duties

A. Maintain control records of all court-martial and claims cases within command.

B. Maintain law library.

C. Examine and distribute incoming correspondence, directives, publications, and other communications.

D. Catalogue and file books, periodicals, newsletters, etc.

E. Maintain records of discipline within command.

F. Administer office budget.

G. Orient new personnel and monitor their training.

IV. Court Reporting

A. Use the steno-mask for recording legal proceedings.

B. Prepare charges to the jury.

C. Mark exhibits as they are entered into evidence.

D. Transcribe and assemble records of the proceeding.

- ***Comment on Paralegal Work in This Area:***

"I have been working for the Office of the Staff Judge Advocate (SJA) at Fort Ord, California. The SJA is the Army's lawyer. We serve a military community of just over 90,000 people. Staff within the SJA consists of a combination of military and civilian attorneys, paralegals, legal clerks and court reporters. I am responsible for claims filed against the federal government under the Federal Tort Claims Act. I am responsible for discovery and investigative efforts, determining legal issues, writing memorandums of law and recommending settlement or denial. Job satisfaction for paralegal professionals is high in the U.S. government. I know that, should I desire to re-enter the civilian work sector, my experience and knowledge of the government legal systems will uniquely qualify me to work for any firm that deals with the government." Richards, *Marching to a Different Drummer: Paralegal Work in the Military*, 2 California Paralegal Magazine 8.

- ***More on This Area of the Law on the Net:***
  - *www.court-martial.com*
  - *www.law.cornell.edu/wex/index.php/Military*
  - *findlaw.com/01topics/45military*

34. Municipal Finance Law[10]

(See also *banking law* and *corporate law*.)

I. Document Preparation

A. Basic documents

1. Prepare first drafts of basic documents, including bonds, indentures of trust, financing agreements, and all other related documents.

2. Attend drafting sessions and note changes required to initial drafts.

3. Prepare second and subsequent drafts by incorporating revisions.

B. Closing documents

1. Prepare first drafts of all closing documents.

2. Prepare second and subsequent drafts by incorporating revisions and red-line changes.

C. Draft official statement/private offering memorandum

1. Prepare first drafts.

2. Attend drafting sessions.

3. Perform due diligence to verify the information and data contained in the offering document.

4. Prepare second and subsequent drafts by incorporating revisions and red-line changes.

II. Coordination

A. Establish timetable and list of participants.

B. Distribute documents to participants.

C. Coordinate printing of bonds and offering documents.

D. File all documents as required.

E. Coordinate publication of notices of meetings and elections, ordinances, public hearing notices, etc.

III. Closing

A. Prepare checklist.

B. Arrange and assist in preclosing and closing.

C. File special documents prior to closing.

D. Secure requisite documents to be prepared or furnished by other participants.

E. Perform all post-closing procedures.

1. File all documents or security agreements.

2. Supervise preparation of closing binders, etc.

IV. Formation of Special Districts

A. Prepare documents necessary to organize the district.

B. File documents with city or county and court.

C. Prepare documents for organizational meeting of district.

V. Elections (Formation of District or Bond Election)

Draft election documents and obtain all necessary election materials.

VI. Develop and Maintain Research Files

A. IDB procedures for municipalities.

B. Home rule charters.

C. Demographic and economic statistics.

D. Memoranda noting statutory changes.

E. Interoffice research memoranda.

F. Checklists for each type of financing.

- ***More on This Area of the Law on the Net:***
  - *www.law.cornell.edu/wex/index.php/ Local_government_law*
  - *www.abanet.org/statelocal/home.html*

35. Oil and Gas Law

Some paralegals who work in the area of oil and gas law are referred to as *land technicians* or *landmen*. (See also *real estate law*.)

I. Collect and analyze data pertaining to land ownership and activities that may affect the procurement of rights to explore, drill for, and produce oil or gas.

II. Help acquire leases and other operating rights from property owners for exploration, drilling, and producing oil, gas, and related substances.

III. Monitor the execution of the leases and other operating agreements by ensuring that contract obligations are fulfilled (e.g., payment of rent).

IV. Help negotiate agreements with individuals, companies, and government agencies pertaining to the exploration, drilling, and production of oil or gas.

V. Assist in acquiring oil and gas producing properties, royalties, and mineral interests.

VI. Process and monitor the termination of leases and other agreements.

VII. Examine land titles.

- *Comment on Paralegal Work in This Area:*

  "As an oil and gas paralegal, my practice encompasses many different areas of law including real estate, litigation, bankruptcy, and securities, as well as contact with various county, state, and federal government agencies. I frequently spend time searching real estate records in counties . . . for information on leases to determine such things as who has been assigned an interest in the lease. I have worked in mechanic's lien foreclosures, partition actions, and bankruptcy cases. While researching regulatory information and oil prices, I have obtained information from the Federal Energy Regulatory Commission offices in Washington. The variety of work requires a working knowledge of several areas of law, and is always challenging and interesting." Hunt, *Oil and Gas*, The Citator (Legal Assistants of Central Ohio).

- *More on This Area of the Law on the Net:*
  - *www.washlaw.edu/subject/oilgaslaw.html*
  - *www.hg.org/natres.html*

36. Parajudge (Lay Judge)

In some states, judges in certain lower courts do not have to be attorneys. Such courts include justice of the peace courts and local magistrates courts.

In New York State, for example, almost 2,000 judges in the state's town and village courts (often called *justice courts*) are not attorneys. "New York is one of about thirty states that still rely on these kinds of local judges, descendants of the justices who kept the peace in Colonial days, when lawyers were scarce."[11]

Administrative agencies, particularly state and local agencies, sometimes allow nonattorneys to conduct administrative hearings within their agencies. The person conducting the hearing (whether an attorney or a nonattorney) is often called an *administrative law judge* (ALJ), *hearing officer*, or *referee*.

- *More on This Area of the Law on the Net:*
  - *www.aalj.org*
  - *www.walja.org*

37. Pro Bono Work

Pro bono work refers to services provided to another person at no charge. Law firms often give their attorneys time off so they can take pro bono cases—for example, to defend a poor person charged with a crime. Paralegals are also encouraged to do pro bono work. This is done on their own time or on law firm time with the permission of their supervisor. Here are examples of the variety of pro bono work performed by paralegals:

I. Abused Women
A. Draft request for protective order.
B. Draft divorce pleadings.

II. AIDS Patients
A. Interview patients and prepare a memorandum of the interview for the attorney on the case.
B. Assist patients with guardianship problems.
C. Draft powers of attorney.

III. Homeless
A. Handle Supplemental Security Income (SSI) claims.
B. Make referrals to shelters and drug programs.

- *Comment on Paralegal Work in This Area:*

  "Asked to share her favorite pro bono experience, Therese Ortega, a litigation paralegal, answered that to choose was too difficult; any time her efforts result in a benefit to the client, 'I get a warm glow.' One occasion she obviously cherishes was the fight on behalf of some low-income kidney dialysis patients whose eligibility for transportation to and from treatment was threatened. 'Perseverance and appeals paid off,' she says. Rides were re-established through the hearing process, then by information conferences. Finally, the cessation notices stopped." *Spotlight on Therese Ortega*, 13 The Journal 3 (Sacramento Ass'n of Legal Assistants).

- *More on This Area of the Law on the Net:*
  - *www.abanet.org/legalservices/probono*
  - *www.corporateprobono.org*
  - *www.probonoinst.org*

38. Public Sector

A paralegal in the *private sector* works in an office whose funds come from client fees or from the budget of the corporate treasury. Every other setting is generally considered the *public sector*. More specifically, the latter refers to those law offices that provide civil or criminal legal services to the poor for free. Often, the services consist of helping clients obtain government benefits such as public housing, welfare, or medical care. Such services are referred to as *public benefits*, and providing such assistance is called the practice of public benefits law. Some of the paralegals who are employed by these offices are called public benefits paralegals. The offices operate with government grants, charitable contributions, and the efforts of volunteers. The offices are called Legal Aid Society, Legal Services Office, Office of the Public Defender, etc. For examples of the kinds of functions performed by paralegals in these offices, see *administrative law, bankruptcy law, civil rights law, criminal law, family law, landlord and tenant law, litigation, pro bono work, social security law, welfare law,* and *workers' compensation law.*

- *Comment on Paralegal Work in This Area:*

  "If someone asked me what I disliked most about my job, I would have to answer: the size of my paycheck. That is the only drawback of working for a nonprofit law firm—[the Community Legal Aid Society which represents elderly and handicapped persons]. Everything else about my job is positive." For example, to "be an integral part of a case where a landlord is forced by the Courts to bring a house up to code and prevent a tenant from being wrongfully evicted is a great feeling." The positive aspects of the job "more than compensate for the size of the paycheck." Hartman, *Job Profile*, Delaware Paralegal Reporter 5 (Delaware Paralegal Ass'n).

"Mr. Watnick stressed that the organization doesn't have the luxury of using paralegals as "xeroxers" or errand runners. Staff paralegals have their own caseloads and represent clients before Administrative Law Judges—with a dramatically high rate of success." Shays, *Paralegals in Human Service*, Postscript 16 (Manhattan Paralegal Ass'n).

- ● *More on This Area of the Law on the Net:*
  - ▪ *www.povertylaw.org*
  - ▪ *findlaw.com/01topics/17govbenefit*
  - ▪ *www.hud.gov*
  - ▪ *www.law.cornell.edu/topics/food_stamps.html*
  - ▪ *www.law.cornell.edu/topics/medicaid.html*

39. Real Estate Law

(See also *banking law*, *contract law*, and *landlord and tenant law*.)

I. General

Assist law firms, corporations, and development companies in transactions involving land, houses, condominiums, shopping malls, office buildings, redevelopment projects, civic centers, etc.

A. Research zoning regulations.
B. Prepare draft of the contract of sale.
C. Title work:
 1. If done outside, order title work from the title company; arrange title insurance.
 2. If done in-house:
  a. Examine title abstracts for completeness.
  b. Prepare a map based on a master title plat or the current government survey map.
  c. Help construct a chain of title noting liens, easements, or other encumbrances.
  d. Obtain releases of liens, payoff statements for existing loans, etc.;
  e. Help draft a preliminary title opinion.
D. Mortgages:
 1. Assist in obtaining financing.
 2. Review mortgage application.
 3. Assist in recording mortgage.
E. Closing:
 1. Arrange a closing time with buyer, seller, brokers, and lender.
 2. Collect the data necessary for closing. Prepare checklist of expenses:
  a. Title company's fee
  b. Lender's fee
  c. Attorney's fee
  d. Taxes and water bills to be prorated
  e. Tax escrow, discharge of liens
 3. Organize the documents for closing:
  a. Deed,
  b. Settlement statement,
  c. Note and deed of trust,
  d. Corporate resolutions,
  e. Performance bond,
  f. Waivers, etc.
 4. Check compliance with the disclosure requirements of the Real Estate Settlement Act.

 5. Arrange for a rehearsal of the closing.
 6. Attend and assist at the closing—e.g., take minutes, notarize documents.
F. Foreclosure:
 1. Order foreclosure certificate.
 2. Prepare notice of election and demand for sale.
 3. Compile a list of parties to be notified.
 4. Monitor publication of the notice.
 5. Prepare bid letter and other sale documents.
G. Eminent domain:
 1. Photograph or videotape the property taken or to be taken by the state.
 2. Prepare inventory of the property taken.
 3. Help client prepare business records pertaining to the value of the property.
 4. Arrange for appraisals of the property.
 5. Order and review soil engineering reports.
 6. Review tax appeal records on values claimed by the property owner.
 7. Mail out notice of condemnation.
H. Office management:
 1. Maintain office tickler system.
 2. Maintain individual attorney's calendar.
 3. Be in charge of the entire client's file (opening it, keeping it up to date, knowing where parts of it are at all times, etc.).
 4. Train other staff in the office system of handling real estate cases.

II. Tax-Exempt Industrial Development Financing
A. Undertake a preliminary investigation to establish facts relevant to:
 1. Project eligibility,
 2. Local issuer, and
 3. Cost estimates of financing.
B. Prepare a formal application to the issuer.
C. Prepare a timetable of approvals, meetings, and all other requirements necessary for closing.
D. Prepare a preliminary draft of portions of the proposal memorandum (relating to the legal structure of the financing) that is submitted to prospective bond purchasers.
E. Obtain confirmation from the Treasury Department that the company is in compliance with the financing covenants of current external debt instruments.
F. Obtain insurance certificates.
G. Write the first draft of the resolutions of the board of directors.
H. Write the preface and recital of documents for the legal opinion of the company.
I. Ask bank to confirm account numbers, amount of money to be transferred, and investment instructions.
J. Prepare a closing memorandum covering the following documents:
 1. Secretary's certificate including resolutions of the board of directors, the certified charter and bylaws of the company, and the incumbency certificate;
 2. UCC-1 financing statements;
 3. Requisition forms;
 4. Certificate of authorized company representative;

5. Deed;
6. Legal opinion of the company;
7. Transfer instruction letter; and
8. Officer's certificate.

K. Confirm that the money has been transferred to the company's account on the day of closing.

L. Order an updated good-standing telegram.

M. Send a copy of the IRS election statement.

N. Assemble, monitor, and distribute documents to appropriate departments.

- *Comment on Paralegal Work in This Area:*

"Although it may look boring to the untrained eye, and sound boring to the untrained ear, for those of us whose livelihoods depend upon it, real estate law is *interesting* and *exciting*. There is always something new to learn or a little flaw to resolve. What can be better than having clients come to you and thank you for your assistance in what would have been a complete disaster without your knowledge and expertise to get them through? I call that total job satisfaction. I am now capable of doing everything in a real estate settlement from opening the file to walking into the settlement room and disbursing the funds. It is not uncommon for me to receive calls from attorneys in the area asking me how certain problems can be solved. That boosts my ego more than any divorce case ever could!" Jaeger, *Real Estate Law Is a Legal Profession Tool*, 14 On Point 9 (Nat'l Capital Area Paralegal Ass'n).

At a paralegal conference, Virginia Henderson made a seminar presentation on her duties as a paralegal. Her "candor and energetic enthusiasm concerning her profession were encouraging and motivating. She was very explicit about her duties as a commercial real estate paralegal, explaining that attorney supervision is lessened once the paralegal assumes more responsibility and exhibits initiative as far as his/her duties are concerned. It was refreshing to listen to a veteran of the paralegal profession speak so optimistically about the profession's limitless potential. Here's to having more paralegals as seminar speakers!" Troiano, *Real Estate*, Newsletter 12 (Western New York Paralegal Ass'n).

"As a foreclosure legal assistant, one of my worst fears is to have a client call and say, 'Remember the Jones property you foreclosed for us last year? Well, we're trying to close on this and it seems there's a problem with the title. . . . ' Oh no, what *didn't* I do! Mortgage foreclosure litigation is fraught with all kinds of pitfalls for the inexperienced and the unwary. An improper or faulty foreclosure could not only be disastrous for the client, it can also be a malpractice nightmare for the law firm." Hubbell, *Mortgage Foreclosure Litigation: Avoiding the Pitfalls*, 16 Facts and Findings 10 (NALA).

- *Quotes from Want Ads:*

"Ideal candidate must possess exceptional organization, communication, writing and research skills and be willing to work overtime." "We need a team player with high energy." "Position requires an ability to work independently on a wide variety of matters and to meet deadlines." "Experience in retail real estate or real estate financing a must." "Should be assertive and have excellent analytical skills." Position requires a "self-motivated person. We seek a TIGER who can accomplish much with a minimum of supervision." "Knowledge of state and federal securities law a plus." "Must be flexible and possess high integrity." Position requires a "self-starter able to deal effectively with executive management, outside counsel, escrow and title companies, brokers, leasing agents, and clients."

- *More on This Area of the Law on the Net:*
  - *www.law.cornell.edu/wex/index.php/ Real_estate_transactions*
  - *www.law.cornell.edu/wex/index.php/Real_property*
  - *www.law.cornell.edu/wex/index.php/Mortgage*
  - *findlaw.com/01topics/33property*

40. Social Security Law

As we will see in chapter 4, paralegals can represent clients (and charge them fees) at social security hearings without attorney supervision. Such representatives are often called *social security representatives;* many have joined the National Organization of Social Security Claimants' Representatives (www.nosscr.org). In chapter 15 we will cover techniques for representing clients at such hearings. (See also *administrative law, public sector,* and *welfare law.*)

I. Problem Identification
A. Person is denied benefits.
B. Recipient is terminated from disability payments.
C. Recipient is charged with receiving overpayment.
D. Medicare denial.

II. Case Preparation
A. Investigate relevant facts.
B. Perform legal research.

III. Representation
A. Engage in informal advocacy with Social Security employees.
B. Represent clients at administrative hearings regarding SSI (Supplemental Security Income).
C. Represent clients at administrative hearings regarding SSD (Social Security Disability).

IV. Appeal
A. Help attorney prepare a court appeal of the Social Security Administration's decision.

- *Comment on Paralegal Work in This Area:*

"Paralegal representation of a claimant in a Social Security Disability hearing is the closest to a judicial setting that a paralegal may expect to become involved in. For the paralegal, this can be a very complex and challenging field. It can also be extremely rewarding, bringing with it the satisfaction of successfully representing a claimant in a quasi-judicial setting." Obermann, *The Paralegal and Federal Disability Practice in Maine*, MAP Newsletter (Maine Ass'n of Paralegals).

- *More on This Area of the Law on the Net:*
  - *www.ssa.gov*
  - *www.naela.com*
  - *www.megalaw.com/top/socsec.php*
  - *www.law.cornell.edu/wex/index.php/Social_Security*

41. Tax Law

(See also *corporate law, employee benefits law, estates law,* and *real estate law.*)

I.   Compile all necessary data for the preparation of tax returns:
A.   Corporate income tax,
B.   Employer quarterly tax,
C.   Franchise tax,
D.   Partnership tax,
E.   Sales tax,
F.   Personal property tax,
G.   Individual income tax,
H.   Estate tax, and
I.   Gift tax.

II. Miscellaneaous Tasks
A.   Obtain missing information from client.
B.   Compile supporting documents for the returns.
C.   Draft extensions-of-time requests for late filings.
D.   Make corrections in the returns based upon new or clarified data.
E.   Compute the tax liability or transfer client information to a computer service that will calculate the tax liability.
F.   Organize and maintain client binder.
G.   Compute cash flow analysis and other calculations needed for proposed real estate syndication.
H.   Compile documentation on the valuation of assets.
I.   Maintain tax law library.
J.   Read looseleaf tax services and other periodic tax data to keep current on tax developments. Let others in office know of such developments.
K.   Supervise and train other nonattorney staff.

● *Comment on Paralegal Work in This Area:*
"A legal assistant with the firm for the past thirteen years, Pat [Coleman] spends a lot of time in her office. She is surrounded by her work, and one gets the idea that Pat knows exactly what is in every file and could put her hand on any information that is needed. Notes are taped next to the light switch; the firm's monthly calendar highlighting important meetings is readily available, and helps her track her many deadlines. Pat is an *Enrolled Agent* (which permits her to practice before the Treasury Department), has a lot of tax background, and is competent in that area as well as bookkeeping. One of her least favorite tax forms is the 990 required of not-for-profit organizations. The 990 tax form is second only to private foundation returns when it comes to being pesky and tricky." Howard, *Patricia Coleman of Chicago Creates Her Niche in Taxes, Trusts and ERISA*, 3 Legal Assistant Today 40. For information on enrolled agents, see the National Association of Enrolled Agents (www.naea.org).

● *More on This Area of the Law on the Net:*
   ■ *www.taxsites.com*
   ■ *www.irs.ustreas.gov*
   ■ *findlaw.com/01topics/35tax*

42. Tort Law

A *tort* is a civil wrong (other than a breach of contract) for which the courts will provide a remedy such as damages. The harm can be to a person or to property. Most paralegals working in tort law, particularly on PI (personal injury) cases, are litigation assistants. The major torts are negligence, defamation, strict liability, and misrepresentation. Paralegals in this area may also be involved in workers' compensation cases for injuries that occur on the job. (See *admiralty law, litigation,* and *workers' compensation.*)

● *Comment on Paralegal Work in This Area:*
"Personal injury/products liability cases can be fascinating, challenging, and educational. They also can be stressful, aggravating and very sad. I have been involved in a great many cases in my career, on both sides of the plaintiff/defendant fence. Some of the cases seemed frivolous and somewhat 'ambulance chasing' in nature. Others were significant cases in which the plaintiff had wrongfully suffered injury. There are many talents a good personal injury/products liability paralegal must have. He or she must be creative, tenacious, observant and able to communicate well with people." Lee, *Personal Injury/Products Liability Cases*, 11 Newsletter 7 (Dallas Ass'n of Legal Assistants).

"Recently, Mary Mann, a paralegal who works on product liability litigation, was asked by her attorney to track down a specific medical article [on a subject relevant to a current case]. The attorney only had a vague description of the article, a possible title, and the name of the organization that might have published it. In her search Mary spoke by phone to people in New York, Atlanta, Washington, and finally to a doctor in Geneva, Switzerland, who spoke very little English. In her effort to make herself understood by the doctor, Mary continued to speak louder and louder in very simplistic and basic English phrases, as people tend to do when confronted by a language barrier. She is sure her efforts to maintain a professional demeanor were humorous to those passing by her office. However, she did succeed in getting the article and in the process gained a friend in Switzerland!" Fisher, *Spotlight: Mary Mann*, 7 The Assistant 14 (Mississippi Ass'n of Legal Assistants).

"Asbestos litigation . . . opened up in the late 1970's with the lawsuits initiated against the Johns-Mansville Corporation. In 1982 Mansville filed a Chapter 11 bankruptcy to protect its assets from the thousands of claims being filed against it." Huge numbers of paralegals were employed in this litigation. For those paralegals working *for* Johns-Mansville on the defense team, "the question of morality arose. I get asked about the morality of my job constantly. For me, personal moral judgment does not enter into it. Our legal system is based on the availability of equal representation for both sides. I think I play a small part in making that system work." Welsh, *The Paralegal in Asbestos Litigation*, 10 Ka Leo O'H.A.L.A. 6 (Hawaii Ass'n of Legal Assistants).

● *Quotes from Want Ads:*
"Medical malpractice law firm seeks paralegal who is a self-starter, has good communication skills, is organized and detail-oriented." Position in PI firm requires "a take-charge person to handle case details from beginning to end." "Prefer person with experience in claims adjustment, medical records, or nursing." Position requires "dynamic, highly-motivated individual who will enjoy the challenge of working independently and handling a wide variety of responsibilities." "Excellent writing skills a must." "Should be able to perform under pressure." Manufacturer of consumer products "seeks paralegal with engineering background." Must be mature enough to handle "heavy client contact." Position requires "ability to read and summarize medical records."

● *More on This Area of the Law on the Net:*
   ■ *www.cpsc.gov*
   ■ *findlaw.com/01topics/22tort*
   ■ *www.toxlaw.com/bookmarks/laws.html*
   ■ *www.hg.org/torts.html*
   ■ *www.law.cornell.edu/wex/index.php/Tort*

43. Tribal Law

Tribal courts on Indian reservations have jurisdiction over many civil and criminal cases in which both parties are Native Americans. Parties are often represented by tribal court advocates who are nonattorney Native Americans. In addition, the judges are often nonattorneys. (See *litigation*.)

- **Comment on Paralegal Work in This Area:**

"Lee's career goal is to become an advocate for the Navajo Nation. In March . . . she will sit for the Navajo Nation Bar exam, something she is permitted to do as a Native American with an associates degree. If she passes, she will be able to become an advocate for the Navajo Nation, practicing much as an attorney would do on the reservation, although she would not be permitted to practice off the reservation. Her work as an advocate would involve quite a bit of dispute resolution and representing Native Americans in their own tribal courts." Jane Roberts, *Unique Specialties* (*Tribal Law*), 23 Legal Assistant Today 65.

As a paralegal, Raylene Frazier "advocates for clients in the Cheyenne River Sioux Tribal Court on a wide range of areas including paternity, custody and probate cases—often against lawyers representing her opposition." Kenya McCullum, *Paralegal Recognized for Work with Native American Community*, 24 Legal Assistant Today 26.

- **More on This Area of the Law on the Net:**
  - *www.law.cornell.edu/topics/indian.html*
  - *findlaw.com/01topics/21indian*

44. Water Law[12]

(See also *administrative law*, *environmental law*, and *real estate law*.)

I. Water Rights

Investigate and analyze specific water rights associated with property:

A. Do research at Department of Water Resources regarding decrees, tabulations, well permits, reservoirs, diversion records, maps, and statements.

B. Communicate in writing and orally with Department of Water Resources personnel regarding status of water rights and wells.

C. Communicate in writing and orally (including interviews) with District Water Commissioners regarding status of water rights and wells, historic use, and use on land.

D. Communicate in writing and orally (including interviews) with property owners and managers, ranch managers, ditch company personnel, etc. regarding status of water rights and wells, historic use, and use on land.

E. Do research at other agencies and offices (such as the Bureau of Land Management, state archives, historical societies, public libraries).

F. Prepare historic use affidavits.

G. Prepare reports, maps, charts, and diagrams on status of water rights and wells, historic use, and use on land.

II. Real Estate Transactions

A. Draft documents for the purchase and sale, encumbrance, or lease of water rights and wells.

B. Perform standup title searches in county clerk and recorder's offices.

C. Perform due diligence investigations.

D. Prepare for and assist at closings.

III. Well Permit Applications

A. Prepare well permit documents for filing: applications, land ownership affidavits, statements of beneficial use, amendments to record, and extensions of time.

B. Coordinate and monitor the well permitting and drilling process.

C. Communicate with Department of Water Resources personnel, well drillers, and client.

IV. Water Court Proceedings

Certain district courts have special jurisdiction over water right proceedings. Proceedings are governed by the Rules of Civil Procedure for District Courts and by local water court and district court rules.

A. Prepare water court documents for filing: applications, statements of opposition, draft rulings and orders, stipulations, withdrawals of opposition, and affidavits.

B. Maintain diligence filing tickler system. Work with client to maintain evidence of diligence.

C. Review, route, and maintain file of term day notices and orders. Prepare attorneys for term day and/or attend term day.

V. Monitor Publications

Read *Reporter* and water court resumes, and register for new water law cases and Department of Water Resources regulations.

- **More on This Area of the Law on the Net:**
  - *www.washlaw.edu/subject/water.html*
  - *www.hg.org/natres.html*

45. Welfare Law (Public Assistance)

(See also *administrative law*, *pro bono work*, *public benefits*, and *social security law*.)

I. Problem Identification

A. Perform preliminary interview:
   1. Identify nonlegal problems for referral to other agencies.
   2. Open a case file or update it.
   3. Using a basic fact sheet (or form), record the information collected during the interview.
   4. Determine next appointment.
   5. Instruct client on what to do next, e.g., obtain medical and birth records.

B. Categorize problems.
   1. Help client learn what benefits exist in programs such as:
      a. Temporary Assistance for Needy Families (TANF)
      b. Social Security
      c. Medicare
   2. Help client fill out application forms.
   3. Help client when department wants to reduce the amount of client's check or terminate public assistance altogether.

II. Problem Resolution

A. Consult with attorney immediately:
   1. Summarize facts for the attorney.
   2. Submit the case record to the attorney.
   3. Obtain further instructions from attorney.

B. Refer nonlegal problems to other agencies:
1. Search for an appropriate agency.
2. Contact agency for the client.
C. Investigate
1. Verify information (call caseworker, visit department office, etc.).
2. Search for additional information.
3. Record relevant facts.
4. Consult with attorney on difficulties encountered.
D. Analyze laws:
1. Check office poverty law manual.
2. Consult with office attorneys.
3. Contact legal service attorneys outside office.
4. Do research in law library.
E. Be an informal advocate (to determine if the problem can be resolved without a hearing or court action).
1. Provide missing information.
2. Pressure the department (with calls, letters, visits, etc.).
3. Maintain records such as current and closed files.
F. Be a formal advocate:
1. Prior hearing (administrative review)
   a. Determine if such hearing can be asked for and when request must be made.
   b. Draft letter requesting such hearing.
   c. Prepare for hearing (see "Fair Hearing" below).
   d. Conduct hearing (see "Fair Hearing" below).
2. Fair Hearing
   a. Determine if the hearing can be asked for and when request must be made.
   b. Draft letter requesting the hearing.
   c. Prepare for the hearing:
      i. In advance of hearing, request that the department send you the documents it will rely on at the hearing.
      ii. Organize other relevant documents such as canceled check stubs.
      iii. Find witnesses.
      iv. Prepare all witnesses (for example, explain what hearing will be about; use role-playing to acquaint them with the format and what you will be seeking from the witnesses).
      v. Make a final attempt to resolve the issues without a hearing.
   d. Conduct the hearing:
      i. Make opening statement summarizing client's case.
      ii. State what relief the client is seeking from the hearing.
      iii. If issue confusion exists, propose a statement of the issue most favorable to the client.
      iv. Complain if department failed to provide requested information in advance of the hearing.
      v. Present the client's case:
         a. Submit documents.
         b. Conduct direct examination of the client's witnesses, including the client.
         c. Conduct re-direct examination of witnesses (if allowed).
         d. Cite the law.
      vi. Rebut case of department:
         a. Raise objections to their documents and their interpretation of the law.
         b. Cross-examine their witnesses.
         c. Re-cross-examine their witnesses (if allowed).
      vii. Make closing statement summarizing the case of the client and repeating the result the client is seeking.
   e. Follow-up:
      i. Request a copy of the transcript of the hearing.
      ii. Consult with attorney to determine whether the hearing result should be appealed in court.
3. Court
   a. Assist the attorney in gathering the documents for appeal; interview the witnesses, etc.
   b. Prepare preliminary draft of the legal argument to be made to the trial court handling the appeal.
   c. Be a general assistant for the attorney in court.
   d. File papers in court.
   e. Serve the papers on opponents.
G. Miscellaneous
1. Train other paralegals.
2. Organize the community around poverty issues.

- *More on This Area of the Law on the Net:*
  - *www.law.cornell.edu/wex/index.php/Welfare*
  - *www.nclej.org*

46. Workers' Compensation Law
(See also *administrative law, labor and employment law,* and *litigation.*)

I. Interviewing
A. Collect and record details of the claim (date of injury, nature and dates of prior illness, etc.).
B. Collect or arrange for the collection of documents, e.g., medical and employment records.
C. Schedule physical examination.

II. Drafting
A. Claim for compensation.
B. Request for hearing.
C. Medical authorization.
D. Demand for medical information in the possession of respondent or insurance carrier.
E. Proposed summary of issues involved.

III. Advocacy
A. Informal: contact (call, visit, write a letter to) the employer and/or the insurance carrier to determine whether the matter can be resolved without a formal hearing or court action.
B. Formal: represent claimant at the administrative hearing.

IV. Follow-up
A. Determine whether the payment is in compliance with the award.
B. If not, draft and file statutory demand for proper payment.
C. If such a statutory demand is filed, prepare a tickler system to monitor the claim.

- *Comment on Paralegal Work in This Area:*
  "I have been working as a paralegal in this area for more than seven years. This is one of the areas of the law [in this state]

in which a paralegal can perform almost all of the functions to properly process a Workers' Compensation claim. A Workers' Compensation practice must be a very high volume in order to be [profitable]. Thus paralegal assistance in handling a large caseload is an absolute necessity. An extensive volume of paperwork is processed on a daily basis. Client contact is a major portion of a paralegal's responsibilities. With a large case load, it is physically impossible for an attorney to communicate with each and every client on a regular basis. It is not unusual for a paralegal in this field to work on several hundred files each week." Lindberg, *Virtually Limitless Responsibilities of a Workers' Compensation Paralegal*, Update 6 (Cleveland Ass'n of Paralegals).

"The Company's two workers' compensation paralegals are responsible for reviewing each claimant's file, prepar-

ing a summary of medical reports, outlining the issues, and reviewing with the adjusters any questions or circumstances of the case before the claimant's deposition. In addition, they draft any necessary subpoenas, witness lists and settlement stipulations for their respective attorneys, and collect information and draft letters to the Special Disability Trust Fund outlining the Company's theory of reimbursement for second injury cases." Miquel, *Walt Disney World Company's Legal Assistants: Their Role in the Show*, 16 Facts and Findings 29 (NALA).

- *More on This Area of the Law on the Net:*
  - *www.law.cornell.edu/wex/index.php/Workers_compensation*
  - *www.dol.gov/dol/topic/workcomp*
  - *www.megalaw.com/top/labor.php*

A Paralegal in the White House

Meg Shields Duke

New Roles in the Law Conference Report 93

[After working as a paralegal on the Reagan-Bush Campaign Committee], I'm a paralegal in the White House Counsel's office. I believe I'm the first paralegal in this office, in the White House. They've had law clerks in the past, but never have they hired a paralegal. There's one paralegal to nine attorneys at the moment. My responsibilities here are varied. Everybody is still trying to determine what their turf is. But for the first couple of months I've worked on a lot of transition matters, which might be expected. I was the coordinator for our transition audit (congressional transition audit), from the Hill which just ended a few weeks ago. I have engaged in drafting correspondence concerning the use of the president's name, the use of his image; our policy on gift acceptance by public employees; drafting standards of conduct for public employees in the White House, job freeze litigation, those few controversial things. The last few weeks of my time have been devoted to the Lefever nomination. It's all been fascinating. Anyway, there are a number of areas that we also get involved in, the ethics of government act, for example. It's the first time it has been applied across the board to a new administration. It has been very, very time consuming for all our staff. I've been assisting in that, reviewing each individual file for high level government employees. As I said, I'm in the counsel's office now and intend to stay for a couple of years. But I would like to start my own paralegal firm. I have a close friend who started her own paralegal firm in Florida and we've talked often in the past of expanding it. I think there is a place for more paralegals in the public sector, at least in the White House. I understand the Department of Justice has many, but I'd like to see it expanded and I'd also like to see more people branching out and trying this independent approach. It's risky, but it's worth it (1982).

[SECTION D]
FINDING A JOB: EMPLOYMENT STRATEGIES

There are many different strategies for finding employment. The strategies discussed in this section are primarily for individuals who have had very little or no employment experience with attorneys. Many of the strategies, however, are also relevant to people who have worked in law offices as secretaries or who are paralegals seeking other employment opportunities in the field.

Before examining these strategies, take a look at your state in appendix E. At the end of the legal materials on the state, you will find specific Web sites that are relevant to finding paralegal jobs in your state.

GENERAL STRATEGIES FOR FINDING EMPLOYMENT
1. Begin now.
2. Start compiling a Job-Hunting Notebook.
3. Organize an employment workshop.
4. Locate working paralegals.
5. Try to have informational interviews.
6. Locate potential employers.
7. Surf the Internet.
8. Prepare a résumé, cover letter, and writing sample(s).
9. Prepare for the job interview.

Strategy 1: Begin Now

You should begin preparing for the job hunt on the first day of your first paralegal class. Do *not* wait until the program is almost over. Although your school will provide you with guidance and leads, you should assume that obtaining a job will be your responsibility. For most students, the job you get will be the job *you* find.

While in school, your primary focus should be on compiling an excellent academic record. *In addition*, you must start the job search now. It is not too early, for example, to begin compiling the lists called for in the Job-Hunting Notebook that we will examine later. When school is over, be prepared to spend a substantial amount of additional time looking for employment, particularly if your part of the country is currently a "buyer's market," where there are more applicants than available jobs.

Being a paralegal requires determination, assertiveness, initiative, and creativity. *Finding* paralegal work may require these same skills. This is not a field for the faint of heart who are easily discouraged.

It may be that you are uncertain about the kinds of employment options that exist. How can you begin looking for a job if you don't yet know what kind of job you would like to have? First of all, many of the suggested steps in this chapter will be helpful regardless of the kind of job you are pursuing. More important, however, the very process of going through these steps will help you clarify your employment objectives. As you begin seeking information and leads, the insights will come to you. At this point, keep an open mind, be conscientious, and begin now.

Strategy 2: Begin Compiling a Job-Hunting Notebook

Later in this chapter, you will find an outline for a Job-Hunting Notebook that you should start preparing now. (See Exhibit 2.15.)

Strategy 3: Organize an Employment Workshop

Exhibit 2.1, at the beginning of this chapter, gave you a list of the major categories (and subcategories) of paralegal employment. As a group project, your class should begin organizing an employment conference or workshop consisting of a panel of paralegals from as many of the categories and subcategories of paralegals as you can locate in your area. Try to find at least one paralegal to represent each category and subcategory. The guest paralegals could be asked to come to an evening or Saturday session to discuss the following topics:

- What I do (what a typical day consists of)
- How I obtained my job
- My recommendations for finding work
- Dos and don'ts for résumés and employment interviews
- What were the most valuable parts of my legal education, etc.

Although you could ask a professor or the director of the program at your school to help you organize the workshop, it is recommended that you make it a student-run workshop. It will be good practice for you in taking the kind of initiative that is essential in finding employment. You might want to consider asking the nearest paralegal association to co-sponsor the workshop with your class.

Have a meeting of your class and select a chairperson to help coordinate the event. Then divide up the tasks of contacting participants, arranging for a room, preparing an agenda for the workshop, etc. You may want to invite former graduates of your school to attend as panel speakers or as members of the audience. The ideal time for such a workshop is a month or two after you begin your coursework. This means that you need to begin organizing immediately.

Strategy 4: Locate Working Paralegals

Perhaps the most significant step in finding employment is to begin talking with paralegals who are already employed. They are the obvious experts on how to find a job! They are probably also very knowledgeable about employment opportunities in their office and in similar offices in the area. (See Job-Hunting Notebook, p. 101.)

Attend paralegal association meetings. See appendix B for a list of paralegal associations. Contact the one nearest you and ask about joining. There may be special dues for students.

Ask if the association has a **job bank** service. Here is what a paralegal who used this service had to say:

> I gained access to an opening to a wonderful job at a law firm exclusively listed in the Minnesota Association of Legal Assistants (MALA) Job Bank . . . I would never have heard about the position if I hadn't been a member of MALA.[13]

job bank A service that lists available jobs, sometimes available only to members of an organization.

Not all associations have job bank services, however, and those that do have them may not make them available to students. Some associations have job banks online. Check the Web sites listed in appendix B.

Try to obtain copies of current and past issues of the monthly or bimonthly newsletters of all the local paralegal associations in your area. Check their Web sites to find out if the newsletters are kept online. Some newsletters give listings of job openings that mention specific employers. If so, try to contact the employers to determine if the position is still open. If it is no longer open, ask if you could send your résumé to be kept on file in the event a position becomes available in the future. Also, try to speak to the paralegal who filled the position in order to ask for leads to openings elsewhere. When you are told that the position is filled, simply ask, "Is there a chance that I could speak for a moment on the phone to the person who was hired? I'd like to get a general idea about working in this area of the law." If the person is hesitant to grant this request, say, "Would you be kind enough to give this paralegal my name and number and ask him (or her) to give me a call so that I could ask a few brief questions? I would really appreciate it."

Ask the local paralegal association if it has a *job-finding manual* for paralegals in your area. The manual may have been created for an employment workshop conducted by the association. Ask the association if such a manual—or any other handouts—is still available from a prior workshop. Also find out if the association has scheduled a future workshop on employment that you can attend.

Go to a general session of the association. Many associations meet once a month. Become a participant. The more active you are as a student member, the more contacts you will make. If there is no paralegal association near you, organize one—beginning with your own student body and past graduates of your school.

Paralegal newsletters often announce **continuing legal education (CLE)** conferences and seminars for practicing paralegals. Similar announcements are found in the newsletters of the major national paralegal associations:

- *National Paralegal Reporter* National Federation of Paralegal Associations (www.paralegals.org)
- *Facts & Findings* National Association of Legal Assistants (www.nala.org/Facts_Findings.htm)
- *@Law* NALS the Association for Legal Professionals (www.nals.org/atlaw)
- *The Alliance Echo* American Alliance of Paralegals (www.aapipara.org/Newsletter.htm)

> **continuing legal education (CLE)** Training in the law (usually short-term) that a person receives after completing his or her formal legal training.

Employed paralegals attend CLE events in large numbers. Hence they are excellent places to meet experienced paralegals.

Paralegals sometimes go to CLE sessions for attorneys conducted by local bar associations, particularly those bar associations where paralegals are allowed to become associate members. (Some of the Web sites in appendix B are to bar associations that allow paralegals to become associate members.) You should also find out if there are associations of legal secretaries and of legal administrators in your area. If so, they might conduct workshops or meetings that you can attend. At such meetings and elsewhere, try to talk with individual legal secretaries and legal administrators about employment opportunities for paralegals where they work.

Strategy 5: Try to Have Informational Interviews

An **informational interview** (sometimes called an *exploratory interview*) is an opportunity to question someone about an area of law or kind of employment. Ideally this is done at the place where the person being interviewed works, although this is not always possible. Unlike a job interview, where you are the one interviewed, *you* do the interviewing in an informational interview. You ask questions that will help you learn what working at that kind of office is like.

> **informational interview** An interview whose primary purpose is to gain a better understanding of an area of law or kind of employment.

> If, for example, you are a real "people" person who finds antitrust theory fascinating, you should listen to antitrust paralegals discussing their day-to-day work. You may hear that most of them spend years in document warehouses with one lawyer, two other paralegals and a pizza delivery man as their most significant personal contacts. That information may influence your decision about antitrust as a career path.[14]

Do *not* try to turn an informational interview into a job interview. While on an informational interview, it is inappropriate to ask a person for a job. Toward the end of the interview, you can delicately ask for leads to employment and you can ask how the person obtained his or her job, but these inquiries should be secondary to your primary purpose of obtaining information about the realities of work at that kind of office. Do not use an informational interview as a subterfuge for a job interview that you are having difficulty obtaining.

Try to interview employed paralegals whom you have met through the steps outlined in Strategy 4. Although some attorneys and legal administrators may also be willing to grant you informational interviews, the best people to talk to are those who were once in your shoes. Simply say to a paralegal you have met, "Would it be possible for me to come down to the office where you work for a brief informational interview?" If he or she is not familiar with this kind of interview, explain its limited objective. Many will be too busy to grant you an interview, but you have nothing to lose by asking. As an added inducement, consider offering to take the paralegal to lunch. In addition to meeting this paralegal, try to have at least a brief tour of the office where he or she works. Observing how different kinds of employees interact with each other and with available technology in the office will be invaluable. If it is not possible to go to an office, try to conduct informational interviews wherever you find working paralegals. For example, go to a paralegal association meeting and ask people at random what kind of work they do. If one mentions an area that interests you, ask the same kinds of questions you would ask if you were interviewing that person in his or her office.

Here are some of the questions you should ask in an informational interview.

- What is a typical day for you in this office?
- What kinds of assignments do you receive?
- How much overtime is usually expected? Do you take work home with you?
- How do the attorneys interact with paralegals in this kind of practice? Who does what? How many different attorneys does a paralegal work with? How are assignment priorities set?
- How do the paralegals interact with secretaries and other support staff in the office?
- What is the hierarchy of the office?
- What kind of education best prepares a paralegal to work in this kind of office? What courses are most effective?
- What is the most challenging aspect of the job? The most frustrating?
- How are paralegals perceived in this office?
- Are you glad you became this kind of paralegal in this kind of office? Would you do it over again?
- What advice would you give to someone who wants to become a paralegal like yourself?

Several of these questions are also appropriate in a job interview, as we will see later. (To learn more, type "informational interview" in Google or any general search engine.)

One final word of caution. Any information you learn about clients or legal matters must be kept confidential, even if the person you are interviewing is casual about revealing such information to you. This person may not be aware that he or she is acting unethically by disclosing confidential information. Carelessness in this regard is not uncommon.

Strategy 6: Locate Potential Employers

There are a number of ways to locate attorneys:

a. Placement office
b. Personal contacts
c. Ads
d. Other paralegals
e. Employment agencies
f. Directories and other lists of attorneys
g. Courts and bar association meetings

(See Job-Hunting Notebook, page 101.)

For every attorney that you contact, you want to know the following:

- Has the attorney hired paralegals in the past?
- If so, is the attorney interested in hiring more paralegals?
- If the attorney has never hired paralegals before, might he or she consider hiring one?
- Does the attorney know of other attorneys who might be interested in hiring paralegals?

The last point is particularly important. Attorneys from different firms often talk with each other about their practice, including their experiences with paralegals or their plans for hiring paralegals. Hence always ask about other firms. If you obtain a lead, begin your contact with the other firm by mentioning the name of the attorney who gave you the lead. You might say, "Mary Smith told me that you have hired paralegals in the past and might be interested in hiring another paralegal," or "John Rodriguez suggested that I contact you concerning possible employment at your firm as a paralegal." If you do not have the name of a contact to mention, you might simply say, "I'm going to be finishing my paralegal training soon [or I've just completed my paralegal training] and I was wondering whether your office employs paralegals." If the response is not encouraging, be sure to ask, "Do you have any suggestions on other offices where I might check?"

a. Placement Office   Start with the placement office of your paralegal school. Talk with staff members and check the bulletin board regularly (e.g., daily). If your school is part of a university that has a law school, you might want to check the placement office of the law school as well. While paralegal jobs are usually not listed there, you may find descriptions of law firms with the number of attorneys and paralegals employed. (See also appendix 2.A at the end of this chapter.) It might be useful for you to identify the major resources for obtaining *attorney* jobs, such as special directories, lists or ads in bar publications, legal newspapers, etc. In particular, try to find the following resource used by unemployed attorneys and law students:

National Directory of Legal Employers National Association for Law Placement

    www.nalp.org

    www.nalpdirectory.com

b. Personal Contacts   Make a list of attorneys who fall into the following categories:

- Personal friends
- Friends of friends
- Attorneys you have hired
- Attorneys your relatives have hired
- Attorneys your former employers have hired
- Attorneys your friends have hired
- Attorneys your church has hired
- Teachers
- Politicians
- Neighbors
- Etc.

You should consider contacting these attorneys about their own paralegal hiring plans as well as for references to other attorneys. Don't be reluctant to take advantage of *any* direct or indirect association that you might have with an attorney. Such contacts are the essence of **networking**, which simply means establishing contacts with people who may be helpful to you now or in the future. The essence of networking is the sharing of information. Here is a fuller definition: "Networking is simply the process by which an individual gathers information and, in turn, shares information with others, creating and enhancing connections for mutual benefit."[15]

networking Establishing contacts with people who might become personal or professional resources

The value of networking is not limited to job hunting. It can be used on the job and throughout your career. If you are diligent, creative, and willing to be a giver as well as a receiver of information, there is a very good possibility that networking:

- Will find you your first job
- Will lead you to resources that will help you perform the jobs you obtain
- Will lead you to other jobs when it is time to move on
- Will find you lots of friends
- Will engage you in the further development of paralegalism as a profession

Of course, networking is not restricted to attorneys. Everyone you meet is a candidate for your network!

c. Ads   You should regularly check the classified pages of your daily and Sunday newspaper as well as the legal newspaper for your area. (See Exhibit 2.4 for some of the common abbreviations used in ads.) If you are seeking employment in another city, the main branch of your public library and the main library of large universities in your area may have out-of-town newspapers. Find out if these newspapers are online by checking the following sites:

- www.newspapers.com
- newslink.org
- www.50states.com/news

Online newspapers often include classified ads. If you have friends in these other cities, they might be willing to send you clippings from the classified ads of their newspapers. Although *national* legal newspapers seldom have ads for paralegal employment, their online editions will usually have "Find a Job" links that will cover paralegal employment. Check:

- *National Law Journal*
  www.nlj.com
- *American Lawyer*
  www.americanlawyer.com
- *Corporate Counsel*
  www.corpcounsel.com

EXHIBIT 2.4	Classified Ad Abbreviations

Abbreviation	Translation	Abbreviation	Translation	Abbreviation	Translation
2+	plus means "or more" (years of experience)	DOE	depending on experience	mgmt	management
acctg	acounting	EOE	Equal Opportunity Employer	ofc	office
advc	advancement	exp nec	experience necessary	opty	opportunity
agcy	agency	exp pfd	experience preferred	ovtm	overtime
appt	appointment	f/pd	fee paid	pd vac	paid vacation
asst	assistant	f/t	full-time	p/t	part-time
begnr	beginner	gd	good	refs	references
bkpg	bookkeeping	inq	inquire	secty	secretary
bnfts	benefits	k	thousands	sr	senior
clk	clerk	LLP	Limited Liability Partnership	w/	with
co	company			w/wo	with or without
col grad	college graduate	loc	location or located	wpm	words per minute
col	college	mfg	manufacturing		

Source: Finding a Job in the Want Ads (New Mexico SOICC).

Law libraries often subscribe to such newspapers. They will also subscribe to local legal newspapers that may have paralegal ads.

As you read online and paper ads, start by looking for paralegal and legal assistant positions. Examples:

PARALEGAL
TRUST ACCOUNTANTS
For details see our ad in
this section headed:
ACCOUNTANT

PARALEGALS Fee Pd. Salary Open. Corporate & Real Estate positions. Superior writing ability is a necessity. Must be able to work under pressure. Superior opportunities. Contact . . .

PARALEGAL
(CORPORATE)
Large Boston law firm seeks expd Corporate Paralegal. Opportunity for responsibility and growth. Must have strong academic background. Computer literacy a plus. Salary commensurate with exp. Send résumé in confidence to: X2935 TIMES

LEGAL ASSISTANT
Large West Palm Beach, Florida firm wishes to employ legal assistant with immigration/ naturalization experience, in addition to civil litigation, research & pleading abilities. Knowledge of Germanic languages helpful. Full fringe benefits. Salary negotiable. Contact . . .

Be alert for "buzzwords" in the ads. These are key words or phrases that indicate what the employer is looking for (e.g., "computer literacy," "work under pressure," "writing," "immigration"). Later, when you write your résumé and cover letter in response to an ad, you should try to use (indeed, emphasize) these buzzwords. For detailed quotes from want ads for a variety of different kinds of paralegal jobs, see Section C in this chapter on paralegal specialties.

The ad may not give the name and address of the employer seeking the paralegal. Instead, it will direct interested parties to an intermediary, such as a newspaper, which forwards all responses to the employer. Such ads are called **blind ads**. Some ads are placed by private employment agencies that specialize in legal placements.

You will find that most want ads seek paralegals with experience in a particular area of practice. Hence, if you are a recent graduate of a paralegal school who is looking for a beginning or entry-level position, you may not meet the qualifications sought in the ads. (See Section F in this chapter, where we discuss the Catch-22 dilemma of no experience/no job faced by graduates seeking their first paralegal job.) Entry-level positions are not often advertised. (Hence they are part of what is sometimes called the *hidden job market*.) The primary means of finding out about such positions are the job-search techniques discussed in this section and the techniques of networking covered at the end of chapter 3. Should you answer ads that specify qualifications such as experience that you do not have? Suppose, for example, that an ad seeks a corporate paralegal with two years of experience. You might consider answering such an ad as follows:

> I am responding to your ad for a corporate paralegal. I do not have the experience indicated in
> the ad, but I did take an intensive course on corporate law at my paralegal school. I am enclosing
> my résumé in the hope that you will consider what I have to offer.

blind ad A classified ad that does not give the name and address of the prospective employer.

When reading want ads, do not limit yourself to the entries for "Paralegal" and "Legal Assistant." Also look for headings for positions that may be law related, such as "Research Assistant," "Legislative Aide," or "Law Library Assistant." For example:

RESEARCH ASSISTANT
IMMEDIATE POSITION

Social Science Research Institute in downtown looking for coder/editor of legal survey instruments. Post Box L3040.

PROOFREADER

Leading newspaper for lawyers has an immediate opening for a proofreader of manuscripts and galleys. Attention to detail, some night work. Past experience preferred. Call Nance, 964-9700, Ext. 603.

LEGISLATIVE ASSISTANT—Good skills essential, dwntwn location, send résumé/sal. requirements to Post Box M 8341.

ADMINISTRATOR—LAW

Medium-size established law firm seeks manager with administrative, financial & personnel experience to supervise all non-legal office activities. Salary will be commensurate with experience. EOE. Applicants should send résumés with salary requirements to Box 9-17-2085.

Of course, some of the above jobs may not be what you are looking for. They may not be directly related to your legal training and experience. Nevertheless, you should read such ads carefully. Some might be worth pursuing.

On most classified pages, you will find many ads for legal secretaries, docket clerks, and word processors. You might want to respond to such ads as follows:

> I saw your ad for a legal secretary. I am a trained paralegal and am wondering whether you have any openings for paralegals. If not, I would greatly appreciate your referring me to any attorneys you know who may be looking for competent paralegals.

Should you ever apply for a position you are not seeking? A distinction should be made between transitional jobs and career jobs. A transitional job is one taken in the hope that it will eventually turn into the job you really want and for which you have been trained. The latter is a career job. Should a paralegal take a clerical job as a transitional position? Many paralegals take the view that this would be a mistake. In a tight employment market, however, some believe that a secretarial or clerical position is a way to "get a foot in the door." Their hope is to perform well and eventually graduate into a position in the office that is commensurate with their paralegal training. This "bloom-where-you-are-planted" course of action is obviously a very personal decision that you must make. Clerical staff *do* sometimes get promoted to paralegal positions in an office, but it is also possible to get stuck in a clerical position. Finally, it is interesting to keep in mind that some attorneys are willing to take paralegal jobs to "get a foot in the door" when there is an oversupply of attorneys looking for work in a particular market.

Should you ever respond to want ads *for attorneys?* Such ads regularly appear in legal newspapers and magazines as well as online. Of course, a paralegal cannot claim to be an attorney. But any office that is looking for attorneys obviously has a need for legal help. Hence, consider these possible reasons for responding to such ads, particularly when they give the name and address of the office seeking the attorney:

- Perhaps the office is *also* looking for paralegal help but is simply not advertising for it (or you have not seen the want ad for paralegals).
- Perhaps the office is having difficulty finding the attorney it is seeking and would consider hiring a paralegal for a temporary period of time to perform paralegal tasks *while* continuing the search for the attorney.
- Perhaps the office has never considered hiring a paralegal *instead of* an attorney but would be interested in exploring the idea.

Many of these employers may be totally uninterested in a response by a paralegal to an ad for an attorney. Yet none of the possibilities just described is irrational. The effort might be productive. Even if you receive a flat rejection, you can always use the opportunity to ask the person you contact if he or she knows of any other offices that are hiring paralegals.

Finally, a word about want ads placed *by a paralegal* seeking employment. Should you ever place an ad in a publication read by attorneys, such as the journal of the bar association or the legal newspaper for your area? Such ads can be expensive and are seldom productive. Nevertheless, if you have a particular skill—for example, if you are a nurse trained as a paralegal and are seeking a position in a medical malpractice firm, an ad might strike a responsive chord.

d. Through Other Paralegals   In Strategy 4 mentioned earlier, we discussed methods to contact working paralegals. Once you talk with a paralegal, you can, of course, obtain information about contacting the employing attorney of that paralegal.

e. Employment Agencies   Most employment agencies find employees who go on the payroll of the offices where they are placed. Another kind is the **staffing agency**. This is an agency that handles the salary, taxes, workers' compensation, and related benefits of the people it places in temporary positions. The office pays the staffing agency, which in turn handles all the financial aspects of the placement. There have always been employment agencies for the placement of attorneys. Many of these agencies also handle placements for full-time and temporary paralegal positions. Recently, a number of agencies have been opened to deal primarily with paralegal placement. To find these agencies on the Internet, see Exhibit 2.7 (More Employment Resources on the Internet) later in the chapter. In this exhibit, check the heading "Temporary Legal Staffing." Many employers will hire temporary workers with the goal of hiring them full-time if they fit in and perform well. (This arrangement is referred to as *temp-to-hire* or *temp-to-perm*.) One placement agency recently used the following ad in a newspaper.

> **staffing agency** An employment agency that places temporary workers, often directly paying the workers and handling all of the financial aspects of the placement.

Help Wanted

Paralegal Agency   **Fee Paid**

Paralegal Placement Experts Recognized by Over 200 Law Firms and Corporations

PENSIONS	**LITIGATION**	**MANAGING CLERK**
Outstanding law firm seeks 1+ yrs pension paralegal exper. Major responsibilities, quality clients & liberal benefits. Salary commensurate w/exper.	SEVERAL positions open at LAW FIRMS for litigation paralegals. Major benefits.	Midtown law firm seeks 1+ yrs exper as a managing clerk. Work directly w/top management. Liberal benefits.

These are just a few of the many paralegal positions we have available.
Call us for professional career guidance.

Look for such ads in the classified pages of general circulation and legal newspapers. Paralegal association newsletters and special paralegal magazines such as *Legal Assistant Today* (www.legalassistanttoday.com) may also have this kind of ad. Check your Yellow Pages under "Employment Agencies." If you are not sure which of the listed agencies cover legal placements, call several at random and ask which agencies in the city handle paralegal placement or legal placement in general. Caution is needed in using such agencies, however. Some of them know very little about paralegals, in spite of their ads claiming to place paralegals. You may find that the agency views a legal assistant or paralegal as a secretary with a little extra training.

All agencies charge a placement fee. You must check whether the fee is paid by the employer or by the employee hired through the agency. Read the agency's service contract carefully before signing. Question the agency about the jobs they have available—for instance, whether evening work is expected or what typing requirements there are, if any.

Most employment or staffing agencies that work with paralegals can place them in temporary or part-time positions. A particular law firm or corporate law department may prefer temporary paralegals because of the low overhead costs involved, the availability of experienced people on short notice for indefinite periods, and the ability to end the relationship without having to go through the sometimes wrenching experience of terminating permanent employees.

f. Directories and Other Lists of Attorneys   Find a directory or list of attorneys. Ask a librarian at any law library or general library in your area. Your Yellow Pages will also list attorneys, often by specialty.

Also check with a librarian about national directories of attorneys. Two of the major directories are:

- *Martindale-Hubbell Law Directory*
  - available in bound volumes
  - available free on the Internet (www.martindale.com)
  - available for a fee at LexisNexis (www.lexis.com)
- *West's Legal Directory*
  - available free on the Internet (lawyers.findlaw.com) (click "Try Name Search")
  - available for a fee at Westlaw (www.westlaw.com)

For an excerpt from the pages of the bound *Martindale-Hubbell Law Directory*, see Exhibit 2.5. *Martindale-Hubbell* gives descriptions of law firms by state and city or county. For each firm, you are given brief biographies of the attorneys (listing bar memberships, college attended, etc.) as well as the firm's areas of practice. (*Martindale-Hubbell* also includes a law digest that summarizes the law of every state and many foreign countries.) For an excerpt from *West's Legal Directory* at its Findlaw site, see Exhibit 2.6. (We will examine Westlaw and LexisNexis in greater detail in chapter 13.)

In addition to these broad-based legal directories, you should try to locate specialty directories of attorneys. Examples include criminal law attorneys, corporate counsel, bankruptcy attorneys, black attorneys, and women attorneys. Here are examples of these associations on the Internet:

- National Bar Association (African-American Attorneys) (www.nationalbar.org)
- Hispanic National Bar Association (www.hnba.com)
- National Asian Pacific American Bar Association (www.napaba.org)
- Hellenic Bar Association (www.hellenicbarassociation.com)
- American Association of Nurse Attorneys (www.taana.org)

Read whatever biographical data is provided on the attorneys. If you have something in common with a particular attorney (for example, you were both born in the same small town or you both went to the same school), you might want to mention this fact in a cover letter or phone conversation.

EXHIBIT 2.5	Excerpt from a Page in Martindale-Hubbell Law Directory

YARBROUGH & ELLIOTT, P.C.
1420 WEST MOCKINGBIRD LANE
SUITE 390, LB115
DALLAS, TEXAS 75247
Telephone: 214-267-1100
Fax: 214-267-1200
URL: www.yarbroughandelliott.com

Corporate Law, Partnership, Real Estate, Civil Litigation, Estate Planning, Family Law.

GEORGE M. YARBROUGH, JR., born Memphis, Tennessee, January 22, 1953; admitted to bar, 1978, Texas. *Education:* University of Mississippi (B.B.A., with honors, 1975); Southern Methodist University (J.D., 1978). Phi Eta Sigma; Phi Kappa Phi; Beta Gamma Sigma; Omicron Delta Kappa. President, Associated Student Body, University of Mississippi, 1974-1975. Member, Student Bar Association Executive Council, 1975-1976. *Member:* Dallas and American Bar Associations; State Bar of Texas (Member, Compensation and Employee Benefits Committee, 1986-1988). *PRACTICE AREAS:* Buying and Selling of Businesses; Limited Liability Company Law; Family Business Law.

NANCY GAIL ELLIOTT, born Corpus Christi, Texas, January 17, 1954; admitted to bar, 1985, Texas. *Education:* University of Texas (B.S., 1975; M.Ed., 1977); Texas Tech University (J.D., 1984). Phi Theta Kappa; Kappa Delta Pi; Phi Delta Phi. *Member:* Dallas Bar Association; State Bar of Texas. *PRACTICE AREAS:* Mechanics Liens; Asset Protection; Estate Planning; Guardianship; Contested Wills.

EXHIBIT 2.6	West's Legal Directory on Findlaw.com (lawyers.findlaw.com)

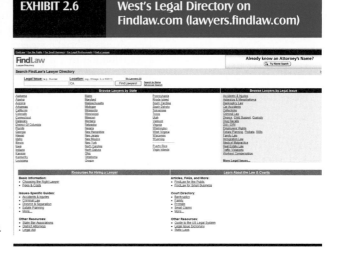

g. Courts and Bar Association Meetings   You can also meet attorneys at the courts of your area—for example, during a recess or at the end of the day. Bar association committee meetings are sometimes open to nonattorneys. The same may be true of continuing legal education

(CLE) seminars conducted for attorneys. When the other strategies for contacting attorneys do not seem productive, consider going to places where attorneys congregate. Simply introduce yourself and ask if they know of paralegal employment opportunities at their firms or at other firms. If you meet an attorney who practices in a particular specialty, it would be helpful if you could describe your course work or general interest in that kind of law. If you are doing some school research in that area of the law, you might begin by asking for some research leads before you ask about employment.

h. Miscellaneous   Look for ads in legal newspapers in which an attorney is seeking information about a particular product involved in a suit that is contemplated or underway. Or read feature stories in a legal newspaper on major litigation that is about to begin. If the area of the law interests you, contact the law firms involved (using the directories just described) to ask about employment opportunities for paralegals. Many firms hire additional paralegals, particularly for large cases.

Find the bar journal of your local or state bar association in the law library. Some bar associations place their journals on the Internet. (See appendix B for the Web sites of state and local bar associations.) Articles in bar journals are often written by attorneys from the state. If the subject of an article interests you, read it and call or e-mail the author. Ask a question or two about the topic of the article and the area of the law involved. Then ask about employment opportunities for paralegals in that area.

Strategy 7: Surf the Internet

Thus far in the chapter, we have mentioned resources on the Internet a number of times. Exhibit 2.7 presents additional resources available in cyberspace.

Strategy 8: Prepare Your Résumé, Cover Letter, and Writing Samples

The cardinal principle of résumé writing is that you *target* the résumé to the job you are seeking. Hence you must have more than one résumé, or you must rewrite your résumé for each particular employer to whom you send it. A targeted résumé, for example, should contain the buzzwords used in the ad for the job you are seeking (e.g., *litigation management* and *office systems*). Word processors make it relatively easy for you to cut and paste whatever portions of the résumé you need for a particular employer.

A résumé is an *advocacy* document. You are trying to convince someone (1) to give you an interview and ultimately (2) to offer you a job. You are not simply communicating information about yourself. A résumé is *not* a summary of your life or a one-page autobiography. It is targeted advertising—a brief *commercial* in which yo u are trying to sell yourself as a person who can make a contribution to a particular prospective employer. Hence the résumé must stress what would appeal to *this* employer. You are advocating (or selling) yourself effectively when the form and content of the résumé have this appeal. Advocacy is required for several reasons. First, there may be more applicants than jobs available. Second, most prospective employers ignore résumés that are not geared to their particular needs.

ASSIGNMENT 2.3

(a) Use some of the Internet sites in Exhibit 2.7 to find a job opening for a paralegal in a city where you hope to work. If you can't find an opening in that city, check openings for the entire state. Where did you find this information on the Internet? What search terms did you use?

(b) Use any of the Internet sites mentioned in Exhibit 2.7 to locate a law firm in your state that employs more than ten attorneys. State the name, address, and phone number of this firm. What kind of law does it practice? Where did you find this information on the Internet? What search terms did you use?

EXHIBIT 2.7	More Employment Resources on the Internet

For many of the employment sites listed below, find out:

- whether specific paralegal jobs are posted (type "paralegal," "legal assistant," or "job bank" in the search boxes provided on these sites, even for those sites that appear to be focused primarily on attorneys),
- whether you can post your résumé on the site for prospective employers to examine,
- whether the service charges a fee, and
- whether guidance is available (directly or through links) on résumé-writing and job-interview strategies.

PARALEGAL JOB SEARCH SITES

- www.paralegalclassifieds.com
- www.lawjobs.com
- www.careers.findlaw.com
- www.paralegalmanagement.org
- paralegals.legalstaff.com
- www.legalstaff.com
- paralegalpost.net

JOB ALERT SITES

(allows you to sign up to be notified of openings)

- www.lawyersweeklyjobs.com
- www.careerbuilder.com
- www.legalstaff.com
- www.usajobs.com

GENERAL LEGAL EMPLOYMENT SEARCH SITES

(for attorneys, paralegals, and other legal staff)

- www.lawcrossing.com
- www.legalemploy.com
- jobs.lawinfo.com
- www.ihirelegal.com
- www.specialcounsel.com

GENERAL EMPLOYMENT SEARCH SITES

(can be used for paralegal searches)

- www.monster.com
- www.hotjobs.com
- www.careerpath.com
- www.indeed.com
- www.simplyhired.com

GENERAL SEARCH ENGINES AS JOB RESOURCES

(in the following engines, type your city, the word *paralegal*, and "jobs search", e.g., Boston paralegal "job search")

- www.google.com
- www.ask.com
- www.yahoo.com
- www.search.msn.com
- www.vivisimo.com

PARALEGAL ASSOCIATIONS AND BAR ASSOCIATIONS

(Go to the Web site of your paralegal association [see appendix B] and your bar association [see appendix C] Find out if the association has a job bank or search feature on its site.)

OTHER SEARCH OPTION

- www.craigslist.org
  (pick your city, then under "Jobs" select "Legal/Paralegal")

FEDERAL GOVERNMENT EMPLOYMENT

- www.usajobs.opm.gov
- www.fedworld.gov/jobs/jobsearch.html

STATE GOVERNMENT EMPLOYMENT

(see your state in appendix 2B at the end of this chapter)

COURT EMPLOYMENT

- www.uscourts.gov (click "Employment")
- www.ncsconline.org/D_KIS/info_court_web_sites.html
  (for the courts in your state, click "Employment Links")

TEMPORARY LEGAL STAFFING

- www.roberthalflegal.com
- www.specialcounsel.com
- www.gibsonarnold.com
- www.cambridgestaff.com
- www.strategicworkforce.com
- www.theassociatesinc.com
- www.juristaff.com
- www.staffwise.com
- www.exclusivelylegal.com
- www.lumenlegal.com

SALARY INFORMATION

- www.salary.com
- www.salaryexpert.com
- www.rileyguide.com/salguides.html

RÉSUMÉ, INTERVIEWING, AND GENERAL JOB SEARCH RESOURCES

- www.hg.org/employment.html
- www.quintcareers.com
- www.acinet.org
- www.rileyguide.com
- www.careeroink.com

FINDING INFORMATION ABOUT LAW OFFICES

- www.martindale.com
- lawyers.findlaw.com
- www.washlaw.edu (click "LawFirms")
- See the Internet sites of law firms in appendix 2.A.

CAUTION

Use caution when responding to any Internet site. Identity thieves have been known to hack into legitimate employment sites,post bogus job offerings, and collect personal information from unsuspecting job hunters.

Before examining sample résumés, we need to explore some general guidelines that apply to *any* résumé.

Guidelines on Drafting an Effective Résumé

1. Be concise and to the point. Generally, the résumé should fit on one page. A second page is justified only if you have a unique education or experience that is directly related to law or to the particular law firm or company in which you are interested. Do not submit a résumé over two pages. Such length is a signal that you don't know how to organize and summarize data. This is not a message that a prospective paralegal wants to convey.

2. Be accurate and cautious. Studies show that about 30 percent of all résumés contain inaccuracies. Recently, a legal administrator felt the need to make the following comment (to other legal administrators) about job applicants: "I'm sure we have all had experiences where an applicant has lied on an application about experience, previous salary scales, length of time with previous employers, training, skills, and anything else they can think of that will make them appear more attractive."[16] While you want to present yourself in the best possible light, it is critical that you not jeopardize your integrity. All of the data in the résumé should be verifiable. Prospective employers who check the accuracy of résumés usually do so themselves, although some use outside credential-checking services. (For example, see www.myreferences.com.) In states where it is illegal to use the *paralegal* (or *legal assistant*) title without meeting specified minimum education or experience requirements (e.g., California), penalties can be imposed for falsifying résumé credentials. Finally, be careful in what you say about yourself online in blogs or social network sites such as *www.myspace.com* and *www.facebook.com*. If someone googles your name, you do not want them to find any character traits or facts that are at odds with what you say or imply in your résumé. The picture of you holding a drink with your eyes rolling may have been a big hit among your circle of friends, but it could lead a prospective employer to doubt whether you would be compatible with the culture of the office.

3. Include personal data—that is, name, street address, zip code, e-mail address, and phone (with area code) where you can be reached. (If someone is not always available to take messages while you are away, use an answering machine.) Do not include a personal photograph or data on your health, height, religion, or political party. You do not have to include information that might give a prospective employer a basis to discriminate against you illegally, such as your marital status. Later we will discuss how to handle such matters in a job interview.

4. Provide a concise statement of your career objective at the top of the résumé. (It should be pointed out, however, that some people recommend that this statement be included in the cover letter rather than in the résumé.) The career objective should be a quick way for the reader to know whether your goal fits the needs of the prospective employer. Hence *the career objective should be targeted to a particular employer* and therefore needs to be rewritten just about every time you send out a résumé to a different employer. An overly general career objective gives the unfortunate effect of a "mass-mailing résumé." Suppose, for example, you are applying for a position as a litigation paralegal at a forty-attorney law firm that is looking for someone to help with scheduling and document handling on several cases going on simultaneously.

   Don't say: **Career Objective**—A position as a paralegal at an office where there is an opportunity for growth.

   Do say: **Career Objective**—A position as a litigation paralegal at a medium-sized law firm where I will be able to use and build on the organizational skills I developed in my prior employment and the case management skills that I have learned to date.

   The first statement is too flat and uninformative. Its generalities could fit just about *any* paralegal job. Even worse, its focus is on the needs of the applicant. The second statement is much more direct. While also referring to the needs of the applicant, the second statement goes to the heart of what the employer is looking for—someone to help create order out of the complexity of events and papers involved in litigation.

5. Next, state your prior education and training if you have not had any legal work experience. If you *have* worked in a law office before, particularly as a paralegal, the next section of the résumé should be work experience, followed by education and training. (See Job-Hunting

Notebook, pages 98 ff.) List each school or training institution and the dates attended. Use a reverse chronological order—that is, start the list with the most current and work backward. Do not include your high school unless you attended a prestigious high school or you are a very recent high school graduate. When you give your legal education:

(a) List the major courses.

(b) State specific skills and tasks covered in your courses that are relevant to the job for which you are applying. Also state major topic areas covered in the courses that demonstrate a knowledge of (or at least exposure to) material that is relevant to the job. For example, if you are applying for a corporate paralegal job, relevant courses could be stated as follows:

> **Corporate Law:** This course examined the formation of a corporation, director and shareholder meetings, corporate mergers, and the dissolution of corporations; we also studied sample shareholder minutes and prepared proxy statements. Grade received: B+.
>
> **Legal Research:** This course covered the basic law books relevant to researching corporate law, including the state code. We also covered the skills of using practice books, finding cases on corporate law through the digests, etc. Grade received: A−.

(c) List any special programs in the school, such as unique class assignments, term papers, extensive research, moot court, internship, or semester projects. Give a brief description if any of these programs are relevant to the job you are seeking.

(d) State any unusually high grades; give overall grade point average (GPA) only if it is distinctive.

List any degrees, certificates, or other recognition that you earned at each school or training institution. Include high aptitude or standard test scores. If the school or institution has any special distinction or recognition, mention this as well.

6. State your work experience. (See Job-Hunting Notebook, pages 96 ff.) List the jobs you held, your job title, the dates of employment, and the major duties that you performed. (Do not state the reason you left each job, although you should be prepared to discuss this if you are granted an interview.) Again, work backward. Start with the most current (or your present) employment. The statement of duties is particularly important. If you have legal experience, emphasize specific duties and tasks that are directly relevant to the position you are seeking—for example, include that you drafted corporate minutes or prepared incorporation papers. Give prominence to such skills and tasks on the résumé. Nonlegal experience, however, can also be relevant. Every prior job says something about you as an individual. Phrase your duties in such jobs in a manner that will highlight important personality traits. (See page 97.) In general, most employers are looking for people with the following characteristics:

- Emotional maturity
- Intelligence
- Willingness to learn
- Ability to get along with others
- Ability to work independently (someone with initiative and self-reliance who is not afraid of assuming responsibility)
- Problem-solving skills
- Ability to handle time pressures and frustration
- Ability to communicate—orally, on paper, and online
- Loyalty
- Stability, reliability
- Energy

As you list duties in prior and current employment settings, do *not* use any of the language just listed. But try to state duties that tend to show that these characteristics apply to you. For example, if you had a job as a camp counselor, state that you supervised eighteen children, designed schedules according to predetermined objectives, prepared budgets, took over in the absence of the director of the camp, etc. A listing of such duties will say a lot about you as a person. You are someone who can be trusted, you know how to work with people, you are flexible, etc. These are the kinds of conclusions that you want the reader of your résumé to reach. Finally, try to present the facts to show a growth in your accomplishments, development, and maturity.

7. Use *action verbs* throughout the résumé.[17] Note that the examples just given used the verbs mentioned in the following lists:

Action Verbs to Use

Creative skills	Financial skills	Management skills	Technical skills
conceptualized	administered	administered	assembled
created	analyzed	analyzed	built
designed	balanced	coordinated	calculated
established	budgeted	developed	designed
fashioned	forecasted	directed	operated
illustrated	marketed	evaluated	overhauled
invented	planned	improved	remodeled
performed	projected	supervised	repaired

Helping skills	Research skills	Communication skills	Administrative skills
assessed	clarified	arranged	arranged
coached	evaluated	addressed	catalogued
counseled	identified	authored	compiled
diagnosed	inspected	drafted	generated
facilitated	organized	formulated	organized
represented	summarized	persuaded	processed
		wrote	systematized

Nonaction Verbs to Avoid

was involved in	had a role in
was a part of	was related to

Nonaction verbs are vague. They give the impression that you are not an assertive person.

8. State other experience and skills that do not fall within the categories of education and employment mentioned above. (See Job-Hunting Notebook, page 97.) Perhaps you have been a homemaker for twenty years, raised five children, worked your way through college, and were the church treasurer, a Cub Scout volunteer, etc. In a separate category on the résumé called "Other Experience," list such activities and state your duties in the same manner mentioned above to demonstrate relevant personality traits. Hobbies can be included (without using the word *hobby*) when they are distinctive and illustrate special talents or achievement.

9. State any special abilities (for example, that you can design a database or speak a foreign language), awards, credentials, scholarships, membership associations, leadership positions, community service, publications, etc., that have not been mentioned elsewhere on the résumé.

10. No one has a perfect résumé. There are facts about all of us that we would prefer to downplay or avoid (e.g., sudden change in jobs, school transfer because of personal or family difficulties, and low aptitude test scores). There is no need to point out these facts, but in a job interview, you must be prepared to discuss any obvious gaps or problems that might be evident from your résumé.

11. Thus far, we have been outlining the format of a **chronological résumé,** which presents your education, training, and experience in a chronological sequence, starting with the present and working backward. (See Exhibit 2.9.) Later we will examine how a **functional résumé** might be more effective than a chronological résumé in handling difficulties such as sudden changes or gaps in employment. (See Exhibit 2.10.) Although we will focus on these two résumé formats, others exist. On the Internet, type "kinds of resumes" in any search engine to locate different styles of résumés.

12. At the end of many résumés, you will find the statement "References available upon request." Some feel that this is a waste of space since it is obvious that you have such a list and that prospective employers can ask for it. Whether or not you include the statement, be sure to have a list of references ready to distribute. On a separate sheet of paper, type the names, work addresses, and phone numbers of people who know your abilities and who could be contacted by a prospective employer. If the latter is seriously considering you for a position, you will probably be asked for the list. This will most likely occur during a job interview. Generally, you should seek the permission of people you intend to use as references. Phone or e-mail them and ask if you can list them as references in

chronological résumé A résumé that presents biographical data on education and experience in a chronological sequence, starting with the present and working backward.

functional résumé A résumé that clusters skills and experience regardless of when they were developed or occurred.

your job search. Verify the contact information you should use on the résumé to allow a prospective employer to reach them. (Also ask if you can include their e-mail address.)

13. Do not state salary requirements or your salary history on the résumé. Leave this topic for the interview. If you are responding to an ad that asks for this history, include it in the cover letter.

14. The résumé should be neatly typed, grammatically correct, and readable. Be sure that there are no spelling errors or smudge spots from erasures or fingerprints. In this regard, if you can't make your résumé *perfect*, don't bother submitting it. (To help you catch errors, print a temporary version of your résumé in a **font** and **point** size that are different from what you used in creating it. Read the text in this new format to see if you find problems that were not initially apparent. Then go back to the font and point size that you will use to submit it.)[17a] Avoid abbreviations except for items such as street, state, degrees earned, etc. Do not make any handwritten corrections; retype or reprint the résumé after you make the corrections. Proofread carefully. Also ask someone else to proofread the résumé for you to see if you missed anything.

> **font** The design or style of printed letters of the alphabet, punctuation marks, or other characters.
>
> **points** A measure of the size of printed letters of the alphabet, punctuation marks, or other characters.

You do not have to use complete sentences in the résumé. Sentence fragments are adequate as long as you rigorously follow the grammatical rule on parallelism. This rule requires that you use a consistent (i.e., parallel) grammatical structure when phrasing logically related ideas in a list. Specifically, be consistent in the use of words ending in *ing*, *ed*, and *tion*. Similarly, be consistent in the use of infinitives, clauses, personal pronouns, and the active voice. For example, say "research*ed* securities issues, draft*ed* complaints, serv*ed* papers on opposing parties." Do not say, "researched securities, drafting complaints, and I served papers on opposing parties." This sentence suddenly changes an "ed" word to an "ing" word and uses the personal pronoun ("I") with only one of the verbs in the list. Also, avoid jumping from past tense to present tense, or vice versa. Do not say "prepared annual budgets and manages part-time personnel." Say "prepare budgets and manage part-time personnel" or "prepared budgets and managed part-time personnel."

Leave one-inch margins around the page. Cluster similar information together and use consistent indentation patterns so that readers can easily skim or scan the résumé and quickly find those categories of information in which they are most interested. Use a conservative font (e.g., Courier New or Times New Roman), do not switch fonts, and do not use anything less than a 12 point font in the résumé.

The résumé should have a professional appearance. If you do not have your own word processor, have your résumé typed on quality white paper (with matching envelopes) by a commercial printing company or word-processing service. Avoid submitting a résumé that was obviously reproduced on a poor-quality photocopy machine at a corner drugstore. The résumé is often the first contact that a prospective employer will have with you. You want to convey the impression that you know how to write and organize data. Furthermore, it is a sign of respect to the reader when you show that you took the time and energy to make your résumé professionally presentable. Law offices are *conservative* environments. Attorneys like to project an image of propriety, stability, accuracy, and order. Be sure that your résumé also projects this image.

15. Again, the résumé concentrates on those facts about you that show you are particularly qualified *for the specific job you are seeking*. The single most important theme you want to convey in the résumé is that you are a person who can make a contribution to *this* organization. As much as possible, the reader of the résumé should have the impression that you prepared the résumé for the particular position that is open. In style and content, the résumé should emphasize what will be pleasing to the reader and demonstrate what you can contribute to a particular office. (See Exhibit 2.8.)

EXHIBIT 2.8	The Résumé as an Advocacy Document

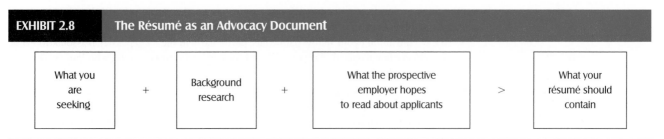

due diligence Reasonable steps that are needed to conduct background factual research or investigation. (See glossary for a more complete definition of *due diligence*.)

The last guideline is very important. You cannot comply with it unless you have done some *background research* on the law office where you are applying. (A background investigation is called doing **due diligence** on an organization or person. Finding out about a prospective employer is sometimes referred to as performing due diligence on it.)

How do you do background research—due diligence—on a prospective employer? There are two kinds of information that you would like to have: public information (facts you can obtain on the Internet or other generally available sources) and private information (facts that usually can be obtained only from an insider).

Public Information

- What kind of office it is? Law firm? Law department of a corporation? Government office? Other?
- If a law firm, what are its major categories of clients? Any specialties? Any recent major victories?
- If a law department, what are the company's main products or services?
- What kinds of personnel does the office have? How many attorneys?
- How long has the office been in existence?
- What does the office say about itself on its Web site? In its own marketing, how does it project itself?

Inside Information

- If the office has an opening for a paralegal, why has it decided to hire one now? What needs or problems prompted this decision?
- How many paralegals does the office have? What specific kinds of work do they do? What are the advantages and disadvantages of working there?
- Has the office experienced a high turnover of personnel? If so, why?
- What's the work culture of the office? Conservative? Demanding? Miserly? Collegial?
- How is the office structured or governed? One individual in charge? A management committee?

Here are some of the techniques you can use to try to find these categories of information:

1. Checking the Web site of the office. Most relatively large law offices have Web sites on which you will find mission statements, kind of law practiced, personnel data, and career options or job openings. To find the office on the Web, simply type its name in any general search engine. See also appendixes 2A and 2B at the end of this chapter for Web addresses of many large law offices and all state government personnel offices.

2. Finding sites for businesses and people. If you are still having difficulty locating specific law offices or individual attorneys or obtaining information about them, try sites such as:
   - www.switchboard.com
   - www.theultimates.com
   - www.llrx.com/features/co_research.htm
   - www.hoovers.com
   - www.business.com

3. Doing a news search. Find out what has been said about the attorney or office in the news. Check news sites such as:
   - news.google.com
   - news.yahoo.com
   - www.altavista.com/news

4. Obtaining an inside perspective. It's not easy to obtain the inside perspective of current and former employees of an office. Here are some techniques to try:
   - Ask around among your fellow paralegals, particularly in the local paralegal association. The chances are fair-to-good that you will find someone who works there, who knows someone who works there, or who once worked there.
   - Check the blogs. A **blog** is an online journal or diary. As we will see in chapter 13, many attorneys (and some paralegals) have blogs on the Internet. (Law blogs are sometimes called *blawgs*.) Some estimate that as many as 20 percent of all law firms publish their own blog.

blog A journal or diary available on the World Wide Web (called *blawg* if the topic is legal).

They cover different aspects of the law or practice (e.g., recent developments in environ-mental law, and tax accounting for corporations). You need to know if anyone working at the office is writing a blog. To find out, type the name of the person or office in standard blog search sites (e.g., blogsearch.google.com or www.blogsearchengine.com) as well as in general search engines such as Google.

• Read the anonymous Web. A popular activity on the Internet is the anonymous posting of comments about organizations, particularly large employers. Some current and former employees take the risk of posting critical information about their bosses (e.g., see the message board at www.greedyassociates.com). Of course, you need to be cautious about relying on such comments. What a disgruntled employee says about an office may be very misleading.

As you can see, obtaining background information about a prospective employer can be hard work. But the effort will be valuable.

A conscientious and organized job search will be good preparation for the career ahead of you. As mentioned earlier, *the same kind of motivation, creativity, and aggressiveness that is needed to find a good job is also needed to perform effectively as a paralegal and to advance in this field.* The cornerstone of achievement and success is a heavy dose of old-fashioned hard work.

Exhibit 2.9 is an example of a *chronological résumé*, the traditional format and the one most commonly used by applicants today. As indicated earlier, this résumé presents your education, training, and work history in reverse chronological sequence, beginning with the most recent events and working backward.

A *functional résumé* clusters certain skills or talents together regardless of the period in which they were developed. See Exhibit 2.10. (Such résumés are sometimes called *skills résumés* or *accomplishments-oriented résumés*.) This style of résumé can be particularly useful when you want to downplay large gaps in education, when you are making a radical change of careers, or when your skills were not gained in paralegal education, training, or employment. The functional résumé should not, however, ignore the chronological sequence of the major training and work events of your life, since a prospective employer will want to know what this sequence is. Note that the functional résumé in Exhibit 2.10 has a skills cluster early in the résumé, followed by the historical overview in reverse chronological order.[18] Using this format puts the emphasis of the résumé on the skills or abilities highlighted at the beginning.

Finally, some employers will allow you to submit an online or electronic résumé over the Internet. (See, for example, Exhibit 2.11.) The employer might ask you a series of detailed online questions, the answers to which would produce the equivalent of your résumé in the format it prefers. Other employers may allow you to e-mail your résumé, usually as an attachment. If so, you will be typing your résumé on a blank screen (like a blank sheet of paper), rather than using preformatted questions. For the résumé to be readable, your e-mail software must be compat-ible with the e-mail software of the recipient. If any difficulties occur, the recipient should be able to tell you what you need to do to make the connection work. Before sending the e-mail to the employer, send it to yourself or to a friend. This will allow you to see how it appears on the screen after it arrives, perhaps suggesting some changes in the way you initially typed or format-ted it. You may find, for example, that you should not use bullets (•) in any of the lists on your résumé because they are translated into some other character when received. Maintain proper formality in whatever you send online. Do not be familiar. Do not address anyone by his or her first name or sign off by using your first name alone. A final word of caution: résumés obviously contain personal information such as your employment history. Identity thieves might find such information useful. You need to make a judgment of whether you are sending the information into a secure environment.

Cover Letter   The **cover letter** is extremely important. "Research done by recruiting firms has shown 10 percent of an employer's attention is spent opening an envelope, 80 percent is used reading a cover letter and the other 10 percent focuses on scanning a resume."[19] Hence you need to use considerable care in composing the letter. In one page, it should state how you learned about the office and should highlight or amplify those portions of the résumé that are relevant to the position you are seeking. Most of a résumé is written in sentence fragments found in tightly compacted lists. The cover letter is your one opportunity to use complete sentences as you explain why you are qualified for the job. Repeat any buzzwords that you picked up from the want ad or from background research you have been able to do

cover letter A letter that tells the recipient what physical items are being sent in the envelope or package. Also called *transmittal letter* or *enclosure letter*.

EXHIBIT 2.9	Sample Chronological Résumé (targeted at a firm seeking a trusts and estates paralegal)

John J. Smith
43 Benning Road SE
Salem, Maryland 21455
(701) 456–0427

CAREER OBJECTIVE
Position as a paralegal at a small law firm working in the area of probate, trusts, and estates.

EDUCATION
Jan. 1999–Jan. 2000, Maynard Paralegal Institute
Courses:
Trusts and Estates:
■ overview of probate procedure and the basics of trusts and estates in Maryland
■ client interviews to identify facts needed to prepare the federal 105 short form

Tax I:
■ basics of estate taxation
■ introduction to personal income taxation
■ fundamentals of accounting
■ valuation of personal and real property

Other Courses:
Introduction to Law, Family Law, Litigation, Legal Research

Internship: Donaldson & Fry, LLP. (Sept. 1999--Dec. 1999)
Tasks performed under supervision of Alex Fry, Esq.:
■ drafted answers to interrogatories in a divorce case
■ maintained the firm's tickler system
■ coded discovery documents
■ cite checked an appellate brief

September 1997–June 1999 Jefferson Community College
Courses:
Business Law; English I, II; Sociology; Creative Writing; French I; Introduction to Psychology

EMPLOYMENT
1995–1998	Teller, Salem National Bank
	Responsibilities: Received deposit and withdrawal requests; trained new tellers; supervised note department in the absence of the assistant manager.
1990–1994	Driver, ABC Biscuit Company

HONORS
1995 Junior Achievement Award for Outstanding Marketing

ASSOCIATIONS
Financial Secretary, Salem Paralegal Association; Regional Representative, National Federation of Paralegal Associations; Member, National Association of Legal Assistants

REFERENCES
Available on request.

---

on why the office is seeking a paralegal. Like the résumé itself, the cover letter should give the impression that you are a professional. It is also important that you communicate a sense of enthusiasm about the position. Try to say something specific in the letter that you learned about the office through your background research. For example, if the office's Web site says that the firm recently merged with another office, you might say at the end of the letter, "From everything I have learned about your firm, including its recent merger with Davis and Kendle, I feel confident that it would be an exciting place to work and that I would be able to make a contribution."

EXHIBIT 2.10	Sample Functional Résumé

Jane Doe
18 East 7th Avenue
Denver, Colorado 80200
303–555–1198

BRIEF SUMMARY OF BACKGROUND

Currently enrolled in paralegal certificate program. Bachelor of Arts and Bachelor of Science (Education) with major in English and minor in Library Science. Taught creative writing and communications to high school seniors; worked several years as research and index assistant in records and research department of large international organization; worked part-time on a volunteer basis in schools and libraries as librarian and reading tutor.

PROFESSIONAL SKILLS

Communication Skills
- taught creative writing to high school seniors
- conducted workshops on library service to employees
- co-led workshops on literacy training
- served as Circulation Representative for *USA Today*

Research Skills
- guided library patrons in use of basic reference materials
- used Internet to obtain sites for county resource manual
- recommended subscription purchases for general circulation library

Organization Skills
- managed all phases of school library
- planned budget requests for library
- supervised paid and volunteer library staff

EMPLOYMENT HISTORY

9/94–Present	Lincoln Elementary School (Denver): Teacher's Aide (part-time)
6/86–6/94	International Church Center, Records and Research Section (Boston): Research and Index Assistant
4/94–6/94	Latin Preparatory School (Dorchester): School Librarian (substitute)
2/93–6/94	James P. O'Reilly Elementary School (Boston): School Librarian (volunteer)
9/84–6/85	Roosevelt High School (St. Paul): English Teacher Aide

EDUCATION

8/06–Present	LaSalle Community College Paralegal Program (expected date of graduation: 7/08)
	Courses: Introduction to Paralegalism, Litigation, Probate, Contracts, Torts, Legal Research and Writing, Law Office Management, Computers in the Law GPA thus far: 3.9
1993–1994	University of Massachusetts, Boston Campus Special courses included: Library and Urban Children; Design Management
1989–1990	Harvard Extension, Problems in Urban Education
1979–1983	University of Minnesota, Minneapolis, B.S., *Major:* English *Minor:* Library Science

SCHOOL ACTIVITIES

National Honor Society, Dramatic Club, Creative Writing Club, YWCA, Minnesota Dance Company.

REFERENCES

Available on request.

Note that the cover letter in Exhibit 2.12 is addressed to a specific person. Try to avoid sending a "To Whom It May Concern" letter unless you are responding to a blind ad. Whenever possible, find out the exact name of the person to whom the résumé should be sent. If you are not sure, call the office and ask. Also check the firm's Internet site to see if it gives the name of the person at the firm in charge of recruitment or personnel.

About a week after you send the résumé and cover letter, consider calling the office to find out if they were received and when you might have a response. Some offices might consider such calls to be annoying, but if you know that an office will probably have many applicants, your call might help demonstrate your initiative.

EXHIBIT 2.11	Example of an Online Résumé/Application

© 2006 Fulbright & Jaworski (www.fulbright.com) L.L.P. All rights reserved.

EXHIBIT 2.12	Cover Letter

43 Benning Road SE
Salem, Maryland 21455
701-456-0427
June 23, 2001

Linda Stenner, Esq.
Stenner, Skidmore & Smith
438 Bankers Trust Bldg
Suite 1200
Salem, Maryland 21458

Dear Ms. Stenner:

I am responding to the ad you placed in the *Daily Telegraph* of June 14 for a trusts and estates paralegal. My résumé is enclosed for your consideration. I am very interested in working in the field of probate, trusts, and estates. The course work that I did at Maynard Paralegal Institute and my prior work at the Salem National Bank provided me with an appreciation of the complexity of this area of the law. I find the field fascinating.

I am fully aware of the kind of attention to detail that a paralegal in this field must have. If you decide to check any of my references, I am confident that you will be told of the high level of discipline and responsibility that I bring to the tasks I undertake. I have read several stories in the *Salem Bar Register* on the Johnson estate case in which your firm represented the petitioners. The description of your firm and its efforts on behalf of the petitioners have been eye-opening. It would be an honor to become a member of your team.

I have two writing samples that may be of interest to you: a draft of a will that I prepared in my course on trusts and estates, and a memorandum of law on the valuation of stocks. These writing samples are available on request.

I would appreciate the opportunity to be interviewed for the paralegal position at your firm. I feel confident that my training and experience have prepared me for the kind of challenge that this position would provide.

Sincerely,

John J. Smith

Enclosure: Résumé

One final, critically important point about the cover letter: it must be grammatically correct and contain no spelling errors. Do you see any problem with the following sentence from a cover letter?

The description of responsibilities in the want ad fit my experience.

This sentence alone might cause a prospective employer to throw the letter, and its accompanying résumé, in the trash can. The subject and verb don't agree. The sentence should read:

The description of responsibilities in the want ad fits my experience.

There must be no lapses in your grammar and spelling. Your standard must be perfection. While this is also true of the résumé, it is particularly true of the cover letter. When the envelope is opened, the first thing that is read is the cover letter. The vast majority of us are *unaware of how poor our grammar is*. We have been lulled into a sense of security because readers of what we write—including some teachers—seldom complain unless we make an egregious error.

In the section on studying at the beginning of this book, there are suggestions for improving your writing skills. In the meantime, proofread, proofread, proofread; and then find others to proof-read everything that you intend to submit to a prospective employer. An additional technique used by careful writers is to read your cover letter (and résumé) *backward*—word by word, punctuation mark by punctuation mark. Of course, when you do this, you are not reading for meaning. You are isolating everything in the sentence in order to force yourself to ask whether anything might be in need of a dictionary or grammar check. Reading backward might help reveal glaring spelling or punctuation errors that you have been glossing over. Spell checkers on popular word processing programs such as Word and WordPerfect can be helpful, but they must be used with caution. They will identify misspelled words, not incorrectly chosen words. For example, a spell checker will tell you that there are no misspelled words in the following sentence: *Their is too choices*. That is true; the sentence has no spelling errors. Yet the sentence should read, *There are two choices*.

When the résumé and cover letter are ready, place them in a large envelope that matches the color of the paper on which you wrote the résumé and letter. Spend the extra money on postage for the envelope so that you do not have to fold the résumé and letter.

ASSIGNMENT 2.4

Find a want ad from a law office seeking an entry-level paralegal. Try to locate an ad as detailed as possible on what the employer is looking for. To find the ad, use general circulation newspapers, legal newspapers, magazines, newsletters, the Internet, etc.

(a) Prepare a résumé for this job. Make it a real résumé except for the following information, which you can make up:
   ■ You can assume that you have already had course work in the areas involved in the job.
   ■ You can assume that you once had a part-time summer position with an attorney, but it was in an area of the law that is different from the area practiced in the law office seeking the paralegal.
   Attach a copy of the ad to the résumé you hand in, and indicate where you obtained it.

(b) Prepare a cover letter to go with this résumé. You can make up identifying information the ad may not provide (e.g., the name and address of the person to whom you will be sending the résumé and letter). Assume that you called to obtain this information.

Writing samples   You should be constantly thinking about writing samples based upon the course work you do and any legal employment or internship experiences you have had. If your writing sample comes from a prior job or internship, be sure that the confidentiality of actual parties is protected by "whiting out" or changing plaintiff and defendant names, addresses, case numbers, and any other identifying information. (Documents altered in this way are referred to as **redacted** documents.) In addition, consider preparing other writing samples *on your own*. For example:

   ■ A brief memorandum of law on the application of a statute to a set of facts that you make up (see chapter 12)
   ■ A pleading such as a complaint (see chapter 10)
   ■ A set of interrogatories (see chapter 10)

redact To edit or prepare a document for publication or release, often by deleting, altering, or blocking out text that you do not want disclosed.

- Articles of incorporation and bylaws for a fictitious corporation
- An analysis of a recent court opinion (see chapters 7 and 11)
- An intake memorandum of law based on an interview that you role-play with another student (see chapter 8)
- A brief article that you write for a paralegal newsletter on an aspect of your legal education or work experience as a paralegal (see appendix B)

Prepare a file or portfolio of all your writing samples. (See Job-Hunting Notebook, page 100.) If possible, try to have a teacher or practicing attorney review each sample. Rewrite it based on their comments. Take the initiative in preparing writing samples and in soliciting feedback from knowledgeable contacts that you make. You need to have a large pool of diverse writing samples from which to choose once you begin the actual job hunt. Start preparing these samples now. Ask your program director for guidance in selecting samples and in obtaining feedback on them.

Strategy 9: The Job Interview

Once you have overcome the hurdles of finding a prospective employer who will read your cover letter and résumé, the next problem is to arrange for a job interview. In your cover letter, you may want to add the following sentence at the end: "Within the next two weeks, I will give you a call to determine whether an interview would be possible." This strategy does not leave the matter entirely up to the prospective employer as to whether there will be further contact with you. Alternatively, you could make such a call without including in the cover letter a statement of your intention to do so.

Job Interview Guidelines

(See Job-Hunting Notebook, page 102.)

> Attired in your best interviewing suit, you nervously navigate your way to the reception area of what you hope will be your future employer's office. You are a comfortable ten minutes early. Upon arrival you are directed to the office of the interviewer, whom you greet with a smile and pleasant handshake. She offers you a cup of coffee, which you wisely refuse, since you may spill it. She then looks you in the eye and poses her first question. "Why are you interested in working for this firm?" [Suddenly you go blank!] All thoughts leave your mind as you pray for the ability to speak.[20]

1. Be sure you have the exact address; room number, and time of the interview. Give yourself sufficient time to find the office. If the area is new to you, be sure you have precise directions. Have in hand a printout of a map and directions from standard Internet map services (e.g., www.mapquest.com and maps.google.com). It would be unfortunate to start your contact with the office by having to offer excuses for being late. Arrive at least ten minutes early. You will probably be nervous and will need to compose yourself before the interview. It is important that you be as relaxed as possible. Be sure that you have turned off your cell phone or pager before the interview.

2. Try to find out in advance who will be interviewing you. If you obtain the name of this person, google him or her. Type his or her name in www.google.com or any general search engine to find out any available information on him or her. Also check if he or she is writing (or is mentioned in) a blog. See the discussion earlier on how to find out. If you will be interviewed by an attorney, check available background information on the attorney in the office's Web site, on *Martindale-Hubbell Law Directory* (see Exhibit 2.5), or on *West's Legal Directory* (see Exhibit 2.6). Don't be surprised, however, if the person who greets you is a substitute for the person originally scheduled to interview you. A number of different kinds of people might conduct the interview depending upon the size of the office: the law office manager, the managing attorney, the supervising attorney for the position, the paralegal supervisor, a staff paralegal, or a combination of the above if you are interviewed by different people on the same day or on different days. The style of the interview may be quite different depending on who conducts it. Someone with management responsibility might stress the interpersonal dimensions of the position, whereas a trial attorney might give you the feeling that you are being cross-examined. Try to determine whether you are being interviewed by the person who has the final authority to hire you. In many large offices, you will be interviewed by someone whose sole task is to screen out unacceptable applicants. If you make it through this person, the next step will usually be an interview with the ultimate decision-maker. You might be lucky enough to talk with someone who has been interviewed by this person before (such as a paralegal now working at the office, another job seeker, or someone at the local paralegal association) so that you can obtain a sense of what to expect.

3. Although relatively uncommon, you may have to face a group interview in which several interviewers question you at once.

4. Make sure that you are prepared for the interview. Review the guidelines discussed above on writing your résumé. In the résumé and in the interview, you are trying to sell yourself. Many of the principles of résumé writing apply to the interview. Know the kinds of questions you will probably be asked. Rehearse your responses. Write down a series of questions (tough ones), and ask a friend to role-play an interview with you. Have your friend ask you the questions and critique your responses. Also take the role of the interviewer and question your friend so that you can gauge both perspectives. Be prepared to handle a variety of questions. (*Biographical* questions seek facts about your life, e.g., when did you graduate? *Behavioral* questions gauge your thought process and values, e.g., when was the last time you faced an ethical dilemma in your everyday life and how did you handle it?) See Exhibit 2.13. Keep in mind, however, that no matter how much preparation you do, you may still be surprised by the course the interview takes. Be flexible enough to expect the unexpected. If you are relaxed, confident, *and prepared*, you will do fine. (For an example of an online mock paralegal interview that you can take, see content.monster.com/articles/3479/18983/1/home.aspx)

5. You are not required to answer potentially illegal questions—for instance, "Are you married?" Some employers use the answers to such irrelevant questions to practice illegal sex discrimination. You need to decide in advance how you will handle them if they are asked. You may want to ask why the question is relevant. Or you may simply decide to steer the interview back to the qualifications that you have and the commitment that you have made to a professional career. A good response might be, "If you're concerned that my marital status may affect my job performance, I can assure you that it will not." Follow this up with comments about dedication and job commitment. It may be the perfect time to offer references.[21] Whatever approach you take, be sure to remain courteous. One commentator suggests the following response to an illegal question: "Gee, that's interesting. I haven't been asked that question before in a job interview."[22] Then continue talking about what makes you a dependable worker without allowing the question to control your response.

6. Avoid being critical of anyone. Do not, for example, "dump on" your prior employer or school. Criticizing or blaming other organizations, even if justified, is likely to give the interviewer the impression that you will probably end up blaming *this* organization if you get the job and difficulties arise.

7. What about being critical of yourself? You will be invited to criticize yourself when you are asked the seemingly inevitable question, "What are your weaknesses?" Interviewers like such questions because your response gives some indication of how you handle yourself under pressure. You may want to pick a *positive* trait and express it as a negative. For example: "I tend to get frustrated when I'm not given enough to do. My goal is not just to collect a paycheck. I want to make a contribution." Or "I think I sometimes have expectations that are too high. There is so much to learn, and I want it all now. I have to pace myself, and realize that the important goal is to complete the immediate task, even if I can't learn every conceivable aspect of that task at the present time." Or "I get irritated by carelessness. When I see someone turn in sloppy work, or work that is not up to the highest standards, it bothers me." If you use any of these approaches, be sure that you are able to back them up when you are asked to explain what you mean.

8. If you have done the kind of background research on the office mentioned earlier, you will have a fairly good idea of the structure and mission of the office. Its Web site, for example, should tell you the kind of law it practices, the location of branches, news of recent judgments won by the office, and public service activities of attorneys at the office such as election to the presidency of the bar association. Web sites often give overviews of areas of the law in which the office specializes. Look for ways to let the interviewer know that you have such information. Interviewers are usually impressed by applicants who have done their homework about the office.

9. A major goal of the interview is to relate your education and experience to the needs of the office. To the extent possible, you want to know what these needs are before the interview so that you can quickly and forcefully demonstrate that you are the person the office is looking for. Most offices decide to hire someone because they have a problem—for example, they need someone with a particular skill, they need someone to help them expand, or they need someone who can get along with a particularly demanding supervising attorney. If you are not sure, ask the interviewer why the office has decided to add a paralegal. Don't wait until the end of the interview when you are asked if you have any questions. Early on in the interview,

EXHIBIT 2.13   The Six Categories of Job Interview Questions

- **Open-Ended Questions** (which are calculated to get you to talk, giving the listener an idea of how you organize your thoughts)
  - (1) Tell me about yourself.
  - (2) What do you know about our firm?
  - (3) Tell me about the kind of position you are seeking.
  - (4) What interests you about this job?
- **Closed-Ended Questions** (which can be answered by one or two words)
  - (5) When did you receive your paralegal certificate?
  - (6) Did you take a course in corporate law?
- **Softball Questions** (which should be fairly easy to answer if you are prepared)
  - (7) What are your interests outside of school and work?
  - (8) What courses did you enjoy the most? Why? Which were least rewarding? Why?
  - (9) Do your grades reflect your full potential? Why or why not?
  - (10) Why did you leave your last job?
  - (11) How have you grown or developed in your prior jobs? Explain.
  - (12) How were you evaluated in your prior jobs?
  - (13) What are your strengths as a worker?
  - (14) Describe an ideal work environment. What would your "dream job" be?
  - (15) What factors make a job frustrating? How would you handle these factors?
  - (16) What do you hope to be doing in ten years? What are your long-term goals?
  - (17) If you are hired, how long are you prepared to stay?
  - (18) Are you interested in a job or a career? What's the difference?
  - (19) Why did you become a paralegal?
  - (20) What problems do you think a paralegal might face in a busy law office? How would you handle these problems?
  - (21) Can you work under pressure? When have you done so in the past?
  - (22) How flexible are you in adapting to changing circumstances? Give examples of your flexibility in the last year.
  - (23) How do you feel about doing routine work?
  - (24) Do you prefer a large or a small law office? Why?
  - (25) What accomplishment in your life are you most proud of? Why?
  - (26) What salary expectations do you have? What was your salary at your last position?
  - (27) What other questions do you think I should ask in order to learn more about you?
  - (28) What questions would you like to ask me about this office?
- **Tension Questions** (which are calculated to put you on the spot to see how you handle yourself; your answers will give the interviewer some insight into your thought process and your values)
  - (29) No one is perfect. What are your weaknesses as a worker?
  - (30) Have you ever been fired from a position? Explain the circumstances.
  - (31) Why have you held so many jobs?
  - (32) Are you a competitive person? If not, why not? If you are, give some examples over the last six months that demonstrate this characteristic.
  - (33) Is there something in this job that you hope to accomplish that you were not able to accomplish in your last job?
  - (34) Do you type? If not, are you willing to learn? What is your typing speed?
  - (35) Where else have you interviewed for a job? Have you been turned down?
  - (36) Why wouldn't you want to become an attorney now?
  - (37) Everyone makes mistakes. What is the biggest mistake that you made in any of your prior jobs and how did you handle it?*
  - (38) No job is perfect. What is the least appealing aspect of the job you are seeking here?
  - (39) There are over fifty applicants for this position. Why do you think you are the most qualified?
  - (40) If you are offered this position, what are the major concerns that you would have about taking it?
  - (41) What would make you want to quit a job?
  - (42) Give some examples of when you have shown initiative over the last six months in school or at your last job.
- **Hypothetical Questions** (in which you are asked how you would handle a stated fact situation)
  - (43) If you were told, "This isn't any good, do it again, and get it right this time," how would you react?
  - (44) If you find out on Friday afternoon that you're expected to come in on Saturday, what would you do?**
  - (45) Assume that you are given the position here and that you work very closely on a day-to-day basis with an attorney. After a six-month period, what positive and negative comments do you think this attorney would make about you as a worker?
  - (46) Name some things that would be unethical for an attorney to do. What would you do if you found out that the attorney supervising you was doing these things?
  - (47) Suppose that your first assignment was to read through and summarize 4,000 documents over an eight-month period. Could you do it? How would you feel about it?
  - (48) Assume that two airplanes crash into each other and that your firm represents one of the passengers who was killed. What kind of discovery would you recommend?
- **Potentially Illegal Questions** (because the questions are not relevant to the candidate's fitness and ability to do most jobs)
  - (49) Are you married? Do you plan to marry?
  - (50) Do you have any children? If so, how old are they? Who takes care of your children?
  - (51) If you do not have any children now, do you plan to have any in the future?
  - (52) How old are you?
  - (53) What is your religion?
  - (54) What is your political affiliation?

*Moralez, *Sample Interview Questions*, 11 Paragram (Oregon Legal Assistant Ass'n, May 1988).

**Wendel, *You the Recruiter*, 5 Legal Assistant Today 31 (September/October 1987).

you want to try to tailor as many of your answers as possible to the specific needs of the office. The success of the interview is directly related to your ability to identify the problem of the office and to demonstrate how you can solve it for them.

10. If the paralegal job is in a certain specialty, such as probate or corporate law, you may be asked questions designed to assess your familiarity with the area. Prior to the interview, spend some time reviewing your class notes. Skim through a standard practice book for that area of the law in the state. Be sure that you can back up anything you said in your résumé about prior involvement with the area in your school or work experience. Such discussions are always an excellent opportunity for you to present writing samples in that field of the law. As indicated, the Web sites of many offices discuss their specialties as part of their effort to entice prospective clients to hire the office. If such discussions exist, read them thoroughly before the interview. Look for opportunities to make specific mention of whatever the Web site says that is relevant to what you have studied and are able to do. You might even ask questions about something said on the site. For example, "I read on your Web site that the firm recently handled the merger of several software companies. Do paralegals at the firm work on such mergers?"

11. Never compromise the truth during an interview. If, for example, you are asked if you know how to prepare trial notebooks, don't say *yes* if you can do little more than define what a trial notebook is. A good answer might be "We studied trial notebooks in our litigation class. I've never prepared one, but I'm a fast learner, and I think that with a good model and clear instructions, I would be able to put together an effective one."

12. Dress traditionally. There is, however, a caveat to this recommendation. "A red, wool crepe suit could work well for a professional woman in Los Angeles, Atlanta, Dallas, and Chicago but might seem too flashy in the financial districts of New York or traditional businesses in Boston or Milwaukee. An interview wardrobe is mostly built in solid colors, which offer a more elegant feeling. Both men and women are advised to dress conservatively for the first interview." Suit up for the interview even if the office is having a casual dress day. "The most important thing to remember is that law firms are generally conservative.... Most firms want to see candidates dressed in traditional, conservative 'Brooks Brothers' looks."[23] You want interviewers to remember what you said, not what you wore.

13. Be sure that you project yourself positively. Take the initiative in greeting the interviewer. A firm handshake is recommended. Address the interviewer as Mr. or Ms., never by first name, unless expressly invited to do so. (Note: "I'm Bob Sheehan" is *not* an express invitation to call the interviewer "Bob.") Maintain good posture and consistent eye contact. While you are talking, do not let your eyes roam around the room. Remember that you are being evaluated. Avoid appearing ill at ease or fidgety. The interviewer will be making mental notes on your body language and forming an opinion of whether you "fit in."

14. Before the interview, find out what you can about paralegal salaries in the area. For example, check recent salary surveys of local and national paralegal associations. (See "Salary Information" in Exhibit 2.7 and the data on salaries in chapter 1.) During the interview, however, try to avoid the topic of salary until the end of the interview when you have completed the discussion of the job itself. Preferably, let the interviewer raise the issue. Think through how you will handle the topic, but try to avoid discussing it until the appropriate time arises. If asked what salary you are seeking, giving a salary range can be an invitation to limit yourself to the lowest figure stated in the range. Try to get the interviewer to give you information about salaries before you answer. For example, you might say, "I will be able to answer that question when I know more about the position and whether there's a mutual fit. It would help me to give a thoughtful answer if I knew the office's salary range for the position. What is the range?"[24] Of course, the office may not have a range. Often a very large office has budgeted a specific salary that is not subject to change. Do the best you can to get the interviewer to tell you what it is. If toward the end of the interview, the topic of salary has not come up, ask, "Can you tell me the salary for the position?"

15. Be enthusiastic, but not overly so. You want to let the office know that you really want the job, not because you are desperate but because you see it as a challenge offering professional development. You are qualified for the job, and you feel that the office is the kind of place that recognizes valuable contributions from its workers.

16. Be yourself. Do not try to overwhelm the interviewer with your cleverness and charm.

17. You might be asked if you intend to go to law school. Some offices may limit their hiring to candidates who want to be career paralegals. It's important that you let the interviewer know you are excited about the paralegal field. If law school might be a possibility for you in the future,

answer the question by leaving your options open. For example, "My focus is on being a paralegal. I want to continue learning everything I can about the law. It's difficult to say what might happen way down the road, but right now my main commitment is to be an outstanding paralegal."

18. Carry a professional-looking portfolio with you to every interview. It should contain copies of:

- Your résumé
- Writing samples
- Your paralegal certificate
- A list of references
- Letters of recommendation
- Your school transcript (if your grades are impressive)
- Performance reviews at other jobs
- Copies of awards or other recognition of achievement
- Proof of attendance at CLE (continuing legal education) sessions
- Statement of membership in professional associations
- Anything else that might have a bearing on your employability

At strategic times during the interview, let the interviewer know that you have items in the portfolio that are relevant to what you are discussing. At the end of the interview, summarize anything in the portfolio that has not been mentioned and ask if the interviewer would like you to leave copies. There is one other item you should have in your portfolio:

- A list of the names of clients and other parties on cases you have worked on in prior employment or volunteer work

We will discuss this list in guideline 22, when we cover avoiding "contamination" of the office.

19. Find out if you can have a brief tour of the office before you leave. Also ask if you can have an opportunity to talk with one or more paralegals currently working at the office. It will be another sign of your seriousness.

20. Try to obtain the business card of everyone you speak to. Accurate names, titles, and addresses will be important for follow-up letters and general networking.

21. Be an active participant in the interview even though you let the interviewer conduct it. Avoid one-word answers. Help keep the discussion going by asking your own questions of the interviewer at appropriate times. In effect, you are interviewing the office as much as the other way around. Come with a written list and don't be afraid to let the interviewer see that you have a checklist of questions that you want to ask. It is a sign of an organized person. There is a great deal of information about the job that you could inquire about. From your background research about the job, you should already have some of this information, but you can now verify what you know. You want to ask pertinent and intelligent questions that will communicate to the interviewer that you are serious about the paralegal field, that you are prepared, and that you grasp what the interviewer has been telling you about the job and the office.

Below are some topics you could cover in your own questions. See also Exhibit 2.14 for more ideas for questions.

- What type of person is the office seeking to hire and what prompted the need for this kind of person? (Ask this now if you were not able to find out earlier in the interview.)
- When you make an offer to someone, is there a probationary period he or she goes through before becoming a permanent employee? If there is, what criteria does the office use to decide whether the person will be permanent?
- Is there a difference between a paralegal and a legal assistant in the office?
- What are some examples of paralegal responsibilities? Will the paralegal specialize in certain tasks or areas of the law? (Ask for a description of a typical workday of a paralegal at the firm.)
- What skills will the paralegal need for the job? Digesting? Investigation? Research? Drafting? Interviewing?
- How many attorneys are in the firm? Is the number growing, declining, or remaining constant?
- How is the firm managed or governed? Managing partner? Management committees? Legal administrator? Is there a policy manual for the firm?
- How many paralegals are in the firm? Is the number growing, declining, remaining constant? Are all the paralegals at the firm full-time? Does the firm use part-time

EXHIBIT 2.14	Checklist of Possible Paralegal Fringe Benefits

Compensation

- Salary increase policy (amount or range? criteria for determining? frequency of review? who reviews?)
- Overtime (frequency? method of compensation?)
- Bonus (method for determining? frequency?)
- Cost-of-living adjustment (frequency? method for determining?)
- Pension/retirement plan (defined benefit? defined contribution? other?)
- Tax-deferred savings plan
- Other investment plan

Insurance

- Basic medical (full coverage? partial?)
- Major medical (full coverage? partial?)
- Dependent medical insurance (fully paid? partially paid?)
- Dental (full coverage? partial?)
- Maternity leave (full coverage? partial?)
- Life insurance (fully paid? partially paid?)
- Disability (short term? long term? full coverage? partial?)
- Sick days (number? carryover of unused sick leave allowed?)

Professional Activities

- Time off for paralegal association events
- Paralegal association dues paid (full? partial?)
- CLE (continuing legal education) paid
- Professional magazine subscription paid (*e.g., Legal Assistant Today*)
- Paralegal association dinner events paid
- Tuition reimbursement for paralegal classes
- Tuition reimbursement for law school
- Notary certification and required notary bond paid

Other

- Vacation (number of days? carry over of unused vacation allowed?)
- Personal leave days (number allowed?)
- Child care assistance
- Paid holidays (number?)
- Parking (fully paid? partially paid?)
- Mileage allowance
- Club membership
- Fitness center
- Sports tickets
- Entertainment allowance
- Free legal advice and representation by the firm on personal matters

Comparability

- Paralegal fringe benefits similar/dissimilar to those of new attorneys?
- Paralegal fringe benefits similar/dissimilar to those of secretaries?

or freelance paralegals? Does the firm have (or has it considered hiring) a paralegal coordinator?

- Is there a career ladder for paralegals in the firm?
- How long has the firm used paralegals? What is the average length of time a paralegal stays with the firm? What are the feelings of firm members on the value of paralegals to the firm? Why is this so? How would firm members describe an ideal paralegal employee? Do all members of the firm feel the same about paralegals? What reservations, if any, do some members of the firm have about paralegals?
- What other personnel does the firm have (secretaries, computer staff, library staff, clerks, messengers, part-time law students, etc.)? What relationship does the paralegal have with each?
- What kind of supervision does a paralegal receive? Close supervision? From one attorney? Several?
- Will the paralegal work for one attorney? Several? Is there a pool of paralegals available to many attorneys on a rotating basis as needed?

- What kind of client contact will the paralegal have? None? Phone? E-mail? Meetings? Interviews? Document inspection at client's office?
- What kind of writing will the paralegal be doing? Memos? Letters that the paralegal will sign? Letters for attorney to sign?
- What opportunities does a paralegal have for further learning? Office training programs? (Do paralegals attend new-attorney training sessions?) Does the firm encourage outside training for paralegals, e.g., from paralegal associations, bar associations, and area schools?
- Will the paralegals be attending staff meetings? Strategy sessions with attorneys?
- How are paralegals evaluated in the office? Written evaluations? Oral? How often?
- Are paralegals required to produce a set number of billable hours? Per day? Per week? Per month? Annually? Is there a **billable hours quota** or billable hour goal? What is the hourly rate at which a paralegal's time is billed to a client? Do different paralegals in the office bill at different rates? If so, what determines the difference?
- How often are paralegals required to record their time? Daily, hourly, in ten-minute segments, etc.?
- What kinds of nonbillable tasks do paralegals perform?
- What secretarial assistance is available to the paralegal? None? Secretary shared with an attorney? With other paralegals? Use of a secretarial pool? Will the paralegal do any typing? Light typing? His or her own typing? Typing for others?
- Does the job require travel?
- What equipment will the paralegal be using? Computer, fax machine, copier, dictaphone? What software does the firm use for its major tasks? Word processing? Database management? Litigation support?
- Does the firm use an **intranet**?
- Office space for the paralegal? Private office? Shared office? Partitioned office?
- Compensation and benefits—see Exhibit 2.14, "Checklist of Possible Paralegal Fringe Benefits."

22. Don't contaminate the law firm! Later, in chapter 5, when we study conflict of interest, you will learn that a new employee can contaminate an entire office by creating a conflict of interest. (Once an office is contaminated, it can be disqualified from continuing to represent a client.) This could occur if a prospective employee once worked or volunteered at an office that represented a client who is an opponent of a current client of the office where the paralegal is seeking employment. Hence before an office hires an experienced paralegal (or an experienced attorney or secretary), the office needs to know the names of clients at offices where he or she has worked or volunteered. When you are seeking employment as a paralegal, therefore, you must be prepared to provide these names if you have had prior legal experience. This disclosure, however, usually does not need to occur until it is clear that the office is very interested in you and asks for a list of such clients. Never volunteer to show the list to anyone. The names of clients are confidential. But limited disclosure will be needed to avoid a disqualification due to a conflict of interest.

23. After you have thoroughly explored the position during the interview, if you still want the job, ask for it. Be sure that you make a specific request. Some interviewers go out of their way to stress the difficult aspects of the job in order to gauge your reaction. Don't leave the interviewer with the impression that you may be having second thoughts if in fact you still want the job after you have had all your questions answered.

24. Thank the interviewer by name. "I want to thank you, Mr. Sheehan, for the opportunity to discuss this position with you."

Follow-up letter   After the interview (within twenty-four hours, if possible), send a follow-up letter to each person at the office who interviewed you. In a surprising number of cases, the follow-up letter is a significant factor in obtaining the job. In the letter:

- Thank the person for the interview.
- Tell the person that you enjoyed the interview and the opportunity to learn about the office. (Personalize this statement by briefly referring to something specific that occurred or was said during the interview, e.g., "I appreciated your detailed description of how employees at the firm are evaluated." "It was very enlightening to hear how your firm handles environmental litigation, particularly in light of the new legislation you mentioned.")
- State that you are still very interested in the position.
- Briefly restate why you are qualified for the position.

billable hours quota
A minimum number of hours expected from a timekeeper on client matters that can be charged (billed) to clients per week, month, year, or other time period.

intranet A private network of computers within a particular firm, company, or other organization, established so that computers can share information online, often using features similar to those of the World Wide Web.

- Clarify any matters that arose during the interview.
- Submit references or writing samples that may have been asked for during the interview.

Keep a copy of all such letters. In a notebook, maintain accurate records on the dates you sent out résumés, the kinds of résumés you sent, the dates of interviews, the names of people you met, your impressions, the dates when you made follow-up calls, etc. (See page 103.)

If you are turned down for a job, find out why. Call the office to try to obtain more information than is provided in standard rejection statements. Politely ask what could have improved your chances. Finally, use the occasion to ask for any leads to other prospective employers.

CLASS EXERCISE 2.A

Role-play an interview in class. The instructor will decide what kind of job the interview will be for and will select students to play the role of interviewer and interviewee. The interviewer should ask a variety of questions such as those presented above in the guidelines for handling a job interview. The interviewee can make up the answers within the guidelines provided by the instructor. The rest of the class will evaluate the interviewee. What were his or her strong points? Were mistakes made? How should the interviewee have dealt with certain questions? Was he or she confident? Overconfident? Did he or she ask good questions of the interviewer? Were these questions properly timed? What impressions did the interviewee convey of himself or herself? Make a list of do's and don'ts for such interviews.

[SECTION E]
THE JOB-HUNTING NOTEBOOK

Purchase a large three-ring, looseleaf notebook for your Job-Hunting Notebook. Include in it the outline of sections presented in Exhibit 2.15. Following the outline, create at least one page for each section.

There are a number of purposes for the Notebook:

- To help you identify your strengths based on past legal or nonlegal employment, training, and other life experience
- To help you organize this data for use in your résumés
- To provide you with checklists of contacts that you should start making immediately
- To help you prepare for job interviews

EXHIBIT 2.15   Outline of Job-Hunting Notebook

Part I. Résumé and Writing Sample Preparation
1. Prior and current nonlegal employment—analysis sheet
2. Prior and current legal employment—analysis sheet
3. Prior and current volunteer activity—analysis sheet
4. Other life experiences—analysis sheet
5. Nonlegal education and training—analysis sheet
6. Legal education and training—analysis sheet
7. Notes on résumé writing
8. Draft of general résumé
9. Drafts of specialized résumés
10. Writing samples
11. Portfolio

Part II. Contacts for Employment
12. Contacts—attorneys you already know or with whom you have any indirect association
13. Contacts—employed paralegals
14. Contacts and tasks—general

Part III. Legwork in the Field
15. Job Interview checklist
16. Job interview—analysis sheet
17. Record keeping

- To provide a place to store copies of résumés, cover letters, writing samples, follow-up letters, notes on job leads and strategies, personal impressions, etc.
- To keep a calendar on all aspects of the job search

The Notebook is your own personal document. No one else will see it unless you choose to share its contents with others.

1. PRIOR AND CURRENT NONLEGAL EMPLOYMENT—ANALYSIS SHEET
2. PRIOR AND CURRENT LEGAL EMPLOYMENT—ANALYSIS SHEET
3. PRIOR AND CURRENT VOLUNTEER ACTIVITY—ANALYSIS SHEET

We begin by analyzing your experience in these three areas: (1) in nonlegal jobs (e.g., cashier, truck driver), (2) in legal jobs (e.g., legal secretary, investigator), (3) and in volunteer activity (e.g., church sale coordinator, or political campaign assistant). Make a list of these jobs and volunteer activities. Start a separate sheet of paper for each entry on your list, and then do the following:

- State the name, address, and phone number of the place of employment or location of the volunteer work.
- State the exact dates you were there.
- State the names of your supervisors there. (Circle the names of supervisors who had a favorable impression of you. Place a double circle around the name of each supervisor who would probably write a favorable recommendation for you, if asked.)
- Make a list of every major task you performed there. Number each task, starting with number 1. (As you write this list, leave a three-inch left-hand margin on the paper. In front of the number for each task, place all of the following letters that apply to that task. When an explanation or description is called for, provide it on attached sheets of paper.)

B	The task required you to conform to a *budget*. (Briefly describe the budget, including its size and who prepared it.)
C	There was some *competition* in the office about who was most qualified to perform the task. (Briefly describe why you were the most qualified.)
E	You were *evaluated* on how well you performed the task. (Briefly describe the evaluation of you.)
EI	To perform the task, you occasionally or always had to *exercise initiative*; you did not just wait for detailed instructions. (Briefly describe the initiative you took.)
ET	You occasionally or frequently had to devote *extra time* to perform the task. (Briefly describe the circumstances.)
J/C	It was not a mechanical task; you had to exercise some *judgment* and/or *creativity* to perform it. (Briefly describe the kind of judgment or creativity you exhibited.)
M	*Math* skills were involved in performing the task. (Briefly describe what kind of math you had to do.)
OD	*Others depended* on your performing the task well. (Briefly describe who had to rely on your performance and why.)
OT	You always or regularly performed the task *on time*.
OW	To perform the task, you had to coordinate your work with *other workers*; you did not work alone. (Briefly describe the nature of your interaction with others.)
P	You had some role in *planning* how the task would be performed; you were not simply following someone else's plan. (Briefly describe your planning role.)
PI	You did not start out performing the task; you were formally or informally *promoted into* it. (Briefly describe what you did before being asked to perform this task and the circumstances of the promotion.)
PP	You are *personally proud* of the way you performed the task. (Briefly describe why.)
R	You made *recommendations* on how the task could be more efficiently performed or better integrated into the office. (Briefly describe the recommendations you made and what effect they had.)
RR	You *received recognition* because of how well you performed the task. (Briefly describe the recognition you received and from whom.)
SE	To perform the task, you had to operate *some equipment* such as computers or motor vehicles. (Briefly describe the equipment and the skills needed to operate it.)

SO To perform the task, you had to *supervise others* or help supervise others. (Briefly describe whom you supervised and what the supervision entailed.)

T You also *trained* others to perform the task. (Briefly describe this training.)

TP You had to work under *time pressures* when you performed the task; you didn't have forever to perform it. (Briefly describe these pressures.)

W Performing the task involved some *writing*. (Briefly describe what kind of writing you did.)

Include other characteristics of the task that are not covered in this list.

4. OTHER LIFE EXPERIENCES—ANALYSIS SHEET

Circle *each* of the following experiences that you have had. Do not include experiences that required schooling, since these experiences will be covered elsewhere in the Notebook. Do not include experiences that involved volunteer work unless you have not already included them elsewhere in the Notebook. Attach additional sheets as indicated and where more space is needed.

- Raised a family alone
- Helped raise a family
- Traveled extensively
- Read extensively in a particular field on your own
- Learned to operate computer programs on your own
- Learned a language on your own
- Learned a craft on your own, such as furniture making or fixing cars
- Learned an art on your own, such as painting or sculpture
- Developed a distinctive hobby requiring considerable skill
- Other life experiences (list each)

Attach a separate sheet of paper for *each* of the life experiences or activities that you listed above. Write the activity at the top of the sheet. Answer the following questions for each activity:

a. How long did you engage in this activity?

b. Have you ever tried to teach this activity to someone else? If so, describe your efforts.

c. Do you think you could teach this activity to others? Explain your answer.

d. Which of the following characteristics do you think are necessary or very helpful in being able to perform the activity competently? Do not focus at this point on whether you possess these characteristics. Simply compile a list of what would be helpful or necessary.

Intelligence	Compassion	Patience
Creativity	Responsibility	Dependability
Perseverance	Punctuality	Determination
Drive	Self-confidence	Stamina
Independence	Poise	Self-control
Talent	Efficiency	Grace
Understanding	Skill	Dexterity
Cleverness	Competitiveness	Sophistication
Spirit	Congeniality	Stick-to-itiveness
Conviction	Judgment	Will power
Fortitude	Strength	Zeal
Ambition	Know-how	Experience
Ability to work with others	Imagination	Others? (list)

e. Ask *someone else* (whom you trust and who is familiar with you) to look at the list. Ask this person if he or she would add anything to the list. Then ask him or her to identify which of these characteristics apply to *you* for this activity.

f. Now it's your turn. Which of these characteristics do *you* think apply to you for this activity?

g. If there are any major differences in the answers to (e) and (f) above, how do you explain the discrepancy? Are you too hard on yourself? Do you tend to put yourself down and minimize your strengths?

5. NONLEGAL EDUCATION AND TRAINING—ANALYSIS SHEET

On a separate sheet of paper, list every school or training program *not* involving law that you have attended or are now attending (whether or not you completed it), starting with the most recent. Include four-year colleges, two-year colleges, vocational training schools, weekend seminars, work-related training programs, internships, church training programs, hobby training programs, self-improvement training, etc. Include everything since high school.

Devote a separate sheet of paper to each school or training program, writing its name at the top of the sheet and answering the following questions for it. If more than one course was taught, answer these questions for two or three of the most demanding courses.

a. What were the exact or approximate dates of attendance?

b. Did you complete it? What evidence do you have that you completed it? A grade? A certificate? A degree? A transcript?

c. Were you required to attend? If so, by whom? If not, why did you attend?

d. How did you finance your attendance?

e. What requirements did you meet in order to attend? Was there competition to attend? If so, describe in detail.

f. Describe the subjects taught. What was the curriculum?

g. How were you evaluated?

h. What evidence of these evaluations do you have? Could you obtain copies of the evaluations? Do you have a transcript of your record?

i. Describe in detail any writing that you had to do, such as exams or reports.

j. What skills other than writing did you cover, such as organization, research, computer use, speaking, reading, operating equipment, managing or supervising people?

k. What evidence do you have or could you obtain that shows you covered these skills and how well you did in them?

l. Did you receive any special award or distinction? If so, describe it and state what evidence you have or could obtain that you received it.

m. Make a list of every favorable comment you can remember that was made about your work. What evidence of these comments do you have or could you obtain?

n. Was the experience meaningful in your life? If so, explain why. How has it affected you today?

o. What, if anything, did you do that called for extra effort or work on your part beyond what everyone else had to do?

p. Have you ever tried to teach someone else what you learned? If so, describe your efforts. If not, could you? Describe what you could teach.

q. List each teacher who knew you individually. Circle the name of each teacher who would probably write you a letter of recommendation if asked.

r. Would any other teacher or administrator be able to write you a letter of recommendation based on the records of the school or program? If so, who?

s. Does the school or program have a reputation for excellence? If so, describe its reputation.

6. LEGAL EDUCATION AND TRAINING—ANALYSIS SHEET

On a separate sheet of paper, list every *legal* course or training program that you have ever taken—formal or informal. Include individual classes, seminars, internships, etc., at formal schools, on the job, or through associations. Devote a separate sheet of paper to each course or program, writing its name at the top of the sheet and answering the following questions for it.

a. What were the exact dates of attendance?

b. Did you complete it? What evidence do you have that you completed it? A grade? A certificate?

c. What requirements did you meet in order to attend? Was there competition to attend? If so, describe in detail.

d. What text(s) did you use? Photocopy the table of contents in the text(s) and circle those items that you covered.

e. Attach a copy of the syllabus and circle those items in the syllabus that you covered.

f. Make two lists: a list of the major themes or subject areas that you were required to *know* or understand (content) and a list of the things that you were asked to *do* (skills).

g. Make a detailed list of everything that you were asked to write for the course or program, such as exams, memos, research papers, other reports. For every written work product other than exams, give the specific topic of what you wrote. Describe this topic in at least one sentence.

h. Which of these written work products could you now *rewrite* as a writing sample? Whom could you ask to evaluate what you rewrite to ensure that it meets high standards?

i. Describe in detail everything else you were asked to do other than mere reading assignments. Examples: role-play a hearing, visit a court, verbally analyze a problem, interview a client, evaluate a title abstract, search a title, operate a computer, find something in the library, find something on the Internet, or investigate a fact.

j. How were you evaluated? What evidence do you have or could you obtain of these evaluations? Do you have a transcript of your record?

k. Did you receive any special award or distinction? If so, describe it and state what evidence you have or could obtain that you received it.

l. Make a list of every favorable comment you can remember that was made about your work. What evidence of these comments do you have or could you obtain?

m. What, if anything, did you do that called for extra work or effort on your part beyond what everyone else had to do?

n. Describe the most valuable aspect of what you learned.

o. Have you ever tried to teach anyone else what you learned? If so, describe your efforts. If not, could you? Describe what you could teach.

p. Describe every individual who evaluated you. Could you obtain a letter of recommendation from these individuals?

7. NOTES ON RÉSUMÉ WRITING

It is important that you have an open mind about résumés. There is no perfect format. Different people have different views. In the best of all worlds, you will be able to do some background research on the law office where you are applying for work and will learn what kind of résumé (in form and content) that office prefers. When this type of research is not possible, you must do the best you can to predict what kind of a résumé will be effective.

On this page in the Notebook, you should collect ideas about résumés from a wide variety of people such as:

Teachers	Program administrators
Working paralegals	Unemployed paralegals
Paralegal supervisors	Legal administrators
Fellow students	Attorneys whom you know
Personnel officers	Authors of books and articles on
Placement officers	finding employment
Legal secretaries	Others?

You want to collect different points of view on questions such as:

- What is an ideal résumé?
- What are the major mistakes that a résumé writer can make?
- What is the best way to phrase a career objective? Should it be placed in the résumé or in the cover letter?
- How long should the résumé be?
- In what order should the data in the résumé be presented?
- How detailed should the résumé be?
- What kind of personal data should be included and omitted?
- How do you phrase educational experiences to make them relevant to the job you are seeking?
- How do you phrase employment experiences to make them relevant to the job you are seeking?
- How do you show that nonlegal experiences (school or work) can be relevant to a legal job?
- How do you handle potentially embarrassing facts, e.g., frequent job changes and low course grades?
- What should the cover letter for the résumé say?

8. DRAFT OF GENERAL RÉSUMÉ

Prepare a general résumé and include it here. We are calling it general because it is not directed or targeted at any specific job. It should be comprehensive with no page limitation. Use the guidelines, questions, and checklists in this Notebook to help you identify your strengths. The résumé you write for actual job searches will be shorter, specialized, and tailored to the job you are seeking. Before you write specialized résumés, however, you should write a general one that will be your main point of reference in preparing these other résumés. The general résumé will probably never be submitted anywhere. Take at least one full day to compile the general résumé after carefully thinking about the data needed for it.

9. DRAFTS OF SPECIALIZED RÉSUMÉS

Every time you write a résumé that is tailored to a specific job, include a copy here. Also include several practice copies of specialized résumés. While taking a course in corporate law, for example, write a résumé in which you pursue an opening at a law office for a corporate paralegal. For each résumé that you write (practice or real), solicit the comments of teachers, administrators, other students, working paralegals, attorneys, etc. Include these comments in this section of the Notebook.

10. WRITING SAMPLES

The importance of collecting a large pool of writing samples cannot be overemphasized. Even if you eventually use only a few of them, the value of preparing them is enormous. The following characteristics should apply to *each* writing sample:

- It is your own work.
- It is clearly and specifically identified. The heading at the top tells the reader what the writing is.
- It is typed (handwritten work should be typed).
- There are no spelling or grammatical errors in it.
- Its appearance is professional.
- Someone whom you respect has evaluated it before you put it in final form.
- You feel that it is a high-quality product.
- It does not violate anyone's right to privacy or confidentiality. (If the sample pertains to real people or events, you have redacted it by disguising all names or other identifying features.)

There are two main kinds of writing samples: those that are assigned in school or at work and those you generate on your own.

Examples of Required Work That You Could Turn into a Writing Sample

- A memorandum of law
- A legal research report or memo
- An answer to a problem in a textbook
- An exam answer
- An intake memorandum of law
- A complaint
- An answer to a complaint
- A motion
- A set of interrogatories
- Answers to a set of interrogatories
- An index to discovery documents
- A digest of one or more discovery documents
- Other memos, studies, or reports
- Articles of incorporation and bylaws

Any of these writing samples could be generated on your own if they are not required in your coursework. Ask your teachers or supervisors to help you identify written pieces that you could create. Also consider writing an article for one of the many newsletters of paralegal associations (see appendix B). The article could cover an aspect of your education or work experience. You could write about why you want to become a paralegal. You might write a response or reaction to someone else's article in a paralegal newsletter or magazine. Even if what you write is not published in a newsletter, it might still become a writing sample if it meets the criteria listed above.

11. PORTFOLIO

Have a portfolio that you carry with you to interviews. It should contain:

- Your résumé
- Writing samples
- Your paralegal certificate
- A list of references
- Letters of recommendation
- Your school transcript (if your grades are impressive)
- Performance reviews at other jobs
- Copies of awards or other recognition of achievement
- Proof of attendance at CLE (continuing legal education) sessions
- Statement of membership in professional associations
- List of clients and other parties (names of clients and other parties on cases you have worked on in prior employment or volunteer work; this list is never shown to anyone until you are close to having an offer)
- Anything else that might have a bearing on your employability

12. CONTACTS—ATTORNEYS YOU ALREADY KNOW OR WITH WHOM YOU HAVE ANY INDIRECT ASSOCIATION

Make a list of attorneys as described in Strategy 6 in this chapter on page 70. Include their names, street and e-mail addresses, and phone numbers. Not only do you want to know whether any of these attorneys are interested in hiring paralegals, but equally important, you also want to know if they can give you any leads to other employers who might be interested in hiring.

13. CONTACTS—EMPLOYED PARALEGALS

You want to talk with as many employed paralegals as you can to obtain leads to possible positions, as well as general guidelines for the job search. Make a list of the names, street and e-mail addresses, and phone numbers of all the paralegals that you contact. Include notes on what they told you. If they have nothing useful to say at the present time, ask them if you could check back with them in several months and if you could leave your name and number with them in the event that they come across anything in the future. See page 68 for ideas on how to locate employed paralegals for this kind of networking.

14. CONTACTS AND TASKS—GENERAL

Below you will find a general checklist of contacts and tasks that you should consider in your job search. Take notes on the results of these contacts and tasks and include these notes here if they are not included elsewhere in the Notebook. Your notes should include what you did, when, whom you contacted, their street and e-mail addresses and phone numbers, what was said, what follow-up is still needed, etc.

General Checklist for Job Search

- Attorneys with whom you already have a direct or indirect association
- Employed paralegals
- Other paralegals searching for work; they may be willing to share leads that were unproductive for them, especially if you do likewise
- Contacts provided by your placement office
- Want ads in general circulation newspapers
- Want ads in legal newspapers
- Want ads and job bank openings listed in paralegal newsletters
- General directories of attorneys, such as *Martindale-Hubbell* and *West's Legal Directory*
- Special directories of attorneys, such as the *Directory of Corporate Counsel*
- Employment agencies specializing in paralegal placement
- Legal staffing agencies specializing in support staff and paralegal placement
- Employment agencies specializing primarily in attorney placement
- Bar association meetings open to the public
- Legal secretaries who may have leads
- Legal administrators who may have leads

- Local attorneys who have written articles in bar journals
- Stories in legal newspapers on recent large cases that are in litigation or are about to go into litigation (page 76)
- Local and national politicians who represent your area
- Service companies and consulting firms (page 39)

15. JOB INTERVIEW CHECKLIST

1. Exact location of interview (Internet street map)
2. Time of arrival
3. Professional appearance in dress
4. Extra copies of résumé
5. Extra copies of writing samples
6. Copies of your transcripts
7. Name of person(s) who will conduct interview
8. Background research on the firm or company so that you know the kind of law it practices, why it might be considering hiring paralegals, etc.
9. Role-playing of job interview in advance with a friend
10. Preparation for difficult questions that might be asked, such as why you left your last job so soon after starting it
11. Preparation of questions that you will ask regarding:

    Responsibilities of the position
    Skills needed for the position
    Methods of supervision
    Office's prior experience with paralegals
    Career ladder for paralegals
    Relationship among paralegals, secretaries, and other clerical staff
    Client contact
    Opportunities for growth
    Methods of evaluating paralegals
    Continuing education opportunities
    Billable hours expected of paralegals
    Nonbillable tasks
    Use of systems in the practice of law
    Working conditions (typing, photocopying, office, etc.)
    Travel
    Overtime
    Computers and other equipment use
    Compensation and fringe benefits (see Exhibit 2.14)

12. Follow-up letter

16. JOB INTERVIEW—ANALYSIS SHEET

Write out the following information *after* each job interview that you have.

1. Date of interview
2. Name, address, and phone number of firm or company where you interviewed
3. Name(s), phone number(s), and e-mail address(es) of interviewer(s)
4. Kind of position that was open
5. Date you sent the follow-up letter
6. What you need to do next (send list of references, send writing samples, provide missing information that you did not have with you during the interview, etc.)
7. Your impressions of the interview (how you think you did, what surprised you, and what you would do differently the next time you have an interview)
8. Notes on why you were not offered the job
9. Notes on why you turned down the job offered

EXHIBIT 2.16	Record Keeping and the Job Search

PERSON/OFFICE CONTACTED

HOW CONTACTED (PHONE, LETTER)

DATE OF CONTACT

ADDRESSES
(STREET, E-MAIL, WEB, PHONE)

NOTES ON THE CONTACT

DATE FURTHER CONTACT NEEDED

DATE RÉSUMÉ SENT/DELIVERED

DATE WRITING SAMPLE SENT/DELIVERED

DATE OF INTERVIEW

NOTES ON INTERVIEW

DATE THANK-YOU (FOLLOW-UP) NOTE SENT

DATE FURTHER CONTACT NEEDED

(Fill out one card per contact; file alphabetically.)

17. RECORD KEEPING

You need a system to keep track of the steps taken to date. See Exhibit 2.16 (Record Keeping and the Job Search). In addition, keep a calendar where you record important future dates, such as when you must make follow-up calls, when the local paralegal association meets, etc. Design your own **tickler** for such dates. It can be as simple as making entries in your standard paper calendar. Online reminder systems also exist. Find out if there is a built-in online calendar in your e-mail system. Microsoft's Outlook, for example, allows you to make entries on future calendar dates. As the dates arrive, Outlook sends you reminders in the form of pop-ups, e-mail messages, or both.

tickler A system designed to provide reminders of important dates.

[SECTION F]

YOUR SECOND JOB

If you examine want ads for paralegals, you will find that most prospective employers want paralegals with experience. The market for such individuals is excellent. But if you are *new* to the field seeking an entry-level position, you are caught in the dilemma of not being able to find a job without experience and not being able to get experience without a job. How do you handle this classic Catch-22 predicament?

- You work even harder to compile an impressive résumé. You make sure that you have collected a substantial writing-sample file. Such writing samples are often the closest equivalent to prior job experience available to you.
- When you talk to other paralegals, you seek specific advice on how to present yourself as an applicant for your first job.
- You consider doing some volunteer work as a way to acquire experience for your résumé. Legal service offices and public interest law firms often encourage volunteer (i.e., pro bono)

work. A recent law school graduate struggling to start a practice may be another option. ("The 1st solo practitioner I approached," commented a person posting on a paralegal listserv, "agreed to allow me to intern with his firm for free. I received a lot of hands-on experience" during the weeks I was there. "That internship was invaluable!") Here are some options for finding volunteer opportunities in the *public* sector:

- Paralegal associations. At the Web site of paralegal associations in your state (see appendix B for addresses), look for pro bono links or type "pro bono" in the search box.
- CASA (court-appointed special advocates). Find the CASA office in your area (www.nationalcasa.org). In family law cases, CASA uses nonattorney volunteers as fact finders, interviewers, and investigators. They gather pertinent information relative to the child's case and report on these findings in court.
- American Bar Association. Check the ABA site for volunteer options in the country (www.abanet.org/legalservices/probono). Many of the programs use attorney and paralegal volunteers. See the "Directory of Local Pro Bono Programs" at the ABA site.
- Legal Services Corporation. Go to the site of the Legal Services Corporation, the federal government agency that funds legal service programs (www.lsc.gov). Click your state on the map or type your state in the search box. Links should lead you to legal service/legal aid programs in the state, many of which welcome pro bono assistance from attorneys and paralegals.
- LawHelp. Find your state at this "gateway to America's nonprofit legal services providers" (www.lawhelp.org). Although this site is primarily for potential clients with specific legal problems, the links to offices providing legal help often use attorney and paralegal volunteers.
- Volunteer Match. At Volunteer Match (www.volunteermatch.org), type in your zip code and click "Justice & Legal" in the "Interest Area." You will be led to organizations seeking people who can provide direct or indirect legal help.
- Search engines. As indicated, many offices that use attorney volunteers also use paralegal volunteers. When you find an office that uses attorneys, contact it to find out if paralegals are used as well. Use general search engines to locate offices that use attorney volunteers. In Google, for example, run a search that contains the name of your city or county, the phrase "pro bono," and the word ~attorney. The tilde (~) before the word *attorney* means you want to include synonyms of attorney such as *lawyer* and *counsel*. Examples: (orlando "pro bono" ~attorney) ("santa clara" "pro bono" ~attorney). If the name of your city or county is common in the United States, add the name of your state to the search.

- Find out from legal staffing and employment agencies (see Exhibit 2.7) if there are any temporary or part-time positions available that match your qualifications.
- Contact a private law firm and offer to perform "runner" services at low or no cost, e.g., delivery of documents, filing, and service of process. Be upfront. For example, say to an attorney, "If I volunteered at your office one afternoon a week, would you have tasks for me that would help me gain practical experience in a law office?"
- You may have to reassess what you will accept for your first job. Perhaps you can eventually turn the first job into a more acceptable position. You might have to treat it as a transitional job in which you gain the experience necessary for landing a better second job.

Once you have had several years of experience and have demonstrated your competence, you will find many more employment options available to you. You will find it substantially easier to negotiate salary and articulate your skills in a job interview. You can also consider other kinds of employment where your legal training, skills, expertise, and experience are valuable. It is not uncommon for a paralegal to be recruited by former or active clients of a first employer. Numerous business contacts are made in the course of a job; these contacts could turn into new careers. In Exhibit 2.17 you will find a list of some of the types of positions that paralegals have taken after they demonstrated their ability and acquired legal experience.

In short, you face a different market once you have acquired a record of experience and accomplishment. You are in greater demand in law firms and businesses. Furthermore, your legal skills are readily transferable to numerous law-related positions.

EXHIBIT 2.17	Positions for Experienced Paralegals

- Paralegal supervisor
- Law office administrator (legal administrator)
- Law firm marketing administrator
- Professional development coordinator
- Paralegal consultant
- Freelance/independent paralegal
- Law librarian/assistant
- Paralegal teacher or co-teacher
- Paralegal school administrator
- Placement officer
- Bar association lawyer referral coordinator
- Court administrator
- Court clerk
- Elected official (e.g., legislator, school board member, or mayor)
- Sales representative for legal publisher/vendor
- Investigator
- Customs inspector
- Compliance and enforcement inspector
- Occupational safety and health inspector
- Lobbyist
- Legislative assistant
- Real estate management consultant
- Real estate specialist
- Real estate portfolio manager
- Land acquisitions supervisor
- Title examiner
- Independent title abstractor
- Abstractor
- Systems analyst
- Computer analyst
- Computer sales representative
- Bank research associate
- Trust officer (trust administrator)
- Trust associate
- Assistant loan administrator
- Fiduciary accountant
- Financial analyst/planner
- Investment analyst
- Assistant estate administrator
- Enrolled agent
- Equal employment opportunity specialist
- Employee benefit specialist/consultant
- Pension specialist
- Pension administrator
- Compensation planner
- Corporate trademark specialist
- Corporate manager
- Securities analyst
- Securities compliance officer
- Insurance adjustor
- Actuarial associate
- Claims examiner
- Claims coordinator
- Director of risk management
- Risk management specialist
- Contracts administrator
- Patient advocate
- Legal journalist
- Legal proofreader
- Environmental specialist
- Editor for a legal or business publisher
- Personnel director
- Recruiter, legal employment agency
- Administrative law judge (ALJ)
- Arbitrator
- Mediator
- Internal security inspector
- Victim witness specialist
- Evidence technician
- Demonstrative evidence specialist
- Fingerprint technician
- Polygraph examiner
- Fraud examiner
- Probation officer
- Parole officer
- Corrections officer
- Bailiff
- Etc.

Chapter Summary

Someone once said that finding a job is a job in itself. The first step is to become informed about where paralegals work and what they do at those locations. The first part of this chapter was designed to provide you with this information. The major employers of paralegals are private law firms, corporations and other businesses, the government, and legal service/legal aid offices. While other settings also exist, these are the largest. Comparisons were made on working conditions that paralegals are likely to face in each setting.

We then looked at forty-six specialties such as bankruptcy and criminal law. Our focus was the identification of paralegal

functions in the specialties and a brief paralegal perspective of what life is like in each. For the specialties where most paralegals work (corporate law, estates, family law, litigation, real estate, and tort law), quotations from job ads identified traits and skills employers often seek.

In the second half of the chapter, we turned to strategies for finding employment. The strategies addressed the following questions: when should you begin the search? How do you compile a Job-Hunting Notebook? How do you organize an employment workshop? How do you locate working paralegals in order to obtain leads to employment? How do you arrange an informational interview? How can you use local paralegal associations as a resource? How do you locate potential employers? How do you do background research ("due diligence") on potential employers? What should your résumé contain? What is an effective cover letter? What kinds of writing samples should you prepare, and when should you start preparing them? How should you prepare for a job in-

terview? What kinds of questions should you anticipate? What kinds of questions should you ask? How can you organize all of the contacts, events, and pieces of paper that are involved in a comprehensive job search?

Finally, we examined alternative career opportunities for paralegals, particularly for those who have gained paralegal experience on the job.

Key Terms

private law firm	pro bono	job bank	point
boutique law firm	special interest group	continuing legal education	due diligence
general counsel	test case	(CLE)	blog (blawg)
civil service	prepaid legal services	informational interview	cover letter
jurisdiction	public defender	networking	redact
paralegal specialist	assigned counsel	blind ad	billable hours quota
indigent	freelance paralegal	staffing agency	intranet
civil	outsourcing	chronological résumé	tickler
IOLTA program	insurance defense	functional résumé	
uncontested	legalman	font	

Review Questions

1. What categories of people sometimes compete for paralegal jobs?
2. What are the nine major categories of paralegal employment?
3. What is a private law firm? A boutique law firm?
4. What are some of the differences between working in large and smaller private law offices?
5. What is an in-house law department? Who runs it?
6. Name four kinds of offices where government parale-gals work.
7. Summarize the major duties of a person in the paralegal specialist series (GS-950) of the federal government.
8. Name some of the ways to find job opportunities in federal, state, and local government.
9. What is a neighborhood legal service office?
10. What are pro bono legal services and IOLTA programs?
11. Give examples of special interest groups that may have legal staffs.
12. What are prepaid legal services?
13. What is the role of public defenders and assigned counsel?
14. What is a freelance paralegal? A virtual assistant? What is meant by *outsourcing*?
15. Name some of the services offered by service companies and consulting firms that use paralegals.
16. What is a legal nurse?
17. Pick any three paralegal specialties in which you might want to work upon graduation and list some of the major paralegal duties in each of the three specialties.
18. When should you start looking for paralegal work?

19. What are the major ways to contact employed paralegals for leads to employment?
20. What is a job bank service?
21. What is the limited purpose of an informational interview?
22. List the major ways to contact potential attorney employers.
23. Explain the meaning and value of networking?
24. What kinds of job titles should you check in online and traditional want ads?
25. What is a blind ad?
26. If you need an entry-level position, how might you respond to an ad seeking someone with paralegal experience?
27. Distinguish between a transitional job and a career job.
28. Why would you consider contacting an office seeking to hire attorneys?
29. Why is caution needed in using employment agencies?
30. What is a staffing agency?
31. In what ways can the Internet help you find a paralegal job?
32. What is the cardinal principle of résumé writing?
33. Summarize guidelines for drafting effective résumés.
34. How can you identify relevant skills that you obtained through nonlegal employment, legal employment, volunteer activity, other life experiences, nonlegal education, and legal education?
35. What nonaction verbs should you avoid using in a résumé?
36. What is meant by *grammatical parallellism*?
37. How do you perform due diligence on a prospective employer?

38. Distinguish between the two major kinds of résumés.
39. Name some techniques of effective cover letter writing.
40. What writing samples should you start collecting now?
41. Summarize guidelines for effective job interviews.
42. How can you try to phrase "negative" traits in a positive way?
43. What are the six major kinds of questions you should be prepared to answer in a job interview?
44. What should you include in a portfolio that you take with you to job interviews?
45. List the major categories of fringe benefits.
46. What kinds of questions should you be prepared to ask the interviewer during a job interview?
47. How can you avoid contaminating a law office where you are seeking employment?
48. What is the function of a follow-up letter after an interview?
49. What data should you keep in a Job-Hunting Notebook?
50. How can you try to overcome the Catch-22 predicament many new paralegals face when looking for entry-level work?
51. What kinds of positions are often available for experienced paralegals?
52. What are some of the reasons you should examine a law firm's Internet site?
53. What are the civil service standards and qualifications for paralegal employment within your state government?

Helpful Web Sites: More on Paralegal Employment

Paralegal Functions

- www.bls.gov/oco/ocos114.htm

Large Law Firms

- www.ilrg.com/nlj250
- www.vault.com/hubs/507/hubhome_507.jsp?ch_id=507
- www.bls.gov/oco/ocos053.htm

Job Interviews

- en.wikipedia.org/wiki/Job_interview
- www1.ctdol.state.ct.us/jcc/viewarticle.asp?intArticle=9

Improper Interview Questions

- www.rileyguide.com/interview.html
- www.laborlaws.com/block4/item426
- humanresources.about.com/od/interviewing/a/interviewtips_2.htm

Outsourcing Legal Services

- www.outsourcing-law.com

Areas of the Law

- www.megalaw.com/top/top.php

Google Searches (run the following searches for more sites)

- paralegal roles
- paralegal profiles
- kinds of law practice
- finding paralegal jobs
- Texas paralegal jobs (insert your state)
- government paralegal jobs
- corporate paralegal jobs
- public sector legal jobs
- improper interview questions
- sample paralegal resume
- paralegal blog listserv weblog
- no experience no job
- outsourcing law legal
- salary topic interviews
- kinds of law practice

25 Things You Should Never Put on a Résumé

- www.hrworld.com/features/25-things-not-to-put-on-resume-121807

Endnotes

1. Andrea Wagner, *Tips & Traps for the New Paralegal*, 8 Legal Assistant Today 78 (March/April 1991).
2. Altman Weil, *2003 Government Legal Agency Management Benchmarks Survey* (www.altmanweil.com), quoted in 22 Legal Management 9 (November/December 2003).
3. U.S. Office of Personnel Management, *Position Classification Standard for Paralegal Specialist Series, GS-0950* (www.opm.gov/fedclass/gs0950.pdf).
4. See Commercial Law League of America, *A Paralegal Approach to the Practice of Commercial Law* (November 14, 1975).
5. J. Stein & B. Hoff, *Paralegals and Administrative Assistants for Prosecutors* (Nat'l District Attorneys Assn 1974); J. Stein, *Paralegals: A Resource for Defenders and Correctional Services* (1976).
6. Rocky Mountain Legal Assistants Assn, *The Use of the Legal Assistant* (1975).

7. Colorado Bar Assn Paralegal Committee (www.cobar.org/ sectandcomms.cfm) (click "Paralegal" then "Guidelines for the Utilization of Paralegals").

8. See endnote 7.

9. C. Berg, *Annual Survey* (San Francisco Assn of Legal Assistants, December 19, 1973).

10. See endnote 7.

11. William Glaberson, *In Tiny Courts of New York, Abuses of Law and Power*, New York Times, September 25, 2006, at A1.

12. See endnote 7.

13. *Merrill Advantage* (Spring 1990).

14. Gainen, *Information Interviews: A Strategy*, Paradigm (Baltimore Assn of Legal Assistants, November/December 1989).

15. Donna Gerson, *Jobs*, Student Lawyer 5 (December 2005).

16. Jacobi, *Back to Basics in Hiring Techniques*, The Mandate 1 (Assn of Legal Administrators, San Diego Chapter, October 1987)

17. U.S. Department of Labor, *Tips for Finding the Right Job* 17 (1991).

17a. Gretchen Rubin and Joanna Young, *The Artful Edit* (2007), quoted at raymondpward.typepad.com/newlegalwriter/ 2007/07/a-simple-trick-.html.

18. See Rocky Mountain Legal Assistant Assn, *Employment Handbook for Legal Assistants* (1979).

19. Judy Waggoner, *Cover Letter as Important as Resume in Job Search*, Appleton Post-Crescent (August 11, 2005) (edit.wisinfo. gannettonline.com/apps/pbcs.dll/article?AID=/20050811/ APC03/51117036/0/APCopinion).

20. Cunningham, *A Planned Approach to Interviewing*, 5 The LAMA Manager 1 (Legal Assistants Management Assn, Fall 1989).

21. Reitz, *Be Steps Ahead of Other Candidates: Understand the Interview Game*, 5 Legal Assistant Today 24, 84 (March/April 1988).

22. Michelle Cottle, *Too Personal at the Interview*, New York Times, April 25, 1999, at BU10.

23. Chere Estrin & Stacey Hunt, *The Successful Paralegal Job Search Guide* 204–5 (2001).

24. Leslie Hilton, *Interview Scenarios*, San Jose Mercury News, January 26, 2003, at 1PC.

Student CD-ROM

For additional materials, please go to the CD in this book.

Online Companion™

For additional resources, please go to http://www.paralegal.delmar.cengage.com

Paralegal Employment in Selected Large Law Offices

After the name of the law firms in this list, you will find two numbers separated by a slash (/). The first number is the number of attorneys employed by the office in the city indicated. The number to the right of the slash is the number of paralegals employed by the office. Some of the names of the offices have been shortened to the first two partner names; commas between names have been omitted. You will also find the Internet site of the offices. Go to these sites to find out what kind of law the office practices (click "Practice Areas," "Practice Groups," or "Services"). The site may also tell you whether the office is currently seeking to hire paralegals (click "Recruitment," "Careers," "Employment" or "Opportunities"). If a search box exists on the site, type *paralegal* or *legal assistant* in the box to try to learn more about nonattorneys at the office. Some firms have special paralegal links, e.g., www.whitecase.com (click "Careers," "North America," "Legal Assistants"). If there is a "Contact Us" option, you might want to send an e-mail inquiring about employment opportunities for paralegals at the office. (You may find that most of the firms on this list seeking paralegals are looking for paralegals with specified experience.) For additional information about specific law firms, see "Finding Information about Law Offices" in Exhibit 2.7.

Alabama (Birmingham)

Baker Donelson Bearman: 63/13 (www.bakerdonelson.com)
Balch Bingham: 129/17 (www.balch.com)
Bradley Arant Rose: 129/56 (www.barw.com)
Burr Forman: 140/74 (www.burr.com)
Haskell Slaughter: 52/10 (www.hsy.com)
Johnston Barton Proctor: 52/6 (johnstonbarton.com)
Maynard Cooper 145/40
Sirote Permutt: 81/26 (www.sirote.com)

Arizona (Phoenix)

Bryan Cave: 75/17 (www.bryancave.com)
Community Legal Services, Inc.: 23/24 (800–852–9075)
Fennemore Craig: 153/31 (www.fclaw.com)
Gallagher Kennedy: 97/15 (www.gknet.com)
Greenberg Traurig: 62/12 (www.gtlaw.com)
Jennings Strouss Salmon: 88/21 (www.jsslaw.com)
Jones Skelton: 70/25 (www.JshFirm.com)
Lewis Roca: 170/40 (www.lewisandroca.com)
Maricopa County Attorney: 330/885 (www.maricopacountyattorney.org)
Osborn Maledon: 43/9 (osbornmaledon.com)
Perkins Coie Brown: 66/17 (www.perkinscoie.com)
Quarles Brady Streich: 112/18 (www.quarles.com)
Shughart Thomson: 23/11 (www.stklaw.com)

Snell Wilmer: 188/27 (www.swlaw.com)
Squire Sanders Dempsey: 70/12 (www.ssd.com)
Steptoe Johnson: 53/11 (www.steptoe.com)
Stinson Morrison Hecker: 37/9 (www.stinsonmoheck.com)

Arizona (Tuscon)

Quarles Brady Streich: 15/4 (www.quarles.com)
Snell Wilmer: 36/6 (www.swlaw.com)

Arkansas (Little Rock)

Barber McCaskill: 22/10 (www.barberlawfirm.com)
Friday Eldredge: 80/20 (www.fridayfirm.com)
Gill Elrod: 16/6 (www.gill-law.com)
Mitchell Williams: 60/20 (www.mitchellwilliamslaw.com)
Quattalbaum Grooms: 30/11 (www.qgtb.com)
Williams Anderson: 23/6 (www.williamsanderson.com)
Wright Lindsey: 57/12 (www.wlj.com)

California (Costa Mesa)

Latham Watkins: 76/24 (www.lw.com)
Paul Hastings: 52/7 (www.paulhastings.com)
Rutan Tucker: 143/15 (www.rutan.com)
Snell Wilmer: 67/12 (www.swlaw.com)

California (Fresno)

Baker Manock: 46/11 (www.bmj-law.com)
Kimble MacMichael: 17/3 (www.kmulaw.com)

California (Irvine)

Gibson Dunn: 70/8 (www.gibsondunn.com)
Knobbe Martens: 133/36 (www.kmob.com)
Palmieri Tyler: 35/8 (www.ptwww.com)

California (Los Angeles)

Akin Gump Strauss: 89/8 (www.akingump.com)
Arnold Porter: 57/10 (www.arnoldporter.com)
Bet Tzedek Legal Services: 20/8 (www.bettzedek.org)
Bingham McCutchen: 112/19 (www.bingham.com)
Christensen Glaser Fink: 106/10 (www.chrisglase.com)
Cox Castle Nicholson: 114/18 (www.coxcastle.com)
Gibson Dunn Crutcher: 210/27 (www.gibsondunn.com)
Greenberg Glusker Fields: 102/11 (www.ggfirm.com)
Heller Ehrman: 65/20 (www.hellerehrman.com)

Hennigan Bennett: 42/12 (www.hbdlawyers.com)
Howrey: 62/12 (www.howrey.com)
Irell Manella: 227/30 (www.irell.com)
Jackson Lewis: 380/51 (www.jacksonlewis.com)
Jeffer Mangels: 142/16 (www.jmbm.com)
Jones Day: 138/15 (www.jonesday.com)
Katten Muchin: 75/13 (www.kattenlaw.com)
Kirkland Ellis: 116/18 (www.kirkland.com)
Latham Watkins: 274/44 (www.lw.com)
Loeb Loeb: 106/15 (www.loeb.com)
Manatt Phelps: 286/41 (www.manatt.com)
Mitchell Silberberg: 113/28 (www.msk.com)
Morrison Foerster: 117/16 (www.mofo.com)
Munger Tolles: 163/46 (www.mto.com)
O'Melveny Myers: 276/46 (www.omm.com)
Paul Hastings: 187/17 (www.paulhastings.com)
Quinn Emanuel: 144/23 (www.quinnemanuel.com)
Sheppard Mullin: 179/19 (www.sheppardmullin.com)
Sidley Austin Brown: 158/30 (www.sidley.com)
Skadden Arps: 119/20 (www.skadden.com)
White Case: 48/7 (www.whitecase.com)
Winston Strawn: 48/12 (www.winston.com)

California (Newport Beach)

O'Melveny Myers: 67/14 (www.omm.com)
Stradling Yocca: 104/21 (www.sycr.com)

California (Palo Alto/Menlo Park/Mountain View)

Cooley Godward: 185/31 (www.cooley.com)
Dechert: 23/13 (www.dechert.com)
DLA Piper Rudnick: 117/23 (www.dlapiper.com)
Fenwick West: 231/49 (www.fenwick.com)
Heller Ehrman: 124/39 (www.hellerehrman.com)
Latham Watkins: 71/14 (www.lw.com)
McDermott Will: 48/14 (www.mwe.com)
Morrison Foerster: 104/19 (www.mofo.com)
Orrick Herrington: 89/27 (www.orrick.com)
Pillsbury Winthrop: 76/19 (www.pillsburylaw.com)
Wilson Sonsini: 413/146 (www.wsgr.com)

California (Riverside)

Best Best Krieger: 162/38 (bbklaw.com)

California (Sacramento)

Attorney-General: 996/130 (www.ag-ca.gov)
Downey Brand: 112/17 (www.downeybrand.com)
Jackson Lewis: 380/51 (www.jacksonlewis.com)
McDonough Holland: 108/14 (www.mhalaw.com)
Orrick Herrington: 29/9 (www.orrick.com)

California (San Diego)

Cooley Godward: 78/20 (www.cooley.com)
DLA Piper Rudnick: 134/20 (www.dlapiper.com)
Fish Richardson: 53/26 (www.fr.com)
Foley Lardner: 39/12 (www.foley.com)
Gordon Rees: 78/14 (www.gordonrees.com)
Heller Ehrman: 46/10 (www.hellerehrman.com)
Latham Watkins: 107/21 (www.lw.com)
Luce Forward: 186/32 (www.luce.com)
Morrison Foerster: 58/14 (www.mofo.com)
Procopio Cory: 80/10 (www.procopio.com)
Public Defender: 180/12 (www.co.san-diego.ca.us/public_defender)
San Diego City Attorney: 144/26 (www.sandiego.gov/city-attorney)

Seltzer Caplan: 57/20 (www.scmv.com)
U.S. Attorney's Office: 115/20 (www.usdoj.gov/usao/cas)

California (San Francisco)

Baker McKenzie: 84/18 (www.bakernet.com/BakerNet)
Bingham McCutchen: 157/22 (bingham.com)
Cooley Godward: 100/18 (www.cooley.com)
DLA Piper Rudnick: 67/11 (www.dlapiper.com)
Drinker Biddle: 32/18 (www.drinkerbiddle.com)
Duane Morris: 69/12 (www.duanemorris.com)
Farella Braun: 120/28 (www.fbm.com)
Gordon Rees: 143/49 (www.gordonrees.com)
Hanson Bridgett: 131/19 (www.hansonbridgett.com)
Heller Ehrman: 186/72 (www.hellerehrman.com)
Howard Rice: 121/33 (www.howardrice.com)
Jackson Lewis: 380/51 (www.jacksonlewis.com)
Latham Watkins: 122/19 (www.lw.com)
Morgan Lewis: 112/27 (www.morganlewis.com)
Morgenstein Jubelirer: 33/14 (www.mjllp.com)
Morrison Foerster: 280/55 (www.mofo.com)
Nixon Peabody: 87/13 (www.nixonpeabody.com)
O'Melveny Myers: 91/16 (www.omm.com)
Orrick Herrington: 179/36 (www.orrick.com)
Paul Hastings: 85/14 (www.paulhastings.com)
Pillsbury Winthrop: 160/22 (www.pillsburylaw.com)
Sidley Austin: 42/10 (www.sidley.com)
Skadden Arps: 22/10 (www.skadden.com)
Thelen Reid: 149/52 (www.thelenreid.com)
Townsend Townsend: 164/52 (www.townsend.com)
Winston Strawn: 41/12 (www.winston.com)

California (San Jose)

County Public Defender: 109/27 (www.sccgov.org)
Thelen Reid: 32/8 (www.thelenreid.com)

California (Santa Monica)

Alschuler Grossman: 94/15 (www.agsk.com)
Greenberg Traurig: 72/17 (www.gtlaw.com)
Perkins Coie: 38/8 (www.perkinscoie.com)

Colorado (Denver)

Baker & Hostetler: 47/9 (www.bakerlaw.com)
Brownstein Hyatt: 113/30 (www.bhf-law.com)
Davis Graham: 109/16 (www.dgslaw.com)
Faegre Benson: 80/14 (www.faegre.com)
Holland Hart: 139/15 (www.hollandhart.com)
Holme Roberts: 135/23 (www.hro.com)
Ireland, Stapleton: 22/9 (www.irelandstapleton.com)
Kutak Rock: 65/11 (www.kutakrock.com)
Otten Johnson: 49/8 (www.ojrnr.com)
Rothgerber Johnson: 72/8 (www.rothgerber.com)
Sherman & Howard: 152/24 (www.shermanhoward.com)
Snell Wilmer: 32/7 (www.swlaw.com)
Wheeler Trigg: 38/19 (www.wtklaw.com)

Connecticut (Hartford)

Bingham McCutchen: 63/15 (www.bingham.com)
Day Berry: 115/23 (www.dbh.com)
Dechert: 14/6 (www.dechert.com)
Edwards Angell: 21/7 (www.eapdlaw.com)
Halloran Sage: 91/9 (halloran-sage.com)
Jackson Lewis: 380/51 (www.jacksonlewis.com)
Murtha Cullina: 130/22 (www.murthalaw.com)
Pepe Hazard: 63/14 (www.pepehazard.com)

Robinson Cole: 226/34 (www.rc.com)
Shipman Goodwin: 110/28 (www.shipmangoodwin.com)
Updike Kelly: 57/8 (www.uks.com)

Connecticut (New Haven)

Tyler Cooper: 64/15 (www.tylercooper.com)
Wiggin Dana: 90/23 (www.wiggin.com)
Withers Bergman: 47/14 (www.withersworldwide.com)

Connecticut (Stamford)

Cummings Lockwood: 70/10 (www.cl-law.com)
Day Berry: 42/9 (www.dbh.com)
Paul Hastings: 64/10 (www.paulhastings.com)

Delaware (Wilmington)

Community Legal Aid Society: 20/15 (www.declasi.org)
DuPont Corporation Law Department: 119/56
    (www2.dupont.com)
Morris James: 52/28 (www.morrisjames.com)
Morris Nichols: 88/17 (www.mnat.com)
Pepper Hamilton: 17/7 (www.pepperlaw.com)
Potter Anderson: 67/19 (www.potteranderson.com)
Richards Layton: 127/28 (www.rlf.com)
Saul Ewing: 21/8 (www.saul.com)
Skadden Arps: 60/22 (www.skadden.com)
Young Conaway: 98/41 (www.youngconaway.com)

District of Columbia

Akin Gump Strauss: 273/42 (www.akingump.com)
Arent Fox: 221/40 (www.arentfox.com)
Arnold Porter: 422/135 (www.arnoldporter.com)
Boies Schiller: 197/83 (www.bsfllp.com)
Covington Burling: 359/72 (www.cov.com)
Crowell Moring: 279/73 (www.crowell.com)
Dickstein Shapiro: 265/54 (www.dicksteinshapiro.com)
Finnegan Henderson: 197/62 (www.finnegan.com)
Hogan Hartson: 493/42 (www.hhlaw.com)
Holland Knight: 173/23 (www.hklaw.com)
Howrey: 238/48 (www.howrey.com)
Hunton Williams: 143/33 (www.hunton.com)
Jackson Lewis: 380/51 (www.jacksonlewis.com)
King Spalding: 112/24 (www.kslaw.com)
Kirkland Ellis: 115/59 (www.kirkland.com)
Kirkpatrick Lockhart: 150/36 (www.klgates.com)
McDermott Will: 210/41 (www.mwe.com)
McKee Nelson: 82/26 (www.mckeenelson.com)
Miller Chevalier: 110/23 (www.millerchevalier.com)
Morgan Lewis: 263/46 (www.morganlewis.com)
Patton Boggs: 248/32 (www.pattonboggs.com)
Pillsbury Winthrop: 219/22 (www.pillsburylaw.com)
Sidley Austin: 232/36 (www.sidley.com)
Skadden Arps: 265/112 (www.skadden.com)
Spriggs Hollingsworth: 71/23 (www.spriggs.com)
Steptoe Johnson: 312/70 (www.steptoe.com)
Sterne Kessler: 72/27 (www.skgf.com)
Venable: 220/23 (www.venable.com)
White Case: 110/30 (www.whitecase.com)
Wiley Rein: 231/34 (www.wrf.com)
Williams Connolly: 215/67 (www.wc.com)
Wilmer Cutler: 248/142 (www.wilmerhale.com)

Florida (Jacksonville)

Akerman Senterfitt: 37/5 (www.akerman.com)
City of Jacksonville, General Counsel: 39/7 (www.coj.net)

Foley Lardner: 43/11 (www.foley.com)
Holland Knight: 53/6 (www.hklaw.com)
McGuire Woods: 26/8 (www.mcguirewoods.com)
Rogers Towers: 101/20 (www.rtlaw.com)
Smith Gambrell: 24/7 (www.sgrlaw.com)

Florida (Miami)

Akerman Senterfitt: 159/27 (www.akerman.com)
Bilzin Sumberg: 94/16 (www.bilzin.com)
Carlton Fields: 80/14 (www.carltonfields.com)
Greenberg Traurig: 85/40 (www.gtlaw.com)
Holland Knight: 104/22 (www.hklaw.com)
Hunton Williams: 60/11 (www.hunton.com)
Miami-Dade County Attorney: 74/32 (www.miamidade
    .gov/Atty)
Shook Hardy: 47/19 (www.shb.com)
Shutts Bowen: 90/22 (www.shutts-law.com)
Stearns Weaver: 77/17 (www.stearnsweaver.com)
Steel Hector: 52/11 (www.steelhector.com)
White Case: 90/12 (www.whitecase.com)

Florida (Orlando)

Akerman Senterfitt: 74/10 (www.akerman.com)
Baker Hostetler: 71/20 (www.bakerlaw.com)
Foley Lardner: 40/9 (www.foley.com)
Greenberg Traurig: 45/20 (www.gtlaw.com)
Holland Knight: 65/12 (www.hklaw.com)
Public Defender: 83/16 (pd.circuit9.org)
Rumberger Kirk: 75/20 (www.rumberger.com)

Florida (Tampa)

Carlton Fields: 90/10 (www.carltonfields.com)
Foley Lardner: 38/10 (www.foley.com)
Fowler White: 115/54 (www.fowlerwhite.com)
Hill Ward: 68/26 (www.hwhlaw.com)
Holland Knight: 76/10 (www.hklaw.com)
Shook Hardy: 19/6 (www.shb.com)
Shumaker Loop: 47/10 (www.slk-law.com)
Trenam Kemker: 68/19 (www.trenam.com)

Florida (West Palm Beach)

Akerman Senterfitt: 40/9 (www.akerman.com)
Edwards Angell: 29/8 (www.eapdlaw.com)
Greenberg Traurig: 42/8 (www.gtlaw.com)
Gunster Yoakley: 51/6 (www.gunster.com)

Georgia (Atlanta)

Alston Bird: 488/52 (www.alston.com)
Arnall Golden: 140/36 (www.agg.com)
Atlanta Legal Aid Society: 45/7 (www.atlantalegalaid.org)
Constangy Brooks: 97/16 (www.constangy.com)
Georgia Legal Services: 63/41 (www.glsp.org)
Greenberg Traurig: 53/10 (www.gtlaw.com)
Holland Knight: 64/10 (www.hklaw.com)
Hunton Williams: 98/22 (www.hunton.com)
Jones Day: 136/14 (www.jonesday.com)
Kilpatrick Stockton: 268/56 (www.kilpatrickstockton.com)
King Spalding: 423/93 (www.kslaw.com)
Mckenna Long: 156/16 (www.mckennalong.com)
Morris Manning: 176/26 (www.mmmlaw.com)
Ogletree Deakins: 263/64 (www.ogletreedeakins.com)
Parker Hudson: 60/14 (www.phrd.com)
Paul Hastings: 94/14 (www.paulhastings.com)
Powell Goldstein: 207/32 (www.pogolaw.com)

Rogers Hardin: 54/17 (www.rh-law.com)
Seyfarth Shaw: 53/15 (www.seyfarth.com)
Smith Gambrell: 164/28 (www.sgrlaw.com)
Sutherland Asbill: 233/45 (www.sablaw.com)
Swift Currie: 89/29 (www.swiftcurrie.com)
Troutman Sanders: 248/31 (www.troutmansanders.com)
Weinberg Wheel: 60/11 (www.wwhgd.com)
Womble Carlyle: 69/27 (www.wcsr.com)

Georgia (Savannah)

Hunter Maclean: 55/11 (www.huntermaclean.com)

Hawaii (Honolulu)

Ashford Wriston: 26/6 (www.ashfordwriston.com)
Cades Schutte: 69/11 (www.cades.com)
Carlsmith Ball: 52/12 (www.carlsmith.com)
Goodsill Anderson: 69/8 (www.goodsill.com)
Ian Mattoch: 7/8 (www.ianmattoch.com)
Legal Aid Society: 33/20 (www.legalaidhawaii.org)
McCorriston Miller: 39/5 (www.m4law.com)

Idaho (Boise)

Holland Hart: 28/8 (www.hollandhart.com)
Stoel Rives: 18/4 (www.stoel.com)

Illinois (Chicago)

Baker McKenzie: 179/23 (www.bakerinfo.com)
Barack Ferrazzano: 79/10 (www.bfkpn.com)
Bell Boyd: 208/18 (www.bellboyd.com)
Brinks Hofer: 122/16 (www.usebrinks.com)
Chapman Cutler: 195/18 (www.chapman.com)
City Department of Law: 260/56 (www.cityofchicago.org/Law)
Cook City Public Guardian: 56/17 (www.publicguardian.org)
Cook City State's Attorney: 955/11 (www.statesattorney.org)
DLA Piper Rudnick: 271/43 (www.dlapiper.com)
Drinker Biddle: 203/29 (www.drinkerbiddle.com)
Fitch Even Tabin: 50/17 (www.fitcheven.com)
Foley Lardner: 148/14 (www.foley.com)
Goldberg Kohn: 84/13 (www.goldbergkohn.com)
Hinshaw Culbertson: 411/55 (www.hinshawlaw.com)
Holland Knight: 148/18 (www.hklaw.com)
Jenner Block: 366/39 (www.jenner.com)
Jones Day: 158/10 (www.jonesday.com)
Katten Muchin: 295/49 (www.kattenlaw.com)
Kirkland Ellis: 525/202 (www.kirkland.com)
Latham Watkins: 124/24 (www.lw.com)
Leydig Voit Mayer: 81/22 (www.leydig.com)
Lord Bissell Brook: 225/24 (www.lordbissell.com)
Mayer Brown: 474/75 (www.mayerbrownrowe.com)
McAndrews Held: 86/31 (www.mhmlaw.com)
McDermott Will: 261/34 (www.mwe.com)
McDonnell Boehnen: 62/18 (www.mbhb.com)
McGuire Woods: 157/19 (www.mcguirewoods.com)
Neal Gerber: 172/33 (www.ngelaw.com)
Pattishall McAuliffe: 28/12 (www.pattishall.com)
Sachnoff Weaver: 141/23 (www.sachnoff.com)
Schiff Hardin: 317/42 (www.schiffhardin.com)
Seyfarth Shaw: 254/27 (www.seyfarth.com)
Sidley Austin: 509/65 (www.sidley.com)
Skadden Arps: 164/31 (www.skadden.com)
Sonnenschein Nath: 229/32 (www.sonnenschein.com)
Vedder Price: 182/32 (www.vedderprice.com)
Wildman Harrold: 222/31 (www.wildmanharrold.com)
Winston Strawn: 445/90 (www.winston.com)

Indiana (Indianapolis)

Baker Daniels: 221/23 (www.bakerdaniels.com)
Barnes Thornburg: 214/28 (www.btlaw.com)
Bingham McHale: 121/14 (binghammchale.com)
Bose McKinney: 118/19 (www.boselaw.com)
Ice Miller: 224/44 (www.icemiller.com)
Krieg DeVault: 101/9 (www.dannpecar.com)
Sommer Barnard: 97/9 (www.sommerbarnard.com)

Iowa (Des Moines)

Belin Lamson: 38/7 (www.belinlaw.com)
Faegre Benson: 12/2 (www.faegre.com)

Kansas (Overland Park)

Stinson Morrison: 17/2 (www.stinsonmoheck.com)
Warden Triplett: 20/5 (www.wardentriplett.com)

Kentucky (Lexington)

Frost Brown: 38/9 (www.frostbrowntodd.com)
Stites Harbison: 48/9 (www.stites.com)
Stoll Keenon Ogden: 92/20 (www.skofirm.com)

Kentucky (Louisville)

Frost Brown: 125/27 (www.frostbrowntodd.com)
Greenebaum Doll: 180/44 (www.greenebaum.com)
Stites Harbison: 240/53 (www.stites.com)
Stoll Keenon Ogden: 57/8 (www.skofirm.com)
Woodward Hobson: 51/21 (www.whf-law.com)
Wyatt Tarrant: 211/36 (www.wyattfirm.com)

Louisiana (Baton Rouge)

Jones Walker: 216/10 (www.joneswalker.com)
Phelps Dunbar: 43/9 (www.phelpsdunbar.com)

Louisiana (New Orleans)

Baker Donelson: 31/7 (www.bakerdonelson.com)
Fisher Phillips: 14/5 (www.laborlawyers.com)
Jones Walker: 216/19 (www.joneswalker.com)
Liskow Lewis: 94/25 (www.liskow.com)
Phelps Dunbar: 91/17 (www.phelpsdunbar.com)
Proskauer Rose: 13/12 (www.proskauer.com)
Stone Pigman: 55/11 (www.stonepigman.com)

Maine (Portland)

Drummond Woodsum: 38/4 (dwmlaw.com)
Perkins Thompson: 27/5 (www.perkinsthompson.com)
Pierce Atwood: 116/20 (www.pierceatwood.com)
Verrill Dana: 91/15 (www.verrilldana.com)

Maryland (Baltimore)

Ballard Spahr: 40/5 (www.ballardspahr.com)
DLA Piper Rudnick: 165/26 (www.dlapiper.com)
Gordon Feinblatt: 71/24 (www.gfrlaw.com)
Miles Stockbridge: 195/27 (www.milesstockbridge.com)
Ober Kaler: 120/23 (www.ober.com)
Saul Ewing: 57/10 (www.saul.com)
Tydings Rosenberg: 48/6 (www.tydingslaw.com)
Venable: 138/27 (www.venable.com)
Whiteford Taylor: 159/22 (www.wtplaw.com)

Massachusetts (Boston)

Bingham McCutchen: 282/41 (www.bingham.com)
Bromberg Sunstein: 34/9 (www.bromsun.com)

Brown Rudnick: 109/19 (www.brownrudnick.com)
Burns Levinson: 40/8 (www.burnslev.com)
Choate Hall: 173/11 (www.choate.com)
Edwards Angell: 180/34 (www.eapdlaw.com)
Fish Richardson: 83/19 (www.fr.com)
Foley Hoag: 216/22 (www.foleyhoag.com)
Goodwin Procter: 444/57 (www.goodwinprocter.com)
Goulston Storrs: 179/24 (www.goulstonstorrs.com)
Greenberg Traurig: 47/9 (www.gtlaw.com)
Holland Knight: 133/14 (www.hklaw.com)
Jackson Lewis: 380/51 (www.jacksonlewis.com)
McDermott Will: 77/10 (www.mwe.com)
Mintz Levin: 295/39 (www.mintz.com)
Nixon Peabody: 158/22 (www.nixonpeabody.com)
Nutter McClennen: 140/17 (www.nutter.com)
Rackemann Sawyer: 40/8 (www.rackemann.com)
Ropes Gray: 435/54 (www.ropesgray.com)
Skadden Arps: 44/19 (www.skadden.com)
Sullivan Worcester: 179/21 (www.sandw.com)
Wilmer Hale: 313/85 (www.wilmerhale.com)
Wolf Greenfield: 41/12 (www.wolfgreenfield.com)

Massachusetts (Concord)

Hamilton Brook: 38/15 (www.hbsr.com)

Massachusetts (Worcester)

Bowditch Dewey: 63/16 (www.bowditch.com)
Fletcher Tilton: 40/50 (www.ftwlaw.com)
Mirick O'Connell: 56/14 (www.modl.com)

Michigan (Bloomfield Hills)

Dickinson Wright: 71/9 (www.dickinsonwright.com)
Dykema Gossett: 68/7 (www.dykema.com)
Howard Howard: 87/12 (www.h2law.com)

Michigan (Detroit)

Bodman: 128/15 (www.bodmanllp.com)
Butzel Long: 206/42 (www.butzel.com)
Clark Hill: 123/12 (www.clarkhill.com)
Dickinson Wright: 85/12 (www.dickinsonwright.com)
Dykema Gossett: 105/16 (www.dykema.com)
Honigman Miller: 147/19 (www.honigman.com)
Miller Canfield: 349/66 (www.millercanfield.com)
Pepper Hamilton: 33/8 (www.pepperlaw.com)

Michigan (Grand Rapids)

Law Weathers: 41/5 (www.lwr.com)
Miller Johnson: 81/18 (www.millerjohnson.com)
Varnum Riddering: 147/15 (www.varnumlaw.com)
Warner Norcross: 180/28 (www.wnj.com)

Michigan (Kalamazoo)

Miller Johnson: 12/19 (www.millerjohnson.com)

Michigan (Lansing)

Foster Swift: 90/21 (www.fosterswift.com)
Honigman Miller: 21/3 (www.honigman.com)

Michigan (Southfield)

Jaffe Raitt: 91/9 (www.jaffelaw.com)
Kupelian Ormond: 21/2 (www.kompc.com)

Minnesota (Minneapolis)

Bassford Remele: 38/5 (www.bassford.com)
Briggs Morgan: 157/26 (www.briggs.com)

Cargill: 29/6 (www.cargill.com)
Dorsey Whitney: 271/53 (www.dorsey.com)
Faegre Benson: 302/47 (www.faegre.com)
Fish Richardson: 33/6 (www.fr.com)
Fredrikson Byron: 181/39 (www.fredlaw.com)
Gray Plant: 131/15 (www.gpmlaw.com)
Halleland Lewis: 44/14 (www.halleland.com)
Hennepin City Attorney: 163/39 (www.hennepinattorney.org)
Jackson Lewis: 380/51 (www.jacksonlewis.com
Leonard Street: 188/31 (www.leonard.com)
Lindquist Vennum: 187/30 (www.lindquist.com)
Maslon Edelman: 79/18 (www.maslon.com)
Merchant Gould: 83/12 (www.merchant-gould.com)
Oppenheimer Wolff: 110/11 (www.oppenheimer.com)
Rider Bennett: 122/18 (www.riderlaw.com)
Robins Kaplan: 152/49 (www.rkmc.com)
Winthrop Weinstine: 80/11 (www.winthrop.com)
Zelle Hofmann: 31/9 (www.zelle.com)

Mississippi (Gulfport)

Balch Bingham: 16/3 (www.balch.com)
Phelps Dunbar: 10/5 (www.phelpsdunbar.com)

Mississippi (Jackson)

Baker Donelson: 55/36 (www.bakerdonelson.com)
Butler Snow: 101/53 (www.butlersnow.com)
Phelps Dunbar: 60/12 (www.phelpsdunbar.com)

Missouri (Columbia)

Missouri State Public Defender: 242/59 (www.publicdefender.
   mo.gov)

Missouri (Kansas City)

Armstrong Teasdale: 37/4 (www.armstrongteasdale.com)
Bryan Cave: 76/11 (www.bryancave.com)
Husch Eppenberger: 67/20 (www.husch.com)
Lathrop Gage: 272/50 (www.lathropgage.com)
Lewis Rice: 129/16 (www.lewisrice.com)
Missouri State Public Defender: 242/59 (www.publicdefender.
   mo.gov)
Polsinelli Shalton: 210/44 (www.pswslaw.com)
Shook Hardy: 316/73 (www.shb.com)
Shughart Thomson: 175/42 (www.stklaw.com)
Sonnenschein Nath: 57/7 (www.sonnenschein.com)
Spencer Fane: 95/16 (www.spencerfane.com)
Stinson Morrison: 186/26 (www.stinsonmoheck.com)

Missouri (St. Louis)

Armstrong Teasdale: 171/24 (www.armstrongteasdale.com)
Blackwell Sanders: 82/14 (www.blackwellsanders.com)
Bryan Cave: 246/47 (www.bryancave.com)
Greensfelder Hemker: 131/28 (www.greensfelder.com)
Husch Eppenberger: 152/67 (www.husch.com)
Polsinelli Shalton: 210/44 (www.pswslaw.com)
Sonnenschein Nath: 45/8 (www.sonnenschein.com)
Spencer Fane: 24/9 (www.spencerfane.com)
Thompson Coburn: 274/45 (www.thompsoncoburn.com)

Montana (Billings)

Holland Hart: 14/4 (www.hollandhart.com)

Nebraska (Omaha)

Kutak Rock: 101/15 (www.kutakrock.com)

Nevada (Las Vegas)

Alverson Taylor: 43/3 (www.alversontaylor.com)
Beckley Singleton: 36/25 (www.beckleylaw.com)
Hale Lane Peek: 46/7 (www.halelane.com)
Jolley Urga Wirth: 18/5 (www.juwws.com)
Kolesar Leatham: 17/4 (www.klnevada.com)
Kummer Kaempfer: 44/10 (www.kkbrf.com)
Lionel Sawyer: 53/9 (lionelsawyer.com)
McDonald Carano: 16/4 (www.mcdonaldcarano.com)
Morris Pickering: 12/2 (www.morrislawgroup.com)
Santoro Driggs: 39/5 (santorodriggs.com)
Snell Wilmer: 25/3 (www.swlaw.com)
U.S. Attorney's Office: 42/8 (www.usdoj.gov/usao/nv)

New Hampshire (Concord)

New Hampshire Public Defender: 74/26 (www.nhpd.org)
Orr Reno: 29/10 (www.orr-reno.com)

New Hampshire (Manchester)

Devine Millimet: 65/21 (www.dmb.com)
McLane Graf: 75/25 (www.mclane.com)
Sheehan Phinney: 60/80 (www.sheehan.com)
Wiggin Nourie: 38/13 (www.wiggin-nourie.com)

New Jersey (Atlantic City)

Fox Rothschild: 28/5 (www.foxrothschild.com)

New Jersey (Bridgewater)

Norris McLaughlin: 86/12 (www.nmmlaw.com)

New Jersey (Florham Park)

Drinker Biddle: 84/14 (www.drinkerbiddle.com)

New Jersey (Hackensack)

Cole Schotz: 88/22 (www.coleschotz.com)

New Jersey (Haddonfield)

Archer Greiner: 124/34 (www.archerlaw.com)

New Jersey (Morristown)

Pitney Hardin: 176/26 (www.pitneyhardin.com)
Porzio Bromberg: 102/102 (www.pbnlaw.com)
Riker Danzig: 171/28 (www.riker.com)

New Jersey (Newark)

Gibbons Del Deo: 136/30 (www.gibbonslaw.com)
Kirkpatrick Lockhart: 37/5 (www.klgates.com)
Latham Watkins: 32/6 (www.lw.com)
McCarter English: 365/95 (www.mccarter.com)
Proskauer Rose: 40/13 (www.proskauer.com)
Sills Cummis: 158/42 (www.sillscummis.com)

New Jersey (Princeton)

Dechert: 31/7 (www.dechert.com)
Fox Rothschild: 64/8 (www.foxrothschild.com)
Pepper Hamilton: 26/4 (www.pepperlaw.com)
Saul Ewing: 22/4 (www.saul.com)

New Jersey (Roseland)

Connell Foley: 101/26 (www.connellfoley.com)
Lowenstein Sandler: 239/37 (www.lowenstein.com)
Lum Danzis: 37/4 (www.lumlaw.com)

New Jersey (Short Hills)

Budd Larner: 98/12 (www.budd-larner.com)
Edwards Angell: 21/4 (www.eapdlaw.com)

New Jersey (Voorhees)

Ballard Spahr: 39/9 (www.ballardspahr.com)

New Jersey (West Orange)

Wolff Samson: 100/9 (www.wolffsamson.com)

New Jersey (Woodbridge)

Greenbaum Rowe: 94/14 (www.greenbaumlaw.com)
Wilentz Goldman: 143/56 (www.wilentz.com)

New York (Buffalo)

Damon Morey: 71/4 (www.damonmorey.com)
Hodgson Russ: 150/47 (www.hodgsonruss.com)
Jaeckle Fleischmann: 60/9 (www.jaeckle.com)

New York (New York)

Cadwalader Wickersham: 369/70 (www.cadwalader.com)
Chadbourne Parke: 253/41 (www.chadbourne.com)
Cleary Gottlieb: 437/83 (www.cgsh.com)
Cravath Swaine: 454/196 (www.cravath.com)
Cullen Dykman: 136/41 (www.cullenanddykman.com)
Davis Polk: 589/85 (www.davispolk.com)
Debevoise Plimpton: 487/67 (www.debevoise.com)
Dewey Ballantine: 291/56 (www.deweyballantine.com)
Fried Frank: 324/105 (www.friedfrank.com)
Greenberg Traurig: 252/47 (www.gtlaw.com)
Hughes Hubbard: 221/98 (www.hugheshubbard.com)
Kasowitz Benson: 157/58 (www.kasowitz.com)
Kaye Scholer: 334/80 (www.kayescholer.com)
Kenyon Kenyon: 189/64 (www.kenyon.com)
Kirkland Ellis: 192/62 (www.kenyon.com)
Kramer Levin: 290/55 (www.kramerlevin.com)
LeBoeuf Lamb: 256/27 (www.llgm.com)
Legal Aid Society of New York City: 427/86 (www.legal-aid.org)
Milbank Tweed: 538/85 (www.milbank.com)
New York City Law Department: 653/189 (www.nyc.gov/html/law)
New York County District Attorney: 442/116 (www.manhattanda.org)
O'Melveny Myers: 219/43 (www.omm.com)
Orrick Herrington: 184/59 (www.orrick.com)
Paul Weiss: 516/169 (www.paulweiss.com)
Proskauer Rose: 424/65 (www.proskauer.com)
Ropes Gray: 194/39 (www.ropesgray.com)
Schulte Roth: 377/87 (www.srz.com)
Simpson Thacher: 723/186 (www.simpsonthacher.com)
Skadden Arps: 763/164 (www.skadden.com)
Stroock Stroock: 274/63 (www.stroock.com)
Sullivan Cromwell: 401/139 (www.sullcrom.com)
Thacher Proffitt: 220/39 (www.tpw.com)
U.S. Attorney: 223/57 (www.usdoj.gov/usao/nys)
Weil Gotshal: 593/82 (www.weil.com)
White Case: 450/77 (www.whitecase.com)
Willkie Farr: 367/74 (www.willkie.com)

New York (Rochester)

Boylan Brown: 36/9 (boylanbrown.com)
Farmworker Legal Services: 1/5 (www.flsny.org)
Harris Beach: 191/54 (www.harrisbeach.com)
Harter Secrest: 104/24 (www.hselaw.com)
Nixon Peabody: 107/49 (www.nixonpeabody.com)

New York (Syracuse)

Bond Schoeneck: 189/43 (www.bsk.com)
Hancock Estabrook: 64/14 (www.hancocklaw.com)

New York (Uniondale)

Rivkin Radler: 125/14 (www.rivkinradler.com)

North Carolina (Chapel Hill)

Southern Environment Law Center: 6/5
    (www.southernenvironment.org)

North Carolina (Charlotte)

Alston Bird: 73/13 (www.alston.com)
Cadwalader Wickersham: 55/22 (www.cadwalader.com)
Culp Elliott: 14/5 (www.ceandc.com)
Dechert: 17/5 (www.dechert.com)
Helms Mulliss: 104/19 (www.hmw.com)
Hunton Williams: 34/8 (www.hunton.com)
Katten Muchin: 27/9 (www.kattenlaw.com)
Kennedy Covington: 123/33 (www.kennedycovington.com)
Kilpatrick Stockton: 28/4 (www.kilpatrickstockton.com)
Legal Services of Southern Piedmont: 4/2 (www.lssp.org)
Mayer Brown: 35/7 (www.mayerbrownrowe.com)
McGuire Woods: 36/4 (www.mcguirewoods.com)
Moore Van Allen: 177/49 (www.mvalaw.com)
Parker Poe: 159/52 (www.parkerpoe.com)
Poyner Spruill: 32/7 (www.poynerspruill.com)
Robinson Bradshaw: 114/17 (www.rbh.com)
Shumaker Loop: 20/6 (www.slk-law.com)
Womble Carlyle: 67/10 (www.wcsr.com)

North Carolina (Greensboro)

Brooks Pierce: 75/15 (www.brookspierce.com)
Smith Moore: 74/18 (www.smithmoorelaw.com)

North Carolina (Morrisville)

Moore Van Allen: 34/5 (www.mvalaw.com)

North Carolina (New Bern)

Ward Smith: 66/51 (www.wardandsmith.com)

North Carolina (Raleigh)

Alston Bird: 10/2 (www.alston.com)
Hunton Williams: 36/9 (www.hunton.com)
Kilpatrick Stockton: 41/11 (www.kilpatrickstockton.com)
Parker Poe: 38/9 (www.parkerpoe.com)
Poyner Spruill: 48/13 (www.poynerspruill.com)
Smith Anderson: 93/18 (www.smithlaw.com)
Smith Moore: 22/3 (www.smithmoorelaw.com)
Womble Carlyle: 62/18 (www.wcsr.com)

North Carolina (Rocky Mount)

Poyner Spruill: 17/7 (www.poynerspruill.com)

North Carolina (Winston-Salem)

Kilpatrick Stockton: 52/14 (www.kilpatrickstockton.com)

Ohio (Akron)

Brouse McDowell: 46/7 (www.brouse.com)
Buckingham Doolittle: 148/39 (www.bdblaw.com)
Roetzel Andress: 66/14 (www.ralaw.com)

Ohio (Cincinnati)

Baker Hostetler: 15/4 (www.bakerlaw.com)
Dinsmore Shohl: 258/42 (www.dinslaw.com)
Frost Brown: 149/31 (www.frostbrowntodd.com)
Graydon Head: 62/9 (www.graydon.com)
Keating Muething: 102/27 (www.kmklaw.com)
Legal Aid Society Cincinnati: 16/9 (lascinti.org)
Procter & Gamble Legal Division: 9/10
    (www.pg.com/jobs)
Strauss Troy: 50/9 (www.strausstroy.com)
Taft Stettinius: 193/34 (www.taftlaw.com)
Thompson Hine: 64/7 (www.thompsonhine.com)
Ulmer Berne: 40/15 (www.ulmer.com)
Vorys Sater: 51/15 (www.vssp.com)

Ohio (Cleveland)

Baker Hostetler: 194/12 (www.bakerlaw.com)
Benesch Friedlander: 96/10 (www.bfca.com)
Calfee Halter: 196/28 (www.calfee.com)
Hahn Loeser: 73/13 (www.hahnlaw.com)
Jones Day: 271/37 (www.jonesday.com)
McDonald Hopkins: 96/27 (www.mcdonaldhopkins.com)
Squire Sanders: 149/31 (www.ssd.com)
Thompson Hine: 145/23 (www.thompsonhine.com)
Ulmer Berne: 116/19 (www.ulmer.com)
Vorys Sater: 34/6 (www.vssp.com)

Ohio (Columbus)

Bailey Cavalieri: 45/6 (www.baileycavalieri.com)
Baker Hostetler: 71/9 (www.bakerlaw.com)
Bricker Eckler: 126/25 (www.bricker.com)
Jones Day: 90/3 (www.jonesday.com)
Kegler Brown: 63/13 (www.keglerbrown.com)
Ohio Attorney General: 353/44 (www.ag.state.oh.us)
Ohio State Legal Services: 33/8 (www.oslsa.org)
Porter Wright: 200/23 (www.porterwright.com)
Schottenstein Zox: 109/10 (www.szd.com)
Squire Sanders: 83/12 (www.ssd.com)
Thompson Hine: 45/11 (www.thompsonhine.com)
Vorys Sater: 250/68 (www.vssp.com)

Ohio (Dayton)

Coolidge Wall: 51/11 (www.coollaw.com)
Porter Wright: 22/4 (www.porterwright.com)
Thompson Hine: 49/10 (www.thompsonhine.com)

Ohio (Toledo)

Anspach Meeks: 35/6 (www.anspachlaw.com)
Eastman Smith: 73/20 (www.eastmansmith.com)
Robison Curphey: 32/5 (www.rcolaw.com)
Shumaker Loop: 161/17 (www.slk-law.com)
Spengler Nathanson: 32/5 (www.spenglernathanson.com)
Legal Aid Western Ohio: 5/3 (www.lawolaw.org)

Oklahoma (Oklahoma City)

Crowe Dunlevy: 90/21 (www.crowedunlevy.com)

Oklahoma (Tulsa)

Doerner Saunders: 42/9 (www.dsda.com)
Gable Gotwals: 57/7 (www.gablelaw.com)
Hall Estill Hardwick: 100/24 (www.hallestill.com)

Oregon (Portland)

Ater Wynne: 55/8 (www.aterwynne.com)
Ball Janik: 46/10 (www.balljanik.com)
Bullivant Houser: 87/19 (www.bullivant.com)
Davis Wright: 92/20 (www.dwt.com)

Dunn Carney: 49/13 (www.dunncarney.com)
Garvey Schubert: 28/6 (www.gsblaw.com)
Holland Knight: 17/5 (www.hklaw.com)
Lane Powell: 47/13 (www.lanepowell.com)
Miller Nash: 80/11 (www.millernash.com)
Multnomah City District Attorney: 84/17 (www.mcda.us)
Perkins Coie: 60/8 (www.perkinscoie.com)
Schwabe Williamson: 124/22 (www.schwabe.com)
Stoel Rives: 162/26 (www.stoel.com)
Tonkon Torp: 68/18 (www.tonkon.com)

Pennsylvania (Harrisburg)

McNees Wallace: 105/15 (www.mwn.com)

Pennsylvania (Lancaster)

Barley Snyder: 70/20 (www.barley.com)

Pennsylvania (Lansdale)

Fox Rothschild: 23/8 (www.foxrothschild.com)

Pennsylvania (Philadelphia)

Akin Gump: 30/9 (www.akingump.com)
Anapol Schwartz: 25/10 (www.anapolschwartz.com)
Ballard Spahr: 242/33 (www.ballardspahr.com)
Blank Rome: 248/39 (www.blankrome.com)
Buchanan Ingersoll: 53/9 (www.buchananingersoll.com)
Community Legal Services: 39/31 (www.clsphila.org)
Cozen O'Connor: 535/143 (www.cozen.com)
Dechert: 327/71 (www.dechert.com)
Defender Association of Philadelphia: 194/9 (www.phila.
   gov/defender)
DLA Piper Rudnick: 43/12 (www.dlapiper.com)
Drinker Biddle: 188/31 (www.drinkerbiddle.com)
Duane Morris: 179/31 (www.duanemorris.com)
Fox Rothschild: 103/15 (www.foxrothschild.com)
Hangley Aronchick: 49/11 (www.hangley.com)
Harkins Cunningham: 33/12 (www.harkinscunningham.com)
Jones Day: 58/10 (www.jonesday.com)
Montgomery McCracken: 147/30 (www.mmwr.com)
Morgan Lewis: 258/29 (www.morganlewis.com)
Pepper Hamilton: 220/54 (www.pepperlaw.com)
Philadelphia District Attorney: 296/106 (www.phila.gov/
   DistrictAttorney)
Reed Smith: 121/28 (www.reedsmith.com)
Saltz Mongeluzzi: 25/12 (www.smbb.com)
Saul Ewing: 266/44 (www.saul.com)
Schnader Harrison: 100/14 (www.schnader.com)
Stradley Ronon: 134/17 (www.stradley.com)
White Williams: 220/58 (www.whiteandwilliams.com)
Wolf Block: 296/36 (www.wolfblock.com)
Woodcock Washburn: 84/40 (www.woodcock.com)

Pennsylvania (Pittsburgh)

Babst Calland: 52/5 (www.bccz.com)
Buchanan Ingersoll: 129/20 (www.buchananingersoll.com)
Cohen Grigsby: 106/24 (www.cohenlaw.com)
Eckert Seamans: 252/57 (www.eckertseamans.com)
Kirkpatrick Lockhart: 260/75 (www.klgates.com)
Klett Rooney: 66/7 (www.klettrooney.com)
LeBoeuf Lamb: 25/13 (www.llgm.com)
McGuire Woods: 38/8 (www.mcguirewoods.com)
Pepper Hamilton: 40/12 (www.pepperlaw.com)
Reed Smith: 206/47 (www.reedsmith.com)
Thorp Reed: 100/16 (www.thorpreed.com)

Pennsylvania (Reading)

Stevens Lee: 178/19 (www.stevenslee.com)

Rhode Island (Providence)

Edwards Angell: 86/22 (www.eapdlaw.com)
Hinckley Allen: 60/16 (www.haslaw.com)
Partridge Snow: 35/13 (www.psh.com)
Shechtman Halperin: 21/18 (www.shslawfirm.com)
Winograd Shine: 10/6 (www.wszlaw.com)

South Carolina (Charleston)

Moore Van Allen: 24/6 (www.mvalaw.com)

South Carolina (Columbia)

Nexsen Pruet: 177/45 (www.nexsenpruet.com)
Turner Padget: 72/32 (www.tpgl.com)

South Carolina (Greenville)

Dority Manning: 18/5 (www.dority-manning.com)
Leatherwood Walker: 57/11 (www.lwtm.com)
Womble Carlyle: 22/8 (www.wcsr.com)
Wyche Burgess: 34/11 (www.wyche.com)

Tennessee (Chattanooga)

Baker Donelson: 36/12 (www.bakerdonelson.com)
Husch Eppenberger: 18/3 (www.husch.com)
Miller Martin: 84/16 (www.millermartin.com)

Tennessee (Knoxville)

Baker Donelson: 19/3 (www.bakerdonelson.com)
Harwell Howard: 29/9 (www.h3gm.org)

Tennessee (Memphis)

Armstrong Allen: 78/15 (armstrongallen.com)
Baker Donelson: 77/16 (www.bakerdonelson.com)
Butler Snow: 37/5 (www.butlersnow.com)
Husch Eppenberger: 32/21 (www.husch.com)
Wyatt Tarrant: 211/36 (www.wyattfirm.com)

Tennessee (Millington)

Navy Judge Advocate General Corps: 740/290 (www.jag.navy.mil)

Tennessee (Nashville)

Adams Reese: 33/4 (www.adamsandreese.com)
Baker Donelson: 77/16 (www.bakerdonelson.com)
Bass Berry: 179/59 (www.bassberry.com)
Boult Cummings: 96/12 (www.boultcummings.com)
Legal Aid Society: 25/10 (www.tba.org/LawBytes/T1_1002.html)
Miller Martin: 48/10 (www.millermartin.com)
Stites Harbison: 45/8 (www.stites.com)
Waller Lansden: 170/27 (www.wallerlaw.com)

Texas (Austin)

Akin Gump Strauss: 50/13 (www.akingump.com)
Andrews Kurth: 32/3 (www.andrewskurth.com)
Baker Botts: 57/10 (www.bakerbotts.com)
Clark Thomas: 123/57 (www.ctw.com)
Dewey Ballantine: 13/5 (www.deweyballantine.com)
DLA Piper Rudnick: 22/5 (www.dlapiper.com)
Fulbright Jaworski: 86/30 (www.fulbright.com)
Graves Dougherty: 64/9 (www.gdhm.com)
Jackson Walker: 56/10 (www.jw.com)
McGinnis Lochridge: 78/15 (www.mcginnislaw.com)

Scott Douglass: 42/9 (www.scottdoug.com)
Strasburger Price: 35/7 (www.strasburger.com)
Vinson Elkins: 81/8 (www.velaw.com)
Wilson Sonsini: 29/6 (www.wsgr.com)
Winstead Sechrest: 46/5 (www.winstead.com)

Texas (Dallas)

Akin Gump Strauss: 130/32 (www.akingump.com)
Andrews Kurth: 80/15 (www.andrewskurth.com)
Baker Botts: 160/23 (www.bakerbotts.com)
Baker McKenzie: 74/16 (www.bakernet.com)
Carrington Coleman: 95/15 (www.carringtoncoleman.com)
Fish Richardson: 45/8 (www.fr.com)
Fletcher Springer: 25/9 (www.fletchspring.com)
Fulbright Jaworski: 111/19 (www.fulbright.com)
Gardere Wynne: 173/24 (www.gardere.com)
Haynes Boone: 192/19 (www.haynesboone.com)
Hughes Luce: 148/14 (www.hughesluce.com)
Hunton Williams: 79/14 (www.hunton.com)
Jackson Walker: 120/13 (www.jw.com)
Jones Day: 184/25 (www.jonesday.com)
Locke Liddell: 178/20 (www.lockeliddell.com)
McKool Smith: 76/17 (www.mckoolsmith.com)
Munsch Hardt: 109/21 (www.munsch.com)
Sidley Austin: 24/10 (www.sidley.com)
Strasburger Price: 106/19 (www.strasburger.com)
Thompson Coe: 126/49 (www.thompsoncoe.com)
Thompson Knight: 210/30 (www.tklaw.com)
Vinson Elkins: 127/15 (www.velaw.com)
Weil Gotshal: 73/17 (www.weil.com)
Winstead Sechrest: 160/36 (www.winstead.com)

Texas (El Paso)

Scott Hulse Marshall: 38/12 (www.scotthulse.com)

Texas (Fort Worth)

Haynes Boone: 18/3 (www.haynesboone.com)
Kelly Hart: 89/12 (www.khh.com)

Texas (Houston)

Akin Gump Strauss: 91/20 (www.akingump.com)
Andrews Kurth: 229/51 (www.andrewskurth.com)
Baker Botts: 271/42 (www.bakerbotts.com)
Baker Hostetler: 65/7 (bakerlaw.com)
Beck Redden: 34/18 (www.brsfirm.com)
Beirne Maynard: 103/33 (www.bmpllp.com)
Bracewell Giuliani: 206/23 (www.bracewellgiuliani.com)
Fulbright Jaworski: 318/64 (www.fulbright.com)
Gardere Wynne: 96/35 (www.gardere.com)
Haynes Boone: 113/16 (www.haynesboone.com)
Howrey Simon: 86/32 (www.howrey.com)
Jackson Walker: 58/14 (www.jw.com)
Johnson Spalding: 25/15 (www.js-llp.com)
King Spalding: 73/17 (www.kslaw.com)
Locke Liddell: 157/16 (www.lockeliddell.com)
Mayer Brown: 60/13 (www.mayerbrownrowe.com)
Porter Hedges: 92/20 (www.porterhedges.com)
Sheehy Serpe: 45/21 (sswpc.com)
Strasburger Price: 47/10 (www.strasburger.com)
Thompson Knight: 99/14 (www.tklaw.com)
Vinson Elkins: 348/83 (www.velaw.com)
Weil Gotshal: 57/15 (www.weil.com)
Winstead Sechrest: 74/11 (www.winstead.com)

Texas (Huntsville)

State Counsel for Offenders: 22/21 (www.tdcj.state.tx.us)

Texas (Richardson)

Haynes Boone: 30/4 (www.haynesboone.com)

Texas (San Antonio)

Akin Gump Strauss: 67/19 (www.akingump.com)
Bracewell Giuliani: 30/10 (www.bracewellgiuliani.com)
Cox Smith Matthews: 122/11 (www.coxsmith.com)
Fulbright Jaworski: 63/29 (www.fulbright.com)
Jackson Walker: 28/7 (www.jw.com)

Utah (Salt Lake City)

Ballard Spahr Andrews: 35/12 (www.ballardspahr.com)
Holland Hart: 33/2 (www.hollandhart.com)
Snell Wilmer: 58/8 (www.swlaw.com)
Stoel Rives: 55/4 (www.stoel.com)
Van Cott Bagley: 45/5 (www.vancott.com)

Vermont (Burlington)

Downs Rachlin: 58/14 (www.drm.com)
Gravel Shea: 22/4 (www.gravelshea.com)

Virginia (Alexandria)

Oblon Spivak: 90/6 (www.oblon.com)

Virginia (Falls Church)

Reed Smith: 53/7 (www.reedsmith.com)

Virginia (Lynchburg)

Virginia Legal Aid Society: 10/6 (www.vlas.org)

Virginia (McLean)

Greenberg Traurig: 40/13 (www.gtlaw.com)
Hogan Hartson: 54/5 (www.hhlaw.com)
Hunton Williams: 42/11 (www.hunton.com)
McGuire Woods: 62/9 (www.mcguirewoods.com)
Pillsbury Winthrop: 96/10 (www.pillsburylaw.com)
Troutman Sanders: 25/7 (www.troutmansanders.com)
Watt Tieder: 69/12 (www.wthf.com)

Virginia (Norfolk)

Willcox Savage: 65/18 (willcoxsavage.com)

Virginia (Reston)

Cooley Godward: 58/12 (www.cooley.com)
DLA Piper Rudnick: 41/4 (www.dlapiper.com)
Finnegan Henderson: 33/4 (www.finnegan.com)

Virginia (Richmond)

Christian Barton: 43/6 (www.cblaw.com)
Hirschler Fleischer: 69/17 (www.hf-law.com)
Hunton Williams: 238/107 (www.hunton.com)
LeClair Ryan: 141/41 (www.leclairryan.com)
McGuire Woods: 210/55 (www.mcguirewoods.com)
Sands Anderson: 68/32 (www.sandsanderson.com)
Troutman Sanders: 124/27 (www.troutmansanders.com)
Williams Mullen: 113/23 (www.williamsmullen.com)

Virginia (Roanoke)

Gentry Locke: 39/15 (www.gentrylocke.com)

Virginia (Virginia Beach)

Troutman Sanders: 26/6 (www.troutmansanders.com)
Williams Mullen: 41/17 (www.williamsmullen.com)

Washington State (Belleview)

Davis Wright: 26/10 (www.dwt.com)

Washington State (Seattle)

Attorney General: 509/120 (www.atg.wa.gov)
Betts Patterson: 22/5 (www.bpmlaw.com)
Bullivant Houser: 42/14 (www.bullivant.com)
Cairncross Hempelmann: 40/8 (www.cairncross.com)
Christensen O'Connor: 43/15 (www.cojk.com)
Davis Wright: 174/23 (www.dwt.com)
Defender Association: 80/11 (www.defender.org)
DLA Piper Rudnick: 22/5 (www.dlapiper.com)
Dorsey Whitney: 71/24 (www.dorsey.com)
Garvey Schubert: 65/14 (www.gsblaw.com)
Heller Ehrman: 102/30 (www.hellerehrman.com)
Hillis Clark Martin: 39/11 (www.hcmp.com)
Karr Tuttle: 61/15 (www.karrtuttle.com)
King City Prosecution: 271/72 (www.metrokc.gov/proAttorney)
Kirkpatrick Lockhart: 150/36 (www.klgates.com)
Lane Powell: 115/40 (www.lanepowell.com)
Ogden Murphy: 26/6 (www.omwlaw.com)
Orrick Herrington: 17/7 (www.orrick.com)
Perkins Coie: 242/72 (www.perkinscoie.com)
Riddell Williams: 56/10 (www.riddellwilliams.com)
Ryan Swanson: 47/13 (www.ryanlaw.com)
Seed IP Law Group: 26/10 (www.seedip.com)
Stoel Rives: 77/14 (www.stoel.com)
Williams Kastner: 70/21 (wkg.com)

Washington State (Tacoma)

Gordon Thomas: 71/25 (www.gth-law.com)

West Virginia (Charleston)

Bowles Rice McDavid: 101/39 (www.bowlesrice.com)
Dinsmore Shohl: 16/4 (www.dinslaw.com)
Spilman Thomas: 65/14 (www.spilmanlaw.com)

West Virginia (Huntington)

Huddleston Bolen: 39/27 (www.huddlestonbolen.com)

Wisconsin (Madison)

Foley Lardner: 66/16 (www.foley.com)
Heller Ehrman: 10/3 (www.hellerehrman.com)
LaFollette Godfrey: 47/10 (www.gklaw.com)
Michael Best: 62/9 (www.mbf-law.com)
Quarles Brady: 35/5 (www.quarles.com)

Wisconsin (Milwaukee)

Davis Kuelthau: 52/8 (www.daviskuelthau.com)
Department of Justice: 88/21 (www.doj.state.wi.us)
Foley Lardner: 224/40 (www.foley.com)
Godfrey Kahn: 185/37 (www.gklaw.com)
Michael Best: 141/15 (www.mbf-law.com)
Quarles Brady: 178/35 (www.quarles.com)
Reinhart Boerner: 185/27 (www.reinhartlaw.com)
von Briesen Roper: 84/17 (www.vonbriesen.com)
Whyte Hirschboeck: 93/16 (www.whdlaw.com)

Wyoming (Cheyenne)

Holland Hart: 13/4 (www.hollandhart.com)

| APPENDIX 2.B | Summary Chart—Survey of State Government Job Classifications for Paralegals | | | |

Government	Position	Responsibilities	Qualifications	Salary
Alabama Personnel Dept. 64 North Union St. Montgomery, AL 36130 334-242-3389 www.personnel. state.al.us	Legal Research Assistant (11503)	• Assist staff attorneys by performing routine research into legal sources and into legal problems arising in connection with the operation of state departments and agencies • At a paralegal level, prepare and interpret basic legal documents • Handle routine administrative duties	• Graduation from an accredited legal assistant or paralegal program. • Possession of a legal assistant or paralegal certificate • 1 year of experience in legal research work OR • Graduation from a recognized school of law and eligibility to be admitted to the Alabama State Bar Examination	$26,620–$46,788 per year

Other position to check in Alabama: Docket Clerk (11501).

Government	Position	Responsibilities	Qualifications	Salary
Alaska Dept. of Administration Div. of Personnel 333 Willoughby Ave. Juneau, AK 99811 907-465-4430 800-587-0430 notes.state.ak.us (click "Workplace Alaska"; click "Job Class Specifications"; click "p")	Paralegal I (P7105)	• Research facts and the law • Prepare preliminary statements of facts • Examine and analyze evidence to determine if a violation, cause of action, or defense exists • Make oral and written recommendations for appropriate courses of action • Draft subpoenas • Serve and/or arrange for service • Assemble exhibits, affidavits, and other legal documents for use in case preparation and trial or administrative hearings	(a) 3 years of journey-level experience as a court clerk, law clerk, law office assistant, or criminal justice technician with the State of Alaska or the equivalent elsewhere; or (b) a bachelor's degree or the equivalent the social or behavioral sciences OR Certification from an American Bar Association–approved state paralegal training and education program OR Graduation from an associate of arts program in paralegal, criminal justice, or legal studies	$2,920–$3,354 per month (for Anchorage area)

Other positions to check in Alaska: Paralegal II (P7106); Investigator II (P7767); Latent Fingerprint Examiner I (P7756).

(continues)

APPENDIX 2.B	Summary Chart—Survey of State Government Job Classifications for Paralegals—*continued*			
Government	**Position**	**Responsibilities**	**Qualifications**	**Salary**
Arizona Dept. of Administration Human Resources Div. 100 N. 15th Ave. Phoenix, AZ 85007 602-542-5482 www.hr.state.az.us	Legal Assistant I (32201)	• Perform legal research • Write drafts of routine legal documents • Interview complainants or witnesses • Perform legal research	4 years of full-time paralegal experience OR Associate's degree in paralegal studies OR Associate's degree in any area PLUS paralegal certification through an accredited program	$29,142–$45,026 per year
Other positions to check in Arizona: Legal Assistant II (32202); Legal Assistant III (32203); Legal Assistant Project Specialist (32204).				
Arkansas Office of personnel Management 1509 West 7th St., Ste 201 Little Rock, AR 72201 501-682-1823 www.state.ar.us/dfa/opm	Legal Assistant (R177)	• Perform legal research • Check court files to inform attorneys of status of cases • Maintain law library • Prepare summaries of documents • File documents in court	1 year of paralegal experience OR 1 year of law school OR Other approved job-related education and/or experience	$20,822–$39,822 per year
California Dept. of Personnel Administration 1515 S. St., Ste 400 Sacramento, CA 94814 916-324-0455 www.dpa.ca.gov www.dpa.ca.gov/jobinfo/class/classification.shtm www.dpa.ca.gov./textdocs/specs/s1/s1820.txt www.dpa.ca.gov/textdocs/specs/s5/s5237.txt www.spb.ca.gov	Legal Assistant (JY66, 1820)	• Assist in reviewing legal documents to determine if they comply with the law • Do preliminary analysis of proposed legislation • Digest and index opinions, testimony depositions, and other trial documents • Perform research of legislative history • Assist in drafting complaints and other pleadings • Help answer inquiries on legal requirements	6 units of paralegal or undergraduate legal courses (3 of which are in legal research) AND 2 years of experience in state gov't in legal clerical or other law-related position OR 3 years as a law clerk or legal secretary in a law office	$3,164–$3,846 per month
	Legal Analyst (JY62, 5237)	• Investigate and analyze facts involved in litigation • Coordinate witnesses • Draft interrogatories and answers to interrogatories • Draft pleadings • Summarize discovery documents	2 years of gov't experience as a legal assistant AND 6 units of paralegal or other legal courses (3 of which are in legal research) OR 2 years of experience as a paralegal in a law firm or elsewhere AND 12 units of paralegal or other legal courses OR equivalent to graduation from college	$3,589–$4,363 per month
Other positions to check in California: Law Indexer (CX20 2957); Legal Documents Examiner (CW65 1829).				

(continues)

APPENDIX 2.B	Summary Chart—Survey of State Government Job Classifications for Paralegals—*continued*			
Government	**Position**	**Responsibilities**	**Qualifications**	**Salary**
Colorado Dept. of Personnel General Support Services State Centennial Bldg. 1313 Sherman St. Denver, CO 80203 303-866-2323 www.gssa.state.co.us	Legal Assistant I (H5E1XX)	• Conduct legal research • Take notes at depositions • Conduct interviews • Identify legal issues • Review documents for legal sufficiency • Monitor status of cases • Provide information on legal procedures	Bachelor's degree and certificate from approved paralegal studies program OR Work experience in the legal services field that provides the same kind, amount, and level of knowledge acquired in the required education. (This experience may substitute for the degree on a year-for-year basis.)	$3,268–$4,713 per month

Other position to check in Colorado: Legal Assistant II (H5E2XX).

Connecticut Personnel Div. Dept. of Administration Services 165 Capital Ave. Hartford, CT 06106 800-452-3451 860-713-5000 www.das.state.ct.us	Paralegal Specialist 1 (6140)	• Act as liaison between legal and clerical staff • Perform legal research • Assist in drafting legal documents • Maintain tickler systems • Present written and oral argument at administrative hearings • Maintain records	2 years of experience working for a lawyer (A paralegal degree or certificate may substitute for this experience.)	$44,428–$55,060 per year

Other position to check in Connecticut: Paralegal Specialist 2 (1641).

Delaware Human Resource Management Haslet Armory 122 William Penn Street Dover, DE 19901 800-345-1789 302-739-4195 delawarepersonnel.com www.state.de.us/spo	Paralegal I (93101)	• Reviews legal documents for completeness • Reviews laws to ensure compliance of legal actions/processes • Sets up case files • Gathers information to satisfy requests under the Freedom of Information Act (FOIA) • Writes and places public notices in qualified newspapers; notifies all involved parties of date/time for hearing, court appearances, etc.	Enough education and/or experience to demonstrate knowledge of (1) legal research, (2) interviewing, (3) record keeping, and (4) document maintenance. Also must have an ability to communicate effectively.	$27,963–$41,945 per year

Other positions to check in Delaware: Paralegal II (93102); Paralegal III (93103); Judicial Assistant (12355)

(continues)

APPENDIX 2.B	Summary Chart—Survey of State Government Job Classifications for Paralegals—*continued*			
Government	**Position**	**Responsibilities**	**Qualifications**	**Salary**
District of Columbia D.C. Office of Personnel 441 4th St. NW Wash, DC 20001 202-442-9700 dcop.dc.gov/main.shtm	Paralegal Specialist (DS-950)	• Prepare litigation/ administrative hearing reports • Summarize the factual situation, the basis of the appeal, legal issues presented, and relevant case law • Gather, sort, classify, and interpret data from various relevant legal sources	Applicant must have 1 year of specialized experience at the next-lower grade level. Specialized experience: experience that equips the applicant with the particular knowledge, skills, and abilities to perform successfully the duties of the position, and that is typically in or related to the work of the position to be filled. To be creditable, at least 1 year of specialized experience must be equivalent to at least the next-lower grade level in the normal line of progression.	$39,421–$50,761 per year
Florida Dept. of Management Services 4050 Esplanade Way Tallahassee, FL 32399 850-488-2786 dms.myflorida.com/ dms/workforce/ human_resource_ management	Paralegal/legal assistant (23–2011)	• Gather research data • Prepare legal documents • Maintain case files • File pleadings • Assist victims and witnesses • Answer routine legal questions • Assist attorneys at depositions and trials	The individual agency or the supervisor determines the level of qualifications preferred. Examples of possible preferences: • Completion of legal assistant or paralegal training • A degree or certificate in legal studies or allied legal services • Graduation from a school of law • 4 years of experience involving paralegal work • 4 years of experience in legal secretarial work	$1,970–$5,120 per month

Other positions to check in Florida: Law Clerks; Judicial Assistants; Legislative Aides (sun6.dms.state.fl.us/owa_broadband/owa/broadband_www. broadband_menu.bb_occ_grp?soc_str=23).

Georgia Georgia Merit System of Personnel Administration 2 Martin Luther King Jr., Drive SE Atlanta, GA 30334 404-656-2705 404-656-5636 www.gms.state.ga.us	Paralegal (95412)	• Draft legal documents for review • Assist in scheduling • Enter case data into computer • Perform legal research	Completion of a program of paralegal studies OR 2 years of experience as a litigation paralegal or judicial clerk.	$25,895–$45,453 per year

Other position to check in Georgia: Legal Assistant (95406).

Hawaii Dept. of Human Resources Development 235 S. Beretania St. Honolulu, HI 96813 808-587-1100 808-587-0977 www.hawaii.gov/hrd	Legal Assistant II (2.141)	• Prepare drafts of legal documents • Perform legal research • Summarize laws • Establish evidence and develop cases	4 years of legal experience OR Graduation from an accredited legal assistant training program.	$38,988–$57,708 per year

Other position to check in Hawaii: Legal Assistant III (2.142).

(continues)

| APPENDIX 2.B | Summary Chart—Survey of State Government Job Classifications for Paralegals—*continued* |

Government	Position	Responsibilities	Qualifications	Salary
Idaho Personnel Commission 700 West State St. Boise, ID 83720 208-334-2263 805-554-5627 www.dhr.state.id.us	Legal Assistant (05910)	• Identify legal issues • Perform legal research • Draft legal documents • Answer Inquiries • Conduct investigative interviews • Assist in discovery • Assist in trial preparation	Good knowledge of legal research method; the court system, court procedures, and legal ethics. Experience interpreting and analyzing laws, preparing legal documents, tracking documents on a computer database, etc.	$28,724–$47,860 per year

Illinois
Dept. of Central
   Management Services
Bureau of Personnel
500 Stratton Office Bldg.
Springfield, IL 62706
217-782-3379
www.state.il.us/cms
www.state.il.us/cms/
   persnl/specs/30860.pdf
	Paralegal Assistant (30860)	• Write legal memoranda and other documents for attorneys
		• Analyze hearing transcripts
		• Excerpt data from transcripts
		• Prepare statistical reports
			Completion of 4 years of college with coursework in areas such as prelegal, medical, English, and statistics
			<u>OR</u>
			Equivalent training and experience
				$2,886–$4,120 per month

Indiana State Personnel Dept. 402 W. Washington St. Indianapolis, IN 46204 317-232-0200 www.state.in.us www.IN.gov/jobs	Legal Assistant (22015/1VAS)	• Perform legal research • Verify citations to be used in memos and decisions • Maintain Files • Schedule hearings • Respond to requests for subpoenas • Supervise clerical staff • Respond to inquires from attorneys on current hearings • Assist attorneys at depositions	3 years of full-time paralegal experience in law office. (Accredited college training in paralegal studies, political science, business administration, prelaw, or a related area can substitute for 2 years of experience.)	$23,400–$39,052 per year

Iowa
Human Resources
   Enterprise
400 East 14th
Des Moines, IA 50319
515-281-3087
das.hre.iowa.gov/
   state_jobs.html
das.hre.iowa.gov/
   jd_legal_labor_
   safety.html
515-281-3087
	Paralegal
	(15004)
	(45004)
	(95004)
		• Prepare drafts of pleadings and motions
		• Conduct fact investigations
		• Perform legal research
		• File legal documents
			Graduation from an accredited paralegal program
			<u>OR</u>
			Experience equal to 2 years of full-time work as a paralegal or in a similar support capacity under the supervision of a practicing attorney.
				$31,678–$45,801 per year

Kansas Dept. of Administration Div. of Personnel Services 900 Jackson, Rm. 9515 Topeka, KS 66612 785-296-4278 da.state.ks.us	Legal Assistant (4093D3)	• Perform legal research • Draft legal documents • Maintain law library • Schedule witnesses • Coordinate subpoenas • Prepare trial notebook	6 months of experience as a legal assistant, paralegal, or legal secretary. Education may be substituted for experience as determined relevant by the agency.	$1,116–$1,495 biweekly

(continues)

APPENDIX 2.B	Summary Chart—Survey of State Government Job Classifications for Paralegals—*continued*			
Government	**Position**	**Responsibilities**	**Qualifications**	**Salary**
Kentucky Personnel Cabinet 200 Fair Oaks Lane. Frankfort, KY 40601 502-564-8030 866-725-5463 Personnel.ky.gov	Paralegal I (9856)	• Conduct analytical research • Investigate cases • Interview complainants and witnesses • Draft documents • Provide general assistance to attorneys in litigation	Bachelor's degree in para-legal science OR Postbaccalaureate certificate in paralegal studies OR Bachelor's degree with a minor in paralegal studies OR Completion of 2-year program in paralegal studies (Paralegal experience can substitute for some of the educations.)	$24,852–$32,924 (midpoint wage) per year

Other positions to check in Kentucky: Paralegal II (9857); Paralegal III (9858); Law Clerk (9801); Victim's Advocate I (9861).

Louisiana Dept. of State Civil Services 1201 North Third Street, Ste. 3-280 Baton Rouge, LA 70802 225-342-8534 www.dscs.state.la.us	Paralegal I (165650) (C1 PA)	• Perform legal research • Draft pleadings • Interview potential trial witnesses • Compose briefs and memoranda • Collect delinquent payments • Index legal opinions • Maintain law library	Completion of a paralegal/legal assistant studies program at a 4-year college, at a junior college, or at an otherwise approved school (Possession of a CLA certification from National Association of Legal Assistants will substitute for the education requirement.)	$24,170–$49,483 per year

Other position to check in Louisiana: Paralegal 2 (113470).

Maine Bureau of Human Resources State Office Bldg. 4 State House Station Augusta, ME 04333 207-624-7761 www.state.me.us/bhr	Paralegal (0884) (CFA8015103) (0699)	• Assist attorneys in completing legal casework • Explain laws and procedures • Summarize legal documents • Prepare pleadings and other legal documents	A bachelor's degree and 2 years of paralegal experience in a law firm, court, or legal services agency OR Graduation from an approved, accredited paralegal program of instruction and 1 year of paralegal experience (Equivalent related experience may be substituted for educa-tion on a year-for-year basis.) (Relevant experi-ence may substitute for educational requirement.)	$28,558–$38,604 per year

Other positions to check in Maine: Paralegal Assistant (0016); Senior Paralegal (0880); Legal Administrator (0885); Workers' Compensation Advocate (5242); Senior Paralegal (0880).

(continues)

APPENDIX 2.B	Summary Chart—Survey of State Government Job Classifications for Paralegals—*continued*			
Government	**Position**	**Responsibilities**	**Qualifications**	**Salary**
Maryland Office of Personnel Services and Benefits State Office Bldg. #1 301 W. Preston St. Baltimore, MD 21201 410-767-4715 800-705-3493 www.dbm.state.md.us	Paralegal I (0844)	• Perform legal research • Conduct investigations • File pleadings • Prepare witnesses • Draft correspondence on routine legal issues	High school diploma or equivalency certificate and 2 years of experience performing legal research or preparing legal documents for an attorney (A certificate in paralegal studies can substitute for the required experience.) Applicants may substitute 1 year of education or a certificate in paralegal studies from an accredited college or university for the required experience.	$26,429–$40,351 per year

Other position to check in Maryland: Paralegal II (0885).

Massachusetts Dept. of Personnel Administration One Ashburton Pl. Boston, MA 02108 617-727-3777 www.state.ma.us/hrd	Paralegal Specialist (10-R39) (Group 31)	• Answer inquiries on agency rules • Analyze statutes • Digest the law • Prepare briefs and answers to interrogatories • Interview parties • Evaluate evidence • Develop case tracking systems • Schedule appointments	2 years of experience in legal research or legal assistant work. (An associate's degree or a higher degree with a major in paralegal studies or one year of law school can be substituted for the required experience.)	$38,530–$55,671 per year

Other positions to check in Massachusetts: Legal Assistant (1291); Legal Assistant II (1292).

Michigan
Dept. of Civil Service
400 South Pine St.
P.O. Box 30002
Lansing, MI 48909
517-373-3048
800-788-1766
www.michigan.gov/mdcs
www.michigan.gov/
  documents/
  Paralegal_ 12243_
	7.pdf	Paralegal 8 (8020403)
		• Perform legal research
		• Conduct investigations
		• Draft legal documents
		• Prepare interrogatories
		• Digest and index laws
		• Serve and file legal papers
			Associate's degree in a paralegal or legal assistant program	

$15.77–$27.53 per hour

Minnesota Dept. of Employee Relations 200 Centennial Bldg. 658 Cedar St ST. Paul, MN 55101 651-259-3637 www.doer.state.mn.us	Paralegal (3611)	• Prepare legal documents according to prescribed procedures • Perform legal research • Collect information from clients for use by the lawyer • Investigate facts and law of cases to determine causes of action and to prepare cases	Completion of a recognized paralegal training program OR Bachelor's degree with a major in paralegal training OR 2 or more years of law school OR 2 years of varied paralegal experience	$32,886–$46,207

Other positions to check in Minnesota: Legal Technician (1541); Legal Analyst (2957).

(continues)

APPENDIX 2.B	Summary Chart—Survey of State Government Job Classifications for Paralegals—*continued*			
Government	**Position**	**Responsibilities**	**Qualifications**	**Salary**
Mississippi State Personnel Board 301 N, Lamar St. Jackson, Ms 39201 601-359-1406 www.spb.state.ms.us	Paralegal Specialist (1848)	• Interpret and explain laws to staff • Assist in preparing legal documents • Review reports • Assist in referring cases for prosecution • Perform research	Bachelor's degree and 1 year of experience in court filings, records, and appeals OR High School or GED plus 5 years related experience (of which 1 year is in court filings, records, and appeals)	$29,861–$52,257 per year
Other positions to check in Mississippi: PS-Paralegal Specialist (4264); Workers' Comp, Legal Assistant (4410).				
Missouri Office of Administration Div. of Personnel 301 West High Street, Rm 430 Jefferson City, MO 65102 573-751-4162 www.oa.mo.gov/pers	Paralegal or legal assistant positions are not found under the Missouri Merit System. Individual agencies not covered by the Merit System, however, may have such positions under the paralegal (9730) class. For example, the Missouri Office of the State Public Defender has a Paralegal Investigator I position. Duties include records retrieval, review of pleadings and transcripts, and investigation of factual claims. Qualifications include graduation from a paralegal program plus two years of paraprofessional experience OR graduation from a four-year institution with a major in criminal justice or paralegal studies. The position pays $2011 per month.			
Montana Dept. of Administration Personnel Div. Mitchell Bldg., Rm, 130 P.O. Box 200127 Helena, MT 59620 406-444-3871 doa.mt.gov hr.mt.gov	Paralegal Assistant I (119004) (249110)	• Perform legal research • Compile citations and references; check cites • Assemble exhibits • Explain laws • Arrange interviews and depositions • File pleadings • Supervise clerical staff	Graduation from an approved paralegal training program plus 3 years of experience as a paralegal assistant or equivalent in a law practice OR 2 years toward a bachelor's degree with courses in business or public administration plus 3 years of experience as a paralegal assistant or equivalent in a law practice OR 6 years of experience as a paralegal assistant or equivalent in a law practice	Grade 11 $21,773–$30,689 per year
Other positions to check in Montana: Paralegal Assistant II (119005); Agency Legal Services Investigator (168155).				

Nebraska
State Personnel Div.
Dept. of Administrative
  Services
301 Centennial Mall South
Lincoln, NE 68509
402-471-2075
www.das.state.ne.us/
  personnel
www.das.state.ne.us/
  emprel/JobSpecs/A/
  A31121.doc
	Paralegal I (A31121)	• Interview witnesses
		• Take sworn statements
		• Summarize depositions
		• Draft interrogatories
		• Draft pleadings
		• Act as law librarian
			2 years associate's degree from business school
			OR
			4-year bachelor's degree
			OR
			post-college course of a paralegal institute (Formal training has no preference over experience and can be freely substituted.)
				$39,237–$56,894 per year

Other positions to check in Nebraska: Paralegal II (V31122); Legal Aide I (C318131); Legal Aide II (C31812).				

Nevada
Dept. of Personnel
209 E. Musser St.
Carson City, NV 89710
775-684-0150
www.dop.nv.govdop.
  nv.gov/specs/2/
  02-159.html
dop.nv.gov/specs/2/
  pdf/02-159.pdf
	Legal Assistant (2.159)	• Perform legal research
		• Summarize cases
		• Draft legal documents, e.g., motions
		• File court documents
		• Answer inquiries on the status of cases
		• Communicate approved legal advice
		• Subpoena witnesses
			Completion of a 2-year paralegal course and 2 years of experience as a legal secretary at the journey level
			OR
			Designation as a Certified Legal Assistant (CLA) by the National Association of Legal Assistants
				$32,155–$47,000 per year

(continues)

APPENDIX 2.B	Summary Chart—Survey of State Government Job Classifications for Paralegals—*continued*			
Government	**Position**	**Responsibilities**	**Qualifications**	**Salary**
New Hampshire Div. of Personnel 25 Capitol St. Concord NH 03301 603-271-3262 www.state.nh.us/hr www.nh.gov/hr/ classspec_p/6793.htm	Paralegal I (6793–16)	• Maintain docket control and file organization • Conduct investigations • Review complaints of alleged violations • Help assess credibility of potential witnesses • Examine legal documents to ensure compliance with law	2 Years of experience in law or a related field AND An associate's degree OR A paralegal certificate from a certified paralegal program or 2 years of college with a major study in law (Substitutions are allowed.)	$26,832–$35,899 per year
Other positions to check in New Hampshire: Paralegal II (6792–19); Legal Assistant (5671–19); Legal Research Assistant (5676–24); Legal Aide (5660–15).				

New Jersey
Dept. of Personnel
44 S. Clinton Ave.
Trenton, NJ 08625
609-292-4144
www.state.nj.us/
   personnel
webapps.dop.state.
   nj.us/jobspec/
   02593.htm
	Paralegal Specialist (02593)	• Gather relevant facts in preparation for trial
		• Perform legal research
		• Assist attorney during trial or hearing
		• Review and answer correspondence
		• Review brief format prior to court submission
		• Interview clients and witnesses
		• Summarize depositions
			Associate's degree as a legal assistant or in paralegal studies, or an associate's or bachelor's degree and a certificate of proficiency in paralegal studies from an approved program
			OR
			2 years of experience preparing drafts of contracts, briefs, motions, affidavits, or other legal documents and/or experience in the analysis of laws and other legal material, and the preparation of summaries of the points of law involved
				$23,500–$33,000 per year

Other positions to check in New Jersey: Paralegal Technician 1 (30462); Paralegal Specialist Stenography (04785). Note: the Legal Assistant position (02275) requires a law degree.				
New Mexico State Personnel Office 2600 Cerrillos Rd. Santa Fe, NM 87505 505-476-7777 505-827-8120 www.state.nm.us/spo	Paralegal and Legal Assistant-B (H2011B) (Basic)	• Help prepare records and other legal instruments • Assist in interviewing clients • Investigate facts • Give clients information about the legal system • Conduct research to support a legal proceeding, formulate a defense, or initiate legal action • Operate copy machines • Prepare and maintain records • Handle routine legal correspondence	4 years of experience as a paralegal AND/OR 4 years experience performing general secretarial duties (College education in the secretarial/legal field may substitute for experience on a month-for-month basis.) Paralegal studies can substitute for 3 years of experience.	$22,610–$40,227 per year
Other positions to check in New Mexico: Paralegal and Legal Assistant-O (H2011O) (Operational); Paralegal and Legal Assistant-A (H2011A) (Advanced).				
New York Dept. of Civil Service 1120 Washington Ave. Albany, NY 12239 518-457-2487 877-697-5627 www.cs.state.ny.us	Legal Assistant 1 (2522210)	• Schedule witnesses • Assemble exhibits • Negotiate and propose preliminary settlements of fines as directed or authorized by the attorney • Cite check legal documents • Answer routine questions from the public	Associate's degree in paralegal studies OR Certificate of satisfactory completion in general practice legal specialty training from an approved school OR Law school graduation	$32,659–$41,705 per year
Other positions to check in New York: Legal Assistant Trainee I (2522230); Legal Assistant 2 (2522210).				

(continues)

APPENDIX 2.B	Summary Chart—Survey of State Government Job Classifications for Paralegals—*continued*			
Government	**Position**	**Responsibilities**	**Qualifications**	**Salary**
North Carolina Office of State Personnel 116 West Jones St. Raleigh, NC 27603 919-733-7108 www.osp.state.nc.us/ ExternalHome	Paralegal I (NC 01422)	• Draft legal instruments • Prepare routine opinions on agency • Handle complaints and inquiries from the public • Administer the law office • Perform legal research	Graduation from a certified paralegal school and 1 year of paralegal experience	$30,045–$45,462 per year

Other positions to check in North Carolina: Paralegal II (NC 1423); Paralegal III (NC 1424).

North Dakota Human Resource Management 600 E. Boulevard Ave., Dept. 113 Bismarck, ND 58505 701-328-3293 www.nd.gov/hrms	Legal Assistant I (0701)	• Draft legal documents • Maintain case files • Answer letters seeking information on laws • Maintain law library • File documents in court • Assist attorneys in litigation	Completion of 2 years of college in legal assistance or prelaw AND 2 years of experience in legal research analysis	$1,679–$2,798 per month

Other position to check in North Dakota: Legal Assistant II (0702).

Ohio Dept. of Administrative Service Div. of Personnel 30 E. Road Street Columbus, OH 43266 www.state.oh.us/das das.ohio.gov/hrd/ cspecs/classp.html	Paralegal/Legal Assistant (63810)	• Perform legal research • Review corporate filings • Prepare responses to legal inquiries • Prepare case summaries • Negotiate settlements • File documents in court • Schedule hearings	Completion of paralegal certification program OR Other evidence showing you have the legal knowl- edge and skills required OR Completion of 1 year law school	$29,453–$34,611 per year

Other positions to check in Ohio: Paralegal/Legal Assistant 2; Certified Paralegal (das.ohio.gov/hrd/cspecs/classpdf/6381s.pdf).

Oklahoma Office of Personnel Management 2101 N. Lincoln Blvd. Oklahoma City, OK 73105 405-521-2177 www.state.ok.us/-opm www.opm.state.ok.us/ jfd/e-specs/e30.htm	Legal Research Assistant (K101 FC: K10) (E30A)	• Perform legal research • Conduct investigations • Assist attorneys in litigation • File pleadings • Maintain law library	Completion of approved legal research assistant program OR Completion of bachelor's degree in legal studies OR Completion of 18 semester hours of law school	$23,211–$38,685 per year

Other positions to check in Oklahoma: Human Rights Representative (C15); Child Support Specialist (#30); Legal Assistant (Office of the Municipal Counselor, Oklahoma City).

Oregon Dept. of Admin. Services Human Resource Services Div. 155 Cottage St. NE Salem, OR 97301 503-378-8344 www.hr.das.state.or.us/ hrsd/class	Paralegal (1524)	• Help prepare written statements of facts • Review case files for sufficiency of docu- mentation • Provide litigation assistance • Manage computer- ized litigation support database • Prepare legal correspondence • Perform legal research • Cite-check briefs	2-year associate's degree in paralegal or legal assistant studies OR 18 months of paralegal experience OR Any combination of train- ing and experience that demonstrates experience in legal work, independent judgment, legal terminol- ogy principles, concepts, systems, and processes	$2,844–$4,184 per month

(continues)

| APPENDIX 2.B | Summary Chart—Survey of State Government Job Classifications for Paralegals—*continued* |

Government	Position	Responsibilities	Qualifications	Salary
Pennsylvania Office of Administration Bureau of State Employment Finance Bldg. Room 110 Harrisburg, PA 17120 717-787-5703 www.bse.state.pa.us	Legal Assistant 1 (07010)	• Review work of field personnel for possible legal implications • Summarize cases • Review files • Prepare reports	3 years of progressively re-sponsible clerical, auditing, enforcement, or investiga-tive experience OR Any equivalent combina-tion of experience and training	$26,386–$39,355 per year

Other positions to check in Pennsylvania: Legal Assistant 2 (07020); Legal Assistant Supervisor (07030).

Government	Position	Responsibilities	Qualifications	Salary

Rhode Island
Office of Personnel
  Administration
1 Capitol Hill
Providence, RI 02908
401-277-2160
www.dlt.state.ri.us/
  webdev/JobsRI/
  statejobs.htm
	Paralegal Aide
	(02461300)
		• Perform legal research
		• Conduct investigations
		• Answer questions by interpreting laws
		• Assist in litigation
		• Maintain files
			Graduation from a senior high school supple-mented by completion of an accredited paralegal training program
			OR
			Considerable employment in a legal office performing various para-professional duties relative to an exten-sive legal services program
				$30,009–$32,597 per year

Other position to check in Rhode Island: Legal Assistant.

Government	Position	Responsibilities	Qualifications	Salary
South Carolina Budget and Control Board Div. of Budget and Analyses Office of Human Resources 1201 Main St. Columbia, SC 29201 803-737-0900 www.state.sc.us/jobs	Administrative Assistant (AA75) [The Paralegal As-sistant classification was combined with about 30 other job titles to create the Administrative Assistant position.]	• Help perform legal research • Draft legal documents • Proofread legal documents	A high school diploma and work experience that is di-rectly related to the area of employment (The employ-ing agency may impose other requirements. Example: 2 years as a para-legal/legal assistant OR a high school diploma and 1 year of training under the supervision of a South Carolina attorney.)	$23,222–$42,963 per year

South Dakota
Bureau of Personnel
500 E. Capital
Pierre, SD 57501
605-773-3148
www.state.sd.us/bop
www.state.sd.us/bop/
  Classification/
  ClassSpecs/11205.htm
	Legal Assistant
	(11205)
		• Conduct legal research
		• Perform investigations
		• Summarize discovery documents
		• Draft correspondence and pleadings
		• Index trial materials
		• Act as client liaison
		• Attend depositions, hear-ings, and trials
			Note: South Dakota has discontinued using minimum qualifications for the majority of its career service positions. The clas-sification standards state the knowledge, skills, and abilities (KSAs) required for a position, but not how they must be obtained.	$24,350–$36,525 per year

(continues)

APPENDIX 2.B	Summary Chart—Survey of State Government Job Classifications for Paralegals—*continued*			
Government	**Position**	**Responsibilities**	**Qualifications**	**Salary**
Tennessee Dept. of Personnel 505 Deaderick St. Nashville, TN 37243 800-221-7345 615-741-4841 www.state.tn.us/ personnel	Legal Assistant (02350)	• Help attorney prepare for trial • Summarize laws and regulations • Maintain law library • Answer routine inquiries on laws and regulations	Associate's degree in para-legal studies, or bachelor's degree in paralegal studies, or a paralegal certificate, or 1 year of law school OR High school graduation (or equivalent) or 2 years of full-time experience in researching legal issues and documenting findings to assist in building case files, settling legal disputes, and/or providing legal counsel to clients	$2,518–$4,029 per month

Other positions to check in Tennessee: Paralegal (27094, 27096, 29720); Legal Aide—Court Administration (27133); Legal Assistant Tennessee Housing Development Agency (28878); Legal Assistant—Treasury (29426).

Government	**Position**	**Responsibilities**	**Qualifications**	**Salary**
Texas Texas State Auditor's Office State Classification Office Robert E. Johnson Building 1501 N. Congress Avenue Austin, TX 78701 512-936-9500 www.hr.state.tx.us www.hr.state.tx.us/ compensation/ jobdescriptions/ r3570.htm	Legal Assistant I (3572)	• Draft pleadings, legal correspondence, and other legal documents • Perform legal research • Coordinate service of subpoenas and notices of deposition • Checks citations, quotations, and footnotes for accuracy • File pleadings with courts • Organize case files • Help draft discover requests	Experience in legal as-sistance work. Graduation from an accredited 4-year college or university with major coursework in law or a related field is generally preferred. Experience and education may be substi-tuted for one another. May require certification as a legal assistant	$29,602–$41,892 per year

Other positions to check in Texas: Legal Assistant II (13574); Legal Assistant III (3576).

Government	**Position**	**Responsibilities**	**Qualifications**	**Salary**
Utah Dept. of Human Resources Management 2120 State Office Bldg. Salt Lake City, UT 84114 801-538-3081 www.dhrm.utah.gov	Legal Assistant (Paralegal) I (85508)	• Draft correspondence and other document • Maintain documents control • Digest trial folders • Conduct record searches • Prepare trial displays and provide other litigation assistance • Conduct interviews to gather or clarify information	Certificate in paralegal studies or equivalent consisting of 60 semester hours (or equivalent quar-ter hours) with 15 hours of substantive legal courses	$14.38–$22.81 per hour

Other positions to check in Utah: Legal Assistant (Paralegal) II (85510); Legal Assistant (Paralegal) III (85512).

(continues)

Government	Position	Responsibilities	Qualifications	Salary
Vermont Department of Human Resources 110 State St., Drawer 20 Montpelier, VT 05620 802-828-3491 www.vermontpersonnel.org	Paralegal Technician I (081800) (CLS 18)	• Assist attorneys in litigation • Conduct investigations • Interview parties • Perform legal research • Audit records • Interpret laws • Draft briefs and legal documents • Advise parties of their rights	High school graduate <u>AND</u> 4 years of experience or above senior clerical level, including 1 year of investigatory, analytical, research, or paralegal duties (30 college credits in legal or paralegal studies can substitute for general experience requirement; a JD degree is considered qualifying.)	$14.89–$23.01 per hour

Other positions to check in Vermont: Paralegal Technician (08230); Workers' Compensation Investigator (038600).

Virginia Dept. of Human Resource Management 101 N. 14th St. Richmond, VA 23219 804-225-2131 www.dhrm.virginia.gov jobs.state.va.us	Administrative and Office Specialist III (19013)	• Act as a specialist in assigned program area • Review and process claims • Gather and provide information • Interpret policies and procedures	High school graduate with at least 4 years of experience in office/business administration or a paralegal certificate	$22,188–$45,539 per year

Other position to check in Virginia: Legal Assistant (21521).

Washington, D.C. (See District of Columbia)

Washington State
Dept. of Personnel
521 Capitol Way S
P.O. Box 47500
Olympia, WA 98504
360-664-1960
hr.dop.wa.gov
hr.dop.wa.gov/lib/hrdr/
  specs/40000/
  46610.htm
	Paralegal 1
	(46610)
		• Organize litigation files
		• Enter data into computer databases
		• Conduct investigations
		• Prepare responses to interrogatories
		• Prepare trial questions
		• Prepare trial notebook
		• Negotiate claims
			2 years of experience as paralegal <u>OR</u> Graduation from 2-year paralegal course <u>OR</u> 4-year college degree plus 9-month paralegal program or 1 year of paralegal experience <u>OR</u> 3 years of legal secretarial experience plus 30 quarter hours of paralegal college courses	$39,732–$52,104 per year

Other positions to check in Washington: Paralegal 2 (46620); Paralegal 3 (46630).

West Virginia
Div. of Personnel
1900 Kanawha Blvd. East
Charleston, WV 25305
304-558-3950
www.state.wv.us./
  admin/personnel
www.state.wv.us/admin/
  personnel/clascomp/
  specs/9500.htm
	Paralegal
	(9500)
		• Perform legal research
		• Summarize evidence
		• Supervise clerical staff
		• Maintain case calendar of attorneys
		• Compose routine correspondence
		• Monitor pending legislation
			Completion of a paralegal assistant training program <u>OR</u> 2 years of paid experience in a legal setting performing legal research, reading and interpreting laws, and preparing legal documents under attorney supervision	$19,392–$35,892 per year

Other positions to check in West Virginia: Child Advocate Legal Assistant (9501); Lead Paralegal (9502).

(continues)

APPENDIX 2.B	Summary Chart—Survey of State Government Job Classifications for Paralegals—*continued*			
Government	**Position**	**Responsibilities**	**Qualifications**	**Salary**
Wisconsin State Employment Relations 101 East Wilson St. P.O. Box 7855 Madison, WI 53707 608-266-9820 oser.state.wi/us/dmrs/ documents/ 19201SPC.pdf	Legal Assistant-Entry (19201)	• Help prepare answers to discovery requests • Identify, locate, and interview witnesses • Prepare and arrange for service of subpoenas • Code litigation documents • Conduct preliminary legal research • Summarize transcripts and other documents, such as medical evidence • Maintain computerized databases	The qualifications required will be determined on a position-by-position basis at the time of recruitment. Hiring will be based on an analysis of the education, training, work, or other life experiences that provide reasonable assurance that the knowledge and skills required for the position have been acquired.	$14.61–$22.32 per hour

Other positions to check in Wisconsin: Legal Assistant Objective (19202); Legal Assistant—Confidential (19211; 19212); Paralegal (9500) (www.state.wv.us/admin/personnel/clascomp/specs/9500.htm); Paralegal (15001) (15010) (15020); Legal Associate (18301), a paraprofessional position.

| **Wyoming**
Human Resources Division
2001 Capitol Ave.
Cheyenne, WY 82002
307-777-7188
personnel.state.wy.us | Legal Assistant
(LG01) | • Prepare pleadings, contracts, forms, and legal memoranda
• Perform legal research
• Cite-check (verify accuracy of cited cases)
• Conduct factual investigations
• Interview witnesses
• Perform case management | 4 years of work experience as a legal assistant
OR
An associate's degree in paralegal PLUS 2 years of work experience as a legal assistant
OR
Certification from the National Association of Legal Assistants as a CLA (certified legal assistant) or CP (certified paralegal) or certification from the National Federation of Paralegal Associations as a PACE registered paralegal. | $3,188–$4,465 per month |

On-The-Job Realities: Assertiveness Training for Paralegals

CHAPTER OUTLINE

[SECTION A]

THE IDEAL

The practice of law is a high-performance arena of challenges, frustrations, and triumphs; it is not for the faint of heart. In this chapter, we will explore some of the major techniques needed to survive and thrive in the practice of law. Before doing so, we pause to examine the ideal.

What is a "perfect" paralegal job? Perhaps it is impossible to describe perfection in its fullest sense, but if we made the attempt, what would the description contain? Exhibit 3.1 presents such an attempt: it identifies forty factors of an ideal paralegal job environment. The factors are not of equal importance, and some of them overlap. Nor would every paralegal agree that all forty are needed. In general, however, these are the factors (not necessarily listed in order of priority) that must be considered according to many working paralegals.

| EXHIBIT 3.1 | Forty Factors That Can Affect Paralegal Job Satisfaction |

1. Your pay and fringe benefits are satisfactory (see Exhibit 2.14 in chapter 2 on possible fringe benefits).
2. You are respected and treated as a professional.
3. Attorneys in the office know how to delegate tasks and work with paralegals.
4. Before you are given a new assignment, your supervisor determines how it fits with other assignments still on your agenda. You are never uncertain about what has priority.
5. You are not in competition with new attorneys or other paralegals for billable hours.
6. Secretaries, office clerks, and other support personnel understand and accept your role. The office functions as a team.
7. There are clear lines of authority in the office. You know who to turn to for help if your immediate supervisor is not available.
8. Your work is adequately supervised.
9. The work you do is challenging.
10. Your paralegal skills are being used by the office; you are delegated meaningful tasks along with your share of mundane work.
11. There is a reasonable variety in the tasks you are asked to perform.
12. Demands on you to perform clerical tasks are reasonable, e.g., you perform them when deadlines must be met or when the office is short staffed.
13. Overtime requirements of the job are reasonable. (Overtime does not interfere with maintaining a work-life balance.)
14. There is no undue pressure to meet billable hour goals or quotas.
15. You look forward to coming to work every day.
16. You feel you are making a contribution to the office.
17. Your contribution to the office is acknowledged.
18. Your performance is regularly and constructively evaluated according to clearly articulated standards.
19. You share the same values as the people with whom you work.
20. The office has high standards of performance.
21. The office follows high standards of ethical and moral responsibility. The office can be aggressive in the practice of law, but its guiding principle is not to "win at all costs." You are encouraged to raise ethical questions about something the office has done and you know where to turn for answers.
22. In addition to being a business, the office demonstrates a commitment to the community through pro bono work and other volunteer activities that benefit society.
23. There is no sexism, racism, ageism, homophobia, or other inappropriate discrimination in the office.
24. You are given financial support and time off to participate in activities of paralegal associations such as CLE (continuing legal education).
25. Your work area and office equipment are satisfactory.
26. You have adequate access to clerical assistance.
27. Your privacy is respected.
28. When you need help in performing a task, you know what resources are available and you are encouraged to use them.
29. You are encouraged to develop new skills.
30. You participate in office training programs for new attorneys, administrative staff, and others when the training is relevant to your job.
31. You have some client contact.
32. You participate in major social events in the office. They are not always attorney-only events.
33. Office politics are manageable.
34. There is a good flow of communication in the office. The grapevine is not the sole source of information.
35. You attend regularly scheduled and well-run staff meetings.
36. People in the office know how to listen.
37. You have good rapport with other paralegals in the office.
38. Office policies and procedures are clearly spelled out.
39. The office has a career ladder for paralegals.
40. You can see (or are told about) the end product of your work even though you may not work on every stage of a case.

ASSIGNMENT 3.1

(a) Select what you feel are the ten most important factors in Exhibit 3.1. Write out your list and make a copy. Indicate whether you have ever had any law office work experience as a secretary, a paralegal, etc.

(b) Give the copy of your list to a person in the class whom your instructor will designate as the statistician. The latter will collect all the copies from the students and make the following tabulations: (1) which factors received the most votes on the "top ten" list by the students who have had prior law office experience; and (2) which received the most votes from the other students.

In class, discuss the results of these tabulations. Are there significant differences in the opinions of the two groups? Can you explain the differences or similarities?

We move now to the *reality* of paralegal employment. The forty factors obviously do not exist in every paralegal job. While most paralegals are satisfied with the career they have chosen, problems can arise in any occupation. Our focus in this chapter will be to identify some of these problems and to suggest resolution strategies. It should be pointed out that many of the problems we will be discussing are not peculiar to paralegalism. Sexism, for example, and the hassles of worker coexistence are certainly not unique to the law office. Indeed, this chapter is probably as much about human nature as it is about the paralegal career.

Some of the discussion will be directed at attorneys and what they must do to solve a particular employment problem. Yet a major concern of this chapter is what the *paralegal* can do to overcome difficulties, even those that appear to be beyond the control of the paralegal. According to Beth King, president of the Oregon Legal Assistant Association:

> Job satisfaction is one of life's most important assets. As such, it is something we should cherish and cultivate. We may blame a lack of job satisfaction on our employer or those with whom we work. In truth, satisfaction with our jobs lies within our control.[1]

[SECTION B]
COMMUNICATION

A busy law office is often a charged environment, particularly if the office is engaged in litigation or has a large caseload with a relatively high turnover.

> It is difficult to explain to outsiders the pressures of a law firm environment. Client demands [seem] never ending, equipment failures send staff into a frenzy, messengers run throughout the city like maniacs, . . . receptionists cannot find various personnel because they did not check in or out, the accounting [department] is complaining about time and billing, and priorities change every minute.[2]

When large projects or huge sums of money are at stake, careers are on the line. Attorneys, not known for their lack of ego, can at times have unrealistic expectations of those around them. In this atmosphere, communication can occasionally break down. According to a recent survey published by the journal *Legal Management*, "14 percent of each 40-hour workweek is wasted due to poor communication between staff and managers—amounting to a stunning seven weeks a year."[3] Here is an example:

> A senior partner thinks he told his paralegal to take care of an important filing. In actuality, all he told the paralegal to do was to *draft* the necessary documents to make the filing. The paralegal drafts the documents and puts them in the senior partner's in-box for his review. The filing deadline is missed. The senior partner blames his paralegal. The worst part of this scenario is that the paralegal is never told what happened or that she is being blamed. Perhaps the senior partner wishes to avoid a confrontation; perhaps he fears being told that the problem is not only his responsibility, but also his fault. In any event, the paralegal's reputation is smeared among the professional staff.[4]

In a case such as this, trying to establish the truth—what actually happened—can sometimes be fruitless. People may simply be in no mood for "explanations."

Source: Sheila Swanson, 14 At Issue 8 (San Francisco Ass'n of Legal Assistants).

The need, of course, is to *prevent* miscommunication. Be aware of the standard factors that contribute to communication problems:

- Distractions
- Time pressures
- Work overload
- Embarrassment over asking for clarification
- Personality conflicts
- Equipment breakdown
- Physical impairment (e.g., hearing difficulty, defective eyeglasses)
- Etc.

You can take specific steps to help avoid miscommunication. For example, immediately after receiving an assignment, repeat back to the supervisor your understanding of what you have been asked to do and find out what priority the task should have. For lengthy or complex assignments, send your supervisor a brief note or e-mail message in which you confirm what you have been asked to do and when it is due. Also, keep a personal **WIP** (work in progress) diary or journal in which you record your current tasks. Later in the chapter, we will examine such diaries or journals in greater detail.

> **WIP** Work in progress. A list of tasks on which you are currently working.

The danger of miscommunication in a busy law office can be quite high. If you are constantly aware of the danger, you'll be in a better position to help avoid a communication breakdown. It is a little like crossing the street. The busier the intersection, the more caution you must use to avoid an accident. Most law offices are very busy intersections.

[SECTION C]
EXPECTATIONS

A fair amount of paralegal frustration on the job can result from unrealistic expectations about the career in general and about a particular job. Frustration is mainly generated by surprise: "I never thought the job would be like this!" For example, most paralegal programs spend a good deal of time teaching students to do legal research. In many law offices, however, paralegals do not do extensive legal research. Research courses are important in your curriculum because of the understanding they give you about the legal system and the language of the law. Although you may eventually be given research assignments, do not enter your first paralegal job expecting to spend a great deal of time in the law library.

One of the objectives of this book is to provide you with information that will help prevent surprise. You need a candid account of what you might find. Chapter 2, for example, outlined steps on doing background investigation (due diligence) on a potential employer *before* you accept a job, such as talking with paralegals who have worked or who still work at the office. Following these steps, whenever possible, should give you a more accurate picture of what lies ahead if you take the job.

If you live in a seller's market where there are more applicants than jobs, you may be so anxious to obtain a job that you will overlook its potential negative aspects. This is unfortunate. It is essential that you walk into a job, or any situation, with open eyes. Not only will accurate information help reduce any frustration that may eventually develop, but the information will also be the foundation for corrective steps you can begin taking as soon as possible.

You need a lot of information. In the best of all possible worlds, you would have information relevant to each of the forty factors listed in Exhibit 3.1 that affect potential job satisfaction. (At a minimum, you would like information on the ten factors that you identified as most important in Assignment 3.1.) Of course, there are limitations on what you can learn now. Furthermore, even the information you receive can at best be a guide to your own prediction of how these factors might apply to you as an individual once you are on the job. This should not deter you, however, from going after whatever information is available about the paralegal field in your area and about particular prospective employers.

Whether the information you are able to gather is extensive or minimal, the healthiest attitude is to expect the unexpected. Be prepared for surprises about what supervisors think you are capable of doing, the level and quantity of assignments you are given, how secretaries and other paralegals in the office respond to you, who in the office will become the major influences on your growth and success as a paralegal, etc. This is not to say that everything you encounter will be a surprise. But it may not be a bad idea to proceed as if it will be. In short, be careful of your preconceptions about what is going to happen. Do not let them block the challenges waiting for you.

[SECTION D]

THE ENVIRONMENT OF A LAW OFFICE

When you walk into a law office, your first impression is likely to be that:

- The office is very formal and organized.
- The people here are set in their ways.

These impressions can be very misleading. A law office is in a state of perpetual *becoming*. The environment is always changing. New people are added, new clients come in, old clients are lost, new computer hardware and software are installed, new ways of doing things are developed, personality conflicts arise—numerous factors interact to produce an office that is in constant transition. Furthermore, *you* go through a process of change along with everyone else as the office continues to grow. On the surface, the office may appear to be a model of stability, but underneath all the layers of order and permanence, there is a *live* office that is in motion.

The consequences of this reality for the paralegal are twofold:

- Do not be deceived by appearances.
- Recognize your own responsibility and ability to help shape the environment in which you are working.

Assume that after being on the job for a while, you become dissatisfied with an issue such as salary, office procedures, or billable hour expectations. Avoid becoming defeatist; look for ways to bring about change. To solve the problem, suggest an alternative that others are likely to accept because it is cost effective and nonthreatening to their priorities. If you receive no response, suggest another alternative. Don't give up. As long as you are competent in performing your work, your supervisors will listen to you. Maybe not immediately. Your first suggestion may not be accepted. It may take six months and five more suggestions before you see improvement. Change usually does *not* occur within the timetable of the person seeking the change. If you are the type of person who wants every possible change made in every area in need of change, and you want all the changes made *now*, you may not have the temperament needed to survive and thrive in a busy law office. Change is possible, and you can play a major role in creating it as long as you are competent, patient, and creative enough to keep looking for ways to try to bring it about.

[SECTION E]

OFFICE POLITICS

Office politics is the interaction among coworkers who do not always have the same goals, expectations, abilities, or timetables for performing the work of the office. Because tension can arise out of this interaction, office politics often has a negative reputation. Everyone dislikes it. Most of us want to work where office politics does not exist. If this is not possible, our instinct is to blame others. We do what is right; others play politics.

These attitudes are illusions and interfere with your chances of bringing about change. "There are three things in life you can always count on: death, taxes, and the inevitability of office politics."[5] Whenever two people work together, politics is involved. When fifty people work together, politics is the order of the day. The "people you work with become your second family, complete with squabbles and jealousies. It is not possible to completely avoid confrontations or politics."[6] People often disagree about minor and major matters. As a result, conscious or unconscious *negotiation* becomes the mechanism by which things get done. Bargaining takes place all the time. More to the point, bargaining in the context of egos takes place all the time. There is simply no alternative to this process.

If there is harmony in an office, it is because people are engaged in *effective* office politics. People are trading what others want. Disharmony usually results from the fact that people are not responding to each other's needs.

Here are some examples of disharmony that can exist in law offices, particularly large ones:

- Rivalry among associates to become partners
- Dissatisfaction by partners over associates who do not log enough billable hours
- Dissatisfaction by associates that they are not receiving enough supervision and mentoring from partners
- Conflict among partners over the direction of the office
- Conflict between the office manager and the secretarial pool

office politics The interaction among coworkers who do not always have the same goals, expectations, abilities, or timetables for performing the work of the office.

Paralegals must be careful not to take sides when such conflict exists. At times, however, the conflict might directly affect them. For example, some recently hired young attorneys might be reluctant to delegate tasks to paralegals because the attorneys feel pressured to increase their own billable hours.

Paralegals need a two-part strategy: first, be competent; and second, publicize your competence. Ultimately, your goal as a practitioner of effective office politics is to demonstrate to others that your competence can help them do their jobs better. To a large extent, the paralegal profession was founded on this principle. Self-promotion by paralegals is not inconsistent with this principle. As you establish your credibility, you need to make sure that others know your worth to them and to the office.

> Blow your own horn: let the attorney know how you saved the client thousands of dollars, how you found the hard-to-locate witness, how you organized a huge file in mere hours, how the information you gathered helped win the case, etc. (Attorneys do this all the time.) Make sure your colleagues know of your special areas of expertise. For example, perhaps you are a good photographer, know everything there is to know about stocks and bonds, or speak several languages. (One paralegal I know dabbles in handwriting analysis; her firm found out and now she is a "handwriting expert.") Show an interest in other matters your firm is handling. Compliment an attorney with whom you are not presently working when you hear he/she won in court, closed a complicated big dollar deal, negotiated brilliantly, etc. . . . Be a real team player.[7]

> Ignoring, or worse, denying the ever-present politics of legal environments can be hazardous to your employment. You must be in-tune with the un-spoken; listen to your intuition and the grapevine. Stay out of gossip groups, keeping your ears open and your mouth shut. Watch how the attorneys interact with each other. Monitor power plays and coalitions. Make an effort to understand each of the attorneys you work with on an individual basis, and by that I mean: writing style, organizational preferences, demeanor. *You* must adapt to each attorney. . . . Strategize yourself when possible: work with other attorneys in your firm, or with outside co-counsel; assist baby lawyers without a demeaning attitude. (Remember that baby lawyers grow up to be associates and associates grow up to be partners.) Enlist help within and without your firm—usually persons you have no control over. You must appeal to them and win them over to help you. But be genuine! Everyone can spot a fake.[8]

What do you think of the following advice from another successful paralegal? "Set your goals and aim for them. Open your mouth and let people know that you're headed up. Search out greater responsibility. Work your tail off—and let everyone know about it."[9] Too extreme? Too risky? People really don't get ahead this way? You don't have to advertise talent because it will eventually be discovered without self-promotion? Maybe. Talk with successful and satisfied paralegals around you. Make inquiries. Take a long look at people you respect in a competitive environment. Try to assess whether their abilities might have gone untapped without a healthy, effective, measured dose of self-assertiveness. You will probably discover that they are comfortable with office politics and are not reluctant to use it to their advantage.

[SECTION F]

SELF-ASSESSMENT AND EMPLOYER EVALUATIONS

None of the techniques and strategies discussed in this chapter can ever be a substitute for your own competence as a paralegal. The techniques and strategies are designed to combat unrecognized and unrewarded competence.

Are you competent? To answer this question, you must evaluate yourself and receive the evaluations of others. Here are some suggestions for making both kinds of evaluations more meaningful, now and on the job.

performance review An analysis of the extent to which a person or program has met designated objectives. Also called *performance appraisal*.

- Carefully read the evaluation form in Exhibit 3.2.[10] (Such evaluations are also called **performance reviews** or performance appraisals.) First, note the standards used to earn a "Superior" rating and a "Very Good" rating in the eight categories being evaluated. These standards should be the day-to-day employment goals of every paralegal. Second, apply the form *now* to your present job or to any of your prior jobs, regardless of the kind of work involved. What ratings would you give yourself in the eight categories? What ratings do you think your supervisor would give you? (If you have never worked in a law office, simply substitute the word *supervisor* every time the word *attorney* is used in the form.)

EXHIBIT 3.2	Paralegal Evaluation Form

Personal and Confidential

Paralegal _____ Hire Date _____
Review Period _____ Department _____
Evaluating Attorney _____ _____

A. **CONTACT.** Indicate the contact you have had with the paralegal during the review period.
   — *Substantial* Regular, daily, or weekly contact. (Included in most attorney briefing/strategy meetings.)
   — *Occasional* Specific assignments and routine maintenance work requiring occasional personal instruction.
   — *Infrequent.* Limited contact.

B. **WORK PERFORMED,** Describe the work performed by the paralegal for you, listing some examples. Specify the degree of difficulty and expertise required.

   _____
   _____
   _____
   _____
   _____
   _____

C. **PERFORMANCE EVALUATION.** Evaluate the paralegal in each of the following eight areas. Check the blank to the left of the rating description that best summarizes the paralegal's performance. Use the space on the back of the last page for additional comments.

   1. **Work Product.** (Consider the paralegal's ability to understand what is required and to provide a work product that is both thorough and complete. Consider the speed and efficiency with which the work product is returned.)
      — *Superior.* In most cases, needs little instruction. Takes initiative in asking questions if aspects of the task are unclear. Is resourceful in developing more efficient ways to complete projects. Demonstrates ability to consider factors not indicated by attorney that make the work product more useful.
      — *Very good.* Needs instruction once or twice. Paralegal completes task thoroughly and keeps attorney informed as to work progress.
      — *Good.* Sometimes needs to do a task several times before he or she feels comfortable. Substantial attorney supervision is necessary during first attempts at a project. Once paralegal is comfortable with the job requirements, he or she does a thorough and complete work product.
      — *Marginal.* Has difficulty understanding what kind of work product is required. Sometimes does an incomplete job and takes more time than should be needed.
      — *Unacceptable.* Seldom masters what is required and hence cannot do a thorough and complete work product.
      — *No opportunity to form an opinion.*

   2. **Efficient Management of Workload.** (Consider the volume of work produced and the efficient use of time in order to meet deadlines.)
      — *Superior.* Highly efficient. Completes all assignments successfully, on time, and without prompting.
      — *Very good.* Efficient. Most assignments completed successfully. Rarely misses deadlines.
      — *Good.* Basically efficient. Assignments are generally completed successfully within a reasonable amount of time.
      — *Marginal.* Needs to improve efficiency. Assignments sometimes go uncompleted. Needs substantial attorney supervision.
      — *Unacceptable.* Inefficient. Deadlines are rarely met. Assignments often uncompleted.
      — *No opportunity to form an opinion.*

   3. **Ability to Work Well under Pressure.** (Consider the ability of the paralegal to make sound judgments and to organize work under pressure.)
      — *Superior.* Nearly always works well under pressure. Maintains organization and control over assignments; continues to make sound judgments.
      — *Very good.* In most cases works well under pressure; rarely makes unsound judgments or becomes disorganized.
      — *Good.* Generally works fairly well under pressure; sometimes makes judgments that are not carefully considered or becomes slightly disorganized.
      — *Marginal.* Frequently fails to work well under pressure. Tends to become disorganized and to exercise poor judgment.
      — *Unacceptable.* Rarely works well under pressure. Allows pressure to interfere with effective management of assignments and often uses poor judgment.
      — *No opportunity to form an opinion.*

   4. **Analytical Skill.** (Consider the paralegal's ability to digest and analyze the facts of a particular case or assignment and the thoroughness of performing factual research.)
      — *Superior.* Is exceptionally thorough in gathering facts and quick to master the facts. Depth of understanding is evidenced by a high-quality work product.
      — *Very good.* Is thorough in gathering information. Masters facts quickly and uses them well in preparation of work product.
      — *Good.* Generally thorough in gathering information. Masters facts over an acceptable period of time. Sometimes needs attorney direction in developing the information required for work product.
      — *Marginal.* Sometimes misses essential information during factual investigation. Knowledge of facts is incomplete. Needs substantial attorney direction in order to analyze facts correctly.
      — *Unacceptable.* Often misses essential information during factual investigation. Knowledge of facts is seriously deficient. Work product needs substantial revision in order to ensure completeness. Sometimes careless in presentation of facts to attorney.
      — *No opportunity to form an opinion.*

(continues)

EXHIBIT 3.2 Paralegal Evaluation Form—*continued*

5. **Professionalism.** (Consider the extent to which the paralegal is personally involved in his or her work; the extent to which he or she takes the job requirements seriously; and the extent to which he or she demonstrates responsibility for high-quality work in all instances.)
   — *Superior.* Exhibits exceptionally high level of personal involvement in assignments and is extremely responsible. Takes initiative.
   — *Very good.* Highly involved in assignments. Demonstrates strong commitment to his or her work. Very dependable.
   — *Good.* Generally dependable and involved in assignments. Demonstrates average commitment to his or her work.
   — *Marginal.* Frequently appears to lack interest in assignments. Needs substantial follow-up by attorney as to both deadlines and quality of work.
   — *Unacceptable.* Unwilling to assume the necessary responsibility.
   — *No opportunity to form an opinion.*

6. **Ability to Work Independently.** (Consider the paralegal's ability to exercise good judgment by making well-reasoned choices and then to maintain necessary communication with attorney.)
   — *Superior.* Considers all options and makes good decisions. Always keeps attorney well informed.
   — *Very good.* In most cases makes good decisions. Occasionally needs attorney assistance in defining options. Keeps attorney well informed.
   — *Good.* Usually considers options before making a decision. May not recognize the need to request attorney assistance in defining options.
   — *Marginal.* Has difficulty making well-reasoned choices after options are defined. Fails to cover necessary material with attorney and does not readily call upon attorney for assistance or explanation.
   — *Unacceptable.* Is not able to make reasonable choices after options are defined. Rarely keeps attorney informed and lacks understanding as to appropriate area of paralegal work as defined by attorney.
   — *No opportunity to form an opinion.*

7. **Quality of Written Work.** (Consider the ability of the paralegal to express himself or herself in clear, precise language; thoroughness; organization; accuracy and neatness; grammar.)
   — *Superior.* Exceptionally clear, precise, and thorough work that is neat and free from errors.
   — *Very good.* In most cases, precise, clear, and thorough.
   — *Good.* Generally acceptable but occasionally needs improvement.
   — *Marginal.* Frequently lacking in one or more respects.
   — *Unacceptable.* Work product is almost always lacking in one or more respects.
   — *No opportunity to form an opinion.*

8. **Outside Contact.** (Consider the extent to which the paralegal is required to work with persons outside the firm, such as co-counsel, clients, state and federal agencies, state and federal court personnel.)
   — *Superior.* Consistently demonstrates ability to readily gain the cooperation and confidence the assignment requires. Establishes excellent working relationships.
   — *Very good.* Generally gains cooperation and confidence. Establishes cooperation and confidence.
   — *Good.* Needs occasional assistance but is able to gain the necessary cooperation and confidence.
   — *Marginal.* Unable to handle outside assignments without substantial attorney assistance. Has difficulty developing necessary confidence and cooperation.
   — *Unacceptable.* No understanding of what is required in order to gain necessary cooperation and confidence. Complaints received with regard to paralegal's behavior.
   — *No opportunity to form an opinion.*

COMMENTS. On the back of this form, space is provided to allow for elaboration of any of the ratings checked under the preceding categories. You are encouraged to provide additional comments on the paralegal's performance: strengths, weaknesses, and suggestions for improvement.

- The ideal evaluation form is one that you and your supervisor design *together*. The goal is to have a form that is specifically geared to the tasks you perform in the office. Even if the office already has an evaluation form, think about ways to adapt it more closely to you as an individual. Make notes on what you would like to see in such a form. Discuss it with your supervisor. Your initiative in this regard will be much appreciated, especially if you make clear that your goal is to use the evaluation to improve communication and to find ways to increase your skills and productivity.
- Start preparing for your evaluation on the first day of your employment *and* on the day after your last evaluation. Do not wait until a few days before the evaluation itself.[11]
- When you work on large projects, ask for a "project evaluation" at the conclusion of the project. This evaluation should be in *addition* to any regularly scheduled evaluations you receive.
- Before a regularly scheduled evaluation, write a pre-evaluation memo and submit it to your supervisor. The memo should list the major cases or projects you have worked on since the last evaluation, your functions on each, names of your supervisors and coworkers on each, special accomplishments, events showing initiative (such as weekend work), written or oral quotations from individuals commenting on your work, etc.[12]
- Before an evaluation, review the criteria by which you will be evaluated, if available.

- Before an evaluation, review your job description. If your duties have been slowly changing, rewrite your job description to reflect these changes. Submit the revision to your supervisor for approval.
- If this is your first formal evaluation by a particular supervisor, try to talk with others in the office who have been evaluated by this supervisor before. Find out what you might expect from this person.
- After an evaluation, set some *measurable* goals. Do not simply pledge that you will "work harder." Establish goals that are more concrete. For example:
  - "Before January, attend a bar-association seminar or a paralegal-association conference covering an aspect of my job."
  - "For the next ten weeks, spend a minimum of ten minutes a day studying paragraph structure in grammar/writing books."
  - "Once a month for the next six months, go to lunch with a paralegal whose professionalism I respect in order to brainstorm techniques for improvement."
  - "Within five weeks, reread the word-processing software manual from cover to cover."
  Note that each of these goals can be placed on a calendar. You can determine whether each has been met. Of course, you should also commit yourself to broader goals, like learning how to digest interrogatories or improving your research skills. Yet be sure to include more objective, short-term, self-measurable goals as well.
- If you receive a negative evaluation, don't react defensively. You might want to ask for a few days to respond so that you can collect your thoughts. Although you will want to correct any factual errors made about you in the evaluation, little can be gained by trying to show that the boss is wrong. The best response is to discuss ways in which you can improve your performance. Before your next regularly scheduled evaluation, you may want to ask for a follow-up evaluation in order to determine whether you have made any progress on what was considered negative.
- Suppose you work in an office that does not have regularly scheduled performance evaluations. It never uses formal written evaluations. Employees are evaluated, but not on an organized, consistent, written basis. You need to become an advocate for a more structured system of evaluation. You will be successful if you can convince your supervisor of two things: structured evaluations have value and will not take too much of the supervisor's time. To save time, use evaluation forms such as the one in Exhibit 3.2. Or design your own evaluation form, as suggested earlier.
- If you are unsuccessful in getting a busy supervisor to give you formal evaluations, ask for brief oral comments on your work covering strengths and areas in need of improvement. Take notes on what the supervisor says, type up the notes, and ask the supervisor to read and sign or initial them. All you need say is, "I want to have something in my files. We are so busy that it's easy to forget six months down the road."
- A large factor in obtaining and learning from evaluations is your ability to handle criticism. Many of us are defensive when someone tells us something negative about our work or our attitude. Here are some suggestions on taking criticism:[13]
  - Listen to all comments without trying to influence or criticize the critic.
  - Be sure you understand the complaint.
  - Admit when you are wrong; it is a sign of strength.
  - Agree with the truth.
  - Admit when you do not know something.
  - Ask for clarification.
  - Ask for instructions or advice; be someone who is teachable.
  - Think of ways you can put the advice into action.

We will have more to say about evaluations later when we discuss ways to support a request for a salary increase.

[SECTION G]
CHARACTERISTICS OF SOME ATTORNEYS

The personality of a particular attorney has a great deal to do with the effectiveness of a paralegal-attorney working relationship. Many paralegals speak in glowing terms about their attorney-supervisor. Not only is the attorney easy to work with, but he or she also provides a challenging environment within which the paralegal can grow. Other attorneys, however, fall short of this standard; they do not function well as the leader of a team. According to two experts on the practice of law, a number of characteristics common to many attorneys do not encourage effective team building:[14]

Autonomy: Attorneys are less likely to collaborate than people in other occupations. Often they adhere to their preferred approach even when another is equally desirable.

Critical: The successful attorney is highly critical. Typically, the focus of the attorney is on what is wrong with an idea. The merits of the idea are often ignored.

Competitive: Like the very nature of the legal system, the attorney is competitive and adversarial. In policy questions and in personal relationships, progress and truth are achieved through varying degrees of confrontation.

Similarly, a professor of psychology studied twenty professions for optimism and reached the following conclusion:

[O]nly one profession demonstrated that success was correlated with pessimism, not optimism—the law. . . . Lawyers are trained to look for negative possibilities, for disasters, for unusual catastrophes. We want them to be diligent for our wills, our companies, our divorces, our contracts. . . . [L]awyers are trained to look for loopholes. This is why they cannot always be reflective listeners. They are listening to find something wrong with your logic. Sometimes they can't be sensitive listeners because they are listening for the rational logic that affects the content.[15]

It may not be easy to work with attorneys who fit these characteristics. The key to survival is assertiveness. According to one expert, many attorneys "prefer to work with assertive paralegals who are competent and knowledgeable. If you are not assertive with attorneys, they will lose confidence in you, and you may find yourself burdened with problems [including] . . . boring work, poor raises, and poor working conditions."[16]

Thus far in the chapter, we have referred to the importance of assertiveness a number of times. We now turn to a closer examination of this topic.

[SECTION H]
ASSERTIVE/NONASSERTIVE/AGGRESSIVE BEHAVIOR

Of the three behaviors discussed here, nonassertive behavior is the easiest to define. It is passiveness or undue silence. A nonassertive person rarely, if ever, complains to a person causing or contributing to a problem.

Aggressive behavior is at the other extreme; it is constant complaining. An aggressive person is a negative person who cannot express dissatisfaction without depressing someone else. Aggressive people may be right in many of the things they are saying, but they are so unpleasant that supervisors and coworkers seldom listen to them.

In between these two extremes is assertive behavior. Successfully assertive people:

- Are competent and display competence.
- Are prepared.
- Show initiative; do not always wait to be told what to do.
- Act like they belong in the office.
- Are always willing to learn.
- Respect the competence of others.
- Are problem solvers.
- Know that one of the best ways to help others solve problems is to provide them with options.
- Appreciate the value of timing; know that "now" is not always the best time to resolve a problem.
- Act like professionals.
- Do not shy away from office politics.
- Know the difference between griping and negotiating.
- Understand the necessity of compromise.
- Know the difference between little concerns and major ones; do not treat every problem as a crisis.

- Know when and how to lose gracefully.
- Advocate with resolve, not fanfare.
- Are self-assured enough to give credit to subordinates.
- Are willing to help others do their job well.
- Are secure enough to be able to say *no*.
- Are not offensive.
- Can express an opinion without putting someone down.

Assertive paralegals make themselves known. The backbone of assertiveness is competence—your work product meets high standards. The trump card of assertiveness is timing—you watch for the right moment to come forward. The foundation of assertiveness is preparation—you have collected all the facts that support your position.

Suppose, for example, you feel that you are not earning what you are worth. What do you do? You can take one of a number of approaches.

Nonassertive

You hope that things will get better, but you don't want to rock the boat. After all, your salary isn't *that* bad; it could be worse. You talk with fellow paralegals about your salary, and you are very frank with your aunt when the two of you talk on the phone about your work. But there's no sense in trying to get the firm to pay you more. The firm probably doesn't earn that much. And Mr. Smith, the head of the firm, is very pleasant to work with. Money isn't that important. Maybe next year will be better.

Aggressive

Three weeks after you begin your job, you tell your supervisor that your salary is ridiculous. "With inflation, how do you expect me to live on this salary?" When your supervisor is not responsive, you send a memo to all the attorneys in the firm demanding that "something be done about paralegal salaries." When you walk the corridors of the firm, you are always visibly angry.

Assertive

- You prepare a fact sheet of paralegal salaries in your area after you talk with paralegals at other firms and examine salary surveys conducted by local and national paralegal associations, such as the following:
  - *National Utilization and Compensation Survey Report* published by the National Association of Legal Assistants (www.nala.org)
  - *Paralegal Compensation and Benefits Report* published by the National Federation of Paralegal Associations (www.paralegals.org)
  - *Annual Compensation Survey for Legal Assistants/Paralegals and Managers* published by the International Paralegal Management Association (www.paralegalmanagement.org)
- You make sure that your supervisors have evaluated you regularly in writing. You summarize these evaluations and add them to the fact sheet.
- You make a list of the projects you have worked on. You highlight special projects, such as helping design part of the office manual or helping to train a new paralegal or attorney.
- You make sure that the decision-makers in the firm know who you are and what you have accomplished.
- You "know your numbers," consisting of (1) the total number of billable hours you have submitted over a designated period, and (2) your **realization rate**, which is calculated on the basis of what the firm actually collects from the billable hours you work.
- You have attempted to find out as much relevant information about the economics of the firm as possible, e.g., the percentage salary increase that the office generally gives employees, the extent to which the office (or your department in the office) was profitable last year and is profitable this year to date, and unusual expenses in the office such as the purchase of new computer equipment. Such events will inevitably have an impact on salary decisions made by the office.[17]
- You make note of every nonbillable task you performed that freed an attorney to devote more of his or her time to billable tasks.
- You discuss strategies for seeking a raise with other paralegals in the firm, with other paralegals in the area, and perhaps with some attorneys in the firm with whom you have developed considerable rapport.
- When others make a favorable comment about your work, you ask them to put it in writing so that it can go into your personnel file.

realization rate The hourly rate that a law office actually collects from the billable hours submitted by an attorney or paralegal.

- You select the right time to meet with your supervisor. You decide to wait until the supervisor is not hassled with a difficult case. But you don't wait until the next regularly scheduled performance review since salary decisions may already have been made by then.
- You may adopt a two-part strategy: you first ask for a meeting with your supervisor to discuss ways of increasing your contribution and productivity. At a follow-up meeting, you bring up the topic of a salary increase.
- Months before you ask for a raise, you ask your supervisor to identify those factors that will be taken into consideration in evaluating your overall performance and in recommending a salary level. In the months that follow, you make sure that you organize your efforts and your notes in accordance with the criteria the supervisor initially identified.
- If you are unsuccessful in obtaining the raise you are seeking, you have a fall-back position ready—for example, you seek a performance bonus in lieu of a raise; additional insurance, educational tuition reimbursement, or other fringe benefits; perhaps a different office setting; or **flextime**.

flextime A system that allows employees some control over aspects of their work schedule such as the times that they arrive at and leave from work during the day.

If you ask successful paralegals about their secret of success (see Exhibit 3.3), one message will come through loud and clear: *Seize the initiative.* No one is going to hand you anything simply because you are smart or because you have a certificate. You must prove yourself. You must be assertive.

EXHIBIT 3.3	**Taking the Initiative: Recommendations of Successful Paralegals**

Tami Coyne:
I have heard this tired refrain many times: "I am a hard worker and just don't get the recognition or the responsibility I deserve." This attitude gets you nowhere. If you believe that it is up to your employer to pick you out of the crowd and reward you just because you do your job, you will be sorely disappointed. In order to advance as a paralegal, you must prove that you are capable of taking on greater responsibility by performing your present duties exceptionally well. Show your initiative by anticipating the next stage of any assignment and completing it before you are asked to do it. Do not wait for recognition or feedback. You must be the one to initiate a feedback discussion after you have completed an assignment.[18]

Renee Sova:
Volunteer to draft the next document. Say, "I can do that; will you let me try?" Patience is a virtue. If the lawyer doesn't accommodate your first request, keep asking. Upon receiving and ultimately completing the assignment, there is nothing wrong with asking: "What could I have done differently to make it better?" This shows you truly care about your work product. Always do more than is expected. Few professionals became successful [by leaving] their careers to fate.[19]

Laurie Roselle:
If you feel like a second-class citizen, that's the way you will be treated—and that's how you should be treated. However, if you want respect in this profession, you must command it. To command this respect, you must be an intelligent professional willing to take on responsibility without having to be asked. Find ways to make yourself even more valuable than you already appear to be. Don't sit and complain about the way things are. Take charge and change them.[20]

Carol Musick:
Stay current on file status. Don't wait to be told to do something. Attorneys don't have time to spoon feed their paralegals. Stay current and find out "what comes next" on your own initiative.[21]

Marian Johnson:
The greatest key to success is something no one can give you—a good attitude! Enthusiasm has nothing to do with noise; it has more to do with motivation. It deals with our attitude. An attitude is something you can do something about. I can choose to be enthusiastic or I can choose not to be. Excitement is infectious. It's sort of like a case of the measles. You can't infect someone unless you have the real thing![22]

Chere Estrin:
Be assertive. Take an attorney to lunch![23]

[SECTION I]

KEEPING A DIARY OR JOURNAL AND A CAREER DEVELOPMENT FILE

Earlier in the chapter, we discussed the importance of having a personal diary or journal in which you regularly record your WIP (work in progress). Specifically, the diary or journal should contain the following:

- Notes on the assignments you are given (e.g., what you were asked to do, date you received the assignment, its due date, feedback received before completion, changes in the assignment made by the supervisor, sources consulted, and date completed)
- Names of the parties on both sides of cases on which you have performed tasks
- Favorable and unfavorable comments (written or oral) on your work
- Total billable hours per day attributable to your work
- Your realization rate
- Dates when you work evenings and weekends
- Dates when you work at home
- Dates you were late, were absent, or had to leave early
- Dates when you came in early or worked through lunch hour
- Names of any clients you referred to the firm
- Time you spent doing your own typing or photocopying
- Time you spend in courses, seminars, or other ventures to improve your skills

You need to have the facts of your employment at your command. The diary or journal is your personal record; you keep it to yourself for use as needed. Not only will the facts be valuable when you are making an argument for a raise, but they might also be essential when misunderstandings arise about what you have or have not done.

The diary or journal may be burdensome for you at first, and you may not make use of it for a while. It is worth the burden and the wait. A law firm respects someone who has the facts, particularly with dates!

In addition, start a *career development file* that contains everything that is relevant to your employment and growth as a paralegal. It should include:

- *Résumés.* A copy of every résumé you have written, including a current one that you should update every two or three months.
- *Job history.* A record of the dates you were hired in previous and current jobs; who hired you; who supervised you; a copy of your job descriptions; starting salary; amounts and dates of raises, bonuses, and other benefits received; dates and reasons you left.
- *Work accomplishments.* A copy of every written evaluation; letters received from clients commenting on your work; verbal comments made about your work by supervisors that you later wrote down.
- *Professional activities.* Evidence of your involvement with paralegal associations; attendance at conferences, seminars, and classes (including names of major teachers, copies of syllabi, etc.); speaking engagements; articles you have written for paralegal newsletters.
- *Conflict-of-interest data.* A list of the cases on which you worked, including the exact names of all clients, opposing parties, and opposing attorneys; a brief description of your role in each case; the dates of your involvement in these cases. (These data may be needed when you seek employment with another law office that wants to avoid being disqualified from a case because of your involvement with a particular party at a prior job. See chapter 5.)

Now you are ready. You have what you need when you sit down with management to discuss the raise for which you have been patiently waiting. If there is a career ladder in the office, you have assembled what will be relevant if the time comes to demonstrate that you deserve the next step up the ladder. Even if you are not looking for another job, you are ready to pursue unexpected opportunities that can't be passed up.[24]

ASSIGNMENT 3.2

To practice keeping a diary or journal, create a school log in which you chronologically list every assignment, the date you received it, what you were asked to do, the due date, the date submitted, and any comments or grade you received. Also record the date and substance of all contacts with your teachers outside of class. Finally, include anything you do to further your education that is not required, e.g., read an article mentioned in the bibliography of one of your textbooks or attend a meeting of the local paralegal association.

[SECTION J]

PARALEGAL CLE

continuing legal education
(CLE) Training in the law (usually short term) that a person
receives after completing his or
her formal legal training.

Elsewhere in this book we have stressed the reality that your legal education never ends. There is always something to learn. This is true for attorneys, and it is certainly true for paralegals. Education after employment is referred to as **continuing legal education (CLE)**. CLE is offered mainly by or through a bar association or a paralegal association. (To locate specific CLE programs for paralegals, see Helpful Web Sites at the end of the chapter.) There are two main ways in which CLE takes place. The traditional way is to go to a brick-and-mortar building such as a downtown hotel facility. The training might occur on a workday afternoon or on a Saturday. Alternatively, a great deal of CLE is now offered online so that the course can be taken at any time during the week. (To find CLE courses in your area, see the sites listed under "Continuing Legal Education" at the end of this chapter.) CLE is significantly different from the paralegal education you initially received. CLE is usually short term; most courses can be completed in one day or less. Because CLE occurs while you are employed, you are able to select seminars that directly and immediately relate to your day-to-day job responsibilities. Here is an example of this reality from Felicia Garant, a paralegal in Maine:

> I had an experience where I attended a half-day title insurance seminar and passed around a memo to attorneys in my section of the firm summarizing what I had learned there. A few minutes after I circulated the memo, an attorney flew out of his office exclaiming, "There's a new law on this subject?" He asked me to help him get a copy of the law since he had a case at that time that would be directly affected. You are the attorney's extra pair of eyes and ears, and you may pick up something at these seminars which will be new to the attorney. Your attendance at seminars, educating yourself, then passing the information on to the attorney not only increases your qualification as a legal assistant, but also makes you a valuable employee.[25]

CLE is not limited to substantive law topics. According to a survey of legal staff, the top CLE subjects were as follows:[26]

68% software training
59% time management
57% getting along with difficult people
42% effective use of e-mail
29% electronic filing (e-filing) of court documents

Often, the employer is willing to pay all or part of your expenses in attending such seminars and to give you time off if they occur during work hours. (See Exhibit 2.14 in chapter 2 for an overview of fringe benefits some paralegals receive.) Even if your employer refuses to pay for them, you should go on your own time and at your own expense. Few things are more important to the professional development of a paralegal than CLE—and what you pay out-of-pocket is tax deductible.[27]

In almost every state, attorneys must attend a designated number of CLE hours per year as a condition of maintaining their license to practice law. As we will see in chapter 4, CLE is required of all paralegals in California. The failure to comply with California's mandatory CLE requirement can lead to a fine and imprisonment! Mandatory CLE for paralegals, however, does not exist in most states.

The voluntary certification programs of the major national paralegal associations (NALA, NFPA, and NALS) require a designated number of CLE hours to maintain the certification earned after passing their examination. (See Exhibit 4.7 in chapter 4.)

[SECTION K]

RESPONSIBILITIES OF SUPERVISORS

What is a good attorney supervisor? The checklist in Exhibit 3.4 lists the factors that constitute effective supervision. You might cautiously consider showing this checklist to your supervisors so that they might evaluate themselves as supervisors. Do not do this, however, until you are well established in your job. Considerable tact is needed when suggesting that a supervisor might be less than perfect.

EXHIBIT 3.4	Checklist for Effective Supervision of Paralegals

(Grade each factor on a scale of 1 to 5 with a 5 indicating that the supervisor is excellent in this factor and 1 indicating an unsatisfactory rating.)

FACTOR	RATING (on a scale of 1–5)
a. You give clear instructions to the paralegal on assignments.	a. _____
b. You do not overburden the paralegal with assignments. Before you give a new assignment, you determine what the paralegal already has to do. If the demands on a paralegal are great, you consider alternatives such as hiring temporary paralegal help.	b. _____
c. You provide reasonable deadlines on assignments, with adequate time built in for review and redrafting where appropriate.	c. _____
d. Whenever possible, you involve the paralegal at the beginning of a case, e.g., at the initial client interview.	d. _____
e. You take affirmative steps to inquire about the paralegal's progress on assignments to determine if you should offer more guidance or if deadline extensions are needed. You do not simply wait for the paralegal to come to you with problems.	e. _____
f. You provide adequate training for each assignment given. You take the time to make sure the paralegal can perform the task.	f. _____
g. You are not afraid to delegate tasks to the paralegal.	g. _____
h. You delegate meaningful tasks, not just routine tasks.	h. _____
i. You make sure that the paralegal has some variety in his or her work.	i. _____
j. You are supportive when the paralegal makes a mistake; your corrective suggestions for the future are constructive.	j. _____
k. You regularly inform the paralegal about the status of a case, even with regard to aspects of the case on which the paralegal is not working.	k. _____
l. You permit paralegals to experience the end product of cases on which they are working, e.g., you give them a copy of the finished product, or you invite them to your court presentation.	l. _____
m. You include the paralegal in strategy meetings on cases.	m. _____
n. You occasionally encourage the paralegal to use the law library in order to increase his or her knowledge and to appreciate the legal context of a case.	n. _____
o. You use the paralegal's skills and regularly look for ways the paralegal can increase his or her skills.	o. _____
p. You encourage paralegals to give their opinion on cases and on office policy.	p. _____
q. You design systems with instructions, checklists, forms, etc., for the performance of tasks involving paralegals.	q. _____
r. You encourage the paralegal to help you write these systems.	r. _____
s. You regularly evaluate the paralegal, informally and in writing.	s. _____
t. You encourage the paralegal to help you design a relevant paralegal evaluation form.	t. _____
u. You encourage the paralegal to evaluate you as a supervisor.	u. _____
v. You give credit to the paralegal where credit is due.	v. _____
w. You make sure others in the firm know about the contribution of the paralegal.	w. _____
x. You lobby with other attorneys who do not use paralegals or do not appreciate their value in order to change their attitude.	x. _____
y. You make yourself aware of any tension that may exist among paralegals, secretaries, and other staff members in the office in order to help end the tension.	y. _____
z. You back the paralegal's reasonable requests on salary and working conditions.	z. _____
aa. You introduce your clients to the paralegal, explain the latter's role, and express your confidence in your employee.	aa. _____
bb. You do not unduly pressure the paralegal about producing a quota of billable hours.	bb. _____
cc. You make sure the paralegal has suitable office space, supplies, secretarial support, access to computer support, etc.	cc. _____
dd. When changes are made in office procedures that affect paralegals, you let them know in advance so that they can make suggestions about the changes.	dd. _____
ee. You support the paralegal's need for financial help (and time off) to attend outside training programs (CLE).	ee. _____
ff. You support the paralegal's need for financial help (and time off) to participate in the activities of paralegal associations.	ff. _____
gg. You recognize that the paralegal, like any employee, will need reasonable time off to attend to pressing personal matters.	gg. _____
hh. You consider letting the paralegal have reasonable time off to do some pro bono work (e.g., time donated to poverty law offices or public interest law firms).	hh. _____
ii. You don't assume that the paralegal is happy about his or her job simply because you have no complaints and the paralegal hasn't expressed dissatisfaction; you take the initiative to find out what is on the paralegal's mind.	ii. _____
jj. You treat the paralegal as an individual.	jj. _____
kk. You treat the paralegal as a professional.	kk. _____

"I'm headed out for a show tonight, and tomorrow I'll be at the golf tournament. I know the report is due tomorrow. I'll ask Helen, my paralegal, to do the report. She needs something to do."

[SECTION L]

RELATIONSHIP WITH SECRETARIES

At one time, many secretaries, particularly those in smaller law offices, resented the hiring of paralegals. This friction arose for a number of reasons, as the following overview points out:

> Historically, the legal secretary was "queen" of her territory. The more competent she was, the more control she had over her immediate environment—how the office looked, how the work was done, how the clients were handled, and for that matter, how the lawyer was trained. The longer she worked with one lawyer, the more responsibility she was given, and the better she got at her job. In the office of the sole practitioner, the practice could go on smoothly even if the lawyer was in court or out of town. She was just about as indispensable as one person could be. There was a relationship of mutual trust and respect between the legal secretary and the lawyer that was practically impenetrable. Then along came the legal assistant, intruding on the legal secretary's territory, doing many of the things that the legal secretary had been doing for years. To add insult to injury, the legal secretary was expected to perform secretarial work for the legal assistant![28]

Fortunately, this problem is less prevalent today. In most law firms, secretaries and paralegals work together smoothly. Yet tension can occasionally surface, particularly over the issue of titles. As we saw in chapter 1, a large number of secretaries have begun to call themselves legal assistants without obtaining additional legal training. An attorney employer might encourage this title switch in order to increase the likelihood of collecting paralegal fees for their work.

Part of the confusion over titles is due to the fact that there is an overlap of functions in many law offices. There are attorneys who perform paralegal tasks, secretaries who perform paralegal tasks, and paralegals who perform attorney tasks. On paper, the three roles are distinct, but in practice, there can be considerable overlap, particularly in smaller law offices. Furthermore, computers on every desk make it possible for individuals to increase the variety of tasks that they perform. In times of pressure (e.g., during a trial or when a large commercial transaction must be completed before a looming deadline), everyone tends to pull together by doing whatever it takes to accomplish the task at hand. During a crisis, you rarely hear anyone say, "That's not my job."

In light of this reality, it is understandable that some legal secretaries are ambivalent about their title. The paralegal occupation grew out of the legal secretary occupation. Before paralegal training programs became commonplace, most paralegals came from the ranks of legal secretaries. Many secretaries were members of NALS, the National Association of Legal Secretaries. As the paralegal field grew, paralegals started forming their own associations. In fact, the National Association of Legal Assistants (NALA) was initially formed as a breakaway association from NALS. Both associations are still headquartered in Tulsa, Oklahoma. NALS, however, does *not* consider itself to be a secretaries-only association. Recently, it changed its name from the National Association of Legal Secretaries to NALS, the Association for Legal Professionals (www.nals.org). In addition to its certification program for legal secretaries, NALS has also launched its own examination for legal assistants and paralegals, leading to certification as a professional paralegal (PP), as we will see in greater detail in chapter 4.

Clearly, the relationship between paralegals and legal secretaries is still evolving.

It is highly unlikely, however, that you will experience turf battles with secretaries. When problems arise, they most likely will be due to normal interoffice tension in a busy environment. On those occasions when you are allowed to have the assistance of a secretary, consider the following recommendations for a smooth working relationship.[29]

- Never assume a legal secretary knows less than you.[30]
- Give the secretary accurate, detailed instructions along with a reasonable timetable for completion.
- Make sure your written instructions are legible.
- Avoid waiting until the last minute to assign work that you know about beforehand.
- Don't pawn off undesirable chores that are rightly yours.
- Limit interruptions.
- Make yourself available to discuss problems or questions that arise during the performance of a task.
- Provide all the tools necessary to complete a job.
- Look for ways to recognize the contribution of secretaries. (The Rhode Island Paralegal Association, for example, conducts an annual secretary-appreciation luncheon.) "Remember that a pat on the back is just a few vertebrae removed from a kick in the pants, but miles ahead in results."[31]
- A cheerful demeanor can go a long way toward making your relationship more pleasant. Treat your secretary the way you wish to be treated, and don't forget basic courtesies, such as saying, "Good morning" and "Have a nice evening."

Paralegals sometimes complain that attorneys do not treat paralegals with respect. How ironic that an insensitive paralegal could become subject to this same criticism.

[SECTION M]

SEXUAL HARASSMENT

Sexual harassment consists of unwelcome sexual advances, requests for sexual favors, and other verbal or physical conduct of a sexual nature when this conduct explicitly or implicitly affects an individual's employment, unreasonably interferes with an individual's work performance, or creates an intimidating, hostile, or offensive work environment. When submission is made a condition of employment or of a benefit of employment (e.g., promotion), the harassment is called **quid pro quo harassment**. If the offending conduct unreasonably interferes with work performance or creates an offensive working environment (even if no conditions are imposed), the harassment is sometimes called **hostile environment harassment**. An example of the latter would be an office that is significantly pervaded by sexual commentary, off-color jokes, offensive pictures, or generalized sexual conduct even if there is no direct trading of sexual favors for employment benefits.[32]

An employer must actively combat sexual harassment by:

- Establishing a written policy against sexual harassment and distributing it throughout the office,
- Investigating all accusations of sexual harassment promptly,
- Establishing appropriate sanctions for employees who commit sexual harassment,
- Informing employees of their right to bring a charge of sexual harassment under Title VII of the Civil Rights Act of 1964, and
- Informing employees how to bring a charge of sexual harassment under Title VII.

It is not a defense for an employer to say he or she did not know that one of the employees engaged in sexual harassment of another employee or that the harassment took place in spite of an office policy forbidding it. If the employer *should have known of the harassing conduct*, the employer must take immediate and appropriate corrective action beyond merely telling all employees not to engage in sexual harassment.

quid pro quo harassment Unwelcome sexual advances, requests for sexual favors, and other verbal or physical conduct of a sexual nature when this conduct explicitly or implicitly is made a condition of employment decisions such as hiring or promotion.

hostile environment harassment Unwelcome sexual advances, requests for sexual favors, and other verbal or physical conduct of a sexual nature when this conduct explicitly or implicitly and unreasonably interferes with an individual's work performance or creates an intimidating, hostile, or offensive work environment.

Studies indicate that the harassment can come from a superior, a colleague, or a client of the law office. See Exhibit 3.5. Here are some concrete examples:

> The paralegal . . . told of one incident in which a partner placed his hand on her knee and asked if she had thought about her future with the firm. "Harassment of women lawyers is only the tip of the iceberg," according to the paralegal. "The support staff has it much, much worse."[33]

> Recently a female paralegal began working with an insecure male lawyer who was a first year associate at the firm. He started "making the moves" on her by constantly asking if she was dating anyone. One day he called her in his office, closed the door, dialed a number on the phone, and handed the receiver to the paralegal. "What I heard was an obscene recording. I laughed, opened the door, and left." She did not believe in pursuing office relationships. Resentment developed when they began working on the same case together. He falsely accused the paralegal of lying and of not completing assignments on time. He made derogatory comments to her co-workers. When she confided in a female lawyer at the firm, she was told that the associate acts that way with all the women at the firm, that the paralegal supervisor and the associate are very good friends, that the partner in charge "sticks to this associate like glue" and does not want to be bothered by "petty personnel problems."[34]

contemporaneous Existing or occurring in the same period of time; pertaining to records that are prepared on events as the events are occurring or shortly thereafter.

When something of this nature happens, make detailed **contemporaneous** notes on who said and did what. Do this immediately after the incident. Should you do anything more? A passive response would be to ignore the problem and hope that it will go away. Another response would be to blame yourself. Phyllis Schlafly told the Senate Labor and Human Resources Committee that "men hardly ever ask sexual favors of women from whom the certain response is *no*."[35] It is highly unlikely, however, that blaming yourself is either correct or productive.

For isolated and less serious problems, all that may be needed is a firm comment to the offender such as:

> Mr. Smith, you know that I respect your ability and authority in the firm. But I want you to know that I do not appreciate the comment you made at that meeting about me as a woman. I did not think it was appropriate or professional.

Unfortunately, this approach may be inadequate when the problem becomes more complicated and persists. Clearly, all possible internal avenues for resolving the problem should be attempted. Hopefully, *somebody* in a position of responsibility will lend a sympathetic ear. Local paralegal associations should be a source of ideas and support. Speak with officers of the association. Go to general meetings. Ask for advice. It is highly likely that you will find others who have had similar experiences and who can provide concrete suggestions.

Equal Employment Opportunity Commission (EEOC) The federal agency that investigates employment discrimination that violates federal law.

If all else fails, you have a powerful weapon at your disposal: the law. Harassment on the basis of sex is a violation of Title VII of the Civil Rights Act of 1964. The federal **Equal Employment Opportunity Commission (EEOC)** (www.eeoc.gov) as well as state departments of civil rights are available to enforce the law.

EXHIBIT 3.5	Incidents of Sexual Harassment in Law Offices

PERCENTAGE OF RESPONDENTS WHO REPORT HAVING EXPERIENCED VARIOUS TYPES OF SEXUAL HARASSMENT ON THE JOB

Incident	By Superior	By Colleague	By Client
Unwanted sexual teasing, jokes, remarks, or questions	36	30	32
Unwanted pressure for dates	8	6	10
Unwanted letters, telephone calls, or materials of a sexual nature	4	3	4
Unwanted sexual looks or gestures	21	11	16
Unwanted deliberate touching, leaning over, cornering, or pinching	14	6	9
Unwanted pressure for sex	6	3	4
Unwanted pressure for sex in return for promotions or business	1	0	1
Actual or attempted rape or assault	1	0	0

Source: *National Law Journal/West Group Survey on Women and Law*, National Law Journal S2 (December 11, 1989).

Violations can lead to severe penalties. In one case, the legal community was shocked by a jury award of $6.9 million in punitive damages against the world's largest law firm, Baker & McKenzie, because of sexual harassment by one of its partners against his legal secretary. With other damages, the award came to $7.1 million. The court later reduced the award to about $3.5 million. The partner dumped candy in the front pocket of the secretary's blouse and fondled her breast. At a luncheon, he grabbed her hips and asked her repeatedly, "What is the wildest thing you have done?" The jury found that the firm was negligent in the way it responded to her allegations against the partner. It was not enough for the firm to transfer the employee to another attorney when she complained of his behavior. The court was not persuaded by the argument that the partner simply had an "overactive imagination." After the trial, the secretary's attorney said that the case should substantially affect law firms across the country. And the chairman of Baker & McKenzie's executive committee said the firm will handle any future complaints of sexual harassment from its employees very differently.[36]

[SECTION N]
WORKING WITH SYSTEMS

Some paralegal employment problems are attributed to the fact that the firm has not carefully examined how paralegals can be effectively used in the office. Paralegals should be part of an attorney-paralegal-secretary team. The difficulty, however, is that the office may not have done the necessary planning to design the *system* that the team will execute.

A system is simply an organized way of accomplishing a task. All participants are supposed to perform those functions that they are capable of handling and for which they are not overtrained. Here is how many systems are created:

- Select the task that is to be systematized. It will usually be a task that the office performs regularly, such as incorporating a business, probating an estate, filing for divorce, or engaging in discovery. (According to some studies, attorneys perform over 75 percent of their tasks more than once.)
- Carefully study the task to identify its various components. What are the pieces that must always be performed? What facts must always be obtained? What letters must always be sent? What forms must always be drafted?
- Prepare a systems or procedural manual containing a description of the task, instructions or checklists of things to be done, standardized letters, pleadings, forms, and other documents that are customarily used for that task. The manual might be placed in a three-ring notebook and/or on a computer.
- Photocopy statutes, court rules, or other laws frequently used to perform the task and place them in a special section of the manual, often in the appendix.
- Delegate the performance of the components of the task to various members of the team.

It takes considerable sophistication to *design* a system. Even more sophistication is sometimes needed to *implement* the system and make it work. The participants must believe in the system and ideally have had a role in its design if it requires changes in their work habits. Many attorneys are notoriously resistant to change, particularly if they believe that the system fails to recognize the role of professional judgment. If you have been doing something the same way for fifteen years, you tend to be suspicious of suggestions that more efficient ways are possible. Furthermore, in the transition from blueprint to operation, the system may have to be modified to work out the "bugs." In short, a precondition for success is a willingness and a determination of the participants to make the new system work.

When paralegals walk into an office for the first time, they may confront any one of a number of situations:

- There are few or no systems; most attorneys practice law in their individualistic ways.
- There is talk of systemization, but no one has yet done any serious design work.
- An ineffective system is in place.
- A system is in place, but the participants do not believe in it.
- A system exists on paper, but no one has expended the time and energy to make the system work.

All these environments can make life difficult for the paralegal. A disorganized office can be frustrating.

As you gain experience on the job, don't be reluctant to try to design your own system. Begin modestly with a system for a portion of one of your tasks. Start out on a small scale by writing instructions or checklists for functions that you regularly perform. Write the system so that a new paralegal would be able to read it and know what to do. Here is an example of how a project led to the creation of a system:

> Diedre Wilton's organizational skills were really put to the test during a recent assignment which required her to file fictitious business name statements for a client in every county in California. "Almost every county had a different form!" lamented Diedre. "And I had to arrange for publication in fifty-eight different newspapers." She is creating an extensive file on the project so that . . . when the filings come up for renewal, the next person won't have to start from scratch.[37]

Supervisors will be *very* impressed by such efforts to create systems. A paralegal with this much initiative will soon become a prized member of the office.

[SECTION O]
CAREER LADDERS

In the early days of the paralegal movement, a common complaint among paralegals was the absence of career ladders. Once a paralegal demonstrates competence by making a significant contribution to the office, what comes next? Higher salaries, a better office, more variety in assignments—these are all helpful, but they are not the same as *promotion*. Yet what can a paralegal be promoted to? The only next step was lawyerdom. But going to law school is a rather drastic step. Taking this step means, of course, leaving the field of paralegalism entirely. Hence, in those early days, the only way up was out!

Although some progress has been made in developing career ladders, the progress has been primarily limited to law offices that employ relatively large numbers of paralegals. Most of the paralegals in small offices still have no career ladder. For this and related reasons, surveys show that between 10 and 15 percent of working paralegals today say that they intend to go to law school—eventually.

Yet other paralegals resent the following question put to them by attorneys: "So when are you going to law school?" or "Why don't you become an attorney?" Here is another example of this mentality:

> One day I accompanied an attorney to a deposition, at the request of our client. When we arrived at the opposing counsel's office, the attorney I was working with introduced me as the paralegal working on the case. The opposing counsel responded with, "Oh, so you're an aspiring attorney." "No," I responded, "I'm an aspiring paralegal."[38]

These paralegals see paralegalism as an end in itself, not necessarily as a stepping-stone to becoming an attorney. Attorneys are not always asked, "When are you going to become a judge?" And nurses do not constantly hear, "When are you going to become a doctor?" Paralegals deserve the same respect. Many wish that they could stop having to answer "the law school question."

The solution, of course, is the creation of meaningful career ladders for paralegals within a particular law office. And at least the larger law offices have responded. As we saw in chapter 1, the International Paralegal Management Association (IPMA; www.paralegalmanagement.org) has defined six levels of paralegal workers from paralegal clerk to paralegal manager.

[SECTION P]
YOUR NEXT JOB

It is extremely important to remember that throughout your current employment, you will be creating a record for your *next* job. While it is possible that you will remain in one position for your entire paralegal career, the likelihood is that you will one day be employed at another law firm, corporation, or law office. You should assume that everyone in a position of authority where you now work will one day be called by a prospective employer who will ask a series of questions about you:

- What kind of a worker were you?
- How did you get along with coworkers?

- Did you show initiative?
- Did you function well under pressure? Etc.

The legal profession is conservative by nature. Attorneys like to stay with winners; they are often reluctant to take chances. The most attractive candidate for a paralegal job is someone who has been successful at a previous paralegal job. Attorneys are hesitant to hire people who have run into difficulty at an earlier job—even if it was not their fault. Hence, *treat all supervisors in the office as potential references.*

[S E C T I O N   Q]

PARALEGAL ASSOCIATIONS AND NETWORKING

Your greatest ally in confronting any of the on-the-job problems discussed in this chapter is the paralegal association at the local and national level. (See appendix B). Not only are the associations a source of excellent information about paralegal practice in your area and across the nation, but they are also a potential gold mine of ideas and strategies. It is probably impossible for you to have a problem on the job that has not been experienced by many other paralegals within an association. Tap into this resource as soon as possible. You can learn a great deal by listening to the problems of others and finding out how they tried to solve them. What worked? Why? What didn't work? Why not? What is the next thing that should be tried? Answers to such questions will be readily available to you through the paralegal associations.

Communication among paralegals is also available online. One of the ways to participate in such communication is through **listservs**, which are Internet computer programs that facilitate receiving and sending messages from and to persons who sign up to be members of a list. A member types a message and then sends it (e-mails it) to every other member on the list. Once received, the message can be opened whenever the recipient goes online to check his or her mail from the list.

> **listserv** A program that manages computer mailing lists automatically, including the receipt and distribution of messages from and to members of the list.

Here are some ways to find listservs relevant to paralegals that you can join:

- Go to the Web site of your local paralegal association (see appendix B for addresses) to find out if it has its own listserv.
- www.legalassistanttoday.com (click "E-Mail Lists" and "LAT Forum").
- www.paralegals.org (type "listserv" in the "Site Search").
- groups.yahoo.com (type "paralegal" in the search box).
- groups.google.com (type "paralegal" in the search box).

Once you have joined a listserv, you can use it to communicate and learn about a wide range of issues that concern you. One member of a popular paralegal listserv, when asked why he had joined, said, "I would like to hear about people's experiences as a paralegal and their specific areas of practice. I'm curious as to how they started, and what led them to the positions they are in now." When a listserv member sends ("posts") a question or comment, it is e-mailed to hundreds and potentially thousands of members of a group. For example, you might type in questions such as the following:

> I'm a paralegal in a law firm that has 75 attorneys and 10 paralegals. With rare exceptions, the firm has never helped paralegals pay fees to attend paralegal association meetings. I'd be interested in hearing whether other paralegals have had this problem and how they have handled it.

> Our Illinois office has a client that incorporated one of its branches in Montana in 1957. I need to find out what the filing fees were in 1957. I was just handed this assignment, and as usual, the attorney needs it yesterday. Anybody got any ideas?

> Does anyone have a copy of the 1976 report of the New York State Bar Association, Committee on Professional Ethics? I think the name of the report is *Guidelines for the Utilization of Lawyers of the Services of Legal Assistants*. My fax number is 619–456–0269.

Within an hour or two of sending such posts, scores of replies are possible. They will be filled with ideas, suggestions, cautions, greetings, and irrelevancies. If you do not wish to send out messages, you can simply "lurk," which means reading what others have posted without posting anything of your own. Listservs are a wonderful new resource for reaching other paralegals and keeping up-to-date about some of the current topics of the day that concern paralegals. Unfortunately, one of the downsides of listservs is that unscrupulous marketers sometimes use them to flood the Internet with unsolicited junk mail (**spam**). Despite the efforts of modern e-mail programs to filter out such messages, they continue to be a problem.

> **spam** Unsolicited e-mail messages, often consisting of commercial advertising; unsolicited junk mail.

networking Establishing contacts with people who might become personal or professional resources.

E-mail communication through listservs is just one of the many ways of engaging in **networking**, which should take place at social gatherings, in businesses, at schools, on the phone, online—in short, wherever and whenever you interact with other people. Networking is the process of establishing a large number of social and professional contacts with people, making notes on what they do and how to reach them, and organizing these notes so that you can renew the contacts in the future as the need arises.

> I discovered first hand the value of networking. Attorneys, legal assistants and legal secretaries alike are all part of this maze we call our legal system. When we develop contacts, exchange ideas and information, reach out for help or lend a hand to someone else, we are creating a map for ourselves and others to navigate that infrastructure more effectively. Networking enables us to expand and diversify our profession, as well as our individual goals and aspirations.[39]

As we saw in chapter 2, there are at least five major benefits of networking. First, it will help you find your first job, particularly in the "hidden market," where available jobs are not advertised. Second, it will lead you to resources that will help you perform the job you obtain (e.g., help you locate a process server in a county you have never worked with before). Third, it will lead you to other jobs when it is time to move on. Fourth, it will connect you with many new personal friends. And fifth, it will involve you in the further development of paralegalism as a profession.

Networking, however, is not self-executing; it does not happen on its own. You need to exercise considerable initiative to build up your network. Step one is to resolve that whenever you attend a group meeting or other gathering, you will network with one or more people at the gathering. Here are concrete suggestions for accomplishing this goal:

- Go up to strangers at a meeting or function and introduce yourself.
- Do not sit with people you already know.
- Ask people you know to introduce you to people you do not know.
- Have some inexpensive business cards made so that you can hand them out (if you do not have a title, simply have the card list your name and how you can be reached).
- At the end of the day, use a notebook to write out the names and addresses of the people you have met that day; indicate what they do, how they can be reached, whether they have any connection to the law, and whether they might be a future lead to employment or other assistance.

See Exhibit 3.6 for a form you can use to keep track of your networking contacts.

Of course, the other side of the networking equation is you. You must make yourself available to go onto the formal and informal networking lists of others, particularly fellow

---

EXHIBIT 3.6	Record Keeping for Networking Contacts

Networking Contacts

Name: _____

Address: _____

(snail mail, e-mail, blog, etc.) _____

Employed at: _____

Date of contact: _____

Special interests: _____

Notes on contact: _____

Follow-up needed: _____

paralegals. Once you gain a reputation as a person who is willing to provide information and contact leads to others, you will find a dramatic increase in the willingness of others to share their resources with you. As one veteran paralegal put it, "I've always believed that if you want to make a connection with someone, you have to demonstrate your worth *to them* and they will remember you for it."[40]

ASSIGNMENT 3.3

Examine the following fact situations. For each situation:

- Identify the problems that you see.
- What strategies do you think would be helpful in resolving the problem or problems? Why?
- What strategies do you think would be counterproductive? Why?
- What do you think could have been done to prevent the problem or problems from occurring in the first place? How could they have been avoided?
- In your responses, specify what you think would be assertive, nonassertive, and aggressive behavior.

(a) Tom has been a paralegal at a firm for three years. His paralegal training in school was in drafting, legal research, investigation, etc. For the entire three years, however, he has been collating and digesting numerous documents in a big antitrust case. It is a very important case, and the firm is reluctant to take him off it due to his familiarity with these documents. The problem, however, is that Tom is becoming bored. He is satisfied with his pay but dreads coming to work each day. He tried to explain this to his supervisor, but he was simply told how important he was to the case. The supervisor said, "If you decide to leave the firm, I hope you will give us six months' lead time so that you can train a replacement." This made Tom all the more depressed, since he does not want to leave.

(b) Ellen is a probate paralegal at a firm. She has worked there two years. At a recent paralegal association meeting, she discovered that other probate paralegals in the city with the same experience are making at least $4,000 more per year than she is. She wants to talk with her supervisor about this but is not sure if this is the right time. The last three months have been difficult for her. She has missed work a lot due to illness. She also recently began work on a new complex case. She is struggling to keep up with the new work involved in the case and must constantly ask her supervisor for help. The supervisor appears to be irritated with her progress on the case. Her next scheduled salary review is ten months away.

(c) Fran is a paralegal in a firm where she works for the senior partner—the most powerful person in the firm. Fran receives excellent pay and fringe benefits. She loves her work. Other paralegals in the firm, however, resent her because their benefits are much lower and they receive less desirable assignments.

(d) Same situation as in (c) above. Fran's supervisor, the senior partner, is currently going through a divorce, and the strain on him has been enormous. One consequence of this is that Fran's workload is increasing. More of his work is being shifted to her. He is extremely sensitive to any criticism about the way he practices law, so Fran is reluctant to talk with him about the extra work—particularly when he is under so much pressure due to the divorce. Yet Fran is worried about her ability to do her job competently in view of the increased work. She hopes that things will get back to normal when the divorce is over.

(e) Mary works in a law firm that charges clients $225 an hour for attorney time and $75 an hour for paralegal time. She and another paralegal, Fred, are working with an attorney on a large case. She sees all of the time sheets that the three of them submit to the firm's accounting office. She suspects that the attorney is padding his time sheets by overstating the number of hours he works on the case. (As we will see in chapter 5, padding is unethically adding something without justification.) For example, he lists thirty hours for a four-day period when he was in court every day on another case. Furthermore, Fred's time is being billed at the full $75-an-hour rate even though he spends about eighty percent of his time typing correspondence, filing, and performing other clerical duties.

(f) Tom has been a paralegal at the firm for six years. He works for three attorneys. One day he is told by a memo from the office administrator that an outside consultant has been hired to study Tom's job in order to find ways "to increase productivity." The letter instructs Tom to

(continues)

ASSIGNMENT 3.3—*continued*

spend the next two days permitting the consultant to follow him around and ask questions about what he does. Tom feels insulted.

(g) Mary has been a paralegal at the firm for two years. She works for one attorney, Mr. Getty. One day a client calls Mary and says, "I'm sending you another copy of the form that Mr. Getty said you lost." This is news to Mary. She works with the client's file every day and knows that she has never lost anything. She pauses, trying to think of what to say to this client over the phone before hanging up.

(h) Veronica works for a law firm where none of the supervisors give formal evaluations of the paralegals. The supervisors feel that formal evaluations would be too time-consuming and too general to be helpful. They are also afraid that they might be sued for making negative comments about employees. Veronica has received yearly raises, and according to her supervisor, this is the best indication of what the firm thinks of her. Veronica is unhappy, however, with the feedback she has gotten about her work.

(i) How would you handle the fact situation involving sexual harassment (questions about dating, obscene recording, etc.) presented on page 150? Assume the paralegal legal does not want to quit and is afraid that she will lose her job if she institutes legal action.

ASSIGNMENT 3.4

Karen considers herself a quiet, nonaggressive person. She has two job offers: (1) a large law firm (seventy-five attorneys and twenty-two paralegals) and (2) a one-attorney/one-secretary office. She likes the type of work both offices do. The pay and benefits in both offices are roughly the same. How would you advise Karen on which job to take?

ASSIGNMENT 3.5

According to Douglas McGregor in *The Human Side of Enterprise* (1960), there are two basic views of human behavior at work. "Theory X" says that a person has a natural dislike of work and will avoid it whenever possible. "Theory Y" says that physical and mental work is as natural to a person as any other activity. Under theory Y, workers do not naturally shy away from responsibility.

- Describe a law office using paralegals that is managed under theory X. How would it function? How would the office handle employee or personnel problems?
- Describe a law office using paralegals that subscribes to theory Y. How would it function? How would the office handle employee or personnel problems?
- Which theory do you think is correct?
- Which theory describes you?

ASSIGNMENT 3.6

What needs does a paralegal or any worker have? What is our "hierarchy of needs"? Rearrange the following needs so that you think they reflect the conscious or unconscious priorities of most human beings: the need to be fulfilled; the need to be respected; the need to eat, sleep, and be clothed; the need to be safe; the need to be admired; the need to belong; the need to have self-worth. See A. Maslow, *Motivation and Personality* (1970) (www.deepermind.com/20maslow.htm).

Chapter Summary

A major theme of chapter 3 is the critical importance of paralegal initiative. Every occupation has its problems. This chapter covered problems in the paralegal arena and how initiative is a primary vehicle for resolving them. After listing forty factors that influence job satisfaction, we turned to topics such as the breakdown of communication in the hectic environment of a law practice, the lack of realistic expectations of what it means to work with attorneys, the characteristics of some attorneys that do not make them good supervisors, assertive strategies for seeking a raise, the inevitability of office politics, the central role of self-evaluation and employer evaluation, the tensions that might exist in the attorney-paralegal-secretary relationship, and the problem of sexual harassment.

While initiative cannot solve all of the problems that may exist, it appears to be a central ingredient in the success of competent paralegals. Such paralegals take advantage of opportunities for continuing legal education (CLE); they know how to work with—and to help create—systems; they know what it means to be prepared; and they understand the value of networking, particularly through paralegal associations.

Key Terms

WIP
office politics
performance review
realization rate
flextime

continuing legal
  education
quid pro quo harassment
hostile environment
harassment

contemporaneous
Equal Employment
  Opportunity
  Commission (EEOC)

listserv
networking
spam

Review Questions

1. What are some of the major factors that paralegals say affect job satisfaction?
2. What are some of the main causes of a breakdown in communication in a law office?
3. What steps should you take to avoid miscommunication in a busy law office?
4. What is the major antidote to job frustration resulting from expectations?
5. Why can it be said that law office environments are neither static nor unchangeable?
6. What is meant by office politics, and why is it unrealistic to wish that it will go away?
7. What effective ways can paralegals use to "publicize" their competence in a law office?
8. What are performance reviews, and why are they essential?
9. When should you ask for an evaluation of your work?
10. What is a pre-evaluation, and how should you prepare for one?
11. Give examples of measurable goals before your next evaluation.
12. Know the characteristics of many attorneys that may not make them effective supervisors and team leaders.
13. Know the differences involved in being assertive, non-assertive, and aggressive in your behavior.
14. What assertive strategies can be used when you are seeking a salary increase?

15. What information should be kept in a diary or journal?
16. What should be kept in a career development file?
17. What are some of the secrets of successful paralegals?
18. Why is CLE important?
19. What are some of the major factors of effective paralegal supervision?
20. What are some of the possible reasons friction might arise between paralegals and secretaries, and how can they be avoided?
21. What are the definitions of the two kinds of sexual harassment that violate the law?
22. What resources should a victim of sexual harassment use?
23. What are the obligations of an employer to prevent sexual harassment?
24. What are law office systems, how are they created, and why are they sometimes difficult to implement?
25. Where are you likely to find career ladders in the law?
26. What is meant by creating a record for your next job while on a current job, and why is it important to do so?
27. What are the advantages of participating in paralegal associations?
28. What are some of the effective techniques of networking?
29. What is the distinction between theory X and theory Y in human behavior at work, and how can either theory affect the way a law office is managed?

Helpful Web Sites: More About On-The-Job Paralegal Realities

Job Surveys

- www.nala.org/survey_table.htm
- www.paralegals.org
  (in "Site Search" type "survey")
- www.utahbar.org/sections/paralegals

Office Politics

- www.officepolitics.com
- www.managementhelp.org/intrpsnl/off_pltc.htm
- www.officepolitics.com/promo_hr/promo_hr_index.html

Employment Discrimination and Sexual Harassment

- www.eeoc.gov
  (see "Discriminatory Practices")
- www.de2.psu.edu/harassment
- www.lawguru.com/faq/16.html

Continuing Legal Education (CLE)

- Go to the Web site of your local paralegal association (see appendix B for addresses) to find out what CLE it sponsors or links to.

- nalacampus.com
- www.paralegals.org (click "CLE")
- www.nals.org
  (Click "Online Learning Center")
- www.cleonline.com
- www.washlaw.edu (click "CLE")
- westlegaledcenter.com (In the CLE pull-down menus, find programs for your state.)
- www.lexisnexis.com/cle
- www.findlaw.com/07cle/list.html
- www.taecan.com
  (Click your state in the pull-down menu)

Listservs
Type "paralegal listserv" in the following search engines:
- www.google.com
- www.ask.com
- clusty.com

Miscellaneous
- www.delmar.cengage.com
- www.lexisnexis.com/paralegal
- estrinlegaled.typepad.com
- www.knowparalegal.com

- paralegalgateway.com
- paralegal.meetup.com
- paralegalonline.blogspot.com
- indianaparalegals.blogspot.com
- counsel.net/chatboards/paralegals
- www.chesslaw.com/paralegalnews.htm
- paralegaltalk.com
- www.greedyassociates.com
  (Click "Message Search," then type "paralegal" or the name of a particular firm in the search box)
- www.vault.com
  (Find "Message Boards" and type "paralegal" in the search box)

Google Searches (run the following searches for more sites)
- office politics
- Utah continuing legal education (Insert your state)
- legal networking
- employee evaluation
- salary raise strategies
- assertiveness
- law office environment culture
- effective supervision

Endnotes

1. Beth King, *President's Message*, 10 Newsletter 1 (Oregon Legal Assistant Ass'n, February 1987).
2. Mary Ryan, Human Resources Consultant.
3. *Poor Communication Devours Seven Workweeks Per Year*, Legal Management 14 (November/December 1998).
4. Sgarlat, *The Scape Goat Phenomenon*, 6 The Journal 10 (Sacramento Ass'n of Legal Assistants, June 1986).
5. Chere Estrin, *Political Aspirations*, 16 Legal Assistant Today 94 (May/June 1999).
6. McLaverty, *Office Politics and Communication*, 24 WALS State Journal 50 (January 1990).
7. Chernowsky, *Toward Greater Visibility*, 15 Reporter (Los Angeles Paralegal Ass'n, August 1986).
8. Michele Boerder, *Four Pointers to Professionalism*, 14 DALA Newsletter 3 (Dallas Ass'n of Legal Assistants, December 1990).
9. Oder, *Paralegal Upward Mobility*, 6 National Paralegal Reporter 6 (Nat'l Federation of Paralegal Associations, Fall/Winter 1981); Los Angeles Paralegal Ass'n, *Reporter* (September 1981).
10. Reprinted with the permission of Heller, Ehrman, White & McAuliffe, San Francisco, California.
11. Wojt, *Making the Most of Your Performance Review*, 38 The Docket 22 (April/May 1990).
12. In some offices, the employee will be asked to fill out a *self-evaluation* form before any formal evaluations by a supervisor take place.
13. Barbara Middleton, *Taking Criticism*, 7 Newsletter 25 (Texas Legal Assistant Division, November 1991).
14. Allen & Williams, *Team-Building Frenzy Reaches Law Firms*, The National Law Journal, December 17, 1990, at 20.
15. Jean Hollands, *Why Lawyers Are Sometimes Unhappy*, Los Altos Town Crier, May 17, 2000, at 47.
16. Andrea Wagner, *Tips & Traps for the New Paralegal*, 8 Legal Assistant Today 78, 82 (March/April 1991).
17. *Negotiating for More Money in a Tough Market*, Estrin LegalEd Newsletter (June 2007) (www.careercoachesinternational.com) (www.estrinlegaled.com/newsletter).
18. Tami Coyne, *Strategies for Paralegal Career Development*, Nat'l Paralegal Reporter 20 (NFPA, Winter 1990).
19. Renee Sova, *Bridging the Gap from Student to Professional*, 7 Legal Professional 47 (January/February 1990).
20. Laurie Roselle, *I Don't Get No Respect!*, 9 Nat'l Paralegal Reporter 2 (NFPA, November/December 1984).
21. Carol Musick, *Productivity*, 5 FWPA Newsletter 3 (Fort Worth Paralegal Ass'n, May 1987).
22. Marion Johnson, *President's Message*, Newsletter 1 (Arizona Paralegal Ass'n, July 1988).
23. Chere Estrin, *10 Easy Steps to Leveraging Your Career*, 10 TALA Newsletter 7 (Toledo Ass'n of Legal Assistants, October 1989).
24. Kunz, *Personal Management File*, WDALA Summons (Western Dakota Ass'n of Legal Assistants, August 1990).
25. Garant, *Speech to USM Paralegal Program Graduates*, Newsletter 3 (Maine Ass'n of Paralegals, April 1990).
26. Special Counsel, *Continuing Education Survey* reported in Legal Management 16 (September/October 2000)
27. Internal Revenue Service, *Tax Benefits for Education* (2005) (www.irs.gov/pub/irs-pdf/p970.pdf).
28. *The Legal Assistant and the Legal Secretary: Friend or Foe*, 8 The Journal 4 (Sacramento Ass'n of Legal Assistants, April 1988).

29. Rosen, *Effective Delegation*, 13 Update 8 (Cleveland Ass'n of Legal Assistants, June/July 1990).

30. Ruth-Ellen Post, *Paralegal Internships* 118 (1999).

31. Guinn, *Personnel Management Techniques*, 8 Legal Assistant Today 56, 58 (March/April 1991).

32. Wapner, *Sexual Harassment in the Law Firm*, 16 Law Practice Management 42, 43 (September 1990); Smith, *Sexual Harassment Discussed at Litigation Sectional*, MALA Advance 19 (Minnesota Ass'n of Legal Assistants, Summer 1989); 29 C.F.R. § 1604.11(a)(3); 47 Federal Register 74,676 (November 10, 1980).

33. Goldberg, *Law's "Dirty Little Secret,"* 76 A.B.A. (34 October 1990).

34. Nat'l Federation of Paralegal Associations, *Harassment: Personnel Problem or Worse?* 9 Nat'l Paralegal Reporter 7 (February 1985).

35. Baca, Speech to Nat'l Capital Area Paralegal Ass'n (April 29, 1981).

36. R. Thompson, *Legal Secretary Awarded Record $7.1 Million in Sexual Harassment*, 12 Legal Assistant Today 14 (November/December 1995).

37. *Paralegal Profile*, 12 Points & Authorities 9 (San Joaquin Ass'n of Legal Assistants, March 1991).

38. Burdett, *Rodney Dangerfield: You're Not Alone*, 12 Nat'l Paralegal Reporter 12 (Nat'l Federation of Paralegal Associations, Spring 1988).

39. Deborah Worthington, *Networking in Action*, 19 DALA Newsletter 7 (Dallas Ass'n of Legal Assistants, February 1996).

40. Denise Templeton, *Networking Isn't a Dirty Word*, 20 Legal Assistant Today 42 (May/June 2003).

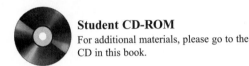

Student CD-ROM

For additional materials, please go to the CD in this book.

Online Companion™

For additional resources, please go to http://www.paralegal.delmar.cengage.com

The Regulation of Paralegals

CHAPTER OUTLINE

A. Kinds of Regulation

B. Unauthorized and Authorized Practice of Law

C. Licensing of Paralegals

D. Should Paralegals Become Part of Bar Associations?

E. Self-Regulation by Paralegals: Certification

F. Fair Labor Standards Act

G. Tort Liability of Paralegals

H. Malpractice Insurance

[SECTION A]

KINDS OF REGULATION

The activities of paralegals could be directly or indirectly regulated in six important ways:

- Laws on the unauthorized practice of law and on the *authorized* practice of law by non-attorneys
- State licensing
- Self-regulation through certification
- Fair Labor Standards Act
- Tort law
- Ethical rules

The first five of these methods of regulation are covered in this chapter. Ethics will be examined in the next chapter. As we explore these methods, you should keep in mind the terminology of regulation outlined in Exhibit 4.1.

[SECTION B]

UNAUTHORIZED AND AUTHORIZED PRACTICE OF LAW

1. DEFINING THE PRACTICE OF LAW

Every state has laws on the **unauthorized practice of law (UPL)**, which simply means the performance of services that constitute the **practice of law** by someone not authorized to provide such services. In many states, it is a *crime* to practice law illegally. It is not a crime to represent yourself, but you risk going to jail if you practice law on behalf of someone else.

unauthorized practice of law (UPL) Conduct by a person who does not have a license to practice law or other special authorization needed for that conduct.

practice of law Using legal skills to assist a specific person in resolving his or her specific legal problem.

160

EXHIBIT 4.1	Terminology of Regulation

Regulation is any governmental or nongovernmental method of controlling conduct.

Accreditation is the process by which an authoritative organization (usually nongovernmental) evaluates and recognizes an institution or a program of study as meeting specified qualifications or standards.

Approval means the recognition that comes from accreditation, certification, licensure, registration, or other form of acknowledgment.

Certification is the process by which a *nongovernmental* organization grants recognition to a person who has met qualifications set by that organization. It is a voluntary process; not having certification usually does not affect the right of the person to engage in a particular career. Three of the most common qualifications for certification are:

- Graduating from a school or training program, and/or
- Passing a standard examination, and/or
- Completing a designated period of work experience

Some prefer the term *certificated* as opposed to *certified* if the recognition is from a paralegal school. (Later, in Exhibits 4.7 and 4.8, we will examine the certification programs of the national and state paralegal associations in the country.) Occasionally a *government* agency will have programs that "certify" individuals. The program may be similar to those described above, or it may in fact be a license program.

Code is any set of rules that regulates conduct (See the glossary for another definition of *code.*)

Ethics are rules that embody standards of behavior to which members of an organization are expected to conform.

Guideline is suggested conduct that will help an applicant obtain accreditation, certification, licensure, registration, or approval. *Guideline* can also refer to a statement of policy or procedure, often with options on carrying it out.

Licensure is the process by which an agency of government grants permission to persons meeting specified qualifications to engage in an occupation and often to use a particular title. This permission is a license. The qualifications are designed to ensure that the person has at least the minimum competency needed for the protection of the public. Licensure is one of the more drastic methods of controlling entry into a career.

Limited licensure (also called specialty licensure) is the process by which an agency of government grants permission to persons meeting specified qualifications to engage in designated activities that are customarily (but not always exclusively) performed by another category of license holder. (If, in the future, paralegals are granted a limited license in a particular state, they will be authorized to sell designated services—now part of the attorney monopoly—directly to the public in that state.)

Registration or enrollment is the process by which individuals or institutions list their names on a roster kept by an agency of government or by a nongovernmental organization. There may or may not be qualifications that must be met before one can go on the list.

Why such a harsh penalty? Legal problems often involve complicated, serious issues. A great deal can be lost if citizens do not receive competent legal assistance. To protect the public, the state requires either a license to practice law or some other special authorization to provide legal assistance. The state will punish anyone who tries to provide it without the license or other special authorization. Such individuals are engaged in UPL.

Unfortunately, however, a finding of UPL is not always easy to make because the definition of the practice of law is so vague. The most common general definition is as follows: *using legal skills to assist a specific person in resolving his or her specific legal problem.* But not all states use this definition. Exhibit 4.2 contains most of the definitions or tests that the courts have used. (For the definition in your state, see appendix E.) Courts, legislatures, and bar associations throughout the country have struggled to try to come up with a more precise definition that will apply to the large variety of cases in which someone is charged with engaging in UPL.

Many states have concluded that it is hopeless to try to formulate an all-encompassing definition that will cover every case. Here is the view of one court in a state that uses the traditional areas test (see Exhibit 4.2):

[I]t is impossible to lay down an exhaustive definition of "the practice of law" by attempting to enumerate every conceivable act performed by lawyers in the normal course of their work. We believe it sufficient to state that those acts, whether performed in court or in the law office, which lawyers customarily have carried on from day to day through the centuries must constitute "the practice of law."[1]

EXHIBIT 4.2	Disagreement over How to Define the Practice of Law

Tests Used by Different Courts to Define the Practice of Law

States differ on how they define the practice of law to determine whether an activity constitutes the unauthorized practice of law. (See appendix E for the definition in your state.) Here are the tests used by different states, some of which overlap. Note, however, that some states use more than one test and that many activities (e.g., arguing a case in court) would constitute the practice of law under all the tests.

Professional judgment test. Does the service require an attorney's professional judgment, meaning the special training and skills of an attorney? If the answer is yes, the service is the practice of law. Example: questioning a witness at a deposition. The professional judgment test is the most widely used test in the country.

General public/personal relationship test. Is the service offered to the general public rather than to a specific person? If the answer is yes, the service is not the practice of law. Example: an author writes a book on how to draft a will but does not provide personal attention to any individual buyer of the book. If, however, the service connects (applies) the law to the facts of a specific person, the service is the practice of law.

Complex/difficult question test. Does the service seek to resolve a complex or difficult question of law that is beyond the capability of the average layperson? If the answer is yes, the service is the practice of law. Example: giving legal advice on an involved commercial transaction.

Important rights/public protection test. Does the service pertain to important legal rights that can be protected only by someone with special legal skills? If the answer is yes, the service is the practice of law. Example: giving legal advice on a divorce.

Traditional areas test. Is the service one that attorneys have traditionally performed? If the answer is yes, the service is the practice of law. Example: drafting a separation agreement in a divorce.

Commonly understood test. Is the service commonly understood to be the practice of law? If the answer is yes, the service is the practice of law. Example: making a motion in court. Preparing tax returns, on the other hand, is not commonly understood to be the practice of law.

Incidental test. Is the service an adjunct to (incidental to) what another business routinely provides? If the answer is yes, the service is not the practice of law. Example: the preparation of a sales contract (using standard forms) by a real estate agent for which a separate fee is not charged.

The following comment presents a similar theme in a state that uses a combination of the professional judgment test and the general public/personal relationship test:

> It is neither necessary nor desirable to attempt the formulation of a single, specific definition of what constitutes the practice of law. Functionally the practice of law relates to the rendition of services for others that call for the professional judgment of a lawyer. The essence of the professional judgment of the lawyer is his educated ability to relate the general body and philosophy of law to a specific legal problem of a client; and thus, the public interest will be better served if only lawyers are permitted to act in matters involving professional judgment. Where this professional judgment is not involved, non-lawyers, such as Court Clerks, Police Officers, Abstractors, and many Governmental employees[,] may engage in occupations that require a special knowledge of law in certain areas. But the services of a lawyer are essential in the public interest whenever the exercise of professional judgment is required.[1a]

attorney in fact One authorized to act in place of or for another, often in a business transaction.

power of attorney 1. A document that authorizes another to act as one's agent of attorney in fact. 2. The authority itself.

Before examining the nature of the practice of law and UPL in greater detail, it is important to distinguish between an attorney at law and an **attorney in fact**. An attorney at law is someone who engages in the practice of law, according to the definitions we have been studying. An attorney in fact, on the other hand, is someone authorized to act in place of or for another, often in a business transaction. Examples might include someone given the authority to sign a deed for another or to sell another's business. (The document that authorizes another to act as an attorney in fact is called a **power of attorney**.) Both attorneys at law and attorneys in fact are agents, but their authority as agents is dramatically different. An attorney at law practices law on behalf of another. An attorney in fact conducts a transaction on behalf of another. Persons who are attorneys in fact (because they have been granted a power of attorney) cannot practice law unless they happen to also be attorneys at law. Phrased another way, giving someone a power of attorney does not grant him or her the right to practice law for the person giving the power.

Let's look more closely at the components of the practice of law. It involves three main categories of service:

- Representing someone in court or in an administrative agency proceeding;
- Drafting legal documents for someone; and
- Giving someone legal advice.

The third category—giving legal advice—usually takes place while performing the other two activities, although legal advice can also be given independently of them. The essence of the practice of law is performing any of the three activities to help a particular person resolve a specific legal problem.

Suppose that you write a self-help book on how to sue your landlord. The book lists all the laws, provides all the forms, and gives precise guidelines on how to use the laws and the forms. Are you practicing law? No, because you are not addressing the *specific* legal problem of a *specific* person. It is not the practice of law to sell law books or similar materials to the general public, even if a member of the public uses them for his or her specific legal problem. Now suppose that you open an office in which you sell the book and even type the forms for customers. Practice of law? No. In most states this is not the practice of law *unless you provide individual help in filling out the forms.* You can type the forms but most states require the customer to do all the thinking about what goes in the forms! Similarly:

- It is proper for a nonattorney to charge citizens a fee to type legal forms in order to obtain a divorce. But in most states it is the UPL to provide personal assistance on how to fill out the forms.
- It is proper for a nonattorney to charge citizens a fee to type their will or trust. But in most states it is the UPL to provide personal assistance on what should go in the will or trust.
- It is proper for a nonattorney to charge citizens a fee to type and file their bankruptcy petition. But in all states, it is the UPL to provide personal assistance on how to fill out the petition. Individuals who provide this kind of assistance are called *bankruptcy petition preparers* (BPPs), as we will see later in the chapter.

Courts have struggled with interactive Internet or computer software programs that are designed to help individuals engage in many legal activities such as preparing their own wills, incorporating their business, and drafting pleadings for their divorce. The question-and-answer format of these programs allows documents to be selected and prepared in response to the specific facts typed in by the users. Some courts have said that this is the equivalent of providing personal assistance on a person's specific legal problem and hence is the practice of law. Most courts, however, have disagreed, on the theory that the Web site or software is nothing more than the equivalent of a more detailed how-to-do-it book.

A distinction should be made between providing *legal information* and providing *legal advice*. According to the American Bar Association;

> Although *the line between legal information and legal advice is blurry*, there are important differences between the two. Anyone can sell or give you legal information. On the other hand, only a licensed lawyer can give you legal advice. Legal information is supposed to be general and not based on a specific set of facts. Legal advice is provided by a trained lawyer who uses his or her knowledge of the law to tell you how the law applies to your specific circumstances. When you get legal advice from a lawyer, you also enter into an "attorney-client relationship" with the lawyer. This gives you certain legal protections. For example, the lawyer cannot tell someone else what you said without your permission. [The attorney-client privilege prevents this.] Your lawyer can't advise or represent someone whose position or interests will conflict with yours. [This would be a conflict of interest.] You do not have these protections when you get legal information from someone.[2]

The following opinion of the attorney general in Maryland explores the distinction between legal information and legal advice in greater depth. You will note that this opinion allows a paralegal (called a *lay advocate*) to provide *some* minimal assistance in filling out court forms ("pointing out where on the form particular information is to be set out"). The reason given is that such assistance does not require much legal skill or knowledge of the law. Be aware, however, that not all states would agree with this Maryland position. In most states, *any* assistance given to specific individuals in completing legal documents would constitute the practice of law.

Opinion of the Attorney General No. 95–056

State of Maryland
80 Opinions of the Attorney General 138 (December 19, 1995)
www.oag.state.md.us/Opinions/1995/95index.htm
1995 Westlaw 783587

You have requested our opinion whether lay advocates who provide certain services to victims of domestic violence engage in the unauthorized practice of law. As you point out, lay advocates often provide important information about medical or social services available outside the court system to victims of domestic violence; activities of this kind raise no significant issue of unauthorized practice of law.

Your concern is with activities that relate to the legal system. Specifically, you ask whether lay advocates may: (i) provide information to domestic violence victims about legal options and remedies available to them; (ii) provide information to victims about court proceedings, including the role of witnesses; (iii) provide assistance to victims in preparing form pleadings, either using their own language or that of the victim; (iv) provide "non-legal assistance" to victims during judicial proceedings; (v) sit at trial table with victims; and (vi) engage in advocacy on behalf of victims' rights before State's Attorneys and other public officials. . . .

I. Scope of the Practice of Law

In general, a person may practice law in Maryland only if admitted to the Bar by the Court of Appeals. §§ 10–206 and 10–601 of the Business Occupations and Professions ("BOP") Article, *Maryland Code*. The unauthorized practice of law is a misdemeanor and is also subject to injunction. BOP §§ 10–606 (a) and 10–406. Moreover, Maryland Rule of Professional Conduct 5.5 (b) prohibits a lawyer from "assist[ing]" a person who is not a member of the bar in the performance of activity that constitutes the unauthorized practice of law."

Yet the comment to this rule recognizes a reality of legal practice: "Paragraph (b) does not prohibit a lawyer from employing the services of paraprofessionals and delegating functions to them, so long as the lawyer supervises the delegated work and retains responsibility for their work." In addition, Rule of Professional Conduct 5.3 identifies a lawyer's responsibilities regarding "nonlawyer assistants." Therefore, this opinion's discussion of the potential for unauthorized practice of law by lay advocates does not apply to the activities of lay advocates that are performed on behalf of a lawyer's client and are supervised by the lawyer. Even if some of these activities might constitute the "practice of law," with proper supervision and accountability they are not the "unauthorized practice of law." See *In re Opinion 24*, 607 A.2d 962 (N. J. 1992).

Our discussion in the balance of this opinion assumes that other lay advocates carry out their activities without a lawyer's supervision. For these lay advocates, the scope of the "practice of law" is crucial.

Exactly what constitutes the practice of law is generally for the courts to decide. *Public Service Comm'n v. Hahn Transportation, Inc.*, 253 Md. 571, 583, 253 A.2d 845 (1969). In Maryland, as elsewhere, however, the legislative and judicial branches have shared this responsibility, reaching a "comfortable accommodation." Id.

Under the General Assembly's definition of "practice of law," the term encompasses giving legal advice, representing another person before a court or other governmental unit, and preparing or assisting in the preparation of a form or document to be filed in courts. BOP §§ 10–101(h). This is an inevitably imprecise definition, leaving construction on a case-by-case basis to the courts. *Hahn,* 253 Md. at 583. See also *Unauthorized Practice Committee v. Cortez,* 692 S.W. 2d 47, 51 (Tex. 1985) (courts have inherent power and duty to determine what constitutes the practice of law in any given case).

The Court of Appeals has construed the statute to preclude a layperson from preparing and filing pleadings in a contested case or appearing and engaging in representation at trial on behalf of another. *Hahn,* 253 Md. at 580–581. Further, the Court of Special Appeals held that even where trial work is not involved, an individual is practicing law if he or she is preparing legal documents, interpreting legal documents, giving legal advice, or "applying legal principles to problems of any complexity." *Lukas v. Bar Association of Montgomery County,* 35 Md. App. 442, 448, 371 A.2d 669 (1977), cert. denied, 250 Md. 733 (1977) (citations omitted). The test, stated generally, is whether the activity requires "more than the most elementary knowledge of law, or more than that which [a layperson] may be deemed to possess." Id. (citation omitted).

The Court in *Lukas* made clear, however, that this prohibition does not extend to "mere mechanical" functions, like filling out forms or performing clerical work. Id. Echoing *Lukas,* an opinion of this office drew the same distinction, finding that "nonlawyers may fill out forms and perform other purely mechanical functions, [but] may not represent [clients] at hearings. . . , nor may they give legal advice, interpret legal documents, or apply legal principles to any problems of complexity for a client." 65 *Opinions of the Attorney General* 28 (1980).

We have also concluded that the simple act of providing information about legal rights, as opposed to offering advice about such rights and what to do about them, is not unauthorized.

In deciding that a social worker may inform a birth parent about his or her statutory right to revoke consent to adoption, we stated that the "mere conveying of information about a provision of law" does not constitute the practice of law. 79 *Opinions of the Attorney General No. 94–14* (March 7, 1994). Observing that a rule to the contrary would grind commerce and government to a halt, we said that "the line of unauthorized practice is potentially crossed when someone who is not a lawyer purports to give professional advice about another person's legal situation or suggests a course of conduct based on an interpretation of the law, [but] the line is not crossed by the unadorned provision of information." *Opinion No. 94–014,* at 3.

II. Prohibited and Permissible Services

Under these principles, some of the services lay advocates provide victims of domestic violence constitute the unauthorized practice of law; others do not. . . .

(continues)

Opinion of the Attorney General No. 95–056—*continued*

A. General Information

Lay advocates may provide information to victims about their potential legal rights and remedies. In doing so, however, they must be careful to limit their activity to the unadorned conveyance of information about what rights and remedies exist. They may not help victims decide, based upon the victims' particular circumstances, whether to invoke any of their rights or pursue any of their potential remedies. Providing this latter assistance would be improperly suggesting a "course of conduct." *Opinion No. 94–014,* at 3. See also *Cortez,* 692 S.W.2d at 50 (advising clients as to whether they qualified to file various petitions and whether they should file various immigration forms required legal skill and was thus unauthorized practice of law).

B. Information about Court Proceedings

Lay advocates may inform victims about purely nonlegal, basic matters such as appropriate attire, where to sit, and so forth. They may also provide a general orientation or overview about the kind of proceeding involved. This kind of information is not legal advice.

Providing any more particular or individualized information about judicial proceedings, such as how to present a case, call witnesses, cross-examine witnesses, introduce documents, and the like, requires a specialized knowledge ordinarily beyond the purview of a layperson. See *Lukas,* 35 Md. App. at 448–49. See also *Matter of Bright,* 171 B.R. 799 (Bkrtcy. E. D. Mich. 1994) (paralegal engaged in unauthorized practice where she advised clients regarding proper testimony and provided them with basic information about local bankruptcy court procedures and requirements). A lay advocate who advised a victim on how her case should be presented or defended would violate BOP § 10–206.

C. Trial Activities

Lay advocates may sit at trial table or stand by the victim in the courtroom, subject to the discretion of the trial judge, provided they do not engage in any activities otherwise prohibited. They may not hold themselves out as representatives of victims or provide victims with any kind of assistance at trial that constitutes unauthorized practice.

D. Preparation of Pleadings

Lay advocates may help a victim fill out a form pleading herself by defining terms in the instructions that might be unclear to the victim or by pointing out where on the form particular information is to be set out. Lay advocates may themselves fill out a form pleading (for a person who is illiterate, for example) only if the assistance is limited to transcribing or recording verbatim the victim's own language. The typing or other transcription of a victim's own words constitutes a "purely mechanical function" permitted by BOP § 10–206. See, e.g., 65 *Opinions of the Attorney General* at 28. See also *Brammer v. Taylor,* 338 S.E. 2d 207, 212 (W. Va. 1985) (merely typing a legal instrument drafted by another person, or merely reducing words of another person to writing, does not constitute the unauthorized preparation of a legal document).

On the other hand, lay advocates may not assist in filling out forms or form pleadings "using their own words," or summarizing information given them by a client. This degree of aid rises impermissibly to the level of applying facts to the law in the "preparation" of a legal document. See *Matter of Bright,* 171 B.R. at 803–04 (deciding where information should be placed on bankruptcy forms and in what format, deciding what property should be listed, and adding language to forms not dictated by clients constitute unauthorized practice); *Akron Bar Association v. Singleton,* 573 N.E.2d 1249, 1250 (Ohio Bd. Unauth. Prac. 1990) (selling of "dissolution kits" is unauthorized practice of law when layperson prepared dissolution of marriage form pleadings based on information sheet completed by clients); *State v. Hunt,* 880 P.2d 96, 100 (Wash. App. 1994) (preparation of legal forms constitutes unauthorized practice).

E. Government Advocacy

Lay advocates may not urge Assistant State's Attorneys or other government employees to follow a particular course of action in an individual case, if the advocate purports to do so on behalf of individual victims. This type of advocacy would be "representing" a client before a governmental unit. See BOP § 10–101 (h) (1) (ii). See also *In re Disciplinary Action Against Ray,* 452 N.W.2d 689, 693 (Minn. 1990) (advising clients in legal matter and attempting to negotiate a settlement constitutes unauthorized practice). However, advocates could speak with governmental representatives on behalf of victims' rights generally, without reference to any particular case or individual. . . .

The prohibition against unauthorized practice undoubtedly furthers an important goal—to "protect the public from being preyed upon by . . . incompetent, unethical, or irresponsible representation." *In re Application of R.G.S.,* 312 Md. 626, 638, 541 A.2d 977 (1988). However, this concern would hardly seem to be paramount in this context. Rather, victims of domestic violence are being "preyed upon" in ways far more threatening than the specter of inadequate representation. Lay advocates could help victims assert legal rights that they would otherwise have no means of pursuing. Battered women need legal assistance desperately and too often cannot find it within the legal community. . . .

[Summary]

1. A lay advocate may:
   (i) provide victims with basic information about the existence of legal rights and remedies;
   (ii) provide victims with basic information about the manner in which judicial proceedings are conducted;
   (iii) assist a victim to prepare a legal pleading or other legal document on her own behalf by defining unfamiliar terms on a form, explaining where on a form the victim is to provide certain information, and if necessary, transcribing or otherwise recording the victim's own words verbatim;
   (iv) sit with a victim at trial table, if permitted by the court; and
   (v) engage in the general advocacy of the rights of battered women as a group.
2. Except under the supervision of an attorney, a lay advocate may not:
   (i) Provide any advice relating to a victim's rights or remedies, including whether a victim's particular circumstances suggest that she should pursue a particular remedy;

(continues)

Opinion of the Attorney General No. 95–056—*continued*

(ii) provide information about the legal aspects of judicial proceedings, such as how to present a case, call witnesses, introduce evidence, and the like;

(iii) use the advocate's own language in preparing or filling out pleadings or other legal documents; or

(iv) engage in advocacy before any governmental representative on behalf of an individual victim.

ASSIGNMENT 4.1

You are a paralegal talking to Mary Smith, who is thinking about filing for divorce. Give several examples of what you might tell this person that would constitute:

(a) Information about her legal rights

(b) Legal advice on her legal rights

For years, attorneys have complained that large numbers of individuals were crossing the line by providing improper personal assistance. Bar associations often asked the state to prosecute many of them. Yet some charged that the attorneys were less interested in protecting the public than in preserving their own monopoly over the practice of law. A famous case involving this controversy is that of Rosemary Furman and the Florida bar.

Rosemary Furman: Folk Hero or Menace?

Rosemary Furman, a former legal secretary, believes that you should be able to solve simple legal problems without hiring an attorney. Hence she established the Northside Secretarial Service in Jacksonville, Florida. She compiled and sold packets of legal forms (for $50) on divorce, name changes, and adoptions. The price *included her personal assistance in filling out and filing the forms.* The Florida Bar Association and the Florida courts moved against her with a vengeance for practicing law illegally. She was convicted and sentenced to thirty days in jail. She never served the sentence, however.

Widespread support for Ms. Furman developed. Her case soon became a cause célèbre for those seeking increased access to the legal system for the poor and the middle class.[3] Many were outraged at the legal profession and the judiciary for their treatment of Ms. Furman.

The CBS program *60 Minutes* did a story that was favorable to her cause. Other national media, including *Newsweek*, covered the case. Warner Brothers considered doing a docudrama on the story. Rosemary Furman struck a responsive chord when she claimed that for every $50 she earned, an attorney lost $500. An editorial in the *Gainesville Sun* said, "Throw Rosemary Furman in jail? Surely not after the woman forced the Florida bar and the judiciary to confront its responsibility to the poor. Anything less than a 'thank you' note would indeed show genuine vindictiveness on the part of the legal profession" (November 4, 1984). There were, however, other views. An editorial in *USA Today* said that what she was doing was illegal. "If she can give legal advice, so can charlatans, frauds, and rip-off artists" (February 2, 1984).

The events in the Rosemary Furman story are as follows:

- 1978 & 1979: The Florida Bar Association takes Rosemary Furman to court, alleging that she is practicing law without a license.
- 1979: The Florida Supreme Court rules against her. She is enjoined from engaging in the unauthorized practice of law.
- 1982: The Florida Bar Association again brings a complaint against her business, alleging that she was continuing the unauthorized practice of law.
- 1983: Duval County Circuit Judge A. C. Soud Jr. finds her in contempt of court for violating the 1979 order. The judge makes this decision in a nonjury hearing. She is then ordered to serve thirty days in jail.
- 1984: The U.S. Supreme Court refuses to hear the case. This has the effect of allowing the state jail sentence to stand. The Court is not persuaded by her argument that she should have been granted a jury trial of her peers rather than having been judged solely by a profession (attorneys and judges) that was biased against her.
- Her attorneys ask the Florida Supreme Court to vacate the jail sentence if she agrees to close her business.
- The Florida Bar Association tells the Florida Supreme Court that the jail term is a fitting punishment and should be served.
- November 13, 1984: The Florida Supreme Court orders her to serve the jail sentence for practicing law without a license. (451 So. 2d 808)

(continues)

Rosemary Furman: Folk Hero or Menace?—continued

- November 27, 1984: Rosemary Furman is granted clemency from the thirty-day jail term by Florida governor Bob Graham and his Clemency Board. She does not have to go to jail.
- Furman and her attorneys announce that they will work on a constitutional amendment defining the practice of law to make it easier for citizens to avoid dependency on attorneys in civil cases. Says Ms. Furman, "I have only begun to fight."

This case has had an impact in Florida and elsewhere in the country. Recently, for example, Florida made a dramatic change in the definition of unauthorized practice of law. Under this definition, it "shall not constitute the unauthorized practice of law for a nonlawyer to engage in limited oral communications to assist a person in the completion of blanks on a legal form approved by the Supreme Court of Florida. Oral communications by nonlawyers are restricted to those communications reasonably necessary to elicit factual information to complete the blanks on the form and inform the person how to file the form."[4] Later in this chapter, we will discuss the even more dramatic concept of *limited licensing* for paralegals, which is being considered in a number of states. Some have referred to these developments as "the long shadow of Rosemary Furman."

ASSIGNMENT 4.2

(a) Define the practice of law in your state. Quote from your state code, court rules, or other official authority that is available. See appendix E.

(b) Would Rosemary Furman have been prosecuted for the unauthorized practice of law in your state today? Why or why not?

The Furman case involved direct competition with attorneys. More indirect competition comes from people engaged in law-related activities, such as accountants, claims adjusters, real estate agents, life insurance agents, and officers of trust departments of banks. For years, bar associations complained about such activities. In many instances, they challenged the activities in court as the unauthorized practice of law. The problem was so pervasive that some bar associations negotiated a **statement of principles** (sometimes called a *treaty*) with these occupations in an attempt to identify boundary lines and methods of resolving difficulties. Most of these treaties, however, have been ineffective in defining the kinds of law-related activities that can and cannot be performed by nonattorneys. A tremendous amount of effort and money is needed to negotiate, monitor, and enforce the treaties. The resources are simply not available. Furthermore, there is a concern that such efforts by attorneys to restrain competition might violate the antitrust laws. In light of all these difficulties, the treaties either have been withdrawn or are being ignored.

statement of principles
Guidelines that try to identify the activities of specified law-related occupations that do not constitute the practice of law.

The Legal Profession: A Bow to the Past—a Glimpse of the Future

by Joseph Sims

[The following speech was delivered by Joseph Sims, the deputy assistant attorney general in the Antitrust Division of the U.S. Department of Justice. He discusses the antitrust implications of the "statements of principles" used by bar associations. The speech also mentions two major changes in the law: (1) the end of the prohibition on advertising by attorneys, and (2) the *Goldfarb* case, which held that the legal profession could no longer impose minimum fee schedules on attorneys, because such schedules operated as a fixed, rigid price floor and therefore constituted price fixing. We will examine advertising and minimum fee schedules in the next chapter on ethics.]

Today, legal services are being advertised on television. That fact alone gives us some idea of how much change has come to the legal profession in the last few years.

That change has not always come easy, but the fact that it has come so far, so fast, tells us quite a bit about what will happen in the future. We lawyers as a group have grumbled and argued, fought and yelled, struggled and been confused—but there are now lawyers advertising on television. Even a casual observer cannot fail to appreciate the significance of this change.

Competition, slowly but surely, is coming to the legal profession. This opening of traditional doors, the breaking of traditional barriers is the result of many forces—the number of new lawyers, the awakening of consumerism, the growing realization that the complexity of our society requires legal assistance in more and more areas. But one contributing factor has been antitrust litigation and the Department of Justice. . . .

[The Supreme Court fired the shot heard 'round the bar in the unanimous decision *Goldfarb v. Virginia State Bar*, 421 U.S. 773 (1975).] The Court held that the minimum fee schedule challenged by the Goldfarbs violated Section 1 of the Sherman Act. This decision broke the dam and released the flood of change that we see engulfing the profession today. For better or worse, the Goldfarbs had set in motion a series of events that were to change the character of the legal profession forever.

The Court decided several things in *Goldfarb*, but the most important was that the legal profession was subject to the antitrust laws—there was no "professional exemption." The response

to *Goldfarb* was fascinating. A large number of private suits were filed challenging various aspects of bar regulation. . . .

[An] area sure to be controversial in the future is unauthorized practice. There is already at least one antitrust challenge, against the Virginia State Bar, seeking to prohibit the bar from promulgating unauthorized practice opinions. This case, which involves title insurance, is a direct challenge to the extraordinary power that the legal profession now has—in most states—to define the limits of its own monopoly. It would be strange indeed for a state to hand over to, say its steel industry, not only the power to regulate entry into the industry and the conduct of those within it, but also the power to define what the industry was. In many states, that is exactly the power the organized bar now has, and that power is being challenged as inconsistent with the antitrust laws.

The heart of this challenge is that lawyers shouldn't be deciding what is the practice of law—defining the scope of the legal monopoly. The papers filed in that case . . . indicate that the objection is not to such a decision being made; the objection is to the State's delegation of that power to the [legal] profession.

In fact, of course, the principle behind this lawsuit could be expanded not only to other subject matter areas, but also to arrangements between the organized bar and other professions which have as their basic result the division of commercial responsibilities.

For example, the American Bar Association [once] entered into "statements of principles" with respect to the practice of law with a variety of other professions and occupations ranging from accountants to claim adjusters, publishers, social workers, and even professional engineers. These documents generally set forth the joint views of the professions as to which activities fall within the practice of law and which activities are proper for members of the other profession. They nearly all provide that each profession will advise its clients to seek out members of the other profession in appropriate circumstances.

As a general rule, two competitors may not agree with each other to allocate markets, or bids, or even functions; if they do, they violate the antitrust laws. At the least, this traditional antitrust principle raises some questions about the legal effect of such "statements of principles."

Some practitioners of law-related occupations have gone directly to the legislature to seek enactment of statutes that authorize what would otherwise be the unauthorized practice of law. In many instances, they have been successful. For example:

Code of Georgia, § 15–19–52. Furthermore, a title insurance company may prepare such papers as it thinks proper or necessary in connection with a title which it proposes to insure, in order, in its opinion, for it to be willing to insure the title, where no charge is made by it for the papers.

Utah Code Ann. § 61–2–20. (1) Principal brokers and associate brokers may fill out any documents associated with the closing of a real estate transaction.

The effect of such statutes is to allow members of designated occupations to perform certain legal tasks that are intimately related to their work without having to hire attorneys or without forcing their clients to hire them.

In 2002, the American Bar Association challenged the future validity of such statutes by proposing a model definition of the practice of law that contained a series of controversial presumptions. Under the proposal, the practice of law would be defined as the

> "application of legal principles and judgment with regard to the circumstances or objectives of a person that require the knowledge and skill of a person trained in the law."[5]

There was nothing dramatically new in this definition. (Indeed, the proposed definition simply restates the professional judgment test that we examined earlier in Exhibit 4.2.) What was new and highly controversial were some presumptions on what activities would constitute the practice of law under the new definition. The Antitrust Division of the U.S. Department of Justice (DOJ) and a similar division of the Federal Trade Commission (FTC) warned the ABA that the proposal had serious monopoly and antitrust implications. The DOJ and FTC were particularly disturbed with provisions that said that a person who engaged in the following activities on behalf of another would be "presumed to be practicing law":

- Selecting, drafting, or completing agreements and other legal documents that affect the legal rights of a person;
- Negotiating legal rights or duties on behalf of a person;
- Representing a person before a body with the authority to resolve a legal dispute (an "adjudicative body"), including, but not limited to, preparing or filing documents or conducting discovery; or
- Giving advice or counsel to persons as to their legal rights or responsibilities or to those of others.

The DOJ and FTC said that these provisions, particularly the first two, were overly broad because they would prohibit nonattorneys from offering a number of limited services they currently provide in competition with attorneys to the benefit of consumers. Here are examples of such services:

- Realtors selecting, explaining, drafting, and negotiating documents used in the sale of real estate;
- Tenants' associations informing renters of landlord and tenant legal rights and duties, often in the context of a particular landlord-tenant problem;
- Experienced nonattorney employees advising their employer about what their company must do to comply with state labor laws or safety regulations;
- Income tax preparers and accountants interpreting federal and state tax codes, family law code, and general partnership laws, and providing advice to their clients based on this legal information;
- Investment bankers and other business planners providing advice to their clients that includes information about various laws;
- Interactive software allowing consumers to select and draft wills, trusts, and other legal documents.

The DOJ and FTC are not arguing that a nonattorney should have the same right to practice law as an attorney. They are simply saying that the ABA has failed to provide evidence of the kind of consumer harm in the above examples that would justify a requirement that only attorneys should be able to provide the services listed. Competition between attorneys and nonattorneys for such services is healthy for the consumer:

> Together, the DOJ and the FTC have become increasingly concerned about efforts to prevent nonlawyers from competing with attorneys in the provision of certain services through the adoption of Unauthorized Practice of Law opinions and laws by state bar agencies, courts, and legislatures. . . . [W]e urge the ABA not to adopt the current proposed Definition, which, in our judgment, is overbroad and could restrain competition between lawyers and nonlawyers to provide similar services to American consumers. If adopted by state governments, the proposed Definition is likely to raise costs for consumers and limit their competitive choices. There is no evidence before the ABA of which we are aware that consumers are hurt by this competition and there is substantial evidence that they benefit from it. Consequently, we recommend that the proposed Model Definition be substantially narrowed or rejected.[6]

Stung by this criticism, the ABA chose to abandon the proposed definition. The ABA did not want to risk an even broader antitrust challenge against the legal profession that the DOJ and FTC appeared to be on the verge of launching.

2. AUTHORIZED PRACTICE OF LAW

Examine the following phrase closely: unauthorized practice of law by nonattorneys. If there is such a thing as the *un*authorized practice of law, then, by implication, there must be an *authorized* practice of law. And indeed there is. First of all, paralegals in law offices throughout the country are practicing law. Every day, they are intimately involved in the resolution of the legal problems of specific persons. This practice, however, is authorized because the paralegals are acting under the supervision of attorneys. Also, the treaties and special-authorization statutes discussed earlier are additional examples of the authorized practice of law by nonattorneys. Furthermore, as we will see, there are other areas where nonattorneys are given a special authorization to practice law. Occasionally, attempts are made to call what they do something other than the practice of law, but these attempts conflict with reality, since the nonattorneys are doing what attorneys usually do for their clients, even if the nonattorneys are acting within a more restricted arena. Why has there been an erosion, however limited, in the attorney's monopoly over the practice of law? A number of reasons account for the existence of the authorized practice of law by nonattorneys.

One reason is the image of the attorney as excessively combative. Most of the public view attorneys as fighters, people who will pursue an issue to the bitter end. While the client for whom an attorney is doing battle may view this trait favorably, many feel that an attorney's aggressive inclinations can be counterproductive. Administrative agencies, for example, are often suspicious of the involvement of attorneys. They are viewed as combatants who want to turn every agency decision into an **adversarial** proceeding. Agencies often see courtroom gymnastics and gimmicks as the attorney's primary mode of operation. The attorney is argumentative to a fault.

Former Chief Justice Rehnquist of the U.S. Supreme Court agrees. In describing a proposal to increase the role of attorneys in administrative hearings, he was concerned that attorneys might turn amicable conferences into protracted controversies. "To be sure, counsel can often perform useful functions . . . they may bring out facts ignored by or unknown to the authorities, or help to work out satisfactory compromises. But this is only one side of the coin. Under our **adversary system**, the role of counsel is not to make sure the truth is ascertained but to advance his client's cause by any ethical means. Within the limits of professional propriety, causing delay and sowing confusion not only are his right but may be his duty. The result [of greater attorney involvement in administrative hearings may] be to turn what might have been a short conference leading to an amicable result into a protracted controversy."[7]

This image of the attorney as someone who complicates matters is best summed up by an old accountants' joke that taxation becomes more and more complex in direct proportion to attempts by attorneys to *simplify* tax law. Whether or not this view of attorneys is correct, it has accounted for some erosion of the legal profession's monopoly over the practice of law.

The unavailability of attorneys has also contributed to this result. A vast segment of our population has legal complaints that are never touched by attorneys. This is due, in part, to the fact that most of these complaints do not involve enough money to attract attorneys. Yet many attorneys in this country are unemployed or underemployed. The logical solution would appear to be for attorneys to lower the cost of their services to meet the demand. This has not happened to any significant extent. Hence the pressure for alternatives continues.

We now turn to a fuller exploration of these themes under the following headings:

a. Court "representation" by nonattorneys
b. Attempted restrictions on the activities of the "jailhouse lawyer" and the broader policy considerations raised by such restrictions
c. Agency representation by nonattorneys

a. Court Representation

In the vast majority of courts in this country, only attorneys can represent someone in a judicial proceeding. There are, however, some limited exceptions.

In some lower courts in the country, particularly in the West, parties can have nonattorneys represent them. Examples include justice of the peace courts, magistrates courts, and small claims courts. Restrictions might be placed on such representation. For example, the nonattorney may be limited to a one-time representation or to cases involving the nonattorney's family or business associates.

adversarial Involving conflict or adversaries.

adversary system A method of resolving a legal dispute whereby the parties (alone or through their advocates) argue their conflicting claims before a neutral decision maker.

When a business is sued, some states allow a nonattorney employee of the business to represent it in court. An example is the conciliation court, which is a small claims court, in Minnesota:

> **Minnesota Statutes Annotated, § 491A.02.** A corporation, partnership, limited liability company, sole proprietorship or association may be represented in conciliation court by an officer, manager, or partner . . . or may appoint a natural person who is an employee . . . to appear on its behalf to settle a claim in conciliation court. . . . [This] representation does not constitute the practice of law. . . .

It strains logic to say that representing someone in court is not the practice of law, even if the court does not hear complicated cases. A more honest approach would be to say that it is the practice of law, but we are simply going to allow it. This is the approach taken by the District of Columbia, which allows a corporation to be defended in court by one of its nonattorney employees in a landlord-tenant action.[8] If the corporation files a **counterclaim**, however, the corporation must be represented by an attorney.

Tribal courts on Indian reservations have jurisdiction over designated civil and criminal matters involving Native Americans. In many of these courts, both parties are represented by nonattorney advocates. (See Tribal Law in Section C of chapter 2.)

Government employees occasionally act in a representative or semirepresentative capacity in court proceedings, even though they are not attorneys. In North Carolina cases involving the termination of parental rights, for example, the U.S. Supreme Court has noted the role of nonattorneys:

> In fact . . . the North Carolina Departments of Social Services are themselves sometimes represented at termination hearings by social workers instead of by lawyers.[9]

A number of states have hired nonattorney court employees to act as advisors or facilitators for **pro se** parties (persons who are representing themselves), particularly in divorce and other family law cases. The employee does not represent the person in court but is available to answer questions about which forms or pleadings to file, how to fill them out or draft them, and where to file them—all classic examples of what attorneys do when practicing law.

Litigation attorneys often spend unproductive time traveling to court and waiting around simply to give documents to the judge and to set dates for the various stages of pretrial and trial proceedings. Another problem is that an attorney may have to be in two different courtrooms at the same time. For example, an early morning hearing may be unexpectedly extended, preventing the attorney from appearing at a previously scheduled mid-morning proceeding in another courtroom on a different case. In such situations, wouldn't it be helpful if the attorney's paralegal could "appear" in court for the limited purpose of delivering papers to the judge, asking for a new date, or presenting some other message? *In most states, such activity is strictly prohibited.*

A Kentucky paralegal learned about this prohibition in a dramatic way. Her attorney was involved in a trial at the Jefferson Circuit Court. He asked the paralegal to go to another courtroom during "Motion Hour," where attorneys make motions and schedule future proceedings on a case. He told her to ask for a hearing date on another case that he had pending. She did so. When the case was called during Motion Hour, she rose, identified herself as the attorney's paralegal, and gave the message to the judge, asking for the hearing date. Opposing counsel was outraged. He verbally assaulted the paralegal in the courtroom and filed a motion to hold the paralegal and her attorney in contempt of court for the unauthorized practice of law. When a hearing was later held on this motion, members of a local paralegal association packed the courtroom. Tensions were high. The judge *denied* the motion, after a hearing on the matter. The audience broke out into loud applause. "Apparently the judge concluded that [the paralegal] had rendered no service involving legal knowledge or advice, but had merely transmitted to the court [the attorney's] message regarding disposition of the motion, that is, she had been performing a function that was administrative, not legal in nature."[10]

A celebrated Illinois opinion, *People v. Alexander*, took a position similar to that of this Kentucky court. In this opinion, the defendant was an unlicensed **law clerk** who appeared before the court to state that his employing attorney could not be present in court at the moment because he was trying a case elsewhere. On behalf of his employer, the law clerk requested a **continuance**. The defendant's actions were challenged. It was argued that *any* appearance by nonattorneys before a court to give information on the availability of counsel or the status of litigation constitutes the unauthorized practice of law. The Illinois court took the unique position

---

counterclaim A claim by one side in a case (usually the defendant) that is filed in response to a claim asserted by an opponent (usually the plaintiff).

pro se (on one's own behalf) Appearing for or representing oneself. Also called *in propria persona, pro per.*

law clerk An attorney's employee who is in law school studying to become an attorney or who has graduated from law school and is waiting to pass the bar examination. (See the glossary for additional definitions of *law clerk*.)

continuance The adjournment or postponement of a proceeding until a later date.

that this was not the practice of law. The reasoning of the court is presented in the following except from the opinion:

People v. Alexander

53 Ill. App. 2d 299, 202 N.E.2d 841 (Appellate Court of Illinois, First District, 1964)

In the case of *People ex rel. Illinois State Bar Ass'n v. People's Stock Yards State Bank*, 344 Ill. 462, at page 476, 176 N.E. 901, at page 907, wherein a bank was prosecuted for the unauthorized practice of law, the following quotation is relied upon:

According to the generally understood definition of the practice of law in this country, it embraces the preparation of pleadings, and other papers incident to actions and special proceedings, and the management of such actions and proceedings on behalf of clients before judges and courts.

Since this statement relates to the appearance and management of proceedings in court on behalf of a client, we do not believe it can be applied to a situation where a clerk hired by a law firm presents information to the court on behalf of his employer.

We agree with the trial judge that clerks should not be permitted to make motions or participate in other proceedings which can be considered as "managing" the litigation. However, if apprising the court of an employer's engagement or inability to be present constitutes the making of a motion, we must hold that clerks may make such motions for continuances without being guilty of the unauthorized practice of law. Certainly with

the large volume of cases appearing on the trial calls these days, it is imperative that this practice be followed.

In *Toth v. Samuel Phillipson & Co.*, 250 Ill. App. 247 (1928) the court said at page 250:

It is well known in this county where numerous trial courts are sitting at the same time the exigencies of such a situation require that trial attorneys be represented by their clerical force to respond to some of the calls, and that the court acts upon their response the same as if the attorneys of record themselves appeared in person.

After that opinion was handed down, the number of judges was substantially increased in the former circuit and superior courts and the problem of answering court calls has at least doubled. We cannot add to the heavy burden of lawyers who in addition to responding to trial calls must answer pretrial calls and motion calls—all held in the morning—by insisting that a lawyer must personally appear to present to a court a motion for a continuance on grounds of engagement or inability to appear because of illness or other unexpected circumstances. To reduce the backlog, trial lawyers should be kept busy actually trying lawsuits and not answering court calls.

It must be emphasized that most states would *not* agree with Kentucky and Illinois. Most states would prohibit nonattorneys from doing what was authorized by the two courts in these two states. Fortunately, however, at least a few additional states have disagreed.

The Allen County Bar Association of Indiana, for example, has taken the bold move of permitting paralegals to perform what hitherto had been considered attorney functions in court. A paralegal is authorized, for example:

- To "file" a motion for a continuance, a motion for a default judgment, a motion to compel discovery, a motion to dismiss the action, a motion to appoint a receiver, etc.
- To receive ("obtain") orders on these motions
- To "set" pretrial conferences and all other hearing dates except trials

The vast majority of attorneys in the country would be amazed to learn what is going on in Allen County. Once the shock subsides, however, these attorneys will probably see the wisdom and common sense of what Allen County has done and begin to think of ways to try it themselves.

The rules of the Allen County program are as follows:

Authority of Attorneys' Employees, Rule 21

Allen County Superior Court (2001)
West's Annotated Indiana Code, Title 34. Appendix Court Rules (Civil)

A. In General. Generally, attorneys' employees who have not been admitted to practice law in Indiana but who assist their employers in Courthouse activities (herein called "legal assistants"), shall be limited to the performance of tasks which do not require the exercise of legal discretion or judgment that affects the legal rights of any person.

B. Trust Account Deposits. Only one legal assistant per law firm shall have the authority to obtain trust account deposits at the Allen County Clerk's Office in the name of his or her employer

firm. The employer law firm shall submit a letter to the Clerk of the Allen Circuit and Superior Courts stating that . . . [s]uch employee is authorized to obtain trust account deposits at the Allen County Clerk's Office in the name of his employer. . . .

C. Legal Documents. All pleadings which the legal assistant presents or files at the Courthouse must contain an attorney's signature, as the attorney for a party, or a statement affixed indicating that the documents were prepared by said attorney.

(continues)

Authority of Attorneys' Employees, Rule 21—*continued*

D. Permitted Acts. Such an employee shall be limited to the following acts:

(1) To file, and obtain orders on all motions described in Local Rule 10(A). [Examples: for a continuance, for a default judgment, to compel discovery, to dismiss the action, to appoint a receiver.]

(2) To set Pre-Trial Conferences and all other hearing dates except trials.

(3) To examine pleadings and chronological case summary sheets and make copies thereof within the Courthouse.

(4) At the discretion of the Court, to obtain approval of orders of the Court from the Judge's Law Clerk for:

(a) Notice of hearings.

(b) Orders to appear and answer interrogatories on the filing of a Verified Motion for Proceedings Supplemental.

(c) Stipulations signed and approved by all parties of record.

(d) Motions to Withdraw Appearance.

E. Acts Not Permitted. Such employee shall not have the authority to perform any acts not specified in Paragraph D of this rule.

F. Termination of Authority. Each employer law firm shall be responsible for notifying in writing the Clerk of the Allen Circuit and Allen Superior Court, and the Allen Superior Court Executive of the termination or revocation of any legal assistant's authority to act on behalf of said law office as covered by this rule.

A similar program exists in the Spokane County District Court and Superior Court in Washington State. Once paralegals are registered with the local bar association, they can present **ex-parte** and **uncontested** orders to the court. Here is the rule for the district court:

ex parte With only one side present; involving one party only. An *ex parte order* is a court order requested by one party and issued without notice to the other party.

uncontested Unchallenged; without opposition.

Paralegals, Rule 10

Spokane County District Court (LARLJ) (2000) West's Washington Local Rules of Court

Paralegals who are currently registered with the Spokane County Bar Association for the purpose of presentation of such orders may personally present agreed, ex-parte and uncontested orders signed by counsel, based solely upon the documents presented and the record in the file. Said privilege may be revoked or limited by the Court for noncompliance with this rule, or other misconduct, regardless of whether the Paralegal is permitted to present orders before other Courts.

b. The Jailhouse Lawyer

A **jailhouse lawyer** (also called a *writ writer*) is an incarcerated nonattorney who helps other prisoners with their legal problems. Jailhouse lawyers clearly practice law, often for fees in the form of cigarettes, cash, etc. Some prisons attempted to prevent jailhouse lawyers from providing this legal assistance even though the prisons provided no meaningful alternatives. This prohibition was struck down, however, by the United States Supreme Court in *Johnson v. Avery* in 1969. The basis of the opinion was that without the jailhouse lawyer, prisoners might not have access to the courts. The concurring opinion of Justice William O. Douglas raises significant questions about justice in our society.

jailhouse lawyer An incarcerated paralegal, usually self-taught, who has a limited right to provide other inmates with legal services if the institution does not provide adequate alternatives to such services.

Johnson v. Avery

United States Supreme Court 393 U.S. 483, 89 S. Ct. 747, 21 L. Ed. 2d 718 (1969)

Mr. Justice DOUGLAS, concurring.

While I join the opinion of the Court [in striking down the prohibition on the activities of jailhouse lawyers] I add a few words in emphasis of the important thesis of the case.

The increasing complexities of our governmental apparatus at both the local and the federal levels have made it difficult for a person to process a claim or even to make a complaint. Social security is a virtual maze, the hierarchy that governs

(continues)

Johnson v. Avery—continued

urban housing is often so intricate that it takes an expert to know what agency has jurisdiction over a particular complaint; the office to call or official to see for noise abatement, for a broken sewer line, or a fallen tree is a mystery to many in our metropolitan areas.

A person who has a claim assertable in faraway Washington, D.C., is even more helpless, as evidenced by the increasing tendency of constituents to rely on their congressional delegation to identify, press, and process their claims.

We think of claims as grist for the mill of the lawyers. But it is becoming abundantly clear that more and more of the effort in ferreting out the basis of claims and the agencies responsible for them and in preparing the almost endless paperwork for their prosecution is work for laymen. There are not enough lawyers to manage or supervise all of these affairs . . . *Yet there is a closed-shop philosophy in the legal profession that [drastically cuts down] active roles for laymen. . . . That traditional, closed-shop attitude is utterly out of place in the modern world where claims pile high. . . .* [Emphasis added.]

> If poverty lawyers are overwhelmed, some of the work can be delegated. . . . New York law permits senior law students

to practice law under certain supervised conditions. Approval must first be granted by the appellate division. A rung or two lower on the legal profession's ladder are laymen legal technicians, comparable to nurses and lab assistants in the medical profession. Large law firms employ them, and there seems to be no reason why they cannot be used in legal services programs to relieve attorneys. . . . Samore, *Legal Services for the Poor*, 32 Albany L. Rev. 509, 515–516 (1968).

The plight of a man in prison may in these respects be even more acute than the plight of a person on the outside. He may need collateral proceedings to test the legality of his detention or relief against management of the parole system or against defective detainers lodged against him which create burdens in the nature of his incarcerated status. He may have grievances of a civil nature against those outside the prison. His imprisonment may give his wife grounds for divorce and be a factor in determining the custody of his children; and he may have pressing social security, workmen's compensation, or veterans' claims.

While the demand for legal counsel in prison is heavy, the supply is light. For private matters of a civil nature, legal counsel for the indigent in prison is almost nonexistent.

Notes

1. "Jailhouse lawyers, or writ writers, as they are sometimes called, have always been part of prison society. But in recent years their numbers as well as the amount of litigation they generate, has increased substantially." One jailhouse lawyer at Soledad Prison "devotes 16 hours a day to his legal work, subscribes to dozens of legal publications (at a cost of $1,800 a year), and files a steady stream of lawsuits." Suing "has become almost a national pastime. Prisoners act no differently from other citizens in a litigious society." M. Kroll, *Counsel Behind Bars: Jailhouse Lawyers*, 7 California Lawyer 34 (June 1987).

2. The *Johnson* opinion stressed that the prison provided *no* alternative to the jailhouse lawyer. If alternatives had been available, the inmate would not be allowed to practice law. In *Williams v. United States Dep't of Justice*, 433 F.2d 958 (5th Cir. 1970), the court held that the presence of law students in the prison could be an alternative, but only if it were demonstrated that the students were meeting the need for inmate legal services. If the inmates had to wait a considerable period of time, for example, before they could be interviewed by the law students, then no adequate alternative would exist and the jailhouse lawyer could not be prevented from helping other inmates.

3. In *Gilmore v. Lynch*, 319 F. Supp. 105 (N.D. Cal. 1970), affirmed by the U.S. Supreme Court in *Younger v. Gilmore*, 404 U.S. 15 (1971), the court held that California had to either satisfy the legal needs of its prisoners or expand the prison law library to include a more comprehensive collection of law books.

4. Finally, the right of an inmate to assist other inmates in legal matters does *not* extend to representing an inmate in court. *Guajardo v. Luna*, 432 F.2d 1324 (5th Cir. 1970). Nor can a nonattorney represent an inmate in court even if this nonattorney is not an inmate himself or herself. This latter point was decided by the U.S. Supreme Court in *Hackin v. Arizona*, 389 U.S. 143 (1967).

5. How far can the rationale of *Johnson* be extended? Suppose, for example, it is demonstrated that many claimants before state administrative agencies are not receiving legal services because they cannot afford attorneys. Would the *Johnson* opinion permit paralegal representation before such agencies even if the latter prohibited it? What is the difference between an inmate's right to have access to the courts and *anyone's* right to complain to an agency? How do you think Justice Douglas would handle the case if it came before him?

"Although the *Johnson* case is admittedly narrow in scope, it does nevertheless, give aid and comfort to the view that whenever lawyers are unavailable for whatever reason, society will sanction alternative systems for the delivery of legal services. The paramount consideration will not be ethics nor the exclusivity of the right to practice law, but rather it will be the facilitation of access routes to the grievance machinery set up for the resolution of claims. If lawyers are not available to assist the citizenry with these claims, then the question arises as to whether skilled non-lawyers represent a viable alternative. The inevitability of this question becomes clear when we listen to the statistics on the demand for the services of a lawyer. Estimates have been made to the effect that if every lawyer devoted full time to the legal needs of the poor, there would still be a significant shortage of lawyers for the poor. If the legal needs of the middle class are added, the shortage of legal services becomes overwhelming." W. Statsky and P. Lang, *The Legal Paraprofessional as Advocate and Assistant: Roles, Training Concepts and Materials*, 49–50 (1971). See also W. Statsky, *Inmate Involvement in Prison Legal Services: Roles and Training Options for the Inmate as Paralegal* (American Bar Association, Commission on Correctional Facilities and Services, Resource Center on Correctional Law and Legal Services, 1974).

c. Agency Representation

A considerable number of administrative agencies will permit a paralegal or other non-attorney to represent clients at the agency. These individuals are usually called *agents, practitioners,* or *representatives*. They engage in both *informal* advocacy (e.g., phoning agency officials on behalf of a client) and *formal* advocacy (e.g., representing a client at an adversarial administrative hearing within the agency). (A proceeding is adversarial if it involves conflict or adversaries, whether or not the other side is represented.) Often the issues before the agency are economic, statistical, or scientific, but legal issues are also involved. It is clear that in conducting some adversarial hearings before an agency, the nonattorney can be practicing law in a manner that is remarkably similar to an attorney's representation of a client in court. Our study of this phenomenon will begin with federal administrative agencies, and then we will cover state agencies. (Later, in chapter 15, we will examine specific techniques of paralegal advocacy within administrative agencies.)

Nonattorney Practice before Federal Administrative Agencies. Congress has passed a statute, the **Administrative Procedure Act (APA)**, that governs procedures before *federal* administrative agencies such as the Social Security Administration and the Federal Trade Commission. The act gives each federal agency the power to decide for itself whether only attorneys can represent clients before it:

> **Administrative Procedure Act,** 5 U.S.C. § 555(b) (2001). A person compelled to appear in person before an agency . . . is entitled to be accompanied, represented, and advised by counsel or, if permitted by the agency, by other qualified representative. (www4.law.cornell.edu/uscode/5/555.html)

When an agency decides to use this power to permit nonattorney representation, it can allow anyone to act as the agent or representative of another before the agency, or it can establish qualifications or standards of admission to practice before it. If the agency takes the latter course, there are a number of qualifications or standards it could impose such as passing a specialized test to demonstrate competency in the subject matter regulated by the agency, minimum educational or experience requirements, registration or enrollment on the agency's approved roster of representatives, and an agreement to abide by designated ethical rules of practice—a violation of which could result in suspension and "disbarment."

The U.S. Patent and Trademark Office (USPTO) has established criteria for individuals to practice before the USPTO as **registered agents** (www.uspto.gov). Their services include drafting applications for patents, filing them with the USPTO, and searching legal opinions on patentability.[11] Over 15 percent of USPTO representatives are nonattorneys. Perhaps the largest use of nonattorneys in federal agencies is at the Internal Revenue Service within the Treasury Department.[12] Any certified public accountant is authorized to practice before the IRS. The American Institute of Certified Public Accountants (www.aicpa.org) has more than 300,000 members, most of whom are not attorneys.[13] In addition, the IRS has enrolled (i.e., registered) thousands of nonattorneys called **enrolled agents** to represent taxpayers at all administrative proceedings within the IRS. (Once a dispute goes to court, however, an attorney must take over.) To become an enrolled agent, an individual must either pass a written IRS examination or prove that he or

Administrative Procedure Act (APA) The statute that governs procedures before federal administrative agencies. (Many states have their own APA for procedures before state administrate agencies.)

registered agent A nonattorney authorized to practice before the United States Patent and Trademark Office.

enrolled agent An attorney or nonattorney who is authorized to represent taxpayers before the Internal Revenue Service.

she once worked at the IRS for five years interpreting and applying tax laws. In most states, there are organizations of enrolled agents; the major national organization is the National Association of Enrolled Agents (www.naea.org).

Although many federal agencies allow nonattorney representation, relatively few nonattorneys actually use the authority they have. A study by the American Bar Association of thirty-three federal administrative agencies reached the following conclusion: "We found that the overwhelming majority of agencies studied permit nonlawyer representation in both adversarial and nonadversarial proceedings. However, most of them seem to encounter lay practice very infrequently (in less than 5% of adjudications), while only a few encounter lay practice as often as lawyer practice. Thus, although universally permitted, lay practice before federal agencies rarely occurs."[14]

One agency where nonattorney representation is fairly high (about 15 percent) is the Social Security Administration (SSA). Paralegals are frequently appointed by clients (see Exhibit 4.3) to represent them before the agency. Here is what the SSA says about the role of representatives:

What a Representative May Do.   Once you appoint a representative, he or she can act on your behalf in most Social Security matters by:

- Obtaining information from your Social Security file;
- Helping you obtain medical records or information to support your claim;
- Coming with you, *or for you*, to any interview, conference, or hearing you have with SSA;
- Requesting a reconsideration, hearing or Appeals Council review; and
- Helping you and your witnesses prepare for a hearing and questioning any witnesses.

The representative also will receive a copy of the decision(s) made on claim(s).[15]

According to the results of a study that compared the success of clients at hearings based on who represented them:

- 72.6 percent of clients represented by attorneys were successful.
- 69.8 percent of clients represented by nonattorneys were successful.
- 52.7 percent of clients who represented themselves were successful.[16]

administrative law judge (ALJ) A hearing officer who presides over a hearing at an administrative agency.

In another study, SSA hearing officers, called **administrative law judges (ALJ)**, were asked to rate the competence of the paralegals and attorneys who represent claimants at the hearings:

- 60 percent rated paralegal representation good or satisfactory.
- 88 percent rated attorney representation good or satisfactory.
- 34 percent rated paralegal competence as better than or about equal to attorney competence.
- 65 percent rated paralegals less or significantly less competent than attorneys.[17]

Social Security representatives have formed the National Organization of Social Security Claimants' Representatives (NOSSCR), consisting of attorneys and "many skilled paralegals" (www.nosscr.org). See chapter 15 on paralegal advocacy on behalf of Social Security claimants.

Attorneys and paralegals can charge fees for their services in representing clients before the SSA, but the agency must specifically approve the fee. This is not to say, however, that attorneys and paralegals are treated alike. If an attorney successfully represents a claimant, the agency will deduct up to 25 percent of the claimant's award, which will be paid directly to the attorney to cover fees. In contrast, if a paralegal successfully represents a claimant, the traditional rule has been that the paralegal must collect the fee directly from the client; the SSA would not deduct anything from the award in such cases. In 2005, however, the SSA began a demonstration project that authorizes direct payment of fees to nonattorney representatives who meet designated criteria such as having experience representing clients before the SSA, passing an examination on Social Security law, and carrying liability insurance to protect clients against malpractice.[18] Paralegals who do not meet these qualifications must collect their fees directly from their clients.

Nonattorney Practice before State Administrative Agencies.   At the *state* level, there is often a similar system for authorizing nonattorneys to provide representation at many state administrative agencies. The state agencies most likely to allow nonattorney representation are those handling unemployment insurance, workers' compensation, public health and public assistance benefits, employment discrimination, and real estate assessments.[19] In New York, for example, a survey found that 70 percent of New York state agencies and 63 percent of New York City agencies permitted some form of nonlawyer representation.[20]

EXHIBIT 4.3	Appointment of Representative

Social Security Administration
Please read the instructions before completing this form.

Form Approved
OMB No. 0960-0527

Name (Claimant) (Print or Type)	Social Security Number ___ - ___ - ___
Wage Earner (If Different)	Social Security Number ___ - ___ - ___

Part I   **APPOINTMENT OF REPRESENTATIVE**

I appoint this person, _____ ,

(Name and Address)

to act as my representative in connection with my claim(s) or asserted right(s) under:

☐ Title II   ☐ Title XVI   ☐ Title XVIII   ☐ Title VIII
(RSDI)   (SSI)   (Medicare Coverage)   (SVB)

This person may, entirely in my place, make any request or give any notice; give or draw out evidence or information; get information; and receive any notice in connection with my pending claim(s) or asserted right(s).

☐ I authorize the Social Security Administration to release information about my pending claim(s) or asserted right(s) to designated associates who perform adminisrtative duties (e.g. clerks), partners, and/or parties under contractual arrangements (e.g. copying services) for or with my representative.

☐ I appoint, or I now have, more than one representative. My main representative is _____ .

(Name of Principal Representative)

Signature (Claimant)	Address
Telephone Number (with Area Code) ( ) —	Fax Number (with Area Code) ( ) —	Date

Part II   **ACCEPTANCE OF APPOINTMENT**

I, _____ , hereby accept the above appointment. I certify that I have not been suspended or prohibited from practice before the Social Security Administration; that I am not disqualified from representing the claimant as a current or former officer or employee of the United States; and that I will not charge or collect any fee for the representation, even if a third party will pay the fee, unless it has been approved in accordance with the laws and rules referred to on the reverse side of the representative's copy of this form. If I decide not to charge or collect a fee for the representation, I will notify the Social Security Administration. (Completion of Part II satisfies this requirement.)

Check one: ☐ I am an attorney. ☐ I am a non-attorney who is participating in the direct fee payment demonstration project.

☐ I am a non-attorney . I am not participating in the direct fee payment demonstration project.

I have been disbarred or suspended from a court or bar to which I was previously admitted to practice as an attorney. ☐ Yes ☐ No

I have been disqualified from participating in or appearing before a Federal program or agency. ☐ Yes ☐ No

I declare under penalty of perjury that I have examined all the information on this form, and on any accompanying statements or forms, and it is true and correct to the best of my knowledge.

Signature (Representative)	Address
Telephone Number (with Area Code) ( ) —	Fax Number (with Area Code) ( ) —	Date

Part III (Optional)   **WAIVER OF FEE**

I waive my right to charge and collect a fee under sections 206 and 1631(d)(2) of the Social Security Act. I release my client (the claimant) from any obligations, contractual or otherwise, which may be owed to me for services I have provided in connection with my client's claim(s) or asserted right(s).

Signature (Representative)	Date

Part IV (Optional)   **WAIVER OF DIRECT PAYMENT**
by Attorney or Non-Attorney Eligible to Receive Direct Payment

I waive only my right to direct payment of a fee from the withheld past-due retirement, survivors, disability insurance or supplemental security income benefits of my client (the claimant). I do not waive my right to request fee approval and to collect a fee directly from my client or a third party.

Signature (Representative Waiving Direct Payment)	Date

Form SSA-1696-U4 (2-2008) ef (2-2008)
Destroy Prior Editions

TAKE OR SEND ORIGINAL TO SSA AND RETAIN A COPY FOR YOUR RECORDS
(4 Copies: File, Claimant, Representative, OHA)

(www.ssa.gov/online/ssa-1696.pdf)

ASSIGNMENT 4.3

Assume that someone in your state wants to challenge:

(a) The denial of workers' compensation

(b) The denial of unemployment compensation

(c) The denial of a license to practice any occupation for which your state requires a license

(d) The assessment of property for purposes of property tax

For any two of these challenges, determine whether the agency involved will allow a nonattorney to represent the person bringing the challenge at the agency.

Challenging Nonattorney Practice before Administrative Agencies.   Of course, the organized bar has never been happy that federal and state administrative agencies have given this special authorization to nonattorneys. Since there are state statutes on who can practice law (and often criminal penalties for nonattorneys who practice law in violation of these statutes), how can an administrative agency allow a nonattorney to engage in activity that is clearly the practice of law? The answer to this question is somewhat different for federal and state agencies.

If the agency permitting nonattorney representation is a *federal* agency (for example, the U.S. Patent and Trademark Office, the Internal Revenue Service, and the Social Security Administration), its authorization takes precedence over any *state* laws that would prohibit it. This principle was established in the U.S. Supreme Court case of *Sperry v. State of Florida ex rel. the Florida Bar.*[21] The case involved a nonattorney who was authorized to represent clients before the U.S. Patent Office (now the U.S. Patent and Trademark Office). The Florida Bar claimed that the nonattorney was violating the state practice-of-law statute. The Supreme Court ruled that the **Supremacy Clause** of the U.S. Constitution gives federal laws supremacy over conflicting state laws. The Court also said,

> Examination of the development of practice before the Patent Office and its governmental regulation reveals that: (1) nonlawyers have practiced before the Office from its inception, with the express approval of the Patent Office and to the knowledge of Congress; (2) during prolonged congressional study of unethical practices before the Patent Office, the right of non-lawyer agents to practice before the Office went unquestioned, and there was no suggestion that abuses might be curbed by state regulation; (3) despite protests of the bar, Congress in enacting the Administrative Procedure Act refused to limit the right to practice before the administrative agencies to lawyers; and (4) the Patent Office has defended the value of nonlawyer practitioners while taking steps to protect the interests which a State has in prohibiting unauthorized practice of law. We find implicit in this history congressional (and administrative) recognition that registration in the Patent Office confers a right to practice before the Office without regard to whether the State within which the practice is conducted would otherwise prohibit such conduct.

> Moreover, the extent to which specialized lay practitioners should be allowed to practice before some 40-odd federal administrative agencies, including the Patent Office, received continuing attention both in and out of Congress during the period prior to 1952. The Attorney General's Committee on Administrative Procedure which, in 1941, studied the need for procedural reform in the administrative agencies, reported that "[e]specially among lawyers' organizations there has been manifest a sentiment in recent years that only members of the bar should be admitted to practice before administrative agencies. The Committee doubts that a sweeping interdiction of nonlawyer practitioners would be wise."[22]

The *Sperry* case involved an unsuccessful attempt by a bar association to prevent nonattorney representation at a federal agency. Suppose, however, that a *state* agency permits nonattorney representation. Can the bar association successfully challenge this authorization? The *Sperry* case would not apply to this question because *Sperry* covered only federal agencies. Determining whether a state agency can allow nonattorney representation depends on who has the *power* to regulate the practice of law in a particular state. If the state legislature has this power, then the agency authorization of nonattorney representation is valid so long as a state statute authorizes it. Suppose, however, that the state *judiciary*, through the highest state court, has the power to regulate the practice of law. If so, a state court might rule that a state agency's authorization of nonattorney representation interferes with the judiciary's right to regulate the practice of law. The court could then invalidate such representation even if a state statute authorized it.

Hence when nonattorney representation at a state agency is challenged, we need to find out who controls the practice of law in the state. The answer is not always clear, particularly in those states where the legislature and judiciary share the power to regulate the practice of law.

Supremacy Clause The clause in the U.S. Constitution (art. VI, cl. 2) that has been interpreted to mean that when valid federal law conflicts with state law, federal law controls.

[SECTION C]
LICENSING OF PARALEGALS

There are two main reasons an occupation may want to be licensed by the government:

- To protect the public
- To enhance the occupation's own image

Occupations such as electricians, brokers, and nurses offer services that require knowledge and skills that most citizens do not have. A license serves as a measure of assurance (although not a guarantee) that license holders are competent to perform their specialized and often technical services. In addition to a desire to protect the public, an occupation may want licensing as a way to enhance its self-image, credibility, and professionalism. The occupation often views licensing as a way to prevent less educated and less skilled individuals from working in the field.

No state requires paralegals to be licensed, although California has come very close. Several states have seriously considered licensing proposals, either *broad-based licensing* covering all paralegals or *limited licensing* covering only one sector of the field.

Before examining these proposals, it should be noted that the proposals sometimes confuse *certification* with *licensure*. Certification is usually a statement by a *non*governmental organization that a person has met certain qualifications. Licensure is a permission or authorization *by a government* to engage in a certain activity. (See Exhibit 4.1.)

BROAD-BASED LICENSING

An example of a broad-based licensing proposal is the Legal Assistant Act that the Michigan legislature considered but did not enact. The purpose of the act was to "regulate the practice of legal assistants." Under this proposal, a nine-member commission would be created to establish the requirements for the "certification" of legal assistants. Even though the proposal uses the word *certification*, it was a licensure program, since it would establish government-enforced requirements for engaging in a particular occupation. If this legislation had been enacted, a person could not be a legal assistant in Michigan without passing a statewide examination and having the educational credentials identified by the commission.

Such licensing schemes have not been enacted primarily because broad-based licensing is not needed to protect the public. The vast majority of paralegals are employees supervised by their attorney-employers. (Such paralegals are called **traditional paralegals**.) The public is protected by this supervision. Why add a vast bureaucratic licensing mechanism that would not increase the protection the public already receives through the attorney's ethical obligation to supervise all law office employees? Many bar associations would agree with the following point of view on paralegal licensing expressed by the North Carolina Bar Association:

traditional paralegal A paralegal who is an employee of an attorney.

> Several states have considered the possibility of adopting a licensing statute for paralegals, but none has done so. Licensing itself is subject to great public and legislative concern at present. So long as the work accomplished by non-lawyers for lawyers is properly supervised and reviewed by a licensed and responsible attorney, there would seem to be no need for a further echelon of licensing for the public's protection. Furthermore, licensing might be more dangerous than helpful to the public. The apparent stamp of approval of a license possibly could give the impression to the public that a person having such a license is qualified to deal directly with and give legal advice to the public. Although the Committee would not attempt to close the door on licensing of paralegals in the future if circumstances change and if, for example, the use of independent, non-lawyer employee paralegals were to become widespread, present conditions, at least, do not call for any program of licensing for paralegals.[23]

ASSIGNMENT 4.4

How would you characterize the opposition to licensure expressed by the North Carolina Bar Association? Do you think there is a conflict of interest in attorneys making these judgments about paralegal control? Explain.

New Jersey almost enacted broad-based licensing in 1999. After five years of study, a Committee on Paralegal Education and Regulation recommended that the Supreme Court of New Jersey adopt a broad-based licensing system run by the judiciary for all paralegals in the state. The system would include minimum educational requirements and an ethics examination. Some paralegal associations endorsed the proposal as enhancing the professionalism of the field and the degree of respect accorded paralegals. Other paralegal associations, however, agreed with the American Bar Association and the New Jersey State Bar Association that the proposal was unnecessary. The New Jersey Supreme Court rejected the plan. The establishment was clearly not in the mood to create the kind of bureaucracy that would be needed to implement and monitor broad-based licensing.

The New Jersey court acknowledged that "many of the tasks conducted by paralegals involve the practice of law." Yet in performing these tasks, paralegals are already subject to oversight by their attorney supervisors. Consequently, "the Court has concluded that direct oversight of paralegals is best accomplished through attorney supervision rather than through a Court-directed licensing system."[24]

In 2000, however, California broke ranks and created a regulatory scheme that has many features of broad-based licensing.[25] This event was a bombshell. No one expected comprehensive regulation from California, particularly since every other state had gone the other way.

The essence of California's radical program was to place restrictions on who can be called a paralegal or legal assistant. From now on, the only individuals who can use these titles in California are those who:

- Work under the supervision of an attorney,
- Meet stringent education qualifications (e.g., complete an approved paralegal program with a designated number of law-related courses or have a baccalaureate degree and one year of law-related experience under the supervision of a California attorney), and
- Attend mandatory **continuing legal education (CLE)** (four hours of ethics training every two years and four hours in general law or the law of a specialty every two years).

continuing legal education (CLE) Training in the law (usually short term) that a person receives after completing his or her formal legal training.

If you do not work under attorney supervision, you cannot call yourself a paralegal or legal assistant in California. Independent paralegals who sell their services directly to the public can no longer call themselves paralegals. This part of the legislation is not new. There are a few other states (e.g., Maine and Florida) where the titles *paralegal* and *legal assistant* are limited to those who work for attorneys. What is dramatically new about the California legislation is the imposition of education qualifications, mandatory CLE, and a government-backed enforcement mechanism to punish violators. Anyone who violates the requirements of California's new law can be fined $2,500 for the first offense and be imprisoned for subsequent offenses! Violation constitutes a misdemeanor.

It is significant to point out what the California legislation did *not* do:

- *It did not expand the scope of what a paralegal is able to do.* The legislation specified what tasks paralegals/legal assistants are able to perform (e.g., case management, legal research, interviewing clients, fact gathering, and drafting legal documents). These tasks, however, are not role expansions. The tasks listed in the legislation are the same tasks that could be performed in California (or in any other state) before the legislation was enacted.
- *It did not require paralegals or legal assistants to pass an examination.* To be a paralegal or legal assistant in California, you need to meet the requisite education or experience qualifications, work under attorney supervision, and attend mandatory CLE. An examination is not required.
- *It did not establish a paralegal code of ethics.* The four hours of ethics training (CLE) that paralegals must attend every two years will, for the most part, be on the code of ethics governing attorneys.
- *It did not set up a judicial or administrative bureaucracy to administer and enforce the program.* There is no central office, agency, or board in the state that administers or enforces any aspect of the regulation governing traditional paralegals. The program does not require registration with anyone. There is no license to obtain. The program is enforced primarily by the threat of criminal prosecution and civil suit. The legislation creates a new crime (illegal use of the title *paralegal* or *legal assistant*) punishable by fine or imprisonment. Violation can also lead to a civil suit: "Any consumer injured by a violation of this chapter may file a complaint and seek redress in any municipal or superior court for injunctive relief, restitution, and damages."[26] A self-policing mechanism is set up for the CLE requirements. Paralegals/legal assistants must keep their own records of CLE attendance. They must demonstrate (i.e., "certify") to their supervising attorneys that CLE obligations have been met. No one else keeps track of CLE hours of attendance. If, however, a criminal charge or civil lawsuit is brought, the paralegal/legal assistant must be prepared to present proof of compliance.

Although the California legislation did not establish a formal licensing system, it did use the force of law to determine who is in and who is out of the paralegal/legal assistant field. That's what licensing does. It is true that most licensing laws prohibit the performance of designated tasks by persons who do not obtain the license. For example, only licensed electricians can wire a house.

California did not take this route. A California attorney can ask a secretary or anyone else in the office to perform any paralegal task (e.g., digest a deposition, interview a client, or perform legal research), but such individuals cannot be called paralegals or legal assistants unless they meet the education and CLE requirements of the law. This, however, does not lessen the dramatic impact of what has occurred in California.

Here are some examples of attorneys and paralegals who have probably violated the California law:

- Charles Kiley, Esq., is a sole practitioner in California. He hires Sally Belmont to be his paralegal. Sally recently graduated from a community college that does not have a paralegal program. Sally has never been formally trained as a paralegal. Kiley wants to train her himself. He does so. Since the day he hired her, Kiley has been very satisfied with the quality of her paralegal work.
- Smith & Smith, a California law firm, promotes one of its veteran secretaries, Mary Adams, to be a paralegal. This secretary has been with the firm for fifteen years and knows more about her specialty than most new attorneys. She does not have a degree and has never attended a paralegal program.
- King, Swenson & Carter, a California law firm, hires Tom Harris to be a paralegal. Tom was a paralegal for ten years in New York before moving to California. The firm where he worked says that he is the finest paralegal the firm has ever had. Tom has a paralegal certificate from a paralegal program in New York, but this program did not have the designated number of law related courses required for a California paralegal.

Sally Belmont, Mary Adams, and Tom Harris are illegal paralegals. They have not met the requirements of California law no matter how competent their employers think they are. Sally, Mary, and Tom run the risk of going to jail. Their employers must stop calling them paralegals.

The new law also made major changes in the lives of the numerous independent paralegals and legal technicians who once sold their services directly to the public without attorney supervision. They had their own paralegal association, called the California Independent Paralegal Association. Working for themselves as **independent contractors**, their ads flooded Yellow Pages throughout the state. Did California abolish their right to exist? No, but they lost the right to call themselves paralegals, legal assistants, or legal technicians. They now had to be called *legal document assistants* (LDAs) and had to meet stringent registration and bonding requirements, as we will see. These changes were justified on the grounds that their former title was sometimes confusing. A citizen, for example, might have thought that an independent paralegal worked for an attorney. Recognizing that a new day had arrived, the California Independent Paralegal Association reluctantly changed its name to the California Association of Legal Document Assistants (CALDA) (www.calda.org).

Many traditional paralegals in California are thrilled with the new law. Its unexpected enactment was largely due to the determined efforts of individual paralegal associations throughout the state, spearheaded by the California Alliance of Paralegal Associations (www.CAPAralegal.org). The front page of the newsletter of the largest local paralegal association in the state proclaimed, "Hear Ye! Hear Ye! The time has finally come. . . . After years of struggling to get recognition and affirmation of the role that paralegals play in the legal industry, our time has finally come."[27] No longer can the boss take anyone off the street or from the copy room and call him or her a paralegal or legal assistant. They can have this title and role only if they meet the requirements of the law. The sponsor of the law in the legislature, Assemblywoman Marilyn Brewer, said that her goal was "to elevate the [paralegal] profession with the recognition it so well deserves."[28]

Not everyone, however, is happy with the new world of paralegalism in California. As expected, independent paralegals were devastated. "I've been robbed of my title," lamented one veteran independent paralegal.

The California program has been criticized as overkill, difficult to enforce, and overly punitive. Preventing independents from calling themselves paralegals (or legal assistants) arguably protects the public by eliminating potential confusion caused by these titles. But how is the public protected by requiring *attorney-supervised paralegals* to meet a new set of education and CLE requirements? The president of the American Association for Paralegal Education (AAfPE) said of the California regulation, "[O]bviously this new law is major news. Frankly, my personal opinion is that the law is unduly restrictive to the paralegal profession."[29] Law firms have lost some flexibility in making personnel decisions about who can be a paralegal or legal assistant in

independent contractor One who operates his or her own business and contracts to do work for others who do not control many of the administrative details of how that work is performed.

their firms. Prior to the enactment of the new law, the California State Bar Association voted against recommending a regulatory scheme that was similar to the one the California legislature eventually adopted. The International Paralegal Management Association (IPMA) opposes mandatory regulation of attorney-supervised paralegals because such regulation "may unnecessarily restrict who is classified as a legal assistant" and "limit the flexibility and discretion employers need in hiring those individuals they believe most closely match the standards and expectations of their businesses and their clients."[30]

It is difficult to predict whether other states will follow the path taken in California. Undoubtedly, there will be increased status and higher salaries for traditional paralegals in California. The question, however, is whether one of the consequences will be higher client fees. When the American Bar Association was expressing its opposition to the New Jersey regulation proposal, the chairwoman of the ABA Standing Committee on Paralegals made the following observation:

> [If the requirements] end up limiting entry into the paralegal field, the net effect could undermine the whole purpose of using paralegals: the ability to delegate work to someone who can perform quality work at a lower cost.[31]

ASSIGNMENT 4.5

Is the California legislation good policy? If so, for whom? Is it likely to increase the availability of legal services?

LIMITED LICENSING

Thus far we have been examining broad-based licensing (and its close equivalent in California), particularly for *traditional paralegals* (i.e., paralegals who are employed and supervised by attorneys). We turn now to the equally controversial topic of limited licensing. This is a government permission to persons meeting specified qualifications to engage in designated activities that are customarily (but not always exclusively) performed by another category of license holder. (See Exhibit 4.1.) Since the day paralegalism came into existence, limited licensing has been a hot issue. Its pros and cons have been debated in hundreds of conferences and paralegal association newsletters throughout the country. Independent paralegals have been particularly active in lobbying for changes in rules governing the practice of law. In some states, there have been demonstrations outside meetings of legislative committees and bar associations.

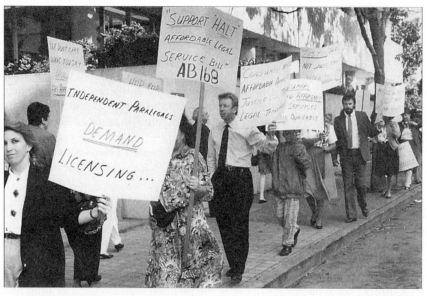

Independent paralegals demonstrating on the issue of limited licensing in California.

Our examination of this issue will cover:

- The role of the American Bar Association,
- Developments in Washington State,
- The positions of NALA and NFPA,
- Increased restrictions on independent contractors,
- Reforms in the practice of law, and
- Steps to take when paralegal regulation in the legislature is proposed.

The Role of the American Bar Association

The ABA does not favor broad-based licensing of all paralegals. In a 1986 report, however, an ABA Commission on Professionalism cautiously suggested—on page 52 of the report—that there be "limited licensing of paralegals" and "paraprofessionals" to perform certain functions such as handling some real estate closings, drafting simple wills, and performing certain tax work. The report argued that such a proposal could help reduce the cost of legal services:

> No doubt, many wills and real estate closings require the services of a lawyer. However, it can no longer be claimed that lawyers have the exclusive possession of the esoteric knowledge required and are therefore the only ones able to advise clients on any matter concerning the law.[32]

This remarkable proposal caused quite a stir. Many refer to the controversy it created as the **page 52 debate**. For years, many attorneys were suspicious of paralegalism because of a fear that paralegals might eventually be licensed and compete with attorneys. Then along comes a report of an ABA commission that recommends licensing! Yet it must be remembered that neither the report nor the commission speaks for the entire ABA. In fact, the proposal in the report "drew the ire" of other ABA members *and was never given serious consideration by the ABA as a whole.*

In 1995, the ABA took a different approach. It established a Commission on Nonlawyer Practice to conduct hearings throughout the country. Its goal was "to determine the implications of nonlawyer practice for society, the client and the legal profession." The commission defined and studied four categories of nonlawyers:

- **Self-represented person** A person who represents himself or herself, with or without assistance from someone else. The self-represented person acts pro se, which means appearing or representing oneself. A pro se litigant, for example, will argue his or her own case in court. This person is proceeding *in propria persona*—in one's own proper person. (The abbreviation is *pro per.*)
- **Document preparer** A person who assists someone in the preparation of forms and documents using information provided by a self-represented person. No advice or substantive information is provided on which forms or documents to use, how to fill them out, or where to file them. The document preparer (also called a **scrivener** or professional copyist) does little more than type.
- **Paralegal** A person who performs substantive work for a client under the supervision of an attorney or for which an attorney is accountable. A paralegal (also called a legal assistant) is an employee of attorneys or is retained by attorneys as an independent contractor. The commission refers to this category as the *traditional paralegal* because an attorney has control of and responsibility for the paralegal's work product.
- **Legal technician** A person (sometimes called an independent paralegal) who provides advice or other substantive legal work to the public without attorney supervision and for which no attorney is accountable.

For two years, the commission studied these individuals, particularly the document preparer and legal technician. It heard the testimony of hundreds of witnesses and received thousands of pages of written testimony. The diversity of points of view presented to the commission was enormous:

> Many suggestions received passionate support and were then opposed with equal vehemence. Experienced lawyers and nonlawyers often testified to diametrically opposed perceptions of consumer needs, risks of harm, nonlawyer capabilities and deficiencies, and the potential economies or effectiveness of any chosen regulatory approach.[33]

Throughout the country, the final report of the commission was eagerly awaited. Supporters of limited licensing were hoping that the report would endorse some form of limited licensing. Some attorneys, however, feared that the commission would move in this direction. At a meeting of bar association leaders, the former president of the New York State Bar Association said, "I will tell you that, unanimously, we reacted in horror to the idea that somehow the ABA might sanction an increase in non-lawyer practice."[34]

page 52 debate A debate on whether there should be limited licensing for paralegals (based on a recommendation in favor of such licensing on page 52 of a report of an American Bar Association commission.)

scrivener A professional copyist; a document preparer.

When the commission issued its final report, however, no dramatic recommendations were made. There was nothing comparable to the "page 52" debate that emerged from the 1986 report. The commission made relatively lukewarm recommendations about expanding the role of the traditional paralegal. What everyone wanted to know was whether the commission was going to conclude that the time was ripe for limited licensing.

Its answer to this volatile question was *maybe*. Rather than make a recommendation one way or another, the commission said that each state should decide the question for itself. The main contribution of the commission was to suggest guidelines or criteria that a state should use in deciding whether the state's current regulation of nonattorney activity was sufficient and, if not, what further regulation was needed, including the option of allowing limited licensing of legal technicians.

First of all, the commission believes a state should ask whether nonattorneys are posing risks to the public. If "there is no serious risk to the consumer even when the nonlawyer's service is poor, then a state may conclude that the activity should be unregulated."[35] The same conclusion might be reached if the state thinks the public is sufficiently able to judge for itself whether a legal technician is qualified to offer his or her services.

Establishing a regulatory scheme is an expensive and often politically explosive undertaking. This is true whether the regulation seeks to ban nonattorneys from performing a particular service or to grant them a limited license to perform it. A state must make an assessment of the public risks involved. For example, assume that a state reaches the following conclusions about the landlord-tenant legal problems of the public:

- There is a serious shortage of help on these problems.
- It is not economical for attorneys to handle all of these cases.
- Legal technicians can help meet the demand for legal services in this area.
- But serious harm can result if a consumer receives erroneous legal services in a landlord-tenant case.
- Because of the complexity of some landlord-tenant problems, the public may not be able to judge which legal technicians are qualified to work on them.
- A limited licensing program can be established that meets these concerns. The program would institute standards for training legal technicians, testing them, requiring them to carry liability insurance, disciplining them for unethical behavior, etc.

The state, however, might also conclude that the benefits of allowing legal technicians to work in this area are outweighed by the cost of setting up the elaborate licensing scheme that would be needed to make sure the public is protected from the substantial harm that can result from incompetent landlord-tenant legal services. Hence the state would reject a program of limited licensing for these kinds of legal problems. This is the kind of analysis the commission says each state must undertake for all unmet legal needs of the public.

The reaction to the commission's report was mixed. Many welcomed the positive comments the report made about the important role paralegals have played in the delivery of legal services. Others, however, were critical of the commission for being so tepid. For example, Merle Isgett, president of the National Federation of Paralegal Associations and a member of the commission, said it was a "cop out" for the commission to send the big issues like limited licensing back to the states instead of making forthright proposals for change. "We should have laid out the rules for state Supreme Courts to adopt. That's what the ABA does. All this says is that states should look at it."[36] "It's going to be put on some shelf somewhere and collect a lot of dust."[37] Unfortunately, President Isgett's prediction has proven to be correct. With the possible exception of Washington State, no state has made any progress in expanding the role of nonattorneys by creating the kind of limited licensing envisioned by the commission. Yet the work of the commission remains significant. Its report is the product of the most comprehensive and sophisticated study in the field of paralegalism to date. When and if the day arrives for limited licensing, the recommendations of the commission will play an important role.

Developments in Washington State

As indicated, a ray of hope exists in Washington State. In 2001, the Supreme Court of Washington State created the Practice of Law Board to:

- Promote expanded access to affordable and reliable legal and law-related services; and
- Make recommendations to the court regarding the circumstances under which nonlawyers may be involved in the delivery of certain types of legal and law-related services

EXHIBIT 4.4	Washington State Guidelines on Proposals for Limited Licensing

Guidelines for Making Recommendations to the Supreme Court Regarding the Provision of Legal and Law-Related Services by Non-Lawyers.

On request of the Supreme Court or any person or organization, or on its own initiative, the [Practice of Law] Board may recommend that non-lawyers be authorized to engage in certain defined activities that otherwise constitute the practice of law. . . . In forwarding a recommendation that non-lawyers be authorized to engage in certain legal or law-related activities that constitute the practice of law . . . the Board shall determine whether regulation under authority of the Supreme Court (including the establishment of minimum and uniform standards of competency, conduct, and continuing education) is necessary to protect the public interest.

Any recommendation that non-lawyers be authorized to engage in the limited provision of legal or law-related services shall be accompanied by a determination:
(A) that access to affordable and reliable legal and law-related services consistent with protection of the public will be enhanced by permitting non-lawyers to engage in the defined activities set forth in the recommendation;
(B) that the defined activities outlined in the recommendation can be reasonably and competently provided by skilled and trained non-lawyers;
(C) if the public interest requires regulation under authority of the Supreme Court, such regulation is tailored to promote access to affordable legal and law-related services while ensuring that those whose important rights are at stake can reasonably rely on the quality, skill and ability of those non-lawyers who will provide such services;
(D) that, to the extent that the activities authorized will involve the handling of client trust funds, provision has been made to ensure that such funds are handled in a manner consistent with the ethics rules of the state, including the requirement that such funds be placed in interest bearing accounts, with interest paid to the Legal Foundation of Washington; and
(E) that the costs of regulation, if any, can be effectively underwritten within the context of the proposed regulatory regime.
Recommendations to authorize non-lawyers to engage in the limited practice of law pursuant to this section shall be forwarded to the Washington State Board of Governors for consideration and comment before transmission to the Supreme Court. Upon approval of such recommendations by the Supreme Court . . . those who meet the requirements and comply with applicable regulatory and licensing provisions shall be deemed to be engaged in the authorized practice of law.

Source: General Rules (GR) 25, Practice of Law Board, Approved by the Washington State Supreme Court (Sept. 1, 2001)

The guidelines established by the court for making these recommendations are presented in Exhibit 4.4.

This is a potentially major development. The mandate of the Practice of Law Board is not simply to investigate the unauthorized practice of law. The board is charged with determining where the role of paralegals and other nonattorneys might be expanded. Although a number of attorney committees and task forces over the years have recommended expansion of nonattorney roles (e.g., see the earlier discussion of the page 52 debate), the Supreme Court of Washington is the most authoritative *governmental* entity that has set in motion a process that might actually lead to such expansion. Of course, everything depends on what the Practice of Law Board recommends and what the Supreme Court of Washington ultimately accepts.

In 2005 the board circulated a proposal for "limited nonlawyer practice," a form of limited licensing. The proposal would allow what it calls "legal technicians" to perform designated tasks (e.g., prepare approved legal documents and advise the client of other documents that may be needed) in discrete areas of the law that the board will identify later. To become a legal technician, an applicant would have to pass an examination and meet specified education and experience qualifications.[38] This historic proposal, if adopted, would expand the scope of what nonattorneys are allowed to do. The California regulation did not go this far.

The Washington State Bar Association opposes the proposal of the board, at least in its present form. Yet the proposal is being taking seriously and may eventually be accepted by the state supreme court.

One reason to be optimistic that Washington State will adopt a form of limited licensing is that such licensing already exists in the state in the position of the **limited practice officer (LPO)**, also called a certified closing officer. An LPO is a nonattorney certified by the Supreme Court of Washington to select and prepare documents that have been approved for use in designated property transactions such as closing a loan, extending credit, or transferring land. The documents include deeds, mortgages, and bills of sale. LPOs are regulated by a Limited Practice Board. Candidates to become LPOs must pass an examination and be "of good moral character" before they can be "admitted" by the Supreme Court of Washington as a limited practice officer.[39] LPOs must follow specific procedures when closing real estate, including identifying

limited practice officer (LPO) A nonattorney in Washington State who has the authority to select and prepare approved legal documents for designated property transactions.

themselves as LPOs and making clear they are not attorneys and not advocates for either party. LPOs are assigned an LPO license number, which they also use when signing documents in their capacity as LPO.

A number of paralegals in Washington State are licensed LPOs. After meeting LPO requirements, such paralegals typically use the title *paralegal/LPO*. An example is Jeanne J. Dawes, a paralegal with the law firm of Gore & Grewe. She appears on the firm stationery and business cards as "Jeanne J. Dawes, Paralegal/LPO."

The Positions of NALA and NFPA

Two of the major national paralegal associations take very different positions on limited licensing. The National Association of Legal Assistants (NALA) opposes proposals for limited licensing on the grounds that the proposals do not provide sufficient guidelines to determine the categories of cases nonattorneys would be competent to handle. Many legal cases presented by clients are complex at the outset or become complex as they unfold. Such cases, argues NALA, require the attention of an attorney. Nonattorneys are not in the best position to determine when a case is beyond their skills. Furthermore, limited licensing might lead to open warfare with attorneys and to public disillusionment with the legal system. "For all practical purposes," limited license holders could "become direct and fierce competitors . . . of lawyers who will not look kindly upon these 'mini-lawyers.' It is only a matter of time . . . [before] the inevitable will occur; the public will have a bad experience working with one of these untrained, inadequately educated non-lawyers and it will become further disillusioned with the legal system. Thus the results will further blacken the public's image of lawyers and the law profession."[40]

The National Federation of Paralegal Associations (NFPA) has a different approach to limited licensing. It has embraced the concept of licensing, particularly if it will expand the scope of tasks paralegals are able to provide. NFPA has proposed its own Model Act for Paralegal Licensure to be called the State Licensed Paralegal Act. The proposal contains a two-tier licensing scheme: an entry-level license for all paralegals and an advanced specialty license that can be obtained four years after obtaining the entry-level license. Each license would require meeting minimum education requirements, completing mandatory continuing legal education (CLE), and passing an examination.[41] To date, no state has adopted the Model Act.

ASSIGNMENT 4.6

Do you agree with the position of NALA on limited licensing or with that of NFPA? Why?

Increased Restrictions on Independent Contractors

Independent contractors such as independent paralegals and legal technicians have been among the most vocal advocates for limited licensing. Although they might eventually achieve some progress in states such as Washington, they face the prospect of a backlash from those who want to see their activities *restricted* rather than expanded. A president of one bar association said of limited licensing, "It's like letting nurses do brain surgery." Here are some other comments from attorneys: "This is the worst thing since the plague!" They think "just about everybody should be able to practice law. I guess they think everybody should be able to slice open a belly and remove an appendix." "I cannot think of anything that would be more injurious to the public." This is an idea "whose time has not yet come." "This is potentially the most fractious and controversial issue ever confronted" by the bar association. Scoffing at the notion that you can carve out tasks that do not require the skills of an attorney, a judge commented, "You never know if you have a simple case until an expert looks at it. It's like a pain in the side. Only an expert can tell whether it should be treated with aspirin or by surgery."[42] Such hostility has in fact led to some restrictive legislation at the state and federal levels.

California has gone the farthest in imposing new restrictions on independent contractors. It has created two titles to cover individuals who sell their services directly to the public without attorney supervision: the *legal document assistant* (whom we briefly examined earlier when discussing California's proposal to regulate traditional paralegals) and the *unlawful detainer assistant*.

- The **legal document assistant (LDA)** provides "self-help" service to a member of the public who is representing himself or herself in a legal matter.
- The **unlawful detainer assistant (UDA)** helps landlords or tenants bring actions or defend actions for the possession of land. (*Detainer* means keeping something in one's custody.)

Here are some of the important controls imposed on these independent contractors:

- LDAs must meet minimum education requirements (e.g., a high school diploma or its equivalent and two years of law-related experience under the supervision of a licensed attorney).
- LDAs are limited to providing self-help services consisting of typing or otherwise completing legal documents in a ministerial manner; the documents must be selected by the person being helped, who is representing him or herself.
- LDAs and UDAs cannot provide any "kind of advice, explanation, opinion, or recommendation to a consumer about possible legal rights, remedies, defenses, options, selection of forms, or strategies."
- LDAs and UDAs must be registered. They must obtain a certificate of registration from the county clerk.
- The application for a certificate of registration must be accompanied by a fee of $175 and a $25,000 bond to ensure compliance with the regulations.
- The certificate or registration must be renewed every two years.
- Once an LDA or UDA is properly registered, the county clerk will issue an identification card that lists the title "*legal document assistant*" or "*unlawful detainer assistant*," the date the registration expires, a photograph of the registrant, and the following two statements: "This person is not a lawyer" and "The county clerk has not evaluated this person's knowledge, experience, or services." See Exhibit 4.5.
- LDAs and UDAs must give their clients a written contract that states the services to be performed and the cost. The contract must also inform the client where he or she may be able to obtain free or low-cost legal services from an attorney and that the LDA or UDA is not an attorney and cannot give advice, explanations, or recommendations on legal matters.
- An LDA or UDA cannot call him or herself a paralegal or legal assistant.
- An LDA or UDA cannot retain in his or her possession any original documents of a client.
- If an LDA or UDA violates these regulations, the unpaid fees could be forfeited and the collected fees could be ordered returned to the client. In addition, the LDA or UDA could be fined up to $2,000 and imprisoned for up to a year.
- Suspended or disbarred attorneys cannot register as an LDA or UDA.[43]

legal document assistant (LDA) A nonattorney in California who is authorized to charge fees for providing "self-help" service (without attorney supervision) to anyone representing himself or herself in a legal matter.

unlawful detainer assistant (UDA) A nonattorney in California who is authorized to charge fees for providing assistance or advice (without attorney supervision) to landlords or tenants to bring or defend actions for the possession of land.

EXHIBIT 4.5	Example of the Identity Card of a Legal Document Assistant (LDA) in California

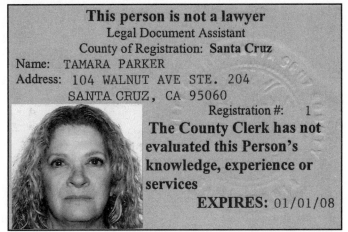

For the Internet site of this LDA, see www.legaldocumentassistant.net (Reprinted with permission of Tamara Parker)

Arizona has also created a new document preparer position. A legal document preparer (LDP) in Arizona is a person who has been certified to "prepare or provide documents" without attorney supervision for citizens engaged in self-representation. More formally, he or she is known as an Arizona certified legal document preparer (AZCLDP). Like the LDA (legal document assistant) in California, Arizona LDPs are subject to significant restrictions on the services they can provide. They can give "general legal information" or "general factual information pertaining to legal rights, procedures, or options," but they:

> may not provide any kind of specific advice, opinion, or recommendation to a consumer about possible legal rights, remedies, defenses, options, or strategies."[44]

They must specifically tell their clients that they are not attorneys. To be certified, LDPs must be at least eighteen years old and be of good moral character. In addition, they must meet minimum educational/experience qualifications. Examples of the latter include graduation from paralegal school, or graduation from law school, or graduation from high school plus two years of legal experience under the supervision of an attorney or another certified LDP. Applicants must pass an exam on the rules governing LDPs. Once certified, they must complete ten hours of continuing legal education (CLE) every year. The program was created by the Arizona Supreme Court and is administered by a Board of Legal Document Preparers (www.supreme.state.az.us/cld/ldp.htm), which consists of eleven members, five of whom must have experience as legal document preparers.

In Florida, the titles of *paralegal* and *legal assistant* are restricted to persons who work under attorney supervision. Nonattorneys can provide direct assistance to the public, but they must give each of their clients a copy of a disclosure that contains the following provisions:

- (Name) told me that he/she is a nonlawyer and may not give legal advice, cannot tell me what my rights or remedies are, cannot tell me how to testify in court, and cannot represent me in court.
- A paralegal is a person who works under the supervision of a member of The Florida Bar and who performs specifically delegated substantive legal work for which a member of The Florida Bar is responsible. Only persons who meet the definition may call themselves paralegals. (Name) informed me that he/she is not a paralegal.
- (Name) told me that he/she may only type the factual information provided by me in writing into the blanks on the form. (Name) may not help me fill in the form and may not complete the form for me. If using a form approved by the Supreme Court of Florida, (Name) may ask me factual questions to fill in the blanks on the form and may also tell me how to file the form.[45]

At the federal level, Congress has imposed severe restrictions on independent contractors who sell bankruptcy services to the public without attorney supervision. At one time, many used the word *paralegal* in their title (e.g., *independent paralegal* or *bankruptcy paralegal*). Today, if they are not supervised by attorneys, they must be called **bankruptcy petition preparers (BPPs)**. Although they are allowed to charge fees to assist a person who is filing bankruptcy documents in federal court, a number of important restrictions apply:

- A BPP shall not use the word "legal" or any similar term in any advertisements. In a recent case, a court ruled that a BPP's ad offering "paralegal services" is illegal since "the term 'paralegal' fosters consumer confusion."[46]
- A BPP must print his or her name, address, and Social Security number on every document he or she prepares.
- A BPP must give the debtor a copy of each document the debtor signs at the time of signing.
- A BPP shall not execute any document on behalf of a debtor.
- A BPP shall not receive any payment from the debtor for court fees in connection with filing the petition.
- Within ten days after the filing of a petition, a BPP shall file a declaration disclosing any fee received from the debtor and any unpaid fee charged to the debtor.
- The bankruptcy court will disallow any BPP fee found to be in excess of the value of services rendered for the documents prepared.
- Each violation of the regulations can lead to a fine of $500, and a BPP can be forced to pay the debtor $2,000 or twice the amount the debtor paid for the BPP's services (whichever is greater) plus the debtor's attorney fees.[47]

bankruptcy petition preparer (BPP) A nonattorney who is authorized to charge fees for preparing (without attorney supervision) a bankruptcy petition or any other bankruptcy document that a debtor will file in a federal court.

Reforms in the Practice of Law

For many Americans, attorneys have priced themselves out of the market. Studies continue to document a vast unmet need for legal services in our society. Here, for example, are some of the conclusions of studies conducted in two large states:

Each year in Illinois, by conservative estimates, 300,000 low-income families face approximately 1,000,000 civil legal problems for which they do not receive legal help.[48]

The poor in New York face nearly 3,000,000 civil legal problems per year without legal help. Not more than 14% of their overall need for legal assistance is being met.[49]

The statistics are even more alarming if the legal needs of the middle class are included. In light of these numbers, critics are calling for drastic reform.

Legislatures and the organized bar have tried to respond to this grim picture by creating some important reforms in the delivery of legal services. (See Exhibit 4.6.) The question, however, is whether these reforms are enough. Should limited licensing programs be added to the list of reforms? Some will continue to argue that limited licensing is a cure worse than the disease and that what is needed is more aggressive enforcement against the unauthorized practice of law by nonattorneys. While the debate continues, underrepresentation remains a critical deficiency—indeed, an embarrassment—of our legal system.

EXHIBIT 4.6	Reforms in the Practice of Law Designed to Increase the Number of People Receiving Legal Services

■ *Pro bono work.* Many law firms and corporations give their attorneys time off to provide **pro bono** legal services to the poor. Some offices do the same for their paralegals. Pro bono means for free (short for *pro bono publico*—concerning what one does for the public good without fee or compensation). For a directory of pro bono links in your state, see the American Bar Association's Access to Justice page (www.abanet.org/legalservices/probono/directory.html). Although the concept of pro bono is usually limited to free legal services, you will occasionally see the concept applied to legal services provided to the needy at a reduced rate.

■ *Simplified forms.* Some courts and bar associations have helped create legal forms that are relatively easy for the public to use without the assistance of an attorney. See, for example, the family law court forms in Maryland (www.courts.state.md.us).

■ *Internet self-help centers.* Many courts have created Internet sites that provide assistance for citizens with legal problems who are representing themselves. See, for example:
www.courtinfo.ca.gov/selfhelp
www.abalawinfo.org

■ *Court facilitators.* In some states, volunteer or paid attorneys or paralegals are available outside courtrooms to provide general guidance (but not legal advice or representation) to parties representing themselves in court cases. See, for example, the program for such individuals in Washington State (www.courts.wa.gov/court_dir/index.cfm).

■ *Prepaid legal services.* Some companies and unions have developed legal insurance plans that enable participants to pay a set amount each month for designated legal services that might be needed while the participant is in the program. They are called **prepaid legal services,** *legal plans,* or *group legal services.* See the American Prepaid Legal Services Institute (www.aplsi.org).

■ *Attorney advertising.* Media advertising by attorneys (which was once prohibited) has arguably made the public more aware of legal services and more inclined to use such services. On attorney advertising, see chapter 5 and the links to your state in the American Bar Association's site on advertising, solicitation, and marketing (www.abanet.org/legalservices/clientdevelopment/adrules).

■ *Publicly funded legal services.* Legal service/legal aid offices receive substantial funding from the government and from IOLTA programs to provide free legal services to the poor. (IOLTA programs—Interest on Lawyers Trust Accounts—are discussed in chapter 2.) Most of the legal service/legal aid offices employ full-time attorneys and paralegals who work for clients who meet the income guidelines of the programs. For a list of such programs in your state, see the Legal Services Corporation (www.lsc.gov).

■ *Modest means panels.* Some states have modest means panels consisting of private attorneys who are willing to provide relatively low-cost (e.g., $60 an hour) legal services in limited areas of the law to low-income individuals who are not poor enough to qualify for free legal services. See *A Blueprint for Lawyer Referral and Information Service Modest Means Panels* (www.abanet.org/legalservices/delivery/blueprint1.html).

■ *Traditional paralegals.* The increased use of paralegals by attorneys can lead to lower client costs because the billing rate for paralegal time is considerably lower than the billing rate for most attorneys. Paralegals can perform many tasks that would otherwise have to be performed by attorneys. (See the discussion of law firm economics and paralegals in chapter 1.)

■ *Limited licensing?* The big question in the reform movement is whether proposals for limited licensing in states like Washington State will be enacted.

Steps to Take When Paralegal Regulation in the Legislature Is Proposed

As you can see from this discussion, licensing is a major issue in paralegalism. We have not seen the last of the proposals for this kind of regulation. It is important that paralegals continue to be intimately involved in shaping these proposals when they surface. Like the California program, the proposals are most likely to emerge from the state legislature. Here are some of the steps that should be taken when you hear about regulation under consideration by the legislature in your state:

1. Obtain a copy of the proposed legislation or bill as soon as possible. If you know the name of the legislator sponsoring the bill, write, call, or e-mail him or her directly. Otherwise contact the office of the speaker of the house, speaker of the assembly, president of the senate, etc. Ask how you can locate the proposed bill.

2. Find out the exact technical status of the bill. Has it been formally introduced? Has it been assigned to a committee? What is the next scheduled formal event on the bill? For example, have hearings been scheduled?

3. Immediately inform the sponsoring legislator(s) and the relevant committee(s) that you want an opportunity to comment on the bill. If hearings have been scheduled, make known your interest in participating in such hearings. Your goal is to slow the process down so that the bill is not rushed into enactment. Be particularly alert to the possibility that the paralegal bill may be buried in proposed legislation on a large number of related or unrelated topics. There is a real danger that the bill will get through relatively unnoticed.

4. Determine why the paralegal bill is being proposed. What is the *public* reason given for the proposal of the bill? More important, what is the underlying *real* reason for the proposal? Perhaps some special interest or small group (real estate agents, for instance) is seeking a special privilege in a law-related field. Yet the language of the bill they are proposing may be so broad that paralegals will be adversely affected. This happened in Montana when legislation sought and obtained by private investigators unexpectedly placed restrictions on investigations conducted by paralegal employees of law offices. It took considerable effort to convince the legislature to amend the legislation in order to remove these restrictions.

5. Alert your local paralegal association. It needs to be mobilized in order to express an organized position on the bill. Contact the major national paralegal associations: NFPA, NALA, and NALS (see appendix B). Do they know about the proposed legislation? Have they taken a position? They need to be activated.

6. If your local bar association has a paralegal committee, seek its support.

7. Launch an e-mail or letter-writing campaign. Make sure that large numbers of paralegals in the area know about the bill and know how to express their opinion to the legislature.

8. Ask local paralegal schools to take a position.

Keep in mind that we are talking about mandatory *licensing* by the state, not voluntary *certification* by entities such as paralegal associations. The certification debate will be covered later in this chapter.

ASSIGNMENT 4.7

(a) Do you favor broad-based licensing for every paralegal? Limited licensing? Will licensing advance or restrict the development of paralegalism?

(b) If all attorneys in the country drastically cut their fees, would there be a need for paralegal licensing?

(c) Paralegals who work for attorneys (traditional paralegals) cannot perform some tasks, such as taking the deposition of a witness. Should there be limited licensing to authorize such tasks?

ASSIGNMENT 4.8

Evaluate the following observation: "The emerging professions and the more established professions have frequently sought greater regulation of their occupational group. They are often motivated, despite the obligatory language on protection of the public interest, to do so in efforts to establish their 'territorial imperative' or to establish barriers to entry into the profession and thereby enhance their economic self-interest." Should paralegals establish such barriers on who can become a paralegal? D. Sapadin, *A Comparison of the Growth and Development of the Physician Assistant and the Legal Assistant*, Journal of the American Association for Paralegal Education: Retrospective 1983, 142 (1983).

[SECTION D]

SHOULD PARALEGALS BECOME PART OF BAR ASSOCIATIONS?

At present, no paralegals are full members of any bar association. In recent years, however, a number of state and local bar associations have invited paralegals to join their organizations in various capacities. The association might allow the paralegals in

- as associate or affiliate members of the entire association, including its committees and sections;
- as associate or affiliate members of committees or sections only; or
- as full members of special paralegal divisions.

The most active example of a division is the Paralegal Division of the State Bar of Texas (www .txpd.org). It has over 2,300 members. The annual voting membership fee is $70. (Other states that include some form of bar membership include Alaska, Arizona, California, Colorado, Connecticut, Florida, Illinois, Kansas, Maryland, Michigan, Minnesota, Missouri, Montana, Nevada, New Jersey, New Mexico, New York, North Carolina, North Dakota, Ohio, Rhode Island, Utah, Virginia, and Wisconsin. See appendix B for the addresses of many of the bar associations that allow such membership.) In some of the bar associations, paralegals are allowed to vote on issues within the section, committee, or division of which they are members. But they cannot vote on general bar association issues.

ASSIGNMENT 4.9

Does the state, city, or county bar association where you live have a membership category for paralegals? If so, what are the eligibility requirements for membership, and what are the benefits of membership? Go to the Web sites of the bar associations in your state (see appendix C for their addresses) and type *paralegal* or *legal assistant* in their search box to find membership options, if any, for nonattorneys. The list of paralegal associations in appendix B also includes bar associations with paralegal membership programs.

What about the major national bar association—the American Bar Association (ABA)? For a long time, many argued that paralegals should become affiliated with the ABA in some way. In 1982, the ABA standing Committee on Paralegals proposed that the ABA create a new category of membership for paralegals. The National Association of Legal Assistants (NALA) warmly endorsed the proposal, while the National Federation of Paralegal Associations (NFPA) opposed it. The ABA accepted the proposal and allowed paralegals to join as ABA associates (www.abanet.org/join).

As indicated, not all paralegals endorsed the concept of associate or affiliate membership in bar associations when the idea was first proposed. Here are some typical comments in opposition:

I haven't been able to understand why paralegals would want to become second class members of an organization that represents the interests of another profession. [Some paralegals view associate membership] as a positive development, while the very idea is enough to raise the blood pressure of other paralegals.[50]

[It is] in the public interest that the allied legal professions remain autonomous. [It is] necessary and advisable that paralegals retain primary control in the development of the paralegal profession.[51]

It is a recognized and uncontested fact that the purpose of any bar association is to promote and protect attorneys and their practice of law, rather than legal assistants. Further, associate members do not participate in the administrative and substantial legal decisions which are made by the Bar Association, e.g., no vote on dues, by-laws, budget or substantive issues of membership requirements. [Avoiding membership in a bar association may] eliminate possible conflicts of interest on issues where attorneys and legal assistants hold differing perspectives and opinions regarding the future of legal practice.[52]

Those who viewed paralegals as an autonomous, self-directed profession tended to disagree with the effort to join bar associations in any form. Yet this point of view is *not* shared by the majority of paralegals today. The momentum is toward more and more bar associations creating membership categories for paralegals. And when this option is made available, many paralegals take advantage of it for a number of reasons. It looks good on a résumé. It fosters a positive relationship between paralegals and attorneys. Employers often pay all or part of the paralegal's membership fee. Bar association meetings can be an excellent place for networking. Members receive newsletters and announcements, thus keeping them better informed about developments in the legal community. This perspective is best summed up in the following comment made by a paralegal before the ABA created the associate membership category:

> It is time our profession stopped being paranoid about ABA Associate Membership and open our eyes to opportunities presented to us. [We should not be spending time] dreaming up reasons to reject a chance for growth and improved relations within the established legal community. No guarantees have been given to assure us that associate membership would be beneficial, but why close *any* doors opened to us? If just a few paralegals would like to take advantage of this opportunity, why slam the door in their faces? The spirit of cooperation and teamwork within the legal community are the key reasons to encourage associate membership.[53]

ASSIGNMENT 4.10

(a) Should paralegals become a formal part of bar associations? What effect do you think associate membership would have on existing paralegal associations? Strengthen them? Weaken them? Is it healthy or unhealthy for paralegals to organize themselves as independent entities? Is it healthy or unhealthy for them to be able to challenge the organized bar? What is the conflict-of-interest argument against associate membership? Do you agree with this argument?

(b) Should a paralegal association allow *attorneys* to become full members of its association? Associate members? Why or why not?

(c) Should a paralegal association allow *secretaries* to become full members of its association? Associate members? Why or why not?

(d) Should a paralegal association allow *paralegal managers* (e.g., nonattorney senior paralegals) to become full members of its association? Associate members? Why or why not?

(e) To become an associate or affiliate member of a bar association, the applicant usually must obtain the signed statement of an attorney-employer asserting or attesting to certain facts about the applicant—for instance, that he or she is a paralegal who works for the attorney. The statement is called an **attorney attestation**. For example, to obtain affiliate membership in the State Bar of Michigan, the attorney must "hereby attest" that the applicant "is employed by me and is recognized as a legal assistant [paralegal] and that he/she, under the supervision and direction of a lawyer, performs the service" specified elsewhere on the application.[54] Some *paralegal* associations require the same kind of attorney attestation as a condition of allowing paralegals to join the paralegal association. Do you think attorney attestation is a good idea for associate/affiliate membership in a bar association? For full membership in a paralegal association? Why or why not?

attorney attestation A signed statement by an attorney that a paralegal applying for membership in an association meets one or more of the criteria of the association.

[SECTION E]
SELF-REGULATION BY PARALEGALS: CERTIFICATION

The most common definition of certification is the process by which a nongovernmental organization grants recognition to a person who has met the qualifications set by that organization. There is a large variety of criteria established by various organizations for granting their certification. The most common are:

- graduation from a school or training program, and/or
- passing a standard examination, and/or
- completing a designated period of work experience

As pointed out in Exhibit 4.1, some prefer the term *certificated* as opposed to *certified* if the recognition is from a school. (Note that *certified* is sometimes broadly used by any organization to mean that someone is in compliance with designated standards or criteria.)

In this section, our primary focus will be on certification programs established by paralegal associations. These programs are a form of self-regulation by the paralegal profession. Paralegal certification is a voluntary process; the failure or refusal of a paralegal to become certified by the programs we will be examining does not affect his or her ability to work as a paralegal.

The majority of paralegals in the country do *not* seek certification. Perhaps the main reason is that in most states employers do not actively encourage certification even though they are generally pleased when a paralegal employee acquires it. But the credential does not immediately lead to a pay increase. One paralegal commented, "When I passed the exam, my employer at the time chose only to increase my hourly billing rate, but not my salary."[55] Paralegals who most often seek certification are those who are active in local, state, or national paralegal associations. Once certified, these paralegals eloquently promote the value of certification as a way to maintain and enhance the professionalism of the field.

Two categories of paralegal certification exist: national and state specific. There are three major national certification programs and eight state-specific certification programs.

We begin with the national programs. Here are the three credentials offered by the three national associations:

- **CLA** or **CP** Meeting the certification requirements of the National Association of Legal Assistants entitles you to call yourself a Certified Legal Assistant (CLA) or a Certified Paralegal (CP). The National Association of Legal Assistants (NALA) is primarily an association of individual paralegals; it also has affiliated local paralegal associations.

- **RP** or **PACE registered paralegal** Meeting the certification requirements of the National Federation of Paralegal Associations entitles you to call yourself a Registered Paralegal (RP) or a PACE Registered Paralegal. The National Federation of Paralegal Associations (NFPA) is primarily an association of local paralegal associations; it also has a small number of individual paralegal members.

- **PP** Meeting the certification requirements of NALS the Association for Legal Professionals entitles you to call yourself a Professional Paralegal (PP). NALS the Association for Legal Professionals is primarily an association of individual paralegals and individual legal secretaries; it also has affiliated local associations. NALS was once called the National Association of Legal Secretaries. Its new name keeps the original NALS letters, but it officially calls itself NALS the Association for Legal Professionals.

There are some major differences among these three certification programs. (See Exhibit 4.7.) For example, only the CLA/CP certification can be achieved without paralegal experience. The other two programs require experience; they are not **entry-level certifications**.

CLA or CP The certification credential bestowed by the National Association of Legal Assistants. CLA stands for Certified Legal Assistant; CP, for Certified Paralegal.

RP or PACE registered paralegal The certification credential bestowed by the National Federation of Paralegal Associations. RP stands for registered paralegal; PACE stands for Paralegal Advanced Certification Examination.

PP The certification credential bestowed by NALS the Association for Legal Professionals. PP stands for professional paralegal.

entry-level certification Certification acquired by meeting eligibility requirements that do not include work experience.

EXHIBIT 4.7	National Certification Examinations: CLA (CP), PACE, and PP		
Name of Exam	Certified Legal Assistant Exam	PACE: Paralegal Advanced Certification Exam	Professional Paralegal Certification Exam
Sponsor	National Association of Legal Assistants (www.nala.org) (click "Paralegal Certification")	National Federation of Paralegal Associations www.paralegals.org (click "PACE/RP")	NALS the Association for Legal Professionals www.nals.org (click "Certification")
Credential	CLA (Certified Legal Assistant) *or* CP (Certified Paralegal) Here is how a person can sign his or her name: Mary Jones, CLA Certified Legal Assistant Mary Jones, CLA Certified Paralegal Mary Jones, CP Certified Legal Assistant Mary Jones, CP Certified Paralegal	PACE Registered Paralegal *or* RP. There are several ways to sign your name: Sam Smith, PACE-Registered Paralegal Sam Smith, RP, Paralegal Sam Smith, RP, Legal Assistant	Professional Paralegal Here is how you would sign your name: Alice Davis, PP (For ethical reasons, nonattorney status should also be indicated by including the words, paralegal, legal assistant, or legal secretary)
Required for Employment?	No. The test is voluntary, although some employers may be impressed by a job applicant who is a CLA.	No. The test is voluntary, although some employers may be impressed by a job applicant who is PACE Accredited.	No. The test is voluntary, although some employers might be impressed by a job applicant who is a PP.
Cost	$275 (if you are not a member of NALA) $250 (if you are a member of NALA)	$225	$250 (if you are not a member of NALS) $200 (if you are a member of NALS) $150 (if you have PLS—professional legal secretary—certification and are a member of NALS)
Date Exam Began	1976	1996	2004

(continues)

EXHIBIT 4.7	National Certification Examinations: CLA (CP), PACE, and PP —*continued*		
Can You Take the Exam Immediately Upon Graduating from School?	Yes, if you apply under Category 1 (see next section). You do not need experience as a paralegal. The CLA exam is entry-level unless you apply under Categories 2 and 3.	No. There are three categories of eligibility to take the test (see next section). Each category includes experience requirements. The PACE exam is not an entry-level exam.	No. There are three categories of eligibility to take the test (see next section). Each category includes experience requirements. The PP exam is not an entry-level exam.
Eligibility to Take Exam	Requirements to take the CLA exam. You do *not* have to be a member of NALA to take the exam. An applicant must fit within one of the following three categories: ■ **Category 1:** You are a graduate of a legal assistant program that (a) grants an associate's degree, (b) grants a bachelor's degree, (c) is a postbaccalaureate certificate program, (d) has a minimum of sixty semester hours, or (e) is ABA approved. ■ **Category 2:** You have a bachelor's degree in any field, plus either (a) one year of experience as a legal assistant, or (b) fifteen semester hours of substantive legal courses. ■ **Category 3:** You have a high school diploma or equivalent, plus seven years of experience as a legal assistant under attorney supervision plus twenty hours of CLE (continuing legal education) within two years prior to taking the test.	Requirements to take the PACE exam. You do *not* have to be a member of NFPA (or one of its affiliate associations) to take the exam. An applicant must fit within one of the following three categories: ■ **Category 1:** You have an associate's degree in paralegal studies from an accredited school and/or from an ABA-approved paralegal education program plus six years substantive paralegal experience. ■ **Category 2:** You have a bachelor's degree in any course of study from an accredited school plus three years of substantive paralegal experience. ■ **Category 3:** You have a bachelor's degree and you have completed a paralegal program with an accredited school (the paralegal program may be embodied in a bachelor's degree) plus two years of substantive paralegal experience.	Requirements to take the PP exam. You do *not* have to be a member of NALS to take the exam. An applicant must fit within one of the following three categories: ■ **Category 1:** You have five years of experience performing paralegal/legal assistant duties. ■ **Category 2:** You have four years of experience performing paralegal/legal assistant duties plus (a) a postsecondary degree, (b) other certification, or (c) a paralegal certificate. ■ **Category 3:** You have three years of experience performing paralegal/legal assistant duties plus a paralegal degree.
Where Given	The exam is given three times a year at locations throughout the country.	The exam is given at one of the 200 Sylvan Technology Centers throughout the country. The Centers are open for testing six days a week during which you can take the exam.	The exam is given twice a year at locations throughout the country.
Length of Exam	8.5 hours over two days	Four hours (taken entirely on a computer) in one day	Seven hours in one day
Is the Exam State Specific?	No. The exam is national in scope. It does not test on the law of any particular state.	No. The exam is national in scope. It does not test on the law of any particular state. In the future, NFPA hopes to develop a Tier II test that *will* test specific state law.	No. The exam is national in scope. It does not test on the law of any particular state.
Topics Tested	(a) 90 minutes: communications (e.g., writing, interviewing, human relations); (b) 150 minutes: judgment and analytical ability; (c) 60 minutes: ethics; (d) 90 minutes: legal research; and (e) 120 minutes: any 4 of the following areas you select: administrative law, bankruptcy, business organizations/ corporations, contracts, family law, criminal law, litigation, probate and estates, and real estate.	(a) administration of client legal matters (e.g., conducting a conflict check): 23% of the test, (b) development of client legal matters (e.g., interviewing clients): 30%, (c) factual and legal research (e.g., validating legal research): 22%, (d) factual and legal writing (e.g., drafting legal documents): 20.5%, and (e) office administration (e.g., maintaining a billing system): 4.5%	Part 1. Written communications: grammar and word usage, spelling, punctuation, number usage, capitalization, composition, and expression. Part 2. Legal knowledge and skills: legal research, citations, legal terminology, the court system, alternative dispute resolution, legal interviewing, investigation, and docketing. Part 3. Ethics and judgment skills. Part 4. Substantive law: all areas of substantive law, e.g., administrative law, bankruptcy law, business organizations, contracts, civil procedure, litigation, criminal law, family law, real property, torts, estate law, labor law, and taxation.

(continues)

EXHIBIT 4.7	National Certification Examinations: CLA (CP), PACE, and PP —*continued*		
Format of Examination	Objective questions (e.g., true/false, multiple choice, matching). Some essay and short answer questions. Examples of Objective Questions: [1] True or False: Federal statutes are printed in codified form in Federal Reporter, 3d. [2] The Model Penal Code was drafted by (a) ABA, (b) American Law Institute, (c) Congress, (d) None of the above [3] "The appellate brief is poorly written, sloppy, and should have been shortened." This sentence: (a) violates parallelism, (b) has too many commas, (c) contains the passive voice, (d) a & b, (e) a & c (f) a, b, & c. Answers: [1] False, [2] (b), [3] (e).	All objective questions: 200 multiple-choice questions. Examples: [1] A case raising an issue for the first time is (a) a primary case, (b) a case of first impression, (c) a jurisdictional case, (d) a case-in-chief. [2] Which one of the following kinds of deeds offers the most protection to the buyer? (a) Quitclaim, (b) Warranty, (c) Trustee, (d) Survivorship. [3] Which federal statute enables any citizen, upon proper request, to obtain documents from a federal agency? (a) Open Records Act, (b) Freedom of Information Act, (c) Administrative Communication Act, (d) Privileged Information Act. Answers: [1] (b), [2] (b), [3] (b).	All objective questions Examples: [1] When researching a court's opinion, a paralegal's main focus should be: (a) a brief statement of the facts of the case, (b) the errors of law of the lower court, (c) a summary of legal issues raised, or (d) the words of the court itself. [2] While some state agencies provide similar services to federal agencies, in the event of a conflict, the federal agency will prevail, because (a) of the Supremacy Clause in the U.S. Constitution, (b) Congress has ordered that federal agencies override state agencies, (c) federal agencies were established before state agencies, or (d) state agencies can blame federal agencies for inequities. [3] The law of torts defines and measures the duty of care in a negligence case as (a) an agreeable person who is well liked in the community, (b) someone who has never been diagnosed with a psychological problem, (c) the standard of behavior expected of a hypothetical reasonable person, or (d) a person who has no special education or training. Answers: [1] (d), [2] (a), [3] (c).
Passing Score	A score of 70% is needed for each section of the exam	Total points possible: 700 Number needed to pass: 550 (Scoring for PACE will be on a scale score like the SAT. The range will be from 300 to 700.)	290 points are needed to pass the exam, a score of approximately 70 percent. (These points can be obtained by either straight-pass or cumulative scoring.)
Continuing Legal Education (CLE) Requirements	The CLA credential must be renewed every five years by attending fifty hours of CLE or of individual study programs. (A Certificate of Attendance must be filed.)	To maintain the PACE credential, paralegals must complete twelve hours of CLE every two years. (At least one of the twelve must be in ethics.)	To maintain the PP credential, paralegals must complete seventy-five hours of CLE every five years. Five of the hours must be in legal ethics, and seventy of the hours must be in substantive areas.
Statistics	Approximately 8% of all working paralegals nationwide are CLAs. Number who have taken CLA exam: over 25,000. Number passed: 13,958 (Almost half of all CLAs are in Florida and Texas.)	Number who have taken the PACE exam: over 1,500. Number passed: 600 (almost 40 percent of whom are in Connecticut, Indiana, New York, Ohio, and Texas).	Number who have taken the PP exam: 400. Number passed: 339 (the largest number of whom are in Texas, Michigan, Alabama, Missouri, and Washington).
Study Materials	*CLA Review Manual* (2d ed.): www.nala.org/cert.htm (click "Study Materials")	*PACE Study Manual;* Online PACE materials: www.paralegals.org (click "PACE/RP") 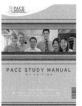	NALS Professional Paralegal Resource Manual: www.nala.org/cert.htm (click "Study Materials") (www.nals.org/education/Legal TrainingCourse/Index.html)

(continues)

Additional Certification	NALA also offers advanced certification: ACP (Advanced Certified Paralegal). The ACP credential can be awarded in designated specialties such as litigation after completing online courses and "test modules" connected with each course. To be eligible for ACP, you must have already passed the basic CLA/CP examination or do so within one year of completing the ACP requirements. The program is called Advanced Paralegal Certification (APC) leading to the ACP credential (www. nala.org/APC.htm).	Eventually, NFPA hopes to develop a second-level certification test (called Tier II) that will test specialty areas of the law. (www.paralegals.org) (click "PACE/RP")	NALS also offers ALS certification and PLS certification examinations. They are primarily for clerical law office personnel (www.nals.org/certification/index.html).

A fourth national certification credential has been added to the field. You can become an AACP (American Alliance Certified Paralegal) by meeting the requirements of the recently created American Alliance of Paralegals Inc. (AAPI). The requirements include at least five years of experience and specified education, but not an examination (www.aapipara.org).

Some states have their own voluntary *state-specific* certification exam, meaning that the exam tests knowledge of the law of a specific state, unlike the national exams of NALA, NFPA, and NALS. Exhibit 4.8 presents an overview of the state-specific certification programs of California, Florida, Texas, Louisiana, and North Carolina:

- CAS (California Advanced Specialist)
- CFLA (Certified Florida Legal Assistant)
- Board Certified Legal Assistant, [name of specialty], Texas Board of Legal Specialization
- LCP (Louisiana Certified Paralegal)
- NCCP (North Carolina certified paralegal)

EXHIBIT 4.8   State-Specific Certification Programs: Testing on the Law and Procedure of a Particular State

	CALIFORNIA	**FLORIDA**	**TEXAS**	**LOUISIANA**	**NORTH CAROLINA**
Name of Exam	California Advanced Specialty Program (The program is currently being revised.)	Certified Florida Legal Assistant Exam	Legal Assistant Specialty Certification Exam	Louisiana Certified Paralegal Exam	North Carolina Certified Paralegal Exam
Sponsors	California Alliance of Paralegal Associations in cooperation with National Association of Legal Assistants. The test is administered by the Commission for Advanced California Paralegal Specialization, Inc. (CACPS) (www.cla-cas.org.).	Paralegal Association of Florida, Inc. (www.pafinc.org/certification.php)	Texas Board of Legal Specialization (www.tbls.org)	Louisiana State Paralegal Association (www.la-paralegals.org)	North Carolina State Bar (www.nccertifiedparalegal.org)
Credential	CAS (California advanced specialist) (For example, John Jones, CAS, Paralegal; or John Jones, CAS, Legal Assistant) The CLA or CP designation can be added since CAS candidates must also meet the requirements for becoming a CLA or CP (see eligibility, below).	CFLA (Certified Florida legal assistant) (For example, Patricia Evans, CFLA, Legal Assistant) The CLA or CP designation can be added since CFLA candidates must also meet the requirements for becoming a CLA or CP (see eligibility, below).	Board certified legal assistant [name of specialty] Texas Board of Legal Specialization (For example, Mary Smith–Board Certified Legal Assistant, Family Law, Texas Board of Legal Specialization)	LCP (Louisiana certified paralegal) (For example, Edward Duffy, LCP, Paralegal) (Note in all the examples of credentials listed in exhibits 4.7 and 4.8 that the words *paralegal* and *legal assistant* must be used along with the letter credential. This meets the ethical requirement of making one's status clear to the public, as we will see in chapter 5.)	NCCP North Carolina Certified Paralegal, North Carolina State Bar Certified Paralegal, Paralegal Certified by the North Carolina State Bar Board of Paralegal Certification (For example, Alice Weston, North Carolina Certified Paralegal)

(continues)

EXHIBIT 4.8	State-Specific Certification Programs: Testing the Law and Procedure of a Particular State— *continued*				
Required for Employment?	No. The test is voluntary.	No. The test is voluntary.	No. The test is voluntary.	No. The test is voluntary.	No. The test is voluntary.
Cost	$150	$125 ($100 for members of Paralegal Association of Florida)	$150	$175 for members of the Louisiana State Paralegal Association ($195 for nonmembers)	$125
Date Started	1995	1983	1994	1996	2005
Eligibility to Take Exam	(a) Passing the CLA exam of NALA. (b) Confirmation by an active California attorney that the applicant has the knowledge, skill, and competence to work at an advanced level in the particular specialty practice area.	(a) Passing the CLA exam of NALA. (b) Having an attorney certify the applicant's employment, awareness of the rules of ethics, and moral character.	(a) Five years of experience as a paralegal, and (b) substantial involvement in the last three years in the specialty area for which certification is being sought, and (c) One of the following: −CLA certification of NALA −a baccalaureate in any field −graduation from an approved paralegal program, or −four additional years of paralegal experience under an attorney.	You already passed the CLA exam of NALA or you take and pass the CLA exam within three years of passing the LCP exam.	(a) Passing the NCCP exam (starting in 2007). (b) One of the following: (i) 5,000 hours of paralegal work in North Carolina, three hours of continuing legal education in ethics, and a high school diploma; (ii) 2,000 hours of paralegal work in North Carolina and already having national certification (e.g., from NALA or NFPA); or (iii) 2,000 hours of paralegal work in North Carolina and a degree in paralegal studies or other approved paralegal coursework. (c) Verification by an attorney of the applicant's credentials.
Topics Tested	Advanced knowledge and proficiency in the following specialty areas of California law: civil litigation, business organization and business law, real estate, trusts and estates, and family law.	Part I: ethics, general Florida law. Part II: you select 6 questions from the Florida substantive law of contracts, corporate law, business law, civil litigation, criminal law, estate/probate law, family law, and real estate law.	Texas civil trial law, criminal law, estate planning and probate, family law, personal injury and trial law, and real estate law.	General Louisiana law, Louisiana civil procedure, Louisiana ethics. You choose four areas from the following: business organizations, contracts, criminal law, evidence, family law, property, torts, and wills/probate/ trusts.	Civil Litigation, Commercial Law, Criminal Law, Ethics, Family Law, Legal Research, Real Property, and Wills, Trusts & Estate Administration. Also: five performance domains.
Length of Exam	Four hours	Three hours	Four hours	$10^{1}/_{2}$ hours over two days	Three hours
Passing Score	70%	70% in each part	A curve method (Norm Reference Testing) is used to calculate the pass/fail results.	70% for each exam section	The passing score will vary for different parts of the exam.
Continuing Legal Education (CLE) Requirements	Seventy hours of CLE every five years. (At least ten hours must be in the specialty area of California certification.)	Thirty hours of CLE on Florida law over five years.	Thirty hours of CLE in the specialty area within three years prior to taking the test; seventy-five hours of CLE in the specialty area every five years thereafter.	2.5 units in Louisiana substantive and/or procedural law and 0.5 unit in ethics every five years.	Six hours of CLE (including one in ethics) every year.
Number Certified to Date	48	130	320	16	2,400

Like the national certification exams, the state exams of these states are voluntary. The Florida program is run by a paralegal association. Recently a new Florida certification program was launched, this time by the Supreme Court of Florida and the Florida Bar Association. It is also voluntary. Under this program, a paralegal can become a *Florida Registered Paralegal* (FRP) if he or she meets designated education requirements, abides by a code of ethics, and registers with the Florida Bar (www.floridasupremecourt.org/decisions/2007/sc06–1622.pdf).

Other states are starting to create their own certification programs. The most recent to do so are Delaware, Ohio, and Pennsylvania:

- Delaware.   To become a DCP (Delaware Certified Paralegal), you must meet minimum education or experience requirements, but there is no examination. To maintain DCP status, eight hours of continuing legal education (CLE) are required every two years.[56]
- Ohio.   To become an OSBA Certified Paralegal of the Ohio State Bar Association (OSBA), you must meet minimum education and experience requirements, submit professional references, pass a written examination, and attend twelve credit hours of continuing legal or paralegal education prior to taking the examination.[57]
- Pennsylvania.   To become a Pa.C.P. (Pennsylvania Certified Paralegal), you must meet education or experience requirements and attend designated continuing legal education (CLE).[57a]

Several years ago the American Bar Association studied the question of certification. Some suggested that the ABA should certify individual paralegals. It declined the invitation, taking the position that certification should be undertaken by a national body that includes paralegals, attorneys, educators, and members of the general public. Furthermore, the ABA favored specialty certification, *not* entry-level certification. It felt that the benefits of entry-level certification would *not* be worth the time, expense, and effort to implement the program.[58]

Nevertheless, the momentum toward certification continues. Paralegals want to control their own future, and many see certification as a practical way to accomplish this goal. Certification, however, will remain controversial as the field continues to debate the following topics:

- Whether enough paralegals are interested in pursuing certification. (The numbers seeking certification to date have been relatively low, primarily because few prospective employers limit their search to individuals who have passed certification exams. If, however, you live in an area of the country where a relatively large number of paralegals are certified (e.g., Florida), the likelihood is increased that prospective employers in that area will give preference to job candidates who have passed certification exams.)
- Whether certification should be entry-level, specialty, or both.
- Whether voluntary certification programs will be confused with mandatory licensing programs. (Will the public think that a certified paralegal is a licensed one?)
- Whether the eligibility requirements to take the certification exam are so high that they will discourage people from entering the profession.

ASSIGNMENT 4.11

(a) Do you favor the certification of paralegals? Why or why not?

(b) If certification exists, should it be entry-level, specialty, or both? Why?

(c) Who should control certification? Paralegals? Attorneys? The government? Why?

(d) When a new local paralegal association is formed, it is often lobbied by NALA and NFPA to become a part of one of these national organizations. The local association will usually make one of three decisions: affiliate with NALA, affiliate with NFPA, or remain unaffiliated. If you were a member of a local association faced with the decision of whether to join NALA or NFPA or to stay unaffiliated, what would your vote be? Why?

(e) Is it a good idea to have more than one national association? Why or why not?

Throughout this book, the importance of paralegal associations has been stressed. They have had a major impact on the development of paralegalism. Many state and local bar associations as well as the ABA have felt the effect of organized paralegal advocacy through the associations.

As soon as possible, you should join a paralegal association. Find out if the association allows students to become members. If an association does not exist in your area, you should form one and decide whether you want to become part of one of the national associations. The paralegal association is your main voice in the continued development of the field. Join one now and become an active member. In addition to networking opportunities, educational benefits, and job placement services that many associations provide, you will experience the satisfaction of helping shape your career in the years to come.

[SECTION F]

FAIR LABOR STANDARDS ACT

Under the federal **Fair Labor Standards Act (FLSA)**,[59] employees are entitled to overtime compensation (one-and-one-half times regular pay) if they (1) are paid on a salary basis, (2) work more than forty hours a week, and (3) earn under $455 a week ($23,600 a year). Most paralegals earn over this amount. Are they also entitled to overtime compensation? In general, the answer is yes *unless they are exempt.*

Before we examine whether paralegals earning over $455 a week are exempt under the FLSA, we need to note two related circumstances that do not involve the FLSA. First, *state* overtime law might be more generous than federal law. Many employees are subject to two wage laws: federal overtime law (the FLSA) and state overtime law. It is possible for an employee to be entitled to overtime law under state law but not under federal law. If so, the law that leads to the higher salary controls. In this area of law, federal law does not **preempt** (i.e., displace or take precedence over) state law. Second, unions may negotiate labor contracts that provide better wage protection than either federal or state law. The following discussion is limited to federal overtime law governing nonunion employees.[60]

The FLSA is enforced by the Wage and Hours Division of the U.S. Department of Labor (DOL). If employees are not exempt under the FLSA, they must be given overtime compensation; they cannot be pressured by their employers to waive this right. Nor can they be retaliated against if they assert a claim for overtime compensation.

There are three main categories of exempt employees: executive, professional, and administrative. (They are referred to as the *white-collar exemptions.*) Do paralegals fit within any of them? The answer depends on their primary duties, meaning the main or most important tasks they perform. It does not depend on their title, which, as we saw in chapter 1, can vary from employer to employer. Furthermore, because paralegals perform a wide variety of tasks in many different settings, the question of whether they are exempt must be determined on a case-by-case basis—one paralegal at a time. It is possible for a paralegal in an office to be exempt while another paralegal in the same office is nonexempt.

Here is an overview of the three exemptions and how they might apply to paralegals:

Executive exemption: The employee (1) manages an enterprise such as a department or subdivision that has a permanent status or function in the office; (2) regularly directs the work of two or more employees; and (3) either has the authority to hire, promote, or fire other employees or can recommend such action and the recommendation is given particular weight.

Most paralegal *supervisors* meet all three tests of the executive exemption. They often manage the paralegal unit of the firm, supervise more than two employees, and have great influence on who is hired, promoted, or fired in their department. The supervisor does not lose this exemption if he or she also works on individual client cases in addition to his or her primary supervisory role. Line paralegals, however, who do not exercise managerial or supervisory responsibility, do not fit within the executive exemption.

Professional exemption: The employee performs work that requires advanced knowledge that is customarily acquired by a prolonged course of specialized intellectual instruction. (Advanced knowledge means work that is predominantly intellectual in character and includes work requiring the consistent exercise of discretion and judgment.) There are two categories of exempt professional employees: learned professionals (whose specialized academic training is a standard prerequisite for entrance into the profession) and creative professionals (who work mainly in the creative arts).

Paralegals do not fit within the professional exemption. They are not "learned professionals" because prolonged specialized instruction is not a standard prerequisite to entering the field. A bachelor's degree, for example, is not a prerequisite to becoming a paralegal. (An example of a support occupation that *would* qualify as a learned profession is the registered nurse because having a specialized advanced degree is a standard prerequisite for becoming a registered nurse.) And paralegals are not "creative professionals" because law is not in the same category as music, theater, or one of the other creative arts.

Administrative exemption: The employee (1) performs office work that is directly related to the management or general business operations of the employer or of the employer's customers, and (2) exercises discretion and independent judgment with respect to matters of significance. The question of whether the administrative exemption applies to paralegals is less clear. Historically, the DOL has argued that this exemption does *not* apply to the vast majority of paralegals.

Fair Labor Standards Act (FLSA) The federal statute that regulates conditions of employment such as when overtime compensation must be paid.

preempt Displace or take precedence over. The noun is *preemption.* Under the Supremacy Clause of the U.S. Constitution, federal laws take precedence over (preempt) state laws when Congress (1) expressly mandates the preemption, (2) regulates an area so pervasively that an intent to preempt the entire field may be inferred, or (3) enacts a law that directly conflicts with state law.

The first test under the administrative exemption is that the employees perform office work that is directly related to the management or general business operations of the employer or of the employer's customers. This means "assisting with the running or servicing of the business" such as working on budgets, purchasing equipment, or administering the office's computer database. Such tasks, however, are not the primary duties of most paralegals, although they may help out in these areas. In the main, paralegals spend most of their time working on individual cases and hence do not meet the first test.

The second test (which also must be met for the administrative exemption to apply) is that the employees exercise "discretion and independent judgment with respect to matters of significance." The phrase "discretion and independent judgment" involves (1) comparing and evaluating possible courses of conduct and (2) acting or making a decision after the various possibilities have been considered. The phrase implies that the employee has authority to make an independent choice, "free from immediate direction or supervision." An employee does *not* exercise discretion and independent judgment if he or she merely uses skills in applying well-established techniques, procedures, or standards described in manuals or other sources.

Do paralegals meet the second test of exercising "discretion and independent judgment with respect to matters of significance"? They certainly work on "matters of significance." Yet it is not clear whether they exercise "discretion and independent judgment." Paralegals are often given some leeway in the performance of their work. Yet if they operate "within closely prescribed limits," they are not exercising discretion and independent judgment.

The DOL has consistently taken the position that paralegals do not have the kind of independence this exemption requires because of the attorney supervision and approval their work must be given under the rules of ethics. As we will see in chapter 5, if paralegals make independent choices on client matters, they run the risk of being charged with engaging in the unauthorized practice of law.

To summarize, only paralegal supervisors are exempt under the executive exemption, most paralegals are not exempt under the professional exemption, and most paralegals are probably not exempt under the administrative exemption. Nonexempt employees must be given overtime compensation under the FLSA if they are salaried and work over forty hours in a week.

For years paralegals debated the desirability of being classified as exempt or nonexempt. The debate was referred to as GOD, the great overtime debate. Those opposed to overtime compensation felt that being classified as exempt gave them increased respect. Attorneys do not receive overtime compensation. Their long hours are rewarded by higher salaries and bonuses. If paralegals were exempt, they arguably would be treated in a similar way. Other paralegals took the position that there is nothing demeaning about receiving overtime and that many firms offered bonuses to both exempt and nonexempt employees. Today the GOD is relatively quiet. It raged during a time when there was doubt on when the law allowed an exemption. Recent clarifications in the law by the Department of Labor have all but eliminated this doubt.

ASSIGNMENT 4.12

If you had a choice, would you want to receive overtime compensation as an entry-level paralegal?

[SECTION G]

TORT LIABILITY OF PARALEGALS

Thus far we have discussed a number of ways that paralegal activities are or could be regulated.

- Criminal liability for violating the statutes on the unauthorized practice of law
- Special authorization rules on practice before administrative agencies and other tribunals
- Licensing
- Self-regulation
- Labor laws

tort A civil wrong (other than a breach of contract) that causes injury or other damage for which our legal system deems it just to provide a remedy such as compensation.

Finally, we come to **tort** liability, which is another method by which society defines what is and is not permissible. A tort action is brought when someone has allegedly caused injury or other damage by committing a civil wrong other than a breach of contract. While a tort is different from a breach of contract and a crime, the same conduct that constitutes a breach of contract or a crime can also constitute a tort.[61]

Two questions need to be kept in mind. First, when are paralegal employees *personally liable* for their torts? Second, when are employers *vicariously liable* for the torts of their paralegal employees? (**Vicarious liability** simply means one person being responsible or liable for what another person does because of the relationship that exists between them.) The short answer to the first question is: *always*. The short answer to the second question is: *when the wrongdoing by the paralegal was within the scope of employment*. After covering both questions, we will then examine the separate question of when malpractice insurance will pay for such liability.

Several different kinds of wrongdoing are possible. The paralegal might commit:

- The tort of negligence
- An intentional tort, such as battery
- An act that is both a crime (such as embezzlement) *and* an intentional tort (such as conversion)

A client who is injured by any of these torts can sue the paralegal in the same manner that a patient in a hospital can sue a nurse. Paralegals are not relieved of liability simply because they work for, and function under the supervision of, an attorney. Every citizen is *personally* liable for the torts he or she commits. If a client suffers harm because of the negligence or other wrongdoing of a paralegal and the client sues the paralegal, it is not a defense that the employee committed the wrongdoing on behalf of someone else (an attorney in a law office).

Next we turn to the employers of paralegals. Are they *also* liable for the wrongdoing committed by their employees? There are four possible theories of employer liability for employee wrongdoing:

- Careless hiring
- Careless supervision
- Participation in the wrongdoing
- Vicarious liability

Under the first theory, the employer was careless in hiring the employee; the employer should have known that the person was likely to commit wrongdoing. (This theory is sometimes called *negligent hiring*.) Under the second theory, the employer was careless in supervising the employee; the wrongdoing by the employee would not have occurred if the employer exercised proper oversight or training of the employee's work. (This theory is sometimes called *negligent supervision*.) Under the third theory, the employer actually participated in the wrongdoing with the employee; the two of them committed the wrongdoing together. Under the fourth theory, the employer is liable for what the employee did solely because of the special relationship that exists between them—an employer-employee relationship. (This theory is called *vicarious liability*.)

Not all wrongdoing of an employee will result in vicarious liability of the employer. Under the doctrine of **respondeat superior**, an employer will be liable for the wrongdoing of his or her employee if the wrongdoing occurred within the **scope of employment**.[62] This means the wrongdoing was foreseeable by the employer and the employee was under the employer's specific or general control at the time. Slandering a client in a law office for failure to pay a law firm bill would be within the scope of employment. It's foreseeable that a paralegal would insult a client for this reason. It's not what the employer would want the paralegal to do, but it is foreseeable and it occurred within the confines and general control of the employer. But the opposite would probably be true if the paralegal has an argument with a client over a football game and punches the client during their accidental evening meeting at a bar. In this example, the client could not sue the paralegal's employer for the intentional tort of battery under the theory of respondeat superior. The battery was not foreseeable by the employer, was not under the employer's control, and was unrelated to the business of the employer. Only the paralegal would be liable for the tort under such circumstances.

When a paralegal's wrongdoing is within the scope of employment (making the paralegal personally liable and the attorney-employer vicariously liable under respondeat superior), the client can sue the paralegal or the attorney, or both. This does not mean that the client recovers twice; there can be only one recovery for a tort. The client is simply given a choice in bringing the suit. In most cases, the primary target of the client will be the employer, who is the so-called **deep pocket**, the one who has resources from which a judgment can be satisfied.

NEGLIGENCE

The most commonly committed tort is **negligence**. This tort occurs when the defendant's failure to use reasonable care causes harm. When a member of an occupation or profession is charged with negligence, reasonable care is determined by the knowledge and skill commonly possessed by members of that occupation or profession in good standing. Attorney negligence is the failure to exercise the reasonable care expected of an attorney in good standing. An attorney is not an insurer, however. Every mistake will not lead to negligence liability even if it causes harm

---

vicarious liability Liability imposed on one party for the conduct of another, based solely upon the status of the relationship between the two (e.g., employer–employee).

respondeat superior Let the master (boss) answer. An employer is responsible (liable) for the wrongs committed by an employee within the scope of employment.

scope of employment That which is foreseeably done by an employee for an employer under the latter's specific or general control.

deep pocket (1) An individual, a business, or another organization with resources to pay a potential judgment. (2) Sufficient assets for this purpose. The opposite of *shallow pocket*.

negligence Harm caused by the failure to use reasonable care.

to the client. The harm must be due to an *unreasonable* mistake, such as forgetting to file an action in court before the statute of limitations runs out.

When a *traditional paralegal* (one employed by an attorney) commits negligence for which the attorney becomes liable under respondeat superior, the same standard applies. Since the work product of this paralegal blends into the work product of the supervising attorney, the attorney becomes as fully responsible for what the paralegal did as if the attorney had committed the negligence. Unreasonableness is measured by what a reasonable attorney would have done, not by what a reasonable paralegal would have done.

An *independent paralegal* (or legal document assistant) would be treated differently from a traditional paralegal. Because independent paralegals do not work under attorney supervision, they will be held to the standard of a reasonable independent paralegal. The standard would be the knowledge and skill commonly possessed by independent paralegals in good standing. If such a paralegal is charged with negligence, he or she will not be held to the standard of a reasonable attorney—unless the paralegal led the client to believe he or she was an attorney or worked under an attorney's supervision.

There have not been many tort cases in which paralegals have been sued for wrongdoing in a law office. Yet as paralegals become increasingly prominent in the practice of law, more are expected to be named as defendants. Michael Martz, general counsel of the Mississippi Bar Association, makes the unsettling point that the prominence of paralegalism means there will be more suits against them. "As paralegals become more and more professional and proficient, they . . . will become better targets for disgruntled clients looking for someone to sue."[63] The most common kinds of cases involving paralegals have occurred when the paralegal was a notary and improperly notarized signatures under pressure from the supervising attorney.

ASSIGNMENT 4.13

Mary Smith is a paralegal at the XYZ law firm. One of her tasks is to file a document in court. She negligently forgets to do so. As a result, the court enters a default judgment against the client. What options are available to the client?

Client victims of negligence must establish that they suffered actual harm. It is not enough to show that a law office failed to use reasonable care. This failure must lead to (i.e., cause) actual harm. Assume that an attorney represents Tom, who wants to sue his employer for $25,000 in back wages. The case is dismissed, however, because his attorney carelessly fails to file the claim before the statute of limitations runs out. Tom now sues the attorney for negligence. What are Tom's damages in this negligence suit? Tom has not lost $25,000 *unless* he can establish that he would have won the case against his employer if it had not been thrown out because of the attorney's filing negligence. If the wage claim was so weak that Tom would have lost it if it had been tried, there was no loss of $25,000. Hence, in a negligence action against an attorney, the client must show (a) that the attorney's conduct fell below the standard of reasonable care expected of attorneys, and (b) that the underlying claim would have been successful if the attorney had not been careless.

There are two other torts we need to consider: malicious prosecution and abuse of process. They involve the misuse of legal **process**. *Process* refers to summons, writs, court orders, or procedures in legal actions.

MALICIOUS PROSECUTION

Nature of the tort: Someone maliciously initiates a civil or criminal case for which there is no probable cause and that is won by the party against whom the case was brought.

Example: A store owner files a criminal complaint for drug dealing against a hated neighbor whom the store owner knows is innocent. The neighbor is eventually found to be innocent. The store owner used the law firm of Adams & Adams for legal advice in bringing the criminal complaint.

ABUSE OF PROCESS

Nature of the tort: Someone uses process for a purpose for which it was not designed.

Example: A father brings a suit for child custody against the mother (his ex-girlfriend) of their child in order to pressure her to pay a business debt she owes the father. In the suit, the father was represented by the law firm of Smith & Smith. Process was abused because the purpose of custody suits is not to collect unrelated debts.

process 1. A summons, writ, or court order, e.g., to appear in court. 2. Procedures or proceedings in an action or prosecution.

malicious prosecution A tort with the following elements: (1) to initiate or procure the initiation of civil or criminal legal proceedings; (2) without probable cause; (3) with malice or an improper purpose; and (4) the proceedings terminate in favor of the person against whom the proceedings were brought.

abuse of process A tort consisting of (1) the use of a civil or criminal process, (2) for a purpose for which the process is not designed, and (3) resulting in actual damage.

In these examples, the neighbor can sue the store owner for malicious prosecution and the mother can sue the father for abuse of process. They will probably try to join as defendants the attorneys used by the store owner and father (Adams & Adams and Smith & Smith, respectively). Such suits against attorneys are seldom successful, however, because attorneys (and their staffs) have a privilege to use the courts on behalf of their clients. It would have to be shown that the attorneys knowingly and maliciously helped their clients misuse process against the neighbor and mother. This is difficult to prove. Yet victims such as the neighbor and mother may be so angry that they will want to join the attorneys as defendants. This is not a position that law offices like to be in. It's never pleasant to be sued, even if you can win the case brought against you.

[SECTION H]
MALPRACTICE INSURANCE

Legal **malpractice** generally refers to wrongful conduct by an attorney for which an injured party (the attorney's client) can receive damages. Just as doctors purchase malpractice insurance against suits by their patients, so, too, attorneys can buy such insurance to cover suits against them by their clients for alleged errors and omissions. (See Exhibit 4.9.) We need to examine how paralegals fit into this picture.

Until the 1940s, not many attorneys bought malpractice insurance because suits by clients were relatively rare. Today, the picture has changed radically; cautious attorneys do not practice law without such insurance against their own malpractice. "Statistically, the new attorney will be subjected to three claims before finishing a legal career."[64] Hence very few attorneys are willing to **go bare**—that is, practice without liability insurance. This change has been due to a number of factors. As the practice of law becomes more complex, the likelihood of error increases. Furthermore, the public is becoming more aware of its right to sue. In spite of disclaimers by attorneys that they are not guaranteeing any results, client expectations tend to be high, and hence clients are more likely to blame their attorney for an unfavorable result. And attorneys are increasingly willing to sue each other. In fact, some attorneys have developed a legal malpractice specialty in which they take clients who want to sue other attorneys. (To find attorneys with this specialty, run this search in Google or another search engine: "suing attorneys.") As malpractice awards against attorneys continue to rise, the market for malpractice insurance has dramatically increased. And so has the cost. There are cities where the premium for insurance can be between $5,000 and $15,000 per year per attorney. This has tempted some attorneys (particularly those in solo or small firms) to go bare or to purchase very low coverage. In some states, attorneys without liability insurance or with coverage below a designated amount (e.g., $100,000) are ethically required to notify their clients (or prospective clients) of this fact.

Typically, legal malpractice claims arise in the context of fee disputes. The sequence is often as follows: a client fails to pay agreed-upon attorney fees, the attorney sues the client for fees, and the client responds by suing the attorney for malpractice and by filing an ethics charge with the bar association alleging the same malpractice.

Two kinds of professional liability insurance policies cover attorney malpractice: occurrence policies and claims-made policies. An **occurrence policy** covers all occurrences (such as negligent error or omission) during the period the policy is in effect, even if the claim on such an occurrence is not actually filed until after the policy expires. Insurance companies are reluctant to write such policies because of the length of time it sometimes takes to uncover the existence of the negligent error or omission. Here's an example: An attorney makes a careless mistake in drafting a will that is not discovered until the person who hired the attorney dies many years later. Under an occurrence policy, the attorney is covered if the mistake occurred while the policy was in effect, even if the actual claim was not filed in court until after the policy terminated. The most common kind of policy sold by insurance companies today is the **claims-made policy** under which coverage is limited to claims actually filed (made) during the period in which the policy is in effect. Covered claims are usually subject to limits on the amount the insurance company will pay per claim and over the life of the policy.

Malpractice policies usually cover all the attorneys *and* the nonattorney employees of the law office. One policy, for example, defines the individuals covered—"the insured"—as follows:

> The insured includes the firm, all lawyers within the firm, and all non-lawyer employees, as well as former partners, officers, directors and employees solely while they acted on behalf of the insured firm.[65]

Such inclusion of employees is not always automatic, however. The policies of some insurance companies do not include paralegals or secretaries unless the law firm specifically requests coverage for them and pays an additional premium for their inclusion. Paralegals should therefore ask their employers if their malpractice policy explicitly covers paralegals.

malpractice Professional misconduct or wrongdoing such as an ethical violation, crime, negligence, battery, or other tort.

go bare To engage in an occupation or profession without malpractice (liabilty) insurance.

occurrence policy Insurance that covers all occurrences (e.g., a negligent error or omission) during the period the policy is in effect, even if the claim is not filed until after the policy expires.

claims-made policy Insurance that covers only claims actually filed ("made") during the period in which the policy is in effect.

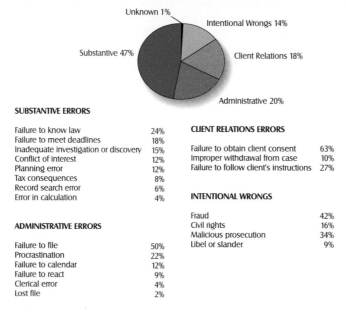

| EXHIBIT 4.9 | Professional Liability Claims Against Law Firms |

SUBSTANTIVE ERRORS

Failure to know law	24%
Failure to meet deadlines	18%
Inadequate investigation or discovery	15%
Conflict of interest	12%
Planning error	12%
Tax consequences	8%
Record search error	6%
Error in calculation	4%

CLIENT RELATIONS ERRORS

Failure to obtain client consent	63%
Improper withdrawal from case	10%
Failure to follow client's instructions	27%

INTENTIONAL WRONGS

Fraud	42%
Civil rights	16%
Malicious prosecution	34%
Libel or slander	9%

ADMINISTRATIVE ERRORS

Failure to file	50%
Procrastination	22%
Failure to calendar	12%
Failure to react	9%
Clerical error	4%
Lost file	2%

Source: St. Paul Fire and Marine Insurance Company (due to rounding, figures don't add up to 100%).

What about independent or freelance paralegals who sell their services to attorneys? Although they may not be considered employees of the firm, they will usually be covered under the firm's policy in the same manner as full-time, in-house paralegal employees. So long as the employing attorney supervises and is responsible for the conduct of the paralegal, the malpractice policy usually provides coverage. In the language of one widely used policy, coverage is provided for "any other person for whose acts, errors or omissions the insured is legally responsible,"[66] which would include independent or freelance paralegals. A sophisticated paralegal would make sure that this is so before undertaking work for an attorney.

Independent or freelance paralegals *who do not work for attorneys* need to purchase their own liability policy if they want protection. Such insurance, however, is expensive and difficult to find. At one time, a company offered "Paralegal Professional Indemnity Insurance" that provided $250,000 in coverage for $1,800 a year. The company offering this policy no longer exists. Most independents today "go bare."

As we saw earlier in the chapter, legal document assistants (LDAs) in California are required to purchase a bond in the amount of $25,000. It costs approximately $500 a year.

Chapter Summary

Criminal prosecution may result from violating statutes on the unauthorized practice of law. Defining the practice of law, however, is sometimes difficult. States do not all use the same definition or test. In general, the law prohibits nonattorneys from appearing for another in a representative capacity, drafting most legal documents, and giving legal advice. In most states, nonattorneys can sell forms and other legal materials but cannot give individual help in using them. They can give (and even sell) legal information, but they cannot give legal advice.

There are some major exceptions to the prohibitions on nonattorney conduct. In a very limited number of circumstances,

nonattorneys are authorized to do what would otherwise constitute the unauthorized practice of law. For example:

- In most states, a real estate broker can draft sales contracts.
- Several specialized courts allow nonattorneys to represent clients in court, although this is rare.
- A few states allow paralegals to appear in court to request a continuance or a new date for the next hearing in a case.
- An inmate can "practice law" in prison such as by drafting documents for and giving legal advice to another inmate if the prison does not offer adequate alternative

methods of providing inmates with legal services that provide access to the courts.

■ Many administrative agencies, particularly at the federal level, allow nonattorneys to represent clients before the agencies.

A number of states have considered broad-based licensing (which would cover all activities of all paralegals) and limited licensing (which in the main would cover specified activities of those paralegals who are not supervised by attorneys). To date, neither kind of licensing has been enacted. Broad-based licensing for traditional paralegals is generally considered unnecessary because the public is sufficiently protected by attorney supervision. A few states place restrictions on who can use the titles of *paralegal* and *legal assistant*. In California, for example, the titles can be used only by individuals who work under attorney supervision, meet minimum educational requirements, and attend a designated number of hours of continuing legal education (CLE).

Independent contractors who work without attorney supervision are called legal document assistants (LDAs) or unlawful detainer assistants (UDAs). In Arizona they are called legal document preparers (LDPs). They are subject to strict regulation, as are bankruptcy petition preparers (BPPs), who can provide limited assistance to citizens undergoing bankruptcy. Washington State may create new limited-licensing positions in the future similar to the position it has already created, the limited practice officer (LPO). NALA opposes limited licensing; NFPA favors it if it will expand the scope of tasks paralegals are allowed to carry out.

To address the problem of underrepresentation, some of the reforms in the practice of law have included pro bono programs, simplified forms, Internet self-help centers, court facilitators, prepaid legal services, attorney advertising, publicly funded legal services, modest means panels, and the use of traditional paralegals. Some argue that creating limited licensing for independent paralegals would be another reform that would help resolve the problem of underrepresentation.

A number of bar associations allow paralegals to become associate or affiliate members. For example, the American Bar Association has a membership category called legal assistant associate.

There are three major national certification programs. NALA offers an entry-level CLA/CP (Certified Legal Assistant/Certified Paralegal) exam, NFPA offers PACE (Paralegal Advanced Certification Exam), and NALS the Association for Legal Professionals offers the PP (Professional Paralegal) exam, the latter two of which require paralegal work experience to take. A number of states have state-specific certification programs: California, Florida, Louisiana, Texas, North Carolina, Delaware, Ohio, and Pennsylvania.

The Fair Labor Standards Act (FLSA) requires employers to pay overtime compensation to employees unless the latter are exempt. There are three categories of exemption: executive, professional, and administrative. Most paralegals (other than some paralegal managers) are not exempt and hence are entitled to overtime compensation. State labor laws and union contracts may provide greater overtime rights than those accorded under the federal FLSA.

If a paralegal commits a tort, such as negligence, he or she is personally liable to the defendant. Under the theory of respondeat superior, the supervising attorney is also liable for the wrong committed by a traditional paralegal if it occurred within the scope of employment. Most attorneys have a claims-made malpractice insurance policy that covers their employees, although paralegals should check whether they are covered by such policies.

Key Terms

unauthorized practice of law	pro se	scrivener	entry-level certification
practice of law	law clerk	legal technician	Fair Labor Standards Act (FLSA)
regulation	continuance	limited practice officer (LPO)	preempt
accreditation	ex parte	legal document assistant (LDA)	tort
approval	uncontested	unlawful detainer assistant (UDA)	vicarious liability
certification	jailhouse lawyer	bankruptcy petition preparer (BPP)	respondeat superior
code	Administrative Procedure Act (APA)	pro bono	scope of employment
ethics	registered agent	prepaid legal services	deep pocket
guideline	enrolled agent	attorney attestation	negligence
licensure	administrative law judge (ALJ)	CLA	malpractice
limited licensure	Supremacy Clause	CP	go bare
registration	traditional paralegal	PP	process
attorney in fact	continuing legal education (CLE)	RP	malicious prosecution
power of attorney	independent contractor	PACE Registered Paralegal	abuse of process
statement of principles	page 52 debate		occurrence policy
adversarial	document preparer		claims-made policy
adversary system			
counterclaim			

Review Questions

1. In what six ways could paralegals be regulated?
2. Define *regulation, accreditation, approval, certification, code, ethics, guideline, licensure, limited licensure,* and *registration* or *enrollment.*
3. Distinguish between *certified* and *certificated.*
4. Why do UPL laws exist, and how are they enforced?
5. What are the major tests used by courts to define the practice of law, and which test is the most commonly used?
6. What is the distinction between an attorney at law and an attorney in fact?
7. What three kinds of activities comprise the practice of law?
8. Distinguish between *legal information* and *legal advice.*
9. Why was Rosemary Furman prosecuted?
10. In what ways can bar associations violate the antitrust laws?
11. What is an adversary system?
12. Give examples of when nonattorneys engage in the authorized practice of law.
13. What did *Johnson v. Avery* decide?
14. What does the Administrative Procedure Act (APA) say about agency representation by nonattorneys?
15. Describe the role of registered agents in the U.S. Patent and Trademark Office and enrolled agents at the Internal Revenue Service.
16. Summarize the rules governing paralegal practice before the Social Security Administration.
17. What case held that federal laws allowing nonattorney practice at federal agencies takes precedence or supremacy over state laws that prohibit such practice?
18. When can a court invalidate a state agency's authorization of paralegal practice before that agency?
19. For what two reasons does an occupation want to be licensed?
20. Distinguish between *broad-based licensing* and *limited licensing.*
21. Why do many attorneys and bar associations oppose paralegal licensing?
22. Why did New Jersey reject broad-based licensing for paralegals in 1999?
23. Describe the paralegal regulation enacted by California in 2000.
24. For what reasons did some individuals and groups oppose the California regulation?
25. What was the *page 52 debate*?
26. State the definitions used by the ABA Commission on Nonlawyer Practice of (1) *self-represented person,* (2) *document preparer,* (3) *paralegal,* and (4) *legal technician.*
27. What recommendations did the commission make about nonattorney practice?
28. What is the function of the Practice of Law Board in Washington State?
29. What is the role of an LPO in Washington State?
30. What are the positions of NALA and NFPA on proposals for limited licensing?
31. What are the following individuals allowed to do and not allowed to do: (1) the LDA and UDA in California, (2) the LDP in Arizona, and (3) a BPP in any state?
32. What are the major reforms in the practice of law that are designed to make legal services more accessible?
33. What steps should you take when a licensing bill is proposed in your state?
34. What different categories of membership do paralegals have in some bar associations?
35. What are the arguments for and against paralegal membership in bar associations?
36. What are the main features of the following certification programs: (1) CLA/CP of NALA, (2) PACE of NFPA, and (3) PP of NALS?
37. What states have state-specific certification programs?
38. What is the position of the ABA on paralegal certification?
39. Under what circumstances are paralegals entitled to overtime compensation?
40. When are paralegals personally liable for their own torts?
41. When are employers vicariously liable for the torts of their paralegals under respondeat superior?
42. What is the basic standard of care in a negligence case?
43. Distinguish between the torts of malicious prosecution and abuse of process.
44. What are the main errors that have led to professional liability insurance claims in the following categories: (1) substantive errors, (2) administrative errors, (3) client relations errors, and (4) intentional wrongs?
45. Why is it dangerous for a paralegal to work for an attorney who is going "bare"?
46. State the difference between an occurrence malpractice policy and a claims-made malpractice policy, and explain why insurance companies prefer the latter.
47. When should paralegals try to purchase their own professional liability insurance policy?

Helpful Web Sites: More on the Regulation of Paralegals

Regulation Links Collected by the National Federation of Paralegal Associations (NFPA)

- www.paralegals.org
  (click "Positions & Issues")

Regulation Links Collected by the National Association of Legal Assistants (NALA)

- www.nala.org
  (click "General Information")

Regulation Links Collected by the International Paralegal Management Association (IPMA)

- www.paralegalmanagement.org
  (type *regulation* in the search box)

Regulation Links Collected by the ABA Standing Committee on Paralegals (SCOP)

- www.abanet.org/legalservices/paralegals
  (click "Information for Lawyers")

Self-Help Resources

- www.wmitchell.edu/resources/ilr.asp?key1=
  Self-Help
  www.abalawinfo.org
- public.findlaw.com
  www.nolo.com

Legal Advice

- "Employee Guide to Legal Advice"
  www.courts.michigan.gov/mji
  (click "Publications" then "Legal Advice")

Legal Malpractice and Liability Insurance

- www.abanet.org/legalservices/lpl/home.html
- www.abanet.org/legalservices/lpl/directory
- www.halt.org/reform_projects/lawyer_accountability/
  legal_malpractice

Overtime Compensation

- www.dol.gov/dol/topic/wages/overtimepay.htm
- www.dol.gov/esa/whd/opinion/FLSA/2005/
  2005_12_16_S4.FLSA.htm

Licensure and Government Regulation of Paralegals

- www.nala.org/licissues.htm

Rosemary Furman Case

- www.law.fsu.edu/library/flsupct/51226/51226.html
- www.law.fsu.edu/library/flsupct/51226/51226brief.pdf

Unauthorized Practice of Law

- "The Case for Repealing Unauthorized Practice of Law
  Statutes" (www.cato.org/pubs/regulation/reg20n1c.html)

Comparison of Certification Programs

- www.nals.org/certification/compchart.html

Legal Document Assistants

- en.wikipedia.org/wiki/Legal_document_assistant

A Jailhouse Lawyer's Manual

- www.columbia.edu/cu/hrlr

Occupational Claims to Professionalism: The Case of Paralegals

- caliber.ucpress.net/doi/abs/10.1525/si.2001.24.3.343

Google Searches (run the following searches for more sites)

- paralegal regulation
- unauthorized practice of law
- overtime paralegal
- paralegal certification
- limited licensing
- nonattorney agency representation
- legal malpractice
- professional liability insurance
- jailhouse lawyer

Endnotes

1. *State Bar of Ariz. v. Arizona Land Title & Trust Co.*, 90 Ariz. 76, 87, 366 P.2d 1, 9 (Ariz.1961).

1a. Ethics Opinion No 2 of the Mississippi State Bar (June 26, 1975) (www.msbar.org/ethic_opinions.php?id=288).

2. Legal Information vs. Legal Advice (www.abanet.org/legalservices/findlegalhelp/faq_legalinfo.cfm) (emphasis added).

3. Peoples & Wertz, *Update: Unauthorized Practice of Law*, 9 Nat'l Paralegal Reporter 1 (Nat'l Federation of Paralegal Associations, February 1985).

4. Rule 10–2.1(a), *Rules Regulating the Florida Bar* (2006). (www.floridabar.org/divexe/rrtfb.nsf/FV/5DE8883FE14988A585256BC2004522AA) See also *The Florida Bar Re Approval of Forms Pursuant to Rule 10–1.1(B) of the Rules Regulating the Florida Bar*, 591 So. 2d 594 (Fla. 1991); *Florida Bar News* 12 (August 1, 1989).

5. American Bar Association, Task Force on the Model Definition of the Practice of Law, *Proposed Model Definition of the Practice of Law* (September 18, 2002).

6. U.S. Department of Justice and Federal Trade Commission, *Comments on the American Bar Association's Proposed Model Definition of the Practice of Law* (December 20, 2002) (www.ftc.gov/opa/2002/12/lettertoaba.htm) (visited April 12, 2006).

7. *Walters v. National Ass'n of Radiation Survivors*, 473 U.S. 305, 325, 105 S.Ct. 3180, 3191 (1985) citing Judge Henry Friendly, *Some Kind of Hearing*, 123 U. Pa. L. Rev. 1267, 1288 (1975) (supreme.justia.com/us/473/305/case.html).

8. *District of Columbia Rules of Court*, D.C. Court of Appeals Rule 49(c)(11) (2001); *Bar Report* (August/September 1993).

9. *Lassiter v. Dep't of Social Services*, 452 U.S. 18, 29 (1981).

10. Winter, *No Contempt in Kentucky*, 7 Nat'l Paralegal Reporter 8 (Nat'l Federation of Paralegal Associations, Winter 1982).

11. 37 C.F.R. § 1.31. (2001). Office of Enrollment and Discipline (www.uspto.gov/web/offices/dcom/gcounsel/oed.htm).

12. 31 C.F.R. § 10.0 (2001); 26 U.S.C. § 7521 (2001).

13. Rose, *Representation by Non-Lawyers in Federal Administrative Agency Proceedings* (Administrative Conference of the United States 1984); Vom Baur, *The Practice of Non-Lawyers before Administrative Agencies*, 15 Federal Bar Journal 99 (1955).

14. ABA Standing Committee on Lawyers' Responsibility for Client Protection, *Report of 1984 Survey of Nonlawyer Practice before Federal Administrative Agencies* (October 19, 1984).

15. Your Right to Representation (www.socialsecurity.gov/pubs/10075.html); "Representing Claimants" (www.socialsecurity.gov/representation).

16. Office of Hearings and Appeals, Office of Policy Planning and Evaluation, Social Security Administration, *Highlights for Fiscal Year 1993* Tables 1, 2 (November 30, 1993).

17. Elaine Tackett, *Paralegal Representation of Social Security Claimants*, 16 Journal of Paralegal Education and Practice 67 (2000).

18. 70 Federal Register 2447–50 (January 13, 2005) (www.ssa.gov/representation/FR108_01_13_2005.txt) (www.ssa.gov/representation/overview.htm). See also 42 U.S.C. § 406(b)(1)(A) (2001).

19. Commission on Nonlawyer Practice, American Bar Association, *Nonlawyer Activities in Law-Related Situations* 146 (1995).

20. Committee on Legal Assistants, New York County Lawyers' Association, *Committee Report* (October 14, 1993).

21. 373 U.S. 379, 83 S. Ct. 1322, 10 L. Ed. 2d 428 (1963).

22. 373 U.S. at 388.

23. North Carolina State Bar Association, *Report of the Special Committee on Paralegals* 3 (1980).

24. Supreme Court of New Jersey, Press Release (May 18, 1999) (www.judiciary.state.nj.us/pressrel/admpara.htm).

25. West's Annotated California Business & Professions Code §§ 6450 et seq. (2000).

26. *Id.* at § 6455(a).

27. Sharlean Perez, *The New Law of the Paralegal Land*, 20 LAPA Reporter 1 (Los Angeles Paralegal Assn, October 2000).

28. *Legislative Report: AB 1761 FAQs*, Recap 7 (California Alliance of Paralegal Associations, Winter 2001).

29. Bob LeClair, AAFPE Listserv message (September 19, 2000).

30. *LAMA Position Paper on Legal Assistant Regulation* (October 9, 1996).

31. Nancy Ritter, *N.J. State Bar Says No*, 16 Legal Assistant Today 16 (March/April 1999).

32. *In the Spirit of Public Service: A Blueprint for Rekindling of Lawyer Professionalism* 52 (ABA, Comm'n on Professionalism, 1986). See 112 F.R.D. 243 (1986) (F.R.D. is the Federal Rules Decisions reporter).

33. Commission on Nonlawyer Practice, American Bar Association, *Nonlawyer Activity in Law-Related Situations* 175 (1995).

34. Mike France, *Bar Chiefs Protect the Guild*, The National Law Journal, August 7, 1995, at A1, A28.

35. ABA, *Nonlawyer Activity*, supra note 31, at 177.

36. Mark Curriden, *The ABA Nonlawyer Practice Report*, 13 Legal Assistant Today 89 (November/December 1995).

37. Mark Curriden, *The ABA Has Spoken: Will the Nonlawyer Practice Report Make a Difference?*, 14 Legal Assistant Today 62 (January/February 1996).

38. Proposed New APR Authorizing Limited Nonlawyer Practice (www.wsba.org/lawyers/groups/practiceoflaw) (www.wsba.org/lawyers/groups/practiceoflaw/legal+technician+rule.htm).

39. Washington State Supreme Court Rule 12(a). To read this rule, go to the court's site (www.courts.wa.gov/court_rules) and type "limited practice officer" in the search box. See also Washington State Bar Association (www.wsba.org/info/lpo.htm).

40. National Association of Legal Assistants, *Statement to . . . State Bar of California* (1991).

41. Model Act for Paralegal Licensure (www.paralegals.org/displaycommon.cfm?an=1&subarticlenbr=341).

42. Judge William Hogoboom, quoted in Harry Krause, *Family Law* 734 (3rd ed. 1990).

43. West's Annotated California Business & Professions Code §§ 6400–6450 (2000).

44. Arizona Code of Judicial Administration, § 7–208 (www.supreme.state.az.us/cld/ldp.htm).

45. Rule 10–2.1(a), Rules Regulating the Florida Bar (2006) (www.floridabar.org/divexe/rrtfb.nsf/FV/5DE8883FE14988A585256BC2004522AA).

46. *In re Moore*, 232 Bankruptcy Reporter 1, 13 (D. Maine 1999).

47. 11 U.S.C.A. § 110 (2001).

48. Illinois State Bar Association and Chicago Bar Association, *Illinois Legal Needs Study* 5 (1989).

49. New York State Bar Association, *New York Legal Needs Study: Draft Final Report* 196 (1989).

50. Whelen, *An Opinion: Bar Association's Paralegal Non-Voting Membership*, 15 At Issue 9 (San Francisco Assn of Legal Assistants, May 1987).

51. *NFPA Findings*, 8 The Journal 3 (Sacramento Assn of Legal Assistants, January 1986).

52. Heller, *Legal Assistant Associate Membership in the ABA*, 14 On Point 1, 14 (Nat'l Capital Area Paralegal Assn, August 1988).

53. Anderson, *ABA Associate Membership: A Different Perspective*, 3 Findings and Conclusions 7 (Washington Assn of Legal Assistants, August 1987).

54. State Bar of Michigan Legal Assistant Section (www.michbar.org/legalassistants); Application (www.michbar.org/legalassistants/pdfs/SectnApp.pdf).

55. Barbara Homles, *PACE Testimonial*, 30 National Paralegal Reporter 29 (October/November 2005).

56. Delaware Certified Paralegal Program (www.deparalegals.org/dcpp.php).

57. Ohio Paralegal Certification Program (www.ohiobar.org/pub/?articleid=785).

57a. Pennsylvania Certified Paralegal Program (keystoneparalegals.org).

58. ABA Standing Committee on Legal Assistants, *Position Paper on the Question of Legal Assistant Licensure or Certification*, 5 Legal Assistant Today 167 (1986).

59. 29 U.S.C.A. §§ 201 et seq. (1976). See also 29 C.F.R. part 541 and U.S. Department of Labor Wage and Hour Division (www.dol.gov/esa/whd).

60. See state labor laws (www.dol.gov/esa/programs/whd/state/state.htm).

61. See William Statsky, *Torts: Personal Injury Litigation* (4th ed. 2001).

62. We are talking here of vicarious *civil* liability or, more specifically, the tort liability of employers because of the torts committed by their employees. In general, employers are not subject to vicarious *criminal* liability. If a paralegal commits a crime on the job, only the paralegal goes to jail (unless the employer actually participated in the crime).

63. Michael Martz, *Ethics, Does a Paralegal Need Insurance?* The Assistant 13 (Mississippi Assn of Legal Assistants, Fall 1993).

64. Ronald Mallen & Jeffrey Smith, *Legal Malpractice* 2 (3d ed. 1989).

65. Home Insurance Companies, Professional Liability Insurance.

66. American Home Assurance Company, Lawyers Professional Liability Policy.

Student CD-ROM

For additional materials, please go to the CD in this book.

Online Companion™

For additional resources, please go to http://www.paralegal.delmar.cengage.com

Attorney Ethics and Paralegal Ethics

[SECTION A]

INTRODUCTION

As you know from the media, the legal profession is under attack. The general public does not have a favorable opinion of attorneys. Elsewhere in this book, we examine some of the reasons for this hostility. (See, for example, the beginning of chapter 8.) Here in chapter 5, we confront one of the main reasons: the perception that attorneys are not very ethical, or, more cynically, the perception that attorneys are ethical only when it doesn't cost them anything.

Courts and legislatures have responded to this problem in different ways. Every law school must offer a required course in legal ethics. Many state bar associations require practicing attorneys to attend annual **continuing legal education (CLE)** courses or seminars on ethical themes. And state disciplinary bodies have hired more attorneys (and paralegals) to investigate claims of ethical violations by practicing attorneys.

Of course, attorneys are not the only individuals under attack for ethical misconduct. Some commentators claim that the problem is rampant throughout society. Our focus here, however, is the legal profession.

As paralegals, you are about to enter a very special work environment. You will meet many different kinds of attorneys: those whose ethical behavior is beyond reproach, those who engage in blatantly unethical behavior, and those who sometimes walk a thin line between ethical and unethical behavior. Which of these categories of attorneys will one day be your employers and supervisors? The short answer, of course, is that you don't know. Hence, you need to prepare yourself for any work environment.

In the abstract, it's easy to be ethical. We all agree that the proper course of conduct is to do the right thing. The problem, however, is that pressures in the real world (particularly financial pressures) can interfere. The niceties of ethics can sometimes give way to the desire to win, the urge to retaliate, or the fear of losing a job or a client. One expert defines *ethics* as "whether you are willing to do the right thing when it costs more than you are willing to pay."[1] Many attorneys, he argues, feel that they don't "have the luxury of living ethically." Pressures "such as billable hours,

continuing legal education (CLE) Training in the law (usually short term) that a person receives after completing his or her formal legal training.

overhead costs, and technology cause people to take shortcuts like extending cases too long and lying about billable hours." Attorneys are guilty of a form of rationalization called the Doctrine of Relative Filth, which says that "as long as there's somebody out there worse than you are, you're not that bad."[2]

With these sobering thoughts in mind, you should begin your paralegal career with the resolution of *becoming an arch-conservative on matters of ethics*. Our goal in this chapter is to provide you with the tools that will enable you to become this kind of conservative. We begin by presenting an overview of some of the most important ethical guidelines that we will study. Carefully read—indeed, memorize—the summary in Exhibit 5.1. In your career, the paramount question must always be "What is the right thing to do?" Answering this question will not always be easy, particularly if you are ever forced to make a choice between your ethics and your job.

EXHIBIT 5.1	Paralegal Ethics: A Summary of Major Guidelines

1. Study the ethical rules governing attorneys in your state, including those on the ethical use of paralegals by attorneys. (See appendix E for the rules that apply in your state.) Read the rules. Reread them. Attend seminars on ethics conducted by bar associations and paralegal associations. If you understand when attorneys are vulnerable to charges of unprofessional conduct, you will be better able to assist them in avoiding such charges.

2. Assume that people outside your office do not have a clear understanding of what a paralegal or legal assistant is. Make sure that everyone with whom you come in contact (clients, prospective clients, attorneys, court officials, agency officials, and the public) understands that you are not an attorney.

3. Never tell anyone who is not working on a case anything about that case. This includes your spouse, your best friend, and your mother!

4. Know what legal advice is. It is the application of laws or legal principles to the facts of a particular person's legal problem. When you are asked questions that call for legal advice, refuse to be coaxed into providing it, no matter how innocent the question appears to be, no matter how clear it is that you know the correct answer, and no matter how confident your supervisor is that you can handle such questions on your own.

5. Never make contact with an opposing party in a legal dispute, or with anyone closely associated with that party, unless you have the permission of your supervising attorney *and* of the attorney for the opposing party, if the latter has one.

6. Don't sign your name to anything if you are not certain that what you are signing is 100 percent accurate and that the law allows a paralegal to sign it. If you are asked to witness someone's signature, for example, be sure that the document you are witnessing is signed in your presence. Your signature as witness should signify that you watched someone sign the document.

7. Never pad your time sheets by recording time that was not in fact spent on a client matter. Insist that what you submit be 100 percent accurate.

8. Disclose your inexperience. Let your supervisor know if all or part of an assignment is new to you and that you may need additional training and supervision to undertake it competently.

9. Know the common rationalizations for misrepresentation and other unethical conduct:
   - ■ It's always done.
   - ■ The other side does it.
   - ■ The cause of our client is just.
   - ■ If I don't do it, I will jeopardize my job.

   Promise yourself that you will not allow any of these rationalizations to entice you to participate in unethical conduct.

10. If what you are asked to do doesn't feel right, don't proceed until it does. Adhere to rigorous standards of professional ethics, even if those standards are higher than those followed by attorneys, paralegals, and others around you.

[SECTION B]
ENFORCING ETHICS

1. ETHICS AND SANCTIONS

ethics Rules that embody standards of behavior to which members of an organization are expected to conform.

sanction (1) Penalty or punishment imposed for unacceptable conduct. (2) Permission or approval.

Ethics are rules that embody standards of behavior to which members of an organization must conform. The organization is often an association of individuals in the same occupation—for example, attorneys, paralegals, stockbrokers, or accountants. The ethical rules of some organizations are enforced by **sanctions**. A sanction is any penalty or punishment imposed for unacceptable conduct, e.g., the sanction of a fine or expulsion from the organization because of fraud. (A very different meaning of sanction is permission or approval, e.g., the motion could not be filed without the sanction of the court.)

All of the major national paralegal associations have adopted ethical rules, as we will see later, in Exhibit 5.4. *None*, however, are enforced by meaningful sanctions. A paralegal association might occasionally throw someone out of the association because of misconduct, but this is rare and it is highly unlikely that an expulsion would interfere with his or her ability to work as a paralegal. Phrased another way, there are no jobs that require a paralegal to be a member in good standing of a paralegal association. This is not to say, however, that paralegal misconduct will go unnoticed. Such conduct may lead to sanctions by employers and the state.

Attorneys, on the other hand, *are* subject to enforceable ethical rules that can affect whether they are allowed to continue practicing law. Attorney ethics are backed by sanctions. The rules attempt to govern everything an attorney does in the practice of law from adding clients to withdrawing from representing clients.

One of the things an attorney does is employ paralegals. Hence there are rules on how an attorney can use a paralegal ethically. Unethical use of paralegals by an attorney can subject the attorney to sanctions. We will spend considerable time in this chapter examining this reality.

2. ATTORNEY CODES

In most states, the regulation of attorneys is primarily under the control of the highest court in the state (often called the *supreme court*), which determines when an attorney can be granted a license to practice law and under what conditions the license will be taken away or suspended because of unethical conduct. The state legislature may also exert some regulatory authority over attorneys, and disputes occasionally arise over which branch of government can control a particular aspect of the practice of law. The judiciary often wins this dispute and becomes the final authority. In practice, however, the judicial branch and the legislative branch usually share regulatory jurisdiction over the practice of law. The state supreme court, for example, might rule that although the legislature has the power to impose minimum standards on attorney conduct, the court can impose standards that are higher than the minimum.

Neither the courts nor the legislature, however, performs the day-to-day functions of implementing the rules governing attorneys. That role is delegated to an entity such as a state bar association and a disciplinary board or grievance commission.

There are four kinds of bar associations:

- National (e.g., the American Bar Association, Hispanic National Bar Association, and American Association of Justice)
- State (e.g., the Illinois State Bar Association and State Bar of Montana)
- Local (e.g., the Boston Bar Association, New York County Bar Association, and San Diego County Bar Association)
- Specialty (e.g., the Academy of Matrimonial Attorneys, American Association of Justice, and National Association of Women Lawyers)

All national, local, and specialty bar associations are voluntary; no attorney is required to be a member. The majority of *state* bar associations in the country, however, are *integrated*, which simply means that membership is required as a condition of practicing law in the state. (**Integrated bar associations** are also referred to as *mandatory* or *unified* bar associations.) There is a state bar association in every state. Most, but not all, are integrated.

Under the general supervision of the state's highest court, the state bar association has a large role in regulating most aspects of the practice of law. For example, dues charged by integrated bar associations are used to fund the state's system of enforcing ethical rules. States that do not have integrated bar associations often have a **registration** requirement. Each attorney in the state registers to practice law and pays a registration fee that is used to fund that state's system of enforcing the ethical rules. A registration state will also have a state bar association. While attorney membership in it is voluntary, the association nevertheless has considerable influence over the regulation of all attorneys in the state. Given this dominant role of bar associations, the method of regulating attorneys in America is essentially that of self-regulation: attorneys regulating attorneys. This is true even in those states that allow nonattorney citizens to serve on boards or commissions that help regulate the legal profession.

There is no national set of ethical rules that applies to every state. Each state can adopt its own state code to regulate the attorneys in that state. The state code may have different names such as code of ethics, canons of ethics, code of professional responsibility, model rules. Yet the rules that the states have adopted are quite similar. The reason for this similarity is the influence of the American Bar Association.

The American Bar Association is a voluntary national bar association; no attorney must belong to it. (As we saw in chapter 4, paralegals can join as ABA associates, www.abanet.org/join.) Yet approximately 55 percent of the attorneys in America do belong to the ABA. It publishes ethical

integrated bar association A state bar association to which an attorney must belong in order to practice law in the state.

registration The process by which individuals or institutions list their names on a roster kept by an agency of government or by a nongovernmental organization.

rules but does *not* discipline attorneys for unethical conduct. The role of the ABA in this area is to write ethical rules and to *propose* to the individual states that they be accepted. A state is free to adopt, modify, or reject the rules. The current recommendation of the ABA is found in a document called the *Model Rules of Professional Conduct*. This document has been very influential throughout the country. Many states adopted it with relatively minor changes. The *Model Rules* is a revision of the ABA's *Model Code of Professional Responsibility*, which a number of states still follow.

Exhibit 5.2 presents an overview of the major ethical codes governing attorney conduct. Most of these codes include provisions that are directly relevant to paralegals and other nonattorneys

EXHIBIT 5.2	**Ethical Codes Governing Attorney Conduct**				
NAME OF DOCUMENT	**DATE**	**AUTHOR**	**STATUS**	**STRUCTURE**	**PARALEGALS**
Model Rules of Professional Conduct	1983	American Bar Association	Current. The *Model Rules* replaces the *Model Code* (see below). The *Model Rules* is not binding on attorneys unless a state has adopted it. Forty-three states and the District of Columbia have adopted the *Model Rules* in whole or with changes.	There are eight main rules in the *Model Rules*. All of the rules are followed by interpretative comments. These rules are available at www.abanet.org/cpr/mrpc/model_rules.html.	Rule 5.3 of the *Model Rules* covers the ethical use of paralegals by attorneys and Rule 5.5 covers the unauthorized practice of law. (We will discuss both later in this chapter.)
Model Code of Professional Responsibility	1969	American Bar Association	The *Model Code* is an earlier version of the *Model Rules*. The *Model Code* is not binding on attorneys unless a state has adopted it. While the ABA now recommends the *Model Rules*, a few states still follow their version of the *Model Code*. These states never adopted the *Model Rules*.	There are nine main canons in the *Model Code*. Within each canon are Disciplinary Rules (DR), which are mandatory statements or rules, and Ethical Considerations (EC), which are behavioral guidelines.	DR 3–101 of the *Model Code* covers the unauthorized practice of law. EC 3–6 covers the proper delegation of tasks to paralegals. (We will discuss DR-3-101 and EC-3-6 later in this chapter.)
State Codes	Varies	The state codes are written by the highest state court in the state. In addition, the state legislature may also pass statutes governing attorney ethics.	This is the code that is binding on every practicing attorney in the state. Most states have based their code on the ABA *Model Rules*. Some, however, still follow their version of the ABA *Model Code*.	Varies. If the state code is based on the *Model Rules*, the state code may have the same structure as the *Model Rules* (eight rules plus comments). If the state code is based on the *Model Code*, the state code may have the same structure as the *Model Code* (DRs and ECs). To find the ethics code of your state online, see appendix E and "Helpful Web Sites" at the end of this chapter.	Varies. May have Rule 5.3 (if the state code is based on the *Model Rules*) or may have DR 3–101 and EC 3–6 (if based on the *Model Code*).
Special Codes	Varies	A separate city, state, regional, or national bar association	These special bar associations may have their own code of ethics.	Varies. To try to find the ethics code of special bar associations, go to the Web site of the association.	Seldom specifically refer to paralegals or other nonattorney personnel.

who work for attorneys. (See the last column of Exhibit 5.2.) Later in the chapter, we will examine these provisions.

3. ACCUSATION OF UNETHICAL CONDUCT

When an attorney is charged with unethical conduct, the case is investigated by a disciplinary body appointed by the state's highest court. The name for this body differs from state to state, e.g., the Grievance Commission, the Attorney Registration and Disciplinary Commission, the Committee on Professional Conduct, or the Board of Professional Responsibility.

A hearing is held to determine whether unethical conduct was committed by the accused attorney. The commission, committee, or board then makes its recommendation to the state's highest court, which makes the final determination of whether to accept this recommendation. A number of sanctions can be imposed by the court. As you can see from Exhibit 5.3, they can range from relatively mild slaps on the wrist (reprimand, admonition) to expulsion from the legal profession itself (disbarment). Some states require attorneys to attend a day of special ethics training (the equivalent of traffic school) as part of the discipline imposed for violating the state's ethical code.

Later in the chapter, we will cover one of the most contentious issues in this area: can a disbarred or suspended attorney continue working in a law office as a paralegal? As we will see, some states say no. The risk is too great that the disciplined attorney will continue to practice law under the guise of being a paralegal. Other states, however, allow it but may do so with restrictions, such as forbidding the attorney paralegal from having any client contact.

4. PARALEGAL CODES AND GUIDELINES

Thus far we have been discussing attorney codes of ethics. Can a *paralegal* be sanctioned for violating these codes? Not directly. With one exception that we will discuss in a moment, the codes apply to attorneys only. Since paralegals cannot join a bar association as full members, they cannot be sanctioned by a bar association or by any other entity set up to monitor attorney conduct. Serious paralegal wrongdoing, however, can lead to severe consequences: the paralegals might be fired by their employer, they might be sued for negligence, they might face criminal prosecution, their supervising attorney might face ethical charges because of the paralegal's wrongdoing, etc. But the paralegals themselves cannot be punished for unethical conduct by the entity that regulates attorneys.

multidisciplinary practice (MDP) A partnership consisting of attorneys and nonlegal professionals that offers legal and nonlegal services.

As indicated, there is an exception to the rule that attorney codes apply to attorneys only. Recently, there has been considerable debate over whether the legal profession should allow attorneys and nonlegal professionals to form a **multidisciplinary practice (MDP)**. This is a

EXHIBIT 5.3	Attorney Sanctions for Unethical Conduct

Disbarment:
The revocation or termination of the right to practice law. Disbarment is often permanent, although some states allow a disbarred attorney to apply for readmission after a designated number of years. If readmitted, conditions may be imposed (see *probation*, below).

Suspension:
The removal of an attorney from the practice of law for a specified minimum period, after which the attorney can apply for reinstatement. An *interim suspension* is a temporary suspension pending the imposition of final discipline. The attorney may be required to notify clients of the suspension. Sometimes the sanction of suspension is imposed but does not go into effect, i.e., the suspension is stayed. The attorney can continue to practice law while operating under a stayed suspension so long as he or she does not commit any further ethical violations. Other conditions might be imposed such as those listed under *probation* below.

Reprimand:
An official declaration that an attorney's conduct was unethical. The declaration does not affect the attorney's right to practice law. A *private reprimand* is not disclosed to the public; a *public reprimand* is. Conditions that might be imposed along with the reprimand are listed under *probation*, below. In some states, a milder form of private reprimand is called an *admonition, private warning,* or *private reproval.*

Probation:
Allowing the attorney to continue to practice but under specified conditions, such as submitting to periodic audits of client funds controlled by the attorney, making restitution to a client whose funds were wrongly taken by the attorney, and obtaining treatment for substance abuse if alcohol or drug use has been a problem. He or she may also be asked to attend additional ethics training and/or to retake the professional responsibility (ethics) portion of the bar exam.

partnership between attorneys and groups such as accountants, doctors, therapists, economists, scientists, and environmental consultants that delivers legal and nonlegal services. In such a partnership, the nonattorney partner *would* be governed by the ethical code that governs attorneys. Only a few states allow such partnerships, although many are studying the possibility of allowing them. These entities would be a major departure from the rule that attorneys must not form a partnership with (or share fees with) nonattorneys. Critics warn that MDPs will lead to a loss of attorney control over the practice of law. The big fear is that companies such as Sears Roebuck and H&R Block will be able to start offering legal services in direct competition with traditional law firms. Proponents argue that MDPs will open up new markets for law firms, particularly in a global economy where large American law firms often compete in countries that authorize MDPs for their own attorneys.

If MDPs ever become widespread in the United States, they will probably not have a significant effect on paralegals. The goal of an MDP is to allow a law firm to expand its scope of business by partnering with individuals who have nonlegal skills and expertise. There is nothing nonlegal about paralegals! They are an intimate part of the attorney's legal team. While it is possible that a state might one day allow an attorney to form an MDP with a paralegal, the likelihood of this happening is relatively small.

paralegal code Rules and guidelines covering ethical issues involving paralegals.

Now we turn to **paralegal codes**. These are sets of rules and guidelines devoted exclusively to issues of paralegal ethics. There are two kinds of paralegal codes: those written by attorneys and those written by paralegals. See Exhibit 5.4 for an overview of both.

Paralegal Codes Written by Attorneys

The ABA has issued the *Model Guidelines for the Utilization of Paralegal Services.* Like the ABA's *Model Rules* and *Model Code* (see Exhibit 5.2), the *Model Guidelines* are recommendations to the states. The ABA itself does not discipline anyone for violating the *Model Guidelines.* (Later in this chapter, you will find a discussion of every major guideline or rule contained in the *Model Guidelines.*) To date, about half the states have their own state paralegal codes that are similar to the *Model Guidelines.* (For a discussion of your state, see appendix E.) Most were adopted by the state bar association or by the committee of the bar association that covers paralegals. Some have been formally approved and adopted by the state's highest court. The *Model Guidelines* and the state paralegal codes are primarily directed to attorneys who use paralegals in their practice. Hence, if there are violations by paralegals, it is the supervising attorney who may be subject to sanctions by the state entity that enforces attorney ethics.

Paralegal Codes Written by Paralegals

The three major national associations (NFPA, NALA, and NALS) have also written paralegal codes. (See Exhibit 5.4 for the titles of these codes and where you can read them online. See also appendix F.) As indicated earlier, these codes are not enforced by meaningful sanctions. The associations might terminate a paralegal's membership in the association for ethical improprieties, but this is rarely done. The associations simply do not have the resources or clout to implement a system of enforcement. This does not mean, however, that the paralegal codes are unimportant. Their main value is to reinforce the critical importance of ethics in the practice of law.

Paralegals are on the front line. *One of their primary responsibilities is to help an attorney avoid being charged with unethical conduct.* A recent seminar conducted by the Los Angeles Paralegal Association was entitled "Law Firm Ethics: How to Keep Your Attorneys off '60 Minutes'!" Hence paralegals must be intimately familiar with ethical rules. Our goal in this chapter is to provide you with that familiarity.

[SECTION C]

ETHICAL RULES

We turn now to an overview of specific ethical rules that apply to attorneys. The overview is based on the ABA's *Model Rules of Professional Conduct.* (See Exhibit 5.2.) The rule numbers used in the discussion (such as Rule 1.5) refer to the *Model Rules.* Since not all states have adopted the

Model Rules, we will occasionally refer to the ABA's *Model Code of Professional Responsibility*, which some states still follow.

Where appropriate, the discussion will include a *paralegal perspective* based on the *ABA Model Guidelines* and the other paralegal codes mentioned in Exhibit 5.4.

One final note before we begin: most ethics charges are brought by disgruntled clients who claim to have been harmed by the attorney's alleged unethical behavior. For example, the client's case was dismissed because the attorney carelessly forgot to file a pleading in court. We need to emphasize, however, that a person who initiates a charge of unethical conduct does *not* have to prove he or she suffered actual harm thereby. Suppose, for example, an attorney represents a client with whom the attorney has a clear conflict of interest. The attorney should never have taken the case. Representing the client in the case is unethical even if the attorney wins the case for the client! Proof of harm is not necessary to establish a violation of the ethical rules, although such harm is usually present.

EXHIBIT 5.4	Paralegal Codes		
NAME OF DOCUMENT	**DATE**	**AUTHOR**	**COMMENTS**
A. Those Written by Attorneys			
ABA Model Guidelines for the Utilization of Paralegal Services	1991	American Bar Association	A series of guidelines recommended by the ABA for adoption by the states on the ethical use of paralegals by attorneys. (Go to www.abanet.org/legalservices/paralegals and click "ABA Model Guidelines.") States are free to adopt, amend, or reject these guidelines.
State Codes and Guidelines	Varies	State Bar Association	About half the states have adopted rules and guidelines on practicing law ethically with paralegals. To find out what exists in your state: ■ See your state in appendix E. ■ At the Web site of your state bar association (see appendix C), type *paralegal* or *legal assistant* in the site's search box. ■ At the Web sites of paralegal associations in your state (see appendix B), check all ethics links.
B. Those Written by Paralegals			
Model Code of Ethics and Professional Responsibility and Guidelines for Enforcement	1993	National Federation of Paralegal Associations	To read the *Model Code* online, go to NFPA's site (www.paralegals.org), click "Positions & Issues," and then click "Ethics."
Code of Ethics and Professional Responsibility	1975 1995	National Association of Legal Assistants	All members of NALA must agree to abide by its *Code of Ethics* (www.nala.org/code.htm). This code is elaborated upon in NALA's *Model Standards and Guidelines for Utilization of Legal Assistants/ Paralegals* (1991) (www.nala.org/98model.htm).
Code of Ethics	1975	NALS the Association for Legal Professionals	To read the *Code of Ethics* online, go to NALS's site (www.nals.org/aboutnals/Code).
Special Codes	Varies	Local, state, or regional paralegal associations	Other paralegal associations have written ethical codes to govern their membership. For example, here are some ethics codes you can read online: ■ California Alliance of Paralegal Associations, *Ethics Guidelines* (caparalegal.org/ethics.html) ■ Kansas Paralegal Association, *Code of Ethics and Professional Responsibility* (www.ksparalegals.org/ethics.html)

1. COMPETENCE

An attorney shall provide competent representation to a client. **Model Rule 1.1**

competent Using the knowledge and skill that are reasonably necessary to represent a particular client. (See the glossary for another meaning.)

A **competent** attorney is one who uses the *knowledge* and *skill* that are reasonably necessary to represent a particular client. What is reasonably necessary depends on the complexity of the case. A great deal of knowledge and skill, for example, will be needed when representing a corporate client accused of complicated antitrust violations.

How do attorneys obtain this knowledge and skill? They draw on the general principles of legal analysis and legal research learned in law school. But more important, they take the time needed to *prepare* themselves. They spend time in the law library. They talk with their colleagues. In some instances, they formally associate themselves with more experienced attorneys in the area. Attorneys who fail to take these steps are acting unethically if their failure means that they do not have the knowledge and skill reasonably necessary to represent a particular client.

Some attorneys have so many clients that they could not possibly give proper attention to each. Always looking for more lucrative work, they run the risk of neglecting the clients they already have. As a consequence, they might miss court dates or other filing deadlines, lose documents, fail to determine what law governs a client's case, etc. Such an attorney is practicing law "from the hip"—incompetently and unethically.

> **Example:** Mary Henderson, Esq. has a large criminal law practice. She agrees to probate the estate of a client's deceased son. She has never had a probate client before and does not investigate how probate cases should be handled. Five years go by. No progress is made in determining who is entitled to receive the estate. If some minimal legal research had been done, Henderson would have been able to close the case within six months of taking it.

Henderson has probably acted unethically. The failure to do basic research on a case is a sign of incompetence. The need for such research is clear in view of the fact that she has never handled a probate case before. Either she must take the time to find out how to probate the estate, or she must contact another attorney with probate experience and arrange to work with this attorney on the case. Not doing either is unethical.

The vast majority of graduates of law schools need considerable on-the-job study and guidance before they are ready to handle cases of any complexity. A law school education gives new attorneys a good theoretical understanding of the law. This is different from the *practical* knowledge and skill needed to work on real cases. Many law schools have **clinical education** programs in which students receive credit for working on actual cases under the supervision of attorneys. For example, the school might operate its own tax clinic for senior citizens or might assign students to work several hours a week on different kinds of cases at a local legal service/legal aid office. Although these clinical programs provide practical experience, they are not a major part of the law school curriculum of every law school. Most new attorneys (including those with clinical experience), therefore, are quite nervous when they face their first client on their first job. The nervousness is based on the fact that they are acutely aware of how much they *don't* know. This doesn't necessarily mean they are incompetent to practice law. It simply means they must take the time to prepare themselves and to draw on the assistance of others where needed.

clinical education A training program in which students work on real cases under attorney supervision.

Continuing legal education (CLE) is another vehicle used by attorneys to achieve competence. Most states require attorneys to participate in a designated number of hours of CLE per year as a condition of maintaining their license to practice law. (This requirement is called MCLE, or *mandatory CLE.*) CLE sessions are designed to help practicing attorneys stay current in their areas of practice. The sessions are often conducted by a CLE institute affiliated with the bar association. Throughout the year, and particularly during bar conventions, attorneys have the opportunity to attend relatively short CLE sessions, e.g., an afternoon. CLE on the Internet is another option that is becoming increasingly popular.

If an attorney is incompetent, he or she can be sanctioned for being unethical. In addition, the incompetence may have other consequences. The client might try to sue the attorney for negligence in a legal malpractice case. (Such suits were discussed in chapter 4.) If the client is a criminal defendant who was convicted, he or she may try to appeal the conviction on the grounds that the attorney's incompetence amounted to a denial of the effective "Assistance of Counsel" guaranteed by the Sixth Amendment of the U.S. Constitution.

Paralegal Perspective:

- It is unethical for an attorney to assign a task to a paralegal without making sure that the paralegal has the training or experience needed to perform that task competently. While the attorney has this supervisory responsibility, paralegals also have a responsibility to maintain their own competence.

- If you are given assignments that are beyond your knowledge and skill, let your supervisor know. Either you must be given training with close supervision, or you must be given other assignments. A "lawyer should explain to the legal assistant that the legal assistant has a duty to inform the lawyer of any assignment which the legal assistant regards as beyond his capability."[3]

- Be wary of the attorney who has so much confidence in your competence that he or she uses your work product with little or no checking. This is extremely dangerous, particularly for paralegals who work for very busy attorneys. The danger is that you will make a mistake that will not be caught until damage is done to the client. No matter how much experience you develop in an area of the law, unique problems often arise. Unless someone is reviewing your work, how will you know whether you have missed one of these problems? Your ego will appreciate the confidence your supervisor expresses in you by delegating so much responsibility, but the attorney still has an ethical obligation to supervise your work. Your competence is not a substitute for this supervision. Paralegals are engaged in the unauthorized practice of law when they perform legal tasks without supervision, as we will see later in the chapter.

- Try to turn assignments into ongoing learning experiences. After a new assignment has been completed, ask your supervisor how it can be improved the next time. You may have to wait until a busy supervisor has time to respond, but don't wait until the year-end evaluation. Every day presents opportunities to increase your competence—if you make it part of your agenda to look for and take those opportunities. Your growth as a paralegal will depend on it, and you will be contributing to the ethical mandate of the office to be competent.

- Find out which attorneys, administrators, paralegals, and secretaries in the office have a reputation for explaining things well. Try to spend time with such individuals even if you do not work with them on a daily basis. Take them to lunch. Find time to sit with them on a coffee break. Ask lots of questions. Let them know you respect high-quality work and appreciate anything they can tell you to help you increase your competence.

- Invest in CLE. Take the initiative in continuing your training after your formal education is over. Do not wait for someone to suggest further training. Ask if you can attend CLE sessions for attorneys in the areas of law that are relevant to your case assignments. CLE is often conducted on a weekday afternoon, on a Saturday, or online. Here are ways to find out what CLE opportunities are available in your area:
  - Go to the Web site of paralegal associations in your area (see appendix B). If CLE is not listed on the homepage, type "continuing legal education" in the search box or send an e-mail to the association inquiring about CLE.
  - Go to the Web site of the bar associations in your area. If CLE is not listed on the homepage, type "CLE" or "continuing legal education" in the search box.
  - Go to any general search engine (e.g., www.google.com, www.yahoo.com) and do a search that includes the name of your state and the phrase "continuing legal education" (e.g., New York "continuing legal education," or Texas "continuing legal education").

  Find the time to attend CLE sessions, even if you must pay for them yourself. Because the law often changes, you need to use resources like CLE to keep current.

  As we saw in chapter 4, continuing legal education is not optional in California. Paralegals and legal document assistants (LDAs) in that state have mandatory CLE requirements. Also, paralegals who have passed the certification exams of the local and state paralegal associations have CLE obligations that must be met in order to maintain their certification status (see Exhibits 4.7 and 4.8 in chapter 4).

- There are many steps you can take on your own to increase your computer skills. See Exhibit 13.1 in chapter 13, "Developing Your Computer Skills: What You Can Do on Your Own Now."
- Review the section in chapter 4 on malpractice insurance. No matter how competent you are, you could be a defendant in a negligence suit brought against a law firm by a disgruntled client. Before you are hired by a firm, find out if the firm has a malpractice policy and whether it covers paralegal employees.

2. DILIGENCE/UNWARRANTED DELAY

Causing unwarranted delay in representing a client is unethical. The attorney must act with reasonable diligence and promptness. Model Rule 1.3

Reasonable efforts must be taken to expedite litigation. Model Rule 3.2

Angry clients often complain that attorneys take forever to complete a case and keep clients in the dark about what is happening. "He never answers my calls." "It took months to file the case in court." "She keeps telling me that everything is fine, but nothing ever gets done." Such complaints do not necessarily indicate unethical behavior by the attorney. Events may be beyond the control of the attorney. For example, the court calendar is crowded or the other side is not responding. Yet this does not excuse a lack of regular communication with clients to keep them reasonably informed about the status of their case.

Other explanations for a lack of diligence and promptness, however, are more serious:

- The attorney is disorganized. The law office has not developed adequate systems to process cases. The delays are due to careless mistakes and a lack of skill.
- The attorney is taking many more cases than the office can handle. Additional personnel should be hired to do the needed work, or new cases should not be accepted.
- The office fails to designate backup attorneys to handle ongoing cases of attorneys who are away on vacation or are otherwise unavailable because of pressing work on other cases.

statute of limitations A law stating that civil or criminal actions are barred if not brought within a specified period of time.

dilatory Causing delay, usually without merit or justification.

Often the failure to use reasonable diligence and promptness causes harm to the client. For example, the attorney neglects to file a suit before the **statute of limitations** has run against the client. Unreasonable procrastination, however, can be unethical even if such harm does not result.

Another problem is the attorney who intentionally causes numerous delays in an effort to wear the other side down. It is unethical to engage in such **dilatory** practices. Attorneys must use reasonable efforts to expedite litigation, consistent with protecting the interests of their clients.

Paralegal Perspective:

- An overloaded attorney probably works with an overloaded paralegal. Successful paralegals often take the initiative by asking for additional work. But reason must prevail. If you have more work than you can handle, you must let your supervisor know. Otherwise, you might find yourself contributing to the problem of undue delay.
- Learn everything you can about office systems, particularly for tasks that the office performs on a regular basis. Find out how systems are created. After you have gained some experience in the office, you should start designing systems on your own initiative. (For example, one component of a system that can be created with relative ease is a folder containing frequently used documents in a divorce or other kind of case the office often handles. The documents in the folder become a source of model documents that can be adapted for future cases of that kind.) Effective office systems substantially reduce the risk of unethical delays in client representation.
- When a busy attorney is in court or cannot be disturbed because of urgent work on another case, someone in the office should be available to communicate with clients who want to know the status of their case. In many offices, the paralegal is in a position to provide this information. This role can be delicate. In addition to asking about the status of their case, clients often ask questions that call for legal advice. Giving such advice may constitute the unauthorized practice of law. Later we will examine in greater depth the temptations and pressures on a paralegal to give legal advice.

3. FEES

Fees for legal services must be reasonable. Model Rule 1.5(a)

There is no absolute standard to determine when a fee is excessive and therefore unreasonable. A number of factors must be considered: the amount of time and labor involved, the complexity of the case, the customary fee in the locality for the same kind of case, the experience and reputation of the attorney, etc. In one case, a court ruled that $500 an hour was excessive in a simple battery case in which there was no trial (the accused pled guilty) and there were no unusual issues to be resolved. In another case, a court concluded that a fee of $22,500 was excessive in an uncomplicated real estate case involving very little attorney time. The case was settled through the efforts of someone other than the attorney.

A fee is not necessarily excessive simply because it is large. Cases exist in which courts have approved fees of hundreds of millions of dollars. An example is the tobacco litigation of the 1990s, in which attorneys brought suits that resulted in multibillion-dollar settlements and judgments. Prior to this time, the tobacco industry had remarkable success in winning personal injury suits brought by sick smokers and by the estates of deceased smokers. In assessing the reasonableness of a fee, a court will consider the odds against winning and the uniqueness of the issues raised in the litigation. By these standards, the attorneys who won the cases against the tobacco industry were entitled to very high fees. When they began, few thought they had much chance of winning anything, let alone winning billions. (Later in the chapter, we will discuss the infamous role of a paralegal, Merrill Williams, in the tobacco litigation.)

The basis of the fee should be communicated to the client before or soon after the attorney starts to work on the case. This is often done in the contract hiring the attorney, called an *attorney-client fee agreement*. (For an example of such an agreement, see Exhibit 8.1 in chapter 8). Kinds of fees are also discussed in greater detail in chapter 14.)

States differ on whether the fee agreement must be in writing. In some states, written agreements are recommended but not required. Oral agreements are acceptable as long as the basis of the fee is adequately explained to the client and nothing misleading is said about fees, costs, and related expenses. For contingent fee cases, however, many states require a written agreement signed by the attorney and the client. (We will examine contingent cases shortly.)

In Exhibit 5.2, we outlined the major attorney codes of ethics. Many bar associations write formal and informal opinions that interpret sections of their code. Attorneys can submit questions to the bar's ethics committee. (To preserve confidentiality, attorneys submit these questions without client names or other identifying information, e.g., "If an attorney represents client A in a case against a local merchant, would it be ethical to...?") The answers to questions are sometimes published as formal or informal opinions so that the entire legal community can benefit from the bar's interpretive advice. For example, in Formal Ethics Opinion 93–379, the American Bar Association addressed the issue of excessive fees through the following three fact situations:

Case I. John Smith, Esq. (who bills by the hour) has two clients who happen to have separate cases in the same court on May 9, each requiring relatively minor attention from the attorney. If the attorney had gone to court on two separate days, each client could have been billed for three hours. On May 9, however, Smith was able to handle both cases. He spent a total of three hours in court. Can he bill each client three hours for the time spent on May 9, since he would have been able to do so if he went on separate days?

Answer: No. Smith did not earn six billable hours on May 9. Billing more than one client for the same time is unreasonable. Savings resulting from scheduling must be passed on to clients.

Case II. Mary Jones, Esq. (who bills by the hour) charges a client five hours transportation time to travel by airplane to a meeting with the client in another city. While on the plane, she skips the in-flight movie in order to spend two hours drafting a motion for a different client on another case. Can she bill the first client five hours and the second client two hours to cover the total of five hours on the plane?

Answer: No. Jones has not earned seven billable hours. Billing more than one client for the same time is unreasonable. Savings resulting from being able to do two things simultaneously (traveling and drafting a motion) for different clients must be passed on to clients.

Case III. George Harris, Esq. (who bills by the hour) bills a client for ten hours to research a problem and draft a memorandum of law covering the issues in the case. Several days later he uses the same memorandum on a different case for another client who happens to have the same legal problem as the earlier client. Can he bill the second client ten hours for the memorandum?

Answer: No. Harris has not earned twenty billable hours. Billing more than one client for the same work product (a research memorandum) is unreasonable. Savings resulting from being able to reuse a work product must be passed on to clients. If Harris needed time to *adapt* the memo to the needs of the second client, he could charge for this time. When billing this client, however, he cannot assume that the prior memo did not exist.

As you can see, ethical opinions such as Formal Ethics Opinion 93–379 can be very helpful in interpreting the rules of ethics. The opinions help give the rules a concrete context. Later we will cover the steps you need to take to locate ethical opinions of the American Bar Association and of state and local bar associations. See also summaries of ethical opinions in your state in appendix E.

At one time, bar associations published a list of "recommended" minimum fees that should be charged for designated kinds of services. A fee below the minimum was considered unethical. These **minimum-fee schedules** have now been prohibited by the U.S. Supreme Court. They constitute illegal price fixing by the bar in violation of the antitrust laws.

Contingent fees can sometimes present ethical problems. A contingent fee is a fee that is paid only if the case is successfully resolved by litigation or settlement.

> **Example:** An attorney agrees to represent a client in an automobile negligence case. If the jury awards the client damages, the attorney will receive 30 percent of the award. If the client loses the case, the attorney receives no fee. Similarly, if the case is settled in the client's favor, the attorney receives 30 percent of the settlement, but no fee if the client obtains nothing in the settlement.

This is a contingent fee because it is dependent on the successful outcome of the negligence case.

The benefit of a contingent fee is that it provides an incentive for an attorney to take the case of a client who does not have funds to pay hourly fees while the case is pending. But contingent fees are not ethical in every case, even if the amount to be received by the successful attorney is otherwise reasonable. A contingent fee in a criminal case, and in most divorce cases, for example, is unethical.

> **Example:** Gabe Farrell is a client of Sam Grondon, Esq. in a criminal case. Gabe is charged with murder. Gabe agrees to pay Grondon $100,000 if he is found innocent. Grondon will receive nothing if Gabe is convicted of any crime.

This fee agreement is unethical. Contingent fees are not allowed in criminal cases. Note the pressures on Grondon. He arguably has no incentive to try to negotiate a guilty plea to a lesser charge, e.g., manslaughter, because such a plea would mean a conviction and, hence, no fee. In such a situation, the attorney's own personal interest (obtaining the $100,000) could conflict with the interest of the client (receiving a lesser penalty through a negotiated plea). Similar inappropriate pressures can arise in family law cases:

> **Example:** Tom Edgers hires an attorney to obtain a divorce from his wife. The fee is $25,000 if the divorce is granted.

As the case develops, suppose a glimmer of hope arises that the husband and wife might reconcile. Here, again, the attorney's interest (obtaining the $25,000) could conflict with the interest of the client (reconciling). This might lead the attorney to discourage the reconciliation or to set up roadblocks to it. Reconciliation obviously removes the possibility of the contingency—obtaining the divorce—from occurring. In family law cases, therefore, contingent fees are unethical if the fee is dependent on securing a divorce or on the amount of alimony or support, or the amount of property settlement in lieu of alimony or support. This is so even if the terms of the contingent fee are otherwise reasonable. Some states have limited exceptions to this rule. For example, a state might forbid a contingent fee when a client is seeking *future* child support but allow it if the client is seeking to collect a support judgment that has already been rendered. If a judgment already exists, the attorney's interest in collecting the contingent fee is less likely to interfere with the continuation or reconciliation of family relationships.

One final theme should be covered: **fee splitting**. The splitting or division of a fee refers to a single client bill covering the fees of two or more attorneys who are not in the same firm. (Fee splitting is also called *fee sharing*.) Sometimes one attorney will pay another a **forwarding fee**

---

minimum-fee schedule A bar association list of the lowest fees an attorney can charge for specific kinds of legal services.

contingent fee A fee that is paid only if the case is successfully resolved by litigation or settlement. (The fee is also referred to as a *contingency*.)

fee splitting A single client bill covering the fees of two or more attorneys who are not in the same firm. Also called *fee sharing*.

forwarding fee A fee received by one attorney from another to whom the first attorney referred a client. Also called *referral fee*.

(also called a *referral fee*) for referring the case. (The forwarding attorney often does no actual work on the case.) Or attorneys from different firms may simply join forces to work on the case.

> **Example:** John Jones, Esq. is hired by a singer who is charging her record company with copyright infringement and breach of contract. Jones calls in Randy Smith, Esq., a specialist in copyright law from another firm. Both work on the case. They share (split) the fees paid by the singer, who receives one bill for the work of both attorneys even though they work for different law firms.

The attorneys are splitting or dividing the fee between them. This arrangement is proper under certain conditions. The total fee must be reasonable, and the client must agree in writing with the compensation arrangement among all the attorneys. The share of the fee received by each attorney must be in proportion to his or her work on the case unless each attorney agrees to joint malpractice responsibility for the case.

Suppose that the attorney splits a fee with a nonattorney.

> **Example:** Frank Martin is a freelance investigator. He refers accident victims to a law firm. For every client he refers to the firm, he receives 25 percent of the fee collected by the firm.

> **Example:** Helen Gregson is a chiropractor. She refers medical malpractice cases to a law firm, which compensates her for each referral.

These are improper divisions of fees with nonattorneys—even if the amount of the division is reasonable and the clients brought in by Martin or Gregson give written consent to their receiving a part of the fee. An attorney cannot share with a nonattorney a portion of a fee *paid by particular clients*. The rationale behind this prohibition is that the nonattorney might exercise some control over the attorney and thereby jeopardize the attorney's independent judgment.

For the same reason, an attorney cannot form a partnership with a nonattorney if any of the activities of the partnership consist of the practice of law. If the office practices law as a corporation, a nonattorney cannot own a shareholder interest or be a director or officer. (Professional corporations are discussed in chapter 14.) As we saw earlier, however, if a state allowed the formation of a multidisciplinary practice (MDP), nonattorneys would be allowed to become partners of the firm and thereby share fees.

When a client has a serious dispute with an attorney over a fee, the client will sometimes dismiss the attorney and ask for a return of the client's file, which may contain many documents such as correspondence, complaints, other pleadings, exhibits, and reports of experts. This file is the property of the client and must be surrendered by the attorney when the client requests it, even if there are unpaid bills for fees and costs. If the attorney has a claim for payment, the remedy is to sue the client for breach of contract; it is unethical for the attorney to hold the file hostage to ensure payment. The attorney can copy the file before turning it over, but at the attorney's own expense. (For more on an attorney's client-file responsibilities at the close of a case, see chapter 14.)

The fees that we have been discussing are separate from the **fee caps** that many states have imposed. A fee cap is an upper limit on the fees that can be charged in traditional or contingent cases. For example, a state may say that in a medical malpractice case, fees cannot exceed 20 percent of what is recovered.

fee cap A maximum amount or maximum percentage that can be charged as a fee in particular kinds of cases.

In addition to paying fees for an attorney's time, clients can also be charged for out-of-pocket expenses incurred by the office in the representation. Examples of expenses include court filing costs, witness fees, and long-distance travel. Clients must not be misled about their payment. If an attorney tells clients that they "pay nothing if they don't win," it must be made clear whether such statements refer to fees only. If clients must pay an attorney's out-of-pocket expenses even if the case is lost, the clients must be made aware of this at the outset of the attorney-client relationship.

Paralegal Perspective:

- Paralegals who work for law firms receive salaries. This does not constitute the unethical sharing of fees with nonattorneys, even though the firm pays salaries out of revenue generated by fees. So long as there is no advance agreement to pay a paralegal all or part of *particular* legal fees, there is no ethical impropriety. Suppose that a paralegal is eligible to become part of the firm's retirement plan, which has a profit-sharing component. Or suppose that the firm has a bonus plan for its paralegals. In most states, the same rule applies. Retirement plans and bonuses are ethical so long as there is no sharing or splitting of a particular client's fees. There is a major difference between:

- A law firm agreeing to pay a paralegal 10 percent of whatever fees are collected in the Davis v. Kelly automobile negligence case on which the paralegal has done good work (unethical in all states) and
- A law firm giving this paralegal a bonus because the firm appreciates the paralegal's good work on all of the negligence cases (including Davis v. Kelly) that resulted in high fees during the year (ethical in most states).

Although the latter is ethical in most states, there are some states that disagree. See, for example, Indiana's Guideline 9.8, which provides that a "legal assistant's compensation may not be contingent, by advance agreement, upon the profitability of the attorney's practice." (See appendix E for a summary of all Indiana's ethical rules.)

- An important related restriction is that an attorney cannot give a paralegal any compensation for referring business to the attorney. With few exceptions, a "lawyer shall not give anything of value to a person for recommending the lawyer's services." "Lawyers are not permitted to pay others for channeling professional work" (Model Rule 7.2(b) and Comment 5).
- Paralegals occasionally speak with prospective clients before an attorney does. When this occurs, paralegals must not set fees or say anything that could be interpreted as accepting or rejecting a case. These are attorney-only functions. Is a paralegal allowed to tell a prospective client what the standard fees of the office are? Probably, since this would be considered communicating information about fees rather than "setting" them. Cautious offices, however, instruct their paralegals to avoid *any* mention of fees except perhaps to state whether there is a fee for an initial consultation.
- Attorneys may charge clients fees for paralegal work on their cases, referred to as **paralegal fees**. Paralegals record their time on time sheets that eventually become the basis of the bills sent to clients. The amount that an attorney bills for paralegal time must be reasonable. Reasonableness is determined by a number of factors, such as the experience of the paralegal, the nature of the tasks the paralegal undertakes, and the market rate for paralegals in the area. Many attorney-client fee agreements state the amount a client will be charged for a paralegal's time. (See Exhibit 8.1.) The fact that the client agrees to a fee, however, does not prove that the fee is reasonable. Factors such as experience and market rate must still be used to determine whether the fee is reasonable. Furthermore, when a client agrees to pay paralegal fees, the fees must be for the performance of paralegal tasks. It is unethical to claim such fees for time the paralegal spent performing clerical duties such as photocopying. A paralegal is allowed to perform such duties, but the office cannot seek paralegal fees from clients for doing so. The costs of secretarial or clerical tasks, like that of rent and the gas bill, are part of overhead for which clients should not be separately charged unless the clients have explicitly agreed otherwise.
- In special **statutory fee cases**, the losing side can be forced to pay the attorney fees (and the paralegal fees) of the winning party in litigation. The same guidelines apply in such cases: the paralegal fees must be reasonable and cannot cover nonparalegal tasks. Some states ask attorneys to submit an affidavit to support the amount claimed for the paralegal's time. The affidavit must give a detailed statement of the time and services rendered by the paralegal, a summary of the paralegal's qualifications, etc. Law firms should avoid **block billing**, in which a single time charge is assigned to multiple tasks. Billing records should provide the actual time spent on individually described tasks.
- Your time records should be **contemporaneous**, that is, made at approximately the same time as the events you are recording. Try to avoid recording time long after you perform tasks that require time records.
- Avoid **double billing**. It is fraudulent to charge a client twice for the same service.

> **Example:** Charles is a litigation paralegal in a law firm. One of his tasks is to digest (i.e., summarize) a deposition. The firm bills the client twenty hours for this task at the paralegal's rate ($65 per hour). The firm also bills the client ten hours of Attorney Bedford's time for digesting the same deposition at the attorney's rate ($150 per hour).

The client is being double billed, a grossly unethical practice. It would be proper for an attorney to charge a client for time spent *supervising* a paralegal's work but not for *performing* the paralegal's work. The related offense of **padding** is also fraudulent. It occurs when you

---

paralegal fee A fee that an attorney can collect for the nonclerical work of his or her paralegal on a client case.

statutory fee case A case applying a special statute that gives a judge authority to order the losing party to pay the winning party's attorney and paralegal fees.

block billing Grouping multiple tasks under a single time charge rather than describing each task separately and assigning the actual time associated with each task.

contemporaneous Existing or occurring in the same period of time; pertaining to records that are prepared on events as they are occurring or shortly thereafter.

double billing Fraudulently charging a client twice for the same service.

padding Adding something without justification; adding unnecessary material in order to make something larger.

add hours to your time sheet that were not in fact spent on the client's case (**time padding**) or bill for added tasks that were not needed (**task padding**).

> **Example:** It takes Charles, the litigation paralegal, twelve hours to digest a deposition. His time sheets, however, say he spent twenty hours on the task.

Padding is a serious problem in the practice of law. Here is what one attorney observed:

> I was routinely told to double and triple bill my time. . . . The lawyers are engaged in pervasive deception of clients, pretending to be doing work that they are not doing, pretending to spend more time than they are spending, pretending that work needs to be done which in fact does not need to be done. The delivery of legal services is conceptualized principally as a billing opportunity to be manipulated and expanded.[4]

Unfortunately, paralegals can find themselves under a similar pressure, which, of course, must be resisted. In many offices, a paralegal's job security depends on the number of billable hours he or she accumulates. Even if the office does not impose a **billable hours quota,** the number of hours billed is closely watched in order to determine how profitable paralegals are to the office. This creates an incentive to engage in double billing and padding.

> One of the most common temptations that can corrupt a paralegal's ethics is to inflate billable hours, since there is often immense pressure in law firms to bill high hours for job security and upward mobility. Such "creative billing" is not humorous; it's both morally wrong and illegal. It's also fraudulent and a plain and simple case of theft.[5]

> Paralegals claim that questionable billing is among the most common unethical practice attorneys ask them to perform. [One commentator] reported incidents where paralegals were ordered to double bill and bill for time they did not spend working.[6]

When you are employed as a paralegal, will you face such pressure? Yes, or at least very probably, if you work in an office where income is generated through hourly fees. The office wants high billings to increase its income. The paralegal wants high billings to demonstrate to the office that he or she is financially valuable to the office. Of course, every paralegal does not submit fraudulent time sheets and billings. But the pressure to do so is real.

A veteran paralegal recently made the following dramatic and troublesome comments about this problem:

> The economic benefits [of using paralegals] to the client are receiving greater attention. From my experience, however, there has been more abuse than benefit. The client is billed for a task traditionally performed by a secretary, doublebilled for redoing a task because it was poorly delegated and is being billed at an attorney's rate for "routine tasks" which can be best handled by a qualified paralegal.[7]

The following case of *Brown v. Hammond* involves a paralegal, Cynthia Brown, who complained about the improper billing practices of her law firm. Like most nonunion employees in the private sector, Brown was an **at-will employee.** The rule governing such employees is that they can be terminated (or they can quit) at any time for any reason. There are, however, some narrow public policy exceptions to this rule. The question in the *Brown* case was whether any of the exceptions applied.

time padding Inflating a client's bill by charging for time that was not spent.

task padding Inflating a client's bill by charging for tasks that were not performed.

billable hours quota A minimum number of hours expected from a timekeeper on client matters that can be charged (billed) to clients per week, month, year, or other time period.

at-will employee An employee who can quit or be terminated at any time and for any reason; an employee who has no union or other contract protection.

Brown v. Hammond

810 F. Supp. 644 (E.D. Pa. 1993)
United States District Court, Eastern District, Pennsylvania

WALDMAN, District Judge.

Plaintiff [Cynthia Brown] is an employee of defendant attorney [Robert Hammond] and his law firm. She is suing for wrongful discharge after having "blown the whistle" on the defendants' allegedly improper billing practices. Jurisdiction is based on diversity of citizenship.* Defendants have moved to dismiss the complaint for failure to state a claim upon which relief can be granted, pursuant to Fed.R.Civ.P. [Federal Rule of Civil Procedure] 12(b)(6).

I.   Legal Standard

The purpose of a Rule 12(b)(6) motion is to test the legal sufficiency of a complaint. . . . In deciding a motion to dismiss for failure to state a claim, the court must "accept as true all the

---

*Plaintiff is a citizen of Texas, and defendants are citizens of Pennsylvania. The amount in controversy exceeds $50,000.

(continues)

Brown v. Hammond—continued

allegations in the complaint and all reasonable inferences that can be drawn therefrom, and view them in the light most favorable to the non-moving party." See *Rocks v. Philadelphia,* 868 F.2d 644, 645 (3d Cir. 1989). Dismissal is not appropriate unless it clearly appears that plaintiff can prove no set of facts in support of his claim which could entitle him to relief. See *Hishon v. King & Spalding,* 104 S. Ct. 2229, 2232. . . . A complaint may be dismissed when the facts pled and the reasonable inferences drawn therefrom are legally insufficient to support the relief sought. . . .

II. FACTS

The pertinent factual allegations in the light most favorable to plaintiff are as follows. From November 4, 1990 to April 4, 1991, plaintiff was employed by defendants at-will as a paralegal and secretary. The time she spent on client matters was billed to clients as "attorney's time" without any notice to such clients that the work was done by a non-lawyer. Her supervisors directed her at times to bill her work directly as attorney's time despite her protests that the practice was improper. She then informed various authorities and affected clients of this practice. Plaintiff does not allege that she had any responsibility for overseeing the firm's billing practices.

Defendants responded by imposing new work rules with respect to hours of employment which applied only to and discriminated against plaintiff. She was subsequently terminated.

In count I, plaintiff asserts that she was terminated in violation of public policy for reporting the wrongful actions of defendants. In count II, she asserts that she was terminated in violation of public policy for refusing to perform wrongful actions. . . .

III. DISCUSSION

It is well established under Pennsylvania law that "absent a statutory or contractual provision to the contrary . . . either party [may] terminate an employment relationship for any or no reason." *Geary v. United States Steel Corp.,* 456 Pa. 171, 175–176, 319 A.2d 174 (1974). An employer may determine, without any fair hearing to an at-will employee, that the employer simply wishes to be rid of him. *Darlington v. General Electric,* 350 Pa. Super. 183, 210, 504 A.2d 306 (1986). An employer's right to terminate an at-will employee has been characterized as "virtually absolute." *O'Neill v. ARA Services, Inc.,* 457 F. Supp. 182, 186 (E.D. Pa. 1978).

Pennsylvania law does recognize, however, a nonstatutory cause of action for wrongful discharge from employment-at-will, but only in the quite narrow and limited circumstance where the discharge violates a significant and recognized public policy. *Borse v. Piece Goods Shop,* 963 F.2d 611, 617 (3d Cir. 1992); *Geary,* supra; *Darlington,* supra. Such a public policy must be "clearly mandated" and of a type that "strikes at the heart of a citizen's social right, duties and responsibilities." *Novosel v. Nationwide Insurance Co.,* 721 F.2d 894, 899 (3d Cir. 1983). *Geary* signals a "narrow rather than expansive interpretation of the public policy exception." *Bruffett v. Warner Communications. Inc.,* 692 F.2d 910, 918 (3d Cir. 1982). Public policy exceptions "have been recognized in only the most limited of circumstances." *Clay v. Advanced Computer Applications, Inc.,* 522 Pa. 86, 89, 559 A.2d 917 (1989).

While courts generally look to constitutional or legislative pronouncements, some courts have found an expression of significant

public policy in professional codes of ethics. See *Paralegal v. Lawyer,* 783 F. Supp. 230, 232 (E.D. Pa. 1992); *Cisco v. United Parcel Services,* 328 Pa. Super. 300, 476 A.2d 1340 (1984). . . .

The court in [the] *Paralegal [v. Lawyer* case] found that the Pennsylvania Rules of Professional Conduct as adopted by the Pennsylvania Supreme Court pursuant to state constitutional powers, Pa. Const. art. 5, § 10(c), could provide the basis for a public policy exception to the at-will employment rule. See *Paralegal [v. Lawyer],* 783 F. Supp. at 232 (finding public policy against falsifying material facts and evidence from rules 3.3(a)(1), 3.4(a), and 3.4(b)). In that case, a paralegal whose employer was being investigated by the state bar was terminated after she learned that the attorney-employer had created a false record to exculpate himself and so informed the lawyer who was representing the employer in disciplinary proceedings.

Taking [Cynthia Brown's] allegations as true, defendants would appear to have violated the Pennsylvania Rules of Professional Conduct by misrepresenting to clients who had performed work for which they were paying or by effectively permitting the unauthorized practice of law by a non-lawyer. See Rule 1.5 (regulating fees); Rule 5.5(a) (prohibiting aiding non-lawyers in unauthorized practice of law); Rule 7.1 (prohibiting false or misleading communications about lawyer's services); 8.4(c) (defining "professional misconduct" to include dishonesty, fraud, deceit or misrepresentation).

Based upon pertinent precedent and persuasive authority, the court must distinguish between gratuitous disclosure of improper employer conduct and disclosures by persons responsible for reporting such conduct or for protecting the public interest in the pertinent area. See *Smith v. Calgon Carbon Corp.,* 917 F.2d 1338, 1345 (3d Cir. 1990) . . . (discharged chemical company employee not responsible for reporting improper emissions or spills); *Field v. Philadelphia Electric Co.,* 388 Pa. Super. 400, 565 A.2d 1170 (1989) (nuclear safety expert discharged for making statutorily required report to federal agency). See also *Hays v. Beverly Enters.,* 766 F. Supp. 350 (W.D. Pa.), aff'd, 952 F.2d 1392 (3d Cir. 1991) (physician's duty does not extend to plaintiff nurse); *Gaiardo v. Ethyl Corp.,* 697 F. Supp. 1377 (M.D. Pa. 1986). aff'd, 835 F.2d 479 (3d Cir. 1987) (plaintiff not supervisor or responsible for quality control).

The court concludes that plaintiff's termination for gratuitously alerting others about defendants' improper billing practice does not violate the type of significant, clearly mandated public policy required to satisfy the new narrow exception to Pennsylvania's rigid at-will employment doctrine.

By her own characterization what plaintiff did was to "blow the whistle" on wrongful conduct by her employer. The Pennsylvania Whistleblower Law, 43 Pa. C.S.A. [Consolidated Statutes Annotated] § 1421 et seq., protects from retaliatory adverse employment action employees of public bodies or entities receiving public appropriations who report wrongdoing.* That Law, which excludes from its protection wholly private employment, has been found not to codify any previously existing legal right or privilege and held not to constitute an expression of clearly mandated public policy in the context of private at-will employment.† See *Smith,* 917 F.2d at 1346; *Cohen v. Salick Health Care, Inc.,* 772 F. Supp. 1521, 1531 (E.D. Pa. 1991) (employee discharged for alerting employer's prospective

(continues)

Brown v. Hammond—continued

contractee of inflated financial projections); *Wagner v. General Electric Co.,* 760 F. Supp. 1146, 1155 (E.D. Pa. 1991) (employee discharged after expressing criticism of employer's product to customers).

On the other hand, courts are less reluctant to discern important public policy considerations where persons are discharged for refusing to violate the law themselves. See *Smith,* 917 F.2d at 1344; *Woodson v. AMF Leisureland Centers, Inc.,* 842 F.2d 699 (3d Cir. 1988) (refusal to sell liquor to intoxicated patron); *Shaw v. Russell Trucking Line, Inc.,* 542 F. Supp. 776, 779 (W.D. Pa. 1982) (refusal to haul loads over legal weight); *McNulty v. Borden, Inc.,* 474 F. Supp. 1111 (E.D. Pa. 1979) (refusal to engage in anti-trust violations). No employee should be forced to choose between his or her livelihood and engaging in fraud or other criminal conduct. To the extent that plaintiff appears to allege that she was also terminated for refusing herself to engage directly in fraudulent billing, her action may proceed. . . .

An appropriate order will be entered.

Order

AND NOW, this 12th day of January, 1992, upon consideration of defendants' Motion to Dismiss Plaintiff's Complaint, consistent with the accompanying memorandum, IT IS HEREBY ORDERED that said Motion is GRANTED in part and DENIED in part in that [count I] of plaintiff's complaint [is] DISMISSED.

---

*While the Whistleblower Law protects covered employees who report impropriety to outside authorities, it does not authorize such employees to voice complaints directly to clients of a public or publicly funded entity.

†Because of the special nature of the attorney-client relationship, an attorney's misrepresentation about the source, quality, nature or cost of work performed is arguably more reprehensible than such misrepresentation to clients and customers by other suppliers of goods and services. It is not, however, sufficiently different in kind therefrom to satisfy the narrow public policy exception to Pennsylvania's stringent at-will employment doctrine.

ASSIGNMENT 5.1

(a) Who won this case? What happens next? In the next proceeding in the case, what does the paralegal have to prove?

(b) Do you think a paralegal has an obligation to report unethical conduct? Should there be a "snitch rule"? If so, to whom should the report be made? See the discussion later in the chapter on an attorney's duty to report misconduct of another attorney. Should paralegals have a similar duty?

(c) Go to Genna H. Rosten, *Wrongful Discharge Based on Public Policy Derived from Professional Ethics Codes,* 52 A.L.R. 5th 405 (1997). You can find A.L.R. 5th in a law library or online if you have access to Westlaw (www.westlaw.com). Does this annotation discuss any decisions written by state courts in your state on the issue of firing someone in circumstances similar to those of Cynthia Brown's? If so, summarize these cases—up to a maximum of three.

4. CRIME OR FRAUD BY AN ATTORNEY

An attorney must not engage in criminal or fraudulent conduct. **Model Rule 8.4**

Sadly, there are attorneys who are charged with criminal conduct, such as theft of client funds, securities fraud, falsification of official documents, or tax fraud. Because such conduct obviously affects the attorney's trustworthiness and fitness to practice law, sanctions for unethical conduct can be imposed in addition to prosecution in a criminal court. Once an attorney is convicted of a serious crime in court, a separate disciplinary proceeding is often instituted to suspend or disbar the attorney for unethical conduct growing out of the same incident.

If an attorney misappropriates a client's funds, the client may be able to receive compensation from a **client security fund** that some state bar associations have established for this purpose.

client security fund A fund (often run by a bar association or foundation) used to compensate victims of designated kinds of attorney misconduct.

Paralegal Perspective:

■ Value your integrity above all else. A paralegal in Oklahoma offers the following advice: "Insist on the highest standards for yourself and for your employer. One small ethical breach can lead to a series of compromises with enormous" disciplinary and "legal malpractice consequences."[8]

■ If your supervisor is charged with criminal conduct, the chances are good that you will be questioned by prosecutors, and you might become a suspect yourself.

■ In the highly charged, competitive environment of a law office, some attorneys may be willing to violate the law in the interest of winning. Be sensitive to the overt and subtle pressure on you to participate in such violations. If you are subjected to this pressure, talk with other paralegals who have encountered this problem. Don't sit in silence. If there is no one in the office with whom you can frankly discuss the elimination of these pressures, you must consider quitting. (See section E of this chapter.)

attestation clause A clause stating that you saw (witnessed) someone sign a document or perform other tasks related to the validity of the document.

insider trading Improperly using material, nonpublic information to trade in the shares of a company.

pirated software Software that has been placed ("loaded") in a computer that is not authorized by the terms of the purchase or lease of the software.

- Paralegals who are also notaries are sometimes asked by their supervisors to notarize documents that should *not* be notarized. In fact, paralegals "are most often named as defendants for false notarization of a signature."[9] Assume that a law office is sued and the paralegal is named as one of the defendants. If the plaintiff wins, who pays the judgment? As we saw in chapter 4, the office may have a malpractice insurance liability policy that will pay judgments against it and its employees. These policies often exclude intentional acts of misconduct, however. (False notarization is usually an intentional act.) Hence, the losing defendants—including the paralegal—must pay the judgments out of their personal pockets. In short, be extremely cautious of what you are asked to sign. The same is true of documents you are asked to witness even if no formal notarization is involved. Don't sign a clause saying you witnessed something being performed or executed (called an **attestation clause**) unless you *actually* witness it.

- Be extremely careful about using any information you learn involving a corporation whose stock is likely to change in value as a result of an event that is not yet known to the public. Assume that Company X is planning to merge with Company Y. The news is not yet public. When it does become public, the value of the stock in Company X is expected to rise dramatically. You work at a law firm that represents Company X, and you find out about the planned merger while at work. If you buy stock in Company X before the announcement of the merger, you would benefit from the increased value of the stock that would result after the announcement. This might be an illegal use of inside information, called **insider trading**. In a dramatic case, a paralegal who worked at a securities law firm in Boston was charged with insider trading by the Securities and Exchange Commission (SEC). While working on a case involving a proposed merger, she learned certain information, which she gave to outside investors who used it to make illegal profits in the stock market. The story made national news. One headline read, "SEC Says Boston Paralegal Gave Tip Worth $823,471." Soon after the incident, she was fired. Criminal prosecution for the crime of insider trading became a very real possibility. All employees of law firms must be extremely careful. Innocently buying stock as a personal investment could turn into a nightmare. One attorney "recommends that any paralegal who would like to buy or sell securities should check first with a corporate attorney in the firm to see if the firm represents the issuer or a company negotiating with the issuer. If it does, an accusation of 'insider trading' might later be made."[10] The same caution applies when a member of the paralegal's immediate family buys or sells such securities.

- Another problem area is the use of so-called **pirated software**. Some businesses buy or lease one copy of computer software and then copy it so that other employees in the office can use it on other terminals. If the software manufacturer has not authorized such copying as part of the original purchase or lease agreement, the copying is illegal and can subject violators to criminal penalties and civil damages.

- In all aspects of your career as a paralegal, adopt the motto "If it doesn't feel right, it probably isn't." (See guideline 10 in Exhibit 5.1 at the beginning of this chapter.)

5. CRIME OR FRAUD BY A CLIENT

If an attorney knows that future conduct of a client would be criminal or fraudulent, the attorney must not advise the client to engage in the conduct nor otherwise assist the client in engaging in it. Model Rule 1.2(d)

The client hires the attorney and controls the purpose of the attorney-client relationship. Furthermore, the client is entitled to know the legal consequences of any action he or she is contemplating. This does not mean, however, that the attorney must do whatever the client wants.

> **Example:** The president of a corporation hires Leo Richards, Esq. to advise the company on how to dump toxic waste into a local river.

Note that the president has not asked Richards *if* the dumping is legal. It would be perfectly ethical for Richards to answer such a question. In the example, the president asks *how* to dump. If Richards feels that the dumping can legally take place, he can so advise the president. Suppose, however, that it is clear to Richards that the dumping would violate the federal or state criminal code. Under such circumstances, it would be unethical for Richards to advise the president on how to proceed with the dumping. The same would be true if the president wanted help in filing an environmental statement that misrepresented the intentions of the company. Such an application would be fraudulent, and an attorney must not help someone commit what the attorney knows is fraudulent conduct.

When attorneys are later charged with unethical conduct in such cases, their defense is often that they did not *know* the conduct proposed by the client was criminal or fraudulent. This defense can be successful. If the law applicable to the client's case is unclear, an attorney can make a good-faith effort to find a legal way for the client to achieve his or her objective. The point at which the attorney crosses the ethical line is when he or she *knows* the client is trying to accomplish something criminal or fraudulent.

In addition to charges of unethical conduct, an attorney could be subjected to civil suits for participating in illegal conduct of a client. For example, as we saw in chapter 4, an attorney could be sued for the torts of **malicious prosecution** (improperly bringing litigation without probable cause) and **abuse of process** (using civil or criminal process for an improper purpose). Participating in the destruction or alteration of evidence (**spoliation**) can also have serious consequences.

One final point on the theme of legal services and illegal conduct. Suppose that a senior citizen goes to an attorney for advice on Medicaid. This is a needs-based program; you have to be poor enough to qualify for its health care benefits. Assume that the client has too many assets to qualify. The attorney then describes how the bulk of the assets could be disposed of (e.g., by gifts to children) so that the client would qualify. The strategy was so widespread that Congress (angry that attorneys were "teaching people how to abuse the system") made it a crime to give such advice! The law became known as the "Send Granny's Lawyer to Jail" law.[10a] The law certainly made it difficult for attorneys to argue that they did not know that they were participating in something illegal with their clients. The advice itself was illegal! The law created an uproar in the legal community and was immediately challenged in court as a violation of free speech under the First Amendment. The issue eventually became moot when the U.S. Attorney General announced that the Department of Justice would not bring prosecutions under the law because of its dubious legality.

Paralegal Perspective:

- An attorney will rarely tell paralegals or other staff members that he or she knows the office is helping a client do something criminal or fraudulent. But you might learn that this is so, particularly if there is a close, trusting relationship between you and your supervising attorney. You must let this attorney or some other authority in the office know you do not feel comfortable working on such a case.

6. FRIVOLOUS LEGAL POSITIONS

An attorney must not bring a frivolous claim or assert a frivolous defense. **Model Rule 3.1**

We often say that we have an **adversary system** of justice. This means that our method of resolving a legal dispute is to have opposing sides fight it out before an impartial decision maker. We believe that truth and fairness are more likely to emerge when each side has an equal chance to present its case forcefully. Within this system, clients have the right to hire an attorney to be a vigorous advocate.

But there are limits on how vigorous an advocate can be. It is unethical, for example, for an attorney to assert **frivolous positions** as claims or defenses. A position is frivolous if the attorney is unable to make a good-faith argument that existing law supports the position or that existing law should be changed or reversed to support the position. A position is not necessarily frivolous simply because the attorney thinks the client will probably lose. The key is whether there is a good-faith argument to support the position. If the attorney can think of no rational support for the position, it is frivolous. Because the law is often unclear, however, it is difficult to establish that an attorney is acting unethically under the test of good faith.

Closely related to asserting frivolous positions is the unethical practice of asserting positions for the purpose of harassing or maliciously injuring someone.

A charge of unethical conduct is not the only consequence for asserting a frivolous position. Under Rule 11 of the Federal Rules of Civil Procedure, for example, whenever an attorney in a federal case submits a motion or pleading to the court, he or she must certify that "it is not being presented for any improper purpose, such as to harass or to cause unnecessary delay or needless increase in the cost of litigation" and that "the claims, defenses, and other legal contentions therein are warranted by existing law or by a nonfrivolous argument for the extension, modification, or reversal of existing law or the establishment of new law." Violating Rule 11 can lead to sanctions by the court (e.g., a fine) in addition to a charge of unethical conduct. Many states have their own version of Rule 11 for state court cases.

Paralegal Perspective:

- In the heat of controversy, tempers can run high. Attorneys do not always exhibit the detachment expected of professionals. They may so thoroughly identify with the interests of their clients that they lose perspective. Paralegals working for such attorneys may get caught up

malicious prosecution A tort with the following elements: (1) to initiate or procure the initiation of civil or criminal legal proceedings, (2) without probable cause, (3) with malice or an improper purpose; and (4) the proceedings terminate in favor of the person against whom the proceedings were brought.

abuse of process A tort consisting of (1) the use of a civil or criminal process, (2) for a purpose for which the process is not designed, (3) resulting in actual damage.

spoliation Intentionally destroying, altering, or concealing evidence.

adversary system A method of resolving a legal dispute whereby the parties (alone or through their advocates) argue their conflicting claims before a neutral decision maker.

frivolous position A position taken on behalf of a client that the attorney cannot support by a good-faith argument based on existing law or on the need for a change in existing law.

in the same fever, particularly if there is a close attorney-paralegal working relationship on a high-stakes case that has lasted a considerable time. The momentum is to do whatever it takes to win. While this atmosphere can be exhilarating, it can also create an environment where less and less attention is paid to the niceties of ethics.

7. SAFEKEEPING PROPERTY

An attorney shall hold client property separate from the attorney's own property. **Model Rule 1.15**

fiduciary One whose duty is to act in the interests of another with a high standard of care. Someone in whom another has a right to place great trust and to expect great loyalty.

client trust account A bank account controlled by an attorney that contains client funds that may not be used for office operating expenses or for any personal purpose of the attorney.

commingling Mixing what should be kept separate, e.g., depositing client funds in a single account with general law firm funds or with an attorney's personal funds.

retainer (1) An amount of money (or other property) paid by a client as a deposit or advance against future fees, costs, and expenses of providing services. (2) The act of hiring or engaging the services of someone, usually a professional. (The verb is *retain*.)

Attorneys are **fiduciaries,** individuals who must exercise a high standard of care on behalf of their clients. This fiduciary responsibility is particularly important when handling client funds.

A law office often receives client funds or funds of others connected with the client's case, e.g., attorneys receive money in settlement of a case or as trustees or escrow agents. Such funds should be held in a **client trust account**. General operating funds of the office should be kept in a separate account. There must be no **commingling** of client funds and office funds. It is unethical to place everything in one account. This is so even if the firm maintains accurate bookkeeping records on what amounts in the single account belong to which clients and what amounts belong to the firm. In a commingled account, the danger is too great that client funds will be used for nonclient purposes.

It is also improper for an office to misuse funds on **retainer**. Clients sometimes deposit funds with an office to cover future fees, costs, and expenses. The office should not draw on these fees before they are earned or withdraw the funds for expenses not yet incurred. This is so even if the funds were never commingled when deposited by the client. For more on the use and abuse of such funds, see Section G in chapter 14.

Client records must also be safeguarded. The client's file is the property of the client. When the attorney's representation of the client is over, the firm cannot discard or destroy the file. The client must be given the opportunity to receive it. The firm can keep copies. In fact, most states require that copies of files be kept in storage a minimum period of time (e.g., five years) after the firm has completed its representation of a client on a matter. When a firm is allowed to destroy files, it must do so without breaching confidentiality. It would probably be unethical, for example, to throw unshredded files containing client names and other case information into regular trash bins.

Paralegal Perspective:

- Use great care whenever your responsibility involves client funds, such as receiving funds from clients, opening bank accounts, depositing funds in the proper account at a bank, and making entries in law firm records on such funds. It should be fairly obvious to you whether an attorney is violating the rule on commingling funds. It may be less clear whether the attorney is improperly using client funds for unauthorized purposes. Attorneys have been known to "borrow" money from client accounts and then return the money before anyone discovers what was done. They might even pay the account interest while using the money. Elaborate bookkeeping and accounting gimmicks might be used to disguise what is going on. Such conduct is unethical even if the attorney pays interest and eventually returns all the funds. In addition, the attorney may eventually be charged with theft or criminal fraud. Of course, anyone who knowingly assists the attorney could be subject to the same consequences.
- Be very careful about signatures. An attorney may want to delegate the task of signing for deposits, transfers, or withdrawals. It some states, it is unethical for an attorney to allow a nonattorney to sign for transactions involving client property, particularly funds in client trust accounts.

8. FALSE STATEMENTS AND FAILURE TO DISCLOSE

(1) An attorney must not knowingly make a false statement of an important or material fact to a court or other tribunal;

(2) An attorney must not knowingly cite incorrect or invalid law to a court or other tribunal;

(3) An attorney must not offer evidence he or she knows is false;

(4) An attorney must tell a court or other tribunal about a material fact when the attorney knows that silence about that fact would assist the client to commit fraud or a crime such as perjury;

(5) If an attorney knows of a law that goes against the claims of his or her own client, the attorney must tell a court or other tribunal about that law if he or she knows that opposing counsel has not done so, usually due to carelessness or incompetence. Model Rule 3.3

One of the reasons the general public holds the legal profession in low esteem is the perception that attorneys seldom comply with the above rules. Our adversary system does not always encourage the participants to cooperate in court proceedings. In fact, quite the opposite is often true. In extreme cases, attorneys have been known to lie to the court, to offer knowingly false evidence, etc. Under Model Rule 3.3, such conduct is unethical.

The argue-against-yourself requirement of Rule 3.3 (see the last provision) is particularly startling.

Example: Karen Singer and Bill Carew are attorneys who are opposing each other in a bitter trial involving a large sum of money. Singer knows about a very damaging but obscure case that goes against her client. But because of sloppy research, Carew does not know about it. Singer never mentions the case, and it never comes up during the trial.

It is certainly understandable why Singer does not want to say anything about the case. She does not want to help her opponent. But she must pay a price for her silence. She is subject to sanctions for a violation of her ethical obligation of disclosure under Model Rule 3.3.

Another controversial part of Model Rule 3.3 that has the effect of forcing an attorney to turn against his or her own client is the requirement that the attorney disclose facts that are needed to avoid assisting the client commit fraud or a crime (see the fourth provision). Because this raises issues of confidentiality, we will discuss such disclosures later when we cover confidentiality.

Paralegal Perspective:

- Be aware that an attorney who justifies the use of deception in one case will probably repeat such deceptions in the future on other cases. To excuse the deception, the attorney will often refer to the necessity of protecting the client or to the alleged evilness of the other side. Deceptions are unethical despite such justifications.
- Chances are also high that employees of such an attorney will be pressured into participating in deception—for example, give a false date to a court clerk, help a client lie (commit perjury) on the witness stand, help an attorney alter a document to be introduced into evidence, or improperly notarize a document.
- Do not compromise your integrity no matter how much you believe in the cause of the client, no matter how much you detest the tactics of the opposing side, no matter how much you like the attorney for whom you work, and no matter how important this job is to you.

9. WITHDRAWAL

An attorney must withdraw from a case: if the client fires the attorney, if continuing on the case violates ethical rules or other laws, or if competent representation is jeopardized because of the attorney's physical or mental health. Withdrawal for these reasons is required unless a court or other tribunal orders the attorney not to withdraw. Model Rule 1.16

Attorneys are not required to take every case. Furthermore, once they begin a case, they are not obligated to stay with the client until the case is over. If, however, the case has already begun in court after the attorney has filed a **notice of appearance**, withdrawal is usually improper without the permission of the court.

In some circumstances, an attorney *must* withdraw from a case that has begun:

- The client fires the attorney. An attorney is an agent of the client. Clients are always free to dismiss their agents.
- Representation of the client would violate ethical rules—for example, the attorney discovers that he or she has a conflict of interest with the client that cannot be **cured** or remedied even with the consent of the client.
- Representation of the client would violate the law—for example, the client insists that the attorney provide advice on how to defraud the Internal Revenue Service.
- The attorney's physical or mental health has deteriorated to the point where the attorney's ability to represent the client has been materially impaired. This may be due to alcohol or drug abuse, marital problems, etc.

These are examples of when the attorney *must* withdraw from the case. There may be other circumstances that do not require withdrawal but that are serious enough to give the attorney the

notice of appearance A formal notification to a court by an attorney that he or she is representing a party in the litigation.

cure To correct or overcome; to remove a legal defect or error.

option of withdrawing without being charged with unethically walking away from or abandoning the client. This option exists, for example, if the client insists on an objective that the attorney considers repugnant or imprudent. Similarly, the attorney has the option of withdrawing if the attorney is experiencing an unreasonable financial burden because of the failure of the client to pay attorney fees.

Withdrawal, if allowed, must be done reasonably. An attorney should not abruptly withdraw on the eve of an important hearing or on the day before the client's cause of action dies because of the expiration of the statute of limitations. The client will need time to find other representation. The attorney should send the client a **letter of disengagement** (also called, pejoratively, a "kiss-off" letter). It formally notifies the client that the attorney will no longer be representing the client. The letter confirms the termination of the attorney-client relationship. It should provide the reason for the withdrawal, a summary of the scope of the representation that was attempted, and a statement of the disposition of funds, if any, remaining in the client's account. (See also chapter 8 for a discussion of the **letter of nonengagement**, which should be sent to someone the attorney has never represented if the attorney declines a request for representation.)

letter of disengagement
A letter sent to a client formally notifying him or her that the law office will no longer be representing the client.

letter of nonengagement
A letter sent to a prospective client that explicitly says that the law office will not be representing him or her.

Paralegal Perspective:

- When you have a close working relationship with an attorney, particularly in a small law office, you become aware of his or her professional strengths and personal weaknesses. Bar associations around the country are becoming increasingly concerned about the *impaired* attorney, someone who is not functioning properly due to substance abuse or similar problems. A paralegal with such an attorney for a supervisor is obviously in a predicament. Seemingly small problems have the potential of turning into a crisis. If it is not practical to discuss the situation directly with the attorney involved, you need to seek the advice of others in the firm.

10. CONFIDENTIALITY OF INFORMATION

An attorney must not disclose information relating to the representation of a client unless (a) the client consents to the disclosure or (b) the attorney reasonably believes the disclosure is necessary (1) to prevent reasonably certain death or substantial bodily harm, or (2) to prevent the client from committing a crime or fraud that is reasonably certain to result in substantial injury to the financial interests of another and in furtherance of which the client has used or is using the attorney's services. Model Rule 1.6.

confidential That which should not be revealed; pertaining to information that others do not have a right to receive.

privileged Protected by a privilege, e.g., does not have to be disclosed.

Information is **confidential** if others do not have a right to receive it. When access to information is restricted in this way, the information is considered **privileged**. After we cover ethics and confidentiality, we need to examine the related topics of the attorney-client privilege and the attorney work-product rule.

Ethics and Confidentiality

The ethical obligation to maintain confidentiality applies to all or almost all information that relates to the representation of a client, whatever its source. One court has said, "[V]irtually any information relating to a case should be considered confidential . . . even unprivileged client information."[11] Note also that the obligation is broader than so-called secrets or matters explicitly communicated in confidence. Information can be confidential even if the client does not refer to it as a secret and even if the client does not ask that it not be revealed. Confidentiality has been breached in each of the following examples:

- At a party, an attorney tells an acquaintance from another town that the law firm is representing Jacob Anderson, who wants to prevent his employer from forcing him to retire. (The identity of a client is confidential. So is the reason the client is seeking legal help.)
- At a bar association conference, an attorney tells an old law school classmate that a client named Brenda Steck is considering a suit against her brother over the ownership of property left by their deceased mother. (The identity of a client and what lawsuits she is considering are confidential.)
- A legal secretary carelessly leaves a client's file open on her desk where a stranger (e.g., another client) briefly reads parts of it. (The contents of a client file are confidential.)

The rule on confidentiality is designed to encourage clients to discuss their case fully and frankly with their attorney, including embarrassing and legally damaging information. Arguably, a client would be reluctant to be open with an attorney if he or she had to worry about whether the attorney might reveal the information to others. The rule on confidentiality makes it unethical for attorneys to do so. Yet this rule is not absolute. There are some important exceptions.

A client can always **consent** to an attorney's disclosure about the client—*if* the client is properly consulted about the proposed disclosure in advance. Well-known trial attorneys who write books about their cases, for example, need to have clear client consent to reveal the otherwise-confidential client information contained in such books. Sometimes disclosure is implicitly authorized because of the nature of the client's case. In a dispute over alimony, for example, the attorney would obviously have to disclose certain relevant financial information about the client to a court or to opposing counsel during the settlement negotiations.

Disclosure can also be ethically permissible to prevent reasonably certain death or substantial bodily harm.

> **Example:** An attorney represents a husband in a bitter divorce action against his wife. During a meeting at the law firm, the husband shows the attorney a gun and says he is going to use it to kill his wife later the same day.

Can the attorney tell the police what the husband said? Yes, if the attorney reasonably believes that the disclosure is necessary to prevent death or substantial bodily harm. That appears to be the case here. The client said he was going to kill his wife and displayed the gun he intended to use.

Assume that an attorney learns that the client is about to harm someone financially, but not bodily. Can the attorney reveal this fact if it is reasonably necessary to prevent the financial harm? Yes, if the client was going to cause the harm through a criminal or fraudulent act and through the use of the attorney's services.

Corporate attorneys who practice before the Securities and Exchange Commission (SEC) are subject to special disclosure laws. If they know about serious securities violations, they must disclose them up-the-ladder to the chief legal officer, the chief executive officer, or the board of directors of the company. Such disclosure will not be considered an unethical breach of confidentiality.

Finally, some disclosures can be proper in suits between attorney and client. Suppose, for example, the attorney later sues the client for nonpayment of a fee or the client sues the attorney for malpractice. In such proceedings, an attorney can reveal information about the client if the attorney reasonably believes disclosure is necessary to present a claim against the client or to defend against the client's claim.

Attorney-Client Privilege

The **attorney-client privilege** serves a function similar to that of the ethical rule on confidentiality in that both doctrines are designed to encourage open communication between attorney and client. The two doctrines overlap, although the ethical duty of confidentiality is much broader than the attorney-client privilege:

> *Ethical duty of confidentiality*: Protects all information (not just client communications) from any source if the information pertains to a client case and was obtained by a law office while representing the client.

> *Attorney-client privilege*: Protects all communications made in confidence between an attorney and client if the purpose of the communication was to obtain legal services from the attorney. A communication is made in confidence if it was intended to be confidential. If it is made in the presence of strangers (e.g., in front of strangers on an elevator) the privilege is lost.

Everything protected by the attorney-client privilege is also protected by the ethical duty of confidentiality. The reverse, however, is not always true. All information protected by the ethical duty of confidentiality is not also protected by the attorney-client privilege. Suppose, for example, that while investigating the finances of a client's company, the attorney learns from minutes of a shareholder meeting that the company considered discontinuing a particular product five years ago. This information is protected from disclosure by the ethical duty of confidentiality. Because, however, the information was not part of a communication between attorney and client, the information is not protected by the attorney-client privilege.

The attorney-client privilege most often arises in court or administrative proceedings in which the attorney or client is asked a question that pertains to a communication between them while the client was seeking legal help. The client can refuse to answer on the ground of privilege. If the attorney is the one being asked the question, he or she *must* refuse to answer on the same ground unless the client gives the attorney consent to answer. Only the client can waive the privilege.

---

consent (1) To waive a right; to agree. (2) Voluntary agreement or permission, express or implied.

attorney-client privilege A client and an attorney can refuse to disclose any communication made between them if the purpose of the communication was to facilitate the provision of legal services for the client.

If an attorney can claim the attorney-client privilege, then his or her paralegals and other employees can do so as well. Here is an example of a statute that specifies this extension of the privilege:

Who May Not Testify without Consent

Colorado Revised Statutes § 13–90–107(1)(b) (1996)

An attorney shall not be examined without the consent of his client as to any communication made by the client to him or [as to] his advice given thereon in the course of professional employment; nor shall an attorney's secretary, paralegal, legal assistant, stenographer, or clerk be examined without the consent of his employer concerning any fact, the knowledge of which he has acquired in such capacity.

The *ethical* rule on confidentiality tells us when sanctions can be imposed on attorneys when they (or their employees) improperly disclose confidential client information to anyone outside the law office. The *attorney-client privilege* tells us when clients and attorneys (or their employees) can refuse to answer questions pertaining to communications involving legal services for a client.

Attorney Work-Product Rule

Suppose that, while working on a client's case, an attorney prepares a memorandum or other in-house document that does *not* contain any confidential communications. The memorandum or document, therefore, is *not* protected by the attorney-client privilege. Can the other side force the attorney to provide a copy of the memorandum or document? Is it **discoverable**, meaning that an opposing party can obtain information about it during discovery at the pretrial stage of a lawsuit? This question leads us to the attorney **work-product rule**.

Under this rule, the *work product* of an attorney is considered confidential. Work product consists of notes, working papers, memoranda, or similar documents and tangible things prepared by the attorney in anticipation of litigation. An example is an attorney's interoffice memorandum that lays out his or her strategy in litigating a case. Attorneys do not have to disclose their work product to the other side. With few exceptions, it is not discoverable.[12] To the extent that such material is not discoverable, it is privileged. (The work-product rule is sometimes referred to as the work-product privilege.)

Inadvertent Disclosure of Confidential Material

The great fear of law office personnel is that the wrong person will obtain material that should be protected by ethics, by the attorney-client privilege, or by the work-product rule. This can have devastating consequences. For example, if a stranger overhears a confidential communication by a client to the attorney or to the attorney's paralegal, a court might rule that the attorney-client privilege has been **waived** on the theory that it is inconsistent to let a stranger or any third party hear what you claim was confidential. Media celebrity Martha Stewart was confronted with this reality when a court ruled in her criminal trial that she had waived the attorney-client privilege covering the contents of an e-mail with her attorney when Stewart mailed a copy of the e-mail to her daughter.[12a] At a recent paralegal conference, a speaker told a stunned audience that a paralegal in her firm accidentally "faxed" a strategy memo on a current case to the opposing attorney! The paralegal punched in the wrong phone number on the fax machine! This could just as easily have occurred by sending an e-mail message or attachment to the wrong address.

Paralegal Perspective:

- Attorneys must take reasonable steps to guard against a breach of confidentiality by their paralegals or other nonattorney employees. This includes instruction on the obligation not to disclose information relating to the representation of a client. When you are hired, the firm may ask you to sign a formal confidentiality agreement in which you promise not to divulge client information to anyone who is not working on the client's case. (For an example, see Exhibit 5.5.) The agreement is simply a device to stress the importance of confidentiality. You, of course, are bound to maintain confidentiality even if your employer does not ask you to sign such an agreement.

---

discoverable Pertaining to information or other materials an opponent can obtain through deposition, interrogatories, or other discovery devices.

work-product rule Notes, working papers, memoranda, or similar documents and tangible things prepared by or for an attorney in anticipation of litigation are not discoverable by an opponent, absent a showing of substantial need.

waiver The express or implied relinquishment of a right or privilege. Examples of an implied relinquishment include failing to claim it at the proper time or acting in a manner that is inconsistent with its existence. The verb is *waive*.

EXHIBIT 5.5	Example of a Confidentiality Agreement

Confidentiality Agreement

While employed by this firm, you will find yourself exposed to many matters that come within what are known as the "attorney-client" and "work product" privileges. These involve communications between clients and the attorneys in the firm, as well as work conducted, strategies employed, and materials prepared in connection with matters on which we are working for clients. Employees are obliged to keep such information and materials strictly confidential and, except under very limited circumstances, cannot disclose such matters to anyone beyond this office.

As a firm employee, you are also obligated to keep absolutely confidential all communications between our office and our clients (and from clients to our office), the work that we are doing for our clients, and information relating to our cases. Such matters may not be discussed or disclosed outside of our office, even with or to your families and friends. You may not even divulge the *existence* of a case or legal matter that the firm is handling or has handled.

This obligation shall continue in the event that you should, for any reasons, leave the firm.

In addition, should you at any time become employed by another law firm, or any legal department, you must refrain from working on or having any contact with any matter in which you or our firm has been involved while working here or that relates to such a matter.

Agreement to these terms and adherence to the "Rules of Professional Conduct" as adopted by the Supreme Court of the State of New Jersey are requirements of your employment by Porzio, Bromberg & Newman, P.C. A copy of the "Rules of Professional Conduct" will be provided at your request.

I agree to the above terms.

_____   _____
Signature   Date

_____
Witness

Source: Reprinted with permission of Porzio, Bromberg & Newman (www.pbnlaw.com).

- As indicated earlier, the major national paralegal associations have their own ethical codes (see Exhibit 5.4). All of these codes stress the importance of maintaining confidentiality:
  - "A legal assistant must protect the confidences of a client and must not violate any rule or statute now in effect or hereafter enacted controlling the doctrine of privileged communications between a client and an attorney." Canon 7. National Association of Legal Assistants, *Code of Ethics and Professional Responsibility*.
  - "A paralegal shall preserve all confidential information provided by the client or acquired from other sources before, during, and after the course of the professional relationship." "'Confidential information' means information relating to a client, whatever its source, that is not public knowledge nor available to the public." Section 1.5. National Federation of Paralegal Associations, *Model Code of Ethics and Professional Responsibility*.
  - "Every member shall [o]bserve rules governing privileged communications and confidential information." "Members of this association shall preserve and protect the confidences and privileged communications of a client." Canon 4. NALS the Association for Legal Professionals, *Code of Ethics*.
- Paralegals face *many* temptations to violate confidentiality. For example, a paralegal inadvertently reveals confidential information:
  - while networking with other paralegals at a paralegal association meeting;
  - during animated conversation with another paralegal in a common area such as a restaurant or an elevator; or
  - after returning home from work during casual discussions with a relative, spouse, or roommate about interesting cases at the office.

  Some paralegals make the mistake of thinking that the rule applies only to damaging or embarrassing information or that the rule simply means you should not reveal things to the other side in the dispute. Not so. The rule is much broader. Virtually all information relating to the representation of a client must not be revealed to *anyone* outside the office.
- In Missouri, the obligation of silence is even broader. The paralegal must not disclose information—"confidential or otherwise"—relating to the representation of the client.[13] In Texas, confidential information includes both privileged information and unprivileged client information. An attorney must "instruct the legal assistant that all information concerning representation of a client (indeed even the fact of representation, if not a matter of

public record) must be kept strictly confidential."[14] In Philadelphia, paralegals are warned that it is "not always easy to recognize what information about your firm's clients or office is confidential. Moreover, a client of your office might be offended to learn that a ... firm employee has discussed the client's business in public, even if the information mentioned is public knowledge. The easiest rule is to consider *all* work of the office to be confidential: do not discuss the business of your office or your firm's clients with any outsider, no matter how close a friend, at any time, unless you are specifically authorized by a lawyer to do so."[15] Under guidelines such as these, there is very little that paralegals can tell someone about their work!

- During the war, sailors were told that "loose lips sink ships." The same applies to law firms. Note that the last clause of the following law firm statement to all paralegals places limits on what can be said to other employees within the same law firm: "Throughout your employment, you will have access to information that must at all times be held in strictest confidence. Even the seemingly insignificant fact that the firm is involved in a particular matter falls within the orbit of confidential information. Unless you have attorney permission, do not disclose documents or contents of documents to anyone, *including firm employees who do not need this information to do their work*."[16]

- If you attend a meeting on a case outside the law office, ask your supervisor whether you should take notes or prepare a follow-up memorandum on the meeting. Let the supervisor decide whether your notes or the memo might be discoverable.[17]

- Be *very* careful when you talk with clients in the presence of third persons. As indicated earlier, overheard conversations might constitute an unintentional waiver of the attorney-client privilege. Cellular phones can sometimes cause problems. The signal in mobile communications is transmitted by frequency over airwaves. Therefore, outsiders can listen to conversations with relative ease. If you are on a cellular phone with a client, warn him or her that confidential information should not be discussed.[18]

- Do not listen to your messages on a phone answering machine when others in the room can hear the messages as well. Clients often leave messages that contain confidential information. When using speaker phones, intercoms, or paging systems, don't broadcast confidential information. Assume that many people will be hearing you on these public systems and that most of them are not entitled to hear what you are saying.

- Make sure your door is closed when discussing a client's case. If there is no door to the office, find out if there is a private room in the firm you can use for the call. If this is not practical, lower your voice when talking on the phone and be alert at all times to the presence of anyone around you who can hear what you are saying. This is particularly important for paralegals who work in open cubicle areas.

- When working on your computer, try to position the monitor so that others cannot read the screen, especially when you need to leave your desk. Computers have programs that automatically make the screen go dark or that add a design graphic after a designated period of time when there is no typing. The screen then reappears when you continue typing. Be sure that this screen saver program is installed on your computer.

- Use a shredding machine when throwing away papers containing confidential information.

- Extra caution is needed when deleting files from a computer. Using the delete key or button may not be enough. A file may be deleted from the computer directories (and from the computer trash bin), but still be present on your hard drive. Find out what steps the office takes (or should take) to delete files *permanently*.

metadata Data about data. Data about a computer document that are hidden within the document itself, e.g., earlier versions of the document.

- Avoid sending inappropriate **metadata**. When you send someone a document online (e.g., a memo created by Microsoft Word that you send as an attachment to an e-mail message), you are sending more than the data that will be read on the screen when the document is opened. Digital documents also contain metadata, which are data about data. They could consist of hidden information about the document such as the text or language you used in earlier drafts of the document or a list of the strengths and weaknesses of your client's position. It may be helpful for you to be able to read these earlier drafts, but it is unlikely you would want the recipients of the document to be able to read them. Yet they can read them if they know how to locate the metadata in what you send. Hence, before you send a document online, you need to find out how the software you used to create it will let you erase the document's metadata. The metadata might contain confidential information. (For more guidance on this topic, type "removing metadata" in Google or any search engine.)

- Standard e-mail messages on the Internet are considered sufficiently secure; it is not a violation of confidentiality to send client information by e-mail. The messages do not have to be **encrypted**. Clients, however, should be warned that e-mail communication is not foolproof. Furthermore, when highly sensitive information must be given to clients, they should be asked to state their preferred method of communication. Confidential information should never be sent through open formats such as bulletin boards and listservs because strangers are easily able to read what is sent over them. We will examine these Internet programs in greater detail in chapter 13.

- Find out if anyone other than the client has access to the client's e-mail. If others have such access and read messages to and from the law firm, the attorney-client privilege might be considered waived.

- E-mail messages are sometimes sent to the wrong persons. To put unintended recipients on notice that the mistake does not mean that the message is no longer confidential, law firms routinely include notices at the bottom of every e-mail message, such as the following:

  > This message is for the intended individual or entity and may contain information that is privileged. If the reader of this message is not the intended recipient, you are hereby notified that any copying, forwarding, or other dissemination of this message is strictly prohibited. If you have received this communication in error, please notify the sender immediately by e-mail or telephone, and delete the original message immediately.

- Follow the three-check rule when sending something electronically. Fax machines and computers often store thousands of phone numbers and e-mail addresses to make it easy for you to find an address when you want to send something. The downside of this convenience is that it is very easy to send something to the wrong person. Hence, before you hit the "send" button, look at the phone number or address you have selected or typed and slowly repeat it to yourself three times.

- When using vendors such as outsider printers (e.g., a company that prints appellate briefs) and copying services, make sure that they sign confidentiality agreements stating that they will not disclose the contents of any of the documents on which they will be working.

- Use a stamp marked *privileged* on documents that contain confidential information.

- When transporting file folders or boxes containing case files (e.g., to and from the courthouse), client names should not be visible on the outside of the folder or box.

- If you have permission to use writing samples from a prior job when looking for a new position, be sure you have omitted—**redacted**—any client names or other confidential information in the samples. And during a job interview, never discuss confidential information about prior cases. It would be very unprofessional to do so. Later, when we cover conflict of interest, we will examine the need to provide a prospective employer with a list of names of parties in cases you have worked on in prior jobs. This must be done with great caution, as we will see.

- One of the most dramatic legal stories of the twentieth century was the tobacco litigation of the 1990s. The cases led to billions of dollars in settlements, judgments, and attorney fees. The litigation is still going on today. A critical event in this drama was a breach of confidentiality by a paralegal. Merrell Williams was a paralegal who once worked at Wyatt, Tarrant & Combs, the largest law firm in Kentucky. The firm represented Brown & Williamson (B&W), maker of Kool and Viceroy. As a $9-an-hour paralegal, Williams was assigned to work on the numerous documents involved in the litigation. The task overwhelmed him. "He was sickened by what he read, as document after document showed the lengths to which the tobacco company executives had gone to cover-up the risks of smoking."[19] He secretly photocopied and distributed confidential internal memos, letters, and other documents exchanged by the law firm and its client. The documents demonstrated that the tobacco manufacturer knew about the danger of smoking but tried to cover it up. The news media made extensive use of this material. No one doubted that Williams had produced the "smoking gun" against the tobacco industry. Here is how a *Los Angeles Times* article described the impact of what Williams had done:

  > Big tobacco is known as a formidable legal adversary, skilled and even ruthless in the courtroom. Yet the industry is being undone by its former secrets. . . . Disclosure of documents [containing these secrets], many dating back forty years, has done enormous damage, outraging citizens and forcing once-helpful politicians to climb on the anti-tobacco bandwagon. . . . The ground shifted in 1994, when an obscure paralegal, who had secretly stolen thousands of pages of documents from a [law firm representing] B&W, leaked the purloined papers to

encrypted Converted into a code that renders it incomprehensible until it is reconverted to a readable format by an authorized recipient.

redact To edit or prepare a document for publication or release, often by deleting, altering, or blocking out text that you do not want disclosed.

Congress and the media. The documents were an instant sensation. In one 1963 memo, for example, the [tobacco] company's former general counsel declared, "We are, then, in the business of selling nicotine, an addictive drug.". . . Now the blood was in the water, and so were the sharks. For 1994 also marked the formation of a powerful alliance of product liability lawyers and state attorneys general, who began filing immense new claims against the industry.[20]

Wyatt, Tarrant & Combs obtained an injunction against Merrell Williams (no longer an "obscure paralegal") to prevent him from continuing to reveal what he learned at the firm. The firm says, "Williams broke his employment contract which requires confidentiality, and stole photocopies of documents from the law office." An ex-smoker himself, Williams has undergone quadruple bypass surgery and has "threatened to seek damages for injuries allegedly caused by smoking and by his exposure during the course of his employment to information that had induced psychological suffering." *Brown & Williamson Tobacco Corp. v. Williams*, 62 F. 3d 408, 411 (D.C. Cir. 1995).

This remarkable saga raises some critical issues. Clearly, Williams violated client confidentiality. Indeed, it is difficult to think of a violation that has had a greater impact. Yet was his violation justified on moral grounds? Tobacco causes the death of thousands every year in this country and hundreds of thousands around the world. Until Williams committed his act, the tobacco industry was all but invulnerable in the legislatures and in the courts of this country. The disclosure of the documents turned the tide. Was Williams a hero or a common thief? Of course, few paralegals during a job interview will tell an interviewer that Williams is one of their heroes. Such an acknowledgment would probably frighten off any potential employer. Furthermore, the Williams case is complicated by allegations that the attorney to whom Williams gave the documents provided Williams with a home, cars, and cash, either outright or as loans. This raised the further ethical and legal issue of whether stolen evidence was being paid for and received. Nevertheless, the question remains: was Merrell Williams engaged in an act of civil disobedience for which anyone who cares about public health should be grateful?

11. CONFLICT OF INTEREST

An attorney should avoid a conflict of interest with his or her client

conflict of interest Divided loyalty that actually or potentially harms someone who is owed undivided loyalty.

Three words strike dread in the heart of a practicing attorney: **conflict of interest**. Why? Because if it exists, it can lead to the disqualification of the attorney (and his or her entire law firm) from representing the particular client with whom the conflict exists—even if the attorney is in the middle of the representation of this client! A conflict of interest means serving two masters. More precisely, it is divided loyalty that actually or potentially harms a person even though you owe that person undivided loyalty. The conflict does not have to lead to actual harm; all that is needed is the *potential* for harm or disadvantage.

Conflicts of interest are not limited to law. They can exist in many settings:

> **Example:** Bill Davenport is a salesman who does part-time work selling the same type of product manufactured by two competing companies.

Davenport has a conflict of interest. How can he serve two masters with the same loyalty? Normally, a company expects the undivided loyalty of people who work for it. How can Davenport apportion his customers between the two companies? There is an obvious danger that he will favor one over the other. The fact that he may try to be fair in his treatment of both companies does not eliminate the conflict of interest. A *potential* certainly exists that one of the companies will be disadvantaged. It may be that both companies are aware of the problem and are not worried. Indeed, both may be thrilled by the profits he generates for them. This does not mean that there is no conflict of interest; it simply means that the affected parties have consented to take the risks involved in the conflict.

Let's look at another example of how widespread these conflicts can be:

> **Example:** Frank Jones is the head of the personnel department of a large company. Ten people apply for a job, one of whom is Frank's cousin.

Frank has a conflict of interest. He has loyalty to his company (pressuring him to hire the best person for the job) and a loyalty to his cousin (pressuring him to help a relative). There is a potential that the company will be disadvantaged because Frank's cousin may not be the best qualified for the job. The conflict exists even if the cousin *is* the best qualified, and even if Frank does *not* hire his cousin for the job, and even if the company *knows* about the relationship but still wants

EXHIBIT 5.6	Conflicts of Interest: Jeopardizing an Attorney's Undivided Loyalty

Here are examples of conflicts of interest in the practice of law. Later in the section, we will discuss the consequences of such conflicts. Every conflict does not necessarily lead to disqualification.

Conflicting Commitment to Win

Example: Smith is suing Jones for negligence. Paul Kiley, Esq. represents both Smith and Jones in the case.

Nature of the Conflict: Kiley must be zealous in representing Smith; he must also be zealous in representing Jones. But how can he zealously argue that Smith should win against Jones and simultaneously argue—zealously—that Jones should win against Smith?

Conflicting Use of Confidential Information (same law firm)

Example: Peterson is suing Davis for breach of warranty. Mary Adams, Esq. represents Peterson. Peterson wins. (Case #1) A year later, Adams, at the same law firm, represents Davis in a case against Peterson for libel. (Case #2)

Nature of the Conflict: In Case #1, Adams learned confidential information about Peterson, e.g., his real financial worth. In Case #2, Adams could use this information against Peterson while representing Davis.

Conflicting Use of Confidential Information (different law firms)

Example: Parker is suing Dower for trespass. Sam Peabody, Esq. represents Parker. Parker wins. (Case #1) A year later, Peabody goes to work for a different law firm. At the new firm, he represents Dower, who is suing Parker for battery. (Case #2)

Nature of the Conflict: In Case #1, Peabody learned confidential information about Parker, e.g., Parker has been sued before by others. In Case #2, Peabody could use this information against Parker while representing Dower.

Conflicting Family Relationship

Example: Bryson is suing Meffert for breach of contract. Helen Yanke, Esq. represents Bryson. Meffert is represented by Harrison, who is Yanke's brother-in-law.

Nature of the Conflict: Yanke must be zealous in representing Bryson, but she also does not want to alienate her husband's brother—Harrison.

Conflicting Financial Interest

Example: Pellson is suing Dooley for conversion. Kevin Sanchez, Esq. represents Pellson. Sanchez owns stock in the shipping company that Dooley founded and still controls.

Nature of the Conflict: Sanchez must be zealous in representing Pellson, but he also does not want the litigation against Dooley to jeopardize his (Sanchez's) investment in Dooley's company. For example, a big award to Pellson might force Dooley to shut down the shipping company.

Conflicting Personal Interest

Example: Philips is suing Dawson for invasion of privacy. Charlene Pace, Esq. represents Philips. Pace becomes romantically involved with Philips (or with Dawson).

Nature of the Conflict: Pace must be zealous in representing Philips, but her interest in preserving and perhaps furthering her emotional life may not be what's best for her romantic partner.

Frank to make the hiring decision. For conflict of interest to exist, all you need is the potential for harm or disadvantage due to *divided loyalties;* you do not have to show that harm or disadvantage actually resulted.

In legal settings, conflict of interest is a major concern. Exhibit 5.6 provides examples of some of the reasons why. To understand these and related examples, the following topics will be covered:

    a. Business transactions with a client
    b. Loans to a client
    c. Gifts from a client
    d. Sex with a client
    e. Personal bias
    f. Multiple representation
    g. Former client/present adversary
    h. Law firm disqualification
    i. Switching jobs and the "Chinese wall"
    j. Conflicts checks

As we examine each of these topics, one of our central concerns will be whether the independence of the attorney's professional judgment is compromised in any way because of conflicting interests.

a. Business Transactions with a Client

Attorneys sell professional legal advice and representation. When they go beyond such services and enter a business transaction with the client, a conflict of interest can arise.

> **Example:** Janet Bruno, Esq. is Len Oliver's attorney. Oliver owns an auto repair business for which Bruno has done legal work. Oliver sells Bruno a 30 percent interest in the repair business. Bruno continues as Oliver's attorney.

Serious conflict-of-interest problems may exist here. Assume that the business runs into difficulties and Oliver considers bankruptcy. He goes to Bruno for legal advice on bankruptcy law. Bruno has dual concerns: to give Oliver competent legal advice and to protect *her own* 30 percent interest in the business. Bankruptcy may be good for Oliver but disastrous for Bruno's investment. How can an attorney give a client independent professional advice when the advice may go against the attorney's own interest? Bruno's concern for her investment creates the potential that Oliver will be placed at a disadvantage. Divided loyalties exist.

This is not to say, however, that it is always unethical for an attorney to enter a business transaction with a client. If certain strict conditions are met, it can be proper.

An attorney can enter a business transaction with a client if:

(i) the terms of the business transaction are fair and reasonable to the client and are fully disclosed to the client in understandable language in writing, and

(ii) the client is given reasonable opportunity to seek advice on the transaction from another attorney who is not involved with the transaction or the parties, and

(iii) the client consents to the business transaction in writing. Model Rule 1.8(a)

In our example, Oliver must be given the chance to consult with an attorney other than Bruno on letting Bruno buy a 30 percent interest in the business. Bruno would have to give Oliver a clear, written explanation of their business relationship. And the relationship must be fair and reasonable to Oliver.

In the 1990s, many start-up companies, particularly dot-com businesses, offered attorneys stock for legal services in lieu of or in addition to a cash fee. This practice is ethical as long as the requirements we have discussed are met.

b. Loans to a Client

An attorney, like all service providers, wants to be paid. Often a client does not have the resources to pay until *after* the case is over.

> **Example:** Harry Maxell, Esq. is Bob Smith's attorney in a negligence action in which Smith is seeking damages for serious injuries caused by the defendant. Since the accident, Smith has been out of work and on public assistance. While the case is pending, Maxell agrees to lend Smith living expenses and court-filing fees.

A debtor-creditor relationship now exists between Smith and Maxell in addition to their attorney-client relationship. The loan covering *living expenses* creates a conflict of interest. Suppose that the defendant in the negligence case makes an offer to settle the case with Smith. Should he accept the offer? There is a danger that Maxell's advice on the offer will be colored by the fact that he has a financial interest in Smith—he wants to have his loan repaid. The amount of the offer to settle may not be enough to cover the loan. Should he advise Smith to accept the offer? Accepting the offer may be in Smith's interest but not in Maxell's own interest. Such divided loyalty is an unethical conflict of interest. Model Rule 1.8(e).

The loan covering *litigation expenses,* such as filing fees and other court costs, is treated differently. Such loans can be ethical. In our example, Maxell's loan to cover the cost of the filing fees is proper.

c. Gifts from a Client

Clients sometimes make gifts to their attorneys or to the spouse or relative of their attorneys. Such gifts rarely create ethical problems except when a document must be prepared to complete the gift.

> **Example:** William Stanton, Esq. has been the family attorney of the Tarkinton family for years. At Christmas, Mrs. Tarkinton gives Stanton a television set and tells him to change her will so that Stanton's ten-year-old daughter would receive funds for a college education.

If a document is needed to carry out the gift, it is unethical for the attorney to prepare that document. Its preparation would create a conflict of interest. In our example, the gift of money for college involves a document—Mrs. Tarkinton's will. Note the conflict. It would be in Mrs. Tarkinton's interest to have the will written so that a set or maximum sum is identified for this gift as well as a cutoff date for its use. Stanton would probably want the will drafted so that there is no maximum amount stated and no cutoff date. One day his daughter may want to go to graduate school. If the language of the will is vague (and no time limits are inserted), an argument could be made that the gift covers both undergraduate and graduate work. Other questions could arise as well, e.g., does the gift cover room and board at college, and what if the daughter does not go to college until after she marries and raises her own children? It is in Stanton's interest to draft the will to benefit his daughter under all these contingencies. This may not be in Mrs. Tarkinton's interest.

Because of this conflict, an attorney cannot prepare a document such as a will, trust, or contract that results in any substantial gift from a client to the attorney or to the attorney's children, spouse, parents, or siblings. If a client wants to make such a gift, *another* attorney who is not part of the same law firm must prepare the document. There is, however, one exception. If the client-donor is *related* to the person receiving the gift, the attorney can prepare the document. Model Rule 1.8(c).

There does not appear to be any ethical problem in taking the gift of the television set from Mrs. Tarkinton. No documents are involved.

Paralegal Perspective:

- Can a paralegal accept a gift from a client, e.g., a Christmas present, a trip, or other bonus from a client who just won a big judgment? First of all, never consider accepting gifts from clients unless your supervising attorney approves. Considerations of which you are unaware may make the gift inappropriate. Suppose, however, it is approved, but the gift involves the preparation of a document, which the attorney prepares. Though technically not the same as the attorney preparing the document for a gift to his or her spouse or children, the similarities certainly create an appearance of impropriety. The attorney will probably want to prepare the document to achieve the maximum advantage for his or her employee. This may not be in the best interest of the client—the giver of the gift.

d. Sex with a Client

One of the more dramatic examples of a conflict of interest is the attorney who develops a romantic relationship with a current client, particularly a sexual relationship. Clients often come to an attorney when they are most vulnerable. Under such circumstances, it is unconscionable for the attorney to take advantage of this vulnerability. An attorney with a physical or emotional interest in a client will be looking for ways to increase that interest and to inspire a reciprocal interest from the client. Needless to say, this may not be what the client needs. But the attorney's own need could well cloud his or her ability to put the client's welfare first. The only way to maintain professional independence is for attorneys—and their paralegals and other employees as well—to avoid these kinds of relationships with current clients. When the case is over and they cease being clients, such relationships are less likely to constitute a conflict of interest.

The ABA prohibits sexual relations between attorney and client, even if consensual, unless the sexual relationship began before the attorney-client relationship began. Model Rule 1.8(j). Surprisingly, however, only a few states specifically mention this subject in their codes of ethics. And those that do are hesitant to impose prohibitions. In Rule 4–8.4 of the Florida code, for example, sexual conduct is prohibited only if it can be shown that the conduct "exploits the lawyer-client relationship." In Rule 3–120 of the California code, a member of the bar shall not:

(B) (1) Require or demand sexual relations with a client incident to or as a condition of any professional representation; or

(2) Employ coercion, intimidation, or undue influence in entering into sexual relations with a client; or

(3) Continue representation of a client with whom the member has sexual relations if such sexual relations cause the member to perform legal services incompetently. . . .

(C) Paragraph (B) shall not apply to . . . ongoing consensual sexual relationships which predate the initiation of the lawyer-client relationship.

e. Personal Bias

Do you think the attorneys in the following cases have a conflict of interest?

- A homosexual attorney represents a parent seeking to deny custody to the other parent because the latter is gay.

- An attorney who believes abortion is immoral works on a case where the client is Planned Parenthood.
- An attorney whose father was murdered ten years ago represents a client charged with murdering his wife.
- An attorney who is opposed to the death penalty is the prosecutor on a case where the state has asked for the death penalty.

bias Prejudice for or against something or someone. An inclination or tendency to think and to act in a certain way. A danger of prejudgment.

disinterested Not working for one side or the other in a controversy; not deriving benefit if one side of a dispute wins or loses; objective.

These attorneys have a prejudice or **bias**, which is an inclination or tendency to think and to act in a certain way. This inclination or tendency creates a danger of prejudgment. The opposite of a biased person is an objective or **disinterested** person.

In our adversary system, as indicated earlier, clients are entitled to vigorous representation within the bounds of law and ethics. If an attorney or paralegal has strong personal feelings that go against what a client is trying to accomplish, there is a likelihood—not a guarantee—that the feelings will interfere with the ability to provide vigorous representation. If there is interference, it is unethical to continue. In New York State, attorneys are cautioned that they "should decline employment if the intensity of personal feelings . . . may impair effective representation of a prospective client."[21] (We will return to the topic of bias in chapter 8 on interviewing.)

f. Multiple Representation

Rarely can a client receive independent professional counsel and vigorous representation in a case of **multiple representation** (also referred to as *common representation*), where the same attorney represents both sides in a dispute.

multiple representation Representing more than one side in a legal matter or controversy.

> **Example:** Tom and Henry have an automobile accident. Tom wants to sue Henry for negligence. Both Tom and Henry ask Mary Franklin, Esq. to represent them in the dispute.

Franklin has a conflict of interest. How can she give her undivided loyalty to both sides? Tom needs to prove that Henry was negligent; Henry needs to prove that he was not negligent, and perhaps that Tom was negligent himself. How can Franklin vigorously argue that Henry was negligent and at the same time vigorously argue that Henry was not negligent? How can she act independently for two different people who are at odds with each other? Since Tom and Henry have **adverse interests**, she cannot give each her independent professional judgment. (Adverse interests are simply opposing purposes or claims.) The difficulty is not solved by Franklin's commitment to be fair and objective in giving her advice to the parties. Her role as attorney is to be a partisan advocate for the client. It is impossible for Franklin to play this role for two clients engaged in a dispute where they have adverse interests. An obvious conflict of interest would exist. In *every* state, it would be unethical for Franklin to represent Tom and Henry in this case.

adverse interests Opposing purposes or claims.

Furthermore, client consent would *not* be a defense to the charge of unethical conduct. Even if Tom and Henry agree to allow Franklin to represent both of them, it would be unethical for her to do so. The presence of adverse interests between the parties makes it unethical for an attorney to represent both sides with or without their consent.

Suppose, however, that the two sides do *not* have adverse interests. Certain kinds of cases must go before a court even though the parties are in agreement about everything.

> **Example:** Jim and Mary Smith have been married for two months. They are now separated and both want a divorce. There are no children and no marital assets to divide. Neither wants nor is entitled to alimony from the other. George Davidson, Esq. is an attorney that Jim and Mary know and trust. They decide to ask Davidson to represent both of them in the divorce.

Can Davidson ethically represent both sides here? A few states *will* allow him to do so, on the theory that there is not much of a conflict between the parties. Jim and Mary want the divorce, there is no custody battle, alimony is not an issue, and there is no property to fight over. All they need is a court to decree that their marriage is legally over. Hence the potential for harm caused by multiple representation in such a case is almost nonexistent. Other states, however, disagree. They frown on multiple representation in so-called friendly divorces of this kind.

There is no absolute ban on all multiple representation in the Model Rules, although such representation is certainly discouraged:

If two persons have adverse interests, it would be a conflict of interest for an attorney to represent both of them unless four conditions are met. First, the attorney must reasonably believe that he or she will be able to provide competent and diligent representation to each client. Second, the multiple representation is not prohibited by law. Third, the multiple representation does not involve the assertion of a claim by one client against another client in the same litigation. Fourth, each client gives informed consent in writing. Model Rule 1.7

In the Smith example, the conditions can probably be met. Such a divorce is little more than a paper procedure; there is no real dispute between the parties. They are not claiming anything against each other. Hence Davidson would be reasonable in believing that he can provide competent and diligent representation to Jim and to Mary. Davidson can represent both of them so long as there is no explicit law in the state prohibiting such representation and so long as Jim and Mary consent to the multiple representation after Davidson explains what risks might be involved.

Nevertheless, attorneys are urged *not* to engage in multiple representation even if it is ethically proper to do so. The case may have been "friendly" at the outset, but years later, when everything turns sour, one of the parties inevitably attacks the attorney for having had a conflict of interest. Cautious attorneys *always* avoid multiple representation.

g. Former Client/Present Adversary

As indicated earlier, clients are encouraged to be very open with their attorney. To be able to evaluate the legal implications of a case, the attorney needs to know favorable and unfavorable information about the client. The more trust that exists between them, the more frank the client will usually be. Assume that such a relationship exists and that the case is eventually resolved. Months later another legal dispute arises between the same parties, but this time the attorney represents the other side!

> **Example:** Helen Kline, Esq. represented Paul Andrews in his breach-of-contract suit against Richard Morelli, a truck distributor. (Morelli was represented by J. L. Quint, Esq.) Andrews claimed that Morelli failed to deliver five trucks that Andrews ordered. A court ruled in favor of Morelli. Now, a year later, Andrews wants to sue Morelli for slander. After accidentally meeting at a conference, they started discussing the truck suit. Morelli allegedly called Andrews a liar and a thief. In the slander suit, Andrews hires Michael Manna, Esq. to represent him. Morelli hires Helen Kline, Esq.

A former client is now an adversary. Kline once represented Andrews; she is now representing a client (Morelli) who is an adversary of Andrews. Is it ethical for Kline to switch sides in this way? In some circumstances, the switch is unethical without the **informed consent** of the former client. It depends on how closely related the two cases are. Model Rule 1.9(a). Consent is needed (a) *when the second case is the same as the first one or when the two are substantially related* and (b) *when the former client and the present client have materially adverse interests in the current case.* The slander suit is substantially related to the breach-of-contract suit, since they both grew out of the original truck incident. Furthermore, in the current slander case, Andrews and Morelli clearly have materially adverse interests, meaning competing positions or claims that are significant.

If the cases are the same or are substantially related, the likelihood is strong that the attorney will use information learned in the first case to the detriment of the former client in the second case. Kline undoubtedly found out a good deal about Andrews when she represented him in the breach-of-contract case. She would now be in a position to use that information *against* him while representing Morelli in the slander case.

Kline had a **duty of loyalty** when she represented Andrews. This duty does not end once the case is over and the attorney fees are paid. The duty continues if the same case arises again or if a substantially related case arises later—even if the attorney no longer represents the client. A conflict of interest exists when Kline subsequently acquires a new client who goes against Andrews in the same case or in a substantially related case. Her duty of undivided loyalty to the second client would clash with her *continuing* duty of undivided loyalty to the former client in the original case.

Suppose, however, that an attorney *can* take the second case against a former client because the second case is totally unrelated to the first. There is still an ethical duty to refrain from using any information relating to the representation in the first case to the disadvantage of the former client in the second case. There is no ethical ban on taking the case, but if the office has any information relating to the first case, that information cannot be used against the former client in the second case. Although this duty might exist, it is not easy to enforce. Think of how difficult

informed consent Agreement to let something happen after obtaining a reasonable explanation of the benefits and risks involved.

duty of loyalty The obligation to protect the interests of a client without having a similar obligation to anyone else that would present an actual or potential conflict.

it might be to prove that the attorney in the second case used information obtained solely from the first case.

h. Law Firm Disqualification

If an attorney is disqualified from representing a client because of a conflict of interest, every attorney in the *same law firm* is also disqualified unless the client being protected by this rule consents to the representation.

> **Example:** Two years ago, John Farrell, Esq. of the law firm of Smith & Smith represented the stepfather in a custody dispute with the child's grandmother who represented herself in the case. The stepfather won the case, but the grandmother was awarded limited visitation rights. The grandmother now wants to sue the stepfather for failure to abide by the visitation order. John Farrell no longer represents the stepfather. The grandmother asks John Farrell to represent her. He declines because of a conflict of interest but sends her to his law partner, Diane Williams, Esq., down the corridor at Smith & Smith.

The *stepfather* would have to consent to the representation of the grandmother by Williams. There would certainly be a conflict of interest if John Farrell tried to represent the grandmother against the stepfather. The custody dispute and the visitation dispute are substantially related. Once one attorney in a firm is disqualified because of a conflict of interest, every other attorney in that firm is also disqualified. This is known as **imputed disqualification** or vicarious disqualification. The entire firm is treated as one attorney. The disqualification of any one **tainted** attorney in the office contaminates the entire firm. Farrell's partner (Williams) is disqualified because Farrell, the tainted attorney, would be disqualified. Model Rule 1.10. Someone is tainted (also called infected) if he or she brings a conflict of interest to a law office, which thereby becomes contaminated.

i. Switching Jobs and the "Chinese Wall"

Finally, we need to consider the conflict-of-interest problems that can arise from changing jobs. We just saw that there can be an imputed disqualification of an entire law firm because one of the attorneys in the firm has a conflict of interest with a client. If that attorney now goes to work for a *new* firm, can there be an imputed disqualification of the new firm because of the same conflict of interest? Yes.

> **Example:** Kevin Carlson, Esq. works at Darby & Darby. He represents Ajax, Inc., in its contract suit against World Systems, Inc. The latter is represented by Polk, Young & West. While the suit is still underway, Carlson quits his job at Darby & Darby and takes a job at Polk, Young & West. Ajax obtains new counsel in its suit against World.

While Carlson was at Darby & Darby, he obviously acquired confidential information about Ajax. Clearly, he cannot now represent World Systems in the contract litigation against Ajax. Blatant side-switching of this kind is highly unethical. But what about other attorneys at Polk, Young & West? Is the *entire* firm contaminated and hence disqualified from continuing to represent World Systems because of the hiring of Carlson? If other attorneys at Polk, Young & West are allowed to continue representing World Systems against Ajax, there would be pressures on Carlson to tell these attorneys what he knows about Ajax. Must Polk, Young & West, therefore, withdraw from the case?

The same question can be asked about **tainted paralegals** and other nonattorney employees who switch jobs:

> **Example:** Ted Warren is a paralegal who works for Mary Winter, Esq. Winter represents Apple in the case of Apple v. IBM. Ted has substantial paralegal responsibilities on this case. While the case is still going on, Ted switches jobs. He goes to work for Quinton & Oran, which represents IBM in the litigation with Apple.

Ted is tainted. He brings a conflict of interest to the firm of Quinton & Oran. While Ted worked for Mary Winter, he obviously acquired confidential information about Apple. There are pressures on him to tell the attorneys at Quinton & Oran what he knows about Apple so that they can use the information to the advantage of their client, IBM, in the litigation against Apple. Is the entire firm of Quinton & Oran, therefore, contaminated so that it must now withdraw from the case?

There are two main ways that contaminated law offices *try* to avoid imputed disqualification due to tainted attorneys or tainted paralegals whose job switching creates a conflict of interest: consent and screening.

imputed disqualification All attorneys in the same firm are ineligible to represent a client because one of the attorneys or other employees in the firm has a conflict of interest with that client.

tainted Having or causing a conflict of interest.

tainted paralegal A paralegal who brings a conflict of interest to a law office because of the paralegal's prior work at another law office.

Consent   The cleanest way a contaminated law office can avoid imputed disqualification is to try to obtain the consent of the party who has the most to lose—the party whose confidentiality is in jeopardy. In most cases, the consent of this person will avoid disqualification.

> **In our example of the tainted attorney:** Kevin Carlson, Esq. once represented Ajax at Darby & Darby in the litigation against World Systems. Carlson now works for Polk, Young & West, which represents World Systems. Ajax could be asked to consent to the continued representation of World Systems by Polk, Young & West even though Carlson now works for Polk, Young & West.
>
> **In our example of the tainted paralegal:** Ted Warren once worked for the law office of Mary Winter, Esq. who represents Apple in the litigation against IBM. Ted now works for Quinton & Oran, which represents IBM. Apple could be asked to consent to the continued representation of IBM by Quinton & Oran even though Ted now works for Quinton & Oran.

It is unlikely that clients will give their consent in such situations. Their current attorney will probably advise them that the risks are too great that the tainted employee will share (or has already shared) confidential information with the new employer. This is true even if the new employer swears that no such information was shared and abides by the requirement that it will screen the tainted employee (see discussion of screening and the Chinese Wall, below) from the ongoing litigation.

Screening   The contaminated law office will often try to avoid imputed disqualification by screening the tainted employee from the case in question. As we will see, however, this attempt is generally more successful if the tainted employees are paralegals than if they are attorneys. The screening is known as a **Chinese Wall** (sometimes called an *ethical wall* or a *cone of silence*) that is built around the tainted employee who brought the conflict of interest into the office. He or she becomes the **quarantined** employee due to a rigid isolation from anything to do with the case that prompted the conflict. The components of the Chinese Wall are outlined in Exhibit 5.7.

Chinese Wall Steps taken to prevent a tainted employee (e.g., attorney or paralegal) from having any contact with the case of a particular client in the office because the employee has created a conflict of interest between that client and the office; a tainted employee shielded by a Chinese Wall becomes a *quarantined* employee.

quarantined Isolated; kept away from information that would disqualify the firm.

EXHIBIT 5.7	**Components of a Chinese Wall**

The following are the most effective guidelines a law office can follow to screen a tainted employee (e.g., attorney, paralegal, investigator, or secretary) who brings a conflict of interest to the office. The goal is to avoid imputed disqualification by isolating the employee from the case in which he or she has the conflict of interest.

1. The screening begins as soon as the tainted employee arrives at the office.
2. At this time, or soon thereafter, the office notifies the opposing party's attorney that the tainted employee has been hired and that comprehensive screening has begun.
3. The office notifies its own client of the screening and the reason for it.
4. The tainted employee signs a statement promising not to discuss what he or she knows about the case with anyone in the office.
5. Those working on the case in the office promise not to discuss it with, or in the presence of, the tainted employee.
6. A written notice is sent to everyone in the office that identifies the tainted employee and the client's case file in question. All employees are told that they are not to discuss any aspect of the case with the tainted employee.
7. The tainted employee will not be assigned to work with any untainted attorney, paralegal, secretary, or other staff member who is handling the case in question.
8. Others not working on the case in the office are told that if they learn anything about the case, they must not discuss it with the tainted employee.
9. The receptionist and mail handlers are instructed not to forward anything about the case to the tainted employee.
10. The tainted employee works in an area that is physically segregated from work on the case in the office. This area is designed to avoid inadvertent access to the case file.
11. The file in the case is locked in cabinets or other storage facilities so that the tainted employee will have no access to the file.
12. Colored labels or "flags" are placed on each document in the file to indicate it is off limits to the tainted employee. For example, a sticker might say, "ACCESS RESTRICTED—DO NOT DISCUSS THIS CASE WITH EMPLOYEE X."
13. If any office files are located on a central computer system to which everyone has access, either the file in question is removed and placed in a separate database to which the tainted employee does not have access and/or the tainted employee is not given the password that grants a user access to the restricted file in the central system.
14. The tainted employee will not directly earn any profit from, participate in the fees of, or obtain any other financial gain from the case.
15. The firm documents all of the above steps that are taken. This documentation will become evidence, if ever needed, to rebut the presumption that the tainted employee had any communication or other involvement with anyone working on the case at the firm.

We said that consent is a clear way to avoid imputed disqualification. What about screening? Can it avoid disqualification if consent cannot be obtained? In this discussion, we are assuming that the tainted employee has not already communicated confidential information to the new employer. If this has happened, screening will not prevent disqualification. Hence, in our examples, if Kevin Carlson tells attorneys at Polk, Young & West anything significant he knows about Ajax, the Polk firm will be disqualified from continuing to represent World Systems. If Ted Warren tells attorneys at Quinton & Oran anything significant he knows about Apple, the Quinton firm will be disqualified from continuing to represent IBM. Screening will never prevent disqualification if the damage has already been done by improper disclosures from the tainted employee. The purpose of the screening is to *prevent* such disclosures.

Suppose that there have been no disclosures. The office discovers that one of its employees is tainted. It then offers to quarantine this employee by building a Chinese Wall around him or her. Will this prevent disqualification in the absence of consent? Not all states answer this question in the same way, and the answer may differ if the tainted employee is an attorney as opposed to a paralegal or other nonattorney.

Tainted Attorneys   In some states, a Chinese Wall will *not* avoid imputed disqualification. These states doubt that the tainted attorney will be able to resist the pressure to disclose what he or she knows in spite of the screening mechanisms of the wall. "Whether the screen is breached will be virtually impossible to ascertain from outside the firm."[22]

Other states, however, do not automatically impose the extreme sanction of disqualification. These states consider three main factors in deciding whether to disqualify. First, how soon did the office erect the wall around the tainted attorney? Courts like to see the wall in place at the outset of the employment transfer. They are more suspicious if the wall was not built until the other side (i.e., the former employer of the tainted attorney) raised the conflict-of-interest objection. Second, how effective was the wall in preventing the tainted attorney from having contact with the case at the new firm? Courts like to see comprehensive screening devices that are scrupulously enforced. (See Exhibit 5.7.) And, third, how involved was the tainted attorney in the case while at the previous firm? If the involvement was relatively minor, the court is less likely to be concerned.

Tainted Paralegals   Courts are more sympathetic to tainted paralegals—so long as they have not actually revealed confidential information to their new employer and are effectively quarantined by a Chinese Wall. Here are some of the major developments in this area:

- In *Phoenix Founders, Inc. v. Marshall*, 887 S.W.2d 831 (Tex. 1994), a paralegal worked on a case at one firm and then switched jobs to work for opposing counsel on the same case. The court said that if a paralegal does any work on a case, there is a conclusive presumption that he or she obtained "confidences and secrets" about that case. There is also a presumption that the paralegal shared this information with her new firm, *but this is a* **rebuttable presumption;** it is not conclusive. The presumption can be rebutted by showing that the new firm took "sufficient precautions . . . to guard against any disclosure of confidences" through a Chinese Wall. At the new firm, "the newly-hired paralegal should be cautioned not to disclose any information relating to the representation of a client of the former employer. The paralegal should also be instructed not to work on any matter on which the paralegal worked during the prior employment, or regarding which the paralegal has information relating to the former employer's representation. Additionally, the firm should take other reasonable steps to ensure that the paralegal does not work in connection with matters on which the paralegal worked during the prior employment." In two circumstances, however, the *Phoenix Founders* case said that disqualification will always be required unless the former client consents to allow the paralegal to continue working at the new firm: "(1) when information relating to the representation of an adverse client has in fact been disclosed, or (2) when screening would be ineffective or the nonlawyer necessarily would be required to work on the other side of a matter that is the same as or substantially related to a matter on which the nonlawyer has previously worked." In effect, there will be disqualification if there is proof the paralegal made actual disclosures of confidential information to the new firm or if there is little chance the screening of the Chinese Wall would be effective.[23]

rebuttable presumption An inference of fact that can be overcome (rebutted) by sufficient contrary evidence.

- What's it like to work behind a Chinese Wall? Calling it a "deadly cone of silence," a Los Angeles paralegal described the experience of being quarantined this way: "I was a problem . . . . I was put behind an ethical wall, and could hardly walk anywhere in the firm without having to shut my eyes and ears or look the other direction."[24]
- Many paralegals change jobs frequently. The market for experienced paralegals is outstanding. Bar associations realize that an overly strict disqualification rule could severely hamper the job prospects for such paralegals. In Informal Opinion 88–1526, the American Bar Association said:

  > It is important that nonlawyer employees have as much mobility in employment opportunity as possible consistent with the protection of clients' interests. To so limit employment opportunities that some nonlawyers trained to work with law firms might be required to leave the careers for which they are trained would disserve clients as well as the legal profession. Accordingly, any restrictions on the nonlawyer's employment should be held to the minimum necessary to protect confidentiality of client information.

- Although such statements are comforting, the reality is that tainted paralegals are in a very vulnerable position. Many contaminated offices *terminate* the tainted paralegal who caused the contamination. Rather than take the risk that a Chinese Wall built around this paralegal will be judged too little and too late, the office will probably take the safer course and let the paralegal go.
- In one dramatic case, a contaminated paralegal caused a San Francisco law firm to be disqualified from representing nine clients in asbestos litigation involving millions of dollars. The sole reason for the disqualification was that the firm hired a paralegal who had once worked for a law firm that represented the opponents in the asbestos litigation. Soon after the controversy arose, the disqualified firm laid off the tainted paralegal who brought this conflict to the firm. He was devastated when he found out that he was being let go. "I was flabbergasted, totally flabbergasted."[25] He has not been able to find work since.[25] The case was widely reported throughout the legal community. A front-page story in the *Los Angeles Daily Journal* said that it "could force firms to conduct lengthy investigations of paralegals and other staffers before hiring them."[26]
- A court rule in one state provides as follows:

  > Rule 20–108. A lawyer is responsible to ensure that no personal, social or business interest or relationship of the paralegal impinges upon, or appears to impinge upon, the services rendered to the client. *Comment.* If a lawyer accepts a matter in which the paralegal may have a conflict of interest, the lawyer will exclude that paralegal from participation in any services performed in connection with that matter. Furthermore, the lawyer must specifically inform the client that a nonlawyer employee has a conflict of interest which, was it the lawyer's conflict, would prevent further representation of the client in connection with the matter. The nature of the conflict should be disclosed. The lawyer will caution the paralegal to inform the lawyer of any interest or association which might constitute or cause such a conflict, or which might give the appearance of constituting or causing such a conflict. In addition, no interest or loyalty of the paralegal may be permitted to interfere with the lawyer's independent exercise of professional judgment. (*West's New Mexico Rules Annotated*, State Court Rules, Rules Governing Paralegal Services.)

- One law firm makes the following statement to all its paralegals: "If you or a temporary legal assistant working under your supervision were formerly employed by opposing counsel, this could be the basis for a motion to disqualify" this law firm. "So also could personal relationships such as kinship with the opposing party or attorney or dating an attorney from another firm. Make your attorney aware of such connections."[27]
- Start compiling your own **career client list** as soon as you start working in a law office in any role (e.g., paralegal, secretary, or investigator) as a volunteer, employee, or independent contractor. The list should have five columns consisting of the names of all the parties involved in each case or matter, the name of the office, the names of the attorneys on both sides, the dates of your involvement, and a brief description of your role. See Exhibit 5.8. When you apply for a new job, your list will be relevant to whether the law firm will be

career client list A confidential list of every client and matter you worked on in any law office from the beginning of your legal career to the present time that can be used to help determine whether any of your future work might create a conflict of interest.

EXHIBIT 5.8	Career Client List

To help determine whether you might create a conflict of interest, keep a confidential list covering the following information for every law office in which you worked or volunteered from the beginning of your career to your current position:

Names of All Parties Involved	Office	Names of Attorneys (both sides)	Dates	Brief Description of Your Role

subject to disqualification if you are hired. You must be careful with the list, however. Do not attach it to your résumé and randomly send it around town! Until employment discussions have become serious, do not show it to the prospective employer. If you are unable to produce such a list, a conscientious office might refuse to hire you on that basis alone rather than take the risk of finding out later that your prior work created a conflict of interest that could have been identified when you were initially considered for employment.

■ Tainted by association? Assume that an attorney in the office is tainted and that the state allows screening to prevent disqualification. Paralegals who work closely with this attorney would probably have to be screened as well. It wouldn't make sense to prevent an attorney from having contact with a particular case but to allow his or her paralegal to have such contact. The paralegal, in effect, would become tainted by association.

■ Freelance or independent paralegals who work for more than one law office on a part-time basis are particularly vulnerable to conflict-of-interest charges. For example, in a large litigation involving many parties, two opposing attorneys might unknowingly use the same freelance paralegal to work on different aspects of the same case or might use two different employees of this freelance paralegal. Another example is the freelance paralegal who worked on an earlier case for a client and now works on a different but similar case in which that client is the opponent. Attorneys who use freelance or independent paralegals, therefore, must be careful. The attorney cannot simply turn over work and be available to answer questions. At a minimum, the attorney must make inquiries about this paralegal's prior client casework for other attorneys in order to determine whether there are any conflicts.[28]

j. Conflicts Checks

A prospective client walks in the door or someone makes a referral of a prospective client. How does the office determine whether any of its attorneys, paralegals, or other employees have a conflict of interest with this prospect? As indicated, a **conflicts check** must be undertaken. To perform this check, the office needs a comprehensive database containing information such as the following about every former and present client of the office:

conflicts check A determination of whether a conflict of interest exists that might disqualify a law firm from representing a client or from continuing the representation.

■ Names of clients (plus any aliases or earlier names before marriage)
■ Names of spouses of clients
■ Names of children of clients
■ Names of key employees of clients (including the chief executive officers and directors of corporate clients)
■ Names of major shareholders in companies in which the client has an interest
■ Names of parent and subsidiary corporations affiliated with the client, plus their chief executive officers and directors
■ Names of members of small associations the client controls or is a member of[29]

It is often an arduous job to find and check this information to determine whether any possible conflict exists. These data are often summarized in the conflicts section of the New File Worksheet that the office fills out when it begins working with a new client or with a new matter of a current client. (See the conflicts section on the New File Worksheet in Exhibit 14.5 in chapter 14.) Some offices have hired paralegals to go through the office's computer files to try to identify conflict problems that must be addressed by senior attorneys in the office. (These paralegals are sometimes called **conflicts specialists**, *conflicts analysts*, or *conflicts researchers*.) Unfortunately, however, many offices perform conflicts checks carelessly or not at all.

conflicts specialist A law firm employee, often a paralegal, who helps the firm determine whether a conflict of interest exists between prospective clients and current or former clients.

lateral hire An attorney, paralegal, or other employee who has been hired from another law firm.

Detailed conflicts information is also needed when the office is thinking about hiring a new attorney or paralegal from another office (called a **lateral hire**). To determine whether they might contaminate the office, the names of the parties in their prior casework must be checked against the office's current and prospective clients.

When a law office applies for malpractice insurance, the insurance carrier will often inquire about the system the office uses for conflicts checks. See Exhibit 5.9 for examples of questions asked by one of the major liability insurance companies. Note question 27 in the exhibit: "Has the firm acquired, merged with, or terminated a formal business relationship with another firm within the last three years?" If, for example, the ABC law firm merges with the XYZ law firm, the malpractice insurance company of the merged firm will want to know if a new group of tainted employees has been created because of the prior and current caseloads of the two firms. Finding out can be a huge undertaking because of the potentially thousands of cases on which the attorneys and paralegals of the two firms have worked or are working.

Some categories of information are sometimes difficult for the office to obtain. For example:

- Whether an employee in the office holds stock in the company of the adversary of a prospective client
- Whether a spouse, relative, or intimate friend of an employee in the office is employed by or holds stock in the company of the adversary of a prospective client
- Whether an employee in the office is related to or has had a romantic relationship with the adversary of a prospective client
- Whether an employee in the office is related to or has had a romantic relationship with anyone in the law office that represents the adversary of a prospective client

To discover this kind of information, the office usually must rely on its employees to come forward and reveal such connections.

Most litigation support software (see chapter 13) has conflicts-checking functions that enable a law firm to comb through the law firm's database(s) to find possible conflicts. See Exhibit 5.10 for an example.

EXHIBIT 5.9	**Questions on Conflict-of-Interest Avoidance on an Application for Malpractice Insurance by a Law Office**

ADMINISTRATIVE SYSTEMS AND PROCEDURES—CONFLICT OF INTEREST

	Yes	No
22. Do you have a written internal control system for maintaining client lists and identifying actual or potential conflicts of interest?	☐	☐
23. How does the firm maintain its conflict of interest avoidance system? ☐ Oral/memory ☐ Single index files ☐ Multiple index files ☐ Computer		
24. Have the firm members disclosed, in writing, all actual conflicts of interest and conflicts they reasonably believe may exist as a result of their role as director, officer, partner, employee or fiduciary of an entity or individual other than the applicant firm?	☐	☐
25. Do firm members disclose to their clients, in writing, all actual conflicts of interest and conflicts they reasonably believe may exist?	☐	☐
26. Upon disclosure of actual or potential conflicts, do firm members always obtain written consent to perform ongoing legal services?	☐	☐
27. Has the firm acquired, merged with or terminated a formal business relationship with another firm within the last three years?	☐	☐
28. Does the firm's conflict of interest avoidance system include attorney-client relationships established by predecessor firms, merged firms and acquired firms?	☐	☐

Source: The St. Paul Fire and Marine Insurance Company, Professional Liability Insurance Application for Lawyers.

| EXHIBIT 5.10 | Example of Conflicts Checking by Computer |

Reprinted with permission of ProLaw Software (www.prolaw.com).

12. COMMUNICATION WITH THE OTHER SIDE

If an opposing party is represented by an attorney, the permission of the party's attorney is needed to communicate with that party concerning the subject of the case. **Model Rule 4.2**

An unrepresented opposing party must not be misled into thinking that you are neutral or uninvolved in the case. The only advice you can give an unrepresented opposing party is to obtain his or her own attorney. **Model Rule 4.3**

anticontact rule An advocate should not contact an opposing party without permission of the latter's attorney; if the party is unrepresented, the advocate must not convey the impression that the advocate is disinterested.

overreaching Taking unfair advantage of another's naiveté or other vulnerability, especially by deceptive means.

ex parte communication Communication with the court in the absence of the attorney for the other side.

The **anticontact rule** requires an attorney to avoid communicating with an opposing party unless the latter's attorney consents. The ethical concern here is **overreaching**—taking unfair advantage of the other side.

> **Example:** Dan and Theresa Kline have just separated and are thinking about a divorce. Each claims the marital home. Theresa hires Thomas Farlington, Esq. to represent her. Farlington calls Dan to ask him if he would like to settle the case.

It is unethical for Farlington to contact Dan about the case if Farlington knows that Dan has his own attorney. Farlington must talk with Dan's attorney. Only the latter can give Farlington permission to communicate with Dan. If Dan does not have an attorney, Farlington can talk with Dan, but he must not allow Dan to be misled about Farlington's role. Farlington works for the other side; he is not *disinterested.* Dan must be made to understand this fact. The only advice Farlington can give Dan in such a situation is to obtain his own attorney.

A related communication rule is that an attorney should not communicate with the court in the absence of the attorney for the other side. Such **ex parte communications** are usually forbidden.

Paralegal Perspective:

- The ethical restrictions on communicating with the other side apply to the employees of an attorney as well as to the attorney. "The lawyer's obligation is to ensure that paralegals do not communicate directly with parties known to be represented by an attorney, without that attorney's consent, on the subject of such representation."[30] You must avoid improper communication with the other side. If the other side is a business or some other large organization, do not talk with anyone there unless your supervisor tells you that it is ethical to do so. Never call the other side and pretend you are someone else in order to obtain information.

- If your office allows you to talk with an opponent who is not represented by an attorney, you cannot give this person any advice other than the advice to secure his or her own attorney.

13. SOLICITATION

There are two main ways that attorneys seek to be hired by prospective clients:

a. *In-person, live telephone, or real-time electronic contact.* Solicitation of clients through such contact is unethical if the attorney's goal is to seek fees or other financial benefit (**"pecuniary** gain") unless the contact is with another attorney or someone with whom the attorney has a family, close personal, or prior professional relationship. Model Rule 7.3

b. *Written, recorded, or standard electronic contact.* Solicitation of clients through such contact is ethical unless (a) the attorney knows that the prospective client does not want to be solicited, (b) the solicitation involves coercion, duress, or harassment, or (c) the solicitation is untruthful or misleading. Model Rule 7.3

People in distress are sometimes so distraught that they are not in a position to evaluate their need for legal services. They should not be subjected to pressures from an attorney who shows up wanting to be hired, particularly if the attorney is not a relative, close friend, or has never represented them in the past. Such in-person **solicitation** of clients is unethical, if the attorney has a monetary or other financial goal such as generating fees.

> **Example:** Rachael Winters, Esq. stands outside the police station and gives a business card to any individual being arrested. The card says that Winters is an attorney specializing in criminal cases.

Winters is obviously looking for prospective clients. Doing so in this manner is referred to as **ambulance chasing,** which is a pejorative term for aggressively tracking down anyone who probably has a legal problem in order to drum up business. (An unkind member of Congress recently told an audience, "If you want to meet a trial lawyer, follow an ambulance."[31]) There is no indication that Winters is related to or is good friends with any of the people going into the police station or that she has any prior professional relationship with them (for example, they are *not* former clients). Winters appears to have one goal: finding a source of fees. Hence her conduct is unethical. Direct, in-person, or live telephone solicitation of clients in this way is not allowed. The same would be true if Winters contacted these individuals through **real-time** electronic communication such as in an Internet chat room. (See chapter 13 for a discussion of real-time communication.) The concern is that an attorney who contacts potentially vulnerable strangers in these ways may use undue pressure to sign them up as clients.

Undue pressure is less likely to occur if the solicitation is through the mail, a recorded telephone message, or a standard (non–real-time) electronic contact such as an e-mail message. This is true even if the recipients are known to need legal services.

> **Example:** An attorney obtains the names of homeowners facing foreclosure and sends them the following letter: "It has come to my attention that your home is being foreclosed. Federal law may allow you to stop your creditors and give you more time to pay. Call my office for legal help."

While critics claim that such solicitation constitutes "ambulance chasing by mail," the technique is ethical in most states as long as the recipients have not made known to the attorney that they do not want to be solicited; the solicitation does not involve coercion, duress, or harassment; and the solicitation is truthful and not misleading. *In-person* (i.e., face-to-face), *live telephone,* or *real-time electronic* solicitation, however, is treated differently because of the added pressure that it imposes. It is "easier to throw out unwanted mail than an uninvited guest."[32]

Some states impose additional regulations on those solicitations that it allows. For example, the state may require the attorney to print the phrase "Advertising Material" on the outside of the envelope or at the top of an electronic message and may prohibit all solicitations to victims and their relatives for a designated number of days after the accident or disaster for which the attorney is offering legal services. Some federal laws impose additional restrictions. For example, Congress

pecuniary Relating to money. A pecuniary interest is a financial interest.

solicitation 1. An appeal or request for clients or business. 2. An attempt to obtain something by persuasion or application.

ambulance chasing Approaching accident victims (or others with potential legal claims) to encourage them to hire a particular attorney.

real-time Occurring now; happening as you are watching; able to respond immediately.

has passed the Aviation Disaster Family Assistance Act, which provides that in the event of an air carrier accident:

> [N]o unsolicited communication concerning a potential action for personal injury or wrongful death may be made by an attorney or any potential party to the litigation to an individual injured in the accident, or to a relative of an individual injured in the accident, before the 30th day following the date of the accident. 49 U.S.C. § 1136 (g)(2).

In extreme cases, client solicitation can constitute the crime of **barratry** in some states. For example, in 1990, three attorneys and an employee of a law firm were indicted in Texas. They were charged with illegally seeking clients at hospitals and funeral homes soon after twenty-one students were killed and sixty-nine others were injured in a school bus accident.[33]

barratry The crime of stirring up quarrels or litigation; persistently instigating lawsuits, often groundless ones. The illegal solicitation of clients.

Paralegal Perspective:

- An unscrupulous attorney may try to use a paralegal to solicit clients for the office.

  > **Example:** Bill Hill is a senior citizen who lives at a home for senior citizens. Andrew Vickers, Esq. hires Bill as his "paralegal." His sole job is to contact other seniors with legal problems and to refer them to Vickers.

  Andrew Vickers is engaging in unethical solicitation through Bill Hill. Attorneys cannot hire a paralegal to try to accomplish what they cannot do themselves. Nor can they use a **runner**—an employee or independent contractor who contacts personal injury victims or other potential clients in order to solicit business for an attorney. If this person uses deception or fraud in the solicitation, he or she is sometimes called a *capper* or a *steerer*. An example would be someone who arranges for an unsuspecting motorist to be involved in a crash with another vehicle, whose driver (by prearrangement with the capper) flees after the collision. The capper then solicits the motorist to hire an attorney for purposes of filing an insurance claim.

runner 1. One who solicits business, especially accident cases. 2. An employee who delivers and files papers.

- See also the earlier discussion of fees in which we covered the related topics of unethically splitting fees with a nonattorney and paying someone to recommend the services of an attorney.

14. ADVERTISING

Attorneys may advertise in the newspaper, on television, on the Internet, or through other media as long as the advertisements are truthful and do not mislead the public such as by creating unjustified expectations of the results the attorney will be able to obtain. The advertisement must include the name and office address of at least one attorney or law firm responsible for its content. Model Rule 7.2

advertising Calling the attention of the public to a service or product for sale. (Advertising on the Internet is sometimes called *netvertising*.)

At one time, almost all forms of **advertising** by attorneys were prohibited. Traditional attorneys considered advertising to be highly offensive to the dignity of the profession. In 1977, however, the U.S. Supreme Court stunned the legal profession by holding that truthful advertising cannot be completely banned.[34] The First Amendment protects such advertising. Furthermore, advertising does not pose the same danger as in-person, live telephone, or real-time electronic solicitation by an attorney. A recipient of advertising is generally under very little pressure to buy the advertised product—in this case, an attorney's services. Hence attorneys can ethically use truthful, nonmisleading advertising to the general public in order to generate business.

Studies have shown that more than one-third of all attorneys in the country engage in some form of advertising. Most of it consists of listings in the Yellow Pages. The use of other marketing tools is also on the rise. Attorneys spend over $300 million every year on television advertising alone, most of it spent by personal injury (PI) attorneys trying to bring in accident cases that often involve high contingency fees and relatively quick settlements. Former U.S. Chief Justice Warren Burger commented that some attorney ads "would make a used-car dealer blush with shame." Proponents of attorney advertising, however, claim that it has made legal services more accessible to the public and has provided the public with a better basis for choosing among available attorneys.

One of the major problems with advertising is that it can be misleading:

Examples of Misleading Ads:

Ad: Flier states, "You pay no fee if we do not win your case."

Problem: The ad may be misleading if the office requires its client to pay costs and expenses even if it loses the case.

Ad: Man in a wheelchair says, "Fenton and Adams won $5,000,000 in my case."

Problem: The ad may raise false expectations. A viewer of the ad may think the law office is saying that it can obtain the same result for the viewer.

Ad: Newspaper box says, "Trust your case to a specialist."

Problem: Some states have specialty (specialization) certification or licensing programs for attorneys. If a particular state doesn't, calling oneself a specialist may be misleading. If it does, references to the specialty in ads usually must comply with specific regulations, e.g., mentioning the full name of the specialty board that granted the specialty credential.

Many law firms today have Internet sites on the Web (see appendix 2.A at the end of chapter 2). Some firms pay search engines to have their sites appear high on the list of results of certain searches. Recently for example, a law firm paid Google $56.24 for *each* click on a search for "mesothelioma" that led to the firm's Web site. Google was paid this amount whether or not the searcher hired the firm. A mere click on the link triggered the payment. The firm was willing to pay Google such a high price because someone using this search term is likely to be looking for an attorney who handles cases of workers exposed to asbestos, a field of practice that can led to unusually high attorney fees.

Most law firm Web sites are designed to provide the public with general information about the firm, particularly the kind of legal services it offers. In addition, some of the firms' Web pages go into detail about an aspect of the law that is relevant to their practice. For example, a family law attorney might have several pages that list the grounds for divorce in the state or the steps to take to establish paternity. Large law firms may have elaborate Web pages that include pictures of attorneys in the firm and the names and e-mail addresses of its attorneys and paralegals. To avoid the charge that a law firm is practicing law on the Internet, a disclaimer will often be printed on the homepage that tells readers that the site is not intended to establish an attorney-client relationship or to provide legal advice. The goal is to make clear that the site is simply advertising the firm. As such, it must meet the ethical requirements for advertising, e.g., be truthful and not misleading. The disclaimer should also warn viewers that the law of each state may differ; that the firm makes no representation, warranty, or claim that the information on the site is current or accurate; and that viewers should not rely on the information provided on the site without consulting local attorneys. There will often be an e-mail address on the site that a viewer or prospective client can use to contact the firm. Care must be taken in responding to such e-mail messages that no legal advice is given, particularly to individuals who live in states where the attorneys in the firm are not licensed to practice law. Furthermore, the sender should be told that the firm cannot maintain the confidentiality of any communications sent through the Web site and that, until a conflicts check is made, the firm cannot agree to represent anyone. One law firm concludes its disclaimer with this blunt statement: "If you send an e-mail to our firm, you agree that sending us an e-mail will not make you a client of our firm. Until we agree to represent you, you are not a client of this firm, and anything you send to us may not be confidential or privileged."[35]

Paralegal Perspective:

- In California, the titles *paralegal* and *legal assistant* cannot be used by freelancers (independent contractors) who do not work under the supervision of attorneys. In their advertising, they must call themselves *legal document assistants* (LDAs) or *unlawful detainer assistants* (UDAs). Similar restrictions exist in a few other states such as Maine and Florida. (See chapter 4.)
- Bankruptcy petition preparers (BPPs) are not allowed to use the word *legal* or any similar term in their advertising. Some courts have concluded that they cannot use the word *paralegal*. (See chapter 4.)

15. REPORTING PROFESSIONAL MISCONDUCT

Attorneys who know that another attorney has violated the ethical rules must report this attorney to the appropriate disciplinary body if the violation is serious enough to cast substantial doubt on the attorney's trustworthiness or fitness to practice law. Model Rule 8.3

Attorneys may pay a price for remaining silent when they become aware of unethical conduct. The failure of an attorney to report another attorney may mean that both attorneys can be disciplined for unethical behavior. This is known as the *rat rule*, the *snitch rule*, or, more euphemistically, the *whistleblower rule*. Not every ethical violation must be reported, however. The ethical violation must raise a substantial question of the attorney's trustworthiness or fitness to practice law.

Paralegal Perspective:

■ Suppose that a paralegal observes his or her supervising attorney commit fraud, steal from client funds, or use perjured testimony. Clearly, the paralegal has an obligation to avoid participating in such conduct. Such assistance could subject the paralegal to criminal and civil penalties. The problem is real; sooner or later unethical attorneys will probably ask or pressure their paralegals to participate in the unethical conduct.

But is the paralegal under an ethical obligation to report the offending attorney to the bar association or other disciplinary body? The National Federation of Paralegal Associations (NFPA) thinks so. In its *Model Code of Ethics and Professional Responsibility*, the obligation is stated as follows in EC-1.2(f):

> A paralegal shall advise the proper authority of non-confidential knowledge of any dishonest or fraudulent acts by any person pertaining to the handling of the funds, securities or other assets of a client. The authority to whom the report is made shall depend on the nature and circumstances of the possible misconduct, (e.g., ethics committees of law firms, corporations and/or paralegal associations, local or state bar associations, local prosecutors, administrative agencies, etc.). Failure to report such knowledge is in itself misconduct and shall be treated as such under these rules.

As pointed out earlier, ethical rules written by paralegals are not binding in the sense that they affect the paralegal's right to work as a paralegal. A paralegal who violates EC.-1.2(f) by failing to report his or her attorney to the bar association might be kicked out of the paralegal association that has adopted NFPA's *Model Code*, but it is highly unlikely that this will affect his or her employment prospects.

What then should a conscientious paralegal do? Here are some guidelines. First and foremost, do not participate directly or indirectly in the unethical conduct. Second, consult with fellow paralegals in the office and in your local paralegal association. Without naming names and without breaching client confidentiality, find out how others have handled similar predicaments on the job. Third, go to a senior officer at the firm, e.g., a partner, and let him or her know that the conduct you have observed is troubling you. You may need to confront the offending attorney himself or herself. Whomever you approach, be sure to have your facts straight! What appears to you to be an ethical violation may simply be aggressive or zealous advocacy that is on the edge but still within the bounds of propriety.

Should you go to the bar association or to a law enforcement agency? This is obviously a very tough question. The answer may depend on whether you have exhausted available routes within the office to resolve the matter to your satisfaction and, more important, whether you think this is the only way to prevent serious harm to a client. (See also "An Ethical Dilemma: Your Ethics or Your Job!" later in the chapter.)

If you do report an attorney in your office and you are fired or retaliated against in some other way, do you have any recourse? Review the case of *Brown v. Hammond* earlier in the chapter.

16. APPEARANCE OF IMPROPRIETY

How would you feel if you were told that, even though you have not violated any rule, you are still going to be punished because what you did *appeared* to be improper? That would be the effect of an obligation to avoid even the appearance of professional impropriety. In some states, it is unethical for attorneys to engage in such appearances. The ABA *Model Rules*, however, does not list appearance of impropriety as an independent basis for determining unethical conduct. To be disciplined in states that have adopted the *Model Rules*, an attorney must violate one of the specific ethical rules. Yet even in these states, conservative attorneys are as worried about apparent impropriety as they are about specific, actual impropriety.

17. UNAUTHORIZED PRACTICE OF LAW

An attorney shall not assist a nonattorney in the unauthorized practice of law (UPL). **Rule 5.5**

In chapter 4, we saw that it is a crime in many states for a nonattorney to engage in the **unauthorized practice of law**. Our main focus in chapter 4 was the nonattorney who works for an office other than a traditional law office. An example would be an independent paralegal who owns a do-it-yourself divorce office that sells kits and typing services. Now our focus is the nonattorney who works under the supervision of an attorney in a law office. We want to explore the

unauthorized practice of law Conduct by a person who does not have a license to practice law or other special authorization needed for that conduct.

ways in which attorneys might be charged with unethically assisting *their own paralegals* in engaging in the unauthorized practice of law. For example, an attorney might allow a paralegal to give legal advice, to conduct depositions, or to sign court documents. These areas will be discussed below along with an overview of other major ethical issues involving paralegals.

18. PARALEGALS

We turn now to a more direct treatment of when attorneys can be disciplined for the unethical use of paralegals. We will cover the following topics:

a. Paralegals, the ABA *Model Code*, and the ABA *Model Rules*
b. Misrepresentation of paralegal identity or status
c. Doing what only attorneys can do
d. Absentee, shoulder, and "environmental" supervision

a. Paralegals, the ABA *Model Code,* and the ABA *Model Rules*

The first major statement by the American Bar Association on the ethical use of paralegals by attorneys came in its *Model Code of Professional Responsibility.* (As we saw earlier in Exhibit 5.2, the *Model Code* is an earlier edition of the ABA's *Model Rules of Professional Conduct.* Some states still follow the *Model Code.*) Here is what the *Model Code* said about nonattorneys:

DR 3-101(A): A lawyer shall not aid a nonlawyer in the unauthorized practice of law.
EC 3-6: A lawyer often delegates tasks to clerks, secretaries, and other lay persons. Such delegation is proper if the lawyer maintains a direct relationship with his client, supervises the delegated work, and has complete professional responsibility for the work product. This delegation enables a lawyer to render legal services more economically and efficiently.

The following 1967 opinion elaborated on these standards:

Formal Opinion 316

American Bar Association, 1967

A lawyer can employ lay secretaries, lay investigators, lay detectives, lay researchers, accountants, lay scriveners, non-lawyer draftsmen or non-lawyer researchers. In fact, he may employ non-lawyers to do any task for him except counsel clients about law matters, engage directly in the practice of law, appear in court or appear in formal proceedings as part of the judicial process, so long as it is he who takes the work and vouches for it to the client and becomes responsible for it to the client. In other words, we do not limit the kind of assistance that a lawyer can acquire in any way to persons who are admitted to the Bar, so long as the non-lawyers do not do things that lawyers may not do or do the things that lawyers only may do.

From these documents we learn that an attorney can hire a paralegal and is responsible for what the paralegal does. There are two levels of this responsibility: civil liability for malpractice and ethical liability for violation of ethical rules. In chapter 4, we discussed civil liability for malpractice under the topic of respondeat superior and negligence. Here in chapter 5 our primary focus is on ethical violations by attorneys based on what their paralegals do or fail to do.

Example: The law firm of Adams & Adams represents Harold Thompson in his negligence suit against Parker Co. At the firm, Elaine Stanton, Esq. works on the case with Peter Vons, a paralegal whom she supervises. Peter neglects to file an important pleading in court and carelessly gives confidential information about Thompson to the attorney representing Parker. All of this causes Thompson great damage.

Stanton is fully responsible to the client, Thompson, who might decide to bring a malpractice suit in court against her. She cannot hide behind the fact that her paralegal was at fault. (See the discussion of malpractice liability and respondeat superior in chapter 4.)

What about ethics? Can Stanton be reprimanded, suspended, or disbarred because of what her paralegal did? Responsibility to a client for malpractice often raises separate issues from responsibility for unethical conduct. The two kinds of responsibility can be closely interrelated because the same alleged wrongdoing can be involved in the malpractice suit and in the disciplinary case. Yet the two proceedings are separate and should be examined separately.

Model Rule 5.3 The rule in the ABA *Model Rules of Professional Conduct* governing the responsibility of different categories of attorneys for the misconduct of paralegals and other nonattorney assistants in a law firm.

The ABA *Model Rules* is more helpful than the ABA *Model Code* in telling us when attorneys are subject to ethical sanctions because of their paralegals. This is done in **Model Rule 5.3,** covering paralegals. All attorneys in the law firm are not treated the same in Rule 5.3. As you read this rule, note that different standards of ethical responsibility are imposed on the following three categories of attorneys:

- An attorney who runs the firm (this can be a partner or an attorney with managerial authority that is comparable to that of a partner)—see sections (a) and (c)(2)
- An attorney in the firm with direct supervisory authority over the paralegal—see sections (b) and (c)(2)
- Any attorney in the firm—see section (c)(1)

Model Rules of Professional Conduct, Rule 5.3. Responsibilities Regarding Nonlawyer Assistants

American Bar Association, 1983

With respect to a nonlawyer employed or retained by or associated with a lawyer:

(a) a partner and a lawyer who individually or together with other lawyer possesses comparable managerial authority in a law firm shall make reasonable efforts to ensure that the firm has in effect measures giving reasonable assurance that the person's conduct is compatible with the professional obligations of the lawyer;

(b) a lawyer having direct supervisory authority over the nonlawyer shall make reasonable efforts to ensure that the person's conduct is compatible with the professional obligations of the lawyer; and

(c) a lawyer shall be responsible for conduct of such a person that would be a violation of the Rules of Professional Conduct if engaged in by a lawyer if:

(1) the lawyer orders or ratifies the conduct involved; or

(2) the lawyer is a partner or has comparable managerial authority in the law firm in which the person is employed, or has direct supervisory authority over the person, and knows of the conduct at a time when its consequences can be avoided or mitigated but fails to take reasonable remedial action.

Comment:

Lawyers generally employ assistants in their practice, including secretaries, investigators, law student interns, and paraprofessionals. Such assistants, whether employees or independent contractors, act for the lawyer in rendition of the lawyer's professional services. A lawyer must give such assistants appropriate instruction and supervision concerning the ethical aspects of their employment, particularly regarding the obligation not to disclose information relating to representation of the client, and should be responsible for their work product. The measures employed in supervising non-lawyers should take account of the fact that they do not have legal training and are not subject to professional discipline . . . . Lawyers with managerial authority within a law firm [are required] to make reasonable efforts to establish internal policies and procedures designed to provide reasonable assurance that nonlawyers in the firm will act in a way compatible with the Rules of Professional Conduct.

ratify 1. To adopt or confirm a prior act or transaction, making one bound by it. 2. To give formal approval.

Let us analyze Rule 5.3 in detail by applying it to Elaine Stanton, Esq. in our example. First of all, under Rule 5.3(c)(1), *any* attorney in the firm who "orders" the paralegal to commit the wrongdoing in question is ethically responsible for that conduct. The same is true if the attorney **"ratifies"** (that is, approves or endorses) the wrongdoing after the paralegal commits it. There is no indication in the example that Stanton or any other attorney in the firm told Peter not to file the pleading in court or told him to give confidential information about Thompson to the other side. Nor is there any indication that an attorney ratified (approved of) Peter's conduct after it occurred. Therefore, Rule 5.3(c)(1) does not apply.

We need to know whether Stanton is a partner in the firm or is an attorney with managerial responsibilities that are comparable to those of a partner. If so, she has an ethical obligation under Rule 5.3(a) to "make reasonable efforts to ensure that the firm has in effect measures giving reasonable assurance" that the paralegal's conduct "is compatible with the professional obligations of the lawyer." Hence a partner (or comparable manager) cannot completely ignore office paralegals in the hope that someone else in the firm is monitoring them. Reasonable steps must be taken by *every partner* (or comparable manager) to establish a system of safeguards. Here are some examples:

- Make sure that all paralegals in the firm are aware of the ethical rules governing attorneys in the state. Have all paralegals sign a statement that they have read the rules.
- Make sure that all paralegals in the firm are aware of the importance of deadlines in the practice of law and of the necessity of using manual or computer date-reminder

(**tickler**) techniques. Ask another attorney or a legal administrator in the office to let you know when every paralegal in the office has completed a brief in-house course on tickler systems.

In the example, Peter Vons is supervised by Elaine Stanton, Esq. Hence she is an attorney with "direct supervisory authority" over Peter. Rule 5.3(b) governs the conduct of such attorneys. This section requires her to "make reasonable efforts to ensure" that the paralegal's conduct "is compatible with the professional obligations of the lawyer."

Assume that Stanton is charged with a violation of Rule 5.3(b) because her paralegal, Peter, failed to file an important pleading in court (raising the ethical issue of competence) and disclosed information about a client (raising the ethical issue of confidentiality). At Stanton's disciplinary hearing, she would be asked a large number of questions about how she supervised Peter. For example:

- How do you assign tasks to Peter?
- How do you know if he is capable of handling an assignment?
- How often do you meet with him after you give him an assignment?
- How do you know if he is having difficulty completing an assignment?
- Has he made mistakes in the past? If so, how have you handled them?

Peter might be questioned by an investigator from the disciplinary board or called as a witness in Stanton's disciplinary hearing. Peter would probably be asked questions such as:

- Why didn't you file the court document on time?
- Describe the circumstances under which you revealed confidential information to the opponent in the Thompson case.
- How were you trained as a paralegal? What legal courses did you take in school?
- What kinds of assignments have you handled in your paralegal career?
- How long have you worked for Elaine Stanton?
- How does she evaluate your work?
- What do you do if you have a question on an assignment but she is not available in the office?

The purpose of asking these questions of Stanton and of Peter would be to find out if Stanton made "reasonable efforts" to ensure that Peter did not violate ethical standards. Note that attorney supervisors do *not* have to guarantee that a paralegal will act ethically. They simply have to "make reasonable efforts" that this will occur. The preceding questions are relevant to whether Stanton exerted such efforts with respect to Peter.

Another basis of ethical liability is Rule 5.3(c)(2). A partner, an attorney with comparable managerial authority, and a supervisory attorney can be subject to discipline if they knew about the paralegal's misconduct yet failed to take reasonable corrective steps at a time when such steps would have avoided or minimized (**mitigated**) the damage. At their disciplinary hearing, these attorneys would be asked such questions as:

- When did you first find out that Peter did not file the court document?
- What did you do at that time? Why didn't you act sooner?
- When did you first find out that Peter spoke to the opposing attorney?
- What did you do at that time? Why didn't you act sooner?

Peter, too, might be asked questions at the hearing such as when did his supervising attorney (Stanton) find out about what he had done—and what did she do when she found out.

b. Misrepresentation of Paralegal Identity or Status

Attorneys know that paralegals working for them are not members of the bar, but it is unwise to assume that everyone else knows. Anyone outside the firm who comes in contact with such paralegals must not be allowed to think that they are attorneys. To learn how to avoid a misrepresentation of status, intentionally or accidentally, we will examine the following issues:

- Titles
- Disclosure of status
- Business cards
- Letterhead
- Signature on correspondence
- Name on court documents

tickler A system designed to provide reminders of important dates.

mitigate To reduce or minimize the severity of impact. To render less painful.

What Title Can Be Used?   In all states, there are no ethical problems with the title *paralegal* or *legal assistant.* No one is likely to think that persons with such titles are attorneys. Some bar associations prefer titles that are even more explicit in communicating nonattorney status—for example, *lawyer's assistant* and *nonattorney assistant.* Yet they are seldom used because of the widespread acceptance and clarity of the titles *paralegal* and *legal assistant.* Some years ago, the Philadelphia Bar Association said that the titles *paralegal* and *legal assistant* should be given only to employees who possessed "the requisite training and education." California imposes restrictions on the use of titles. In that state, only individuals who work under the supervision of attorneys (and meet specified educational requirements) can call themselves paralegals or legal assistants. (See chapters 1 and 4.) A few other states (e.g., Maine and Florida) impose similar title restrictions.

It is unethical to call a paralegal an "associate" or to refer to a paralegal as being "associated" with a law firm. The title *paralegal associate,* for example, should not be used. The common understanding is that an associate is an attorney. In a moment, we will discuss the related question of the ethical use of abbreviations (e.g., CLA) that indicate certification from a paralegal association.

Note on Disbarred or Suspended Attorney as Paralegal   When attorneys have been disbarred or suspended from the practice of law for ethical improprieties, they may try to continue to work in the law as paralegals for attorneys willing to hire them. Some states will not allow this because it shows disrespect for the court that disciplined the attorney and because the individual is highly likely to engage in the practice of law by going beyond paralegal duties. Other states are more lenient but might impose other restrictions, such as not allowing a disbarred or suspended attorney to have any client contact while working as a paralegal.

Should Paralegals Disclose Their Nonattorney Status to Clients, Attorneys, Government Officials, and the General Public?   Yes, this disclosure is necessary. The more troublesome questions are: what kind of disclosure should you make, and when must you make it? Compare the following communications by a paralegal:

- "I work with Ward Brown at Brown & Tams."
- "I am a paralegal."
- "I am a legal assistant."
- "I am not an attorney."

The fourth statement is the clearest expression of nonattorney status. (Online disclaimers that informally emphasize this fact are sometimes abbreviated as IANAA—I am not an attorney, or IANAL—I am not a lawyer.) The first ("statement") is totally unacceptable because you have said nothing about your status. For most contacts, the second and third statements will be ethically sufficient to overcome any misunderstanding about your nonattorney status. Yet some members of the public may be confused about what a paralegal or legal assistant is. If there is any possibility of doubt, use the magic words "I am not an attorney." Do not assume that a person with whom you come in contact for the first time knows you are not an attorney; the safest course is to assume the opposite!

May a Paralegal Have a Business Card?   Every state allows paralegals to have their own *business cards* as long as their nonattorney status is clear. (See Exhibit 5.11. and appendix H.) At one time, some states wanted the word "nonlawyer" used along with the paralegal's office title. This is rarely required today. Because paralegals are not allowed to solicit business for their employer, the card may not be used for this purpose. The primary focus of the card must be to identify the paralegal rather than the attorney for whom the paralegal works. Finally, there must be nothing false or misleading printed on the card.

May the Letterhead of Law Firm Stationery Print the Name of a Paralegal?   States differ in their answer to this question, although most now agree that nonattorneys' names can be printed on *law firm letterhead* if their title is also printed so that their nonattorney status is clear. (See Exhibit 5.12.) Before 1977, almost all states did *not* allow attorney stationery to print the names of nonattorney employees. The concern was that the letterhead would be used as a form of advertising by packing it with names and titles to make the office look impressive. This concern evaporated in 1977, however, when the Supreme Court held that a state could not ban all forms of attorney advertising.[36] After this date, most states withdrew their objection to the printing of paralegal names on attorney letterhead as long as no one would be misled into thinking that the paralegals were attorneys. In Michigan, it was recommended, but not required, that attorney and nonattorney names be printed on different sides of the stationery to "enhance the clarification that

EXHIBIT 5.11	Paralegal Business Card

HINCKLEY, ALLEN & SNYDER LLP
Attorneys at Law

DAWN E. OSTIGUY
Paralegal

1500 FLEET CENTER
PROVIDENCE, RI 02903-2393
401 274-2000
FAX: 401 277-9600

E-MAIL: dostiguy@haslaw.com

EXHIBIT 5.12	Example of Law Firm Letterhead with Paralegal Name

---

HOLLAND & HART LLP
ATTORNEYS AT LAW

DENVER • ASPEN	SUITE 3200	TELEPHONE (303) 295-8000
BOULDER • COLORADO SPRINGS	555 SEVENTEENTH STREET	FACSIMILE (303) 295-8261
DENVER TECH CENTER	DENVER, COLORADO 80202-3979	www.hollandhart.com
BILLINGS • BOISE	MAILING ADDRESS	
CHEYENNE • JACKSON HOLE	P.O. BOX 8749	CAROL J. LEFFLER
SALT LAKE CITY	DENVER, COLORADO 80201-8749	PARALEGAL
WASHINGTON, D.C.		(303) 295-8551
		(303) 713-6223 Fax
		cleffler@hollandhart.com

---

the paraprofessional is not licensed to practice law." A few states adhere to the old view that only attorney names can be printed on law firm letterhead. Yet, to the extent that this view is still based on a prohibition of attorney advertising, it is subject to challenge. Though ethically permissible in most states, it should be pointed out that not many law firms in the country print nonattorney names on their law firm letterhead.

May a Paralegal Write and Sign Letters on Attorney Stationery?   There is never an ethical problem with a paralegal writing a letter that will be reviewed and signed by an attorney. Suppose, however, that the attorney wants the paralegal to sign his or her own name to the letter. Most states will permit this if certain conditions are met. For example, a title must be used that indicates the signer's nonattorney status, and the letter must not give legal advice.

The following closing formats are proper:

Sincerely,	Sincerely,	Sincerely,
Leonard Smith	Pauline Jones	Jill Strauss
Paralegal	Legal Assistant	Legal Assistant for the Firm

The following closing format, however, is improper:

Sincerely,

William Davis

The lack of a title could mislead the reader into thinking that William Davis is an attorney.

We saw in chapter 4 that paralegals who pass certification exams such as those of the National Association of Legal Assistants and the National Federation of Paralegal Associations are entitled to use the letters that indicate their achievement: CLA, CP, RP. (See Exhibit 4.7 in chapter 4.) In most states, however, it would not be appropriate to use these letters alone (e.g., David Johnson, CLA; Mary Adams, CP; and Karen Vickers, RP). The general public would not understand what these letters mean, or worse, knowing that they work in a law office, might think they are attorneys. Hence a title should be used along with the letters. For example:

David Johnson, CLA	Mary Adams, CP	Karen Vickers, RP
Certified Legal Assistant	Certified Paralegal	Paralegal

In most states, there are no limitations on the persons to whom a paralegal can send letters. Yet, in a few states (e.g., New Jersey), only an attorney can sign a letter to a client, to an opposing attorney, or to a court. A very minor exception to this rule would be "a purely routine request to a court clerk for a docket sheet." A paralegal can sign such a letter. This is also an extreme position. So long as the paralegal's nonattorney status is clear, and so long as an attorney is supervising the paralegal, restrictions on who can be the recipient of a paralegal-signed letter make little sense. Most states impose no such restrictions.

May an Attorney Print the Name of a Paralegal on a Court Document? Formal documents that are required in litigation, such as appellate briefs, memoranda supporting a motion, complaints, or other pleadings, must be signed by an attorney representing a party in the dispute. With rare exceptions, the document cannot be signed by a nonattorney, no matter how minor the formal document may be. In most states, a paralegal can sign a letter on a routine matter to a clerk or other nonjudge, but formal litigation documents require an attorney's signature.

Suppose, however, that the attorney wishes to print on a document the name of a paralegal who worked on the document *in addition to* the attorney's name and signature. The attorney may simply want to give a measure of recognition to the efforts of this paralegal. Most states permit this as long as there is no misunderstanding as to the paralegal's nonattorney status and no attempt is made to substitute a nonattorney's signature for an attorney's signature.

Occasionally, a court opinion will recognize the contribution of a paralegal. Before the opinion begins, the court lists the names of the attorneys who represented the parties. The name of a paralegal might be included with these attorneys. Here, for example, is the list of attorneys that includes the name of a paralegal (Becky M. Strickland, who is a CLA or certified legal assistant) in the case of *United States v. Sanders*, 862 F.2d 79 (4th Cir. 1988):

> Michael W. Patrick (Haywood, Denny, Miller, Johnson, Sessoms & Patrick, Durham, N. C., on brief), for defendant-appellant.
>
> John Warren Stone Jr., Asst. U. S. Atty. (Robert H. Edmunds, Jr., U. S. Atty., Greensboro, N. C., Becky M. Strickland, CLA Paralegal Specialist, on brief), for plaintiff-appellee.
>
> Before PHILLIPS and WILKINSON, Circuit Judges, and BOYLE, District Judge for the Eastern District of North Carolina, sitting by designation.

c. Doing What Only Attorneys Can Do

There are limitations on what attorneys can ask their paralegals to do. We just examined one such limitation: paralegals should never be asked to sign court documents. The failure to abide by these limits might subject the attorney to a charge of unethically assisting a nonattorney to engage in the unauthorized practice of law. The areas we need to examine are as follows:

- Legal advice
- Nonlegal advice
- Drafting documents
- Real estate closings
- Depositions
- Executions of wills
- Settlement negotiations
- Court appearances
- Counsel's table
- Administrative hearings

May a Paralegal Give Legal Advice?   Attorneys use their skills in the **practice of law** to help clients solve legal problems. Giving them **legal advice** is perhaps the most important of these skills. Legal advice is the application of laws and legal principles to the facts of a particular person's legal problem. (See the discussion in chapter 4 on the distinction between legal advice and legal information.)

A paralegal who gives legal advice is engaged in the unauthorized practice of law. A number of paralegals have pointed out how easy it is to fall into the trap of giving legal advice:

- Paralegals should be alert to all casual questions [since your answers] might be interpreted as legal advice.[37]
- Most of us are aware of the obvious, but we need to keep in mind that sometimes the most innocent comment could be construed as legal advice.[38]
- A . . . typical scenario, particularly in a small law office where paralegals have a great deal of direct client contact, is that the clients themselves will coax you to answer questions about the procedures involved in their cases, and lead you into areas where you would be giving them legal advice. Sometimes this is done innocently—because the attorney is unavailable and they are genuinely unaware of the difference between what you can do for them and what their legal counsel [must] do. . . . They will press you for projections, strategy, applicable precedents—in short, legal advice. Sometimes you are placed in situations where you are not adequately supervised and your own expertise may be such that you know more about the specialized area of law than the attorney does anyway. . . . We have all walked the thin line between assisting in the provision of legal services and actually practicing law.[39]

An attorney who permits a paralegal to give legal advice or who fails to take the preventive steps required by Model Rule 5.3 is aiding the paralegal in the unauthorized practice of law—and hence is acting unethically.

The consequences can be extremely serious. In addition to the sanctions described in Exhibit 5.3, insurance problems may exist. Suppose a client sues and alleges that the firm's paralegal gave legal advice. Will the firm's malpractice insurance policy cover this suit? No, according to the General Counsel of the Mississippi Bar Association. "No available insurance policy will cover judgments resulting from a civil suit brought by an angry client based on the theory that a paralegal gave the client legal advice. In fact, if the paralegal gives legal advice, the predominant rule is that coverage is void for such act. Therefore, the paralegal is warned not to give the client advice (even if the paralegal knows the answer) even though it may be an emergency situation. Why? Giving legal advice constitutes the unauthorized practice of law, and the unauthorized practice of law is not covered."[40]

There are a number of situations, however, in which a paralegal *can* give legal advice. First, a paralegal can tell a client precisely what the attorney tells the paralegal to say, even if the message constitutes legal advice. The paralegal, however, cannot elaborate on, interpret, or explain this kind of message from the attorney. Second, the paralegal may be working in an area of the law where nonattorneys are authorized to represent clients, such as Social Security hearings. (See chapter 4.) In such areas, the authorization includes the right to give legal advice.

May a Paralegal Give a Client Nonlegal Advice?   Yes. An attorney may allow a paralegal to render specialized advice on scientific or technical topics. For example, a qualified paralegal can give accounting advice or financial advice. The danger is that the nonlegal advice might also contain legal advice or that the client might reasonably interpret the nonlegal advice as legal advice.

May a Paralegal Draft Legal Documents?   Yes. A paralegal can draft any legal document as long as an attorney supervises and reviews the work of the paralegal. Some ethical opinions say that the document must lose its separate identity as the work of a paralegal and must leave the office as the work product of an attorney. In West Virginia, for example, "anything delegated to a nonattorney must lose its separate identity and be merged in the service of the lawyer." The key point is that an attorney must stand behind and be responsible for the document.

May a Paralegal Attend a Real Estate Closing?   The sale of property is finalized at an event called a real estate **closing**. Many of the events at the closing are formalities, such as signing and exchanging papers. Occasionally, however, some of these events turn into more substantive matters where negotiation, legal interpretation, and legal advice are involved.

In most states, paralegals are allowed to attend closings in order to assist their attorney-supervisor. Can paralegals attend *alone* and conduct the closing themselves? Chicago has one of the most liberal rules. There, paralegals can conduct the closing without the attorney-supervisor being present if no legal advice is given, if all the documents have been prepared in advance, if the attorney-supervisor is available by telephone to provide help, and if the other attorney consents.

practice of law Using legal skills to assist a specific person in resolving his or her specific legal problem.

legal advice The application of laws and legal principles to the facts of a particular person's legal problem.

closing The meeting in which a transaction is finalized. Also called *settlement*.

In some states, additional conditions must be met before allowing paralegals to act on their own. For example, the closing must take place in the attorney-supervisor's law office with the attorney readily accessible to answer legal questions. It must be noted, however, that this is a minority position. Many states would say that it is unethical for an attorney to allow a paralegal to conduct a real estate closing alone regardless of where the closing is held.

May a Paralegal Conduct a Deposition?   No. Paralegals can schedule **depositions**, can assist in preparing a witness who will be **deposed** (called the *deponent*), can take notes at the deposition, and can summarize deposition transcripts, but they cannot conduct the deposition. Asking and objecting to deposition questions are attorney-only functions.

May a Paralegal Supervise the Execution of a Will?   In Connecticut, the execution of a will must be supervised by an attorney. A paralegal can act as a witness to the execution, but an attorney must direct the procedure. Most other states would probably agree, although few have addressed this question.

May a Paralegal Negotiate a Settlement?   A few states allow a paralegal to negotiate with a nonattorney employee of an insurance company, such as a claims adjuster, as long as the paralegal is supervised by an attorney. Most states, however, limit the paralegal's role to exchanging messages from the supervising attorney and do not allow any actual give-and-take negotiating by the paralegal.

May a Paralegal Make a Court Appearance?   In the vast majority of courts, a paralegal cannot perform even minor functions in a courtroom, such as asking a judge to schedule a hearing date for an attorney. As we saw in chapter 4, very few exceptions to this rule exist. Only attorneys can act in a representative capacity before a judge. There are, however, a small number of specialized courts, like the small claims courts of some states, where you do not have to be an attorney to represent parties. This exception, however, is rare. And, as mentioned earlier, a paralegal should not sign a formal court document that is filed in litigation.

May a Paralegal Sit at Counsel's Table during a Trial?   In many courts, only attorneys can sit at counsel's table during a trial. Yet, in some courts, a paralegal is allowed to sit with the attorneys if permission of the presiding judge is obtained. The paralegal does not take an active role in the trial. He or she provides general assistance for the attorney, e.g., note taking, organizing exhibits, and doing quick database searches for documents and discovery testimony if laptop computers are allowed in the courtroom and if such information is in the database. While at the table, the paralegal is sometimes said to be sitting in the **second chair**. This phrase, however, is more accurately used to refer to another attorney who assists the lead attorney, who is in the "first chair." When a nonattorney such as a paralegal is allowed to sit at counsel's table, it might be more accurate to refer to him or her as being in the "third chair."

May a Paralegal Represent Clients at Administrative Hearings?   Yes, when this is authorized at the particular state or federal administrative agency. (See chapters 4 and 15.)

d. Absentee Supervision, Shoulder Supervision, and "Environmental" Supervision

It is difficult to overestimate the importance of attorney supervision in the arena of ethics. According to the supreme court of one state, "Without supervision, the work of the paralegal clearly constitutes the unauthorized practice of law."[41] Almost every ethical opinion involving paralegals (and almost every attorney malpractice opinion involving paralegals) stresses the need for effective supervision. The justification for the very existence of perhaps 95 percent of paralegal activity is this supervision. Indeed, one of the main reasons many argue that paralegal licensing is not necessary is the protective cover of attorney supervision.

What is meant by supervision? The extremes are easy to identify. *Absentee supervision* refers to the attorney who is either never around or seldom available. Once tasks are assigned, paralegals are essentially on their own. At the other extreme is *shoulder supervision*, practiced by attorneys who are afraid to delegate. When they do get up enough courage to delegate something, they constantly look over the shoulder of the paralegal, who is rarely left alone for more than two-minute intervals. Such attorneys suffer from *delegatitis*, the inordinate fear of letting anyone do anything for them.

Both kinds of supervision are misguided. If you work for an attorney who practices absentee supervision, the potential for disaster is high. For example, unsupervised or minimally supervised paralegals are not likely to find out about errors they have made until after the errors have caused

---

deposition A method of discovery by which parties and their prospective witnesses are questioned outside the courtroom before trial. A pretrial question-and-answer session to help parties prepare for trial. The person questioned is called the *deponent*.

depose Ask questions of a witness in a deposition.

second chair A seat at the counsel's table in the courtroom used by an assistant to the trial attorney during the trial.

harm to clients. You may feel flattered by the confidence placed in you; you may enjoy the challenge of independence; you may be highly compensated because of your success. But you are working in an office that is traveling 130 miles per hour in a 50-mile-per-hour zone. Any feeling of safety in such an office is illusory. Shoulder supervision, on the other hand, provides safety at the expense of practicality. Perpetual step-by-step surveillance will ultimately defeat the economy and efficiency motives that originally led the office to hire paralegals.

Perhaps the most effective kind of supervision is *"environmental" supervision*, or what might be called *holistic supervision*. It is far broader in its reach than the immediate task delegated to a paralegal. It addresses this essential question: what kind of law office environment is likely to lead to a high-quality paralegal work product without sacrificing economy or ethics? The components of this kind of supervision are outlined in Exhibit 5.13. "Environmental" supervision requires *hiring*

EXHIBIT 5.13	"Environmental" Supervision: The Ethical Ideal (What kind of law office environment is likely to lead to high-quality paralegal work without sacrificing economy or ethics?)

1. Before paralegals are hired, the office undertakes a study of its practice in order to identify what tasks paralegals should perform and what level of ability will be required to perform those tasks.

2. As part of the job interview process, the office conducts background checks on applicants for paralegal jobs in order to ensure that competent people are hired who already have the needed skills or who are trainable so that they can acquire these skills on the job.

3. A program of orientation and training is created to introduce paralegals to the office and to prepare them for the tasks ahead.

4. Before the paralegal is hired, the office conducts a "conflicts check" to determine whether he or she might have a conflict of interest with any current client of the office. These conflicts might result from the paralegal's prior legal work as well as from his or her family and business connections with anyone who might oppose current clients. Once hired, a similar conflicts check is conducted for every new client or prospective client.

5. Paralegals are given a copy of the ethical rules governing attorneys in the state, special guidelines (if any) that govern an attorney's use of paralegals, and state ethical opinions (if any) that are relevant to paralegals in the practice of law. In addition to reading these rules, they are given training on the meaning of this material.

6. Paralegals are told what to do if they feel that an ethical problem exists. Lines of authority are identified if the paralegal needs to discuss the matter with someone other than, or in addition to, his or her immediate supervisor.

8. An attorney reviews all paralegal work. Although paralegals may be given discretion and asked to exercise judgment in the tasks assigned, this discretion and judgment are always subjected to actual attorney review. A paralegal is not reluctant to say to a busy attorney, "I would appreciate it if you would look this over when you can before it goes out" even if this attorney is inclined to say, "I'm sure it's fine" and not check it.

9. No task is assigned that is beyond the capacity of the paralegal. Specialized instruction always accompanies tasks the paralegal has not performed before.

10. Once a task is assigned, the paralegal is told where to receive assistance if the immediate supervisor is not available.

11. For tasks that the office performs on a recurring basis, there are manuals, office procedures, checklists, or other written material available to the paralegal to explain how the tasks are performed and where samples or models can be found. If such *systems* material does not currently exist, the office plans to create it.

12. To cut down on misunderstanding, every paralegal assignment includes the following information:
    - *A specific due date.* ("Get to this when you can" is unacceptable and unfair.)
    - *A priority assessment.* ("Should everything else be dropped while I do this assignment?")
    - *A context.* ("How does this assignment fit into the broader picture of the case?") and
    - *A financial perspective.* ("Is this billable time?" "What resources can be used, e.g., fee-based online research?" and "What support services will be available, e.g., the secretary?")

13. At reasonable times before the due date of selected assignments, the supervisor monitors the progress of the paralegal to ensure that the work is being done professionally and accurately.

14. A team atmosphere exists at the office among the attorneys, paralegals, secretaries, and other employees. Everyone knows each other's functions, pressures, and potential as resources. A paralegal never feels isolated.

15. Evaluations of paralegal performance are constructive. Both the supervisor and paralegal act on the assumption that there will always be a need and opportunity for further learning.

16. The office sends the paralegal to training seminars conducted by paralegal associations and bar associations to maintain and to increase the paralegal's skills.

17. The office conducts periodic surveys to monitor compliance with ethical rules.

18. The office knows that an unhappy employee is prone to error. Hence the office makes sure that the work setting of the paralegal encourages personal growth and productivity. This includes matters of compensation, benefits, work space, equipment, and advancement.

the right people, *training* those people, *assigning* appropriate tasks, *providing* the needed resources, *monitoring* the progress, *reviewing* the end product, and *rewarding* competence.

Unfortunately, many law offices do *not* practice "environmental" supervision as outlined in Exhibit 5.13. The chart represents the ideal. Yet you need to know what the ideal is so that you can advocate for the conditions that will help bring it about.

Thus far, our discussion on supervision has focused on the traditional paralegal who works full-time in the office of an attorney. We also need to consider the freelance or independent paralegal who works part-time as an independent contractor for one attorney or for several attorneys in different law firms. Very often this freelancer works in his or her own office at home. (See appendix J and Exhibit 2.2 in chapter 2.) How can attorneys fulfill their ethical obligation to supervise such paralegals?

Example: Gail Patterson has her own freelance business. She offers paralegal services to attorneys who hire her for short-term projects, which she performs in her own office.

Attorneys who hire Gail often do not provide the same kind of supervision that they can provide to a full-time paralegal who works in their office. Suppose, for example, that Gail commits an ethical impropriety such as revealing confidential communications. Because she works in her own office, the attorney who hired her may not learn about this impropriety in time to avoid or mitigate its consequences. Conflict of interest is another potential problem. Gail works for many different attorneys and hence many different clients of those attorneys. It is possible that she could accept work from two attorneys who are engaged in litigation against each other without either attorney knowing that the other has hired Gail on the same case. (See the earlier discussion of this problem on page 246, when we covered conflict of interest and the tainted paralegal.)

What kind of supervision is needed to prevent such problems? There is no clear answer to this question. It is not enough that the attorney vouches for, and takes responsibility for, the final product submitted by the freelance paralegal. Ongoing supervision is also needed under Model Rule 5.3. This is particularly true at a time when some law firms are exploring whether **outsourcing** paralegal functions to a foreign country is feasible. Suppose, for example, that a company in India is hired to summarize (digest) a **transcript** of testimony from a deposition or trial. The transcript can easily be sent to India as an e-mail attachment. Yet how can the attorney be sure that the same company is not doing work for an opponent of the attorney's client? Not many states, however, have addressed this area of ethics. In the future, we will probably see the creation of new standards to govern this kind of paralegal.

outsourcing Paying an outside company or service to perform tasks usually performed by one's own employees.

transcript A word-for-word account. A written copy of oral testimony.

[SECTION D]

ETHICAL CODES OF THE PARALEGAL ASSOCIATIONS

As indicated at the beginning of this chapter, there are no binding ethical rules published by paralegal associations. Yet the major national associations have written ethical codes that you should know about. See Exhibit 5.4 for an overview of their structure and functions. For excerpts from these codes, see appendix F.

[SECTION E]

AN ETHICAL DILEMMA: YOUR ETHICS OR YOUR JOB!

Throughout this chapter, we have stressed the importance of maintaining your integrity through knowledge of and compliance with ethical rules. There may be times, however, when this is much easier said than done. First of all, you may not be sure whether an ethical violation has been or is being committed. Like so many areas of the law, ethical issues can be complex. Or consider these possibilities: (1) no one seems to care about whether an ethical problem exists, or worse, (2) your supervisor appears to be the one committing the ethical impropriety, or (3) the entire office appears to be participating in the impropriety.

Compounding the problem is the fact that people often do not appreciate being told that they are unethical. Rather than acknowledge the fault and mend their ways, they may turn on the accuser, the one raising the fuss about ethics. (That is apparently what happened to Cynthia Brown, the paralegal who complained about unethical billing practices in her office. See the case of *Brown v. Hammond,* discussed earlier in the chapter.) Once the issue is raised, it may be very difficult to continue working in the office.

You need someone to talk to. In the best of all worlds, it will be someone in the same office. If this is not practical, consider contacting a teacher whom you trust. Paralegal associations are also an excellent source of information and support. A leader in one paralegal association offers the following advice:

> I would suggest that if the canons, discipline rules, affirmations, and codes of ethics do not supply you with a clear-cut answer to any ethical question you may have, you should draw upon the network that you have in being a member of this association. Getting the personal input of other paralegals who may have been faced with similar situations, or who have a greater knowledge through experience of our professional responsibilities, may greatly assist you in working your way through a difficult ethical situation.[42]

Of course, you must be careful not to violate client confidentiality during discussions with someone outside the office. Never mention actual client names or any specific information pertaining to a case. You can talk in hypothetical terms. For example, "an attorney working on a bankruptcy case asks a paralegal to. . . ." Once you present data in this sterilized fashion, you can then ask for guidance on the ethical implications of the data.

If handled delicately, most ethical problems that bother you can be resolved without compromising anyone's integrity or job. Yet the practice of law is not substantially different from other fields of endeavor. There will be times when the clash between principle and the dollar (or egos) cannot be resolved to everyone's satisfaction. You may indeed have to make a choice between your ethics and your job.

[SECTION F]
DOING RESEARCH ON AN ETHICAL ISSUE

1. See the ethics material for your state in appendix E.
2. For general Internet sites on ethics and professional responsibility, see "Helpful Web Sites" at the end of the chapter.
3. Go to the Internet site of your state bar association (see appendix C). If you can't find a link to "ethics" or "professional responsibility," type these words in any available search box on the site. You will often be led to the full text of the ethics code and ethics opinions.
4. On the state bar site, type "paralegal" or "legal assistant" in any available search box. Look for guidelines or opinions on the use of paralegals by attorneys in the state.
5. Go to the Internet site of every paralegal association in the state (see appendix B). If you can't find a link to "ethics" or "professional responsibility," type these words in any available search box on the site.
6. Go to the Internet site of the highest state court in your state. Try to find a link to "ethics" or "professional responsibility." If none is available, type these words in any available search box on the site.
7. In Google or any major search engine, do a search that contains the name of your state, and the words *ethics, attorney,* and *lawyer* (e.g., Florida ethics attorney lawyer). If your state's name consists of two words, place them in quotes (e.g., "New York" ethics attorney lawyer).
8. At a law library, ask where the following materials are kept:
   - The code or rules of ethics governing attorneys in your state
   - The ethical opinions that interpret the code or rules
   - The ABA's *Model Rules of Professional Conduct*
   - The ethical opinions that interpret these *Model Rules*, as well as the earlier *Model Code of Professional Responsibility* of the ABA
9. Examine the *ABA/BNA Lawyers' Manual on Professional Conduct.* This is a looseleaf book containing current information on ABA ethics and the ethical rules of every state.
10. Other material to check in the library:
    - C. Wolfram, *Modern Legal Ethics* (1986)
    - G. Hazard and W. Hodes, *The Law of Lawyering: A Handbook on the Model Rules of Professional Conduct* (2d ed. 1992)
    - L. Bierwat and R. Hunter, *Legal Ethics for Management and Their Counsel* (1999)

- American Law Institute, *Restatement (Third) of the Law Governing Lawyers* (1998)
- *National Reporter on Legal Ethics and Professional Responsibility* (1982)
- *The Georgetown Journal of Legal Ethics* (periodical)
- *Lawyers' Liability Review* (newsletter)

11. Either Westlaw or LexisNexis will enable you to do computerized legal research on the law of ethics in your state. (See chapter 13.) Here, for example, is a query (question) you could use to ask Westlaw to find cases in your state in which a paralegal was charged with the unauthorized practice of law:

    paralegal "legal assistant" /p "unauthorized practice"

    After you instructed Westlaw to turn to the database containing the court opinions of your state, you would type this query at the keyboard in order to find out if any such cases exist. For many states, there are separate databases devoted to ethics.

12. See chapter 11 on finding legal materials on ethics in legal encyclopedias, legal treatises, legal periodicals, and ALR annotations, and through digests.

ASSIGNMENT 5.2

(a) What is the name of the code of ethics that governs attorneys in your state? (See appendix E.)
(b) To what body or agency does a client initially make a charge of unethical conduct against his or her attorney in your state?
(c) List the steps required to discipline an attorney for unethical conduct in your state. Begin with the complaint stage and conclude with the court that makes the final decision. Draw a flow chart (timeline) that lists these steps.

ASSIGNMENT 5.3

Paul Emerson is an attorney who works at the firm of Rayburn & Rayburn. One of the firm's clients is Designs Unlimited, Inc. (DU), a clothing manufacturer. Emerson provides corporate advice to DU. Recently, Emerson made a mistake in interpreting a new securities law. As a consequence, DU had to postpone the issuance of a stock option for six months. Has Paul acted unethically?

ASSIGNMENT 5.4

(a) Three individuals in Connecticut hire a large New York law firm to represent them in a proxy fight in which they are seeking control of a Connecticut bank. They lose the proxy fight. The firm then sends these individuals a $358,827 bill for 895 hours of work over a one-month period. Is this bill unethical? What further facts would you like to have to help you answer this question?
(b) Victor Adams and Len Patterson are full partners in the law firm of Adams, Patterson & Kelly. A client contacts Patterson to represent him on a negligence case. Patterson refers the case to Victor Adams, who does most of the work. (Under an agreement between them, Patterson will receive 40 percent and Adams will receive 60 percent of any fee paid by this client.) Patterson does not tell the client about the involvement of Adams in the case. Any ethical problems?
(c) An attorney establishes a bonus plan for her paralegals. A bonus will be given to those paralegals who bill a specified number of hours in excess of a stated minimum. The amount of the bonus will depend on the amount billed and collected. Any ethical problems?

ASSIGNMENT 5.5

Mary works in a law firm that charges clients $225 an hour for attorney time and $75 an hour for paralegal time. She and another paralegal, Fred, are working with an attorney on a large case. She sees all of the time sheets that the three of them submit to the firm's accounting office. She suspects that the attorney is padding his time sheets by overstating the number of hours he works on the case. For example, he lists thirty hours for a four-day period when he was in court every day on another case. Furthermore, Fred's time is being billed at the full $75-an-hour rate even though he spends about 80 percent of his time typing correspondence, filing, and performing other clerical duties. Mary also suspects that her attorney is billing out Mary's time at the attorney rate rather than the paralegal rate normally charged clients for her time. Any ethical problems? What should Mary do?

ASSIGNMENT 5.6

Smith is an attorney who works at the firm of Johnson & Johnson. He represents Ralph Grant, who is seeking a divorce from his wife, Amy Grant. In their first meeting, Smith learns that Ralph is an experienced carpenter but is out of work and has very little money. Smith's fee is $150 an hour. Because Ralph has no money and has been having trouble finding work, Smith tells Ralph that he will not have to pay the fee if the court does not grant him the divorce. One day while Smith is working on another case involving Helen Oberlin, he learns that Helen is looking for a carpenter. Smith recommends Ralph to Helen, and she hires him for a small job. Six months pass. The divorce case is dropped when the Grants reconcile. In the meantime, Helen Oberlin is very dissatisfied with Ralph's carpentry work for her; she claims he didn't do the work he contracted to do. She wants to know what she can do about it. She tries to call Smith at Johnson & Johnson but is told that Smith does not work there anymore. Another attorney at the firm, Georgia Quinton, Esq., helps Helen. Any ethical problems?

ASSIGNMENT 5.7

(a) John Jones is a paralegal working at the XYZ law firm. The firm is handling a large class action involving potentially thousands of plaintiffs. John has been instructed to screen the potential plaintiffs in the class. John tells those he screens out (using criteria provided by the firm) in writing or verbally that "unfortunately, our firm will not be able to represent you." Any ethical problems?

(b) Mary Fenton is a paralegal who works for Tom Orson, Esq., a solo practitioner. Mary works extensively on workers' compensation cases. Tom has been tied up for months in a complicated mass tort case. One day a workers' compensation client calls Mary to ask whether his injury qualifies for extended benefits under the state's workers' compensation law. She puts him on hold and calls Tom during a recess of the tort trial. When she asks him the question, he replies, "I don't remember the answer to that, but it's in the code. Just check under injuries or filings and tell the client what you find. Besides, you know more about this area of law than I do." Mary does so. Any ethical problems?

ASSIGNMENT 5.8

A paralegal quits the firm of Smith & Smith. When she leaves, she takes client documents she prepared while at the firm. The documents contain confidential client information. The paralegal is showing these documents to potential employers as writing samples.

(a) What is the ethical liability of attorneys at Smith & Smith under Model Rule 5.3?
(b) What is the ethical liability of attorneys at law firms where she is seeking employment under Model Rule 5.3?
(c) What is the paralegal's liability?

ASSIGNMENT 5.9

subpoena A command to appear at a certain time and place.

(a) Mary is a paralegal at the ABC law firm. She has been working on the case of Jessica Randolph, a client of the office. Mary talks with Ms. Randolph often. Mary receives a subpoena from the attorney of the party that is suing Ms. Randolph. (A **subpoena** is a command to appear at a certain time and place. Here the subpoena was to give testimony in court.) On the witness stand, Mary is asked by this attorney what Ms. Randolph told her at the ABC law office about a particular business transaction related to the suit. Randolph's attorney (Mary's supervisor) objects to the question. Does Mary have to answer?

(b) Before Helen became a paralegal for the firm of Harris & Derkson, she was a chemist for a large corporation. Harris & Derkson is a patent law firm where Helen's technical expertise in chemistry is invaluable. Helen's next-door neighbor is an inventor. On a number of occasions, he discussed the chemical makeup of his inventions with Helen. Now the government has charged the neighbor with stealing official secrets to prepare one of these inventions. Harris & Derkson represents the neighbor on this case. Helen also works directly on the case for the firm. In a prosecution of the neighbor, Helen is called as a witness and is asked to reveal the substance of all her conversations with the neighbor concerning the invention in question. Does Helen have to answer?

ASSIGNMENT 5.10

Bob and Patricia Fannan are separated, and they both want a divorce. They would like to have a joint-custody arrangement in which their son would spend time with each parent during the year. The only marital property is a house, which they agree should be sold, with each to get one-half of the proceeds. Mary Franklin, Esq. is an attorney whom Bob and Patricia know and trust. They decide to ask Franklin to represent both of them in the divorce. Any ethical problems?

ASSIGNMENT 5.11

George is a religious conservative. He works for a law firm that represents Adult Features, Inc., which runs an X-rated Internet site. The client is fighting an injunction sought by the police against its business. George is asked by his supervisor to do some research on the case. Any ethical problems?

ASSIGNMENT 5.12

Peter is a paralegal at Smith & Smith. One of the cases he works on is *Carter v. Horton.* Carter is the client of Smith & Smith. Peter does some investigation and scheduling of discovery for the case. Horton is represented by Unger, Oberdorf & Simon. The Unger firm offers Peter a job working in its law library and in its computer department on database management. He takes the job. While at the Unger firm, Peter can see all the documents in the *Carter v. Horton* case. At lunch a week after Peter joins the firm, he tells one of the Unger attorneys (Jack Dolan) about an investigation he conducted while working for Smith & Smith on the *Carter* case. (Jack is not one of the Unger attorneys working on *Carter v. Horton.*) Two weeks after Peter is hired, the Unger firm decides to set up a Chinese Wall around Peter. He is told not to discuss *Carter v. Horton* with any Unger employee, all Unger employees are told not to discuss the case with Peter, the files are kept away from Peter, etc. The wall is rigidly enforced. Nevertheless, Smith & Smith makes a motion to disqualify Unger, Oberdorf & Simon from continuing to represent Horton in the *Carter v. Horton* case due to Peter's presence at the Unger firm. Should this motion be granted?

ASSIGNMENT 5.13

Alice is a freelance paralegal (independent contractor) with a speciality in probate law. One of the firms she has worked for is Davis, Ritter & Boggs. Her most recent assignment for this firm has been to identify the assets of Mary Steck, who died six months ago. One of Mary's assets is a 75 percent ownership share in the Domain Corporation. Alice learns a great deal about this company, including the fact that four months ago it had difficulty meeting its payroll and expects to have similar difficulties in the coming year.

Alice's freelance business has continued to grow because of her excellent reputation. She decides to hire an employee with a different specialty so that her office can begin to take different kinds of cases from attorneys. She hires Bob, a paralegal with four years of litigation experience. The firm of Jackson & Jackson hires Alice to digest a series of long deposition documents in the case of *Glendale Bank v. Ajax Tire Co.* Jackson & Jackson represents Glendale Bank. Peterson, Zuckerman & Morgan represents Ajax Tire Co. Alice assigns Bob to this case. Ajax Tire Co. is a wholly owned subsidiary of the Domain Corporation. Glendale Bank is suing Ajax Tire Co. for fraud in misrepresenting its financial worth when Ajax Tire Co. applied for and obtained a loan from Glendale Bank. Any ethical problems?

ASSIGNMENT 5.14

Assume that you owned a successful freelance business in which you provided paralegal services to over 150 attorneys all over the state. How should your files be organized in order to avoid a conflict of interest?

ASSIGNMENT 5.15

Joan is a paralegal who works for the XYZ law firm, which is representing Goff in a suit against Barnard, who is represented by the ABC law firm. Joan calls Barnard and says, "Is this the first time that you have ever been sued?" Barnard answers, "Yes it is. Is there anything else that you would like to know?" Joan says *no* and the conversation ends. Any ethical problems?

ASSIGNMENT 5.16

Mary is a paralegal who is a senior citizen. She works at the XYZ legal service office. One day she goes to a senior citizens center and says the following:

All of you should know about and take advantage of the XYZ legal service office where I work. Let me give you just one example why. Down at the office there is an attorney named Armanda Morris. She is an expert on insurance company cases. Some of you may have had trouble with insurance companies that say one thing and do another. Our office is available to serve you.

Any ethical problems?

ASSIGNMENT 5.17

(a) What restrictions exist on advertising by attorneys in your state? Give an example of an ad on TV or in the newspaper that would be unethical. On researching an ethical issue, see the list in Section F.

(b) In *Bates v. State Bar of Arizona*, 433 U.S. 350 (1977), the U.S. Supreme Court held that a state could not prohibit all forms of lawyer advertising. Has *Bates* been cited by state courts in your state on the advertising issue? If so, what impact has the case had in your state? To find out, **shepardize** *Bates.* For the steps to take, see Exhibit 11.28 in chapter 11 ("Checklist for Shepardizing Opinions, Statutes, Administrative Regulations, and Other Cited Materials").

shepardize To use Shepard's citations (in book form, on CD–ROM, or online) to obtain validation and other data on whatever you are shepardizing.

ASSIGNMENT 5.18

Mary Jackson is a paralegal at Rollins & Rollins. She is supervised by Ian Gregory. Mary is stealing money from the funds of one of the firm's clients. The only attorney who knows about this is Dan Roberts, Esq., who is not a partner or manager at the firm and who does not supervise Mary. Dan says and does nothing about Mary's actions. What ethical obligations does Dan have under Model Rule 5.3?

ASSIGNMENT 5.19

John Smith is a paralegal who works for the firm of Beard, Butler, and Clark. John's immediate supervisor is Viola Butler, Esq. With the full knowledge and blessing of Viola Butler, John Smith sends a letter to a client of the firm (Mary Anders). Has Viola Butler acted unethically in permitting John to send out this letter? The letter is as follows:

Law Offices of
Beard, Butler, and Clark
310 High St.
Maincity, Ohio 45238
512-663-9410

Attorneys at Law	***Paralegal***
Ronald Beard	**John Smith**
Viola Butler	
Wilma Clark	May 14, 2005

Mary Anders
621 S. Randolph Ave.
Maincity, Ohio 45238

Dear Ms. Anders:

Viola Butler, the attorney in charge of your case, has asked me to let you know that next month's hearing has been postponed. We will let you know the new date as soon as possible. If you have any questions, don't hesitate to call me.

Sincerely,

John Smith
Legal Intern

JS:wps

ASSIGNMENT 5.20

Under what circumstances would it be appropriate for you to refer to a client of the office where you work as "my client"?

ASSIGNMENT 5.21

John Jones is a paralegal who works for an attorney named Linda Sunders. Linda is away from the office one day and telephones John, who is at the office. She dictates a one-line letter to a client of the office. The letter reads, "I advise you to sue." Linda asks John to sign the letter for her. The signature line at the bottom of the letter reads as follows:

Linda Sunders
by John Jones

Any ethical problems?

ASSIGNMENT 5.22

Sam is a paralegal in the law firm of Orsen and Jacobs. Rachel, a prospective client, calls one day. Sam answers the phone. Any ethical problems based on the following conversation?

Rachel: How much does the firm charge to take a case?

Sam: $200 an hour. What kind of a case is it?

Rachel: I was injured as a passenger in an automobile accident.

Sam: Then the firm will probably take the case on a contingency, meaning that you pay nothing unless we win.

ASSIGNMENT 5.23

Mary is a paralegal who works at the XYZ law firm. She specializes in real estate matters at the firm. Mary attends a real estate closing in which her role consists of exchanging documents and acknowledging the receipt of documents. Are there ethical problems in allowing her to do so? Answer this question on the basis of the following variations:

(a) The closing takes place at the XYZ law firm.

(b) The closing takes place at a bank.

(c) Mary's supervising attorney is not present at the closing.

(d) Mary's supervising attorney is present at the closing.

(e) Mary's supervising attorney is present at the closing except for 30 minutes, during which time Mary continued to exchange documents and acknowledge the receipt of documents.

(f) During the closing, the attorney for the other party says to Mary, "I don't know why my client should have to pay that charge." Mary responds, "In this state that charge is always paid in this way."

ASSIGNMENT 5.24

John is a paralegal who works for the XYZ law firm, which is representing a client against the Today Insurance Company. The Company employs paralegals who work under the Company's general counsel. One of these paralegals is Mary. In an effort to settle the case, Mary calls John and says, "We offer you $2,000." John says, "We'll let you know." Any ethical problems?

ASSIGNMENT 5.25

John Smith is a paralegal who works for Beard, Butler, and Clark. He sends out the following letter. Any ethical problems?

John Smith
Paralegal
310 High St.
Maincity, Ohio 45238
512-663-9410

June 1, 2005

State Unemployment Board
1216 Southern Ave
Maincity, Ohio 45238

Dear Gentlepeople:

I work for Beard, Butler, and Clark, which represents Mary Anders, who has a claim before your agency. A hearing originally scheduled for June 8, 2005, has been postponed. We request that the hearing be held at the earliest time possible after the 8th.

Sincerely,
John Smith

JS:wps

ASSIGNMENT 5.26

In Section C of chapter 2, there is a long list of tasks that paralegals have performed and comments by paralegals working in the specialties covered. Identify any three tasks or paralegal comments that *might* pose ethical problems or problems of unauthorized practice. Explain why.

ASSIGNMENT 5.27

Draft your own paralegal code as a class project. Use any of the material in chapter 5 as a resource. First, have a meeting in which you make a list of all the issues that you think should be covered in the code (e.g., what job titles can be used, when a job title must be disclosed, and what tasks a paralegal can and cannot perform). Divide up the issues by the number of students in the class so that every student has roughly the same number of issues. Each student should draft a proposed rule on each of the issues to which he or she is assigned. Accompany each rule with a brief commentary on why you think the rule should be as stated. Draft alternative versions of the proposed rule if different versions are possible and you want to give the class the chance to examine all of them. The class then meets to vote on each of the proposed rules. Students will make presentations on the proposed rules they have drafted. If the class is not happy with the way in which a particular proposed rule was drafted by a student, the latter will redraft the rule for later consideration by the class. One member of the class should be designated the "code reporter," who records the rules accepted by the class by majority vote.

After you have completed the code, invite attorneys from the local bar association to your class in order to discuss your proposed code. Do the same with officials of the closest paralegal association in your area.

Chapter Summary

Ethics are the standards of behavior to which members of an organization must conform. Begin your paralegal career by committing yourself to becoming an ethical archconservative.

Attorneys are regulated primarily by the highest court in the state, often with the extensive involvement of the state bar association. Because paralegals cannot practice law and cannot become full members of a bar association, they cannot be punished by the bar association (or other attorney regulatory body) for a violation of the ethical rules governing attorneys. The American Bar Association is a voluntary association; no attorney must be a member. The ABA publishes ethical rules that the states are free to adopt, modify, or reject.

The current rules of the ABA are found in its *Model Rules of Professional Conduct*. These ethical rules require attorneys to be competent, to act with reasonable diligence and promptness, to charge fees that are reasonable, to avoid conduct that is criminal and fraudulent, to avoid asserting claims and defenses that are frivolous, to safeguard the property of clients, to avoid making false statements of law and fact to a tribunal, to disclose legal authority that might harm the attorney's own client (if the other side fails to present it), to withdraw from a case for appropriate reasons, to maintain the confidentiality of client information (except when necessary to avoid designated harm), to avoid conflicts of interest, to avoid improper communications with an opponent, to avoid improper solicitation of clients, to avoid improper advertising, to report serious professional misconduct of other attorneys, to avoid assisting nonattorneys in engaging in the unauthorized practice of law, and to supervise paralegal employees appropriately.

Ethical opinions, rules, or guidelines exist in almost every state on the proper use of a paralegal by an attorney. All states agree that the title used for this employee must not mislead anyone about his or her nonattorney status, and that the employee must disclose his or her nonattorney status when necessary to avoid misunderstanding. Rules also exist on other aspects of the attorney-paralegal relationship, but not all states agree on what these rules should be. The following apply in most states.

If there is no misrepresentation of status, paralegals in most states:

- Can have their own business cards
- Can have their names printed on law firm letterhead
- Can sign law firm correspondence
- Can give nonlegal advice
- Can draft legal documents
- Can attend a real estate closing
- Can represent clients at agency hearings if authorized by the agency

With few exceptions, paralegals in most states:

- Cannot give legal advice
- Cannot conduct a deposition
- Cannot sign formal court documents
- Cannot supervise the execution of a will
- Cannot make an appearance in court

Separate ethical rules and guidelines have been adopted by all the major national and some of the local paralegal associations.

Key Terms

continuing legal education
   (CLE)
ethics
sanction
integrated bar association
registration
multidisciplinary practice
   (MDP)
paralegal code
disbarment
suspension
reprimand
probation
competent
clinical education
statute of limitations
dilatory
minimum-fee schedule
contingent fee
fee splitting
forwarding fee
fee cap
paralegal fee
statutory fee case
block billing
contemporaneous

double billing
padding
task padding
time padding
billable hours quota
at-will employee
client security fund
attestation clause
insider trading
pirated software
malicious prosecution
abuse of process
spoilation
adversary system
frivolous position
fiduciary
client trust account
commingling
retainer
notice of appearance
cure
letter of disengagement
letter of nonengagement
confidential
privileged
consent

attorney-client privilege
discoverable
work-product rule
waiver
metadata
encrypted
redact
conflict of interest
bias
disinterested
multiple representation
adverse interests
informed consent
duty of loyalty
imputed disqualification
tainted
tainted paralegal
Chinese Wall
quarantined
rebuttable presumption
career client list
conflicts check
conflicts specialist
lateral hire
anticontact rule
overreaching

ex parte communication
pecuniary
solicitation
ambulance chasing
real-time
barratry
runner
advertising
unauthorized practice of
   law (UPL)
Model Rule 5.3
ratify
tickler
mitigate
practice of law
legal advice
closing
deposition
depose
second chair
outsourcing
transcript
subpoena
shepardize

Review Questions

1. Summarize the ten major ethical guidelines for paralegals.
2. What are ethics, and how are rules of ethics enforced?
3. Name four kinds of bar associations.
4. Distinguish between the ABA *Model Rules* and *Model Code*.
5. What sanctions can be imposed on attorneys for unethical conduct?
6. What consequences might result from unethical conduct by a paralegal?
7. What is a multidisciplinary practice (MDP)?
8. What kinds or categories of paralegal codes exist?
9. What standard is used to determine attorney competence?
10. What is the function of clinical education and CLE?
11. In what ways can paralegals maintain their competence?
12. How should an attorney comply with the obligation to act with diligence and promptness in representing a client?
13. When are fees reasonable?
14. Why are minimum-fee schedules illegal?
15. When and why are contingent fees unethical?
16. When is fee splitting between attorneys unethical?
17. When are attorney payments to paralegals unethical?
18. What are fee caps?
19. What is block billing?
20. Give examples of double billing, time padding, and task padding.
21. What were the holdings in *Brown v. Hammond*?
22. What is the attorney's obligation concerning crimes or fraud of his or her clients?
23. Give an example of insider trading by a paralegal.
24. Describe our adversary system.
25. What is a frivolous claim or defense?
26. What is a client trust account?
27. Give an example of commingling.
28. When must attorneys disclose positions that hurt their own clients?
29. When is an attorney required to withdraw from representation? When is it optional?
30. When is an attorney allowed to breach client confidentiality?
31. Distinguish between confidentiality and the attorney-client privilege.
32. What is the attorney work-product rule?
33. List steps paralegals can take to avoid breaching client confidentiality.
34. What is a conflict of interest?

35. When can an attorney (1) enter a business transaction with a client, (2) make a loan to a client, (3) accept a gift from a client, (4) have a romantic relationship with a client, and (5) engage in multiple representation?
36. Give examples of personal bias that is unethical.
37. When can an attorney represent someone opposed to a former client?
38. When will imputed disqualification be ordered?
39. What are the components of a Chinese Wall?
40. When can a tainted paralegal cause imputed disqualification?
41. How can an independent paralegal create a conflict of interest?
42. What does a comprehensive conflicts check entail?
43. What ethical dangers are posed by lateral hires?
44. When can an office communicate with an opposing party?
45. When is client solicitation ethical and unethical?
46. When is attorney advertising ethical and unethical?
47. What ethical dangers do attorney Internet sites pose?
48. When must one attorney report unethical conduct by another?
49. What is an appearance of impropriety?
50. Summarize the contents of (1) DR 3–101 (A), (2) EC 3–6, and (3) ABA Formal Opinion 316.
51. What are the ethical duties of the three categories of attorneys in Model Rule 5.3?
52. What paralegal titles are ethical and unethical?
53. What ethical dangers exist when a disbarred or suspended attorney functions as a paralegal?
54. When must paralegals disclose their nonattorney status?
55. Can paralegals (1) have business cards, (2) have their names on law firm stationery, and (3) sign letters on law firm stationery?
56. What is legal advice, and when can a paralegal give it?
57. When is it ethical for a paralegal to (1) draft legal documents, (2) attend a real estate closing, (3) attend a deposition, (4) execute a will, (5) negotiate a settlement, (6) make a court appearance, (7) sit at counsel's table, or (8) represent clients at administrative hearings?
58. Describe a comprehensive system of paralegal supervision by attorneys.
59. What should paralegals do when they suspect ethical violations?
60. List some of the main print and online resources that will allow you to research an ethical issue.

Helpful Web Sites: More on Ethics and Professional Responsibility

Finding the Rules of Ethics in Your State:
A State-by-State Directory
- www.abanet.org/cpr/links.html
- www2.law.cornell.edu/ethics
- www2.law.cornell.edu/ethics/listing.html
- www.sunethics.com/other_states.htm

ABA Ethics Codes and Ethics Opinions
- www.abanet.org/cpr
- www.abanet.org/cpr/ethicsearch/resource.html
- www.abanet.org/cpr/pubs/ethicopinions.html

Guides to Legal Ethics on the Internet
- www.findlaw.com/01topics/14ethics/index.html
- www.virtualchase.com/topics/ethics.shtml
- www.megalaw.com/top/ethics.php
- library.law.miami.edu/ethicsguide.html
- www.law.duke.edu/lib/researchguides/legale.html
- www.lexisone.com/legalresearch/legalguide/practice_areas/ethics_and_the_law.htm
- www.ethicsandlawyering.com
- www.legalethics.com

A Basic Guide for Paralegals: Ethics, Confidentiality, and Privilege
- www.cfpainc.com/images/paralegal_Guide-Ethics.pdf

ABA Model Rules (complete text)
- www.abanet.org/cpr/mrpc/mrpc_home.html
- www.law.cornell.edu/ethics/aba/index.htm

ABA Model Code (complete text)
- www.law.cornell.edu/ethics/aba/mcpr/MCPR.HTM

Ethics Links of NALA (National Association of Legal Assistants)
- www.nala.org/links.htm

Advertising, Solicitation, and Marketing
- www.abanet.org/legalservices/clientdevelopment/adrules

Directory of Attorney Disciplinary Agencies
- www.abanet.org/cpr/regulation/scpd/disciplinary.html

State-by-State "Report Card" on the Adequacy of Attorney Discipline
- www.halt.org/reform_projects/lawyer_accountability/report_card_2006
- www.halt.org/reform_projects/lawyer_accountability/report_card

National Lawyer Regulatory Databank
- www.abanet.org/cpr/regulation/databank.html

ABA/BNA Lawyers' Manual on Professional Conduct
- www.bna.com/products/lit/mopc.htm

Conflicts of Interest
- www.freivogelonconflicts.com

Legal Ethics Blog
- www.legalethicsblog.com

Association of Professional Responsibility Lawyers

- www.aprl.net

National Organization of Bar Counsel

- www.nobc.org

National Client Protection Organization

- www.ncpo.org

Lexis (LexisNexis)

- www.lexis.com
- (Go to the ethics databases for your state in Lexis, e.g., CAL library CAETOP file, ETHICS file, or CABAR file)

Westlaw

- www.westlaw.com
- (Go to the ethics databases for your state in Westlaw, e.g., CAETH–EO database, CAETH–CS database, or CA–RULES database)

Google Searches (run the following searches for more sites)

- attorney ethics professional responsibility
- paralegal ethics professional responsibility
- "model rule 5.3"
- attorney discipline "New York" (insert your state)
- paralegal guidelines
- attorney paralegal fees
- unauthorized practice of law (insert your state)
- "insider trading" paralegal
- confidentiality attorney
- "conflict of interest" attorney
- "attorney client privilege"
- imputed disqualification
- "Chinese Wall" attorney
- solicitation advertising attorney

Endnotes

1. Michael Josephson quoted in *We're All in This Together*, 29 Arizona Attorney 28 (August/September 1992).
2. R. Bruenderman, *Ethics Expert Josephson Visits Louisville*, 55 Kentucky Bench & Bar 28 (Summer 1991).
3. *New Mexico Rules Governing the Practice of Law*, § 20–110, Committee Commentary (Judicial Pamphlet 16).
4. Lisa Lerman, *Scenes from a Law Firm*, 50 Rutgers Law Review 2153, 2159 (1998).
5. Smith, *AAfPE National Conference Highlights*, 8 Legal Assistant Today 103 (January/February 1991).
6. Sonia Chan, *ABA Formal Opinion 93–379: Double Billing, Padding and Other Forms of Overbilling*, 9 Georgetown Journal of Legal Ethics 611, 615 (1996).
7. C. Paddelford, 7 RECAP 2 (California Alliance of Paralegal Associations, Fall 1992).
8. Tulsa Ass'n of Legal Assistants, *Hints for Helping Your Attorney Avoid Legal Malpractice*, TALA Times (August 1989).
9. Race, *Malpractice Maladies*, Paradigm 12 (Baltimore Ass'n of Legal Assistants, July/August 1989).
10. Shays, *Ethics for the Paralegal*, Postscript 15 (Manhattan Paralegal Ass'n, August/September 1989).
10a. 42 U.S.C. § 1320a–7b (a) (6) provides as follows: "Whoever . . . for a fee knowingly and willfully counsels or assists an individual to dispose of assets (including by any transfer in trust) in order for the individual to become eligible for medical assistance under a State plan under subchapter XIX of this chapter, if disposing of the assets results in the imposition of a period of ineligibility for such assistance under section 1396 (p) (c) of this title, shall . . . be guilty of a misdemeanor and upon conviction thereof fined not more than $10,000 or imprisoned for not more than one year, or both." (seniorlaw.com/reno.htm)
11. *Phoenix Founders, Inc. v. Marshall*, 887 S.W. 2d 831, 834 (Tex. 1994).
12. An exception exists if the "party seeking discovery has substantial need of the materials in the preparation of the party's case" and is unable to obtain the substantial equivalent of the materials without undue hardship by other means. This test, however, is rarely met. Federal Rule of Civil Procedure 26 (b) (3).
12a. *United States v. Stewart*, 287 F. Supp. 2d 461 (S.D.N.Y. 2003).
13. Missouri Bar Ass'n, *Guidelines for Practicing with Paralegals* (1987).
14. State Bar of Texas, *General Guidelines for the Utilization of the Services of Legal Assistants by Attorneys* (1981); Rule 1.01, Texas Disciplinary Rules of Professional Conduct (1990).
15. Professional Responsibility Committee of the Philadelphia Bar Ass'n, *Professional Responsibility for Nonlawyers* (1989) (emphasis added).
16. *Orientation Handbook for Paralegals* 2 (Lane, Powell, Moses & Miller, 1984) (emphasis added).
17. Daniels, *Privileged Information for Paralegals*, 17 At Issue 15 (San Francisco Ass'n of Legal Assistants, November 1990).
18. Betty Reinert, *Cyberspacing around Cowtown*, 13 Cowtown Paralegal Reporter 10 (March/April 1995).
19. Adam Levy, . . . *Demise of the Tobacco Settlement*, 2 Journal of Health Care Law and Policy 1, 9 (1998).
20. Myron Levin, *Years of Immunity and Arrogance Up in Smoke*, Los Angeles Times, May 10, 1998, at D1, D17.
21. New York State Bar Association, Ethical Consideration 2–30, *Lawyer's Code of Professional Responsibility* (2005) (www.law.cornell.edu/ethics/ny/code).
22. Charles Wolfram, *Modern Legal Ethics* § 7.6.4 (1986).
23. The court in *Phoenix Founders* said that we need to determine "whether the practical effect of formal screening has been achieved." To make this determination, several factors should be considered. They include "the substantiality of the relationship between the matter on which the paralegal worked at the old firm and the matter she worked on at the new firm; the time elapsing between the matters; the size of the firm; the number of individuals presumed to have confidential information; the nature of their involvement in the former matter; and the timing and features of any measures taken to reduce the danger of disclosure." *Phoenix Founders*, 887 S.W. 2d at 836.

24. Susan L. Order, *Beware of Deadly Cone of Silence*, 18 Pre§edents 25 (San Diego Ass'n of Legal Assistants, July/August 1994).

25. Motamedi, *Landmark Ethics Case Takes Toll on Paralegal's Career, Family*, 7 Legal Assistant Today 39 (May/June 1990); *In re Complex Asbestos Litigation*, 232 Cal. App. 3d 572, 283 Cal. Rptr. 732 (1991).

26. M. Hall, *S.F. Decision on Paralegal Conflict May Plague Firms*, Los Angeles Daily Journal, September 25, 1989, at 1, col. 2.

27. *Orientation Handbook for Paralegals* 3 (Lane, Powell, Moses & Miller, 1984).

28. See *In re Opinion No. 24*, 128 N.J. 114, 607 A. 2d 962 (1992).

29. David Vangagriff, *Computing Your Conflicts*, 10 The Compleat Lawyer 42 (Fall 1993).

30. *New Mexico Rules Governing the Practice of Law*, Section 20–104, Committee Commentary (Judicial Pamphlet 16).

31. *Health Plans Depict Lawyers as Threat*, New York Times, October 8, 1999, at A22.

32. Metzner, *Strategies That Break the Rules*, National Law Journal 16 (July 15, 1991).

33. *Four Said to Have Used Bus Crash to Get Business for Law Firm*, New York Times, April 7, 1990, at 8.

34. *Bates v. State Bar of Arizona*, 433 U.S. 350, 97 S. Ct. 2691, 53 L. Ed. 2d 810 (1977).

35. See (www.ssh–intl–law.com/disclaimer.htm).

36. *Bates*, supra endnote 34.

37. King, *Ethics and the Legal Assistant*, 10 ParaGram 2 (Oregon Legal Assistants Ass'n, August 1987).

38. DALA Newsletter 2 (Dallas Ass'n of Legal Assistants, December 1990).

39. Spiegel, *How to Avoid the Unauthorized Practice of Law*, 8 The Journal 8–10 (Sacramento Ass'n of Legal Assistants, February 1986).

40. Michael Martz, *Ethics: Does a Legal Assistant Need Insurance?* The Assistant 13 (Mississippi Ass'n of Legal Assistants, Fall 1993).

41. *In re Opinion No. 24 of Committee on Unauthorized Practice of Law*, 128 N.J. 114, 121, 607 A. 2d 962, 965 (1992).

42. Harper, *Ethical Considerations for Legal Assistants*, Compendium (Orange County Paralegal Ass'n, April 1987).

Student CD-ROM

For additional materials, please go to the CD in this book.

Online Companion™

For additional resources, please go to http://www.paralegal.delmar.cengage.com

Introduction to the Legal System

CHAPTER OUTLINE

A. Federalism, Checks and Balances, and Paralegals

B. Common Law and Our Adversarial System

C. Law and Equity

D. Judicial Systems

E. Administrative Agencies

F. The Legislative Process

[SECTION A]

FEDERALISM, CHECKS AND BALANCES, AND PARALEGALS

What are the components of the legal system and what kind of laws do they produce? These are the concerns of this chapter as we continue to explore the role of the paralegal.

Our legal system consists of three levels of government:

- The federal government (also called the national government and the United States [U.S.] government; the phrases "United States" and U.S. often mean *federal*)
- Fifty state governments (plus the District of Columbia, which is often treated like a state)
- Local governments (called counties, cities, townships, etc.)

Our primary focus will be on federal and state governments. To a large extent, local governments are dependent on (even though, in many respects, they are separate from) state governments.

A division of powers exists between the federal government and the state governments. Some powers are limited to one level. Only the federal government, for example, has the power to declare war, whereas only a state government has the power to issue a marriage license or a divorce decree. Some powers are shared among these levels of government. In the area of public assistance or welfare, for example, both the federal government and the state governments play major roles. The term **federalism** refers to the division of powers between the federal government and the state governments. Federalism simply means that we live in a society where some powers are exercised by the federal government, others by the state governments, and still others by both the federal and the state governments.

Within the federal, state, and local levels of government, there are three *branches:* one that makes or enacts laws (**legislative branch**), one that carries out, executes, or administers laws (**executive branch**), and one that interprets laws by resolving disputes that arise under them (**judicial branch**). The categories of law that these three branches of government write are outlined in Exhibit 6.1. Collectively these laws contain or reflect the **public policy** of each level of government.

federalism The division of powers between the federal government and the state governments.

legislative branch The branch of government with primary responsibility for making or enacting the law.

executive branch The branch of government with primary responsibility for carrying out, executing, or administering the laws.

judicial branch The branch of government with primary responsibility for interpreting laws by resolving disputes that arise under them.

public policy Principles inherent in customs and societal values that are embodied in a law.

EXHIBIT 6.1	Kinds of Primary Authority

Primary authority is any law that a court could rely on in reaching a decision. (Secondary authority, any nonlaw a court can rely on in its decision, will be covered in chapter 11, Exhibit 11.10.)

CATEGORY	DEFINITION	WHO WRITES THIS KIND OF LAW?	EXAMPLE
a. Opinion	A court's written explanation of how it applied the law to the facts before it to resolve a legal dispute. Also called a *case*. (The word *case* has two other meanings: a pending matter on a court calendar and a client matter handled by a law office.)	Courts—the judiciary. The vast majority of opinions are written by courts of appeal, also called appellate courts. Occasionally, trial courts also write opinions.	In the *Bradshaw* opinion, the U.S. Supreme Court sent the death penalty issue back to the lower court for further proceedings. *Bradshaw v. Stumpf,* 545 U.S. 175 (2005)
b. Statute	A law passed by the state or federal legislature that declares, commands, or prohibits something. Also called *act* and *legislation*. (Statute, act, and legislation are sometimes used in a broader sense to include laws passed by any legislature, which would include ordinances passed by a city council.)	The legislature. Some states allow the electorate to participate in the enactment of statutes (and constitutional provisions) by popular vote through the *initiative* and *referendum* process (see these terms in the glossary).	§ 200 of title 4 of the statutory code requires corporations to file biannual finance statements with the secretary of state. 4 U.S.C. § 200 (2004)
c. Constitution	The fundamental law that creates the branches of government, allocates power among them, and defines some basic rights of individuals.	Varies. Often a combination of the legislature and a vote of the people. Another option might be a constitutional convention.	§ 7 of Article I of the U.S. Constitution provides that all bills for raising revenue shall originate in the House of Representatives. § 7 U.S. Cont., Art. I § 7
d. Administrative regulation	A law written by an administrative agency designed to explain or carry out the statutes, executive orders, or other regulations that govern the agency. Also called an *administrative rule*.	Administrative agency.	§16 of title 27 of the administrative code provides that all finance statements filed pursuant to § 200 of the statutory code shall be accompanied by a $75 filing fee. 27 C.F.R. § 16 (2006)
e. Administrative decision	An administrative agency's resolution of a controversy (following a hearing) involving the application of the regulations, statutes, or executive orders that govern the agency. Also called an *administrative ruling*.	Administrative agency.	In the *Trojan* decision, the National Labor Relations Board ruled that the union had been validly certified. *Trojan Transp., Inc.,* 249 N.L.R.B. 642 (1980)
f. Charter	The fundamental law of a municipality or other local unit of government authorizing it to perform designated governmental functions.	Varies. The state legislature often writes charter provisions for cities in the state. The local government itself may be able to create and change the charter.	Section 22 of the charter was amended at the last session to establish a new department in the agency. N.Y. City Charter 2, §22 (1989)
g. Ordinance	A law passed by the local legislative branch of government (e.g., city council) that declares, commands, or prohibits something. (Same as statute, but at the local level of government.) See statute above on the broader meaning of statute and legislation.	The local legislature (e.g., city council, county commission).	Section 5-2.206 of the municipal code allows the city to levy service fees for using the city's tree removal unit. Beverly Hills, Cal., Code § 5-2.206 (1999)
h. Rules of court	The procedural laws that govern the mechanics of litigation (practice and procedure) before a particular court. Also called *court rules*.	Varies. The legislature and/or the highest court in the jurisdiction.	The scope of discovery under rule 56.01 of the Missouri Supreme Court rules of civil procedure does not include privileged material. Mo. R. Civ. P. 56.01 (b)

(continues)

EXHIBIT 6.1	Kinds of Primary Authority—*continued*		
CATEGORY	**DEFINITION**	**WHO WRITES THIS KIND OF LAW?**	**EXAMPLE**
i. Executive order	A law issued by the chief executive pursuant to specific statutory authority or to the executive's inherent authority to direct the operation of governmental agencies.	President (for U.S. government); governor (for state government); mayor (for local government).	Executive Order No. 22,796 directs the Department of Education to complete its review within six months. Exec. Order No. 22,796, 3 C.F.R. 359 (1992)
j. Treaty	A formal agreement between two or more nations. Also called a *convention.*	The president makes treaties by and with the consent of the U.S. Senate. (If the president has the authority to enter the agreement without Senate approval, it is called an *executive agreement.*)	Upon reading the text of the treaty in U.S.T. (United States Treaties and other International Agreements), you will find that Japan was within its rights to impose the additional requirement for entry. Treaty of Friendship, Commerce and Navigation, U.S.-Japan, Art. vi, May 24, 1953, 4 U.S.T. 2063
k. Opinion of the attorney general	Formal legal advice given by the chief law officer of the government to another government official or agency. (Technically, this is *not* a category of law, but it is often relied on as a source of law.)	Attorney general (sometimes called legal counsel)	In 2005, the U.S. Attorney General concluded that the Office of the Comptroller requires special congressional authorization to conduct biannual audits. 69 Op. Att'y Gen 126 (2005)

Here is an overview of our three levels of government and the three branches that exist at each level:

Federal Government

Legislative branch: The Congress

Executive branch: The president and the federal administrative agencies (see the chart in appendix D).

Judicial branch: The U.S. Supreme Court, the U.S. Courts of Appeals, the U.S. District Courts, and other federal courts (see Exhibits 6.3 and 6.4)

State Government

Legislative branch: The state legislature

Executive branch: The governor and the state administrative agencies

Judicial branch: The state courts (see Exhibit 6.2)

Local Government

Legislative branch: The city council or county commission

Executive branch: The mayor or county commissioner and the local administrative agencies

Judicial branch: The local courts (some local courts, however, are considered part of the state judiciary)

In addition to the division of power *between* the federal and state levels of government, there is a division of power *among* the three branches—legislative, executive, and judicial—within each level. This division is called the system of **checks and balances** and is designed to prevent any one branch from becoming too powerful. The system allocates governmental powers among the three branches. One branch is allowed to review, block, or otherwise check another branch so that a balance of powers is maintained among the branches. Let's look at an example.

The legislative branch has the primary responsibility for writing or enacting the law. By majority vote, the legislature creates what are called *statutes* (see Exhibit 6.1). But there are significant checks on this power. First of all, the chief executive must give final approval to a proposed law before it can become a statute. He or she can veto (i.e., reject) the proposed law. The legislature, however, has another power that operates as a countercheck on the chief executive's power to veto proposed laws. The legislature can override (i.e., nullify) the chief executive's veto by a two-thirds vote. These are some of the ways that the legislative and executive branches check each other.

checks and balances An allocation of governmental powers whereby one branch of government can block, check, or review what another branch wants to do (or has done) in order to maintain a balance of power among the legislative, executive, and judicial branches.

judicial review The power of a court to determine the constitutionality of a statute or other law, including the power to refuse to enforce it if the court concludes that it violates the constitution.

The judiciary branch has a similar function. Courts can check the legislative and executive branches through the power of **judicial review**. This is the power to refuse to enforce a law because it is in conflict with the *constitution*. In turn, the judicial branch can be checked by the other branches. For example, the chief executive often nominates persons to be judges and the legislature confirms or rejects the nominations.

The result of all these checks and counterchecks is a *balance* of power among the three branches so that no one branch becomes too powerful.

How do paralegals fit within these levels and branches of government? First of all, many paralegals are civil service employees of government, particularly in federal, state, and local administrative agencies (see appendix 2.B in chapter 2). To a more limited extent, paralegals are also employees of legislatures and courts. Second, paralegals help attorneys solve the legal problems of clients by applying the different kinds of law outlined in Exhibit 6.1 to the facts presented by client cases. These laws could be written by different levels and branches of government.

For example:

Linda Thompson applies for unemployment compensation benefits after being terminated from her job. Her former employer says the termination was due to a slowdown in business at the company. Linda believes she was let go because she is a woman and because she is HIV positive. You are a paralegal working for Sims & Sims, which represents her. Your supervisor may ask you to undertake a variety of tasks: interviewing, investigation, research, analysis, drafting, law office administration, etc. A central focus of everything the attorney and paralegal do on such a case is the application of laws to the facts of the case. The laws are written by different branches of government at the different levels of government. Here are some examples of laws that might apply to Linda Thompson's case:

- The Fourteenth Amendment of the U.S. Constitution guaranteeing equal protection of the law
- Federal statutes on civil rights, sex discrimination, disability discrimination, evidence and civil procedure in federal courts, etc.
- Opinions of federal courts on civil rights, sex discrimination, disability discrimination, evidence, civil procedure in federal courts, etc.
- Administrative regulations on sex discrimination of the U.S. Equal Employment Opportunity Commission and other federal administrative agencies
- The Equal Rights Amendment of the state constitution prohibiting sex discrimination
- State statutes on unemployment compensation, civil rights, sex discrimination, evidence and civil procedure in state courts, etc.
- State court opinions on unemployment compensation, civil rights, sex discrimination, evidence and civil procedure in state courts, etc.
- Administrative regulations on unemployment compensation of the state unemployment compensation commission

These are the kinds of laws that might have to be found and applied by a law office that represents a client such as Linda Thompson. Note the different levels and branches of government that could be involved. This interaction gives us the definition of our legal system. It is *an organized method of resolving legal disputes and achieving justice through the interpretation and enforcement of laws written by different levels and branches of government*. To participate, paralegals need to have a basic understanding of the essential components of this process. The chapters in part II of this book are designed to provide this understanding.

ASSIGNMENT 6.1

(a) Exhibit 6.1 presents the main categories of law. As we will see later in chapters 11 and 13, a great deal of this law is available on the Internet. Even before studying those chapters, however, you should be able to find some of this law now. If, for example, you wanted to find a statute written by the Florida legislature or by Congress, you could type the search "Florida statute" or "federal statute" or "United States statute" in any search engine (e.g., www.google.com). Using this general guide, find one example of each of the following material on the Internet. When asked for state material, use the state where you will be working as a paralegal. Give the name of what you found and the Internet address where you found it: (1) a federal court opinion; (2) a state court opinion; (3) a federal statute; (4) a state

(continues)

statute; (5) a clause in the U.S. Constitution; (6) a clause in a state constitution; (7) an administrative regulation of a federal agency; (8) an administrative regulation of a state agency; (9) an administrative decision of a federal agency; (10) a city or county charter; (11) a city, county, or town ordinance; (12) a rule of court of a federal court; (13) a rule of court of a state court; (14) an executive order of the president; (15) an executive order of a governor; (16) a treaty signed by the United States; (17) a federal opinion of the attorney general; and (18) a state opinion of the attorney general.

(b) Find a recent article in your local general newspaper that meets the following criteria: (1) it refers to more than one kind of law listed in Exhibit 6.1, and (2) it refers to more than one level of government. The article will have no formal citations to laws, so do the best you can to guess what kinds of law and levels of government are involved. Clip out the article. In the margin, next to each reference to a law, place the appropriate abbreviation: FO (if you think the reference is to a federal court opinion); SO (if you think the reference is to a state court opinion); FS (federal statute); SS (state statute); FC (U.S. Constitution); SC (state constitution); FAR (administrative regulation of a federal agency); SAR (administrative regulation of a state agency). Make up your own abbreviations for any other kind of law listed in Exhibit 6.1. If the article refers to the same law more than once, make a margin note only the first time the law is mentioned. (We'll have an informal contest to see which student can find the article with the most different kinds of laws involving more than one level of government.)

[SECTION B]

COMMON LAW AND OUR ADVERSARIAL SYSTEM

Before examining the components of our judicial system, we need to understand two of its critical characteristics: it is based on the common law and it is adversarial.

The phrase **common law** has at least four meanings, the last of which will be our primary concern in this book:

- At the broadest level, common law simply means case law—court opinions—as opposed to statutory law. In this sense, all case law develops and is part of the common law.
- Common law also refers to the legal system of England and the United States. Common law originated in England during the early Middle Ages when judges in the king's courts created law based on customs and well-established principles. At the time, a unique feature of this law was that it was enforced throughout England—it was *common* throughout the realm. The English legal system (later adopted and adapted in the United States) had its foundation in the decided cases containing this common law. The counterpart of the common law system is the **civil law system** of many Western European countries other than England. The origin of civil law includes the jurisprudence of the Roman Empire set forth in the Code of Justinian. Many civil codes in Europe (other than England) have been greatly influenced by the Code Napoléon of France. Both the common law system and the civil law system rely on statutory codes and on case law. The difference is primarily one of emphasis. In a common law system, the role of case law is greater than it is in a civil law system. On the other hand, in a civil law system, statutory or code law has greater prominence than it does in a common law system. Forty-nine states in the United States have a common law system. Louisiana is unique in that its law is largely based on civil law due to the historical importance of France in that state. (An entirely different meaning of civil law is any noncriminal law. Under this meaning, a civil wrong is a transgression other than a crime.)
- More narrowly, common law refers to all of the case law *and* statutory law in England and in the American colonies before the American Revolution. The phrase **at common law** often refers to this colonial period.
- Judge-made law in the absence of controlling statutory law or other higher law.

The fourth definition is the most important. Courts are sometimes confronted with disputes for which there is no applicable law. There may be no constitutional provisions or statutes governing the dispute. When this occurs, the court will apply—and if necessary, create—common law to resolve the controversy. This is judge-made law created in the absence of statutory law or of

common law (1) Court opinions; all of case law. (2) The legal system of England and of those countries such as the United States whose legal system is based on England's. (3) The case law and statutory law in England and in the American colonies before the American Revolution. (4) Judge-made law in the absence of controlling statutory law or other higher law.

civil law system The legal system of many Western European countries (other than England) that places a greater emphasis on statutory or code law than do countries (such as England and the United States) whose common law system places a greater emphasis on case law.

at common law All the case law and statutory law in England and in the American colonies before the Revolution.

other higher law needed to resolve the case at hand. In creating the common law, the court relies primarily on the unwritten customs and values of the community from time immemorial. Very often these customs and values are described and enforced in old opinions that are heavily cited by modern courts in the continuing process of developing the common law.

The common law grows slowly, case by case. Radical changes are not encouraged and, therefore, are relatively rare. Once a court decides a case, it becomes a potential **precedent** that can be helpful as a standard or guide for the resolution of similar cases that arise in the future. Under the doctrine of **stare decisis**, a court will decide similar cases in the same way (i.e., it will follow available precedents) unless there is good reason for the court to do otherwise. Courts are most comfortable when they can demonstrate that their decisions are rooted in precedent. Knowing this, attorneys and paralegals study precedents in order to try to predict how a court might resolve a current case.

Suppose, for example, that a law firm is representing a client who is being sued for battery, which is a common law **cause of action**. He took a baseball bat and forcefully hit the handle bars of a bicycle on which the plaintiff was riding at the time. The bat did not touch the plaintiff's body. This case raises the question of whether you can batter someone without making contact with his or her body. One of the steps the law firm will take in representing this client is to do legal research in order to try to find precedents for this kind of case. Assume that on the shelves of the law library (or in an online legal database), the attorney or paralegal finds the prior case of *Harrison v. Linner*. This case decided that the defendant committed a battery when he knocked over a plate being held by the plaintiff even though the defendant never touched any part of the plaintiff's body. Is *Harrison v. Linner* a precedent for the bicycle case? Is hitting a bicycle handle with a bat sufficiently similar to knocking a plate out of someone's hand? The law firm must predict whether a court will apply *Harrison v. Linner* to the bicycle case. Making such a prediction requires legal analysis, which we will be studying in chapter 7. For our purposes, the example illustrates how precedent is used in our common law system. When the bicycle case goes before the court, the attorneys for both sides will be spending a good deal of time trying to convince the court that *Harrison v. Linner* is or is not a precedent.

Note that the fourth definition of common law says judge-made law in the absence of controlling statutory law or other higher law. There is a hierarchy in the categories of law. Constitutional law, for example, is higher in authority than statutory law. So, too, statutory law is higher in authority than common law. Assume that the courts have created common law in an area where no controlling statutes existed. This does not mean that statutes can never play a role in this area. The legislature can now decide to step in and create statutes that change the common law in this area. Such statutes are said to be *in derogation of the common law.*

One of the best examples of the interplay between common law and statutory law can be found in the area of contracts. A great deal of contract law was created by the courts as common law. Centuries ago, for example, the courts created the principle that a contract was not enforceable unless it was supported by **consideration**. Over the years, statutes have been written to change many common law contract principles. In some kinds of contracts, for example, statutes have changed the common law of consideration. For commercial contracts, the greatest statutory changes were brought about by the Uniform Commercial Code (UCC). Many other contract statutes in derogation of the common law also exist. Today, contract law consists of a mix of statutes and those common law principles that have not been changed by legislatures or indeed by the courts themselves, who are always free to change their own common law. This evolution of the common law has been taking place for centuries and has given us what commentators call the "seamless web" of the common law.

The second critical characteristic of our judicial system is that it is **adversarial**. An **adversary system** is a form of head-to-head combat. If a dispute arises, you get everyone in the same room and have them fight it out—in the open. This approach is based on the theory that justice and truth have a greater chance of being achieved when the parties to a controversy appear (on their own or through a representative or advocate) before a neutral judge to present their conflicting positions. We don't expect the judge to control the case by calling and questioning the witnesses. By and large, we leave this to the parties and their representatives. Ideally, the parties have an equal opportunity to present their case to the decision maker.[1] Unfortunately, the system is often criticized for failing to live up to this ideal. In many disputes between a citizen and a corporation, for example, the citizen cannot afford the kind of representation available to the corporation. Not all countries use an adversary system. Civil law countries, for example, often follow an **inquisitorial system**

---

precedent A prior decision covering a similar issue that can be used as a standard or guide in a later case.

stare decisis ("stand by things decided") Courts should decide similar cases in the same way unless there is good reason for the court to do otherwise. In resolving an issue before it, a court should be reluctant to reject precedent—a prior opinion covering a similar issue.

cause of action A legally acceptable reason for suing. Facts that give a party the right to judicial relief.

derogation A partial repealing or abolishing of a law, as by a subsequent act that limits its scope or force.

consideration A bargained-for promise, act, or forbearance. Something of value exchanged between the parties.

adversarial Involving conflict or adversaries.

adversary system A method of resolving a legal dispute whereby the parties (alone or through their advocates) argue their conflicting claims before a neutral decision maker.

inquisitorial system A method of resolving a legal dispute in some civil law countries in which the judge has a more active role in questioning the witnesses and in conducting the trial than in an adversary system.

in which the judge has a more active role in questioning the witnesses and in conducting the trial than in an adversary system.

[SECTION C]

LAW AND EQUITY

One final point about the common law. At one time in our history, most states had two separate state court systems: *common law courts* (also called *law courts* or *courts of law*) and *courts of equity* (also called *equity courts* and *Chancery courts*). Common law courts applied the common law (referred to as "legal" principles of law or, in shorthand, as the "law"). Courts of equity applied **equity** (referred to as "equitable" principles of law).

A major reason courts of equity were developed was to provide parties with more flexible remedies and greater fairness than common law courts could sometimes provide. In a common law court, for example, a victim of a breach of contract would be limited to recovering a money judgment (i.e., damages) from the wrongdoer. In some cases, this remedy was inadequate (and, in fact, was referred to as an *inadequate remedy at law*). Suppose, for example, that Tom breaches his contract to sell Mary a painting that Mary's uncle painted before she was born. In a common law court, she would be limited to winning damages from Tom. In a court of equity, however, she might be able to obtain the equitable remedy of **specific performance**, which would direct Tom to perform the contract as promised and turn over the painting to her. If Tom tried to sell the painting overseas, Mary could seek an **injunction** that orders him not to remove the painting. An injunction is another equitable remedy that she could not obtain in a court of law. She would undoubtedly consider such remedies to be fairer than a mere award of damages; her goal was the painting itself, not cash.

In most states today we no longer have separate common law and equity courts. Parties can request the application of equitable principles in whatever courts they are in. There has been what is called a *merger of law and equity*, meaning that the same court can apply legal and equitable principles.

[SECTION D]

JUDICIAL SYSTEMS

There are two main kinds of courts: **constitutional courts** (those created within the constitution) and **legislative courts** (those created by the legislature). The lifeblood of both kinds of courts is its **jurisdiction**. After examining the nature of jurisdiction, our goal in this section will be to identify the major courts that exist and how they are interrelated.

At the broadest level, jurisdiction has two main meanings. First, and most importantly, it refers to the *power* of a court to decide a matter in dispute. When, for example, we say, "The court has jurisdiction over labor strikes," we are referring to a court's power to resolve legal issues involving labor strikes. Second, it refers to the *geographic area* over which a particular court has authority. When, for example, we say, "The court can act in the jurisdiction of New York," we are referring to a place—the state of New York. Our primary concern in this section will be the power definition of jurisdiction. As we will see, there are several subdivisions of this power.

1. JURISDICTION

There are fifty state court systems and one main federal court system. (In addition, the District of Columbia has its own court system.) Each court within a system is identified by its jurisdiction to **adjudicate** (i.e., resolve judicially) a legal dispute brought before it. Here we are referring to the power definition of jurisdiction. There are two categories of this power.

First, there is the power over the persons or over the property involved in the litigation. Power over the person is called **personal jurisdiction** (also, in personam jurisdiction). If the court is not able to obtain personal jurisdiction over the defendant, it still may be able to make an order over a particular thing or status (called the *res*) located within the territory over which the court has authority. An example of a res would be land. The jurisdiction that a court needs to render a judgment over such a res is called **in rem jurisdiction**. Everyone with an interest in the res (e.g., anyone who claims to own all or a part of it), and not just those over whom the court has personal

---

equity Justice administered according to fairness in a particular case, as contrasted with strictly formalized rules once followed by common law courts.

specific performance An equitable remedy that orders the performance of a contract according to the precise terms agreed upon by the parties.

injunction An equitable remedy that orders a person or organization to do or to refrain from doing something.

constitutional court A court created within the Constitution. (At the federal level, they are called Article III courts because they are created within Article III of the U.S. Constitution.)

legislative court A court created by the legislature. (At the federal level, they are called Article I courts because Article I of the U.S. Constitution gives Congress the authority to create special courts.)

jurisdiction 1. The power of a court to decide a matter in controversy. 2. The geographic area over which a particular court system or other government unit has authority. 3. The scope of power or authority that a person or entity can exercise. (For a definition of the closely related term *venue*, see chapter 10, and the glossary.)

adjudicate To hear and resolve a legal matter judicially. To judge. The noun is *adjudication*; the adjective is *adjudicative*.

personal jurisdiction A court's power over a person to adjudicate his or her personal rights.

in rem jurisdiction The court's power over a particular thing or status ("res") located within the territory over which the court has authority.

quasi-in-rem jurisdiction A court's power over a person, but restricted to his or her specific interest in property within the territory over which the court has authority.

subject matter jurisdiction The court's power to resolve a particular kind or category of dispute.

jurisdiction, must obey the judgment of a court with in rem jurisdiction. If only designated or named individuals must obey the judgment on the res, the court's power to issue the judgment would be called **quasi-in-rem jurisdiction**.

The second kind of power that enables a court to adjudicate a dispute is its power over the subject matter of the dispute. By *subject matter*, we mean the particular kind or category of case involved (e.g., copyright infringement, manslaughter, or divorce). This power is called **subject matter jurisdiction**. The most common classifications of subject-matter jurisdiction are as follows:

- Limited jurisdiction
- General jurisdiction
- Exclusive jurisdiction
- Concurrent jurisdiction
- Original jurisdiction
- Appellate jurisdiction

a. Limited Jurisdiction

limited jurisdiction The court's power to hear only certain kinds of cases. Also called *special jurisdiction*.

A court of **limited** (or special) subject matter **jurisdiction** can hear only certain kinds of cases. A criminal court is not allowed to take a noncriminal case, and a small claims court is authorized to hear only cases in which the plaintiff claims an amount of money as damages from the defendant that is below the maximum set by statute. If a plaintiff brings a civil case in a criminal court or seeks damages in a small claims court that are above the maximum, the defendant can challenge the court's subject matter jurisdiction.

b. General Jurisdiction

general jurisdiction The power of a court to hear any kind of civil or criminal case, with certain exceptions.

state questions Issues that arise from or are based on the state constitution, state statutes, state administrative regulations, state common law, or other state laws.

federal questions Issues that arise from or are based on the federal constitution, federal statutes, federal administrative regulations, or other federal laws.

A court of **general jurisdiction** can, with some exceptions, hear any kind of civil or criminal case. (Here, the word *civil* simply means noncriminal.) A state court of general jurisdiction can hear any case that raises **state questions** (i.e., questions arising from or based on the state constitution, state statutes, state regulations, state common law, or other state laws); a federal court of general jurisdiction can hear any case that raises **federal questions** (i.e., questions arising from or based on the federal constitution, federal statutes, federal regulations, or other federal laws). In this context, the word *federal* means United States. The U.S. government is the federal government, U.S. law is federal law, U.S. courts are federal courts, etc.

c. Exclusive Jurisdiction

exclusive jurisdiction The power of a court to hear a particular kind of case, to the exclusion of other courts.

A court of **exclusive jurisdiction** is the only court that can handle a certain kind of case. For example, a juvenile court may have exclusive jurisdiction over all cases involving children under a designated age who are charged with acts of delinquency. If this kind of case is brought in another court, there could be a challenge on the grounds that the court lacked subject matter jurisdiction over the case.

d. Concurrent Jurisdiction

concurrent jurisdiction The power of a court to hear a particular kind of case, along with other courts that could also hear it.

Sometimes two courts have jurisdiction over a case; the case could be brought in either court. In such a situation, both courts are said to have **concurrent jurisdiction** over the case. For example, a family court and a county court may have jurisdiction to enforce a child-support order.

e. Original Jurisdiction

original jurisdiction The power of a court to be the first to hear a case before it is reviewed by another court.

A court of **original jurisdiction** is one with the power to be the first to hear a case before it is reviewed by another court. It is also called a *trial court* or a *court of first instance*. In addition, it is a court of limited jurisdiction (if it can try only certain kinds of cases), or of general jurisdiction (if it can try cases involving any subject matter), or of exclusive jurisdiction (if the trial can take place only in that court), or of concurrent jurisdiction (if the trial can take place either in that court or in another court).

f. Appellate Jurisdiction

appellate jurisdiction The power of an appellate court to review and correct the decisions of a lower tribunal.

A court with **appellate jurisdiction** can hear appeals from lower tribunals (e.g., a lower court, an administrative agency) to determine whether the lower tribunal committed any error of law. For example, at the federal level, the U.S. Supreme Court has appellate jurisdiction to review a decision of a U.S. Court of Appeals. Similarly, at the state level, the New York Court of Appeals has appellate jurisdiction to review a decision of a lower New York state court. The reexamination of what the lower tribunal has done is called a **review**. Sometimes a party who is dissatisfied with a lower court ruling can appeal as a matter of right to the appellate court (the court must hear the appeal); in other kinds of cases, the appellate court has discretion as to whether it will hear the appeal. If the appellate court uses its discretion to hear the appeal, the court issues a **writ of certiorari** (abbreviated cert.). This writ orders the lower court to certify the record of the lower court proceeding and send it up to the appellate court for review. If the appellate court uses its discretion to refuse to hear the appeal, the lower court's decision is final.

review The power of a court to examine the correctness of what a lower tribunal has done. Short for *judicial review*.

writ of certiorari (cert.) An order (or writ) by a higher court that a lower court send up the record of a case because the higher court has decided to use its discretion to review that case.

2. STATE COURT SYSTEMS

First, we examine state judicial systems—our state courts. States may differ in the names of their courts and in the number of appellate courts that they have, as we will see in Exhibit 6.2.

a. State Courts of Original Jurisdiction

A court of original jurisdiction is a trial court. A state may have one or more levels or tiers of trial courts (referred to as tier I and tier II in Exhibit 6.2). Trial courts hear the dispute, determine the facts of the case, and make the initial determination or ruling. In addition, they may sometimes have the power to review cases that were initially decided by an administrative agency.

EXHIBIT 6.2	State Judicial Systems

NOTE: The names of state courts differ from state to state. The chart here in Exhibit 6.2 presents an overview of the names that exist. For the specific names of state courts in your state, go to:

- www.ncsconline.org (click "Court Web Sites" and "State Court Structure Charts")
- www.govengine.com (click "Your State")
- www.google.com (type the abbreviation for your state and "Court System" [in quotes], e.g., CA "Court System")

Level of Court	Name(s) of Court at this Level in Different States	Function of Court at this Level	Lines of Appeal
Trial courts: tier I	Superior court, circuit court, district court, court of common pleas (in New York, the trial court at this level is called the supreme court)	■ Tier I trial courts are courts of original jurisdiction—trial courts. ■ Tier I trial courts have general jurisdiction.	Cases from tier I trial courts are appealed to the intermediate appellate courts in the state if the state has intermediate appellate courts. If the state does not have such courts, cases are appealed to the court of final resort.
Trial courts: tier II (interior courts)	Probate court, small claims court, family court, municipal court, county court, district court, justice of the peace court, police court, city court, water court (trial courts at this level are sometimes called *inferior courts*)	■ Tier II trial courts are courts of original jurisdiction—trial courts. A tier II trial court is considered a lower (inferior) level of trial court than a tier I trial court. ■ Tier II trial courts have limited or special jurisdiction. *Examples:* The Probate Court (also called Surrogate Court) hears estate cases of deceased or incompetent persons; the Small Claims Court hears cases involving small amounts of money (damages); the Family Court hears divorce, custody, and other domestic relations matters; the Municipal Court hears traffic cases and those involving petty crimes.	Cases from tier II trial courts (those of limited or special jurisdiction) are often appealed to tier I trial courts of general jurisdiction. Some, however, are appealed to the intermediate appellate courts (if they exist) or to the court of final resort.
Intermediate appellate courts (exist in about half the states)	Court of appeals, court of civil appeals, court of criminal appeals, appellate court, appeals court, district court of appeals, intermediate court of appeals, court of special appeals, appellate division of superior court	■ Intermediate appellate courts are courts of appellate jurisdiction.	An intermediate appellate court hears appeals from trial courts in the state. If the state does not have intermediate appellate courts, appeals go directly from the trial court to the court of final resort.
The court of final resort—the highest court in the state court system	Supreme court, supreme judicial court, supreme court of appeals, court of appeals	■ The court of final resort has appellate jurisdiction.	The court of final resort hears appeals from lower courts in the state. If the state has intermediate appellate courts, appeals are heard from these courts. If intermediate appellate courts do not exist in the state, the court of final resort hears appeals directly from trial courts.

inferior court A trial court of
limited or special jurisdiction.
(A broader meaning of inferior
court is any court that is subordinate to the court of final
resort.)

The most common arrangement is a two-tier system of trial courts. At the lower level are courts of limited or special jurisdiction, the so-called **inferior courts**. Local courts, such as city courts, county courts, small claims courts, or justice of the peace courts, often fall into this category. These courts may have original jurisdiction over relatively minor cases, such as violations of local ordinances and lawsuits involving small sums of money. Also included in this category are special courts that are limited to specific matters, such as surrogate courts or probate courts that hear matters involving the estates of deceased or mentally incompetent persons.

Immediately above the trial courts of limited jurisdiction are the trial courts of general jurisdiction, which usually handle more serious cases, such as lawsuits involving large sums of money. (See "Trial courts: tier I" in Exhibit 6.2.) The name given to the trial courts at this second level varies greatly from state to state. They are known as superior courts, circuit courts, district courts, or courts of common pleas. New York is especially confusing. There, the trial court of general jurisdiction is called the *supreme court*, a label reserved in most states for the court of final appeals, the highest court in the system.

Not all states have a two-tier trial system. Some states do not have inferior courts of limited jurisdiction; they have only one court of original jurisdiction. Moreover, the individual levels may be segmented into divisions. A court of general jurisdiction, for example, may be broken up into specialized divisions such as landlord-tenant, family, juvenile, and criminal divisions.

b. State Courts of Appellate Jurisdiction

appellate brief A document
submitted (filed) by a party to
an appellate court (and served
on the opposing party) in which
arguments are presented on
why the appellate court should
affirm (approve), reverse, or
otherwise modify what a lower
court has done.

panel A group of judges, usually
three, who decide a case in a
court with a larger number of
judges. (See the glossary for
other meanings of *panel*.)

en banc By the entire court.

court of final resort The
highest court within a judicial
system.

An appellate court has appellate jurisdiction that allows it to review decisions of a lower tribunal, usually a lower court. The goal of the review is to determine whether the lower court committed any errors of law by incorrectly interpreting or applying the law to the facts of the dispute. In this review process, appellate courts do *not* make their own findings of fact. No new evidence is taken, and no witnesses are called. The court limits itself to an analysis of the trial court record (consisting of transcripts of testimony, copies of the various documents that were filed, etc.) to determine if that lower court made any errors of law. Attorneys submit **appellate briefs** containing their arguments on the correctness or incorrectness of what the lower court did.

An appellate court often consists of an odd number of justices, e.g., 5, 7, 9, 11, 15. This helps avoid tie votes. Some of these courts hear cases in smaller groups of judges, usually three. These groups are called **panels**. Once a panel renders its decision, the parties have the right to petition for an **en banc** review by the same court. If granted, a much larger number of appellate judges on the court (often all of them) will review the case.

Many states have only one level of appellate court to which trial court judgments are appealed. About half the states have two levels or tiers of appellate courts. The first level is the intermediate appellate court, sometimes called the *court of middle appeals*. The decisions of this court can in turn be reviewed by the court of final appeals. This latter court, often known as the supreme court, is the **court of final resort**. About half the states do not have intermediate appellate courts. Appeals from trial courts in such states go directly to the court of final resort.

ASSIGNMENT 6.2

(a) Redo Exhibit 6.2 so that your chart includes all the state courts of your state. Identify each level of state court in your state, using Exhibit 6.2 as a guide. Give the complete name of each court you include and a one-sentence description of its subject matter jurisdiction. Indicate the lines of appeal among these courts. To find out what state courts exist in your state, check the Internet sites presented at the beginning of Exhibit 6.2.

(b) Select any state trial court of general jurisdiction in your state. Give its name, address, and phone number. Include the e-mail address and the World Wide Web site if the court has either. Also give the name, phone number, and fax number of the chief clerk of this court.

(c) Give the name, address, and phone number of the court to which decisions of the trial court you selected are appealed. Include the e-mail address and the World Wide Web site if the court has either. Also give the name, phone number, and fax number of the chief clerk of this appellate court.

3. FEDERAL COURT SYSTEM

The federal court system, like the state systems, consists of two basic kinds of courts: courts of original jurisdiction (trial courts) and courts of appellate jurisdiction (appellate courts). See Exhibit 6.3.

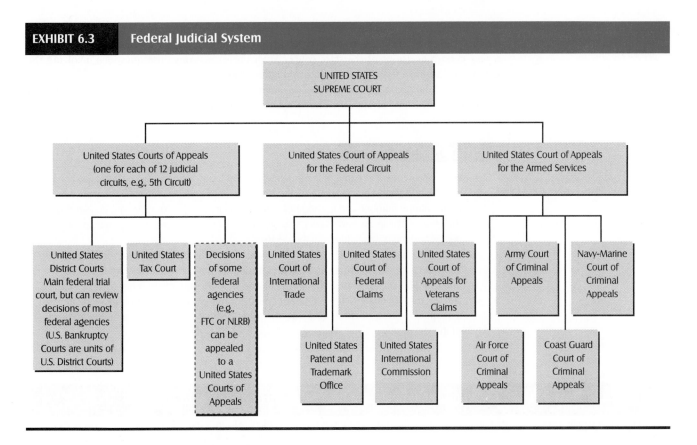

| EXHIBIT 6.3 | Federal Judicial System |

a. Federal Courts of Original Jurisdiction

The main federal court at the trial level is the **U.S. District Court**. It hears two main categories of cases: those that raise *federal questions* (e.g., whether an employer has violated the National Labor Relations Act) and those that involve **diversity of citizenship** (e.g., a citizen of Ohio sues a citizen of Idaho claiming $80,000 for a breach of contract). There are federal districts throughout the country, with at least one for every state, the District of Columbia, Guam, the Virgin Islands, and Puerto Rico. The district courts exercise general, original jurisdiction and also serve as courts of review for many cases initially decided by federal administrative agencies. U.S. Bankruptcy Courts are units of the U.S. District Courts. (U.S. bankruptcy judges hear those bankruptcy cases that are referred to them by U.S. district judges.)

In addition to the U.S. District Courts, several federal courts exercise limited, original jurisdiction over specialized cases. Such courts include the U.S. Court of Federal Claims (which hears contract and other non tort claims against the federal govenment), the U.S. Court of International Trade, and the U.S. Courts of Appeals for Veterans Claims.

b. Federal Courts of Appellate Jurisdiction

The federal system, like almost half of the fifty state judicial systems, has two levels or tiers of appellate courts: intermediate appellate courts and the court of final resort. The primary courts at the intermediate appellate level are the **U.S. Courts of Appeals** (formerly called *circuit courts of appeals*). There are twelve of these courts, one for each of the twelve judicial circuits in the country. Eleven of the circuits are made up of groupings of various states and territories. The District of Columbia has its own circuit. The main function of the U.S. Courts of Appeals is to review the decisions of the federal courts of original jurisdiction, primarily the district courts and the tax court. In addition, decisions of certain federal agencies, e.g., the Federal Trade Commission (FTC) and the National Labor Relations Board (NLRB), are reviewed directly by a court of appeals without first going to a district court. There is a specialized court of appeals called the *court of appeals for the federal circuit*. This court reviews (1) decisions from the U.S. Court of International Trade, the U.S. Court of Federal Claims, the U.S. Court of Appeals for Veterans Claims, the U.S. Patent and Trademark Office, the U.S. International Commission; and (2) some decisions of the district courts where the U.S. government is a defendant. Finally, the U.S. Court of Appeals for the Armed Services reviews decisions of the courts of criminal appeals within the branches of the military.

U.S. District Court The main trial court in the federal judicial system.

diversity of citizenship The disputing parties are citizens of different states and the amount in controversy exceeds $75,000. This diversity gives jurisdiction to a U.S. District Court.

U.S. Court of Appeals The main intermediate appellate court in the federal judicial system.

U.S. Supreme Court The court of final resort in the federal judicial system.

The federal court of final resort is, of course, the **U.S. Supreme Court**, which provides the final review of the decisions of all federal courts and agencies. The Supreme Court may also review certain decisions of the state courts when these decisions raise questions involving the U.S. Constitution, a federal statute, or other federal law.

Exhibit 6.4 illustrates the division of the federal court system into twelve circuits. Each circuit has its own U.S. Court of Appeals. The U.S. District Courts exist within these circuits.

ASSIGNMENT 6.3

(a) What is the complete name of the federal trial court that covers where you live? Give its address and phone number. Include the e-mail address and the Web site. Also state the name, phone number, and fax number of the chief clerk of this court. Are the decisions of this court available on its Web site? If so, pick a recent decision, and give the names of the parties and the online address of the decision.

(b) What is the name of the U.S. Court of Appeals to which decisions of your federal trial court are appealed? Give its address and phone number. Include the e-mail address and the Web site. Also state the name, phone number, and fax number of the chief clerk of this appellate court. Are the decisions of this court available on its Web site? If so, pick a recent decision, and give the names of the parties and the online address of the decision.

EXHIBIT 6.4   The Eleven U.S. Courts of Appeals and the U.S. District Courts within Them

(The dotted lines within a state indicate boundary lines for the district courts; If no dotted lines exist in a state, the district court covers the entire state.)

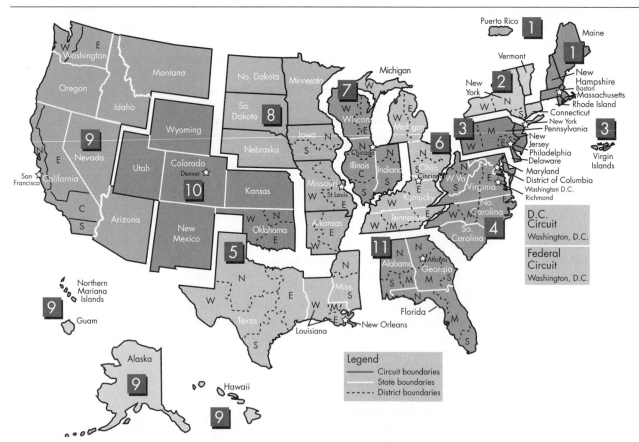

Source: Administrative Office of the United States Courts, January 1983 (www.uscourts.gov/courtlinks)

[SECTION E]

ADMINISTRATIVE AGENCIES

An **administrative agency** is a governmental body, other than a court or legislature, that carries out (i.e., administers or executes) the statutes of the legislature, the executive orders of the chief executive, and its own regulations. At the federal level, the chief of the executive branch of government is the president; at the state level, it is the governor; and at most local levels, it is the mayor. As we will see in a moment, many agencies do more than carry out or execute the law; they also have rule-making and dispute resolution responsibilities.

Administrative agencies can have a wide variety of names. Here are some examples:

- Fire Department
- Board of Licenses and Occupations
- Civil Service Commission
- Agency for International Development
- Department of Defense
- Office of Management and Budget
- Legal Services Corporation
- Bureau of Taxation
- Internal Revenue Service
- Division of Child Support and Enforcement
- Social Security Administration

Certain types of agencies exist at all three levels of government. For example, there is a separate tax collection agency in each of the federal, state, and local governments. Other agencies, however, are unique to one of the levels. For example, only the federal government has a Department of Defense (DOD) and a Central Intelligence Agency (CIA). Nothing comparable exists at the state and local levels of government. The latter have police departments and the highway patrol, but their roles are significantly different from those of the DOD and CIA.

For a list of some of the most important federal agencies, see appendix D.

There are three main kinds of administrative agencies:

- Executive department agencies
- Independent regulatory agencies
- Quasi-independent regulatory agencies

Executive department agencies exist within the executive branch of the government, often at the cabinet level. Examples include the Department of Agriculture and the Department of Labor. These agencies are answerable to the chief executive, who usually has the power to dismiss them for any reason. The chief executive does not have to establish **cause** for doing so.

Independent regulatory agencies exist outside the executive department and, therefore, outside the day-to-day control of the chief executive. Examples include the Securities and Exchange Commission and the Public Utilities Commission. Their function is usually to regulate an aspect of society—often a particular industry such as securities or public utilities. To insulate these agencies from politics, those in charge usually cannot be removed at the whim of the chief executive; *cause* must be established.

A **quasi-independent regulatory agency** is a hybrid agency, often with characteristics of the two kinds just described. It has more independence than an executive department agency, yet it might exist within the executive department. An example is the Federal Energy Regulatory Commission, which exists within the U.S. Department of Energy.

In a category all its own is the **government corporation**. This is a government-owned entity that has characteristics of a business corporation and a government agency. It is designed to have considerable flexibility and independence in carrying out a predominantly business function in the public interest. Examples include the Tennessee Valley Authority, the U.S. Post Office, and the Corporation for Public Broadcasting. The government establishes this entity and usually provides its initial funding. Often, however, a substantial portion of its ongoing budget comes from fees and private charitable giving. Members of the boards of directors of federal government corporations are usually appointed by the president and confirmed by the Senate.

---

administrative agency A governmental body, other than a court or legislature, that carries out (i.e., administers or executes) the statutes of the legislature, the executive orders of the chief executive, and its own regulations.

executive department agency An administrative agency that exists within the executive branch of government, often at the cabinet level.

cause A legally sufficient reason to do something. Sometimes referred to as *just cause* or *good cause*.

independent regulatory agency An administrative agency that regulates an aspect of society. It often exists outside the executive branch of government.

quasi-independent regulatory agency An administrative agency that has characteristics of an executive department agency and an independent regulatory agency.

government corporation A government-owned entity that is a mixture of a business corporation and a government agency created to serve a predominantly business function in the public interest.

Many administrative agencies have three functions: execution, rule making, and dispute resolution:

- **quasi-legislation** An administrative regulation enacted by an administrative agency that has some characteristics of the legislation (statutes) enacted by the legislature.

- ■ *Execution.* The primary function of the agency is to execute (i.e., carry out or administer) the statutes and executive orders governing the agency as well as the administrative regulations created by the agency itself. This is the agency's executive function.
- ■ *Rule making.* The agency often has the authority to write administrative regulations (also called administrative rules). (See Exhibit 6.1 for a definition of administrative regulation.) In so doing, the agency is "making law" like a legislature. Indeed, such laws are often referred to as **quasi-legislation**. When considering a new regulation, the agency often publishes it in a register (e.g., the *Federal Register* for federal agencies) in order to give the public an opportunity to comment on the proposed regulation. Once finalized, the regulation is often published in a code (e.g., the *Code of Federal Regulations* for federal agencies).
- ■ *Dispute resolution.* The agency has the authority to interpret the statutes and regulations that govern it. Furthermore, it often has the authority to resolve disputes that arise over the application of such laws. It will hold administrative hearings and issue decisions. (See Exhibit 6.1 for a definition of administrative decision.) In this sense, the agency is acting like a court when the latter adjudicates (i.e., resolves) disputes. The dispute resolution power of the agency is therefore called a quasi-judicial power. The phrase **quasi-adjudication** refers to a written decision of an administrative agency that resolves a legal dispute in a manner that is similar to the way a court resolves such a dispute. An agency exercises its quasi-judicial power at several levels. At the first level is a *hearing*, which is similar to a trial in a court of original jurisdiction. The presiding agency official—known variously as hearing examiner, trial examiner, or **administrative law judge (ALJ)**—will, like the judge in a trial court, take testimony of witnesses, examine other evidence, determine the facts of the case, and apply the law to those facts in order to render a decision. In many agencies, the findings of fact and the decision of the hearing officer constitute only a recommendation to the director, commissioner, secretary, or other high official who will make the decision at this level. Like the courts, many agencies then provide a second, "appellate" level where a body such as a board or commission reviews the decision of the hearing examiner (or other official) to correct errors. After the parties to the dispute have used all these avenues of redress within the agency, they have **exhausted administrative remedies** and may then appeal the final administrative decision to a court. For federal and many state administrative agencies, the procedures that must be followed within the agencies are defined in the **Administrative Procedure Act** (APA).

- **quasi-adjudication** An administrative decision written by an administrative agency that has some characteristics of an opinion written by a court.

- **administrative law judge (ALJ)** A government officer who presides over a hearing at an administrative agency.

- **exhaust administrative remedies** To go through all dispute-solving avenues that are available in an administrative agency before asking a court to review what the agency did.

- **Administrative Procedure Act (APA)** The statute that governs procedures before federal administrative agencies. Many states have their own APA for procedures before state administrative agencies.

Here is an example of an agency using all three powers:

Securities and Exchange Commission (SEC)

- ■ *Execution.* The SEC accepts filings of registration statements containing financial data on issuers of securities. This is done to carry out the statutes of Congress requiring such registration. When an agency carries out a statute, it is administering or executing that statute.
- ■ *Rule making.* The SEC writes regulations that provide greater detail on what the registration statements must contain.
- ■ *Dispute resolution.* The SEC holds a hearing to decide whether a corporation has violated the registration requirements laid out in the statutes and administrative regulations. The end product of the hearing can be an administrative decision.

ASSIGNMENT 6.4

Give the name, street address, phone number, fax number, e-mail address, World Wide Web address, and function (stated briefly) of:

(a) Three federal agencies with offices in your state.

(b) Five state agencies in your state.

(c) Five city or county agencies with offices in your city or county.

[SECTION F]

THE LEGISLATIVE PROCESS

- **bill** A proposed statute. Legislation under consideration by a legislature. (Occasionally, *bill* means a statute, e.g., the GI Bill.)

The legislative process consists of the steps that a bill must go through before it becomes a statute. (A **bill** is simply a proposed statute.) Exhibit 6.5 outlines these steps for the federal

EXHIBIT 6.5   The Legislative History of a Federal Statute—How a Bill Becomes a Law

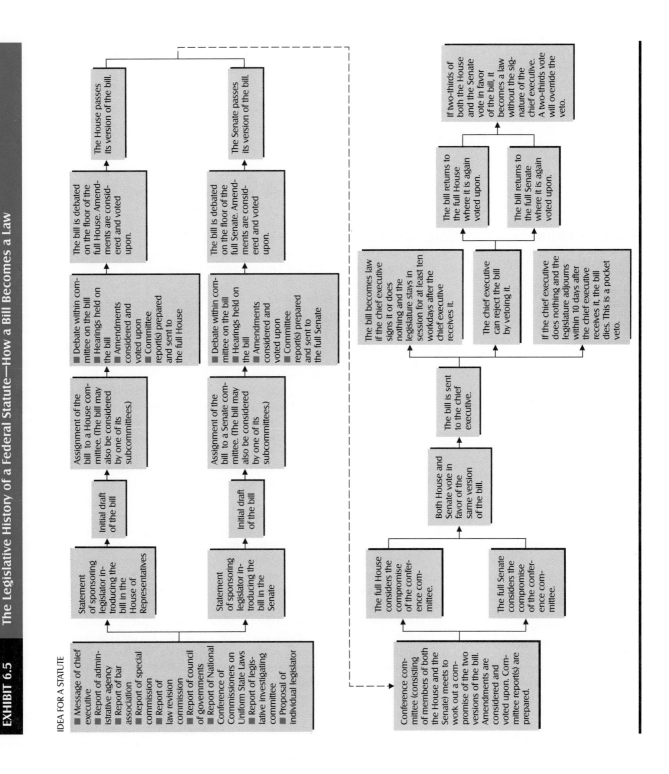

legislature—Congress. The chart in Exhibit 6.5 assumes that the same idea for a bill is introduced simultaneously in both chambers of Congress, the House of Representatives and the Senate. It is, of course, also possible for a bill to be introduced in one chamber, go through all the steps for passage in that chamber, and *then* be introduced in the other chamber. The conference committee step outlined in the chart occurs only when both chambers have enacted their own version of the bill.

bicameral Having two houses or chambers in the legislature.

unicameral Having one house or chamber in the legislature.

Congress is **bicameral**, meaning that it consists of two chambers, the House of Representatives and the Senate. In some state legislatures, the chambers have different names, such as the Assembly and the House of Delegates. Legislatures with one chamber are called **unicameral**. The only state legislature that is unicameral is the Nebraska legislature. Local legislatures, however, such as city councils, are often unicameral.

The process of enactment can involve six major stages:

- Proposal
- Initial committee consideration
- Floor debate
- Conference committee consideration
- Floor debate
- Response of the chief executive

legislative history Hearings, debates, amendments, committee reports, and all other events that occur in the legislature before a bill is enacted into a statute.

The **legislative history** of a statute is what occurs at each of these stages.

a. *Proposal.* A member of the legislature must formally introduce the bill. Where do the ideas for proposed laws originate? There are many possible sources. The chief executive of the government (for example, the president or governor) may initiate the process by sending the legislature a message stating the reasons for a proposed law. Frequently, an administrative agency has made a study of a problem, which is the impetus for the proposal. The agency will usually be the entity with responsibility for administering the proposal if it is enacted into law. The bar association might prepare a report to the legislature calling for the new legislation. The legislature or chief executive may have established a special commission to study the need for changes in the law and to propose changes where appropriate. The commission might consist of members of the legislature and outside experts. Some states have ongoing law revision commissions that frequently make proposals for legislation. In many areas, a council of governments made up of neighboring governments studies problems and proposes legislative changes. The National Conference of Commissioners on Uniform State Laws (www.nccusl.org) is an organization with members from each state. The conference makes proposals to the state legislatures for the enactment of uniform state laws where it deems uniformity to be desirable.

Most ideas for legislation come from within the legislature itself. One or both houses may have established an investigating committee to examine a particular problem and propose legislation where needed. Individual legislators can also generate ideas for bills, and often do so to fulfill promises made during the campaign that led to their election. Can private citizens propose a bill? No. They must convince an individual legislator to sponsor their idea for a bill. (As we saw in Exhibit 6.1, however, voters can participate in the enactment of statutes through the **initiative** and **referendum** process.)

initiative The electorate's power to propose and directly enact a statute or change in the constitution or to force the legislature to vote on the proposal.

referendum The electorate's power to give final approval to an existing provision of the constitution or statute of the legislature.

session 1. A continuous sitting of a legislature or court. 2. Any time in the day during which such a body sits.

transcript A word-for-word account. A written copy of oral testimony. *Transcribed* means taken down in a word-for-word account.

b. *Initial committee consideration.* When a member of the legislature introduces a bill, he or she usually accompanies it with a statement on why the bill should be enacted. As bills are introduced, they are assigned a consecutive number (e.g., S 250 is the 250th bill introduced in the Senate during the current **session**; HR 1753 is the 1753rd bill introduced in the House of Representatives during the current session).

Once the bill is introduced, it follows a similar procedure in each chamber. The bill is sent to the committee with responsibility over the subject matter of the bill—for example, a bill to change the criminal law might go to the Judiciary Committee. If the bill is complex, different portions of it may be sent to different committees. Often a committee will send the bill to one of its subcommittees. Hearings are held, first within the subcommittee and later within the full committee. Citizens and public officials give testimony for or against the bill. In some legislatures, a **transcript** (word-for-word account) is made of this testimony. The comments of the committee members are also *transcribed*. While the bill is being deliberated, members can offer amendments to the bill that are then voted on.

If the full committee votes in favor of the bill, it issues a report summarizing why the bill is needed and what its major provisions are. If there is disagreement on the committee, a minority report is often prepared.

c. *Floor debate.* The bill with its accompanying report(s) then goes to the floor of the chamber of which the committee is a part. The bill is debated by the full chamber. During the debate, which will be transcribed, members ask questions about the meaning of certain provisions in the bill: what is covered and what is not. Amendments are often made from the floor and voted upon. The final version of the bill accepted by the chamber is called the **engrossed bill**.

d. *Conference committee consideration.* Because both chambers act independently of each other in considering the bill, it is rare that they both produce exactly the same bill. Inevitably, the amendment process leads to different versions of the proposed law. To resolve these differences, a **conference committee** is established, consisting of key members of both chambers, such as the chairpersons of the committees that initially considered the bill or the members who first introduced or sponsored the bill. A compromise is attempted in the conference committee. Amendments are considered and a final report of the conference committee is issued. Dissenting members of the committee might prepare a minority report. The majority report summarizes the major terms of the compromise and explains why it should be enacted by each chamber.

e. *Floor debate.* The conference committee compromise then goes back to the floor of each chamber where more debate, explanations, and amendments are considered. Again, everything is transcribed. If both chambers pass the same version of the bill, usually by a majority vote, it goes to the chief executive. This version of the bill is called the **enrolled bill**.

f. *Response of chief executive.* There are three main ways for the bill to become law after it reaches the chief executive. First, he or she can sign it. Second, the chief executive can do nothing. If the legislature stays in session for at least ten weekdays after he or she receives it, the bill automatically becomes law—without requiring a signature. Third, if the chief executive rejects or **vetoes** the bill, it can still become law if both chambers of the legislature **override** the veto by a two-thirds vote.

There are two main ways for the chief executive to reject a bill. First, he or she can explicitly veto the bill. It then goes back to the legislature, often with the chief executive's reasons for the rejection. Second, he or she can do nothing. If the legislature adjourns within ten days after the chief executive receives it, the bill automatically dies. This is known as a **pocket veto**. Because the legislature is no longer in session, the pocket veto deprives the legislature of the opportunity to override the veto.

engrossed bill The version of a bill passed by one of the chambers of the legislature after incorporating amendments or other changes.

conference committee A temporary committee consisting of members of both chambers of the legislature that seeks to reach a compromise on two versions of the same bill each chamber passed.

enrolled bill A bill that is ready to be sent to the chief executive after both chambers of the legislature have passed it.

veto A rejection by the chief executive of a bill passed by the legislature.

override To supersede or change a result. To approve a bill over the veto of the chief executive.

pocket veto The chief executive's "silent" rejection of a bill by not acting on it within ten days of receiving it if the legislature adjourns during this period.

ASSIGNMENT 6.5

(a) Redraw Exhibit 6.5 so that your chart includes the steps needed for a bill to become a statute in your *state* legislature.

(b) Give the name, political party, street address, phone number, e-mail address, and fax number of the chief legislator in each chamber of your legislature, e.g., speaker of the house and president of the senate. (If your state legislature is unicameral [Nebraska], answer these questions for the one chamber that exists.)

(c) What is the World Wide Web address of your state legislature? On this site, can you find current statutes in the code? Current bills in the legislature? Explain what is available.

(d) What is the full name of the legislative committee in each chamber (e.g., judiciary committee) with primary authority to consider laws that directly affect your state courts, such as procedural laws that govern the conduct of litigation? Give the name, political party, phone number, e-mail address, and fax number of the current chairperson of each of these committees.

(e) What is the name of the *local* legislature in your city or county? Give the name, political party, street address, phone number, e-mail address, and fax number of the chief legislator of this body. (If you have both a city and a county legislature, answer this question for both.)

(f) What is the World Wide Web address of your local city legislature? Of your local county legislature? On these sites, can you find current ordinances or other laws in force? Current bills in the legislature? Explain what is available.

Chapter Summary

Our legal system consists of three levels of government (federal, state, and local) and three branches of government (executive, legislative, and judicial) within each level. Federalism is the division of powers between the federal or national government and the state governments. To keep any one branch from becoming too powerful, our system imposes checks and balances among the three branches.

There are ten main categories of laws: opinions, statutes, constitutions, administrative regulations, administrative decisions, charters, ordinances, rules of court, executive orders, and treaties. (In a special category are opinions of the attorney general.) These laws are written by one of the three branches of government (legislative, executive, and judicial) that exist within the three levels of government (federal, state, and local).

Ours is a common law legal system. The main definition of common law is judge-made law in the absence of controlling statutory law or other higher law. The method of resolving legal disputes is adversarial. The opposing sides go before a neutral decision maker who listens to the arguments of each side before rendering a decision. At one time, there were two separate court systems consisting of common law courts and courts of equity. Today the two systems have been merged so that the same court can issue legal and equitable remedies.

An understanding of jurisdiction is key to understanding our judicial system. To render a decision, a court must have jurisdiction over the persons (personal jurisdiction) or over the particular thing (res) involved in the litigation (e.g., in rem jurisdiction). The court must also have subject matter jurisdiction, which specifies the kinds of cases over which a court can exercise its power. There are six main kinds of subject matter jurisdiction: limited, general, exclusive, concurrent, original, and appellate. Courts of original jurisdiction are the trial courts.

There may be two levels or tiers of trial courts within a judicial system. There may also be two levels or tiers of courts with appellate jurisdiction.

There are three main kinds of administrative agencies: executive department agencies, independent regulatory agencies, and quasi-independent regulatory agencies. (Government corporations are special entities that are a mixture of business corporation and government agency.) Agencies serve three main functions: to carry out statutes and executive orders, to write rules and regulations, and to resolve disputes that arise under laws for which the agency has responsibility.

The federal legislature (Congress) and most state legislatures are bicameral; that is, they consist of two chambers. For a bill to become a statute, it must go through approximately six stages. First, the bill is proposed by being introduced into one of the chambers of the legislature. It may be introduced into the other chamber simultaneously or at a later date. Second, a committee of each chamber gives the bill initial consideration. If the committee votes in favor of the bill, it goes to the next stage. Third, all of the members of each chamber are given the opportunity to debate and vote on the bill. Fourth, a conference committee, usually made up of members of both chambers, considers the bill. The role of this committee is to try to reconcile any differences in the two versions of the bill passed by each chamber. Fifth, the bill goes back to the full membership of each chamber for a vote on what the conference committee produced. Sixth, the chief executive signs or vetoes the bill. If he or she explicitly vetoes the bill, it can still become a statute if two-thirds of each chamber vote to override the chief executive. The legislative history of a statute consists of what happens during these six stages.

Key Terms

federalism	civil law system	quasi-in-rem jurisdiction	diversity of citizenship
legislative branch	at common law	subject matter jurisdiction	United States Court of
executive branch	precedent	limited jurisdiction	Appeals
judicial branch	stare decisis	general jurisdiction	United States Supreme
public policy	cause of action	state questions	Court
opinion	derogation	federal questions	administrative agency
statute	consideration	exclusive jurisdiction	executive department agency
constitution	adversarial	concurrent jurisdiction	cause
administrative regulation	adversary system	original jurisdiction	independent regulatory
administrative decision	inquisitorial system	appellate jurisdiction	agency
charter	equity	review	quasi-independent regula-
ordinance	specific performance	writ of certiorari	tory agency
rules of court (court rules)	injunction	inferior court	government corporation
executive order	constitutional court	appellate brief	quasi-legislation
opinion of the attorney	legislative court	panel	quasi-adjudication
general	jurisdiction	en banc	administrative law
checks and balances	adjudicate	court of final resort	judge (ALJ)
judicial review	personal jurisdiction	United States District	exhaust administrative
common law	in rem jurisdiction	Court	remedies

Administrative Procedure
   Act (APA)
bill
bicameral

unicameral
legislative history
initiative
referendum

session
transcript
engrossed bill
conference committee

enrolled bill
veto
override
pocket veto

Review Questions

1. Define federalism.
2. What are the three levels of government and the three branches within each level?
3. What is public policy?
4. Define
   (1) opinion,
   (2) statute,
   (3) constitution,
   (4) administrative regulation,
   (5) administrative decision,
   (6) charter,
   (7) ordinance,
   (8) rules of court,
   (9) executive order,
   (10) treaty, and
   (11) opinion of the attorney general.
5. Give examples of how
   (1) the legislative and executive branches check and balance each other, and
   (2) the judicial branch checks the legislative and executive branches.
6. What is judicial review?
7. Give four meanings of common law.
8. What is stare decisis?
9. What is a statute in derogation of common law?
10. Describe our adversary system.
11. What is meant by adjudicate?
12. Distinguish between common law courts and courts of equity.
13. What is meant by the merger of law and equity?
14. How do constitutional courts differ from legislative courts?
15. What are
    (1) jurisdiction,
    (2) geographic jurisdiction,
    (3) personal (in personam) jurisdiction,
    (4) subject matter jurisdiction,
    (5) limited jurisdiction,
    (6) general jurisdiction,
    (7) exclusive jurisdiction,
    (8) concurrent jurisdiction,
    (9) original jurisdiction, and
    (10) appellate jurisdiction?
16. Distinguish between state questions and federal questions.
17. Describe the hierarchy of courts in a typical state court system of trial and appellate courts.
18. What are some of the different names a state trial court may have in different states?
19. What is a probate or surrogate court?
20. What is an intermediate appellate court?
21. What are some of the different names a state court of final resort may have in different states?
22. What is an appellate brief?
23. What is meant by a panel of appellate judges?
24. What happens when a case is heard en banc?
25. What is the hierarchy of courts in the federal court system of trial and appellate courts?
26. What is diversity of citizenship?
27. Define administrative agency.
28. State three main functions of many administrative agencies.
29. Define
    (1) executive department agency,
    (2) independent regulatory agency,
    (3) quasi-independent regulatory agency, and
    (4) government corporation.
30. Define quasi-legislation and quasi-adjudication.
31. What is an administrative law judge?
32. What is meant by exhausting administrative remedies?
33. What is the Administrative Procedure Act (APA)?
34. Define bill.
35. Distinguish between unicameral and bicameral legislatures.
36. What steps must a federal bill go through before it becomes a statute?
37. Distinguish between initiative and referendum.
38. Distinguish between an engrossed bill and an enrolled bill.
39. What is meant by legislative history?

Helpful Web Sites: More on Our Legal System

Understanding the Federal Courts
- www.uscourts.gov/about.html
- www.uscourts.gov/journalistguide/welcome.html

Comparing Federal and State Court Systems
- www.uscourts.gov/outreach/resources/comparefedstate.html
- www.uscourts.gov/outreach/resources/comparingcts.gif

National Center for State Courts
- www.ncsconline.org

How Our Laws Are Made (Congress)
- thomas.loc.gov/home/lawsmade.toc.html
- thomas.loc.gov/home/holam.txt

How a Bill Becomes a Law (Example of state legislation: Minnesota)

- www.leg.state.mn.us/leg/howbill.asp

How a Bill Becomes a Law (Example of county ordinances: Baltimore)

- www.baltimorecountycouncil.org/howbill.htm

Administrative Agency Links (Federal)

- www.usa.gov
- www.fedworld.gov

Administrative Procedures Act (APA)

- www.oalj.dol.gov (click "APA")
- usgovinfo.about.com/library/bills/blapa.htm
- en.wikipedia.org/wiki/Administrative_Procedure_Act

Constitutional Law

- www.law.cornell.edu/wex/index.php/Constitutional_law
- www.megalaw.com/top/constitutional.php
- en.wikipedia.org/wiki/Constitutional_law

State and Local Government on the Net

- www.statelocalgov.net

Google Searches (run the following searches for more sites)

- federalism
- "kinds of laws"
- "common law" equity
- adversary system
- stare decisis
- "kinds of jurisdiction"
- federal government overview
- Florida government overview (insert your state)
- Oregon court system (insert your state)
- Kentucky "administrative agencies" (insert your state)
- federal "administrative agencies"
- Hawaii "how our laws are made" (insert your state)
- "North Carolina" legislature (insert your state)
- Congress

Endnote

1. William Burnham, *Introduction to the Legal System of the United States* 78 (2d ed. 1999).

Student CD-ROM

For additional materials, please go to the CD in this book.

Online Companion™

For additional resources, please go to http://www.paralegal.delmar.cengage.com

PART II

The Skills of
a Paralegal

Introduction to Legal Analysis

CHAPTER OUTLINE

[SECTION A]
INTRODUCTION

Throughout society, people constantly apply rules to facts. For example:

When Fred tells his soon-to-be seventeen-year-old daughter, "We can't afford that car for you," he is applying rules to facts. In this instance, the rules are budgetary rules on how household funds are to be spent. The facts consist of his daughter's desire to have a particular car on the dealer's lot. When she responds, "But you allowed Tommy to have one like that when he turned seventeen," the discussion will probably heat up and focus on fairness rules that may or may not have been part of this family's history. When she further urges, "And I'll need a car to get to my part-time job," she is telling her father that the fact of her employment means he should apply an exception to the earlier-announced rule on when she can have a car.

The vast majority of rule applications and rule conflicts in our society never enter the legal system. Most disputes are settled privately or are simply ignored. Fred and his daughter will not be resolving their car dispute in court. While our focus in this chapter will be those disputes that *do* enter the legal system, the method by which the law resolves such disputes is quite similar to the way in which rules are applied to facts in all kinds of conflict throughout society. There is no magic process of conflict resolution used in the law. The process that the law uses may at times be complicated, but it is remarkably similar to how every other segment of society identifies its rules and resolves its conflicts over them.

Attorneys become involved only when rules of law are applied to facts that raise legal disputes. In this arena, the heart of what the attorney does is called **legal analysis** or legal reasoning. It is

legal analysis The application of one or more rules of law to the facts of a client's case in order to answer a legal question that will help (1) keep a legal dispute from arising, (2) resolve a legal dispute that has arisen, or (3) prevent a legal dispute from becoming worse. Also called *legal reasoning.*

the application of rules of law to facts in order to answer a legal question or issue. There are three interrelated goals of legal analysis:

1. To keep a legal dispute from arising (e.g., "Will I get into trouble with the Federal Trade Commission if we merge with our main competitor?")
2. To resolve a legal dispute that has already arisen (e.g., "I feel the deduction I took was legitimate, but the IRS has notified me that I now owe interest and penalties because of it.")
3. To prevent a legal dispute from becoming worse (e.g., "The police are on the way to question me about the fight I was in. What should I tell them?")

Paralegals need to study legal analysis for two main reasons. First, many paralegals are given assignments that in varying degrees call for legal analysis. Secondly, and perhaps more importantly, since attorneys talk the language of legal analysis all the time (issues, rules, exceptions, elements, briefing, reasoning, etc.), a paralegal who knows the basics of legal analysis will be better equipped to understand and communicate with attorneys.

[SECTION B]
THE STRUCTURE OF LEGAL ANALYSIS

The basic structure or format of legal analysis is demonstrated in Exhibit 7.1 containing a relatively simple example. Note the process outlined in this exhibit:

EXHIBIT 7.1	The Basic Structure of Legal Analysis: Rule, Facts, Issue, Application, and Conclusion					
RULE	+	**FACTS**	+	**ISSUE**	+	**APPLICATION** (connecting rule and facts) = **CONCLUSION**
§ 10. "Any business within the city must apply for and obtain a license to do business within the city limits."		Bill and his neighbors have formed a downtown food co-op through which members buy their food collectively from a wholesale company. All funds received by the co-op go for expenses and the purchase of more food to sell.		Is a food co-op a "business" within the meaning of § 10 requiring a license "to do business"?		The city argues that the co-op is a business in the city. The co-op concedes that it is in the city but argues that it does not "do business," since the co-op does not earn a profit.	The co-op has the better argument. § 10 was not intended to cover nonprofit ventures. Hence, the co-op does not have to have a license.

- You start with a specific rule, such as a statute or regulation. (For the definition for these and other categories of rules of law, see Exhibit 6.1 in chapter 6.) You quote the relevant language exactly.
- You state the major facts.
- You phrase the legal issue in terms of specific language in the rule and specific facts that raise a question or controversy about that language.
- You draw the *connection* between specific language in the rule and specific facts. The substance of the analysis *is* this connection. Another term for connection is **application**— applying the rules to the facts.
- You reach a conclusion based on these steps.

Here is a more detailed statement of the analysis referred to as the "connection" in Exhibit 7.1. Section 10 provides as follows:

"Any business within the city must apply for and obtain a license to do business within the city limits." There are two main elements of § 10:

1. Any business
2. Within the city limits

application Connecting facts to a rule in order to determine whether the rule applies to the facts. (Later we will see that the focus is on the relevant portion or element of the rule. *Application* means providing an explanation of how the element of a rule applies or does not apply to the facts.)

When the facts fit within these two elements, the entity in question must apply for and obtain a license to do business. The consequence of the rule is the need to be licensed. This consequence is mandated once both elements apply to the facts.

1. *Any business.* The city claims that the co-op is a business. It does not matter to the city that the co-op does not earn profits in the traditional sense. According to the city, the co-op members are "selling" goods to each other. A business is any ongoing entity that engages in any form of selling.

   The co-op, on the other hand, argues that § 10 was not intended to cover co-ops. A business is an enterprise that seeks to earn a profit over and above expenses. Nothing of this kind occurs in the co-op. Everything taken in by the co-op goes out in the form of food purchases and expenses. Hence, the co-op is not a business and does not have to have a license.

2. *Within the city limits.* There is no dispute between the parties on this element. The city and the co-op agree that the downtown co-op operates within the city limits. The only dispute in this case concerns the first element: whether the co-op is a business.

If you had included legal research data on the meaning of § 10, the analysis might have contained the following:

- A discussion of court opinions, if any, that interpret § 10
- A discussion of administrative regulations, if any, that implement § 10
- A discussion of the legislative history, if available, of § 10
- A discussion of constitutional provisions, if any, that affect the applicability of § 10
- A discussion of **secondary authority** (e.g., legal periodical literature or legal treatises), if any, that interprets § 10

Later, in chapter 11, we will examine how to find opinions, administrative regulations, legislative history, constitutional provisions, and secondary authority.

An important guide to remembering the major components of legal analysis is called **IRAC**. This is an acronym beloved of generations of attorneys who were introduced to IRAC during their first year of law school. (Watch the smile on the face of supervising attorneys when you tell them that you've studied IRAC or that you're going to "IRAC" a problem.) The acronym IRAC stands for *issue, rule, application* (or sometimes *analysis*), and *conclusion:*

Issue:	Identify the legal issue to be resolved in the client's case.
Rule:	State the portion (element) of the rule that is at the center of the dispute.
Application:	Apply (connect) the rule to the facts of the client's case. Do this from the perspective of the client and from the perspective of the client's opponent. (The latter perspective is the *counteranalysis*, which is the position of the other side on how the rule applies to the facts.) By *connect* we mean a two-step process: first, you quote specific language from a portion (element) of the rule and second, you show how that language does or does not apply to the facts. Suppose, for example, that the client is having trouble claiming a certain benefit for her Honda Odyssey under § 100.7 of a state statute. You point out that § 100.7 covers "motor vehicles" in the state. You then simply argue that the client's Honda Odyssey is a "motor vehicle" within the meaning of the statute. If you anticipate any disagreement with this position (e.g., the phrase "motor vehicle" was not intended to cover foreign-made cars such as Hondas), you discuss it as a counteranalysis.
Conclusion:	State the conclusion on whether the rule applies to the facts.

If a problem in the client's case involves more than one issue, each is "IRAC-ed" in the same manner. (In a moment we will discuss FIRAC and RFIAC, which are variations of the IRAC format.)

IRAC can be used in memos, in essay exam answers, or in your head—in short, whenever you are doing legal analysis. If you write out your analysis in a law office, you usually do so in a document known as a **memorandum of law** (also called a *legal memorandum*). Often the memorandum of law (*memo* for short) is organized in four parts corresponding to the four components of IRAC. Some of the essay examinations you take in school can follow the same organizational format, although your examination answer may not be as formally structured as a memo. Even less formal will be the legal analysis you will do in your head. Whenever and wherever you do legal analysis, you can use the same analytical IRAC structure. Keep in mind, however, that IRAC is only a guide. There is no rigid formula for doing legal analysis. What is important is to make sure

---

secondary authority Any *non-law* that a court could rely on in reaching a decision. Authority that describes or explains, but does not constitute, the law. (Authority that consists of laws, e.g., a statute or administrative regulation, is called *primary authority*.)

IRAC An acronym that stands for the components of legal analysis: issue (I), rule (R), application of the rule to the facts (A), and conclusion (C). IRAC provides a structure for legal analysis.

memorandum of law A written explanation of how the law might apply to the fact situation of a client.

that you cover the essentials somewhere in your analysis. The essentials are issue, rule, application (connections), and conclusion.

Let us look at another example. Assume that a statute (§ 12) provides that additional punishment can be imposed "when a weapon is used by the accused in the commission of a drug offense." John Smith is convicted of selling heroin to his brother. When John Smith was arrested, the police found a gun in his back pocket. The question is whether he can be subjected to additional punishment under § 12. Here is a skeleton overview of how this problem might be analyzed with IRAC as a guide in a memorandum of law. Before going through IRAC, note that we begin with a statement of the facts. Whenever legal analysis begins with a statement of facts, it is more accurate to refer to the IRAC guide as FIRAC: facts, issue, rule, application, and conclusion. (A further variation would be RFIAC, if you begin with the statement of the rule.) The example below uses the FIRAC format:

FACTS

On December 12, 2007, John Smith was arrested at 465 East 8th Street, South Boston, at midnight. He was observed selling a substance to another adult, his brother Richard Smith. The substance was later determined to be heroin. When John Smith was arrested immediately after the sale, Officer Frank Doyle searched him and found a gun in his back pocket. Doyle was not aware of the presence of the gun until this search. At the trial, Smith was convicted of selling heroin. During sentencing, the prosecution asked for additional punishment under § 12 because he used a weapon in the commission of a drug crime. Smith objected on the ground that he did not use the weapon within the meaning of § 12 because the gun had nothing to do with the heroin.

ISSUE

Has a person "used" a weapon in committing a drug offense under § 12 when he is found with a gun in his back pocket at the time he is arrested for selling heroin even though the gun played no active role in the drug sale?

RULE

Section 12 provides as follows:

§ 12. A judge may impose additional punishment when a weapon is used by the accused in the commission of a drug offense.

APPLICATION

There are four elements of § 12:

1. Weapon
2. Is used
3. By the accused
4. In the commission of a drug offense

If these four elements apply, a judge can impose additional punishment on the defendant under § 12. (The additional punishment is the *consequence* of the four elements applying.) There is no dispute between the parties on the first, third, and fourth elements. Both John Smith and the prosecutor will agree that the gun is a "weapon," that it was found on the "accused" (Smith), and that selling heroin is the "commission of a crime." The question is whether the second element applies—whether Smith "used" this weapon in the commission of a crime.

The parties will disagree over the definition of "used." The prosecution will argue that it means having it in one's possession ready for employment as needed. Under this definition, Smith "used" the gun. A person with a gun in his pocket possesses the gun. Furthermore, Smith was in possession of the gun while Smith was selling heroin. Hence he used the weapon in the commission of a crime.

Smith, on the other hand, will argue that the prosecution's definition is too broad. When the legislature passed § 12, it intended the word *used* to mean actively employing a weapon in the actual commission of the drug offense for which the defendant was arrested. The legislature could have used the word *possessed* if it merely wanted the weapon to be present during the commission of a drug offense. But instead the legislature wrote the word *used*, which has a more active meaning than *possessed*. Smith argues that he did nothing more than possess the weapon. Furthermore it was concealed. He was not going to use it on his own brother. When Smith sold heroin to his brother, he never took out his gun. There is no evidence that his brother knew he was armed.

John Smith never actively employed the gun by brandishing it, displaying it, striking anyone with it, or threatening to fire it. Hence he never "used" the gun. Merely possessing it is not enough under § 12. If the weapon played no role in the commission of the drug offense, the legislature did not intend defendants to suffer additional punishment.

CONCLUSION

Smith has the stronger argument. The word *used* suggests activity beyond concealed, passive possession.

_____

If relevant court opinions existed that interpreted § 12, they would be included under the "A" component of IRAC to help us interpret the meaning of "used" in § 12 in the Smith case. Similarly, this section of the analysis might include:

- A discussion of other rules (e.g., constitutional provisions), if any, that affect the applicability of § 12
- A discussion of the legislative history, if available, of § 12
- A discussion of secondary authority, if any, that interprets § 12, such as legal periodical literature and legal treatises

_____

Next, we examine three skills that are often involved in IRAC:

- *Element identification skill.* This skill allows you to break any rule into its elements.
- *The skill of phrasing issues.* This skill allows you to identify which elements of a rule are in contention. Each element in contention will be the basis of a separate issue.
- *The definitions skill.* This skill allows you to determine if an element in contention can be defined broadly and narrowly. The application of the element will discuss these competing definitions.

Mastering these three skills will go a long way toward equipping you to use IRAC in legal analysis.

[SECTION C]

THE ELEMENT IDENTIFICATION SKILL

element A portion of a rule that is a precondition of the applicability of the entire rule.

Step one in applying a rule is to break it down into its pieces or **elements**. Before the consequences of a rule can apply, you must demonstrate that all of the elements of that rule apply.

Rules have different kinds of consequences. There are rules that:

- Authorize something
- Prohibit something
- Impose punishments
- Require payments
- Require safety steps to be taken
- Institute procedures
- Make statements of policy
- Declare definitions of important concepts
- Carry out a combination of the above consequences

The element identification skill requires you to answer two questions: what is the consequence of the rule you are applying, and what must happen before this consequence will be imposed or go into effect? When you answer the second question, you will have identified the elements of the rule. An element is a portion of a rule that is a precondition of the applicability of the entire rule. If you can show that all of the elements of a rule apply to a fact situation, then the rule itself—and its consequence—applies. The failure of any *one* of the elements to apply means that the entire rule cannot apply.

As you identify the elements of a rule, keep the following guidelines in mind: (1) each element must be a precondition to the consequence of the entire rule, and (2) you should be able to discuss each element separately with relative ease. Both guidelines apply regardless of the length of the rule you are examining.

Let us look at some examples:

§ 971.22. Change of place of trial. The defendant may move for a change of the place of trial on the ground that an impartial trial cannot be had in the county. The motion shall be made at the time of arraignment.

Step one is to break the rule into its elements. The effect or consequence of this rule is to change the place of the trial. Ask yourself what must happen before this consequence will follow. What conditions or preconditions must exist before the result will occur? The answer will provide you with the elements of the rule:

1. Defendant
2. May move for a change of the place of trial
3. On the ground that an impartial trial cannot be had in the county
4. The motion must be made at the time of the arraignment

Hence, there are four elements to § 971.22. All four must exist before the place of the trial will be moved. Suppose that the *plaintiff* or the *prosecutor* asks the court to change the place of the trial and can demonstrate that an impartial trial cannot be had in the county. Does § 971.22 apply? No. The first element says, "defendant." A plaintiff or prosecutor might be able to have the trial moved under some other law. Section 971.22 requires that the change be sought by the defendant. If one element of a rule does not apply, the consequence of that rule cannot apply no matter how many of the other elements fit the facts.

Suppose you are analyzing the following statute:

§ 25–403. A pharmacist must not sell prescription drugs to a minor.

The effect or consequence of this rule is that something is prohibited—the selling of prescription drugs. Ask yourself what conditions must exist before § 25–403 applies. Your answer will consist of its elements:

1. Pharmacist
2. Must not sell
3. Prescription drugs
4. To a minor

No violation exists unless all four elements of the statute are established. If, for example, a pharmacist sells simple aspirin (a nonprescription drug) to a minor, he or she has not violated the statute. The third element cannot be established. Hence there is no violation because one of the elements (preconditions) cannot be met. Similarly, if a nonpharmacist (e.g., a barber) sells prescription drugs to a minor, the statute has not been violated. The first element of § 25–403 is "pharmacist." If a barber or any other nonpharmacist sells prescription drugs to a minor, some other statute might be violated, but not § 25–403 since the facts do not fit the first element of this statute—the first element does not apply. If any single element of a rule does not apply, the entire rule cannot apply.

For a number of reasons, rules such as statutes and regulations can be difficult to break into elements. For example, the rule may be long or may contain:

- Lists
- Alternatives
- Exceptions or provisos

Nevertheless, the same process is used. You must take the time to dissect the rule into its component elements. Examine the following rule as we try to identify its elements:

§ 5. While representing a client in connection with contemplated or pending litigation, a lawyer shall not advance or guarantee financial assistance to his client, except that a lawyer may advance or guarantee court costs, expenses of investigation, expenses of medical examination, and costs of obtaining and presenting evidence provided the client remains ultimately liable for such expenses.

The elements of § 5 are:

1. A lawyer
2. Representing a client in connection with contemplated litigation or in connection with pending litigation
3. Shall not advance financial assistance to his client or guarantee financial assistance to his client, except that the following is proper:
   a. Lawyer advances or guarantees court costs provided the client remains ultimately liable for them, or
   b. Lawyer advances or guarantees expenses of investigation provided the client remains ultimately liable for them, or

    c. Lawyer advances or guarantees expenses of medical examination provided the client remains ultimately liable for them, or

    d. Lawyer advances or guarantees costs of obtaining and presenting evidence provided the client remains ultimately liable for them.

When an element is stated in the alternative, list all the alternatives within the same element. Alternatives related to one element should be kept within the phrasing of that element. The same is true of exception or proviso clauses. State them within the relevant element when they are intimately related to the applicability of that element. In our § 5 example, the most complicated element is the third—(3). It contains lists, alternatives, an exception, and a proviso. But they all relate to the same point—the propriety of financial assistance. None of the subdivisions of the third element should be stated as a separate element.

Sometimes you must do some unraveling of a rule in order to identify its elements. This certainly had to be done with the third element of § 5. Do not be afraid to pick the rule apart in order to cluster its thoughts around unified themes that should stand alone as elements. Diagram the rule for yourself as you examine it.

If more than one rule is involved in a statute, administrative regulation, constitutional provision, charter, ordinance, etc., treat one rule at a time. Each rule should have its own elements, and, when appropriate, each element should be subdivided into its separate components, as in the third element of § 5.

Once you have broken the rule down into its elements, you have the structure of the analysis in front of you. Each element becomes a separate section of your analysis. You discuss one element at a time, concentrating on those that pose difficulties.

Element identification has many benefits in the law, as demonstrated in Exhibit 7.2. For example, knowing the elements of rules can help give direction to interviewing and investigation.

EXHIBIT 7.2	The Benefits of Element Identification

- **Identifying legal issues.** Once you identify the elements of a rule, the next step is to find the *elements* that are most likely to be in contention. These elements become the basis of legal issues (as we shall see in the next section).

- **Drafting a complaint.** When drafting a legal complaint, you often organize your factual allegations around the *elements* of each important rule in the controversy. (The most important rule is called the *cause of action*, which is a legally acceptable reason for suing someone. More concretely, it is a set of facts that give a person a right to judicial relief. Negligence is an example of a cause of action.)

- **Drafting an answer.** When drafting an answer to a complaint, you often state your defenses by alleging facts that support the *elements* of each defense. (Many *defenses*, such as the statute of limitations, are nothing more than rules designed to defeat the claims of another.)

- **Organizing an interview of a client.** One of the goals of interviewing a client is to obtain information on facts relevant to each of the *elements* of the potential causes of action and defenses in the case. Element analysis, therefore, helps you organize the interview and give it direction.

- **Organizing an investigation.** One of the goals of investigation is to obtain information on facts relevant to each of the *elements* of the potential causes of action and defenses in the case. Element analysis, therefore, helps you organize the investigation and give it direction.

- **Conducting a deposition.** During a deposition, many of the attorney's questions are designed to determine what facts the other side may be able to prove that support the *elements* of the potential causes of action and defenses in the case. Element analysis, therefore, helps the attorney organize the deposition and give it direction.

- **Organizing a memorandum of law.** One of the purposes of a memorandum of law is to tell the reader what rules might apply to the case, what *elements* of these rules might be in contention, and what strategy should be undertaken as a result of this analysis. As we saw earlier, a memo is often organized in an IRAC format. The "A" (application or analysis) of IRAC almost always includes breaking down each rule (the "R" of IRAC) into its elements and concentrating on those elements in contention.

- **Organizing an examination answer.** Many essay examinations in school are designed to find out if the student is able to identify and define the major *elements* of the rules that should be analyzed.

- **Charging a jury.** When a judge charges (i.e., instructs) a jury, he or she will go over each of the *elements* of the causes of action and defenses in the case in order to tell the jury what standard to use to determine whether facts in support of those elements have been sufficiently proven during the trial. Element analysis, therefore, helps the judge organize the charge and give it direction.

While performing these tasks, you are often looking for relevant facts. How do you know which facts are relevant? One of the ways is to identify the elements of the potentially applicable rules that both sides may be arguing in the litigation. Facts are relevant if they help show that those elements apply or do not apply. As you can see from Exhibit 7.2, element identification will also help identify issues, draft complaints and answers, conduct depositions, organize memos and exam answers, and even charge the jury.

To a very large extent, legal analysis proceeds by *element analysis*. A major characteristic of sloppy legal analysis is that it does not clearly take the reader (or listener) through each element of rule that must be analyzed.

ASSIGNMENT 7.1

Break the following rules into their elements:

(a) § 200. Parties to a child custody dispute shall attempt mediation before filing for a custody order from the court.

(b) § 75(b). Lawyers shall not enter into a business transaction with a client if they have differing interests therein and if the client expects the lawyer to exercise his or her professional judgment therein for the protection of the client.

(c) § 38. A person or agency suing or being sued in an official public capacity is not required to execute a bond as a condition for relief under this section unless required by the court in its discretion.

(d) § 1.2. A lawyer may not permit his or her legal assistant to represent a client in litigation or other adversary proceedings or to perform otherwise prohibited functions unless authorized by statute, court rule or decision, administrative rule or regulation, or customary practice.

(e) § 179(a)(7). If at any time it is determined that application of best available control technology by 1988 will not assure protection of public water supplies, agricultural and industrial uses, and the protection and propagation of fish, shellfish, and wildlife, and allow recreational activities in and on the water, additional effluent limitations must be established to assure attainment or maintenance of water quality. In setting such limitations, EPA (the Environmental Protection Agency) must consider the relationship of the economic and social costs of their achievement, including any economic or social dislocation in the affected community or communities, the social and economic benefits to be obtained, and determine whether or not such effluent limitations can be implemented with available technology or other alternative control strategies.

[SECTION D]

THE SKILL OF PHRASING ISSUES

After you have broken a rule into its elements, the next step is to identify the **element in contention**. That element then becomes the basis of a **legal issue**. An element is in contention when you can predict that the other side in the controversy will probably not agree on the definition of the element, whether the facts fit within the element (i.e., within its definition), or both. If a rule has five elements and you anticipate disagreement over all of them, phrase five separate issues. If, however, only one of the five elements will probably be in contention, phrase only one issue. There is no need to waste time over elements that will most likely not be the basis of disagreement.

During informal discussions in a law office, you will often find that attorneys and paralegals phrase legal issues very broadly, almost in shorthand. For example:

- Was Tom negligent?
- Does § 12 apply?
- Can we use the trespass defense?

While broad issue statements such as these can be good starting points for discussion, you need to be able to provide a more *comprehensive* statement of the issue. This is done by including in your issue:

- A brief quote from the element in contention and
- Several of the important facts relevant to that contention

element in contention The portion of a rule about which the parties cannot agree. The disagreement may be over the definition of the element, whether the facts fit within the element, or both.

legal issue A question of law. A question of what the law is, or what the law means, or how the law applies to the facts. Also called *legal question* or *question of law*. If the dispute is over the truth or falsity of the alleged facts, it is referred to as a *question of fact* or a *factual issue*.

For example, suppose that you are analyzing the following rule and facts:

§ 92. The operator of any vehicle riding on a sidewalk shall be fined $100.
Facts: Fred rides his ten-speed bicycle on the sidewalk. He is charged with violating § 92.

The element breakdown and issue statement would be as follows:
Elements of § 92:

1. Operator
2. Any vehicle
3. Riding
4. On a sidewalk

Issue: Is a ten-speed bicycle a "vehicle" under § 92?

The parties will probably agree that Fred rode his bicycle on a sidewalk and that Fred was the operator of his bicycle. The first, third, and fourth elements, therefore, should not be made into legal issues. The only disagreement will be over the second element. Hence, it is the basis of an issue. Note the quotation marks around the element in contention (vehicle) and the inclusion of an important fact that is relevant to this contention (it was a ten-speed bicycle).

ASSIGNMENT 7.2

Provide a shorthand and a comprehensive phrasing of the legal issue or issues in each of the following situations:

(a) *Facts:* Tom owns a 1999 Ford. One day it stalls on a hill; the engine stops running. He wants to get the car off the street. He, therefore, pushes the car so that it glides off the street and onto the sidewalk. While pushing the car on the sidewalk, a police officer stops him.
Statute: § 92. The operator of any vehicle riding on a sidewalk shall be fined $100.

(b) *Facts:* Harry Franklin works for the XYZ Agency. In one of the agency's personnel files is a notation that Paul Drake, another agency employee, was once arrested for fraud. Harry obtains this information from this file and tells his wife about it. (She also knows Paul.) Harry is unaware that Paul has told at least three other employees about his fraud arrest.
Regulation: 20(d). It shall be unlawful for any employee of the XYZ Agency to divulge confidential material in any file of the agency.

(c) *Facts:* Jones has a swimming pool in his backyard. The pool is intended for use by the Jones family members and guests who are present when an adult is there to supervise. One hot summer night, a neighbor's child opens an unlocked door of a fence that surrounds the Jones's yard and goes into the pool. (There is no separate fence around the pool.) The child knows that he should not be there without an adult. No one else is at the pool. The child drowns.
Statute: § 77. Property owners are liable for the foreseeable harm that occurs on their property.

(d) *Facts:* Dr. Carla Jones is the family physician of the Richardson family. After an appointment with Mary Richardson, age sixteen, Dr. Jones prescribes birth control pills. Mary tells Dr. Jones that she can't afford the pills and does not want her parents to know she is taking them. Dr. Jones says she will give her a supply of the pills at no cost in exchange for an afternoon of office clerical work at Dr. Jones's office.
Statute: § 12(c). It is illegal to sell prescription drugs to a minor.

(e) *Facts:* Victor and Cathy Moseley own a lingerie store called Victor's Little Secret in a small town in Kentucky. The multinational company, Victoria's Secret, objects to the name of this store on the ground that it can confuse the public and thereby dilute the value of its well-known mark. (A *mark* is any language or symbols used to identify or distinguish one's product or service.)
Statute: § 43. The owner of a famous mark shall be entitled to an injunction for its dilution.

[SECTION E]

THE DEFINITIONS SKILL

Language can frequently be defined broadly or narrowly. Assume that an apartment complex has a restrictive rental policy. "Families Only," its literature announces. The rental application of a gay couple, Ted and Bob, is denied because they are not a family. (They are not married and neither has any children.) Ted and Bob assert that they have been a family for years. The question then becomes: what is the definition of a family?

Broad Definition: Family means persons living together who have a close personal relationship.
Narrow Definition: Family means persons living together who are related by blood or marriage.

The same dynamic is found when interpreting ambiguous language within elements in contention. Recall the bicycle example discussed in the preceding section:

§ 92. The operator of any vehicle riding on a sidewalk shall be fined $100.

Facts: Fred rides his ten-speed bicycle on the sidewalk. He is charged with violating § 92.
Issue: Is a ten-speed bicycle a "vehicle" under § 92?

This controversy may well turn on whether "vehicle" should be defined broadly or narrowly. Fred will argue that it should be interpreted narrowly, whereas the government will argue for a broad definition:

Broad Definition: Vehicle means any method of transportation.
Narrow Definition: Vehicle means any motorized method of transportation.

Whenever you have an element in contention that contains ambiguous language, you should put yourself in the shoes of each person in the controversy and try to identify what definition of the language each would propose. Think of a broad and a narrow definition, and state which side would argue which definition.

To help resolve a definition dispute, you would undertake some legal research—for example, you would try to find cases interpreting "vehicle" under § 92 and trace the legislative history of § 92. Often, however, you will *not* find the answer in the library. The precise question may never have arisen before. This is particularly true of recent statutes and administrative regulations.

ASSIGNMENT 7.3

In each of the following problems, identify any ambiguous language in elements in contention. Give broad and narrow definitions of this language, and state which side would argue which definition. Do not do any legal research.

(a) *Facts:* Alice Anderson is nine months pregnant. A police officer gives her a ticket for driving in a carpool lane in violation of § 101. The officer said he gave her the ticket because she was alone in the car at the time.
Regulation: § 101. Carpool lanes can be used only by cars in which there is at least one passenger with the driver.

(b) *Facts:* Mary is arrested for violating § 55. She is charged as a felon. She forced open the lock on the driver's side of a van at 5 P.M. Mary didn't know that the door on the passenger side was unlocked. She went into the back of the van and fell asleep on the floor. The police arrested her after waking her up at 9 P.M. The owner of the van claims that a $20 bill is missing. Mary had a $20 bill on her, but she said it was her own.
Statute: § 55. A person who breaks and enters a dwelling at night for the purpose of stealing property therein shall be charged as a felon.

ASSIGNMENT 7.4

Analyze the problem in the following situations. Do not do any legal research. Simply use the facts and rules you are given. Be sure to include in your analysis what you have learned about elements, issues, and definitions. Use IRAC for each issue. As a guide, use the South Boston drug and weapon example involving John Smith at the end of Section B earlier in the chapter.

(continues)

(a) Susan is arrested for carrying a dangerous weapon. While in a hardware store, she got into an argument with another customer. She picked up a hammer from the counter and told the other customer to get out of her way. The customer did so, and Susan put the hammer back. She was later arrested and charged with violating § 402(b), which provides, "It is unlawful for anyone to carry a dangerous weapon."

(b) It is against the law in your state "to practice law without a license" (§ 39). Fred is charged with violating this law. He told a neighbor that a certain parking ticket received by the neighbor could be ignored because the police officer was incorrect in issuing the ticket. In gratitude, the neighbor buys Fred a drink. (Assume that what Fred told the neighbor about the ticket was accurate and that Fred is *not* an attorney.)

(c) Ted and Ann are married. Ted is a carpenter and Ann is a lawyer. They buy an old building that Ted will repair for Ann's use as a law office. Ted asks Ann to handle the legal aspects of the purchase of the building. She does so. Soon after the purchase, they decide to obtain a divorce. Ted asks Ann if she will draw up the divorce papers. She does so. Ted completes the repair work on the building for which Ann pays him a set amount. Has Ann violated § 75(b) that you found earlier in problem (2) of Assignment 7.1?

[SECTION F]
FACTOR ANALYSIS

factor One of the circumstances or considerations that will be weighed in making a decision, no one of which is conclusive.

Thus far we have concentrated on the analysis of elements in rules. Elements are preconditions to the applicability of the entire rule. If one element does not apply, the entire rule does not apply. We now turn to a closely related but different kind of analysis: *factor* analysis. A **factor** is simply *one* of the circumstances or considerations that will be weighed in making a decision, no one of which is conclusive.

Elements and factors are not limited to the application of rules to facts. Many of the important decisions we make in everyday life involve the equivalent of elements and factors, e.g., picking someone to marry, buying a car or a house. When people look for a house, they consider space, neighborhood, area schools, affordability, etc. If an item is essential, it is an element. Suppose, for example, that you will not buy a house with less than three bedrooms. Then this is a precondition to the entire purchase in the same manner as any single element of a rule is a precondition to the applicability of the entire rule. A house hunter may also want a large yard and a bus line within walking distance. But if these are not preconditions, they are simply factors to be considered, no one of which is dispositive or essential. If the bus line is a factor, the house hunter may decide to buy a particular house even though the bus line is not within walking distance. Why? Because this negative fact was examined in the light of everything else about the house (e.g., it had a very large yard and it was the right color) and, on balance, the decision was to make the purchase. The bus line problem did not outweigh all of the other factors.

Factors often play an important role in legal analysis as well. Assume that § 107 provides that a quotation from a copyrighted work is not an infringement or violation of the copyright if the quotation constitutes "fair use." To determine whether "fair use" exists, § 107 says that a court will consider the following factors:

- The purpose and character of the use, including whether such use is of a commercial nature or is for nonprofit educational purposes;
- The nature of the copyrighted work;
- The amount and substantiality of the portion used in relation to the copyrighted work as a whole; and
- The effect of the use upon the potential market for or value of the copyrighted work.

These four considerations are factors that the court will assess to decide whether someone has made "fair use" of a copyrighted work. Because they are factors, no one of them will be conclusive or determinative. Each one will be considered and balanced against the others.

Assume that Mary O'Brien has a three-page explanation of the energy crisis in the introduction to her seventy-page copyrighted book that she sells. Ted Kelly decides to quote the entire explanation in a brochure that he compiles for a charity fundraising event for an environmental organization. He does not obtain the permission of O'Brien. Did Kelly infringe her copyright? We need to determine whether his quotation for the brochure constituted "fair use."

This requires a factor analysis because § 107 tells us that "fair use" is determined by an assessment of factors.

The first factor is the purpose and character of the use. (In general, a use is more likely to be fair if the purpose of the use is not for profit.) Kelly was not trying to sell anything. He was engaged in a nonprofit activity—raising funds for an environmental charity. The second factor is the nature of the copyrighted work. (In general, a use is more likely to be fair if the copyrighted work does little more than collect facts, as opposed to a work that is creative in nature.) O'Brien's work explained the energy crisis. Explaining something is a creative undertaking. The third factor is the amount used in the quote. (In general, the greater the amount used, the more likely the use is unfair.) Kelly used the entire explanation, consisting of three pages from O'Brien's seventy-page book. The fourth factor is the effect of the use on the potential market of the copyrighted work. (In general, the more a use would tend to hurt the sale of the copyrighted work, the more likely the use would be deemed unfair.) To assess the fourth factor, we must investigate whether the use of the quotation in the brochure hurt the sale of O'Brien's book containing her explanation of the energy crisis.

Some of the factors suggest that the use was fair, e.g., the brochure was not used for commercial purposes. Other factors suggest an unfair use, e.g., three pages from a short book is a fairly large percentage. No one factor is determinative. The "totality of the circumstances" must be examined and weighed. The court will balance all the factors in order to determine whether Kelly made "fair use" of O'Brien's work. This is the nature of a factor analysis.

While every rule has elements, not every rule has factors. To determine whether factors are present in a rule, look for the word *factor* in the rule itself. (Section 107 in our example used this word.) If the word *factor* is not in the rule, look for words such as *consider, assess,* or *evaluate* preceded or followed by a list. For example:

> § 20. To determine whether the penalty will be waived, the agency shall consider the amount of the harm, the timing of the violation, and the extent to which the act was performed intentionally or accidentally.

The word *consider* in § 20 followed by a list suggests that a factor analysis is required. Be careful, however. There are no magic words that will always signal the need for a factor analysis. You must examine the rule carefully in order to determine whether you are being told that several items mentioned in the rule must be weighed in order to decide whether the rule applies.

Once you find factors in a rule, you simply examine the factors one at a time by connecting the facts you have (or must investigate) to each factor. Further investigation is often called for because of the large number of facts that are usually needed to assess each of the factors mentioned in the rule. One of the benefits of this kind of analysis is that it will help the office identify these investigation needs.

What is the relationship between elements and factors? As indicated, all rules have elements. Sometimes the applicability of an element is determined by the definition of that element. (See the definitions skill in the preceding section.) At other times, however, the applicability of an element is determined by factors. "Fair use" is one of the elements of § 107. But there is no traditional definition available for this element. Its applicability is determined by a factor analysis.

ASSIGNMENT 7.5

(a) Rachel Sanderson is running for mayor. In a campaign speech, she tells her audience that the city must not neglect the poor. She gives ten examples of the kinds of poor families she means, each of which has experienced a different kind of poverty, e.g., poverty resulting from divorce and poverty resulting from illness. Harry Smith finds out that Sanderson's speech took numerous quotes from an article he wrote for a college magazine some years ago. Smith is a mail carrier in the city where Sanderson is running for mayor. His article was entitled "The Faces of the Downtrodden." It contained fifteen categories of families in distress. Sanderson used ten of them in her speech. She used his labels for the ten categories. He devoted two paragraphs to each category in his article. Sanderson's speech used at least one full paragraph, word for word, for each category from Smith's article. Was Sanderson's speech a "fair use" of Smith's article? Do a factor analysis on the applicability of § 107. In your analysis, you will need to identify further facts that should be investigated. State how such facts might be relevant to your factor analysis.

(continues)

brief A summary of the main or essential parts of a court opinion. (Brief also sometimes refers to a trial brief or to an appellate brief.)

trial brief 1. An attorney's personal notes on how to conduct a trial. Also called *trial manual* and *trial book*. 2. An attorney's presentation to a trial court of the legal issues and positions of his or her client. Also called *trial memorandum*.

appellate brief A document submitted (filed) by a party to an appellate court (and served on an opposing party) in which arguments are presented on why the appellate court should affirm (approve), reverse, or otherwise modify what a lower court has done.

below Pertaining to a lower court in the judicial system. (*Below* also directs a reader to text printed later in a document.)

memorandum of points and authorities A document submitted to a trial court that makes arguments with supporting authorities for something a party wishes to do, e.g., have a motion granted.

reporter A volume (or set of volumes) of court opinions. Also called *case reports*. (See the glossary for other meanings of *reporter*.)

unofficial reporter A reporter printed by a commercial publishing company without special authority from the government. (An *official reporter* is printed under the authority of the government, often by a government printing office.)

(b) Section 100 provides as follows: "Motorists shall be liable for the foreseeable harm or damage caused by their driving. To determine foreseeability, the court must consider road conditions, speed, weather, visibility, and any other circumstance that would affect the likelihood of the harm or damage occurring." Charles Wilson ran his truck into the side of a parked car when he came to an abrupt stop at an intersection. There was some oil on the road. Wilson's car skidded on the oil at the time of his attempt to stop. The incident occurred at 7 P.M., just after rush hour. Was the damage caused by Wilson foreseeable? Do a factor analysis on the applicability of § 100. In your analysis, identify further facts that you would need to investigate. State how such facts might be relevant to your factor analysis.

[SECTION G]

BRIEFING COURT OPINIONS

The word *brief* has several meanings.

First, to **brief** a court opinion is to summarize its major components (e.g., key facts, issues, reasoning, disposition). Such a brief (sometimes called a *case brief*) is your own summary of the opinion for later use. This section of the chapter covers the skill of briefing opinions; the next section covers the more important skill of applying opinions. As you will see, you cannot apply an opinion unless you know how to brief it. Second, the word *brief* refers to a **trial brief**, which is an attorney's personal notes on how he or she will conduct the trial. The notes (often placed in a trial notebook) will be on the opening statement, witnesses, exhibits, direct and cross-examination, closing argument, etc. This trial brief is sometimes called a trial manual or trial book. (Trial brief has other meanings as well. In some states, for example, when an attorney submits a written argument in support of a motion during a trial, the writing is called a trial brief.) Third, the **appellate brief** is a document submitted (filed) by a party to an appellate court (and served on an opposing party) in which arguments are presented on why the appellate court should affirm (approve), reverse, or otherwise modify what a lower court has done. The focus of the appellate brief is on the claimed errors made **below** by the lower court. (If the written presentation is being made to a *trial* court, it is often called a **memorandum of points and authorities**.)

Here our concern is the first meaning of the word *brief*—a summarization of the essential components of a court opinion. It should be pointed out that paralegals do not spend a lot of time on the job briefing opinions. Yet learning this skill has important benefits. Briefing is an excellent way to increase your understanding of legal analysis as used by judges and advocates in the life of the law. It will also give you a greater appreciation of how appellate courts and trial courts interrelate within the court system.

We will be studying an opinion as it might appear in a library volume called a **reporter**. The opinion is *People v. Bruni*, referred to in the discussion as the *Bruni* case or opinion, or simply as *Bruni*. (Names of cases appear in italics.) The publisher of this reporter is West Group.

Whenever you are going to brief an opinion, read it through at least once before you start the actual brief. Obtain an overview. Who is suing whom for what? Who won? Then go back to pick apart the opinion in order to identify the components of the opinion for your brief. After our examination of *Bruni*, we will outline these components in Exhibit 7.3.

A Detailed Look at a Court Opinion

(The circled numbers in the explanation correspond to the circled numbers in the *Bruni* opinion itself. When the word *Bruni* is in italics, the reference is to the opinion; when it is not in italics, the reference is to the party in the opinion, Ronald James Bruni.)

---

citation A reference to any legal authority printed on paper or stored in a computer database that will allow you to locate the authority. As a verb, to *cite* something means to give its location (e.g., volume number and/or Web address) where you can read it. It is the paper or online "address" where you can read something. (See the glossary for other meanings of *citation*.)

① The *California Reporter* (abbreviated Cal. Rptr.) is an **unofficial reporter** of state opinions in California. The "100" indicates the volume number of the reporter. An unofficial reporter is a collection of cases printed by a private or commercial printer/publisher (here, West Group) without specific authorization from the government. (If the opinion had such authorization, it would be considered an *official* reporter.)

② The *Bruni* opinion begins on page 600. The **citation** (also called *cite*) of this opinion is *People v. Bruni*, 25 Cal. App. 3d 196, 100 Cal. Rptr. 600 (1972). The official cite is given at the top of the first column above the word PEOPLE. (An official cite is a reference to the opinion printed in its official reporter. An unofficial cite would be a reference to the same opinion printed in an unofficial reporter.)

③ When the *People* or the state brings an action, it is often a criminal law opinion. *People v. Bruni* is an appellate court decision. Trial court decisions are appealed to the appellate court. The **appellant** is the party bringing the appeal because of alleged errors in the ruling or decision of the lower court. The state of California brought the case as the plaintiff and prosecutor in the lower court (Superior Court, County of San Mateo) and is now the appellant in the higher court (Court of Appeal, First District, Division 1).

④ Ronald James Bruni was the defendant in the lower court because he was being sued or, in this case, charged with a crime. The appeal is taken against him by the People (appellant) because the people believed that the lower court was in error when it ruled in favor of *Bruni*. The party against whom a case is brought on appeal is called the **respondent**. Another word for respondent is *appellee*.

⑤ "Cr. 10096" refers to the **docket** or calendar number of the case. "Cr." stands for *criminal*. (Docket numbers are not used in the citation of **reported** opinions. *Reported* here means printed in a reporter. See number 7, below.)

⑥ Make careful note of the name of the court writing the opinion. As soon as possible, you must learn the hierarchy of state courts in your state. (See Exhibit 6.2 in chapter 6.) In many states, there are three levels of courts: trial level, intermediate appellate level, and supreme level. (Opinions in such states are appealed from the trial court to the intermediate appellate level and then to the supreme level. If a state has only two levels of courts, opinions are appealed from the trial court to the supreme court level.) Here, we know from the title of the court that wrote *People v. Bruni* (Court of Appeal) that it is an appellate court. It is not the supreme court because in California the highest court is the California Supreme Court.

The name of the court is significant because of legal authority. If the court is the highest or supreme court of the state, then the opinion would govern similar cases in the future throughout the state. An intermediate appellate court opinion, however, applies only in the area of the state over which it has jurisdiction. When you see that the opinion was written by a trial or intermediate appellate court, you are immediately put on notice that you must check to determine whether the opinion was appealed subsequent to the date of the case. The two main systems for checking the subsequent history of an opinion are Shepard's Citations and KeyCite. As we will see in chapter 11, these systems are called **citators**.

⑦ When a reported opinion is being cited, only the year (here 1972) is used, not the month or day (April 27). (If the opinion has not yet been reported, the month, day, and year are used—along with the docket number.) Sometimes the text of the reported opinion will also give you other

appellant The party bringing an appeal because of alleged errors made by a lower tribunal. Sometimes called *petitioner*.

respondent The party against whom an appeal is brought. Also called the appellee.

docket A court's list of its pending cases. Also called *calendar*. (See the glossary for another meaning of *docket*.)

reported Printed in a reporter.

citator A book, CD–ROM, or on-line service containing lists of citations that can (1) help you assess the current validity of an opinion, statute, or other item; and (2) give you leads to additional relevant materials.

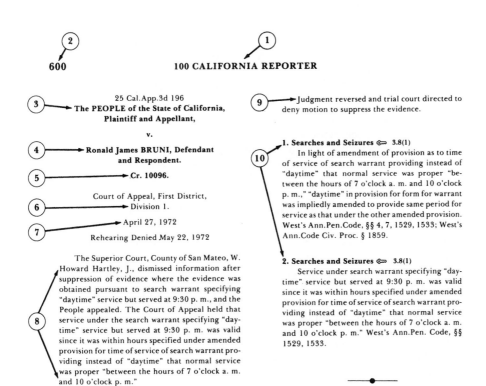

100 CALIFORNIA REPORTER

600

25 Cal.App.3d 196
The PEOPLE of the State of California, Plaintiff and Appellant,

v.

Ronald James BRUNI, Defendant and Respondent.

Cr. 10096.

Court of Appeal, First District, Division 1.

April 27, 1972

Rehearing Denied May 22, 1972

The Superior Court, County of San Mateo, W. Howard Hartley, J., dismissed information after suppression of evidence where the evidence was obtained pursuant to search warrant specifying "daytime" service but served at 9:30 p. m., and the People appealed. The Court of Appeal held that service under the search warrant specifying "daytime" service but served at 9:30 p. m. was valid since it was within hours specified under amended provision for time of service of search warrant providing instead of "daytime" that normal service was proper "between the hours of 7 o'clock a. m. and 10 o'clock p. m."

Judgment reversed and trial court directed to deny motion to suppress the evidence.

1. Searches and Seizures ⟊ 3.8(1)
In light of amendment of provision as to time of service of search warrant providing instead of "daytime" that normal service was proper "between the hours of 7 o'clock a. m. and 10 o'clock p. m.," "daytime" in provision for form for warrant was impliedly amended to provide same period for service as that under the other amended provision. West's Ann.Pen.Code, §§ 4, 7, 1529, 1533; West's Ann.Code Civ. Proc. § 1859.

2. Searches and Seizures ⟊ 3.8(1)
Service under search warrant specifying "daytime" service but served at 9:30 p. m. was valid since it was within hours specified under amended provision for time of service of search warrant providing instead of "daytime" that normal service was proper "between the hours of 7 o'clock a. m. and 10 o'clock p. m." West's Ann.Pen. Code, §§ 1529, 1533.

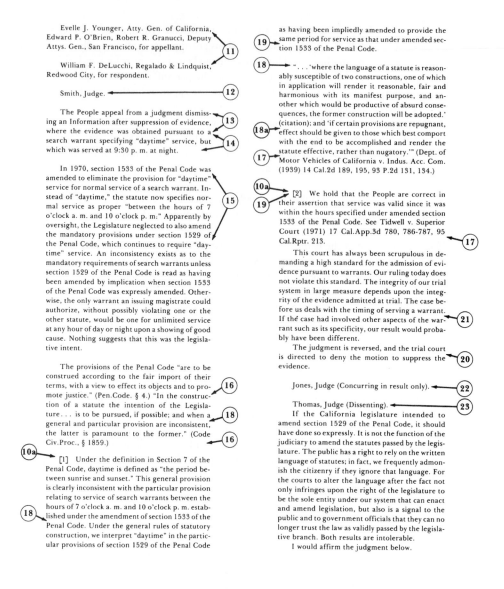

dates (e.g., the date when a request for a rehearing was denied). The year of the decision is still the critical one for citation purposes.

⑧ Here you are provided with a summary (**syllabus**) of what the opinion says. The summary provides the procedural background of the case, a few of the major facts, and what the court "held." The last item refers to the holdings of the opinion. Recently the publisher of these reporters (West Group) has separated the syllabus into two parts: *background* (consisting mostly of the procedural steps leading up to the present opinion) and *holdings* (summarizing the holdings of the opinion). Very few courts write these summaries. For most court opinions, the summaries are written by editors. Hence the summaries should not be quoted or relied on. They are merely aids to the reader who can quickly skim the summary to determine whether the opinion covers relevant areas of law. This summary paragraph is often called the syllabus. Note that the syllabus of the *Bruni* opinion tells you what the court of appeals "held."

⑨ Here continues the unofficial summary, providing the reader with what procedurally must happen as a result of the April 27 opinion.

⑩ These are editor's **headnotes**, which are short-paragraph summaries of portions of the opinion. Headnotes are printed before the opinion begins. When the editors first read the opinion, they decide how many major topics are covered in the opinion. Each of these topics is summarized in a headnote, all of which are then given consecutive numbers, here 1 and 2. These numbers correspond with the bracketed numbers [1] and [2] in the opinion itself. (See 10a.) If, for example, you wanted to read the portion of the opinion that was summarized in the second headnote of opinion, you would go to the text of the opinion that begins with the bracketed [2].

syllabus A brief summary or outline. Also called a *case synopsis*. The syllabus is printed before the opinion begins. It is usually a summary of the entire opinion.

headnote A short-paragraph summary of a portion of a court opinion (usually covering a single legal issue) printed before the opinion begins.

The headnotes also have a **key number**, which consists of a topic and a number, here "Searches and Seizures ☞ 3.8(1)." Each headnote will also be printed in the **digests** of West Group. Its digests are volumes that contain nothing but the headnotes of court opinions. You can find out what other courts have said about the same or similar points by going to the West Group digest volumes, looking up the key numb`er of a headnote (e.g., Searches and Seizures ☞ 3.8(1)), and reading summary paragraphs from many court opinions such as our opinion, *People v. Bruni*.

Caution is needed in reading the syllabus and headnotes of opinions. They are not written by the court and therefore should never be relied on or quoted. They are merely preliminary guides to what is in an opinion. To understand the opinion, you must carefully study the language of the opinion itself through the process called *briefing*. Do not follow the example of what is pejoratively called a *headnote lawyer*, someone who overly relies on the summaries of an opinion found in its headnotes without taking the time to brief it in its entirety.

⑪ Here are the attorneys who represented the appellant and respondent on appeal. Note that the attorney general's office represented the People. The attorney general or the district attorney's office represents the state in criminal cases.

⑫ The opinion begins with the name of the judge who wrote the opinion, Judge Smith. In this spot you will sometimes find the words *Per Curiam, Per Curiam Opinion,* or *Memorandum Opinion:* A **per curiam opinion** is a court opinion that does not mention the individual judge who wrote the opinion. Such opinions are usually short because they cover relatively simple issues. (There are exceptions to this. For example, the famous case of *Bush v. Gore*, 121 S. Ct. 525 (2001), which led to the election of President George W. Bush, was a per curiam opinion. The name of the justice who wrote the *Bush* opinion was not given, but the issue resolved in the opinion could not be called simple.) Memorandum opinions, like per curiam opinions, do not name the judge who wrote the opinion. A **memorandum opinion** will briefly state the conclusion (holding) of the opinion or the disposition of the case with few or no supporting reasons.

⑬ In reading or briefing an opinion, make note of the history of the litigation to date. The lower court rendered a judgment dismissing the information (similar to an indictment) against Bruni after certain evidence was suppressed and declared inadmissible. (This is the *prior* proceeding.) The People have now appealed the judgment. (This appeal is the *present* proceeding.)

If the words *information* and *suppression* are new to you, look them up in a legal dictionary. Do this for every new word. (In this book, also check the definitions of such words in the glossary.)

⑭ It is critical to state the facts of the opinion accurately. Here the facts are relatively simple: A search warrant that said "daytime" service was served at 9:30 P.M., and evidence was taken pursuant to this search warrant. Defendant objected to the admission of this evidence at trial. In most opinions, the facts are not this simple. The facts may be given at the beginning of the opinion, or they may be scattered throughout the opinion. If you confront the latter situation, you must carefully read the entire opinion to piece the facts together. Ultimately, your goal is to identify the **key facts** of the opinion. A key fact is simply one that was essential or very important to the result or holding of the court.

⑮ The next step in reading an opinion is to state the issue (or issues) that the court was deciding. When phrasing an issue, make specific reference to the language of the rule in controversy (e.g., a statute) along with important facts that raise this controversy. The issue in *Bruni* is as follows: When § 1533 was amended to allow service up to 10:00 P.M., did the legislature impliedly also amend § 1529, which continues to require "daytime" service, so that evidence obtained pursuant to a warrant served at 9:30 P.M. can be admitted into evidence? See the discussion earlier in the chapter (Section D) on phrasing issues, particularly phrasing them comprehensively.

⑯ The court refers to other statutes to support the conclusion it will reach. Note the interrelationship of the statutory sections. One statute is interpreted by interpreting other statutes. Section 4 of the Penal Code ("Pen. Code") says that the sections of the Penal Code are to be interpreted ("construed") rationally in order to carry out their purpose or objective and to promote justice. Section 1859 of the Code of Civil Procedure ("Code Civ. Proc.") says that when a general and a particular section are inconsistent, the latter is preferred.

The interrelationship of the statutes in this opinion is as follows:

- Section 1529 of the Penal Code still says, "daytime."
- Section 7 of the Penal Code defines daytime as sunrise to sunset.

---

key number A general topic (e.g., Searches and Seizures) and a number for one of its subtopics (e.g., 3.8(1)). Key numbers are used by West Group to organize millions of cases by topic in its digests.

digest An organized summary or abridgment. A set of volumes that contain brief summaries (sometimes called *abstracts* or *squibs*) of court opinions, arranged by topic and by court or jurisdiction.

per curiam opinion (an opinion "by the court" as a whole) A court opinion, usually a short one, that does not name the judge who wrote it.

memorandum opinion (mem.) The decision of a court with few or no supporting reasons, often because it follows established principles. Also called *memorandum decision.*

key fact A critical fact; a fact that is essential or very important to the conclusion or holding of a court.

- Section 1533 of the Penal Code, as amended, says between 7:00 A.M. and 10:00 P.M.
- Section 4 of the Penal Code and § 1859 of the Code of Civil Procedure provide principles of interpreting statutes that are inconsistent.

precedent A prior decision or opinion covering a similar issue that can be used as a standard or guide in a later case.

reasoning An explanation of why the court resolved a legal issue the way it did—why it reached the particular holding for that issue.

⑰ In the same manner, a court will refer to other opinions to support its ruling. In this way, the court argues that the other opinions are **precedents** for the issues before the court. The court in *People v. Bruni* is saying that *Dept. of Motor Vehicles of California v. Indus. Acc. Com.* and *Tidwell v. Superior Court* are precedents for its own ruling.

⑱ Here is the **reasoning** of the court to support its ruling: If there is a general statute (such as § 7 and § 1529) and a specific statute (such as § 1533) that are inconsistent, the specific is paramount and is preferred. Hence the legislature probably intended to amend the more general statute—§ 1529—when it amended § 1533.

⑱a Note the word "citation" within parentheses, which appears in a quotation of another opinion used by the court. More precisely, it is a quotation within a quotation, as you can tell by the use of single quotes (') within double quotes ("). Whenever a court inserts "(citation)" inside or at the end of a quote, it is simply telling the reader that the quote contained a citation, which the quoting court decided not to include in its use of the quote.

holding A court's answer to one of the legal issues in the case. Also called a *ruling*.

⑲ The result, or **holding**, of the court's deliberation of the issue must then be identified. The holding is that § 1529 was impliedly amended to authorize service up to 10:00 P.M. The holding is also called the court's ruling.

⑳ The consequences of the court's resolution of the issue are then usually stated, as here, toward the very end of the opinion. The judgment of the lower court is reversed. The lower court cannot continue to suppress (i.e., declare inadmissible) the evidence seized at the 9:30 P.M. search. This is the **disposition** of the court.

disposition The final order of a court reached as a result of its holding(s).

vacate To cancel or set aside. (See the glossary for another meaning of *vacate*.)

remand To send back a case to a lower tribunal with instructions from a higher tribunal (e.g., an appellate court) on how to proceed.

An appellate court could take a number of positions with respect to a lower court's decision. It could affirm the decision, meaning to accept and confirm the decision; it could modify the decision by reversing or **vacating** it in whole or in part; or the appellate court could **remand** the case (send it back to the lower court) with instructions on how to proceed, such as how to retry the case.

㉑ In theory, a judge must be very precise in defining the issue before the court—and in resolving only that issue. The judge should not say more than *must* be said to decide the case. This theory, however, is sometimes not observed. This can make your job more difficult; you must wade through the language of the court to identify (1) the precise issues, (2) the key facts for those issues, (3) the holdings for each issue, and (4) the reasoning for each holding. The worst tangent that a judge can stray into is called **dictum**. Dictum is a judge's or court's view of what the law is, or might be, on facts that are *not* before the court. (The plural of dictum is dicta.) Judge Smith indicated that the result of the case might be different if the warrant were not specific, e.g., if it did not name the individual to be searched or what the investigator was looking for. This was not the situation in *Bruni*; therefore, Judge Smith's commentary or speculation is dictum.

dictum A statement made by a court that was not necessary to resolve the legal issues growing out of the specific facts before the court. A court's comments on the law that applies (or that might apply) to facts that are not before the court. Dictum is short for *obiter dictum*, "something said in passing." (See the glossary for another meaning of *dictum*.)

㉒ On any court there may be several judges. They do not always agree on what should be done. The majority controls. (The majority consists of at least half the judges plus one who agree on the result and reasoning.) In *Bruni*, Judge Smith wrote the **majority opinion**. A **concurring opinion** is one that votes for the result reached by the majority but for different reasons. In *Bruni*, Judge Jones concurred but specified that he accepted only the result of Judge Smith's opinion. Normally, judges in such situations will write an opinion indicating their own point of view. Judge Jones did not choose to write an opinion. He simply let it be known that he did not necessarily agree with everything Judge Smith said; all he agreed with was the conclusion that the warrant was validly served. To reach this result, Judge Jones might have used different reasoning, relied on different opinions as precedent, etc. If all the judges on the bench agree on the result and reasoning, the opinion is called a unanimous opinion. If a majority of the judges cannot agree, a **plurality opinion** might be written in which the largest number of judges—short of a majority—agree on the result and reasoning. (Assume, for example, that there are seven judges on the bench, four of whom cannot agree. If any three *can* agree, their opinion would be the plurality opinion.)

majority opinion The opinion whose result and reasoning are supported by at least half plus one of the judges on the court.

concurring opinion The opinion written by less than a majority of the judges on the court that agrees with result reached by the majority but not with all of its reasoning.

plurality opinion The controlling opinion that is joined by the largest number of judges on the bench short of a majority.

㉓ A **dissenting opinion** disagrees with part or with all of the result and reasoning in the opinion of the majority or of the plurality. Dissenting opinions are sometimes heated. Of course, the dissenter's opinion is not controlling. It is often valuable to read, however, in order to determine what the dissenter thinks that the majority or plurality decided.

dissenting opinion An opinion of one or more judges that disagrees with the result and the reasoning of the majority or plurality opinion.

We turn now to the ten components found in a comprehensive brief of a court opinion (Exhibit 7.3) followed by a ten-part brief of *Bruni* that conforms to the guidelines of briefing presented in Exhibit 7.3. (You should keep in mind, however, that not everyone follows the same briefing format or uses the same labels for the different components of a brief.)

EXHIBIT 7.3	Comprehensive Brief of a Court Opinion

I. Citation
Where can the opinion be found? Provide a full *citation* to the opinion you are briefing, e.g., the volume number of the reporter, the abbreviation of the name of the reporter, the page on which the opinion begins, the date of decision.

II. Parties
Who are the *parties*? Identify the lead parties, their relationship to each other, their litigation status "below" when the case began (e.g., defendant), and their litigation status "here" in the case you are now reading and briefing (e.g., appellant).

III. Objectives of Parties
When the litigation began, what were the parties seeking? State the ultimate *objectives of the parties* in terms of the end result they want from the litigation (e.g., to convict someone, to force someone to pay for injuries suffered). At this point, do not focus on tactical or procedural objectives.

IV. Theories of the Litigation
What legal *theories* are the parties using? At the trial level of a civil case, name the *cause of action* (e.g., negligence, breach of contract, violation of § 65) and the main *defenses*. In a criminal case, state what the prosecution was for and the response of the defendant. If the opinion is now on appeal, briefly state the main theory of each party. Where relevant, always refer to specific rules.

V. History of the Litigation
What happened below—what are the prior proceeding(s)? For each *prior proceeding*, briefly state the nature of the proceeding, the party initiating it, the name of the court or agency involved, and the result of the proceeding. For the *present proceeding*, briefly state the nature of the proceeding, who initiated it, and the name of the court or agency involved.

VI. Facts
What are the facts? Specifically, state the *key facts*. A key fact is a critical fact, one that was essential or very important to the conclusion(s) or holding(s) reached by this court. This is one of the most significant parts of the brief. For each holding, identify the facts that were most important to the court. Note the facts that the court emphasized by repetition or by the use of adjectives such as "material" or "crucial." You know you have identified a key fact if you can say that the holding would probably have been different if that fact had not been in the opinion.

VII. Issue(s)
What are the questions of law now before the court? Provide a comprehensive statement of each *issue* by quoting specific language of the rule in controversy (e.g., a statute) along with important facts that raise this controversy.

VIII. Holding(s)
What are this court's answers to the issues? If you have stated each issue comprehensively, its *holding* will be a simple YES or NO response.

IX. Reasoning
Why did the court answer the issues the way it did? State the *reasons* for each holding.

X. Disposition
What order did this court enter as a result of its holding(s)? State the *disposition*, i.e., the consequences of the court's resolution of the issue(s).

Comprehensive Brief of *People v. Bruni*

CITATION:	*People v. Bruni*, 25 Cal. App. 3d 196, 100 Cal. Rptr. 600 (1972).
PARTIES:	People of California/prosecution/plaintiff below/appellant here v. Bruni/accused/defendant below/respondent here
OBJECTIVES OF PARTIES:	The people want to convict and punish Bruni for alleged criminal conduct. Bruni wants to avoid conviction and punishment.
THEORIES OF THE LITIGATION:	1. TRIAL: The People sought to prosecute Bruni for alleged commission of a crime. (The legal theory that justifies the bringing of the prosecution is the alleged commission of a crime. The opinion does not tell us which crime.) Because Bruni is resisting the prosecution, we can assume that the basis and theory of his case is simply that he did not commit the crime. At the trial this was probably his main defense. 2. APPEAL: Bruni says that the state violated the requirement in § 1529 of a "daytime" service when the search warrant was served at 9:30 P.M. The People say § 1529 was impliedly amended by § 1533, which allows service up to 10:00 P.M.

(continues)

Comprehensive Brief of *People v. Bruni—continued*

HISTORY OF THE LITIGATION	1. TRIAL: A criminal prosecution was brought by the People (the state) in the Superior Court (San Mateo).
Prior Proceeding:	RESULT: Judgment for Bruni dismissing the information after the court granted a motion to suppress the evidence obtained from the search warrant.
Present Proceeding:	2. APPEAL: The People now appeal the dismissal of the information to the Court of Appeals (First District).
FACTS:	A search warrant that said "daytime" service was served at 9:30 P.M. Evidence was obtained during this search, which the People unsuccessfully attempted to introduce during the trial.
ISSUE:	When § 1533 was amended to allow service up to 10:00 P.M., did the legislature impliedly also amend § 1529, which continues to require "daytime" service, so that evidence obtained pursuant to a warrant served at 9:30 P.M. can be admitted into evidence?
HOLDING:	YES.
REASONING:	If there is a general statute (such as § 1529) and a specific statute (such as § 1533) that are inconsistent, the specific statute is paramount and is preferred. Hence the legislature probably intended to amend the more general statute—§ 1529—when it amended § 1533.
DISPOSITION:	The trial court's judgment dismissing the information is reversed. When the trial resumes, the court must deny the motion to suppress the evidence based on the time of the service.

At the end of your brief, you should consider adding some notes that cover the following topics:

- What has happened to the opinion since it was decided? Has it been overruled? Has it been expanded or restricted by later opinions? You can find the later history of an opinion and its treatment by other courts by using Shepard's Citations or KeyCite. (See Exhibit 11.28 in chapter 11.)
- Summary of concurring opinions, if any.
- Summary of dissenting opinions, if any.
- Interesting dicta, if any, in the majority opinion.
- Your own feelings about the opinion. Was it correctly decided? Why or why not?

A *thumbnail brief* is, in effect, a brief of a brief. It is a shorthand version of the ten-part comprehensive brief. A thumbnail brief includes abbreviated versions of six of the components (citation, facts, issues, holdings, reasoning, and disposition) and leaves out four of the components (parties, objectives, theories, and history of the litigation). By definition, you must know how to do a comprehensive brief before you can do a shorthand one. Many students fall into the trap of doing *only* shorthand briefs.

Thumbnail Brief of *People v. Bruni*

CITATION:	*People v. Bruni*, 25 Cal. App. 3d 196, 100 Cal. Rptr. 600 (1972).
FACTS:	A "daytime" search warrant served at 9:30 P.M. uncovers evidence that the People unsuccessfully attempt to introduce during the trial.
ISSUE:	Did § 1533 (which allows service up to 10:00 P.M.) impliedly amend § 1529 (which requires "daytime" service), so that evidence obtained from a 9:30 P.M. search warrant is admissible?
HOLDING:	Yes.
REASONING:	A specific statute (§ 1533) is preferred over an inconsistent general one (§ 1529).
DISPOSITION:	Dismissal of the information is reversed; motion to suppress the 9:30 P.M.–obtained evidence must be denied.

It takes considerable time to do a comprehensive brief. It is highly recommended, however, that early in your career you develop the habit and skill of preparing briefs comprehensively. Without this foundation, your shorthand briefs will be visibly superficial. Shorthand briefs are valuable time savers when communicating with colleagues, but they are not substitutes for comprehensive briefs.

At the beginning of the chapter, we said that *IRAC* stands for the components of legal analysis: issue, rule, application, and conclusion. What is the relationship between IRAC (or its variations such as FIRAC) and a court opinion? Judges certainly provide legal analysis in their opinions. Do the judges follow IRAC? Yes they do, although often in highly stylized formats. In almost every court opinion, judges:

- identify the legal issues to be resolved (the I of IRAC);
- interpret statutes and other rules (the R of IRAC);
- provide reasons why the rules do or do not apply to the facts (the A of IRAC); and
- conclude by answering the legal issues through holdings and a disposition (the C of IRAC).

Each issue in the opinion goes through this process. A judge may not use all of the language of IRAC, may use different versions of IRAC, and may discuss the components of IRAC in a different order. Yet IRAC is the heart of the opinion. It is what opinions do: they apply rules to facts to resolve legal issues.

ASSIGNMENT 7.6

Prepare a comprehensive and a thumbnail brief of each of the following opinions:

(a) *United States v. Kovel,* printed below.

(b) *Brown v. Hammond,* printed in chapter 5 toward the beginning of Section C on fees.

ASSIGNMENT 7.7

Read the following facts taken from an opinion. Then read a quote by the judge who wrote this opinion. What is dictum in this quote and why?

Facts in the opinion: Plaintiff sues a cable company for an injury to his foot allegedly caused by a gap or hole the company left in the sidewalk. He claims that it was dark out at the time and that he was unconscious after he fell. When he woke up, he saw the gap or hole. His leg was twisted, and he saw that his sneaker had come off. The company asked the court to dismiss the complaint because the plaintiff had failed to produce enough evidence of where he fell and what caused the fall.

Quote of judge writing this opinion: "The cable company's position lacks merit. It is true that negligence claims will be dismissed if causation is based on pure speculation. In this case, however, plaintiff did in fact identify the cause and location of his accident. While he could not recall the exact manner in which his foot became entrapped in the alleged defect, and could not describe the way it looked on the night of the accident prior to his fall, he repeatedly identified the gap/hole between the sidewalk and the depressed cable vault cover as the condition that trapped his foot and caused him to fall. Plaintiff also specifically identified, by circling and initialing on a photographic exhibit, the exact location and condition that caused his fall. The company's position would have merit if the accident had been caused by a transitory condition such as ice or a slippery liquid of nebulous nature. Here, plaintiff woke up with his leg twisted, then saw the gap, and even saw his sneaker off."

United States v. Kovel

296 F.2d 918 (2d Cir. 1961)
United States Court of Appeals for the Second Circuit

FRIENDLY, Circuit Judge.

This appeal from a sentence for criminal contempt for refusing to answer a question asked in the course of an inquiry by a grand jury raises an important issue as to the application of the attorney-client privilege to a non-lawyer employed by a law firm.

Kovel is a former Internal Revenue agent having accounting skills. Since 1943 he has been employed by

(continues)

United States v. Kovel—continued

Kamerman & Kamerman, a law firm specializing in tax law. A grand jury in the Southern District of New York was investigating alleged Federal income tax violations by Hopps, a client of the law firm; Kovel was subpoenaed to appear on September 6, 1961. The law firm advised the Assistant United States Attorney that since Kovel was an employee under the direct supervision of the partners, Kovel could not disclose any communications by the client or the result of any work done for the client, unless the latter consented; the Assistant answered that the attorney-client privilege did not apply to one who was not an attorney. . . .

On September 7, the grand jury appeared before Judge Cashin. The Assistant United States Attorney informed the judge that Kovel had refused to answer "several questions . . . on the grounds of attorney-client privilege"; he proffered "respectable authority . . . that an accountant even if he is retained or employed by a firm of attorneys, cannot take the privilege." The judge answered "You don't have to give me any authority on that." A court reporter testified that Kovel, after an initial claim of privilege had admitted receiving a statement of Hopps' assets and liabilities, but that, when asked "what was the purpose of your receiving that," had declined to answer on the ground of privilege "Because the communication was received with a purpose, as stated by the client"; later questions and answers indicated the communication was a letter addressed to Kovel. After verifying that Kovel was not a lawyer, the judge directed him to answer, saying "You have no privilege as such." The reporter then read another question Kovel had refused to answer, "Did you ever discuss with Mr. Hopps or give Mr. Hopps any information with regard to treatment for capital gains purposes of the Atlantic Beverage Corporation sale by him?" The judge again directed Kovel to answer reaffirming "There is no privilege—You are entitled to no privilege, as I understand the law."

Later on September 7, they and Kovel's employer, Jerome Kamerman, now acting as his counsel, appeared again before Judge Cashin. The Assistant told the judge that Kovel had "refused to answer some of the questions which you had directed him to answer." A reporter reread so much of the transcript heretofore summarized as contained the first two refusals. The judge offered Kovel another opportunity to answer, reiterating the view, "There is no privilege to this man at all." Counsel referred to New York Civil Practice Act, § 353, which we quote in the margin,* . . .

Counsel reiterated that an employee "who sits with the client of the law firm . . . occupies the same status . . . as a clerk or stenographer or any other lawyer . . . "; the judge was equally clear that the privilege was never "extended beyond

---

*"An attorney or counselor at law shall not disclose, or be allowed to disclose, a communication, made by his client to him, or his advice given thereon, in the course of his professional employment nor shall any clerk, stenographer or other person employed by such attorney or counselor . . . disclose, or be allowed to disclose any such communication or advice."

the attorney." The court held [Kovel] in contempt, sentenced him to a year's imprisonment, ordered immediate commitment and denied bail. Later in the day, the grand jury having indicted, Kovel was released until September 12, at which time, without opposition from the Government, I granted bail pending determination of this appeal.

Here the parties continue to take generally the same positions as below—Kovel, that his status as an employee of a law firm automatically made all communications to him from clients privileged; the Government, that under no circumstances could there be privilege with respect to communications to an accountant. The New York County Lawyers' Association as *amicus curiae* has filed a brief generally supporting appellant's [Kovel's] position.

Decision under what circumstances, if any, the attorney-client privilege may include a communication to a nonlawyer by the lawyer's client is the resultant of two conflicting forces. One is the general teaching that "The investigation of truth and the enforcement of testimonial duty demand the restriction, not the expansion, of these privileges," 8 Wigmore, *Evidence* (McNaughton Rev. 1961), § 2192, p. 73. The other is the more particular lesson "That as, by reason of the complexity and difficulty of our law, litigation can only be properly conducted by professional men, it is absolutely necessary that a man . . . should have recourse to the assistance of professional lawyers, and . . . it is equally necessary . . . that he should be able to place unrestricted and unbounded confidence in the professional agent, and that the communications he so makes to him should be kept secret . . . ," Jessel, M. R. in *Anderson v. Bank,* 2 Ch.D. 644, 649 (1876). Nothing in the policy of the privilege suggests that attorneys, simply by placing accountants, scientists or investigators on their payrolls and maintaining them in their offices, should be able to invest all communications by clients to such persons with a privilege the law has not seen fit to extend when the latter are operating under their own steam. On the other hand, in contrast to the Tudor times when the privilege was first recognized, the complexities of modern existence prevent attorneys from effectively handling clients' affairs without the help of others; few lawyers could now practice without the assistance of secretaries, file clerks, telephone operators, messengers, clerks not yet admitted to the bar, and aides of other sorts. "The assistance of these agents being indispensable to his work and the communications of the client being often necessarily committed to them by the attorney or by the client himself, the privilege must include all the persons who act as the attorney's agents. 8 Wigmore *Evidence,* § 2301; Annot, 53 A.L.R. 369 (1928).

Indeed, the Government does not here dispute that the privilege covers communications to non-lawyer employees with "a menial or ministerial responsibility that involves relating communications to *an attorney.*" We cannot regard the privilege as confined to "menial or ministerial" employees. Thus, we can see no significant difference between a case where the attorney sends a client speaking a foreign language to an interpreter to make a literal translation of the client's story; a second where

(continues)

United States v. Kovel—continued

the attorney, himself having some little knowledge of the foreign tongue has a more knowledgeable non-lawyer employee in the room to help out; a third where someone to perform that same function has been brought along by the client, and a fourth where the attorney, ignorant of the foreign language, sends the client to a non-lawyer proficient in it with instructions to interview the client on the attorney's behalf and then render its own summary of the situation, perhaps drawing on his own knowledge in the process, so that the attorney can give the client proper legal advice. All four cases meet every element of Wigmore's famous formulation, § 2292, "(1) Where legal advice of any kind is sought (2) from a professional legal advisor in his capacity as such (3) the communications relating to that purpose, (4) made in confidence (5) by the client, (6) are at his instance permanently protected (7) from disclosure by himself or by the legal advisor, (8) except the protection be waived," ... Section 2301 of Wigmore would clearly recognize the privilege in the first case and the Government goes along to that extent; § 2301 would also recognize the privilege in the second case and § 2301 in the third unless the circumstances negated confidentiality. We find no valid policy reason for a different result in the fourth case, and we do not read Wigmore as thinking there is. Laymen consulting lawyers should not be expected to anticipate niceties perceptible only to judges—and not even to all of them.

This analogy of the client speaking a foreign language is by no means irrelevant to the appeal at hand. Accounting concepts are a foreign language to some lawyers in almost all cases, and to almost all lawyers in some cases. Hence the presence of an accountant, whether hired by the lawyer or by the client, while the client is relating a complicated tax story to the lawyer, ought not destroy the privilege, any more than would that of the linguist in the second or third variations of the foreign language theme discussed above; the presence of the accountant is necessary, or at least highly useful, for the effective consultation between the client and the lawyer which the privilege is designed to permit. By the same token, if the lawyer has directed the client, either in the specific case or generally, to tell his story in the first instance to an accountant engaged by the lawyer, who is then to interpret it so that the

lawyer may better give legal advice, communications by the client reasonably related to that purpose ought fall within the privilege; there can be no more virtue in requiring the lawyer to sit by while the client pursues these possibly tedious preliminary conversations with the accountant than in insisting on the lawyer's physical presence while the client dictates a statement to the lawyer's secretary or is interviewed by a clerk not yet admitted to practice. What is vital to the privilege is that the communication be made *in confidence* for the purpose of obtaining *legal* advice *from the lawyer.* If what is sought is not legal advice but only accounting service, or if the advice sought is the accountant's rather than the lawyer's, no privilege exists. We recognize this draws what may seem to some a rather arbitrary line between a case where the client communicates first to his own accountant (no privilege as to such communications, even though he later consults his lawyers on the same matter, *Gariepy v. United States,* 189 F.2d 459, 463 (6th Cir. 1951)),‡ and others, where the client in the first instance consults a lawyer who retains an accountant as a listening post, or consults the lawyer with his own accountant present. But that is the inevitable consequence of having to reconcile the absence of a privilege for accountants and the effective operation of the privilege of client and lawyer under conditions where the lawyer needs outside help. We realize also that the line we have drawn will not be so easy to apply as the simpler positions urged on us by the parties—the district judges will scarcely be able to leave the decision of such cases to computers; but the distinction has to be made if the privilege is neither to be unduly expanded nor to become a trap.

The judgment is vacated and the cause remanded for further proceedings consistent with this opinion.

---

‡We do not deal in this opinion with the question under what circumstances, if any, such communications could be deemed privileged on the basis that they were being made to the accountant as the client's agent for the purpose of subsequent communication by the accountant to the lawyer; communications by the client's agent to the attorney are privileged, 8 Wigmore, *Evidence,* § 2317–1.

[SECTION H]

APPLYING COURT OPINIONS

A court opinion can have two impacts. First, it resolves the legal dispute between the specific parties within the opinion. Their controversy is over. Under the doctrine of **res judicata,** they will not be allowed to relitigate any issue that was resolved **on the merits.** Second, the opinion might become a precedent for future cases. The rest of the world can read the opinion to assess whether its conclusions (holdings) can be applied to the legal disputes of others. Under the doctrine of **stare decisis,** similar cases should be decided the same way. Hence, when a client walks into a law office and presents facts that raise legal issues, the office must determine whether any prior cases (opinions) are precedents for the client's case. The process of finding out is called *applying court opinions.* Our goal in applying an opinion is to determine whether the opinion is **analogous** to the facts presented by a client's case. An opinion is analogous if it is sufficiently similar to justify a similar outcome or result.

res judicata ("a thing adjudicated") A final judgment on the merits will preclude the same parties from later relitigating the same claim and any other claim based on the same facts or transaction that could have been raised in the first suit but was not. Also called *claim preclusion.*

on the merits Pertaining to a court decision that is based on the facts and on the substance of the claim, rather than on a procedural ground.

stare decisis ("stand by things decided") Courts should decide similar cases in the same way unless there is good reason for the court to do otherwise. In resolving an issue before it, a court should be reluctant to reject precedent—a prior opinion covering a similar issue.

analogous Sufficiently similar to justify a similar outcome or result. (See the glossary for other meanings of *analogous*.)

enacted law Any law that is not created within litigation. Law written by a deliberative body such as a legislature or constitutional convention after it is proposed and often debated and amended.

prospective Governing future events; effective (having an effective date) in the future.

common law Judge-made law in the absence of controlling statutory law or other higher law. (See the glossary for other meanings of *common law*.)

Before we cover the techniques of applying opinions, we need to briefly examine the two main kinds of rules that courts interpret and apply in their opinions: enacted law and common law.

Enacted law is any law that is not created within litigation. Enacted laws include constitutions, statutes, administrative regulations, and ordinances. See Exhibit 6.1 in chapter 6 for the definitions of these rules and who writes them. The verb *enact* means to pass or adopt a rule after someone has proposed it. (The noun is *enactment*, which refers to the result of the process—e.g., a statute—or to the process itself.) The proposal is often debated by a deliberative body such as a legislature or city council, commented on by the public and by experts, amended, and eventually voted up or down. Most enacted laws are intended to cover broad categories of people or entities (e.g., taxpayers, motorists, or businesses). With few exceptions, the reach of an enacted law is **prospective**—it governs future events that will occur after the rule is enacted. A statute, for example, might provide that after a certain date, all motorcycle riders in the state must wear helmets.

Common law is significantly different. It is judge-made law in the absence of controlling statutory law or other higher law such as the constitution. Common law is created by the courts within litigation. It applies to and grows out of litigation involving specific parties; in the main, it covers events that have already occurred (e.g., an automobile accident, an allegedly discriminatory firing). Examples of common law include negligence, breach of contract, and self-defense. (See chapter 6 for the relationship between statutes and the common law, particularly the power of a statute to change the common law.)

The opinions you will be examining interpret and apply (1) enacted law, (2) common law, or (3) both. Your job is to read and brief these opinions in order to determine if their holdings apply to the facts presented by a client or by a teacher in an assignment. (We will refer to client or assignment facts as the *problem facts*.)

Two sets of comparisons must be made when applying opinions: a rule comparison and a fact comparison.

RULE COMPARISON

The rule that was interpreted and applied in the opinion was one or more enacted laws or common laws. Don't try to apply this opinion to new facts unless the problem facts involve the same enacted laws or the same common laws.

Assume, for example, that your client in the problem facts is charged with failing to make "estimated payments" as required by § 23 of the estate tax. One of your first steps is to go to the law library or to an online database and find this rule (§ 23) in the state code. You will also try to find opinions that have interpreted and applied § 23. You would not waste time looking for opinions that have interpreted housing or pollution rules. You focus on opinions that cover the *same* rule involved in the client's case—§ 23. This is also true of common law rules. If, for example, the client has a negligence case involving an attractive nuisance (a rule covering the duty owed to children), you search for negligence opinions interpreting the attractive nuisance rule.

Suppose, however, that you cannot find opinions interpreting the same rule. Occasionally, you *can* use opinions applying different rules, but only if they are similar in language and purpose. In the first example we just examined, the problem facts involved the failure to pay "estimated taxes" under § 23 of the rules governing estate taxes. Assume that you cannot find any opinions interpreting § 23, but that you can find an *income* tax opinion applying § 100, which also uses the phrase "estimated taxes." Can you use such an opinion? Usually not. If, however, you carefully compare the language used in the two rules (§ 23 and § 100) and the reason (purpose) the legislature had in writing them, you may be able to argue that the opinion interpreting § 100 can be helpful in interpreting § 23. To be able to do so, the language and purpose of the two rules must be sufficiently similar.

FACT COMPARISON

Now we come to the most important part of the application process: fact comparison. In a fact comparison, you will be identifying fact similarities, fact differences, and fact gaps.

Checklist for Fact Comparisons when Applying Opinions

1. Identify factual similarities, factual differences, and factual gaps between the facts in the opinion and the problem facts.
2. Identify the key facts in the opinion you are applying.

(continues)

Checklist for Fact Comparisons when Applying Opinions—*continued*

3(a). If you want a holding to apply to the problem facts, try to show that there is a substantial similarity between all the key facts in the opinion for that holding and the problem facts.

3(b). If you do not want a holding to apply to the problem facts, try to show that there is a substantial difference between at least one of the key facts for that holding and the problem facts.

4. If you can't fill a factual gap, do the best you can to assess its significance.

---

1. Identifying factual similarities, differences, and gaps

Identify factual similarities, factual differences, and factual gaps between the facts in the opinion and the problem facts. The heart of your analysis begins when you start comparing the facts in the opinion with the problem facts. Specifically, you need to identify factual similarities, factual differences, and factual gaps. For example:

Your Facts (problem facts)	**The Opinion: *Smith v. Apex Co.***
Client sees an ad in the newspaper announcing a sale at a local store. He goes to the back of the store and falls into a pit. There was a little sign that said "Danger" near the pit. The client wants to sue the store owner, J. Jackson, for negligence in failing to use reasonable care in preventing his injury. The law office assigns a paralegal to research the case. The paralegal finds the case of *Smith v. Apex Co.* and wants to argue that it applies.	This case involved a man (Tom Smith) who is looking for an address. He is walking down the street. He decides to go into an office building to ask someone for directions. While coming down the corridor, he slips and falls on a wet floor. There was a small sign in the corridor that said "Wet floor," which Smith saw. Smith sued the owner of the building (Apex Co.) for negligence. The court held that the owner was negligent for failure to exercise reasonable care for the safety of users of the building. The cite of the opinion is *Smith v. Apex Co.*, 223 Mass. 578, 78 N.E.2d 422 (1980).

First, identify all factual similarities:

- The client was in a public place (a store). Smith was also in a public place (an office building).
- Both situations involved some kind of warning (the *danger* sign and the *wet floor* sign).
- The warning in both situations was not conspicuous (the *danger* sign was "little"; the *wet floor* sign was "small").

Next, identify all factual differences:

- The client was in a store, whereas Smith was in an office building.
- The client's case involved a hole or pit, whereas *Smith v. Apex Co.* involved a slippery surface.
- The client was there about a possible purchase, whereas Smith was looking for directions and therefore not trying to transact any business in the office building.

Next, identify any factual gaps:

- Smith saw the *wet floor* sign, but we do not know whether the client saw the *danger* sign.

Ninety percent of your legal analysis is complete if you have been able to make these three categories of fact identification: factual similarities, factual differences, and factual gaps. Many students either ignore the categories or do a superficial job of laying them out. They do not carefully pick apart the facts in order to identify similarities, differences, and gaps.

2. Identifying key facts in the opinion.

Identify the key facts in the opinion you are applying. When you briefed the opinion, you began to identify the key facts for each holding in the opinion. As we saw earlier, a key fact is one that was essential or very important to the holding or conclusion reached by the court. In a divorce opinion, for example, it probably will not be a key fact that the plaintiff was thirty-three years old. The court would have reached the same result if the plaintiff had been thirty-two or thirty-four. Age may have been irrelevant or of very minor importance to the holding. What *may* have been key is the fact that the plaintiff beat his wife, because without this fact the court might not have reached the conclusion (holding) that cruelty existed as a ground for divorce. Carefully comb the opinion to read what the judge said about the various facts. Did the judge emphasize certain facts in the opinion? Repeat them? Label them as crucial or important? These are the kinds of questions you must ask yourself to determine which facts in the opinion were key. (See "Facts" in Exhibit 7.3 earlier in the chapter.)

3. Comparing key facts in the opinion with the problem facts

(a) If you want a holding to apply to the problem facts, try to show that there is a substantial similarity between all the key facts in the opinion for that holding and the problem facts. (b) If you do not want a holding to apply to the problem facts, try to show that there is a substantial difference between at least one of the key facts for that holding and the problem facts.

If a holding in an opinion is favorable to your client in the problem facts and you want the holding to apply, you emphasize the similarities between the problem facts and the key facts for that holding in the opinion. They must be substantially similar for the holding to apply. If any of your problem facts differ from a fact in the opinion, you try to point out that this is not significant because the latter was not a key fact in the opinion. If a holding in an opinion is not favorable to your client in the problem facts and you do not want that holding to apply, you emphasize the differences between the problem facts and the key facts for that holding in the opinion. If some of the problem facts are similar to a key fact in the opinion, you try to point out that this is not significant because there is still a dissimilarity with at least one key fact for that holding in the opinion. For a holding to apply, *all* its key facts must be substantially similar to the problem facts.

When you want a holding to apply, the best opinion to find is one that is **on all fours** with the problem facts. The facts in such an opinion are exactly the same as the problem facts, or almost so. Such opinions, however, are relatively rare. Most opinions will have a mixture of similar and dissimilar facts, requiring you to go through the kind of analysis described above.

on all fours Exactly the same, or almost so; being a very close precedent.

4. Handling fact gaps

If you can't fill a factual gap, do the best you can to assess its significance. If the factual gap is in the facts of your client's case, you simply go back to the client and ask him or her about the fact. In our negligence example, the paralegal asks the client whether he saw the "danger" sign. Suppose, however, that the factual gap is in the opinion itself. Assume that your client was running when he fell into the pit but that the opinion does not tell you whether Smith was running, walking, etc. You obviously cannot go to Smith or to the judge who wrote the opinion and ask. You must make a guess of what the judge would have done in the opinion if Smith was running at the time he slipped on the corridor floor. You may decide that it would have changed the result or that this additional fact would have made no difference to the holding of the court.

―――――――――

We turn now to an overview of how *Smith v. Apex Co.* would be applied to the client's case in a memorandum of law. The latter, as we have seen, is simply a written analysis or explanation of how the law might apply to a fact situation.

The client's case and the *Smith* opinion involve exactly the same rule—the law of negligence. Assume that the part of this rule that is in contention (the *element in contention*) between the client and the store owner, J. Jackson, is the requirement that "reasonable care" be used.

roadmap paragraph An overview or thesis paragraph at the beginning of a memorandum of law that tells the reader what issues will be covered and briefly states the conclusions that will be reached.

The following example of a memorandum of law begins with an introduction containing a **roadmap paragraph**. It gives the reader an overview of the issues and briefly states the conclusion that will be reached in the memo. Later in chapter 12, we will discuss additional components of the following memo such as the heading. The memo in chapter 12 (Exhibit 12.5) will also add a Recommendations section. For now, our focus is on the legal analysis involved in applying an opinion.

Office Memorandum of Law

TO : Leona Adams, Esq.
FROM : Rachael Parker, Paralegal
DATE : June 30, 2008
CASE : Client v. J. Jackson
Office File Number : 08–557

RE : Whether the store owner, J. Jackson, was negligent

A. Introduction

This memorandum addresses the question of whether a store used "reasonable care" for the safety of its occupants. My conclusion is that it did not.

B. Issue and summary conclusion

Issue: Was a store owner negligent for failure to use "reasonable care" toward someone who is injured by a pit in the store when the only available warning was a small *danger* sign near the pit?

Summary conclusion: Yes.

C. Facts

The client saw an ad in a newspaper announcing a sale. He went to the back of store and fell into a pit. There was a small sign that said "Danger" near the pit.

D. Analysis

An opinion on point is *Smith v. Apex Co.*, 233 Mass. 578, 78 N.E.2d 422 (1980). In this opinion, the holding of the court was that the owner of an office building was liable for negligence when Smith slipped on a wet corridor floor in the building. There was a small *wet floor* sign in the corridor. This opinion is substantially similar to our own client's case. Both were in public buildings where owners can expect people to be present. In both situations, the warning was insufficient. The *wet floor* sign in the opinion was "small." The *danger* sign in our situation was "little." Because of all these important similarities, it can be argued that the holding in *Smith v. Apex Co.* applies.

It is true that in the opinion the judge pointed out that Smith saw the sign. Our facts do not state whether the client saw the *danger* sign in the store. This, however, should not make any difference. The judge in the opinion would probably have reached the same holding if Smith had not seen the *wet floor* sign. In fact, the case would probably have been stronger for Smith if he did *not* see the sign. The building was dangerous in spite of the fact that users of the building such as Smith could see the sign. Obviously, the danger would be considered even greater if such users could not see the sign. We should find out from our client whether he saw the *danger* sign, but I do not think that it will make any difference in the applicability of the holding in *Smith v. Apex Co.*

The store owner will try to argue that the opinion does not apply. The argument might be that a pit is not as dangerous as a wet floor because a pit is more conspicuous than a wet floor and hence not as hazardous. A user is more likely to notice a hole in the floor than to know whether a floor is slippery enough to fall on. Our client could respond by pointing out that the pit was in the back of the store where it may not have been very noticeable. Furthermore, the wet floor in the opinion was apparently conspicuous (Smith saw the *wet floor* sign), yet in the opinion the judge still found the defendant liable.

E. Conclusion

Our client has the stronger argument on whether the store was negligent in failing to use reasonable care by providing adequate warning of the danger posed by the pit in the store.

ASSIGNMENT 7.8

In the following situations, point out any factual similarities, differences, and gaps between the client facts and the facts of the opinion.

(a) *Client facts:* Jim is driving his car 30 mph on a dirt road at night. He suddenly sneezes and jerks the steering wheel slightly, causing the car to move to the right and run into Bill's fence. Bill sues Jim for negligence.

Opinion: A pedestrian brings a negligence action against Mary. Mary is driving her motorcycle on a clear day. A page of a newspaper unexpectedly flies into Mary's face. Because she cannot see where she is going, she runs into a pedestrian crossing the street. The court finds for Mary, ruling that she did not act unreasonably in causing the accident.

(b) *Client facts:* Helen is the mother of David, age four. The state is trying to take David away from Helen on the ground that Helen has neglected David. Helen lives alone with David. She works part-time and leaves David with a neighbor. Helen's job occasionally requires her to travel. Once she was away for a month. During this period, David was sometimes left alone because the neighbor had to spend several days at the hospital. When David was discovered alone, the state began proceedings to remove David from Helen on the ground of neglect.

Opinion: The state charged Bob Thompson with the neglect of his twins, aged ten. The state wishes to place the twins in a foster home. Bob is partially blind. One day he accidentally tripped and fell on one of the twins, causing severe injuries to the child. Bob lives alone with the twins but refuses to hire anyone to help him run the home. The court ruled that Bob did not neglect his children.

Finally, we need to relate IRAC to our discussion of applying opinions. IRAC (covered at the beginning of the chapter) is an acronym for the structure of legal analysis: *issue, rule, application* (sometimes called *analysis*), and *conclusion*. We said that when you are analyzing any rule such as a statute, you break it down into its elements, create issues out of the elements in contention, and connect the facts to those elements. We also said that if you found any court opinions in your research, you would include them in your analysis. Opinions are examined in the "A" component of IRAC. That is what we did in the example of the client who fell into a pit and sued the store owner for negligence. The element in contention was "reasonable care," which became the basis of this issue: did the store use "reasonable care" for the safety of users of the store when the only warning of a pit in the store was a small danger sign near the pit? To help answer this question, we applied *Smith v. Apex Co.* through the comparisons we have outlined. If other opinions were potentially relevant, they would have to be argued in the same manner.

ASSIGNMENT 7.9

(a) Before Helen became a paralegal for the firm of Harris & Derkson, she was a chemist for a large corporation. Harris & Derkson is a patent law firm where Helen's technical expertise in chemistry is invaluable. Helen's next-door neighbor is an inventor. On a number of occasions, he discussed the chemical makeup of his inventions with Helen. The neighbor is being charged by the government with stealing official secrets in order to prepare one of these inventions. Harris & Derkson represents the neighbor on this case. Helen also works directly on the case for the firm. In a prosecution of the neighbor, Helen is called as a witness and is asked to reveal the substance of all her conversations with the neighbor concerning the invention in question. Does Helen have to answer? Apply *United States v. Kovel* to this question. Do not do any legal research. Limit yourself to the application of this one opinion based on the guidelines of this section. The text of the *Kovel* opinion is at the end of Section G of this chapter.

(b) Anthony Bay is a paralegal who works for Iverson, Kelley, and Winters in Philadelphia. He is an at will employee. His supervising attorney is Grace Swenson. One day Bay notices that Swenson deposited a client settlement check in the general law firm account. Bay calls the bar association disciplinary committee and charges Swenson with commingling funds unethically. (Attorneys have an ethical obligation to keep client funds and general law firm funds in separate accounts. Commingling or mixing these funds in one account is unethical, as we saw in chapter 5.) Bay is fired for disloyalty. In the meantime, the bar investigates the charge of commingling and finds that the charge is accurate. Swenson is eventually disciplined. Can Bay sue Swenson and Iverson, Kelley, and Winters for wrongful dismissal? Apply *Brown v. Hammond* to answer this question. Do not do any legal research. Limit yourself to the application of this one opinion based on the guidelines of this section. The text of the *Brown* opinion is at the beginning of Section C (on fees) of chapter 5.

Chapter Summary

Legal analysis is the process of connecting a rule of law to a set of facts in order to answer a legal question or issue for the purpose of avoiding or resolving a legal dispute or preventing it from becoming worse. IRAC presents the structure of legal analysis: *issue* (a question that arises out of the facts of the problem), *rule* (the statute, common law, or other rule that is being applied), *application* (the connection of the facts to the rule), and *conclusion* (a statement of which side has the better argument of how the rule applies to the facts).

An important skill in legal analysis is the ability to break a rule down into its elements. An element is simply a component or portion of a rule that is a precondition of the applicability of the entire rule. If all the elements apply to a fact situation, then the rule applies to the fact situation. If any one element does not apply, then the rule does not apply. A legal issue is often phrased to ask whether one of the elements applies to the facts. (This element is referred to as the element in contention.) The answer may depend on whether the element is to be interpreted (defined) broadly or narrowly.

Sometimes the applicability of a rule (or an element within a rule) will be determined by an assessment of factors. A factor is one of the circumstances or considerations that will be weighed, no one of which is conclusive.

To brief an opinion means to identify its ten major components: citation, parties, objectives of the parties, theories of the litigation, history of the litigation, facts, issues, holdings, reasoning, and disposition. In addition, it is often essential to determine the subsequent history of the opinion.

A thumbnail brief is a shorthand brief of an opinion consisting of the citation, facts, issues, holdings, reasoning, and disposition.

Opinions interpret enacted law, common law, or both kinds of law. There are two main steps in applying an opinion to a set of facts from a client's case. First, you compare the rule (which will be either an enacted law or a common law) that was interpreted in the opinion with the rule you are considering in the client's case. With limited exceptions, the opinion cannot apply unless these two rules are the same. Second, you compare the key facts in the opinion with the facts of the client's case. In general, the opinion will apply if these facts are the same or are substantially similar.

Key Terms

legal analysis	memorandum of points and	digest	plurality opinion
application	authorities	per curiam opinion	dissenting opinion
secondary authority	reporter	memorandum opinion	res judicata
IRAC	unofficial reporter	key fact	on the merits
memorandum of law	citation	precedent	stare decisis
element	appellant	reasoning	analogous
element in contention	respondent	holding	enacted law
legal issue	docket	disposition	prospective
factor	reported	vacate	common law
brief	citator	remand	on all fours
trial brief	syllabus	dictum	roadmap paragraph
appellate brief	headnote	majority opinion	
below	key number	concurring opinion	

Review Questions

1. What are the three interrelated goals of legal analysis?
2. What is the basic structure or format of legal analysis?
3. What kinds of legal research data might be included in a memorandum that is analyzing a statute?
4. What is the distinction between secondary and primary authority?
5. What is the meaning of IRAC (or its variations, FIRAC and RFIAC)?
6. What is a memorandum of law?
7. What kind of authority would you discuss in the application component of IRAC if you were to include the results of legal research?
8. What is an element of a rule?
9. Name some of the consequences that a rule can have.
10. Why are rules sometimes difficult to break into elements?
11. How does element identification help in identifying legal issues, drafting a complaint, drafting an answer, organizing an interview, organizing an investigation, conducting a deposition, organizing a memorandum of law, organizing an examination answer, and charging a jury?
12. What is the relationship between an element in contention and a legal issue?

13. What is the distinction between a shorthand and a comprehensive statement of a legal issue?
14. What are the two ways that definitions of elements in contention can often be phrased?
15. What is the distinction between an element and a factor?
16. How do you do a factor analysis in determining the applicability of a rule?
17. Give three different meanings of the word *brief*.
18. What is the distinction between an unofficial and an official reporter?
19. What are the meanings of the following terms: *appellant, respondent, docket, appellee, citation, reported, citator, syllabus, headnote, key number, digest, per curiam opinion, memorandum opinion, key fact,* and *stare decisis?*
20. What happens when a court remands a case?
21. When is something in an opinion considered dictum?
22. Define the following kinds of opinions: *majority, concurring, plurality, unanimous,* and *dissenting.*
23. What are the functions of the following components of a brief: citation, parties, objectives of the parties, theories of the litigation, history of the litigation, key facts, issue(s), holding(s), reasoning, and disposition?

24. What is the distinction between a thumbnail and a comprehensive brief?
25. What two impacts can an opinion have?
26. Distinguish between res judicata and stare decisis.
27. What are the differences between enacted law and common law?
28. What are the guidelines for rule comparison when applying an opinion?

29. What are the guidelines for fact comparison when applying an opinion?
30. How should fact gaps be handled when applying an opinion?
31. When is an opinion on all fours?
32. When following IRAC, where do you discuss opinions?
33. What is the function of a roadmap paragraph, and where is it placed in a memorandum of law?

Helpful Web Sites: More on Legal Analysis

Legal Analysis
- www.onlineasp.org/analysis/index.htm
- ga.essortment.com/basicsoflegal_ritg.htm

IRAC
- www.lawnerds.com/guide/irac.html
- law.slu.edu/academic_support/irac.html
- en.wikipedia.org/wiki/IRAC

How to Brief a Case
- www.cjed.com/brief.htm
- www.lawnerds.com/guide/reading.html
- www.lib.jjay.cuny.edu/research/brief.html
- www.people.virginia.edu/~rjb3v/briefhow.html
- www.law.umkc.edu/faculty/profiles/glesnerfines/bateman.htm

Taking Examinations
- www.law.umkc.edu/faculty/profiles/glesnerfines/bgf-ed5.htm

Google Searches (run the following searches for more sites)
- "legal analysis"
- "legal reasoning"
- IRAC school
- "how to brief a case"
- "memorandum of law" write
- "applying court opinions"

Student CD-ROM
For additional materials, please go to the CD in this book.

Online Companion™
For additional resources, please go to http://www.paralegal.delmar.cengage.com

Legal Interviewing

[SECTION A]
CLIENT RELATIONS IN AN ERA OF LAWYER BASHING

Before beginning our study of interviewing, we need to examine some preliminary matters that often influence client relationships today.

Some of the clients you will be working with may be hiring an attorney for the first time. Their image of the legal profession is often heavily influenced by the portrayal of attorneys in the media. The media can be very negative about attorneys. In a steady stream of commercials, cartoons, and jokes, attorneys are sometimes held up to public ridicule. Indeed, there is so much unfavorable publicity that many bar associations have accused the media of lawyer bashing and have urged their members to take affirmative steps to improve the image of the profession. Improvement is clearly needed. Almost two-thirds of Americans think lawyers are necessary but are overpaid, about half think they do more harm than good, and four in ten think they are dishonest, according to a nationwide survey commissioned by Columbia Law School.[1]

This may be the environment in which a paralegal comes into contact with clients. How they perceive you matters a great deal. The way you dress, how you communicate, and how you perform your job can reinforce the negativism or help reverse it. Whether you are interviewing the client or have roles that require no client contact, it is extremely important that you project yourself as a professional. There is no better way to combat negative stereotypes of attorneys than for everyone in the office to maintain a high level of integrity and competence.

You should act on the assumption that every large or small task you perform on a client's case is of critical importance. Even if you have only a small role in a particular client's case, you should assume that how you perform your role will help determine whether the client is satisfied with the services rendered by the entire office and whether he or she will readily recommend the office to relatives, friends, and business associates. This is particularly important because about 40 percent of a law office's new business comes from referrals and recommendations of satisfied clients.[2]

Admittedly, you cannot single-handedly correct the public's perception of attorneys. It is due to forces beyond your control. To a significant extent, the public does not have a clear understanding of the role of attorneys in society. A federal judge recently made the following comment about the legal profession and how lawyers are trained to think: "From the first day of law school, would-be lawyers learn not how to seek the truth, but how to advocate effectively for a client's *version* of the truth, expressed as a legal position."[3] Some citizens find this reality difficult to accept, as reflected in the question attorneys are often asked, "Would you represent a guilty person?"

Attorneys sometimes take unpopular cases such as defending people charged with committing heinous crimes. When interviewed on TV or radio, these attorneys seldom generate much sympathy when they suggest that the accused is the victim. Attorneys are frequently injected into the middle of bitter disputes where they become lightning rods for underlying and overt hostility. Opponents often accuse the other attorney of causing the hostility or of setting up roadblocks to resolution in order to increase fees. Although you cannot eliminate these perceptions, you can perform your job in such a way that the client feels that his or her case is the most important case you are working on and that you are doing everything possible to help the office keep costs to a minimum. This kind of professionalism will be a significant step in the direction of correcting public misconceptions about the practice of law.

[SECTION B]

HIRING THE FIRM

retainer (1) The act of hiring or engaging the services of someone, usually a professional. (The verb is *retain*.) (2) An amount of money (or other property) paid by a client as a deposit or advance against future fees, costs, and expenses of providing services.

There are several ways in which an attorney-client relationship is created and formalized. Both sides usually sign an attorney-client fee agreement. See Exhibit 8.1 for an example. (It might also be called a **retainer** agreement, retainer contract, contract of representation, or, simply, fee agreement.) The document covers the scope of services to be provided as well as the payments the client will be making for those services. The payments will be for attorney fees, paralegal fees, court costs (e.g., filing fees), and any other expenses (e.g., witness fees and travel costs) that may be involved in the representation. The noun *retainer* has several meanings. It is the act of hiring or engaging the services of someone, usually a professional. (The verb is *retain*.) Retainer also refers

---

EXHIBIT 8.1	Example of an Attorney-Client Fee Agreement

_____, 20 ___

This ATTORNEY-CLIENT FEE CONTRACT ("Contract") is entered into by and between
_____ ("Client") and _____ ("Attorney")

1. CONDITIONS. This Contract will not take effect, and Attorney will have no obligation to provide legal services, until Client returns a signed copy of this Contract and pays the deposit called for under paragraph 3.

2. SCOPE AND DUTIES. Client hires Attorney to provide legal services in connection with _____. Attorney shall provide those legal services reasonably required to represent Client, and shall take reasonable steps to keep Client informed of progress and to respond to Client's inquiries. Client shall be truthful with Attorney, cooperate with Attorney, keep Attorney informed of developments, abide by this Contract, pay Attorney's bills on time, and keep Attorney advised of Client's address, telephone number, and whereabouts.

3. DEPOSIT. Client shall deposit $ _____ by _____. The sum will be deposited in a trust account, to be used to pay:
___ Costs and expenses only.
___ Costs and expenses and fees for legal services.
Client hereby authorizes Attorney to withdraw sums from the trust account to pay the costs or fees or both that Client incurs. Any unused deposit at the conclusion of Attorney services will be refunded.

4. LEGAL FEES. Client agrees to pay for legal services at the following rates:
partners—$_____ an hour; associates—$_____ an hour; paralegals—$ _____ an hour;
law clerks—$_____ an hour; and for other personnel as follows:

Note that paragraph 2 is careful to state that "reasonable" steps will be taken. The attorney's standard of performance will be reasonableness. The office's obligation is to do what is reasonable, not to guarantee any specific results. This disclaimer is made more explicit in paragraph 10.

Paragraph 3 refers to a client trust account, which will be covered in chapter 14. The money in this account should not be mixed (i.e., commingled) with general law office funds. See chapter 5. Once it is earned by the office, however, it can be commingled.

(continues)

EXHIBIT 8.1	Example of an Attorney-Client Fee Agreement

If services to Client require extensive word processing work for documents in excess of 15 pages, Client will be charged $_____ a page.
Attorneys and paralegals charge in minimum units of 0.2 hours.

5. COSTS AND EXPENSES. In addition to paying legal fees, Client shall reimburse Attorney for all costs and expenses incurred by Attorney, including, but not limited to, process servers' fees, fees fixed by law or assessed by courts or other agencies, court reporters' fees, long-distance telephone calls, messenger and other delivery fees, postage, in-office photocopying at $_____ a page, parking, mileage at $_____ a mile, investigation expenses, consultants' fees, expert witness fees, and other similar items. Client authorizes Attorney to incur all reasonable costs and to hire any investigators, consultants, or expert witnesses reasonably necessary in Attorney's judgment, unless one or both of the clauses below are initialed by Client and Attorney.
____ Attorney shall obtain Client's consent before incurring any cost in excess of $ ___
____ Attorney shall obtain Client's consent before retaining outside investigators, consultants, or expert witnesses.

6. STATEMENTS. Attorney shall send Client periodic statements for fees and costs incurred. Client shall pay Attorney's statements within _____ days after each statement's date. Client may request a statement at intervals of no less than 30 days. Upon Client's request, Attorney will provide a statement within 10 days.

7. LIEN. Client hereby grants Attorney a lien on any and all claims or causes of action that are the subject of Attorney's representation under this Contract. Attorney's lien will be for any sums due and owing to Attorney at the conclusion of Attorney's services. The lien will attach to any recovery Client may obtain, whether by arbitration award, judgment, settlement, or other means.

8. DISCHARGE AND WITHDRAWAL. Client may discharge Attorney at any time. Attorney may withdraw with Client's consent or for good cause. Good cause includes Client's breach of this Contract, Client's refusal to cooperate with Attorney or to follow Attorney's advice on a material matter; or any other fact or circumstance that would render Attorney's continuing representation unlawful or unethical.

9. CONCLUSION OF SERVICES. When Attorney's services conclude, all unpaid charges shall become immediately due and payable. After Attorney's services conclude, Attorney will, upon Client's request, deliver Client's file to Client, along with any Client funds or property in Attorney's possession.

10. DISCLAIMER OF GUARANTEE. Nothing in this Contract and nothing in Attorney's statements to Client will be construed as a promise or guarantee about the outcome of Client's matter. Attorney makes no such promises or guarantees. Attorney's comments about the outcome of Client's matter are expressions of opinion only.

11. EFFECTIVE DATE. This Contract will take effect when Client has performed the conditions stated in paragraph 1, but its effective date will be retroactive to the date Attorney first provided services. The date at the beginning of this Contract is for reference only. Even if this Contract does not take effect, Client will be obligated to pay Attorney the reasonable value of any services Attorney may have performed for Client.

"Attorney"

By: _____

"Client"

_____

Source: Pamela I. Everett, *Fundamentals of Law Office Management*, 196–7 (1994).

Paragraph 4 makes clear that fees for paralegal services are separate and additional to fees charged by attorneys and law clerks. (The latter are individuals who are still in law school or who have completed law school and are waiting to pass the bar examination.)

Note that paragraph 9 does *not* say that the client's file will be returned only when all fees and costs are paid. Such a condition would be unethical. See chapter 5.

to the amount of money (or other property) paid by a client as a deposit or advance against future fees, costs, and expenses of providing services.

Another method of formalizing the attorney-client relationship is for the attorney to send the prospective client an **engagement letter** that specifies the scope of the professional services to be rendered. At the end of the letter there is space for the prospective client to sign, indicating agreement with the terms stated in the letter.

Suppose, however, the attorney decides *not* to accept the case. This may happen for a number of reasons. There may be a conflict of interest because the law office once represented the opponent of the prospective client (see chapter 5). The attorney may feel that the case lacks merit because there is no legal justification for what the client wants to accomplish. More commonly, the attorney will refuse to take the case for economic reasons. The client may not be able to afford the anticipated legal fees, and the party the client wants to sue may not have enough cash or other resources to pay a winning judgment. (Such an opponent is said to lack a **deep pocket**.) Whatever the reason, it is very important for the office to document its rejection of prospective clients by sending them a letter explicitly stating that the office will not be representing them. The document is called a **letter of nonengagement** or a **declination** letter. Its purpose is to avoid any misunderstandings if the person later claims to have been confused about whether the office had agreed to take the case. This person may try to assert that he or she took no further action on the case because of the belief that the office was going to provide representation. The ultimate nightmare occurs when this person loses the case by default because no one showed up in court at a scheduled hearing or because the **statute of limitations** ran out before any action was taken to bring the claim. One way to avoid this predicament is by sending him or her an emphatic letter of nonengagement (sometimes humorously referred to in the office as the "Dear Not Client Letter"). The letter will often conclude with a statement such as the following: "While our office cannot represent you, we urge you to protect your rights by seeking other counsel."

[SECTION C]

THE CONTEXT OF INTERVIEWING IN LITIGATION

There are three main kinds of legal interviews:

- The initial client interview
- The follow-up client interview
- The field interview of someone other than the client

In the initial client interview the attorney-client relationship is established and legal problems are identified as the fact collection process begins. Follow-up interviews occur after the initial interview. The client is asked about additional facts and is consulted on a variety of matters that require his or her attention, consent, and participation. The field interview is conducted during investigation. The interviewer, as investigator, will contact individuals outside the office in order to try to verify facts already known and to uncover new relevant facts. Investigation will be examined in the next chapter. Here our focus will be the initial and follow-up client interviews.

Interviewing is among the most important skills used in a law office. Many assume that this skill is relatively easy to perform (all you need is a person to interview [the **interviewee**], a pleasing personality, and some time). Yet interviewing is much more than good conversation. To avoid incomplete and sloppy interviewing, the interviewer must establish a relationship with the client that is warm, trusting, professional, and goal-oriented as the office goes about its mission of identifying and solving legal problems. The materials in this chapter, particularly the charts and checklists, are designed to help you achieve such a relationship.

Paralegals in different settings have varied duties and authority. In a private law office, an attorney will usually conduct the initial interview and may assign the paralegal the task of gathering detailed information from the client in a follow-up interview. For example, a paralegal may be asked to help a bankruptcy client obtain details on debts and assets by listing them on a worksheet. Some attorneys ask their paralegals to sit in and take detailed notes on the interview conducted by the attorney. If an office handles many cases of the same kind (e.g., divorce, bankruptcy, or DWI [driving while intoxicated]), it may have a streamlined interview process. The North Carolina law firm of Harris, Mitchell & Hancox, for example, represents many clients charged with DWI. "When a new client arrives . . . a receptionist obtains client information, including address, telephone numbers, court location and appearance date, and other data concerning the charge. . . . Next a paralegal takes a client through a 15-page preliminary interview form covering all aspects of the arrest. . . . Only after these preparatory stages does the client meet an attorney."[4]

---

engagement letter A letter that identifies the scope of services to be provided by a professional and the payments to be made for such services.

deep pocket (1) An individual, business, or other organization with resources to pay a potential judgment. (2) Sufficient assets for this purpose. The opposite of *shallow pocket*.

letter of nonengagement A letter sent to a prospective client that explicitly states that the law office will not be representing him or her.

declination A formal rejection.

statute of limitations A law stating that civil or criminal actions are barred if not brought within a specified period of time.

interviewee The person being interviewed.

Paralegals in government agencies or publicly funded legal aid offices are often given more interviewing responsibilities. For example, a paralegal might conduct the initial interview with a client and remain the primary contact with the client throughout the resolution of the case.

The *initial client interview* is critical because it sets the foundation for the entire litigation process. (See Exhibit 8.2.) The facts obtained from this interview are further pursued through *field investigation;* subsequent or *follow-up interviews* are often needed to clarify new facts and pursue leads uncovered during investigation; the laws governing the facts are *researched* in a traditional law library or online; the facts and the governing law are informally argued between counsel for the parties in an effort to *settle* the case through *negotiation;* if there is no settlement, a *trial* is held in which the facts are formally established; and, finally, the process may end with an *appeal.* Everything begins with the facts obtained through the initial client interview. A poor job done at this stage can have major negative consequences throughout the remaining steps of the litigation.

EXHIBIT 8.2	Interviewing in the Context of Litigation

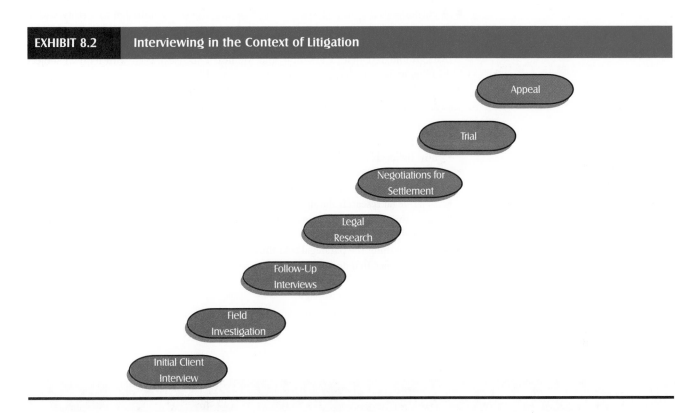

[SECTION D]

THE FORMAT OF AN INTAKE MEMO

Before analyzing the interviewing process, we should look briefly at one of the end products of the interview—a document that is sometimes called the **intake memo**. It summarizes the interviewer's notes on the interview. The intake memo goes first to the supervisor and then into a newly opened case file on the client. The memo often has five parts:

1. *Heading.* The heading provides the following information at the top of the first page:
   - The name of the person who wrote the memo
   - The supervisor in charge of the case to whom the memo is addressed
   - The date the memo was written
   - The date the interview was conducted
   - The name of the case
   - The office file number of the case
   - The kind of case (general area of the law, e.g., mortgage foreclosure, child custody)
   - The notation **Re**, which means concerning or in reference to. After Re, you provide a more specific statement of what is covered in the memo.

intake memo A memorandum that summarizes the facts given by a client during the initial client interview.

Re Concerning (*In re* in the title of a court opinion means "in the matter of.")

2. *Personal data:*
   - Name of the client
   - Home address (mailing address, if different)
   - Phone numbers where the client can be reached; e-mail address(es)
   - Age of client
   - Marital status
   - Place of employment of the client
   - Etc.
3. *Statement of the assignment.* The first paragraph of the memo should state the precise objective the paralegal was given in conducting the interview. It is a more detailed statement of what was listed under *Re* in the heading.
4. *Body of the memo.* Here the facts are presented in a coherent, readable manner according to a number of possible organizational principles:
   - A chronological listing of the facts so that the events are unfolded as a story with a beginning, middle, and end
   - A categorizing of the facts according to the major topics or issues of the case (e.g., Background, Accident, Causation, and Medical Expenses), each with its own subject heading under which the relevant facts are placed
   - Any other format called for by the supervisor
5. *Conclusion.* Here different kinds of information could be included. Examples:
   - The paralegal's impressions of the client, such as
     - how knowledgeable the client appeared to be
     - how believable the client appeared to be
   - A list of the next steps, for example:
     - What further facts should be sought through investigation
     - What legal research should be undertaken
     - Any other recommendations on what should be done on the case based on what was learned during the interview
   - A list of anything the paralegal told the client to do, such as
     - Bring in specified documents relevant to the case.
     - Check on further facts and call back.
     - Return for another interview.

Exhibit 8.3 shows a sample of the introductory parts of an intake memo.

EXHIBIT 8.3	**Beginning of an Intake Memo**

Intake Memo

To: Ann Fuller, Supervisor	**Case:** John Myers vs. Betsy Myers
From: Jim Smith, Paralegal	**File Number:** 09–102
Date of Memo: March 13, 2009	**Kind of Case:** Child Custody
Date of Interview: March 12, 2009	**Re:** Intake Interview of John Myers

Personal Data
Name of Client: John Myers
Address: 34 Main Street, Salem, Massachusetts 01970
Phone: 966–3954 (H) 297–9700 (x301) (W)
E-mail: jmyers@aol.com
Age: 37
Marital Status: Married but separated from his wife, Betsy Myers
Employment: ABC Construction Co., 2064 South Street, Salem, Massachusetts 02127

You asked me to conduct a comprehensive intake interview of John Myers, our client, in order to obtain a listing of his assets and the facts surrounding his relationship with his children.

   A. ASSETS
     John Myers owns...

[SECTION E]

WHAT FACTS DO YOU SEEK? GUIDES TO THE FORMULATION OF QUESTIONS

Unless you know what to accomplish in an interview, valuable time will be wasted. For example, suppose a client is being interviewed concerning the **grounds** for a divorce. You do not simply write down *all* the facts about the marriage and the client's problems in it. The facts must be clustered or arranged in categories that are relevant to the grounds for divorce. Unless you have this objective in mind before and during the interview, you may end up with a confusing collection of facts and may have to conduct a second interview to go over matters that should have been covered initially. (As all-star Yankee catcher Yogi Berra once said, "If you don't know where you are going, when you get there you'll be lost.") This does not mean that you cannot talk about anything other than what is directly related to the objective, but it does mean that each interview must have a definite *focus*.

There are six major ways to achieve focus in the formulation of questions to be asked of a client:

- Instructions of the supervisor for the interview
- Checklists
- Legal analysis
- Fact particularization
- Common sense
- Flexibility

These methods overlap; at various times during an interview, you may be using all six. The goal of the methods is to help you avoid all the following examples of an *ineffective* interview:

- You fail to seek the information that the supervisor wanted you to obtain.
- You miss major relevant facts.
- You fail to probe for greater details about unpleasant or unflattering facts that the client glossed over.
- You fail to ask questions about the extent to which the client was sure *or unsure* about the major facts the client gives you.
- You fail to pursue leads the client provides about other relevant themes or topics that may not have been part of the supervisor's explicit instructions or may not have been within the scope of your initial questions.

INSTRUCTIONS OF THE SUPERVISOR FOR THE INTERVIEW

The instructions of the supervisor control what you do in the interview. You may be asked to do a limited interview or a comprehensive one. Be sure to write down what the supervisor wants from the interview.

One concern that frequently arises is the amount of detail desired. Attorneys like facts. During three years of law school, they were constantly asked by their law professors, "What are the facts?" The likelihood is that the attorney for whom you work will want considerable detail from the interview. Even if you are told to limit yourself to obtaining the basic facts from the client, you may find that the supervisor wants a lot of detail about those basic facts. When in doubt, the safest course is to be detailed in your questioning. If possible, try to sit in on an interview conducted by your supervisor to observe his or her method of questioning and the amount of detail sought. Also, examine some closed or open case files that contain intake memos. Ask the supervisor if any of these memos is exemplary, and if so, why. A factually detailed memo can be useful as a guide.

CHECKLISTS

The office where you work may have checklists that are used in conducting interviews. For some kinds of cases, such as probate or bankruptcy, the checklists may be extensive. If such checklists are not available, you should consider writing your own for the kinds of cases in which you acquire experience.

Caution is needed in using checklists:

- You should find out why individual questions were inserted in the checklist.
- You should be flexible enough to ask relevant questions that may not be on the checklist.

By definition, a checklist is nothing more than a standard form. Use it as a guide that must be adapted to the case and client in front of you, rather than as a rigid formula from which there can

ground A reason that is legally sufficient to obtain a remedy or other result.

be no deviation. There is a danger of being so tied to a checklist that you fail to hear and respond to what the client is saying.

LEGAL ANALYSIS

legal analysis The application of one or more rules to the facts of a client's case in order to answer a legal question that will help (1) keep a legal dispute from arising, (2) resolve a legal dispute that has arisen, or (3) prevent a legal dispute from becoming worse.

relevant (1) Logically tending to establish or disprove a fact. Pertinent. (2) Contributing to the resolution of a problem or issue.

Extensive **legal analysis** does not take place while the interview is being conducted. Yet *some* legal analysis may be needed to conduct an intelligent interview. (See chapter 7 for an overview of legal analysis.)

Most of the questions you ask in the interview should be legally **relevant** or be reasonably likely to lead to something that is legally relevant. A question is legally relevant if the office needs the answer to determine whether a particular legal principle governs. At least a general understanding of legal analysis is needed to be able to apply the concept of legal relevance intelligently. It could be dangerous to ask questions by rote, even if checklists are used. The question-and-answer process is a little like a tennis match—you go where the ball is hit or it passes you by.

Suppose that you are interviewing a client on an unemployment compensation claim. The state denied the claim because the client is allegedly not "available for work," as required by statute. You cannot conduct a competent interview unless you know the legal meaning of this phrase. From this understanding, you can formulate questions that are legally relevant to the issue of whether the client has been and is "available for work." You will ask obvious questions such as:

> Where have you applied for work?
> Were you turned down, and if so, why?
> Did you turn down any work, and if so, why?
> What is your present health?

Suppose that during the interview, the client tells you the following:

> There were some ads in the paper for jobs in the next town, but I didn't want to travel that far.

You must decide whether to pursue this matter by inquiring about the distance to the town, whether public transportation is available, the cost of such transportation, whether the client owns a car, etc. Again, legal analysis can be helpful. What did the legislature mean by the phrase "available for work"? As we saw in chapter 7, one of the central questions asked in legal analysis is how broadly or narrowly legal terms can be defined. Does "available for work" mean available anywhere in the county or state (broad), or does it mean available within walking distance or by easily accessible public transportation (narrow)? Is one *un*available for work because of a refusal to make efforts to travel to an otherwise available job in another area? Questions such as these must go through your mind as you decide whether to seek more details about the ads for work in the other town. These are questions of legal analysis. *You must be thinking while questioning.* Some instant mental analysis should be going on all the time. This does not mean you must know the answer to every legal question that comes to mind while interviewing the client. But you must know something about the law and must be flexible enough to think about questions that should be generated by unexpected facts provided by the client.

When in doubt about whether to pursue a line of questions, check with your supervisor. If he or she is not available, the safest course is to pursue it. As you acquire additional interviewing experience in particular areas of the law, you will be better equipped to know what to do. Yet you will never know everything. There will always be fact situations that you have never encountered before. Legal analysis will help you handle such situations.

FACT PARTICULARIZATION

fact particularization A fact-gathering technique to generate a large list of factual questions (who, what, where, how, when, and why) that will help you obtain a specific and comprehensive picture of all available facts that are relevant to a legal issue.

Fact particularization is one of the most important concepts in this book. To *particularize a fact* means to ask an extensive series of questions about that fact in order to explore its uniqueness. Fact assessment is critical to the practice of law; fact particularization (FP) is critical to the identification of the facts that must be assessed. FP is a fact collection technique. It is the process of viewing every person, thing, or event as unique—different from every other person, thing, or event. Every important fact a client tells you in an interview should be particularized. You do this by asking a large number of follow-up questions once you have targeted the fact you want to explore. (See Exhibit 8.4.)

> **Example:** You are working on an automobile negligence case. Two cars collide on a two-lane street. They were driven by Smith and Jones. Jones is a client of your law office. One of the facts alleged by Jones is that Smith's car veered into Jones's lane moments before the collision. Your

EXHIBIT 8.4	Fact Particularization (FP)

You *particularize* a fact you already have:

1. by assuming that what you know about this fact is woefully inadequate,
2. by assuming that there is more than one version of this fact, and
3. by asking a large number of basic who, what, where, how, when, and why questions about the fact, which, if answered, will provide as specific and as comprehensive a picture of that fact as is possible at this time.

job is to particularize this fact by trying to obtain a much more detailed picture of the alleged veering. This is done by seeking a comprehensive elaboration of this fact. Using FP, you ask the following commonsense questions: who, what, where, how, when, and why.

- What does Jones mean by veering into the other lane?
- How much veering was done? An inch? A foot? Did the entire car come into the other lane? How much of an angle was there?
- Who saw this happen? According to Jones, Smith's car veered. Did Jones see this happen himself? Who else saw it, if anyone? Any passengers in Jones's car? Any passengers in Smith's car? Were there any bystanders? Has the neighborhood been checked for witnesses, e.g., people who live or work in the area, people who frequently sit on public benches in the area?
- Were the police called after the accident? If so, who was the officer? Was a report made? If so, what does it say, if anything, about the car veering into the other lane? Where is this report? How can you obtain a copy?
- What time of day was it when it occurred?
- Why did Smith's car veer according to Jones or anyone else who alleges that this occurred?
- How fast was Jones's car going at the time of the veering? Why was Jones going at this speed? Who would be able to substantiate the speed? Who might have different views of how fast Jones was going?
- How fast was Smith's car going at the time of the veering? Why was Smith going at this speed? Who would be able to substantiate the speed? Who might have different views of how fast Smith was going?
- Have there been other accidents in the area? If so, how similar have they been to this one?
- What was the condition of the road at the time Smith started to veer? At the time of the collision?
- What was the weather at the time?
- How was visibility?
- What kind of a road is it? Straight? Curved at the area of the collision? Any inclines? Any hills that could affect speed and visibility?
- What kind of area is it? Residential? Commercial?
- Is there anything in the area that would distract drivers, e.g., potholes?
- Where is the nearest traffic light, stop sign, or other traffic signal? Prepare a diagram or obtain an online street map (e.g., through maps.google.com or www.mapquest.com) on which you note their location. How, if at all, did they affect traffic at the time of the accident?
- What is the speed limit of the area?
- What kind of car was Smith driving? Were there any mechanical problems with the car? Would these problems help cause the veering? What prior accidents has Smith had, if any?
- What kind of car was Jones driving? Were there any mechanical problems with the car? What prior accidents has Jones had, if any?
- Etc.

FP can be a guide in formulating factual questions that need to be asked in different settings:

- In a client interview (our focus in this chapter)
- In investigations (see chapter 9)
- In interrogatories (written questions sent to an opponent prior to trial; see Exhibit 10.6 in chapter 10)
- In a deposition (an out-of-court session in which questions are asked of an opponent or of a potential witness of the opponent prior to trial)
- In an administrative or court hearing (in which witnesses are formally questioned; see chapters 10 and 15)

In legal interviewing, the starting point for the FP process is an important fact that the client has told you during the interview. Here are additional examples: "I tried to find work"; "the car hit me from the rear"; "the pain was unbearable"; "the company was falling apart"; "he told me I would get the ranch when he died"; "he fired me because I am a woman." Then you ask the client the basic who-what-where-how-when-why questions that we used in the Smith and Jones driving example. As a guide to help you organize these questions, Exhibit 8.5 presents eight categories of questions that need to be asked in order to achieve competent FP.

EXHIBIT 8.5	Categories of Questions for Fact Particularization (FP)

FACT PARTICULARIZATION

Steps: Begin by obtaining a general picture of what happened. Next, particularize every important fact you obtain by seeking comprehensive details on that fact through who-what-where-how-when-why questions that are relevant to the following interrelated categories:

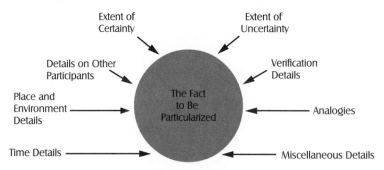

The eight categories are not mutually exclusive, and all eight categories are not necessarily applicable to every fact that you will be particularizing. The questions need not be asked in any particular order as long as you are comprehensive in your search for factual detail. The point of FP is simply to get the wheels of your mind rolling so that you will think of a large number of questions and avoid conducting a superficial interview.

Date and Time Details

When did the fact occur or happen? Find out the precise date and time. The interviewer should be scrupulous about all dates and times. If more than one event is involved, ask questions about the dates and times of each. If the client is not sure, ask questions to help jog the memory and ask the client to check his or her records or to contact other individuals who might know. Do not be satisfied with an answer such as "It happened about two months ago." If this is what the client says, record it in your notes, but then probe further. Show the client a calendar and ask about other events going on at the same time in an effort to help him or her be more precise.

Place and Environment Details

Be equally scrupulous about geography. Where did the event occur? Where was the thing or object in question? Where was the client at the time? Ask the client to describe the surroundings. Ask questions with such care that you obtain a verbal photograph of the scene. If relevant, ask the client to approximate distances between important objects or persons. You might want to have the client draw a diagram, or you can draw a diagram on the basis of what you are told and ask the client if the drawing is accurate. (Also consider printing one of the online maps mentioned earlier.) Ask questions about the weather or about lighting conditions. You want to know as much as you can about the environment or whatever the client could observe about the environment through the senses of sight, hearing, smell, and touch.

Details on Other Participants

Who else was involved? Ask questions about who they were, their roles, their ages, appearance, etc., if relevant. Where were they at the time? When did they act? Why did they act? Why did they fail to act? Could you have anticipated what they did or failed to do? Why or why not? Have they ever acted or failed to act in this way before? Ask questions designed to obtain a detailed picture of who these other participants were and their precise relationship to the fact being particularized.

Extent of Certainty and Uncertainty

Everything the client tells you can be placed somewhere on the *spectrum of certainty:*

Absolutely Certain	Substantially Certain	Fairly Certain	Have a Vague Certainty	Unsure	Only a Guess

It would be a big mistake, for example, to record that the client said a letter was received two weeks ago when in fact the client said, "I think it came two weeks ago." Do not turn uncertainty into certainty by sloppy listening and sloppy recording in your notes and intake memo of what the client said. Of course, it may be possible for a client to be uncertain about a fact initially but then become more certain of it with the help of your questioning. If so, record this transition by saying, "The client at first did not remember who else was present, but then said she thought Fred was 'probably' there."

At the outset, explain to the client how critical it is for you to obtain accurate information. Encourage the client to say, "I'm not sure" when that is the case. Not everyone wants to make such admissions, particularly about facts that are favorable to what they are trying to accomplish. Clients must be relaxed and unthreatened before they will be this honest and frank about what they know and, equally important, about what they do not know. A lot depends on the attitude of the interviewer in asking questions and in reacting to answers. Let the client know that when you ask a question, you are looking for no more than the best of his or her recollection. Never be irritated or disappointed when a client cannot answer a question with absolute certainty. Do not keep saying, "Are you sure?" after every client answer. Probing will often be necessary in order to find out where on the spectrum of certainty a fact falls. Yet this probing must be undertaken with sensitivity. Repeating back what the client has said in the form of a question can be a tactful way to reinforce the importance of obtaining precise dates and times (e.g., "You said the delivery was made at 1:30 in the afternoon?"). We will cover similar interviewing techniques in Exhibit 8.10 on attentive listening later in the chapter.

Verification Details

The fact that the client tells you something happened is *some* evidence that it happened. Verification details are *additional* evidence that supports what the client has said. Always pursue verification details. Ask yourself how you would establish the truth of what the client has said if the client suddenly disappeared and you had to rely exclusively on other sources. Inquire about documents (such as letters or check stubs) that support the client's statements. Inquire about other people who might be available to testify to the same subject. Ask the client questions that will lead you to such verification details. This approach does not mean that you do not trust the client or that you think the client is lying. It is simply a good practice to view a fact from many perspectives. You are always seeking the strongest case possible. This calls for probing questions about verification details.

Analogies

Some facts that you are particularizing (e.g., "the pain was unbearable"; "I was careful"; "it looked awful"; "I was scared") are difficult to pin down. In the interview, you should ask the client to explain such statements. Sometimes it is helpful to ask the client to use **analogies** to describe what is meant. When you ask a client to use an analogy, you are simply asking him or her to explain something by comparing it to something else. For example:

> What would you compare it to?
> Was it similar to anything you have ever seen before?
> Have you observed anyone else do the same thing?
> Have you ever been in a similar situation?
> Did it feel like a dentist's drill?

analogy A comparison of similarities and differences.

First, you ask the client to compare the fact to something else. Then you ask about the similarities and differences. Through a series of directed questions, you are encouraging the client to analogize the fact he or she is describing to some other fact. This is done in a further attempt to obtain as comprehensive a picture as possible of what the client is saying.

Miscellaneous Details

Here, you simply ask about any details that were not covered in the previous categories of questions. Include questions on anything else that might help in particularizing the fact under examination.

CLASS EXERCISE 8.A

In this exercise, FP will be role-played in class. One student will be selected to play the role of the client and another, the role of the paralegal interviewer. The rest of the class will observe and fill out the FP Score Card on the interview.

Instructions to interviewer. You will not be conducting a complete interview from beginning to end. You will be trying to particularize a certain fact that is given to you. Go through all the categories of FP outlined in Exhibit 8.5. Use any order of questioning you want. Probe for comprehensiveness. Your instructor will select one of the following facts to be used as the basis of the interview:

(a) "I was hit in the jaw by Mary."
(b) "He neglects his children."
(c) "I have not been promoted because I am a woman."
(d) "The computer system the store sold me is useless."
(e) "I'm buried in debt."

Your opening statement to the client will be "Tell me what happened" after the client makes one of these five statements to you. Then use the process of FP to particularize the statement.

Instructions to client. The interviewer will ask you what happened. Simply make one of the five statements above as selected by the instructor. Then the interviewer will ask you a large number of questions about the statement. Make up the answers—ad lib your responses. Do not, however, volunteer any information. Answer only the questions asked.

Instructions to class. Observe the interview. Use the following score card to assess how well you think the interviewer particularized the fact.

FP Score Card

	5	4	3	2	1	
Effective in obtaining date and time details						Weak in obtaining date and time details
Effective in obtaining place and environment details						Weak in obtaining place and environment details
Effective in obtaining details on other participants						Weak in obtaining details on other participants
Effective in finding out where the client's statements fall on the spectrum of certainty						Weak in finding out where the client's statements fall on the spectrum of certainty
Effective in seeking verification details						Weak in seeking verification details
Effective in using analogies to obtain greater detail						Weak in using analogies to obtain greater detail
Effective in obtaining miscellaneous details						Weak in obtaining miscellaneous details

Following the interview, put a check on the appropriate number for each of the preceding categories of assessment. A "5" score means you thought the interview was very precise or effective in fulfilling the goal of the particular FP category being assessed; a "1" score means the opposite. Also, make notes of questions you think the interviewer *should have asked*. These questions, and your scores, will be discussed in class after the interview.

COMMON SENSE

Common sense is another major guide to determining what questions to ask, achieving comprehensiveness, and giving the interview a focus. Though law is full of legalisms and technicalities, good judgment and common sense are still at the core of the practice of law. It is common sense, for example, to organize an interview by having the client tell the relevant events chronologically in the form of a story with a beginning, middle, and end. It is common sense to ask further questions that follow up on a potentially important topic the client mentions even though you had not anticipated the topic. If the client says something you do not understand, common sense dictates that you ask what the client means before continuing with the interview. At times, it may be common sense to stop the interview for a moment to obtain further guidance from your supervisor.

FLEXIBILITY

In the previous discussion, the importance of flexibility was mentioned a number of times. The best frame of mind an interviewer can have is to be prepared but to expect the unexpected. Although you lead the interview and give it direction, you must be ready to go where the interview takes you. It could be a serious mistake to block out topics that arise simply because they were not part of your game plan in conducting the interview or are not on your checklist. As with so many areas of the law, you may not know what you are looking for until you find it. In interviewing a client about incorporating a business, for example, you may stumble across a lead from something the client says that could involve fraud or criminal prosecution on a matter unrelated to the incorporation. Don't block this out. Pursue what appears to be reasonably related to the law office's relationship with the client. Check with your supervisor. Again, let common sense be your guide. Flexibility is one of the foundations of common sense.

[SECTION F]
WHAT DOES THE CLIENT WANT?

A number of points can be made about many clients, particularly new ones:

- They are not sure what they want.
- They change their minds about what they want.
- They are not aware of all legal and nonlegal options.
- The legal problem they tell you about involves other legal problems that they are not aware of and that even you may not be aware of at the outset.

Suppose Tom Kelly walks into the office and says, "I want to declare bankruptcy." The following observations *might* be possible about Kelly:

1. He has an incorrect understanding of what a bankruptcy is.

2. He says he wants to declare bankruptcy because he thinks this is the only remedy available to solve his problem.

3. If he knew that other options exist (e.g., credit counseling, and free mentoring advice from the Small Business Administration), he would consider them.

4. What really troubles Kelly is that he is under pressure from organized crime in the neighborhood; bankruptcy is the only way he thinks he can escape the pressure.

If any of these observations is correct, think of how damaging it would be for someone in the office to take out the standard bankruptcy forms and start filling them out immediately after the client says, "I want to declare bankruptcy." Kelly needs a consultation with an attorney in order to find out (1) what bankruptcy entails and (2) what alternatives to bankruptcy should be considered.

This is not to say that a law office must psychoanalyze every client or that it should distrust everything clients say when they first seek legal help.

It is rather a recognition of the fact that *most people are confused about the law and make requests based on misinformation about what courses of action are available to solve problems.* Common sense tells us to avoid taking all statements at face value. People under emotional distress need to be treated with sensitivity. We should not expect them to be able to express their intentions with clarity all the time in view of the emotions involved and the sometimes complicated nature of the law.

ASSIGNMENT 8.1

During an interview, the client makes the following statements. What areas do you think need to be probed to make sure the office does not misunderstand what the client wants?

(a) I want to institutionalize my sick father.
(b) I want my boss arrested for assaulting me.
(c) I want to file for divorce.

[SECTION G]
ASSESSING YOUR OWN BIASES

bias An inclination or tendency to think and to act in a certain way. A danger of prejudgment. Prejudice for or against something or someone.

You need to be aware of how your personal feelings might affect your work on a case. Such feelings are the foundation of **bias**, which is an inclination or tendency to think and to act in a certain way. How would you answer the following question: "Am I objective enough that I can assist a person even though I have a personal distaste for what that person wants to do or what that person has done?" Many of us would quickly answer "yes" to this question. We all like to feel that we are levelheaded and not susceptible to letting our prejudices interfere with the job we are asked to accomplish. Most of us, however, have difficulty ignoring our personal likes and dislikes.

ASSIGNMENT 8.2

In the following fact situations, to what extent might an individual be hampered in delivering legal services because of personal reactions toward the client? Identify potential bias.

(a) Mr. Smith, the client of your office, is being sued by his estranged wife for custody of their two small children. Mr. and Mrs. Smith live separately, but Mr. Smith has had custody of the children during most of their lives while Mrs. Smith has been in the hospital. Mrs. Smith has charged that Mr. Smith often yells at the children, leaves them with neighbors and day care centers for most of the day, and is an alcoholic. Your investigation reveals that Mrs. Smith will probably be able to prove all these allegations in court.

(b) Mrs. Jones is being sued by Mr. Jones for divorce on the ground of adultery. Mrs. Jones is the client of your office. Thus far your investigation has revealed that there is considerable doubt over whether Mrs. Jones did in fact commit adultery. During a recent conversation with Mrs. Jones, however, she tells you that she is a prostitute.

(c) Jane Anderson is seeking an abortion. She is not married. The father of the child wants to prevent her from having the abortion. Jane comes to your office for legal help. She wants to know what her rights are. You belong to a church that believes abortion is murder. You are assigned to work on the case.

(d) Paul and Victor are a gay couple who want to adopt Sammy, a six-month-old baby whose parents recently died in an automobile accident. Sammy's maternal grandmother is not able to adopt him because of her age and health. She opposes the adoption by Paul and Victor because of their lifestyle. Your office represents Paul and Victor. You agree with the grandmother's position but have been assigned to work on the case.

(e) Tom Donaldson is a client of your office. His former wife claims that he has failed to pay court-ordered alimony payments and that the payments should be increased substantially because of her needs and his recently improved financial status. Your job is to help Tom collect a large volume of records concerning his past alimony payments and his present financial worth. You are the only person in the office who is available to do this record gathering. It is clear, however, that Tom does not like you. On a number of occasions, he has indirectly questioned your ability.

objectivity The state of being dispassionate; the absence of a bias.

Having analyzed the fact situations in Assignment 8.2, do you still feel the same about your assessment of your own **objectivity**? Clearly, we cannot simply wish our personal feelings away or pretend that they do not exist. Nor are there any absolute rules or techniques that apply to every situation you will be asked to handle. Nor are the following admonitions very helpful: "Be objective," "be dispassionate," "don't get personally involved," "control your feelings." Such admonitions are too general, and when viewed in the abstract, they may appear not to be needed, since we want to believe that we are always objective, detached, and in control.

We must recognize, however, that there are facts and circumstances that arouse our emotions and tempt us to impose our own value judgments. Perhaps if we know where we are vulnerable, we will be in a better position to prevent our reactions from interfering with our work. It is not desirable for you to be totally dispassionate and removed. A paralegal who is cold, unfeeling, and incapable of empathy is not much better than a paralegal who self-righteously scolds a client. It is clearly not improper for a paralegal to express sympathy, surprise, and perhaps even shock at what unfolds from the client's life story. If these feelings are genuine and if they would be normal reactions to the situation at a given moment, then they should be expressed. The problem is *how to draw the line* between expressing these feelings and reacting so judgmentally that you interfere with your ability to communicate with the client now and in the future. Again, there are no absolute guidelines. As you gain experience in the art of dealing with people, you will develop styles and techniques that will enable you to avoid going over that line. The starting point in this development is to recognize how easy it is to go over the line.

Some paralegals apply what is called the "stomach test." If your gut tells you that your personal feelings about the case are so intense that you may not be able to do a quality job for the client, you need to take action.[5] Talk with your supervisor. You may have some misunderstandings about the case that your supervisor can clear up. You may be able to limit your role in the case or be reassigned to other cases. Contact your local paralegal association to try to talk with other paralegals who have handled similar situations. They may be able to give you some guidance. Be very careful, however, in what you say about a law office case to someone outside the office. Do not act unethically by breaching client confidentiality. Never say anything about a case that would allow an outsider to identify what client or clients you are talking about. The names of current clients and everything you know about their cases must be kept confidential.

Attorneys often take unpopular cases involving clients who have allegedly done things that run the gamut from being politically incorrect to being socially reprehensible. As professionals, attorneys are committed to the principle that *everyone* is entitled to representation. Paralegals need to have this same commitment.

But attorneys and paralegals are human beings. No one can treat every case identically. In the final analysis, you need to ask yourself whether your bias is so strong that it might interfere with your ability to give the needs of the client 100 percent of your energy and skill. If such interference is likely, you have an obligation not to work on the case. As we saw in chapter 5, the failure to recognize the presence of this kind of bias can have ethical implications. It is unethical for you to be working on a case to which you cannot devote 100 percent of your professional skills. There should not be a conflict of interest between your personal feelings or belief system and the client's need for vigorous representation from every member of the legal team.

ASSIGNMENT 8.3

Think about your past and present contacts with people who have irritated you the most. Make a specific list of what bothered you about these people. Suppose that you are working in a law office where a client did one of the things on your list. Could you handle such a case?

[SECTION H]

COMMUNICATION SKILLS

INTRODUCTION

You have probably been interviewed hundreds of times in your life. You may also have interviewed others frequently. The next assignment and the class exercise that follows it are designed to identify what you already know about interviewing in general.

ASSIGNMENT 8.4

Write down your answers to the following questions. When you have finished this chapter, come back to what you have written and ask yourself whether your perspective has changed.

(a) List some of the times you have interviewed someone. List some of the times you have been interviewed by someone.

(continues)

(b) Describe what you feel are the central ingredients of a good interview in any setting.

(c) Describe a bad interview. From your experience, what are some of the worst mistakes an interviewer can make?

(d) Describe what you think are some of your strong and weak points as an interviewer. What can you do to improve?

The following exercise involves an interview role-played in class. After watching this interview, you will be asked to deduce some principles of communication for interviewing.

CLASS EXERCISE 8.B

In this exercise, two students will role-play a legal interview in front of the class. The rest of the class will observe the interview and comment on it.

Instructions to client. You will role-play the part of a client. A month ago you sprained your back while lifting a computer and carrying it from one room to another. You are an accountant. When you came to work that day, you found the computer on your desk. It did not belong there, and you did not know how it got there. You decided to move it to another desk. That was when you sprained your back.

You have come to the law office for legal advice. You have already seen an attorney in this office who has agreed to take your case. An interviewer has been assigned to conduct an interview with you to obtain a complete picture of what happened. This interview will now be role-played in front of the class.

The basic facts involve the accountant and the computer. You can make up all other facts to answer the interviewer's questions. Make up the name of the company for which you work, the details surrounding the accident, etc. You can create *any* set of facts as long as your answers are reasonably consistent with the basic facts given to you above.

Instructions to interviewer. You will play the role of the interviewer in the case involving the sprained back. You are a paralegal in the office. All you know about the case thus far is that the client's back was injured in a work-related accident. You have been assigned to interview the client for detailed information about the client and about the accident. Start off by introducing yourself and stating the purpose of the interview. Then proceed to the questions. Take notes on the client's answers.

You do not need to know any law in order to conduct the interview. Let common sense be your guide. Your goal is to compile as comprehensive a picture of the facts as you can prompt this client to convey. Consult the material on fact particularization (FP) as you prepare and formulate questions. Be sure to listen carefully to the answers so that you can ask appropriate follow-up questions that seek more details on the facts contained in the answers.

The class will observe you in order to assess the manner and content of the interview. A good deal of constructive criticism may develop from the class discussion. As you listen to the criticism, try to be as objective as you can. It is difficult to conduct a comprehensive interview and probably impossible to conduct one flawlessly. For every question that you ask, there may be ten observations on how you could have asked it differently. Hence, try not to take the comments personally.

Instructions to class. You will be watching the interview involving the sprained back. You have two tasks:

(1) Read through the Legal Interviewing Communications Score (LICS) form. Then close your book so that you will give your complete attention to the interview. After the interview, fill out the LICS form. The teacher will ask you to state the total score you gave the interview or to submit this score to someone who will calculate the average score from all students' scores.

(2) Identify as many dos and don'ts of interviewing as you can. If you were writing a law office manual on *How to Interview*, what would you include? What guidance would you give an interviewer on taking notes during the interview, asking follow-up questions, maintaining eye contact with the client, etc.? After you observe the interview, discuss specific suggestions on what an interviewer should or should not do. Ideas will also come to mind while you are filling out the LICS form.

Legal Interviewing Communications Score (LICS)

How to Score:

You will be observing the role-playing of a legal interview and evaluating the interviewer on a 100-point scale. These 100 points will be earned in the four categories listed below. The score is not based on scientific data. It is a rough approximation of someone's oral communication skills in a legal interview. A score can be interpreted as follows:

90–100 Points: Outstanding Interviewer
80–89 Points: Good Interviewer
60–79 Points: Fair Interviewer
0–59 Points: A Lot More Work Needs to Be Done

(Of course, the LICS does *not* assess the interviewer's ability to *write* an intake memo for the file. See Exhibit 8.3 and the discussion of the intake memo at the beginning of this chapter.)

Category I: Role Identification

On a scale of 0–5, how well did the interviewer explain his or her role and the purpose of the interview?
(A 5 score means the interviewer took time to explain clearly what his or her job was in the office and what he or she hoped to accomplish in the interview. A low score means the interviewer gave little or no explanation or mumbled an explanation without being sensitive to whether the client understood.)

Category I Score: ☐

Category II: Factual Detail

On a scale of 0–80, how would you score the interviewer's performance in asking enough questions to obtain factual comprehensiveness? How well was FP performed?
(An 80 score means the interviewer was extremely sensitive to detail in his or her questions. A low score means that the interviewer stayed with the surface facts, with little or no probing for the who-what-where-how-when-why details. The more facts you think the interviewer did not obtain, the lower the score should be.)

Category II Score: ☐

Category III: Control

On a scale of 0–10, how would you score the interviewer's performance in controlling the interview and in giving it direction?
(A 10 score means the interviewer demonstrated excellent control and direction. A low score means the interviewer rambled from question to question or let the client ramble from topic to topic.)

Category III Score: ☐

Category IV: Earning the Confidence of the Client

On a scale of 0–5, how would you score the interviewer's performance in gaining the trust of the client and in setting him or her at ease?
(A 5 score means the interviewer appeared to do an excellent job of gaining the trust and confidence of the client. A low score means the client seemed to be suspicious of the interviewer and probably doubted his or her professional competence. The more the interviewer made the client feel that he or she was genuinely concerned about the client, the higher the score. The more the client obtained the impression that the interviewer was "just doing a job," the lower the score.)

Category IV Score: ☐

Total Score: ☐

ANALYSIS OF A LEGAL INTERVIEW

Introduction

We will now examine portions of a **hypothetical** interview involving Sam Donnelly, who walks into the law office of Day & Day seeking legal assistance. Last month he was a passenger in a car that collided with a truck.

Our goal in this analysis is to identify guidelines that can help you conduct competent interviews. In particular, we want to increase your sensitivity to the large variety of factors that affect the quality of the communication between a client and an interviewer. Earlier in the chapter, we discussed fact particularization as an important technique in achieving factual comprehensiveness in the interview. Here our focus will be the broader context of interviewing land communication.

hypothetical Not actual or real but presented for purposes of discussion or analysis.

Assume that Mr. Donnelly is in the office of William Fenton, Esq., one of the partners of Day & Day. During their meeting, the law firm agrees to represent Mr. Donnelly. The arrangement is confirmed in the attorney-client fee agreement that Mr. Donnelly signs. (See Exhibit 8.1 for a sample agreement.) At the conclusion of the meeting, Mr. Fenton calls his paralegal, Jane Collins. He asks her to come to his office so that he can introduce her to Mr. Donnelly.

Attorney:	*[As the paralegal walks into Mr. Fenton's office, he says]* Mr. Donnelly, I want to introduce you to Jane Collins who will be working with me throughout the case. I have asked her to schedule an appointment with you to do a comprehensive interview that will cover the facts you and I began to discuss today. Jane will be an additional contact for you throughout the case. If at any time you can't reach me, let Jane know what concerns, questions, or needs you have. I will be reviewing all of Jane's work and will be meeting with her regularly. Jane is a trained paralegal. She is not an attorney and therefore can't give legal advice, but she can do many things to help me represent you.
Client:	Nice to meet you.
Paralegal:	*[Jane walks over to where Mr. Donnelly is sitting and, with a smile, extends her hand to offer a firm handshake.]* I'm very pleased to meet you, Mr. Donnelly. I look forward to working with you on the case. Let me give you one of my cards so that you'll know how to reach me.
Client:	Thank you.
Attorney:	I've already explained to Mr. Donnelly that you will be doing an in-depth interview with him on the case.
Paralegal:	Yes. . . . Before you leave today, Mr. Donnelly, let's discuss when it would be convenient for you to have the interview. Or if you need to check your calendar, I can call you.

It is extremely important to note that the supervising attorney, Mr. Fenton, has taken the initiative to introduce the client to the paralegal. This sets the tone for the client-paralegal relationship. Many clients have little more than a general understanding of what a paralegal is. Here, the introduction by the supervising attorney is very specific in identifying Jane as a nonattorney who has been trained to help attorneys represent clients. She will also act as a liaison between the attorney and the client.

Note also the manner in which the paralegal treats the client. She walks toward the client to greet him with a firm handshake and a smile. She tells the client that she looks forward to working with him. She gives him her business card. (This is often appreciated because the client is probably meeting several new faces during the first few visits to the law office.) She is very deferential to the client in asking when it would be convenient for him to schedule an interview with her. These are signs of a paralegal who is willing to go out of her way to make the client feel important and at ease.

Preparing for the Interview

How do you get ready for an interview? Exhibit 8.6 lists some of the major steps you should take to prepare. The list assumes that this is one of the first legal interviews you have conducted.

In addition to the suggestions in Exhibit 8.6, try to observe someone interview a client. Find out if anyone else in the office will be conducting an interview soon. If so, ask permission to sit in. Watching others interview can be very instructive. Another way to prepare is to read some intake memos or other reports written after interviews in other cases. They can be found in the open or closed files of other clients. Pay particular attention to the amount and kind of information obtained in those cases.

Your mental attitude in preparing for the interview is very important. You need to approach each interview as if it is going to be a totally new experience for you. It is dangerous to think that you know what the client is going to say, no matter how many times you have worked on a particular kind of case before. The danger is that you will not be listening carefully to what the client is saying. An interviewer who has an I've-heard-it-all-before attitude may block out what is unique about the facts of *this* client's case.

The hallmark of the *professional* is to view every client, every problem, and every incident as different and potentially unique ("There's never been one like this before"). A professional interviewer, therefore, keeps probing for more facts to try to show that this case is not like all the rest.

EXHIBIT 8.6	Preparing for an Interview

- Schedule the interview during a time when you will not be rushed or constantly interrupted.
- Schedule the interview at a location that will be private and convenient for the client.
- Find out from your supervisor if the client has any special needs such as wheelchair accessibility.
- Call or write the client in advance to confirm the date and place of the interview. Give an estimate of how long the interview will take. If the directions are complex, offer to send or fax a map (hand-drawn if necessary). Remind the client of anything you want him or her to bring to the interview, e.g., insurance policies, copies of tax returns.
- Anticipate and prepare for the client's comfort, e.g., a comfortable chair, a pad and pencil in case the client wants to take notes, and a supply of tissues. Also, know where you can quickly obtain fresh water or coffee after offering them to the client early in the interview.
- Before the interview, read everything in the office file on the client. Bring any documents in the file that you may want to question the client about or have the client review during the interview.
- Have a final brief meeting (or phone conversation) with your supervisor to make sure you understand the goals of the interview.
- Find out if the office has any checklists you should use in asking questions. If none exist, prepare an outline of about a dozen major questions you will ask the client. You will have many more questions in the interview, but you can use this outline as a guide.
- Spend a little time in the law library (or online) doing some general background research in the area of the law involved in the client's case to obtain an overview of some of the major terminology and legal issues. This overview may suggest additional questions you will want to ask during the interview.
- Prepare any forms you may want to ask the client to sign during the interview, e.g., consent to release medical information, or authorization to obtain employment history records.
- Have your own supplies ready for note taking. Some interviewers recommend using different colored pens so that you can switch colors when the client is telling you something you want to give particular emphasis in your notes.[6]
- Walk into the interview with the attitude that the client will be telling you a story that you have never heard before. Do not assume you know what the client is going to say even if you have handled many cases of this kind before.

The goal of the professional is to find out what makes this case stand out. The inclination of the *bureaucrat*, on the other hand, is to see the similarities in clients, problems, and incidents ("These cases are a dime a dozen"). The bureaucrat clusters things together into coherent groupings and patterns so that time can be saved and efficiency achieved. The bureaucrat feels that chaos could result if we viewed everything as potentially unique. An interviewer who has a bureaucratic attitude usually does not spend much time probing for facts; his or her goal is to fit this case into a category of similar cases handled in the past.

We all have within us professional and bureaucratic tendencies that are sometimes at war with each other.[7] Our bureaucratic self is very practical; our professional self can be a bit extreme in its search for uniqueness. When conducting legal interviews, however, or engaging in any task in the representation of a client, our goal is to try within reason to let our professional selves dominate.

Environment

You need to consider the impact of the physical setting or environment in which you conduct the interview. It will usually take place in the office of the interviewer. If this office is not private enough, however, try to reserve the conference room or borrow an available office from someone else if it would be more private than your own. In our example, let us assume that Jane Collins's office is suitable for her interview with Sam Donnelly.

[There is a knock at Jane Collins's door. She gets up from her chair, goes over to the door, opens it, and says, as she extends her hand].

Paralegal: Hello, Mr. Donnelly. I'm Jane Collins, Mr. Fenton's paralegal. It's good to see you again. Won't you come in?... Did you have any trouble finding the office?

Client: No, I had to use the bus, but it worked out fine.

Paralegal: Let me take your coat for you. Please have a seat. *[The paralegal points the client toward a chair on the opposite side of the desk from where she sits. They face each other.]*

Note the seating arrangement the paralegal selects as illustrated in diagram A. ("I" stands for interviewer and "C" stands for client.)

Diagram A

A number of other seating arrangements could have been used:

Diagram B   Diagram C   Diagram D

The chairs can be arranged so that the interviewer and the client sit on opposite sides of a desk (diagram A), diagonally across a desk (diagram B), on the same side of a desk (diagram C), or in another part of the room away from the desk altogether (diagram D). Seating arrangements are usually made at the convenience of the "owner" of the office. Rarely is enough thought given to how a particular arrangement may help or hurt the flow of communication. Sometimes the seating arrangement will create an austere and official atmosphere; other settings may be close and warm.

Of the four seating arrangements diagrammed above, which do you think would be most effective? Which would you feel most comfortable with? Which do you think the client would be most comfortable with? A number of factors can help you answer these questions. First, there is probably no single seating arrangement that will be perfect for all situations. The interviewer must be flexible enough to experiment with different arrangements. For most legal interviews, you will be taking extensive notes as the client answers your questions. If you are going to make any notes about the client that you may not want him or her to see (e.g., "appears reluctant to answer"), you will want to select a seating arrangement that does not allow the client to read what you are writing.

To some extent, seating arrangements can be a reflection of your personality. How do you want to project yourself? As an authority figure? If so, you might be inclined toward the seating arrangement in diagram A. Do you, on the other hand, want the client to feel closer to you and not to have the impression that you are hiding behind a desk? If a particular arrangement is used for the initial interview, do you think a different arrangement might ever be appropriate for follow-up interviews with the same client? When clients look up, do you want them to be looking straight at you (diagram A) or do you think that it might be more comfortable for them to be able to face in other directions (diagram B) without appearing to scatter their attention?[8]

Of course, an office is much more than an arrangement of desks and chairs. Describe the potential benefits or disadvantages of the following:

- Numerous posters on the wall display political slogans, e.g., "Down with the Republicans!" or "Pro Choice IS Pro Family."
- A copy of the latest issue of the *Rush Limbaugh Newsletter* is on the desk.
- The desk is cluttered with papers, books, and half-eaten food.
- A sign on the wall says, "Don't even think of smoking here."

You want the office to help you project a professional image of yourself. A messy desk usually suggests the opposite. Be careful about explicit messages around the room. Your political views may clash with those of the client. Do not broadcast your politics by having partisan literature on the walls or the desk. What do you think of the no-smoking sign? Courtesy would suggest a more friendly way of letting clients know that they should not smoke in your room, e.g., a sign that says, "Thank you for not smoking."

Getting Started

Note that the paralegal, Jane Collins, went to the door to greet the client. Suppose that, instead, she had remained in her chair and called, "Come in," in a loud voice. Do you think it makes any difference whether the interviewer walks over to the client? When you walk into a room with someone, you are communicating the message "Come share my room with me." If, however, you are seated at your desk and call the visitor in, the message to the visitor is likely to be: "This is my room; I control it; you have my permission to enter." Although this is not necessarily an inappropriate message, it is not as friendly and warm as going to the door to escort the client in.

Notice, however, that the paralegal apparently did *not* go out to the front entrance of the law firm to greet the client. Here is what may have happened: the client came to the front door, was greeted by a receptionist, was told to wait in the reception area, and was then given directions to find the paralegal's office on his own. If this is what happened, it was a mistake. The paralegal should have left instructions with the receptionist to call her when the client arrived, and the paralegal then should have gone out to the reception area to greet the client and personally walk him back to her office. This would be the most courteous approach. Furthermore, you do not want clients roaming around offices—even if they know the way. A wandering client may overhear confidential conversations between other members of the firm or see open files of other clients on the desks of secretaries. This danger is minimized if the paralegal escorts the client from the front door to her office.

Note that the paralegal reintroduced herself to the client: "Hello, Mr. Donnelly. I'm Jane Collins, Mr. Fenton's paralegal. It's good to see you again." She does not expect the client to remember who she is. It is a sign of courtesy to reintroduce yourself at the beginning of a second meeting. And never call a client by his or her first name unless expressly invited to do so by the client.

Paralegal:	Thank you for coming in today, Mr. Donnelly. Are you ready for today's session?
Client:	Ready as I can be.
Paralegal:	Good. . . . How have you been?
Client:	Not bad considering all this mess. I can't believe all this is happening.
Paralegal:	Being involved in an accident can be very upsetting. It must be very hard for you. . . . Our office has handled cases like this before. While no one can predict how a case will turn out, you can rest assured that we will be doing everything possible to help lessen the burden on you.
Client:	Thank you.
Paralegal:	Let me ask you, Mr. Donnelly, is there anything that you want to cover now before we begin?
Client:	This letter came in the mail this morning. It looks like the truck company has its lawyers on the case.
Paralegal:	*[She takes the letter from Mr. Donnelly and spends a few moments reading it.]* This is a letter from the attorney representing the truck company seeking information from you. They obviously don't know yet that we represent you. Once they know you are represented, it is improper for them to contact you directly. They need to go through your attorney. I'll let Mr. Fenton know about this letter right away. Why don't I photocopy it before you leave so that you can keep a copy for your records. After Mr. Fenton sees this, we'll let you know if there is anything you need to do about the letter. For now, let us take care of it.

Early on, the paralegal thanked the client: "Thank you for coming in today." Throughout the case, the office may ask the client to do many things such as come to meetings, sign documents, and collect information. Each time, you should express appreciation for doing what was asked. Never expect the client to thank *you*, although this may occur. You do not want the client to have the impression that you are doing the client a favor. The reverse is always true. Hence, constantly be appreciative.

Soon after inviting the client in, the paralegal asked, "Did you have any trouble finding the office?" And a little later, "How have you been?" It is a good idea to begin the interview at a personal level with some small talk about the weather, how the client is doing, or a recent sports event the client might know something about. (Within reason, of course, since clients are being charged by

contingency case A case in which clients pay attorney and paralegal fees only if they win through litigation or settlement.

breach of contract A cause of action in which a party seeks a court remedy for the alleged failure of a party to perform the term(s) of an enforceable contract.

the hour unless they have a **contingency case** with the office.) Small talk helps put the client at ease. The client may still be a bit nervous about the accident or whatever led to the conflict and the involvement of attorneys. Being a little lighthearted and personal for a few moments at the beginning of the interview may help break the ice.

When clients are particularly stressed or overwhelmed, you need to provide reassurance that the office will be actively working on the case and that the situation is manageable. The paralegal did that here when she told the client the office has handled similar cases in the past and would be doing everything possible to help lessen the burden on him. Comments such as these should help reassure the client. Of course, many clients want to be told they are going to win their cases. Avoid making any statement that could be interpreted as a promise or guarantee of success. Otherwise, the office could be sued for **breach of contract** if the case is not successful. Instead of telling a client, "You've got a great case," say something like the following: "There is no way of telling how a case will turn out. You've got a lot of good points in your favor, and we're going to work as hard as we can for you."

The paralegal also told the client, "Being involved in an accident can be very upsetting. It must be very hard for you." Here, the paralegal is expressing understanding and empathy for the client's predicament. This is extremely important. The comment tells the client that the paralegal is *listening* to what the client is saying. Mr. Donnelly refers to the "mess" he is in and says, "I can't believe all this is happening." Rather than ignoring this comment, the paralegal lets the client know that she has heard what he said. This is comforting for clients. On the other hand, you don't want to be patronizing or condescending. A comment such as "You poor fellow" would obviously fall into this category.

Interviewers often learn a large number of highly personal facts about the client's life. Think of how you would feel if you were revealing such facts about yourself to a stranger. Think of how you would want this person to react to what you are revealing. At such a vulnerable time, clients need understanding and compassion. This does not mean that you should lose your objectivity. As indicated earlier, if it would be natural for you to express an emotion in response to what a client tells you, express the emotion. For example, "I'm very sorry to hear that" or "I can understand why you'd be angry." At the same time, you need to have an appropriate professional distance from the emotions and drama of the client's story.

Some clients will be understandably reluctant to talk about certain topics. Indeed, as an interviewer, you may feel uncomfortable delving into them. Examples might be prior bankruptcies a client has gone through, violence engaged in by the client in the past, or the client's sexual history with his or her spouse. If, however, these topics are relevant to the legal services sought by the client, they must be covered. The client will be looking for signs that you are not embarrassed by such topics and that you can talk about them with appropriate sensitivity.

Of course, never be judgmental of the client. Do not ask the client, "Why did you do that?" if your tone is one of suspicion or disbelief. Clients should not feel that they are required to justify their actions or inactions to you. This obviously would not encourage open communication between interviewer and client.

Also important was the paralegal's question "[I]s there anything that you want to cover now before we begin?" Early in the interview, find out if the client has any immediate concerns or questions on his mind. This should be done not only as a matter of courtesy but also as a technique to make sure the client has your undivided attention. On the way into the law office, the client may have been thinking of several things he wants to ask about. He may be worried that he will forget them. Or he may be a little embarrassed about asking his questions. Give the client a chance to express anything on his mind at the outset before you begin your barrage of questions. In our example, this technique worked. Mr. Donnelly did have something on his mind—the letter he received from opposing counsel.

Paralegal:	Our goal today is to obtain a comprehensive statement of the facts of the accident. It will take at least an hour, maybe a little more. As Mr. Fenton told you, I am a paralegal, not an attorney. I'll be able to help on the case in many ways, but I won't be able to give you legal advice. That will have to come from Mr. Fenton. If anything comes up today that calls for legal advice, I'll bring it to Mr. Fenton's attention so that we can get you the response you need. Since I work for an attorney, you should know that everything you tell me is protected by the attorney-client privilege.
Client:	Fine.

Paralegal:	Before we begin, Mr. Donnelly, you mentioned that you had to take the bus in. Is there a problem with your car? Was it involved in the accident with the truck?
Client:	No, no. . . . I let my brother borrow my car today.
Paralegal:	All right. . . . I want to start by getting an overview of what happened on the day of the accident. Then we'll go back and fill in the details. I'll be taking detailed notes to make sure that I remember everything you say. . . . OK, what happened that day?

This is the second meeting between the paralegal and Mr. Donnelly. Although the supervising attorney, Mr. Fenton, told Mr. Donnelly that Jane Collins was not an attorney, it is a good idea for the paralegal to reinforce this point herself. Paralegals who have contact with clients are sometimes pressured by clients to give legal advice. Making it clear at the outset that this is inappropriate can cut down on this pressure, although, unfortunately, it will not eliminate it.

The paralegal also told the client that what he tells her "is protected by the attorney-client privilege." The client needs to know this, but *not* in this way. The phrase *attorney-client privilege* is legal **jargon**. It is technical language that does not have an everyday meaning. Avoid jargon unless the client needs to know it and you explain it in language the client can understand. When you use jargon or confusing terms, do not interpret the client's lack of questions to mean that the client understands the jargon. Do not wait for the client to ask you to explain unfamiliar terms. Take the initiative to provide explanations. In our example, it probably would have been sufficient to tell Mr. Donnelly that what he tells her will be confidential rather than using the more technical phrase *attorney-client privilege*.

jargon Technical language; words that do not have an everyday meaning.

Another useful technique for beginning an interview is to briefly state the major goal of the interview—here, to obtain a comprehensive statement of the facts of the accident. Give the client an overview of what you hope to accomplish and how long it may take. Do this even if you gave the client this information when you set up the appointment.

Let the client know you will be taking notes so you will have an accurate record of what he says during the interview. As indicated earlier, the document that contains the detailed report of the interviewer is sometimes called the *intake memo* (see Exhibit 8.3). This will be prepared after the interview based on the interviewer's notes.

Some interviewers recommend against taking detailed notes, particularly at the beginning of the interview when you want to maintain eye contact and establish rapport. If you follow this advice, at least some notes should be taken at the outset as reminders of the topics you need to come back to later for detained questioning and notetaking.

Occasionally, your supervisor will want you to tape-record the interview. Be sure the client consents to the recording. At the beginning of the interview, say, "This is Jane Collins, a paralegal in the law office of Day & Day. Today's date is March 23, 2008. I am in our law office with Mr. Samuel Donnelly. Mr. Donnelly, have you agreed to have this interview tape-recorded?" The latter question will help disprove any allegations that you secretly recorded the interview. On the tape, also state the names of other persons, if any, who are in the room during the taping.

A good interviewer is always listening for clues to other legal or relevant nonlegal problems. There is always a danger that an interviewer will block out anything that does not fit within the topics scheduled for discussion. In our example, the paralegal said to Mr. Donnelly, "[Y]ou mentioned that you had to take the bus in. Is there a problem with your car?" While the car apparently has nothing to do with the case, it was worth inquiring into. Suppose, for example, the client is not driving because of injury to his eyes caused by an eye doctor. Or perhaps the client has had a contract dispute with an auto mechanic. It is a good idea to listen for suggestions or clues to other problems provided by a client. If you do not want to cover the matter immediately, make a note to raise it later in the interview at a more appropriate or convenient time.

The major techniques and guidelines for beginning an interview are summarized in Exhibit 8.7.

Kinds of Questions

One of the early questions the paralegal asked the client was "[W]hat happened that day?" This is known as an **open-ended question**. It is a broad, relatively unstructured question that rarely can be answered in one or two words. An open-ended question gives the client more control over the kind and amount of information to be provided in response. It also gives the interviewer an opportunity to size up the ability of the client to organize his or her thoughts in order to present a coherent response. Here are some other examples of open-ended questions: "What brings you in today?" and "What led to the crisis at the bank?" One of the most frequently used categories

open-ended question A broad, unstructured question that rarely can be answered in one or two words.

EXHIBIT 8.7	Beginning the Interview

- Introduce yourself by name and title. If this is your second meeting with the client, reintroduce yourself.
- Do not call a client by his or her first name unless invited to do so by the client. Do not ask the client for permission to use his or her first name. Wait to be asked to do so.
- Express appreciation each time the client does something the office asks, e.g., come in for an interview, or read and sign a document.
- Make sure the client understands that you are not an attorney and cannot give legal advice.
- Start at a personal level (e.g., with some small talk) rather than launching right into the task at hand.
- Review the goals of the interview with the client (based on the assignment from your supervisor), and provide an estimate of how long the interview will take.
- Make the client feel that his or her case is special. Avoid giving the impression that you are engaged in anything boring or routine.
- Never tell a client how busy you are. It suggests to the client that he or she is bothering you and might give the impression that the office is disorganized.
- Express understanding and empathy for the client's predicament without being condescending.
- Do not be judgmental.
- Make sure the client understands that what he or she tells you is confidential.
- Find out if there are immediate concerns that the client wants to raise.
- Avoid legal jargon unless the client needs to become familiar with the jargon and you provide clear definitions and explanations.
- Let the client know you will be taking notes, and why.
- Listen for clues to other legal and relevant nonlegal problems that the office may need to explore.
- Begin new topics with open-ended questions. (See Exhibit 8.9 on the kinds of questions an interviewer can ask.)
- Spend the first few minutes obtaining an overview/outline of the entire event or transaction. Then go back to obtain the details.
- Encourage the client to give you the facts chronologically as a story with a beginning, middle, and end. If more than one event is involved in the case, cover them separately in the same chronological way. Then go into how the events are interconnected.
- If the client appears overwhelmed or unusually distressed, try to provide reassurance by letting him or her know that the office is actively working on the case and is doing everything it can. Do not, however, promise results or say anything that a client could interpret as a promise or even as a prediction of what the outcome of the case will be.

overview question an open-ended question that asks for a summary of an event or condition.

of open-ended questions is the **overview question**, which asks for a summary of something such as an important event. For example, "What happened during your first year in college?" or Jane Collins's question, "[W]hat happened that day?" An open-ended *request* (e.g., "Tell me about the problem") invites the same kind of broad response but is phrased as a request rather than as a question.

Open-ended questions (or requests) invite the person questioned to give a long and potentially rambling answer. Hence they should not be overused. These questions are often most effective when beginning a new topic in the interview.

closed-ended question A narrowly structured question that usually can be answered in one or two words. Also called a *directed question*.

At the opposite extreme is the **closed-ended question**, which is a narrowly structured question that usually can be answered in one or two words. Examples: "How old are you?" "What time did the accident occur?" and "Did you receive the letter?" Closed-ended questions give the interviewer more control over the interview because they let the client know precisely what information is sought.

If the facts of a case are relatively complex, you should consider spending the first few minutes asking overview questions in order to obtain an outline of the entire event or transaction, and then going back to obtain the details. Once you have the big picture, you will be better able to see connections among the individual facts. The paralegal in our example took this approach when she said, "I want to start by getting an overview of what happened on the day of the accident. Then we'll go back and fill in the details." She followed this up with the open-ended overview question, "[W]hat happened that day?"

chronological question A question designed to encourage the interviewee to describe what happened in the order in which events occurred—by date, step by step.

Both the request for an overview and the detailed questioning should be designed to encourage the client to tell the events of the case *chronologically*. The case may have many confusing aspects. The client may be inclined to talk about four or five things simultaneously—the accident, the hospitalization, the events leading up to the accident, the deceitfulness of the other side, etc. The best way to conduct an orderly interview is to help the client structure the case as a *story* with a beginning, middle, and end. Hence you should regularly ask **chronological questions** such as

"What happened next?" or "What did you do then?" If the client says something substantially out of chronological sequence, politely say, "Could we get to that in a moment? First I want you to finish telling me what happened after. . . ." Although you want to see the interconnections among the various events of the case, the discussion may become tangled and confusing unless you cover one topic at a time in the same methodical manner. In most instances, the most methodical way is chronologically.

Drawing a **timeline** as the client speaks is sometimes helpful when a story involves some complexity. The simplest format of a timeline is usually a straight line that lists significant events chronologically along the line. Each event might be drawn within a separate box that includes the date when the event occurred (see Exhibit 8.8). A diagram such as this gives the client a visual overview of what occurred and may prompt further questions and clarifications.

timeline A chronological presentation of significant events, often organized as a straight-line diagram.

EXHIBIT 8.8	Example of a Timeline

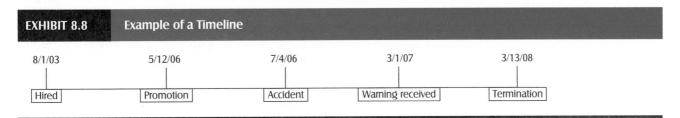

In general, you should avoid asking **leading questions** in which the answer is suggested in the question. For example, "You didn't return the call, did you?" "Did he tell you about the defect in the engine after you already said you would buy it?" The danger of a leading question is that a nervous client or witness will simply give you the answer you appear to want. Leading questions might sometimes be useful when trying to challenge something that a hostile witness is saying, but this approach should obviously not be needed with your own client. If a client is having difficulty remembering something (e.g., the weather on a particular day), a leading question might help jog the memory (e.g., "Was it raining that day?"). If a client needs constant prodding through leading questions, however, you may have reason to doubt the client's entire story.

leading question A question that suggests an answer within the question.

Another category is the **corroborative question**, which seeks to verify (or corroborate) facts beyond the word of the client or witness. For example, "Were there any passengers in the car who will back that up?"

corroborative question A question designed to verify (corroborate) facts by seeking information beyond what is provided by the interviewee.

In general, you should avoid **combination questions**—those with more than one part. They can confuse the person being interviewed. There are two kinds of combination questions: multiple-choice and add-on. A **multiple-choice question** asks the client or witness to choose among options presented by the interviewer. It is an "or" question. For example, "Did you personally review the balance sheet, *or* did you rely exclusively on what the accountant told the committee?" The interviewee may not remember both options and respond only to the last part of the question. An **add-on question** is simply several questions phrased as one. It is an "and" question. For example, "When did you arrive in Boston, *and* how long did you stay there?" Two questions asked at once are sometimes referred to as *double-barreled questions*. Of course, add-on questions could have more than two parts: for example, "What was your salary when you began work at the company, at the time of the accident, *and* on the date you were terminated?" Avoid add-on questions for the same reason you should avoid most multiple-choice questions; they can be confusing.

combination question A question that has more than one part.

multiple-choice question A question that asks the interviewee to choose among two or more options stated in the question.

add-on question A question that stacks one or more additional questions within it.

There are some combination questions that are relatively simple. For example, "Was he driving a car *or* a truck?" and "What is your husband's name, *and* where was he born?" Yet the danger of confusion still exists, and the better practice is to break all combination questions into individual questions that are asked separately.

The final question that should always be asked at the end of the interview (or at the end of a separate topic during the interview) is the **wrap-up question**. It asks whether the interviewee thinks everything has been covered. "OK, before we conclude, have we gone over everything you wanted to say about. . . .?" This gives clients the opportunity to raise or reinforce anything of particular importance to them.

wrap-up question A question asked at the end of the interview (or at the end of a separate topic within the interview) in which the interviewee is asked if there is anything he or she thinks has been left out or inadequately covered.

See Exhibit 8.9 for an overview of the major kinds of questions an interviewer can ask.

Attentive Listening

Studies have shown that clients rate "evidence of concern" as being more significant than the results they obtain from a law office.[9] This is a remarkable conclusion. Of course, clients want to win their cases. Yet they are also desperate for a sympathetic ear. Being involved in a legal dispute is often traumatic for them. In addition to being treated competently as a plaintiff or defendant, clients want a law office that is genuinely concerned about them as persons.

One of the best ways to demonstrate concern is through **attentive listening**. This simply means that you take affirmative steps to let the client know that you have heard what he or she has said and that you consider every meeting with the client important. Unfortunately, listening is not a skill that comes naturally to us. "Too many times in today's society, what passes for listening is merely waiting quietly for your turn to talk."[10] According to the International Listening Association (www.listen.org), when we are going through the motions of listening to someone, we are in fact preoccupied with something else about 75% of the time. To help combat this problem, Exhibit 8.10 summarizes some of the major techniques of attentive listening.

Some experienced paralegals often handle the same kind of case over and over. Clients, however, want to feel that their case deserves and will get *individual* attention; they do not want their cases handled in an assembly-line or mass-production manner. They appreciate having experienced attorneys and paralegals working for them, but they are particularly pleased when they feel that the office is treating their case as special.

Comprehensiveness

A major goal of most legal interviews is to achieve factual comprehensiveness; you want to obtain as many relevant facts as the client is able to give. The most important technique in accomplishing this goal is *fact particularization*, discussed earlier in the chapter. (See Exhibits 8.4 and 8.5.) Also important are *corroborative questions* that ask about documents or other individuals who can support the version of the facts the client is relating. (See Exhibit 8.9.)

attentive listening Taking affirmative, ongoing steps to let an interviewee know that you have heard what he or she has said and that you consider the meeting with him or her to be important.

EXHIBIT 8.9	Kinds of interview Questions

Here are some of the major categories of questions, some of which overlap:

- *Open-ended questions.* Those that are broad and relatively unstructured, allowing the client or witness to express what is on his or her mind. They rarely can be answered by one or two words. Examples: "What can we do for you today?" "Tell me what happened on the day of the accident?" and "What kind of a marriage did you have?"
- *Closed-ended questions.* Those that narrowly focus the attention of the client or witness and call for a very brief answer, often one or two words such as yes or no. Examples: "Are you seeking a divorce?" "Were you wearing your glasses when you saw the accident?" and "Did your husband ever hit you?"
- *Overview questions.* Those that seek a summary of a major event or condition. Examples: "Would you first give me a general picture of what happened?" "What are the major incidents that led to the dismissal?" and "Could you start me off by giving a brief description of what happened at the party before the shooting?"
- *Chronological questions.* Those designed to get the client or witness to tell the story of what happened chronologically—step by step. Examples: "Then what happened?" "What did he say after he saw the accident?" and "What happened next?"
- *Leading questions.* Those in which the answer is suggested in the question. Examples: "Where was the fender dented?" "The car wasn't damaged when you received it, was it?" and " You were traveling 75 mph?"
- *Corroborative questions.* Those designed to verify (corroborate) facts by seeking information beyond the word of the client or witness. Examples: "Who else saw the accident?" "Were you the only one who complained?" and "Do you have receipts?"
- *Combination questions.* Those that contain more than one part. Examples: "Did you accept the offer, reject it, or ask for more time to respond?" (multiple choice) and "What school does your child attend and are you satisfied with how well he is doing there?" (add on).
- *Wrap-up questions.* Those asked at the end of the interview (or at the end of separate topics within the interview) in which the interviewee is asked if there is anything else he or she wants to add. Examples: "Have we covered everything?" and "Anything more on the phone calls you received?"

Most clients want to give you facts that support their case. You need to encourage them to tell you negative as well as positive facts. Let them know how important it is for the attorney to know *all* the facts. The attorney for the other side may find out about negative facts. Indeed, one of the preoccupations of the other side is to find the facts that will hurt the client. The client's attorney must know all the facts in advance so that he or she can prepare a response when these facts come out, as they inevitably do.

Interviewers must also carefully distinguish between *observed data* and **inferences**.[11] Observed data are what the client directly experienced through the senses (e.g., "I saw the car weaving back and

inference A deduction or conclusion reached from facts.

EXHIBIT 8.10	Attentive Listening

- Make it obvious to the client that he or she has your full attention. If a receptionist answers incoming calls to the office, let the client hear you tell the receptionist that you are in an interview and do not wish to be disturbed. If you know that there might be an interruption during the interview, alert the client and apologize in advance.
- Occasionally lean forward toward the client as he or she speaks.
- Avoid being fidgety or appearing nervous.
- Take notes. This is an obvious sign that you think what the client is saying is important. (As indicated earlier, however, some interviewers avoid extensive notetaking at the beginning of an interview in order to help establish rapport through concentrated attention.)
- Maintain eye contact whenever you are not taking notes.
- As the client speaks, give frequent *yes* nods. Also say, "Ah hum," "ok," or "I see" when the client momentarily pauses while answering your questions. Connecting or reinforcing words such as these let the client know that you are following what he or she is saying.
- Several times during the interview, use the client's name, e.g., "Mr. Jones, was that the first time you spoke to your accountant last year?" and "Did I hear you say, Mrs. Phillips, that you lease the car rather than own it outright?"
- Periodically let the client know he or she is providing useful information. Make comments such as "That could be very important" or "I'm glad you recall the event in such detail."
- In addition to listening to the words of the client, "listen" to the feelings the client is expressing through body language. Words are not the only way a client lets you know that he or she is anxious, suspicious, worried, or in pain. Frowns, hand gestures, eye contact, and a lack of eye contact are examples of body language—nonverbal communication.
- At appropriate times, restate a feeling the client is trying to describe, e.g., "The stress you were under must have been overwhelming." You may want to do this in the form of a question, e.g., "You were really angry when you found out, weren't you?"
- Occasionally read something from your notes out loud to the client and ask if you have correctly recorded what he or she has said. This reinforces the value of precision in the practice of law as well as letting the client know how important this interview is.
- Recap regularly. Often during the interview, paraphrase and summarize what the client has said and ask if your paraphrase or summary is correct. ("Let me see if I understood what you have said . . . .")
- Occasionally (or often if needed), ask the client to clarify or elaborate on something he or she has said.
- Ask spontaneous questions that occur to you while listening to an answer of the client. This helps demonstrate that you are not trying to fit the client's answers into your preconceived notions about the case. Rather, you are following the client's train of thought.
- Refer back to what the client said earlier, e.g., "When we were discussing the purchase, you said that your father wanted his brother to manage the property. Could you tell me what you meant?"
- Never express impatience, no matter how frustrated you are at the client's failure to answer what you feel should be an easy question.
- While a client is answering a question, try to avoid interrupting unless he or she is rambling and you need clarification before the client moves to another point.
- Do not finish the client's sentences for him or her no matter how certain you are of what the client is trying to say. Finishing someone's sentences demonstrates your impatience and is condescending.

forth over the center line" and "I smelled alcohol on his breath"). An inference is a deduction or conclusion from facts (e.g., "He was driving carelessly" and "He was drunk"). Part of being comprehensive in an interview is to uncover all the observed data that led to the inferences made by a client. This is not always easy to do. Opinionated clients sometimes confuse facts and opinions. They may state an opinion but think it is a fact because they "swear" it is true. But opinions are mere inferences. Let a client express them during an interview and record them in your notes, but follow up with probing questions that identify underlying observed data. Fact particularization will help you achieve this goal.

Earlier we said that checklists of questions can be helpful in preparing for an interview. Be careful in using checklists, however. Although they can provide guidance on what to cover in the interview, you must be flexible enough to deviate from the checklist when relevant topics come up that are not on the checklist. Use any checklist (whether written by others or prepared on your own) as no more than a starting point. Suppose, for example, you are interviewing a client about her financial assets. You are working from a checklist of questions on wages, real estate holdings, stocks, bonds, etc. During the interview, the client happens to mention an ailing grandparent who is very fond of the client. This suggests the possibility of another possible asset: inheritance from this grandparent. Suppose, however, the checklist contains no questions about future inheritances. Common sense (one of the guides to formulating questions discussed earlier in the chapter) should tell you to ask whether the client thinks she might be a beneficiary in someone's will. Hence, if you have a checklist of questions, use it, but don't be so tied to the checklist that you fail to hear or respond to something the client says that does not fit into the checklist.

Take accurate notes on the facts the client gives you. Recall that one of the components of fact particularization is to record the extent of the certainty and uncertainty a client expresses about a fact. Suppose the client tells you, "I'm not sure" how fast an approaching car was going, but then says it was "about 50 mph." Your final report based on your notes should say,

> When I asked the client how fast the other car was going, he said he was "not sure." Then he estimated, "About 50 mph."

This lets the supervising attorney know that the client may be vulnerable as a witness in court if questioned about the matter of speed. An interviewer does not achieve the desired factual comprehensiveness unless he or she asks about and records the extent to which the client is certain or uncertain about the facts conveyed.

Finally, creative interviewers realize that a brief demonstration, drawing, or exhibit can sometimes be helpful in eliciting greater factual detail. One interviewer who works on many automobile negligence cases has a set of toy cars at her desk. She will occasionally line them up on the desk and ask the client to explain what happened by using the toy cars. "People love visual demonstrations. As powerful as words can be, charts, maps, graphs, re-enactments, diagrams, timelines, and other visual aids" can be very effective in communicating information.[12]

The techniques for obtaining factual comprehensiveness are summarized in Exhibit 8.11.

EXHIBIT 8.11	Achieving Factual Comprehensiveness

- Apply the technique of fact particularization to all the major facts the client tells you and that you need to cover. (See Exhibits 8.4 and 8.5.)
- Ask corroborative questions. (See Exhibit 8.9.)
- Encourage the client to tell you about negative facts.
- Probe beneath client opinions to obtain the underlying facts.
- Follow available checklists of questions, but be prepared to ask questions not on the checklist if they pertain to relevant topics that come up during the interview.
- Ask questions to determine the extent to which the client is certain or uncertain about an important fact.
- Where appropriate, use demonstrations and exhibits to elicit further information. For an example, see the timeline in Exhibit 8.8.
- After each separate topic is covered during the interview (and at the end of the entire interview), ask a wrap-up question to determine if the client thinks anything has been left out or has not been covered adequately.

Ethical Concerns

Paralegal: *[Telephone rings.]* Excuse me, Mr. Donnelly. "Yes, hello. How are you? . . . No, the Jackson case has been resolved. Mr. Jackson decided not to go through with his suit after McDonald made its offer. . . . You're welcome." Sorry, Mr. Donnelly, let's get back to the. . . .

A legal interview must be conducted competently *and ethically.* Unfortunately, there are more than a few opportunities for an interviewer to run afoul of ethical rules.

Mr. Donnelly has just heard the paralegal discuss the Jackson case on the phone. This is a violation of the paralegal's ethical obligation to preserve client confidentiality. Even though Mr. Donnelly may not have understood anything about the Jackson and McDonald case, he was not entitled to hear what he heard. He should not even know that Jackson or McDonald is a client of Day & Day. Revealing information about a client is a breach of confidentiality, whether it is done intentionally or carelessly. Mr. Donnelly may now have the impression that the paralegal will be as careless about discussing *his case* in front of strangers.

Client: A friend of mine told me that if another car rams into you and commits a clear traffic violation, their negligence is automatic. Is that true?

Paralegal: I'll take that question up with Mr. Fenton and get back to you. All legal questions like that need to be dealt with by an attorney.

Another major ethical danger that can arise during an interview is giving legal advice. As we saw in chapters 4 and 5, legal advice consists of applying laws or legal principles to the facts of a particular client's case. The more contact a paralegal has with clients, the greater the likelihood the paralegal will be asked to give legal advice. This is especially true during legal interviews. Clients are often hungry for answers. Mr. Donnelly is no exception. He asked the paralegal whether a traffic violation makes one's negligence "automatic." Even general questions about the law could be interpreted as questions that call for legal advice. Mr. Donnelly is probably trying to understand how the courts will handle his case.

Suppose the paralegal knows the correct answer. Think of how tempting it would be for her to answer the question. It takes a lot of will power for her to refrain from answering. She wants to appear intelligent. We all want to show off what we know. Be conservative, however, about ethics. (See Exhibit 5.1 in chapter 5.) To be safe, avoid giving an answer. The paralegal told Mr. Donnelly that she would "get back" to him after consulting with Mr. Fenton. This is better than coldly saying, "I'm not allowed to answer that question." When she said, "All legal questions like that need to be dealt with by an attorney," she is also helping to train the client about the limitations inherent in the paralegal's role. This may cut down on pressures in the future from Mr. Donnelly's attempts to ask her for legal advice.

Some of the major areas of ethical concern are summarized in Exhibit 8.12.

EXHIBIT 8.12   Avoiding Ethical Problems during Interviews

- If you cannot avoid phone interruptions or visits by others to your office during the interview, be sure that you do not discuss the facts of other clients' cases. Never mention the names of clients (or their opponents) in front of another client even if you are certain that the latter will not recognize these names. Excuse yourself and leave the room if you must discuss anything about other cases.
- While talking to the client, do not have open files of other clients on the desk.
- Do not let the client wander in the corridors of the office, e.g., to go to the coffeepot. You do not want the client to overhear conversations about other cases among attorneys, paralegals, secretaries, or other employees.
- Make sure the client understands you are not an attorney.
- Resist pressures from the client to give legal advice. When in doubt about whether a question you are asked calls for legal advice, do not answer. Refer the matter to your supervising attorney.
- If the client says anything during the interview that suggests the possibility of a conflict of interest (e.g., the client tells you that the opposing side's spouse was once represented by your law firm), stop the interview and check with your supervisor about whether you should continue.
- Do not discuss fees with a client.

Ending the Interview

The interview is over when you have accomplished the objectives of the interview or when the client is not able to provide you with any additional information. The client may need to check some of his records at home or contact a family member or business associate in order to answer some of your questions. The missing data can probably be communicated on the phone or through the mail.

Use wrap-up questions to give the client the opportunity to raise anything that *he* thinks should have been covered. For example, you could say, "Before we end today's session, let me ask you if there is anything you think we haven't covered or haven't covered enough." If the client raises anything, you may want to take some additional time now to go over the client's areas of concern, or you may have to tell the client that you'll get back to him on when you will be able to go over those concerns. The important point is to find out how the client feels about what was discussed during the interview and to respond to any of his concerns.

Often the client needs to sign documents that authorize the office to obtain confidential information about the client, e.g., a consent to release medical information. Be sure to explain the document clearly to the client and give him some time to read through what he is being asked to sign. Do not simply hand the client a document and say, "I'll need your signature on this form that will allow us to get your medical records." Here is a more appropriate approach:

Paralegal: *[Handing the document to him.]* Mr. Donnelly, I want you to take a look at this document. It's a consent to release medical information. We'll use it to ask doctors, hospitals, or other medical providers to give us information about your medical condition. Would you please take a moment to read through it and let me know if you have any questions about it. If not, there's a space at the end of the document for your signature.

Client: OK.

Paralegal: Once you sign it, I'll keep the original and get you a copy for your records.

The client will want to know what is going to happen next—after the interview. Remind the client of any scheduled appointments, e.g., doctor visits or depositions. If there are none, simply tell the client that you will be preparing a report for the attorney on the case and that the office will be getting back to the client. Also, summarize anything you asked the client to do during the interview, e.g., call you to provide the exact address of a former employer.

Begin preparing a draft of your intake memo soon after the interview is over, while the data and your notes are fresh in your mind. (See Exhibit 8.3.) Do this even if you need to obtain additional facts to include in your memorandum by follow-up interviewing or investigation. Modern word processing makes it relatively easy to make additions to memos or other documents. (See chapter 13.) Do not wait until you have all the facts before you start writing.

Also, make a notation in the client's file that you conducted the interview, even before you complete the intake memo. If the file does not have a summary form on which events can be recorded, simply place a brief note in the file stating the date and place of the interview. Someone else in the office working on the case (e.g., supervising attorney, law clerk, or secretary) should be able to look at the file and know what has been done to date.

For a summary of these and similar steps to take at the end of an interview, see Exhibit 8.13.

EXHIBIT 8.13   Ending the Interview

- Ask the client to sign any standard forms needed by the office, e.g., consent to release medical information, or authorization to obtain employment history records. Before doing so, clearly explain what the document is designed to do and give the client the opportunity to ask any questions about the document before he or she signs it.
- Use wrap-up questions to ask the client if there is anything else on his or her mind that he or she would like to raise before the interview is concluded.
- Let the client know precisely what the next step will be in the office's representation of the client, e.g., the attorney will call the client, or the paralegal will schedule a medical examination of the client.
- Remind the client how to reach you. Have additional copies of your business card on the desk.
- Thank the client for the interview.
- Start preparing a draft of your intake memo.
- In the client's file, make a brief note of the fact that you conducted the interview. Include the date and place of the interview.

Personality Observations

After conducting an interview, you should formulate some preliminary observations about the client's personality, particularly as they pertain to his or her sincerity, credibility, and persuasiveness. Here is how one attorney described this aspect of the interview:

> "Assess the client's personality" and whether you think the office "can work with this person." "Watch for red flags or danger signals, including the client who is emotionally distraught or vengeful; is inconsistent with the story or avoids answering questions; has unrealistic objectives; suggests use of improper influence or other unethical or illegal conduct; rambles, wanders off the subject, or constantly interrupts you"; tells the office "how to run the case; has already discharged or filed disciplinary complaints against other lawyers; has a personality disorder; or is flirtatious."[13]

In your intake memo to your supervisor, include your observations and assessments relevant to concerns such as these.

Improving Your Interviewing Skills

There are many ways you can improve your interviewing skills. They are summarized in Exhibit 8.14. Be a perpetual student of the law. Always be inquisitive. Never be totally comfortable with any of your skills. One of the fascinating aspects of working in a law office is the availability of infinite opportunities to grow and improve.

THE "DIFFICULT" CLIENT

Most clients are relatively easy to work with. Occasionally, however, you will encounter clients who can be troublesome. Here are some examples.

EXHIBIT 8.14	Improving Your Interviewing Skills

- There is a good deal of literature on legal interviewing. Check legal periodicals and legal treatises. Ask a law librarian for leads to such literature. On the Internet, run searches such as "interview skills" or "the art of interviewing" on general search engines (e.g., *www.google.com* and *search.msn.com*). Even though some of the results of such searches will lead you to sites on job interviewing, you may find techniques covered that apply to many interview settings.
- Try to attend seminars that include the topic of legal interviewing, e.g. CLE (Continuing Legal Education) seminars for attorneys conducted by bar associations or CLE seminars conducted by paralegal associations.
- Ask someone you respect in the office to observe you interview a client and then give you a critique. (You will need the advance permission of the client for this person to sit in.)
- Ask someone you respect in the office to read your intake memo and critique it. An experienced interviewer will be able to see if there appear to be any gaps in what you covered in your memo.
- Try to sit in when others in the office are interviewing clients. Read their memos on the interview and ask them questions about their interviewing techniques. (To observe someone else's interview, you will need the consent of the interviewer and of the client interviewee.)
- Ask attorneys and other paralegals about their interviewing experiences even if you are not able to watch them conduct an interview.

The Client Who Knows All the Law

Some clients are quick to tell the office that they know the law. They may have been in litigation before, have taken courses on law, have a close relative who is an attorney, or have read a good deal about the law on the Internet. The difficulty arises if such clients are always second-guessing the way the office is handling their case or are unduly critical of anyone trying to help them. Ultimately, the attorney in charge of the case must decide if the office can continue to work with such clients. All clients, of course, are entitled to their opinions about the legal system and about anyone trying to help them. (Indeed, clients have the right to fire their attorneys at any time.) The central question is whether a client is prepared to listen to the advice provided by the attorney. The client is not obligated to follow every recommendation, but there may be no point in continuing with the attorney-client relationship if the client does not trust the attorney's professional judgment. Paralegals working with such clients must be careful to avoid arguing with them or giving them legal advice. If a client starts lecturing a paralegal about the law, the best response is to listen respectfully and then respond by saying, "I'll be sure to let the attorney know what you have said."

As with all client contacts, make a brief note in the file on this exchange, indicating the date of the contact, what the client wanted, and what you said or did in response.

The Angry Client

Some clients can be very angry. They may feel outrage at the injustice someone has allegedly committed against them. It is important that such clients be given a chance to express themselves. At the very least, they need to know that the office they have hired understands what they have been through and how they feel. They need an opportunity to vent. If, however, they continue to be angry after they have had this opportunity, the office may have difficulty providing them with effective representation. As indicated earlier, it is important to show empathy for a client by making comments such as "This must be a very difficult time for you" or "I can understand why that would be upsetting." These comments can have a settling effect on clients without immersing the interviewer into the middle of an emotional thicket. You do not want to lose your professionalism by adopting the same pessimistic or hostile frame of mind as the client.

The Demanding or Suspicious Client

Some clients have difficulty believing that everyone in the office is not preoccupied with their case. They demand instant attention and results ("Why is it taking so long? I want this thing over!"). They may interpret delays as a tactic by the office to run up fees. An obvious response is to explain that the courts and the legal system often work at a slow pace unless an extreme emergency exists. Generally, it is not very helpful to point out that there are other clients who also need the attention of the attorneys and paralegals in the office. One possibly effective approach is to keep the demanding clients constantly informed of the status of their case. The office may want to send them copies of documents as these are prepared for them, and send periodic reports on the status of their case. During the initial interview, the office needs to head off or offset any unrealistic client expectations about how much time the case will take by providing a time range such cases often take for completion. The client also needs to be told that complications (e.g., new counterdemands by the opponent) almost always create additional delays.

The Client Who Lies

There is a difference between clients who give facts a favorable interpretation and clients who lie. Assume, for example, that an office represents a husband who is seeking sole custody of his children in a bitter divorce case. It is understandable that he will attempt to portray himself as a loving father. He may glowingly describe the positive effect he has had on his children by attending sports events with them and by helping them with their homework. Careful questioning and further investigation will help determine whether he has exaggerated his role. If he has, an experienced legal team will know how to present his case in a favorable light without compromising the truth. Suppose, however, that the father goes beyond exaggeration. For example, he may falsely claim that he does not use corporal punishment on the children, or he may deny that he takes illegal drugs in front of them in spite of evidence to the contrary. Of course, if any of these facts can reasonably be interpreted in the father's favor, the office has an obligation to present this interpretation to the court. Yet it may eventually become clear to the office that the client has a tendency to lie. Serious ethical problems can arise in such cases. As we saw in chapter 5, an attorney has an ethical obligation to avoid telling the court something that is not true and to avoid allowing a client to lie to the court when the attorney knows that this is what the client has done or is about to do. An attorney's withdrawal from a case is justified when continued representation of the client will cause the attorney to violate an ethical obligation. Furthermore, it may be impossible for the attorney to provide competent representation without knowing all available facts. The client must be told that the attorney cannot rebut negative facts without knowing what those facts are before someone else reveals them. The client cannot make those facts go away by lying about them or concealing them. If the office cannot convince the client of this reality, the likelihood of representing the client effectively and ethically is low.

CLASS EXERCISE 8.C

Form a circle of chairs with a single chair in the middle. The student sitting in the middle will play the role of the client. The students in the circle (numbering about 10) will be the interviewers, in rotation. The instructor will ask one of the students to begin the interview. As this student runs into difficulty during the interview, the student to his or her right picks up the interview, tries to resolve the difficulty in his or her own way, and then proceeds with the interview. If *this* student cannot resolve the difficulty, the student to his or her right tries, and so on. The objective is to identify as many diverse ways of handling difficulties as possible in a relatively short period. No interviewer should have the floor for more than a minute or two at any one time. The student playing the role of the client is given specific instructions about how to play the role. For example, sometimes he or she is asked to be shy; other times, demanding. The client should not overdo the role, however. He or she should respond naturally within the role assigned. Here are four sets of instructions for this "interview in rotation."

(a) The interviewer greets the client and says, "I am a paralegal." The client is confused about what a paralegal is. The interviewer explains. The client is insistent upon a comprehensive definition that he or she can understand.

(b) The client comes to the law office because he or she is being sued for negligent driving. The interviewer asks the client if he or she must wear eyeglasses to drive. The answer is *yes*. The interviewer then asks if he or she was wearing eyeglasses during the accident. The client is very reluctant to answer. (In fact, the client was not wearing glasses at the time.) The client does not appear to want to talk about this subject. The interviewer persists.

(c) The client is being sued by a local store for $750.00 in grocery bills. The client has a poor memory, and the interviewer must think of ways to help him or her remember. The client wants to cooperate but is having trouble remembering.

(d) The client wants to sue an auto mechanic. The client gives many opinions, conclusions, and judgments (such as "The mechanic is a crook," "I was their best customer," or "The work done was awful"). The interviewer is having difficulty encouraging the client to state the facts (observed data) underlying the opinions. The client insists on stating conclusions.

After each exercise, the class should discuss principles, guidelines, and techniques of interviewing.

CLASS EXERCISE 8.D

Below are two additional role-playing exercises to be conducted in class.

(a) The instructor asks the class if anyone was involved, in any way, in a recent automobile accident. If someone says *yes,* this student is asked if he or she would be willing to be interviewed by another class member whose job is to obtain as complete a picture as possible of what happened. At the outset, the interviewer knows nothing other than that some kind of an automobile accident occurred. The interviewee can make up any sensitive facts if he or she wishes to keep some of the actual events confidential.

(b) The instructor asks the class if anyone has recently had trouble with any government agency (like the post office or sanitation department). If someone says *yes,* this student is asked if he or she would be willing to be interviewed by another class member whose job is to obtain as complete a picture as possible of what happened. The interviewer at the outset knows nothing other than the fact that the person being interviewed has had some difficulty with a government agency. The interviewee can make up any sensitive facts if he or she wishes to keep some of the actual events confidential.

CLASS EXERCISE 8.E

When an office represents a debtor, one of the paralegal's major responsibilities may be to interview the client in order to write a comprehensive report on the client's assets and liabilities. Assume that your supervising attorney has instructed you to conduct a comprehensive interview of the client in order to write such a report. Assets are everything the client *owns* or has an interest in. Liabilities are everything *owed;* they are debts. These are the only definitions you need; you do not need any technical knowledge of law to conduct this interview. All you need is common sense in the formulation of questions.

Your instructor will role-play the client in front of the room. It will be a collective interview. Everyone will ask questions. Take detailed notes on the questions asked by every student (not just your own) and the answers provided in response. You will have to write your individual report based on your own notes.

Raise your hand to be recognized. Be sure to ask follow-up questions when needed for factual clarity and comprehensiveness. You can repeat the questions of other students if you think you might elicit a more detailed response. Any question is fair game as long as it is directly or indirectly calculated to uncover assets or liabilities. There may be information the client does not have at this time, such as bank account numbers. Help the client determine how such information can be obtained later. In your notes, state that you asked for information that the client did not have and state what the client said he or she would do to obtain the information. To achieve comprehensiveness, you must obtain factual detail. This means that you go after names, addresses, phone numbers, dates, relevant surrounding circumstances, verification data, etc. In short, we want fact particularization (FP). (See also Exhibit 8.11.)

The heading of your report will be as follows:

Office Memorandum

To: [name of your instructor]
From: [your name]
Date: [date you prepared the report]
RE: Comprehensive Interview of_____
Case File Number: _____

(Make up the case file number.) The first paragraph of your report should state what your supervisor has asked you to do in the report. Simply state what the assignment is. Organization of the data from your notes is up to you. Use whatever format you think will most clearly communicate what you learned from the client in the interview.

Chapter Summary

Projecting competence and professionalism is an essential ingredient in performing any task on behalf of a client. The fee agreement or engagement letter establishes the scope of the attorney-client relationship. If the office decides not to represent the prospective client, it should send him or her a letter of nonengagement.

Interviewing is structured conversation for the purpose of obtaining information. In a law office, legal interviewing is designed to obtain facts that are relevant to the identification and eventual resolution of a legal problem. These facts are often reported in a document called an intake memo. Six major guides exist to the kinds of questions that should be asked during a legal interview. The most important is the instructions of the supervisor on the goals of the interview. Other guides include checklists for certain kinds of interviews, legal analysis to help you focus on relevance, fact particularization as a device to achieve comprehensiveness, and, finally, common sense and flexibility to help you remain alert and responsive as the interview unfolds.

Determining what the client wants often takes probing and presentation of options. Otherwise, the office might fail to identify client objectives. Most of us are not fully aware of how our prejudices affect our performance. Detecting interviewer bias may not be easy; it is sometimes difficult to distance our personal feelings from the client's objectives.

The supervising attorney helps set the tone for an effective interview by introducing the client to the paralegal and explaining the latter's role. The professional interviewer strives to uncover facts that make the case of each client unique. There are many ways to prepare for an interview such as scheduling the interview at a convenient time, reading everything in the file, having supplies available, and preparing initial questions. The seating arrangement should facilitate communication. The walls, desk, and overall appearance of the office should project a professional image. Go out to greet the client when he or she arrives at the reception desk.

Always be appreciative of what the client does. Some small talk at the beginning of the interview can help decrease client tension. Avoid making any promises of what the office can accomplish. Express empathy without being condescending or losing objectivity. Find out if there are any immediate concerns on the client's mind. Avoid legal jargon unless the client needs to know about it and clear explanations are given. Briefly restate the purpose of the interview for the client. Let the client know why you are taking notes. Listen for clues to other problems the office should know about.

The following are the major kinds of questions an interviewer can ask (some of which overlap): open-ended, overview, closed-ended, chronological, leading, corroborative, combination, and wrap-up. One of the most important ways of building a relationship with the client is through attentive listening techniques such as maintaining eye contact and repeating back what the client has told you. Ask questions that will ferret out whatever observed data helped lead to the inferences drawn by the client so that facts and opinions can be clearly identified and differentiated. Factual comprehensiveness is achieved through fact particularization, corroborative questions, probing, etc. The interviewer must be alert to potential ethical problems such as breaching confidentiality and giving legal advice.

At the conclusion of the interview, ask the client to read and sign needed forms, find out if the client has any concerns not addressed during the interview, tell the client what next steps are planned, and make sure the client knows how to reach you. As soon as possible, make a note to the file that you conducted the interview. Begin writing the report or intake memo soon after the interview, making note of any personality characteristics relevant to working with the client that you observed. To improve your interviewing technique, read literature and attend CLE seminars on interviewing, seek the critique of others, try to observe others interview, etc.

Special sensitivity is needed when working with potentially difficult clients such as those who claim to know all the law, who are angry, who are demanding, or who lie. Every effort should be made to work with such clients while maintaining professionalism, but ultimately the office may have to decide whether continued representation is feasible or ethically appropriate.

Key Terms

retainer
engagement letter
deep pocket
statute of limitations
letter of nonengagement
declination
interviewee
intake memo
Re
ground
legal analysis

relevant
fact particularization
analogy
bias
objectivity
hypothetical
breach of contract
contingency case
jargon
open-ended question
overview question

closed-ended question
chronological question
timeline
leading question
corroborative question
combination question
multiple-choice question
add-on question
wrap-up question
attentive listening
inference

Review Questions

1. What can paralegals do to help combat the negative perception of attorneys in the minds of many in the public?
2. What are some of the reasons this negative perception exists?
3. Define *retainer*.
4. Why might an attorney decide not to take a case?
5. What is a deep pocket?
6. What is the function of a letter of nonengagement?
7. What are the three kinds of legal interviews?
8. What roles can paralegals have in client interviewing?
9. What is an intake memo? Name its five parts.
10. In what six ways can a paralegal achieve focus in the formulation of questions in an interview?
11. State five reasons why interviews can be ineffective.
12. In interviewing, what is the role of (1) legal analysis, and (2) fact particularization (FP)?
13. What kinds of questions allow you to particularize a fact?
14. Why do some clients have difficulty stating what they want?
15. How can bias interfere with effective interviewing?
16. What steps are needed to prepare for an interview?
17. Distinguish between a professional and a bureaucratic perspective or attitude.
18. How can the seating arrangement in a law office affect communication in an interview?
19. List techniques and guidelines for beginning an interview.
20. What could a paralegal tell a client that might result in a breach-of-contract suit against the law office?
21. How does a paralegal maintain professional objectivity without being insensitive to a client's emotional story?
22. How should legal jargon be handled during the interview?
23. What role is played by the following kinds of questions: (1) open-ended, (2) overview, (3) closed-ended, (4) leading, (5) chronological, (6) corroborative, (7) multiple-choice combination, (8) add-on combination, and (9) wrap-up?
24. How does a paralegal engage in attentive listening?
25. List techniques and guidelines for achieving factual comprehensiveness during an interview.
26. Distinguish between observed data and inferences.
27. What are some of the major ethical problems that can arise during an interview? How can they be avoided?
28. List techniques and guidelines for ending an interview.
29. List techniques and guidelines for improving your legal interviewing skills.
30. Identify different kinds of difficult clients. List techniques and guidelines for dealing with them.

Helpful Web Sites: More about Interviewing

Interviewing: Selected Articles
- www.rongolini.com/Interviewing.html

Basics of Legal Interviewing
- courses.washington.edu/civpro03/resources/interviewing.doc

Attentive Listening
- www.chass.ncsu.edu/ccstm/scmh/morelisten.html
- www.businesslistening.com/listening_skills-3.php
- www.everyonenegotiates.com/negotiation/attentivelisteningskillspt1.htm

Public Perceptions of Attorneys
- www.abanet.org/litigation/lawyers/publicperceptions.pdf
- en.wikipedia.org/wiki/Attorneys (click "media images")

International Listening Association
- www.listen.org

Google Searches (run the following searches for more sites)
- fee agreements attorney
- lawyer bashing
- intake memo
- "legal interviewing"
- interviewing clients
- attentive listening
- "kinds of questions"
- "difficult clients"

Endnotes

1. *Americans Find Lawyers Necessary, but Overpaid and Dishonest* (2002) (writ.lp.findlaw.com/dorf/20020417.html) (www.montanabar.org/montanalawyer/junejuly2002/columbiastudy.html).
2. Brent Roper, *Practical Law Office Management* 121 (1995).
3. Jeremy Fogel, *"Justice Denied" Is a National Problem*, San Jose Mercury-News, February 12, 2006, at 3P.
4. David Vandagriff, *Take My Breath Away*, 80 American Bar Association Journal 95 (May 1994).
5. Shari Caudron, *Crisis of Conscience*, 12 Legal Assistant Today 73, 75 (September/October 1994).
6. Denise Clemens, *Client Interviewing*, 11 California Paralegal Magazine 12, 13 (October/December 1991).

7. William P. Statsky & Philip C. Lang, *The Legal Paraprofessional as Advocate and Assistant: Roles, Training Concepts, and Materials* (Center on Social Welfare Policy & Law, 1971).

8. See also White, *Agricultural Suggestions for a Law Office Building*, 2 Practical Lawyer 66 (No. 8, 1956).

9. H. Freeman & H. Weihofen, *Clinical Law Training, Interviewing and Counseling* 13 (1972).

10. Jim Calloway, *The Initial Client Interview*, Oklahoma Bar Association (www.okbar.org/members/map/articles/interview.htm).

11. Kenney F. Hegland, *Introduction to the Study and Practice of Law*, 161 (4th ed. 2003).

12. Claire Summerhill, *Imagine This*, Legal Assistant Today 78 (July/August 2004).

13. *The Initial Interview*, 12 Family Advocate 6 (Winter 1990).

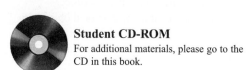

Student CD-ROM
For additional materials, please go to the CD in this book.

Online Companion™
For additional resources, please go to http://www.paralegal.delmar.cengage.com

Investigation in a Law Office

CHAPTER OUTLINE

[SECTION A]

INTRODUCTION

For relatively large and important cases, law offices often hire private investigators or investigators with a specialty. Examples of specialty areas include **forensic** accounting (involving tasks such as examining corporate records for evidence of fraud or embezzlement) and data forensics (involving the collection and analysis of information on computers, cell phones, PDAs, and other electronic devices). In practices such as criminal law, insurance law, or mass torts, the office may have its own investigators on staff. In the vast majority of cases, however, investigative work is performed by attorneys and paralegals as part of their regular duties. Lana Clark, a litigation paralegal, says, "Many of us have been approached by our attorneys at the last minute to interview a witness and 'Find out what he knows.'"[1]

There are many different kinds of investigation assignments that a paralegal might be given. Here are some examples:

- Contact all witnesses to an accident and obtain a witness statement from each;
- Verify information given by a witness;

forensic 1. Pertaining to the use of scientific techniques to discover and examine evidence. 2. Belonging to or suitable in courts of law. 3. Concerning argumentation. 4. Forensics: ballistics or firearms evidence.

- Go to the scene of an accident and photograph the area;
- Order aerial photographs;
- Determine the registered agent of a company for service of process;
- Find out if a company is publicly traded or privately held;
- Obtain the names of the board of directors and shareholders of a company;
- Find out if a national corporation headquartered in another state has any assets in your state;
- Obtain a "D&B" on a prospective client (D&B is the abbreviation for Dun & Bradstreet, a company that provides financial information on businesses; www.dnb.com);
- Help conduct **due diligence** on a company, including the fair market value of its assets, its income and profit history, and its actual and potential exposure to liability from customers, competitors, or staff;
- Determine whether any judgments have been filed against a potential client;
- Find out if there is any pending litigation against a particular individual or company;
- Determine whether someone has a criminal record;
- Locate an expert witness;
- Research the background of an opposing witness;
- Find an automobile engine of the same make and year as one destroyed in a collision that a client had with the defendant;
- Trace the ownership and repair history of a motor vehicle through its VIN number.

In the movie *Erin Brockovich*, based on a true story, Julia Roberts won an Academy Award for her role as a nonattorney employee who was given a major investigation assignment in the law office where she worked. She investigated the link between a highly toxic antirust chemical agent (chromium-6) used by a major public utility and the life-threatening diseases suffered by residents in the area where the utility had dumped the agent. Their water supply had become contaminated. Brockovich's work led to a $333 million dollar settlement for the victims and, eventually, to a $1 million dollar bonus for herself from her grateful supervising attorney. Of course, most paralegal investigation assignments will not be this dramatic. Yet the movie certainly highlighted the importance of investigation and the critical role that nonattorneys can have in this arena of fact gathering.

Many paralegals look forward to their investigation assignments, particularly in an era when so much can be accomplished on the Internet. "One of the things I enjoy most in the profession is the investigative part of cases. I take it as a personal challenge to see how much I can find out about a person [the other side] inadvertently or deliberately left out of their answers to discovery. It becomes an even bigger challenge when that person is out of state."[2] Whether you are "diving deep for information on a multinational corporation" or "just checking the background of a witness," good investigative skills can be a major asset in a paralegal's professional development.[3]

[**S E C T I O N B**]

THE NATURE AND CONTEXT OF LEGAL INVESTIGATION

Legal investigation is the process of gathering additional facts and verifying presently known facts in order to advise a client on how to avoid or solve a legal problem. A **fact** is an actual event or occurrence or one that someone alleges to be actual. It can be an incident or a state of mind such as an intention or emotion. Our study of investigation will focus on three main topics:

- The nature of investigation
- The techniques of investigation
- Evidence law and investigation

In chapter 8, on legal interviewing, we examined six major guides to fact gathering:

- Instructions of the supervisor
- Checklists
- Legal analysis
- Fact particularization (FP)
- Common sense
- Flexibility

You should review these guides now because they are equally applicable to investigation. Fact particularization (FP) is especially important.

due diligence Reasonable efforts to find and verify factual information needed to carry out an obligation, to avoid harming someone, or to make an important decision, e.g., to determine the true market value of a potential investment.

legal investigation The process of gathering additional facts and verifying presently known facts in order to advise a client on how to solve or avoid a legal problem.

fact 1. An actual event; a real occurrence. Anything that is alleged to exist or that can be shown to exist, e.g., an incident, a relationship, an intention, an opinion, or an emotion. 2. An event or state of mind that can lead to (but that is separate from) its legal consequences.

We begin our study of legal investigation with some general observations about its nature and context:

1. *Investigative techniques are very individualistic.* Styles, mannerisms, and approaches to investigation are highly personal. Through a sometimes arduous process of trial and error, the investigator develops effective techniques. Some of these techniques come from the suggestions of fellow investigators. Most, however, are acquired from on-the-job experience.

2. *It is impossible to overemphasize the importance of hustle, imagination, and flexibility.* If there is one characteristic that singles out the effective investigator, it is a willingness to dig. Many investigation assignments are relatively straightforward. For example:

   ■ Check court records to find out if a particular doctor has any other malpractice cases pending against him or her
   ■ Find out if someone has filed a workers' compensation claim
   ■ Obtain a copy of an ambulance report
   ■ Photograph the ceiling of a bathroom that a tenant claims is falling down

   Other assignments are potentially more involved because they are open-ended (e.g., find out what property or other assets of the defendant may be available to pay a judgment). An extensive range of options and conclusions is possible in such assignments. The answer is not always there for the asking. For such assignments, investigators must be prepared to identify and pursue leads, be unorthodox, and let their feelings, hunches, and intuition lead where they will. In short, the formal principles of investigation must give way to hustle, imagination, and flexibility.

   A good example is the case recently worked on by Edna Wallace, an Indianapolis paralegal. She needed to find out the name of the bank of a company that was avoiding payment of a judgment that her firm had obtained against it. Her strategy was to have dinner at one of the company's restaurants and to pay by check. Once it was cashed and returned to her, she was able to determine where the company banked and what its account number was. Her firm immediately put a freeze on the company's bank account.[4]

   Good investigators are always in pursuit. They are on the offensive and do not wait for the facts to come to them. They know that legwork is required. They know that 50 percent of their leads will turn out to be dead ends. They are not frightened by roadblocks and therefore do not freeze at the first hurdle. They know that there are no perfect ways of obtaining information. They know that they must take a stab at possibilities and that it takes persistent thinking and imagination to come up with leads. At the same time, good investigators are not fools. They do not pursue blind alleys. After being on the job for a while, they have developed "a feel" for whether a possibility or lead is reasonable. They have been able to develop this feel because, when they first started investigating, they had open minds and were not afraid to try things out.

3. *Investigators may not know what they are looking for until they find it.* Investigation, like interviewing and legal research, sometimes takes on a life of its own, particularly in open-ended assignments where you may be walking into the unknown. You may not know what you are looking for until you find it. Suppose, for example, that the law firm has a client who is charging his employer with racial discrimination. In the process of working on the case, the investigator discovers that this employee had a managerial job at the company and that several of the workers under him have complained that *he* practiced racial discrimination against them. The investigator had no idea that she would uncover this until it was uncovered. In short, an open mind is key when undertaking an assignment.

4. *Investigation and interviewing are closely related.* The interviewer conducting the initial client interview has two responsibilities: to help identify legal problems and to obtain from the client as many relevant facts on those problems as possible. The starting point for the investigator is the report or intake memo (see Exhibit 8.3) prepared by the interviewer on what the client said. The investigation needs may be clear from this report, or they may become clear only after the investigator and his or her supervisor have defined them more precisely.

   The investigator should approach the interview report with a healthy skepticism. Thus far, all the office may know is what the client has said. The perspective of the office is therefore narrow. Without necessarily distrusting the client's word, the investigator's job is to verify the facts given during the interview and to determine whether new facts exist that were unknown or improperly identified during the interview. The interview report should not be taken at face value. New facts may be revealed or old facts may for the first time be seen in a context that gives them an unexpected meaning. The investigator must approach a case almost as if the office knows nothing about it or as if what the office knows is invalid. By adopting this attitude, the investigator will be able to give the case an entirely different direction when the product of the investigation warrants it.

5. *The investigator must be guided by goals and priorities.* The starting point in an investigation assignment is a set of instructions from the supervisor. These instructions determine the investigator's goals and priorities. Unfortunately, supervisors are not always clear on what these goals and priorities are. For example:

- Supervisors may have a very definite idea of what they want.
- Supervisors may think they know what they want but are not sure.
- Whatever conception supervisors have about what they want, they are not effective in explaining it to the investigator.
- Supervisors have no idea what they want other than a desire to obtain as many facts about the case as possible.

The first responsibility of the investigator is to establish communication with the supervisor. With as much clarity as possible, determine what the supervisor wants to accomplish through the investigation.

6. *Investigation, negotiation, and trial are closely related.* There are two ultimate questions that should guide the investigator's inquiry into every fact being investigated:

- How will this fact assist or hurt the office in attempting to settle or negotiate the case without a trial?
- How will this fact assist or hurt the office in presenting the client's case at trial?

A large percentage of legal claims never go to full trial. Opposing counsel hold a number of bargaining sessions in which they attempt to hammer out a **settlement** acceptable to their clients. Very often they discuss the law that they think will be applicable if the case goes to trial. Even more often they present each other with the facts that they think they will be able to establish at trial. Here, the investigator's report becomes invaluable. As a result of this report, the attorney should be able to suggest a wide range of facts that could be used at trial ("we have reason to believe . . ." or "we are now pursuing leads that would tend to establish that . . ." etc.). The attorney's bargaining leverage is immeasurably increased by a thorough investigation report.

If negotiations do not produce a settlement, the investigator's report can help the attorney:

- Determine whether to go to trial
- Decide what witnesses to call
- Choose questions to ask of witnesses
- Decide how to **impeach** (i.e., contradict or attack the credibility of) opposing witnesses
- Anticipate how the other side might try to impeach your client and witnesses
- Determine what tangible or physical evidence to introduce
- Decide how to attack the tangible or physical evidence the other side will introduce

The investigator should be familiar with the standard, pretrial **discovery** devices: depositions, interrogatories, requests for admissions, medical examination reports, etc. A **deposition** is a pretrial question-and-answer session conducted outside court, usually in the office of one of the attorneys. The attorney asks questions of the other party (or of a witness of the other party) in order to obtain facts that will assist in preparing for trial. Depositions are often **transcribed** so that typed copies of the session are available. **Interrogatories** are used for the same purpose, but differ in that the questions and answers are usually provided in writing rather than in person. An interrogatory is simply a question submitted by one party to another. A **request for admission** is a request by one party that another party admit the substance of a statement (usually a statement of fact). Those that are admitted do not have to be proven at trial. A request for a medical examination will be granted by the judge when the examination will help resolve a medical issue in the trial, such as the extent of the plaintiff's alleged injuries.

Investigators can be of assistance during this discovery stage by helping the attorney decide what questions to ask in a deposition or in an interrogatory, what admissions to request, whether to ask for a medical examination, etc.

After the discovery devices have been used, the investigator should carefully study all the facts these devices disclose in order to:

- Cross-check or verify these facts, and
- Look for new leads (names, addresses, incidents) that could be the subject of future investigation.

settlement An agreement resolving a dispute without full litigation. (See glossary for other meanings of *settlement*.)

impeach To challenge; to attack the credibility of.

discovery Compulsory pretrial disclosure of information related to litigation by one party to another party. Discovery can also be used in post-judgment enforcement proceedings.

deposition A method of discovery by which parties and their prospective witnesses are questioned before trial. A pretrial question-and-answer session to help parties prepare for trial.

transcribed Taken down in a word-for-word account. The account is called a *transcript*.

interrogatories A method of discovery consisting of written questions sent by one party to another to assist the sender to prepare for trial.

request for admission A method of discovery in which one party asks another to admit or deny the substance of a statement, e.g., a statement of fact or of the application of law to fact.

7. *It is important to distinguish between proof of a fact and evidence of a fact.* **Evidence** is anything that could be offered to prove or disprove an alleged fact. **Proof** is enough evidence to establish the truth or falsity of a fact. Investigators are looking for evidence. They should not stop looking simply because they have not found proof. It is the role of the judge and jury to determine truth and falsity. The function of investigators is to identify reasonable options or fact possibilities. To be sure, they can speculate on whether a judge or jury would ever believe an alleged fact to be true. But the presence or absence of proof is not the test that should guide them in their investigations. The tests that an investigator should apply in determining whether to investigate a fact possibility are:

- Am I reasonable in assuming that a particular fact will help establish the case of the client? Am I reasonable in assuming that the specific evidence of that fact I am investigating might be accepted as true by a judge or jury?
- Am I reasonable in assuming that a particular fact will help to challenge or discredit the case of the opposing party? Am I reasonable in assuming that the specific evidence of that fact I am investigating might be accepted as true by a judge or jury?

It is important to be able to approach the case from the perspective of the opponent, even to the point of assuming that you work for the other side! What facts will the opponent go after to establish its case? What is the likelihood that such facts will be accepted?

8. *The investigator must know some law.* Investigators do not have to be experts in every area of the law or in any particular area of the law in order to perform their job. For their fieldwork to have a focus, however, they must have at least a general understanding of evidence, civil procedure, and the **substantive law** governing the facts of the client's case. They must know, for example, what *hearsay* and *relevance* mean. They must understand basic procedural steps in litigation in order to see how facts can be used in different ways at different steps in the litigation process. Some substantive law is also needed. In a negligence case, for example, the investigator should know the basic elements of a negligence cause of action in the state. The same kind of basic information is needed for every area of the law involved or potentially involved in the client's case. Such knowledge can be obtained:

- In paralegal courses or seminars
- Through brief explanations from the supervisor
- By talking to experienced attorneys and paralegals whenever they have time to give you an overview of the relevant law
- By reading a chapter in a legal treatise or a section in a legal encyclopedia that provides an overview of the relevant law. For a checklist of techniques for finding summary overviews of any legal topic, see Exhibit 11.18 in chapter 11.

9. *The investigator must know the territory.* When you are on the job as an investigator, it is important to begin acquiring a detailed knowledge of the makeup of the city, town, or state where you will be working. Such knowledge should include:

- The political structure of the area: Who is in power? Who is the opposition?
- The social and cultural structure of the area: Are there racial problems? Are there ethnic groupings that are diffused or unified? Are there different value systems at play?
- The contacts that are productive: If you want something done at city hall, whom do you see? Which court clerk is most helpful? Does the director of a particular agency have control over the staff? What agencies have "real services" available?

It is usually very difficult for the investigator to acquire this knowledge in any way other than going out into the field and obtaining it through experience. Others can provide guidance, and often will. In the final analysis, however, you will probably discover that what others say is biased or incomplete. You must establish your own network of contacts and sources of information. First and foremost, you must establish your credibility in the community. People must get to know and trust you. Simply announcing yourself as an investigator (or presenting a printed card indicating title and affiliation) will not be enough to win instant cooperation from the community. You must *earn* this cooperation. If you gain a reputation as arrogant, dishonest, opportunistic, or insensitive, you will quickly find that few people want to deal with you. An investigator could be in no worse predicament.

Often the best way to learn about an area and begin establishing contacts is by being casual and unassuming. Have you ever noticed that insurance agents often spend time talking about the weather, sports, politics, the high cost of housing, etc., *before* coming to their sales pitch? Their intent is to relax you, to find out what interests you, to show you that they

---

evidence Anything that could be offered to prove or disprove an alleged fact. Examples include testimony, documents, and fingerprints. (A separate determination must be made on whether a particular item of evidence is relevant or irrelevant, and admissible or inadmissible.)

proof Enough evidence to establish the truth or falsity of a fact.

substantive law Nonprocedural laws that define or govern rights and duties.

are human. Then they hit you with the benefits of buying their insurance. The investigator can use this approach not only in establishing contacts at agencies and in the community generally, but also in dealing with prospective witnesses on specific cases.

[SECTION C]

FACT ANALYSIS: ORGANIZING THE OPTIONS

One of the hallmarks of a good investigator, and indeed of all paralegals, is the ability to organize facts, or more accurately, to organize *versions* of facts. Carolyn Saenz, a veteran Ohio paralegal, says, "I've become quite good at reading body language and listening to people. It's amazing how many different versions of one story can be told."[5]

A number of fundamental characteristics of facts should be kept in mind:

- Events take place.
- Events mean different things to different people.
- Different people, therefore, can have different versions of events.
- Inconsistent versions of the same event do not necessarily indicate fraud or lying.
- Although someone's version may claim to be the total picture, it probably will contain only a piece of the picture.
- In giving a version of an event, people usually mix statements of *why* the event occurred with statements of *what* occurred. Or worse, they may tailor their description of what happened to fit the version that they *wish* occurred.
- Whenever it is claimed that an event occurred in a certain way, one can logically expect that certain signs, indications, or traces (evidence) of the event can be found.

Given these truisms, you should plan an investigation along the lines indicated in Exhibit 9.1. It is possible for a single client's case to have numerous individual facts that are in dispute. Furthermore, facts can change, or people's versions of facts can change in the middle of a case. Each new or modified fact requires the same comprehensive process of fact analysis outlined in Exhibit 9.1.

EXHIBIT 9.1	Planning an Investigation: Fact Versions

Starting Point

All the facts you currently have on the case:
- Arrange the facts chronologically.
- Place a number before each fact that may have to be established in a legal proceeding.

State the Following Versions of Each Fact

Version I: The client's
Version II: The opponent's (as revealed to you or as assumed)
Version III: A witness's
Version IV: Another witness's
Version V: Any other reasonable version (e.g., from your own deductions)

As to Each Version

- State precisely (using quotes if available) what the version is.
- State the evidence or indications that tend to support the version according to persons presenting the version.
- State the evidence or indications that tend to contradict this version.
- Determine how you will verify or corroborate the evidence or indications.

Of course, every fact will not necessarily have multiple versions. It is recommended, however, that you assume there will be more than one version until you have demonstrated otherwise to yourself. Obtaining different versions of a fact is sometimes difficult because the differences may not be clear on the surface. Undoubtedly, you will have to do some probing to uncover the versions that exist. Better to do so now than to be confronted with a surprise at trial or at an agency hearing.

People will not always be willing to share their accounts or versions of facts with you. If you are not successful in convincing them to tell their story, you may have to make assumptions of what their story is *likely* to be and then check out these assumptions.

[SECTION D]

DISTORTIONS IN INVESTIGATION

Investigators are not mere newspaper reporters or photographers who simply report what they see, hear, or otherwise experience. You have a much more dynamic role. In a very significant sense, you sometimes have the power to influence what someone else says about the facts. This can have both positive and negative consequences.

Be alert to the danger of asking questions in such a manner that you are putting words into someone's mouth. The primary technique that can bring about this result is the **leading question**. A leading question is one that suggests an answer in the statement of the question. For example, "You were in Baltimore at the time, isn't that correct?" "You earn over $200 a week?" "Would it be fair to say that when you drove up to the curb, you didn't see the light?" (For more on the different kinds of questions that can be asked, see Exhibit 8.9 in chapter 8.)

Questions can intentionally or unintentionally manipulate someone's answer by including a premise that has yet to be established. It sometimes takes an alert person to say to such questions, "I can't answer your question (or it is invalid) because it assumes another fact that I haven't agreed to." In the following examples of questions and answers, the person responding to the question refuses to be trapped by the form of the question:

Q: How much did it cost you to have your car repaired after the accident?
A: It's not my car and it wasn't an accident; your client deliberately ran into the car that I borrowed.

Q: Have you stopped beating your wife?
A: I never beat my wife!

Q: Can you tell me what you saw?
A: I didn't see anything; my brother was there and he told me what happened.

The last leading question containing the unestablished premise can be highly detrimental. Suppose the question and answer went as follows:

Q: Can you tell me what you saw?
A: The car was going about 70 mph

In fact, the person answering the question did not see this himself; his brother told him that a car was traveling at this speed. This person may have failed to tell the investigator that he did not see anything first-hand for a number of reasons:

- Perhaps he did not hear the word "saw" in the investigator's question.
- He may have wanted the investigator to think that he saw something himself; he may want to feel important by conveying the impression that he is special because he has special information.
- He may have felt that correcting the investigator's false assumption was not important; he may have thought that the investigator was more interested in *what* happened than in *who* saw what happened.

Whatever the reason, the investigator has carelessly put himself or herself in the position of missing a potentially critical fact, namely, that the person is talking from second-hand knowledge. Before asking what the person "saw," the investigator should ask, "Were you there?" and if so, "Did you see anything?"

Also, be careful about the way you phrase a question. "Research indicates the wording of questions to witnesses significantly affects their recall. For example, more uncertain or 'don't know' responses are given if a witness is asked about an indefinite item (e.g., 'Did you see *a* knife?') than occurs when the question contains a definite article ('Did you see *the* knife?')."[6]

Communication is often blurred when the questioner concentrates on some themes to the exclusion of others. If you do not ask questions about certain matters, intentionally or otherwise, you are likely to end up with a distorted picture of a person's version of the facts. For example, assume that Smith and Jones have an automobile collision. The investigator, working for the attorney who represents Jones, finds a witness who says that she saw the accident. The investigator asks her to describe what she saw, but fails, however, to ask her where she was at the time she saw the collision. In fact, she was sitting in a park more than two blocks away and could see the collision only through some shrubbery. The investigator did not ask questions to uncover this information; it was not volunteered. The investigator, therefore, walks away with a potentially distorted idea of

leading question A question that suggests an answer in the question.

how much light this individual can shed on what took place. This is similar to the distortion that can result from the use of questions that contain an unestablished premise.

Yet, in some instances, these techniques may have beneficial results. For example, a leading question can sometimes help jar someone's memory, making the person better able to recall the facts. If, however, this person constantly needs leading questions in order to remember, you have strong reason to suspect that, rather than being merely shy, inarticulate, or in need of a push now and then, the person knows little or nothing.

Suppose that the witness being questioned is uncooperative or has a version of the facts that is damaging to the client of the investigator's office. It may be that the techniques described in this section as normally improper can be used to challenge a version of the facts. A leading question with an unestablished premise, for example, may catch an individual off guard and give the investigator reasonable cause to believe that the person is not telling the truth.

If you have reason to doubt someone's willingness to tell you what he or she knows, a leading statement or question might be helpful in prompting communication:

> A technique I've found very successful is to ask a question I feel will evoke a factual answer. For example, I would ask Mr. John Doe, "Mr. Doe, you claim that you are a witness to the accident when, in fact, I understand you were not in a position to see everything that happened." Often, the person will respond with a defensive answer similar to, "I was in a position to see everything," and then continue to tell me their location and what they saw.[7]

[SECTION E]

SOURCES OF EVIDENCE/SOURCES OF LEADS

As we have seen, evidence is anything offered to prove or disprove an alleged fact. Two major categories of evidence are **parol evidence** (oral) and **tangible evidence** (physical). Exhibit 9.2 presents a partial checklist of some of the standard sources of parol and tangible evidence—or

parol evidence Evidence of an oral statement.

tangible evidence Evidence that can be seen or touched; evidence that has a physical form. *Intangible evidence* is evidence without physical form such as a right that a person has. Such rights, however, are usually embodied or evidenced by something physical, e.g., a written contract.

EXHIBIT 9.2	**Checklist of the Standard Sources of Evidence and Leads**

(Some of the records in this list are online. For Web addresses, see "Helpful Web Sites" at the end of the chapter.)

- Statements of the client
- Documents the client brings or can obtain
- Information from the attorneys involved with the case in the past
- Accounts of eyewitnesses
- Hearsay accounts
- Interrogatories, depositions, other discovery devices; letters requesting information
- Pleadings (such as complaints) filed thus far in the case
- Newspaper accounts (check online and public libraries)
- Notices in the media requesting information
- General records of municipal, state, and federal administrative agencies
- Business records (such as canceled receipts)
- Employment records, including job applications
- Photographs
- Hospital records
- Informers or the "town gossip"
- Surveillance of the scene
- Reports from the police and other law enforcement agencies (See Exhibit 9.3.)
- Fingerprints
- School records
- Military records
- Information that may be voluntarily or involuntarily provided by the attorney for the other side

- Use of alias
- Bureau of vital statistics and missing persons
- Court records
- Workers' compensation records
- Office of politicians
- Records of Better Business Bureaus and consumer groups
- Telephone book
- *Polk Directory*
- Reverse phone directory
- Boat registry
- Automobile registry (DMV)
- County assessor (for real property)
- Tax assessor's office
- County election records
- Post Office (record of forwarding addresses)
- Object to be traced (such as an auto)
- Credit bureaus
- Reports of investigative agencies
- Associations (trade, professional, etc.)
- *Who's Who* directories
- Insurance Company Clearing House
- Standard and Poor's *Register of Directors and Executives*
- Telling your problem to a more experienced investigator and asking for other leads
- Shots in the dark

leads to such evidence. Of course, once evidence is identified, it often becomes its own lead to further evidence.

[SECTION F]

GAINING ACCESS TO RECORDS

Often the simplest way to obtain a record or other information is to ask for it. Gaining access to some records, however, can sometimes be difficult. There are four categories of records you may need to examine on behalf of a client:

1. Those already in the possession of a client or an individual willing to turn them over to you on request
2. Those in the possession of a governmental agency (see Exhibits 9.3 and 9.4) or of a private organization and available to anyone in the public
3. Those in the possession of a governmental agency or of a private organization and available only to the client or to the individual who is the subject of the records

---

EXHIBIT 9.3	Request for Copy of Peace Officer's Accident Report

(On the value of this report in the investigation of an accident, see the beginning of the article on *Auto Accident Analysis* later in the chapter.)

REQUEST FOR COPY OF PEACE OFFICER'S ACCIDENT REPORT
(PLEASE SUBMIT IN DUPLICATE)

Statistical Services   Date of Request _____
Texas Department of Public Safety
P.O. Box 15999   Claim or Policy No. _____
Austin, Texas 78761–5999

Enclosed is a (check)(money order) payable to the Texas Department of Public Safety in the amount of $ _____ for (check service desired):

☐ Copy of Peace Officer's Accident Report – $4.00 each

☐ Certified Copy of Peace Officer's Accident Report – $8.00 each

for the accident listed below:

Please provide as accurate and complete information as possible.

ACCIDENT DATE _____
          MONTH   DAY   YEAR

ACCIDENT LOCATION _____ _____ _____
          COUNTY   CITY   STREET OR HIGHWAY

WAS ANYONE
KILLED IN THE ACCIDENT? _____ If So, Name of Deceased _____

INVESTIGATING AGENCY AND/OR OFFICER'S NAME (IF KNOWN)

| | DRIVER INFORMATION (If Available) | | |
DRIVER'S FULL NAME	DATE OF BIRTH	TEXAS DRIVER LICENSE NO.	ADDRESS
1. _____			
2. _____			
3. _____			

Texas Statutes allow the investigating officer 10 days in which to submit his report. **Requests should not be submitted until at least 10 days after the accident date to allow time for receipt of the report.**

The Law also provides that if an officer's report is not on file when a request for a copy of such report is received, a certification to that effect will be provided in lieu of the copy and the fee shall be retained for the certification.

Mail To _____

Mail Address _____

City _____ State _____ Zip _____

Requested by _____ Phone # _____

EXHIBIT 9.4	Guidelines for Gaining Access to Records

1. Write, phone, or visit the organization and ask for the record.

2. Have the client write, phone, or visit and ask for it.

3. Draft a letter for the client to sign that asks for it.

4. Have the client sign a form stating that he or she gives you authority to see any records that pertain to him or her and that he or she specifically waives any right to confidentiality with respect to such records.
   (For special rules and forms pertaining to the privacy of medical records, see *www.hhs.gov/ocr/hipaa*.)

5. Find out if one of the opposing parties has the record, and if so, ask his or her attorney to send you a copy.

6. Find out if others have it (such as a relative of the client or a co-defendant in this or a prior court case) and ask them if they will provide you with a copy.

7. For records available generally to the public, find out where these records are and go use them. For government records, check the Internet site of the government agency that has the records. Find out if they are available online at this site.

8. If you meet resistance, make a basic fairness pitch to the organization as to why you need the records.

9. Find out (by legal research) if there are any statutes, administrative regulations, or cases that arguably provide the client with the right of access to records kept by government agencies—for example, through the Freedom of Information Act (FOIA) of Congress covering federal agencies. (See Exhibit 9.5.) Many states have their own FOIA for state agencies. Before making a FOIA request, go to the Internet site of the federal or state agency that has the records you need. Find out if the site gives you any specific instructions on filing a FOIA request at that agency. See the Freedom of Information sites in "Helpful Web Sites" at the end of the chapter.

10. If the person who initially turns down the request for access is a line officer, appeal the decision formally or informally to his or her supervisor, and up the chain of command to the person with final authority.

11. Solicit the intervention of a politician or some other respectable and independent person in trying to gain access.

12. Let the organization know that your office is considering (or is preparing) a suit to establish a right to the record (when this is so). Once a lawsuit has begun, it is often possible to obtain copies of records through discovery devices such as a *request for production* (see chapter 10).

EXHIBIT 9.5	Sample FOIA Letter

Agency Head or FOIA Officer
Title
Name of Government Agency
Address of Agency
City, State, Zip

                                        Re: Freedom of Information Act (FOIA) Request.

Dear FOIA Officer:

Please send me copies of [describe the documents or information you seek in as much detail as possible. Include any file names or file numbers, if applicable.]

I agree to pay all necessary costs associated with this request.

[or]

I agree to pay all necessary costs up to the amount of $xx.00. Please contact me if you expect that the costs will exceed that amount.

If you deny all or any part of this request, please cite each specific exemption you think justifies your refusal to release the information and notify me of appeal procedures available under the law.

Sincerely,

Your name, address, and phone

Adapted from foi.missouri.edu/foialett.html; www.fas.usda.gov/info/FOIA/sample.html; www.foia.cia.gov/sample_request_letter.asp

4. Those in the possession of a governmental agency or of a private organization and claimed to be confidential except for in-house staff

Obviously, there should be no difficulty in gaining access to the first category of records unless they have been misplaced or lost, in which event the person who once had possession would ask the source of the records to provide another copy. As to records in the latter three categories, the checklist in Exhibit 9.4 should provide some guidelines on gaining access, including use of the **Freedom of Information Act** (FOIA) for government records.

> **Freedom of Information Act**
> A statute that gives citizens access to certain information in the possession of the government.

[SECTION G]
EVALUATING EVIDENCE

At all times, you must make value judgments on the usefulness of the evidence that you come across. A number of specific criteria can be used to assist you in assessing the worth of what you have. The checklists in Exhibits 9.6 and 9.7 may be helpful in determining this worth.

EXHIBIT 9.6	Checklist on Assessing the Validity of Parol (Oral) Evidence

CHECKLIST IF THE WITNESS IS SPEAKING FROM FIRST-HAND (EYEWITNESS) INFORMATION

- How long ago did it happen?
- How good is the memory of this witness?
- How far from the event was the witness at the time?
- How good is the sight of the witness?
- What time of day was it and would this affect vision?
- What was the weather at the time and would this affect vision?
- Was there a lot of commotion at the time and would this affect vision or ability to remember?
- What was the witness doing immediately before the incident?
- How old is the witness?
- What was the last grade of school he or she completed?
- What is the witness's employment background?
- What is the reputation of the witness in the community for truthfulness?
- Was the witness ever convicted of a crime? Are any criminal charges now pending against him or her?
- Does the witness have technical expertise or other qualifications relevant to what he or she is saying?
- Is the witness related to, an employee of, or friendly with either side in the litigation? Would it be to this person's benefit, in any way, to see either side win?
- Does any direct evidence exist to corroborate (confirm) what this witness is saying?
- Does any hearsay evidence exist to corroborate it?
- Is the witness willing to sign a statement covering what he or she tells the investigator? Is he or she willing to say it in court?
- Is the witness defensive when asked about what he or she knows?
- Are there any inconsistencies in what the witness is saying?
- How does the witness react when confronted with the inconsistencies? Defensively?
- Are there any gaps in what the witness is saying?
- Does the witness appear to exaggerate?
- Does the witness appear to be hiding or holding anything back?

CHECKLIST IF WITNESS IS RELAYING WHAT SOMEONE ELSE (THE DECLARANT) SAID (HEARSAY)

- How well does the witness remember what was told to him or her by the other person (the declarant) or what the witness heard him or her say to someone else?
- How is the witness sure that it is exact?
- Is the declarant now available to confirm or deny this hearsay account of the witness? If not, why not?
- Under what conditions did the declarant allegedly make the statement (for example, was declarant ill)?
- Is there other hearsay testimony that will help corroborate (confirm) this hearsay?
- Does any direct evidence exist to corroborate this hearsay?
- How old is the witness? How old is the declarant?
- What are the educational and employment backgrounds of both?
- What is their reputation in the community for truthfulness?
- Was either ever convicted of a crime? Are any criminal charges pending against either?
- Does the witness or the declarant have technical expertise or other qualifications relevant to what was said?
- Is the witness or the declarant related to, an employee of, or friendly with either side in the litigation? Would it be to the benefit of the witness or the declarant to see either side win?
- Is the witness willing to sign a statement covering what he or she tells the investigator concerning the declarant? Is the witness willing to say it in court?
- Is the witness defensive when asked about what he or she was told by the declarant or what he or she heard the declarant say to someone else?
- Are there any inconsistencies in what the witness is saying?
- How does the witness react when confronted with the inconsistencies? Defensively?
- Are there any gaps in what the witness is saying?
- Does the witness appear to exaggerate?
- Does the witness appear to be hiding or holding anything back?

EXHIBIT 9.7	Checklist on Assessing the Validity of Physical (Tangible) Evidence

CHECKLIST FOR WRITTEN MATERIAL

- Who wrote it?
- Under what circumstances was it written?
- Is the original available? If not, why not?
- Is a copy available?
- Who is available to testify that the copy is in fact an accurate copy of the original?
- Is the author of the written material available to testify on what he or she wrote? If not, why not?
- Is there any hearsay testimony available to corroborate (confirm) the authenticity of the writing?
- Is there any other physical evidence available to corroborate the authenticity of the writing?
- What hearsay or direct evidence is available to corroborate or contradict what is said in the writing?
- Can you obtain sample handwriting specimens of the alleged author?
- Who found it and under what circumstances?

CHECKLIST FOR NONWRITTEN MATERIAL

- Where was it found?
- Why would it be where it was found? Was it unusual to find it there?
- Who is available to identify it?
- What identifying characteristics does it have?
- Who owns it? Who used it?
- Who owned it in the past? Who used it in the past? Who has had possession?
- Who made it?
- What is its purpose?
- Does it require laboratory analysis?
- Can you take it with you?
- Can you photograph it?
- Is it stolen?
- Is there any public record available to trace its history?
- What facts does it tend to establish?
- Was it planted where it was found as a decoy?

[SECTION H]
INTERVIEWING WITNESSES

Francis Ritter, a seasoned investigator, tells us that there are six parts to every conversation: three for the speaker and three for the listener. For the *speaker:*

- What the speaker wants to say,
- What the speaker actually says, and
- What the speaker thinks he or she said.

For the *listener:*

- What the listener wants to hear,
- What the listener actually heard, and
- What the listener thinks he or she heard.[8]

The following guidelines apply to all witness interviews:

1. *Whenever possible, interview a witness with no other potential witnesses present.* If other people are in the room when you interview a witness, they are likely to be influenced by what the witness says. If two people have different versions of an event, you are often more likely to find this out if you talk to each one separately than if they are together. Of course, this may not always be possible. A witness may be uncomfortable talking with you alone and, indeed, you may feel safer if others are present. Do the best you can under such circumstances. Later you may be able to telephone them individually to ask that they clarify something they said earlier. This might increase the chance you will obtain an account that is uninfluenced by what others have said.

2. *Know what image you are projecting of yourself.* In the minds of some people, an investigator is often involved in serious and dangerous undertakings. How would you react if a stranger introduced himself or herself to you as an investigator? This might cause many people to be guarded and suspicious, so you may not want to call yourself an investigator. You may want to say, "My name is _____, I work for (name of law office) and we are trying to get information on _____."

   Can you think of different people who would respond more readily to certain images of investigators? The following is a partial list of some of the images that an investigator could be projecting by dress, mannerisms, approach, and language:

   - A professional
   - Someone who is just doing a job
   - Someone who is emotionally involved in what he or she is doing

- A neutral bystander
- A friend
- A manipulator or opportunist
- A salesperson
- A wise person
- An innocent and shy person

You must be aware of (a) your own need to project yourself in a certain way, (b) the way in which you think you are projecting yourself, (c) the way in which the person to whom you are talking perceives you, and (d) the effect that all this is having on what you are trying to accomplish.

Here is how one paralegal, Janet Jackson, describes her approach:

[The] basic techniques are to approach the person as a friend, make him or her feel comfortable talking, and gain his or her trust. One simple way of doing this is using the principle that people respond to their names. I address the contact by name several times throughout the interview. I also use a friendly, soft, nonthreatening, inquisitive tone of voice. The first few moments . . . are always the most difficult and the most important. Usually in these few moments the contact makes the decision whether to talk. So, a strong opening is needed. I plan, write out, and practice my opening so I can deliver it smoothly and quickly in a friendly, confident voice. . . . I say, "Hello, Mr. Jones, my name is Janet Jackson and I work for the law firm of X, Y & Z. We have been retained by the T. Company to represent them in a lawsuit brought against them by Mr. John Smith. I would like to ask you a few questions about the lawsuit. . . ." I then identify myself as a legal assistant and explain that I am collecting information. Often I have found that saying that I am a legal assistant, not an attorney, causes people to relax and let down their guard.[9]

3. *There are five kinds of witnesses: hostile, skeptical, friendly, disinterested or neutral, and a combination of the above.* Hostile witnesses want your client to lose; they may try to set up roadblocks in your way. Skeptical witnesses are not sure who you are or what you want in spite of your explanation of your role. They are guarded and unsure whether they want to become involved. Friendly witnesses want your client to win and will cooperate fully. **Disinterested** or neutral witnesses do not care who wins. They have information that they are usually willing to tell anyone who asks. Hostile and friendly witnesses have probably prejudged the case. They may be incapable of examining all the facts dispassionately; they are already inclined to think or act in a certain way. They have a **bias**.

If the hostile witness is the opposing party who has retained counsel, it is unethical for the investigator to talk directly with this person without going through his or her attorney (see chapter 5). If the opposing party is not represented by an attorney, check with your supervisor on how, if at all, to approach this party. Never do anything to give an unrepresented party the impression that you are disinterested.

To complicate matters, it must be acknowledged that witnesses are seldom totally hostile, skeptical, friendly, or neutral. At different times during the investigation interview, and at different times throughout the various stages of the case, they may shift from one attitude to another. Although it may be helpful to determine the general category witnesses fit into, it would be more realistic to view any witness as an individual in a state of flux in terms of what he or she is capable of saying and what he or she wants to say. In view of this reality, it is usually recommended that a witness statement be taken soon after the incident in question whenever possible. (Witness statements are discussed later in the chapter.) This helps offset the danger of a witness changing his or her story at a later date.

4. *The investigator must have the trust of the witness.* You have the sometimes difficult threshold problem of sizing up the witness from whom you are trying to obtain information. Here are some of the states of mind that witnesses could have:

- They want to feel important.
- They want to be "congratulated" for knowing anything, however insignificant, about the case.
- They want absolute assurance from you that they will not get into trouble by talking to you. They shy away from talk of courts, lawyers, and law.
- They are willing to talk only after you have given full assurance that you will not reveal the source of the information they give you.

disinterested Not working for one side or the other in a controversy; not deriving benefit if one side of a dispute wins or loses; objective.

bias Prejudice for or against something or someone. An inclination or tendency to think and to act in a certain way. A danger of prejudgment.

- They are willing to talk to you only in the presence of their friends.
- If they know your client, they want to be told that you are trying to keep the client out of trouble.
- They want the chance to meet you first and then have you go away so they can decide whether they want to talk to you again.
- They are not willing to talk to you until you fulfill some of their needs—for example, listen to their troubles or act in a fatherly or motherly manner.

In short, the investigator must gain the trust of individuals by assessing their needs and by knowing when they are ready to tell you what they know. To establish communication, sensitivity to such undercurrents is often required. The most effective approach may not be to take out your notebook immediately upon introducing yourself. What is often needed is persistence, the right tone, and the right language. This is amply demonstrated by Minnesota paralegal Deborah Rohan, who describes how she handles someone who is initially reluctant to talk with her: "I tell him I'm not going to try to sway him to either side of the issues. I say . . . I just want to get the facts. If that doesn't work, I say 'Okay, I won't formally interview you, but could I ask you a few questions?' Often the person will consent to that."[10] Similarly, D. Andrews, a New Jersey paralegal, says she obtains better results when she avoids using the word *witness*. "Do not ask if the person was a witness—simply ask what they know of the incident."[11]

5. *The investigator must assess how well the witness would do under direct examination and cross-examination.* As witnesses talk, ask yourself a number of questions:

- Would they be effective on the witness stand if they agreed to testify or if they were **subpoenaed**?
- Do they know what they are talking about?
- Do they have a reputation for integrity and truthfulness in the community?
- Are they defensive?
- Would they know how to say "I'm not sure" or "I don't understand the question," as opposed to giving an answer for the sake of giving an answer or to avoid being embarrassed?
- When they talk, are they internally consistent?
- Do they know how to listen as well as talk?
- Do they understand the distinction between right and wrong, truth and lying?

subpoenaed 1. Commanded to appear in a court, agency, or other tribunal. 2. Ordered to turn over or produce something.

[SECTION I]

SPECIAL INVESTIGATIVE PROBLEMS: SOME STARTING POINTS

JUDGMENT COLLECTION

The person who wins a money judgment in court is called the **judgment creditor**. Unfortunately, collecting that judgment can be a difficult undertaking. An investigator may be asked to assist the law firm in ascertaining the financial assets of a particular individual or corporation against whom the judgment was obtained, called the **judgment debtor**.

One of the best starting points for such an investigation is government records. The following is a partial list of records available from the county clerk or court office:

judgment creditor The person to whom a court-awarded money judgment (damages) is owed.

judgment debtor The person ordered by a court to pay a money judgment (damages).

- Real property records (check grantee and grantor indexes)
- Real and personal property tax assessments
- Filings made under the Uniform Commercial Code (UCC)
- Federal tax liens
- Court dockets—to determine whether the judgment debtor has been a plaintiff or defendant in prior litigation (check the abstract-of-judgment index)
- Inheritance records—to determine whether the judgment debtor has inherited money or other property (determined by checking records of the surrogate's court or probate court, which handles inheritance and trust cases)

Such records could reveal a good deal of information on the financial status of the party under investigation. You might find out whether he or she owns or has an interest in valuable personal or business property. Even though tax records often undervalue the property being taxed, they are some indication of a person's wealth. Another indication is the existence of past suits against the party.

If a party has been sued in the past, someone made a determination that he or she probably had a **deep pocket** at that time, meaning sufficient assets to satisfy a judgment.

For corporations that are judgment debtors, check the records of state and federal government agencies (such as the state Secretary of State and the federal Securities and Exchange Commission) with whom the corporation must file periodic reports or disclosures on its activities and finances. You should also check with people who have done business with the corporation (customers or other creditors) as well as with its competitors in the field. These records and contacts could provide leads.

A great deal of this information is now online so that it can be searched through computers. For resources available on the World Wide Web (paid and free), see "Helpful Web Sites" at the end of the chapter. Here are some of the major databases and libraries available on Westlaw and LexisNexis, the two largest fee-based online commercial research services. Even if you do not have access to these services (they are very expensive to use), reading the following overview will give you a good idea of the kinds of data that law firms try to obtain.

deep pocket An individual, business, or other organization with resources to pay a potential judgment. (2) Sufficient assets for this purpose. The opposite of *shallow pocket*.

Westlaw

Examples of databases that can be searched on Westlaw:

Asset Locator (ASSET). Identifies major property holdings of a person or business including real estate, stocks, aircraft, watercraft, business equipment, and inventory.

Executive Affiliation Records (EA–ALL). Provides name, title, business address, and phone number of millions of executives nationwide.

Combined Uniform Commercial Code (UCC), Liens/Civil Judgment Filings (ULJ–ALL). Provides information on UCC filings, liens, and civil judgments relating to businesses and individuals.

Dun & Bradstreet Business Records Plus (DUNBR). Provides information on a company's history, operations, and financial performance as well as intracompany relationships for 20 million companies worldwide.

Combined Corporate & Limited Partnership Records (CORP–ALL). Provides abstracts of corporate, limited partnership, and limited liability company filing information.

Combined Bankruptcy Records (BKR–ALL). Provides abstracts of filings in U.S. bankruptcy courts. Includes business filings in all 50 states and personal filings in selected states.

Lawsuits (LS). Provides abstracts of civil lawsuits filed in selected state and local courts.

Dow Jones–All Plus Wires (ALLNEWS–PLUS). Provides documents from all wires, newspapers, magazines, journals, newsletters, and transcripts as provided by Dow Jones & Company, Inc.

LexisNexis

Examples of databases (called *files*) that can be searched on LexisNexis:

ASSETS (ALLTOWN). Provides data that will allow you to discover the location and assessed value of corporate and individual real estate, locate hidden assets, find elusive parties and witnesses, determine current tax mailing addresses for service of process, assess the collectibility of judgments, and locate property for judgment lien attachment.

Bankruptcy (INSOLV) (ALLBKT). Provides access to current business and consumer bankruptcy petitions, dismissal, and discharge data under chapters 7, 11, 12, and 13 from most districts of the U.S. bankruptcy court in all 50 states.

Business Filings (INCORP). Provides access to state and local business filings, including corporate registrations, limited partnership registrations, limited liability company registrations, county d/b/a (doing business as) filings, and professional licenses.

Business Reports (BUSRPT) (D&BRPT). Provides business reports from Dun & Bradstreet and Experian that will help establish company existence, identify expert witnesses, assess financial performance, ascertain client solvency, and confirm company ownership for potential conflicts of interest.

Courts (DOCKET). Provides information from civil and criminal court indices and dockets from various local and federal jurisdictions, judgments and liens, bankruptcy petitions, EPA (Environmental Protection Agency) Civil Docket, and OSHA inspection reports.

Liens (ALLUCC) (ALLIEN). Provides information on Uniform Commercial Code (UCC) liens, state and federal tax liens, and judgments from state courts. The data contain debtor names, addresses, secured parties, assignees, and types of collateral pledged.

License (LICNSE). Provides information on professional licenses, liquor licenses, driver licenses, pilots, and tax practitioners.

This information allows you to locate self-employed individuals, verify their license status, locate business assets, and conduct due diligence research.

Personal Property (P–PROP). Provides information on personal property from boat, motor vehicle, and aircraft registrations.

Verdicts and Settlements (ALLVER). Provides information on recent civil verdicts and settlements from the databases of the Association of Trial Lawyers of America (ATLA); National Jury Verdict Review & Analysis (NTLREV); Verdicts, Settlement & Tactics (VERST); National Law Review Annual Review (NLJVR); and Medical Litigation Alert (MDALRT).

> **due diligence** Reasonable efforts to find and verify factual information needed to carry out an obligation, to avoid harming someone, or to make an important decision, e.g., to determine the true market value of a potential investment.

This kind of data is valuable when conducting **due diligence** investigations, such as when you need to verify the information given by a prospective business associate.

MISSING PERSONS

An investigator may be asked to locate a missing heir, a relative of a client, a person who must be served with process in connection with current litigation, etc. A missing person is generally not difficult to locate—unless this person does not want to be found.

John Lehe, a legal investigator, suggests that you begin with the easily available resources: telephone books, directory assistance operators, and cross-reference directories. "In contacting directory assistance operators, ask for telephone numbers for anyone with the same last name on the street of the last-known address. It is possible for relatives to live on the same street and they may be able to provide the [missing person's] current address or place of employment."[12] Local neighborhood libraries often have a telephone reference section that should be checked. Find out if they have any old telephone directories available.

Your local library may have a cross-reference directory (sometimes called a reverse or criss-cross directory). If all you have is the address of a person, you may be able to use this resource to find out who lives at that address, plus his or her surrounding neighbors.

Try sending a registered letter to the person's last-known address, "return receipt requested," which asks the post office to send you back a notice with the signature of the person who signed to receive the letter.

> **skiptracing** Efforts to locate persons (e.g., debtors) or assets.

A number of effective locator or **skiptracing** services are available online. For Internet resources, see the section on "Finding People or Businesses" in "Helpful Web Sites" at the end of the chapter. The commercial databases also have powerful finding tools:

Westlaw: People Finder (PEOPLE-FIND)
LexisNexis: FINDER (EZFIND, P-TRAK, P-FIND, B-FIND, P-SEEK)

The Social Security Administration will not give you personal information on recipients. Knowing the person's number, however, might provide a clue. The first three digits of a social security number indicate the state in which the card was issued. For example:

545–573 California	010–034 Massachusetts	540–544 Oregon
602–626 California	362–386 Michigan	159–211 Pennsylvania
261–267 Florida	468–477 Minnesota	449–467 Texas
589–595 Florida	135–158 New Jersey	627–645 Texas
318–361 Illinois	050–134 New York	387–399 Wisconsin
212–220 Maryland	268–302 Ohio	

People who "disappear" sometimes return to the state where they grew up—often the state where they obtained their social security card.

Other possible sources of information:

- Relatives and friends
- Former landlord, neighbors, mail carrier, and local merchants in the area of the last-known address
- Professional associations such as unions and other job-related groups (people often retain membership in local chapters as they move around the country)
- Local credit bureau
- Police department, hospitals
- References listed on employment applications
- Naturalization certificate, marriage record, driver's license, car registration
- Newspaper indexes (central and university libraries often keep such indexes; check obituary columns, local interest stories, etc.)

BACKGROUND INVESTIGATIONS

Exhibit 9.8 presents a form used by a large investigative firm for its general background investigations on individuals. The first part of the form seeks information regarding identification of the subject. The antecedent data cover prior history.

EXHIBIT 9.8	Background Investigations

Identification of Subject

1. Complete Name _____ Age _____ SS# _____ Marital Status _____
   Spouse's Name; Pertinent Info _____

   Children's Names and Ages _____

2. Current Residence Address and Type of Neighborhood _____

   Prior Residence Info _____

3. Business Affiliation and Address, Position, Type of Bus. _____

Antecedent History

1. Place & Date of Birth _____
   Parents' Names & Occupations _____

   Where Did They Spend Their Youth? _____

2. Education—Where, Which Schools, Dates of Attendance _____

   Degree? What Kind? _____ Any Other Info Pertaining to Scholastic Achievement, Extracurric.
   Activities _____

3. First Employer, to Present—F/T or P/T, Position or Title, Job Description, Exact Dates of Employment, Type of Company _____

(continues)

EXHIBIT 9.8	Background Investigations—*continued*

4. Relationship with Peers, Supervisors, Subordinates—Where Do Subj.'s Abilities Lie? Any Outside Activities? Reputation for Honesty, Trustworthiness, Integrity? Does Subj. Work Well under Pressure? Anything Derogatory? Reasons for Leaving? Would They Rehire? Salaries? Health? Reliability? Job Understanding? Willingness to Accept Responsibility?

_____

_____

_____

_____

_____

_____

_____

_____

If Self-Employed—What Was the Nature of the Business? With Whom Did Subj. Deal? Corp. Name?

_____

Date & Place of Incorporation _____

Who Were Partners, If Any? _____

What % of Stock Did Subj. Own? ____ Was Business Successful? _____ What Happened to it? _____

If Sold, to Whom? _____

Any Subsid. or Affiliates? _____

_____

5. What is Subj.'s Character or Personality Like? Did Informer Know Subj. Personally?

_____

Hobbies? _____

Family Life? _____

Even-Tempered? _____ Loner or Joiner? _____

Introverted, Extroverted? _____ Written or Oral Abilities? _____

Does Informer Know Anyone Else Who Knows Subj.? _____

_____

6. Credit Information _____

_____

_____

7. Subj.'s Involvement in Litigation _____ Civil _____ Criminal _____ Bankruptcy _____

State _____ Federal _____ Local _____

_____

_____

8. Banking—Financial: Bank _____

Types of Accounts—Average Bal. _____

How Long Did Subj. Have Accounts? _____ Any Company Accounts? _____

Is Subj. Personally Known to Officers of the Bank? _____ Any Borrowing? _____

Secured or Unsecured? _____ If Secured, by What? _____

Do They Have Financial Statement on the Subj.? _____

What Is Net Worth of Subj.? _____ Other Assets? Real Estate _____

Stocks _____

Equity in Subj.'s Co., etc. _____

AUTOMOBILE ACCIDENTS

Auto Accident Analysis

by Dale W. Felton, 27 Trial Magazine 60 (February 1991)[13]

Accidents don't just happen. Except in instances of mechanical failure or acts of God, vehicle collisions occur because of driver negligence. If a collision is properly investigated and analyzed, who was at fault can usually be determined. If the analysis reveals the defendant was negligent, demonstrative evidence can be used to show jurors how the defendant's negligence caused the collision.

Every law office handling vehicle-accident cases would benefit from learning effective methods of investigation and accident analysis. Many of these cases could be settled if insurance adjusters were shown definitive or scientific facts demonstrating that fault lies with the [defendant] insured and not with the plaintiff. Insurance adjusters—like jurors—are receptive to scientific analysis of liability. . . .

An analysis of negligence should not be attempted without first conducting a thorough investigation. It is important to investigate as quickly as possible. Accident scenes change and witnesses move. Of course, you often do not get a case until months after the accident occurred. Even then, the investigation should be started immediately. Bits of evidence and many helpful facts may still be available.

Reports

Begin the investigation by getting a complete statement of facts from the client. Then, get a police report of the collision. [See Exhibit 9.3.] This report will include the officer's estimate of the damage to each vehicle as well as the location of the damage. Often the report will list names, addresses, and telephone numbers of the witnesses and usually the statements that each party gave to the officer at the scene. The report will also show who was ticketed and why. Reports often include a sketch of the accident scene as well as the officer's analysis of the factors contributing to the collision.

Sometimes, however, these drawings may be inaccurate. The officer's analysis of contributing factors may not make sense. In fact, in most instances where an insurance company denies liability, it is because an investigating officer indicated that the plaintiff was in some way at fault. Here the law office must prove that the police officer's analysis was not correct.

In serious collisions, investigating police officers will often keep notes, take photographs, and make a scale drawing of the scene. You can obtain these by subpoena.

After obtaining a police report, take witness statements, being careful that each statement includes all facts the witness knows. [See Exhibit 9.10.] The vehicles involved and the accident scene should be photographed as soon as possible because vehicles may be repaired quickly and accident scenes may change due to construction, resurfacing, installation of traffic control devices, etc. A full investigation also includes taking appropriate measurements and determining the point of impact from physical evidence at the scene, the police report, and the witness statements.

Photographs

Law offices should own and know how to use a [good quality] camera, even if they employ full-time investigators or photographers. Many times, if you wait for someone else to take a photograph, the accident scene will have changed.

Know what photographs you need and make sure that the proper ones are taken. The only way to be sure to get the *right* photograph is to ensure that plenty are taken. The late Axel Hanson, one of the greatest investigators who ever lived, once said that he took 211 photographs of a vehicle involved in a fatality, and *one* proved to be the key to liability.

Photographers should move around the vehicle in a circle, taking photographs "every five minutes on the hands of a clock." Photographers should also take close-ups of damaged areas and use a flash to ensure that shadows do not obscure these areas.

Photographers should take shots from beneath the damaged part of the vehicle, an area that will often reveal the severity of the impact. Photographs taken while focusing straight down on the damaged area are needed because they will reveal the angle of impact. Photographers should carry ladders or, if they are allowed to, stand on the vehicle itself to get these shots. Downward shots of the vehicle involved in a collision can be matched to illustrate the angle at which the vehicles collided.

The photographer should also take pictures of any internal damage to the vehicle, including the speedometer and seats. In a rear-end collision the seats will often be bent backward or broken off at the frames. Jurors can readily understand that an impact strong enough to break seats would be severe enough to injure a human being.

A 50 mm lens best approximates the view as seen by the human eye. To illustrate what each driver saw, photographers should work from as far back as 1,000 feet from the point of collision. (If drivers did not travel 1,000 feet on the road in question before impact, photos should be taken starting from the point where each driver entered the roadway.) Photographs should be taken every 100 feet until 300 feet from the collision site; then every 50 feet until 100 feet from the point of impact; then every 25 feet to the point of impact. Only in this way can photographs show what the driver of each vehicle could see when approaching the collision site.

In photographing a crash scene, the photographer should obtain the same types of vehicles that were in the actual accident from a used-car lot or car dealership. Measurements should be made to determine driver's-eye height. Photographers can set tripods at this height to take approach shots. If a bus or truck is involved, it will be necessary to measure driver's-eye height in the same type of vehicle. In these instances, photographers must use ladders to get eye-height shots of what the drivers could see as they approached the collision site. A foot or two can make a world of difference in what a driver can see. These photographs should show any obstructions to a driver's view.

Photographs should also be taken of all road signs, not only to show their wording but also to show their location. At the point of impact, photos should be taken of gouge marks, scrapes, and any other damage the vehicles caused to the road

(continues)

Auto Accident Analysis

by Dale W. Felton, 27 Trial Magazine 60 (February 1991)—*continued*

surface or surrounding area. Both distance and close-up shots should be taken to pinpoint the damage. For close-up shots, it is often advisable to include a ruler or a pencil in order to indicate the scale.

Light Bulbs

Examining the light bulbs near a vehicle's damaged area will reveal whether they were operating at the time of the crash. During a collision, a heated light filament will stretch or break, while an inoperative cool filament will not. A bulb with a stretched or broken filament can easily be compared with a new bulb to show whether the bulb in question was functioning at the time of the collision. This principle applies to taillights; brake lights; turn indicators (front, back, or side); and to headlights.

The person examining the vehicles should *always* consider whether lighting could have been a factor in the collision and, if so, examine the appropriate bulbs. For example, in all rear-end collisions at night, tail lights are a factor. Brake lights and turn signals may be factors day or night. If bulbs figured in the crash, they should be removed by an investigator and retained. It may be many months before the plaintiff's lawyer learns that the defendant is claiming that the plaintiff did not have the appropriate lights on or failed to give a turn signal.

Photographers should document the removal of bulbs, which should be placed in a padded, labeled box. It is important to indicate the vehicle they came from, their location on the vehicle, the person who removed them, and the date and time of removal. In *Golleher v. Herrera*, the court ruled that to introduce expert testimony concerning whether a vehicle's light bulb was functioning at the time of a collision, not only must the bulb be put into evidence but there must also be testimony that the bulb was the one that came from a particular location on one vehicle in the collision. 651 S.W. 2d 329, 333–34 (Tex. Ct. App. 1983).

Skid Marks

Careful measurements of all skid marks at the scene are essential.* Before measuring them, the investigator should ensure that the skid marks were laid down in the collision in question. To avoid measuring the wrong marks, it is best to have someone who can definitely identify the marks—the client, a witness, or an ambulance driver—at the scene for the investigation. Of course, this also applies for measuring gouges, scrapes, and other physical damage at the accident site. Formulas can be used to determine the minimum speed of the vehicle before the driver applied the brakes.

Straight-skid speed formula. Often a vehicle traveling at a high rate of speed leaves only a few feet of skid marks because the brakes were not applied until the instant before impact. In those instances, determining the speed from skid marks may not be possible. But where skid marks were laid down over a long distance, the straight-skid speed formula

may reveal that the colliding vehicle was traveling at excessive speed.

Yaw mark formula. A yaw mark is left on a road surface by the sideward motion of a tire when the driver turned the wheel sharply, usually to avoid a collision or to take a curve at excessive speed. A yaw mark will reveal the speed at the time the vehicle made the mark. A yaw mark should not be confused with a skid mark. It is a scuff mark made while the tire is rotating. It is easily identified by striations left on the roadway by the tire sidewall.

Flip-vault formula. If an object was thrown from either vehicle because of the impact, the investigator can calculate the minimum speed of the colliding vehicle if the exact point of impact of the vehicles and the exact point where the item first contacted the ground are known. The calculation is done using the flip-vault formula. Therefore, when examining the scene, the investigator should look for anything that may have been thrown from either vehicle.

For example, if a toolbox was thrown from the back of a truck and it can be determined exactly where it hit the ground, applying the flip-vault formula can determine the speed of the colliding vehicle at impact. In one case, a screwdriver with the driver's name taped to the handle was thrown from the colliding vehicle, and the screwdriver stuck blade-first into the ground many feet away from where the vehicles collided. The investigator applied the flip-vault formula to determine speed.

Fall formula. Investigators can use the fall formula to determine the speed of a vehicle that ran off an embankment. The investigator must measure the horizontal distance that the vehicle traveled before hitting the ground and then measure the vertical distance that the vehicle dropped. This formula can be helpful in proving whether a vehicle that went off an embankment was speeding.

Drag Factor

Investigators cannot determine speed from skid marks or yaw marks unless they know the drag factor of the roadway. The drag factor is the coefficient-of-friction, plus or minus grade. It is that percentage of the weight of an object that is required to push or pull it along a surface. The grade takes into account whether or not the object was going uphill or downhill.

To determine speed from skid marks, investigators must measure the drag factor accurately. Many books and other publications give drag-factor ranges for dry concrete, wet concrete, dry asphalt, wet asphalt, gravel and ice.‡ These ranges are best used only to get a general idea of what might be expected for each surface. The drag factor can vary greatly, even on the same roadway. Speed from skid marks or a yaw mark can only be determined by conducting a drag-factor test at the specific point where the marks were made. Just as important, the test must be conducted in the same direction that the vehicle was traveling to take into account the plus or minus grade.

---

*J. Baker, *Traffic Accident Investigation Manual* 216–27 (1975).

‡L. Fricke, *Traffic Accident Reconstruction* 62–14 (1990); "How to Use the Traffic Template and Calculator," Traffic Institute Northwestern University, at 19 (1984); R. Rivers, *Traffic Accident Investigators' Handbook* 157 (1980).

(continues)

Auto Accident Analysis

by Dale W. Felton, 27 Trial Magazine 60 (February 1991)—*continued*

Measurements and Scale Drawings

In examining a collision scene, the investigator should take all measurements relative to a fixed reference point located close to the point of impact like a telephone pole or a corner of a building. The best method is to use a north-south, east-west grid and locate each distance measured north, south, east, or west of the reference point. Using this method, investigators can make an infinite number of measurements and plot each point on a scale drawing of the scene. Triangulation could also be used in measuring a scene, but it requires many times the number of measurement and is much more time-consuming. However, where the roadway is curved, roadway edges are uneven, or an object some distance off the roadway must be pinpointed, triangulation is the only method that will work. The grid method is simplest for most situations.

Besides the obvious distances that must be measured—such as the width of each roadway and the location of all traffic signs—the exact locations of any buildings or obstructions to clear view between the vehicles should be precisely determined.

A 1:20 scale is one scale to use for drawings in almost all these cases. The drawing helps in performing a time and distance analysis, as well as in seeing the entire collision process on paper. Along with minimum speed calculations, a scale drawing of the accident scene can be persuasive when presented to an insurance adjuster. If the case does not settle, a scale drawing can be used to prove a plaintiff's case at trial.

Time and Distance Analysis

Once the investigation is complete and a scale drawing made, the collision can be analyzed.

Time and distance must be taken into account in every collision or vehicle-pedestrian accident. Every moving mass is traveling at a certain speed that converts to either miles per hour or feet per second. To determine the feet per second a vehicle was traveling, multiply miles per hour times 1.47. If you convert miles per hour to feet per second, you can work backward from the point of impact and place the vehicles at the various points on the scale drawing for each second or even one-tenth of a second before the collision occurred. With the scale drawing and the locations of each vehicle at different intervals before impact, you can see the view each driver had of the scene and of each other, determine to what extent speed of each driver was a factor, and determine what action or actions could have been taken by either driver to avoid a collision.

Of course, the miles-per-hour figure may come from the testimony of the driver. In many instances, a defendant driver will say in deposition that the vehicle was going at a slower rate of speed than it actually was. The statement may hurt the defense because at the lower speed the defendant would have had more time to see plaintiff's vehicle and come to a stop or turn in order to avoid a collision.

Time and distance can also be used to refute contributory negligence on the part of the plaintiff. For example where the defendant pulled out in front of the plaintiff or made a left turn into the plaintiff's path, time and distance calculations can be used to show that the legal speed at which the plaintiff was traveling did not allow stopping before colliding with the defendant. In many instances, taking into account the judicially accepted three-quarters-of-a-second reaction time will show that the plaintiff did not even have time to apply the brakes.

Example 1: Safe   Example 2: Too Fast   Example 3: Delayed Perception

(continues)

Auto Accident Analysis

by Dale W. Felton, 27 Trial Magazine 60 (February 1991)—*continued*

Example 4: Wrong Evasive Tactic   Example 5: Failure to Yield   Example 6: Combination of Mistakes

A time and distance analysis is especially helpful in pedestrian cases. Pedestrians have a normal walking speed of about three miles per hour. At this speed it takes several seconds to walk just a few steps. It can usually be shown that in those several seconds the driver had more than ample time to avoid striking the pedestrian.

The flip-vault formula can also be applied in pedestrian cases. If the point of impact and the point where a pedestrian hit the ground after impact are known, the speed of the striking vehicle can be determined. Often, doing a time and distance analysis and applying the flip-vault formula will clearly demonstrate a driver's fault.

Determining Negligence

In Example 1, the driver (S) was traveling at a speed (25 mph) that was safe for the circumstances (an uncontrolled intersection ahead with a view obstruction on the right). The driver looked to the right and as soon as an approaching vehicle (T) was observed, applied the brakes and yielded the right-of-way.

In Example 2, the driver (S) was traveling at a speed too great for existing conditions. At 35 miles per hour, even though the driver maintained a proper lookout and saw the approaching vehicle (T), he could not stop in time to avoid colliding with it.

In Example 3, the driver (S) was traveling at a safe speed (25 mph) but was not looking to see if a vehicle was approaching from the right. By the time she saw the approaching vehicle (T), it was too late. Failure to keep a proper lookout was the cause of the collision.

In Example 4, the driver (S) was traveling at a speed (25 mph) that was safe for conditions and kept a proper lookout. However, he chose the wrong evasive tactic. The driver tried to turn left in front of the approaching vehicle (T) rather than apply the brakes and yield the right-of-way to the vehicle.

In Example 5, the driver (S) was traveling at a safe speed (25 mph), kept a proper lookout, but did nothing to avoid the collision. She simply failed to apply the brakes.

Example 6 shows a combination of errors. The driver (S) was traveling at a greater speed (35 mph) than existing conditions permitted and failed to keep a proper lookout.

A similar analysis on your scale drawing will clearly illustrate to an insurance adjuster, a defense lawyer, and—if those two are hardheaded—a jury, precisely what the defendant did wrong. After seeing and understanding this type of accident analysis, jurors are less likely to fall for the defendant who testifies, "I don't know where he came from. He just came out of nowhere."

What about a rear-end collision? Where the rear-ended vehicle is stopped, the colliding driver may have been negligent in speed, lookout, or brakes application. But what about a rear-end collision that occurs as two cars are traveling down a roadway at about the same speed and the first car has to stop for some unexpected reason?

Alleging that speed caused the collision is faulty, because the first driver was traveling at the same rate of speed as the second. If the second driver testifies that the instant he saw the first driver's brake lights come on he slammed on his brakes, he is probably telling the truth. Usually this type of rear-end collision is not the result of negligent speed, lookout, or brakes application. It is the result of following too closely.

Analysis Works

Accident analysis really works, but it will not work unless law offices put their best efforts into it. If they ensure that a proper investigation is done and perform an accident analysis in each case, the results will be rewarding.

ASSIGNMENT 9.1

Which of the following statements do you agree or disagree with? Why? How would you modify the statements you disagree with to reflect your own view?

(a) There is a great difference between investigation conducted by the police and that conducted by a paralegal working for a law office.

(b) An investigator is an advocate.

(c) It is impossible for the investigator to keep from showing his or her own personal biases while in the field investigating.

(d) There is often a need for a separate investigation to verify the work of another investigation.

(e) A good investigator will probably be unable to describe why he or she is effective. There are too many intangibles involved.

(f) It is a good idea for an investigator to specialize in one area of the law, such as automobile negligence cases.

(g) If someone is willing to talk to and cooperate with an investigator, there is reason to suspect that this person has a bias.

ASSIGNMENT 9.2

If you were Tom in each of the following situations, what specific things would you do to deal with the situation?

(a) Sam owes Tom $50,000. When Tom asks for his money, Sam tells him that he is broke. Tom suspects differently.

(b) Tom's uncle once lived in Boston. After spending two years in the army, he started traveling across the country; he has not been heard from for five years. Tom wants to locate his uncle.

(c) A welfare department has told a client that it is going to terminate public assistance because the client's boyfriend is supporting her and her family. The client denies this. Tom is assigned to the case.

(d) A client has been to the office seeking help in obtaining custody of his children from their mother (to whom he is not married). He claims that she is not taking proper care of the children. Tom is assigned to the case.

ASSIGNMENT 9.3

Select any corporation that has its home office or headquarters in your state, has a Web address, has a large number of employees, and is publicly traded (i.e., has shareholders who are members of the general public). Answer the following questions about this company using the suggestions covered in the chapter thus far, as well as the Internet sources listed in "Helpful Web Sites" at the end of the chapter.

(a) What is the name of the company? What are its street and Internet addresses?

(b) What kind of corporation is it?

(c) What are the names of the five major officers of the corporation?

(d) Give a biographical summary of the president.

(e) What are the names of the members of the board of directors of the corporation?

(f) What is the earnings history of the corporation over the last five years?

(g) What major litigation has been brought by or against the corporation over the last ten years?

ASSIGNMENT 9.4

Using the suggestions covered in the chapter thus far, as well as the Internet resources listed in "Helpful Web Sites" at the end of the chapter, how would you find the following information?

(a) The average life span of a lobster.

(b) The maiden name of the wife of the first married governor of your state.

(c) The assessed property tax value of the tallest commercial building in your city in 1980.

(d) The weather in your state capital at noon on January 1 of last year.

(e) The number of vehicles using diesel fuel that drove in or through the state last month.

(f) At the largest airport in the state, the salary of the air traffic controller with the most seniority on duty on the day last year when the airport experienced the largest rainfall of the year.

Note on the Need for a License

In some states, investigators must be licensed. What about paralegals who are assigned investigation tasks by their supervising attorneys? A literal reading of the licensing statute might lead to the conclusion that such paralegals must be licensed along with traditional, self-employed private investigators. Often, however, the legislature will make an exception to the licensing requirement for employees of attorneys who engage in investigation under the attorney's supervision. Paralegal associations have been successful in seeking these exemptions for paralegals. The main opposition to such exemptions has come from organizations of private investigators, who allegedly seek to impose roadblocks to paralegal investigation in order to secure more business for themselves.

[SECTION J]

EVIDENCE LAW AND INVESTIGATION

INTRODUCTION

We turn now to a closer look at the relationship between investigation and the law of evidence. One of the goals of investigation is to uncover and verify facts that will be admissible in court. Admissibility is determined by the law of evidence.

During a trial, each party attempts to establish its version of the facts. There are four main ways that this can be done:

- Admission
- Judicial notice
- Presumption
- Evidence without aid of the above three

Admission

admission An assertion of the truth of a fact. (See the glossary for another meaning.)

Paula sues Dan for negligence following an automobile accident. Paula claims that Dan has prescription eyeglasses and that he was not wearing them at the time of the accident. Before the trial, Dan concedes that he has glasses but denies that he was not wearing them at the time of the accident. Dan's statement that he needs glasses is an **admission**—an assertion of the truth of a fact. Here Dan has acknowledged the truth of a fact that an opponent wants to prove. One of the ways in which such acknowledgments are made during discovery is through a *request for admission*. As we have seen, this is a discovery device that asks a party to affirm or deny the truth of a particular statement, usually one of fact. Those facts that are admitted as true do not have to be proven in the trial. A less formal way to accomplish the same result is by **stipulation**, which is simply an agreement between the parties about a particular matter. For example, the parties can stipulate that there were no passengers in Dan's car at the time of the accident. (We will return to the topic of admission later when we discuss admission by a party opponent as an exception to the hearsay rule.)

stipulation An agreement between opposing parties about a particular matter.

Judicial Notice

judicial notice A court's acceptance of a well-known fact without requiring proof of that fact.

Some facts are so well accepted that the court can acknowledge them—i.e., take **judicial notice** of them—without requiring either party to prove those facts. An example is that water freezes at 32 degrees Fahrenheit or that there are 31 days in July.

Presumption

presumption An assumption or inference that a certain fact is true once another fact is established.

A **presumption** is an assumption or inference that a certain fact is true once another fact is established. If a party proves that fact A exists, then fact B is established. For example, proof that a person has disappeared for seven years raises the presumption that he or she is dead. Also, proof that a letter was properly addressed and mailed raises the presumption that the addressee received it. Most presumptions are **rebuttable**, meaning that evidence to the contrary can be introduced. The presumption of death after a disappearance of seven years, for example, is rebuttable in most states. Therefore, evidence that the missing person may still be alive could be introduced. An example of such evidence might be that someone recently used the Social Security number of a person who has been missing for eight years. If the court will not consider evidence to the

rebuttable Not conclusive; evidence to the contrary is admissible.

contrary, the presumption is **irrebuttable**. An example of an irrebuttable presumption is that a child under seven years of age is presumed incapable of forming the intent necessary to commit a crime. This is a conclusive presumption. Evidence that a six-year-old child has the intelligence of a teenager, therefore, would not be admitted.

irrebuttable Conclusive; evidence to the contrary is inadmissible. Nonrebuttable.

Evidence

Most facts are established by the introduction of evidence without the aid of admissions, judicial notice, or presumptions.

EVIDENCE IN GENERAL

Evidence is anything that could be offered to prove or disprove an alleged fact. **Admissible** evidence is evidence that the judge will permit the jury to consider. Admissible evidence does not mean that the evidence is true. It simply means that there are no valid objections to keep the evidence out. The jury is free to conclude that it does not believe the evidence that the judge ruled admissible. Two important categories of evidence can be admissible:

admissible Allowed into court to determine its truth or believability.

Direct evidence is evidence (based on personal observation or knowledge) that tends to establish a fact (or to disprove a fact) without the need for an inference.

Circumstantial evidence is evidence of one fact from which another fact (not personally observed or known) can be inferred.

direct evidence Evidence (based on personal knowledge or observation) that tends to establish a fact (or to disprove a fact) without the need for an inference. Also called *positive evidence*.

circumstantial evidence Evidence of one fact from which another fact (not personally observed or known) can be inferred. Also called *indirect evidence*.

Example: The police officer says, "I saw skid marks at the scene of the accident." This statement is:

Direct evidence	▪ that the police officer spoke these words.
	▪ that skid marks were at the scene of the accident.
Circumstantial evidence	▪ that the driver of the car was speeding (this is the inference that can be drawn from the officer's statement).

Examples of *direct* evidence that someone was speeding would be an admission by the driver that he or she was speeding and testimony of people who saw the car being driven.

Investigation Guideline:

Direct evidence is preferred over circumstantial, although both kinds of evidence may be admissible. Identify the inference in the circumstantial evidence. Then try to find direct evidence of whatever was inferred.

RELEVANCE

Relevant evidence is evidence that logically tends to establish or disprove a fact. Phrased another way, evidence is relevant when it reasonably tends to make the existence of a fact more probable or less probable than it would be without that evidence. Relevancy is a very broad concept. It simply means that the evidence *may* be helpful in determining the truth or falsity of a fact involved in a legal dispute. The test of relevancy is common sense and logic. If, for example, you want to know whether a walkway is dangerous, it is relevant that people have slipped on this walkway in the immediate past. Prior accidents under the same conditions make it more reasonable for someone to conclude that the workway is dangerous.

relevant Logically tending to establish or disprove a fact. Pertinent. (See the glossary for an additional definition.)

All relevant evidence, however, is not necessarily admissible evidence. Some highly relevant evidence is considered so potentially inflammatory or prejudicial that a judge will rule it to be inadmissible. An example might be evidence of a defendant's prior convictions for the same kind of crime for which the defendant is currently being tried. Similarly, it would be very relevant to know that the defendant told his attorney he was driving 80 mph at the time of the accident, yet the attorney-client privilege would make such a statement inadmissible. Also, relevant evidence is not necessarily conclusive evidence even if it is admissible. The jury will usually be free to reject relevant evidence it does not believe. Relevancy is simply a *tendency* of evidence to establish or disestablish a fact. It may be a very weak tendency. Prior accidents may be relevant to show danger, but the jury may still conclude, in the light of all the evidence, that there was no danger.

Investigation Guideline:

Let common sense be your main guide in pursuing relevant evidence. So long as there is some logical connection between the fact you are pursuing and a fact that must be established at trial, you are on the right track.

ASSIGNMENT 9.5

Examine the following four situations. Discuss the relevance of each item of evidence being introduced.

(a) Mrs. Phillips is being sued by a department store for the cost of a gas refrigerator. Mrs. Phillips claims that she never ordered and never received a refrigerator from the store. The attorney for Mrs. Phillips wants to introduce two letters: (1) a letter from Mrs. Phillips's landlord stating that her kitchen is not equipped to handle gas appliances and (2) a letter from another merchant stating that Mrs. Phillips bought an electric refrigerator from him a year ago.

(b) Phil Smith has been charged with burglary in Detroit on December 16, 2007. His attorney tries to introduce testimony into evidence that on December 7, 15, and 22, 2007, the defendant was in Florida.

(c) Al Neuman is suing Sam Snow for negligence in operating his motor vehicle. Al's attorney tries to introduce into evidence the fact that Snow currently has pending against him four other automobile negligence cases in other courts.

(d) Jim is on trial for the rape of Sandra. Jim's attorney wants to introduce into evidence (1) the fact that Sandra is the mother of Jim's child, who was born three years ago when they were dating (they separated in bitterness five months after the birth and never married), (2) the fact that Sandra has a page on myspace.com on which she has posted provocative pictures of herself boasting of having multiple boyfriends, and (3) the fact that Sandra is a member of Alcoholics Anonymous.

COMPETENCE OF WITNESSES

competent Allowed to give testimony because the person understands the obligation to tell the truth, has the ability to communicate, and has knowledge of the topic of his or her testimony. (See the glossary for another meaning of competent.)

credibility The extent to which something is believable.

A witness is **competent** to testify if the witness:

- understands the obligation to tell the truth,
- has the ability to communicate, and
- has knowledge of the topic of his or her testimony.

Children or mentally ill persons are not automatically disqualified. They are competent to testify if the judge is satisfied that the above criteria are met.

The competence of a witness must be carefully distinguished from the **credibility** of the witness. Once a court rules that a witness is competent, he or she is allowed to give testimony; competency is simply a ticket into the trial. The witness's testimony becomes admissible once he or she is declared competent. The actual impact of the testimony given by a competent witness depends on the credibility or believability of the witness. Credibility goes to the *weight* of the evidence. This weight is assessed by the trier of fact—usually the jury. Competence goes to whether that witness will be allowed to testify at all, a decision made by the judge. The jury may decide that everything said by a competent witness has little weight and therefore is unworthy of belief.

LAY OPINION EVIDENCE

opinion An inference from a fact. (See the glossary for other meanings of opinion.)

An **opinion** is an inference from a fact. For example, after you watch George stagger down the street and smell alcohol on his breath, you come to the conclusion that he is drunk. The conclusion is the inference. The facts are the observation of staggering and the smell of alcohol on his breath. Technically, a lay witness should not give opinion evidence. He or she must state the facts and let the trier of fact form the opinions. (Expert witnesses, on the other hand, *are* allowed to give opinions on technical subjects not within the understanding of the average layperson.) The problem with the lay opinion rule, however, is that it is sometimes difficult to express oneself without using opinions, as when a witness says it was a sunny day or the noise was loud. Courts are therefore lenient in permitting opinion testimony by lay witnesses when the witness is talking from his or her own observations and it would be awkward for the witness not to express the opinion. If people regularly use opinions when discussing the topic in question, it will be permitted.

Investigation Guideline:

Know when a person is stating an opinion. Even though an opinion may be admissible, you should assume that it will *not* be admissible. Pursue all of the underlying facts that support the inference in the opinion. In the event that the person is not allowed to testify by using the opinion, be prepared by having admissible evidence of the underlying facts the person relied on for the opinion.

ASSIGNMENT 9.6

Make a list of the questions that you would ask in order to uncover the underlying facts that formed the basis of the following opinions:

(a) He was insane.
(b) She couldn't see.
(c) It was cold out.
(d) He was traveling very fast.

HEARSAY

Hearsay is what one learns from another rather than from first-hand knowledge. More specifically, hearsay is an out-of-court statement offered to prove the truth of the matter asserted in the statement.[14] There are four conditions to the existence of hearsay: (1) a witness in court gives testimony, (2) about a statement made out of court by a person (called the declarant), (3) in order to establish the truth of the matter in the statement, (4) so that the value of the statement depends on the credibility of the declarant.[15] If evidence is hearsay, it is inadmissible unless one of the exceptions to the hearsay rule applies.

hearsay An out-of-court statement offered to prove the truth of the matter asserted in the statement.

Example: Sam, a witness in court, says, "Fred told me on Elm Street that he was speeding."

Note that Sam is telling us what he learned from someone else—Fred. Fred is known as the **declarant**, the person who has made a declaration or statement. The problem of hearsay arises when someone tries to give testimony about what a declarant has said or communicated. Is Sam's testimony hearsay? It depends on whether the four conditions for hearsay can be met:

declarant A person who makes a declaration or statement.

Testimony in court	The witness, Sam, is on the stand.
Statement made out of court	The statement by Fred (the declarant) was made on Elm Street, not in court.
Offered to assert the truth of the matter in the statement	Assume that the purpose of the attorney questioning Sam is to show that Fred was speeding—that is, that the statement is true.
The value of the statement depends on the credibility of the out-of-court declarant	Fred is the out-of-court declarant. The value of the statement depends on how believable or credible Fred is.

If the statement is not offered to prove the truth of the matter asserted in the statement, it is not hearsay. Suppose, for example, that the attorney wants to prove that Fred was alive immediately after the accident—that death was not instantaneous. The above statement would be admitted to prove that Fred actually said something, i.e., that Fred was alive enough to make a statement. If the testimony of the witness is offered to prove simply that the words were spoken by Fred rather than to prove that Fred was speeding, then the statement is not hearsay. The testimony that "Fred told me on Elm Street that he was speeding" would therefore be admissible. The jury would have to be cautioned to examine the testimony for the limited purpose for which it is offered and not to consider it evidence that Fred was speeding.

Conduct intended as a substitute for words (called assertive conduct) can also be hearsay. For example, the witness is asked "What did Fred say when you asked him if he was speeding?" The witness answers, "He nodded his head yes." This testimony is hearsay if it is offered to prove that Fred was speeding. Conduct—nodding the head—was intended as a substitute for words.

Investigation Guideline:
Know when hearsay exists so that you can try to find alternative, nonhearsay evidence to prove the truth of the assertions made in the hearsay. See also the second column of Exhibit 9.6 for a checklist on assessing the validity of hearsay evidence.

ASSIGNMENT 9.7

Is hearsay evidence involved in the following situations? Examine the four conditions of hearsay in each.

(a) Tom is suing Jim for negligence. On the witness stand, Tom says, "Jim was speeding at the time he hit me."

(b) Tom is suing Jim for negligence. While Tom is on the stand, his attorney introduces into evidence a mechanic's bill showing that the repair of the car cost $578.

(c) Mary and George were passengers in Tom's car at the time of the collision with Jim. George testifies that just before the collision, Mary shouted, "Look out for that car going through the red light!"

(d) He told me he was God.

There are a number of exceptions to the hearsay rule that have the effect of making evidence admissible even though it fulfills all the conditions of hearsay. Here are some examples:

1. *Admission by Party Opponent.* An admission by a party opponent is an earlier statement by a party that is now offered in court by an opponent. Example: Mary sues Sam for negligence. While Mary is presenting her case, she introduces a statement that Sam made to Paul in which Sam said, "I screwed up big time." This statement is admissible as an admission by a party opponent—Sam. (Note, however, that many states and the federal rules declare such statements by party opponents to be admissible because they are nonhearsay rather than as an exception to the hearsay rule.)

2. *Statement against Self-Interest.* A statement against self-interest is an out-of-court statement, made by a nonparty (who is now unavailable as a witness) that was against the financial interest of the declarant at the time it was made. Example: A nonparty tells a friend at a ball game, "I still owe the bank the money."

3. *Dying Declaration.* A dying declaration is an out-of-court statement concerning the causes or circumstances of death made by a person who is conscious of his or her imminent death. Example: Tom dies two minutes after he was hit over the head. Seconds before he dies, he says, "Linda did it." Many states limit the dying-declaration exception to criminal cases. Some states, however, would also allow it to be used in a civil case, such as in a civil battery or wrongful death case against Linda.

4. *Excited Utterance.* An excited utterance is an out-of-court statement relating to a startling event or condition made while the declarant was under the stress of excitement caused by the event or condition. Example: Fred says, "I heard John say, 'Oh my God, the truck just hit a child.'"

5. *Statement of Present Sense Impression.* A statement of present sense impression is an out-of-court statement describing or explaining an event or condition made while the declarant was perceiving the event or condition or immediately thereafter. Example: Janice says, "As the car turned the corner, a bystander turned to me and said, 'That car will never make it.'"

6. *Statement of Existing Physical or Mental Condition.* A statement of existing physical or mental condition is an out-of-court statement of a then-existing physical or mental condition. Example: Bob says, "A second before Sheila fell, she said to me, 'I feel dizzy.'"

7. *Declaration of Existing State of Mind.* A declaration of existing state of mind is an out-of-court statement made about the person's present state of mind. Example: Len says, "The manager said she knows about the broken railing and will fix it."

8. *Business Record.* A business record is a record kept in the course of a regularly conducted business activity. This also applies to nonprofit organizations such as universities. Example: A hospital record containing a description of a patient's condition upon entering the emergency room.

ASSIGNMENT 9.8

Smith is being sued for assaulting Jones, who later died. Smith is on the stand when the following exchange occurs.

Counsel for Smith: Did you strike the decedent, Jones?
Smith: Yes.
Counsel for Smith: Did Jones say anything to you before you struck him?
Counsel for Jones's estate: Objection, your honor, on the grounds of hearsay. Smith cannot give testimony on what the decedent said, since the decedent is obviously not subject to cross-examination.

(a) If Smith is allowed to answer the last question, he will say, "Yes, Jones told me that he was going to kill me." Would this statement be hearsay?
(b) If so, under what circumstances, if any, can it be admissible?

PRIVILEGE

A **privilege** in the law of evidence is the right to refuse to testify or the right to prevent someone else from testifying on a matter.

1. *Privilege against Self-Incrimination.* Under the privilege against self-incrimination, an accused person cannot be compelled to testify in a criminal proceeding or to answer questions that directly or indirectly connect the accused to the commission of a crime, i.e., incriminating questions.

2. *Attorney-Client Privilege.* Under the **attorney-client privilege**, a client and an attorney can refuse to disclose any communication between them if its purpose was to facilitate the provision of legal services for that client. The attorney cannot disclose the communication without the permission (consent) of the client. Closely related to the attorney-client privilege is the **work-product rule**. Under the latter, an attorney's work in preparation for litigation is privileged. With rare exceptions, the other side's request to be shown this work will be denied. Work in preparation for litigation includes notes, working papers, memoranda, and tangible things.

3. *Doctor-Patient Privilege.* Under the doctor-patient privilege, a patient and doctor can refuse to disclose any confidential (private) communications between them that relate to medical care. The doctor cannot disclose the communication without the consent of the patient.

4. *Clergy-Penitent Privilege.* Under the clergy-penitent privilege, a penitent and a member of the clergy can refuse to disclose any confidential (private) communications between them that relate to spiritual counseling or consultation. The minister, priest, or rabbi cannot disclose the communication without the consent of the penitent.

5. *Marital Communications.* A husband and wife can refuse to disclose confidential (private) communications between them during the marriage. One spouse can also prevent the other from making such disclosures. Both spouses must consent to the disclosure. The marital communications privilege does not apply, however, to litigation between spouses, e.g., divorce litigation.

6. *Government Information.* Some information collected by the government about citizens is confidential and privileged. Examples include most adoption and tax records. The privilege would not prevent use of the information to prosecute the citizen in connection with the citizen's duty to provide accurate information. It would, however, prevent third parties from gaining access to the confidential information.

Investigation Guideline:
When a privilege applies, look for alternative, nonprivileged sources of obtaining the information protected by the privilege.

BEST EVIDENCE RULE

To prove the contents of a private (nonofficial) writing, the **best evidence rule** requires you to produce the original writing unless it is unavailable through no fault of the person now seeking to introduce a copy of the original, e.g., it was destroyed in a sudden storm.

---

privilege A special legal benefit, right, immunity, or protection. (See the glossary for another meaning of *privilege*.)

attorney-client privilege A client and an attorney can refuse to disclose any communication between them if the purpose of the communication was to facilitate the provision of legal services to the client.

work product rule Notes, working papers, memoranda, or similar things prepared by or for an attorney in anticipation of litigation are not discoverable by an opponent, absent a showing of substantial need. They are protected by privilege.

best evidence rule To prove the contents of a private writing, the original writing should be produced unless it is unavailable.

authentication Evidence that a writing or other physical item is genuine and is what it purports to be.

testator One who has died leaving a valid will.

parol evidence rule Prior or contemporaneous oral statements cannot be introduced to alter or contradict the terms of a written document if the parties intended the written document to be a complete statement of the agreement.

contemporaneous Existing or occurring in the same period of time.

evidence log An ongoing record that provides identification and other data about documents and other tangible objects that might eventually be introduced into evidence.

AUTHENTICATION

Authentication is evidence that a writing (or other physical item) is genuine and that it is what it purports to be—for example, the testimony of witnesses who saw a **testator** sign a document when the testimony is offered to prove that the testator in fact signed the document and, while doing so, stated that it was his or her last will and testament.

PAROL EVIDENCE RULE

The **parol evidence rule** provides that prior or **contemporaneous** oral statements cannot be introduced to alter or contradict the terms of a written document if the parties intended the written document to be a complete statement of the agreement.

[SECTION K]
EVIDENCE LOG

There are times that attorneys come into possession of documents and other tangible things that might eventually be introduced into evidence, e.g., a defective consumer product or the will of an ancestor. One investigation-related task that paralegals sometimes perform is to help prepare and monitor the **evidence log** for such items. The log is an ongoing record that provides identification and other data about documents and other tangible objects that might eventually be introduced into evidence. The office needs to keep careful records on what the evidence is, how the office came into possession of it, and to whom it was released either before trial (e.g., to an expert for examination) or at the conclusion of the litigation. The evidence log is one way to manage this important information (see Exhibit 9.9).

EXHIBIT 9.9	Evidence Log

EVIDENCE LOG

CASE	FILE NAME	EVIDENCE COLLECTED	DESCRIPTION/ IDENTIFYING MARKS	PERSON WHO COLLECTED THE EVIDENCE	DATE COLLECTED	CIRCUMSTANCES LEADING TO COLLECTION	RELEASED TO/ DATE	REASON RELEASED	CURRENT CUSTODIAN/ LOCATION

[SECTION L]
TAKING A WITNESS STATEMENT

There are four major kinds of witness statements:

1. Handwritten statement
2. Recorded statement in question-and-answer format (on audio- or videotape)
3. Responses to a questionnaire that is mailed to the witness to answer
4. Statement taken in question-and-answer format with court reporters

The most common kind of statement is the first, which we shall consider here.

In a handwritten statement, the investigator writes down what the witness says, or the witness writes out the statement himself or herself. There is no formal structure to which the written statement must conform. The major requirements for the statement are clarity and accuracy.

Here is how one paralegal explains the process to the witness:

"What I'd like to do today is take a written statement from you. After we talk about what you recall about the accident, I'd like to write it down, then have you review it, verifying with your signature that this statement is indeed what you have said about the matter."[16]

From whom should you take a witness statement? "Many people feel that a witness can only be someone who has actually viewed the event or occurrence. Obviously, this is not true. Quite often the so-called **occurrence witness** cannot offer as significant a contribution in testimony as the **pre-occurrence witness** or **post-occurrence witness**. An alert, intelligent post-occurrence witness can shed a great deal of light upon the matter in dispute by testifying as to physical facts such as positions of cars or skid marks. He or she could also testify as to statements made immediately after the occurrence by a party to the lawsuit. The pre-occurrence witness can testify as to the condition of premises or machinery immediately before the accident. Therefore, the paralegal should be interested in interviewing witnesses who can set the stage for the scene of the accident, in addition to those who actually witnessed the occurrence."[17]

> **occurrence witness** Someone who actually observed an event.
>
> **pre-occurrence witness** Someone who did not observe an event but who can give a first-hand account of what happened before the event.
>
> **post-occurrence witness** Someone who did not observe an event but who can give a first-hand account of what happened after the event.

Suppose that a person says he or she knows nothing. Should a "witness" statement be taken of this person? Some recommend that you *should* take a "negative statement" to discourage this person from coming back later to claim "remembered information." Here's an example of such a statement:

"I was not at xxx address on xxx date and did not see a traffic accident at the time. I did not see anything happen at xxx location. I did not hear anything. I talked to no one about this accident nor did I hear anyone say anything about it."[18]

A written statement should begin by identifying (1) the witness (name, address, place of work, names of relatives, and other identifying data that may be helpful in locating the witness later); (2) the date and place of the taking of the statement; and (3) the name of the person to whom the statement is being made. See the example of the beginning of a witness statement in Exhibit 9.10.

EXHIBIT 9.10	Witness Statement

Statement of Patricia Wood

I am Patricia Wood. I am 42 years old and live at 3416 34th Street, N.W., Nashua, New Hampshire 03060. I work at the Deming Chemical Plant at Region Circle, Nashua. My home phone is 966–3954. My work phone is 297–9700 × 301. My e-mail address is pwood@pacbell.com. I am married to John Wood. We have two children, Jessica (fourteen years old) and Gabriel (eleven years old). I am making this statement to Rose Thompson, a paralegal at Fields, Smith and Farrell. This statement is being given on March 13, 2002 at my home, 3416 34th Street, NW.

On February 15, 2002, I was standing on the corner of . . .

Then comes the body of the statement, in which the witness provides information about the event or occurrence in question (an accident that was observed, what the witness did and saw just before a fire, where the witness was on a certain date, etc.). Be sure that the statement includes facts relevant to the ability of the witness to observe, e.g., amount of light available, weather conditions, obstructions. This lends credibility to the statement. It is often useful to have the witness give the facts in chronological order, particularly when many facts are involved in the statement.

At the end of the statement, the witness should say that he or she is making the statement of his or her own free will, without any pressure or coercion from anyone, (e.g., "I have carefully read all ___ pages of this statement. To the best of my knowledge, everything in it is accurate. I have made this statement of my own free will without coercion or pressure from anyone.") The witness then signs the statement and writes the date next to his or her signature. The signature goes on the last page. Each of the other pages is also signed or initialed. If others have watched the witness make and sign the statement, they should also sign an **attestation clause**, which simply states that they observed the witness sign the statement.

> **attestation clause** A clause stating that a person saw someone sign a document or perform other tasks related to the validity of the document.

Before the witness signs, he or she should read the entire statement and make any corrections that need to be made. Each correction should be initialed by the witness. Each page should be numbered with the total number of pages indicated each time. For example, if there are four pages, the page numbers would be 1 of 4, 2 of 4, 3 of 4, and 4 of 4. Each of these page numbers should be initialed and dated by the witness. The investigator should not try to correct any spelling or grammatical mistakes made by the witness. The statement should exist exactly as the witness spoke or wrote it.

rebut To refute or oppose.

Investigators sometimes use tricks of the trade to achieve a desired effect. For example, if the investigator is writing out the statement as the witness speaks, the investigator may *intentionally* make an error of fact, e.g., write "2004" when the witness said "2005." When the witness reads over the statement, the investigator makes sure that the witness catches the error and initials the correction. This becomes added evidence that the witness carefully read the statement. The witness might later try to claim that he or she did not read the statement. The initialed correction helps **rebut** this position.

Try to make sure that every page of the witness statement (other than the last) ends in the middle of a sentence or somewhere before the period. This is to rebut a later allegation that someone improperly added pages to the witness statement after it was signed. The allegation is somewhat difficult to support if the bottom line of one page contains a sentence that is continued at the top of the next page.

Witness statements are generally not admitted into evidence at the trial. If, however, a witness is giving testimony in court that is inconsistent with what he or she said in a witness statement, the statement might be allowed into evidence to demonstrate the inconsistency. The main value of witness statements is thoroughness and accuracy in case preparation. Trials can occur years after the events that led to litigation. Witnesses may disappear or forget. Witness statements taken soon after the event can sometimes be helpful in tracking down witnesses, helping them recall the details of the event, and, as mentioned earlier, discouraging them from changing their story.

ASSIGNMENT 9.9

Select any member of the class and take a witness statement from this person. The statement should concern an accident of any kind (e.g., a serious mishap at work, a highway collision) in which the witness was a participant or an observer. (The witness, however, should not be a party to any litigation growing out of the accident.) You write out the statement from what the witness says in response to your questions. Do not submit a statement handwritten by the witness except for his or her signature, initials, or corrections, if any. Use complete paragraphs in your report. Do not simply write out the question-and-answer exchanges between you and the person you interviewed. Assume that you (the investigator-paralegal) work for the law firm of Davis and Davis, which represents someone else involved in the accident.

[SECTION M]
THE SETTLEMENT WORK-UP

settlement work-up A summary of the major facts in the case presented in a manner designed to encourage the other side (or its insurance company) to settle the case. Also called a *settlement brochure*.

One of the end products of investigation is the **settlement work-up**, which is a summary of the major facts obtained through investigation, client interviewing, answers to interrogatories, deposition testimony, etc. It is also called a *demand package* and *settlement brochure*. The work-up, in one form or another, is used in negotiation with the other side or with the other side's liability insurance company in an effort to obtain a favorable settlement in lieu of trial. In addition to the presentation of the facts of a case, the settlement work-up might also summarize the law that will govern those facts.

Exhibit 9.11 shows a memo containing data for a proposed settlement work-up.[19] Note its precision and attention to detail. Excellent FP (fact particularization; see Exhibit 8.5 in chapter 8) had to be used as the basis of this report.

EXHIBIT 9.11	**Draft of a Proposed Settlement Work-Up**

Office Memorandum

To: Mary Jones, Esq
From: Katherine Webb, Paralegal
Date: October 12, 1995
Re: Joseph Smith vs. Dan Lamb
   Case Summary—Settlement Work-Up

(continues)

EXHIBIT 9.11 Draft of a Proposed Settlement Work-Up—*continued*

I. Facts of Accident

The accident occurred on September 6, 1993, in Orange, California. Joseph Smith was driving westbound on Chapman Avenue, stopped to make a left turn into a parking lot, and was rear-ended by the one-half-ton panel truck driven by Dan Lamb.

The defendant driver, Mr. Lamb, was cited for violation of Vehicle Code Sections 21703 and 22350, following too close, and at an unsafe speed for conditions.

II. Injuries

Severe cervical and lumbar sprain, superimposed over pre-existing, albeit asymptomatic, spondylolisthesis of pars interarticulus at L5–S1, with possible herniated nucleus pulposus either at or about the level of the spondylolisthesis; and contusion of right knee.

Please see attached medical reports for further details.

III. Medical Treatment

Mr. Smith felt an almost immediate onset of pain in his head, neck, back, and right knee after the accident and believes that he may have lost consciousness momentarily. He was assisted from his car and taken by ambulance to the St. Joseph Hospital emergency room, where he was initially seen by his regular internist, Raymond Ross, M.D.

Dr. Ross obtained orthopedic consultation with Brian A. Ewald, M.D., who reviewed the multiple X-rays taken in the emergency room and found them negative for fracture. Lumbar spine X-rays did reveal evidence of a spondylolisthesis defect at the pars interarticulus of L5, but this was not felt to represent acute injury. Dr. Ewald had Mr. Smith admitted to St. Joseph Hospital on the same day for further evaluation and observation.

On admission to the hospital, Mr. Smith was placed on complete bed rest, with a cervical collar and medication for pain. On September 10, neurological consultation was obtained with Michael H. Sukoff, M.D., who, although he did not find any significant objective neurological abnormality, felt that there might be a herniated disc at L4–L5, with possible contusion of the nerve roots.

Drs. Ewald and Sukoff followed Mr. Smith's progress throughout the remainder of his hospitalization. He was continued on bed rest, physiotherapy, and medication, and fitted with a lumbosacral support. He was ultimately ambulated with crutches and was discharged from the hospital on September 25, 1993, with instructions to continue to rest and wear his cervical collar and back brace.

On discharge from the hospital, Mr. Smith was taken by ambulance to the Sky Palm Motel in Orange, where his wife and children had been staying during his hospitalization. Arrangements were made for home physiotherapy and rental of a hospital bed. Mr. Smith was taken by ambulance on the following day to his residence in Pacific Palisades.

After returning home, Mr. Smith continued to suffer from headaches, neck pain, and severe pain in his lower back, with some radiation into both legs, especially the right. He was totally confined to bed for at least two months following the accident, where he was cared for by his wife. Daily physical therapy was administered by Beatrice Tasker, R.P.T.

Mr. Smith continued to receive periodic outpatient care with Dr. Ewald. By the end of December 1993, Mr. Smith was able to discontinue the use of his cervical collar and was able to walk, with difficulty, without crutches. At the time of his office visit with Dr. Ewald on December 21, he was noted to be having moderate neck discomfort, with increasingly severe low back pain. At the time, Dr. Ewald placed Mr. Smith on a gradually increasing set of Williams exercises and advised him to begin swimming as much as possible.

Mr. Smith continued to be followed periodically by Dr. Ewald through March 1994, with gradual improvement noted. However, Mr. Smith continued to spend the majority of his time confined to his home and often to bed, using a cane whenever he went out. In addition, he suffered periodic severe flareups of low back pain, which would render him totally disabled and would necessitate total bed rest for several days at a time.

During this period of time, Mr. Smith also experienced headaches and blurred vision, for which Dr. Ewald referred him to Robert N. Dunphy, M.D. Dr. Dunphy advised that the symptoms were probably secondary to his other injuries and would most likely subside with time.

On April 1, 1994, Mr. Smith consulted Dr. Ewald with complaints of increased back pain following an automobile ride to San Diego. Dr. Ewald's examination at that time revealed bilateral lumbar muscle spasm, with markedly decreased range of motion. Due to his concern about the extremely prolonged lumbar symptoms, and suspecting a possible central herniated nucleus pulposus, Dr. Ewald recommended that Mr. Smith undergo lumbar myelography. This was performed on an inpatient basis at St. Joseph Hospital on April 4, 1994, and reported to be within normal limits.

Mr. Smith continued conservative treatment with Dr. Ewald, following the prescribed program of rest, medication, exercise, and daily physiotherapy administered by his wife. He was able to graduate out of his lumbosacral support by approximately October 1994, resuming use of the garment when he experienced severe flareups of low back pain.

In his medical report dated January 2, 1995, Dr. Ewald stated that he expected a gradual resolution of lumbar symptomatology with time. However, in his subsequent report, dated January 10, 1995, Dr. Ewald noted that since his original report, Mr. Smith had suffered multiple repetitive episodes of low back pain, secondary to almost any increase of activity. At an office visit on February 25, Mr. Smith was reported to have localized his discomfort extremity well to the L5–S1 level, and range of motion was found to have decreased to approximately 75%. Since his examination in February, Dr. Ewald has discussed at length with both Mr. Smith and his wife the possibility of surgical intervention, consisting of lumbar stabilization (fusion) at the L5–S1 level, secondary to the spondylolisthesis present at that level. Dr. Ewald has advised them of the risks, complications, and alternatives with regard to consideration of surgical stabilization, noting that surgery would be followed by a 6-to-9-month period of rehabilitation, and further warning that even if the surgical procedure is carried out, there is no guarantee that Mr. Smith will be alleviated of all of his symptomatology.

As stated in Dr. Ewald's medical report dated March 10, 1995, Mr. Smith is himself beginning to lean toward definite consideration with regard to surgery, although he is presently continuing with conservative management.

(continues)

EXHIBIT 9.11	Draft of a Proposed Settlement Work-Up—*continued*

Dr. Ewald recommends that in the event Mr. Smith does choose to undergo surgery, a repeat myelogram should be performed in order to rule out, as much as possible, the presence of a herniated nucleus pulposus either above or at the level of the spondylolisthesis.

IV. Residual Complaints

Mr. Smith states that his neck injury has now largely resolved, although he does experience occasional neck pain and headaches. However, he continues to suffer from constant severe pain in his low back, with some radiation of pain and numbness in the right leg.

Mr. Smith notes that his low back pain is worse with cold weather and aggravated by prolonged sitting, walking, driving, or nearly any form of activity. He finds that he must rest frequently and continues to follow a daily regimen of swimming, Williams exercises, pain medication, and physiotherapy administered by his wife. He has also resumed the use of his lumbosacral brace.

Mr. Smith was an extremely active person prior to the accident, accustomed to working 12 to 16 hours per day and engaging in active sports such as tennis. Since the accident, he has had to sell his business and restrict all activities to a minimum, because he has found that any increase in activity will trigger a flareup of low back pain so severe that he is totally incapacitated for several days at a time.

As stated by Dr. Ewald, Mr. Smith is now seriously considering the possibility of surgical stabilization, despite the risks and complications involved. He has always viewed surgery as a last resort but is now beginning to realize that it may be his only alternative in view of his prolonged pain and disability. However, he currently intends to delay any definite decision until after the summer, during which time he intends to increase his swimming activity and see if he can gain any relief from his symptomatology.

V. Specials

(Copies of supporting documentation are attached hereto.)

A. Medical

1. Southland Ambulance Service (9/6/93)	$937.00
2. St. Joseph Hospital (9/6/93–9/25/93)	22,046.29
3. Raymond R. Ross, M.D. (Emergency Room, 9/6/93)	2,025.00
4. Brian A. Ewald, M.D. (9/6/93–4/28/95)	1,604.00
5. Michael H. Sukoff, M.D. (9/10/95–9/22/95)	1,140.00
6. Wind Ambulance Service (9/25/95)	939.50
7. Wind Ambulance Service (9/26/95)	989.00
8. Beatrice Tasker, R.P.T. (9/21/93–10/22/93)	1,825.00
9. Abbey Rents (Rental of hospital bed and trapeze bar, 9/25/93–11/25/93)	422.00
10. Allied Medical & Surgical Co. (Purchase of cane, 1/10/93)	30.45
11. Rice Clinical Laboratories (2/1/94)	114.00
12. Robert N. Dunphy, M.D. (2/1/94–4/15/94)	895.00
13. St. Joseph Hospital (X-rays and lab tests, 2/9/94)	756.00
14. St. Joseph Hospital (Inpatient myelography, 4/23/94–4/24/94)	851.60
15. Medication	1,357.70
Total Medical Expenses	$35,932.54

B. Miscellaneous Family Expenses

(During plaintiff's hospitalization, 9/6/93–9/25/95.)

1. Sky Palm Motel (Lodging for wife and children)	$2,050.50
2. Taxicab (9/6/93)	12.45
Total Miscellaneous Expenses	$2,062.95

C. Wage Loss

At the time of the accident, Mr. Smith was employed as president and co-owner, with Mr. George Frost, of the Inter Science Institute, Inc., a medical laboratory in Los Angeles. As stated in the attached verification from Mr. Mamikunian, Mr. Smith was earning an annual salary of $48,000, plus automobile, expenses, and fringe benefits.

In a telephone conversation with Mr. Smith on May 6, 1995, he advised me that the Inter Science Institute had grossed $512,000 in 1993 and $700,000 in 1994. He further confirmed that prior to the accident of September 6, 1993, both he and Mr. Frost had been approached on at least two to three different occasions by companies, including Revlon and a Canadian firm, offering substantial sums of money for purchase of the business. On the basis of the foregoing, both Mr. Smith and Mr. Frost place a conservative estimate of the value of the business at $2,000,000.

Due to injuries sustained in the subject accident, Mr. Smith was unable to return to work or perform the necessary executive and managerial functions required in his position as president and part owner of the business. As a result, on or about October 26, 1993, while still totally incapacitated by his injuries, Mr. Smith was forced to sell his 50% stock interest in the Inter Science Institute for a total sum of $300,000.

On the basis of the prior estimated value of the business at $2,000,000, *Mr. Smith sustained a loss of $700,000 in the sale of his one-half interest in Inter Science Institute, Inc., in addition to the loss of an annual salary of $48,000, plus automobile, expenses, and fringe benefits.*

Even if one were to assume that the sale of his interest in the business was reasonable value, Mr. Smith has sustained a loss—in salary only—in the sum of *$84,000* to date, based on an annual salary of $48,000 up to October 12, 1995.

ASSIGNMENT 9.10

Assume that the settlement work-up in Exhibit 9.11 is not successful. The case must now go to trial. Prepare a report for the attorney litigating the case of all the evidence that should be collected and considered for use at the trial.

(a) List all possible witnesses your side (representing Joseph Smith) might call and give a summary of what their testimony is likely to be.

(b) List all possible witnesses the other side (representing Dan Lamb) might call and give a summary of what their testimony is likely to be.

(c) List all possible physical evidence your side should consider using and give a summary of what each item might establish.

(d) List all possible physical evidence the other side is likely to consider using and give a summary of what each item might establish.

(e) What further facts do you think need to be investigated?

[SECTION N]

THE ETHICAL INVESTIGATOR

When carrying out an investigation assignment, great care must be used to comply with all of the ethical obligations discussed in chapter 5 that govern law offices. For example:

- Do not communicate with an opponent or an employee of an opponent unless the opponent's attorney allows you to do so. If you are not sure whether someone has attorney representation, ask him or her.
- If the opponent is unrepresented, do not allow him or her to think that you are disinterested; it is deceptive to allow someone to think you are neutral.
- Do not lie about your identity.
- Do not allow anyone to think you are an attorney even if you have made no affirmative misrepresentations about your status.
- Do not give any other false statements of fact while communicating with a potential witness.
- Do not expressly or implicitly promise someone something of value (e.g., money) if he or she agrees to bring or drop a lawsuit.
- Do not expressly or implicitly encourage someone to alter or destroy evidence.
- Do not expressly or implicitly encourage someone to leave the area so that a court would not be able to reach him or her with **process** (e.g., service of process).
- Do not secretly record a conversation with someone.
- Do not reveal personal information about other people.

process 1. A summons, writ, or court order, e.g., to appear in court. 2. Procedures or proceedings in an action or prosecution.

Finally, avoid careless waiver of the attorney-client privilege. While working on a client's case, you undoubtedly will learn a great deal of information that is protected by the attorney-client privilege. Be very careful about mentioning any of this information while talking with a witness. As we saw in chapter 5, the disclosure of such confidential information may result in a waiver of the privilege, even if the witness is friendly to your side.[20]

Chapter Summary

The goal of investigation is to obtain new facts and to verify facts already known by the office. It is a highly individualistic skill where determination, imagination, resourcefulness, and openness are critical. A good investigator has a healthy suspicion of preconceived notions of what the facts are because such notions might interfere with uncovering the unexpected. In the search for the facts, the investigator is concerned with truth in the context of the evidence that will be needed to establish that truth in court. But the standard that guides the search is not truth or proof; the guideline of the investigator is to pursue whatever evidence that is reasonably available.

People often have different perspectives on what did or did not happen, particularly in regard to emotionally charged events. When different versions of facts exist, the investigator must seek them out.

Competent investigation requires an understanding of the kinds of distortions that can occur in an investigation, a knowledge of the standard sources of information, an ability to use the techniques of gaining access to records, and an ability to evaluate the trustworthiness of both oral and physical evidence.

Investigators must be aware of the image they project of themselves, be prepared for witnesses with differing levels of factual knowledge, be ready for witnesses who are unwilling to cooperate, and be able to gain the trust of witnesses.

The law of evidence is an important part of the investigator's arsenal. This should include an understanding of the following: the four ways a version of the facts can be established at the trial, admissibility, the distinction between direct evidence and circumstantial evidence, the nature of relevance, when a witness is competent to give testimony and to state an opinion, the nature of hearsay, and the major exceptions that allow hearsay to be admitted. Investigators need to understand the effect of the privilege against self-incrimination, the attorney-client privilege, the doctor-patient privilege, the clergy-penitent privilege, the privilege for marital communications, and the confidentiality of some government information. They should also understand the best evidence rule, the authentication of evidence, the parol evidence rule, and the function of an evidence log.

Two important documents that are the products of competent investigation are a witness statement, which is taken to preserve the testimony of an important witness, and a settlement work-up, which is an advocacy document that compiles and organizes facts in an effort to encourage a favorable settlement.

Ethical investigators do not improperly contact an opposing party who has attorney representation, lie about their identity, allow anyone to think they are attorneys, make false statements of fact, make promises in exchange for an agreement to bring or drop a lawsuit, encourage anyone to alter evidence or avoid process, secretly record an interview, or reveal personal information about others. They are also careful to avoid carelessly waiving the attorney-client privilege.

Key Terms

forensic	parol evidence	presumption	best evidence rule
due diligence	tangible evidence	rebuttable	authentication
legal investigation	Freedom of Information	irrebuttable	testator
fact	Act (FOIA)	admissible	parol evidence rule
settlement	disinterested	direct evidence	contemporaneous
impeach	bias	circumstantial evidence	evidence log
discovery	subpoenaed	relevant	occurrence witness
deposition	judgment creditor	competent	pre-occurrence witness
transcribed	judgment debtor	credibility	post-occurrence witness
interrogatories	deep pocket	opinion	attestation clause
request for admission	due diligence	hearsay	rebut
evidence	skiptracing	declarant	settlement work-up
proof	admission	privilege	process
substantive law	stipulation	attorney-client privilege	
leading question	judicial notice	work-product rule	

Review Questions

1. What is forensic accounting?
2. Name some investigation tasks commonly performed by paralegals.
3. What is a legal investigation?
4. What is an open-ended investigation assignment?
5. What is the relationship between the initial client interview and investigation?
6. How can the investigator assist the attorney who is trying to negotiate a settlement of a case?
7. What is the goal of impeaching someone?
8. Name and define four discovery devices.
9. How can an investigator be of assistance during the discovery stage of litigation?
10. What is the distinction between proof of a fact and evidence of a fact?
11. What tests should an investigator use in determining whether to pursue a fact possibility?
12. Where can a paralegal learn the law that will often be helpful in conducting an investigation?
13. What are some of the fundamental characteristics of facts and of peoples' perceptions of facts?
14. How should an investigator plan an investigation via fact versions?
15. What are the dangers and advantages of leading questions in investigation?
16. What is the distinction between parol evidence and tangible evidence?
17. List some of the standard sources of evidence and leads.
18. List four categories of records to which you may want to obtain access.
19. What are some of the major techniques of gaining access to records in the face of resistance from those in possession of the records?
20. What is a FOIA letter?
21. Give examples of major questions you would ask yourself to determine the validity of eyewitness evidence.
22. Give examples of questions you would ask yourself to determine the validity of hearsay evidence.

23. Give examples of questions you would ask yourself to determine the validity of written physical evidence.
24. Give examples of questions you would ask yourself to determine the validity of nonwritten physical evidence.
25. Why should you try to interview someone with no other potential witnesses present during the interview?
26. What are the different images you might project of yourself when you investigate?
27. Name five kinds of witnesses.
28. What is a disinterested witness?
29. Name some of the states of mind witnesses can have.
30. What are some of the questions investigators must ask themselves when evaluating how well a witness might do on direct examination and on cross-examination?
31. What do we mean when we say that a witness has a deep pocket?
32. Name some of the kinds of information that a judgment creditor might try to seek online (from free and paid services) about the financial condition of a judgment debtor.
33. Name some of the major techniques of investigation in attempting to locate a missing person.
34. Name some of the kinds of information an investigator will pursue when conducting a background investigation.
35. When investigating an automobile accident, what are some of the guidelines the investigator should follow when taking photographs?
36. Describe one technique for determining the speed of a vehicle just before an accident.

37. Name and briefly describe four ways a party can establish its version of the facts.
38. What is the difference between a rebuttable and irrebuttable presumption?
39. What is the consequence of evidence being declared admissible?
40. What is the difference between direct evidence and circumstantial evidence?
41. What is the difference between relevant evidence and admissible evidence?
42. What three conditions determine the competency of a witness?
43. What is the difference between the competency of a witness and the credibility of a witness?
44. What is opinion evidence and when is it admissible?
45. What are the four conditions for the existence of hearsay?
46. What are the major exceptions to the hearsay rule?
47. What are the major evidentiary privileges?
48. What is the best evidence rule?
49. What is the function of authentication?
50. What is the parol evidence rule?
51. What is the function of an evidence log?
52. Define a pre-occurrence witness, an occurrence witness, and a post-occurrence witness.
53. How should a witness statement be taken?
54. What are the components of a settlement work-up?
55. Name the major dos and don'ts of ethical investigators.

Helpful Web Sites: More about Investigation

Investigator's Guide to Sources of Information
- nilesonline.com/data
- www.gao.gov/special.pubs/soi.htm
- virtualprivatelibrary.blogspot.com/Finding%20People.pdf
- law.richmond.edu/jolt/v12i4/article17.pdf

Conducting Background Investigations
- www.ojr.org/ojr/law/1028842909.php
- www.privacyrights.org
- www.privacyrights.org/workplace.htm
- www.ussearch.com/consumer/index.jsp

Freedom of Information
- www.usdoj.gov/oip/foi-upd.htm
- www.tncrimlaw.com/foia_indx.html
- www.sba.gov/foia/guide.html
- www.nfoic.org

Finding People or Businesses
- www.switchboard.com
- www.bigbook.com
- www.bigfoot.com
- www.people.yahoo.com
- www.whowhere.com
- www.accurint.com
- www.iaf.net
- www.four11.com

- www.merlindata.com
- www.zabasearch.com
- www.555-1212.com

Finding Assets
- www.knowx.com
- www.ussearch.com
- www.tracerservices.com
- www.members.tripod.com/proagency/ask8.html

Finding Information about Businesses
- www.sec.gov/edgar.shtml (SEC filings; Edgar)
- www.edgar-online.com
- www.annualreports.com
- www.bloomberg.com
- www.hoovers.com
- www.onesource.com
- www.dnb.com
- www.choicepoint.net
- www.corporateinformation.com
- www.thecorporatelibrary.com

Business Directories and Search Engines
- www.yellowpages.com
- www.dexonline.com
- www.corporateinformation.com

BP Free Access to Government Records

- www.brbpub.com/pubrecsitesStates.asp (click your state)

Birth, Death, Marriage, and Divorce Records

- www.cdc.gov/nchs/howto/w2w/w2welcom.htm
- www.vitalrec.com
- www.vitalchek.com

State Secretaries of State Records Links

- www.nass.org

Other Major Public Records Search Sites and Resources for Court Documents, Occupational Licenses, Property Assessments, Etc.

- www.brbpub.com
- www.publicrecordfinder.com
- www.50states.com/publicrecords
- www.netronline.com/frameset.asp?StateID=37
- www.searchsystems.net
- www.virtualchase.com/topics/introduction_public_records.shtml
- www.oatis.com/publicrecords.htm
- www.pretrieve.com
- www.knowx.com
- www.dr-rec-fac.com
- www.ancestry.com/search/rectype/military/main/main.htm
- www2.genealogy.com/ssdi_cgi/gen_foot4.html

Government Statistics

- www.census.gov
- www.census.gov/compendia/statab/
- www.fedstats.gov
- www.library.law.pace.edu/government/statistics.html
- www.cdc.gov/nchs/products/pubs/pubd/vsus/vsus.htm

Expert Witness Directory

- www.tasanet.com
- www.expertlaw.com
- www.exemplaris.com
- www.juryverdicts.com/experts/index.html
- www.idex.com
- www.expertpages.com

Maps and Aerial Photos

- maps.google.com
- www.mapblast.com
- www.atlapedia.com
- encarta.msn.com/encnet/features/MapCenter/map.aspx

News Searches

- news.google.com
- www.altavista.com/news
- news.yahoo.com
- www.onlinenewspapers.com

Climate Reports

- www.noaa.gov
- www.ncdc.noaa.gov

Medical Information and Research

- www.nlm.nih.gov
- www.med.yale.edu/library
- library.umassmed.edu/index.cfm

Investigation Services

- www.blackbookonline.info
- www.vitalrec.com/links6.html
- www.ussearch.com
- www.thepiregister.com
- www.ottolabs.com

Alternative Culture Directory

(tracking disinformation)

- www.sourcewatch.org
- en.wikipedia.org/wiki/Disinformation
- www.disinfo.com
- www.zenzibar.com
- www.pantheon.org/mythica.html

Miscellaneous: Facts on the Internet

- www.refdesk.com

Google Searches (run the following searches for more sites)

- "legal investigation"
- due diligence
- freedom of information
- witness interviews
- finding assets
- locating missing persons
- background investigation
- accident investigation
- Wyoming evidence rules (insert your state)
- hearsay evidence
- evidence privilege
- "witness statement"
- "settlement brochure"

Endnotes

1. Lana Clark, *Developing a Strategy for Witness Interviews*, 10 Legal Assistant Today 65 (January/February 1993).

2. Tracy Girrens, *Paralegal Profession the Best*, KLAS ACTION 9 (Kansas Paralegal Association, May 1998).

3. Neal Bevans, *Diving Deep*, 22 Legal Assistant Today 70 (September/October 2004).

4. See Edna M. Wallace, *Regulation: The Good, the Bad and the Ugly* (www.paralegals.org/displaycommon.cfm?an=1&subarticlenbr=343) (2006).

5. Carolyn Saenz, *Paralegal, P.I.*, 16 Legal Assistant Today 56 (May/June 1999).

6. A. Daniel Yarmey, *The Psychology of Eyewitness Testimony* 9 (Free Press, 1979); E. Loftus et al., *Powerful Eyewitness Testimony*, Trial Magazine 64–66 (April 1988).

7. Byron Keith, *Dealing Smartly with Different Witnesses*, The Legal Investigator 38 (November 1991).

8. Francis Ritter, *The Art of Hearing between the Lines*, The Legal Investigator 9 (February 1992).

9. Janet Jackson, *Interviewing Witnesses*, At Issue 1 (San Francisco Association of Legal Assistants April 1994).

10. Julie Bassett, *Hot Tips for Interviewing Witnesses*, 9 Legal Assistant Today 23, 27 September/October 1991).

11. D. Andrews, *Ask the Experts*, SJPA Reporter (South Jersey Paralegal Association, July 1991).

12. John Lehe, *Techniques for Locating Missing Parties*, 11 Legal Assistant Today 80, 81 (January/February 1994).

13. Reprinted with the permission of *Trial* (February 1991) © copyright The Association of Trial Lawyers of America.

14. Roger Haydock and John Sonsteng, *Trial* 209 (1991).

15. E. Cleary, ed., *McCormick's Handbook of the Law of Evidence* 584 (1972).

16. K. Wilkoff, *Writing Witness Statements That Win Cases*, 12 Legal Assistant Today 51, 52 (September/October 1994).

17. Yetta Blair, *Interviewing Witnesses and Securing Their Signed Written Statements*, 14 Points and Authorities 10 (San Joaquin Association of Legal Assistants, May 1992).

18. Kathryn Andrews, *Interviews and Statements* 10 (Oregon Legal Assistants Association, October 1988).

19. Adapted from Katherine Webb, Legal Assistant at Cartwright, Sucherman, Slobodin & Fowler, San Francisco, California.

20. Beth L. King, *The Successful Witness Interview*, 29 National Paralegal Reporter 6 (National Federation of Paralegal Associations October/November 2004).

Student CD-ROM

For additional materials, please go to the CD in this book.

Online Companion™

For additional resources, please go to http://www.paralegal.delmar.cengage.com

Litigation Assistantship

CHAPTER OUTLINE

A. Overview of Litigation

B. Alternative Dispute Resolution (ADR)

C. Litigation Assistantship: Pretrial Stage

D. Litigation Assistantship: Trial Stage

E. Litigation Assistantship: Appeal Stage

F. Litigation Assistantship: Enforcement Stage

[SECTION A]

OVERVIEW OF LITIGATION

litigious 1. Prone to engage in disputes and litigation. Quarrelsome.

litigation 1. The formal process of resolving a legal dispute through the courts. 2. A lawsuit.

America is a **litigious** society, meaning we are prone to engage in disputes and **litigation**. Every year over 100 million new cases are filed in state courts and over 350,000 in federal courts (not including 1.6 million bankruptcy filings).[1] Litigation is the formal process of resolving legal controversies through the courts. Administrative agencies can also resolve some legal disputes through the exercise of their quasi-judicial power. (Quasi-judicial means acting like or similar to a court in resolving disputes. See chapter 6.)

Paralegals can perform many functions in assisting attorneys who are litigating cases. Before studying what these functions are, read the following overview of litigation, which will provide a context for understanding the roles of the attorney and paralegal. The overview is presented in the form of a story—the litigation woes of Michael Brown, who finds himself embroiled in a civil trial, a criminal trial, and an administrative dispute. At the end of the story, you will find most of this overview in outline form in Exhibits 10.2 and 10.3.

There are two broad categories of litigated disputes: civil and criminal. A **civil dispute** consists of:

civil dispute A legal controversy in which (1) one private person or entity (e.g., a business) sues another, (2) a private person or entity sues the government, or (3) the government sues a private person or entity for a matter other than the commission of a crime.

- One private person or entity (e.g., a business) sues another private person or entity (e.g., Jones sues Smith for negligence after an automobile collision; Ajax, Inc. sues Tomas Vine Co. for breach of contract), or
- One private person or entity sues the government (e.g., a senior citizen sues the Social Security Administration for denial of disability benefits; an inmate sues a state prison for violation of civil rights), or
- The government sues a private person or entity for a matter other than the commission of a crime (e.g., the state department of revenue sues the Dayglow Restaurant for the failure to deduct state taxes from the wages of waiters).

criminal dispute A legal controversy in which the government alleges the commission of a crime.

A **criminal dispute** is a legal controversy in which the government alleges the commission of a crime.

THE LEGAL ODYSSEY OF MICHAEL BROWN: AN ANATOMY OF THE LITIGATION PROCESS

Michael Brown is a truck driver for the Best Bread Company. Several years ago, as Brown was walking home from work, Harold Clay, an old friend from the past, stopped and offered him a ride. They had not seen each other since Clay had moved cross-country a number of years ago. They carried on an excited conversation as Clay drove. After a few blocks, a car driven by George Miller, a resident of a neighboring state, ran through a red light and struck Clay's car. All three individuals were seriously injured and were taken to a local hospital. Clay died two weeks later from injuries received in the crash.

Several days after the accident, Brown's boss, Frank Best, wrote Brown a letter. In it, Best said he had learned that the police had found about half an ounce of heroin under the front passenger seat of Clay's car and were planning to charge Brown with possession of narcotics with intent to distribute. Best also stated that several thefts had occurred at the company warehouse recently and that he now suspected Brown of having been involved in them. For these reasons, he decided to fire Brown, effective immediately.

At least three different legal disputes involving Brown could arise out of this fact situation:

1. A dispute among Brown, Miller, and Clay's estate regarding civil liability for the accident.
2. A dispute between Brown and the government regarding the criminal drug charge.
3. A dispute among Brown, the Best Bread Company, and the State Unemployment Compensation Board concerning Brown's entitlement to unemployment compensation benefits.

Each of these disputes could lead to a number of court decisions. The third dispute might involve an administrative decision, possibly followed by one or more court decisions, all concerning Brown's claim for unemployment compensation.

1. Civil Liability

Brown suffered substantial injury as a result of the crash. From whom could he collect *damages?* Who was *liable* for the accident? Was Miller at fault? Clay? Was each of them *jointly* and *severally* liable?

Damages: An award of money paid by the wrongdoer to compensate the person who has been harmed.

Liable: Legally responsible.

Joint and several liability: Legally responsible together and individually. Each wrongdoer is individually responsible for the *entire* judgment; the plaintiff can choose to collect from one wrongdoer or from all of them until the judgment is satisfied.

Brown retained Brenda Davis, Esq. to represent him. Once Brown paid the agreed-upon *retainer,* Davis would later enter an *appearance* and become the *attorney of record.*

Retainer: (1) An amount of money (or other property) paid by a client as a deposit or advance against future fees, costs, and expenses of providing services. (2) The act of hiring or engaging the services of someone, usually a professional. The verb is *retain.*

Appearance: Formally coming before a tribunal as a party or as a representative of a party. The attorney usually appears by filing a *notice of appearance* in court, which is often accomplished through a *praecipe.* A praecipe is a formal request to the court (usually made through the court clerk) that something be done. Here, the request is that the attorney become the attorney of record.

Attorney of record: The attorney noted in the court files as the attorney representing a particular party. Attorneys of record sometimes cannot withdraw from the case without court permission.

The attorney explained that a number of factors had to be considered before deciding on the *forum* in which to sue Miller and Clay's *estate.* Brown might be able to bring the suit in a number of places: (1) in a state trial court where Brown lives, (2) in a state trial court where Miller lives, (3) in a state trial court where Clay's estate is located, (4) in the federal trial court sitting in

Brown's state, (5) in the federal trial court sitting in Miller's state, or (6) in the federal trial court sitting in the state where Clay's estate is located. The reason Brown could sue in a federal court is the existence of *diversity of citizenship*. Davis advised Brown to sue in federal court. The suit would be brought in the U.S. District Court sitting in Brown's own state, since this would be the most convenient *venue* for Brown.

Forum: The court where the case is to be tried.

Estate: All of the assets and liabilities of a decedent (one who has died) after he or she dies. When we say that an estate is sued (or brings a suit), we are referring to the decedent's representative who is authorized to resolve claims involving the decedent's assets and debts. (For other meanings of *estate*, see the glossary.)

Diversity of citizenship: The disputing parties are citizens of different states and the amount in controversy exceeds $75,000. This diversity gives jurisdiction to a U.S. District Court.

Venue: The proper county or geographical area in which a court with jurisdiction may hear a case. The place of the trial. In most judicial systems, there is more than one trial court. For example, there may be one for each county or district. The selection of a particular trial court within a judicial system is referred to as a *choice of venue*.

Having decided on a court, Davis was ready to begin the lawsuit. She instructed her paralegal, Ted Alexander, to prepare the first draft of the *complaint*, naming Brown as the *plaintiff* and *stating a cause of action* for negligence against Miller and Clay's estate as *codefendants*. The complaint was the first *pleading* of the case. In the complaint, Davis stated the facts she felt constituted a cause of action for negligence. Some of the factual *allegations* were based on Brown's personal knowledge, while others were based on *information and belief*. The prayer for relief in the complaint contained an *ad damnum clause* that asked for $100,000. When Davis finished drafting the complaint, she signed it. Since this was not to be a *bench trial*, she included a written demand for a *jury trial* and instructed her paralegal to *file* the complaint and a *civil cover sheet* with the clerk of the court.

Complaint: 1. A plaintiff's first pleading stating a cause of action against the defendant. Also called *petition*. 2. A formal criminal charge.

Plaintiff: The person who initiates a civil action in court.

Cause of action: A legally acceptable reason for suing. Facts that give a party the right to judicial relief.

Stating a cause of action: Including facts in a pleading (e.g., a complaint) that, if proved at trial, would entitle the party to the judicial relief sought (assuming the other party does not plead and prove any defenses that would defeat the effort).

Codefendant: One of two or more defendants sued in the same civil case or prosecuted in the same criminal case.

Pleadings: Formal litigation documents filed by parties that state or respond to claims or defenses of other parties. The major pleadings are the complaint and answer.

Allegation: A claimed fact; a fact that a party will try to prove at trial.

Information and belief: A standard legal term used to indicate that the allegation is not based on the first-hand knowledge of the person making the allegation but that the person, nevertheless, believes in good faith that the allegation is true.

Ad damnum clause: A clause stating the damages claimed. (See "prayer for relief" in Exhibit 10.5 later in the chapter.)

Bench trial: A trial without a jury. Also called *nonjury trial*.

Jury trial: A trial in which a group of citizens resolve the issues or questions of fact. The judge decides the issues or questions of law. If there is no jury at the trial, the judge decides both the questions of law and the questions of fact.

File: To deliver a document to a court officer so that it can become part of the official collection of documents in a case. To deliver a document to a government agency.

Civil cover sheet: A cover sheet filed in federal court along with the complaint indicating the names and addresses of the parties and their attorneys, the kind of action being filed, etc.

Service of process came next. It was accomplished when a copy of the complaint, along with the *summons*, was served on both Miller and the legal representative of Clay's estate. Davis did not serve these parties herself. She used a *process server*, who then had to file with the court a *proof of service* indicating the circumstances under which service was achieved. Service was made before the *statute of limitations* on the negligence cause of action had run out. Once the defendants were properly served, the court acquired *personal jurisdiction* over them.

> **Service of process:** A formal delivery of notice to a defendant that a suit has been initiated to which he or she must respond. The most common method of service of process is to place the complaint and summons in the hands of the defendant.
>
> **Summons:** A notice directing the defendant to appear in court and answer the plaintiff's complaint or face a default judgment. The summons is *served* on the defendant.
>
> **Process server:** Someone with the authority to serve or deliver process. *Process* is a summons, writ, or court order.
>
> **Proof of service:** Evidence that a summons or other process has been served on a party in an action. Also called *certificate of service*, or *return of service*.
>
> **Statute of limitations:** A law stating that civil or criminal actions are barred if not brought within a specified period of time.
>
> **Personal jurisdiction:** A court's power over a person to adjudicate his or her personal rights. Also called *in personam jurisdiction*. More limited kinds of jurisdiction include the court's power over a person's interest in specific property (*quasi in rem jurisdiction*) or over the property itself (*in rem jurisdiction*).

Both Miller and Clay's estate filed *motions to dismiss* for *failure to state a cause of action*. The motions were denied by the court.

> **Motion to dismiss:** A request, usually made before the trial begins, that the judge dismiss the case because of lack of jurisdiction, insufficiency of the pleadings, or the reaching of a settlement.
>
> **Failure to state a cause of action:** Failure of a party to allege enough facts that, if proved, would entitle the party to judicial relief. Even if the party proved every fact he or she alleges, the facts would not establish a cause of action entitling the party to recover against his or her opponent. The motion to dismiss for failure to state a cause of action is sometimes referred to as (a) a *demurrer* or (b) a *failure to state a claim upon which relief can be granted*.

Because the case had been filed in a federal court, the *procedural law* governing the case would be found in the *Federal Rules of Civil Procedure*. (The *substantive law* of the case would be the state law of negligence.) According to the Federal Rules of Civil Procedure, Miller and Clay's estate were each required to file an *answer* to Brown's complaint within 20 days. Miller filed his answer almost immediately. Since Clay was dead and unable to tell his attorney what had happened at the accident, the attorney for the estate had some difficulty preparing an answer and was unable to file it within the 20 days. To avoid a *default judgment* against the estate, the attorney filed a *motion* asking for an extension of 30 days within which to file the answer. The motion was granted by the court, and the answer was filed within the new deadline.

> **Procedural law:** The rules that govern the mechanics of resolving a dispute in court or in an administrative agency.
>
> **Federal Rules of Civil Procedure (Fed. R. Civ. P.):** The technical rules governing the manner in which civil cases are brought in and progress through the U.S. District Courts, which are the main federal trial courts. (www.law.cornell.edu/rules/frcp)
>
> **Substantive law:** Nonprocedural laws that define or govern rights and duties (such as the duty to use reasonable care).
>
> **Answer:** The first pleading of the defendant that responds to the plaintiff's claims. (See the glossary for an additional definition of answer.)
>
> **Default judgment:** A judgment against a party for failure to file a required pleading or otherwise respond to an opponent's claim.
>
> **Motion:** An application or request made to a court or other decision-making body seeking to obtain a favorable action or ruling, e.g., a motion to dismiss. The party making the motion is called the *movant*. The verb is *move*, as in "I move that the court permit the demonstration" or "I move that the case be dismissed."

The answer filed on behalf of Clay's estate denied all allegations of negligence and raised an *affirmative defense* of contributory negligence against Brown on the theory that if Clay had been partially responsible for the collision, it was because Brown had carelessly distracted him through his conversation in the car. Finally, the answer of Clay's estate raised a *cross-claim* against the co-defendant Miller, alleging that the accident had been caused by Miller's negligence. The estate asked $1,000,000 in damages.

> **Defense:** An allegation of fact (or a legal theory) offered to offset or defeat a claim or demand. The word *defense* also means the defendant and his or her attorney.

> **Affirmative defense:** A defense raising new facts that will defeat the plaintiff's claim even if the plaintiff's fact allegations are proven.

> **Cross-claim:** A claim brought by one defendant against another defendant or by one plaintiff against another plaintiff in the same action. Also called a *cross action*.

Miller's answer also raised the defense of contributory negligence against Brown and stated a cross-claim against Clay's estate, alleging that the accident had been caused solely by the negligence of Clay, or of Clay and Brown together. On this same theory (that Brown together with Clay had negligently caused the accident), Miller's answer also stated a *counterclaim* against Brown, to which Brown immediately filed a *reply*. Miller sought $50,000 from Brown and $50,000 against Clay's estate as damages.

> **Counterclaim:** A claim by one side in a case (usually the defendant) that is filed in response to a claim asserted by an opponent (usually the plaintiff).

> **Reply:** A plaintiff's response to the defendant's counterclaim, plea, or answer.

For a time, Miller and his attorney considered filing a *third-party complaint* against his own automobile insurance company, since the company would be liable for any judgment against him. They decided against this strategy because they did not want to let the jury know that Miller was insured. If the jury knew this fact, it might be more inclined to reach a verdict in favor of the plaintiff and for a high amount of damages. The strategy was also unnecessary because there was no indication that Miller's insurer would *contest* its obligation to compensate Miller (within the policy limits of his insurance) for any damages that he might have to pay Brown or Clay's estate in the event that the trial resulted in an *adverse judgment* against him.

> **Third-party complaint:** A defendant's complaint against someone who is not now a party on the basis that the latter may be liable for all or part of what the plaintiff might recover from the defendant.

> **Contest:** To challenge; to raise a defense against a claim.

> **Adverse judgment:** A judgment or decision against you.

At this point, five claims had been filed by the parties. A sixth, Miller's third-party claim against his insurer, had been considered but ultimately had not been filed. These claims and their relationship to each other are illustrated in Exhibit 10.1.

1. Plaintiff Brown's complaint for negligence against Miller
2. Plaintiff Brown's complaint for negligence against Clay's estate (the estate and Miller are codefendants)
3. Defendant Miller's counterclaim for negligence against plaintiff, Brown
4. Defendant Miller's cross-claim for negligence against his codefendant, the estate
5. Defendant estate's cross-claim for negligence against its codefendant, Miller
6. Third-party complaint that defendant Miller considered but ultimately decided *not* to file against his insurance company

Once the pleadings were filed, all three parties began to seek *discovery*. Each attorney first served *interrogatories* on the opposing parties. These were followed by *depositions* and *requests for admissions*. Miller was also served with a *subpoena duces tecum*, which ordered him to bring his driver's license and car registration to his attorney's office, where his deposition took place. He complied with this order. During the deposition, however, Miller refused to answer several questions. As a result, Brown's attorney had to file a discovery motion in court, seeking an *order* compelling Miller to answer. A court *hearing* was subsequently held on the motion. After listening to arguments by all of the attorneys, the judge granted the motion in full, ordering Miller to answer the questions. Faced with the court's order, Miller answered the remaining questions.

Exhibit 10.1	Diagram of the Claims in the Brown/Miller/Clay's Estate Litigation

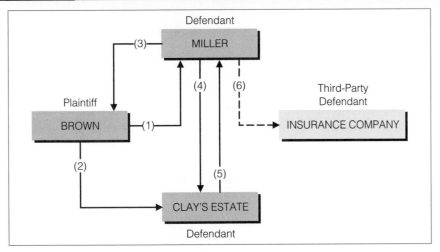

Each party then filed a *motion for summary judgment*. The judge denied these motions, and the case was ready for trial.

Discovery: Compulsory pretrial disclosure of information related to litigation by one party to another party. The major pretrial discovery devices are *interrogatories, deposition, production of documents and things, physical or mental examination,* and *requests for admission*. (For an overview of all these devices, see Exhibit 10.6 later in the chapter.)

Interrogatories: A method of discovery consisting of written questions about a lawsuit submitted by one party to another to help the sender prepare for trial.

Deposition: A method of discovery by which parties and their prospective witnesses are questioned outside the courtroom before trial. A pretrial question-and-answer session to help parties prepare for trial. The person who is *deposed* is called the *deponent*. A recording or transcript—a word-for-word account—is made of the deposition.

Request for admission: A method of discovery in which one party asks another to admit the truth of any matter relating to facts or the application of law to facts.

Subpoena duces tecum: A command that a witness appear at a certain time and place and bring specified things such as documents or records. (If ordered to give testimony, the subpoena would be called a *subpoena ad testificandum*.)

Order: An official command by the court requiring, allowing, or forbidding some act to be done.

Hearing: A proceeding designed to resolve issues of fact or law. Usually, an impartial officer presides, evidence is presented, etc. The hearing is *ex parte* if only one party is present; it is *adversarial* if both parties are present. Hearings occur in court as well as in administrative agencies.

Motion for summary judgment: A *summary judgment* is a judgment of the court that is rendered without a full trial because of the absence of conflict on any of the material facts. A motion for a summary judgment is a request by a party that a decision be reached on the basis of the submitted documents without going through a full trial. A summary judgment is normally allowed only when there is no dispute between the parties as to any of the material or significant facts. Summary judgment can be granted on the entire case or on individual claims or defenses within the case. The word *summary* means done relatively quickly and informally without going through an entire adversary hearing or a full trial.

As the trial date neared, each of the attorneys received a notice asking them to appear before a *magistrate* for a *pretrial conference*. On the appointed day, the attorneys met with the magistrate to prepare the case for trial. During the conference, the magistrate, with the help of the attorneys, prepared a pretrial statement for the trial judge on the case. It contained a statement of the facts that had been *stipulated* by the attorneys and the facts that were still *in issue*. It also listed the *tangible evidence* and witnesses that each attorney intended to *introduce* at the trial.

> **Magistrate:** A judicial officer having some but not all of the powers of a judge. In the federal trial courts (the U.S. District Courts), the magistrate may conduct many of the preliminary or pretrial proceedings in both civil and criminal cases.
>
> **Pretrial conference:** A meeting of the attorneys and the judge (or magistrate) before the trial to attempt to narrow the issues, to secure stipulations, and to make a final effort to settle the case without a trial. Also called a *trial management conference*.
>
> **Stipulated:** Agreed to. Once the parties have reached a *stipulation* (sometimes referred to in shorthand as a *stip*) about a fact, neither side is required to offer evidence as to the existence or nonexistence of that fact at trial.
>
> **In issue:** In dispute or question. If an *issue of fact* exists, then the existence or nonexistence of that fact must be established at trial. (An issue of fact is also called a factual issue, a factual question, or a question of fact.) If an *issue of law* exists, then the judge must rule on what the law is, what the law means, or how the law applies to the facts. (An issue of law is also called a legal issue, a legal question, or a question of law.)
>
> **Tangible evidence:** Evidence that can be seen or touched; evidence that has a physical form. *Intangible* evidence is evidence without physical form, such as a right that a person has. Such rights, however, are usually embodied or evidenced by something physical, e.g., a written contract.
>
> **Introduce evidence:** To place evidence formally before a court or other tribunal so that it will become part of the record for consideration by the judge, jury, or other decision-maker.

After some delay, the case was finally *set for trial*. All of the parties and their attorneys assembled in the courtroom. The judge entered, took the bench, and ordered the *bailiff* to summon a *jury panel* for the trial. Once the potential or prospective jurors were seated in the courtroom, *voir dire* began. Several jurors were *challenged for cause* and dismissed—one because she worked for the insurance company that had issued the policy on Miller's car. The position as to this prospective juror was that she might be *biased*. Several other jurors were dismissed as a result of *peremptory challenges*. Twelve jurors plus two *alternates* were eventually *impaneled* and seated in the jury box.

> **Set for trial:** To schedule a date when the trial is to begin.
>
> **Bailiff:** A court employee who keeps order in the courtroom and renders general administrative assistance to the judge.
>
> **Jury panel:** A group of citizens who have been called to jury duty. From this group, juries for particular trials are selected. Also called *venire*.
>
> **Voir dire:** ("to speak the truth") A preliminary examination of prospective jurors for the purpose of selecting persons qualified to sit on a jury.
>
> **Challenge for cause:** A request from a party to a judge that a prospective juror *not* be allowed to become a member of this jury because of specified causes or reasons.
>
> **Bias:** Prejudice for or against something or someone. An inclination or tendency to think or to act in a certain way. A danger of prejudgment.
>
> **Peremptory challenge:** A request from a party to a judge asking that a prospective juror *not* be allowed to become a member of this jury without stating a reason for this request. Both sides are allowed a limited number of peremptory challenges, but they will be granted as many challenges for cause as they can establish.
>
> **Alternate:** An extra juror who will take the place of a regular juror if one becomes incapacitated during the trial.
>
> **Impaneled:** Selected and sworn in (referring to a jury) (also spelled empaneled).

Before the jury was brought into the courtroom, Brown's attorney made a *motion in limine*. She wanted to prevent the other attorneys from introducing into evidence any reference to a case five years ago when Brown had been sued for negligently causing a brush fire in his neighborhood. The judge granted the motion.

When the jury was seated, Brown's attorney told the judge that she wanted to invoke the *rule on witnesses*. The judge agreed to *sequester* them. The bailiff led all of the witnesses (except for the parties themselves) out of the courtroom. Brown's attorney then began the trial with her *opening statement* to the jury. When she finished, Miller's attorney also delivered an opening statement. The attorney for Clay's estate, however, decided to reserve his opening statement until it was time for him to present the estate's case.

> **Motion in limine:** A request for a ruling on the admissibility of evidence prior to or during trial but before the evidence has been offered.
>
> **Rule on witnesses:** A rule that requires certain witnesses to be removed from the courtroom until it is time for their individual testimony so that they will not be able to hear each other's testimony.
>
> **Sequester:** To separate or isolate a jury or witness. (*Sequester* also means to seize or take and hold funds or other property.) Sometimes called *sequestrate*.
>
> **Opening statement:** An attorney's statement to the jury made before presenting evidence that summarizes the case he or she intends to try to establish during the trial.

Brown's attorney, whose client had the *burden of proof*, called her first witness, a 10-year-old boy who had seen the accident. Miller's attorney immediately rose and requested a *bench conference*. When all the attorneys had gathered around the bench, he stated that he *objected* to the witness on the basis of *competency*. The judge then *excused the jury* temporarily while he conducted a brief *examination* of the witness. The judge *overruled* the objection upon being satisfied that the boy was old enough to understand the obligation to tell the truth and had the ability to communicate what he knew.

> **Burden of proof:** The responsibility of proving a fact at the trial. Generally, the party making the factual allegation has the burden of proof as to that allegation.
>
> **Bench conference:** A discussion between the judge and the attorneys held at the judge's bench so that the jury cannot hear what is being said. Also called a *sidebar conference*.
>
> **Objection:** A formal challenge usually directed at the evidence that the other side is trying to pursue or introduce.
>
> **Competency:** Being allowed (having the legal capacity) to give testimony because the person understands the obligation to tell the truth, has the ability to communicate, and has knowledge of the topic of his or her testimony.
>
> **Excused the jury:** Asked the jury to leave the courtroom.
>
> **Examination:** Questioning, asking questions of.
>
> **Overrule:** To decide against or deny. (*Overrule* also means to reject or cancel an earlier opinion as precedent by rendering an opposite decision on the same question of law in a different litigation.)

The jury was brought back into the courtroom, and Brown's attorney began her *direct examination*. After a few questions, Miller's attorney again objected, this time on the *grounds* that the child's answer had been *hearsay*. The judge *sustained* the objection and, after instructing the jury to disregard the boy's answer, ordered it *stricken from the record*. Brown's attorney continued her examination of the witness for a few minutes before announcing that she had no further questions. The attorney for the estate then rose to conduct a brief *cross-examination* of the boy. He was followed by Miller's attorney, whose cross-examination was also brief. There was no *redirect examination* and, therefore, no *recross-examination*.

> **Direct examination:** The first questioning of a witness by the party who has called the witness. Also called *examination in chief*.
>
> **Grounds:** A reason that is legally sufficient to obtain a remedy or other result.
>
> **Hearsay:** An out-of-court statement offered to prove the truth of the matter asserted in the statement.
>
> **Sustain:** To uphold or agree with. (See the glossary for additional meanings of *sustain*.)
>
> **Strike from the record:** To remove the testimony or evidence from the written record or *transcript of the trial*.
>
> **Cross-examination:** Questioning a witness by an opponent after the other side called and questioned that witness. Generally, the person conducting the cross-examination must limit

himself or herself to the topics or subject matters raised during the direct examination of this witness by the other side.

Redirect examination: Another direct examination of a witness after he or she was cross-examined. The attorney who conducted the direct examination conducts the redirect examination.

Recross-examination: Another cross-examination of a witness after redirect examination. The attorney who conducted the cross-examination conducts the recross-examination.

Brown's attorney, Davis, called several other witnesses who had seen the accident occur. Each witness was examined and cross-examined in much the same fashion as the boy had been. Davis was about to call her fourth witness, Dr. Hadley, when the judge announced a brief recess for lunch. The judge admonished the jury not to discuss the case with anyone, even among themselves, and ordered everyone to be back in the courtroom by 2:00 P.M.

Dr. Hadley was called to the stand immediately after the lunch recess. Brown's attorney began her direct examination with a series of questions about the doctor's medical training and experience in order to *qualify* him as an *expert witness*. She then moved that Dr. Hadley be recognized as an expert witness. The *court*, with no objections by either defense counsel, granted the motion.

Qualify: To present evidence of a person's education and experience sufficient to convince the court that the witness has expertise in a particular area.

Expert witness: A person qualified by scientific, technical, or other specialized knowledge or experience to give an expert opinion relevant to a fact in dispute.

Court: Here refers to the judge trying the case.

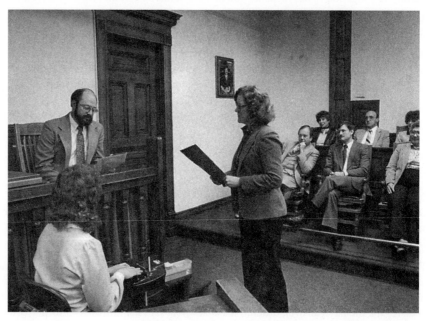

Attorney Davis conducts a direct examination of Dr. Hadley, the doctor who treated plaintiff Brown.

Brown's attorney then asked the doctor to testify as to the nature and extent of the injuries that the plaintiff, Brown, had suffered as a result of the accident. In addition to multiple cuts and bruises, the doctor stated that Brown had suffered a broken knee. The knee, in the doctor's opinion, had been permanently injured, and Brown would continue to suffer periodic pain and stiffness due to the injury. To show the expense that these injuries had cost Brown, the attorney produced the original copies of the bills that the doctor had sent to Brown. She handed the bills to the *clerk*, who marked them as plaintiff's *exhibit* number one. After allowing defense counsel to inspect the bills, Brown's attorney handed them to the doctor, who promptly identified them. The attorney then *moved the bills into evidence* and turned the witness over to defense counsel for cross-examination.

Clerk: The court employee who assists the judge with record keeping at the trial and other administrative duties.

Exhibit: A document, chart, or other object offered or introduced into evidence.

Move . . . into evidence: To request that the items be formally declared *admissible*. This is not the same as declaring them to be true. Admissible means that the items will be admitted simply for consideration as to their truth or believability.

It was late in the afternoon when Brown's attorney finished with her final witness, Brown himself. The judge did not want to recess for the day, however, until the attorneys for the defendants completed their cross-examination of Brown. After about an hour, all the defense attorneys completed their questioning of Brown, and Brown's attorney *rested her case*. She had concluded her *case-in-chief*. The judge *adjourned* the trial until the following morning.

Rest one's case: To announce formally that you have concluded the presentation of evidence (through the introduction of tangible evidence, through direct examination of your own witnesses, etc.). While the other side presents its case, however, you will be entitled to cross-examine its witnesses.

Case-in-chief: The presentation of evidence by one side, not including the evidence it introduces to counter the other side.

Adjourn: To halt the proceedings temporarily.

On the following morning, the attorney for Clay's estate advised the judge that he had a preliminary matter to bring up before the jury was brought into the courtroom. He then proceeded to make a motion for a *judgment as a matter of law* in favor of the estate on Brown's claim of negligence. The judge listened to arguments by the attorneys on the motion. He decided that he would neither deny nor grant the motion but would *take it under advisement*. Miller's attorney also moved for a judgment as a matter of law on the negligence claim of Clay's estate against Miller. After hearing the arguments on this motion, the judge denied it because Clay's estate had introduced sufficient evidence to make out a *prima facie case* of Miller's negligence. Hence he would allow this claim of negligence to go to the jury.

Judgment as a matter of law: A judgment on an issue in a federal jury trial (and in some state jury trials) that is ordered by the judge against a party because there is no legally sufficient evidentiary basis for a reasonable jury to find for that party on that issue. A judgment as a matter of law may be rendered before or after the verdict. In some state courts, this judgment is called a *directed verdict* if it is rendered before the jury reaches a verdict and is called a *judgment notwithstanding the verdict* if it is rendered after the jury reaches a verdict.

Take under advisement: To delay ruling on the motion until another time.

Prima facie case: A case, as presented, that will prevail unless contradicted and overcome by contrary evidence. The party's evidence, if believed by the jury, would be legally sufficient to support a verdict in favor of that party—that is, the party has introduced evidence that, if believed, would include all the facts necessary to establish a cause of action. If the plaintiff *fails* to establish a prima facie case, the judge will decide the case in favor of the defendant without any further proceedings. If the judge finds that there *is* a prima facie case, the defendant will be allowed an opportunity to produce contrary evidence. The case will then go to the jury to decide which version of the facts meets the *standard of proof* (see definition below).

The jury was summoned into the courtroom and seated in the jury box for the second day of the trial. The attorney for the estate began his case by making an opening statement to the jury, reserved from the previous day. He then proceeded to call his witnesses. He had only a few witnesses and was able to conclude his case just before noon, at which time he introduced Clay's death certificate into evidence. The judge then declared a recess for lunch.

Miller's attorney began to present his case in the afternoon, and by late afternoon, he, too, had rested his case. The judge dismissed the jury until the following morning and told the attorneys to be prepared for *closing arguments* at that time. He also asked them to submit any *jury instructions* they would like to request so that he could review them. Brown's attorney requested an instruction that the codefendants had to overcome a *presumption* of negligence against them. The judge denied this request. Finally, he announced that he had decided to deny the estate's earlier motion for a judgment as a matter of law.

Closing argument: The final statements by opposing trial attorneys to the jury (or to the trial judge if there is no jury) summarizing the evidence and requesting a favorable decision. Also called *final argument*, *summation*, or *summing up*.

Jury instructions: A statement of the guidelines and law given to the jury by the judge for use in deciding the issues of fact in its verdict. The instructions to the jury are also referred to as the *charge* to the jury. The attorneys are usually allowed to submit proposed instructions for consideration by the judge.

Presumption: An assumption or inference that a certain fact is true once another fact is established. A *rebuttable* presumption is an assumption that can be overcome (rebutted) or changed if the other side introduces enough facts to overcome it. If the other side does not rebut the presumption, then the assumption stands. An *irrebuttable* presumption cannot be overcome no matter how convincing the evidence of the other side against the assumption.

Closing arguments began late the following morning. Each attorney carefully reviewed the evidence for the jury and argued for a *verdict* in favor of his or her client. Following a brief recess for lunch, the judge thanked the alternate jurors for their time and dismissed them. He then began to instruct the remaining twelve jurors as to the law they were to follow in finding the facts and in reaching a verdict. He said that they, as jurors, were the finders of fact and were to base their decision solely upon the testimony and exhibits introduced during the trial. He explained the concept of burden of proof and stated which party had to carry this burden as to each of the various *elements* of negligence. Each element had to be proved by a *preponderance of evidence*. This was the *standard of proof* for this kind of case. Finally, he described the manner in which they should compute the amount of damages, if any, suffered by the parties. The jury was then led out of the courtroom to deliberate on its verdict. The judge retired to his chambers, and the attorneys settled back with their clients to wait.

Verdict: The final conclusion of the jury.

Elements: Here, the components of a cause of action. (An element is a portion of a rule that is a precondition of the applicability of the entire rule.)

Preponderance of evidence: The burden of proof that is met when the evidence establishes that it is more likely than not that the facts are as alleged. Also called *fair preponderance of evidence*.

Standard of proof: A statement of how convincing a version of a fact must be before the trier of facts (usually the jury) can accept it as true. The main standards of proof are proof *beyond a reasonable doubt* (in criminal cases only), proof *by clear and convincing evidence*, and proof by *preponderance of evidence*.

After about an hour, the judge received a note from the foreman of the jury, asking that the jury be allowed to view several of the exhibits. The items requested were the medical bills allegedly incurred by Brown and Clay. The attorneys for Brown and for the estate took this as a good sign—the jury had probably decided the case against Miller and was now trying to compute damages.

A second note arrived in another hour, announcing that the jury had reached a verdict. The bailiff summoned everyone back to the courtroom, and the jury came in a few minutes later. At the clerk's request, the foreman rose to read the verdict. On Brown's original complaint against Miller for negligence, the jury found for Brown and against Miller, awarding Brown $30,000 in damages. However, on Brown's complaint against Clay's estate (the codefendant), the jury decided in favor of the estate, finding that Clay had not been negligent. The jury found for the estate on its cross-claim against its codefendant, Miller, awarding $750,000 in damages to the estate. Finally, the jury found against Miller on his own cross-claim against the estate, as well as on his counterclaim against Brown. The judge entered a *judgment* against Miller in the amounts awarded by the jury. After denying a motion by Miller for a judgment as a matter of law, he thanked the jurors and dismissed them.

Judgment: The final conclusion of a court that resolves a legal dispute or that specifies what further proceedings are needed to resolve it. Many judgments order the losing party to do something (such as pay damages) or to refrain from doing something. A *declaratory judgment* establishes the rights and obligations of the parties, but it does not order the parties to do or refrain from doing anything.

Miller's attorney immediately made a *motion for a new trial*, arguing several possible grounds. When this motion was denied by the trial judge, he moved for a reduction of the verdict on the grounds that the amounts awarded were excessive. This motion was also denied, and the attorney announced his intention to *appeal*. The judge did, however, grant Miller a *stay* of the judgment, conditioned upon his filing a *timely notice of appeal* and posting the appropriate *bond*.

Motion for a new trial: A request that the judge set aside the judgment and order a new trial on the basis that the trial was improper or unfair due to specified prejudicial errors that occurred.

Appeal: Asking a higher tribunal to review or reconsider the decision of an inferior tribunal.

Stay: The suspension of a judgment or proceeding.

Timely: Within the time set by contract or law.

Notice of appeal: Notice given to a court (through filing) and to the opposing party (through service) of an intention to appeal.

Bond: An obligation to perform an act (e.g., payment of a sum of money) upon the occurrence or nonoccurrence of a designated condition. Here the bond secures the payment of the judgment.

Miller asked his attorney what the $30,000 verdict against him meant. Since Brown had originally sued for $100,000, could Brown later sue Miller again for the rest of the amount he claimed? The attorney explained that, because of the stay granted by the judge, Miller would not have to pay anything until a decision on appeal had been reached. Furthermore, Brown could not sue Miller again on the same cause of action because Brown had received a *judgment on the merits* that would be *res judicata* and would *bar* any later suit based on the same facts. This would also be true of a later action by Clay's estate against Miller.

Judgment on the merits: A judgment, rendered after evidentiary inquiry and argument, determining which party is in the right, as opposed to a judgment based solely on a technical point or procedural error.

Res judicata: ("a thing adjudicated") A final judgment on the merits will preclude the same parties from later relitigating the same claim and any other claim based on the same facts or transaction that could have been raised in the first suit but was not. Also called *claim preclusion*.

Bar: Prevent or stop.

Miller's attorney filed his notice of appeal with the U. S. Court of Appeals and posted bond the following week. As attorney for the *appellant*, it was also his duty to see to it that the *record*, including *transcripts* and copies of exhibits, was transmitted to the court of appeals and that the case was *docketed* by the clerk of that court. Miller's attorney then had 40 days in which to draft and file his *appellate brief* with the court of appeals. He served copies of the brief on the attorneys for the *appellees* (Brown and Clay's estate) who in turn filed their appellate briefs concerning the *issues on appeal*.

Appellant: The party bringing an appeal because of alleged errors made by a lower tribunal. Sometimes called *petitioner*.

Record: The official collection of all the trial pleadings, exhibits, orders, and word-for-word testimony that took place during the trial.

Transcript: A word-for-word account. A written copy of oral testimony. The court reporter prepares this transcription, which is paid for by the parties requesting it.

Docket: A court's list of its pending cases. Also called *calendar*. Once all the necessary papers have been filed, the appeal is "docketed" by the clerk—that is, placed on the court's official calendar.

Appellate brief: A document submitted (filed) by a party to an appellate court (and served on an opposing party) in which arguments are presented on why the appellate court should affirm (approve), reverse, or otherwise modify what a lower court has done. Both the appellant and the appellee prepare appellate briefs. If the appellant responds to the appellate brief of the appellee, it is often called a *reply brief*.

Appellee: The party against whom the appeal is brought (also called the *respondent*). Often, the appellee is satisfied with what the trial court did and wishes the appellate court to approve of or *affirm* the trial court's rulings.

Issues on appeal: The claimed errors of law committed by a lower court. The appellate court does not retry the case. No witnesses are called, and no testimony is taken by the appellate court. The court examines the record and determines whether errors of law were committed by the lower court.

Several months passed before the attorneys finally received a notice from the clerk of the court of appeals that the appeal had been scheduled for *oral argument* before a three-judge *panel* of the court. The arguments were heard a few weeks later. Six months after oral argument, the attorneys received the decision of the court in its written *opinion*. By a vote of two to one (one judge *dissenting*), the court *affirmed* the judgments against Miller. The only error that the majority found was the admission of certain testimony offered through Brown's expert witness. However, because Miller's attorney had not objected to this testimony at trial, the opinion stated, he had *waived* this defect.

Oral argument: A spoken presentation to the court on a legal issue, e.g., telling an appellate court why the rulings of a lower tribunal were valid or were in error.

Panel: The group of judges, usually three, who decide a case in a court with a larger number of judges. (For other meanings of panel, see the glossary.)

Opinion: A court's written explanation of how it applied the law to the facts to resolve a legal dispute. (An opinion is also called a case.) One case can contain several opinions: a majority opinion, a concurring opinion (see the definition that follows), and a dissenting opinion. Opinions are often collected in official and unofficial *reporters*.

Dissent: A judge's vote against the result reached by the judges in the *majority* on a case. If a judge agrees with the result reached by the majority but disagrees with the reasons the majority used to support that result, the judge would cast a *concurring* vote and might write a separate concurring opinion. A *plurality* opinion is the controlling opinion that is joined by the largest number of judges on the bench short of a majority. There can be concurring and dissenting votes (and opinions) against the plurality.

Affirm: To agree with or uphold the lower court judgment. If the appellate court *remanded* the case, it would be sending it back to the lower tribunal with instructions on how to proceed, e.g., instructions on correcting the errors made by the lower tribunal. If the appellate court *reversed* the court below, it would have changed the result reached below.

Waive: To lose or relinquish a right or privilege expressly or by implication. Examples of the latter include failing to claim it at the proper time or acting in a manner inconsistent with its existence. Here, the court is referring to the rule that failure to object during trial is an implied waiver of the right to complain about the alleged error on appeal.

Miller, undaunted, *petitioned* for a *rehearing* by the court *en banc*. The petition was denied. Miller then discussed the possibility of further appeal with his attorney. The attorney explained that Miller could, if he desired, try to appeal to the U. S. Supreme Court. He cautioned Miller, however, that he could not *appeal as a matter of right* in this case but would be limited to a petition for a *writ of certiorari*. He advised Miller that it was extremely unlikely that the Supreme Court would grant the petition and that it probably would not be worth the expense. Miller agreed, and no further appeal was attempted. Shortly thereafter the court of appeals issued its *mandate*, and the case was returned to the district court, where Miller, through his insurance company, *satisfied* the judgment.

Petition: A formal request or motion. (The word *petition* is sometimes synonymous with the word *complaint*, the plaintiff's pleading that attempts to state a cause of action.)

Rehearing: A second hearing by a court to reconsider the decision it made after an earlier hearing.

En banc: By the entire court. The *panel* of judges that heard the first appeal may have consisted of only three judges, yet the number of judges on the full court may be much larger.

Appeal as a matter of right: The appeal of a case that an appellate court must hear; it has no discretion on whether to take the appeal.

Writ of certiorari: (cert.) An order (or writ) by a higher court that a lower court send up the record of a case because the higher court has decided to use its discretion to review that case. The writ is used in a case in which the appellate court has discretion to accept or reject the appeal. If the writ is denied, the court refuses to hear the appeal, and, in effect, the judgment below stands unchanged. If the writ is granted, the lower court "sends up" the record and the appeal proceeds.

Mandate: The order of the court. Here, the mandate of the appellate court was to affirm the trial court's judgment.

Satisfy: To comply with a legal obligation (here, to pay the judgment award).

2. Criminal Liability

As Brown was leaving the hospital after having recovered from his injury, he was met at the door by two police officers. The officers produced a *warrant* and advised Brown that he was under arrest. After he was read his rights, he was taken to the police station. Hence, in addition to suing Clay's estate and Miller, Brown was now defending himself in a criminal *prosecution*.

> **Warrant:** An order from a judicial officer authorizing an act, e.g., the arrest of an individual, the search of property.

> **Prosecution:** The bringing and processing of legal proceedings against someone; usually a criminal proceeding, but the word includes civil proceedings as well. (The verb is *prosecute*.) The words *prosecution* and *prosecutor* also refer to the attorney who represents the government in a criminal case.

The following morning Brown was taken before a judge for his *initial appearance*. The judge advised Brown that he had been charged with a *felony*, possession of narcotics with intent to distribute. He then advised Brown of his rights, including his right to be represented by an attorney. Since Brown was unemployed and without adequate funds to pay an attorney, the judge asked him if he would like the court to appoint an attorney to handle the case. Brown said yes and was given *assigned counsel* to represent him. The judge, at the attorney's request, then agreed to give Brown a chance to confer with his new attorney before continuing the hearing.

> **Initial appearance:** The first court appearance by the accused during which the court (a) informs him or her of the charges, (b) makes a decision on bail, and (c) determines the date of the next court proceeding.

> **Felony:** Any crime punishable by death or by imprisonment for a term exceeding a year; a crime more serious than a *misdemeanor*.

> **Assigned counsel:** An attorney (usually in private practice) appointed by the court to represent an *indigent* person in a criminal or civil case. If the attorney is a government employee handling criminal cases, he or she is often called a *public defender*. *Indigent* means without funds to hire a private attorney; or impoverished.

When the case was recalled, Brown and his court-appointed attorney again approached the bench and stood before the judge. The attorney handed the clerk a praecipe formally entering his name as attorney of record for Brown and advised the judge that he was prepared to discuss the matter of *bail*. He proceeded to describe for the judge the details of Brown's background—his education, employment record, length of residence in the city, etc. He concluded by asking that he be released on *personal recognizance*. The prosecutor was then given an opportunity to speak. He recommended a high bond, pointing out that the defendant was unemployed and had no close relatives in the area. These facts, he argued, coupled with the serious nature of a felony charge, indicated a very real risk that the defendant might try to flee. The judge nevertheless agreed to release Brown on his personal recognizance and set a date for a *preliminary hearing* the following week.

> **Bail:** Money or other property deposited with the court as security to ensure that the defendant will reappear at designated times. Failure to appear forfeits the security. *Bail* also means the release of the defendant upon posting this security.

> **Personal recognizance:** Pretrial release of a defendant in a criminal case without posting a bond, based solely on a promise to appear. Also called *release on own recognizance* (ROR).

> **Preliminary hearing:** A pretrial criminal proceeding to determine if *probable cause* (see definition below) exists that the defendant has committed a crime. Also called *probable cause hearing*.

The only witness at the preliminary hearing was the police officer who investigated the accident. The officer testified that when he helped pull Brown out of the car, he noticed a small paper sack sticking out from under the passenger's side of the front seat. Several glassine envelopes containing a white powdery substance, the officer said, had spilled out of the sack. The substance, totaling about one-half ounce, was tested and proved to be 80 percent pure heroin. Brown's attorney cross-examined the officer briefly, but little additional information came out. The judge found that there was *probable cause* to hold the defendant and ordered the case *bound over* for *grand jury* action. He continued Brown's release on personal recognizance.

Probable cause: A reasonable belief that a specific crime has been committed and that the accused committed the crime.

Bound over: Held or transferred for further court proceedings.

Grand jury: A jury of inquiry (not a trial jury) that receives accusations in criminal cases, hears the evidence of the prosecutor, and issues *indictments* (see definition below) when satisfied that a trial should be held.

Shortly after the preliminary hearing, Brown's attorney went to the prosecutor to see if he could work out an informal disposition of the charge. He tried to convince the prosecutor to enter a *nolle prosequi* on the charge, explaining that Brown had simply been offered a ride home and was not aware that the heroin was in the car. The prosecutor was unwilling to drop the charge. However, he was willing to "nolle" the felony charge of possession with intent to distribute if Brown would agree to *plead* guilty to the lesser offense of simple possession of a dangerous drug, a *misdemeanor*. The attorney said he would speak to his client about it.

Nolle prosequi: A statement by the prosecutor that he or she is unwilling to prosecute the case. The charges, in effect, are dropped.

Plead: To file a pleading, enter a plea, or argue a case in court. In a criminal case, to plead means to admit or deny the charges made by the prosecutor.

Misdemeanor: A crime, not as serious as a felony, punishable by fine or by detention in an institution other than a prison or penitentiary.

He spoke to Brown that same afternoon, told him about the *plea bargaining* session, and advised him of the prosecutor's offer. Brown was not interested. He felt he was innocent and was unwilling to plead guilty, even to a misdemeanor.

Plea bargaining: Negotiations whereby an accused pleads guilty to a lesser included offense or to one of multiple charges in exchange for the prosecution's agreement to support a dismissal of some charges or a lighter sentence. Also called *negotiated plea*.

Several weeks went by before Brown's attorney was notified that the grand jury had returned an *indictment* against his client. The next step would be the *arraignment* on the following Monday. On this date, Brown and his attorney appeared before the judge, and Brown was formally notified of the indictment. He entered a plea of not guilty to the charge. The judge set a trial date ten weeks from that day and again agreed to continue Brown's release on personal recognizance.

Indictment: A formal document issued by a grand jury accusing the defendant of a crime. (If the state has no grand jury, the accusation is often contained in a document called an *information*.)

Arraignment: A court proceeding in which the defendant is formally charged with a crime and enters a plea. Arrangements are then made for the next proceeding.

The day for the trial arrived. Brown's attorney and the prosecutor announced that they were ready. Voir dire was held, and a jury was impaneled. The trial itself was relatively uneventful, lasting less than a day. The prosecutor, following a brief opening statement, presented only two witnesses: the police officer who had been at the scene and an expert from the police lab who identified the substance as heroin. He then rested his case. Brown's attorney made his opening statement and presented his only witness, Brown himself. The jury listened attentively as Brown, on direct examination, explained the events leading up to the accident and his subsequent arrest. Not only had he been unaware of the heroin, he testified, but he had never even seen it, since he had been knocked unconscious by the accident and had not revived until he was in the ambulance. Brown had a previous conviction for shoplifting, and the prosecutor on cross-examination attempted to use this conviction to *impeach* Brown's testimony. Brown's attorney successfully objected, arguing that the conviction, which had occurred eight years previously, was too remote to be *relevant*. The judge agreed and prohibited any mention of the prior conviction. After a few more questions, the prosecutor concluded his cross-examination, and the defense rested its case.

Impeach: To challenge; to challenge the credibility of.

Relevant: Logically tending to establish or disprove a fact. Pertinent. Relevant evidence is evidence having any tendency to make the existence of a fact more probable or less probable than it would be without the evidence.

Both sides presented their closing arguments following the lunch recess. The judge then instructed the jury; he described the elements of the offense and explained that the burden of proof in a criminal case is on the *government*. That burden, he continued, is to prove each element of the offense *beyond a reasonable doubt*. The jury took less than 45 minutes to reach its verdict. All parties quickly reassembled in the courtroom to hear the foreman announce the verdict *acquitting* Brown of the offense. A *poll* of the jury, requested by the prosecutor, confirmed the result, and the judge advised Brown that he was free to go.

Government: Here, the prosecutor.

Beyond a reasonable doubt: The standard of proof required for conviction in a criminal case. If any reasonable doubt exists as to any element of the crime, the defendant cannot be convicted. Reasonable doubt is such doubt as would cause prudent persons to hesitate before acting in matters of importance to themselves.

Acquit: To declare that the accused is innocent of the crime.

Poll: To ask each member of a body (e.g., a jury) that has just voted to state how he or she individually voted. (*Poll* also means to seek a sampling of opinions.)

Generally, criminal cases in which the defendant is acquitted may not be appealed by the prosecutor. Hence, in this case, there was no appeal of the trial judgment. If a defendant is convicted, he or she is sentenced. A convicted defendant *does* have the right to appeal.

3. Administrative Dispute

The day after his indictment on the felony charge, Brown went down to the state employment office to apply for **unemployment compensation**. After being interviewed by a clerk, he filled out an application form. The clerk told Brown that he would receive a letter in about a week notifying him of the agency's initial determination of his eligibility. If he were eligible, his benefits would start in ten days.

Brown received the letter a few days later. It advised him that, although he was otherwise eligible for benefits, a routine check with his former employer had disclosed that he had been fired for misconduct. For this reason, the letter stated, he would be deemed disqualified for a nine-week period. Moreover, the benefits due for those nine weeks would be deducted from the total amount he would otherwise have been entitled to receive. If he wished to appeal this decision, the letter went on, he could request an *administrative hearing* within ten days.

Unemployment compensation: Temporary income from the government to persons who have lost their jobs (for reasons other than misconduct) and are looking for work.

Administrative hearing: A proceeding at an administrative agency presided over by a hearing officer (e.g., an administrative law judge) to resolve a controversy. The hearing is usually conducted less formally than a court hearing or trial.

Brown felt that he needed some legal advice, but he was still out of work and broke. (The lawsuit in the civil action had not been filed yet—it would be well over a year before the case would be tried, the appeal completed, and the judgment award actually paid.) Brown, therefore, decided to obtain help from the local legal aid office. He explained his problem to a receptionist and was introduced to the paralegal who would be handling his case. The paralegal, an expert in unemployment compensation law, interviewed Brown and helped him fill out a form requesting a hearing. He said he would let Brown know as soon as the date was set. Brown left and the paralegal, after consulting with his supervisor, began to research and draft a *memorandum* to submit to the *hearing examiner* on Brown's behalf.

Memorandum: Here, a written presentation of a party's arguments on the facts and legal issues in the case. (This memorandum is referred to as an external memorandum of law, one addressed to someone outside the law office. See Exhibit 12.3 in chapter 12.)

Hearing examiner: One who presides over an administrative hearing and makes findings of fact and rulings of law, or who recommends such findings and rulings to someone else in the agency who will make the final decision. (The examiner is also called *administrative law judge, referee,* or *hearing officer.*)

In Brown's state, a claimant can have nonattorney representation at unemployment compensation hearings. Therefore, the paralegal at the legal aid office was allowed to represent Brown at

> **unemployment compensation**
> Temporary income from the government to persons who have lost their jobs (for reasons other than misconduct) and are looking for work.

his hearing. The only witnesses at the hearing were Brown and his former boss, Frank Best. Best told the examiner about Brown's arrest and about the thefts from the warehouse. Taken together, he argued, these events make it impossible for him to trust Brown on the job any longer. Brown, in turn, denied any participation in the thefts and maintained his innocence on the drug charge. (Brown had not yet been acquitted of the felony.) The hearing examiner, at the close of the proceedings, thanked the parties and promised a decision within a few days.

The hearing examiner's decision arrived shortly thereafter in a document labeled *Proposed Findings and Rulings.* The last paragraph contained the examiner's recommended decision. The hearing examiner agreed with Brown that his boss's mere suspicion that Brown was involved in the thefts was not enough to justify a finding of misconduct. However, the decision went on, the pending criminal charges for a drug-related offense did provide the employer with good cause to fire Brown, since drug involvement could affect his ability to operate a truck safely. The paragraph concluded by recommending a finding of misconduct and the imposition of a nine-week penalty period.

> **Proposed findings and rulings:** Recommended conclusions presented to someone else in the administrative agency who will make the final decision.

A second letter arrived ten days later containing the *administrative decision* of the agency. The letter, signed by the director of the local agency, adopted the recommended decision of the hearing examiner. This decision, the letter concluded, could be appealed within fifteen days to the State Unemployment Compensation *Board of Appeals.* Brown immediately appealed.

> **Administrative decision:** An administrative agency's resolution of a controversy (follow-ing a hearing) involving the application of the regulations, statutes, or executive orders that govern the agency. (See Exhibit 6.1 in chapter 6.)
>
> **Board of appeals:** The unit within an administrative agency to which a party can appeal a decision of the agency.

Copies of the hearing transcript along with memoranda from both sides were filed with the Board of Appeals. The board, exercising its *discretion,* refused to allow oral arguments before it and reversed the decision reached *below.* It issued a short administrative decision stating that, while Best may have had cause to be suspicious of Brown, there was not sufficient evidence of actual misconduct on Brown's part. The Board, in this final administrative decision, ordered the local office to begin paying benefits immediately, including back benefits to cover the period since Brown had first applied.

> **Discretion:** The power to choose among various courses of conduct based solely on one's reasoned judgment or preference.
>
> **Below:** Pertaining to a lower tribunal (here, the office of the hearing examiner). (See the glossary for an additional definition.)

Best decided to appeal this administrative decision in a state court. He was allowed to do so, since he had *exhausted* his *administrative remedies.* He filed a complaint in the county court seeking review of the Board's decision. He submitted the entire record from the proceedings below and asked the court for a *trial de novo.* Brown, now represented by an attorney from the legal aid office, filed his answer and immediately made a motion for summary judgment. The court, upon a review of the record and the pleadings, granted the motion and affirmed the judgment of the Board of Appeals. Best, after discussing the case at length with his attorney, decided against a further appeal of the case to the state court of appeals.

> **Exhaust administrative remedies:** To go through all dispute-solving avenues that are available in an administrative agency before asking a court to review what the agency did. A court generally will not allow a party to appeal an administrative decision until adminis-trative remedies are exhausted.
>
> **Trial de novo:** A new trial as if a prior one had not taken place.

Many of the steps described in the litigation woes of Michael Brown, which you have just read, are outlined in Exhibit 10.2 (overview of civil litigation) and in Exhibit 10.3 (overview of criminal litigation).

EXHIBIT 10.2	Overview of Civil Litigation

(Possible proceedings where administrative decisions, court rulings, and opinions could be written. The events and their sequence presented here are examples only.)

EVENT	DECISIONS, RULINGS, AND OPINIONS	DEFINITIONS	POSSIBLE PARALEGAL ROLES
I. Agency Stage 1. Someone protests an action taken by the *administrative agency* 2. *Administrative hearing* 3. *Intra-agency appeal* to a commission, board of appeals, director, or secretary within the agency. (If no agency is involved, the litigation begins in court at the pretrial stage.)	■ A mid-level agency official (e.g., hearing examiner), writes a recommended decision. ■ The commission, board of appeals, director, or secretary writes an *administrative decision*.	*Administrative agency:* a governmental body, other than a court or legislature, that carries out (i.e., administers or executes) the statutes of the legislature, the executive orders of the chief executive, and its own regulations. *Administrative decision:* an administrative agency's resolution of a controversy (following a hearing) involving the application of the regulations, statutes, or executive orders that govern the agency. *Administrative hearing:* a proceeding at an administrative agency presided over by a hearing officer (e.g., hearing examiner) to resolve a controversy. *Intra-agency appeal:* a review by an agency of an earlier decision within the same agency to determine if the earlier decision was correct.	**a.** Open case file. **b.** Interview client or do follow-up interview. **c.** Interview witnesses **d.** Conduct investigation. **e.** Organize and help manage the case file. **f.** Draft correspondence to agency. **g.** Represent client at agency hearing (if authorized to do so).
II. Pretrial Stage 4. Plaintiff files a *complaint* 5. Court clerk issues a *summons* 6. *Service of process* on defendant 7. Defendant files an *answer* 8. Compulsory *mediation* 9. *Discovery* by *interrogatories* 10. *Discovery* by *deposition* 11. Other discovery 12. Pretrial *motions* 13. *Settlement* efforts 14. *Voir dire*	■ The trial court often makes rulings concerning these events but rarely writes an opinion on any of the rulings. ■ Occasionally, a party may be allowed to appeal a pretrial ruling to an appeals court, which may write an opinion affirming, modifying, or reversing the ruling. Such an appeal is called an *interlocutory appeal*. It takes place before the trial court reaches a final judgment.	*Complaint:* a plaintiff's first pleading, stating a claim against the defendant (also called *petition*). *Summons:* a notice directing the defendant to appear in court and answer the plaintiff's complaint or face a default judgment. *Service of process:* a formal delivery of notice to a defendant that a suit has been initiated to which he or she must respond. *Answer:* the first pleading of the defendant that responds to the plaintiff's claims. *Compulsory mediation:* in some kinds of cases (e.g., medical malpractice), the parties are required to try to resolve their dispute by mediation (see definition in next section) before proceeding with their case in court. *Discovery:* compulsory exchanges of factual information between parties in litigation. *Interrogatories:* a discovery device consisting of written questions about a lawsuit submitted by one party to another. *Deposition:* a discovery device by which parties or their prospective witnesses are questioned outside the courtroom before trial. *Motion:* an application or request made to a court or other	**a.–d.** Same as above if the case begins in court rather than in an administrative agency. **e.** Perform legal research. **f.** Help draft complaint and other pleadings. **g.** Schedule discovery. **h.** Draft discovery requests and motions. **i.** Draft responses to discovery requests and motions. **j.** Summarize (digest) facts obtained through discovery. (For other discovery tasks, see Exhibit 10.6 later in the chapter.) **k.** Assemble trial notebook. **l.** Help prepare and coordinate trial exhibits. **m.** Draft voir dire questions for prospective jurors. **n.** Help evaluate prospective witnesses during voir dire.

(continues)

EXHIBIT 10.2	Overview of Civil Litigation—*continued*		

EVENT	DECISIONS, RULINGS, AND OPINIONS	DEFINITIONS	POSSIBLE PARALEGAL ROLES
		decision-making body seeking to obtain a favorable action or ruling (example: motion to dismiss). *Settlement:* an agreement resolving a dispute without full litigation. *Voir dire:* a preliminary examination of prospective jurors to sit on a jury (not all cases are tried by a jury). *Interlocutory appeal:* an appeal that occurs before the trial court reaches its final judgment; an interim appeal.	

III. Trial Stage
 	
15. *Opening statement* of plaintiff
16. *Opening statement* of defendant
17. Plaintiff presents its case:
  a. *evidence* introduced
  b. *direct examination*
  c. *cross-examination*
18. *Motions* to dismiss
19. Defendant presents its case:
  a. *evidence* introduced
  b. *direct examination*
  c. *cross-examination*
20. Closing arguments to jury by attorneys
21. Jury instructions by judge
22. *Verdict* of jury
23. *Judgment* of court
	■ The trial court often makes rulings concerning these events, but rarely writes an opinion on any of the rulings.
	■ After the trial, the trial court delivers its judgment. Usually, no *opinion* (explaining the judgment) is written.
	■ Several trial courts, however, such as federal trial courts (United States District Courts) and New York State trial courts, do sometimes write trial court opinions.
		Opening statement: an attorney's statement to the jury made before presenting evidence that summarizes the case he or she intends to try to establish during the trial. *Evidence:* anything that could be offered to prove or disprove an alleged fact. *Direct examination:* the first questioning of a witness by the party who has called the witness; also called *examination in chief.* *Cross examination:* questioning a witness by an opponent after the other side called and questioned that witness. *Jury instructions:* a statement of the guidelines and law given to the jury by the judge for use in deciding the issues of fact in its verdict; also called the *charge.* *Verdict:* the final conclusion of the jury. *Judgment:* the final conclusion of a court that resolves a legal dispute or that specifies what further proceedings are needed to resolve it. *opinion:* a court's written explanation of how it applied the law to the facts before it to resolve a legal dispute.	**a.** Coordinate scheduling of witnesses.
			b. Take notes during trial.
			c. Assist attorney with documents and exhibits.
			d. Perform last-minute legal research.
			e. Compare a trial witness's testimony with what he or she said in a deposition or in an answer to an interrogatory.
			f. Perform other tasks needed by the attorney conducting the trial.

IV. Appeal Stage 24. Filing of *notice of appeal* 25. Filing of *appellant's appellate brief* 26. Filing of *appellee's appellate brief* 27. Filing of appellant's *reply brief* 28. Oral argument by attorneys 29. *Judgment* of court	■ An opinion of the intermediate appellate court is often written. ■ This opinion of the middle appeals court might be further appealed to the highest court, in which event another opinion could be written. [Note that in some states there is no intermediate appeals court; the appeal goes directly from the trial court to the highest state court. See Exhibit 6.2 in chapter 6.]	*Notice of appeal:* notice given to a court (through filing) and to the opposing party (through service) of an intention to appeal. *Appellant:* the party bringing an appeal because of alleged errors made by a lower tribunal appeal. *Appellee,* the party against whom the appeal is brought; also called *respondent.* *Appellate brief:* a document submitted by a party to an appellate court in which arguments are	**a.** Draft and file the notice of appeal. **b.** Order the trial transcript. **c.** Summarize (digest) trial testimony relevant to issues to be raised on appeal. **d.** Cite check the appellate brief (e.g., making sure all citations are in proper form, Shepardizing or KeyCiting all laws cited to make sure they have not been repealed or overruled, etc.).

(continues)

EXHIBIT 10.2	Overview of Civil Litigation—*continued*		

EVENT	DECISIONS, RULINGS, AND OPINIONS	DEFINITIONS	POSSIBLE PARALEGAL ROLES
		presented on why the appellate court should affirm (approve), reverse, or otherwise modify what a lower court has done *Reply brief:* an appellate brief of the appellant that responds to the appellate brief of the appellee; any appellate brief that responds to an opponent's appellate brief.	
V. Enforcement Stage 30. *Posttrial discovery* 31. *Execution* by the sheriff	■ Court opinions or rulings are not common at this stage unless the parties disagree about something that requires a decision from a judge.	*Posttrial discovery:* compulsory disclosure of information between parties after a trial to help the party who won a money judgment (called the *judgment creditor*) against the losing party who must pay such a judgment (called the *judgment debtor*). An example would be a deposition of the judgment debtor to help identify his or her assets. *Execution:* the process of carrying into effect the decisions in a judgment, e.g., a command or writ to a court officer (e.g., sheriff) to seize and sell the property of the losing litigant in order to satisfy the judgment debt.	**a.** Investigate judgment debtor's assets. **b.** Schedule posttrial discovery of judgment debtor. **c.** Arrange for sheriff to begin execution of the judgment.

EXHIBIT 10.3	Overview of Criminal Litigation

(Possible proceedings where court rulings and opinions could be written. The events and their sequence presented here are examples only.)

EVENT	RULINGS AND OPINIONS	DEFINITIONS	POSSIBLE PARALEGAL ROLES
I. Pretrial Stage 1. *Arrest* 2. *Booking* 3. *Initial appearance* before a judge or a magistrate 4. *Preliminary hearing* 5. *Indictment* by grand jury 6. *Arraignment* 7. Plea bargaining 8. Discovery 9. Pretrial motions 10. *Voir dire*	■ The trial court often makes rulings concerning these events, but rarely writes an opinion on any of the rulings. ■ Occasionally, a party may be allowed to appeal a pretrial ruling immediately to an appeals court, which may write an opinion affirming, modifying, or reversing the ruling. This *interlocutory appeal* takes place before the trial court reaches a final judgment.	*Arrest:* taking someone into custody to answer a criminal charge. *Booking:* entering charges against someone on a police register. *Initial appearance:* the first court appearance by the accused during which the court (a) informs him or her of the charges (b) makes a decision on bail, and (c) determines the date of the next court proceeding. *Preliminary hearing:* a pretrial criminal proceeding to determine if probable cause exists that the defendant has committed a crime; also called *probable cause hearing.* *Indictment:* a formal document issued by a grand jury accusing the defendant of a crime. (If no	**a.** Conduct investigation of the charges (assuming the paralegal works for the defense attorney). **b.** Prepare facts needed to argue for a low bail or release on personal recognizance (ROR). **c.** Help draft motions, e.g., motion to suppress. **d.** Draft discovery requests and motions. **e.** Summarize (digest) facts obtained through discovery. (For other discovery tasks, see Exhibit 10.6 later in the chapter.) **f.** Assemble trial notebook **g.** Help prepare and coordinate trial exhibits. **h.** Help evaluate prospective witnesses during voir dire.

(continues)

EXHIBIT 10.3	Overview of Criminal Litigation—*continued*		
EVENT	**RULINGS AND OPINIONS**	**DEFINITIONS**	**POSSIBLE PARALEGAL ROLES**
		grand jury is involved in the case, the accusation is contained in a document called an *information*.) *Arraignment*: a court proceeding in which the defendant is formally charged with a crime and enters a plea. Arrangements are then made for the next proceeding. *Voir dire* ("to speak the truth") preliminary examination of prospective jurors for the purpose of selecting persons qualified to sit on a jury (not all cases are tried by a jury). *Plea bargaining:* negotiations whereby an accused pleads guilty to a lesser included offense or to one of multiple charges in exchange for the prosecution's agreement to support a dismissal of some charges or a lighter sentence (not all cases are tried by a jury).	

II. Trial Stage
 	
11. *Opening statements* of attorneys
12. Government presents its case against the defendant:
  a. *evidence* introduced
  b. *direct examination*
  c. *cross-examination*
13. Motions to dismiss
14. Defendant presents its case:
  a. *evidence* introduced
  b. *direct examination*
  c. *cross-examination*
15. Closing arguments to jury by attorneys
16. *Charge* to jury by judge
17. *Verdict* to jury
18. *Judgment* of court, including the sentence if defendant is convicted
	■ The trial court often makes rulings concerning these events, but rarely writes an opinion on any of the rulings.
	■ After the trial, the trial court delivers its judgment. Usually, no opinion (explaining the judgment) is written.
	■ Several trial courts, however, such as federal trial courts (U.S. District Courts) and New York State trial courts, do sometimes write trial court opinions.
		Opening statements: an attorney's statement to the jury made before presenting evidence that summarizes the case he or she intends to try to establish during the trial.
		Evidence: anything that could be offered to prove or disprove an alleged fact.
		Direct examination: the first questioning of a witness by the party who has called the witness; also called *examination in chief.*
		Cross-examination: questioning a witness by an opponent after the other side called and questioned that witness.
		Jury instructions: a statement of the guidelines and law given to the jury by the judge for use in deciding the issues of fact in its verdict; also called the *charge.*
		Verdict: the final conclusion of the jury.
		Judgment: the final conclusion of a court that resolves a legal dispute or that specifies what further proceedings are needed to resolve it.
			a. Coordinate scheduling of witnesses.
			b. Take notes during trial.
			c. Assist attorney with documents and exhibits.
			d. Perform last-minute legal research.
			e. Compare a trial witness's testimony with what he or she said in discovery.
			f. Perform other tasks needed by the attorney conducting the trial.

III. Appeal Stage 19. Filing of *notice of appeal* 20. Filing of *appellant's appellate brief* 21. Filing of *appellee's appellate brief* 22. Filing of appellant's *reply brief*	■ An opinion in the intermediate appellate court will often be written. ■ This opinion in the middle appeals court might be appealed to the highest court, in which event another opinion could be written.	*Notice of appeal:* notice given to a court (through filing) and to the opposing party (through service) of an intention to appeal. *Appellant:* the party bringing an appeal because of alleged errors made by a lower tribunal.	**a.** Draft and file the notice of appeal. **b.** Order the trial transcript. **c.** Summarize (digest) trial testimony relevant to issues to be raised on appeal.

(continues)

EXHIBIT 10.3	Overview of Criminal Litigation—*continued*		
EVENT	**RULINGS AND OPINIONS**	**DEFINITIONS**	**POSSIBLE PARALEGAL ROLES**
23. Oral argument by attorneys 24. Judgment of court	[Note that in some states, there is no intermediate appeals court; the appeal goes directly from the trial court to the highest state court. See Exhibit 6.2 in chapter 6.]	*Appellee:* the party against whom the appeal is brought; also called *respondent.* *Appellate brief:* a document submitted by a party to an appellate court in which arguments are presented on why the appellate court should affirm (approve), reverse, or otherwise modify what a lower court has done. *Reply brief:* an appellate brief of the appellant that responds to the appellate brief of the appellee; any appellate brief that responds to an opponent's appellate brief.	d. Cite check the appellate brief (e.g., making sure all citations are in proper form, Shepardizing or KeyCiting all laws cited to make sure they have not been repealed or overruled, etc.).

[SECTION B]
ALTERNATIVE DISPUTE RESOLUTION (ADR)

As you can see, litigation can be an involved and costly process. If the parties cannot resolve the dispute on their own, an increasingly popular option is **alternative dispute resolution (ADR)**. Persons engaged in a dispute (i.e., *disputants*) can try ADR before resorting to traditional litigation. In some kinds of cases, e.g., medical malpractice, disputants may be required to try ADR before being allowed to have a court trial.

Some forms of ADR such as arbitration (defined below) are used extensively. One paralegal points out that we "live in an age when everything from your bank account to the forms you fill out in a doctor's office contain a clause requiring any dispute that arises to be resolved by arbitration. As such, the modern paralegal is far more likely to help prepare for arbitration than for trial [since] only a small minority of cases go to trial, and that is partly because more and more disputes are governed by arbitration."[2]

There are several different kinds of ADR:

Arbitration: Both sides agree to submit their dispute to a neutral third person who will listen to the evidence and make a decision. The arbitrator is usually a professional arbitrator hired through organizations such as the American Arbitration Association. (www.adr.org). An arbitration proceeding is not as formal as a court trial. Generally, the decision of an arbitrator is not appealable to a court. If a party is dissatisfied, he or she must go to court and start all over again rather than appealing a particular arbitration decision.

Mediation: Both sides agree to submit their dispute to a neutral third person who will help the disputants reach a negotiated settlement on their own. The mediator does not render a decision, although sometimes he or she may make suggestions or recommendations.

Rent-a-Judge: When the arbitrator or mediator is a retired judge, the arbitration or mediation is often called **private judging** or private adjudication. It is sometimes misleadingly referred to as *rent-a-judge* or *rent-a-judging*. The name is misleading because the retired judge has no more authority or power than any other arbitrator or mediator.

Med-Arb: First, mediation is tried. If it is not successful, the proceeding becomes an arbitration, and the mediator switches roles. He or she then makes a decision as an arbitrator.

Neighborhood Justice Center (NJC): In many localities, an NJC exists to offer mediation and arbitration services for disputes involving ongoing relationships in the community, such as between landlord and tenant or among neighbors. The NJC could be sponsored by the government, a foundation, or an existing community organization.

alternative dispute resolution (ADR) A method or procedure for resolving a legal dispute without litigating it in a court or administrative agency.

arbitration A method of alternate dispute resolution (ADR) in which the parties avoid litigation by submitting their dispute to a neutral third person (the arbitrator) who renders a decision resolving the dispute.

mediation A method of alternate dispute resolution (ADR) in which the parties avoid litigation by submitting their dispute to a neutral third person (the mediator) who helps the parties resolve their dispute; he or she does not render a decision resolving it for them.

private judging A method of alternative dispute resolution consisting of arbitration or mediation in which the arbitrator or mediator is a retired judge. Sometimes called *rent-a-judge*.

med-arb A method of alternative dispute resolution (ADR) in which the parties first try mediation, and if it does not work, they try arbitration.

neighborhood justice center (NJC) A government or private center where disputes can be resolved by mediation or other method of alternative dispute resolution (ADR).

summary jury trial A method of alternative dispute resolution (ADR) in which the parties present their evidence and arguments to an advisory jury, which renders a nonbinding verdict.

neutral evaluation A method of alternative dispute resolution (ADR) in which both sides hire an experienced attorney or an expert in the area involved in the dispute who will listen to an abbreviated version of the evidence and arguments of each side and offer an evaluation in the hope that this will stimulate more serious settlement discussions. Sometimes called *case evaluation*.

Summary Jury Trial: The parties use an advisory jury, for a summary jury trial (sometimes called a *mock trial* or a *minitrial*). The jurors for this trial often come from the regular pool of jurors in the county. The attorneys present their evidence and arguments to this jury in an abbreviated (i.e., summary) format. The jury deliberates and renders a nonbinding advisory verdict. Attorneys then question the jurors on the strengths and weaknesses of each side's presentation. The parties use all of this information in deciding whether they should settle, and if so, for what.

Neutral Evaluation: Both sides might hire an experienced attorney or an expert in the area (e.g., a chemist for a patent dispute) to listen to an abbreviated version of the evidence and arguments of each side and offer an evaluation in the hope that this will stimulate more serious settlement discussions.

Parties also have the opportunity to engage in alternative dispute resolution online. One settlement site (www.cybersettle.com) claims to have settled over $1 billion in disputes since it became available online. Internet sites offering online mediation (e.g., www.mediationnow.com) and online arbitration (e.g., www.e-arbitration-t.com) are available. Except for relatively small claims, however, online ADR is not extensively used.

Paralegals have many roles in assisting attorneys who have cases in ADR. For example, a paralegal can organize files, schedule discovery and ADR, conduct investigations, summarize or digest data from discovery, help prepare the client for ADR, and assist the attorney during the ADR proceeding in much the same fashion as paralegals assist attorneys during regular trials. Paralegals often prepare mediation summaries (particularly in personal injury cases) that outline the issues of the case, present the facts (including a description of the incident), list the medical expenses and lost wages incurred by the client, summarize medical records, and state the costs incurred by the law firm to date. "Some firms use a form for this where you simply 'plug in' the information."[3] One paralegal helps her attorney prepare for mediation by scanning all documents and supportive evidence into the attorney's laptop computer and making a PowerPoint presentation of this data that the attorney can use during the mediation session. If ADR leads to a resolution of the case, paralegals can be involved in finalizing the settlement such as by preparing a draft of the document that lays out the terms of the agreements reached.

In addition, some paralegals have become arbitrators and mediators themselves. In most states, you do not have to be an attorney to conduct arbitration or mediation. Service companies are available that offer arbitration and mediation services to parties involved in disputes. A few of these companies hire people with paralegal training and experience to be arbitrators or mediators.

[SECTION C]
LITIGATION ASSISTANTSHIP: PRETRIAL STAGE

For a list of paralegal functions in litigation, see "Paralegal Specialties: A Dictionary of Functions" in Section C of chapter 2. Note the separate entry on litigation (page 57). as well as the trial and other litigation tasks listed under most of the specialty entries presented in this section of chapter 2. Trial work can be challenging because of the high stakes and high energy involved. Litigation paralegal Jennifer Swails "assists lawyers with everything from submitting the first draft of discovery to following through to the end of a trial." Recalling her first trial, she remembers experiencing "every possible emotion." "I was scared to death, nervous, and tired."[4] Not all paralegals have the same responsibility during litigation. Some, like Jennifer, perform a broad range of tasks. Others are given more narrow litigation tasks. We now turn to a more detailed look at this variety of paralegal roles during litigation.

At the *pretrial* stage, we will examine paralegal tasks under the following topics:

1. Drafting pleadings
2. Service of process and court filings
3. Calendar control and scheduling
4. Discovery
5. Preparing the trial notebook
6. Settlement

7. Expert witnesses
8. Interviewing
9. Investigation
10. Legal research

The remainder of the chapter will cover most of these tasks, particularly those at the beginning of the list. Some are also discussed in chapter 8 on interviewing, chapter 9 on investigation, chapter 11 on legal research, chapter 13 on computers in the law, and chapter 14 on law office administration.

I. DRAFTING PLEADINGS

The major pleadings in litigation are the complaint and the answer. Very often you will use standard forms as the starting point in drafting pleadings. Closely examine the guidelines in Exhibit 10.4 on using standard forms.

EXHIBIT 10.4	How to Avoid Abusing a Standard Form

1. A standard form is an example of the document or instrument that you need to draft, such as a pleading, contract, or other agreement.
2. Standard forms are found in a number of places—for example, in formbooks, in manuals, in practice texts, in some statutory codes, and in some court rules. Some standard forms are available through a computer database either as stand-alone software or online. The word processing programs, WordPerfect and Word, have templates that can help you prepare standard documents such as complaints. On the Internet, see www.USCourtForms.com and the sites listed in Helpful Web Sites at the end of the chapter. Searches such as "negligence form" or "contract form" on Google and other general search engines will often lead to standard forms that can be purchased or used for free.
3. Most standard forms are written by private attorneys. Occasionally, however, a standard form will be written by the legislature or by the court as the suggested or required format to use.
4. Considerable care must be exercised in the use of a standard form. Such forms can be deceptive in that they appear to require little more than filling in the blanks. The intelligent use of these forms usually requires much more.
5. The cardinal rule is that you must always adapt the form to the particulars of the client's case. You fit the form to the client's case, not the client's case to the form.
6. Do not be reluctant to change the preprinted language in the form if you have a good reason. Whenever you make such a change, be sure to alert your supervisor so that it can be approved.
7. You should never use a standard form unless and until you have satisfied yourself that you know the meaning of every word and phrase on the form. This includes *boilerplate*, which is standard language commonly used in the same kind of document. The great temptation of most form users is to ignore what they do not understand because the form has been used so often in the past without any apparent difficulty. Do not give in to this temptation. Find out what everything means by:

   - Using a legal dictionary (often a good starting point)
   - Asking your supervisor
   - Asking other knowledgeable people
   - Doing other legal research

8. Once you have found a form that appears useful, look around for another form that attempts to serve the same purpose. Analyze the different or alternative forms available. Which one is preferable? Why? Keep questioning the validity and effectiveness of any form.
9. Do not leave any blank spaces on the form. If a question does not apply, make a notation to indicate this, such as N.A., meaning not applicable.
10. If the form was written for another state, be sure that the form can be adapted and is adapted to the law of your state. Be aware that an out-of-state form may be unadaptable to your state because of the substantial differences in the laws of the two states.
11. Occasionally, you may go to an old case file to find a document that might be used as a model for a similar document that you need to draft on a current case. All the above cautions apply to the adaptation of documents from closed case files.

Here, we will concentrate on drafting a complaint through an examination of its basic structure:

- Caption
- Designation of the pleading
- Statement of jurisdiction
- Body
- Prayer for relief
- Subscription
- Verification

Not all complaints follow this format. You need to check the requirements in the statutes and court rules that govern the structure for complaints in the court where you are filing the action. Detailed requirements may exist on matters such as size, weight, and type of paper that can be used; permissible margins; font and type size; line spacing and numbering, and the use of a colored backing to which the complaint must be fastened. Exhibit 10.5 presents a sample complaint[5] that follows the basic structure listed above.

EXHIBIT 10.5	Structure of a Complaint

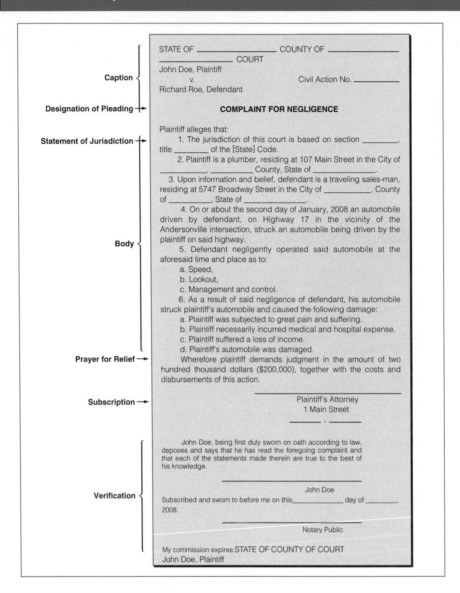

Computers can be used to help draft complaints and other pleadings. In addition to special software that can be purchased for this purpose, standard word processors can also be used. For example, **templates** in Corel's WordPerfect or Microsoft Word automatically lay out a complaint's standard features such as the heading or caption, spacing, and line numbering. A template is simply a set of formulas that allows you to perform a designated task. Of course, these templates will not be keyed to the particular rules of your state. The templates simply provide a framework that you will have to adapt in the manner outlined in Exhibit 10.4 on standard forms.

template A set of formulas created to perform a designated task.

Caption of Complaint

A **caption** of a complaint is the heading that provides identifying information, such as the kind of document it is, the name of the court, the name of the parties, and, if available, the docket number assigned to the case by the court (see top of Exhibit 10.5).

caption The heading or introductory part of a pleading, court opinion, memo, or other document that identifies what it is, the names of the parties, the court involved, etc.

Designation of the Pleading

The title of the pleadings should be clearly stated at the top as part of the caption. The pleading for our example in Exhibit 10.5 is a Complaint for Negligence.

Statement of Jurisdiction

If the court requires a statement of the court's **subject matter jurisdiction**, the citation to the statute or other law conferring this jurisdiction must be included. (This jurisdiction is the power or authority of the court to hear a particular kind or category of dispute). The main federal trial courts—U.S. District Courts—require a statement of subject-matter jurisdiction in complaints. Rule 8 of the Federal Rules of Civil Procedure provides that a claim for relief shall contain "a short and plain statement of the grounds upon which the court's jurisdiction depends." Not all states have the same requirement. Some state courts require a statement of subject matter jurisdiction; others do not.

For purposes of determining **venue**—the place of the trial—the complaint may also have to allege the residence of the parties, where the accident or wrong allegedly occurred, etc.

subject matter jurisdiction The court's power to resolve a particular kind or category of dispute.

venue The proper county or geographical area in which a court with jurisdiction may hear a case. The place of the trial.

Body

The claims or causes of action of the plaintiff are presented (stated) in the *body* of the complaint. A cause of action is a set of facts that gives a party the right to judicial relief; it is a legally acceptable reason for suing. Every separate cause of action used by the plaintiff should be stated in a separate "count," e.g., Count I, Count II, or simply as First Cause of Action, Second Cause of Action, etc. (This is not done in Exhibit 10.5 because only one cause of action is alleged in this complaint—negligence.) The paragraphs should be consecutively numbered. Each paragraph should contain a single fact or a closely related grouping of facts.

With what factual detail must the complaint state the cause of action? There are two main schools of thought on this question: fact pleading versus notice pleading.

1. *Fact Pleading*. In **fact pleading**, there must be a statement of the *ultimate facts* that set forth the cause of action. Not every detail that the plaintiff intends to try to prove at trial is pleaded. The complaint need not contain a catalog of the evidence that the plaintiff will eventually introduce at the trial. Only the ultimate facts are pleaded. There is, however, no satisfactory definition of an ultimate fact. Generally, it is one that is essential to the establishment of an element of a cause of action.

    The complaint should *not* state conclusions of law, such as "Jones assaulted Smith" or "Jones violated section 23 of the state code." The problem, however, is that it is sometimes as difficult to define a conclusion of law as it is to define an ultimate fact. Some statements are mixed statements of fact and law—for example, "Jones negligently drove his car into . . ." As a matter of common sense and practicality, if the conclusion of law (here, "negligently") is also a convenient way of stating facts, it will be permitted.

2. *Notice Pleading*. In federal courts under the Federal Rules of Civil Procedure and in states that have followed the lead of the federal courts, the goal of the complaint is to say enough to notify or inform the defendant of the nature of the claims against him or her. This is the essence of **notice pleading**. There is no requirement that ultimate facts be alleged. The plaintiff must simply provide "a short and plain statement of the claim showing that the pleader is entitled to relief." Rule 8(a)(2). Federal Rules of Civil Procedure.

    It is not improper to fail to plead an ultimate fact. The critical point is that the complaint will not be thrown out if it *fails* to plead an ultimate fact or if it *includes* conclusions of law—as long as the complaint gives adequate notice of the nature of the claim. The technicalities of pleading facts, conclusions of law, etc., are unimportant in notice pleading.

    Notice pleading does not necessarily require a different kind of pleading from fact pleading; notice pleading is simply more liberal or tolerant in what is acceptable.

fact pleading A statement of every ultimate fact. A fact is ultimate if it is essential to establish an element of a cause of action.

notice pleading A short and plain statement of the claim showing the pleader is entitled to relief.

When the plaintiff lacks personal knowledge of a fact being alleged, the fact should be stated upon **information and belief**, as in the third paragraph of Exhibit 10.5.

There are times when the law requires specificity in the pleading. For example, allegations of fraud must be stated with specificity or particularity. Also, when **special damages** are required in defamation cases, the facts must be pleaded with some specificity.

information and belief Good faith belief as to the truth of an allegation, not based on first-hand knowledge.

special damages Actual and provable economic losses, e.g., lost wages.

Prayer for Relief

In the **prayer for relief**, the complaint asks for a specific amount of damages or for some other form of relief such as an injunction against a nuisance. (If the prayer asks for damages, the clause requesting it is called the *ad damnum clause*.) In the event that the defendant fails to appear and answer the complaint, a default judgment is entered against the defendant. The relief given the plaintiff in a default judgment cannot exceed what the plaintiff asked for in the prayer for relief.

prayer for relief A request for damages or other form of judicial relief.

subscription A signature; the act of signing one's name.

Subscription

A **subscription** is someone's signature. If an attorney prepared the complaint, his or her subscription is required. If the plaintiff wrote the complaint and is acting as his or her own attorney in the case, the plaintiff signs.

Verification

verification An affidavit stating that a party has read the pleading and swears that it is true to the best of his or her knowledge.

A **verification** is an affidavit that is submitted with the pleading. It is signed by a party on whose behalf the pleading was prepared, who swears that he or she has read the pleading and that it is true to the best of his or her knowledge. (Not all states require that complaints be verified.)

2. SERVICE OF PROCESS AND COURT FILINGS

substituted service Service by an authorized method (e.g., by mail) other than personal service. Also called *constructive service.*

subpoena A command to appear at a certain time and place.

subpoena duces tecum A command that a witness appear at a certain time and place and bring specified things such as documents or records.

subpoena ad testificandum A command to appear at a certain time and place to give testimony.

The lawsuit begins with service of process—the delivery of the complaint and summons to the defendant. This is often done in person, although there are circumstances when the law allows **substituted service** such as by registered mail. Another service task involves witnesses who are called to appear for a deposition, for a court hearing, or for the trial itself. To compel witnesses to appear, they are often served with a **subpoena**, which is a command to appear at a certain time and place. (If the command is to bring documents or things, it is a **subpoena duces tecum**; if the command is to give testimony, it is a **subpoena ad testificandum**.) A paralegal may be asked to serve process or to serve a subpoena. Alternatively, the law firm may decide to hire a service company that is a professional process server. If so, a paralegal may have the responsibility of hiring and monitoring the company.

Completing a service yourself takes preparation and care. You have to know the local rules on how to serve someone properly. In addition, you need to anticipate the kinds of difficulty you might encounter "on the street." Here is how paralegal David Busch describes his first service assignment.

> "I was given a subpoena to serve on a lady for a hearing the next day. I rushed to the courthouse to pick up the subpoena and immediately proceeded to the address given to me by the attorney. I spent over an hour looking for the address when I realized that it was a bad address. I frantically [tried to call] the lawyer." He was in court. His secretary "gave me a work address. I rushed to the work address to find out that she was on vacation for two weeks beginning yesterday. . . . This was frustrating. This was my first service and I could not even find the lady." I realized that process serving is not as easy as handing someone a copy of a lawsuit.[6]

Filing documents in court also requires careful preparation and compliance with court rules. In federal court filings, for example, the complaint must be accompanied by a *civil cover sheet* that indicates the names and addresses of the parties and their attorneys, the kind of action being filed, etc. Court clerks usually have little sympathy for filers who fail to comply with such requirements:

> There are few things more frustrating to the legal assistant than getting something to the courthouse for filing, often on the very last day it is due, and having it returned, not filed, because of a technical error or oversight. Since the legal assistant is the "last checkpoint" for pleadings and other documents being sent to the courthouse, it falls on him or her to ensure those documents are complete and acceptable.[7]

This observation is from litigation paralegal Erin Schlemme, who recommends the following basic steps for successful filings.

docket number A consecutive number assigned to a case by the court and used on all documents filed with the court during the litigation of that case.

- Know the correct address of the court where the filing must be made.
- Phone in advance or check the court's online Web site to determine the exact hours when the clerk's office will be open to accept filings.
- Place the correct court number on what you are filing (this may be the **docket number** or a special computer coding number provided by the court's file management system).
- Use the correct format including the proper size of paper, content of the cover sheet, etc.
- Have the correct fees (know whether the clerk can accept a personal check or will accept only cash or a law firm check).
- Obtain an official statement indicating that you have made the filing, e.g., a dated receipt or a copy of what you have filed that has the clerk's court stamp on it.

Similar care is needed when filing in courts that allow facsimile filing. Under this method, pleadings are "faxed" directly to the court, eliminating the need to go to the court yourself or to hire a delivery service. The special procedures instituted by the court to use this method of filing must be scrupulously followed.

The same is true of courts that allow electronic filing, referred to as **e-filing**. In the federal courts, for example, the e-filing system is CM/ECF, case management/electronic case files (pacer. psc.uscourts.gov/cmecf). Documents to be e-filed are converted into an image or digital format acceptable by the court, the most popular being **PDF** (portable document format). The documents are then filed over the Internet. A document in a PDF file is a digital document that preserves all the features or elements of the document before it was converted into a digital file. When you read a PDF file, you are reading an exact duplicate of the original document. A special code in the program allows a user to insert a digital signature that verifies the authenticity of the document you are sending. To read PDF files, you need a program such as Adobe Acrobat, a version of which is available free on the Internet. PDF files can also be easily exchanged as e-mail attachments so that they can be read online. The PDF standard is not the only format used in e-filing systems. Another is the XML (extensible markup language) standard.

Courts that allow e-filing have their own procedures on how it is accomplished. Paralegals must check the court's specific rules (usually posted on the court's Web site) on e-filing. In one state, for example:

> "Any document that is electronically filed with the court after the close of business on any day shall be deemed to have been filed on the next court day. 'Close of business,' as used in this paragraph, shall mean 5 P.M. or the time at which the court would not accept filing at the court's filing counter, whichever is earlier."[8]

Furthermore, while a document that is filed electronically will often have the same legal effect as an original paper document, a printed form of the document (containing any required signatures) may have to be kept in the attorney's files and made available upon request by the court or any party involved in the litigation.

Public access to court records through the Internet is increasing dramatically. Many federal courts, for example, use **PACER** (Public Access to Court Electronic Records). Subscribers to PACER can obtain case and docket information from federal courts via the Internet (pacer.psc.uscourts.gov). Clearly, we are moving in the direction of the paperless (or almost paperless) courtroom.

3. CALENDAR CONTROL AND SCHEDULING

Here are five words that a paralegal (and everyone else in a law office) should never be heard saying: "Oh, was that due today?"[9] The clock is a dominant presence in every well-run law office. Calendars are filled with events such as dates for:

- Client meetings
- Filing a lawsuit before the statute of limitations expires
- Sending a **demand letter** to an insurance company setting out terms for a settlement
- Requesting a jury trial
- Filing interrogatories
- Filing requests for production of documents
- Responding to discovery requests from opposing parties
- Filing pretrial motions
- Hearings
- Etc.

Numerous events must take place according to specified deadlines, sometimes at the risk of losing important rights. One of the most common grounds for legal malpractice claims against attorneys, for example, is allowing the statute of limitations to run on a cause of action. The failure to file a lawsuit within the time allowed by law can result in the permanent loss of a client's right to assert a cause of action, no matter how good a case the client would have had.

A major method of achieving calendar control is the office **tickler**, which is used to record important dates and to remind everyone to take appropriate action on these dates. A key responsibility of many paralegals is to operate and monitor these tracking or calendar systems. Attorneys need constant reminders of due dates, particularly when they are working on more than one case or when more than one attorney is working on a single case.

Ticklers operate in different ways. Most offices use computer programs that have reminder or tickler systems built into them. Case management and calendar software programs can easily be set up to send out e-mail reminders automatically as the date of a calendared event approaches. Once

e-filing Electronic filing in court of pleadings and other documents.

PDF (portable document format) A file format consisting of an electronic image of a document that preserves the features or elements of the document (e.g., its line spacing, photographs, and font size) that existed before it was converted into a digital document.

PACER (Public Access to Court Electronic Records) An electronic public access service that allows subscribers to obtain case and docket information from federal courts via the Internet.

demand letter An advocacy letter that asks the recipient to take or refrain from specific action affecting the client.

tickler A system designed to provide reminders of important dates.

you insert future events in the online calendar, you can receive pop-up reminders (and beep sounds) prior to and on the due dates indicated in the calendar. Personal digital assistants (PDAs) help users keep track of their appointments in addition to functioning as cell phones and fax senders.

Some offices still operate their tickler system by hand or manually, relying primarily on paper reminders. Suppose, for example, that an attorney must conduct a deposition on May 23. Weeks before this date, the attorney's paralegal will enter this date on a specially designed, multipart form. One of the parts of the form is torn off and sent to the attorney as a reminder of the deposition. Another part will be torn off and sent to the attorney as a further reminder a few days before May 23.

As additional protection against missed deadlines, there may be a centralized calendar system for the entire office and an individual calender system for each attorney. Most attorneys carry their own daily planner or PDA everywhere they go. The same is true of many litigation paralegals.

"My greatest challenge," comments one paralegal, "is staying on top of schedules. The attorney I work for . . . is incredibly overloaded and the amount of juggling I have to do sometimes makes me feel like I should be in Ringling Brothers and Barnum & Bailey instead of a law office."[10] You must be prepared for any scheduling eventuality. Another paralegal recalls the time when the judge unexpectedly postponed a trial that was about to begin. "Here we are—three days before trial," and everything comes to an abrupt halt. The parties had subpoenaed over twenty witnesses, rooms had been reserved, equipment had been rented, expert witnesses had been prepared, and numerous exhibits were ready to be used. Suddenly the judge's clerk calls to announce a two-month postponement.[11] In the environment of a busy, high-stages law office where calendars and scheduling play such a large role, flexibility is a critical survival skill.

4. DISCOVERY

To help a party prepare for trial, the following discovery devices are available:

- interrogatories
- deposition
- production of documents and things; entry on land for inspection and other purposes
- physical or mental examination
- request for admission

Discovery devices are compulsory exchanges of factual information between parties in litigation. The information exchanged can consist of answers to questions (e.g., What doctors treated you in the last five years?), documents (e.g., bank records), **e-evidence** (e.g., e-mail messages, online spreadsheets, Web pages, database records), etc. When e-evidence is sought in discovery, the process is known as *e-discovery* or *electronic data discovery* (EDD).

The computer age has created not only new kinds of evidence, but also new ways for it to be exchanged. The traditional setting for depositions, for example, is the conference room of one of the attorneys in the litigation. Although this is still the most common method used today, alternatives are now available. An electronic deposition (*e-deposition*), for example, can occur over the Internet with the questioner being in one location and the person being questioned (the deponent) being in another—both seeing each other on their computer screens.

There are many tasks paralegals can perform during the discovery stage of litigation. For example, when responding to discovery requests, they can help prepare the **privilege log** that lists all of the information or documents that the office will refuse to disclose because of a claim of privilege such as:

- the *attorney-client privilege* (if the information sought consists of communications between attorney and client involving the legal services being rendered) and
- the *work-product privilege* (if the information sought consists of notes, memoranda, and the like prepared by an attorney for the litigation).

If only part of a document is protected by privilege, the paralegal can be assigned the task of **redacting** (blocking out or shielding) the part that is not **discoverable** so that the rest can be disclosed. For an overview of discovery and paralegal tasks, see Exhibit 10.6.

Perhaps one of the most frequently performed discovery tasks is **digesting** or summarizing transcripts and documents, particularly depositions. Here is how Dana Nikolewski describes a recent experience with this seemingly never-ending task:

> It's Thursday and I'm on page 20 of a 300-page deposition, which I really should have finished summarizing last week. The phone rings and I relish the thought of this brief interruption, until I recognize the voice on the other end as none other than our local courier announcing the arrival of 200 more depositions which I know need to be summarized ASAP.[12]

e-evidence Evidence generated or stored in a computer such as e-mail messages, online spreadsheets, Web pages, and database records.

privilege log A list of information or documents claimed to be covered by privilege and, therefore, protected from disclosure in discovery or during trial.

redact To edit or prepare a document for publication or release, often by deleting, altering, or blocking out text that you do not want disclosed.

discoverable Pertaining to information or other materials an opponent can obtain through deposition, interrogatories, or other discovery device.

digesting Summarizing transcripts and documents, often in preparation for litigation.

EXHIBIT 10.6	Overview of Discovery and Paralegal Roles	
DISCOVERY DEVICE	**WHO MUST SUBMIT TO DEVICE?**	**POSSIBLE PARALEGAL ROLES**
1. Interrogatories A method of discovery consisting of written questions about a lawsuit submitted by one party to another. (Referred to informally as "Roggs.") (For the law governing interrogatories in federal trial courts, see Rule 33 of the Federal Rules of Civil Procedure; www.law.cornell.edu/rules/frcp/Rule33.htm)	Parties only. Nonparty witnesses do not have to answer and cannot send interrogatories.	**a.** Prepare a draft of the interrogatories. **b.** Prepare a draft of answers to interrogatories received from the other side. **c.** Read all pleadings, interview reports, and investigation reports as background for the drafting tasks listed in (a) and (b) above. **d.** Arrange conference with client to go over questions and answers. **e.** Prepare the privilege log. **f.** Draft a motion to compel a response to interrogatories. **g.** Draft a motion to have matters not answered be deemed admitted. **h.** Digest interrogatories and answers for office file. **i.** Enter due dates in office tickler to serve as reminders of the dates interrogatories must be sent and must be answered.
2. Deposition A method of discovery by which parties or their prospective witnesses are questioned outside the courtroom before trial. If the party being deposed (called the *deponent*) has not seen the questions before they are asked, the deposition is called a *deposition upon oral examination.* (Such questions are always asked by an attorney.) If the deponent is given the questions in writing, the deposition is called a *deposition upon written questions.* (Such questions are often asked by a stenographer or court reporter rather than by an attorney.) (For the law governing depositions in federal trial courts, see Rules 30 and 31 of the Federal Rules of Civil Procedure) (www.law.cornell.edu/rules/frcp/#chapter_v)	A deposition can be taken of a party to the suit. It is also possible to take the deposition of a nonparty witness.	**a.** Schedule time and place for the deposition. **b.** Prepare the subpoena, which orders a nonparty to come to the deposition to be deposed, and the subpoena duces tecum, which requires the deponent (the witness being deposed) to bring specified things (e.g., documents) with him or her. **c.** When your client is being asked to bring things to the deposition under a subpoena duces tecum, prepare the privilege log. **d.** Prepare a list of suggested questions for the attorney to ask the deponent. (This is done after reading everything in the file to date, e.g., complaint, answer, interview reports, investigation reports, and answers to interrogatories.) **e.** Arrange for scheduling and payment of stenographer or reporter. **f.** Order transcript of deposition. **g.** Take notes at the deposition. **h.** Prepare motion to force compliance by other side. **i.** Prepare motion to have matters not answered deemed admitted. **j.** Read transcript of deposition to digest it, compare it to interrogatory answers, look for inconsistencies, etc. **k.** Make entries in office tickler on due dates for scheduled depositions and related court motions.
3. Production of documents and things; entry on land for inspection and other purposes A method of discovery by which a party can force another party to produce documents or other things or to allow entry on land. This can be for purpose of copying, photographing, measuring, or otherwise inspecting the items designated. (For the law governing production and entry in federal trial courts, see Rule 34 of the Federal Rules of Civil Procedure; www.law.cornell.edu/rules/frcp/Rule34.htm)	This device is directed at parties only. The party must be in possession or control of the document, thing or land in question. If you want a *nonparty* to turn over documents and other materials you can seek a deposition of this nonparty and use a *subpoena duces tecum* to specify what should be brought to the deposition.	**a.** Prepare a draft of a request for production of documents, things, etc. specifying what you want to copy, inspect, or test, and when you want to do so. **b.** Arrange who will do the inspecting, copying, etc., payment of costs involved, etc. **c.** Draft a motion to compel the inspection, copying, etc. **d.** File, digest, and index the report(s) based on the inspection, copying, etc. **e.** Enter scheduled dates for inspection, copying, etc. in the officer tickler. **f.** Prepare the privilege log.

(continues)

EXHIBIT 10.6   Overview of Discovery and Paralegal Roles—*continued*

4. Physical or mental examination A method of discovery by which a party can obtain a court-ordered independent examination of a person whose physical or mental condition is in controversy. The exam is referred to as an IME—independent medical examination. (For the law governing IMEs in federal trial courts, see Rule 35 of the Federal Rules of Civil Procedure; www.law.cornell.edu/rules/frcp/Rule35.htm)	Limited to parties only and to persons under the control of parties e.g., the child of a party. (In a few courts, the employees of a party can also be forced to undergo a physical or mental examination.)	**a.** Schedule doctor's appointment and payment. **b.** Prepare court motion to order the examination. **c.** Prepare court motion to have matters relevant to the examination be deemed admitted for failure to submit to examination. **d.** Enter dates pertaining to the examination in office tickler.
5. Request for admissions (RFA) A method of discovery in which one party asks another to admit the truth of any matter relating to facts or the application of law to facts. (For the law governing requests for admission in federal trial courts, see Rule 36 of the Federal Rules of Civil Procedure; www.law.cornell.edu/rules/frcp/Rule36.htm)	Limited to parties only.	**a.** Read everything in the file (pleadings, interview and investigation reports, interrogatory answers, deposition transcript, etc.) in order to prepare a list of facts the other side will be requested to admit. **b.** File, index, and digest the responses from the other side in the office file. **c.** Enter due dates in office tickler. **d.** Prepare the privilege log.

depo summarizer An employee whose main job is digesting (summarizing) discovery documents, particularly depositions.

digest An organized summary or abridgment. (See the glossary for an additional definition.)

Bates stamp A desk tool used to place a sequential number on a page. After using the stamp on a page, it automatically advances to the next number, ready to stamp the next page.

page/line digest A summary of a deposition transcript that indicates the pages and lines of the deponent's answers in the order in which the questions were asked.

chronological digest A summary of a deposition transcript that presents the events described in the deponent's answers in their chronological order.

topical digest A summary of a deposition transcript organized by specific topics covered in the answers of the deponent.

Litigation paralegals do indeed spend a good deal of time digesting. Occasionally, you will see a want ad for paralegals to digest depositions full-time. Such individuals are sometimes called **depo summarizers**. While all litigation paralegals do not perform the task full-time, the experience of Dana Nikolewski is not unusual.

Before digesting can occur, every page of a discovery document may have to be sequentially numbered. The **digests** will refer to specific page numbers in these documents. You will be inserting the page numbers. A variety of numbering formats are possible (e.g., 1, 2, 3, 4; or 0001, 0002, 0003, 0004; or ABC-1, ABC-2, ABC-3, ABC-4). You can combine names with numbers. The pages of the Jackson deposition, for example, might be numbered Jackson01, Jackson02, Jackson03, Jackson04, etc. Page numbering is often performed with a desk tool called a **Bates stamp**. Each time a page number is stamped using this tool, the number on the tool automatically advances so that the next page will be stamped with the next number. Whoever is inserting or stamping the page numbers does not have to advance the number on the Bates stamp manually. Numbering pages with this tool is referred to as Bates numbering. If the transcript document being discovered is an electronic or digital file (e.g., a PDF file), it can be sequentially numbered by using special Bates stamping software.

At a deposition, a reporter is present to record everything that is said. The attorneys then purchase a transcript (word-for-word account of the deposition questions and answers) from the reporter. Many reporters are able to make the transcript available on a disk so that the law office can immediately load the deposition directly into their litigation software.

Once the law office receives the transcript of the deposition from the reporter (either a paper or a digital transcript), paralegals are often asked to digest them. Three major kinds of digests can be prepared: page/line, chronological, and topical.

A **page/line digest** summarizes the answers given by the deponent in the order in which the questions were asked. The digest includes the page and line number of each answer. (The lines on every page are numbered sequentially with each page beginning with the number "1.") A **chronological digest** is a summary of a deposition transcript that presents the events described in the deponent's answers in their chronological order. Finally, a **topical digest** is a summary of a deposition transcript organized by specific topics covered in the answers of the deponent. For examples of these different styles of digests, see Exhibit 10.7.

As a rule of thumb, every ten pages of a deposition can be digested into one page. The ten-to-one ratio, of course is not absolute. The length of the digest depends on what the supervisor wants summarized and on the complexity of the testimony being summarized.[12a]

Many software programs are available (sold separately or as part of a litigation management package, e.g., Summation iBlaze) to facilitate the creation of deposition digests. When transcripts are on disk, searching for specific topics is relatively easy with this software. You simply run a "find"

Exhibit 10.7	Examples of Different Styles of Deposition Digests

PAGE/LINE DIGEST

Page/Lines	Summary	Topic
1:1–35	John Smith, 12 Main St. Buffalo NY 14202. 716–456–9103	Personal Data
1:36–40	Mechanic, Acme Factory. Began work 9/23/90. Became supervisor 5/99.	Employment
2:1–28	Met Adams (coworker) 7/29/94. Supervised Adams on odd jobs; trained him to operate equipment	Relationship to plf (Adams)
2:29–47	Was working at Combine #7 on date of the injury; Adams saw plank fall on Smith	Accident
Etc.		

CHRONOLOGICAL DIGEST

Date	Page	Topic
3/13/43	12	Mary Smith's date of birth
1950	15	Father died; mother returned to work
1950–1964	12	Attended Buffalo parochial schools
1964–1966	12, 14	Attended Bayling Community College
May 1965	13	First job—Elway Mall
6/23/68	13	Married John Smith
Etc.		

TOPICAL DIGEST

Topic	Page	Topic
Education	1, 3	John Smith grew up/was educated in Buffalo pub schools (1940s); took evening auto body courses (approx 1951)
Prior Employment	3, 5	First job: assistant on milk delivery truck (1954); day laborer (1957–1960); used car salesman (1960–63)
Prior Medical History	2, 5, 6	Rheumatic heart trouble as teenager—brief hosp in Syracuse; minor cuts and bruises in HS football—treated by school nurse; began seeing MD about kidney stones in 1982—last incident was 1990.
Accident	6–10	Foreman asks Smith to work early shift; arrives two hours earlier than normal. Floor was wet from a recent mopping. Plank needed to be moved because of malfunction of one at regular location. Smith asks foreman for help. Vague response. Smith attempts to move it himself. Falls on his foot.
Etc.		

search for whatever you need, e.g., every mention of "Giles, MD" in the entire transcript. For more on the use of computers in the law office for such tasks, see chapter 13.

Of course, depositions are not the only discovery devices that a paralegal may be asked to summarize. Answers to interrogatories, medical reports, on-site inspection reports, and responses to requests for admission can also be summarized. A paralegal may be asked to examine all of these documents to summarize specific topics, to look for inconsistencies, and to identify gaps in information that could require further discovery or investigation. Exhibit 10.8 provides general guidelines for all these digesting tasks.

EXHIBIT 10.8	Guidelines for Digesting Discovery Documents

1. Obtain clear instructions from your supervisor. What precisely have you been asked to do? What kind of digest is required? What have you expressly or by implication been told not to do? How much time do you have to complete the digest? It is a good idea to write down the supervisor's instructions. If you have never worked with a particular supervisor before, show him or her your work soon after you begin the assignment to make sure you have understood the instructions.
2. Know the difference between paraphrasing testimony and quoting testimony. To *paraphrase* is to phrase the testimony partly or entirely in your own words. To quote is to use the exact words of the witness even though you may leave out part of what the witness said. Supervisors may not want you to do any paraphrasing. They may want to do their own paraphrasing. Again, you need to know precisely what is expected.
3. Do not "editorialize," i.e., inject your personal comments. For example, do not say that the response of a witness whose testimony you are digesting is "unbelievable."
4. Know the case inside and out. You cannot digest something you do not understand. You must have a general understanding of the causes of action and the defenses so that you can grasp the context of the testimony. Read the client file, including interview and investigation reports, pleadings, interrogatory answers, other discovery documents, etc.

(continues)

EXHIBIT 10.8   Guidelines for Digesting Discovery Documents—*continued*

5. The answers given in a deposition often ramble. (The same may be true of some interrogatory answers.) Given this reality, act on the assumption that the same topic is covered in more than one place in the discovery document. Look for this diversity and record it in your summary by pointing out *each* time the same topic is mentioned.

6. Do not expect the answers to be consistent—even from the same witness. Do not consciously or unconsciously help the witness by blocking out potential inconsistencies. If on page 45 the witness said she saw a "car" but on page 104 said she saw a "van," do not blot out the distinction by saying she saw a "motor vehicle," or by failing to mention both. The danger of doing this is more serious than you may think, particularly when you are reading hundreds of pages and are getting a little red in the eyes.

7. Always think in terms of categories as you summarize. When appropriate, use these categories as topic headings for your summaries. The categories may be as broad as the name of a given witness. Other categories include:

-   Background information
-   Education
-   Past employment
-   Present employment
-   Medical history

-   Insurance
-   Prior claims
-   Pre-accident facts
-   Accident facts

-   Post-accident facts
-   Medical injuries from this accident
-   Damage to property
-   Prior statements made

    Your supervisor will usually tell you what categories or topics to use in organizing your summaries. If not, use your common sense and create your own.

8. Each summary should include the specific document you used (e.g., deposition), the page, and, for depositions, the lines on the page that are the basis of the summary.

9. Find out if the law firm has an office manual that gives you instructions on digesting. If not, check closed case files for samples of the kind of digesting that the firm has done in the past. Ask your supervisor if you should use such samples as models.

10. Update the summaries. After you finish your digest, more facts may become known through further investigation and discovery. Ask your supervisor if you should add these facts to your earlier summary reports.

11. Keep a list (or know where to find a list) of every piece of paper in a file. Some digesting assignments will require you to examine everything in the file.

5. PREPARING THE TRIAL NOTEBOOK

trial notebook A collection of documents, arguments, and strategies that an attorney plans to use during a trial.

A **trial notebook**, also called a trial book, is a collection of documents, arguments, and strategies that an attorney plans to use during a trial. It is often organized in a looseleaf binder with tabbed sections for easy use by the attorney (see Exhibit 10.9). The notebook becomes the attorney's checklist for conducting the trial.

EXHIBIT 10.9   Example of a Trial Notebook

LawFiles Trial Notebook. Courtesy of Bindertek, Sausalito, California (www.bindertek.com)

Not all trial notebooks are organized the same way. Litigation assistant Pam Robtoy cautions us that "[j]ust as each attorney has different preferences on how they want you to perform different tasks, each notebook you organize will be different, depending on which attorney will be utilizing the notebook and the particular requirements of the case. For example, a trial notebook for a medical malpractice case would likely contain a section for medical research regarding the surgical procedure, medication, etc. that is the focus of the case."[13] A trial notebook for a breach-of-contract case would not.

Many trial notebooks contain the following sections:[14]

- Table of Contents of the trial notebook
- Things to Do
- Trial Schedule/Deadlines
- Trial Team (street addresses, phone numbers, e-mail addresses)
- Case Outline
- Statement of Facts
- Pleadings
- Trial Briefs/Trial Memoranda outlining the facts and law of the case (submitted to the court)
- Law
- Outline of Liability
- Our Exhibits
- Opposition Exhibits
- Our Witnesses
- Opposition Witnesses
- Witness Statements
- Requests for Production and Responses
- Requests for Admission and Responses
- Direct Examination Outline of Questions
- Anticipated Cross-Examination Questions
- Outline of Damages
- Motions
- Deposition Summaries
- Voir Dire Questions
- Juror Information
- Jury Chart
- Records
- Opening Statements
- Plaintiff Testimony
- Requests for Jury Instructions
- Defendant Testimony
- Closing Arguments
- Settlement Proposals

It's often the paralegal's job to collect the material that will go into the notebook, organize it, keep it current, and help make it useful to the attorney as a vehicle for trial preparation and trial management. Specifically, the paralegal might do the following:

- Prepare summaries of deposition testimony.
- Prepare a list of all parties and witnesses plus people who are expected to be mentioned during testimony; index this list to the rest of the trial notebook.
- Prepare sample questions to ask witnesses, particularly when needed to lay the foundation for evidence to be introduced.
- Prepare a summary description or log of all the exhibits to be used.
- Prepare an abstract of the contents of every document.
- State the location of documents and exhibits that will not be contained in the trial notebook itself.
- Cross-index material on particular witnesses or on legal theories.
- Summarize all information known about each juror from voir dire.
- Prepare end tabs for each section of the notebook.
- Color-code different kinds of documents and information, such as using blue sheets for citations to authorities that support claims and yellow sheets for deposition testimony and other statements of the opposing party.

Of course, you need to adapt these tasks to the particulars of your case. One paralegal recently color-coded all the tabs (green for exhibits, orange for discovery data, etc.) before she discovered that the attorney using the trial notebook was color blind!

6. SETTLEMENT

Throughout the pretrial stage of litigation, the opposing attorneys often engage in efforts to negotiate a settlement of the case in order to avoid a trial. One of the formal documents the parties sometimes use during negotiations is the **settlement work-up**, also called a settlement brochure. It contains a summary of the major facts in the case presented in a manner designed to encourage the other side (or its liability insurance company) to settle the case. Paralegals often have a large role in helping draft this document. For a sample settlement work-up, see Exhibit 9.11 in chapter 9.

settlement work-up A summary of the major facts in the case presented in a manner designed to encourage the other side (or its liability insurance company) to settle the case.

7. EXPERT WITNESSES

Paralegals often have an important role in working with expert witnesses that the trial attorney may want to use. The first task is to locate potential experts for consideration. Many can be located online. A paralegal can use free and paid Internet resources to locate specific kinds of experts. If, for example, the office has a products liability case involving an allegedly defective steering wheel on a 1997 Buick, it is often relatively easy to use these online resources to find experts who have testified on this or a related defect in the past. Once you find such an expert, the next step is to use other online resources to check that expert's credentials and to obtain recommendations by contacting the law offices that have used the expert before. See the sites on expert witnesses in the sections at the Helpful Web Sites at end of chapter 9 and at the end of this chapter.

Once an expert is selected, he or she is sent a formal engagement letter. Patricia Gustin, a paralegal who has helped draft such letters, recommends that the letter include:[15]

- Confirmation of all past discussions (by phone, e-mail, letter, in-person meetings) about hiring the expert
- A summary of the case, including the case name and docket number, if the case has already been filed in court
- Anticipated dates for the expert's testimony at deposition, at trial, or at both
- The scope of the expert testimony to be provided
- A list of articles or documents enclosed in the letter that the expert should review
- Names of the primary contacts in the office that the expert should use
- A list of support people and available resources in the law office for the witness
- A summary of the financial terms for hiring the expert

After the expert is hired, the paralegal may be asked to monitor the ongoing relationship with him or her. This often includes keeping a detailed log on everything sent to the expert for review. The log will note what was sent (e.g., memos, scientific studies, exhibits, and fee payment checks), the format used for the communication (e.g., disk, e-mail, and paper), and the dates these items were sent.

[SECTION D]

LITIGATION ASSISTANTSHIP: TRIAL STAGE

The role of paralegals at trials depends, in part, on the involvement that they have had with the case up to trial. If the involvement has been minimal, then they may not have much to do to assist the attorney at trial. If, on the other hand, they have been working closely with the attorney on the case all along, their role at trial could include a number of tasks:

- Monitoring all the files, documents, and evidence that the attorney will need to plan and to replan strategy as outlined in the trial notebook.
- Doing some spot legal research on issues that come up during the trial that require an answer fairly quickly.
- Preparing preliminary drafts of certain motions and other documents that are required during the course of the trial.
- Visiting the courtroom in advance of the trial to determine the location of the following items within the courthouse itself and within walking distance of the courthouse building: telephones, photocopy machines, fax machines, food take-out facilities, vending machines, stationery supply stores, public restrooms, and points from which Internet access can be obtained. If the trial will be out of town, the paralegal might be asked to set up a secure hotel conference room (sometimes called a "war room") where the litigation team can regularly meet between trial sessions.
- Assuring the presence of witnesses; assisting the attorney in preparing them for direct examination and in anticipating what might be asked of them on cross-examination.
- Taking notes on the testimony of witnesses. These notes can be taken on a laptop computer if the trial judge allows computers at counsel's table. The attorney may be able to use these notes in preparing for other segments of the trial (e.g., closing argument). A transcript (typed or digital) of the testimony may not be available until after the trial.
- Monitoring the reactions of the jury as the trial unfolds. For example, if juror #7 lights up when the attorney makes a certain point or if juror #10 does not appear to be paying attention, the paralegal will let the attorney know about these reactions during a recess or at the end of the day so that the attorney can decide if anything should be emphasized or if a different strategy is needed when the trial resumes.[16]

- Making suggestions to the attorney on what questions to ask a witness based on the paralegal's close following of what has happened thus far in the trial and based on his or her involvement with the documents and files prepared during the pretrial stage.
- Assisting with trial exhibits.
- Obtaining copies of laws that the attorney wants to check during the trial. These laws might be obtained at the closest law library or, if allowed by the court, on an Internet connection on a laptop the paralegal has in the courtroom.

Trial exhibits can include photographs, x-rays, medical illustrations, video presentations, anatomical models, surgical appliances, computer reenactments, etc. Some paralegals are able to design exhibits. See, for example, the graphic designed by Kathleen Evans, a litigation paralegal, in Exhibit 10.10. Notice that the graphic contains a **timeline** that shows when significant events occurred in a birth case where the graphic was used. The head was delivered at 1:47 and the baby at 1:53, indicating a total of six minutes when the baby was deprived of oxygen. Timelines can help the jury visualize the impact of crucial facts.

timeline A chronological presentation of significant events, often organized as a straight-line diagram. (For another example of a timeline, see Exhibit 8.8 in chapter 8.)

EXHIBIT 10.10	Timeline Trial Graphic Designed by a Paralegal

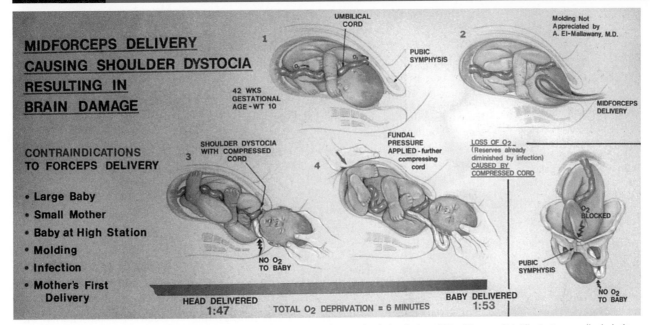

Timeline illustration created by paralegal Kathleen Evans of Litigation Visuals, Inc., that helped win a $3.9 million verdict. "Illustrations really do help the jury know where they are going in calculating damages." 11 *Legal Assistant Today* 28 (November/December, 1993).

Here are some additional examples of paralegal work creating trial exhibits:

- In a case brought against Wal-Mart, paralegal Susan Sharp designed "a 5-foot long by 3.5 foot tall poster board filled with one-sixteenth of an inch squares, each representing $1 million, to graphically illustrate Wal-Mart's wealth."[17] Her poster board was used by the trial attorney during the damages stage of the trial.
- Paralegal Catherine Astl created a calendar chart "wherein we painstakingly . . . thumbed through literally stacks of records, making a list of all therapy visits, doctor visits, pain injection procedures and hospitalizations. We then color coded these events, such as all therapy visits color blocked in blue, all hospitalizations in green, etc. We then gave this information to our exhibit vendor where they shaded in each appropriate box, each of which represented a day on the calendar, for the particular event. For example, if March 4–8 was a hospitalization event, those days were shaded in green. When completed, the jury could visually see the amounts of 'greens' or hospitalizations over several years, the number of 'blues' spent in therapy, the amount of time spent in doctor offices, and the total number of days this poor soul spent in agony after a treatment."[18]

Different versions of the chart created by Catherine Astl are often used as exhibits in personal injury cases. One of the most popular is the life activity calendar that presents a day-in-the-life video or chart on the plaintiff. The exhibit carefully catalogs the minute-by-minute activities of the plaintiff in order to help demonstrate the impact of the injury.

If the office hires a litigation consultant to create such graphics, the role of the paralegal might be to help monitor the work of the consultant. Computer graphics presentation programs such as Microsoft's PowerPoint are available to help create graphics. They can generate slides that contain text, pictures, drawings, and maps. PowerPoint also allows videos or movies to be integrated into the presentation. (For more on these computer programs, see chapter 13.) To display exhibits at trial, the paralegal may have to obtain permission from clerks, the judge's secretary, or other court personnel for the in-court use of devices such as computers, overhead projectors, video players, magnetic boards, blackboards, and chart holders.

In some courtrooms, a judge will allow a paralegal to sit with the attorney at counsel's table during the trial. If laptops are allowed at the table, they may provide online access to earlier deposition testimony given by a witness who is now on the witness stand. As the attorney examines this witness on a topic at the trial, the paralegal can help the attorney quickly find earlier deposition testimony of this witness on the same topic. Here is how one attorney describes the benefits of having paralegals close at hand:

> At trial, the paralegal sitting with counsel can be extremely helpful. Paralegals should be trained to take notes while counsel is examining witnesses and to monitor the admission of exhibits. Thereafter, they can prepare a binder of all exhibits for subsequent trial days and can digest the transcripts. At the end of a day of trial, the file may be out of order, and paralegals can reorganize it for the next day. Finally, paralegals can assist the attorney by calling witnesses to arrange testimony, meeting witnesses in the hall, and talking with the client and his family. Generally, the attorney has so much to concentrate on in trial that paralegals can give the client the needed attention while providing a "buffer" between lawyer and client.[19]

second chair A seat at counsel's table in the courtroom used by an assistant to the trial attorney during the trial. (When paralegals provide this assistance, their role is sometimes referred to as sitting *third chair*.)

For more on the role of the paralegal sitting **second chair** (or "third chair") during the trial, see page 260 in chapter 5.

If the office is about to begin a very important and potentially complex trial, it may decide to conduct a mock trial to give the participants stand-up practice and feedback. A mock trial is a pretend trial staged by one side to operate as close as possible to the upcoming real trial. The office will hire strangers to play the role of jurors. Attorneys in the office will play the role of opposing counsel. Paralegals and secretaries might be asked to play the role of witnesses. After each "side" presents its case, the jury renders its "verdict" and makes itself available to critique the strength of the evidence and the performance of the attorneys. This can be very helpful to the attorney who will be trying the upcoming trial. The exercise is the equivalent of assembling a focus group to obtain reactions to a product or presentation.

shadow jurors Persons hired by one side to observe a trial as members of the general audience and, as the trial progresses, to give feedback to a jury consultant hired by the attorney of one of the parties, who will use the feedback to assess strategy for the remainder of the trial.

Another option is to use **shadow jurors**. These are persons hired by one side to observe a trial as members of the general audience. Typically a law firm will use a jury consultant to select citizens as close demographically to the actual jury as possible. During recess and at the end of the day, these "jurors" will tell the consultant what they thought of the physical evidence, the witnesses, and the performance of the trial attorneys. The consultant will give this information to the attorney who hired the consultant and shadow jurors. Based on this feedback, the attorney will decide whether any shift in trial strategy is warranted for the remainder of the trial. Paralegals might be used to help coordinate the work of the jury consultant as the trial progresses.

[SECTION E]
LITIGATION ASSISTANTSHIP: APPEAL STAGE

Once the trial is over, the central question becomes whether to appeal. (The party bringing the appeal is the *appellant*; the party against whom the appeal is brought is the *appellee* or *respondent*.) In some cases, both sides might decide to appeal if neither party obtained everything it wanted at the trial. Attorneys must review all of the documents and transcripts from the trial in order to identify grounds for an appeal. A paralegal may be asked to go back over the record and do the following:

- Make a list of every time the trial attorney objected to something during the trial. Include the page number where the objection is found, a brief summary of what the objection was, and the ruling of the judge on the objection.
- Make a list of every time opposing counsel made reference to a particular topic, such as the plaintiff's prior involvement in other litigation.
- Make a list of every time the judge asked questions of witnesses.

This information will be critical when the attorney prepares the appellate brief. Arguments made in the brief must refer the judge to specific parts of the trial record and transcript that are relevant to the arguments being made. (These references to specific pages in the trial record are called *record cites*.) The office must be scrupulous in ensuring that references to the record are accurate, particularly quotations from trial transcripts.

Other important paralegal roles on the appellate brief are preparing the table of authorities and cite checking. The **table of authorities** is a list of every primary authority (e.g., cases and statutes) and secondary authority (e.g., legal periodical articles and legal treatises) that a writer has cited in a document such as an appellate brief and indicates where they are mentioned in the document. (For an excerpt from a table of authorities, see Exhibit 12.8 in chapter 12. In chapter 13, we will also examine software used to help create these tables.) The task of **cite checking** the appellate brief is performed by examining every citation in the brief to determine whether the format of the citation is correct, cross-checking the accuracy of every quote, and making sure that any cited laws have not been overruled, repealed, or otherwise modified. We will cover the skill of cite checking (including the use of major **citators** such as Shepard's and KeyCite) in chapter 11.

Once the appellate brief is complete, paralegals can be asked to help monitor its printing (in-house or through an outside printing vendor), filing in court, and service on the opposing side.

When an opponent's appellate brief is received by the office (e.g., the reply brief), the paralegal might be asked to check the accuracy of all quotes to the record and to use the standard citators to determine whether any of the laws cited in the opponent's brief have been overruled, repealed, or otherwise modified.

Some highly skilled paralegals are also given responsibility for drafting part of an appellate brief itself, particularly if the appeal involves an issue the office has often litigated in the past. For example, the appellate office of a public defender might often appeal search-and-seizure issues in criminal cases. A paralegal who works for such an office might be asked to locate earlier briefs on this issue in the office's **brief bank** and to adapt it to the facts of the particular case currently on appeal.

[SECTION F]
LITIGATION ASSISTANTSHIP: ENFORCEMENT STAGE

If a money judgment was awarded to the client, considerable work may be required in collecting it from the **judgment debtor**, the party obligated by the court to pay the judgment. (The person who won the judgment and must be paid is the **judgment creditor**.) The paralegal can arrange for the sheriff to begin **execution**, which is the process of carrying out or enforcing a judgment. The judgment debtor may be ordered by the court to submit to an examination on his or her assets. Investigation work will probably be required to determine what assets exist, where they are, and how they might be reached (see chapter 9 on investigation). In some cases, the attorney may be able to petition the court for a finding of contempt against the judgment debtor for noncompliance with court orders. The paralegal can help by assembling the factual basis to support this charge and in drafting some of the court papers involved.

table of authorities (TOA) A list of primary authority (e.g., cases and statutes) and secondary authority (e.g., legal periodical articles and legal treatises) that a writer has cited in an appellate brief or other document. The list includes page numbers where each authority is mentioned in the document.

cite checking Examining citations in a document to assess whether the format of the citation is correct, whether quoted material is accurately quoted, and whether the law cited is still valid.

citator A book, CD-ROM, or online service with lists of citations that can help assess the current validity of an opinion, statute, or other authority and that give leads to additional relevant material.

brief bank A collection of appellate briefs and related documents drafted in prior cases that might be used as models and adapted for current cases.

judgment debtor The person ordered by a court to pay a money judgment (damages).

judgment creditor The person to whom a court-awarded money judgment (damages) is owed.

execution The process of carrying into effect the decisions in a judgment. A command (via a writ) to a court officer (e.g., sheriff) to seize and sell the property of the losing litigant in order to satisfy the judgment debt.

Chapter Summary

Civil litigation begins with the filing of a complaint, to which the defendant responds with an answer. In these pleadings, the parties state their causes of action and defenses. The next major event is discovery, which can include interrogatories, depositions, requests for admission, etc. If motions for summary judgment are denied, the trial proceeds. After voir dire and opening statements to the jury, the party with the burden of proof puts on its case through the introduction of evidence and the direct examination of witnesses. The latter can be cross-examined by the other party. When the first party rests, the other goes through the same steps. A motion for a judgment as a matter of law (known as a motion

for a directed verdict in some courts) will be granted if there is no legally sufficient evidentiary basis for a reasonable jury to find for the party against whom the motion is made. After closing statements to the jury and the instructions of the judge, the case goes to the jury. Its verdict (if accepted by the court) becomes the basis of the court's judgment.

If dissatisfied with the judgment, the appellant files a notice of appeal and an appellate brief. The appellee also files an appellate brief. After oral argument, the appellate court affirms, reverses, or otherwise modifies what the lower court has done. A further appeal to a higher appellate court might also be possible.

Criminal litigation often begins with an arrest warrant, followed by an initial appearance. Once the decision on bail is made, the prosecution proceeds to the preliminary hearing to determine whether probable cause exists. If so, the grand jury will then determine whether to issue an indictment. The arraignment is next. If plea bargaining is unsuccessful, the case goes to trial, where guilt must be established beyond a reasonable doubt. The criminal trial then proceeds in a manner similar to a civil trial: voir dire, opening statements, etc. The appeal process is also similar: notice of appeal, appellate briefs, etc.

In an administrative hearing, a hearing examiner makes a decision on the dispute within the agency. His or her decision will usually be in the form of a recommendation to a higher official or body within the agency. When a party has exhausted administrative remedies, he or she can appeal the agency's decision to a court.

Alternatives to litigation can include arbitration, mediation, private judging, med-arb, neighborhood justice centers, summary jury trial, and neutral evaluation.

Among the roles fulfilled by paralegals during litigation are the following: drafting complaints, and other pleadings, serving and filing documents, maintaining the calendar, digesting discovery transcripts and documents, helping prepare the trial notebook, assisting with settlement efforts, coordinating trial exhibits, working with expert witnesses, providing assistance as needed during the trial, retrieving and digesting facts in preparation for appeal, and providing general assistance in collecting a judgment.

Key Terms

litigious
litigation
civil dispute
criminal dispute
damages
liable
joint and several liability
retainer
appearance
attorney of record
forum
estate
diversity of citizenship
venue
complaint
plaintiff
cause of action
stating a cause of action
codefendants
pleading
allegation
information and belief
ad damnum clause
bench trial
jury trial
file
civil cover sheet
service of process
summons
process server
proof of service
statute of limitations
personal jurisdiction
motion to dismiss
failure to state a cause of action
procedural law
Federal Rules of Civil Procedure (FRCP)

substantive law
answer
default judgment
motion
defense
affirmative defense
contest
adverse judgment
discovery
interrogatories
deposition
request for admission
subpoena duces tecum
order
hearing
motion for summary judgment
magistrate
pretrial conference
stipulated
in issue
tangible evidence
introduce evidence
set for trial
bailiff
jury panel
voir dire
challenge for cause
bias
peremptory challenge
alternate
impaneled
motion in limine
rule on witnesses
sequester
opening statement
burden of proof
bench conference
objection

competency
excused the jury
examination
overrule
direct examination
ground
hearsay
sustain
strike from the record
cross-examination
redirect examination
recross examination
qualify (a witness)
expert witness
court
clerk
exhibit
move into evidence
rest one's case
case in chief
adjourn
judgment as a matter of law
take under advisement
prima facie case
closing argument
jury instructions
presumption
verdict
elements
preponderance of the evidence
standard of proof
judgment
judgment notwithstanding the verdict
motion for a new trial
appeal
stay
timely

notice of appeal
bond
judgment on the merits
res judicata
bar
appellant
record
transcript
docket
appellate brief
appellee
issues on appeal
oral argument
panel
opinion
dissent
affirm
waive
petition
rehearing
en banc
appeal as a matter of right
writ of certiorari
mandate
satisfy
warrant
prosecution
initial appearance
felony
assigned counsel
bail
personal recognizance
preliminary hearing
probable cause
bound over
grand jury
nolle prosequi
plead
misdemeanor

plea bargaining
indictment
arraignment
impeach
relevant
government
beyond a reasonable doubt
acquit
poll
unemployment
    compensation
administrative hearing
memorandum
hearing examiner
proposed findings and rulings
administrative decision
board of appeals
discretion
below

exhaust administrative
    remedies
trial de novo
alternative dispute
    resolution (ADR)
arbitration
mediation
private judging
med-arb
neighborhood justice
    center (NJC)
summary jury trial
neutral evaluation
template
caption
subject matter jurisdiction
venue
fact pleading
notice pleading

information and belief
special damages
prayer for relief
subscription
verification
substituted service
subpoena
subpoena duces tecum
subpoena ad testificandum
docket number
e-filing
PACER
PDF
demand letter
tickler
e-evidence
privilege log
redact
discoverable

digesting
depo summarizer
digest
Bates stamp
page/line digest
chronological digest
topical digest
trial notebook
settlement work-up
timeline
second chair
shadow jurors
table of authorities
cite checking
citator
brief bank
judgment debtor
judgment creditor
execution

Review Questions

1. What is a litigious society?
2. What are the three categories of civil disputes?
3. What are damages?
4. What are the consequences of joint and several liability?
5. What are the forum choices when citizens of two different states have a legal dispute involving negligence?
6. How does a lawsuit begin?
7. How does a party state a cause of action?
8. Describe the steps involved when serving process.
9. Define three different kinds of jurisdiction.
10. What procedural and substantive law apply in diversity-of-citizenship cases?
11. Distinguish complaint, counterclaim, cross-claim, and third-party complaint.
12. When is a subpoena duces tecum used?
13. When will a court grant a motion for summary judgment?
14. What kinds of challenges can be made against prospective jurors during voir dire?
15. What is the function of opening and closing statements?
16. How does the court resolve a competency challenge to a prospective witness?
17. Describe the sequence of examining witnesses during trial.
18. What motions can be made when both sides rest their case?
19. What is a standard of proof?
20. What are the components of res judicata?
21. What is an appellate brief?
22. What are the options available to an appellate court after it has heard an appeal?
23. What is a writ of certiorari?
24. What is the distinction between an appeal as a matter of right and a writ of certiorari?

25. In a criminal case, what happens at the initial appearance, preliminary hearing, and arraignment?
26. Distinguish between the standard of proof in civil and criminal cases.
27. What is the function of an administrative hearing?
28. How does an administrative agency reach a final conclusion when it has a legal dispute with a citizen?
29. At the agency stage of civil litigation, define the procedural steps involved and state some roles for paralegals at this stage.
30. At the pretrial stage of civil litigation, define the procedural steps involved and state some roles for paralegals at this stage.
31. At the trial stage of civil litigation, define the procedural steps involved and state some roles for paralegals at this stage.
32. At the appeals stage of civil litigation, define the procedural steps involved and state some roles for paralegals at this stage.
33. At the enforcement stage of civil litigation, define the procedural steps involved and state some roles for paralegals at this stage.
34. At the pretrial stage of criminal litigation, define the procedural steps involved and state some roles for paralegals at this stage.
35. At the trial stage of criminal litigation, define the procedural steps involved and state some roles for paralegals at this stage.
36. At the appeals stage of criminal litigation, define the procedural steps involved and state some roles for paralegals at this stage.
37. What are the major kinds of alternative dispute resolution (ADR) and how do they differ?
38. What steps should be taken to avoid abusing a standard form?

39. What are the major components of a complaint?
40. State paralegal roles in service of process and court filings.
41. What is the function of a tickler and what different kinds exist?
42. What are the major methods of discovery and how do paralegals assist attorneys with them?
43. What are the three styles of deposition digests and how do they differ?
44. What guidelines apply to digesting discovery documents?
45. What is the function of a trial notebook and what role do paralegals play in its preparation?
46. What is the function of a settlement work-up?
47. How do paralegals assist attorneys with expert witnesses?
48. How do paralegals assist attorneys at trial?
49. How do paralegals assist attorneys in preparing for an appeal?
50. How do paralegals assist attorneys in the enforcement stage of litigation?

Helpful Web Sites: More on Civil Procedure and Litigation

State and Federal Courts
- www.ncsconline.org/D_KIS/info_court_web_sites.html
- www.uscourts.gov

Trial Overviews (jury handbooks)
- www.mnd.uscourts.gov/jury_handbook.htm
- www.state.ak.us/courts/forms/j-180.pdf
- www.wicourts.gov/services/juror/docs/handbook.pdf

Alternative Dispute Resolution
- www.adr.org
- www.cpradr.org
- www.mediate.com
- www.thecourthousesteps.com

Rules of Procedure and Evidence in Federal Courts
- www.law.cornell.edu/rules/frcp/index.html
- www.law.cornell.edu/rules/fre/index.html
- www.law.cornell.edu/rules/frcrmp

Court Forms
- forms.lp.findlaw.com
- www.USCourtForms.com
- www.lectlaw.com/forma.htm
- www.blumberg.com/forms/index.html

Electronic Court Filing
- www.abanet.org/tech/ltrc/research/efiling/home.html
- www.legaldockets.com
- www.lexisnexis.com/courtlink/online
- www.pacer.psc.uscourts.gov

Electronic Discovery
- discoveryresources.org

Internet Depositions
- www.I-Dep.com

Deposition Summaries
- deposummary.com
- www.dminfo.com/deposition-summary.html
- www.deposums.com/depositionsummaries.html

Expert Witnesses
- www.jurispro.com
- www.seakexperts.com/index.aspx
- www.lectlaw.com/pexp.htm
- www.witness.net
- www.lecg.com
- www.experts.com
- www.tasanet.com

Famous Trials
- www.law.umkc.edu/faculty/projects/ftrials/ftrials.htm

Current Trials
- www.courttv.com

Google Searches (run the following searches for more sites)
- "steps in a trial"
- litigation process
- civil litigation overview
- federal court procedure
- Missouri court procedure (Insert your state)
- trial discovery process
- pretrial procedure
- alternative dispute resolution
- paralegal trial roles

Endnotes

1. National Center for State Courts (www.ncsconline.org/D_Research/csp/CSP_Main_Page.html) and the Federal Judiciary (www.uscourts.gov/judbus2004/front/caseload.pdf).
2. Jane Heath, *Alternative to Trial* 20 Legal Assistant Today 81 (July/August 2003).
3. Catherine Astl, *Inside the Bar*, 78 (iUniverse 2003).
4. Rachel Campbell, *Above and Beyond*, 21 Legal Assistant Today 60 (November/December 2003).
5. Adapted from MacDonald, Pick, DeWitt, and Volz, *Wisconsin Practice Methods* § 1530, at 239 (2d ed. 1959).
6. David Busch, *A Job and an Adventure*, 12 AAPLA Advocate 3 (Alamo Area Professional Legal Assistants, October/November 1993).
7. Erin Schlemme, *Courthouse Etiquette*, 11 The TALA Times 4 (Tulsa Ass'n of Legal Assistants, February 1993).
8. California Civil Procedure Code § 1010.6(a).
9. Christofer French, *The Professional Paralegal Job Search* 18 (1995).

10. Alan Gelb & Karen Levine, *A Survival Guide for Paralegals* 6 (Thomson Delmar Learning 2003).

11. E-mail post on a paralegal listserv (Paralegals@yahoogroups.com) from "lil mermaid" (September 29, 2003).

12. Dana Nikolewski, *Just Call Me Dorothy*, 13 Newsletter 5 (Dallas Ass'n of Legal Assistants, April 1989).

12a. Oliver Gierke, *Deposition Digests*, 24 Legal Assistant Today 86 (September/October 2006).

13. Pam Robtoy, *Preparing Trial Notebooks*, 14 Legal Paraphernalia 5 (St. Louis Ass'n of Legal Assistants, July/August 1994).

14. Hollins, *Assignment: Trial Prep*, 2 California Paralegal 30 (April/June 1990); Feder, *Translating Professional Competence into Performance Competence*, 15 Legal Economics 44 (April 1989).

15. Patricia Gustin, *Making the Expert Witness Part of the Legal Team*, 27 Facts & Finding 14 (November 2000).

16. Debra Martinelli, *A Winning Team*, 19 Legal Assistant Today 54 (July/August 2002).

17. Lee Scheier, *A Very Sharp Legal Team*, 19 Legal Assistant Today 68 (July/August 2002).

18. Catherine Astl, *Behind the Bar* 84 (iUniverse 2003).

19. Lynne Z. Gold-Bikin et al. *Use of Paralegals in a Matrimonial Practice*, 16 FAIR$hare 9 (September 1996).

Student CD-ROM
For additional materials, please go to the CD in this book.

Online Companion™
For additional resources, please go to
http://www.paralegal.delmar.cengage.com

Legal Research

[SECTION A]

INTRODUCTION

This chapter does not cover every aspect of legal research, nor does it treat every conceivable legal resource that could be used in a law library. Rather, the chapter examines the major components of legal research with the objective of identifying effective starting points.

A great deal of information is provided in the pages that follow. You should first skim the chapter to obtain an overview and to see where some concepts are covered in more than one place. Then you should begin collecting the terminology called for in Assignments 11.1 and 11.2. The best way to avoid becoming overwhelmed is to start becoming comfortable with terminology as soon as possible.

When you walk into a law library, your first impression is likely to be one of awe. You are confronted with row upon row of books, most of which seem unapproachable; they do not invite browsing. The same is true of **online** legal materials on the **Internet**. The amount of law that is available online is overwhelming. To be able to use brick-and-mortar or online law libraries, you need to learn the techniques of legal research and understand the limitations of the law library.

A major misunderstanding about the law library is that it contains the answer to every legal question. In many instances, legal problems have no definitive answers. The researcher often operates on the basis of "educated guesses" of what the answer is. To be sure, your guess is supported by what you uncover through legal research. The end product, however, is only the researcher's opinion of what the law is, rather than the absolute answer. No one will know for sure what the "right" or final answer is until the matter is litigated in court. If the problem is never litigated, then the "right" answer will be whatever the parties accept among themselves through negotiation or settlement. The researcher will not know what answer carries the day for the client until the negotiation process is over.

Many simple problems, however, can be answered by basic (easy) legal research. Suppose, for example, you want to know the name of the government agency in charge of incorporating a business or the maximum number of weeks one can receive unemployment compensation. Finding the answer is not difficult if you know what books or other resources to go to and how to use their indexes or other points of access. Many legal research problems, however, are not this simple.

Perhaps the healthiest way to approach the law library is to view it not so much as a source of answers as a storehouse of ambiguities that are waiting to be identified, clarified, manipulated, and applied to the facts of a client's case. You may have heard the story of a client who walked into a law office and asked to see a one-armed attorney. When asked why he required an attorney meeting such specifications, he replied that he was tired of presenting problems to attorneys and having them constantly tell him that "on the one hand" he should do this but "on the other hand" he should do that; he hungered for an attorney who would give him an answer. This concern is well taken. A client is entitled to an answer, to clear guidance. At the same time (or, on the other hand), part of the attorney's job is to identify alternatives or options and to weigh the benefits and disadvantages of each option. Good attorneys are so inclined because they understand that our legal system is infested with unknowns and ambiguities. Good paralegals also have this understanding. They are not frightened by ambiguities; they thrive on them.

In school, you will learn a good deal of law. Eventually, you will probably forget most of it. If you don't, you should! No one can know all of the law, even in a specialty. Furthermore, the law is always changing. Nothing is more dangerous than someone with out-of-date "knowledge" of the law. Law cannot be practiced on the basis of the rules learned in school. Those rules may no longer be valid by the time you try to use them in actual cases. Thousands of courts, legislatures, and administrative agencies spend considerable time writing new laws and changing or adapting old ones. In light of this reality, you need to focus on the *techniques* of doing legal research covered in this chapter. These techniques will remind you to distrust the law you think you know and will equip you to find out what the law is *today*.

The law library and the techniques of legal research are the indispensable tickets of admission to current law. School teaches you to think. *You teach yourself the law through the skill of legal research*. Every time you walk into (or "click on") a law library, you are your own professor. You must accept nothing less than to become an expert on the topic of your research, no matter how narrow or broad the topic. The purpose of the law library is to enable you to become an expert on the current law

online 1. Connected to another computer or computer network, often through the Internet. 2. Residing on a computer and available for use; activated and ready for use on a computer.

Internet A worldwide electronic network of networks on which millions of computer users can share information. A network is a group of computers linked or connected by telephone lines, fiber-optic cables, satellites, or other systems. (The Internet is covered in this chapter and in chapter 13.)

A paralegal in the law library

of your topic. Do not fall into the trap of thinking that you must be an expert in an area of the law to research it properly. The reverse is true. A major way for you to become an expert in an area is by discovering on your own what the law library can teach you about that area.

Never be reluctant to undertake legal research on a topic simply because you know very little about the topic. Knowing very little is often a beneficial starting point for the researcher. Preconceptions about the law can sometimes lead you away from avenues in the library that you should be traveling.

Becoming an expert through comprehensive legal research does not necessarily mean that you will know everything about a particular topic or issue. An expert has answers *and* knows how to *formulate the questions that remain unanswered even after comprehensive legal research*. An expert is someone who can say:

This is what the current law says, and these are the questions that the law has not yet resolved.

Of course, you cannot know what is unresolved until you know what is resolved. The law library will help tell you both.

[SECTION B]
FRUSTRATION AND LEGAL RESEARCH

You are in the position of the king who sadly discovered that there is no royal road to geometry. If he wanted to learn geometry, he had to struggle through it like everyone else. Legal research is a struggle and will remain so for the rest of your career. The struggle will eventually become manageable and even enjoyable and exciting—but there is no way to avoid the struggle no matter how many shortcuts you learn. The amount of material in a law library is simply too massive for legal research to be otherwise, and the material is growing every day with new laws, new formats for law books, new technology, and new publishers offering new services that must be mastered.

Unfortunately, some cannot handle the pressure that the law library sometimes seems to donate in abundance. Too many attorneys, for example, stay away from the library and consequently practice law "from the hip." They act on the basis of instinct and bravado rather than on the basis of the most current law uncovered through comprehensive legal research. Such attorneys need to be sure that they have adequate malpractice insurance!

Legal research will be difficult for you at the beginning, but with experience and the right attitude, you will overcome the difficulties. The most important advice is *stick with it*. Spend a lot of time in the library. Be inquisitive. Ask a lot of questions of fellow students, teachers, librarians, attorneys, paralegals, legal secretaries, etc. Be constantly on the alert for tips and techniques. Take strange books from the shelf and try to figure out what they contain, what they try to do, how they are used, and how they duplicate or complement other law books with which you are more familiar. Do not wait to be taught how to use sets of books that are new to you. Strike out on your own. Do the same online. Visit research sites often. Take advantage of **hypertext** to click your way around the site you are on and the sites to which you are led.

> **hypertext** A method of displaying and linking information found in different locations on the same site or on different sites of the World Wide Web.

We will be saying a good deal about computers in this chapter and in chapter 13. Computers can be very helpful, but they do not eliminate the need to learn the basics. The struggle does not disappear if you study or work where computers are available. Intelligent use of computers requires an understanding of the fundamental techniques of legal research. Furthermore, computer legal research can be expensive. A good deal of free legal information is now available on the Internet, but as we will see, it is not always as current or accurate as information available in traditional library volumes and in commercial (fee-based) computer research services.

At this stage of your career, most of the frustration will center on the question of how to *begin* your legal research of a topic. Once you overcome this frustration, the concern will then become how to *end* your legal research. After locating a great deal of material, you will worry about when to stop. In this chapter, our major focus will be the techniques of beginning. Techniques of stopping are more troublesome for the conscientious researcher. It is not always easy to determine whether you have found everything that you should find. Although guidelines do exist and will be examined (in Section Y, later in the chapter), a great deal of experience with legal research is required before you can make the judgment that you have found everything available on a given topic. Yet the techniques you need will come with time and practice. Don't be too hard on yourself. You will not learn everything now; you can only begin the learning that must continue throughout your career.

Keep the following "laws" of legal research in mind:

1. *The only books that will be missing from a shelf are those that you need to use immediately.*
2. *A vast amount of information on law books and research techniques exists, most of which you will forget soon after learning.*
3. *Each time you forget something, relearning it will take half the time it previously took.*
4. *When you have relearned something for the fourth time, you own it.*

At times, you will walk away from a set of law books that you have used and wonder what you have just done—even if you obtained an answer from the books. At times, you will go back to a set of books that you have used in the past and draw a blank on what the books are and how to use them again. These occurrences are natural. You will forget and you will forget again. Stay with it. Be willing to relearn. You cannot master a set of books after using them only a few times. Learning legal research is a little like learning to play a musical instrument: a seat is waiting for you in the orchestra, but you must practice. A royal road does not exist. Computers will help, but their availability requires you to know another "law" of legal research:

5. *The computer will become your best friend only when you have acquired the techniques of traditional book (i.e., paper) legal research that will allow you to find what you need without a computer.*

[SECTION C]

ORGANIZATION OF THE CHAPTER

This chapter has two main parts. The second half covers checklists and strategies for finding the ten main categories of **primary authority** (laws) that might be needed to resolve a legal issue. The ten categories are as follows:

> **primary authority** Any law that a court could rely on in reaching its decision. *Secondary authority* is any nonlaw (e.g., a legal periodical article) that a court could rely on in reaching its decision.

Opinions	Charters
Statutes	Ordinances
Constitutions	Rules of court
Administrative regulations	Executive orders
Administrative decisions	Treaties

For definitions of these categories (plus a special eleventh category—the opinions of the attorney general), see Exhibit 6.1 in chapter 6.

Before we learn how to find these categories of law, we will do two things: cover some of the *basics* needed to perform any research task and study the major *research resources*. These will be our goals in the first half of the chapter.

BASICS

The basics include the following topics:

- Terminology of legal research
- Kinds of legal authority
- Citation of legal authority
- Indexes

Once we have grasped these fundamentals, we turn to the research resources.

RESEARCH RESOURCES

The major research resources we will use to find the law needed to resolve a legal issue are as follows:

Catalogs	Legal periodicals
Digests	Legal encyclopedias
Annotations	Treatises
Shepard's	Phone and e-mail
Looseleaf services	Computers

Our approach in this chapter, therefore, will be as follows: first, we will cover the basics and the research resources; then, we will use this material to find the ten major categories of primary authority.

[SECTION D]

TERMINOLOGY OF LEGAL RESEARCH: TWO CHECKLISTS

This section contains two lists. The first is a list of essential research terms that you need to understand before you start doing any legal research (see Exhibit 11.1 and Assignment 11.1). The second is a more comprehensive list of terms that you need to understand by the time you finish studying legal research (see Exhibit 11.2 and Assignment 11.2). All of the terms in the essentials list (Exhibit 11.1) are also in the comprehensive list (Exhibit 11.2). Do Assignment 11.1 now. Assignment 11.2 should be completed by the end of the course. You need to learn the language of legal research as well as how to do legal research. Assignments 11.1 and 11.2 will help you start acquiring this language.

Do not be intimidated by the comprehensive list. You are not expected to grasp everything in it right away. Begin collecting definitions now. When you start solving research problems in the library, the terms will have increased meaning for you.

Both lists contain numbers in parentheses after each entry. They are page numbers in the book where the terms are covered. Check the index for other pages where they are covered.

EXHIBIT 11.1   The Terminology of Legal Research: A Checklist of Essentials

1. act (456)
2. administrative code (456)
3. administrative decision (276)
4. administrative regulation (276)
5. advance sheet (for reporters) (456)
6. ALR Index (532)
7. American Jurisprudence 2d (458)
8. American Law Reports (457)
9. analogous/on point (488)
10. annotated (458)
11. annotation (458)
12. authority (primary/secondary; mandatory/persuasive) (486ff)
13. bill (458)
14. brief of a case (459)
15. caption (of a case) (496)
16. CARTWHEEL (516)
17. CD–ROM (454)
18. citator (465)
19. cite/citation (465)
20. cited material/citing material (478)
21. code (465)
22. common law (279)
23. constitution (567)
24. Corpus Juris Secundum (466)
25. cumulative (466)
26. Current Law Index (466)
27. digests (for reporters) (466)
28. docket number (500)
29. enacted law (318)
30. headnote (472)
31. Index to Legal Periodicals and Books (472)
32. Internet (443)
33. key number (467)
34. legal encyclopedia (474)
35. legal periodical (475)
36. legal treatise (475)
37. legislation (475)
38. legislative history (458)
39. looseleaf service (454)
40. National Reporter System (476)
41. notes of decisions (558)
42. opinion (case) (459)
43. ordinance (276)
44. parallel cite (465)
45. pocket part (477)
46. precedent (488)
47. primary authority (445)
48. public domain citation (477, 496)
49. regional reporter (462)

(continues)

EXHIBIT 11.1	The Terminology of Legal Research: A Checklist of Essentials—*continued*	
50. register (477) 51. reporter (regional, official/ unofficial) (459, 462) 52. rules of court (478)	53. search engine (639) 54. secondary authority (486) 55. series/edition (478) 56. session law (456)	57. shepardize (478) 58. statute (276) 59. statutory code (482) 60. U.S. Code (483)

EXHIBIT 11.2	The Terminology of Legal Research: A Comprehensive Checklist	
1. abstract (455)	49. case of first impression (492)	103. Findlaw (450)
2. act (456)	50. cause of action/defense (402, 404)	104. first impression (492)
3. administrative code (276)	51. CD–ROM (454)	105. freestyle (627)
4. administrative decision (276)	52. Century Digest (468)	106. full faith and credit (489)
5. Administrative Procedure Act (569)	53. C.F.R. Index and Finding Aids (563, 570)	107. full-text search (623)
6. administrative regulation (276)	54. CFR Parts Affected (571)	108. General Digest (468)
7. advance session law service/ legislative service (456)	55. charter (276)	109. generic citation (502)
8. advance sheet (456)	56. citator (465)	110. GlobalCite (465)
9. A.L.R. Bluebook of Supplemental Decisions (532)	57. cite checking (510)	111. handbook/hornbook/practice manual/form book (552)
10. ALR Digest (532)	58. cite/citation (465)	112. headnote (472)
11. ALR Federal Tables (533)	59. cited material/citing material (478)	113. historical note (of a statute) (557)
12. ALR Index (532)	60. CLE materials (465)	114. history of a case/treatment of a case (500)
13. A.L.R.2d Later Case Service (532)	61. code (official, unofficial) (482)	115. holding (312)
14. ALR Table of Laws, Rules, and Regulations (533)	62. Code of Federal Regulations (466)	116. hornbook (472)
15. ALWD Citation Manual (457)	63. codify (465)	117. hypertext (445)
16. American Digest System (457, 468)	64. committee report (522)	118. id. (513)
17. American Jurisprudence 2d (458)	65. common law (279)	119. Ilinois Decisions (463)
18. American Law Reports (457)	66. conference committee (291)	120. Index to Legal Periodicals and Books (472)
19. amicus curiae brief (459)	67. conflict of laws (489)	121. Infra (512)
20. analogous/on point (488)	68. Congressional Information Service (CIS) (465)	122. in re (500)
21. annotated (458)	69. Congressional Record (466)	123. Interfiling (515)
22. annotated bibliography (458)	70. constitution (567)	124. Internet (443, 474)
23. annotated reporter (458)	71. construed/construction (561)	125. Iinterstate compact (474)
24. annotated statutory code (458)	72. Corpus Juris Secundum (466)	126. Jurisdictional Table of Cited Statutes and Cases (532)
25. annotation (458)	73. cumulative (466)	127. KeyCite (465)
26. Annotation History Table (532)	74. Current Law Index (466)	128. key number (467)
27. annotation (superseded/ supplemented) (533)	75. Decennial Digest (468)	129. KF call number (526)
28. appellate brief (459)	76. Descriptive Word Index (529)	130. law directory (476)
29. appellant/appellee (respondent) (309)	77. deskbook (466)	131. law review/law journal (475)
30. Atlantic Digest (458)	78. dictum (plural: dicta) (490)	132. legal dictionary (474)
31. Atlantic 2d (458)	79. digest paragraph (528)	133. legal encyclopedia (474)
32. authority (primary/secondary; mandatory/persuasive) (486ff)	80. digests (for A.L.R.) (532)	134. legal newsletter (474)
33. Auto-Cite (458, 465)	81. digests (for Martindale- Hubbell) (476)	135. legal newspaper (474)
34. Bankruptcy Reporter (462)	82. digests (for reporters) (466)	136. legal periodical (475)
35. bill (458)	83. docket number (500)	137. Legal Resource Index (549)
36. black letter law (551)	84. e-CFR (466)	138. legal thesaurus (475)
37. Black's Law Dictionary (458)	85. ejusdem generis (561)	139. LegalTrac (475)
38. Blue and White Book (459)	86. enabling statute (569)	140. legal treatise (475)
39. Bluebook: A Uniform System of Citation, The (458)	87. enacted law (318)	141. legislation (475)
40. Boolean search/natural language search (627)	88. Encyclopedia of Associations (553)	142. legislative history (458)
41. brief of a case (459)	89. et al. (500)	143. legislative intent (487)
42. bulletin (459)	90. ex rel. (500)	144. LexisNexis (476)
43. California Reporter (459)	91. et seq. (545)	145. Library of Congress (LC) Classification System (526)
44. CALR (454)	92. executive agreement (574)	146. listserv (641)
45. caption (of a case) (496)	93. executive order (276)	147. Loislaw (450)
46. CARTWHEEL (516)	94. Federal Appendix (462, 471)	148. looseleaf service (454)
47. casebook (464)	95. Federal Claims Reporter (462)	149. LSA: List of Sections Affected (571)
48. case note (548)	96. federal depository library (449)	150. Martindale-Hubbell Law Directory (476)
	97. federalism (275)	151. MEDLINE (550)
	98. Federal Practice Digest 4th (468)	152. memorandum opinion (311)
	99. Federal Register (471)	
	100. Federal Reporter 3d (462)	
	101. Federal Rules Decisions (462)	
	102. Federal Supplement 2d (462)	

(continues)

153. microforms (microfilm/ultrafiche) (454)
154. Military Justice Reporter (462)
155. National Reporter Blue Book (498)
156. National Reporter System (476)
157. New York Supplement 2d (463)
158. nominative reporter (501)
159. North Eastern 2d (476)
160. North Western Digest (476)
161. North Western 2d (476)
162. notes of decisions (558)
163. nutshell (476)
164. on all fours (320)
165. online (454)
166. opinion (case) (459)
167. opinion (majority/plurality/ concurring/dissenting) (312)
168. opinion of the attorney general (277)
169. opinion (unpublished) (461)
170. ordinance (276)
171. overrule/reverse/override (291, 538)
172. Pacific Digest 2d (476)
173. Pacific 3d (477)
174. parallel cite (465)
175. Parallel Table of Authorities and Rules (563)
176. pattern jury instructions (477)
177. per curiam opinion (311)
178. pinpoint cite (502)
179. plaintiff/defendant table (in digests) (530)
180. plagiarism (492)
181. pocket part (477)
182. popular name table (562)
183. precedent (488)
184. primary authority (445)
185. private law (475)
186. public domain citation (477, 496)
187. public law (475)

188. quick index (532)
189. record (477)
190. regional digest (469)
191. regional reporter (477)
192. register (477)
193. remand (312)
194. reporter (regional, official/ unofficial) (459, 462)
195. reports (477)
196. Restatements (477)
197. root expander (!) (628)
198. rules of court (478)
199. search engine (639)
200. secondary authority (486)
201. section (§) (557)
202. series/edition (478)
203. session law (456)
204. shepardize (478)
205. Shepard's (asterisk/delta) (537)
206. Shepard's (history of the case/ treatment of the case) (537, 538)
207. Shepard's Case Name Citator (497)
208. Shepard's Code of Federal Regulations Citations (480)
209. Shepard's Federal Citations (479)
210. Shepard's Federal Statute Citations (480)
211. Shepard's United States Citations (479)
212. short-form citation (494)
213. slip law (456)
214. slip opinion (460)
215. South Eastern Digest (481)
216. South Eastern 2d (481)
217. Southern 2d (481)
218. South Western 3d (481)
219. special edition state reporter (462)
220. stare decisis (488)
221. star paging (481)

222. statute (276)
223. statutes at large (456, 541)
224. statutory code (482)
225. supra (512)
226. Supremacy Clause (489)
227. Supreme Court Reporter (461)
228. syllabus (in reporters) (310)
229. table of authorities (511)
230. Table of Courts and Circuits (532)
231. Table of Jurisdictions Represented (532)
232. Table of Key Numbers (530)
233. Table of Laws and Rules (552)
234. TAPP (520)
235. term of art (515)
236. thomas.loc.gov (563)
237. treaty (277)
238. uniform laws (483)
239. uniform resource locator (637)
240. universal character (*) (628)
241. U.S. Code (483)
242. U.S. Code Annotated (483)
243. U.S. Code Congressional and Administrative News (483)
244. U.S. Code Service (483)
245. U.S. Law Week (461)
246. U.S. Reports (461)
247. U.S. Statutes at Large (483)
248. U.S. Supreme Court Digest (484)
249. U.S. Supreme Court Reports, Lawyers' Edition (461)
250. U.S. Tax Court Reports (462)
251. validation research (574)
252. Veterans Appeals Reporter (462)
253. West Group (462, 466)
254. Westlaw (625)
255. WilsonWeb (549)
256. writ of certiorari (501)
257. Words and Phrases (484)

ASSIGNMENT 11.1

For each of the words and phrases in Exhibit 11.1, prepare a three-by-five-inch index card on which you include the following information:

- The word or phrase
- The pages in this text where the word or phrase is discussed (begin with the page number given in parentheses; then add other page numbers as the word or phrase is discussed elsewhere in the text, as well as in the glossary)
- The definition or function of the word or phrase
- Other information about the word or phrase that you obtain as you use the law library
- Comments by your instructor in class about any of the words and phrases

Keep the cards in alphabetical order. The cards will become your own file system on legal research that you can use as a study guide for the course and as a reference tool when you do legal research in the library.

ASSIGNMENT 11.2

Do Assignment 11.1 for the list in Exhibit 11.2. Turn in this assignment when you complete your study of legal research.

[SECTION E]

FINDING LAW LIBRARIES

We begin with brick-and-mortar law libraries. The availability of such libraries depends to a large degree on the area where you live, study, or work. Rural areas, for example, have fewer possibilities than larger cities or capitals.

Begin your search for a law library by entering the following search terms—using the name of your state—in Google (www.google.com) or any other general search engine such as Microsoft search (www.live.com):

> Texas "law library"
> Massachusetts "law library"
> "New York" "law library"

Then reenter the search by adding the name of the largest city near you:

> Dallas Texas "law library"
> Boston Massachusetts "law library"
> Albany "New York" "law library"

These searches should lead you to online libraries (discussed below) and to some of the following eleven categories of brick-and-mortar libraries:

- Law school library
- General university library (may have a law section)
- Law library of a bar association
- State law library (in the state capital and perhaps in branch offices in counties throughout the state)
- Local public library (may have a small law section)
- Law library of the legislature or city council
- Law library of the city solicitor or corporation counsel
- Law library of the district attorney or local prosecutor
- Law library of the public defender
- Law library of a federal, state, or local administrative agency (particularly in the office of the agency's general counsel)
- Law library of a court

Some of these libraries are open to the general public. Others provide restricted or no access. Find out if any of them are **federal depository libraries**. These are public or private libraries that receive free federal government publications (e.g., the statutes of Congress) to which they must allow access by the general public without cost. Many states have comparable programs for state government publications. State depository libraries (different names may be used) receive free state government publications to which the general public must be given access without cost.

federal depository library
A public or private library that receives free federal government publications to which it must allow access by the general public without cost. (In some states, there is a comparable program for state government publications.)

Finding a Federal Depository Library

catalog.gpo.gov/fdlpdir/FDLPdir.jsp

Finding a State Depository Library

- On the Web site of *federal* depository libraries, you will often be directed to *state* depository libraries, if any exist.
- Run the following search in Google or any general search engine (using the name of your state):

Florida depository library

Another option is an online law library. As we will stress throughout this book, however, caution is needed when using any online resources, particularly those that are free. The material you find online, with some major exceptions, may not be reliable or current. We will have more to say on this concern later.

In chapter 13, we will cover fee-based and free online law library resources. Here is a preview of some of the major ones (some of which consist of links to sites that contain the legal materials):

Major Online Legal Resources (free)

For a more comprehensive list, see Exhibit 13.11 in chapter 13.

www.loc.gov/law/public/law.html
www.washlaw.edu
www.law.indiana.edu/v-lib
www.findlaw.com
www.law.cornell.edu
www.lawresearch.com
www.hg.org
www.lawguru.com

Major Online Legal Resources (fee-based)

www.westlaw.com
www.lexis.com
loislaw.com
www.versuslaw.com

Major Online Legal Resources for Your State

Run the following search in Google or any major search engine (using your state's name):

Texas "legal research"
Massachusetts "legal research"
"New York" "legal research"

[SECTION F]
CATEGORIES OF RESEARCH MATERIALS

The research materials that you will use in your legal career fall into four categories based on their function:

- Materials that contain the full text of the law
- Materials that help you locate the law
- Materials that help you understand and interpret the law
- Materials that help you determine the current validity of the law

The four main columns of Exhibit 11.3 classify research materials by these four functions. As we will see, some materials can serve more than one function. Legal periodicals, for example, can help you find the law as well as understand it. Exhibit 11.3 is our point of departure. All of the material mentioned in Exhibit 11.3 will be examined in detail later in the chapter.

EXHIBIT 11.3	The Four Functions of Research Materials			
Kind of Law	**Materials That Contain the Full Text of This Kind of Law**	**Materials That Can Be Used to Locate This Kind of Law**	**Materials That Can Be Used to Help Understand This Kind of Law**	**Materials That Can Be Used to Help Determine the Current Validity of This Kind of Law**
(a) Opinions	Reports Reporters Advance sheets Looseleaf services Slip opinions CD–ROM Internet: Fee-Based (Ex: Westlaw and LexisNexis) Internet: Free (Ex: www.gpoaccess .gov/cfr)	Digests Annotations in A.L.R. Shepard's Legal periodicals Legal encyclopedias Legal treatises Looseleaf services Words and Phrases Internet search engines and directories (Ex: www.google.com and www.hg.org)	Legal periodicals Legal encyclopedias Legal treatises Legal newsletters Annotations in A.L.R. Looseleaf services	Shepard's KeyCite GlobalCite

(continues)

EXHIBIT 11.3	The Four Functions of Research Materials—*continued*			
Kind of Law	**Materials That Contain the Full Text of This Kind of Law**	**Materials That Can Be Used to Locate This Kind of Law**	**Materials That Can Be Used to Help Understand This Kind of Law**	**Materials That Can Be Used to Help Determine the Current Validity of This Kind of Law**

(b) Statutes	Statutory Code
	Statutes at Large
	Session Laws
	Compilations
	Consolidated Laws
	Slip Laws
	Acts & Resolves
	Laws
	Legislative Services
	CD–ROM
	Internet: Fee-Based
	  (Ex: Westlaw and
	  LexisNexis)
	Internet: Free
	  (Ex: thomas.loc.gov)
		Index volumes of
		  statutory code
		Looseleaf services
		Footnote references
		  in other materials
		Internet search engines
		  and directories
		  (Ex: www.yahoo.com
		  and www.findlaw.com)
			Legal periodicals
			Legal encyclopedias
			Legal treatises
			Legal newsletters
			Annotations in A.L.R.
			Looseleaf services
				Shepard's
				KeyCite
				GlobalCite

(c) Constitutions	Statutory Code
	Separate volumes
	  containing the
	  constitution
	CD–ROM
	Internet: Fee-Based
	  (Ex: Westlaw and
	  LexisNexis)
	Internet: Free
	  (Ex: www.usconstitution
	  .net)
		Index volumes of
		  statutory code
		Looseleaf services
		Footnote references
		  in other materials
		Internet
		  (Ex: www.law.cornell
		  .edu)
			Legal periodicals
			Legal encyclopedias
			Legal treatises
			Legal newsletters
			Annotations in A.L.R.
			Looseleaf services
				Shepard's
				KeyCite

(d) Administrative Regulations	Administrative Code
	Separate volumes
	  containing the
	  regulations of some
	  agencies
	Looseleaf services
	CD–ROM
	Internet: Fee-Based
	  (Ex: Westlaw and
	  LexisNexis)
	Internet: Free
	  (Check the Web site
	  of the administrative
	  agency)
		Index volumes of the
		  administrative code
		Looseleaf services
		Footnote references
		  in other materials
		Internet: Run the
		  following search in
		  Google or another
		  search engine (substi-
		  tuting your state):
		  Florida "administrative
		  regulations"
			Legal periodicals
			Legal treatises
			Legal newsletters
			Annotations in A.L.R.
			Looseleaf services
				Shepard's
				KeyCite
				GlobalCite
				List of Sections Affected
				  (www.gpoaccess
				  .gov/lsa)

(e) Administrative Decisions	Separate volumes of
	  decisions of some
	  agencies
	Looseleaf services
	Internet: Fee-Based
	  (Ex: Westlaw and
	  LexisNexis)
	Internet: Free
	  (Check the Web site
	  of the administrative
	  agency)
		Looseleaf services
		Index to (or digest
		  volumes for) the
		  decisions
		Footnote references
		  in other materials
			Legal periodicals
			Legal treatises
			Legal newsletters
			Annotations in A.L.R.
			Looseleaf services
				Shepard's
				KeyCite

(continues)

EXHIBIT 11.3	The Four Functions of Research Materials—*continued*			
Kind of Law	Materials That Contain the Full Text of This Kind of Law	Materials That Can Be Used to Locate This Kind of Law	Materials That Can Be Used to Help Understand This Kind of Law	Materials That Can Be Used to Help Determine the Current Validity of This Kind of Law
(f) Charters	Separate volumes containing the charter Municipal Code Register State session laws Official journal Internet: Fee-Based (Ex: Westlaw and LexisNexis) Internet: Free (Check the Web site of the municipality or county)	Index volumes to the charter or municipal code Footnote references in other materials	Legal periodicals Legal treatises Annotations in A.L.R.	Shepard's
(g) Ordinances	Municipal code Official journal Legal newspaper Internet: Fee-Based (Ex: Westlaw and LexisNexis) Internet: Free (Check the Web site of the municipality or county)	Index volumes of municipal code Footnote references in other materials Internet (Ex: www.municode.com)	Legal periodicals Legal treatises Annotations in A.L.R.	Shepard's
(h) Rules of Court	Separate rules volumes Statutory code Practice manuals Deskbook CD–ROM Internet: Fee-Based (Ex: Westlaw and LexisNexis) Internet: Free (Ex: www.supreme-courtus.gov/ctrules/ctrules.html)	Index to separate rules volumes Index to statutory code Index to practice manuals Index to deskbook Footnote references in other materials Internet (Ex: www.11rx.com/courtrules)	Practice manuals Legal periodicals Legal treatises Legal newsletters Annotations in A.L.R. Legal encyclopedias Looseleaf services	Shepard's KeyCite
(i) Executive Orders	Federal Register Code of Federal Regulations Weekly Compilation of Presidential Documents U.S. Code Congressional and Administrative News U.S.C./U.S.C.A./U.S.C.S. Internet: Fee-Based (Ex: Westlaw, LexisNexis) Internet: Free (Ex: www.gpoaccess.gov/wcomp)	Index volumes to the sets of books listed in the second column Footnote references in other materials Internet (Ex: www.whitehouse.gov)	Legal periodicals Legal treatises Legal newsletters Annotations in A.L.R. Looseleaf services	Shepard's KeyCite

(continues)

EXHIBIT 11.3	The Four Functions of Research Materials—*continued*			
Kind of Law	**Materials That Contain the Full Text of This Kind of Law**	**Materials That Can Be Used to Locate This Kind of Law**	**Materials That Can Be Used to Help Understand This Kind of Law**	**Materials That Can Be Used to Help Determine the Current Validity of This Kind of Law**
(j) Treaties	Statutes at Large (up to 1949) United States Treaties and Other International Agreements Department of State Bulletin International Legal Materials Internet: Fee-Based (Ex: Westlaw and LexisNexis) Internet: Free (Ex: thomas.loc.gov/home/treaties/treaties.htm)	Index within the volumes listed in second column World Treaty Index Current Treaty Index Footnote references in other materials Internet (Ex: www.state.gov/s/l/treaty)	Legal periodicals Legal treatises Legal newsletters Annotations in A.L.R., A.L.R.2d, A.L.R. Fed. Legal encyclopedias Looseleaf service	Shepard's
(k) Opinions of the Attorney General	Separate volumes containing these opinions Internet: Fee-Based (Ex: Westlaw and LexisNexis) Internet: Free (Ex: www.usdoj.gov/olc/opinions.htm)	Digests Footnote references in other materials		

[SECTION G]

FORMATS OF LEGAL RESEARCH MATERIALS

The legal community in the United States spends over $5.5 billion a year to be able to read the research materials listed in Exhibit 11.3. The availability of free material on the Internet has not lowered this cost; it has simply made more options available. A great deal of choice is available. You can read a court opinion or a statute, for example, in a book, online, on a disk, or on microform. Variety exists even within these media categories. Here is an overview of available formats:

Legal Research Media

1. Paper
   a. Pamphlet
   b. Hardcover, fixed pages
   c. Hardcover, looseleaf

2. Online (CALR)
   a. Fee-based
   b. Free

3. CD–ROM

4. Microform
   a. Microfilm
   b. Ultrafiche

The trend in legal research is toward **CALR** (computer-assisted legal research). As indicated earlier, however, knowing how to use the other formats (particularly traditional law books) is one of the foundations of competent CALR. Furthermore, many clients cannot afford the high cost of the most sophisticated CALR that is available. Attorneys and paralegals working for such clients must know how to use the alternatives.

PAPER

Traditional library books are pamphlets or hardcover volumes made of paper. Very often the pamphlets are considered temporary. They tend to contain recent legal research material that will eventually be printed in more permanent hardcover volumes. When the latter become available, the law library throws away the pamphlets.

Most hardcover volumes contain pages that you cannot remove without ripping the book. A looseleaf book, in contrast, is a hardcover book with removable pages. A **looseleaf** service is a lawbook with a binding (often three ringed) that allows easy inserting and removal of pages for updating.

Inserting pages into a looseleaf service

ONLINE (CALR)

In legal research, the most common meaning of *online* is being connected to other computers, primarily through the Internet. Such research is called computer-assisted legal research (CALR). The major commercial (i.e., fee-based) providers of CALR are Westlaw, LexisNexis, and Loislaw. Some online services are free. When online (or offline) material is in the **public domain**, it is not protected by copyright or patent and hence is available to anyone without fee. The major examples of online legal material in the public domain are statutes found on the sites of legislatures and opinions found on the sites of courts. (A broader meaning of *online* is residing on a computer and available for use whether or not the computer is connected to other computers.)

CD-ROM

CD-ROM (compact disk read-only memory) is a compact disk that stores data in a digital format. It is an optical information-storage system that operates much like a compact disk sold in music stores. Through your computer system, you gain access to the vast amount of information stored on the disk. Up to 150 large volumes of law books can be stored on one disk! Users cannot add any information to the disk: they can only read the information on it through their computer screen or monitor (hence the phrase *read only*). Unlike Internet-based computer-assisted legal research systems, you do not need a modem or wireless connection to use a CD-ROM. (As we will see in chapter 13, there are other kinds of compact disks that *do* allow the reader to write to the disks as well as read what is on them. An example is a CD-RW (compact disk re-writable).)

Examples of CD-ROM products

MICROFORM

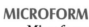

Microforms are images or photographs that have been reduced in size. Among the materials stored on microforms are pages from reporters, codes, treatises, periodicals, etc. Vast amounts of material can be stored in this way. An entire volume of a 1,000-page law book can fit on a single plastic card. Special machines (*reader-printers* and *fiche readers*) magnify the material so that it can be read. These machines are sometimes awkward to use. The major value of microforms is the space savings that can result by storing (i.e., archiving) a large quantity of materials that no longer need to take up shelf space. In general, these are older materials that researchers do not use on a regular basis. Several kinds of microforms are available. *Microfilm* stores the material on film reels or cassettes. *Ultrafiche* is microfiche with a considerably greater storage capacity, providing a reduction factor of 100 or more.

Example of ultrafiche (a microform) that contains an entire reporter volume

[SECTION H]

GLOSSARY OF RESEARCH MATERIALS

We turn now to an overview of the major research terms and research materials that we will encounter throughout the remainder of the chapter. The overview is presented in the form of a glossary. At the end of the glossary, you will find a chart (Exhibit 11.9 on page 484) that summarizes most of the materials introduced in the glossary. Later in the chapter, we will focus on how to *use* the materials listed in this glossary. At this stage, our goal is more modest: identifying what exists.

One final caution about definitions before we begin. There are standard definitions of most terms used in legal research, but there are a few dramatic exceptions. For example:

- The phrase *Supreme Court* means the highest court in our federal judicial system (the United States Supreme Court) and the highest state court in many state judicial systems (e.g., California Supreme Court). In New York, however, one of the main *lower* courts is called the Supreme Court.
- The word *digest* usually refers to a set of volumes that contain brief summaries of court opinions. In Minnesota, there is a digest that fits this definition—it gives brief summaries of Minnesota court opinions. There is another digest in Minnesota, however, called *Dunnell Minnesota Digest*, that is a legal encyclopedia rather than a traditional digest. Furthermore, we will see that the word *digest* can refer to other kinds of research materials as well.

Although standard definitions are generally available, you should be prepared to find variations such as these.

ASSIGNMENT 11.3

The glossary on pages 455–484 contains over eighty photographs of books and pamphlets, not counting the photos of page excerpts. Some of the photos contain more than one volume. In this assignment, you are to go to the most comprehensive law library or libraries near you and find the books and pamphlets depicted in the photographs (or close substitutes). There are several reasons why you may not be able to find the exact book or pamphlet in one of the photos:

- The library may not have purchased or subscribed to the book or pamphlet.
- The library has the book or pamphlet, but not the volume number or issue depicted in the photo. (Some pamphlets, for example, are thrown away when bound volumes come out that include the material in the pamphlets.)
- The library has the book or pamphlet, but the one you want is simply not on the shelf. (It may be in use or have been misshelved.)
- The photograph is not clear enough to allow you to make out the volume number or other identifying information about the book or pamphlet in the photo.

If any of these reasons applies, try to find as close a substitute as possible in the law library. A close substitute might be a different volume number in the same set, a different title in the same category of book, or the same category of book but for a different state. Proceed as follows:

(a) Make a list of every book or pamphlet photographed in the glossary on pages 455–484 (not including photos of page excerpts). If more than one book or pamphlet is depicted in a photo, list each separately.

(b) Place a check mark (✔) in front of a book or pamphlet on the list if you found it *exactly* as pictured in the photograph, e.g., the same volume number. Include a one-sentence description of the kind of material found in that book or pamphlet.

(c) Place an **(s)**, meaning substitute, in front of a book or pamphlet on the list if you substituted another book or pamphlet for the one in the photo for any of the reasons listed above. State why you had to use a substitute and make clear what your substitute is. Include a one-sentence description of the kind of material found in the book or pamphlet.

(d) Place an **(x)** in front of a book or pamphlet on the list if you were not able to find it or a substitute. State why this was so. Still include a one-sentence description of the kind of material found in the book or pamphlet you were seeking.

Abstract   An **abstract** is a summary of the important points made in a document or other text; it is an overview. Summaries of opinions are sometimes called *abstracts* or *squibs*. One of the major places they are printed is in **digests**, which are volumes that contain brief summaries of court opinions, arranged by subject matter and by court or jurisdiction.

Act   An **act** is a law passed by the state or federal legislature that declares, commands, or prohibits something. Also called statute or legislation. A *bill* (which is a proposed statute) becomes an act once the legislature enacts it into law. Acts can be printed in several formats: as a **slip law** (which is one act of the legislature printed in a single pamphlet), as part of the *session laws* (which is an uncodified collection of every private and public act—*uncodified* means arranged chronologically rather than by subject matter), and as part of the *statutory code* (which is a collection of every public act arranged by subject matter). Session laws are also called *statutes at large* and *laws*.

Administrative Code   An **administrative code** is a collection of regulations (organized by subject matter) of one or more administrative agencies. Generally, the regulations of state and local administrative agencies are poorly organized and difficult to find. Not so for the regulations of *federal* administrative agencies, as we will see when we cover the *Code of Federal Regulations* (C.F.R.). A distinguishing feature of a code is that the material in it is organized by subject matter rather than chronologically. A subject matter organization would mean that all or many regulations on the environment, for example, are together in one place in the code. A chronological printing, however, would mean that laws on totally different subject matters could follow each other, depending on the order in which the laws were passed. Two sets of laws that often have a subject matter organization are administrative codes (that print administrative regulations) and statutory codes (that print statutes).

Advance   In general, the word *advance* or **advance sheet** refers to a pamphlet that comes out prior to (in advance of) a thicker pamphlet or a hardcover volume. Very often the material in the advance publication is later reprinted in the thicker pamphlet or hardcover volume so that the advance publication can be thrown away. Here are three examples of publications that have this advance feature:

1. Advance sheet for a reporter. A **reporter** is a volume (or set of volumes) of court opinions. Also called *reports*. (The word *reporter* has two other meanings: the person in charge of reporting the decisions of a court and the person who takes down and transcribes proceedings.) A reporter advance sheet prints opinions soon after they are written by the courts. Once several reporter advance sheets are available, the opinions in them are all printed in a hardcover volume so that all the advance sheets can be thrown away.

2. Advance sheet for Shepard's (shorthand for the *citator* called *Shepard's Citations*). A *citator* is a book, CD–ROM, or online service with lists of citations that can help assess the current validity of an opinion, statute, or other authority and give leads to additional relevant material. A major citator is *Shepard's Citations*. The advance sheet for Shepard's contains early citator information—the citations—which is later reprinted in larger pamphlets and hardcover volumes. Once the library receives the larger publication, the advance sheet is thrown away.

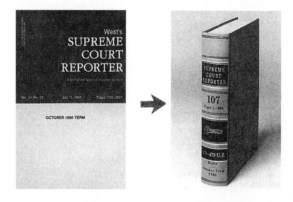

Advance sheet for a reporter (here the *Supreme Court Reporter*). An advance sheet contains the full text of court opinions that will later be printed in a hardcover reporter volume.

3. Advance sheet for a statutory code. The most current statutes are often first published in a special pamphlet that may be called a **legislative service** or **advance session law service**. Most libraries throw these pamphlets away once they are published in hardcover session law volumes and (if they are public laws) in a bound statutory code.

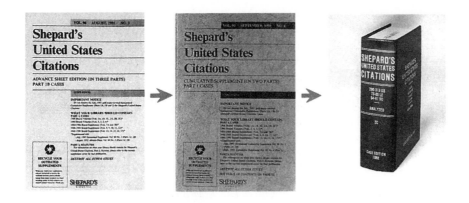

Advance sheet for Shepard's (here the *Shepard's United States Citations*). The first photo is the advance sheet, the material from which is later reprinted in a thicker supplement pamphlet (middle photo) and finally in a hardcover volume (third photo).

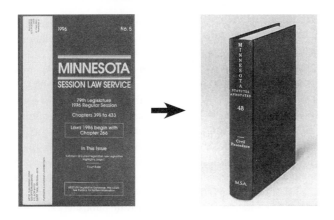

Advance sheet for a statutory code (here the *Minnesota Session Law Service*). The first photo is the advance sheet. Many of the statutes of the Minnesota Legislature are first printed chronologically in this advance sheet. Later they are printed by subject matter in the statutory code for the state, *Minnesota Statutes Annotated.*

A.L.R., A.L.R.2d, A.L.R.3d, A.L.R.4th, A.L.R.5th, A.L.R.6th, A.L.R.Fed., A.L.R.Fed.2d

- A.L.R.: *American Law Reports, First Series*
- A.L.R.2d: *American Law Reports, Second Series*
- A.L.R.3d: *American Law Reports, Third Series*
- A.L.R.4th: *American Law Reports, Fourth Series*
- A.L.R.5th: *American Law Reports, Fifth Series*
- A.L.R.6th: *American Law Reports, Sixth Series*
- A.L.R. Fed.: *American Law Reports, Federal, First Series*
- A.L.R.Fed.2d: *American Law Reports, Federal, Second Series*

These eight sets of books contain the complete text of *selected* court opinions along with extensive commentaries, which are, in effect, research papers on issues within the opinions selected. The research papers are called **annotations**. (An annotation is a note or commentary that summarizes or provides explanation.) The sets of books are, therefore, called **annotated reporters** because they print the full text of opinions plus commentary on them. They are published by West Group. As we shall see later, annotations are excellent case finders. (Although the abbreviation *A.L.R.* refers primarily to the First Series, it also commonly refers to all eight sets collectively.) Many annotations have been placed online (on Westlaw) so that they can now be found and read on a computer screen (see Exhibit 11.24 later in the chapter on finding annotations).

ALWD Citation Manual   The citation guide published by the Association of Legal Writing Directors. It is the major competitor to *The Bluebook: A Uniform System of Citation.*

American Digest System   The American Digest System consists of three sets of digests that provide summaries of court opinions written by every federal and every state court that publishes its opinions. The three digests (printed by West Group) are the *General Digest* (containing the most recent summaries), the *Decennial Digests* (containing summaries covering ten-year periods), and the *Century Digest* (containing summaries for cases written prior to 1897). As we will see later, the volumes of the *General Digest* (which update the most recent *Decennial Digest*) are thrown away when the next *Decennial Digest* is printed.

Example of a volume of *American Law Reports, Fifth Series*. All A.L.R. volumes print several opinions plus extensive annotations on selected issues in these opinions.

Example of a volume of
American Jurisprudence 2d,
a national legal encyclopedia

American Jurisprudence 2d (Am. Jur. 2d)   Am. Jur. 2d is a national **legal encyclopedia** published by West Group. (Am. Jur. 2d is the second edition of Am. Jur. First.) A legal encyclopedia is a multivolume set of books that summarizes every major legal topic, arranged alphabetically. (Am. Jur. 2d is also available online through Westlaw and LexisNexis.) The other major national legal encyclopedia is *Corpus Juris Secundum* (C.J.S.), also from West Group.

There are three main uses of national legal encyclopedias such as Am. Jur. 2d and C.J.S.: (1) they are useful as background reading before you begin legal research in a new area of the law, (2) they are good case finders because of their extensive footnotes to court opinions, and (3) they provide cross-references to other publications of West Group on whatever topic you are reading in the encyclopedia. In addition to these two national encyclopedias, several states have state encyclopedias devoted to the law of one state (e.g., California, Florida, and Michigan).

American Law Reports (A.L.R.)   *American Law Reports* is an annotated reporter. It prints the full text of selected opinions and extensive annotations based on issues in those opinions.

Annotation   An *annotation* is a note or commentary that summarizes or provides explanation. The main volumes containing annotations are the eight sets of *American Law Reports*: A.L.R., A.L.R.2d, A.L.R.3d, A.L.R.4th, A.L.R.5th, A.L.R.6th, A.L.R.Fed, and A.L.R.Fed.2d. The annotations are research papers that are based on selected court opinions in these volumes. When a supervisor asks you to "find out if there are any annotations," you are being sent to A.L.R., A.L.R.2d, etc.

The verb is **annotate**. If materials are annotated, they contain notes or commentaries. An **annotated statutory code** prints statutes by subject matter and includes research references such as historical notes and summaries of court opinions that have interpreted the statutes (often called **notes of decisions**. The abbreviation for annotated is Ann. (e.g., Del. Code Ann. for *Delaware Code Annotated*) or A. (e.g., U.S.C.A. for *United States Code Annotated*). An *annotated reporter*, such as A.L.R., prints court opinions along with notes or commentaries on them called annotations. An *annotated bibliography* contains a list of research references along with a brief comment on each reference.

With rare exceptions, annotations are written by private publishers and authors. They are not official documents of courts, legislatures, or agencies.

Atlantic Digest   A regional digest that summarizes state court opinions in the *Atlantic Reporter*. See research link A and Exhibit 11.6.

Atlantic Reporter 2d (A.2d)   A regional reporter of West Group that prints state court opinions of nine states and Wash. D.C. (Conn., Del., D.C., Me., Md., N.H., N.J., Pa., R.I., and Vt.). A.2d is the second series of this reporter. The first series is Atlantic Reporter (A.). See Exhibit 11.5.

Opinions in *Atlantic 2d* (A.2d)   *Atlantic Digest*

RESEARCH LINK A

Every opinion in the *Atlantic 2d* reporter written by the state courts in the atlantic region (Conn., Del., D.C., Me., Md., N.H., N.J., Pa., R.I., and Vt.) is digested (summarized) in *Atlantic Digest*.

Auto-Cite   **Auto-Cite** is an online citator of LexisNexis that will tell you whether an opinion you are checking is good law. For example, you will be told whether the opinion has been overruled or criticized by another opinion. Auto-Cite also provides parallel cites and other citing material.

Bill   A **bill** is a proposed statute (one that has not yet been enacted into law). The steps a bill goes through before it becomes a statute (e.g., hearings, debates, and amendments) are known as its **legislative history**.

Black's Law Dictionary   A single-volume legal dictionary.

Bluebook   The phrase **bluebook** (sometimes spelled *blue book*) usually refers to one of the following four books or sets of books:

- *The Bluebook: A Uniform System of Citation*
  This is a small blue pamphlet published by the law reviews of several law schools. The pamphlet covers the "rules" of citation form. It is considered by many to be the bible of citation form, although as we will see, not everyone follows it and a competing bible (the *ALWD Citation Manual*) has recently emerged.

Example of a bill introduced in the House of Representatives of Congress. A bill is a proposed statute.

The Bluebook: A Uniform System of Citation, providing guidelines on proper citation form

- *National Reporter Blue Book*

  This set of books, published by West Group, enables you to find a *parallel cite* to a court opinion. A parallel cite is simply an additional reference to printed or online sources where you will be able to read the same material word for word. A parallel cite to an opinion would be a reference to another reporter that prints the entire text of the opinion. The *National Reporter Blue Book* covers every state. Some states have a *Blue and White Book*, which covers parallel cites for the opinions of one state only.

- *A.L.R. Blue Book of Supplemental Decisions*

  This set of books allows you to update the annotations in *A.L.R. First Series*.

- A directory of government offices and employees. Many states have a directory or manual that gives names, addresses, telephone numbers, and e-mail addresses of their state agencies. They may also include information about the functions of each agency. Many of these directories are called *bluebooks*.

National Reporter Blue Book, providing parallel cites to court opinions

Brief   As we saw in chapter 7, the word **brief** has several meanings:

- *Brief of a court opinion*   A summary of the major components of a court opinion (e.g., key facts, issues, reasoning, and disposition). See Exhibit 7.3 in chapter 7.

- *Trial brief*   An attorney's personal notes on how he or she will conduct a trial. Also called a *trial manual* or *trial book*. (In some states a trial brief is a written argument presented to a court in support of a motion.)

- ***Appellate brief***   A document submitted (filed) by a party to an appellate court (and served on an opposing party) in which arguments are presented on why the appellate court should affirm (approve), reverse, or otherwise modify what a lower court has done. If a nonparty is given special court permission to file an appellate brief with its views on the case before the court, the brief is called an **amicus curiae** (friend-of-the-court) **brief**. Many appellate briefs are available in large public law libraries and online from fee-based services such as Westlaw and LexisNexis.

Bulletin   A bulletin is an ongoing (e.g., monthly) publication that prints documents of administrative agencies chronologically (Ex: *Internal Revenue Bulletin*). Also called a *register, gazette,* or *journal.*

California Reporter (Cal. Rptr.)   An unofficial court reporter of West Group that prints opinions of California state courts.

Front cover (title page) of an appellate brief submitted to the United States Supreme Court. An appellate brief asks the appellate court to affirm (approve), reverse, or otherwise modify what a lower court has done.

Cases   The word *case* has three meanings. First, a case is a court **opinion**, which is a court's written explanation of how it applied the law to the facts before it to resolve a legal dispute. (See Exhibit 6.1 in chapter 6.) Opinions are printed in volumes called reporters or reports. The words *case* and *opinion* are often used interchangeably. For example, you will hear researchers say that they "read a case" or that they "read an opinion." Second, *case* means a pending matter before a court—a matter that is still in litigation. (Every trial and appellate court, for example, has a **docket** that lists pending cases on its calendar. The docket is also referred to as the *calendar*.) Third, *case* means any client matter in a law office, whether or not litigation is involved. (A large law office, for example, may have hundreds of cases in its active case file and thousands in its closed case files.)

The first meaning of case—an opinion—is our primary concern in this chapter. Every year well over 100,000 opinions are written by hundreds of courts throughout the United States. Our study of this vast array of law will focus on three major themes:

- Where can you read these opinions?
  (We will cover this theme now.)
- How do you find them?
  (We will cover this theme later, in Section P of the chapter.)
- How do you read (i.e., brief) and apply them?
  (We covered these themes in chapter 7.)

For many opinions, there are 11 possible places where you can read them. They are outlined in Exhibit 11.4. The most common is the unofficial reporter. (See the fourth option in Exhibit 11.4.) An **official reporter** is a reporter printed under the authority of the government, often by a government printing office. An **unofficial reporter** is a reporter printed by a commercial publishing company without special authority from the government. As we will see, West Group is the major publisher of unofficial reporters, particularly through its National Reporter System. Unofficial does not mean unreliable. In fact, West Group's unofficial reporters are so reliable that many states have discontinued their own official reporters. In such states, most people, including judges, rely almost exclusively on the unofficial reporter.

EXHIBIT 11.4	Eleven Possible Places to Read the Same Court Opinion

Category	Description	Currency (How soon is the opinion available in this format after the court writes it?)	Frequency of Use (How often do researchers read the opinion in this format?)	Editorial Enhancements (How many features are available in this format in addition to the text of the opinion?)
1. Slip Opinion	A single opinion printed by the court.	Very current	Seldom	Almost none
2. Advance Sheet	A pamphlet (containing several opinions) printed in advance of a hardcover reporter volume.	Very current	Very often	Many (e.g., headnotes with key numbers)
3. Reporter (official)	A volume (or set of volumes) of court opinions. Sometimes called *Reports*. An official reporter is one printed under the authority of the government, often by the government itself.	Not very current	Not very often	Not many
4. Reporter (unofficial)	A volume (or set of volumes) of court opinions. Sometimes called *Reports*. An unofficial reporter is one printed by a commercial publishing company (e.g., West Group) without special authority from the government.	Fairly current	Very often	Many (e.g., headnotes with key numbers)
5. Looseleaf Service	A lawbook with a binding (often three ringed) that allows easy inserting and removal of pages for updating.	Very current	Fairly often	Many (e.g., suggestions on practicing law)
6. Legal Newspaper	A newspaper (published daily, weekly, etc.) devoted to legal news; may print opinions of local courts.	Very current	Fairly often	Almost none
7. Legal Newsletter	A special-interest publication (printed monthly, bimonthly, etc.) covering a particular area of law; may print opinions in that area.	Fairly current	Fairly often	Some
8. Microforms (e.g. ultrafiche)	Images or photographs that have been reduced in size.	Very current	Not often	Many (if the images are from unofficial reporters such as those of West Group)
9. CD–ROM	A compact disk that stores data (e.g., court opinions) in a digital format.	Fairly current	Not very often (although increasing)	Many
10. Online: Fee-Based	The major fee-based online services that sell access to legal materials such as court opinions are Westlaw, LexisNexis, and Loislaw.	Very current	Fairly often	Many
11. Online: Free	Many courts have Web sites that provide access to their opinions at no cost. For links to these sites, see www.findlaw.com/casecode.	Very current	Fairly often	Almost none

Courts do not formally publish every opinion they write. An **unpublished opinion** is an opinion that the court has designated as not for official publication, meaning generally that it should not be cited as authority even though you may be able to read it online or in special reporters. Unpublished opinions of some U.S. Courts of Appeals are printed in an unofficial reporter of West Group called *Federal Appendix* (F. App'x.) Many unpublished opinions can also be read online on Westlaw and LexisNexis.

We turn now to an overview of the major reported opinions, focusing first on federal court opinions and then on state court opinions.

Federal Court Opinions   Federal court opinions are written by the U.S. Supreme Court, U.S. Courts of Appeals, U.S. District Courts, and several special federal courts (see Exhibit 6.3 for an overview of federal courts).

U.S. Supreme Court Opinions

Name	Description	Abbreviation
United States Reports	Official opinions of the U.S. Supreme Court	U.S.
Supreme Court Reporter	Unofficial opinions of the U.S. Supreme Court (West Group)	S. Ct.
United States Supreme Court Reports, Lawyers' Edition; United States Supreme Court Reports, Lawyers' Edition, 2d	Unofficial opinions of the U.S. Supreme Court (LexisNexis)	L. Ed., L. Ed. 2d
United States Law Week	Unofficial opinions of the U.S. Supreme Court published as a looseleaf service (Bureau of National Affairs—BNA) (www.bna.com)	U.S.L.W.
Court Web site	Free online (www.supremecourtus.gov)	
Findlaw	Free online (www.findlaw.com/casecode)	
Legal Information Institute	Free online (supct.law.cornell.edu/supct)	
LexisOne	Free online (www.lexisone.com)	
LexisNexis	Fee-based online (www.lexis.com)	
Westlaw	Fee-based online (www.westlaw.com)	WL
Loislaw	Fee-based online (www.loislaw.com)	
VersusLaw	Fee-based online (www.versuslaw.com)	

Three major reporters containing opinions of the United States Supreme Court. The first one (*United States Reports*) is the official reporter. The other two are unofficial.

Federal Reporter, Third Series (F.3d). Currently contains the full text of the opinions written by the United States courts of appeals.

Federal Supplement 2d (F. Supp. 2d) Currently contains the full text of opinions written by United States district courts.

Example of an official state reports volume

The opinions of lower federal courts (e.g., U.S. Courts of Appeals and U.S. District Courts) can also be found in a variety of sources:

Lower Federal Court Opinions

Name	Description	Abbreviation
Federal Reporter; *Federal Reporter, 2d;* *Federal Reporter, 3d;*	Opinions of the U.S. courts of appeals (West Group)	F., F.2d, F.3d
Federal Appendix	Unpublished opinions of some U.S. courts of appeals (West Group)	F. App'x.
Federal Supplement; *Federal Supplement 2d*	Opinions of U.S. district courts (West Group)	F. Supp., F. Supp. 2d
Federal Rules Decisions	Opinions of the some U.S. district courts on procedural issues (plus related materials, e.g., speeches)	F.R.D.
Bankruptcy Reporter	Opinions of U.S. bankruptcy courts and district courts on bankruptcy issues)	B.R.
United States Tax Court Reports	Opinions of the U.S. Tax Court	T.C
Federal Claims Reporter	Opinions of the U.S. Court of Federal Claims	Fed. Cl.
Military Justice Reporter	Opinions of the U.S. Court of Appeals for the Armed Forces	M.J.
Veterans Appeals Reporter	Opinions of the U.S. Court of Veterans Appeals	Vet. App.
Court Web site	Free online (www.law.emory.edu/FEDCTS) (www.uscourts.gov/links.html)	
LexisOne	Free online (www.lexisone.com)	
LexisNexis	Fee-based online (www.lexis.com)	
Westlaw	Fee-based online www.westlaw.com)	WL
Loislaw	Fee-based online www.loislaw.com)	
VersusLaw	Fee-based online www.versuslaw.com)	

State Court Opinions At one time, all states had official reporters containing the opinions of their highest state courts. As indicated earlier, however, a large number of states have discontinued their official reports. For such states, the unofficial reporters are the main source for opinions of their state courts.

The major publisher of unofficial state reports is West Group through its *National Reporter System*. There are seven **regional reporters** in the System. (West Group's other reporters are also part of the National Reporter System.) A regional reporter is simply an unofficial reporter that contains state court opinions of several states within one of seven regions of the country. (See Exhibit 11.5.)

If a law office subscribes to a regional reporter covering its own state, the office is also receiving opinions of other states in the same region. These other opinions may be of little practical value to the office. West Group, therefore, publishes special state editions for over half the states. These **special edition state reporters** (sometimes called *offprint reporters*) contain only the opinions of an individual state that are also printed in the regional reporter. For example, the opinions of the highest court in Kansas are printed in the *Pacific Reporter*. A Kansas attorney who does not want to subscribe to the *Pacific Reporter* can subscribe to the special edition Kansas reporter, called *Kansas Cases*. (See research link B.)

Regional Reporter   Special Edition State Reporter (offprint reporter)

RESEARCH LINK B

The seven regional reporters each contain the opinions of several states. If all of the opinions of one of these states are taken out and also printed in a separate reporter, the latter is called a special edition state reporter (or an offprint reporter).

EXHIBIT 11.5	Seven Regional Reporters in the National Reporter system

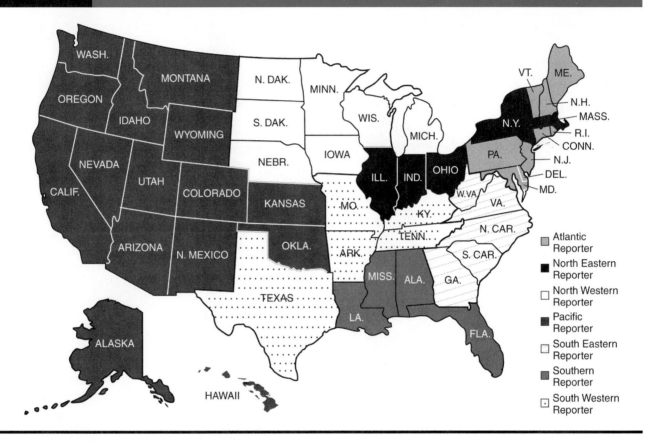

Atlantic Reporter
North Eastern Reporter
North Western Reporter
Pacific Reporter
South Eastern Reporter
Southern Reporter
South Western Reporter

Finally, West Group publishes three separate reporters containing state court opinions of New York, California, and Illinois. The current series of these reporters containing the most recent state court opinions are as follows:

- *New York Supplement 2d* (N.Y.S.2d)
- *California Reporter 3d* (Cal. Rptr. 3d)
- *Illinois Decisions* (Ill. Dec.)

Each contains the opinions of the highest court in the state as well as selected opinions of its lower state courts. Keep in mind that these are unofficial reporters of West Group, a private publishing company. Each of these states has its own official reporters containing the same opinions.

Major Characteristics of West Group Reporters

- The reporters contain the full text of court opinions.
- The opinions are arranged in roughly chronological order according to the date of the decision; they are not arranged by subject matter. In a regional reporter, for example, a murder case could follow a tax case.
- The reporters have advance sheets that come out before the hardcover volumes. When the hardcover reporter volume comes out, all the advance sheets are thrown away.
- A table of cases appears at the beginning of each reporter volume.
- Many reporters have a statutes table listing the statutes construed (i.e., interpreted) within an individual reporter volume.

A volume of *Kansas Cases* (a special edition state reporter) containing all the Kansas opinions printed in *Pacific Reporter 2d*.

■ There is no traditional index to the opinions in a reporter volume. How then do you find opinions? Later we will see that digests are one of the major ways of locating what is in reporters. A digest is a separate set of volumes that contain summaries of opinions. In effect, the digest acts as an index to the opinions in reporter volumes.

■ Each opinion is summarized in a series of short paragraphs called **headnotes**. A headnote is a short paragraph summary of a portion of a court opinion printed before the opinion begins. Headnotes are written by West Group editors, not by the court.

Of course, West Group reporters are not the only way to read a court opinion. See Exhibit 11.4 for other options.

Regional Reporters

Atlantic Reporter, Second Series (A.2d). The opinions of state courts in Conn., Del., D.C., Me., Md., N.H., N.J., Pa., R.I., Vt.

North Eastern Reporter, Second Series (N.E.2d). The opinions of state courts in Ill., Ind., Mass., N.Y., Ohio.

North Western Reporter, Second Series (N.W.2d). The opinions of state courts in Iowa, Mich., Minn., Neb., N.D., S.D., Wis.

Pacific Reporter, Second Series (P.2d). The opinions of state courts in Alaska, Ariz., Cal., Colo., Haw., Idaho, Kan., Mont., Nev., N.M., Okla., Or., Utah, Wash., Wyo.

South Eastern Reporter, Second Series (S.E.2d). The opinions of state courts in Ga., N.C., S.C., Va., W. Va.

Southern Reporter Second series (So. 2d). The opinions of state courts in: Ala., Fla., La., Miss.

South Western Reporter, Second Series (S.W.2d). The opinions of state courts in Ark., Ky., Mo., Tenn., Tex.

Example of a casebook used in a law school classroom

Casebook   A **casebook** is a law school textbook. It consists mainly of a collection of edited court opinions and other materials relating to a particular area of the law, e.g., Lockhart, Kamisar, Choper, and Shiffrin, *Constitutional Law: Cases, Comments, Questions.* Casebooks are not used for legal research; they are classroom texts.

CD–ROM   CD–ROM (compact disk read-only memory) is a compact disk that stores data in a digital format. See the discussion of this medium in Section G of this chapter.

Century Digest   The *Century Digest* is one of the three digests in the American Digest System published by West Group. The *Century Digest* contains short-paragraph summaries of court opinions written prior to 1897. The other two digests in the American Digest System are the *Decennial Digests* and the *General Digest*.

CIS   *CIS* is the abbreviation for the Congressional Information Service. It is one of the major publishers of information that will allow you to trace the legislative history of a federal statute.

Citation   A **citation** (also called a *cite*) is a reference to any authority (e.g., opinion, statute, or legal periodical article) printed on paper or stored in a computer database that will allow you to locate that authority. The citation is the "address" where you can find and read the authority. Most citations are to printed materials; such citations consist of information such as volume number, page number, and date. As we will see later in Section J, there are citation guidelines for citing different kinds of legal materials. One of the major publications containing citation guidelines is *The Bluebook: A Uniform System of Citation*, which we saw earlier. Law school teachers and legal periodical publishers love the *Bluebook*. But many courts do not follow it: they may have their own official citation rules that must be followed. (In Section J, we will also examine the *ALWD Citation Manual*, another citation guide that is a recent competitor to *The Bluebook*.)

A **parallel cite** is an additional citation where you can find the *same* written material in the library or online. Here, for example, is the citation to an opinion with a parallel cite:

Coleman v. City of New York, 91 N.Y.2d 821, 689 N.E.2d 523 (1997)

The same text of the *Coleman* opinion is found, word for word, on page 821 of volume 91 of *New York Reports 2d* (N.Y.2d) and on page 523 of volume 689 of *North Eastern Reporter 2d* (N.E.2d.). Later, we'll be spending a great deal of time on such citations.

Citator   A **citator** is a book, CD–ROM, or online service that contains lists of citations that can (1) help you assess the current validity of an opinion, statute, or other item and (2) give you leads to other relevant materials. It is an organized list of citations to legal materials that have referred to (i.e., cited) whatever you are checking. For example, if you are checking the validity of an opinion, the citator will tell you what the courts have said about that opinion and what legal periodical articles have mentioned it. The same is true if you want to check the validity of a statute, constitutional provision, administrative regulation, rule of court, etc. (see research link C). The two main reasons to use a citator are to assess the validity of what you are checking and to locate additional laws or other materials on the issues covered in what you are checking. A major citator in legal research is *Shepard's Citations*. You can find *Shepard's Citations* in a set of printed volumes (pamphlets and hardcover), on CD–ROM, and online in LexisNexis. The other major online citators are KeyCite (found in Westlaw), Auto-Cite (found in LexisNexis), and GlobalCite (found in Loislaw).

Citators (Shepard's) (KeyCite) (Auto-Cite) (GlobalCite)	opinion, statute, constitutional provision, administrative regulation, rule of court, etc.

RESEARCH LINK C
A citator will help you determine the current validity of an opinion, statute, constitutional provision, administrative regulation, rule of court, etc. The citator will also lead you to additional relevant materials.

CLE Materials   **CLE materials** are continuing legal education texts, videos, Web sites, or other materials for use in continuing legal education CLE. CLE is training in the law (usually short term) that a person receives after completing his or her formal legal training. Many states require attorneys to participate in a designated number of CLE hours per year. Most paralegal certification programs also require CLE to maintain certification status (see Exhibits 4.7 and 4.8 in chapter 4). A few states like California require CLE of all paralegals. Materials for CLE programs often contain checklists, sample forms, and the full text of recent cases, statutes, and administrative regulations that would be of practical value to an attorney or paralegal working in a particular specialty. To find out about CLE materials and programs in your area, type *CLE paralegal* plus the name of your state (e.g., CLE paralegal Colorado) in Google or any major search engine.

Code   A **code** is a collection of laws or rules organized by subject matter regardless of when they were enacted. To **codify** something means to rearrange it by subject matter. *Un*codified material is arranged chronologically by date of enactment; *codified* material is arranged by subject matter or topic regardless of when passed or enacted. When a statute or act is first passed by the legislature, it appears initially as a *slip law* (which is a single act printed as a small pamphlet) and then is printed in uncodified books called session laws or statutes at large. Finally, statutes of general interest are later codified in statutory codes.

Sample volumes of the *Code of Federal Regulations* (C.F.R.), which contain many current administrative regulations of federal agencies

Code of Federal Regulations (C.F.R.)   The C.F.R. is an administrative code in which many of the current administrative regulations of federal agencies are organized by subject matter. The C.F.R. is printed by the United States government in a large number of pamphlets that are reissued each year in a different color. It is also possible to read the C.F.R. online on the free Internet (www.gpoaccess.gov/cfr/index.html). The most recent changes to the C.F.R. can be read without cost in the unofficial **e-CFR**, the *Electronic Code of Federal Regulations* (www.gpoaccess.gov/ecfr). The C.F.R. is also available on fee-based online services (e.g., Westlaw, LexisNexis, and Loislaw). Before a federal administrative regulation is adopted and printed in the C.F.R., it must be proposed and printed in the daily *Federal Register* (Fed. Reg.) (see research link D).

| *Federal Register* (Fed. Reg.) | *Code of Federal Regulations* (C. F. R.) |

RESEARCH LINK D

Before a federal administrative regulation is adopted and printed in the *Code of Federal Regulations* (C.F.R.), it is proposed in the daily *Federal Register* (Fed. Reg.).

Congressional Record   The *Congressional Record* (Cong. Rec.) is an official record of the proceedings and debates of the U.S. Congress. It is one source of legislative history for federal statutes. It also contains many relatively trivial items that are relevant only to the districts of individual legislators.

Corpus Juris Secundum (C.J.S.)   *Corpus Juris Secundum* is a national legal encyclopedia published by West Group. (It is the second edition of *Corpus Juris*.) *A legal encyclopedia* is a multivolume set of books that summarizes every major legal topic, arranged alphabetically. (C.J.S. is also available online through Westlaw.) The other major national legal encyclopedia is Am. Jur. 2d, also from West Group. There are three main uses of national legal encyclopedias such as C.J.S. and Am. Jur. 2d: (1) they are useful as background reading before you begin legal research in a new area of the law, (2) they are good case finders because of their extensive footnotes to court opinions, and (3) they provide cross-references to other publications of West Group on whatever topic you are reading in the encyclopedia. In addition to these two national encyclopedias, several states have state encyclopedias devoted to the law of one state (e.g., Florida and Michigan).

Sample volumes of *Corpus Juris Secundum*, a national legal encyclopedia

Cumulative   **Cumulative** means that which repeats earlier material and consolidates it with new material in one place or unit. A cumulative supplement, for example, is a pamphlet or volume that repeats, updates, and consolidates all earlier pamphlets or volumes. Because of the repetition, the earlier pamphlets or volumes can be thrown away. Similarly, pocket parts (containing supplemental material at the end of a book) are often cumulative. When the most recent pocket part comes out, the old one can be thrown away.

Current Law Index   *Current Law Index* (CLI) is the most comprehensive general index to legal periodical literature available. (The other major one is the *Index to Legal Periodicals and Books*.) The CLI comes out in a paper version (consisting of pamphlets and hardcover volumes), on CD–ROM, and in an online version where it is known as LegalTrac. (On Westlaw and LexisNexis, it is called Legal Resource Index.)

Decennial Digest   The *Decennial Digest* is one of the three digests in the American Digest System published by West Group that contains summaries of court opinions written by every federal and state court that publishes its opinions. Each *Decennial Digest* covers a ten-year period. (Recent decennials are published in two five-year parts.) The other two digests in the American Digest System are the *Century Digest* and the *General Digest*.

UNITED STATES CODE ANNOTATED

Title 28
Judiciary and Judicial Procedure
§§ 171 to 1250

Cumulative Annual Pocket Part

For Use in 2007

Replacing prior pocket part in back of volume

Example of a cumulative pocket part in a statutory code

Deskbook   A **deskbook** is a one- or two-volume collection of the rules of procedure for one or more courts, usually in the same judicial system. These rules of procedure are called court rules or rules of court.

Digests   Our goals in this section are to define *digest*, to identify the major digests, and to explain the relationship between digests and reporters. Later in this book, we will cover the techniques of using digests in research (see Section O).

Digests are a set of volumes that contain brief summaries (sometimes called *abstracts* or *squibs*) of court opinions, arranged by subject matter and by court or jurisdiction. The primary purpose of digests is to act as case finders. The major publisher of digests are West Group. They can be found in print (hardcover and pamphlet) and online. First we will examine the print digests of West Group.

The West Key Number System® is the organizational principle used to classify the millions of short-paragraph summaries in the digests. Here is how this principle works. West Group divides all of law into over more than 400 general topics such as Arson, Infants, Marriage, Negligence, and Obscenity. Each of these general topics is further classified into subtopics, and each subtopic is then assigned a number. The phrase **key number** refers to two things: the general topic and the number of the subtopic. Examine the following examples of subtopics under the general topic of Negligence:

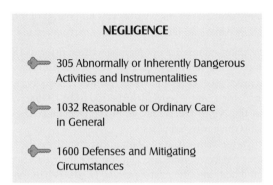

NEGLIGENCE

305 Abnormally or Inherently Dangerous Activities and Instrumentalities

1032 Reasonable or Ordinary Care in General

1600 Defenses and Mitigating Circumstances

Examples of key numbers

The second key number in this example is referred to as "Negligence 1032." (It is *not* referred to as "1032 Reasonable or Ordinary Care in General.") The key number must include the general topic. You usually do not have to state what the subtopic is; giving the general topic and the number is enough. If a supervisor asks you to check Negligence 1032 in a West Group digest, you simply go to the N volume of the digest, where you will check number 1032 under Negligence.

Once you find a key number (consisting of a general topic and a number) that is relevant to your research problem, you will find summaries of court opinions under that key number. For example, the following excerpt from a digest contains opinions that are summarized (or digested) under key number Obscenity 1 and key number Obscenity 2:

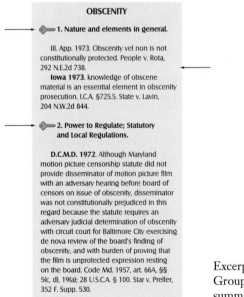

OBSCENITY

1. Nature and elements in general.

Ill. App. 1973. Obscenity vel non is not constitutionally protected. People v. Rota, 292 N.E.2d 738.

Iowa 1973. knowledge of obscene material is an essential element in obscenity prosecution. I.C.A. §725.5. State v. Lavin, 204 N.W.2d 844.

2. Power to Regulate; Statutory and Local Regulations.

D.C.M.D. 1972. Although Maryland motion picture censorship statute did not provide disseminator of motion picture film with an adversary hearing before board of censors on issue of obscenity, disseminator was not constitutionally prejudiced in this regard because the statute requires an adversary judicial determination of obscenity with circuit court for Baltimore City exercising de nova review of the board's finding of obscenity, and with burden of proving that the film is unprotected expression resting on the board. Code Md. 1957, art. 66A, §§ 5(c, d), 19(a); 28 U.S.C.A. § 100. Star v. Preller, 352 F. Supp. 530.

Excerpt from a West Group digest containing summaries of opinions

Beneath each summary paragraph is a citation to the case being summarized. For example, see the citation for *People v. Rota* in the first paragraph listed.

Where do these summary paragraphs come from? They come from the *headnotes* of court opinions in West Group reporters. (For an example of two headnotes at the beginning of an opinion, see the *Bruni* opinion in Section G of chapter 7.) As we saw earlier, a headnote is a short-paragraph summary of a portion of the opinion that is printed before the opinion begins.

We now turn to an overview of the following four kinds of West Group digests:

- A national digest covering most state and federal courts
- Federal digests covering only federal courts
- Regional digests covering courts whose opinions are printed in regional reporters
- Digests of individual states

These digests are called *key number digests* because they organize the case summaries within them according to the key number system.

National Digest   West Group publishes one national digest: the American Digest System. This massive set (containing over 100 volumes) gives you summaries of the court opinions of most state and federal courts. The American Digest System has three main units:

- *Century Digest*, covering summaries of opinions written prior to 1897.
- *Decennial Digests*, covering summaries of opinions written during ten-year periods starting in 1897. The more recent Decennials are printed in two five-year parts. Part 1 of the Eleventh Decennial, for example, covers the period from 1996 to 2001. Part 2 covers 2001 to 2004. (Prior to the Ninth Decennial, all of the Decennial Digests were issued in one part only—covering the entire ten years.)
- *General Digests*, covering summaries of opinions written since the last Decennial was published. The *General Digest* volumes are kept on the shelf only until they are eventually consolidated (cumulated) into the next *Decennial Digest*. When the latter arrives, all of the *General Digest* volumes are thrown away.

Here are examples of volumes from each of the three units of the American Digest System:

Example of a *Century Digest* volume

Example of a *Decennial Digest* volume

Example of a *General Digest* volume

Federal Digests Covering Only Federal Courts   West Group publishes five large digests that cover the three main federal courts: the U.S. Supreme Court, the U.S. Courts of Appeals, and the U.S. District Courts. The five digests are as follows:

- *Federal Digest*
- *Modern Federal Practice Digest*
- *Federal Practice Digest 2d*
- *Federal Practice Digest 3d*
- *Federal Practice Digest 4th*

The last digest listed—*Federal Practice Digest 4th*—is the most important because it covers the most recent period; it digests federal cases from the mid-1980s to the present. The other four cover earlier time periods and are therefore used less frequently.

Finally, West Group publishes a number of special digests that cover specific courts or specific topics:

- *West's Bankruptcy Digest*
- *West's Education Law Digest*
- *West's Military Justice Digest*
- *West's Veterans Appeals Digest*
- *United States Supreme Court Digest* (West Group)

Federal Practice Digest 4th. Gives summaries of federal court opinions.

United States Supreme Court Digest.

Pacific Digest, one of the regional digests. Gives summaries of opinions in the *Pacific Reporter.*

Regional Digests   A **regional digest** contains summaries of those court opinions that are printed in full in its corresponding regional reporter. The opinions in the *Pacific Reporter,* for example, are digested in the *Pacific Digest.* As we shall see in Exhibit 11.6, only four of the seven regional reporters have corresponding regional digests. Those digests are *Atlantic Digest, North Western Digest, Pacific Digest,* and *South Eastern Digest* (see research link E). Regional digests for the other three regions either do not exist or have been discontinued.

Four Regional Reporters:
Atlantic 2d (A.2d), *North Western 2d* (N.W.2d), *Pacific 2d* (P.2d), *South Eastern* (S.E.2d)

Four Regional Digests:
Atlantic Digest, North Western Digest, Pacific Digest, South Eastern Digest

RESEARCH LINK E
The opinions in four of the regional reporters (A.2d, N.W.2d, P.2d, and S.E.2d) are summarized (digested) in their corresponding regional digests.

EXHIBIT 11.6	Reporters and Digests: A Checklist	
Name of Reporter	**The Courts Whose Opinions Are Currently Printed in Full in this Reporter**	**The Digests That Contain Summaries of the Opinions in this Reporter**
United States Reports (U.S.) *Supreme Court Reporter* (S. Ct.) *United States Supreme Court Reports, Lawyers' Edition* (L. Ed.) *United States Law Week* (U.S.L.W.)	U.S. Supreme Court	American Digest System *United States Supreme Court Digest* (West Group) *Federal Practice Digest 4th* Individual state digest (for Supreme Court cases relevant to that state)
Federal Reporter 2d (F.2d) *Federal Reporter 3d* (F.3d)	U.S. Courts of Appeals	American Digest System *Federal Practice Digest 4th* Individual state digest (for U.S. court of appeals cases relevant to that state)
Federal Supplement (F. Supp.) *Federal Supplement 2d* (F. Supp. 2d)	U.S. District Courts	American Digest System *Federal Practice Digest 4th* Individual state digest (for U.S. district court cases relevant to that state)
Atlantic Reporter 2d (A.2d)	State courts in Conn., Del., D.C., Me., Md., N.H., N.J., Pa., R.I., Vt.	American Digest System *Atlantic Digest* Individual state digest for Conn., D.C., Me., Md., N.H., N.J., Pa., R.I., Vt. (There is no individual state digest for Delaware.)
North Eastern Reporter 2d (N.E.2d)	State courts in Ill., Ind., Mass., N.Y., Ohio	American Digest System Individual state digests for Ill., Ind., Mass., N.Y., Ohio (There is *no* North Eastern Digest.)

(continues)

EXHIBIT 11.6	Reporters and Digests: A Checklist—*continued*	
Name of Reporter	**The Courts Whose Opinions are Currently Printed in Full in this Reporter**	**The Digests that Contain Summaries of the Opinions in this Reporter**
North Western Reporter 2d (N.W.2d)	State courts in Iowa, Mich., Minn., Neb., N.D., S.D., Wis.	American Digest System *North Western Digest* Individual state digests for Iowa, Mich., Minn., Neb., N.D., S.D., Wis.
Pacific Reporter 3d (P.3d)	State courts in Alaska, Ariz., Cal., Colo., Haw., Idaho, Kan., Mont., Nev., N.M., Okla., Or., Utah, Wash., Wyo.	American Digest System *Pacific Digest* Individual state digests for Alaska, Ariz., Col., Colo., Haw., Idaho, Kan., Mont., N.M., Okla., Or., Wash., Wyo. (There are no individual state digests for Nevada and Utah.)
South Eastern Reporter 2d (S.E.2d)	State courts in Ga., N.C., S.C., Va., W.Va.	American Digest System *South Eastern Digest* Individual state digests for Ga., N.C., S.C., Va., W.Va. (Virginia and West Virginia have a combined digest.)
Southern Reporter 2d (So. 2d or S.2d)	The highest state court and some intermediate appellate courts in Ala., Fla., La., Miss.	American Digest System Individual state digests for Ala., Fla., La., Miss. (There is *no* Southern Digest.)
South Western Reporter 3d (S.W.3d)	The highest state court and some intermediate appellate courts in Ark., Ky., Mo., Tenn., Tex.	American Digest System Individual state digests for Ark., Ky., Mo., Tenn., Tex. (There is *no* South Western Digest.)

Digests of Individual States   An individual state digest contains summaries of the opinions of the state courts within that state, as well as the opinions of the federal courts that are relevant to that state. Almost every state has its own digest. (The main exceptions are Delaware, Nevada, and Utah. Also, Virginia and West Virginia are merged in a single digest.)

To summarize, examine Exhibit 11.6, where you will find a list of reporters, the names of the courts whose full opinions are currently printed in those reporters, and the names of the digests that give summaries of those opinions.

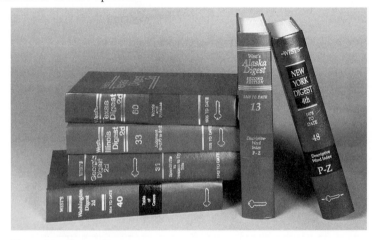

Examples of state digests

Digests Online   All of the digests we have been discussing are printed in hardcover volumes. West Group also makes its digests available online through Westlaw. Earlier we looked at key numbers Negligence 1032, Obscenity 1, and Obscenity 2 as they would appear in a digest volume. One of the ways to find them on Westlaw is to use a special Westlaw "k" number assigned to each of over 400 general topics in the West Group digest system. For example, Negligence is k number 272 and Obscenity is k number 281. To find Negligence 1032, Obscenity 1, and Obscenity 2 in Westlaw, you would type:

272k1032
281k1
281k2

If you are using hardcover digest volumes and want to look at the potentially thousands of cases summarized under Negligence 1032, you would go to the N volume of the digest and find number 1032 under Negligence. If, however, you are online on Westlaw, you would simply type 272k1032 at the keyboard after selecting the database you want. This would lead you to the potentially thousands of cases summarized under 272k1032. See research link F. Later we will cover both kinds of searches in greater depth.

West Group's digest volumes:
key number

Westlaw (online):
k number

RESEARCH LINK F

Every key number in a bound West Group digest volume (which allows you to find cases summarized under a particular topic) has a corresponding k number in Westlaw (which allows you to find the same cases summarized under that k number online).

Federal Appendix (F. App'x.)   A West Group reporter that prints unpublished opinions of some U.S. Courts of Appeals.

Federal Cases   *Federal Cases* is the name of the West Group reporter that contains very early opinions of the federal courts (up to 1880), before F., F.2d, F.3d, F. Supp., and F. Supp. 2d came into existence.

Federal Practice Digest 2d; Federal Practice Digest 3d; Federal Practice Digest 4th   See Exhibit 11.6.

Federal Register (Fed. Reg.)   The *Federal Register* is a daily publication of the federal government that prints proposed federal regulations, notices of agency hearings, executive orders, and related information about federal agencies. Many of the proposed regulations that are adopted by the federal agencies are later printed in the *Code of Federal Regulations* (C.F.R.). See research link D.

Examples of the *Federal Register* and the *Code of Federal Regulations*. The C.F.R. prints regulations that were first proposed in the Fed. Reg.

Federal Reporter (F.); Federal Reporter (F.2d); Federal Reporter (F.3d)   West Group reporters. Currently, F.3d contains opinions of the U.S. Courts of Appeals.

Federal Rules Decisions (F.R.D.)   A West Group reporter containing opinions of some U.S. District Courts on issues of civil and criminal procedure, plus articles, speeches, and conference reports on federal procedural issues.

Federal Supplement (F. Supp.); Federal Supplement 2d (F. Supp. 2d)   West Group reporters. Currently, F. Supp. 2d contains opinions of the U.S. District Courts.

Example of a form book

Form Book   A **form book** is a collection of sample or model forms, often with practical guidance on how to use them. Form books are usually written by private individuals, although a court might issue its own set of required or recommended forms. A form book is sometimes called a practice manual.

General Digest   The *General Digest* is one of three digests within the American Digest System published by West Group. The other two are the *Century Digest* and the *Decennial Digests*. All three digests contain summaries of court opinions by every federal and state court that publishes its opinions. The *General Digest* covers opinions written since the date of the last *Decennial Digest*. Eventually, every *General Digest* volume will be thrown away, and the material in them will be consolidated into the next *Decennial Digest* (see research link G).

General Digest (the most recent digest of the American Digest System)	*Decennial Digest* (the largest digest of the American Digest System)

RESEARCH LINK G

The *General Digest* is a multivolume digest that summarizes (digests) opinions of every state and federal court. All *General Digest* volumes will eventually be thrown away. The material in them will be printed in the next *Decennial Digest* covering a ten-year period (currently printed in two five-year parts).

Headnote   A *headnote* is a short-paragraph summary of a portion of an opinion, printed just before the opinion begins. Most headnotes are written by a private publisher such as West Group. (A few courts, however, ask one of their clerks or other employees to write them.) In West Group reporters, each headnote has two numbers. First is a consecutive number. In an opinion with four headnotes, for example, the headnotes will be numbered 1, 2, 3, and 4. Second, each headnote is assigned a key number, which consists of a general topic and a number. These headnotes with key numbers are also printed in digests. (When a headnote is printed in a digest, it is sometimes called a *digest paragraph*.) Here is an example of the third headnote from an opinion that has the key number "Libel and Slander 28":

The third headnote from an opinion in a West Group, reporter

> **3. Libel and Slander** 🗝 **28**
>
> One may not escape liability for defamation by showing that he was merely repeating defamatory language used by another person, and he may not escape liability by falsely attributing to others the ideas to which he gives expression.

For another example, see the headnotes at the beginning of the *Bruni* opinion in Section G of chapter 7. Again, all headnotes from opinions in reporters are also printed in West Group digests that cover those reporters. See Exhibit 11.6 for a checklist of what digests cover what reporters. West Group is not the only publisher with headnotes, although it is the only publisher of headnotes with key numbers. As indicated, some courts have their clerks or other employees write headnotes for their opinions. If West Group publishes the same opinions, it will give you the court's headnotes plus its own key number headnotes. The other major publisher of headnotes is LexisNexis. For the opinions that LexisNexis publishes online (www.lexis.com), it writes headnotes (abbreviated *HN*) that serve the same function as the other headnotes we have been discussing.

Hornbook   A **hornbook** is a legal treatise designed primarily for the law school student. The treatise summarizes an area of the law that is often covered within a single law school course.

Index to Legal Periodicals and Books (ILP)   *Index to Legal Periodicals and Books* (ILP) is one of the two major general indexes to legal periodical literature. (The other is the *Current Law Index*.) The ILP is available in paper (consisting of pamphlets and hardcover volumes) and online.

Internet   The Internet is a worldwide electronic network of networks on which millions of computer users can share information. It is not run or controlled by any single government

Examples of hornbooks

or organization. A *network* is a group of computers connected by telephone lines, fiber-optic cables, satellites, or other systems. The members of the network can communicate with each other to share information that is placed on the network. Vast quantities of data are available on the networks of the Internet, including legal information. Examples include court opinions, statutes, administrative regulations, treaties, court addresses, and directories of attorneys. For example, on the Web site of the New Jersey State Legislature (www.njleg.state.nj.us), you gain access to New Jersey statutes and bills, names of legislators, the current legislative calendar, etc. And on the Web site of the federal courts (www.uscourts.gov), you find links to the opinions of every federal court, their dockets, biographies of the judges, federal rules of court, etc. Exhibit 11.7 presents a Web page that provides links to the law of every state.

EXHIBIT 11.7	Internet Links to the Law of Every State

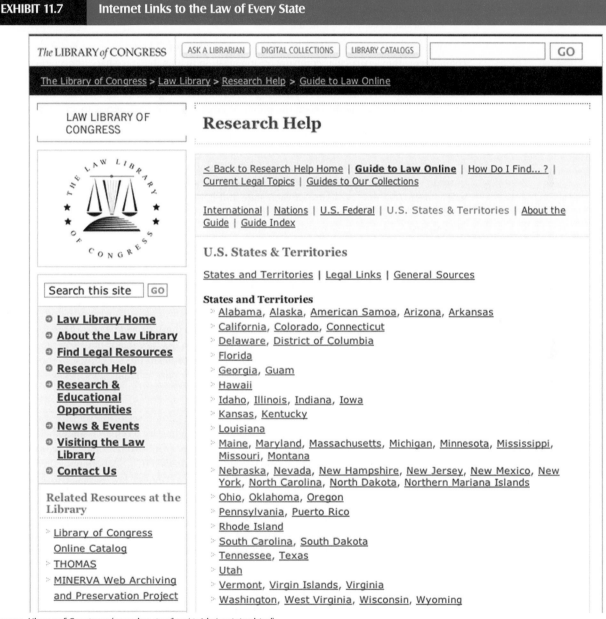

Source: Library of Congress (www.loc.gov/law/guide/usstates.html)

(We will cover such sites in greater detail later in chapter 13.) As indicated earlier, a great deal of the information you can obtain on these sites is free once you are connected to the Internet. Often, however, this information is not as current or accurate as the information available in traditional library volumes and on commercial (fee-based) databases such as Westlaw, LexisNexis, and Loislaw.

One of the best ways to find information on the Internet is through the **World Wide Web**, which is a system of sites on the Internet that can be accessed through **hypertext** links. Hypertext is a method of displaying and linking information found in different locations on the same site or on different sites of the World Wide Web. For example, if you are in a document that contains the court opinions of your state, you may be able to "click" the phrase *state statutes* to switch to another document or site that contains information on the statutes of your state.

Here, for example, is a description of a research resource available from Georgetown University Law Center. Note the extensive amount of material available by hypertext linking:

> We invite you to take a look at our web site (www.ll.georgetown.edu). It contains links to many sources of law and law-related information. State coverage, for example, is provided through a clickable list of links to the law of each state. In addition, an "A–Z Legal Topics" list will lead you to comprehensive materials on subjects as diverse as bankruptcy, civil rights, family law, legal ethics, and sexual orientation and the law.

You need to distinguish the Internet from an **intranet**. The latter is a private network of computers within a particular company or organization that enable it to share information online, often using features similar to those on the World Wide Web. A law office with branch offices, for example, might have an intranet for sharing appellate briefs, legal memoranda, personnel manual, or other data. Unlike the Internet, the public at large does not have access to an intranet. If an office with an intranet allows selected outside individuals (e.g., clients) to connect to some of the data on its intranet, that part of the system is called an *extranet*.

Interstate Compact   An interstate compact is an agreement between two or more states governing a problem of mutual concern, such as the resolution of a boundary dispute. The compact is passed by the legislature of each state and is therefore part of the statutes of the states involved. Congress must give its approval. Hence the compact also becomes part of the statutes of Congress.

KeyCite   KeyCite is an online citator of Westlaw (www.westlaw.com). As we saw when we examined citators, its main competitors are Shepard's Citations and GlobalCite. KeyCite and GlobalCite exist online only. Shepard's Citations exists online and in paper volumes.

Black's Law Dictionary

Legal Dictionary   A **legal dictionary** contains definitions of words and phrases used in the law. Examples include *Black's Law Dictionary* (West Group), *Ballentine's Law Dictionary* (West Group), and *Statsky's Legal Thesaurus/Dictionary* (West Group). The major multivolume legal dictionary is *Words and Phrases* from West Group. The definitions in this set consist of thousands of excerpts from court opinions that have treated the word or phrase. Hence this massive dictionary can also serve as an excellent case finder.

Legal Encyclopedia   A *legal encyclopedia* is a multivolume set of books that summarizes every major legal topic. It is valuable (1) as background reading for a research topic that is new to you and (2) as a case finder (due to its extensive footnotes). The two national encyclopedias are *American Jurisprudence 2d* (Am. Jur. 2d) and *Corpus Juris Secundum* (C.J.S.), both published by West Group. A number of states have their own encyclopedias covering the law of that state, e.g. *Florida Jurisprudence* and *Michigan Law and Practice*.

Legal Newsletter   A **legal newsletter** is a special interest legal periodical (published daily, weekly, etc.) covering practical suggestions and current developments in a particular area of the law (e.g., *AIDS Policy and Law* and *Product Liability Daily*). Most are available in paper, although an increasing number are also online.

Example of a national legal newspaper

Legal Newspaper   A **legal newspaper** is a newspaper (published daily, weekly, etc.) devoted primarily to legal news. There are two kinds of legal newspapers: local and national. Local legal newspapers are usually published weekly or every business day. They print court dockets (calendars), the full text of selected opinions of local courts, information on new rules of court, job announcements, etc. Some large cities have their own legal newspaper. Examples: *New York Law Journal*, *Chicago Daily Law Bulletin*, and *San Francisco Daily Journal*. There are several national legal newspapers such as the weekly *National Law Journal* (www.nlj.com). They cover more than one state on topics such as law firm mergers and dissolutions, salary surveys, careers of prominent attorneys, trends in federal areas of the law, etc.

Legal Periodical   In the broadest sense, a **legal periodical** is a pamphlet on a legal topic that is usually sold by subscription and issued at regular intervals. All periodicals are first printed as pamphlets (called *issues*) and then are often placed in hardcover volumes if the law library considers them sufficiently important. This broad definition of legal periodical would include legal newspapers and legal newsletters. More commonly, however, the phrase legal periodicals refers to three categories of periodicals:

■ Academic legal periodicals (often called *law reviews* or *law journals*) are published by law schools and hence are scholarly in nature. Law students are selected to do some of the writing and all of the editing for most academic legal periodicals. (It is a mark of considerable distinction for a student to be "on law review.") Most academic legal periodicals are general in scope, covering a wide variety of legal topics. Others are special-interest legal periodicals that concentrate on specific subject areas such as women's rights or environmental law.

■ Commercial legal periodicals are published by private companies. They tend to be more practice-oriented, specialized, and expensive than the academic legal periodicals.

■ Bar association legal periodicals are published by national, state, or local bar associations. Their focus is on practical articles and features of interest to the membership.

There are two major general indexes to legal periodical literature:

■ *Current Law Index* (CLI)
■ *Index to Legal Periodicals and Books* (ILP)

See research link H. In addition to these general indexes, there are special indexes to legal periodical literature on topics such as tax law.

Examples of academic legal periodicals

Current Law Index (CLI) Index to Legal Periodicals and Books (ILP)	Legal Periodicals Examples: *Yale Law Journal, Marquette Law Review, Harvard Law Review, Ecology Law Quarterly, ABA Journal, Boston Bar Journal*

RESEARCH LINK H
A great deal of literature exists in the three kinds of legal periodicals (academic, commercial, and bar association). The two major indexes to this literature are the *Current Law Index* (CLI) and the *Index to Legal Periodicals and Books* (ILP).

Legal Thesaurus   A **legal thesaurus** provides word alternatives for words used in legal writing. The thesaurus may also be helpful when you need word alternatives to form queries for computer-assisted legal research (see chapter 13). Example: Statsky's *Legal Thesaurus/Dictionary: A Resource for the Writer and Legal Researcher* (West Group).

LegalTrac   **LegalTrac** is a major general index to legal periodical literature. It is the online version of the *Current Law Index*, the most comprehensive general index to legal periodical literature available.

Legal Treatise   A **legal treatise** (not to be confused with treaty) is any book written by a private individual (or by a public official writing as a private citizen) that provides an overview, summary, or commentary on a legal topic. The treatise will usually attempt to give an extensive treatment of that topic. Hornbooks, handbooks, and form books are also treatises. Some treatises (e.g., hornbooks) are designed primarily as study aids for students. Treatises are printed in single volumes, multivolumes, and looseleafs.

Statsky's Legal *Thesaurus/Dictionary*

Legislation   **Legislation** is the process of making statutory law by the legislature. The word *legislation* also means the statutes themselves. (Legislation sometimes refers to constitutions and treaties as well as to statutes. More commonly, however, legislation refers to statutes alone. For the definition of statute and other categories of primary authority, see Exhibit 6.1 in chapter 6.)

There are two main categories of statutes:

■ **Public law**s (also called *public statutes*): statutes that apply to the general public or to a segment of the public and have permanence and general interest. Example: a statute defining a crime. Such statutes are published as slip laws, as session laws, and as codified laws.

■ **Private laws** (also called *private statutes*): statutes that apply to specifically named individuals or groups and have little or no permanence or general interest. Example: a statute naming

Examples of looseleaf service

Martindale-Hubbell Law Directory

Examples of nutshells (the two pamphlets) and hornbooks

a bridge after a deceased senator. These statutes are published as slip laws and as session laws; they are not codified.

LexisNexis   One of the major commercial fee-based computer-assisted legal research services (www.lexisnexis.com). Its main competitor is Westlaw.

Looseleaf Service   A **looseleaf service** is a lawbook with a binding (often three ringed) that allows easy inserting and removal of pages for updating. As new material is written on the topic of the looseleaf service, it is placed in the binder, often replacing the pages that the new material has changed or otherwise supplemented. Looseleaf updating can occur as often as once a week. Examples of looseleaf services include *Environmental Reporter, Employment Practices Guide, Standard Federal Tax Reports, United States Law Week, Criminal Law Reporter, Family Law Reporter, Media Law Reporter, Labor Relations Reporter.*

Martindale-Hubbell Law Directory   The *Martindale-Hubbell Law Directory* is a multivolume set of books that serves three major functions by providing:

- An alphabetical listing of attorneys and law firms by state and city—this is the **law directory**, which is the main component of the set
- Short summaries of the law of all fifty states (in its separate Digest service)
- Short summaries of the law of many foreign countries (in its separate Digest service)

The *Martindale-Hubbell Law Directory* is also available on the Internet (www.martindale.com). The major competing online law directory is the West Legal Directory (lawyers.findlaw.com) See Exhibits 2.5 and 2.6 in chapter 2.

National Reporter System   The reporters of the West Group that cover the opinions of state courts (e.g., the seven regional reporters such as A.2d) and federal courts (e.g., S. Ct., F.3d). The reporters use key numbers to classify the issues in the opinions.

New York Supplement 2d   (N.Y.S.2d) A reporter of West Group that publishes court opinions of state courts in New York.

North Eastern Reporter 2d (N.E.2d)   A regional reporter of West Group that prints state court opinions of five states (Ill., Ind., Mass., N.Y., and Ohio). N.E.2d is the second series of this reporter. The first series is North Eastern Reporter (N.E.). See Exhibit 11.5.

North Western Digest   A regional digest of West Group that gives summaries of opinions in the North Western Reporter. See research link I and Exhibit 11.6.

Opinions in *North Western 2d* (N.W.2d)   *North Western Digest*

RESEARCH LINK I

Every opinion in the *North Western 2d* reporter written by the state courts in the northwestern region (Iowa, Mich., Minn., Neb., N.D., S.D., and Wis.) is digested (summarized) in *North Western Digest.*

North Western Reporter 2d (N.W.2d)   A regional reporter of West Group that prints state court opinions of seven states (Iowa, Mich., Minn., Neb., N.D., S.D., and Wis.). N.W.2d is the second series of this reporter. The first series is North Western Reporter (N.W.). See Exhibit 11.5.

Nutshell   A **nutshell** is a legal treatise written in pamphlet form. It summarizes a topic that is often covered in a law school course. Nutshells, therefore, are primarily used as study aids by law students. Nutshells are similar to hornbooks in function, although nutshells are usually smaller and are always printed as pamphlets. Nutshells are published by West Group.

Pacific Digest 2d   A regional digest of West Group that gives summaries of opinions in the Pacific Reporter. See research link J and Exhibit 11.6.

Opinions in *Pacific 3d* (P.3d)   *Pacific Digest 2d*

RESEARCH LINK J

Every opinion in the *Pacific 3d* reporter written by the state courts in the pacific region (Alaska, Ariz., Cal., Colo., Haw., Idaho, Kan., Mont., Nev., N.M., Okla., Or., Utah, Wash., and Wyo.) is digested (summarized) in *Pacific Digest 2d.*

Pacific Reporter 3d (P.3d)   A regional reporter of West Group that prints state court opinions of fifteen states (Alaska, Ariz., Cal., Colo., Haw., Idaho, Kan., Mont., Nev., N.M., Okla., Or., Utah, Wash., and Wyo.). P.3d is the third series of this reporter. The second series is Pacific Reporter (P.2d). The first series is Pacific Reporter (P.). See Exhibit 11.5.

Pattern Jury Instructions   Toward the end of a jury trial, the judge must give the jury *instructions* (also called the *charge*) on the law that will govern its deliberations. In some states and judicial systems, there are suggested instructions that can be adapted to the specifics of a particular trial. The instructions are called model jury instructions or, more commonly, **pattern jury instructions**. They are printed in hardcover volumes and are often available online.

Pocket Part   A pocket part is a pamphlet inserted into a small pocket built into the inside back (and occasionally front) cover of a hardcover volume. The pamphlet contains text that supplements or updates the material in the hardcover volume. The pocket part is published after the hardcover volume is published. The purpose of a pocket part is to update the material in the hardcover volume. Pocket parts are critically important in legal research. You may be reading something in the hardcover volume without being aware that it is no longer valid. One of the ways to check its validity is to check the pocket part for that volume. (For a list of law books that often have pocket parts, see Exhibit 11.15, later in the chapter.)

Example of a law book with a pocket part

Public Domain Citation   A citation that is medium neutral (meaning that it can be read in a paper volume or online) and vendor neutral (meaning that it does not contain volume, page, or other identifying information created by particular vendors such as a commercial publisher). Also called *generic citation*. Here is an example of a public domain citation that we will study later in the chapter:

Pine Ridge Realty, Inc. v. Massachusetts Bay Ins. Co., 2000 ME 106 ¶ 3.

Record   When referring to a trial, the record is the official collection of what happened during the trial. It includes a word-for-word transcript of what was said, the pleadings, and all the exhibits. *See also* Congressional Record.

Regional Digest   A digest that summarizes cases in a regional reporter. See Exhibit 11.6. See also research links A, E, I, J, and L.

Regional Reporter   A West Group reporter that contains state court opinions of states within a region of the country. West Group has divided the country into seven regions. See Exhibit 11.5.

Register   A **register** is a regularly published collection of regulations and other documents of administrative agencies and the chief executive, e.g., the *Federal Register*.

Reporter   A reporter is a volume (or set of volumes) of court opinions. An *official reporter* is printed under the authority of the government, often by a government printing office. (Official reporters are sometimes called reports, e.g., *United States Reports*.) An *unofficial reporter* is a reporter printed by a private or commercial publisher without specific authority from the government. (The word *reporter* is also sometimes used in other kinds of publications as well, e.g., in sets of administrative regulations and in looseleaf services.) See Exhibits 11.5 and 11.6 for lists of reporters.

Restatements   Restatements are scholarly publications of the American Law Institute (ALI) (www.ali.org) that attempt to formulate (that is, restate) the existing law of a given area. Occasionally, the Restatements also state what the ALI thinks the law *ought* to be.

Examples of Restatements:

Example of a Restatement

Restatement of Agency   *Restatement of the Law Governing Lawyers*
Restatement of Conflicts of Law   *Restatement of Property*
Restatement of Contracts   *Restatement of Restitution*
Restatement of Foreign   *Restatement of Security*
   Relations Law   *Restatement of Torts*
Restatement of Judgments   *Restatement of Trusts*

Because the Restatements are written by a private organization (ALI) rather than by an official government entity, they are not laws. However, because of their scholarly content, they have great prestige in the courts. Judges frequently rely on them in their opinions. One of the reasons this is so is the elaborate procedure the ALI follows before issuing one of its Restatements. First, a renowned scholar in the field prepares an initial draft of the Restatement. This draft is reviewed by a committee of advisors consisting of other scholars and specialists in the field. A council of the

ALI then reviews and revises the draft. This leads to a *tentative draft* that is considered by the ALI at one of its annual meetings. After further editing and revision, the final version is approved by the ALI. You can read the Restatements in bound volumes and online in Westlaw and LexisNexis.

Example of rules of court volumes

Rules of Court **Rules of court**, also called *court rules*, are the laws of procedure that govern the mechanics of litigation before a particular state or federal court. (For the definition of rules of law and other primary authorities, see Exhibit 6.1 in chapter 6.) Rules of court are often found in the statutory code and in separate volumes or pamphlets, called *deskbooks*.

Series A new **edition** is usually a revision of an earlier version of a book or set of books. A new **series,** in contrast, refers to a new numbering order for new volumes within the *same* set of books. Reporters, for example, come in series. *Federal Reporter, First Series* (F.) has 300 volumes. After volume 300 was printed, the publisher decided to start a new series of the same set of books—*Federal Reporter, Second Series* (F.2d). The first volume of F.2d is volume 1. F.2d has 999 volumes. After volume 999 was printed, the publisher decided to start a new series of the same set of books—*Federal Reporter, Third Series* (F.3d). After a large number of F.3d volumes are printed, we will undoubtedly see an F.4th, which will begin again with volume 1. There is no consistent number of volumes that a publisher will print before deciding to start a new series for a set of books.

Session Law **Session laws** are uncodified statutes enacted during a particular session (often lasting two years) of the legislature. (Individual session laws are printed as *slip laws*.) Session laws are printed chronologically rather than by subject matter. Session laws are sometimes called Statutes at Large (e.g., *United States Statutes at Large*). Session laws contain both *public statutes*—also called *public laws* (which are statutes that apply to the general public or to a segment of the public and have permanence and general interest)—and *private statutes*—also called *private laws* (which are statutes that apply to specifically named individuals or groups and have little or no permanence or general interest). Only public statutes or laws are later *codified*, which means they are placed in statutory codes and arranged by subject matter. See research link K.

Slip Law (a single public or private statute)
Session Laws (arranged by date)
(public and private statutes)

Statutory Code (arranged by subject matter)
(public statutes only)

RESEARCH LINK K

After public and private statutes are first printed as *slip laws*, they are printed in volumes of *session laws* where they are arranged chronologically (by date of enactment). The public statutes are then arranged by subject matter and printed in a *statutory code*.

Excerpt from a page in a Shepard's volume (Shepard's Citations is also available online: law.lexisnexis.com/shepards).

Shepard's Citations Our goal here is to provide a brief overview of Shepard's and shepardizing by identifying the major sets of Shepard's volumes that exist. Later, in Section O of this chapter, we will learn how to use Shepard's—how to **shepardize.**

Shepard's Citations is a citator, which is a book, CD–ROM, or online service containing lists of citations that can (1) help you assess the current validity of an opinion, statute, or other item; and (2) give you leads to additional relevant materials. To shepardize something simply means that you use any of the formats of *Shepard's Citations* to accomplish these ends. See research link C.

What can you shepardize? Here is a partial list:

- Court opinions
- Statutes
- Constitutions
- Some administrative regulations
- Some administrative decisions
- Ordinances
- Charters

- Rules of court
- Some executive orders
- Some treaties
- Patents, trademarks, copyrights
- Restatements
- Some legal periodical literature

It is important to distinguish between **cited material** and **citing material** within Shepard's. The cited material is always what you are checking or shepardizing. Everything on the above list is cited material. It refers to that which is mentioned—cited—by something else. What do we call the materials that *do* the citing? Answer: cit*ing* materials. Here are some examples:

- Assume you are shepardizing *Smith v. Smith*, 100 N.E.2d 458 (Mass. 1980). You find out through Shepard's that this case was once mentioned by the case of *Jones v. Jones*, 105 N.E.2d 62

(Mass. 1982). What was cited? The *Smith* case. Therefore, it is the cited material. Who did the citing? The *Jones* case. Therefore, it is the citing material.

- Assume you are shepardizing section 100 of the state statutory code. You find out through Shepard's that this statute was once mentioned by the case of *Kiley v. New York*, 296 N.E.2d 222 (N.Y. 1982). What was cited? Section 100. Therefore, it is the cited material. Who did the citing? The *Kiley* case. Therefore, it is the citing material.

As you can see from the first example, an opinion can be the cited material—what you are shepardizing—and another opinion can be the citing material for what you are shepardizing.

In Exhibit 11.8, there is an overview of some of the major opinions, statutes, and administrative regulations that can be shepardized, with the appropriate set of *Shepard's Citations* that you would use to do so.

EXHIBIT 11.8   Examples of Opinions, Statutes, and Administrative Regulations That Can Be Shepardized

Assume that you want to shepardize an opinion of the U.S. Supreme Court:

Supreme Court Reporter

Here is a volume from the set of Shepard's you use to shepardize an opinion of the U.S. Supreme Court:

Shepard's United States Citations

Assume that you want to shepardize opinions found in *Federal Reporter, 3d:*

Federal Reporter 3d (F.3d)

Here is a volume from the set of Shepard's you use to shepardize an F.3d opinion:

Shepard's Federal Citations

Assume that you want to Shepardize opinions found in *Federal Supplement 2d:*

Federal Supplement 2d (F. Supp. 2d)

Here is a volume from the set of Shepard's you use to shepardize an F. Supp. 2d opinion:

Shepard's Federal Citations

(continues)

EXHIBIT 11.8	Examples of Opinions, Statutes, and Administrative Regulations That Can Be Shepardized—*continued*

Assume that you want to shepardize a federal statute of Congress: a statute found in U.S.C.A. (*United States Code Annotated*) or in U.S.C.S. (*United States Code Service*) or in U.S.C. (*United States Code*):

Here is a volume from the set of Shepard's you use to shepardize a federal statute:

United States Code Annotated (U.S.C.A.)

Shepard's Federal Statute Citations

Assume that you want to shepardize a regulation of a federal agency found in C.F.R.:

Here is a volume from the set of Shepard's that will enable you to shepardize a regulation in C.F.R.:

Code of Federal Regulations (C.F.R.)

Shepard's Code of Federal Regulations Citations

Assume that you want to shepardize opinions found within the following regional reporters:

    Atlantic Reporter 2d
    Pacific Reporter 2d
    South Western Reporter 2d
    South Eastern Reporter 2d
    North Eastern Reporter 2d

At the right are volumes from the sets of Shepard's that you use to shepardize to opinions in these regional reporters.

(continues)

EXHIBIT 11.8	Examples of Opinions, Statutes, and Administrative Regulations That Can Be Shepardized—*continued*

Assume that you want to shepardize the following:

A Rhode Island court opinion
A Rhode Island statute
A Rhode Island constitutional provision
A New Hampshire court opinion
A New Hampshire statute
A New Hampshire constitutional provision

Here are volumes from the sets of Shepard's that you would use:

Note: Every state has its own set of Shepard's similar to *Shepard's Rhode Island Citations and Shepard's New Hampshire Citations* above.

Slip Law   A slip law is a single act passed by the legislature and printed in a single pamphlet. It is the first official publication of the act. All slip laws are later printed chronologically in volumes that may be called session laws or statutes at large. Finally, if the slip law is a public law (public statute), it is also printed in a **statutory code**, where the arrangement is by subject matter.

Slip Opinion   When a court first announces a decision, it is usually published in what is called a **slip opinion** or slip decision. It is the first printing of a single court opinion. The slip opinions are later printed in advance sheets for reporters, which in turn become hardcover reporters.

South Eastern Digest   A regional digest of West Group that gives summaries of opinions in the South Eastern Reporter. See research link L and Exhibit 11.6.

Example of a slip law

Opinions in *South Eastern 2d* (S.E.2d)	*South Eastern Digest*

RESEARCH LINK L

Every opinion in the *South Eastern 2d* reporter written by the state courts in the southeastern region (Ga., N.C., S.C., Va., and W.Va.) is digested (summarized) in *South Eastern Digest*.

South Eastern Reporter 2d   (S.E.2d) A regional reporter of West Group that prints state court opinions of five states (Ga., N.C., S.C., Va., and W.Va.). S.E.2d is the second series of this reporter. The first series is South Eastern Reporter (S.E.). See Exhibit 11.5.

Southern Reporter 2d   (So. 2d) A regional reporter of West Group that prints state court opinions of four states (Ala., Fla., La., and Miss.). So. 2d is the second series of this reporter. The first series is Southern Reporter (So.). See Exhibit 11.5.

South Western Reporter 3d   (S.W.3d) A regional reporter of West Group that prints state court opinions of five states (Ark., Ky., Mo., Tenn., and Tex.). S.W.3d is the third series of this reporter. The second series is South Western Reporter 2d (S.W.2d). The first series is South Western Reporter (S.W.). See Exhibit 11.5.

Example of a slip opinion

Star Paging   A special notation (e.g., an asterisk or an inverted T) that is placed next to text in a book or online database that will tell you on what page that same text can also be found in another book or edition. When you find this notation in the text of an unofficial reporter, you will know on what page that text also appears in an official reporter (its parallel cite). When you find this notation in the text of an online database (e.g., in Westlaw), you will know on what page that text also appears in a traditional (i.e., paper) reporter volume.

Example of star paging. This excerpt is from page 658 of a reporter. Note the special mark (an inverted T) telling you that the same text will begin on page 378 of another reporter.

658

to determine which crimes have been punished too leniently, and which too severely. § 994(m). Congress has called upon the Commission to exercise its judgement about which $\perp_{378}$ types of crimes and which types of criminals are to be considered similar for the purposes of sentencing.

Statutes at Large   An uncodified printing of statutes. Statutes at Large (abbreviated Stat.) are session laws.

Example of a state statutory code

Statutory Code   Statutes are first published as *slip laws*, then in *session law* volumes, and finally, if they are of general public interest, in a *statutory code*. A statutory code is a collection of statutes of the legislature organized by subject matter. For example, the statutes on murder are together, the statutes on probate are together, etc. An **official statutory code** is one printed under the authority of the government, often by the government itself. An **unofficial statutory code** is one printed by a commercial publishing company without special authority from the government. Statutory codes are often annotated (particularly unofficial codes), meaning that notes or commentaries accompany the full text of the statutes. The notes might include summaries of cases (often called *notes of decisions*) that have interpreted the statute and information on the legislative history of the statute, such as the dates of earlier amendments. Statutes are published in printed volumes, on CD–ROMs, online through fee-based services (e.g., Westlaw, LexisNexis, and Loislaw), and online through free Internet sites that we will examine later.

The three major *federal* statutory codes containing the statutes of Congress are:

U.S.C.—*United States Code* (published by the U.S. Government Printing Office) (official)
U.S.C.A.—*United States Code Annotated* (published by West Group) (unofficial)
U.S.C.S.—*United States Code Service* (published by LexisNexis) (unofficial)

Availability and updating of these three sets:

- U.S.C. is available for free online (www.gpoaccess.gov/uscode).
- U.S.C. is available on fee-based services such as Westlaw, LexisNexis, and Loislaw.
- U.S.C. (print version) is updated by Supplement volumes.
- U.S.C.A. is available on Westlaw.
- U.S.C.A. (print version) is updated by pocket parts.
- U.S.C.S. is available on LexisNexis.
- U.S.C.S. (print version) is updated by pocket parts.

The three major federal statutory codes: U.S.C., U.S.C.A, and U.S.C.S.

Supreme Court Reporter (S. Ct.) An unofficial reporter of West Group that prints opinions of the U.S. Supreme Court. Before the final volumes are printed, it comes out in pamphlet advance sheets and in hardcover *Interim Edition* volumes.

Ultrafiche A microform consisting of images or photographs that have been reduced by a factor of 100 or more on a single sheet of film.

Uniform Laws Uniform laws are laws proposed to state legislatures in areas where uniformity is deemed appropriate. Each state can adopt, modify, or reject the proposals. The main organization submitting these proposals is the National Conference of Commissioners on Uniform State Laws (www.nccusl.org). Examples of uniform laws that many states have adopted are the Uniform Commercial Code (UCC) and the Uniform Child Custody Jurisdiction Act (UCCJA). Sometimes the proposals are called *model acts*. An example is the Model Penal Code (MPC) of the American Law Institute (www.ali.org).

United States Code (U.S.C.) The official statutory code published by the U.S. Government Printing Office containing federal statutes of Congress.

United States Code Annotated (U.S.C.A.) An unofficial statutory code published by West Group containing federal statutes of Congress.

United States Code Congressional and Administrative News (U.S.C.C.A.N.) U.S.C.C.A.N., published by West Group will enable you to:

- Obtain the complete text of public laws or statutes of Congress before they are published in U.S.C./U.S.C.A./U.S.C.S. (All of the recent Statutes at Large of Congress—its session laws—are published in U.S.C.C.A.N.)
- Obtain the complete text of some congressional committee reports (important for legislative history).
- Translate a Statute at Large cite into a U.S.C./U.S.C.A./U.S.C.S. cite (through Table 2).
- Obtain leads to the legislative history of federal statutes (primarily through Table 4).

Table 4
LEGISLATIVE HISTORY

Bill numbers in parentheses ( ) are companion bills reported either in the Senate or the House

Public Law		BH Stat. Page	Bill No.	Report No. 91-		Comm. Reporting		Cong.Rec.Vol. 116 (1970) Dates of Consideration and Passage	
No.91-	Date App.			House	Senate	House	Senate	House	Ser
191	Feb. 5	5	S.J.Res. 121	810	853	FA	FR	Jan. 29	M
192	Feb. 6	6	H.J.Res.	none	647	none	J	Jan. 26	
193					76	none	none	Feb. 7	
						App	App	Dr	
							J		
						467			

- Obtain the complete text of some federal agency regulations (duplicating what is found in the *Federal Register*—Fed. Reg.—and in the *Code of Federal Regulations*—C.F.R.).
- Obtain the complete text of executive orders and other executive documents.
- Obtain the complete text of all current *United States Statutes at Large* (see below).

United States Code Service (U.S.C.S.) An unofficial statutory code published by LexisNexis containing federal statutes of Congress.

United States Law Week (U.S.L.W.) U.S.L.W. is an unofficial looseleaf service that prints opinions of the U.S. Supreme Court. U.S.L.W. also contains other data on cases in the Supreme Court and summarizes important cases from other courts.

United States Reports (U.S.) An official reporter for opinions of the U.S. Supreme Court. The advance sheets for *United States Reports* are called **preliminary prints**.

United States Statutes at Large (Stat.) The session laws of Congress are printed in volumes called *United States Statutes at Large* (Stat.). They contain the full text of every public law or statute and every private law or statute of Congress. (A private law or private statute applies to specifically named individuals or to groups and has little or no permanence or general interest, unlike a public law or public statute.) The statutes within Stat. are printed chronologically. See research link M. All current statutes at large are now also printed in *U.S. Code Congressional and Administrative News* as well as in separate Stat. volumes. (The public laws of general interest are later codified and printed in each of the three sets of codified federal statutes: U.S.C., U.S.C.A., and U.S.C.S.)

United States Statutes at Large (Stat.) (public and private statutes of Congress arranged by date)	*United States Code* (U.S.C.) (public statutes of Congress arranged by subject matter) *United States Code Annotated* (U.S.C.A.) (public statutes of Congress arranged by subject matter) *United States Code Service* (U.S.C.S.) (public statutes of Congress arranged by subject matter)

RESEARCH LINK M

All public and private statutes of Congress are printed chronologically as session laws in *United States Statutes at Large* (Stat.). If they are public statutes, they are also codified and printed by subject matter in the three codes containing federal statutes: U.S.C. (official), U.S.C.A. (unofficial), and U.S.C.S. (unofficial).

Words and Phrases, a multi-volume legal dictionary

United States Supreme Court Digest   A digest of West Group that gives summaries of opinions of the U.S. Supreme Court.

United States Supreme Court Reports, Lawyers' Edition 2d   (L. Ed. 2d) An unofficial reporter of LexisNexis that prints opinions of the U.S. Supreme Court. This is the second series (L. Ed. 2d.). The first series is *United States Supreme Court Reports, Lawyers' Edition* (L. Ed.).

Westlaw   One of the major fee-based computer-assisted legal research services (www .westlaw.com). Its main competitor is LexisNexis.

Words and Phrases   A multivolume legal dictionary. Most of the definitions in this dictionary are quotations from court opinions.

OUTLINE

For a summary of many of the glossary entries we have been examining, see Exhibit 11.9.

EXHIBIT 11.9   **Major Legal Reference Materials: An Outline**

BOOKS OF LAW

Federal Statutes . . . .
- *U.S. Statutes at Large*
- *U.S. Code*
- *U.S. Code Annotated*
- *U.S. Code Service*

State Statutes . . . .
- Session laws
- State statutory codes

Federal Court Opinions

U.S. Supreme Court . . . .
- *U.S. Reports*
- *Lawyers' Edition 2d*
- *Supreme Court Reporter*
- *U.S. Law Week*

U.S. Courts of Appeals . . . .
- *Federal Reporter 3d*

U.S. District Courts . . . .
- *Federal Supplement 2d*

Specialty or Topical Reporters . . . .
- *Federal Rules Decisions*
- *Military Justice Reporter*
- *Bankruptcy Reporter*
- *Federal Claims Reporter*
- *Veterans Appeals Reporter*

(continues)

EXHIBIT 11.9   Major Legal Reference Materials: An Outline—*continued*

**BOOKS OF
LAW
(cont.)**

State Court Opinions

    Regional Reporters of the
    National Reporter System . . . .

- *Atlantic Reporter 2d*
- *North Eastern Reporter 2d*
- *North Western Reporter 2d*
- *Pacific Reporter 3d*
- *South Eastern Reporter 2d*
- *Southern Reporter 2d*
- *South Western Reporter 3d*

        Others . . . .

- Official state reporters
- Special edition state reporters (offprint reporters)

Federal and State Constitutions . . . .

- Within statutory code

Federal Administrative Regulations . . . .

- *Federal Register*
- *Code of Federal Regulations*

State Administrative Regulations . . . .

- State register
- State administrative code

Charters and Ordinances . . . .

- Municipal code

**BOOKS OF
SEARCH
AND/OR
INTERPRETATION**

Digests . . . .

- American Digest System
  - *Century Digest*
  - *Decennial Digests*
  - *General Digests*
- U.S. Supreme Court Digest
- Regional digests
- Individual state digests
- *Federal Practice Digest 4th*
- *Bankruptcy Digest*
- *Education Law Digest*
- *Military Justice Digest*
- *Veterans Appeals Digest*

Legal Encyclopedias . . . .

- *American Jurisprudence 2d*
- *Corpus Juris Secundum*

Legal Periodicals . . . .

- *Index to Legal Periodicals and Books*
- *Current Law Index*
- *LegalTrac*
- *WilsonWeb*

Annotations . . . .

- *American Law Reports*
- *American Law Reports 2d*
- *American Law Reports 3d*
- *American Law Reports 4th*
- *American Law Reports 5th*
- *American Law Reports 6th*
- *American Law Reports Fed.*
- *American Law Reports Fed. 2d*

Others . . . .

- Looseleaf services
- Legal treatises
- Legal newsletters
- Legal newspapers

(continues)

| EXHIBIT 11.9 | Major Legal Reference Materials: An Outline—*continued* |

COMPUTER RESEARCH . . . .
- Fee-based (e.g., Westlaw, LexisNexis, and Loislaw)
- Free (e.g., official sites of courts, legislatures, chief executives, and administrative agencies)

CITATORS . . . .
- Shepard's Citations
- KeyCite (Westlaw)
- Auto-Cite (LexisNexis)
- GlobalCite (Loislaw)

PARALLEL CITATION TABLES . . . .
- *National Reporter Blue Book*
- *Blue and White Book*

LEGAL DICTIONARIES . . . .
- *Black's Law Dictionary*
- *Ballentine's Law Dictionary*
- *Statsky's Legal Theasurus/ Dictionary*
- *Words and Phrases*

CITATION GUIDELINES . . . .
- *Bluebook: A Uniform System of Citation*
- *ALWD Citation Manual*

[SECTION I]

AUTHORITY IN RESEARCH AND WRITING

1. INTRODUCTION

The purpose of legal research is to find the law that will help a client solve a legal dispute, prevent such a dispute from arising, or prevent a dispute from getting worse. All three are accomplished by analyzing the facts of the client's case and by applying any existing *mandatory primary authority* to these facts. Our goal in this section is to identify what we mean by this kind of authority and to explore what must be done if such authority cannot be found. First, some definitions.

Authority is any source that a court can rely on in reaching its decision.

Primary and Secondary Authority

Primary authority is any *law* that the court can rely on in reaching its decision. Examples include statutes, administrative regulations, constitutional provisions, executive orders, charters, ordinances, treaties, and other court opinions (see Exhibit 6.1 in chapter 6).

Secondary authority is any *nonlaw* that the court can rely on in reaching its decision. Examples include legal and nonlegal periodical literature, legal and nonlegal encyclopedias, legal and nonlegal dictionaries, and legal and nonlegal treatises. (See Exhibit 11.10, later in this section.)

Mandatory Authority and Persuasive Authority

Mandatory authority, also called *controlling authority*, is whatever the court *must* rely on in reaching its decision. Only primary authority—such as another court opinion, a statute, or a constitutional provision—can be mandatory authority. A court is never required to rely on secondary authority, such as a legal periodical article or legal encyclopedia. Secondary authority cannot be mandatory authority.

Persuasive authority is whatever the court relies on when it is not required to do so. There are two main kinds of persuasive authority: (1) a prior court opinion that the court is not required to follow but does so because it finds the opinion persuasive and (2) any secondary authority that the court finds persuasive.

---

authority Any source that a court could rely on in reaching its decision.

primary authority Any *law* that a court could rely on in reaching its decision.

secondary authority Any *nonlaw* a court can rely on in its decision. Writings that describe or explain, but do not constitute, the law.

mandatory authority Any authority that a court must rely on in reaching its decision. Also called *controlling authority*.

persuasive authority Any authority a court relies on in reaching its decision that it is not required to rely on.

Nonauthority

Nonauthority is (1) any primary or secondary authority that is not on point because it is not relevant and does not cover the facts of the client's problem; (2) any invalid primary authority, such as an unconstitutional statute; or (3) any materials that are solely finding aids (e.g., digests) or validating tools (e.g., citators).

2. MANDATORY AUTHORITY

Courts *must* follow mandatory authority. There are two broad categories of mandatory authority: (1) **enacted law** such as a statute, a constitutional provision, an ordinance, or an administrative regulations; and (2) other court opinions. (See chapter 7 for a discussion of the meaning of enacted law.) Each category will be considered separately.

enacted law Any law that is not created within litigation. Law written by a deliberative body such as a legislature or constitutional convention after it is proposed and often debated and amended.

Enacted Law as Mandatory Authority

Any enacted law is mandatory authority and must be followed if the following three tests are met:

- The enacted law is being applied in a geographic area over which the authors of the law have power or jurisdiction (e.g., a Florida statute being applied to an event that occurred in the state of Florida).
- It was the intention of the authors of the enacted law (e.g., the legislature that wrote the statute) to cover the kinds of facts that are currently before the court.
- The application of this enacted law to these facts does not violate some other law that is superior in authority (e.g., the statute does not violate the constitution).

If an enacted law such as a state statute meets these three tests, it is mandatory authority in every state court in the state.

For example, assume that § 14 of the Florida statutory code says, "It shall be a felony to break and enter a dwelling for the purpose of stealing property therein." Smith is charged with violating § 14 after being arrested for knocking down the door of a Miami apartment and taking jewelry from the apartment. Is § 14 mandatory authority in a Florida criminal court where Smith is being prosecuted? Yes. The author of § 14 is the Florida legislature. The alleged crime occurred in Miami, a geographical area over which the Florida legislature clearly has power or jurisdiction. The first test is met. There is little doubt that an apartment is a "dwelling." Hence the legislature intended § 14 to cover stealing from an apartment. The second test is met. There is no indication that § 14 violates the state constitution or any other higher authority. Assuming there is no such violation, the third test is met. Therefore, § 14 is mandatory authority in the criminal trial of *Florida v. Smith*.

Suppose, however, that Smith is arrested for breaking into a *car* and stealing valuables from the glove compartment. Is § 14 mandatory authority in this case? We need to know whether a car is a "dwelling" for purposes of § 14. (In part, it might depend on whether the owner of the car ever slept in it.) To answer this question, we need to ask whether the Florida legislature intended to include motor vehicles within the meaning of "dwelling" in § 14. This is a question of **legislative intent**. If the statute was not intended to cover these facts, it is not applicable; it cannot be mandatory authority. In this instance, it would be nonauthority.

legislative intent The design or purpose of the legislature in passing (enacting) a particular statute.

Furthermore, even if the enacted law *was* intended to cover the facts before the court, it is not mandatory authority if it violates some higher law. The authors of an administrative regulation, for example, may intend to cover a particular individual's activities. If, however, this regulation is inconsistent with the statute that the regulation is supposed to be carrying out, the regulation is not mandatory authority. The regulation violates a higher law—a statute—and therefore is invalid; it is nonauthority. Similarly, a statute may clearly cover a given set of facts but be invalid because the statute is unconstitutional. For example, a statute that prohibits marriage between the races is clearly intended to prevent interracial marriage, but the statute is not mandatory authority because it is in violation of the constitution. The statute violates a higher law—the constitution—and therefore is invalid; it is nonauthority.

State enacted law (e.g., a state statute, a state administrative regulation) is usually mandatory only in the state that enacted that law. Suppose, however, that a state court is considering a *federal* enacted law.

Federal enacted law (e.g., the U.S. Constitution, a federal statute, and a federal administrative regulation) can sometimes be mandatory authority in *state* courts. The U.S. Constitution is the highest authority in the country. If a provision of this Constitution applies, it controls over any state law to the contrary. Federal statutes and the regulations of federal administrative agencies are also superior in authority to state laws in those areas entrusted to the federal government by the U.S. Constitution, such as interstate commerce, patents, bankruptcy, or foreign affairs. Federal statutes and regulations in these areas are mandatory authority in state courts.

Court Opinions as Mandatory Authority

When is a court *required* to follow an opinion, so that the opinion is mandatory authority? Two conditions must be met:

- The opinion is **analogous**.
- The opinion was written by a higher court that is superior to the court currently considering the applicability of the opinion.

By *analogous*, we mean that that the facts and issues in the opinion are sufficiently similar to the facts and issues in the dispute now before the court to justify reaching the same result in the dispute that was reached in the opinion. If the opinion is analogous, the first condition of classifying the opinion as mandatory authority has been met.

The second condition is that the opinion was written by a higher court. To understand this condition, we need to examine the relationship between the court that wrote the opinion and the court that is currently considering that opinion. We will briefly cover six variations:

1. The highest court in the judicial system is considering an opinion written by a lower court in the same judicial system.
2. A lower court is considering an opinion written by the highest court in the same judicial system.
3. A court is considering an opinion written in the past by the same court.
4. A state court is considering an opinion written by a court from another state.
5. A state court is considering an opinion written by a federal court.
6. A federal court is considering an opinion written by a state court.

In each of these six situations, a court is attempting to determine whether the conclusion or holding in a prior opinion is binding in the dispute currently before the court. Assume that the opinion is analogous.

1. *The highest court in the judicial system is considering an opinion written by a lower court in the same judicial system.*

    A higher court is never required to follow an opinion written by a lower court in the same judicial system, whether or not the opinion is analogous. The California Supreme Court, for example, does not have to follow the holding in an opinion written by a California Superior Court, one of the lower courts in the California judicial system. Similarly, the U.S. Supreme Court does not have to follow the holding in an opinion written by a U.S. District Court, the trial court in the federal judicial system. If the opinion is analogous, it can only be persuasive authority; the higher court can follow the holding if it chooses to do so.

2. *A lower court is considering an opinion written by the highest court in the same judicial system.*

    An opinion written by the highest court in a judicial system *is* mandatory on every lower court in the same judicial system—if the opinion is analogous. An analogous opinion by the Supreme Court of Montana, for example, must be followed by every lower state court in Montana.

3. *A court is considering an opinion written in the past by the same court.*

    Does a court have to follow its *own* prior opinions? If, for example, the Florida Supreme Court wrote an opinion in 1970, is the holding in that opinion mandatory authority for the Florida Supreme Court in 2002 if the opinion is analogous? No. A court is always free to **overrule** and in effect invalidate its own prior opinions. This, however, rarely happens. A court is reluctant to change holdings in prior opinions unless there are good reasons to do so. This reluctance is known as **stare decisis**. Stated more positively: if a **precedent** exists, a court will follow it in a later similar case unless there are good reasons for the court to change the precedent. A precedent is simply a prior decision that can be used as a standard in a later similar case. To maintain fairness and stability, stare decisis means that courts should decide similar cases in the same way unless there is good reason to do otherwise.

    The Florida example involved the highest state court considering an earlier opinion written by the same court. Suppose the opinion had been written by an intermediate or middle appeals court. Sometime later, this same court is asked to follow its own prior opinion because the previous opinion is analogous to the case currently before the court. Does it have to? No. *Any* court can later overrule itself and reach a holding that differs from the holding it reached in the earlier opinion.

4. *A state court is considering an opinion written by a court from another state.*

    A state court generally does not have to follow an opinion written by a state court in another state, no matter how similar or analogous the cases are. An Idaho court, for example, does not have to follow an opinion written by a Texas court.

---

analogous Sufficiently similar to justify a similar outcome or result. (See the glossary for other meanings of *analogous*.)

overrule 1. To decide against or deny. 2. To reject or cancel an earlier opinion as precedent by rendering an opposite decision on the same question of law in a different litigation.

stare decisis ("stand by things decided") Courts should decide similar cases in the same way unless there is good reason for the court to do otherwise. In resolving an issue before it, a court should be reluctant to reject precedent—a prior opinion covering a similar issue.

precedent A prior decision covering a similar issue that can be used as a standard or guide in a later similar case.

There are two main exceptions to the principle that an opinion of one state is not mandatory authority in another state. The first involves conflict of laws and the second, full faith and credit:

- **Conflict of laws**. Suppose that an accident occurs in New York between a New York citizen and an Ohio citizen. The New Yorker decides to sue for negligence in a state court in Ohio, where the defendant lives. Assume that the Ohio court has **subject matter jurisdiction** over the dispute (meaning that the court has the power to hear this kind of dispute) and **personal jurisdiction** over the parties (meaning that the court has the power to render a decision that would resolve or adjudicate the personal rights of these particular parties). What negligence law does the Ohio court apply? Ohio negligence law or New York negligence law? The negligence law of the two states may differ in significant respects. This is a conflict-of-law problem, which arises whenever there is an inconsistency between the laws of two different, coequal legal systems such as two states. Under the principles of the conflict of law, a court of one state may be *required* to apply the law of another state. For example, the law to be applied may be the law of the state where the injury occurred or the law of the state that is at the center of the dispute. If this state is New York, then the Ohio court will apply New York negligence law. Analogous opinions of New York courts on the law of negligence will be mandatory authority in the Ohio court.

- **Full faith and credit**. The United States Constitution provides that "Full Faith and Credit shall be given in each State to the public Acts, Records, and judicial Proceedings of every other State" (art. IV, § 1). Suppose that Richards sues Davis for breach of contract in Delaware. Davis wins. Richards cannot go to another state and bring a breach-of-contract suit against Davis arising out of the same facts. If the Delaware court had proper jurisdiction (subject matter and personal) when it rendered its judgment, the Delaware opinion must be given full faith and credit in every other state. The case cannot be relitigated. The Delaware opinion is mandatory authority in every other state.

5. *A state court is considering an opinion written by a federal court.*

Most litigation in state court raises only state issues. Occasionally, however, a federal issue can arise in litigation under way in state court. Assume, for example, that Adams sues Peterson in state court for negligence, a state issue. Assume further that the court in this suit must define the phrase *public accommodations* that appears in a federal statute. Now we have a federal issue arising in a state court case. If there are federal court opinions defining this phrase, they would be mandatory authority in the state litigation between Adams and Peterson. Under the **Supremacy Clause** of the U.S. Constitution, state courts must follow federal law on federal issues such as the meaning of a valid federal statute. Federal court opinions are mandatory authority in state courts when federal issues are raised. On all *state* issues, however, a state court would not have to follow any federal court opinions.

6. *A federal court is considering an opinion written by a state court.*

Most litigation in federal court raises only federal issues. Occasionally, however, a state issue can arise in litigation under way in federal court. Assume, for example, that Smith sues Jackson in federal court for copyright infringement, a federal issue. Assume further that the court in this suit must define *compulsory* under the state law of Georgia, where Smith lives. Now we have a state issue arising in a federal court case. If there are Georgia state court opinions defining this term, they would be mandatory authority in the federal litigation between Jackson and Smith. State court opinions are mandatory authority in federal courts when state issues are raised. On all *federal* issues, however, a federal court would not have to follow any state court opinions.

There is one other category of case in which a federal court must apply state law. Recall the facts discussed earlier in which a New York citizen sues an Ohio citizen in an Ohio state court for negligence based on an accident that occurred in New York. Let's change the **forum** of the suit. Suppose that the New Yorker decides to sue for $100,000 in a *federal* court in New York rather than a state court in Ohio. Because of **diversity of citizenship**, a federal court has jurisdiction to hear this case. *Diversity* means that the disputing parties are citizens of different states and the amount in controversy exceeds $75,000. What law will a federal court apply in diversity cases? It will apply federal *procedural* law (e.g., the law on how many days a party has to file an answer to a complaint) but state *substantive* law (e.g., the negligence law on the duty of a motorist to drive reasonably). Hence a state court opinion on negligence could be mandatory authority in a diversity case when the federal court is resolving a dispute raising state issues.

3. PERSUASIVE AUTHORITY

We turn next to persuasive authority, which is any authority (law or nonlaw) that a court decides to follow because of its persuasiveness rather than because of a mandate or duty to follow

---

conflict of laws Differences in the laws of two coequal legal systems (e.g., two states) involved in a legal dispute. The choice of which law to apply in such disputes.

subject matter jurisdiction The court's power to resolve a particular kind or category of dispute.

personal jurisdiction A court's power over a person to adjudicate his or her personal rights. Also called *in personam jurisdiction*.

full faith and credit One state must recognize and enforce valid public acts of other states, e.g., a valid court judgment. U.S. Constitution, art IV, § 1.

Supremacy Clause The clause in the U.S. Constitution (art. VI, cl. 2) that has been interpreted to mean that when valid federal law and state law conflict, federal law controls.

forum The court where the case is to be tried.

diversity of citizenship The disputing parties are citizens of different states and the amount in controversy exceeds $75,000. This diversity gives jurisdiction to a U.S. District Court.

it. The most common categories of persuasive authority we need to consider are (1) other court opinions and (2) secondary authority.

Court Opinions as Persuasive Authority

Review the two conditions mentioned earlier on when an opinion is mandatory authority: The opinion must be analogous, *and* the opinion must have been written by a court that is superior to the court currently considering that opinion. If both these tests are not met, the opinion can't be mandatory authority, but it might be *persuasive authority*.

Suppose that you are reading an opinion that is analogous but not mandatory because of one of the following:

- It was written by an inferior court and is now being considered by a court within the same judicial system that is superior to the court that wrote the opinion; or
- It was written by a court from a different judicial system such as a Texas court considering a Virginia opinion. (Assume that there are no conflict-of-interest or full-faith-and-credit issues.)

If either of these two situations exists, the court, as we have seen, does *not* have to follow the opinion; it is not mandatory authority. If, however, the opinion is analogous, the court would be free to adopt the opinion as persuasive authority.

A number of factors go into a court's determination of whether a prior opinion is persuasive enough to adopt. A judge is usually interested in knowing how many other courts have adopted the conclusion (the holding) of this opinion. Is there a "majority rule" or school of thought that has developed around that conclusion? Has the opinion been frequently cited with approval? (To find out, citators such as Shepard's and KeyCite would be checked.) How well reasoned is the opinion? These considerations will help a judge decide whether to adopt an opinion as persuasive. Finally, it is human nature for judges to gravitate toward opinions that are most in tune with their personal philosophies and biases—although preferences on this basis are never acknowledged.

dictum A statement or observation made by a judge in an opinion that is not essential to resolve the issues before the court; comments that go beyond the facts before the court. Also called *obiter dictum*.

holding A court's answer to one of the legal issues in the case. Also called a *ruling*.

Finally, we need to consider **dictum** as persuasive authority. Dictum is a statement made by a court that was not necessary to resolve the narrow question or issue before the court. Assume that a tenant (Mr. Kiley) sued his landlord (ABC Properties, Inc.) for failing to repair the main elevator in the building. The landlord claimed the tenant should repair it. The court rendered its decision in the opinion of *Kiley v. ABC Properties, Inc.*, ruling in favor of the tenant. In the *Kiley* opinion, the court says, "Landlords have an obligation to maintain elevators as well as all common passageways in the rented premises." The court's statement about the elevator is its **holding**; its statement about common passageways, however, is dictum. (A holding is a court's answer to a specific question or issue that arises out of facts before the court.)

The narrow issue before the court was whether the landlord must repair the elevator. The court's answer to this issue is its holding. Everything else is dictum. There was no need for the court to tell us about the landlord's legal obligation concerning *passageways*. The law governing passageways should be resolved in a future case when the dispute before the court involves parties fighting over who must maintain passageways. To be sure, it was convenient for the court in the *Kiley* opinion to add its observation about passageways; they seem to be similar in function to elevators. But in our legal system, we prefer that courts stick to the disputes arising from the facts before them. Occasionally, they don't, leading to dictum.

Now assume that, years later, another landlord-tenant case comes before the court. Jackson (the tenant) is being sued by Weber (the landlord) over repair of the passageway in the building where Jackson lives. Is *Kiley v. ABC Properties, Inc.*, mandatory authority? No. Jackson is very happy about the language in *Kiley* that says landlords must maintain passageways. But the *Kiley* opinion is not mandatory authority on the issue of a landlord's responsibility to maintain passageways because this issue was never before the *Kiley* court. The language about passageways in *Kiley* was dictum. Does this mean that the court in the Jackson/Weber case must ignore the dictum in *Kiley* on passageways? No. The court can decide to adopt the *Kiley* statement on passageways because it finds the statement persuasive. It is not required to follow the *Kiley* statement but may decide to do so as persuasive authority.

Secondary Authority as Persuasive Authority

Secondary authority such as a legal treatise or a legal periodical article is not the law itself. It is not written by the legislature, a court, an agency, a city council, etc. Secondary authority can never be mandatory authority; it can only be persuasive. The chart in Exhibit 11.10 provides an overview of the major kinds of secondary authority that a court could decide to rely on in reaching its conclusion.

Almost all secondary authorities quote from the law itself; they quote primary authority. For example, here is an excerpt from page 321 of the third edition of a 1990 legal treatise called *Administrative Law and Process in a Nutshell* by Ernest Gellhorn and Ronald M. Levin. Note that this excerpt quotes from § 553(b)(3)(B) of the Administrative Procedure Act (APA), which is within title 5 of the United States Code Annotated (U.S.C.A.):

> The final exemption to the APA's notice-and-comment procedures applies when "notice and public procedure . . . are impracticable, unnecessary, or contrary to the public interest." 5 U.S.C.A. § 553(b)(3)(B). In practice this exception applies primarily when delay in the issuance of the rule would frustrate the rule's purpose. Ernest Gellhorn & Ronald M. Levin, *Administrative Law and Process in a Nutshell* 321 (3d ed. 1990).

EXHIBIT 11.10	Categories of Secondary Authority	
Kind	**Contents**	**Examples**
1a. Legal Encyclopedias	Summaries of the law, organized by topic	*Corpus Juris Secundum* *American Jurisprudence 2d*
1b. Nonlegal Encyclopedias	Summaries of many topics on science, the arts, history, etc.	*Encyclopaedia Britannica*
2a. Legal Dictionaries	Definitions of legal terms taken almost exclusively from court opinions	*Words and Phrases*
2b. Legal Dictionaries	Definitions of legal terms that come from a variety of sources	*Black's Law Dictionary* *Statsky's Legal Thesaurus/Dictionary*
2c. Nonlegal Dictionaries	Definitions of all words in general use	*Webster's Dictionary*
3a. Legal Periodicals (academic)	Pamphlets (often later bound) containing articles on a variety of legal topics	*Harvard Law Review* *Utah Law Review* *Yale Journal of Law and Feminism*
3b. Legal Periodicals (commercial)	Pamphlets (often later bound) containing articles on a variety of legal topics	*Case and Comment* *Practical Lawyer*
3c. Legal Periodicals (bar association)	Pamphlets (often bound) containing articles on a variety of legal topics	*American Bar Association Journal* *California Lawyer* *Wisconsin Bar Bulletin*
3d. Nonlegal Periodicals	Pamphlets (often later bound) containing articles on a variety of mainly nonlegal topics	*Newsweek* *Foreign Affairs*
4a. Legal Treatises	Summaries of and commentaries on areas of the law	*McCormick on Evidence* Johnstone and Hopson, *Lawyers and Their Work*
4b. Nonlegal Treatises	Summaries of and commentaries on a variety of mainly nonlegal topics	Samuelson, *Economics*
5. Form Books, Manuals, Practice Books	Same as legal treatises with a greater emphasis on the "how-to-do-it" practical dimensions of the law	Dellheim, *Massachusetts Practice* Moore's *Federal Practice* *Am. Jur. Pleading and Practice Forms Annotated*
6. Looseleaf Services	A lawbook with a binding (often three ringed) that allows easy inserting and removal of pages for updating	*State Tax Guide* (CCH) *Labor Relations Reporter* (BNA)
7a. Legal Newspapers	Daily or weekly information relevant to a law practice	*Chicago Law Bulletin* *National Law Journal*
7b. Nonlegal Newspapers	General-circulation newspapers	*New York Times* *Detroit Free Press*
8. Legal Newsletters	Weekly, biweekly, or monthly practical information on a specific area of the law	*Appellate Counselor* *The School Law Newsletter*

If you want to quote § 553(b)(3)(B) in your memorandum or other writing, do *not* do it solely by quoting a secondary authority such as this legal treatise. Go directly to the current U.S. Code (using U.S.C., U.S.C.A., or U.S.C.S.) and quote from § 553(b)(3)(B) itself. Do not rely solely on the Gellhorn/Levin quotation of § 553(b)(3)(B). You may *also* want to cite the Gellhorn/Levin observation that includes the quote from § 553(b)(3)(B) but not as a substitute for a direct quote. As a general rule, *you should never use someone else's quotation of the law*. Quote *directly* from the primary authority. Use the secondary authority to bolster your arguments on the interpretation of the primary authority. This is one of the main functions of secondary authority: to help you persuade a court to adopt a certain interpretation of primary authority. You are on very dangerous ground when you use secondary authority as a substitute for primary authority.

Even if you never use secondary authority in your writing, it may still be of value to you. For example, the footnotes in a legal treatise, encyclopedia, or periodical might give you leads to the primary authority that you need to analyze. Furthermore, if you are doing research in an area of the law that is new to you, some background reading in a legal treatise, encyclopedia, or periodical often provides an excellent introduction to the area, as we will see later in Exhibit 11.18. Armed with some basic definitions and a general understanding, you will be better equipped to launch your research and analysis into the specific issues before you.

Suppose you want to use an excerpt from a secondary authority in your legal writing. You may, for example, want to quote from a treatise to bolster your argument on the interpretation of a statute or other primary authority. As such, you are asking the court to accept the secondary authority as persuasive authority. What steps are necessary to do so properly? What is the proper foundation for the use of secondary authority in legal writing? Exhibit 11.11 presents this foundation. To avoid the charge of **plagiarism**, be sure to provide a complete citation to any secondary authority that you quote.

plagiarism Using another's original ideas or expressions as one's own.

| EXHIBIT 11.11 | The Foundation for Using a Quote from a Legal Treatise or Any Other Secondary Authority in Your Legal Writing as Possible Persuasive Authority |

1. The quote from the legal treatise (or other secondary authority) must never be a substitute for a direct quote from the court opinion, statute, or other primary authority. When you need to tell the reader what the primary authority says, you do not do so solely through secondary authority.
2. The quote from the legal treatise (or other secondary authority) that you want to use does not contradict mandatory case law, statutory law, or any other primary authority that exists in the jurisdiction where the client is in litigation. Stated more simply, there must be no contrary mandatory authority.
3. If the quote from the legal treatise (or other secondary authority) *does* contradict case law, statutory law, or any other primary authority, you cannot use the quote unless the court (before which the client is in litigation) has the power to invalidate or otherwise change the law that contradicts what the legal treatise (or other secondary authority) says and, in effect, to adopt a new interpretation of the law in the jurisdiction.

Most well-written and comprehensively researched legal memoranda and appellate briefs make relatively few references to secondary authority. Experienced advocates know that judges are suspicious of secondary authority. It is true that some secondary authorities are highly respected, such as *Prosser on Torts* or any of the Restatements of the American Law Institute. Yet even these must be used with caution. The preoccupation of a court is with primary authority. Before you use secondary authority in your writing, you must be sure that (1) the secondary authority is not used as a substitute for the primary authority; (2) the secondary authority is not unduly repetitive of the primary authority; (3) the secondary authority will be helpful to the court in adopting an interpretation of primary authority, particularly when there is not a great deal of primary authority on point; (4) you discuss the secondary authority after you have presented the primary authority; and (5) the foundation for the use of secondary authority (see Exhibit 11.11) can be demonstrated if needed.

Courts are most receptive to secondary authority when the authority discusses *novel* issues—those that have never arisen in your jurisdiction. There is no primary authority resolving the issues because they are being raised for the first time. Such issues are called issues of **first impression**. (A case raising such issues is called a *case of first impression*.) You are on relatively safe ground in using such discussions in your legal writing. Courts are often willing to adopt secondary authority as persuasive authority when novel questions or issues are involved.

first impression New; that which has come before the court for the first time.

ASSIGNMENT 11.4

Are the following statements true or false? If false, explain why.

(a) All primary authority is mandatory authority because primary authority consists of statutes, constitutional provisions, or other laws.

(b) Secondary authority can be mandatory authority.

(c) An invalid state statute can be persuasive authority if a court decides to follow the statute even though it does not have to.

(d) A federal administrative regulation can be mandatory authority in a state court.

(e) An opinion of the U.S. District Court can be mandatory authority for the U.S. Supreme Court.

(f) Because dictum is a comment by the court that was not necessary to resolve the issues before the court, dictum is nonauthority.

(g) An opinion in one state cannot be mandatory authority in the court of another state.

(h) A federal court can overrule an opinion of a state court.

(i) If your library does not have a copy of the statute you need to cite, you can cite the language of the statute that is printed in a scholarly analysis of the statute in a legal periodical article.

(j) A dissenting opinion can be persuasive authority.

[SECTION J]

CITATION FORM

A *citation*, or *cite*, is a reference to any legal authority printed on paper or stored in a computer database that will allow you to locate the authority. The cite gives you the "address" where you can go in the library or online to find whatever is cited.

Are there any consistent rules on citation form? If you pick up different law books and examine the citations of similar material within them, you will notice great variety in citation form. You will find that people abbreviate things differently, do not include the information in the same order in the cite, use parentheses differently, use punctuation within the cite differently, include different amounts of information in the same kind of cite, etc. There does not appear to be any consistency. Yet, in spite of this diversity and confusion, you may be admonished for failing to use "proper citation form." What, you may well ask, is "proper"?

Start by checking the rules of court or statutes governing the court that will have jurisdiction over the problem you are researching. They may or may not contain *official citation rules*, that tell you how you must cite legal authorities within documents submitted to courts in the state. If official citation rules exist, they must obviously be followed no matter what any other citation guidebook may say. These are, in effect, citation *laws*.

Suppose, however, that there are no official citation laws in your state or that such laws exist but do not cover the kind of authority you are trying to cite. In such circumstances, *ask your supervisor what citation form you should use*. You may be told, "Use the *Bluebook*" or to **bluebook it**. A job ad recently posted on a paralegal manager's site (www.paralegalmanagement.org) called for an individual with "exceptional blue booking skills." This is a reference to *The Bluebook: A Uniform System of Citation*, which we looked at earlier. It is a small blue pamphlet (although in earlier editions, white covers were used). The *Bluebook* is published by a group of law students on the law reviews of their law schools.

Caution is needed in using the *Bluebook*. It is a highly technical and sometimes difficult-to-use pamphlet because it packs so much information into a relatively small space. Primary users of the *Bluebook* are the law reviews of law schools that have special styles and formats that they follow. For example, law reviews often use large and small caps when they abbreviate a set of books in a footnote (e.g., FLA. STAT.), whereas everyday memorandum and brief writing in a law office use a standard cap format (Fla. Stat.). While the *Bluebook* will also cover everyday writing of this kind, keep in mind that we are not the main audience of the *Bluebook*. Also, be aware that many courts do *not* follow the *Bluebook* even if there are no court rules on citation form for their courts. Judges often simply use their own "system" of citation without necessarily being consistent.

Until recently, the *Bluebook* had no serious competition. In 2000, a major competitor emerged, the *ALWD Citation Manual* by the Association of Legal Writing Directors and Darby Dickerson. Many schools have begun to adopt this alternative. It is difficult to determine what impact the ALWD guidebook will have. Most of your older attorney supervisors spent countless law school

bluebook it Cite an authority according to the rules in *The Bluebook: A Uniform System of Citation.*

hours poring over and applying the *Bluebook*. They may have little tolerance for anything new. Life without *Bluebook* rules is unimaginable for such attorneys. You may find, however, that some of the more recent graduates from law school have joined the ALWD bandwagon and expect their paralegals to be able to cite the ALWD way. Consequently, you must be prepared to use *Bluebook* and ALWD citation formats. Because the *Bluebook* is still dominant, all of the examples in this section will follow *Bluebook* format. Many of the major differences with ALWD will be noted in brackets [*ALWD*:].

Before we begin, review general citation guidelines in Exhibit 11.12.

EXHIBIT 11.12	General Citation Guidelines

1. Find out if there are citation laws in the rules of court or in statutes that you must follow. The following two sites will let you know if such laws exist in your state:
   - www.law.cornell.edu/citation
     (Click "Cross Reference Tables," then "State-Specific Practices")
   - www.alwd.org/cm
     (Click "Appendices," then "Appendix 2")
2. Ask your supervisor if he or she has any special instructions on citation form. What guidelines should you follow? *Bluebook*? ALWD? Others?
3. Consult the specific citation guidelines presented below (I-VIII). Most of these rules are based on the *Bluebook*. Where ALWD differs, the ALWD rule or example will be provided [in brackets].
4. Remember that the *functional* purpose of a citation is to enable readers to locate your citation in a library or online. You must give enough information in the cite to fulfill this purpose. Courtesy to the reader in providing this help is as important as compliance with the niceties of citation form—so long as you are not violating any explicit citation law.
5. Often a private publisher or a book will tell you how to cite the book. ("Cite this book as. . . .") Ignore this instruction! Instead, follow guidelines 1–4 above.
6. When in doubt about whether to include something in a citation after carefully following guidelines 1–4 above, resolve the doubt by including it in the cite.

SPECIFIC CITATION GUIDELINES

I.   Citing Opinions
II. Citing Constitutions and Charters
III. Citing Federal Statutes
IV. Citing State Statutes
V.   Citing Administrative Regulations and Decisions
VI. Citing Documents of Legislative History
VII. Citing Secondary Authority
VIII. Citing Internet Sources

Our focus will be on providing complete or full citations for each of these categories. Later we will also learn how to provide a **short form citation**, which is an abbreviated citation of an authority that you have already cited in full earlier in your memorandum or other writing.

short form citation An abbreviated citation format of an authority for which you have provided a complete citation elsewhere in what you are writing.

I. Citing Opinions

Examine Exhibit 11.13 at the top of the next page for the typical citation format of a court opinion. Not all opinions are cited in the same way, however. The citation format that you use depends on the kind of court that wrote the opinion. Before examining the guidelines that explain these differences, here is an overview:

Example A: Format of a citation to an opinion of the highest federal court (the United States Supreme Court):

> *Taglianetti v. United States*, 394 U.S. 316 (1969)
> [ALWD: *Taglianetti v. U.S.*, 394 U.S. 316 (1969)]

Example B: Format of a citation to an opinion of a federal middle appeals court (the U.S. Court of Appeals for the Second Circuit):

> *Podell v. Citicorp Diners Club, Inc.*, 112 F.3d 98 (2d Cir. 1997)

EXHIBIT 11.13 Components of a Typical Citation of an Opinion: *Cashen v. Spann*, 66 N.J. 541, 334 A.2d 8 (1975)

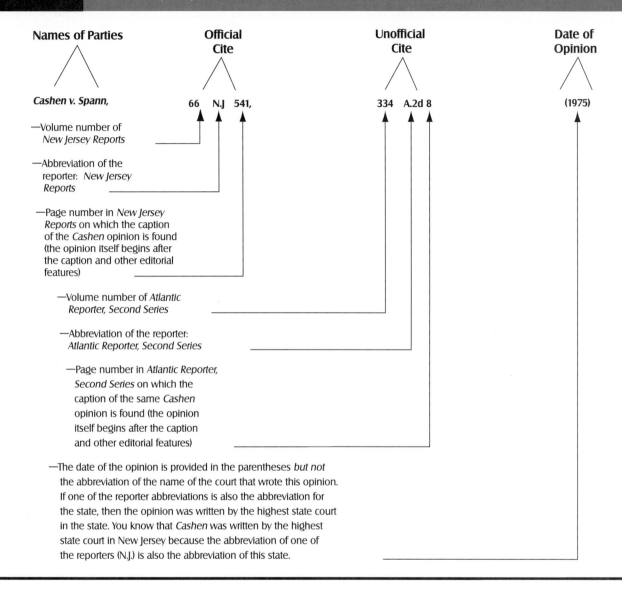

Example C: Format of a citation to an opinion of a federal trial court (the U.S. District Court for the District of Pennsylvania):

Stratton v. Marsh, 71 F. Supp. 2d 476 (E.D. Pa. 1999)

Example D: Format of a citation to an opinion of the highest state court (New Jersey Supreme Court) (assume that a **parallel cite** is required):

Petlin Associates, Inc. v. Township of Dover, 64 N.J. 327, 316 A.2d 1 (1974)

Example E: Format of a citation to an opinion of a lower state court (Connecticut Superior Court, Appellate Session) (assume that a parallel cite is required):

Huckabee v. Stevens, 32 Conn. Supp. 511, 338 A.2d 512 (Super. Ct. 1975)

parallel cite An additional citation where you can find the same written material in the library or online.

public domain citation
A citation that is medium neutral (meaning that it can be read in a paper volume or online) and vendor neutral (meaning that it does not contain volume, page, or other identifying information created by particular vendors such as a commercial publisher). The public domain citation in Example F (2000 ME 106, ¶ 3) does not use the volume or page numbers of any particular vendor such as West Group. The traditional Atlantic 2d parallel cite (A.2d) *does* use them.

Example F: Format of citation that includes a **public domain citation** (Supreme Court of Maine) (assume that a parallel cite is required):

> *Pine Ridge Realty, Inc. v. Massachusetts Bay Ins. Co.*, 2000 ME 106, ¶ 3, 752 A.2d 595, 599

Example G: Format of a citation to an administrative decision (National Labor Relations Board):

> *Standard Dry Wall Products, Inc.*, 91 N.L.R.B. 544 (1950).

Example H: Format of a citation to an opinion of the Attorney General:

> 40 Op. Att'y Gen. 423 (1945)

Guidelines for Citing Opinions

1. The names of the parties in a case should be italicized (if your printer has this capacity) or *underlined* (i.e., underscored). If you are able to use italics, an example would be as follows:

   Steck v. Farrell, 479 F.2d 1129 (7th Cir. 1990)

   If you cannot italicize the names of the parties, underline (underscore) them:

   Steck v. Farrell, 479 F.2d 1129 (7th Cir. 1990)

2. You will note that some of the citations in the above boxed examples have parallel cites (see examples D, E, and F) and some do not. Before examining the rules of providing parallel cites and the techniques of finding such cites, some basics need to be covered.

   The same opinion can be printed in more than one place. (See Exhibit 11.4 for 11 possibilities in traditional reporters, CD–ROM, and online services.) A parallel cite is an additional citation where you can find the *same* written material in the library or online; it is a second "address" for whatever is being cited. If there is a parallel cite to an opinion, you will be able to find that opinion (word for word) in at least two different reporters or databases. Note that in example D, the *Petlin* opinion can be found in *New Jersey Reports* (abbreviated N.J.) and in *Atlantic Reporter 2d* (A.2d). Similarly, both the *Huckabee* opinion in example E and the *Pine Ridge* opinion in example F have a parallel cite. The other opinions cited in examples A, B, C, G, and H do not have parallel cites.

3. Do not confuse parallel cite with the "same case on appeal." Examine the citations of the following two opinions:

   Jarrett v. Jarrett, 64 Ill. App. 3d 932, 382 N.E.2d 12 (1978)
   Jarrett v. Jarrett, 78 Ill. 2d 337, 400 N.E.2d 421 (1979)

   - Note that each opinion has its own parallel cite. The first *Jarrett* opinion begins on page 932 of volume 64 of *Illinois Appellate Court Reports, Third Series* (Ill. App. 3d) *and* also on page 12 of volume 382 of *North Eastern Reporter, Second Series* (N.E.2d). The second *Jarrett* opinion begins on page 337 of volume 78 of *Illinois Reports, Second Series* (Ill. 2d) *and* also on page 421 of volume 400 of *North Eastern Reporter, Second Series* (N.E.2d).
   - The 1979 *Jarrett* opinion is the *same case on appeal* as the 1978 *Jarrett* opinion. In fact, the 1979 opinion reversed the 1978 opinion. "Same case on appeal" means that the opinions are part of the same litigation. The first *Jarrett* opinion is *not* a parallel cite of the second *Jarrett* opinion. Although part of the same litigation, the 1978 opinion and the 1979 opinion are totally separate opinions, each of which has its own parallel cite.
   - Assume that you wanted to cite the 1978 opinion. As we will see later, you need to tell the reader about anything significant that has happened to an opinion on appeal, such as a reversal. Here is how you would do this for the *Jarrett* opinions:

   Jarrett v. Jarrett, 64 Ill. App. 3d 932, 382 N.E.2d 12 (1978), *rev'd*, 78 Ill. 2d 337, 400 N.E.2d 421 (1979)

4. There are six main techniques of finding a parallel cite. See research link N on page 498.

   - Check the top of the caption. Go to the reporter that contains the opinion. At the beginning of the opinion, there is a *caption* giving the names of the parties, the name of the court that wrote the opinion, the date of the decision, and other information about the litigation that led to the opinion. See if there is a parallel cite at the top of the caption. This technique does not always work, but it is worth a try. It works primarily when you check the captions of the opinions printed in the seven regional reporters we examined in Exhibit 11.5. Here is an example from the *North Western Reporter*, one of the seven regional reporters:

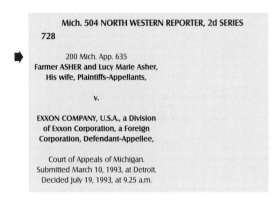

Mich. 504 NORTH WESTERN REPORTER, 2d SERIES

728

200 Mich. App. 635
**Farmer ASHER and Lucy Marie Asher,
His wife, Plaintiffs-Appellants,**

v.

**EXXON COMPANY, U.S.A., a Division
of Exxon Corporation, a Foreign
Corporation, Defendant-Appellee,**

Court of Appeals of Michigan.
Submitted March 10, 1993, at Detroit.
Decided July 19, 1993, at 9.25 a.m.

Finding a parallel cite by checking the top of the caption. If you go to 504 N.W.2d 728 and check the top of the caption of *Asher v. Exxon Co., U.S.A.*, you are told that its parallel cite is 200 Mich. App. 635.

■ Shepardize the case in the standard sets of *Shepard's Citations*, such as *Shepard's Southwestern Reporter Citations*. To *shepardize* a case means to obtain the validation and other data on that case provided by any of the three versions of *Shepard's Citations* (paper, CD–ROM, or online). Among the data provided for a court opinion are available parallel cites. The first cite in *Shepard's Citations* found in parentheses is the parallel cite. If you find no cite in parentheses, it means (1) that no parallel cite exists, (2) that the reporter containing the parallel cite has not been printed yet, or (3) that the parallel cite was given in one of the earlier volumes of Shepard's and was not repeated in the volume you are examining.

```
— 756 —          702SW̄910
E. I. Du          707SW̄²375
Pont de           707SW̄²392
Nemours and         Cir. 8
Co. v. Dillaha    d758F2d⁴1303
1983              789F2d²614
                  909F2d²1155
(280Ark477)       923F2d⁵1289
669SW̄³464         dPR¶ 10340
685SW̄⁴811         PR¶ 10822
695SW̄⁵835         PR¶ 10970
697SW̄⁴889
699SW̄¹743
```

Using *Shepard's Citations* to find a parallel cite. If you shepardized the *E.I. DuPont* case (that begins on page—756—), you are told that its parallel cite is volume 280, page 477 of *Arkansas Reports* (280Ark477).

■ Use the *Shepard's Case Names Citator*. Shepard's also has a separate set of citators called *Case Name Citator*. Its sole function is to give you parallel cites. Court opinions are listed alphabetically by party names along with the parallel cites.

ILLINOIS CASES NAMES CITATOR

Wil-Win

Wilson v. Parker 132 Ill App. 2d 5, 269 NE2d
   523 (1971)

Wilson v. Peters 343 Ill App. 354, 99 NE2d
   150 (1951)

Wilson, Renson v 335 Ill App.7, 80 NE2d
   381 (1948)

Wilson v. Reevels Red-E-Mix Concrete
   Products 29 Ill App 3d NE2d S21 (1975)

Wilson & Tavridges Inc. v. inductrial
   Commission 32 Ill 2d 355, 204 NE24 556 (1965)

Wilson Enterpries Inc., Thakkar v. 120 Ill
   App 34 878, 76 Ill Dec 331, 458 NE2d 95 (1983)

Using *Shepard's Case Names Citator* to find a parallel cite. The parallel cites for *Wilson v. Peters* are 343 Ill App. 354 and 99 NE2d 150.

- The *National Reporter Blue Book*, published by West Group, can be used to find parallel cites. This set of books will also tell you which official reporters have been discontinued. If your state has a *Blue and White Book*, you can also use it to try to find a parallel cite.
- Check the table of cases in a digest. Go to every digest that gives summaries of court opinions for the court that wrote the opinion, e.g., the American Digest System. Go to the table of cases in these digests. See if there is a parallel cite for your case. In the following excerpt from a digest table of cases, you find two cites for *Ames v. State Bar*—106 Cal. Rptr. 489 and 506 P.2d 625:

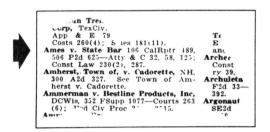

Finding a parallel cite by checking the Table of Cases in digests.

- Use computer databases. When you call up your case on any of the major online, fee-based computer systems (e.g., Westlaw and LexisNexis) you will be given any parallel cites that exist. The free Internet might also work. On any general search engine, type the cite that you have in quotation marks. Recall the *Cashen* case we looked at in Exhibit 11.13. One of its cites is 334 A.2d 8. In Google, type this cite in the search box with quotation marks ("334 A.2d 8"). Note that you are led to several documents that contain this cite and its parallel cite (66 N.J. 541).

Six Techniques for Finding a Parallel Cite of an Opinion:
- Top of the caption
- Shepardize
- *Shepard's Case Names Citator*
- *National Reporter Blue Book*
- Table of cases in digests
- Westlaw, LexisNexis and Loislaw and free Internet

Opinion
(assume that you are looking for the parallel cite of this opinion)

RESEARCH LINK N

You have the citation to one reporter where you can read an opinion. You now want a parallel cite so that you can read the same opinion—word-for-word—in another reporter. There are six major techniques you can use to try to find a parallel cite. For example, assume you know the cite of the *Smith* case in New York Reports, but you don't know its cite in the *North Eastern Reporter*. Use the six techniques to try to find the N.E.2d parallel cite.

5. If you are citing an opinion in your memorandum or other writing, are you required to give a parallel cite? The answer to this question will differ depending on what court wrote the opinion and where you are trying to use the citation. Recall that many opinions have:

- an official cite to an *official reporter* (an official reporter is a reporter printed under the authority of the government, often by the government itself) and
- an unofficial cite to an *unofficial reporter* (an unofficial reporter is a reporter printed by a commercial printing company without special authority from the government)

When must you provide both the official cite and the unofficial cite of an opinion? Here are the guidelines to follow:

- For *federal* opinions, do not use parallel cites. See examples A B, and C at the beginning of the section covering the citation of the major federal courts. None of the citations to the federal cases in these examples have parallel cites.
- For *state* opinions, provide a parallel cite if the local rules of the court to which you are submitting a document (e.g., an appellate brief) require the use of parallel cites.

- If the state has adopted public domain cites, you may be required to provide the public domain cite and the parallel cite to the unofficial reporter. See example F, which includes the public domain cite and the unofficial cite to A.2d. (We will examine public domain cites in greater detail later.)
- If the local rules do not require parallel cites, it is generally sufficient to cite only the unofficial reporter.

Let's look more closely at citations with and without parallel cites. As you see, the following citation does not include a parallel cite:

Nace v. Nace, 790 P.2d 48 (Ariz. 2003)

Note the abbreviation Ariz. just before the date in the parentheses. This is an abbreviation of the court that wrote the opinion. When the abbreviation is the abbreviation of the state itself, you know that the opinion was written by the highest state court in the state. If you did not provide this abbreviation, someone looking at the cite would not know what court wrote it. The general rule is to provide an abbreviation of the court that wrote the opinion unless the identity of this court is unambiguously clear by looking at the abbreviation of any of the reporters in the cite. The reporter in this cite is *Pacific Reporter 2d* (P.2d). Looking at the cite of this reporter certainly does not tell you what court wrote *Nace*. (Many states are covered in P.2d. See Exhibit 11.5 and research link J.) Hence you must abbreviate the court in the parentheses before the date.

Suppose, however, that you need to provide the parallel cite to the *Nace* case. Assume that the case begins on page 411 of volume 162 of *Arizona Reports* (abbreviated Ariz.), the official state reporter. Here is how you would cite the case:

Nace v. Nace, 162 Ariz. 411, 790 P.2d 48 (2003)

Note that there is no need to include the abbreviation of the court that wrote the opinion in the parentheses before the date. As we have seen, if the abbreviation of a reporter is the abbreviation of a state, you can assume that the case was written by the highest state court in that state. Hence there is no need to abbreviate the court in the parentheses with the date. You can tell by looking at the abbreviation of the official reporter (162 Ariz. 411) that the highest state court in Arizona wrote the case because Ariz is the abbreviation of the state.

6. When a parallel cite is required, the official cite goes first, as in the second *Nace* example above and in examples D and E at the beginning of the section.

7. Include only the last name of parties who are people. For example, if the parties are listed as "Frank Taylor v. Mary Smith" in the caption, your cite should list them as *Taylor v. Smith* in your citation.

8. When a party is a business or organization, you need to determine whether to abbreviate part of the party's name. There are eight words that are almost always abbreviated: and (&), Association (Ass'n), Brothers (Bros.), Company (Co.), Corporation (Corp.), Incorporated (Inc.), Limited (Ltd.), and Number (No.). The abbreviation of other words in a party's name depends on whether the citation is a stand-alone citation or is part of a sentence. Here is an example of a stand-alone citation:

Erie R.R. Bldg. Preservation Ass'n v. Smith Co., 100. F.3d 23 (5th Cir. 1998)

Here is an example of the same citation that is part of a sentence:

> In *Erie Railroad Building Preservation Ass'n v. Smith Co.*, 100 F.3d 23 (5th Cir. 1998), the court discussed the reversion doctrine.

Note that the words "Association" and "Company" are abbreviated in both examples. They are among the eight that are almost always abbreviated. The abbreviation of "Railroad" and "Building," however, differs in the examples. The *Bluebook* gives a list of words that you must abbreviate in stand-alone citations but not when you use them in a citation that is part of a sentence (which the *Bluebook* refers to as a citation "in a textual sentence"). The list includes words such as Authority (Auth.), Board (Bd.), Building (Bldg.), Committee (Comm.), Department (Dep't), Education (Educ.), Government (Gov't), Railroad (R.R.), and University (Univ.). The general rule is as follows: abbreviate these words only in stand-alone citations.

ALWD and the *Bluebook* do not agree on some abbreviations. For example:

	Bluebook	**ALWD**
Association	Ass'n	Assn.
Commission	Comm'n	Commn.
Department	Dep't	Dept.
Government	Gov't	Govt.
National	Nat'l	Natl.
University	Univ.	U.

9. When the United States is a party, can you use the abbreviation U.S.? No, according to the *Bluebook*; you must spell it out. Yes, according to *AWLD*. See example A (*Taglianetti v. United States*).

10. Assume that Maine is a party. Your cite should say "State" (rather than "State of Maine" or "Maine") *if and only if* the opinion was written by a Maine state court. Suppose, however, that Maine is a party in an opinion written by an Ohio court. In such a case, use "Maine" (not "State of Maine" or "State") in your cite as the name of this party. This same guideline applies for the words "Commonwealth" and "People." These words are used alone in a cite only if the court that wrote the opinion you are citing is in the same state referred to by the words "Commonwealth" and "People." Example: You are citing an opinion of the California Supreme Court, whose caption describes the parties as follows:

People of California v. Gabriel S. Farrell

Your cite of this opinion would be *People v. Farrell*.

11. Sometimes you will be citing an opinion of an appellate court that combined or consolidated more than one litigation in the same appeal because of a similarity of issues raised in the litigations. A supreme court, for example, may use one opinion to resolve similar issues raised in several different lower court cases. The caption of such an opinion will probably list all the parties from these different lower court cases. For example, the caption might say *A v. B; C v. D; E v. F*. When you cite this opinion, include only the *first* set of parties listed in the caption—here, *A v. B*. If the caption says **et al.** (meaning "and others") after the name of a party, do not include the phrase *et al.* in your cite.

12. Often the court will tell you the **litigation status** of the parties, such as plaintiff, defendant, appellant, or appellee. Do not include this information in your cite.

13. Titles of individual parties (such as administrator or secretary) should be omitted from your cite. One exception is the Commissioner of Internal Revenue. Cite this party simply as "Commissioner"—for example, *Jackson v. Commissioner*.

14. When the caption of an opinion contains the phrase **In re** (meaning "in the matter of"), include this phrase in your cite—for example, *In re Jones*.

15. If the government is bringing the suit in the name of another (the real party in interest), the phrase **ex rel.** is used after the government's name. Example:

Illinois ex rel. Madigan v. Telemarketing Associates, Inc.

16. Include the year of the decision at the end of the cite in parentheses. If more than one date is given in the caption of the opinion, use the year from the date the opinion was decided.

17. Do not include the **docket number** of the case in the cite unless the case is still pending. (The docket number is the number assigned to a case by the court.)

18. Know the distinction between the *treatment of a case* and the *history of a case*. Once an opinion is written, it is often commented upon by other opinions. For example, the case of *Smith v. Jones* might be followed or distinguished by the case of *Adams v. Lincoln*. This subsequent commentary on an opinion is called the *treatment of a case*. It consists of what courts in different litigation have said about an opinion. Of course, subsequent events can also occur in the same litigation. For example, the case of *Smith v. Jones* might be affirmed or reversed on appeal, leading to further opinions in the same litigation. What happens to an opinion within the same litigation is referred to as the *history of a case*. (As we saw earlier, further appeals are also referred to as the *same case on appeal*.) This brings

et al. And others.

litigation status The procedural category of a party during any stage of litigation, e.g., plaintiff, defendant, or appellant.

In re In the matter of.

ex rel. (ex relatione) Upon relation or information. A suit ex rel. is brought by the government in the name of the real party in interest (called the *realtor*).

docket number A consecutive number assigned to a case by the court and used on all documents filed with the court during the litigation of that case.

us to the citation question: when you cite an opinion, do you include any of its history or treatment?

Important events in the history of a case *should* be included in the citation of an opinion. Here is an example:

Herbert v. Lando, 568 F.2d 974 (2d Cir. 1977), *rev'd*, 444 U.S. 111 (1979)

It would obviously be important to let the reader know that the *Herbert* case was reversed (*rev'd*) on appeal. For very recent opinions (e.g., decided within the last two years), you would also want to let the reader know whether the case was affirmed (*aff'd*) on appeal and whether an appellate court accepted certiorari (*cert. granted*) or denied certiorari (*cert. denied*). (Certiorari refers to the **writ of certiorari**. This is an order by an appellate court requiring a lower court to send up the record of a lower court proceeding to the appellate court, which has decided to use its discretion to review the lower court decision.) For older cases, however, a reader would usually not be interested in knowing whether an appellate court accepted or denied certiorari. What about the treatment of a case? Do you include any of the treatment of a case in its citation? The answer is: almost never. A major exception is when a court **overrules** one of its earlier opinions. For example, over fifty years after the U.S. Supreme Court wrote *Plessey v. Ferguson*, 163 U.S. 537 (1896), the Court overruled it in *Brown v. Bd. of Education*, 347 U.S. 483 (1954). If you were citing *Plessey*, it would obviously be important to tell the reader about this treatment by *Brown*. Here is how you would cite *Plessey*:

Plessey v. Ferguson, 163 U.S. 537 (1896), *overruled by Brown v. Bd. of Education*, 347 U.S. 483 (1954)

19. The reporter volumes that contain current opinions are conveniently arranged by volume number. All the volumes of the same set have the same name, e.g., *Atlantic Reporter 2d*. At one time, however, life was not this simple. Volumes of opinions were identified by the name of the individual person who had responsibility for compiling the opinions written by the judges. These individuals were called reporters. "7 Cush. 430," for example, refers to an opinion found on page 430 of volume 7 of Massachusetts cases when Mr. Cushing was the official reporter. When he ended his employment, Mr. Gray took over, and the cite of an opinion in the volume immediately after "7 Cush." was "1 Gray." By simply looking at the cover of the volume, you *cannot* tell what court's opinions are inside unless you happen to be familiar with the names of these individuals and the courts for which they worked. These volumes are called **nominative reporters** because they are identified by the name of the individual person who compiled the opinions for the court.

20. Assume that all you know are the names of the parties and the name of the court that wrote the opinion. How do you obtain the full cite so that you can find and read the opinion? Here are some techniques to use:

   - Go to every digest that covers that reporter. See Exhibit 11.6 for a list of what digests cover what reporters. Check the table of cases in the digests.
   - Call the court clerk for the court that wrote the opinion. (The clerk's number will usually be available on the court's Web site.) If it is a recent case, the clerk may be able to send you a copy. Occasionally, the clerk will give you the cite of the case. (It will help if you can tell the clerk the docket number of the case.)
   - Go to the reporter volumes that cover the court that wrote the opinion. Because you do not have a volume number, you cannot go directly to the volume that has the opinion. If you can *approximate* the date of the case, however, you can check the table of cases in each reporter volume that probably covers that year. You may have to check the table of cases in ten to fifteen volumes before achieving success. The opinions are printed in the reporters in roughly chronological order.
   - Use *Shepard's Case Names Citator* referred to (and excerpted) earlier.
   - On the Internet, type the name of the case in any search engine. Or go directly to the site maintained by the court that wrote the opinion. (See Exhibit 11.38, later in the chapter.) You may be led to the full text of the opinion.
   - If you have access to fee-based online services (e.g., Westlaw, LexisNexis, or Loislaw), enter the name of the case in the appropriate database or file. This will lead you to the opinion with all available parallel cites.

writ of certiorari (cert.) An order (or writ) by a higher court that a lower court send up the record of a case because the higher court has decided to use its discretion to review that case.

overrule 1. To decide against or deny. 2. To reject or cancel an earlier opinion as precedent by rendering an opposite decision on the same question of law in a different litigation. To *reverse* means to overturn on appeal.

nominative reporter A reporter volume that is identified by the name of the person responsible for compiling and printing the opinions in the volume.

pinpoint cite A reference to material on a specific page number within a document (e.g., a court opinion or legal periodical article) as opposed to the page number on which the document begins. Also called a *jump cite*. In some court opinions, the pinpoint reference is to a specific paragraph number in the opinion.

21. When you are quoting specific language in an opinion or in a legal periodical article, you need to give two page numbers: first, the page number on which the opinion or legal periodical article begins; and second, the page number on which the quote is found. This is known as a **pinpoint cite** (or *jump cite*) which is a reference to material on a specific page in a document, as opposed to the page on which the document begins. The page on which the quote is found is the "pinpointed" number. For opinions, this number goes immediately after the page number on which the opinion begins, separated by a comma. Assume that you want to quote from an opinion that has a parallel cite. Hence your quote will be found in the opinion printed in both reporters, but on different page numbers. A pinpoint cite of this opinion would state the page number in each reporter where the opinion begins *plus* the page number in each reporter on which your quote is found. In the following example, the *Bridgeton* opinion begins on page 17 of *Maryland Reports* (Md.) and on page 376 of the *Atlantic Reporter 2d* (A.2d). The quote from the *Bridgeton case*, however, is found on page 20 and on page 379 of these reporters, respectively:

"Even though laches may not apply, one must use reasonable promptness when seeking of judicial protection." *Bridgeton Educ. Ass'n v. Board of Educ.*, 147 Md. 17, 20, 334 A.2d 376, 379 (1975).

In some documents, all of the paragraphs are separately numbered. In such documents, the pinpoint can be to a paragraph number rather than to a page number.

22. Most opinions are read in reporters published by vendors such as West Group, e.g., *Supreme Court Reporter, North Western Reporter 2d*. For example, here is a cite to a South Dakota Supreme Court opinion that directs the reader to a quote on pinpoint page 332:

Davis v. Cardiff, 402 N.W.2d 327, 332 (S.D. 2001)

Because this cite relies on a volume number (402) and page numbers (327 and 332) that are assigned by the vendor (West Group), it is called a vendor-specific citation. Here is the citation to the same opinion that is vendor neutral:

Davis v. Cardiff, 2001 SD 22, ¶ 74

Davis is the 22d opinion decided by the South Dakota Supreme Court in 2001. Every paragraph in the opinion is sequentially numbered. Our quote is in the 74th paragraph of the *Davis* opinion. Note the differences in the two formats. A vendor-neutral cite:

- Does not contain abbreviations of any reporters
- Uses a year instead of a volume number and places the year immediately after the names of the parties
- Tells you in what order the opinion was decided that year
- Does not tell you the page number on which the opinion begins
- Gives the pinpoint reference as a paragraph number rather than as a page number

Vendor-neutral cites are also medium neutral because they can be found and read in any medium (e.g., paper or online) using the same identifying numbers. Cites that are vendor neutral and medium neutral are called **public domain citations** or *generic citations*.

public domain citation A citation that is medium neutral (meaning that it can be read in a paper volume or online) and vendor neutral (meaning that it does not contain volume, page, or other identifying information created by particular vendors such as a commercial publisher). Also called *generic citation*.

Courts that have adopted public domain citations include state courts in Arizona, Colorado, Florida, Louisiana, Maine, Mississippi, Montana, New Mexico, North Dakota, Oklahoma, Pennsylvania, South Dakota, Utah, Wisconsin, and Wyoming, and the U.S. Court of Appeals for the Sixth Circuit. The public domain citation systems used in these jurisdictions may differ slightly from each other, although the format described here for South Dakota contains the basics.

When a public domain citation is required, you should *also* provide the traditional vendor-specific cite if it is available. Hence our cite to the *Davis* opinion would be:

Davis v. Cardiff, 2001 SD 22, ¶ 74, 402 N.W.2d 327, 332

If no pinpoint reference is needed, the cite would be:

Davis v. Cardiff, 2001 SD 22, 402 N.W.2d 327

See also example F at the beginning of this section for another example of a public domain cite. For a report on the Internet that gives the details of vendor-neutral systems adopted by specific courts, see www.aallnet.org/committee/citation.

II. Citing Constitutions and Charters

Constitutions and charters are cited to (a) the abbreviated name of the constitution or charter, (b) the article, and (c) the section.

U.S. Const. art. I, § 9
N.M. Const. art. IV, § 7

When citing constitutions and charters currently in force, do not give the date of enactment.

III. Citing Federal Statutes

1. All federal statutes of Congress are collected in chronological order of passage as session laws in the *United States Statutes at Large* (abbreviated "Stat."). Session laws are statutes of the legislature that are organized chronologically by date of enactment rather than by subject matter. If the statute is of general public interest, it is also printed in *each* of three codes in which the statutes *are* organized by subject matter:

   - *United States Code* (U.S.C.)
   - *United States Code Annotated* (U.S.C.A.)—West Group
   - *United States Code Service* (U.S.C.S.)—LexisNexis

   The preferred citation format is to U.S.C., which is the official code. (In the following example, the number before the abbreviation of the code—42—is the title number. This is where title numbers are placed in all citations to federal statutes.)

   42 U.S.C. § 3412(a)(2000)

   or

   Narcotic Rehabilitation Act of 1966, 42 U.S.C. § 3412(a)(2000)

   Although it is not necessary to give the **popular name** of the statute (as in the second version of the above example), citing the popular name when known is often helpful.

   > **popular name** A phrase or short title identifying a particular statute.

2. A new edition of the U.S.C. comes out every six years. The date you use in citing a statute in U.S.C. is the date of the edition you are using unless your statute is found in one of the annual Supplements to the U.S.C., which come out in between editions. If your statute is in a Supplement, you cite the volume and year of this Supplement. Suppose your statute is found in the sixth Supplement published in 1983. Your cite would be as follows:

   29 U.S.C. § 169 (Supp. VI 1983)

   The date you use in citing a statute in U.S.C. is not the year the statute was enacted or passed by the legislature. Nor is it the year the statute became effective. The date you use is the date of the edition of the code or of the Supplement you are using.

3. Although citation to U.S.C. is preferred, it is not uncommon to find citations to the other codes: U.S.C.A. and U.S.C.S. (There is never a need, however, to cite more than one of the three codes.) The format is as follows:

   29 U.S.C.A. § 169 (West 1983)
   29 U.S.C.S. § 169 (LexisNexis 1982) [ALWD: (Lexis 1982)]

   In parentheses before the date, include the name of the publisher. Use the year that appears on the title page of the volume, or its latest copyright year, in this order of preference. If your statute is in one of the annual pocket parts of either of these two codes, include "Supp." and give the year of the pocket part—for example: (West Supp. 1998).

4. There is one instance in which you *must* cite to the *United States Statutes at Large* (Stat.) rather than to U.S.C. The rule is as follows: cite to the statute in *Statutes at Large* if (a) there is a difference in the language of the statute between Stat. and U.S.C. and (b) the statute in U.S.C. is in a title that has *not* been enacted into positive law by Congress.

It is highly unlikely that you will find a difference in language between Stat. and U.S.C. Yet the conscientious researcher must check this out before relying on any statutory language. All the statutes in U.S.C. fall within one of 50 titles—for example, title 11 on Bankruptcy, title 39 on the Postal Service. If Congress goes through all the statutes in a particular title and formally declares that all of them are valid and accurate, then that title has been enacted into positive law. You can rely exclusively on the language of such statutes even if the language is different from the statute as it originally appeared in *Statutes at Large*. At the beginning of the first volume of U.S.C., you will be told which titles of the U.S.C. have been enacted into positive law.

5. A *Statute at Large* cite, when needed, should include:

- The popular name of the statute if one exists; if one does not exist, include "Act of" and give the full date of enactment—month, day, and year
- The Public Law (Pub. L.) number of the statute or its chapter number
- The section of the statute you are citing
- The volume number of the *Statutes at Large* used
- The abbreviation "Stat."
- The page number on which your statute is found in the Stat. volume
- In parentheses, the year the statute was enacted or passed by the legislature. Do not include the year, however, if you used the "Act of" option referred to in the first bullet.

Narcotic Addict Rehabilitation Act, Pub. L. No. 80–793, § 9, 80 Stat. 1444 (1966)

Note again that the year in parentheses at the end of the cite is the year the statute was passed. Guideline 2 above said that you do not use the date of enactment when citing a statute in U.S.C. The rule is different when giving a Stat. cite.

This example referred you to section number (§) 9 of this public law (Pub. L.). The statute might also have several title numbers. If so, § 9 would be found within one of these titles. Assume, for example, that § 9 is in title III of the public law. It is important to remember that these sections and the title numbers are found in the original *session law* edition of the statute. When this statute is later printed in U.S.C. (assuming it is a public law of general interest), it will *not* go into § 9 of the third title. The U.S.C. has its own title and section number scheme. (For example, title III, § 9 of the above statute might be found in title 45, § 1075(b) of the U.S.C.) This can be very frustrating for the researcher new to the law. If you are reading a statute in its original session or public law form, you will not be able to find this statute under the same title and section number in U.S.C. You must translate the public law or Stat. cite into a U.S.C. cite. Phrased another way, you must translate the session law cite into a code cite. Later we will see that this is done by using one of two tables: Table III in a special Tables volume of U.S.C./U.S.C.A./U.S.C.S. or Table 2 in *United States Code Congressional and Administrative News* (U.S.C.C.A.N.). See research link O.

Session Law: *United States Statutes at Large* (Stat.)	To find a session law in a code, check: · Table III in the Tables volume of U.S.C./U.S.C.A./U.S.C.S. · Table 2 in U.S.C.C.A.N.

RESEARCH LINK O

If you have a federal statute with a Stat. (session law) cite and you want to read this statute in one of the three federal codes, you need a way to translate a Stat. cite into a U.S.C./U.S.C.A./U.S.C.S. cite. Use Table III and Table 2.

Rarely will you need to cite a session law when its codified cite is available. The latter is usually all that is needed. If, however, you need to cite a session law that has already been codified, let the reader know where it will found in the code, i.e., give both the session law *and* the codified cite. Here is an example:

Health Insurance Portability Act of 1996, Pub. L. No. 104–191, § 102, 110 Stat. 1936 (codified at 42 U.S.C.A. § 300gg (West Supp. 1997))

6. Of course, if the statute is a private law that is deemed to be of no general public interest, it will not be printed in the U.S.C. or the U.S.C.A. or the U.S.C.S. It will be found only in *Statutes at Large* (Stat.).

7. The *Internal Revenue Code* (I.R.C.) is within the *United States Code* (U.S.C.). Hence, to cite a tax statute, use the guidelines presented earlier on citing U.S.C./U.S.C.A./U.S.C.S.

26 U.S.C. § 1278 (1976)

There is, however, another option that is acceptable:

I.R.C. § 1278 (1976)

8. There is a special format for citing the Federal Rules of Civil Procedure, Federal Rules of Criminal Procedure, Federal Rules of Appellate Procedure, and Federal Rules of Evidence:

Fed. R. Civ. P. 15
Fed. R. Crim. P. 23(l)
Fed. R. App. P. 3
Fed. R. Evid. 310

IV. Citing State Statutes

1. Like federal statutes, the statutes of the various states are compiled in two kinds of collections: state *codes* (arranged by subject matter) and *session laws* (arranged in chronological order of enactment).
2. Citations to state codes vary from state to state. Exhibit 11.14 shows examples of standard *Bluebook* citation formats. If there are variations between the *Bluebook* and *ALWD* formats, the *ALWD* format is presented in brackets beneath the *Bluebook* citation. Use these as guides unless local rules of court dictate otherwise. The year at the end of the cite should be the year that appears on the spine of the volume, or the year that appears on the title page, or the latest copyright year—in this order of preference.

EXHIBIT 11.14   Examples of Bluebook and ALWD Formats for Citing State Statutory Codes

An asterisk (*) indicates the official code. Bluebook examples of state statutory citations are followed in brackets by those that follow ALWD format. Note, however, that if a state has its own citation rules that differ from *Bluebook* and ALWD formats, the state's own rules must be followed.

Alabama:	Ala. Code § 37–10–3 (1977)*		Fla. Stat. Ann. § 23.8911 (West 1986)
	[Ala. Code § 37–10–3 (West 1977)*]		[Fla. Stat. Ann. § 23.8911 (West 1986)]
	Ala. Code § 15–4–75 (LexisNexis 1977)		Fla. Stat. Ann. § 4.73 (LexisNexis 1986)
	[Ala. Code § 15–4–75 (Lexis 1977)]		[Fla. Stat. Ann. § 4.73 (Lexis 1986)]
Alaska:	Alaska Stat. § 22.10.110 (1962)*	Georgia:	Ga. Code Ann. § 15–11–28 (1973)*
	[Alaska Stat. § 22.10.110 (Lexis 1962)*]		[Ga. Code Ann. § 15–11–28 (1973)*]
Arizona:	Ariz. Rev. Stat. Ann. § 37–4312 (1956)*		Ga. Code Ann. § 7–6–539 (West 1977)
	[Ariz. Rev. Stat. Ann. § 37–4312 (West 1956)*]		[Ga. Code Ann. § 7–6–539 (West 1977)]
	Ariz. Rev. Stat. § 44–1621 (LexisNexis 1956)	Hawaii:	Haw. Rev. Stat. § 351–32 (1988)*
	[Ariz. Rev. Stat. § 44–1621 (Lexis 1956)]		[Haw. Rev. Stat. § 351–32 (1988)*]
Arkansas:	Ark. Code Ann. § 5–1–09 (1968)*		Haw. Rev. Stat. Ann. § 66–2256 (LexisNexis 1988)
	[Ark. Code Ann. § 5–1–09 (Lexis 1968)*]		[Haw. Rev. Stat. Ann. § 66–2256 (Lexis 1988)
	Ark. Code Ann. § 12–64–844 (West 1968)	Idaho:	Idaho Code Ann. § 18–3615 (1987)*
	[Ark. Code Ann. § 12–64–844 (West 1968)]		[Idaho Code Ann. § 18–3615 (Lexis 1987)*]
California:	Cal. Prob. Code § 585 (West 1956)*	Illinois:	5 Ill. Comp. Stat. 100/5–80 (1993)*
	[Cal. Prob. Code Ann. § 585 (West 1956)*]		[5 Ill. Comp. Stat. 100/5–80 (1993)*]
	Cal. Prob. Code § 23 (Derring 1956)		5 Ill. Comp. Stat. Ann. 65/2–15(c) (LexisNexis 1993)*
	[Cal. Prob. Code Ann. § 23 (Lexis 1956)]		[5 Ill. Comp. Stat. Ann. 65/2–15(c) (Lexis 1993)*]
Colorado:	Colo. Rev. Stat. § 32–7–131 (1971)*		5 Ill. Comp. Stat. Ann. 9/14–444 (West 1993)
	[Colo. Rev. Stat. § 32–7–131 (Lexis 1971)*]		[5 Ill. Comp. Stat. Ann. 9/14–444 (West 1993)]
	Colo. Rev. Stat. Ann. § 6–11–67 (West 1971)	Indiana:	Ind. Code § 9–8–1–13 (1976)*
	[Colo. Rev. Stat. Ann. § 6–11–67 (West 1971)]		[Ind. Code § 9–8–1–13 (1976)*]
Connecticut:	Conn. Gen. Stat. § 34–29 (1989)*		Ind. Code Ann. § 55–17–6–332 (West 1976)
	[Conn. Gen. Stat. § 34–29 (1989)*]		[Ind. Code Ann. § 55–17–6–332 (West 1976)]
	Conn. Gen. Stat. Ann. § 2–108(a) (West 1972)		Ind. Code Ann. § 4–67–9–121 (LexisNexis 1979)
	[Conn. Gen. Stat. Ann. § 2–108(a) (West 1972)]		[Ind. Code Ann. § 4–67–9–121 (Lexis 1983)]
Delaware:	Del. Code Ann. tit. 18, § 2926 (1974)*	Iowa:	Iowa Code § 455.92 (1958)*
	[Del. Code Ann. tit. 18, § 2926 (Lexis 1974)*]		[Iowa Code § 455.92 (1958)*]
District of Columbia:	D.C. Code § 16–2307 (1981)*		Iowa Code Ann. § 94.14 (West 1984)
	[D.C. Code § 16–2307 (West 1981)*]		[Iowa Code Ann. § 94.14 (West 1984)]
	D.C. Code Ann. § 4–555 (LexisNexis 1981)	Kansas:	Kan. Stat. Ann. § 38–1506 (1986)*
	[D.C. Code Ann. § 4–555 (Lexis 1981)]		[Kan. Stat. Ann. § 38–1506 (1986)*]
Florida:	Fla. Stat. 2.314 (1986)*		Kan. Corp. Code Ann. § 17–6303 (West 1995)
	[Fla. Stat. 2.314 (1986)*]		[Kan. Corp. Code § 17–6303 (West 1995)]

(continues)

EXHIBIT 11.14	Examples of Bluebook and ALWD Formats for Citing State Statutory Codes—*continued*

Kentucky:	Ky. Rev. Stat. Ann. § 208.060 (West 1988)*		N.C. Gen. Stat. Ann. § 2–442 (West 1988)
	[Ky. Rev. Stat. Ann. § 208.060 (West 1988)*]		[N.C. Gen. Stat. Ann. § 2–442 (West 1988)]
	Ky. Rev. Stat. Ann. § 44.072 (LexisNexis 1986)	North Dakota:	N.D. Cent. Code § 23–12–11 (1989)*
	[Ky. Rev. Stat. Ann. § 44.072 (Lexis 1986)]		[N.D. Cent. Code § 23–12–11 (1989)*]
Louisiana:	La. Rev. Stat. Ann. § 15:452 (1982)*	Ohio:	Ohio Rev. Code Ann. § 2835.03 (LexisNexis 1979)*
	[La. Rev. Stat. Ann. § 15:452 (1982)*]		[Ohio Rev. Code Ann. § 2835.03 (Lexis 1979)*]
	La. Civ. Code Ann. art. 3132 (1961)*		Ohio Rev. Code Ann. § 429.131 (West 1996)
	[La. Civ. Code Ann. art. 3132 (1961)*]		[Ohio Rev. Code Ann. § 429.131 (West 1996)]
Maine:	Me. Rev. Stat. Ann. tit. 36, § 1760 (1964)*	Oklahoma:	Okla. Stat. tit. 42, § 130 (1979)*
	[36 Me. Rev. Stat. Ann. § 1760 (1964)*]		[Okla. Stat. tit. 42, § 130 (1979)*]
Maryland:	Md. Code Ann., Fam. Law § 7–106 (LexisNexis 1984)*		Okla. Stat. Ann. tit. 21, § 491 (West 1983)
	[Md. Fam. Law Code Ann. § 7–106 (1984)*]		[Okla. Stat. Ann. tit. 21, § 491 (West 1983)]
	Md. Code Ann., Real Prop. § 23–654 (West 1957)	Oregon:	Or. Rev. Stat. § 450.870 (1987)*
	[Md. Ann. Code Art. 23, § 654 (1999)*]		[Or. Rev. Stat. § 450.870 (1987)*]
Massachusetts:	Mass. Gen. Laws ch. 106, § 318 (1984)*		Or. Rev. Stat. Ann. § 32.7771 (West 1987)
	[Mass. Gen. Laws ch. 106, § 318 (1984)*]		[Or. Rev. Stat. Ann. § 32.7771 (West 1987)]
	Mass. Gen. Laws Ann. ch. 156, § 37 (West 1970)	Pennsylvania:	1 Pa. Cons. Stat. § 1991 (1972)*
	[Mass. Gen. Laws Ann. ch. 156, § 37 (West 1970)]		[1 Pa. Consol. Stat. Ann. § 1991 (1972)*]
	Mass. Ann. Laws ch. 123, § 15 (LexisNexis 1988)		18 Pa. Cons. Stat. Ann. § 3301 (West 1983)
	[Mass. Ann. Laws ch. 123, § 15 (Lexis 1988)]		[18 Pa. Consol. Stat. Ann. § 3301 (West 1983)]
Michigan:	Mich. Comp. Laws § 550.1402 (1980)*		22 Pa. Stat. Ann. § 708 (West 2002)
	[Mich. Comp. Laws § 550.1402 (1980)*]		[Pa. Stat. Ann. tit. 22, § 708 (West 2002)]
	Mich. Comp. Laws Ann. § 211.27 (West 1986)	Puerto Rico:	P.R. Laws Ann. tit. 7, § 299 (1985)*
	[Mich. Comp. Laws Ann. § 211.27 (West 1986)]		[7 Laws P.R. Ann. § 299 (1985)*]
Minnesota:	Minn. Stat. § 336.1 (1988)*	Rhode Island:	R.I. Gen. Laws § 34–1–2 (1956)*
	[Minn. Stat. § 336.1 (1988)*]		[R.I. Gen. Laws § 34–1–2 (1956)*]
	Minn. Stat. Ann. § 104.08 (West 1987)	South Carolina:	S.C. Code Ann. § 16–23–10 (1976)*
	[Minn. Stat. Ann. § 104.08 (West 1987)]		[S.C. Code Ann. § 16–23–10 (1976)*]
Mississippi:	Miss. Code Ann. § 19–13–57 (1972)*	South Dakota:	S.D. Codified Laws § 15–6–54(c) (1984)*
	[Miss. Code Ann. § 19–13–57 (Lexis 1972)*]		[S.D. Codified Laws § 15–6–64(c) (1984)*]
	Miss. Code Ann. § 5–8–705 (West 1972)	Tennessee:	Tenn. Code Ann. § 33–1–204 (1984)*
	[Miss. Code Ann. § 5–8–705 (West 1972)]		[Tenn. Code Ann. § 33–1–204 (Lexis 1984)*]
Missouri:	Mo. Rev. Stat. § 545.010 (1986)*		Tenn. Code Ann. § 12–7–12(c) (West 1998)
	[Mo. Rev. Stat. § 545.010 (1986)*]		[Tenn. Code Ann. § 12–7–12(c) (West 1998)]
	Mo. Ann. Stat. § 334.540 (West 1989)	Texas:	Tex. Penal Code Ann. § 19.06 (Vernon 1989)*
	[Mo. Rev. Stat. Ann. § 334.540 (West 1989)]		[Tex. Penal Code Ann. § 19.06 (1989)*]
Montana:	Mont. Code Ann. § 37–5–313 (1989)*	Utah:	Utah Code Ann. § 41–3–8 (1953)*
	[Mont. Code Ann. § 37–5–313 (1989)*]		[Utah Code Ann. § 41–3–8 (Lexis 1953)*]
Nebraska:	Neb. Rev. Stat. § 44–406 (1983)*		Utah Code Ann. § 12–25–167 (West 1976)
	[Neb. Rev. Stat. § 44–406 (1983)*]		[Utah Code Ann. § 12–25–167 (West 1976)]
	Neb. Rev. Stat. Ann. § 7–222 (LexisNexis 1995)	Vermont:	Vt. Stat. Ann. tit. 19, § 708 (1987)*
	[Neb. Rev. Stat. Ann. § 7–222 (Lexis 1986)]		[Vt. Stat. Ann. tit. 19, § 708 (1987)*]
Nevada:	Nev. Rev. Stat. § 463.150 (1987)*	Virginia:	Va. Code Ann. § 18.1–265 (1950)*
	[Nev. Rev. Stat. § 463.150 (1987)*]		[Va. Code Ann. § 18.1–265 (Lexis 1950)*]
	Nev. Rev. Stat. Ann. § 679B.180 (LexisNexis 1986)		Va. Code Ann. § 7.01–312 (West 2003)
	[Nev. Rev. Stat. Ann. § 679B.180 (Lexis 1986)]		[Va. Code Ann. § 7.01–312 (West 2003)]
New Hampshire:	N.H. Rev. Stat. Ann. § 318:25 (1984)*	Washington:	Wash. Rev. Code § 7.48A.010 (1987)*
	[N.H. Rev. Stat. Ann. § 318:25 (West 1984)*]		[Wash. Rev. Code § 7.48A.010 (1987)*]
	N.H. Rev. Stat. Ann. § 45:119 (LexisNexis 1988)		Wash. Rev. Code Ann. § 11.17.110 (West 1967)
	[N.H. Rev. Stat. Ann. § 45:119 (Lexis 1988)]		[Wash. Rev. Code Ann. § 11.17.110 (West 1967)]
New Jersey:	N.J. Stat. Ann. § 40:62–127 (West 1961)*		Wash. Rev. Code Ann. § 9.04.266 (LexisNexis 1967)
	[N.J. Stat. Ann § 40:62–127 (West 1961)*]		[Wash. Rev. Code Ann. § 9.04.266 (Lexis 1967)]
	N.J. Rev. Stat. § 14A:5–20 (1969)	West Virginia:	W. Va. Code § 23–1–17 (1985)*
	[N.J. Rev. Stat. § 14A:5–20 (1969)]		[W. Va. Code § 23–1–17 (1985)*]
New Mexico:	N.M. Stat. § 31–6–2 (1978)*		W. Va. Code Ann. § 16–5–3 (LexisNexis 1998)
	[N.M. Stat. § 31–6–2 (1978)*]		[W. Va. Code Ann. § 16–5–3 (Lexis 1998)]
	N.M. Stat. Ann. § 4–88–657 (West 1978)		W. Va. Code Ann. § 16–5–3 (West 1998)
	[N.M. Stat. Ann. § 4–88–657 (West 1978)]		[W. Va. Code Ann. § 16–5–3 (West 1998)]
	N.M. Stat. Ann. § 29–231–12 (LexisNexis 1978)	Wisconsin:	Wis. Stat. § 52.28 (1967)*
	[N.M. Stat. Ann. § 29–231–12 (Lexis 1978)]		[Wis. Stat. § 52.28 (1967)*]
New York:	N.Y. Penal Law § 151.05 (McKinney 1988)*		Wis. Stat. Ann. § 341.55 (West 1971)
	[N.Y. Penal Law § 151.05 (McKinney 1988)*]		[Wis. Stat. Ann. § 341.55 (West 1971)]
	N.Y. Ins. Law § 224.128 (Consol. 1978)*	Wyoming:	Wyo. Stat. Ann. § 26–18–113 (1977)*
	[N.Y. Ins. Law § 224.128 (Consol. 1978)*]		[Wyo. Stat. Ann. § 26–18–113 (1977)*]
	N.Y. Gen. Mun. Law § 115.331 (Gould 1978)*		
	[N.Y. Gen. Mun. Law § 115.331 (Gould 1978)*]		
North Carolina:	N.C. Gen. Stat. § 15A–1321 (1988)*		
	[N.C. Gen. Stat. § 15A–1321 (Lexis 1988)*]		

V. Citing Administrative Regulations and Decisions

1. Federal administrative regulations are published in the *Federal Register* (Fed. Reg.). Many of these regulations are later codified by subject matter in the *Code of Federal Regulations* (C.F.R.). See research link D.

2. Federal regulations that appear in the *Code of Federal Regulations* are cited to (1) the title number in which the regulation appears; (2) the abbreviated name of the code—C.F.R.; (3) the number of the particular section to which you are referring; and (4) the date of the code edition that you are using.

    29 C.F.R. § 102.60(a)(2007)

3. Federal regulations that have not yet been codified into the *Code of Federal Regulations* are cited to the *Federal Register* using (1) the volume in which the regulation appears, (2) the abbreviation "Fed. Reg.," (3) the page on which the regulation appears, and (4) the year of the *Federal Register* you are using. (*ALWD* requires the full date, not just the year.)

    27 Fed. Reg. 2092 (1962)
    [*ALWD*: 27 Fed. Reg. 2092 (March 13, 1962)]

4. Federal regulations are often divided into several parts in the *Federal Register*. If you are not citing the entire regulation, give the page in the *Federal Register* where the regulation begins *and* the pinpoint cite, which would be the page that contains the part to which you are referring.

    27 Fed. Reg. 2092, 2094 (1962)
    [*ALWD*: 27 Fed. Reg. 2092, 2094 (March 13, 1962)]

    Often the *Federal Register* will tell you where in the *Code of Federal Regulations* a particular regulation will also be found. If so, tell the reader by giving both the Fed. Reg. cite and the codified cite.

    58 Fed. Reg. 7185 (1996) (to be codified at 14 C.F.R. § 39.13)
    [*ALWD*: 58 Fed. Reg. 7185 (April 22, 1996)(to be codified at 14 C.F.R. § 39.13)]

5. The format for citing *state* administrative regulations is similar to the format used for federal administrative regulations. Both the *Bluebook* and AWLD have a table that gives the name of the administrative code and register of every state. To see examples of citations of state administrative regulations for your state, go to:

    www.law.cornell.edu/citation
    (Click "Cross Reference Tables," then "State-Specific Practices")

6. On citing administrative decisions, see example G at the beginning of this section.

VI. Citing the Documents of Legislative History

1. **Legislative history** consists of all the events that occur in the legislature before a bill is enacted into a statute. The main documents of legislative history are hearings, debates, amendments, and committee reports.

2. Bills are cited by reference to (1) the number assigned to the bill by the House of Representatives or Senate, (2) the number of the Congress during which the bill was introduced, and (3) the year of the bill.

    H.R. 3055, 94th Cong. (1976)
    S. 1422, 101st Cong. (1989)
    [*ALWD*: Sen. 1422, 101st Cong. (1989)]

3. Reports of congressional committees are cited by reference to (1) the abbreviation of the House (H.) or Senate (S. in the *Bluebook*, Sen. in *ALWD*) where the report was written, (2) the number of the Congress and the number of the report connected by a hyphen, (3) the page number of the report to which you are referring, and (4) the year in which the report was published. If the report is also printed in the set of books called *United States Code Congressional and Administrative News* (U.S.C.C.A.N.), include the volume number of

legislative history Hearings, debates, amendments, committee reports, and all other events that occur in the legislature before a bill is enacted into a statute.

U.S.C.C.A.N. (which will be a year), the page number in U.S.C.C.A.N. where the report begins, and the specific page number of the report to which you are referring.

H.R. Rep. No. 92–238, at 4 (1979)
S. Rep. No. 92–415, at 6 (1971), *as reprinted in* 1971 U.S.C.C.A.N. 647, 682
[*ALWD*: Sen. Rpt. No. 92–415, at 6 (1971), *reprinted in* 1971 U.S.C.C.A.N. 647, 682]

4. Hearings held by congressional committees are cited by reference to (1) the title of the hearing, (2) the number of the Congress during which the hearing was held, (3) the number of the page in the published transcript to which you are referring, and (4) the year in which the hearing was held.

Hearings on H.R. 631 Before the Subcomm. on Labor of the Senate Comm. on Labor and Public Welfare, 92d Cong. 315 (1971)

5. The *Congressional Record* is issued on a daily basis and later collected into bound volumes. The *bound* volumes are cited by referring to (1) the number of the volume in which the item appears, (2) the abbreviation Cong. Rec., (3) the number of the page on which the item appears, and (4) the year. The *daily* volumes are cited in the same manner except that (1) the page number should be preceded by the letter "H" or "S" to indicate whether the item appeared in the House pages or the Senate pages of the volume; (2) the date should include the exact day, month, and year; and (3) the phrase "daily ed." should go before the date.

Bound volumes:

103 Cong. Rec. 2889 (1975)

Daily volumes:

122 Cong. Rec. S2395 (daily ed. Feb. 26, 1976)
132 Cong. Rec. H1385 (daily ed. Mar. 13, 1990)

VII. Citing Secondary Authority

legal treatise A book written by a private individual (or by a public individual writing as a private citizen) that provides an overview, summary, or commentary on a legal topic.

1. **Legal treatises** are cited to (1) the number of the volume being referred to (if part of a set); (2) the full name of the author; (3) the full title of the book as it appears on the title page; (4) the number of the section or page to which you are referring; (5) the edition of the book, if other than the first; and (6) the date of publication. The title of the book should be italicized or underscored. *ALWD* requires the name of the publisher in the parentheses at the end of the cite; the *Bluebook* almost never does. If the treatise has more than one volume, the volume number goes at the beginning of the cite (*Bluebook*) or after the name of the treatise (*ALWD*).

Alice W. Rand, *International Tribunals* 370 (2d ed. 1970)
[*ALWD*: Alice W. Rand, *International Tribunals* 370 (2d ed., Princeton U. Press 1970)]
6 Melvin M. Belli, *Modern Trials* § 289 (1963)
[*ALWD*: Melvin M. Belli, *Modern Trials* vol. 6, § 289 (West 1963)]

legal periodical A pamphlet on legal topics that is issued at regular intervals. Major examples include law reviews and bar journals.

2. **Legal periodical** articles are cited by reference to (1) the full name of the author; (2) the title of the article; (3) the number of the volume in which the article appears; (4) the abbreviated name of the legal periodical; (5) the number of the page on which the article begins; and (6) the year of publication. The title of the article should be italicized or underscored.

Robert Catz & Susan Robinson, *Due Process and Creditor's Remedies*, 28 Rutgers L. Rev. 541 (2004)

William P. Statsky, *The Education of Legal Paraprofessionals: Myths, Realities, and Opportunities*, 24 Vand. L. Rev. 1083 (1971)

If you are referring to material on a specific page in an article, you need to add a pinpoint cite that will give the page number containing that material. The page number you are pinpointing goes immediately after the page number on which the article begins. Suppose, for example, that you were quoting from page 550 of the above *Rutgers Law Review* article. The cite would be:

Robert Catz & Susan Robinson, *Due Process and Creditor's Remedies*, 28 Rutgers L. Rev. 541, 550 (2004)

3. Legal periodical *notes* and *comments* written by law students are cited in the same manner as articles (see guideline 2) except that the *Bluebook* requires the word *Note* or *Comment* to be placed after the author's name, whereas *ALWD* wants the phrase *Student Author* placed after his or her name.

4. **Legal encyclopedias** are cited by reference to (1) the number of the volume, (2) the abbreviated name of the encyclopedia, (3) the subject heading to which you are referring—in italics or underscored, (4) the number of the section to which you are referring, and (5) the date of publication of the volume you are citing.

> **legal encyclopedia** An alphabetical summary of every important legal topic.

83 C.J.S. *Subscriptions* § 3 (2006)
77 Am. Jur. 2d *Vendor and Purchaser* § 73 (2007)

5. **Restatements** of the law published by the American Law Institute (www.ali.org) are cited by reference to (1) the title of the Restatement, (2) the edition being referred to (if other than the first edition), (3) the number of the section being referred to, and (4) the date of publication.

> **restatements** Treatises of the American Law Institute that state the law and indicate changes in the law that the Institute would like to see implemented.

Restatement (Second) of Agency § 37 (1957)

6. **Annotations** in A.L.R., A.L.R.2d, A.L.R.3d, A.L.R.4th, A.L.R.5th, A.L.R.6th, A.L.R. Fed., and A.L.R. Fed.2d are cited by (1) the full name of the author, if available; (2) the title of the annotation—in italics or underscored; (3) the volume number; (4) the abbreviation of the A.L.R. unit; (5) the page number where the annotation begins; and (6) the date of the volume. After the author's name, the *Bluebook* requires the word *Annotation*; ALWD does not.

> **annotation** 1. A note or commentary that summarizes or provides explanation. 2. The research papers in American Law Reports.

James J. Watson, Annotation, *Attorney's Fees: Cost of Services Provided by Paralegals*, 73 A.L.R.4th 938 (1989)
[*ALWD*: James J. Watson, *Attorney's Fees: Cost of Services Provided by Paralegals*, 73 A.L.R.4th 938 (1989)]

VIII. Citing Internet Sources

When you do want to cite something on the Internet, provide (1) the name of the author, if given; (2) the title or top-level heading of the material you are citing; (3) the **Uniform Resource Locator (URL),** which is its Internet address; and (4) the date of the site, if available. If the date of the site is not available, give the date you "last visited" the site. (ALWD says "accessed" rather than "last visited").

> **Uniform Resource Locator (URL)** The address of a resource on the Internet.

Bluebook

National Federation of Paralegal Associations, *What Is a Paralegal?*, http://www.paralegals.org (last visited May 21, 2007)

Peter W. Martin, *Introduction to Basic Legal Citation*, http://www.law.cornell.edu/citation (last visited December 10, 2007)

ALWD

National Federation of Paralegal Associations, *What Is a Paralegal?*, http://www.paralegals.org (accessed May 21, 2007)

Peter W. Martin, *Introduction to Basic Legal Citation*, http://www.law.cornell.edu/citation (accessed December 10, 2007)

If material is available in a traditional print source and on the Internet, provide only the traditional citation unless including the Internet parallel cite will substantially help a reader gain access to the material. When providing the online parallel cite, indicate that the material is "available at" the Internet address. The *Bluebook* places the phrase "available at" in italics; ALWD does not. Also, only ALWD places the entire URL in parentheses.

Bluebook

Toledo, Ohio, Mun. Code § 115.02 (2006), *available at* http://www.amlegal.com/toledo_oh

ALWD

Toledo, Ohio, Mun. Code § 115.02 (2006) (available at http://www.amlegal.com/toledo_oh)

ASSIGNMENT 11.5

Each of the following citations has one or more things wrong with it. Describe the errors and gaps in format. For example, a parallel cite is missing or something is abbreviated incorrectly. You do not have to go to the library to check any of these cites. Simply use the guidelines presented above. (If the *Bluebook* and the ALWD differ in any of your answers, state the differences.) For some of the cites, you will need additional information to determine the accuracy of the format of the cite. For example, you may need to know where the cite will be used. If you need further information, state what you need and why you need it.

(a) *Smith v. Jones,* 135 Mass. 37, 67 N.E. 2d 316, 320 (1954).
(b) *Paul Matthews v. Edward Foley, Inc.,* 779 F. 2d 729 (W.D.N.Y., 1979).
(c) *Jackson v. Jackson,* 219 F.Supp. 1276, 37 N.E. 2d 84 (1980).
(d) *Davis v. Thompson, et al,* 336 P. 2d 691, 210 N.M. 432 (1976).
(e) *Washington Tire Company v. Jones,* 36 N.J. Super. 222, 351 A. 2d 541 (1976).
(f) *State of New Hampshire v. Atkinson,* 117 N.H. 830, 228 A. 2d 222 (N.H.Super., 1978).
(g) *Richardson v. U.S.,* 229 U.S. 220 (1975).
(h) American Law Institute, *Restatement of Torts* (2d ed 1976).
(i) U.S. Const. Art. III (1797).
(j) Smith, F., Products Liability (3rd ed. 1985).
(k) 42 USC 288 (1970).
(l) 17 U.S.C.A. 519 (1970).
(m) 40 Fed. Reg. § 277 (1976).

ASSIGNMENT 11.6

(a) Find out if there are any special citation rules that must be followed in your state:
www.law.cornell.edu/citation
(Click "Cross Reference Tables," then "State-Specific")
www.alwd.org/cm
(Click "Appendices," then "Appendix 2")
If such rules exist in your state, redo Assignment 11.5 by stating which, if any, of the citations in (a) to (m) would have to be changed to conform to these special citation rules, and how.
(b) Find any court opinion written by the highest state court in your state. Locate this opinion by using the regional reporter for your state. (See Exhibit 11.5.) Pick an opinion that is at least ten pages long.
  (i) Write down every citation in this opinion (up to a maximum of twenty-five).
  (ii) State whether these citations conform to the citation rules outlined in this section. Point out any differences.
  (iii) State whether these citations conform to the special citation rules, if any, you identified in answering question (a) above. Point out any differences.

[SECTION K]

CITE CHECKING

cite checking Examining citations in a document to assess whether the format of the citation is correct, whether a parallel cite is needed, whether quoted material is quoted accurately, and whether the law cited is still valid.

When an assignment involves **cite checking**, you are given a document written by someone else and asked to check the citations provided by the author of the document. The assignment is quite common in law firms, particularly when the document to be checked is an appellate brief. Students on law review in law school also do extensive cite checking on the work of fellow students and outside authors.

Although our focus in this section will be cite checking documents written by others, the guidelines discussed here are in large measure equally applicable to your own writing. (Subjecting what you have written to your own criticism and review is what is known as *self-editing.*)

GUIDELINES FOR CITE CHECKING

The first step is to obtain clear instructions from your supervisor on the scope of the assignment. Should you do a "light check" that merely checks the format of the citations? Or should you do a comprehensive check that could include checking citation format, finding and inserting needed parallel cites, checking quotation accuracy, and determining the current validity of the laws cited?

The following guidelines assume that you have been asked to undertake a comprehensive check.

1. Make sure that you have a *copy* of the document on which you can make comments. Avoid using the original.

2. If the pages of the document already have pencil or pen markings made by others (or by the author who made last-minute insertions), use a pencil or pen that is a different color from all other markings on the pages. In this way, it will be clear to any reader which corrections, notations, or other comments are your own. If you find that you do not have enough room to write in the margins of the pages, use separate sheets of paper. You can increase the size of the margins by photocopying the document on a machine that will reduce the size of what is copied.

3. It is also possible to do a cite check entirely on the computer without any markings on a paper document. Start by making a digital copy of the document. On the copy, use red print (or some other bright color) to indicate every addition you have made to the document. Use the strike-out key (~~key~~) for whatever you want to remove from the document. These format elements make it very easy for the writer of the document to scroll through it and find your additions and omissions. The "Track Changes" feature of word-processing programs such as Word will automatically insert these format elements for you. The programs also allow you to include unobtrusive comments that can explain why you made any of the changes. In the remainder of these guidelines, we will assume that you are doing the cite check in the traditional way—on paper—rather than entirely on the computer.

4. If the document will be submitted to a court, be sure that you are using the official citation rules, if any, that must be followed for all citations in documents submitted to that court. If official citation rules do not exist, find out what rules or guidelines on citation format the supervisor wants you to use. The *Bluebook*? *ALWD*?

5. Before you begin, try to find a model. By going through the old case files of the office, you may be able to locate a prior document, such as an old appellate brief, that you can use as a general guide if it still has the markings and notations on it made by the person who cite-checked it. Ask your supervisor to direct you to such a document. Although it may not cover all the difficulties you will encounter in your own document, you will at least have a general guide approved by your supervisor.

6. Check the citation form of *every* cite in the document written by the author of that document. This includes any cites in the body of the text, the footnotes, the appendix material, and the introductory pages of the document, such as the **table of authorities (TOA)** at the beginning of a brief. (A table of authorities is a list of the primary and secondary authority the writer is using in an appellate brief or other document. The table will indicate on what page(s) in the document each authority is discussed or mentioned. See chapter 12.)

7. For long documents, you need to develop your own system for ensuring the completeness of your checking. For example, you might want to circle every cite that you have checked and found to be accurate, and place a small box around (or a question mark next to) every cite that is giving you difficulties. You will want to spend more time with the latter, seeking help from colleagues and your supervisor.

8. When you find errors in the form of the citation, make the corrections in the margin of the pages where they are found.

9. For some errors, you will not be able to make the corrections without obtaining additional information, such as a missing date or a missing parallel cite. If you can obtain such data by going to the relevant library books (or available online resources), do so. Otherwise, make a notation in the margin of what is missing or what still needs correction.

table of authorities (TOA) A list of primary authority (e.g., cases and statutes) and secondary authority (e.g., legal periodical articles and legal treatises) that a writer has cited in an appellate brief or other document. The list includes page numbers where each authority is cited in the document.

10. Consistency in citation format is extremely important. On page 2 of the document, for example, the author may use one citation format, but on page 10, he or she may use a completely different format for the same kind of legal material. You need to point out this inconsistency and make the consistency corrections that are called for.

11. Often your document will quote from opinions, statutes, or other legal materials. Check the accuracy of these quotations. Go to the material being quoted, find the quote, and check it against the document line by line, word by word, and punctuation mark by punctuation mark. Be scrupulous about the accuracy of quotations.

12. Use standard citators (e.g., *Shepard's Citations*, KeyCite, or GlobalCite) to check the current validity of all primary authority. Here are examples of what you want to find out through the citator:

   ■ Whether any of the cited opinions has been overruled or reversed.

   ■ Whether any of the cited statutes has been repealed or amended by the legislature, or has been invalidated by a court.

supra Above; mentioned earlier in the document.

13. Check the accuracy of every **supra** reference.

   The word *supra* means "above" or "earlier." It refers to something already mentioned (and cited) in the document you are cite checking. For example, assume that footnote 8 on page 23 of the document contains the following cite:

   ⁸Robert G. Danna, *Family Law* 119 (1992).

   The particular reference is to page 119 of Danna's book. Now assume that 10 pages later—in footnote 17—the document again refers to Danna's book, this time to page 35. A full citation to this page would be as follows:

   ¹⁷Robert G. Danna, *Family Law* 35 (1992).

   But a full citation is not needed. You can use a *short-form citation*. This is an abbreviated citation of an authority that you use after you have already given a full citation of that authority earlier in the document. For the short-form citation of a legal treatise such as the Danna *Family Law* book, use the author's last name followed by the *supra* reference:

   ¹⁷Danna, *supra* note 8, at 35.

   [*ALWD*: ¹⁷Danna, *supra* n. 8, at 35.]

   This means that the full cite of Danna's book was already given earlier (*supra*) in the document in footnote 8. There is no need to repeat the full cite. The cite checker must simply go to footnote 8 and make sure that the full cite of the book is provided there.

   Finally, assume that Danna's book was cited in full in the body of the text of the document rather than in a footnote. A later footnote reference to the same book would be as follows:

   ¹⁷Danna, *supra*, at 35.

   The accuracy of this reference is checked in the same way: make sure that the full cite of Danna's book is in fact provided earlier in the body of the text of the document.

infra Below; mentioned or referred to later in the document.

   Infra means "below" or "later" and refers to something that will come later in the document. In the same manner as you checked the *supra* references, you must determine whether the *infra* references are accurate.

14. Check the accuracy of all of short-form *case* citations.

   Assume that the document you are cite checking gives the following reference early in the document:

   Sierra Club v. Sigler, 695 F.2d 957, 980 (5th Cir. 1983).

   The cite is to page 980 of the *Sierra Club* opinion, which begins on page 957 of the *Federal Reporter, Second Series*. Now assume that the author wants to refer to page 962 of the same opinion later in the document. As with the Danna book example, there is no need to repeat the entire citation. The following short form may be used:

   Sierra Club, 695 F.2d at 962.

To check the accuracy of this cite, you must go back in the document to make sure that the *Sierra Club* opinion has already been cited in full.

Do not, however, use *supra* when you are citing court opinions. *Supra* can be used for many items, such as legal treatises and legal periodicals. With rare exceptions, however, do not use it in citations to court opinions. When you wish to avoid repeating the full citation of an opinion, follow the example of the *Sierra Club* short-form citation.

15. All **id**. references should also be checked. *Id.* means the same as something previously mentioned. Use *id.* when you are citing an authority that is also the *immediately preceding* authority cited in a footnote. (*Id.* is more specific than *supra*; the latter means above or earlier. *Id.*, however, means *immediately* above.) Assume, for example, that footnote 21 in the appellate brief you are cite checking says:

> [21]*Kohler v. Tugwell*, 292 F. Supp. 978 (E.D. La. 1968).

And footnote 22 says:

> [22]*Id.* at 985.

The *Id.* reference means that here in footnote 22 you are referring to the immediately preceding authority—the *Kohler* opinion in footnote 21.

Be careful about *id.* references. A writer cannot use *id.* if more than one authority is cited in the preceding footnote. Suppose, for example, that footnote 21 cited *Kohler* and another opinion:

> [21]*Smith v. Harris*, 260 F.2d 601 (2d Cir. 1956); *Kohler v. Tugwell*, 292 F. Supp. 978 (E.D. La. 1968).

If footnote 22 cited *Kohler*, it could not use *id.* because there is more than one authority in footnote 21. Footnote 22 should use the short-form citation as follows:

> [22]*Kohler*, 292 F. Supp. at 985.

16. For more information about cite checking and citation in general, see:

- library.law.wisc.edu/guides/citecheckers
- lib.law.washington.edu/ref/citecheck.html
- www.legalcitation.net

id. The same as the immediately preceding cited authority.

ASSIGNMENT 11.7

In chapter 5 on page 223 you will find the opinion of *Brown v. Hammond* by Judge Waldman. Assume that this opinion in chapter 5 is only the first draft of the judge's opinion. After writing it, Judge Waldman hands it to you and asks you to cite check it. Make sure all the citations are in proper form according to the guidelines presented in this section. Check the accuracy of every quote. Check other references as well. If, for example, the text cites an opinion and summarizes what is in the opinion, check whether the summary is accurate. If you cannot check some of the cites, point out why (e.g., the library you are using does not have whatever you need to check a particular cite).

[SECTION L]

COMPONENTS OF MANY LAW BOOKS

Many law books are similar in structure. To be sure, some books, such as *Shepard's Citations*, are unique. In the main, however, the texts follow a pattern. The following components are contained in many:

1. *Outside Cover*. On the outside cover, you will find the title of the book, the author(s) or editor(s), the name of the publisher (usually at the bottom), the edition of the book (if more than one edition has been printed), and the volume number (if the book is part of a set or series of books). After glancing at the outside cover, you should ask yourself the following questions:

   - Is it a book *containing* law (written primarily by a court, a legislature, or an administrative agency), or is it a book *about* the law (written by a scholar who is commenting on the law)? Is the book a combination of both? (For an overview of the four main functions of books and other legal materials, see Exhibit 11.3.)

- Is this book the most current available? Look at the books on the shelf in the area where you found the book that you are examining. Is there a replacement volume for your book? Is there a later edition of the book? Check your book in the card or computer catalog to see if other editions are mentioned. Also go to the online catalog of the Library of Congress (catalog.loc.gov). In "Basic Search," type the name of the publication to find out about other editions, if any. This is a way to determine if another edition exists even if the library you are using does not have it.

2. *Publisher's Page*. The first few pages of the book often include a page or pages about the publisher. The page may list other law books published by the same company.

3. *Title Page*. The title page repeats most of the information contained on the outside cover: title, author or editor, publisher.

4. *Copyright Page*. The **copyright** page (often immediately behind the title page) has a copyright mark © plus a date or several dates. The most recent date listed indicates the timeliness of the material in the volume. Given the great flux in the law, it is very important to determine how old the text is. If the book has a pocket part (see item 13 below), it has been updated to the date on the pocket part.

copyright (©) The exclusive right for a fixed number of years to print, copy, sell, or perform original works. 17 U.S.C. § 101.

> COPYRIGHT © 1979, 1983, 1989, 1994, 1998 WEST GROUP
> COPYRIGHT © 2007
> By
> WEST GROUP

The dates on this copyright page indicate that the material in the book is current up to 2007, the latest copyright date. Caution, however, is needed in reaching this conclusion. Publishers like to have their books appear to be as current as possible. A book with a 2007 copyright date may in fact have been published *at the beginning* of 2007 or *at the very end* of 2006! A 2002 date does not necessarily mean that you are current up to December of that year. We will return to this concern later when we discuss pocket parts.

5. *Foreword and/or Preface*. Under such headings, you may find some basic information about the book, particularly material on how the book was prepared and guidance on how to use it.

6. *Summary Table of Contents*. On one or two pages, you may find the main topics treated in the book.

7. *Detailed Table of Contents*. When provided, the detailed table of contents can be very extensive. The major headings of the summary table of contents are repeated, and detailed subheadings and sub-subheadings are listed. Use this table as an additional index to the book.

table of cases An alphabetical list of all the opinions printed or referred to in the volume, and where they are found in the volume.

8. *Table of Cases*. The **table of cases** lists, alphabetically, every opinion that is printed or referred to in the text, with the page(s) or section(s) where the opinion is found or discussed. This table is sometimes printed at the end of the book.

table of statutes A list of all the statutes printed or referred to in the volume, and where they are found in the volume.

9. *Table of Statutes*. The **table of statutes** gives the page numbers or section numbers where every statute is interpreted or referred to in the text. This table is sometimes printed at the end of the book.

10. *List of Abbreviations*. The abbreviation list, if provided, is critical. A reader who is unfamiliar with law books should check this list immediately. It may be the only place in the book that spells out the abbreviations used in the body of the text. Suppose, for example, you see a "j" next to a citing case in *Shepard's Citations*. Unless you check the abbreviation list or table at the beginning of the Shepard's volume you are using, you would not know that the "j" means *dissenting opinion*.

11. *Body of the Text*. The fundamental characteristic of the body of many legal texts is that it is arranged according to units such as parts, subparts, divisions, subdivisions, chapters, subchapters, sections, subsections, etc. Often each unit covers a similar subject matter and is numbered or lettered in sequence. You should thumb through the entire book to obtain a feel for the numbering and classification system used by the author or editor.

12. *Footnotes*. Footnotes are very important in law books; researchers place great emphasis on them. They often give extensive citations to cases and other cross-references, and hence can be an excellent lead to additional law.

pocket part A pamphlet inserted into a small pocket built into the inside back (and occasionally front) cover of a hardcover volume. The pamphlet contains text that supplements or updates the material in the hardcover volume.

13. *Pocket Parts and Other Updating Features*. A unique and indispensable feature of many law books is the **pocket part**. It is a pamphlet addition to the text, usually placed in a specially devised pocket built into the inside of the rear cover. The pocket part is published after the

book is printed and is designed to bring the book up to date with the latest developments in the field covered by the book. Of course, a pocket part can also grow out of date. Normally, it is replaced once a year. On the front cover of the pocket-part booklet, there is a date telling you what period is covered. The title page (see item 3 above) may say that the last edition of the book was published in 1990, but the front page of the pocket part may say "for use during 2007–2008." Again, however, use caution in interpreting these dates. The publisher may have prepared this pocket part at the end of 2007 or at the beginning of 2008. You cannot assume that the material in the pocket part is current up to December of 2008.

Normally, the organization of the pocket part exactly parallels the organization of the main text. For example, to find out if there has been anything new in the area covered by chapter 7, part 2, section 714 of the main text, you go to chapter 7, part 2, section 714 of the pocket part. If you find nothing there, then nothing new has happened. If changes or additions have occurred, they will be found there. The changes may appear in different formats. <u>All new text might appear underlined</u>. Or in some pocket parts, you can assume that any text that appears in the pocket part is new text.

Pocket parts are **cumulative** in that, whenever a pocket part is replaced by another pocket part, everything in the earlier pocket part is consolidated into the most recent one. The earlier pocket part is thrown away.

Not all law books have pocket parts. For an overview, see Exhibit 11.15.

How is new material added to law books that do not have pocket parts—the ones listed in the second column of Exhibit 11.15? Shepard's is kept current by advance sheets and supplemental pamphlets; the American Digest System by adding *General Digest* volumes, which are thrown away when the next *Decennial Digest* is published; looseleaf services by inserting pages with new material into the binders and removing pages with outdated material (a process called *interfiling*). For the other items in the second column of Exhibit 11.15—West Group reporters, session laws, etc.—new material is added simply by adding new volumes or issues.

> **cumulative** That which repeats earlier material and consolidates it with new material into one place or unit. A cumulative supplement, for example, contains new supplemental material and repeats earlier supplemental material.

EXHIBIT 11.15 Pocket Parts

LAW BOOKS THAT ALWAYS OR OFTEN HAVE POCKET PARTS:	LAW BOOKS THAT NEVER HAVE POCKET PARTS:
■ State statutory codes (e.g., *Georgia Code Annotated)*	■ Shepard's (e.g., *Shepard's Federal Citations)*
■ Unofficial federal codes (e.g., U.S.C.A. and U.S.C.S.)	■ American Digest System (*Century Digest, Decennial Digests, and General Digests*)
■ Annotated reporters (e.g., A.L.R. 5th)	■ Looseleaf Services (e.g., *United States Law Week*)
■ Legal encyclopedias (e.g., C.J.S. and Am.Jur. 2d)	■ West Group Reporters (e.g., regional reporters, S. Ct., F.3d, F. Supp. 2d)
■ State digests (e.g., *Illinois Digest 2d*)	■ Session Laws (e.g., *United States Statutes at Large*)
■ Regional digests (e.g., *Pacific Digest*)	■ Legal Periodicals (e.g., *Boston College Law Review*)
■ Federal digests (e.g., *Federal Practice Digest 4th*)	■ Legal Newspapers (e.g., *San Francisco Daily Journal*)
■ Legal treatises written for practitioners (e.g., C.Z. Nothstein, *Toxic Torts*)	■ Legal Newsletters (e.g., *The Guardian*)

Some sets of books use a variety of methods to bring them up to date: pocket parts, supplement pamphlets, supplement volumes, reissued volumes, revised volumes, etc. The newest method of updating is the Internet. If the material is on the Internet (particularly on commercial fee-based services), updating is automatic. What you read online either is always current or gives you links to other online pages or sites that will provide the latest updates. Also, at the beginning or end of a volume, you may be given a World Wide Web address where you can go for additional material on the book (often including an **errata page** listing errors that were not caught until after the volume was published).

> **errata page** A list of corrections to a transcript or document.

14. *Appendix*. The text may include one or more appendixes at the end. Normally, they include tables, charts, or the entire text of statutes or regulations, portions of which are discussed in the body of the book.

15. *Glossary*. The book may include a glossary, which is a dictionary that defines a selected number of words (particularly **terms of art**) used in the body of the book.

> **term of art** A word or phrase that has a special or technical meaning.

16. *Bibliography*. A brief or extended bibliography of the field covered by the book may be included at the end of each chapter or at the end of the book.

17. *Index*. The index is a critical part of the book. Unfortunately, some books either have no index or have a poorly prepared index. The index is arranged alphabetically and should

refer the reader to the page number(s) or to the section number(s) where topics are treated in the body of the text. The index is found at the end of the book. If there are many volumes in the set, you may find more than one index. For example, there may be a *general index* for the entire set and a series of smaller indexes covering individual volumes.

[SECTION M]

THE CARTWHEEL

CARTWHEEL A technique designed to help you think of a large variety of words and phrases to check in indexes, tables of contents, and online search engines.

Most people think that using an *index* is a relatively easy task—until they start trying to use indexes of law books! These indexes are often poorly written because they are not comprehensive. To be comprehensive, an index might have to be as long as the text it is indexing.

Because of this reality, one of the most important skills in legal research is the creative use of indexes in law books. When you master this skill, 70 percent of the research battle is won. The **CARTWHEEL** is a word-association technique designed to assist you in acquiring the skill by giving you a method of generating words and phrases. See Exhibit 11.16. (The skill can also be used when checking tables of contents and using online search engines.) Professor Roy Steele, a veteran teacher of legal research, made the following observation about new students:

EXHIBIT 11.16	The CARTWHEEL: Using the Index of Law Books

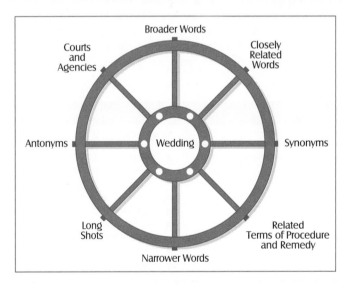

1. Identify all the *major words* from the facts of the client's problem, e.g., wedding (most of these facts can be obtained from the intake memorandum written following the initial interview with the client). Place each word or small set of words in the center of the CARTWHEEL.
2. In the index, look up all of these words.
3. Identify the *broader categories* of the major words.
4. In the index, look up all of these broader categories.
5. Identify the *narrower* categories of the major words.
6. In the index, look up all of these narrower categories.
7. Identify all *synonyms* of the major words.
8. In the index, look up all of these synonyms.
9. Identify all of the *antonyms* of the major words.
10. In the index, look up all of these antonyms.
11. Identify all words that are *closely related* to the major words.
12. In the index, look up all of these closely related words.
13. Identify all terms of *procedure* and *remedy* related to the major words.
14. In the index, look up all of these procedural and remedial terms.
15. Identify all *courts* and *agencies*, if any, that might have some connection to the major words.
16. In the index, look up all of these courts and agencies.
17. Identify all *long shots*.
18. In the index, look up all of these long shots.

Note: The above categories are not mutually exclusive.

I think it is important for students to understand that they cannot just walk into a library and start pulling books off the shelf. That is the quickest way to become frustrated. Legal research requires thoughtful planning. A student must determine which resources will be checked. It is not enough that a student knows [that] a certain resource has an index or table of contents. The student must know what he/she is looking for. This requires the student to develop a list of search terms. Some people would call the development of this list *brainstorming*. However, brainstorming is somewhat hit or miss; it lacks structure and organization. The CARTWHEEL is one of the most effective ways of systematically developing a list of search terms. [It is] a method of analyzing a legal problem and developing a list of descriptive words, which can be used to search indexes.

The objective of the CARTWHEEL can be simply stated: to develop the habit of phrasing every major word involved in the client's problem *fifteen to twenty different ways!* When you go to the index (or to the table of contents) of a law book, you naturally begin looking up the words and phrases that you think should lead you to the relevant material in the book. If you do not find anything relevant to your problem, two conclusions are possible:

- There is nothing relevant in the law book.
- You looked up the wrong words in the index.

Although the first conclusion is sometimes accurate, nine times out of ten, the second conclusion is the reason you fail to find material that is relevant to the client's problem. The solution is to be able to phrase a word in as many different ways and in as many different contexts as possible—hence the CARTWHEEL.

Suppose the client's problem involved, among other things, a wedding. The first step would be to look up the word *wedding* in the index of any law book you are examining. Assume that you are not successful with this word, either because the word is not in the index or because the page or section references do not lead you to relevant material in the body of the book. The next step is to think of as many different phrasings and contexts of the word *wedding* as possible. This is where the eighteen steps of the CARTWHEEL can be useful.

If you applied the steps of the CARTWHEEL to the word *wedding*, here are some of the words and phrases that you might check:

1. *Broader words:* celebration, ceremony, rite, ritual, formality, festivity, union, etc.
2. *Narrower words:* civil wedding, church wedding, golden wedding, proxy wedding, sham wedding, shotgun wedding, formal wedding, informal wedding, etc.
3. *Synonyms:* marriage ceremony, nuptial, etc.
4. *Antonyms*: alienation, annulment, divorce, separation, legal separation, judicial separation, etc.
5. *Closely related words*: license, blood test, contract, minister, matrimony, monogamy, inter-marriage, marital, conjugal, domestic, husband, wife, bride, anniversary, custom, children, premarital, spouse, relationship, family, home, consummation, cohabitation, sexual relations, betrothal, espousal, hand, wedlock, oath, community property, name change, domicile, residence, troth, etc.
6A. *Terms of procedure*: action, suit, statute of limitations, complaint, discovery, defense, petition, jurisdiction, etc.
6B. *Terms of remedy*: damages, divorce, injunction, partition, rescission, revocation, specific performance, etc.
7. *Courts and agencies*: trial court, appellate court, superior court, county court, court of common pleas, court of appeals, supreme court, justice of the peace court, magistrate court, bureau of vital statistics, county clerk, department of social services, Social Security Administration, license bureau, secretary of state, etc.
8. *Long shots:* dowry, common law, single, blood relationship, fraud, religion, illegitimate, remarriage, antenuptial, alimony, bigamy, polygamy, pregnancy, gifts, chastity, impotence, incest, virginity, support, custody, consent, paternity, etc.

If the CARTWHEEL can generate this many words and phrases from a starting point of just one word (wedding), potentially thousands more can be generated when you subject all of the important words from the client's case to the CARTWHEEL. Do you check them all in the index volume of every code, digest, encyclopedia, practice manual, and treatise? No. You can't spend your entire legal career in the law library working on one case! Common sense will tell you when you are on the right track and when you are needlessly duplicating your efforts. You may get lucky and find what you are after in a few minutes. For important tasks in any line of work (or play), however, being comprehensive is usually time-consuming.

The categories of the CARTWHEEL in Exhibit 11.16 may overlap; they are not mutually exclusive. There are two reasons for checking antonyms: they might cover your topic, and they might give you a cross-reference to your topic. It is not significant whether you place a word in one category or another so long as the word comes to your mind as you comb through all available indexes. The CARTWHEEL is, in effect, a *word-association game* that should become second nature to you with practice. Perhaps some of the word selections seem a bit far-fetched. You will not know for sure, however, whether a word is fruitful until you try it. Be imaginative, and take some risks.

As indicated, the CARTWHEEL can also be helpful for generating search terms when you are doing online searches in search engines such as Google. In addition to typing words generated by the CARTWHEEL into an online search box, find out what method is used by the search engine itself to generate additional terms. For example, in Google, if you place a tilde (~) immediately in front of the word, Google will automatically search for synonyms of that word. Hence a search for sites on the police (~police) will give you sites that mention police *and* those that mention the synonyms *cops*, *law enforcement*, and *officer*.

Indexes and tables of contents are often organized into *headings*, *subheadings*, *sub-subheadings*, and perhaps even sub-sub-subheadings. Examine the following excerpt from an index. Note that "Burden of proof" is a sub-subheading of "Accidents" and a subheading of "Unavoidable accident or casualty." The latter is a subheading of "Accidents," which is the main heading of the index entry.

ASSIGNMENT 11.8

CARTWHEEL the following words or phrases:

(a) Paralegal
(b) Woman
(c) Rat bite
(d) Rear-end collision
(e) Monopoly

If you were looking for law on burden of proof, you might be out of luck unless you *first* thought of looking up "accidents" and "unavoidable accident."

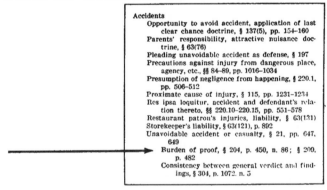

Suppose that you identify the following words to check in an index:

minor	sale
explosion	warranty
car	damage

The index may have no separate heading for "minor," but "minor" may be a subheading under "sale." If so, you would not find "minor" unless you first thought of checking "sale." Under each of the above six words, you should be alert to the possibility that the other five words may be subheadings for that word. Hence the process of pursuing these six words in an index (or table of contents) would involve checking the main words one at a time plus each of the other five to see if any are subheadings of the main words:

Car	Damage	Explosion	Minor	Sale	Warranty
damage	car	car	car	car	car
explosion	explosion	damage	damage	damage	damage
minor	minor	minor	explosion	explosion	explosion
sale	sale	sale	sale	minor	minor
warranty	warranty	warranty	warranty	warranty	sale

ASSIGNMENT 11.9

One way to gain an appreciation for the use of indexes is to write one of your own. When you write an index for this assignment, be sure to use headings, subheadings, sub-subheadings, etc., in each index.

(a) Write a comprehensive index of your present job or the last job that you had.

(b) Pick one area of the law that you have covered in class or read about. Write your own comprehensive index on what you have learned.

(c) Write a comprehensive index of the following statute:

§ 132. Amount of force. The use of force against another for the purpose of effecting the arrest or recapture of the other, or of maintaining custody of him, is not privileged if the means employed are in excess of those which are reasonably believed to be necessary.

ASSIGNMENT 11.10

Examine the index from a legal encyclopedia in Exhibit 11.17. It is an excerpt from the heading of "Evidence." "Death" is the subheading of "Evidence." What sub-subheadings or sub-sub-subheadings of "Evidence" would you check to try to find material on the following:

(a) Introducing a death certificate into evidence.

(b) The weight that a court will give to the personal conclusions of a witness.

(c) Introducing the last words of a decedent into evidence.

(d) A statement by the person who died disclaiming ownership of land around which he or she had placed a fence.

OTHER INDEX SEARCH SYSTEMS

The CARTWHEEL is not the only technique for using indexes (and tables of contents) effectively. Others include descriptive words and TAPP.

Descriptive Words

West Group suggests a five-part descriptive word framework for generating search terms: Parties, Places or Things, Basis of Action or Issue, Defenses, and Relief Sought. By trying to identify terms that fall into these categories, you will be generating numerous words to check in the indexes (and tables of contents) of law books you are examining.

Parties   Identify persons of a particular class, occupation, or relation involved in the problem you are researching (e.g., commercial landlords, children born out of wedlock, physicians, sheriffs, aliens, or collectors). Include any person who is directly or indirectly necessary to a proper resolution of the legal problem.

Places or Things   Identify all significant objects—those places and things perceptible to the senses that are involved in the problem being researched (e.g., automobiles, sidewalks, derricks, garages, or office buildings). An object is significant if it is relevant to the cause of action or dispute that has arisen. (A cause of action is a set of facts that give a party a right to judicial relief; it is a legally acceptable reason for suing.)

Basis of Action or Issue   Identify the alleged wrong suffered or infraction (e.g., negligence, loss of goods, assault, failure to pay overtime, or sex discrimination).

Defenses   Identify those reasons in law or fact why there arguably should be *no* recovery (e.g., assumption of the risk, failure of consideration, act of God, or infancy).

Relief Sought   Identify the legal remedy being sought (e.g., damages, injunction, or annulment).

EXHIBIT 11.17	Excerpt from an Index in a Legal Encyclopedia (Corpus Juris Secundum)

Example At a professional wrestling match the referee was thrown from the ring in such a way that he struck and injured the plaintiff, who was a front-row spectator. The following descriptive words for this problem should be checked:

Parties—spectator, patron, arena owner, wrestler, referee, promoter
Places and things—wrestling match, amusement place, theater, show
Basis of action or issue—negligence, personal injury to spectator, liability
Defense—assumption of risk, contributory negligence, comparative negligence
Relief sought—damages

TAPP

Another system of generating search terms is to think of TAPP categories: Things, Acts, Persons, or Places involved in the problem you are searching.

Things—automobile, pool, knife, blood, etc.

Acts—swimming, driving, rescuing, accounting, etc.

Persons—mother, pedestrian, driver, etc.

Places—state freeway, residence, etc.

A variation is TARPP, in which an R category is added to prompt you to think of relief or remedy words to check.

Relief/Remedy—suit, damages, litigation, injunction, specific performance

ASSIGNMENT 11.11

This assignment asks you to identify as many index (and table of contents) entries as you can that may cover designated topics. Use the CARTWHEEL, descriptive words, TAPP, and TARPP systems. Go to the indexes (and tables of contents) in the sets of books indicated. Make a notation of *every* index (and table of contents) entry that appears to cover the topic. Try to find multiple entries in the indexes (and tables of contents) for the topic you are searching. In class, the teacher may call on you to indicate what entries you found that appeared to be successful so that others in the class can compare their entries with yours.

(a) Rape. Books to use: your state statutory code.

(b) Race discrimination. Books to use: the state digest that covers your state courts.

(c) Suicide. Books to use: *American Jurisprudence 2d.*

(d) Divorce. Books to use: *Corpus Juris Secundum.*

(e) Pollution. Books to use: *Index to Annotations.*

[SECTION N]

THE FIRST LEVEL OF LEGAL RESEARCH: BACKGROUND

There are three interrelated levels of researching a problem:

Background Research. Provides you with a general understanding of the area of law involved in your research problem.

Specific Fact Research. Provides you with primary and secondary authority that covers the specific facts of your research problem.

Validation Research. Provides you with information on the current validity of all the primary authority you intend to use in your research memorandum on the problem.

At times, all three levels of research go on simultaneously. If you are new to legal research, however, it is recommended that you approach your research problem in three separate stages or levels. Our concern in this section is the first level: background research. See Exhibit 11.18. The other two levels are covered throughout the remainder of this chapter.

Let us assume you are researching a topic that is totally new to you. Where do you begin? What law books do you take off the shelves, or what computer databases or files do you start checking? More specifically:

- Should you start looking for federal law or state law?
- Should you begin looking for statutes or for court opinions?
- Should you check constitutional law?
- Should you check procedural law?
- Should you check administrative law?
- Should you check ordinances or other local laws?

By definition, you don't know the answers to such questions—we are assuming that you have never researched a problem like the one now before you. Of course, you will want to ask your supervisor for direction on where to begin. Also, you should try to seek out a colleague who may have some time to provide you with initial guidance. But suppose that such assistance is fairly minimal or is simply not available. Where do you begin?

Start with some of the ten techniques for doing background research outlined in Exhibit 11.18. Spend an hour or two (depending on the complexity of the problem) doing some read-

EXHIBIT 11.18	Techniques for Doing Background Research on a Topic: Getting the Big Picture

1. **Legal Dictionaries**

   Your research problem will have a vocabulary consisting of all the legal terms that will be involved. A legal dictionary is one way to begin collecting definitions of these terms. The definitions in dictionaries are not as authoritative as the definitions you may eventually find in statutes, regulations, and opinions. But the legal dictionary is a good place to start. Here are examples of dictionaries:

   ▪ *Black's Law Dictionary*
   ▪ *Oran's Law Dictionary*
   ▪ *Statsky's Legal Thesaurus/Dictionary*

   The Internet can also be used as a legal dictionary. In Google, for example, type the word you want defined (e.g., libel) immediately after a colon and the word *define* (define:libel) to obtain sites that will give you definitions. Other online legal dictionaries include:

   ▪ dictionary.lp.findlaw.com
   ▪ dictionary.law.com
   ▪ www.jurist.law.pitt.edu/dictionary.htm
   ▪ www.lectlaw.com/def.htm

2. **Legal Encyclopedias**

   Find discussions of your topic in the major national *legal encyclopedias:*

   > *American Jurisprudence 2d*
   > *Corpus Juris Secundum*

   Also check encyclopedias, if any, that cover only your state. Use the CARTWHEEL to help you use their indexes. You should also consider checking online encyclopedias such as Wikipedia (en.wikipedia.org). They may not have in-depth, reliable treatment of every topic, but their extensive network of links on legal and nonlegal topics is impressive.

3. **Legal Treatises**

   Find discussions of your topic in *legal treatises.* Go to your card or computer catalog in the library. Use the CARTWHEEL to help you locate treatises such as hornbooks, nutshells, handbooks, form books, practice manuals, scholarly studies, etc. Many of these books will have *KF call numbers.* If there are open stacks in the library, go to the KF section to browse through what is available on the shelves. Use the CARTWHEEL to help you use the indexes of these books.

4. **Annotations**

   Find discussions of your topic in the *annotations* of A.L.R. (A.L.R. 1st), A.L.R.2d, A.L.R.3d, A.L.R.4th, A.L.R.5th, A.L.R.6th, A.L.R. Fed., and A.L.R.Fed.2d. Use the CARTWHEEL to help you find these discussions through indexes such as the *ALR Index.*

5. **Legal Periodical Literature**

   Find discussions of your topic in *legal periodical* literature. The three main indexes to such literature are:

   > *Index to Legal Periodicals and Books* (ILP)
   > *Current Law Index* (CLI)
   > *LegalTrac* (the online version of CLI)

   Use the CARTWHEEL to help you use these indexes to locate legal periodical literature on your topic.

6. **Agency Reports/Brochures**

   If your research involves an administrative agency, contact the agency to determine what agency reports, brochures, or newsletters are available to the public. The Web site of most agencies has a search box. Type in the topic of your research to find out what is available online. Agency literature often provides useful background information.

7. **Committee Reports**

   Many research projects involve one or more statutes. Before statutes are passed, committees of the legislature often write *committee reports* that comment on and summarize the legislation. (See Exhibit 6.5 in chapter 6.) In addition to being good sources of legislative history on the statute, the reports are excellent background reading:

   ▪ For federal statutes, go to the Web site of the Library of Congress (thomas.loc.gov), and click "committee reports" to find out what reports are available online. (On library shelves, check the volumes of *U.S. Code Congressional and Administrative News* [U.S.C.C.A.N.], which prints many committee reports.)
   ▪ For state statutes, go to the homepage of your state legislature and look for links to committee reports.

8. **Reports/Studies of Special Interest Groups**

   There are *special interest* groups for almost every area of the law, e.g., unions, bar associations, environmental associations, tax associations, insurance and other business associations. They often have position papers and studies that may be available. Although one-sided, such literature should not be ignored. The best place to find this literature is on the Web site of the organization. Want an overview of adoption law? Check the many reports and policy statements of the National Council for Adoption (www.adoptioncouncil.org). Want an overview of tobacco litigation? Check the Web site of a tobacco manufacturer (www.altria.com) and of an antismoking organization (www.tobacco.neu.edu). A wealth of links and information is available, waiting to be sifted through.

(continues)

| EXHIBIT 11.18 | Techniques for Doing Background Research on a Topic—*continued* |

9. Martindale-Hubbell Law Digest

The Law Digest within *Martindale-Hubbell Law Directory* provides concise summaries of the law of the fifty states and many foreign countries. Unfortunately, the volume edition of the Law Digest has been discontinued. Check with your library to see if it has the CD–ROM or online edition or whether it keeps the older volume (paper) edition on its shelf.

10. Law-Dash Searches on the Internet

We have already mentioned ways to use the Internet to do background research by going to the Web sites of specific agencies, legislatures, and special interest groups. In addition, try *law-dash* searches on any general or legal search engine. A law-dash search begins with the word *law* and connects key words by dashes. You may be led to sites that provide the kind of overview you need when you begin legal research on a topic that is new to you. Examples of law-dash searches:

- law-abortion
- law-manslaughter
- law-civil-rights
- law-guardianship
- law-attractive nuisance

Some of the results of such searches will be to Web sites of attorneys practicing in these areas of the law. In addition to self-promotion on the sites, the attorneys may give summaries of the law and relevant links that can be useful.

ing in law books and Web sites you will be led to by these techniques. This will give you an overview or "big picture" of the area(s) of law involved in your research problem. With this general understanding (including the relevant *terms of art*), you will be in a better position to be able to identify the major questions or issues you need to address. Of course, while doing this background research, you will probably also come up with leads that will be helpful in the second and third levels of research.

Most of this background research will be in secondary authority—legal dictionaries, legal encyclopedias, legal treatises, legal periodical literature, etc. Use these materials for the limited purposes of (1) doing background reading and (2) providing leads to primary authority—particularly through footnotes. You will not have time to use all of the ten techniques of background research presented in Exhibit 11.18. Usually, two or three are sufficient for the limited purpose of providing an overview and getting you started. Of course, the first technique on the legal dictionary will be one that you will use throughout all stages of your research.

Exhibit 11.19 illustrates the kind of information you should be able to derive from background research.

ASSIGNMENT 11.12

Fill out the checklist in Exhibit 11.19 for the following research questions. Assume that the individuals involved in each of these questions live in your state.

(a) Can a woman agree (for a fee) to bear the child of another woman using in vitro fertilization?

(b) Can a doctor assist a patient to commit suicide?

(c) Can a private citizen lend money for a fee on the Internet?

(d) Can a church be forced to pay taxes on profits from its bingo games?

[SECTION O]
CHECKLISTS FOR USING NINE MAJOR SEARCH RESOURCES

We have said that the main objective of legal research is to locate mandatory primary authority. There are three levels of government—federal, state, and local. Exhibit 11.20 presents an overview of their primary authority.

For definitions of these primary authorities (constitution, statute, opinion, etc.), see Exhibit 6.1 in chapter 6.

EXHIBIT 11.19	Checklist of Information to Try to Obtain through Background Research

MAJOR AREAS OF LAW THAT MAY BE INVOLVED IN THE RESEARCH PROBLEM
(circle those that preliminarily seem applicable)

antitrust	corporations	immigration	sales
bankruptcy	criminal law	insurance	sea
children	employment	international	securities
civil procedure	environment	labor relations	sports
civil rights	estates and probate	landlord-tenant	taxation
commercial	ethics	military	torts
communications	evidence	municipalities	trademarks
constitutional law	family	partnership	transportation
consumer	fraud	patents	women
contracts	gifts	public benefits	other
copyright	health	real estate	

JURISDICTIONS THAT MAY NEED TO BE CHECKED
(circle those that preliminarily seem applicable)

Federal	State	Local	International

PRIMARY AUTHORITY THAT MAY NEED TO BE CHECKED
(circle those that preliminarily seem applicable; see Exhibit 6.1 in chapter 6)

opinions	administrative decisions	executive orders
statutes	charters	treaties
constitutions	ordinances	
administrative regulations	rules of court	

MAJOR CAUSES OF ACTION AND DEFENSES THAT NEED TO BE EXPLORED

MAJOR TERMS OF ART THAT APPEAR TO BE CRITICAL AND THAT NEED TO BE DEFINED

CITATIONS TO MAJOR STATUTES THAT MIGHT BE APPLICABLE

CITATIONS TO MAJOR ADMINISTRATIVE REGULATIONS THAT MIGHT BE APPLICABLE

CITATIONS TO MAJOR COURT OPINIONS THAT MIGHT BE APPLICABLE

How do you find the law outlined in Exhibit 11.20? The main ways are to use the following nine search resources or tools:

Catalogs	Legal periodical literature
Digests	Legal encyclopedias
Annotations	Legal treatises
Shepard's	E-mail
Looseleaf services	

EXHIBIT 11.20	Kinds of Primary Authority

Federal Level of Government	State Level of Government	Local Level of Government (City, County, etc.)
U.S. Constitution	State constitution	Charter
Statutes of Congress	State statutes	Local ordinances
Federal court opinions	State court opinions	Local court opinions
Federal administrative regulations	State administrative regulations	Local administrative regulations
Federal administrative decisions	State administrative decisions	Local administrative decisions
Federal rules of court	State rules of court	Local rules of court
Executive orders of the president	Executive orders of the governor	Executive orders of the mayor
Treaties		

(For the definitions of these primary authorities, see Exhibit 6.1 in chapter 6.)

A tenth overlapping resource is the computer. In the remainder of the chapter, we will continue to refer to research that can be performed on free and fee-based Internet sites. Extensive coverage of online research will also be provided in chapter 13 on computers in the law.

Because the nine search resources can often be used to find more than one category of primary authority, they are presented together here in Section O. Later in the chapter, we will be referring back to this section often. In short, the search resources are extremely important. Indeed, they can be considered the foundation of legal research itself.

TOPICS FOR SECTION O ASSIGNMENTS 11.13 TO 11.22

The following topics will be used for the assignments in section O. You will be referred back to these topics throughout our study of the nine search resources covered in this section. In each assignment, you are to assume that your legal research problem involves the topic indicated in (a) to (o) below. Use the CARTWHEEL to help you locate material in whatever search resources the assignment is asking you to check.

For these assignments, your instructor may require you to do all of the topics (a to o) or selected ones.

TOPICS

(a) A local government uses its zoning laws to try to close a bar that features topless dancers.

(b) A minor daughter challenges the validity of a deceased parent's will that leaves everything to the parent's pet cat.

(c) A newspaper falsely prints that an individual had been convicted of child molestation.

(d) A client is angry at his attorney for revealing to the police that the client fantasized about killing the president of the United States.

(e) A civil suit against a homeowner is brought by a burglar for injuries received when the burglar fell because of a defective floor in the house being burglarized.

(f) A high school teacher is disciplined for using a Scientology workbook in class.

(g) A husband is arrested after his wife accuses him of raping her.

(h) A father wants to revoke the adoption of a child he did not know existed at the time of the adoption; the mother told him the baby died in childbirth.

(i) A man sues to prevent an abortion from being performed on the woman he impregnated; the woman is a mentally retarded, unmarried adult living with her parents, who are arranging the abortion.

(j) A lesbian sues the Girl Scouts organization that turned down her application to be a volunteer because of her sexual orientation.

(k) A parent seeks to invalidate the marriage of his thirteen-year-old daughter who married her first cousin, also thirteen years old.

(l) A paralegal is charged with insider trading after buying stock in a company that is a client in the law firm where the paralegal works.

(m) A patient wants to prevent his doctor from telling the patient's health insurance company about the patient's AIDS status.

(n) A person wants to cancel a contract to buy a house because the seller failed to disclose that there had recently been a murder in the house.

(o) A patient is scheduled for surgery where her right arm is to be amputated; by mistake, the surgeon amputates the left arm.

---

1. CATALOGS

A well-organized catalog is one of the researcher's best friends. Many large law libraries have computerized their catalogs. Some are available on the Internet for free. Examples of Internet catalogs of law libraries:

catalog.loc.gov
ringding.law.yale.edu
gull.georgetown.edu
lib.law.washington.edu

You should also know how to use a traditional manual card catalog. You may be using a library that does not have a sophisticated online catalog. Furthermore, knowing how to use a card catalog will increase your competence in using online catalogs. Most law libraries use the *Library of Congress (LC) classification system.* Under this system, many law books have KF call numbers. Here is an example of a card from a card catalog:

Most law libraries have open stacks, meaning that users are free to browse through all or some of the shelves. Take advantage of this opportunity when it exists. Go to the KF section to do some browsing. Here are some examples of topics (with their beginning KF call numbers) that you might want to explore to find out what your library has available on the shelves:

Civil Procedure Law: KF 8810   Domestic Relations: KF 501
Constitutional Law: KF 4501   Paralegals: KF 320L
Corporate Law: KF 1384   Real Property Law: KF 560
Criminal Law: KF 9201   Tort Law: KF 1246
Ethics: KF 300   Trials: KF 8910
Lawyers: KF 297   Wills and Trusts: KF 728

If you are browsing the aisles of a library that uses the Dewey Decimal Classification (DDC) system, many of the law-related books are found in the aisles that begin with number 340. (Civil procedure and courts, for example, are found at 347.) Exhibit 11.21 presents guidelines on using the catalog effectively.

2. DIGESTS

We have already examined the major digests and the names of reporters whose opinions are summarized (in brief paragraphs) in the digests. You should review this material now. See Exhibit 11.6. See also research links A, E, I, J, and L earlier in the chapter on the relationship between regional reporters and regional digests.

EXHIBIT 11.21	Checklist for Using the Catalog

1. Find out what kind of catalog your library uses. A card (paper) catalog? Computer? Locate the description of how to use the catalog. (The how-to material for computerized catalogs may be online or available through a HELP key on the keyboard.) If the library still uses the card catalog, there may be more than one available. For example, one set of cards may alphabetize all books by author name, while another may alphabetized them by book title.
2. Select several entries from the catalog at random. Pick ones that appear to contain different kinds of information. Try to figure out why they are different. If you can't, ask a staff member of the library for a brief explanation of the differences.
3. Be sure you understand the information in the catalog that tells you where the books are located in the library. Some books may be on reserve, in special rooms, or in other buildings.
4. Select several KF entries at random, particularly on books housed in different locations within the same building. Try to

find these books on the shelves. Ask for help if you cannot locate them.
5. Now try the reverse process. Select at random three different kinds of books from the library shelves (not the same books you looked at in step 4 above). Take these books to the catalog and try to find the entries for them. Your goal is to become as proficient in the structure and use of the catalog as possible. Steps 2–5 are designed to help you achieve this goal *before* you experience the pressure of actual research.
6. Ask a staff member what kinds of research material, if any, are *not* cataloged, such as microfilm, ultrafiche, appellate briefs, or old exams.
7. Ask whether the library can obtain books for you at other libraries through interlibrary loan.
8. Some law books received by the library are serial subscriptions, e.g., a legal periodical, a looseleaf service.

(continues)

EXHIBIT 11.21	Checklist for Using the Catalog—*continued*

The subscription can include units such as pocket parts, supplemental pamphlets, insert pages, and new hardcover volumes received throughout the year. When you use the library's catalog, are you told what is the most recent unit of the subscription received by the library? (Check any serial subscription at random.) If not, ask a librarian how you can find out. (Simply looking at what is on the shelf may not tell you since the latest unit may have been misshelved or may be in use.)

9. When a library decides to cancel a serial subscription, it does not always remove from the shelves the issues or volumes in the subscription that arrived before the cancellation. This may mislead you into thinking that what is on the shelves

is current. You need to know what the library is no longer updating. There may be a sign on the shelf that says something like "Subscription Discontinued in 2005." The surest way to find out is the catalog. It should indicate whether a particular subscription has been discontinued and, if so, as of what date.

10. When using any catalog, the CARTWHEEL will help you think of words and phrases to check.

11. Never antagonize the employees of a law library. You are going to need all the help you can get! Do not abuse their availability. Do not ask any questions until you first try to find the answer on your own.

ASSIGNMENT 11.13

(a) Use the catalog of a law library near you to find the call number (e.g., a KF number) of one law book that might be helpful in researching each of the topics for the Section O assignments (see page 525). Most of the law books you will select will be legal treatises or looseleaf services, but you are not limited to these categories of books. You can use any law book so long as you locate it through the catalog. Pick one per topic. Give the citation of each book and place a check mark next to the citation to indicate that you were able to locate the book on the shelves of the library. (If you can't locate the book, pick a different one from the catalog.) If the title of the book you select does not indicate that the book probably covers the topic, give the heading of a chapter, section, or page in the book showing that the topic is probably covered in the book. At the top of your answer sheet, give the name and address of the law library you used.

(b) Repeat section (a), with the following modifications: use an Internet catalog (e.g., catalog.loc. gov), and select books that are different from the ones you selected for section (a). You do not need to indicate whether the books you find in the catalog exist on the shelves of the library.

Our focus here is on the digests of West Group. The thousands of opinions summarized in these digests are organized by the *key number system*. Every important issue examined in an opinion is summarized in a short paragraph (called a *headnote*) and assigned a topic and number (called a *key number*) by West Group editors. As we will see, these paragraphs are printed in several places, such as in the digests of West Group. Paragraphs with the same key number are printed together in the digests. This enables a researcher to find numerous opinions on the same point of law. For example, the constitutionality of capital punishment is assigned to the topic of Sentencing and Punishment, key number 1612. You can go to any West Group digest, take down the "S" volume, find Sentencing and Punishment, and turn to number 1612 to try to find a potentially large number of different opinions that covered this issue.

The beauty of the West Group digests is that once you know how to use one of the digests, you know how to use them all. To demonstrate this, we begin by following the journey of a court opinion (and its headnotes) from the time the opinion arrives at West Group. (See Exhibit 11.22.)

EXHIBIT 11.22	Journey of a Court Opinion and Its Headnotes

Journey of a State Court Opinion, e.g., California

1. The California Supreme Court sends a copy of its opinion to West Group in Minnesota.
2. West Group editors write brief paragraph *headnotes* for the opinion. Each headnote is a summary of a portion of the opinion.

Journey of a Federal Court Opinion, e.g., a U.S. Court of Appeals

1. The U.S. Court of Appeals sends a copy of its opinion to West Group in Minnesota.
2. West Group editors write brief paragraph *headnotes* for the opinion. Each headnote is a summary of a portion of the opinion.

(continues)

| EXHIBIT 11.22 | Journey of a Court Opinion and Its Headnotes—*continued* |

Journey of a State Court Opinion, e.g., California	Journey of a Federal Court Opinion, e.g., a U.S. Court of Appeals
3. The headnotes are printed at the beginning of the full text of the opinion in the reporter—here, the *Pacific Reporter* 3d (P.3d). The editors assign each of these headnotes a key number, which consists of a topic and a number, e.g., Criminal Law 🔑 1064(5).	3. The headnotes are printed at the beginning of the full text of the opinion in the reporter—here, the *Federal Reporter* 3d (F.3d). The editors assign each of these headnotes a key number, which consists of a topic and a number, e.g., Appeal and Error 🔑 336.1.
4. This headnote is also printed in the appropriate digests of West Group. (When a headnote is printed in a digest, it is sometimes called a *digest paragraph.*) The above examples will go in the "C" volume of these digests where "Criminal Law" is covered. The headnote will be placed under key number 1064(5) of Criminal Law, along with summaries of other opinions on the same or similar areas of law. In what digests will such headnotes from a recent California opinion be printed? The list follows:	4. This headnote is also printed in the appropriate digests of West Group. (When a headnote is printed in a digest, it is sometimes called a *digest paragraph.*) The above example will go in the "A" volume of these digests where "Appeal and Error" is covered. The headnote will be placed under key number 336.1 of Appeal and Error, along with summaries of other opinions on the same or similar areas of law. In what digests will such headnotes from a recent F.3d opinion be printed? The list follows:
■ All headnotes of P.3d cases go into the American Digest System. First, the headnote goes into a *General Digest* volume. After a ten-year period (in two five-year intervals), all the *General Digests* are thrown away, with the material in them printed in the next *Decennial Digest.*	■ All headnotes of F.3d cases go into the American Digest System. First, the headnote goes into a *General Digest* volume. After a ten-year period (in two five-year intervals), all the *General Digests* are thrown away, with the material in them printed in the next *Decennial Digest.*
■ All headnotes of P.3d cases are also printed in its regional digest—the *Pacific Digest* 2d.	■ All headnotes of F.3d cases are also printed in the most current federal digest—the *Federal Practice Digest 4th.*
■ All headnotes of California cases in P.3d are also printed in the individual state digest—the *California Digest 2d.*	■ If our F.3d case dealt with a particular state, the headnotes of the F.3d case will also be printed in the individual state digest of that state.
5. Hence, the headnote from the opinion of the California Supreme Court will be printed:	5. Hence, the headnote from the opinion of the U.S. Court of Appeals will be printed:
■ at the beginning of the opinion in P.3d.	■ at the beginning of the opinion in F.3d.
■ in the American Digest System (first in the *General Digest* and then in the *Decennial Digest*).	■ in the American Digest System (first in the *General Digest* and then in the *Decennial Digest*).
■ in the regional digest—*Pacific Digest 2d.*	■ in the *Federal Practice Digest 4th.*
■ in the individual state digest—*California Digest 2d.*	■ in a state digest if the F.3d case dealt with a particular state.
In all the above digests, the headnote will be printed in the "C" volume for Criminal Law under number 1064(5), along with headnotes from other opinions on the same or similar area of the law.	In all the above digests, the headnote will be printed in the "A" volume for Appeal and Error under number 336.1, along with headnotes from other opinions on the same or similar area of the law.
6. Finally, West Group publishes all of these opinions and headnotes on Westlaw, its computer research system. (See research link F on the need to translate a digest key number into a Westlaw k number so that you can find cases digested online under the same topics.)	6. Finally, West Group publishes all of these opinions and headnotes on Westlaw, its computer research system. (See research link F on the need to translate a digest key number into a Westlaw k number so that you can find cases digested online under the same topics.)

Keep the following points in mind about Exhibit 11.22:

■ All state court opinions printed in West Group's reporters from the 50 states go through the process or journey outlined in the *first* column of Exhibit 11.22 for California. Of course, different states have their own reporters and digests (see Exhibit 11.6), but the process is the same.

■ All U.S. District Court opinions printed in *Federal Supplement* (F. Supp. 2d) go through the process or journey outlined in the *second* column of Exhibit 11.22. for U.S. Court of Appeals opinions.

■ All U.S. Supreme Court opinions printed in *Supreme Court Reporter* (S. Ct.) go through the process or journey outlined in the *second* column of Exhibit 11.22. (For additional digests that summarize all U.S. Supreme Court opinions, see Exhibit 11.6.)

Assume that you are doing research on the right of a citizen to speak in a public park. You find that the digests of West Group cover this subject under the following key number:

Constitutional Law 🔑 211

West Group publishes about sixty digests—state, federal, and national. (See Exhibit 11.6.) You can go to the "C" volume of *any* of these sixty digests, turn to "Constitutional Law," and look for number "211" under it. Do you want only Idaho case law? If so, go to Constitutional Law 🔑 211 in the *Idaho Digest.* Do you want only case law from the states in the western United States? If so, go to

Constitutional Law 211 in the *Pacific Digest 2d*. Do you want only current federal case law? If so, go to Constitutional Law 211 in the *Federal Practice Digest 4th*. Do you want only U.S. Supreme Court cases? If so, go to Constitutional Law 211 in the *U.S. Supreme Court Digest* (West Group). When you check a key number in multiple digests such as these, you are **tracing a key number**. Do you want the case law of *every* court in the country? If so, trace Constitutional Law 211 through the three units of the American Digest System:

- Go to Constitutional Law 211 in every *General Digest* volume.
- Go to Constitutional Law 211 in every *Decennial Digest*.
- Go to the equivalent number for Constitutional Law 211 in the *Century Digest*.

To trace a key number through the American Digest System means to find out what case law, if any, is summarized under its topic and number in every unit of the American Digest System. (For the *Century Digest*, you will need an equivalent number because there are no key numbers in the *Century Digest*. See step 7 in the checklist in Exhibit 11.23.)

tracing a key number Finding out what case law, if any, is digested (summarized) under a particular key number in different digests of West Group.

Excerpt from a West Group Digest
(this excerpt contains two key numbers: Aliens 54.3(4) and Aliens 54.3(4))

54.3(3) ALIENS

N.D.Ill. 1996. District court's review in case denying visa petition is limited to determination whether Immigration and Naturalization Service's (INS) denial of visa petition was abuse of discretion.—Grimson v. I.N.S., 934 F.Supp. 965.

54.3(4). — Evidence and questions of law or fact.

C.A.D.C. 1996. Standard of review for equal protection challenge to immigration statute is that statute will be upheld if based on facially legitimate and bona fide reason. U.S.C.A. Const.Amend. 5.—Miller v. Christopher, 96 F.3d 1467, 321 U.S.App.D.C. 19.

C.A.5 1996. Determination that elements of crime constitute moral turpitude for purposes of deportation is question of law, which Court of Appeals reviews de novo. Immigration and Nationality Act, § 241(a)(2)(A)(i), 8 U.S.C.A. § 1251(a)(2)(A)(i).—Hamdan v. I.N.S., 98 F.3d 183.

C.A.9 1996. Because neither immigration judge (15) nor Board of Immigration Appeals (BIA) made explicit finding on credibility of petitioner, Court of Appeals would accept petitioner's testimony as credible.—Prasad v. I.N.S., 101 F.3d 614. Court of Appeals will uphold Board of Immigration Appeals (BIA) determination unless evidence compels contrary conclusion.—Id.

C.A.9 1996. Court of Appeals reviews for substantial evidence Board of Immigration Appeals (BIA) determination of eligibility for asylum. Immigration and Nationality Act, § 208(a), as amended, 8 U.S.C.A. § 1158(a).—Lopez-Galarza v. I.N.S., 99 F.3d 954.

EXHIBIT 11.23 **Checklist for Using the Digests of West Group**

1. Locate the right digests for your research problem. This is determined by identifying the kind of case law you want to find. State? Federal? Both? Review Exhibit 11.6 on the American Digest System, the four regional digests, the major federal digests, the digest for U.S. Supreme Court cases, and the individual state digests. You must know what kind of case law is summarized in each of these digests.
2. Find key numbers that cover your research problem. There are hundreds of topics and subtopics in West's digests. How

do you find the ones relevant to your research problem? There are eight techniques:
- Descriptive Word Index (DWI). Every digest has a **DWI**. Use the CARTWHEEL to help you locate key topics in the DWI.
- Table of Contents. There are over 400 main digest topics (e.g., Constitutional Law, Criminal Law), which are covered throughout the volumes of the digest you are using. At the beginning of each main topic, you will find a table of contents. If you can find one of these main topics in the

(continues)

EXHIBIT 11.23   Checklist for Using the Digests of West Group—*continued*

general area of your research, you then use its table of contents to locate specific key numbers. These tables of contents have different names: "*Scope Note,*" "Analysis," or "Subjects Included." Use the CARTWHEEL to help you locate key numbers in them.

■ Headnote in West Group Reporter. Suppose that you already have an opinion on point. You are reading its full text in a West Group reporter. Go to the most relevant headnotes at the beginning of this opinion. (For example, see the search and seizure headnotes at the beginning of the *Bruni* opinion in chapter 7.) Each headnote has a key number. Use this key number to go to any of the digests to try to find more case law under that number.

■ Table of Cases in the Digests. Suppose again that you already have an opinion on point. You are reading its full text in a West Group reporter. Go to the table of cases in the American Digest System or in any other digest that covers the reporter your opinion is in. Look up the name of the opinion in this table of cases. (If you can't find it, check this table in the pocket part of the volume you are using. Not all digest volumes, however, have pocket parts.) If you find your opinion in the table, you will be told what key numbers that opinion is digested under in the digest. Go to those key numbers in the body of the digest to find that opinion summarized, along with other opinions under the same key numbers. (Note: the table of cases in some West Group digests is called *plaintiff-defendant table* or *defendant-plaintiff table,* depending on which party's name comes first. The defendant-plaintiff table is useful if you happen to know only the name of the defendant or if you want many opinions where the same party was sued, e.g., General Motors. Defendant-plaintiff tables usually refer you back to the plaintiff-defendant table, where the key numbers are listed.)

■ Library References in a West Group Statutory Code. After West Group prints the full text of statutes in the statutory codes it publishes, it also provides research references, such as historical note, cross references, library references, and notes of decisions. The library references give you key numbers on topics covered in the statutes. For an example, see Exhibit 11.39 containing an excerpt from a statutory code (§ 146). After the text of the statute, there are library references to two key numbers: Prisons 13, and Reformatories 7. Hence a West Group statutory code has given you a lead to a key number, which you can take to any of the West Group digests to find case law.

■ Leads in Legal Encyclopedias. Both of the national legal encyclopedias, *Corpus Juris Secundum* (C.J.S.) and *American Jurisprudence 2d* (Am. Jur. 2d), will include leads to key numbers of West Group digests on those topics.

■ Leads in A.L.R. Annotations, Recent volumes of *American Law Reports 5th* and *6th* and *American Law Reports Fed.* will give you leads to key numbers as part of the annotations in these volumes.

■ Westlaw. One of the searches you can make on Westlaw is a digest field search, which will give you almost instant access to the millions of headnotes printed in West Group digests. (See research link F on the need to translate a digest key number into a Westlaw k number.)

3. Assume that while using the Descriptive Word Index (DWI) in any of the digests, you come across a key number that appears to be relevant to your research problem. But when you go to check that number in the body of the digest, you find no case law. The DWI has, in effect, led you to nonexistent

case law. The editors are telling you that there are no cases digested under this key number *at this time,* Go to the table of contents for the main topic you are in. Check the "Analysis" or "Scope Note" there to see if you can find a more productive key number. Or, go to a different digest to see if you will have more luck with your original key number.

4. West Group editors occasionally add new topics and numbers to the key number system. Hence you may find topics and numbers in later digests that are not in earlier digest volumes.

5. West Group digests obviously duplicate each other in some respects. The American Digest System, for example, contains everything that is in all the other digests. A regional digest will duplicate everything found in the individual state digests covered in that region. (See the chart in Exhibit 11.6) It is wise, nevertheless, to check more than one digest. Some digests may be more up to date than others in your library. You may miss something in one digest that you will catch in another.

6. Be sure you know all the units of the most comprehensive digest—the American Digest System: *Century Digest, Decennial Digests, General Digest.* These units are distinguished solely by the period of time covered by each unit. Know what these periods of time are: *Century Digest* (1658–1896), *Decennial Digests* (ten-year periods, although since the *Ninth Decennial* they come in two five-year parts), *General Digest* (the period since the last *Decennial Digest* was printed).

7. At the time the *Century Digest* was printed, West Group had not invented the key number system. Hence topics are listed in the *Century Digest* by *section* numbers rather than by key numbers. Assume that you started your research in the *Century Digest.* You located a relevant section number and you now want to trace this number through the *Decennial Digests* and the *General Digest.* To do this, you need a corresponding *key* number. There is a parallel table in volume 21 of the *First Decennial* that will tell you the corresponding key number for any section number in the *Century Digest.* Suppose, however, that you started your research in the *Decennial Digests* or the *General Digest.* You have a key number and now want to find its corresponding section number in the *Century Digest.* In the *First Decennial* and *Second Decennial,* there is a "see" reference under the key number that will tell you the corresponding section number in the *Century Digest.*

8. Tricks of the trade are also needed in using the *General Digest,* which covers the most recent period since the last *Decennial Digest* was printed. When the current ten-year period is over, all the *General Digest* volumes will be thrown away. The material in them will be consolidated or cumulated into the next *Decennial Digest* (which is issued in two five-year parts beginning with the *Ninth Decennial*). When you go to use the *General Digest,* there may be twenty to thirty bound volumes on the shelf. To be thorough in tracing a key number in the *General Digest,* you must check *all* these bound volumes. There is, however, a shortcut. Look for the *Table of Key Numbers* within every tenth volume of the *General Digest.* This table tells you which *General Digest* volumes contain anything under the key number you are searching. You do not have to check the other nine *General Digest* volumes.

9. For an overview of digests and their use, see:
   ■ www.ll.georgetown.edu/lib/guides/digests.html
   ■ www.ll.georgetown.edu/tutorials/cases/index.cfm
   ■ www.bu.edu/lawlibrary/research/guides/digests.html
   ■ lawlibrary.uoregon.edu/guides/westdig.html
   ■ www.law.syr.edu/Pdfs/0WestCaseRepsAndDigs.pdf
   ■ www.law2.byu.edu/Law_Library/Digital_Collections/ Legal_Res_Guides/Leg_Res_Guide2.html

One final point: The headnotes and digests we are discussing are written by a private publishing company—West Group. You never quote headnotes or digests in your legal writing. They *cannot* be authority—primary or secondary. They are mere leads to case law.

ASSIGNMENT 11.14

Go to any West Group digest that covers cases of your state courts. (See Exhibit 11.6.) Find any two key numbers that might be helpful in researching each of the topics for the Section O assignments (see page 525). Pick two per topic. Under both key numbers, find a case written by a state court in your state or by a federal court that sits in your state. If you cannot find a case written by such a court in either of the key numbers, select a different key number until you are able to find one. Give the key number, the citation of the case, and a statement of why you think the case might cover the problem. Also specify which digest you used.

3. ANNOTATIONS

An annotation is a note or commentary that summarizes or provides explanation. The most extensive annotations are those of West Group in the following eight sets of books:

A.L.R. (A.L.R.1st)	A.L.R.5th
American Law Reports, First	*American Law Reports, Fifth*
A.L.R.2d	A.L.R.6th
American Law Reports, Second	*American Law Reports, Sixth*
A.L.R.3d	A.L.R. Fed.
American Law Reports, Third	*American Law Reports, Federal*
A.L.R.4th	A.L.R. Fed. 2d
American Law Reports, Fourth	*American Law Reports, Federal 2d*

All eight sets are reporters in that they print opinions in full. They are *annotated reporters* in that notes or commentaries are provided with each opinion in the form of an annotation. Unlike the regional reporters of West Group, the annotated reporters contain only a small number of opinions. The editors select opinions raising novel or interesting issues, which then become the basis of an annotation. The following is an example of the beginning of an annotation found on page 1015 of Volume 91 of A.L.R.3d:

One of the joys of legal research is finding an annotation **on point**. A wealth of information is contained in annotations, such as a comprehensive, state-by-state survey of law on an issue. A single annotation often contains hundreds of citations to court opinions. Picture yourself having the capacity to hire your own team of researchers to go out and spend days finding just about all the case law that exists on a particular point of law. Though none of us is likely to have this luxury, we do have a close equivalent in the form of annotations in the eight sets of *American Law Reports*. They are a gold mine of research references. There are hundreds of volumes in these eight sets, so the chances are very good that you will find an annotation that is *on point*, i.e., that is relevant to the issues of your research problem.

Most of the references in the annotations are to case law; their primary service is to act as a case finder. Hence, they serve the same function as digests. The annotations of A.L.R. and the key number system of digests are both designed to help you find relevant court opinions. And, as we

on point Raising or covering the same issue as the one before you. Relevant to the issues of a research problem.

saw earlier, when you are reading current annotations in A.L.R., you will be given references to key numbers so that you can check digests on the same topics covered in the annotation.

The annotations cover both federal and state law. A.L.R.1st, A.L.R.2d, and most of A.L.R.3d cover both state and federal law. The later volumes of A.L.R.3d and all of A.L.R.4th, 5th, and 6th cover mainly state law. A.L.R. Fed. and A.L.R. Fed.2d cover only federal law. The annotations in these eight sets do not follow any particular order. There may be an annotation on zoning, for example, followed by an annotation on defective wheels on baby carriages. The annotations in A.L.R.1st and A.L.R.2d are older than the annotations in the other sets, but this is not significant because all of the annotations can be updated.

We turn now to the two major concerns of the researcher:

- How do you find an annotation on point?
- How do you update an annotation that you have found?

The major ways of finding annotations on point are outlined in Exhibit 11.24. As you can see, the eight sets of A.L.R. do not all have the same index or finding systems. Note that a fee-based database (Westlaw) is also listed as a way to find annotations.

EXHIBIT 11.24	How to Find an Annotation		
Finding annotations in A.L.R.1st	**Finding annotations in A.L.R.2d**	**Finding annotations in A.L.R.3rd, A.C.R.4th A.L.R.5th, and A.L.R.6th**	**Finding annotations in A.L.R. Fed. and A.L.R. Fed. 2d**
■ *ALR First Series Quick Index* ■ *ALR Digest* ■ Westlaw	■ *ALR Index* ■ Westlaw ■ *ALR Digest*	■ *ALR Index* ■ *ALR Quick Index 3d, 4th, 5th, 6th* ■ Westlaw ■ *ALR Digest*	■ *ALR Index* ■ *ALR Federal Quick Index* ■ Westlaw ■ *ALR Digest*

As indicated earlier, some of the annotations in the eight sets are very long and comprehensive. How do you find the law of a *particular* state or court within an annotation without having to read the entire annotation? At the beginning of each annotation, look for a table that is organized by state, by court, or by jurisdiction. The table might be called:

- Table of Jurisdictions Represented
- Table of Courts and Circuits
- Jurisdictional Table of Cited Statutes and Cases

This table will help determine where in the annotation your state or court is covered.

Suppose that you have found an annotation on point. It has led you to very useful law. This annotation, however, may be ten, twenty, thirty, or more years old. How do you *update* this annotation to find the most current law on the points covered in the annotation? Of course, any opinion or statute found within the annotation can be shepardized or KeyCited as a technique of finding more law. But our focus here is the updating systems within A.L.R. itself. Exhibit 11.25 outlines these systems.

The easiest way to update an annotation is to check the pocket part of the volume that contains the annotation. This method works for all eight sets *except* for A.L.R.1st and A.L.R.2d. There are no pocket parts for these two sets. Updating annotations in them requires checking the separate volumes listed in Exhibit 11.25.

EXHIBIT 11.25	How to Update an Annotation	
Updating an Annotation in A.L.R.1st	**Updating an Annotation in A.L.R.2d**	**Updating an Annotation in A.L.R.3d, A.L.R.4th, A.L.R.5th, A.L.R.6th, A.L.R. Fed., and A.L.R. Fed. 2d**
■ *A.L.R. Blue Book of Supplemental Decisions* ■ Annotation History Table in the last volume of *ALR Index*	■ *A.L.R.2d Later Case Service* ■ Annotation History Table in the last volume of *ALR Index*	■ Pocket part of volume containing the annotation ■ Annotation History Table in the last volume of *ALR Index*

Note: Any opinion or statute you find is an annotation can also be updated by Sheparding or KeyCiting that opinion or statute.

Tables Printed at the Beginning of Annotations That Tell You Where Your State or Court Is Covered in the Annotation

TABLE OF JURISDICTIONS REPRESENTED
Consult POCKET PART in this volume for later cases

US: §§ 2[b], 3, 4[a], 5[b], 6[a], 7[a], 10[b]
Ala: §§ 2[b], 4[a], 6[a], 7[a], 8, 10[b]
Cal: §§ 4[a, b], 7[a], b], 10[b], 11
Fla: §§ 5[a]
Ga: §§ 3, 4[b], 5[b], 6[b], 10[a]
Ill: §§ 4[b], 5[a, b], 6[a, b], 10[a]
Ind: §§ 4[a], 5[b], 6[a], 7[a, b], 8, 9, 10[b]
Iowa: §§ 7[a], 8
Ky: §§ 3, 4[a], 5[b]
La: §§ 5[b], 7[a, b]
Me: §§ 5[b], 7[a], 10[b]
Md: §§ 4[b]
Mich: §§ 4[a], 10[b]

Miss: §§ 4[a]
Mo: §§ 4[a], 6[a], 10[b]
NH: §§ 3, 4[b]
NC: §§ 7[a]
Ohio: §§ 4[a, b], 6[a], 7[a, b], 10[b]
Or: §§ 4[a], 10[b]
Pa: §§ 4[a], 7[a], 10[b]
Tenn: §§ 4[a], 5[b], 6[a]
Tex: §§ 4[a], 7[a], 10[b]
Vt: §§ 9
Wash: §§ 6[a], 7[a], 8
Wis: §§ 7[a], 8, 10[b], 11

TABLE OF COURTS AND CIRCUITS
Consult POCKET PART in this volume for later cases and statutory changes

Sup Ct: §§ 2[a], 3[a], 5, b, 14
First Cir: §6 5[b], 6[b], 15[b], 16[a], 18[a]
Second Cir: §§ 2[b], 3[a, b], 5[a], 12[a], 16[a], 18[a]
Third Cir: §§ 3[a], 5[a], 7, 11[b], 12[b], 13[a], 15[b]
Fourth Cir: §§ 2[b], 3[a], 4[b], 5[a, b], 8, 9, 10[b], 12[a, b], 13[b], 14, 15[a, b], 16[a], 17, 18[a]
Fifth Cir: §§ 3[a], 5[a, b], 8, 10[a], 11[a, b], 13[a], 15[a], 16[b], 18[b]

Sixth Cir: §§ 5[b], 6[b], 10[a, b], 12[a], 13[a], 15[b]
Seventh Cir: §§ 2[a], 4[b], 5[b], 10[b], 15[b]
Eighth Cir: §§ 3[a], 4[a, b], 5[a, b], 6[a], 12[a], 13[a], 15[b], 16[a], 17, 19
Ninth Cir: §§ 2[a, b], 3[a], 4[a], 5, a, 6[b], 7, 8, 10[a], 11[a, b], 12[a, b], 13[a, b], 15[a, b], 16[b], 17, 18[a, b]
Tenth Cir: §§ 2[b], 3[a], 5[a, b], 6[a, b], 9, 11[a, b], 12[a], 14, 17, 18[b]
Dist Col Cir: §§ 3[a], 5[b], 6[b], 10[a, b]
Ct Cl: § 16[a]

Jurisdictional Table of Cited Statutes and Cases

ALABAMA

A R Civ P, Rule 60(a). See §§ 4[a], 14[a]
Alabama R Civ P, Rule 60(a). see § 5[b]
Antepenko v Antepenko (1991, Ala Civ App) 584 So 2d 836–§ 4[a]
Cornelius v Green (1988, Ala) 521 So 2d 942–§ 5[b]
Merchant v Merchant (1992, Ala Civ App) 599 So 2d 1198–§ 14[a]

ARIZONA

16 A R S R Civ P, Rule 60(a). See § 10[b]
Harold Laz Advertising Co. v Dumes (1965) 2 Ariz App 236, 407 P2d 777–§ 10[b]

CALIFORNIA

Cal Code Civ Proc § 473. See §§ 6[a, b], 7[b], 10[a]
Cal Code Civ Proc § 579. See § 10[a]
Bastajian v Brown (1941) 19 Cal 2d 209, 120 P2d 9–§ 10[a]
Benway v Benway (1945) 69 Cal App 2d 574,159 P2d 682–§ 4[a]

Of course, if you are reading an annotation online through Westlaw, you are automatically given the most current cases for the annotation. You do not have to check more than one computer screen to obtain the most updated version of the annotation.

One final updating feature must be covered: the Annotation History Table. Note that Exhibit 11.25 lists this table as a further method of updating annotations in all eight sets of A.L.R. The law in some annotations may become so outdated that it is replaced by another annotation. The outdated annotation is called a *superseded annotation*, which should no longer be read. If, however, an annotation is substantially updated but not totally replaced by another annotation, the older annotation is called a *supplemented annotation*, which can be read along with the newer annotation. There are two ways to find out which annotations have been superseded or supplemented. Check the Annotation History Table found in the last volume of the *ALR Index*. Another way to find out is to check the standard method for updating annotations in A.L.R.1st (the *Blue Book*), in A.L.R.2d (*Later Case Service*), in A.L.R.3d (pocket parts), in A.L.R.4th (pocket parts), in A.L.R.5th (pocket parts), in A.L.R.6th (pocket parts), in A.L.R. Fed. (pocket parts), and in A.L.R. Fed. 2d (pocket parts).

Finally, there are two important two important ALR resources you should know about:

- *ALR Table of Laws, Rules and Regulations*
- *ALR Federal Tables*

Check these resources if you already have a statute or administrative regulation and you want to know whether any of the annotations have discussed them.

ASSIGNMENT 11.15

Find one annotation that might be helpful in researching each of the topics for the Section O assignments (see page 525). Locate one per topic. In each annotation, find a case written by a state court of your state or by a federal court that sits in your state. If you cannot find a case written by such a court, select a different annotation that does contain one. Give the citation of the annotation and of the case that it cites.

4. SHEPARD'S

There have been four great research inventions in the law:

- The key number system of the West Group digests
- The annotations in A.L.R. (A.L.R.1st), A.L.R.2d, A.L.R.3d, A.L.R.4th, A.L.R.5th, A.L.R.6th, A.L.R. Fed., and A.L.R. 2d Fed.

■ CALR (computer-assisted legal research), particularly the free Internet and major fee-based services such as Westlaw, LexisNexis, and Loislaw.
■ Shepard's

We have just examined the first two. CALR is covered here in chapter 11 and in chapter 13. We turn now to the fourth invention—Shepard's.

Shepardize

shepardize To use *Shepard's Citations* (in book form, on CD–ROM, or online) to obtain validation and other data on whatever you are checking or shepardizing.

The main meaning of the verb **shepardize** is to use the volumes (or CD–ROM or online version) of *Shepard's Citations* to obtain validation and other data on the primary authority you are checking. (The word *Shepard's* is shorthand for *Shepard's Citations*.) You can also shepardize some secondary authorities, such as legal periodical articles, although this is not as common as shepardizing primary authority. When you shepardize opinions, statutes, and other primary authorities, Shepard's will help you answer questions such as the following:

■ Is this opinion that I just found still good law? Is it still valid? Have other courts followed it or rejected it?
■ How can I find other opinions like it?
■ Is this statute that I found still good law? Is it still valid? Has it been changed by the legislature? How have the courts interpreted it?

Before we examine how Shepard's provides you with this kind of information, review Exhibit 11.8 in Section H, containing photographs of the major items that can be shepardized.

citator A book, CD–ROM, or online service containing lists of citations that can (1) help you assess the current validity of an opinion, statute, or other item; and (2) give you leads to additional relevant materials.

Shepard's is a **citator**, which is a book, CD–ROM, or online service that contains lists of citations that can help you assess the current validity of an item and can give you leads to additional relevant materials. We will examine Shepard's as a citator through the following topics:

a. The units of a set of Shepard's
b. Determining whether you have a complete set of Shepard's
c. The distinction between cited material and citing material
d. Abbreviations in Shepard's
e. Shepardizing a case (court opinion)
f. Shepardizing a statute
g. Shepardizing a regulation

We will limit ourselves to shepardizing cases, statutes, and regulations. Knowing how to shepardize these items, however, will go a long way toward equipping you to shepardize other primary authorities as well, such as constitutions, administrative decisions, charters, and rules of court.

The Units of a Set of Shepard's

By "set of Shepard's," we mean the group of volumes of Shepard's that cover whatever you are trying to shepardize. Every set of Shepard's includes two main units: (1) *hardcover* red volumes and (2) white, gold, blue, gray, yellow, or red *pamphlet* supplements. The hardcover volumes and the pamphlet supplements are sometimes broken into parts, e.g., Part 1, Part 2. The white pamphlet is the advance sheet that is later thrown away and *cumulated* (or consolidated) into a larger pamphlet. Eventually, all the pamphlets are thrown away and cumulated into hardcover red volumes. The pamphlet supplements contain the most current shepardizing material.

Example of a set of *Shepard's Citations*

Determining Whether You Have a Complete Set of Shepard's

Shepard's Citations comes in three formats: paper (pamphlets and hardcover volumes), CD–ROM, and online (through LexisNexis). The CD–ROM and online versions are the easiest to use. In most instances, you simply enter what you want to shepardize in order to call up all available citing materials on the computer screen. Paper Shepard's, which most researchers use, is not as easy.

As indicated, Shepard's comes in sets, e.g., the set for Illinois, the set for federal statutes. For some sets, there may be ten hardcover or bound volumes and 3 or 4 pamphlet supplements. Before you start sheparardizing, you must determine whether you have a complete set in front of you on the shelf. To determine whether your set is complete, go through the following steps:

1. Pick up the most recently dated pamphlet supplement—usually the advance sheet— that the library has received for that set of Shepard's. The date is at the top of the supplement. Be careful, however; the pamphlet supplement you find on the shelf may *not* be the most recent; someone else may be using it, or it may have been misshelved. To determine the most recent Shepard's supplement received by the library, check the library's computer catalog. Type in the name of the set of Shepard's. Among the information provided, the computer should tell you the most recent supplement received by the library. If it does not, ask a librarian how you can determine what is the most recent.

2. Once you are satisfied that you have the most recent unit, find the following statement on the front cover: WHAT YOUR LIBRARY SHOULD CONTAIN. This will tell you what is a complete set of Shepard's for the set you are using. Go down the list and make sure everything you are told should be on the shelf is indeed there. (The last entry on the list should be the pamphlet supplement that contains the list you are reading.)

Assume, for example, that today's date is January 2008. You want to shepardize a Wisconsin state case and a Wisconsin state statute. You go to *Shepard's Wisconsin Citations*. On the front cover of a January 2008 advance sheet for this set of Shepard's, you find the following:

WHAT YOUR LIBRARY SHOULD CONTAIN

1999 Bound Volumes 1 and 2, Cases*
1999 Bound Volume 3, Statutes*
1999 Bound Volume 4, Case Names*

Supplemented with:
–April, 2007 Annual Cumulative Supplement
  Vol. 90 No. 4
–January, 2008 Advance Sheet Vol. 91 No. 1

Destroy ALL OTHER ISSUES

To be complete, therefore, the following units of *Shepard's Wisconsin Citations* should be on the shelf:

- a 1999 bound volume (vol. 1) of *Shepard's Wisconsin Citations* covering cases; and
- a 1999 bound volume (vol. 2) of *Shepard's Wisconsin Citations* covering cases; and
- a 1999 bound volume (vol. 3) of *Shepard's Wisconsin Citations* covering statutes; and
- a 1999 bound volume (vol. 4) of *Shepard's Wisconsin Citations* covering case names; and
- an April 2007 Annual Cumulative Supplement pamphlet (vol. 90, no. 4) of *Shepard's Wisconsin Citations* covering cases, statutes, and case names; and
- a January 2008 Advance Sheet pamphlet (vol. 91, no. 1) of *Shepard's Wisconsin Citations* covering cases, statutes, and case names.

The last item on the list is always the pamphlet that contains the list you are reading. Hence the above list is found on the January 2008 Advance Sheet (vol. 91, no. 1) of *Shepard's Wisconsin Citations*.

Occasionally, the list can become quite involved. For example, you may find two lists on the pamphlet. One list tells you what should be on the shelf before a certain hardbound Shepard's volume is received by the library, and a second list tells you what should be on the shelf after that hardbound volume is received by the library. Yet the same process is followed. Carefully go through the list (or lists) one unit at a time, checking to see if what the list says should be on the shelf is there.

Why do you need to take the time to be sure that the set of Shepard's you want to use is complete? Because failure to do so might result in your missing vital information about what you are shepardizing. Assume you are in the library reading the case of *Smith v. Smith* decided in 1990. At the time you are reading this case, you are not aware that it was overruled in 1995. The reporter containing the opinion does not give you this information because the overruling occurred after the reporter volume was printed. Before you rely on a case, you must shepardize it. You go to the right set of Shepard's and check the *Smith* case in every hardbound volume and pamphlet supplement on the shelf. None of them, however, tell you that there are problems with the case. Unfortunately, the pamphlet that says *Smith* was overruled is not on the shelf. Someone else may be using it in another room of the library or it may have been misshelved. Careless researchers would not even know that the pamphlet was missing. Careful researchers, however, make it their business to know what should be on the shelf. They do this by checking the WHAT YOUR LIBRARY SHOULD CONTAIN list. When you do this, as a conscientious researcher, you realize that you cannot complete your shepardizing of *Smith* until you find the missing pamphlet. You go from table to table in the library looking for it. If this does not work, you ask a librarian for help in locating it.

The Distinction between Cited Material and Citing Material

cited material The case, statute, regulation, or other document that you are shepardizing.

citing material The case, article, or annotation that mentions, treats, or discusses whatever you are shepardizing, i.e., that mentions, treats, or discusses the cited material.

- **Cited material** is whatever you are shepardizing, such as a case, statute, or regulation.
- **Citing material** is whatever mentions, treats, or discusses the cited material, such as another case, a legal periodical article, an annotation in A.L.R., etc.

Suppose you are shepardizing the case found in 75 F.3d 107 (a case that begins on page 107 of volume 75 of *Federal Reporter 3d*). While reading through the columns of Shepard's, you find the following cite: f56 S.E.2d 46. The *cited* material is 75 F.3d.107. The *citing* material is 56 S.E.2d 46, which followed (f) or agreed with the decision in 75 F.3d 107.

Suppose you are shepardizing a statute: 22 U.S.C. § 55.8 (section 55.8 of title 22 of the United States Code). While reading through the columns of Shepard's, you find the following cite: 309 U.S. 45. The *cited* material is 22 U.S.C. § 55.8. The *citing* material is 309 U.S. 45, which interpreted, treated, or mentioned 22 U.S.C. § 55.8.

Shepard's indicates the cited material by the bold print along the top of every page of Shepard's and by the bold print numbers that are the volume or section numbers of the cited material. In the following excerpt, the cited material is 404 P.2d 460. The citing material follows the number –460–:

Citing Material for a Cited Case in Shepard's

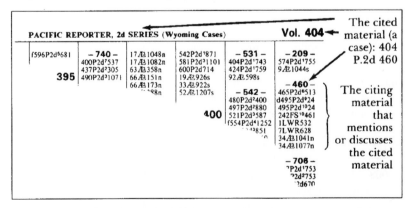

In the following excerpt, the cited material is a statute: § 37–31, which is in Article (Art.) 2 of the Wyoming Statutes. The citing material is indicated beneath § 37–31.

Citing Material for a Cited Statute in Shepard's

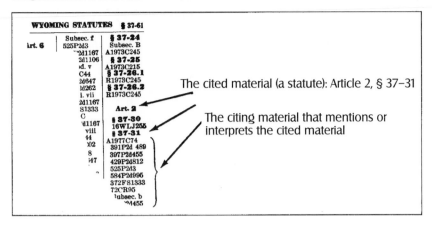

The cited material (a statute): Article 2, § 37-31

The citing material that mentions or interprets the cited material

Abbreviations in Shepard's

Shepard's packs a tremendous amount of information (the cites) into every one of its pages. Each page contains up to eight columns of cites for the cited and the citing materials. For the sake of economy, Shepard's uses many abbreviations that are peculiar to Shepard's. For example:

FS → means *Federal Supplement*

A3 → means *American Law Reports 3d*

* → (asterisk) means that the year next to the citing case is the year of the cited statute or administrative regulation; it is not the year of the citing case

Δ → (delta symbol) means that the year next to the citing case is the year of the citing case; it is not the year of the cited statute or administrative regulation

You are not expected to know the meaning of every abbreviation and symbol used by Shepard's. *But you must know where to find their meanings.* There are two places to go:

- The abbreviations tables at the beginning of most units of Shepard's.
- The preface or explanation pages found at the beginning of most units of Shepard's.

Many researchers neglect the latter. Buried within the preface or explanation pages may be an interpretation of an abbreviation or symbol that is not covered in the abbreviation tables.

Shepardizing a Case (Court Opinion)

Almost every reporter has a corresponding set of Shepard's that will enable you to shepardize cases in that reporter (see Exhibits 11.5 and 11.8 in Section H). For example, if the case you want to shepardize is 40 N.Y.2d 100, you go to the set of Shepard's that covers cases in New York—*Shepard's New York Citations.* If the case you want to shepardize is 402 F.2d 1064, you go to the Shepard's that covers F.2d cases—*Shepard's Federal Citations.*

Of course, many cases have parallel cites—the case is found word for word in more than one reporter. You can shepardize most cases with parallel cites through either reporter. Assume you want to shepardize the following case:

Welch v. Swasey, 193 Mass. 364, 79 N.E. 745 (1907)

This case is found in two reporters: *Massachusetts Reports* and *North Eastern Reporter.* Hence you can shepardize the case and obtain similar citing material from two different sets of Shepard's: *Shepard's Massachusetts Citations* and *Shepard's Northeastern Citations.* A thorough researcher will shepardize his or her case by using *both* sets of Shepard's.

To shepardize a *case* means to obtain the following six kinds of information about the cited case (the case you are shepardizing):

1. The *parallel cite* of the case. The first entry in parentheses is the parallel cite.
2. The *history of the case.* Here, you will find all cases that are part of the same litigation, e.g., appeals, reversals.

3. The *treatment of the case*. Here, you will find all citing cases that have analyzed or mentioned the cited case, e.g., followed it, distinguished it, criticized it, or just mentioned it.

4. Citing legal periodical literature (law review article, case note, etc.) that has analyzed or mentioned the cited case.

5. Citing annotations in A.L.R. (A.L.R. 1st), A.L.R.2d, A.L.R.3d, A.L.R.4th, A.L.R.5th, A.L.R.6th, A.L.R. Fed., and A.L.R. Fed. 2d that have analyzed or mentioned the cited case.

6. Citing opinions of the attorney general that have analyzed or mentioned the cited case.

A *parallel cite* (item 1 above) is an additional reference where you will be able to read the same material word for word. There are two main reasons you may need a parallel cite. First, the rules of citation may require you to include a parallel cite (see Section J). Second, the cite to a case you have may be to a reporter your library does not subscribe to; a parallel cite may lead you to a reporter your library does have.

The *history of the case* (item 2) gives you every case that was part of the same litigation as the case you are shepardizing. For example, you will be given abbreviations that tell you whether the case went up on appeal where it was affirmed (a), dismissed (D), modified (m), reversed (r), etc. Citations to each of these cases are provided. If one of the cases is so recent that its traditional citation is not yet available, Shepard's will give you the **docket number** of the decision. (A docket number is the consecutive number assigned to a case by the court and used on all documents filed with the court during the litigation of that case.) The most obvious reason you need the history of a case is that you do not want to cite a case that is no longer valid.

The *treatment of the case* (item 3) tells you how other cases in unrelated litigation have responded to (treated) the case you are shepardizing. For example, you will be given abbreviations that tell you whether the case has been criticized (c), questioned (q), explained (e), followed (f), overruled (o), etc., by other cases—the *citing cases*. You need to know how a case has been treated in order to assess how much weight it can be given. A case that has been ignored or criticized is obviously of less weight than one that other cases have cited with approval (followed—f).

Note that one of the history options is *reversed*, which should be distinguished from the treatment option of being *overruled*. To **reverse** an opinion means to change its holding on appeal in the same litigation. **Overrule** means to reject or cancel an earlier opinion as precedent by rendering an opposite decision on the same question of law in a different litigation.

As you can see, both the history and the treatment of a case help you perform the third level of legal research, validation research, which we introduced in Section N and will examine again in Section Y.

The great value of Shepard's as a case finder comes through items 3 to 5. If a citing case (item 3) analyzes or mentions the cited case (which you are shepardizing), the two cases probably deal with similar facts and law. All citing cases, therefore, are potential leads to more case law on point. Similarly, a citing legal periodical article (item 4) or a citing A.L.R. annotation (item 5) will probably discuss a variety of cases in addition to the cited case. Hence, again, you are led to more case law through Shepard's.

Let's look more closely at some of the information you will learn when shepardizing an opinion. Assume that you want to shepardize the case of *Parratt v. Taylor*, 451 U.S. 527 (1981), an opinion of the U.S. Supreme Court. Exhibit 11.26 contains an excerpt from one of the columns in the set of Shepard's you would use to shepardize this case, *Shepard's United States Citations*.

Shepardizing a Statute

You shepardize a *statute* to try to find the following seven kinds of information:

1. A parallel cite of the statute (found in parentheses immediately after the section number of the statute). The parallel cite (if given) is to the session law edition of the statute.

2. The history of the statute in the legislature, such as amendments, added sections, repealed sections, renumbered sections, etc.

3. Citing cases that have analyzed or mentioned the statute, declared it unconstitutional, etc.

docket number A consecutive number assigned to a case by the court and used on all documents filed with the court during the litigation of that case.

reverse To overturn a holding on appeal in the same litigation.

overrule To reject or cancel an earlier opinion as precedent by rendering an opposite decision on the same question of law in a different litigation.

(cont. on page 540)

EXHIBIT 11.26	Excerpt from the Set of Shepard's You Would Use to Shepardize *Parratt v. Taylor*, 451 U.S. 527 (1981): *Shepard's United States Citations*

–527–
Parratt v
Taylor
1981
(68LE2d420)
(101SC1908)

The cited case (*Parratt v. Taylor*) begins on page—527—. Shepard's places this number in large bold print between two dashes at the beginning of the references that Shepard's will provide for this case. Not shown in this excerpt is the volume number of the cited case, which Shepard's places in a box:

451

Shepard's prints this box in front of the first case in this volume that can be shepardized. (*Parratt* is not the first case in volume 451.)

In parentheses, Shepard's gives parallel cites to the cited case beneath the year. The parallel cites of *Parratt* are (68LE2d420) and (101SC1908). If you did not know the meaning of these abbreviations, you would check the abbreviations tables in the beginning of this set of Shepard's. There you would be told that LE2d means United States Supreme Court Reports, Lawyers' Edition, Second Series and that SC means Supreme Court Reporter. The full cite of *Parratt*, with these parallel cites, would be *Parratt v. Taylor*, 451 U.S. 527, 101 S. Ct. 1908, 68 L. Ed. 2d 420 (1981). The official cite (U.S.) is always given first. The parallel cites to the two unofficial reporters should be written in the order indicated.

s) 620F2d307
527US643
Cir. 2
239F3d496
130FS2d433
Cir. 3
2003USDist
[LX16305
98FS2d679

The **s)** notation alerts you to history-of-the-case information. The abbreviations tables in Shepard's will tell you the meaning of **s)** and other history notations. The **s)** notation means that 620 F.2d 307 is part of the same litigation as the *Parratt* case. The case at 620 F.2d 307 was probably appealed to the U.S. Supreme Court, leading to *Parratt*, our cited case. Other notations will give you additional critical information about the history of the cited case. Examples: **r)** (the cited case was reversed on appeal), **v)** (the cited case was vacated or withdrawn on appeal), **S)** (the cited case was superseded or substituted upon reconsideration or rehearing), etc.

Many of the citing cases have no special notations next to them. See, for example, the citing case of 239 Federal Reporter 3d 496 (239F3d496). There are no notations such as **f)** or **q)** next to it. This indicates that the citing case mentioned the cited case without giving it much attention. The court in the citing case may have simply said that the cited case covered similar facts.

f) 107FS2d619
112FS2d433
Cir. 6
98FS2d843
102FS2d436
Cir. 7
f) 24FS2d885
63FS2d912

The **f)** notation alerts you to treatment-of-the-case information. The abbreviations tables in Shepard's will tell you what **f)** and other treatment notations mean. The **f)** notation means that the citing case followed (agreed with) the cited case. The citing case is 107 Federal Supplement 2d 619 (107FS2d619). This citing case followed the cited case, *Parratt*. The same is true of 24 Federal Supplement 2d 885 (24FS2d885). Other notations will give you additional critical information about the treatment of the cited case. Examples: **q)** (the cited case was questioned by the citing case), **c)** (the cited case was criticized by the citing case), **e)** (the cited case was explained by the citing case), **d)** (the cited case was distinguished by the citing case), etc. *Distinguished* means that the citing case pointed out that there were differences between the facts or rule in the cited case and the facts or rule in the citing case.

Above most of the citing cases, we are told what jurisdictions decided the citing cases. There are citing cases in Exhibit 11.26 from the following jurisdictions: the federal second circuit (Cir. 2), the federal third circuit (Cir. 3), the federal sixth circuit (Cir. 6), the federal seventh circuit (Cir. 7), and Washington State (Wash.). Another jurisdiction of a citing case is the U.S. Supreme Court itself: 527 U.S. 643

q) 82FS2d
[918
300FS2d680
wash

The **q)** notation, as indicated, tells you that the citing case questioned the cited case. The citing case may have doubted the validity of the cited case or its value as precedent. The citing case is 82 Federal Supplement 2d 918 (82FS2d918).

200SW3d810

Note the page numbers of all the citing cases. See, for example, 200 South Western 3d 810 (200SW3d810). The page number given for this citing case is 810. This is *not* the page on which the citing case begins. It is the page of the citing case that mentions the cited case. Hence if you went to page 810 of volume 200 of South Western 3d, you would find a mention of *Parratt*, our cited case.

86VaL932

Citing materials include citing legal periodical literature. Our cited case (*Parratt*) was mentioned in a law review article: 86 Virginia Law Review 932 (86VaL932).

159ARF44n

Citing materials include citing annotations in ALR. Our cited case (*Parratt*) was mentioned in an annotation: 159 American Law Reports Federal 44 (159ARF44).

ASSIGNMENT 11.16

Pick any case that you found while doing any one of the parts of Assignments 11.14 or 11.15. Do questions (a)–(g) below on this case.

(a) What set of *Shepard's Citations* would you use to shepardize this case?

(b) Is this set of *Shepard's Citations* on the shelf complete? List everything that should be on the shelf. Place a check mark next to each unit that is on the shelf and an "x" next to each unit that is missing.

(c) List the parallel cites, if any, for this case provided by Shepard's.

(d) State the history of this case according to Shepard's. Give the meaning of abbreviations of all symbols that Shepard's uses to indicate this history. If there is no history of the case provided by Shepard's, redo this assignment until you find a case that does have such a history.

(e) In the treatment of the cited case, find a citing case written by a state court in your state. Give the meaning of abbreviations of all symbols, if any, that Shepard's uses to indicate this treatment. If there is no citing case written by a state court of your state, redo this assignment until you find a cited case that does have such a citing case. Give the citation of the citing case. (The cited case must have both history and treatment information as specified in questions (d) and (e).)

(f) Go to the reporter that prints the full text of the citing case you found in (e). Find the citing case in it and quote the sentence from the case that refers to the cited case.

(g) Question (a) asked you to identify a set of Shepard's that you would use to shepardize the case you selected, and question (c) asked you if the case had a parallel cite.

    (i) If there is a parallel cite, is there another set of Shepard's that would allow you to shepardize your case? If so, what is the name of this set of Shepard's?

    (ii) Go to this other set of Shepard's. Is it complete? Redo question (b) for this set.

    (iii) Can you find the same information in this set that you found when answering questions (c), (d), and (e) for the other set? If not, what is different?

(Information Obtained when Shepardizing a Statute—cont.)

4. Citing administrative decisions, such as agency decisions that have analyzed or mentioned the statute.

5. Citing legal periodical literature, such as law review articles that have analyzed or mentioned the statute.

6. Citing annotations in A.L.R. (A.L.R.1st), A.L.R.2d, A.L.R.3d, A.L.R.4th, A.L.R.5th, A.L.R.6th, A.L.R. Fed., and A.L.R. Fed. 2d that have analyzed or mentioned the statute.

7. Citing opinions of the attorney general that have analyzed or mentioned the statute.

To learn how to shepardize a statute, you must first learn the distinction between a statute's session law cite and its codified cite. First, let's review some basics.

A statute is a law passed by the legislature declaring, commanding, or prohibiting something. The official document that contains the statute is called an act. There are two main kinds of statutes:

- *Public laws*, which are statutes that apply to the general public or to a segment of the public and have permanence and general interest (example: a statute changing welfare eligibility)

- *Private laws*, which are statutes that apply to specifically named individuals or groups and have little or no permanence or general interest (example: a statute that names a Wyoming post office building after a recently deceased senator)

Statutes can be found in three major formats printed in the following order:

- *Slip law*: A single statute (public or private law) that is printed separately, often in a small pamphlet.

- *Session law*: A single statute (public or private law) that is printed in chronological order along with every other statute passed during a particular session of the legislature, usually lasting one or two years. (If, for example, the legislature passes a bankruptcy statute and a murder statute on the same day, they will be printed in the session laws one after the other.) Other names for session laws include *Acts*, *Laws*, and, most commonly, *Statutes at Large*. The major set of federal session laws is called *United States Statutes at Large* (abbreviated Stat.). The citation to a session law is called its **session law cite**.

- *Code*: A collection of statutes (public laws only) that are printed by subject matter regardless of when the legislature passed them. When we say a statute has been *codified*, we mean that it has been printed in a code where the rules or laws in it are printed by subject matter rather than chronologically. (For example, all of the bankruptcy statutes are printed together, and all of the murder statutes are printed together elsewhere in the code.) The citation to a statute in a code is called its **codified cite**.

session law cite The citation to a statute that has not been printed in a code and therefore is organized chronologically. If it is a public law, it will eventually be printed in a code. See also *codify*.

codified cite The citation to a statute (or other enacted law) that has been printed in a code and, therefore, is organized by subject matter.

Every private law will have only a session law cite because it will not be printed in a code. Every public law, however, will have both a session law cite *and* a codified cite. Here are examples of session law and codified law cites of a state statute (Ohio) and of a federal statute, both of which are public laws:

Session Law Cite of a Statute	Codified Cite of the Same Statute
1975 Ohio Laws, C. 508 ⟷	Ohio Rev. Code Ann. § 45 (1978)
87 Stat. 297 (1965) ⟷	34 U.S.C. § 18(c) (1970)

Notice the totally different numbering system in the codified and session law cites—yet they are the same statutes. Section 45 of the Ohio Revised Code Annotated is found word for word in Chapter (C.) 508 of the 1975 session laws of Ohio. And section 18(c) of title 34 of the U.S. Code is found word for word in volume 87 of Statutes at Large (Stat.) on page 297. Notice also the different years for the same statute. The year in the session law cite is the year the legislature passed the statute. The year in the codified cite, however, is usually the year of the edition of the code.

Assume that you want to shepardize a statute. (The cited material will be a cited statute.) When do you shepardize a statute through its session law cite, and when do you shepardize through its codified cite?

There are two instances when you *must* shepardize the statute through its session law cite:

- If the statute will never be codified because it is a private law and therefore of no general public interest
- If the statute has not yet been codified because it is so recent (codification will come later)

If the statute *has* been codified, you must shepardize it through its latest codified cite. But suppose you know only the session law cite of the statute. How do you find its codified cite? Go to the current code that should contain your statute. Look for special tables at the beginning or end of the code. For federal statutes in the U.S. Code, for example, there is a *Tables volume* in which you will find Table III. (See research link O on page 504). Table III will enable you to translate a session law cite into a codified law cite. (The same Tables volume exists for U.S.C.A. and for U.S.C.S.) You can also make the translation through Table 2 in *United States Code Congressional and Administrative News* (U.S.C.C.A.N.).

Shepard's has its own abbreviation system for session laws. Suppose that you are shepardizing Kan. Stat. Ann. § 123 (1973)—a codified cite. Section 123 is the *cited statute*—what you are shepardizing. In the Shepard's columns for Kansas statutes, you might find:

§ 123

(1970C6)
A1972C23
Rp1975C45

The *parallel cite* in parentheses is 1970C6, which means chapter 6 of the 1970 Session Laws of the state of Kansas. The mention of a year in Shepard's for statutes usually refers to the session laws for that year. (You find the meaning of "C" by checking the abbreviations tables at the beginning of the Shepard's volume.)

Immediately beneath the parentheses in the above example for section 123 (the cited statute), you find two other references to session laws:

| A1972C23 | This means that in chapter 23 of the 1972 Session Laws of Kansas, there was an amendment to section 123 (which is what "A" means, according to Shepard's abbreviations tables). | Rp1975C45 | This means that in chapter 45 of the 1975 Session Laws of Kansas, section 123 was repealed in part (which is what "Rp" means, according to Shepard's abbreviations tables). |

You will note that Shepard's does *not* tell you what the amendment was or what was repealed in part. How do you find this out? Two ways. First, you go to the actual session laws if your library has them. Second, you go to the cited statute (§ 123) in the codified collection of the statutes (here the *Kansas Statutes Annotated*). At the bottom of the statute in the code, there may be historical or legislative history notes that will summarize amendments, repeals, etc. For an example of this kind of information on a New York statute, see Exhibit 11.39, later in the chapter. (Be sure to check these notes for the cited statute in the pocket part of the code volume you are using.)

Other citing material given in Shepard's for a statute is less complicated. For example, there are cites to citing cases, citing legal periodical articles, etc., that follow a pattern very similar to that of the citing material for cases you are shepardizing.

Assume that you want to shepardize a federal statute in the *United States Code* (U.S.C.). The set of Shepard's you would use is *Shepard's Federal Statute Citations* (see Exhibit 11.8 in Section H). There are two major kinds of citing cases that analyze or mention a federal cited statute. Both kinds give you a year in front of the citing case, but the year can have two very different meanings:

- When there is an asterisk (*) in front of the year, Shepard's is telling you that the court that wrote the citing case specified the year of the U.S.C. in which the cited statute is found. The year following the asterisk is the year *of the U.S.C.* that contains the cited statute, not the year of the citing case. In an asterisk cite, you are not told the year of the citing case.
- When there is a delta (Δ) in front of the year, Shepard's is telling you that the court that wrote the citing case did *not* specify the year of the U.S.C. in which the cited statute is found. The year following the delta is the year *of the citing case*, not the year of the U.S.C. In a delta cite, you are not told the year of the U.S.C. that contains the cited statute.

Assume, for example, that the federal statute you are shepardizing—the cited statute—is section 2506 in title 22 of the *United States Code* (22 U.S.C. § 2506). Exhibit 11.27 contains an excerpt from one of the units of *Shepard's Federal Statute Citations* that you would use to shepardize this statute.

The first citing case is 37FedCl 426. The abbreviations tables at the beginning of Shepard's tell you that FedCl means the Federal Claims Court. On page 426 of volume 37 of this reporter, you will find that the court analyzed or mentioned the cited statute, 22 U.S.C. § 2506. Note the year 1997 following the delta. This means that the court that wrote the citing case did not specify the year of 22 U.S.C. § 2506. Hence 1997 is the year of the citing case, 37FedCl 426; it is not the year of 22 U.S.C. § 2506.

The next citing case is 38FedCl 603. Again, the abbreviations tables tell you that this is a Federal Claims Court case. On page 603 of volume 38 of this reporter, you will find that the court analyzed or mentioned the cited statute, 22 U.S.C. § 2506. Note the year 1980 following the asterisk. This means that the court that wrote the citing case *did* specify the year of 22 U.S.C. § 2506. Hence 1980 is the year of 22 U.S.C. § 2506; it is not the year of the citing case, 38FedCl 603.

ASSIGNMENT 11.17

(a) Go to your state statutory code. Pick any statute in this code that might be helpful in researching any *one* of the topics for the Section O assignments. (See page 525.) Which topic did you select, (a) to (o)? Give the citation of the statute. Give a brief quote from this statute indicating that it might be relevant to the topic you selected.

(continues)

(b) What set of *Shepard's Citations* would you use to shepardize this statute?

(c) Is this set of *Shepard's Citations* on the shelf complete? List everything that should be on the shelf. Place a check mark next to each unit that is on the shelf and an "x" next to each unit that is missing.

(d) According to Shepard's, have there been any amendments, or has the legislature taken any other action on this statute? If so, give the meaning of abbreviations of all symbols that Shepard's uses to indicate this action. (Be sure to check every unit of Shepard's for this set.)

(e) Find a citing case written by a state court in your state. Give the meaning of abbreviations of all symbols, if any, that Shepard's uses to indicate how this citing case treated the cited statute. If there is no citing case written by a state court of your state, redo this assignment until you find a cited statute that *does* have such a citing case. Give the citation of the citing case.

(f) Go to the reporter that prints the full text of the citing case you found in (e). Find the cited statute in it and quote the sentence from the case that refers to the cited statute.

EXHIBIT 11.27	Excerpt from the Set of Shepard's You Would Use to Shepardize a Federal Statute, 22 U.S.C. § 2506: *Shepard's Federal Statute Citations*

Sheperdizing an Administrative Regulation

You cannot shepardize administrative regulations of state agencies. No sets of Shepard's cover state regulations. You can, however, shepardize federal regulations in the *Code of Federal Regulations* (C.F.R.). This is done through *Shepard's Code of Federal Regulations Citations*. It will also allow you to shepardize presidential proclamations, executive orders, and reorganization plans.

To shepardize a C.F.R. regulation means to obtain the following three kinds of information about the *cited regulation* (the regulation you are shepardizing):

1. The history of the regulation in the courts—for example, citing cases that have invalidated or otherwise discussed the cited regulation.
2. Citing legal periodical literature that has analyzed or mentioned the cited regulation.
3. Citing annotations in A.L.R. (A.L.R.1st), A.L.R.2d, A.L.R.3d, A.L.R.4th, A.L.R.5th, A.L.R.6th, A.L.R. Fed., and A.L.R. Fed. 2d. that have analyzed or mentioned the cited regulation.

The C.F.R. comes out in a new edition every year. All the changes that have occurred during the year are incorporated in the new yearly edition. (Each year is printed in a different color.) Two kinds of changes can be made:

- Those changes made *by the agency* itself, e.g., amendments, repeals, renumbering—this is the history of the regulation in the agency.
- Those changes forced on the agency *by the courts*, e.g., declaring a section of the regulation invalid—this is part of the history of the regulation in the courts.

Unfortunately, Shepard's will give you only the history of the regulation in the courts (plus references to the regulation in legal periodical literature and in annotations). The columns of Shepard's will *not* give you the history of the regulation in the agency. (As we will see later, to obtain the latter, you must check elsewhere, e.g., the CFR Parts Affected tables in the *Federal Register*.) The main value of Shepard's for C.F.R. is that it will lead you to what the courts have said about the regulation (plus the periodical and annotation references).

When shepardizing through *Shepard's Code of Federal Regulations Citations*, the cited material, of course, is the federal regulation—which we refer to as the cited regulation. Shepard's provides two categories of *citing* material:

- Citing cases, periodicals, and annotations that refer to the cited regulation *by year*, that is, by C.F.R. edition.
- Citing cases, periodicals, and annotations that refer to the cited regulation *without* specifying the year or edition of the regulation in the C.F.R.

To indicate the first kind of citing material, Shepard's prints an asterisk just before a given year. If, for example, the cited regulation you were shepardizing is 12 C.F.R. § 218.111(j), you might find the following:

§218.111(j)
420F2d90*1965

The citing material is a citing case—420 F.2d 90. The asterisk means that this case specifically identified the year of the cited regulation—1965. This year is *not* the year of the citing case. It is the year of the cited regulation. We are not given the year of the citing case.

Now let us examine the second kind of citing material mentioned above. There may be citing material that mentions the regulation but does *not* tell us the specific year or edition of that regulation. Shepard's uses a delta (Δ) in such situations. If, for example, the cited regulation you were shepardizing is 12 C.F.R. § 9.18(a)(3), you might find the following:

§9.18(a)(3)
274FS628Δ1967

The citing material is a citing case—274 F. Supp. 628. The delta means that the citing case did not refer to the year or edition of section 9.18(a)(3). When this occurs, the year following the delta is the year of the citing case and *not* the year of the cited regulation. The citing case of 274 F. Supp. 628 was decided in 1967.

The techniques for shepardizing opinions, statutes, and administrative regulations are summarized in Exhibit 11.28.

EXHIBIT 11.28	Checklist for Shepardizing Opinions, Statutes, Administrative Regulations, and Other Cited Materials

General Guidelines for Shepardizing Any Cited Material

1. Begin by making sure that you have the correct set of Shepard's to shepardize the cited material. (For lists and photographs of the major sets of Shepard's, see Exhibit 11.8.)
2. Once you have the correct set, find the latest pamphlet in the set. On the front cover of this pamphlet, go down the list of WHAT YOUR LIBRARY SHOULD CONTAIN to make sure that you have a complete set of Shepard's on the shelf. Do not try to shepardize with an incomplete set of Shepard's.
3. Know where to find the meaning of abbreviations. Check the preface and the tables in front of the pamphlet and hardcover volumes of the set of Shepard's you are using.
4. The general rule is that you must check the cited material (opinion, statute, or administrative regulation) in every unit of the set of Shepard's you are using—every pamphlet and every hardcover volume. You can, however, bypass any unit of the set if the front cover of the unit clearly indicates that it does not cover the volume or title of your cited material or if the front cover clearly indicates that it covers a time period prior to the date your cited material was decided or enacted.

(continues)

EXHIBIT 11.28	Checklist for Shepardizing Opinions, Statutes, Administrative Regulations, and Other Cited Materials—*continued*

5. When Shepardizing, work *backward* by examining the most recent Shepard's pamphlets first so that you start by obtaining the latest citing material.
6. Suppose that in one of the units of a set of Shepard's, you find nothing listed for the cited material. This could mean one of three things:
   - You are in the wrong set of Shepard's.
   - You are in the right set of Shepard's, but the Shepard's unit you are examining does not cover the particular volume or title of your cited material. (See guideline 4 above.)
   - You are in the right set of Shepard's. The silence in Shepard's about your cited material means that since the time of the printing of the last unit of Shepard's for that set, nothing has happened to the cited material—there is nothing new for Shepard's to tell you.
7. There is a toll-free number you can call (800–899–6000) to speak with a Shepard's editor on the Shepard's Support Line. You can ask about a feature of the citator that is troubling you. You can also obtain an update of an annotation covering the period since the date of the most recent pamphlet your library has received.
8. If you have access to LexisNexis, you can shepardize cited material online (law.lexisnexis.com/shepards). Shepardizing online, although expensive, is infinitely easier than using paper Shepard's. When online, there are no multiple units. The history and treatment information appears on one screen with links to other pages that explain what has occurred to your cited material.
9. KeyCite is the major competing citator to Shepard's. KeyCite is available only online through Westlaw (www.westlaw.com).

Shepardizing Opinions

10. If the case you want to shepardize (the cited case) has a parallel cite, you can usually shepardize the case through each set of Shepard's that covers the reporters in the parallel cites. When this is so, shepardize through both sets of Shepard's even though a good deal of the citing material will be repeated in the two sets. You may be able to find information in one set that is not available in another.
11. Know the six kinds of information you can try to obtain when shepardizing a case: parallel cites, history of the cited case, treatment of the cited case (found in the citing cases), citing legal periodical literature, citing annotations, and citing opinions of the attorney general.
12. Parallel cites, if any, are given in parentheses. If you do not find a parallel cite in parentheses, several conclusions are possible: your cited case will never have a parallel cite, the reporter volume containing the parallel cite has not been printed yet, or the parallel cite was already given in an earlier unit of the set of Shepard's you are using and is not repeated in later units.
13. Pay close attention to the history of the cited case. You want to know about appeals, particularly whether this case has been reversed.
14. The page number listed for citing cases is the page on which the cited case is mentioned. It is not the page on which the citing case begins.
15. A small "n" to the right of the page number of citing annotations (e.g., 23ALR198n) means the cited case is mentioned within an annotation. A small "s" to the right of the page number of citing annotations (e.g., 78ALR589s) means the cited case is mentioned in a supplement to (or pocket part of) the annotation.
16. You can also shepardize a case online through LexisNexis. Online shepardizing is substantially easier than using the pamphlet and hardcover units of Shepard's. You simply enter the cite of the case you want to shepardize (the cited case) to begin accessing all available citing materials. (For more on LexisNexis, see chapter 13.)

Shepardizing Statutes

17. If the statute has been codified, shepardize it through its latest codified cite. If you have only the session law cite of the statute, translate it into a codified cite by using the tables in the current code. For federal statutes, go to Table III of the Tables volume of U.S.C./U.S.C.A./U.S.C.S. and Table 2 in *United States Code Congressional and Administrative News* (U.S.C.C.A.N.). For state statutes, look for comparable tables in the state's session volumes and in the state's statutory code.
18. If the statute has not been (or will not be) codified, check the set of Shepard's covering statutes to determine whether you can shepardize through its session law cite.
19. Know the seven kinds of information you can try to obtain by shepardizing a statute: parallel cite (not always given), history of the statute in the legislature, citing cases, citing administrative decisions, citing legal periodical literature, citing annotations, and citing opinions of the attorney general.
20. At the top of a Shepard's page, and in its columns, look for your statute by the name of the code, year, article number, chapter number, title number, or section number. Repeat this for every unit of Shepard's.
21. An asterisk or a delta symbol may appear next to the year in citing material:
   - The asterisk (*) means that the citing material referred to the specific year of the cited statute. Hence the year is the year of the cited statute, not of the citing material.
   - The delta symbol (Δ) means that the citing material did not refer to the specific year of the cited statute. Hence the year is the year of the citing material, not of the cited statute.
22. The history of the statute in the legislature is given in session law form, e.g., A1980C45. This refers to an amendment (A) printed in the 1980 Laws of the legislature, Chapter (C) 45. Another example: A34St.654. This refers to an amendment (A) printed in volume 34, page 654, of the Statutes at Large. If you want to locate these session laws, check the Web site of the legislature to see if they are online. The site for federal statutes is thomas.loc.gov. Also find out if your library keeps session laws. Finally, at the end of the statute in a code, there often is an historical note that will give information on the session law cite of the statute. This may help you locate the latter.
23. The notation *et seq* means "and following" (*et sequens*). The citing material may be analyzing more than one statutory section.
24. If your state code has gone through revisions or renumberings, read the early pages in the statutory code and the preface material in the Shepard's volumes to try to obtain an explanation of what has happened. This information may help you interpret the data provided in the Shepard's units for your state code.

(continues)

EXHIBIT 11.28	Checklist for Shepardizing Opinions, Statutes, Administrative Regulations, and Other Cited Materials—*continued*

Shepardizing Administrative Regulations

25. For federal administrative regulations, go to *Shepard's Code of Federal Regulations Citations.* (For a photo, see Exhibit 11.8.)
26. Know the three kinds of information you can obtain when shepardizing a federal regulation: history of the regulation in the courts, citing legal periodical literature, and citing annotations.
27. At the top of a Shepard's page, and in its columns, look for your regulation by the name of the code, year, article number, chapter number, title number, or section number. Repeat this for every unit of Shepard's.
28. An asterisk or a delta symbol may appear next to the year in citing material:

   ■ The asterisk (*) means that the citing material referred to the specific year of the cited regulation. Hence the year is the year of the cited regulation, not of the citing material.
   ■ The delta symbol (Δ) means that the citing material did not refer to the specific year of the cited regulation. Hence the year is the year of the citing material, not of the cited regulation.

29. The set of Shepard's for C.F.R. does not directly tell you what amendments, revisions, or other changes were made *by the agencies* to the administrative regulations. You are told only what *the courts* have said about the regulations. (To find out what the agencies have done to the regulations, you must check sources such as the CFR Parts Affected tables in the *Federal Register.*)
30. All regulations in C.F.R. are based on statutes of Congress. (A statute that is the basis or authority for the actions of an agency is called an **enabling statute**. (It is the statute that allows (enables) an administrative agency to carry out specified delegated powers.) As we will see later, you can find out what statutes in the U.S. Code are the authority for particular administrative regulations in the C.F.R. by checking the "authority" reference under many of the regulations in the C.F.R. Once you know the statute that is the basis for the regulation, you might want to shepardize that enabling statute for more law in the area.
31. The above checklist on shepardizing administrative regulations covered *federal* regulations. Shepard's has nothing comparable for *state* administrative regulations.

More on Shepard's and Shepardizing

   ■ www.fcsl.edu/library/resources/startingpoints/Shepards-Print.pdf
   ■ www.bc.edu/schools/law/library/research/researchguides/shepards.html
   ■ lib.law.washington.edu/ref/oncite.html
   ■ www.bu.edu/lawlibrary/research/updating/index.html
   ■ www.lectlaw.com/files/lwr17.htm
   ■ www.law.syr.edu/Pdfs/0TipsForShepardizingCases.pdf

5. LOOSELEAF SERVICES

Inserting pages into a looseleaf service

A looseleaf service is a lawbook with a binding (often three ringed) that allows easy inserting and removal of pages for updating. If the updating pages can be placed anywhere within the volumes of the set (not just at the end), the looseleaf service is called an *interfiled looseleaf service.* If, however, the updating pages are placed only at the end, it is called a *newsletter-type looseleaf service.* When you subscribe to a looseleaf service, pages regularly arrive in the mail with detailed instructions on which old pages to remove and/or which new ones to add. The task of carrying out such instructions, sometimes performed by paralegals, is referred to as *looseleaf filing.*

Here is a sample list of looseleaf services to give you an idea of the kinds of topics they cover:

AdLaw Bulletin	*Labor Arbitration Awards*
Antitrust & Trade Regulation Daily	*Pension Coordinator*
Corporate Compliance Library	*Product Liability Daily*
Employment Discrimination Report	*Tax Planning Review*
Environmental Due Diligence Guide	*United States Law Week*
Health Law Reporter	

The features of these looseleaf services can include:

   ■ Recent court opinions or summaries of opinions
   ■ Relevant legislation—usually explained in some detail
   ■ Administrative regulations and decisions, or summaries of them (some of this material may not be readily available elsewhere)
   ■ References to relevant studies and reports
   ■ Practice tips

In short, looseleaf services can be extremely valuable. The major publishers include Commerce Clearing House (CCH) (www.cch.com), the Bureau of National Affairs (BNA) (www.bna.com), and

Research Institute of America (RIA) (ria.thomson.com). Given the broad scope of topics covered in looseleaf services, you should assume that one or more looseleaf services exist on the general topic of your research until you prove to yourself otherwise.

Unfortunately, looseleaf services are sometimes awkward to use, particularly the interfiled looseleaf services. To compound the problem, it is not uncommon for library users to misfile pages that they take out for photocopying.

There is no standard structure for looseleaf services. You might find the following variations:

- One volume or a multivolume set
- Organization by page number, organization by section number, organization by paragraph number, or a combination
- Different colored pages to indicate more recent material
- Indexes at the end, in the middle, at the beginning of the volumes, or a combination
- Bound volumes that accompany the three-ring volumes
- Transfer binders that contain current material

Some sets combine the features of interfiled and newsletter-type looseleaf services. In short, you should approach the structure of each looseleaf service as a small puzzle sitting on the shelf waiting to be understood.

The techniques for finding and using looseleaf services are summarized in Exhibit 11.29.

EXHIBIT 11.29	Checklist for Finding and Using Looseleaf Services

1. Divide your research problem into its major topics, such as family law, tax law, antitrust law, etc. Assume that one or more looseleaf services exist for these topics until you demonstrate otherwise to yourself.
2. Find out where the looseleaf services are located in your library. Are they all together? Are they located in certain subject areas? Does the library have a separate list of them?
3. Check the library's card or online catalog. Look for subject headings on your topics to see if looseleaf services are mentioned. Some catalogs may not use the word "looseleaf" in the description of their entries. Be sure to include searches under the names of the major publishers of looseleaf services: Commerce Clearing House (CCH), Bureau of National Affairs (BNA), and Research Institute of America (RIA).
4. Ask library staff members if they know of looseleaf services on the major topics of your research.
5. Call other law libraries in your area. Ask the staff members there if they know of looseleaf services on the major topics of your research. See if they can identify looseleaf services that you have not yet found.
6. Once you have a looseleaf service in front of you, you must figure out how to use it:
   a. Read any preface or explanatory material in the front of the volumes of the looseleaf service.
   b. Ask library staff members to give you some help.
   c. Ask attorneys or paralegals who are experts in the area if they can give you a brief demonstration of its use.

d. Read print or online pamphlets or promotional literature by the publishers on using their looseleaf services. For each looseleaf service, you need to know the following:
   - What it contains and what it does not contain
   - How it is indexed
   - How it is supplemented (updated)
   - What its special features are
   - How many volumes or units it has and the interrelationship among them

You obtain this information through techniques (a) to (d) above.

7. Looseleaf services often contain the complete text of cases, statutes, administrative regulations, and administrative decisions. You should not cite these laws as they appear in a looseleaf service unless they are not readily available elsewhere. When you want to cite the law (primary authority), cite traditional publications such as reporters and codes. You can, however, cite the looseleaf service for its other features such as commentary on the law or practice suggestions.
8. For an overview of looseleaf services and their use, see:
   - www.ll.georgetown.edu/guides/lls.cfm
   - www.law.syr.edu/Pdfs/1LooseLeafs.pdf
   - www.ll.georgetown.edu/lib/guides/lls.html
   - www.fcsl.edu/Library/Startpoints/legal%20looseleafs.htm
   - www.bc.edu/schools/law/library/meta-elements/pdf/researchguides/looseleaf.pdf

ASSIGNMENT 11.18

Find one looseleaf service that might be helpful in researching each of the topics for the Section O assignments (see page 525). Locate one per topic. In each looseleaf service, find a case written by a state court in your state or by a federal court that sits in your state. If you cannot find a case written by such a court, use a different looseleaf service until you find one. Give the citation of the looseleaf service and of the case.

6. LEGAL PERIODICAL LITERATURE

Legal periodical literature consists of the following:

- Lead articles and comments written by individuals who have extensively researched a topic
- **Case notes** that provide relatively brief commentary on recent court opinions
- Book reviews

case note A relatively brief commentary on a recent court opinion.

There are three major publishers of periodicals: academic institutions, including almost all of the nation's law schools (where the students running the periodicals have the prestige of being "on law review"); commercial companies; and bar associations. Legal periodicals are either general, covering a wide variety of legal topics, e.g., *Harvard Law Review*, or specialized, e.g., *Family Law Journal*. The large number of available legal periodicals provides researchers with a rich source of material.

How can you locate legal periodical literature on point? What index systems will allow you to gain access to the hundreds of legal periodicals and the tens of thousands of articles, comments, case notes, book reviews, and other material in them? Two major general index systems exist:

- *Index to Legal Periodicals and Books* (ILP) published by H.W. Wilson Co.
- *Current Law Index* (CLI) published by Information Access Corporation

Of the two, the CLI is more comprehensive because it indexes more legal periodicals. Both are available in three different versions: a paper version (consisting of pamphlets and hardcover volumes), a CD–ROM version, and an online version. Few law libraries subscribe to all the legal periodicals indexed in the ILP and the CLI. Hence you may be obtaining leads to periodicals that your library does not have. If so, check other libraries in the area.

Examples of the paper versions of the *Index to Legal Periodicals and Books* (ILP) and the *Current Law Index* (CLI). Both are also available online and on CD–ROM.

Index to Legal Periodicals and Books (ILP)

- The ILP first comes out in pamphlets that are later consolidated (i.e., cumulated) into bound volumes.
- You must check each ILP pamphlet and each ILP bound volume for whatever years you want.
- The ILP regularly adds new periodicals that are indexed.
- Every recent ILP pamphlet and bound volume has four indexes:
    - (1) A Subject and Author Index
    - (2) A Table of Cases commented on
    - (3) A Table of Statutes commented on
    - (4) A Book Review Index
- Abbreviation tables appear at the beginning of every pamphlet and bound volume.
- The Subject and Author Index in the ILP is easy to use. You simply go to the topic on which you are seeking periodical literature, e.g., abortion or smoking. If you have the name of an

author and want to know if he or she has written anything on the topic of your research, you simply check that author's last name in this index.

- Toward the end of every ILP pamphlet and hardcover volume is a Table of Cases. Suppose that elsewhere in your research you come across an important case, and you now want to know if that case was ever commented on (i.e., noted) in the legal periodicals. Go to the ILP pamphlet or hardcover volume that covers the year of the case and check the Table of Cases. (See research link P.)
- The Table of Statutes serves the same function for statutes. This table will tell you where you can find periodical literature commenting on certain statutes that are important to your research, e.g., the Pregnancy Leave Act. (See research link Q.)
- At the end of every pamphlet and hardcover ILP volume is a Book Review Index. If you are looking for a review of a law book you have come across elsewhere in your research, go to the ILP pamphlet or hardcover volume that covers the year of publication of the book for which you are seeking reviews.
- In addition to its print version (pamphlet and hardcover), the ILP is available:
  - on WilsonWeb, the publisher's online database (www.hwwilson.com/Databases/legal.htm)
  - on CD–ROM
  - on Westlaw and on LexisNexis

Current Law Index (CLI)

The CLI is more comprehensive than ILP because of the larger number of legal periodicals indexed.

- The CLI first comes out in pamphlets that are later consolidated (i.e., cumulated) into hardcover volumes.
- You must check each CLI pamphlet and each annual CLI issue for the years you want.
- There are four indexes within each CLI unit:
    (1) A Subject Index
    (2) An Author-Title Index
    (3) A Table of Cases
    (4) A Table of Statutes
- Abbreviation tables appear at the beginning of every CLI unit.
- The Subject Index gives full citations to periodicals under a topic (e.g., child welfare or zoning) and under an author's name.
- Book reviews are included under the Author-Title Index along with cites to periodical literature by the authors.
- The Table of Cases is valuable if you already know the name of a case located elsewhere in your research. To find out if that case was commented on, check the Table of Cases in the CLI unit that covers the year of the case. (See research link P.)
- The Table of Statutes is equally valuable. If you already have the name of a statute from your other research (such as the California Fair Employment Practices Act), look for the name of that statute in the Table of Statutes for the CLI unit that covers the approximate time the statute was passed. (See research link Q.)
- In addition to its print version (pamphlet and hardcover), the CLI is available:

  - on LegalTrac, an online version of CLI (www.gale.com/title_lists)
  - on CD–ROM
  - on Westlaw and on LexisNexis (where the CLI is known as the Legal Resource Index)

| Case in a Reporter
Federal Case, e.g., a federal case in
Federal Reporter 3d.
State Case, e.g., a state case in
Pacific 3d. | Table of Cases in ILP

Table of Cases in CLI |

RESEARCH LINK P

If you have found a federal or state case in a reporter that is important to your research, you should check if that case has been commented on in a case note in legal periodical literature. To find out, check the tables of cases in ILP and CLI.

Statute in a Code		Table of Statutes in ILP
Federal Statute in the United States Code.		Table of Statutes in CLI
State Statute, e.g., a state statute in the Iowa Code Annotated.		

RESEARCH LINK Q

If you have found a federal or state statute in a code that is important to your research, you should check if that statute has been commented on in a legal periodical literature. To find out, check the tables of statutes in ILP and CLI.

Other Index Systems

A number of other periodical index systems exist:

- Index to Federal Tax Articles
- Index to Foreign Legal Periodicals
- MEDLINE, an index of biomedical journals
  gateway.nlm.nih.gov/gw/Cmd
  www.ncbi.nlm.nih.gov

Legal Periodicals on the Internet

You can find a great deal of legal periodical literature on fee-based services such as Westlaw, LexisNexis, and WilsonWeb. They contain complete (referred to as *full-text*) articles, comments, notes, etc. On the free Internet, however, you are more limited. Although there are some full-text periodicals on the free Internet, you are more likely to find only summaries or abstracts and tables of contents of periodical literature. For an overview of what is available, check:

law.usc.edu/library/resources/journals.cfm
www.lawreview.org
www.hg.org/journals.html
stu.findlaw.com/journals

The techniques for finding legal perodical literature are found in Exhibit 11.30.

EXHIBIT 11.30   Checklist for Finding Legal Periodical Literature

1. Use legal periodical literature mainly for background research and for leads to primary authority, particularly through the extensive footnotes in this literature.
2. One of the major indexes to legal periodical literature is the *Index to Legal Periodical Literature and Books* (ILP). It is available:
   - in print (pamphlets and hard cover)
   - on WilsonWeb (www.hwwilson.com/Databases/legal.htm)
   - on CD–ROM
   - on Westlaw and on LexisNexis
3. Another major indexes to legal periodical literature is the *Current Law Index* (CLI). It is available:
   - in print (pamphlets and hard cover)
   - on LegalTrac, an online version of CLI (www.gale.com/title_lists)
   - on CD–ROM
   - on Westlaw and on LexisNexis (on both of these services, the CLI is known as the Legal Resource Index)
4. The CARTWHEEL will help you locate material in ILP and CLI.
5. Both ILP and CLI also contain separate indexes. You should become familiar with all these internal index features.
6. Start with the subject indexes within ILP and CLI.
7. Identify the name and date of every important case that you have found in your research thus far. Go to the table of cases in ILP and in CLI to find out if any periodical literature has commented on these cases. (Go to the ILP and CLI units that would cover the year the case was decided. To be safe, also check their units for two years after the date of the case.) See research link P.

8. If you are researching a statute, find out if any periodical literature has commented on the statute. (See research link Q.) This is done in two ways:
   a. Check the tables of statutes in ILP and CLI.
   b. Break your statute down into its major topics. Check these topics in the subject indexes of ILP and CLI to see if any periodical literature on these topics discusses your statute.
9. If you have the name of an author who is known for writing on a particular topic, you can also check for literature written by that author under his or her name in ILP and CLI.
10. Ask library staff members if the library has any other indexes to legal periodical literature, particularly in specialty areas of the law.
11. It is possible to shepardize some legal periodical literature. If you want to know whether the periodical article, note, or comment was ever mentioned in a court opinion, go to *Shepard's Law Review Citations*.
12. If you have the citation of a legal periodical article, find out if you can read it on the free Internet. Type the name of the periodical in Google or in any general search engine. For a list of periodicals available online, check sites such as: law.usc.edu/library/resources/journals.cfm
13. For an overview of legal periodicals and their use, see:
   - www.ll.georgetown.edu/tutorials/second/index.cfm
   - www.ll.georgetown.edu/guides/articles.cfm
   - library.law.smu.edu/resguide/periodicals.htm
   - law.lib.buffalo.edu/departments/info-services/research/bibliographies/PeriodicalIndex.pdf

ASSIGNMENT 11.19

Find one legal periodical article that might be helpful in researching each of the topics for Section O assignments (see page 525). Choose one per topic. In each article, scan the footnotes to find a case written by a state court in your state or by a federal court that sits in your state. If you cannot find a case written by such a court, choose a different legal periodical article until you find one. Give the citation of the article. Quote the sentence (or footnote) from the article that mentions this case.

7. LEGAL ENCYCLOPEDIAS

The major multivolume legal encyclopedias are *Corpus Juris Secundum* (C.J.S.), a dark blue set, and *American Jurisprudence 2d* (Am. Jur. 2d), a green set. Both are published by West Group. In many law libraries, they are among the most frequently used secondary authorities because they are easy to use and are comprehensive. If you know how to use a general encyclopedia, you know how to use a legal encyclopedia. The volumes contain hundreds of alphabetically arranged topics on almost every major area of the law. For each topic, you are given explanations of the basic principles of law and extensive footnote references supporting these principles. The vast majority of the references are to cases, although for certain topics, such as federal taxation, there are references to statutes as well. Legal encyclopedias have two main values. They are excellent as background research in a new area of the law. (See Exhibit 11.18.) They are also valuable as leads to primary authority, particularly case law. In addition to the national legal encyclopedias, some states have state-specific encyclopedias devoted to the law of one state, e.g., *Florida Jurisprudence*.

For a sample page from C.J.S., see Exhibit 11.31. Every section begins with a summary of that section in bold print. The phrase **black letter law** has come to mean any statement of a fundamental or basic principle of law.

At the end of both C.J.S. and Am. Jur.2d is a huge *general index*. There are also extensive topic indexes within individual volumes. See Exhibit 11.32.

American Jurisprudence 2d,
a national legal encyclopedia

black letter law A statement of a fundamental or basic principle of law.

EXHIBIT 11.31	**Excerpt from a Page in** *Corpus Juris Secundum*

§§ 22–23 BURGLARY

c. Use of Instrument, Explosives, or Torch

In order to constitute burglary, entry need not be made by any part of accused's body, but entry may be made by an instrument, where the instrument is inserted for the purpose of committing a felony.

In order to constitute a burglary, it is not necessary that entry be made by any part of the body; it may be by an instrument,[5] as in a case where a hook or other instrument is put in with intent to take out goods, or a pistol or a gun with intent to kill.[6] It is necessary, however, that the instrument shall be put within the structure, and that it shall be inserted for the immediate purpose of committing the felony or aiding in its commission, and not merely for the purpose of making an opening to admit the hand or body, or, in other words, for the sole purpose of breaking.

A statute making it an offense to break and enter a building with intent to commit a crime, and defining "enter" as including insertion into the building of any instrument held in defendant's hand and intended to be used to detach or remove property, does not require that the offender intend the detachment or removal of property to occur at the moment of insertion only, and the intended detachment or removal relates to a later times as well. . .

5. Cal.—People v. Walters, 57 Cal.Rptr.484, 249 C.A.2d 547. Del.—
   Bailey v. State, 231 A.2d 469.
Me.—State v. Liberty, 280 A.2d 805.
N.M.—State v. Tixier, 551 P.2d 987, 89 N.M. 297.
Or.—Terminal News Stands v. General Cas. Co., 278 P.2d 158, 203 Or. 54.
Tenn.—State v. Crow, 517 S.W.2d 753.
Tex.—Tanner v. State, Cr., 473 S.W.2d 936.
6. N.J.—Corpus Juris Secundum quoted in State v. O'Leary,
   107 A.2d 13, 16, 31 N.J.Super. 411.
Tex.—Stroud v. State, 60 S.W.2d 439, 124 Tex.Cr.56.

ASSIGNMENT 11.20

(a) Find one section in C.J.S. that might be helpful in researching each of the topics for the Section O assignments (see page 525). Find one per topic. Within this section, find a case cited in the footnotes written by a state court in your state or by a federal court that sits in your state. If you cannot find a case written by such a court, choose a different section of C.J.S. until you find one. Give the citation of the C.J.S. section you used. Quote the sentence (or footnote) from the section that mentions this case.

(b) Repeat part (a), this time using Am. Jur. 2d.

Corpus Juris Secundum,
a national legal encyclopedia

EXHIBIT 11.32   Checklist for Using Legal Encyclopedias

1. Use the two national legal encyclopedias (Am. Jur. 2d and C.J.S.) for the following purposes:

   a. For background research on areas of the law that are new to you.

   b. For leads in their extensive footnotes to primary authority, such as cases and statutes.

2. Both legal encyclopedias have multivolume general indexes at the end of their sets. Use the CARTWHEEL to help you locate material in them. In addition to these general indexes, Am. Jur. 2d and C.J.S. have separate indexes in many of the individual volumes.

3. Neither Am. Jur. 2d nor C.J.S. includes a table of cases.

4. Both Am. Jur. 2d and C.J.S. have a separate volume called *Table of Laws and Rules*. Check this table if you have found a relevant statute, regulation, or rule of court from your other research that you want to find discussed in Am. Jur. 2d. or C.J.S.

5. Am. Jur. 2d and C.J.S. are published by West Group. Within these legal encyclopedias, the publisher provides library references to other research books that it publishes, e.g., annotations in A.L.R. (A.L.R. 1st), A.L.R. 2d, A.L.R.3d, etc.

6. Both encyclopedias also have references to key numbers so that you can find additional case law in West Group digests.

7. Find out if your library has a *local* encyclopedia that is limited to the law of your state. States with such encyclopedias include California, Florida, Illinois, Kentucky, Maryland, Michigan, Minnesota, New York, Ohio, Pennsylvania, and Texas.

8. Am. Jur. 2d is available online through LexisNexis and Westlaw.

9. For an overview of legal encyclopedias and their use, see:
   - www.ll.georgetown.edu/tutorials/second/index.cfm
   - www.law.du.edu/library/guides/39legalencyclopedias.pdf
   - www.bu.edu/lawlibrary/research/guides/encyclopedias.html
   - www.law.harvard.edu/library/services/research/guides

8. LEGAL TREATISES

legal treatise A book written by a private individual (or by a public individual writing as a private citizen) that provides an overview, summary, or commentary on a legal topic.

A **legal treatise** is any book written by private individuals (or by public officials writing in a private capacity) on a topic of law. Some treatises are scholarly; others are more practice oriented. The latter are often called hornbooks, handbooks, form books, and practice manuals. Treatises give overview summaries of the law, plus references to primary authority. There are single-volume treatises such as *Prosser on Torts*, as well as multivolume treatises such as *Moore's Federal Practice*, *Collier on Bankruptcy*, etc. See Exhibit 11.33.

EXHIBIT 11.33   Checklist for Finding and Using Legal Treatises

1. Always look for legal treatises on the topics of your research problem. Assume, until you prove otherwise to yourself, that three or four such treatises exist and are relevant to your problem.

2. Treatises are useful for background research and for leads to primary authority.

3. Many treatises are updated by pocket parts or supplemental volumes. (If the legal treatise is printed as a looseleaf service, it may be updated by insert pages.)

4. Start your search for treatises in the Card or computer catalog (see Exhibit 11.21 on using the catalog).

5. Check with experts in the area of law in which you are interested, e.g., teachers, for recommendations on treatises you should examine. See Exhibit 11.34.

6. If your library has open stacks, find the treatise section. For example, go to the section of the stacks containing books with KF call numbers. Locate the section of the stacks containing treatises on your topic. Browse through the shelves to try to find additional treatises. Some treatises that you need, however, may be on reserve rather than in the open stacks.

7. You can also browse legal treatises in some online catalogs. For example:
   - Go to the online catalog of the Library of Congress (catalog. loc.gov)
   - Click "Basic Search"
   - Type a legal topic, e.g., "paralegal" or "hearsay"
   - Click the title of any of the books listed
   - Click the KF or other call number of the book you select
   - You will then be able to see all of the books that are on the shelf next to that call number

8. Once you have found a treatise, check that author's name in the *Index to Legal Periodicals and Books* (ILP) or the *Current Law Index* (CLI) to try to find periodical literature on the same topic by this author. (See Exhibit 11.30 on finding legal periodical literature.)

9. For an overview of legal treatises and their use, see:
   - www.ll.georgetown.edu/tutorials/second/index.cfm
   - law.wustl.edu/library/index.asp?id=1348
   - www.law.harvard.edu/library/services/research/guides

ASSIGNMENT 11.21

Find one legal treatise that might be helpful in researching each of the topics for the Section O assignments (see page 525). Find one per topic. The legal treatise you select must be different from any of the legal treatises you may have used in Assignments 11.13 and 11.18. In each legal treatise, find a citation to a case written by a state court in your state or by a federal court that sits in your state. If you cannot find a case written by such a court, choose a different legal treatise until you find one. Give the citation of the legal treatise and of the case. Quote the sentence (or footnote) from the legal treatise that mentions this case.

9. E-MAIL AS A RESEARCH TOOL

E-mail can be an excellent research tool, particularly for brief questions that seek factual information, general guidance, or leads. Here are examples of the kinds of questions you can ask by e-mail:

- Do you know of any studies that have been conducted on the relationship between osteoarthritis and repetitive hand motion?
- I'm looking for the total amount of attorney fees awarded in asbestos cases in Oregon in 2003.
- How would I obtain a copy of a criminal complaint filed (but dismissed the day it was filed) against a Franklin County, Georgia, car dealership (Jasper Chevrolet) that is no longer in business?
- Our case involves a 1961 Ford Galaxie that was demolished in an accident. We believe it may have had a gasket that was defectively designed. I need to locate and examine an intact vehicle of the same make and model.
- I need a copy of the environmental regulations on pesticides that were in effect in Boise, Idaho, in 1957 before the city rewrote its municipal code.

To pursue answers to such questions, see the checklist in Exhibit 11.34.

EXHIBIT 11.34   **Checklist for Using E-Mail as a Research Tool**

1. *Before contacting someone by e-mail.*

   Before you contact someone by e-mail, use general search engines such as Google (www.google.com) and MSN Live Search (search.live.com) to try to find the answer on your own. (On phrasing search queries, see Exhibit 13.9 in chapter 13.) For your search terms, type the main concepts of what you are seeking. Examples:
   - osteoarthritis "repetitive hand motion"
   - complaint jasper georgia
   - 1961 ford galaxie gasket
   - pesticide Boise regulation

2. *Finding sources to contact by e-mail.*
   - Online librarians. Many libraries allow you to e-mail research questions to members of their staff. To find such librarians, type the following search in any search engine: "online librarian." Many of the libraries offering this service do not require you live within their area or be a member of their organization.
   - Administrative agencies. If your question involves a federal, state, or local government agency, go to the Web site of that agency. Such sites almost always have a "Contact Us" link to e-mail addresses where you can ask your research question pertaining to that agency.
   - Federal and state legislators. If your question involves recent federal, state, or local legislation or if it could involve proposed legislation, e-mail your representative in the legislature. If you have two representatives in the legislature, e-mail both of them as well as the office of the leader of the legislative body (e.g., senate president or assembly speaker). Ask each of them for information that pertains to the specific or general topic of your question.
   - To find the e-mail addresses of members of Congress:
     - www.congress.org/congressorg/home
     - www.visi.com/juan/congress
   - To find the e-mail addresses of members of your state legislature, type the name of your state and the word "legislature" (e.g., Texas legislature) in any search engine. Then follow member links to try to obtain e-mail addresses.

   - Online groups and listservs. Find out if there are any online discussion groups or listservs that cover the topic of your research question. You may find that members of such groups have discussed the exact question that you have. Find out if there is an archives link that the group uses to store prior communications among group members. Also, consider joining the group to ask your question by e-mail. Ways to locate online groups:
     - Google groups (groups.google.com)
     - Yahoo groups (groups.yahoo.com)
   - Authors. In your research so far, you may have come across the name of a person who has written about the topic of your research question. Try to find the e-mail address of this author. (On locating individuals, see "Helpful Web Sites" at the end of chapter 9 and the search resources in Exhibit 13.10 in chapter 13.)
   - Associations. Find an association that has some involvement with the specific or general topic of your research question. Such associations almost always have "Contact Us" links on their Web sites. To find associations:
     - Check the online (or print) *Encyclopedia of Associations.* Many local public libraries subscribe to this resource and make it available to its patrons.
     - In any search engine, type the subject of your research and the word *association* (examples: civil rights association, adoption association, and cancer association).

3. *Etiquette when making contact by e-mail.*
   - Keep your question brief. The recipient of your e-mail message is more likely to ignore a question that is long and rambling than if it consists of a few sentences.
   - Be humble. Don't write as if you expect an answer, or worse, as if you are entitled to one.
   - The most effective way to express a question is to say, "I'm looking for leads on . . ."
   - The last two lines of your message should say, "I would appreciate any suggestions you may have or any leads to individuals or organizations where I might inquire. Thanks for any help you can provide."

ASSIGNMENT 11.22

Give the names, affiliations, and e-mail addresses of two experts you would try to contact because they might be helpful in researching each of the topics for the Section O assignments (see page 525). Give two per topic. State why you think they might be helpful and where you obtained the information on how to contact them.

[SECTION P]

FINDING CASE LAW

In chapter 7, we covered the structure of a court opinion, the briefing of an opinion, and the application of an opinion to a set of facts. Here, our focus is on *finding* these opinions in the library—finding case law.

In searching for case law, you will probably find yourself in one or more of the following situations:

■ You already have one case *on point* (or close to being on point), and you want to find additional ones. (Something is on point if it raises or covers the same issue as the one before you.) See Exhibit 11.35.

EXHIBIT 11.35	Techniques for Finding Case Law When You Already Have One Case On Point

1. *Shepardize the case that you have.* (See Exhibit 11.28 on shepardizing cases.) In the columns of Shepard's, look for cases that have mentioned your case. Such cases will probably cover similar topics. (You can also shepardize a case online through LexisNexis.)
2. *Shepardize cases cited by the case you have.* Almost every court opinion discusses or at least refers to other opinions. Is this true of the case you already have? If so, shepardize every case your case cites that might be relevant to your research. (See Exhibit 11.28 on shepardizing cases.)
3. *KeyCite your case.* If you have access to Westlaw, do a KeyCite check on the case you already have. KeyCite (like Shepard's) will lead you to any cases that have cited the case you have.
4. *Use the West Group digests.* There are two ways to use these digests to find additional case law when you already have one case on point:
   a. Go to the Table of Cases in all the digests covering the court that wrote the case you already have, such as the Table of Cases in the American Digest System. The Table of Cases will tell you what key numbers your case is digested under in the main volumes of the digest. Find your case digested under those key numbers. Once you have done so, you may find other relevant case law under the same key numbers.
   b. Go to the West Group reporter that contains the full text of the case you already have. At the beginning of this case in the reporter, find the headnotes and their key numbers. Take the key numbers that are relevant to your problem into any of West Group's digests to find more case law. (See Exhibit 11.23 on using digests.)

5. *Find an annotation.* First identify the main topics or issues in the case you already have. Look up these topics in the *ALR Index* and in the other index systems for finding annotations in the eight sets of A.L.R. (e.g., A.L.R.6th and A.L.R. Fed. 2d). (For a description of these annotation index systems, see Exhibit 11.24.) Another way to try to find annotations is by shepardizing the case you have. Annotations are among the citing materials of Shepard's. Once you find an annotation, you will be given extensive citations to more case law.
6. *Find a discussion of your case in the legal periodicals.* Go to the Table of Cases in the *Index to Legal Periodicals and Books* (ILP) and the *Current Law Index* (CLI). There you will be told if your case was analyzed (noted) in the periodicals. If so, the discussion may give you additional case law on the same topic. (See Exhibit 11.30 on finding legal periodical literature. See also research link P in Section O.)
7. *Go to Words and Phrases.* Identify the major words or phrases that are dealt with in the case you have. Check the definitions of those words and phrases in the multivolume legal dictionary called *Words and Phrases*. By so doing you will be led to other cases defining the same words or phrases.
8. *Try a search engine.* Type the name of the case you have (e.g., "Jackson v. Ford" or "Baker v. Carr") in search engines such as Google (www.google.com), Live Search (www.live.com), or Yahoo (www.yahoo.com). You may be led to a discussion of the case that includes references to similar cases.

■ You are looking for cases interpreting enacted laws such as a statute, constitution, charter, ordinance, court rule, or regulation that you already have. See Exhibit 11.36.
■ You are starting from square one. You want to find case law when you do *not* have a case, statute, or other law to begin with. You may be looking for cases interpreting common law or for cases interpreting enacted law you have not found yet. See Exhibits 11.37 and 11.38.

| EXHIBIT 11.36 | Techniques for Finding Case Law Interpreting a Statute |

1. *Shepardize the statute that you have.* (See Exhibit 11.28 on shepardizing statutes.) In the columns of Shepard's, look for cases that have mentioned your statute. (You can also shepardize a statute online through LexisNexis.)
2. *KeyCite your statute on Westlaw.* If you have access to KeyCite on Westlaw, do a KeyCite check on the statute you have. KeyCite (like Shepard's) will lead you to available case law interpreting your statute.
3. *Examine the Notes of Decisions for your statute in the statutory code.* At the end of your statute in many state and federal annotated statutory codes, there are paragraph summaries of cases (often called Notes of Decisions) that have interpreted your statute. (For an example, see Exhibit 11.39 later in the chapter.) Look for these summaries in the bound volume of the code, in the pocket part of this volume, and in any supplemental pamphlets at the end of the code. (For federal statutes, the codes to check are U.S.C.A. and U.S.C.S. The U.S.C. will *not* have such case summaries.)
4. *Find an annotation on your statute.* There are several ways to find out if there is an annotation the eight sets of A.L.R. (e.g., A.L.R.6th and A.L.R. Fed. 2d) that mentions your statute. First, shepardize that statute. Such annotations are among the citing materials of Shepard's. Second, KeyCite your statute on Westlaw. You will be told if there are any annotations that mention your statute. Third, check the volume called ALR Table of Laws, Rules, and Regulations. It will tell you which annotations mention your statute. The annotation on your statute will cite cases interpreting the statute.
5. *Final legal periodical literature on your statute.* Law review articles on statutes often cite cases that interpret the statutes. There are three ways to find such articles:
   a. Shepardize the statute. Citing material for a statute will include citing legal periodical literature.
   b. KeyCite your statute on Westlaw. You will be told if there is any legal periodical literature that covers your statute.
   c. Check the Table of Statutes in the *Index to Legal Periodicals and Books* (ILP) and in the *Current Law Index* (CLI). (See research link Q and Exhibit 11.30 legal periodicals.)
6. *Go to looseleaf services on your statute.* Find out if there is a looseleaf service on the subject matter of your statute. Such services often give extensive cites to cases on the statute. (See Exhibit 11.29 on looseleaf services.)
7. *Go to legal treatises on your statute.* Most major statutes have treatises on them that contain extensive cites to cases on the statute. (See Exhibit 11.33 on legal treatises.)
8. *Shepardize or KeyCite any cases you found through techniques 1–7 above.* Once you have found one good case that interprets your statute, shepardizing or KeyCiting that case may lead to additional cases interpreting the statute.
9. *Try a general search engine.* Many statutes have a popular name (e.g., Civil Rights Act of 1964 or the Uniform Child Custody Jurisdiction Act). If you know a statute's popular name, type it in search engines such as Google (www.google.com) or Live Search (www.live.com). You may be led to a discussion of the statute that includes cites to cases interpreting it.

| EXHIBIT 11.37 | Techniques for Finding Case Law When You Do Not Have a Case or Statute to Begin With |

1. *West Group digests.* In the Descriptive Word indexes (DWI) of the West Group digests, try to find key numbers on the topics of your research. (See Exhibit 11.23 on using the West Group digests.)
2. *Annotations.* Try to locate annotations on the topics of your research through the index systems for the eight sets of A.L.R. (e.g., A.L.R.6th and A.L.R. Fed. 2d). (See Exhibit 11.24 on finding annotations.)
3. *Legal treatises.* Try to find treatises on the topics of your research in the card or online catalog. (See Exhibit 11.33 on finding treatises.)
4. *Looseleaf services.* Find out if there are looseleaf services on the topics of your reaearch. (See Exhibit 11.29 on finding looseleaf services.)
5. *Legal periodical literature.* Try to find legal periodical literature on the topics of your research in the subject indexes of ILP and CLI. (See Exhibit 11.30 on finding legal periodical literature.)
6. *Legal encyclopedias.* Go to the indexes for Am. Jur. 2d and C.J.S. Try to find discussions in these legal encyclopedias on the topics of your research. (See Exhibit 11.32 on using legal encyclopedias.)
7. *E-mail as a research tool.* E-mail can often be useful when you are having difficulty locating your first case. (See Exhibit 11.34 on e-mail as a research tool.)
8. *Words and Phrases.* Identify all the major words or phrases from the facts of your research problem. Look up these words or phrases in the multivolume legal dictionary *Words and Phrases*, which gives definitions from court opinions.
9. *Shepardizing and KeyCiting.* If techniques 1–8 led you to any good cases, shepardize or KeyCite that case to try to find additional cases. On shepardizing cases, see Exhibit 11.28.
10. *Internet.* Exhibit 11.38 presents Internet sites where you can try to find case law. For sites on this list that have search boxes, enter the topics of your research to try to find cases on those topics.

| EXHIBIT 11.38 | Case Law on the Internet |

The sites in this chart may provide links to (1) the full text of all or some cases, (2) the current docket of the court, (3) the court's rules of court, and (4) administrative information such as the address of the court, names of court personnel, filing instructions, etc.

All Federal Courts
www.uscourts.gov/links.html
www.loc.gov/law/guide/usjudic.html
www.law.emory.edu/FEDCTS

(continues)

EXHIBIT 11.38	Case Law on the Internet—*continued*

www.washlaw.edu
www.findlaw.com/casecode
www.usa.gov/Agencies/Federal/Judicial.shtml
www.pacer.psc.uscourts.gov
www.plol.org

All State Courts
www.law.cornell.edu/opinions.html#state
www.ncsconline.org/D_KIS/info_court_web_sites.html
www.loc.gov/law/guide/usstates.html
www.findlaw.com/casecode
www.washlaw.edu
www.hg.org/usstates.html
www.plol.org

The search techniques in Exhibits 11.35 to 11.38 are not necessarily listed in the order in which they should be tried. Your goal is to know how to use all of them. In practice, you can vary the order.

Assignment 11.23 assumes that you already have one case on point and you now want to try to find additional cases (using the techniques in Exhibit 11.35). You may have found your first case after following some of the background research steps outlined in Exhibit 11.18 in Section N.

ASSIGNMENT 11.23

Go to the regional reporter that covers your state. (See Exhibit 11.5 in Section H). Pick any opinion in this reporter that meets the following criteria: it was decided by the highest state court of your state, it is at least twenty years old, and it has at least five headnotes in it. Assume that this case is relevant to your research problem. What is the citation of this case? Find *additional* cases by using the techniques in Exhibit 11.35. Try to find one additional case through each technique. Describe each of the techniques you used. Explain how you used it and give the cite to the additional case it led you to. If you were not able to use any of the techniques, explain why (e.g., your library did not have the materials (or computer facilities) you needed for the technique).

Assignment 11.24 assumes that you already have a statute and you now want to try to find case law interpreting that statute (using the techniques in Exhibit 11.36). Many of these techniques will be the same when seeking case law interpreting constitutions and regulations.

ASSIGNMENT 11.24

Go to the state annotated statutory code for your state. Pick any statute in this code that meets the following criteria: it is printed in the bound volume rather than in a pocket part or supplement, and there are at least ten court opinions interpreting this statute summarized beneath the statute (Notes of Decisions). Assume that this statute is relevant to your research problem. What is the citation of this statute? Find cases interpreting this statute using the techniques in Exhibit 11.36. Try to find one case through each technique. Describe each of the techniques you used. Explain how you used it, and give the cite to the case it led you to. If you were not able to use any of the techniques, explain why (e.g., your library did not have the materials (or computer facilities) you needed for the technique).

Assignment 11.25 asks you to use the techniques of Exhibit 11.37. It assumes that you are starting from scratch. You are looking for case law, and you do not have a starting case or statute with which to begin. You may be looking for cases interpreting common law or for cases interpreting a statute or other enacted law you have not found yet.

ASSIGNMENT 11.25

Go to today's general-circulation newspaper. Select any topic in any of the stories in the newspaper that interests you. Select one that you think is related to the law in some way. Assume that you want to do legal research on this topic, starting with case law. What topic did you select? Find cases on this topic by using the techniques in Exhibit 11.37. Try to find one case through each technique. Describe each of the techniques you used. Explain how you used it and give the cite of the case it led you to. If you were not able to use any of the techniques, explain why (e.g., your library did not have the materials (or computer facilities) you needed for the technique). If the topic you selected has never been involved in court cases, select another topic from the newspaper after describing the steps you took with the techniques that were unsuccessful.

[SECTION Q]

READING AND FINDING STATUTES

Statutes are laws written by legislatures that declare, command, or prohibit something. Statutes are among the most important primary authorities you will research. The vast majority of court opinions interpret and apply one or more statutes or administrative regulations based on those statutes. Indeed, one of the reasons there are so many opinions is that people constantly disagree over the meaning of statutes.

In the hierarchy of laws, constitutional law is the highest form of primary authority. (For the definition of the categories of law, see Exhibit 6.1. in chapter 6.) Next in the hierarchy are statutes. As long as a statute does not violate the constitution, the statute controls. Courts cannot change a statute, but they can declare it unconstitutional. Courts create common law, yet legislatures can change the common law by enacting statutes in derogation of the common law. In short, statutes play a central role in our legal system.

READING STATUTES

In Exhibit 11.39, there is an excerpt from an annotated New York statutory code. When we say it is a code, we mean that the laws within it are organized by subject matter rather than chronologically. When we say that it is annotated, we mean that notes or commentary accompany the laws. In statutory codes, these notes are mainly research references. Here is an explanation of the circled numbers in Exhibit 11.39:

① This is the section number of the statute. The symbol "§" before "146" means section.

② This is a heading summarizing the main topic of the statute. Section 146 covers who can visit state prisons in New York. This summarization was written by the private publishing company, not by the New York state legislature.

③ Here is the body of the statute written by the legislature.

④ At the end of a statutory section, you will often find a reference to session laws, which are statutes enacted during a particular session of the legislature and printed in chronological order rather than by subject matter. Phrased another way, session laws (also called statutes at large) are uncodified statutes because they are not organized by subject matter. The reference to session laws will use abbreviations such as L. (laws), P.L. or Pub. L. (Public Law), Stat. (Statutes at Large), etc. Here, you are told that in the Laws (L.) of 1962, chapter (c.) 37, § 3, this statute was amended. The Laws referred to are the session laws. See the Historical Note ⑥ below for a further treatment of this amendment.

⑤ The amendment to § 146 was effective (eff.) on February 20, 1962. The amendment may have been passed by the legislature on an earlier date, but the date on which it became the law of New York was February 20, 1962. It is important to know the effective date of a statute. Attorneys sometimes take cases that involve facts that occurred prior to the effective date of an otherwise applicable statute. Unless the statute is retroactive, you must locate the earlier version of the statute. Although no longer in effect, the earlier version may be the statute that governs the client's case.

⑥ The Historical Note provides the reader with some of the legislative history of § 146. First, the reader is again told that § 146 was amended in 1962. Note that early in the body of the statute, there is a reference to the title "commissioner of general services." The 1962 amendment simply changed the title from "superintendent of standards and purchase" to "commissioner of general services." The Historical Note was written by the private publisher, not by the New York state legislature.

EXHIBIT 11.39   **Excerpt from a Statutory Code (New York State)**

§ 146.   Persons authorized to visit prisons

The following persons shall be authorized to visit at pleasure all state prisons: The governor and lieutenant-governor, commissioner of general services, secretary of state, comptroller and attorney-general, members of the commission of correction, members of the legislature, judges of the court of appeals, supreme court and county judges, district attorneys and every minister of the gospel having charge of a congregation in the town wherein any such prison is situated. No other person not otherwise authorized by law shall be permitted to enter a state prison except under such regulations as the commissioner of correction shall prescribe. The provisions of this section shall not apply to such portion of a prison in which prisoners under sentence of death are confined.

As amended L.1962, c. 37, § 3, eff. Feb. 20, 1962.

Historical Note

L.1962, c. 37, § 3, eff. Feb. 20, 1962, substituted "commissioner of general services" for "superintendent of standards and purchase".

Derivation. Prior to the general amendment of this chapter by L.1929, c. 243, the subject matter of this section was contained in former Prison Law, § 160; originally derived from R.S., pt. 4, c. 3, tit. 3, § 159, as amended L.1847, c. 460.

Cross References

Promoting prison contraband, see Penal Law, §§ 205.20, 205.25.

Library References

Prisons ⌘13.
Reformatories ⌘7.

C.J.S. Prisons §§ 18, 19.
C.J.S. Reformatories §§ 10, 11.

Notes of Decisions

1. Attorneys

Warden of maximum security prison was justified in requiring that interviews of prisoners by attorney be conducted in presence of guard in room, in view of fact that attorney, who sought to interview 34 inmates in a day and a half, had shown no retainer agreements and had not stated purpose of consultations. Kahn v. La Vallee, 1961, 12 A.D.2d 832, 209 N.Y.S.2d 591.

Supreme court did not have jurisdiction of petition by prisoner to compel prison warden to provide facilities in prison which would not interfere with alleged violation of rights of prisoner to confer in private with his attorney. Mummiani v. La Vallee, 1959, 21 Misc.2d 437, 199 N.Y.S.2d 263, affirmed 12 A.D.2d 832, 209 N.Y.S.2d 591.

Right of prisoners to confer with counsel after conviction is not absolute but is subject to such regulations as commissioner of correction may prescribe, and prisoners were not entitled to confer with their attorney privately within sight, but outside of hearing of a prison guard, when warden insisted on having a guard present in order to insure against any impropriety or infraction of prison rules and regulations during interview. Id.

⑦ Also part of the Historical Note is the *Derivation* section. This tells the reader that the topic of § 146 of the Corrections Law was once contained in § 160 of the Prison Law, which dates back to 1847. In 1929, there was another amendment.

⑧ The *Cross References* refer the reader to other statutes that cover topics related to § 146.

⑨ The *Library References* refer the reader to other texts that address the topic of the statute. On the left-hand side, there are two key numbers (Prisons ⌘ 13 and Reformatories ⌘ 7) that can be used to find case law in the digests of West Group. In the right column, the library reference is to specific sections of C.J.S. (*Corpus Juris Secundum*), a legal encyclopedia.

⑩ The most important research resource in an annotated code is the Notes of Decisions. It includes a series of paragraphs that briefly summarize every court opinion that has interpreted or applied § 146. For later opinions, the reader must look to the pocket part of this code volume and to any supplemental pamphlets that have been added to the code. (Another way to find more recent opinions interpreting the statute is to shepardize or KeyCite the statute.) The first opinion that you are given in Exhibit 11.39 is *Kahn v. La Vallee*. Next is *Mummiani v. La Vallee*. At the end of the final paragraph, you will find *Id.*, which means that the paragraph refers to the case cited in the immediately preceding paragraph, the *Mummiani* case.

With this perspective of what a statute in an annotated code looks like, we turn to some general guidelines on understanding statutes:

1. *The organization of a statutory code is often highly fragmented because it contains a large number of units and subunits.* A statutory code can contain anywhere from 5 to 150 volumes. If you are unfamiliar with a code, you should examine the first few pages of the first volume. There you will usually find the subject matter arrangement of all the volumes.

   An individual subject in a code may be further broken down into titles, parts, articles, or chapters, which are then broken down into sections and subsections. Here is an example of a possible categorization for the state of "X" covering the topic of corporations:

   > X State Code Annotated
   > Title 1. Corporations
   > Chapter 1. Forming a Corporation
   > Section 1. Choosing a Corporate Name
   > Subsection 1(a). Where to File the Name Application
   > Subsection 1(b). Displaying the Name Certificate
   > Subsection 1(c). Changing the Corporate Name
   > Section 2...
   > Chapter 2...
   > Etc.

   Of course, each state uses its own classification terminology. What is called a chapter in one state may be called a title in another.

   You also need to be sensitive to the internal context of a particular statutory section. A section is often a sub-sub-subunit of larger units.

   > Example: Examine § 1183 in Exhibit 11.40.
   > Note that § 1183 is within Part II, which is within Subchapter II, which is within Chapter 12, which is within Title 8.

   Each section (§) of a statute is part of several units. The meaning of specific statutory language in a section sometimes depends on what unit it is in. Often you will see introductory phrases in a section such as,

   - For purposes of this Title, . . .
   - As used in this Article or Chapter, . . .
   - For purposes of this Subchapter, . . .
   - For purposes of this Part, . . .
   - As used in this article, . . .

   This kind of language tells you that the law contained in the section you are reading may be limited to the unit of which that section is a part.

   Occasionally, a legislature may completely revise its labeling system. What was once "Prison Law," for example, may now fall under the topic heading of "Correction Law." What was once section 73(b) of "Corporations Law" may now be section 13(f) of "Business and Professions Law." If such a revision has occurred, you should be able to find out about it either in a transfer or conversion table at the beginning of one of the code volumes or in the Historical Note at the bottom of the section. One of the advantages of CARTWHEEL (see Exhibit 11.16 in Section M) is that you are less likely to miss such statutes in the index of the code; the CARTWHEEL forces you to think of synonyms and broader/narrower categories of every word you are checking in an index.

2. *Statutes on administrative agencies often follow a common sequence.* A large number of statutes in a code cover administrative agencies. In fact, statutes are carried out mainly by administrative agencies. These statutes are sometimes organized in the following sequence:

   - The agency is created and named.
   - The major words and phrases used in this cluster of statutes are defined.

EXHIBIT 11.40 Sections, Parts, Subchapters, Chapters, and Titles in a Statutory Code

§ 1183 is within Part II of Subchapter II of Chapter 12 of Title 8

- The legislature's purpose in creating the agency is stated.
- The agency's powers are defined.
- The major administrators of the agency are given titles and powers.
- The budgetary process of the agency is specified.
- The method by which the public first comes into contact with the agency is established, such as applying for the benefits or services of the agency.
- The way in which the agency must act when a citizen complains about the agency's actions is established.
- How the agency must go about terminating a citizen from its services is established.
- The way in which a citizen can appeal to a court, if not satisfied with the way the agency handled his or her complaint, is established.

3. *All statutes must be based on some provision in the constitution that gives the legislature the power to pass the statute.* Legislatures have no power to legislate without constitutional authorization. The authorization may be the general constitutional provision vesting all legislative powers

in the legislature; more often, it will be a specific constitutional provision such as the authority to raise revenue for designated purposes.

4. *Check to see if a statutory unit has a definition section.* At the beginning of a cluster of statutes, look for a definition section. If it exists, the section will define a number of words used in the remaining sections of the unit. Here is an example of such a definition section:

> **§ 31.   Definitions.**—As used in this article, unless the context shall require otherwise, the following terms shall have the meanings ascribed to them by this section:
>
> 1. "State" shall mean and include any state, territory or possession of the United States and the District of Columbia.
>
> 2. "Court" shall mean the family court of the state of New York; when the context requires, it shall mean and include a court of another state defined in and upon which appropriate jurisdiction has been conferred by a substantially similar reciprocal law.
>
> 3. "Child" includes a step child, foster child, child born out of wedlock or legally adopted child and means a child under twenty-one years of age, and a son or daughter twenty-one years of age or older who is unable to maintain himself or herself and is or is likely to become a public charge.
>
> 4. "Dependent" shall mean and include any person who is entitled to support pursuant to this article.

5. *Find the statutes of construction.* Many codes have statutes that give you guidelines on how to interpret the statutes in the code. (**Construction** simply means interpretation.) For example, there may be a statute of construction on how to interpret à statute that contains a list of specific items followed by a general item. The rule of construction is that the general item should be construed (interpreted) as being of the same kind (**ejusdem generis**) as the specific items. Suppose § 100 of a statute prohibits "hunting, fishing, horse racing, and other public events." What does "other public events" mean? The ejusdem-generis statute of construction says you are to interpret a general item as being of the same kind as the specific items in the list. This would lead to the conclusion that "other public events" in § 100 means other *outdoor sporting* events, not any public event or even any sporting event. Why? Because all of the specific items in the list are outdoor sporting events. Hence, under this interpretation, § 100 would prohibit ocean swimming races but not necessarily indoor swimming races. Statutes of construction such as these can be very helpful in understanding statutes.

construction Interpretation (the verb is *construe*).

ejusdem generis Where general words follow a list of particular words, the general words will be interpreted as applying only to things of the same class or category as the particular words in the list.

ASSIGNMENT 11.26

Each of the following problems consists of a statute and a set of facts. Determine whether ejusdem generis is helpful in deciding whether the statute applies to the facts.

(a) *Statute:* § 88. An injunction can be obtained against any person who, by circular, advertisement, or otherwise, falsely claims to be the inventor of a product. *Facts:* George is writing letters to people in which he falsely states that he invented the portable radio.

(b) *Statute:* § 608.7. Evidence of abandonment shall include exposure of the child in a street, field, or other place with the intent to leave the child there indefinitely. *Facts:* Roger took his infant child to the church rectory. When no one was looking, he left the child in a corner of the hallway, ran out, and left the state.

6. *Ask yourself the core questions about every statute.* The following essential questions should be asked about every statute you are examining:
   a. What is the citation of the statute? (On citing statutes, see Exhibit 11.14.)
   b. What are the *elements* of the statute? (See discussion of elements in chapter 7.)
   c. To whom is the statute addressed? Who is the audience? (Everyone? The director of an administrative agency? Citizens who want to apply for a permit? Etc.)
   d. What condition(s) make the statute operative? (Many statutes have "when" or "if" clauses that specify condition(s) for the applicability of the statute.)
   e. Is the statute mandatory or discretionary? A **mandatory statute** requires that something happen or be done ("must," "shall"). A **discretionary statute** permits something to occur but does not impose it ("may," "can").
   f. What is the internal statutory context of the statute? To what other statutes, if any, does your statute refer?

mandatory statute A statute that requires something to be done.

discretionary statute A statute that permits something to be done but does not require or mandate it.

g. What is the effective date of the statute?

h. Has the statute been amended in the past? (Check the Historical Notes beneath the statute in annotated codes. Briefly summarize major relevant changes.)

i. Has the statute been declared valid or invalid by the courts? (Check Notes of Decisions beneath the statute in annotated codes, and shepardize or KeyCite the statute.)

j. Do administrative regulations exist that interpret and carry out the statute? (On finding regulations based on statutes, see research link S later in the chapter. Give citations to any such regulations.)

7. *Statutory language tends to be unclear.* Seldom, if ever, is it absolutely clear what a statute means or how it applies to a given set of facts. For this reason, statutory language regularly requires close scrutiny and interpretation.

8. *Statutes are to be read line by line, pronoun by pronoun, punctuation mark by punctuation mark.* Statutes cannot be speed read. They should be read with the same care that you would use if you were translating a foreign language to English. Sentences sometimes appear endless. Occasionally, so many qualifications and exceptions are built into a statute that it appears incomprehensible. Do not despair. The key is perseverance and a willingness to tackle the statute slowly, piece by piece—through its elements.

FINDING STATUTES

We turn now to techniques for finding statutes in traditional legal materials (Exhibit 11.41) and on the Internet (Exhibit 11.42) and the further research steps that should be taken before using or relying on a statute that you have found (Exhibit 11.43).

EXHIBIT 11.41   Techniques for Finding Statutes

1. Go to the statutory code in which you are interested. Some states have more than one statutory code. (See Exhibit 11.14.) For federal statutes, there are the *United States Code* (U.S.C.), the *United States Code Annotated* (U.S.C.A.), and the *United States Code Service* (U.S.C.S.). Know how to use all available statutory codes that cover the same set of statutes. Although they contain the same statutes, the index and research features may differ.

2. Read the explanation or preface pages at the beginning of the first volume of the statutory code. Also read the comparable pages at the beginning of the Shepard's volumes that will enable you to shepardize statutes in that code. These pages can be very helpful in explaining the structure of the code, particularly if there have been new editions, revisions or renumberings.

3. Most statutory codes have general indexes at the end of the set as well as individual indexes for separate volumes. Use the CARTWHEEL to help you use these indexes. Also check any tables of contents that exist. Some statutes have popular names, such as the Civil Rights Act of 1964. If you know the popular name of a statute, you can find it in the statutory code by checking that name in the general index to the code. The code may also have a Popular Name Table that lists the name and location of every statute that has a popular name.

4. While reading one statute in the code, you may be given a cross-reference to another statute within the same code. Check out these cross-references.

5. Update any statute that you find in the statutory code by checking the pocket part of the volume you are using; supplement pamphlets at the end of the code; bound supplement volumes; session law pamphlets; advance legislative services; and online resources such as Westlaw, LexisNexis, and Loislaw.

6. Looseleaf services. Find out if there is a looseleaf service on the topic of your research. Such services will give extensive references to applicable statutes. (See Exhibit 11.29 on finding and using looseleaf services.)

7. Legal treatises. Find out if there are legal treatises on the topics of your research. Such treatises will often give extensive references to applicable statutes. (See Exhibit 11.33 on finding and using legal treatises).

8. Legal periodical literature. Consult the Index to Legal Periodicals and Books (ILP) and the Current Law Index (CLI). Use these indexes to locate periodical literature on the topics of your research. This literature will often give extensive references to applicable statutes. (See Exhibit 11.30 on finding legal periodical literature.)

9. Legal encyclopedias. Occasionally, legal encyclopedias such as Am. Jur. 2d and C.J.S. will summarize statutes in the text and refer you to statutes in the footnotes. (See Exhibit 11.32 on using legal encyclopedias.)

10. Internet. Federal and state statutes are available on free Internet sites of federal and state legislatures (see Exhibit 11.42) and at fee-based services such as Westlaw, LexisNexis, and Loislaw.

11. E-mail. When you are having difficulty locating a statute, particularly a very recent one, e-mail contacts might be fruitful. (See Exhibit 11.34 on using e-mail as a research resource.)

12. Occasionally, in your research, you will come across a statute that is cited in its session law form. To find this statute in the statutory code, you must translate the session law cite into the codified cite. This is done by trying to find transfer or conversion tables in the statutory code. For federal statutes, a session law or *Statutes at Large* cite is translated into a U.S.C./U.S.C.A./ U.S.C.S. cite by:
    a. Checking Table III in the Tables volume of U.S.C./U.S.C.A./ U.S.C.S.
    b. Checking Table 2 in *U.S. Code Congressional and Administrative News* (U.S.C.C.A.N.)
    See research link O in Section J. Some session laws, however, are never printed in the statutory code. Hence there is no codified cite for such statutes. You must go directly to the session laws in the library—if the library has them. (For federal statutes, the session laws are in *United State Statutes at Large.*)

EXHIBIT 11.42	Finding Statutes on the Internet

The following sites will lead you to federal and state statutes on the Internet, most of which have search boxes that allow you to search for statutes on topics that you enter. In addition, most of the sites provide links to pending bills, legislative history, and individual members of the legislatures.

UNITED STATES (federal statutes of Congress):

www.gpoaccess.gov/uscode/index.html
thomas.loc.gov
uscode.house.gov/search/criteria.shtml
findlaw.com/casecode/uscodes
www4.law.cornell.edu/uscode
www.ilrg.com/codes.html
www.plol.org

ALL STATES (statutes of state legislatures; click the link to your state):

www.llsdc.org/sourcebook/state-leg.htm
www.prairienet.org/~scruffy/f.htm

www.ncsl.org/public/leglinks.cfm
www.law.cornell.edu/states/listing.html
www.findlaw.com/casecode/#state
www.findlaw.com/11stategov
www.washlaw.edu
www.statelocalgov.net
www.loc.gov/rr/news/stategov/stategov.html
www.ilrg.com/codes.html
www.plol.org

Once you have found a statute that is relevant to your research problem, you need to do further research on the statute before you rely on it. See Exhibit 11.43.

EXHIBIT 11.43	Techniques for Further Research on Statutes You Have Found

1. Make sure the statute is still valid:
   - Check your statute in the pocket part of the volume where you found the statute.
   - Check your statute in supplement pamphlets and the hardcover supplements that go with the code.
   - Shepardize the statute. (See Exhibit 11.28 on shepardizing statutes.)
   - KeyCite the statute on Westlaw.
2. Check all cross-references with in the statute. If the statute refers to other statutes in the code, check them for their relevance to your research.
3. Find cases interpreting the statute:
   - Check *notes of decisions* following the statute in annotated codes.
   - Shepardize the statute. Among the citing materials are cases that have analyzed or mentioned the statute. (See technique 1 above.)
   - KeyCite the statute on Westlaw to find cases interpreting the statute.
4. Find administrative regulations based on the statute. Many statutes are carried out by administrative regulations. The statute is considered the *authority* for such regulations. It is the enabling statute, which is a statute that is the basis or authority for what an agency does. To find federal regulations based a federal statute, check the "Parallel Table of Authorities and Rules" in the volume called *CFR Index and Finding Aids*, which is part of the

Code of Federal Regulations (C.F.R.). This table will tell you if your statute is the enabling statute for any regulations in the C.F.R. See research link S later in the chapter. (To reverse the process, if you are starting with a regulation and want to identify its enabling statute, check the "Authority" reference beneath the regulation in the C.F.R. See research link R later in the chapter.)
5. Find annotations on the statute.
   - If you shepardize the statute, the citing materials include annotations in the eight sets of A.L.R. (e.g., A.L.R.6th and A.L.R. Fed. 2d)
   - If you KeyCite the statute on Westlaw, you may find annotations that cover the statute.
   - Check the *ALR Table of Laws, Rules, and Regulations*
6. Find legal periodical comments or other periodical literature on the statute. Check the tables of statutes in the ILP and CLI. (See Exhibit 11.30 and research link Q.)
7. Find out if there are any looseleaf services that cover the statute. (See Exhibit 11.29.)
8. Find out if there are any legal treatises that cover the statute. (See Exhibit 11.33.)
9. Find a discussion of your statute in *Corpus Juris Secundum* or *American Jurisprudence 2d.* See the separate volume called *Table of Laws and Rules* that is part of C.J.S and Am.Jur.2d. (See Exhibit 11.32.)
10. Review the legislative history of the statute. See Exhibits 11.44 and 11.45

[SECTION R]

LEGISLATIVE HISTORY

In chapter 6, we examined the six stages of the legislative process through which a bill is enacted into a statute. (See Exhibit 6.5 in chapter 6.) The documents and events that occur during this process constitute the **legislative history** of a statute. Here, we consider two themes: the importance of legislative history and how to find it.

legislative history Hearings, amendments, committee reports, and all other events that occur in the legislature before a bill is enacted into a statute.

WHY SEARCH FOR LEGISLATIVE HISTORY: ADVOCACY OBJECTIVES

To understand why researchers try to find the legislative history of a statute, let's look at an example:

> In 1975, the state legislature enacts the Liquor Control Act. Section 33 of this Act provides that "[l]iquor shall not be sold on Sunday or on any day on which a local, state, or federal election is being held." The Fairfax Country Club claims that § 33 does not apply to the sale of liquor on Sunday or on election day *by membership clubs*; it applies only to bars that provide service to any customers that come in off the street. The question, therefore, is whether the legislature intended to include membership clubs within the restrictions of § 33. The state liquor board says that it did. The Fairfax Country Club argues that it did not.

How can the legislative history of § 33 help resolve this controversy? An advocate has two objectives when researching the legislative history of a statute:

- To determine whether the specific facts currently in controversy were ever discussed by the legislature when it was considering the proposed statute and
- To identify the broad or narrow purpose that prompted the legislature to enact the statute and to assess whether this purpose sheds any light on the specific facts currently in controversy

For example, when the legislature was considering § 33, was there any mention of country or membership clubs in the governor's message, in committee reports, in floor debates, etc.? If so, what was said about them? What was said about the purpose of § 33? Why was it enacted? What evil or mischief was it designed to combat? Was the legislature opposed to liquor on moral grounds? Did it want to reduce rowdyism that comes from the overuse of liquor? Did it want to encourage citizens to go to church on Sunday and to vote on election day? Were complaints made to the legislature about the use of liquor by certain groups in the community? If so, what groups? Answers to such questions might be helpful in formulating arguments on the meaning and scope of § 33. The advocate for the Fairfax Country Club will try to demonstrate that the legislature had a narrow objective when it enacted § 33: to prevent neighborhood rowdyism at establishments that serve only liquor. The legislature, therefore, was not trying to regulate the more moderate kind of drinking that normally takes place at membership clubs where food and liquor are often served together. The opponent, in contrast, will argue that the legislature had a broader purpose in enacting § 33: to decrease the consumption of liquor by all citizens on certain days. The legislature, therefore, did not intend to exclude drinking at a membership club.

FINDING LEGISLATIVE HISTORY

In tracing legislative history, you are looking for documents such as bills, hearing transcripts, proposed amendments, and committee reports. It is often very difficult to trace the legislative history of *state* statutes. The documents are sometimes poorly preserved, if at all. See Exhibit 11.44.

EXHIBIT 11.44   Techniques for Tracing the Legislative History of State Statutes

1. Examine the historical data beneath the statute in the statutory code (see Exhibit 11.39). Amendments are usually listed there.
2. For an overview of codification information about your state, check the introductory pages in the first volume of the statutory code, or the beginning of the volume where your statute is found, or the beginning of the Shepard's volume that enables you to shepardize the statutes of that state.
3. Ask your librarian if there is a book or service (sometimes called a legislative service) that covers your state legislature. If one exists, it will give the bill numbers of statutes, proposed amendments, names of committees that considered the statute, etc. If such a text does not exist for your state, ask the librarian how someone finds the legislative history of a current state statute in your state.
4. Find your state at State Legislative History on the Web.
   - www.law.indiana.edu/library/services/sta_leg.shtml
5. Check the Internet site of the state legislature. (See Exhibit 11.42.) It may have links to sources of legislative history, such as an archives link or a legislative research link. A particularly useful site is that of the National Conference of State Legislatures (www.ncsl.org). It has links to every state legislature (www.ncsl.org/public/leglinks.cfm). On sites that allow you to trace or track proposed legislation currently before the legislature (e.g., www.llrx.com/columns/roundup13.htm), you may find links that will help you locate the legislative history of statutes already on the books. Some sites have an e-mail address to which you can send specific questions. If your state has such an address, send an e-mail asking for a lead to the legislative history of the state statute you are researching.
6. Contact the committees of both houses of the state legislature that considered the bill. The office of your local state representative or state senator might be able to help you identify these committees. If your statute is not too old, staff members on these committees may be able to give you leads to the legislative history of the statute. Ask if any committee reports (or committee prints) were written. Ask about amendments, etc.

(continues)

EXHIBIT 11.44	Techniques for Tracing the Legislative History of State Statutes—*continued*

7. If there is a law revision commission in your state, its Web site may have information on researching legislative history. If the site has a "Contact Us" link, you may be able to inquire about such research by e-mail. On Google or another search engine, type the name of your state and "law revision commission" (e.g., Oregon "law revision commission").

8. If the statute deals with a particular state agency, go to the Web site of the agency to find out if it has any of the legislative history of that statute online. A "Contact Us" link may allow you to ask for specific leads to this history.

9. Is there a state law library in your area? If so, contact it for leads. (For the state law library in your state, see Appendix I at the end of the book.)

10. Check the law library and drafting office of the state legislature for leads.

11. Online law librarians ("Ask a Librarian") are often an excellent source of leads to legislative history. On locating such librarians, see Exhibit 11.34.

12. Cases interpreting the statute sometimes give the legislative history of the statute, or portions of it. To find cases interpreting a statute, check the Notes of Decisions after the statute in the statutory code (see Exhibit 11.39), KeyCite the statute (if you have access to Westlaw), and shepardize it (see Exhibit 11.28 on shepardizing a statute).

13. You may also find leads to the legislative history of a statute in legal periodical literature on the statute (see Exhibit 11.30), in annotations on the statute (see Exhibit 11.24), in treatises on the statute (see Exhibit 11.33), and in looseleaf services on the statute (see Exhibit 11.29).

14. For links to state legislative history, check:
    - www.llsdc.org/sourcebook/state-leg.htm
    - www.ll.georgetown.edu/states/index.cfm
    - www.lexisnexis.com/infopro/zimmerman/disp. aspx?z=1962

It is easier to trace the legislative history of a *federal* statute because the documents are generally more available. See Exhibit 11.45.

EXHIBIT 11.45	Techniques for Tracing the Legislative History of Federal Statutes

1. For an overview of the legislative materials published by the federal government, see:
    - Legislative Branch Resources on GPO Access (www.gpoaccess.gov/legislative.html)
    - Congressional Resources: Thomas (thomas.loc.gov/links)

2. Examine the historical data at the end of the statute in the *United States Code* (U.S.C.), in the *United States Code Annotated* (U.S.C.A.), and in the *United States Code Service* (U.S.C.S.).

3. You will also find the PL (Public Law) number of the statute at the end of the statute printed in U.S.C./U.S.C.A./U.S.C.S. This PL number will be important for tracing legislative history. (Note that each amendment to a statute will have its own PL number.)

4. Step one in tracing the legislative history of a federal statute is to find out if the history has already been compiled (collected) by someone else. To find out:
    - Ask your law librarian.
    - Check:
        - *Union List of Legislative Histories* (www.llsdc.org/sourcebook/about-union-histories.htm)
        - LexisNexis (e.g., LexisNexis Congressional)
        - Westlaw (e.g., LH database)
        - *Compiled Legislative Histories* by Nancy Johnson
    - If the statute deals with a particular federal administrative agency, go to the Web site of the agency to find out if it has any of the legislative history of that statute online. A "Contact Us" link may allow you to ask for specific leads to this history.
    - Contact special interest groups or associations that are directly affected by the statute. They may have compiled all or part of the legislative history. One way to try to locate such organizations is to run a *lobby* search on Google or another search engine (e.g., lobby tobacco). See also the suggestions in Exhibit 11.34 on e-mail as a research tool.

5. The *Congressional Record* gives you the transcript of the conversations between legislators on the floor of the House and Senate while the bill is being debated. These conversations (though sometimes later altered—"amended"—by participating legislators) may cover the meaning of particular clauses in a bill. The conversations are often used by advocates when citing legislative history. The *Congressional Record* is published by Congress in daily pamphlets and later in permanent hardbound volumes. It is also available online on fee-based services such as Westlaw and LexisNexis and on the free Internet (www.gpoaccess.gov/crecord/index.html).

6. The following materials are also useful in tracing the legislative history of federal statutes:
    - *United States Code Congressional and Administrative News* (contains committee reports of important bills; see its Table 4, which is a status table providing leads to legislative history). U.S.C.C.A.N. is a good place to begin your search for federal legislative history.
    - *Monthly Catalog of U.S. Government Publications* acts as an index to tell you which committee hearings have been published) (catalog.gpo.gov/F)
    - *Congressional Index* from Commerce Clearing House (contains digest of bills, status tables, voting records, current news, etc.).
    - The paper, CD-ROM, microform, and online products of CIS (Congressional Information Service) contain reprints of legislative history documents, abstracts, indexes, and other finding tools (www.lexisnexis.com/academic/3cis/cisMnu.asp). The CIS materials include:
        - *CIS/Index to Publications of the United States Congress* (CIS/index)
        - *CIS/Legislative Histories*
        - *CIS/Annual Abstracts*

(continues)

EXHIBIT 11.45   Techniques for Tracing the Legislative History of Federal Statutes—*continued*

- *United States Congressional Serial Set* (committee reports, legislative studies, and other legislative documents) (www. gpoaccess.gov/legislative.html).

- *Congressional Weekly* (contains a legislative history table and a status table on current major bills) (www.cqpress.com/product/1157.html).

7. Contact both committees of Congress that considered the legislation. (www.senate.gov) (www.house.gov). They may be able to send you:

   - committee reports (summaries of the bill and a statement of the reasons for and against its enactment)

   - committee prints (a miscellaneous compilation of information prepared by committee staff members on a bill consisting of statistics, studies, reports, comparative analysis of related bills, etc.)

   - hearing transcripts (includes a word-for-word account of the testimony given by witnesses).

   - copies of the bill and amendments to it

     If you have any difficulty, ask staff members in the office of your U.S. senator and representative for help in obtaining what you need from the relevant committees. Their contact numbers (and e-mail addresses) should be available through links on their Web sites. Also, standard phone directories often give phone numbers of the local offices of U.S. senators and representatives.

8. Cases interpreting the statute sometimes give the legislative history of the statute. To find cases interpreting the statute, check the Notes of Decisions after the statute in the U.S.C.A.

and in the U.S.C.S. Also, KeyCite or shepardize the statute (see Exhibit 11.28 on shepardizing a statute).

9. Find out if there is an annotation on the statute. (see Exhibits 11.24 and 11.25 on annotations.)

10. You may also find leads to the legislative history of a statute in legal periodical literature (see Exhibit 11.30), in legal treatises on the statute (see Exhibit 11.33), in looseleaf services on the statute (see Exhibit 11.29).

11. To try to find a discussion of your statute in the C.J.S. or Am. Jur. 2d legal encyclopedias, check a separate volume called *Table of Laws and Rules*. (See Exhibit 11.32.)

12. Examine your statute in its session law form in *United States Statutes at Large* for possible leads (www.gpoaccess.gov/statutes/index.html).

13. Check legislative histories online through, services such as Westlaw, LexisNexis, and LEGI-SLATE.

14. Check the Internet. Sites that can provide useful leads include:

    - www.loc.gov/rr/law/leghist.html
    - www.lib.umich.edu/govdocs/legchart.html
    - www.llsdc.org/sourcebook/fed-leg-hist.htm
    - law-library.rutgers.edu/resources/fedleghist.php
    - www.columbia.edu/cu/lweb/indiv/usgd/leghis.html
    - www.law.harvard.edu/library/services/research/guides
    - www.lib.unc.edu/instruct/legis_history/histories/histories_print.html

    Sites for finding current statutes may provide leads to sources for legislative history. See Exhibit 11.42.

[SECTION S]

MONITORING PROPOSED LEGISLATION

Occasionally, you will be asked to monitor a bill currently before the legislature that has relevance to the caseload of the law office where you work. To monitor a bill means to determine its current status in the legislature and to keep track of all the forces that are trying to enact, defeat, or modify the bill. See Exhibit 11.46. If you work for a corporation, you may be asked to monitor bills that affect the business of the company. Large corporations often hire lobbyists whose sole function is to monitor and try to influence the content of proposed legislation.

EXHIBIT 11.46   Techniques for Monitoring Proposed Legislation

1. Familiarize yourself with the publications of the legislature on current bills before it (see Exhibits 11.42, 11.44, and 11.45). For state legislation, go to the homepage of the state legislature. For federal legislation, check:

   - Legislative Branch Resources on GPO (www.gpoaccess.gov/legislative.html)

   - Congressional Resources: Thomas (thomas.loc.gov/links)

2. Find out what committee in each chamber of the legislature is considering the proposed legislation you are monitoring. Also determine whether more than two committees are considering the entire bill or portions of it.

3. Ask committee staff members to send you copies of the bill in its originally proposed form and in its amended forms.

4. Determine whether the committees considering the proposed legislation have written any reports on it and, if so, whether copies are available.

5. Determine whether any hearings have been scheduled by the committees on the bill. If so, try to attend. For hearings already conducted, see if they have been transcribed (recorded word for word).

6. Find out the names of people in the legislature who are working on the bill: legislators "pushing" the bill, legislators opposed to it, staff members of the individual legislators working on the bill, and staff members of the committees working on the bill. Ask for copies of any position papers or statements. Many important committees have their own Web sites on which they post announcements, calendars, and reports.

7. The local bar association may have taken a position on the bill. Call the association. Find out what committee of the bar is involved with the subject matter of the bill. This committee may have written a report on the bar's position on the bill. If so, try to obtain a copy. Check the Web site of the bar to see if anything is available on the bill. (The relevant committee may have its own Web site.)

8. Is an administrative agency of the government involved with the bill? Identify the agency with jurisdiction over the subject matter of the bill. Find out who in the agency is working on the bill and whether any written reports of the agency are available. Also find out what is available on the agency's Web site. Determine whether the agency has a legislative liaison office.

(continues)

| EXHIBIT 11.46 | Techniques for Monitoring Proposed Legislation—*continued* |

9. Who else is lobbying for or against the bill? What organizations are interested in it? Find out if they have taken any written positions.
10. What precipitated consideration of the bill by the legislature? Was there a court opinion that prompted the legislative action? If so, you should know what the opinion said.
11. Are any other legislatures in the country contemplating similar legislation? Some of the ways of finding out include the following:
    a. Look for legal periodical literature on the subject matter of the bill (see Exhibit 11.30).
    b. Check looseleaf services, if any, covering the subject matter of the bill (see Exhibit 11.29). These services often cover proposed legislation in the various legislatures.
    c. Check legal treatises on the subject matter of the bill (see Exhibit 11.33).
    d. Organizations such as bar associations, public interest groups, business associations, etc., often assign staff

members to perform state-by-state research on what the legislatures are doing. Such organizations may be willing to share this research with you.
    e. Find out if there is a council of governments in your area. It may have done the same research mentioned in (d) above.
    f. Contact an expert for leads to what other legislatures are doing (see Exhibit 11.34).
12. For more monitoring resources and leads on the Internet, see:
    - www.ncsl.org/nalit/billtrack.htm
    - www.llrx.com/columns/roundup13.htm
    - www.GalleryWatch.com
    - Westlaw (e.g., US-BILLTRK)
    - LexisNexis (e.g., BLKTRCK)

To find out what bill-monitoring services are available covering your state legislature, run a search on tracking in Google or another search engine (e.g., "tracking legislation" Iowa).

[S E C T I O N T]

READING AND FINDING CONSTITUTIONAL LAW

READING CONSTITUTIONAL LAW

The **constitution** sets out the fundamental ground rules for the conduct of the government in the geographical area over which the government has authority or jurisdiction. The constitution creates the branches of government, allocates power among them, and defines some basic rights of individuals. (See Exhibit 6.1 in chapter 6.) The U.S. Constitution does this for the federal government, and the state constitution does it for the state government. In reading the constitution, keep the following guidelines in mind:

constitution The fundamental law that creates the branches of government, allocates power among them, and defines some basic rights of individuals.

1. *Thumb through the headings of all the sections or articles of the constitution, or glance through the table of contents.* How is the document organized? What subjects did the framers want covered by the constitution? A quick scanning of the section headings or table of contents is a good way to obtain an overview of the structure of the text.

2. *The critical sections or articles are those that establish and define the powers of the legislative, judicial, and executive branches of government in the geographic area covered by the constitution.* Who passes, interprets, and executes the law? For the U.S. Constitution, "all legislative Powers granted herein shall be vested in a Congress" (art. I, § 1); "the judicial Power of the United States, shall be vested in one supreme Court, and in such inferior Courts as the Congress may from time to time ordain and establish" (art. III, § 1); and "the executive Power shall be vested in a President of the United States of America" (art. II, § 1). The exact scope of these powers, as enunciated elsewhere in the Constitution, has been and continues to be an arena of constant controversy and litigation.

3. *The amendments to the constitution change or add to the body of the text.* The main vehicle for changing the constitution is the amendment process, which itself is defined in the constitution. Some constitutions, for example, can be amended by a vote of the people in a general election. A condition for most amendments is that they must be approved by one or more sessions of the legislature. Constitutional amendments usually appear at the end of the document.

4. *Constitutions are written in very broad terms.* A common characteristic of many provisions in constitutions is their broad language. How would you interpret the following language of the First Amendment?

Congress shall make no laws respecting an establishment of religion, or prohibiting the free exercise thereof; or abridging the freedom of speech, or of the press; or of the right of the people to assemble, and to petition the Government for a redress of grievances.

How many words in this provision do you *not* understand? What is an "establishment"? If the school board requires a "moment of silence" at the beginning of each day, is the school board establishing a religion? What does "abridging" mean? If a government official leaks secret documents to the press and the government tries to sue the press to prevent publication of the documents, has the "freedom" of the press been abridged? If the people have a right to "assemble," could the government pass a law prohibiting all gatherings of three or more people at any place within 1,000 yards of the White House gates? The questions arising from the interpretation of constitutional law are endless; tens of thousands of court opinions exist on questions such as these. The broader the language, the more ambiguous it is, and, therefore, the greater the need for interpretation.

5. *One of the central questions for the interpreter of constitutional law is: what meaning did the authors intend?* Common sense dictates that when language is ambiguous, the ambiguity may be resolved in part by attempting to determine what the author of the language intended by it. What was the author's meaning? In what context was the author writing? Does the context shed any light on what was meant? This kind of analysis is fundamental to legal reasoning, whether the document is a constitution, a statute, a regulation, or a court opinion. It is particularly difficult to do, however, for a constitution written and amended over two hundred years ago.

Some judges and legal scholars take the view that the authors of the constitution intended it to be a "living" document that must be interpreted in light of the needs of modern society. The danger in this view is that too much can be read into the constitution based on the personal philosophies of individual judges. The charge is that judges rewrite the constitution under the guise of interpreting it to fit modern society. This debate, of course, adds to the controversy and the volume of constitutional law.

FINDING CONSTITUTIONAL LAW

The techniques for finding constitutional law are summarized in Exhibit 11.47.

EXHIBIT 11.47	Techniques for Finding Constitutional Law

1. Start with the text of the constitution itself. It is usually found at the beginning of the statutory code of the jurisdiction. (The federal Constitution is in U.S.C./U.S.C.A./U.S.C.S.)
2. Use the CARTWHEEL to help you use the general index of the statutory code and the separate index for the constitution itself. (See Exhibit 11.16.) Also check the table of contents material for the constitution in the statutory code.
3. Following the text of individual constitutional provisions in annotated codes there are often *Notes of Decisions* containing summaries of cases interpreting the constitution. Some of these notes can run hundreds of pages. Check any available index or table of contents covering these notes.
4. Annotations. Find annotations in the eight sets of A.L.R. (e.g., A.L.R. 6th and A.L.R. Fed. 2d). on the constitutional provisions in which you are interested. (See Exhibit 11.24 on annotations.)
5. Digests. Go to West Group's *United States Supreme Court Digest* and the American Digest System, which covers all courts. Use the Descriptive Word Index (DWI) to locate relevant key numbers. (See Exhibit 11.23 on using West Group digests.)
6. Legal treatises. Find legal treatises on the entire constitution or on the specific portions of the constitution in which you are interested. Numerous such treatises exist. (See Exhibit 11.33 on finding legal treatises.)
7. Legal periodical literature. Go to the two indexes to legal periodical literature, ILP and CLI. Use them to help you locate what you need among the vast periodical literature on the constitution. (See Exhibit 11.30 on finding legal periodical literature.)
8. Looseleaf services. Find out if there are looseleaf services on the area of the constitution in which you are interested. (See Exhibit 11.29 on looseleaf services.)
9. *Words and Phrases.* Identify specific words or phrases within the constitutional provision you are examining. Find court definitions of these words or phrases in the multivolume legal dictionary *Words and Phrases.*
10. Legal encyclopedias. Find discussions of constitutional law in Am. Jur. 2d and in C.J.S. (See Exhibit 11.32 on legal encyclopedias.)
11. Once you have found a constitutional provision relevant to your research, shepardize or KeyCite the provision to find case law interpreting it. The set of Shepard's you use to shepardize the constitution is the same set of Shepard's you would use to shepardize a statute. (See Exhibit 11.28.) Also, any case that you find should be shepardized or KeyCited to try to find additional cases.
12. LexisNexis and Westlaw contain the full text of the U.S. Constitution and every state constitution. They also can lead you to extensive case law interpreting these constitutions and legal periodical literature analyzing them.
13. For a list of constitutions on the Internet, see:
    - www.constitution.org/cons/usstcons.htm
    - www.findlaw.com/11stategov/indexconst.html
    - www.prairiente.org/~scruffy/f.htm
    Also check the Internet site for the state statutes of your state. See Exhibit 11.42. Most of these sites will also lead you to the constitution of your state.
14. For *Constitutions of the Countries of the World* online, see www.oceanalaw.com/main_product_details.asp?ID=341.

ASSIGNMENT 11.27

(a) Go to your state constitution. Find any provision in it that grants powers to your governor. Select one of the powers. Quote a sentence from the provision and give its citation.

(b) Go to the set of Shepard's that will allow you to shepardize this constitutional provision. Pick any citing case. Go to the reporter that contains this citing case. Quote the sentence from the case that cites this provision. Give the citation of your quote. (If there are no citing cases, redo part (a) of this assignment until you find a constitutional provision that does have a citing case.)

(c) Go back to the set of books you used in part (a). Are there Notes of Decisions in this set? If so, find the case you used for part (b). Photocopy this page and circle the case in these notes.

(d) Go to your main state digest. In this digest, find the case you used for part (b). Under what key number(s) was this case digested? On what page(s) of the digest volume (or its supplement) did you find this case digested?

(e) Go to the American Digest System. Find the case you used for part (b). Under what key number(s) was this case digested? In what units of the American Digest System and on what page(s) did you find this case digested?

[SECTION U]

FINDING ADMINISTRATIVE LAW

Many agencies write **administrative regulations**, but few have coherent systems of organizing and distributing the regulations. See Exhibit 6.1 in chapter 6. A major exception is the federal agencies, whose regulations are first published in the *Federal Register*. Many are then codified in the *Code of Federal Regulations*. (See research link D in Section H.) A large number of states follow this pattern of a separate register and code for the regulations of state administrative agencies. The state register and code, however, are not as sophisticated as the *Federal Register* and the *Code of Federal Regulations*.

Normally, an agency does not have the power to write regulations unless it has specific statutory authority to do so. An examination of the statute giving the agency this authority can be helpful in understanding the regulations themselves. In theory, the statutes of the legislature establish the purpose of the agency and define its overall policies but leave to the agency (through its regulations) the task of filling in the specifics of administration. Regulations, therefore, tend to be very detailed.

The other major kind of administrative law is the **administrative decision**. This is a resolution of a controversy between a party and an administrative agency involving the application of the regulations, statutes, or executive orders that govern the agency. (It is also called an administrative ruling. See Exhibit 6.1 in chapter 6.) Not many agencies publish their decisions in any systematic order; some agencies do not publish them at all. Regulatory agencies, such as the Federal Communications Commission and state environmental agencies, often do a better job at publishing their decisions than other agencies.

The federal government and most states have an **Administrative Procedure Act** (APA). This is a statute that governs the steps that an agency must take to write a regulation or issue an administrative decision. Examples of these steps include publishing a notice of a proposed regulation and allowing affected parties to participate in a hearing that leads to an administrative decision. Part of legal research in administrative law should address the question of whether the agency properly complied with the Administrative Procedure Act on such steps.

When looking for an administrative regulation, you must simultaneously be looking for the **enabling statute** that is the authority for the regulation. (An enabling statute is a statute that allows [enables] an administrative agency to carry out specified delegated powers, often through administrative regulations.) With very few exceptions, agencies do not have their own independent power. In large measure, the very reason for the existence of the agency is to carry out the statutes of the legislature that created the agency and gave it specific responsibilities. Consequently, two questions always confront the researcher:

- Is there an administrative regulation on point?
- If so, does the regulation go beyond what its enabling statute authorizes the agency to do? In other words, is the administrative regulation within the scope of the enabling statute?

administrative regulation A law written by an administrative agency designed to explain or carry out the statutes, executive orders, or other regulations that govern the agency.

administrative decision An administrative agency's resolution of a controversy (following a hearing) involving the application of the regulations, statutes, or executive orders that govern the agency. Sometimes called an administrative *ruling*.

Administrative Procedure Act (APA) The statute that governs procedures before federal administrative agencies. Many states have their own APA for procedures before state administrative agencies.

enabling statute The statute that allows (enables) an administrative agency to carry out specified delegated powers.

To answer the second question, of course, you need to find the enabling statute. Often the lead you need to find this statute will be within the administrative code that contains the regulation.

Assume that you have found a federal administrative regulation in the *Code of Federal Regulations* (C.F.R.) that is on point. You now want to check the authority for that regulation in the enabling statute, which for federal statutes would be within the *United States Code* (U.S.C.) or the *United States Code Annotated* (U.S.C.A.) or the *United States Code Service* (U.S.C.S.). To find the statute, you would check the "Authority" reference within the C.F.R. itself. Beneath the regulation you are reading (or at the beginning of the cluster of regulations of which your regulation is a part), find an "Authority" reference that will tell you what federal statutes are the authority for the regulation. See research link R.

| Administrative regulation in *Code of Federal Regulations* (C.F.R.) (Check "Authority" reference) | Enabling statute in *United States Code* (U.S.C.) or *United States Code Annotated* (U.S.C.A.) or *United States Code Service* (U.S.C.S.) |

RESEARCH LINK R

If you have found a federal administrative regulation, and you now want to find the enabling statute that is the authority for that regulation, check the "authority" reference beneath the regulation in C.F.R. (or at the beginning of the cluster of regulations of which your regulation is a part). There you will be given the cite in U.S.C. (or U.S.C.A. or U.S.C.S.) to the federal statute that is the authority for the regulation.

Suppose you have not yet found any administrative regulations, but you have found a statute that is on point. You want to determine whether there are any administrative regulations based on that statute. To find out, check the "Parallel Table of Authorities and Rules" in the pamphlet called *CFR Index and Finding Aids* that is part of the C.F.R. set. See research link S. For techniques in finding administrative law, see Exhibit 11.48.

| Enabling statute in *United States Code* (U.S.C.) or *United States Code Annotated* (U.S.C.A.) or *United States Code Service* (U.S.C.S.) | Administrative regulation in *Code of Federal Regulations* (C.F.R.) (Check "Parallel Table of Authorities and Rules" in *CFR Index and Finding Aids*) |

RESEARCH LINK S

You have found a federal statute in U.S.C. (or U.S.C.A. or U.S.C.S.) and you now want to know whether there are any administrative regulations in C.F.R. that are based on that statute. To find out, check the "Parallel Table of Authorities and Rules" in the pamphlet called *CFR Index and Finding Aids* that is part of the C.F.R. set. This pamphlet will tell you if your statute is an enabling statute for any administrative regulations.

EXHIBIT 11.48   **Techniques for Finding Administrative Law**

General: Federal and State Administrative Law

1. Begin by obtaining an overview of federal and state administrative law. Run the following searches in Google or another search engine:
   - "federal administrative law"
   - "Pennsylvania administrative law" (use the name of your state)
2. Go to the Web site of the administrative agency whose law you are researching. This site will often list regulations, decisions, and reports of the agency that are online. To obtain a list of all federal and state administrative agencies, run the following searches in Google or another search engine:
   - "federal administrative agencies"
   - "New York" "administrative agencies") (use the name of your state)
   In addition, sites that include links to every state agency include:
   - www.usa.gov (click "A-Z Agency Index")
   - www.statelocalgov.net
   - www.govengine.com

Federal Administrative Regulations

3. Many university libraries in your area subscribe to the *Code of Federal Regulations* (C.F.R.) and the *Federal Register* (Fed. Reg.). If these libraries are *federal depository libraries*, you must be given access to this set as well as to other subscriptions the library receives free from the federal government, e.g., the *United States Code* and the *Congressional Record*. If there is a university library that you want to use, call its reference desk and ask if it is a federal depository library. Also check the online list of every depository library in the country (catalog.gpo.gov/fdlpdir/FDLPdir.jsp).
4. Many federal administrative regulations are printed in the *Code of Federal Regulations* (C.F.R.), which are usually printed first in their proposed form in the *Federal Register* before they are enacted by the agency. The C.F.R. comes out in a new edition—and a new color—every year. See research

(continues)

EXHIBIT 11.48   Techniques for Finding Administrative Law—*continued*

link D in Section H. There are seven main ways to locate regulations in the C.F.R.

  a. GPO Access. This is a free online service of the federal government that allows you to search the C.F.R. by subject (www.gpoaccess.gov/cfr/index.html).

  b. The *C.F.R. Index and Finding Aids* volume. This is a single-volume pamphlet that is reissued every year.

  c. The *Index to the Code of Federal Regulations* published by Congressional Information Service (CIS).

  d. Looseleaf services. As indicated earlier, there are numerous looseleaf services covering many federal agencies and some state agencies. These services usually give extensive references to administrative regulations and decisions. (See Exhibit 11.29.)

  e. The *Federal Register*. Although the *Federal Register* (Fed. Reg.) contains proposed regulations, a subject matter search in the *Federal Register* may lead you to regulations currently in force in the C.F.R. To search the *Federal Register*, use GPO Access (www.gpoaccess.gov/fr/index.html).

  f. Fee-based online services. You can also search for regulations in the C.F.R. databases of the fee-based services (e.g., Westlaw, LexisNexis, and Loislaw).

  g. Statutes. If you already have the cite to a federal statute and you want to find regulations in the C.F.R. that implement that statute, check the Parallel Table of Authorities and Rules in a volume called *CFR Index and Finding Aids*, which accompanies the C.F.R. See research link S.

5. Once you have found a federal regulation on point in the C.F.R., do the following:

  a. Shepardize the regulation. (See Exhibit 11.28 on shepardizing a regulation.)

  b. KeyCite the regulation on Westlaw to find information about the regulation comparable to what Shepard's would reveal.

  c. Find the enabling statute that is the authority for that regulation. Read this statute in U.S.C./U.S.C.A./U.S.C.S. Make sure the regulation does not contradict, go beyond the scope of, or otherwise violate the statute that the regulation is supposed to implement. If you have a regulation and want to find out what statute is the authority for that regulation, look for the "Authority" reference beneath the regulation in the C.F.R. (or at the beginning of the cluster of regulations in C.F.R. of which your regulation is a part). See research link R.

6. Once you have found a regulation in the C.F.R., you must find out if the regulation has been affected in any way (changed revoked, added to, renumbered) by subsequent material printed in the *Federal Register*. This is done as follows:

  ■ Check your C.F.R. cite in the monthly pamphlet called *LSA: List of Sections Affected*. This pamphlet is also available on the Internet (www.gpoaccess.gov/lsa/browse.html).

  ■ Check your C.F.R. cite in the "CFR Parts Affected" table in the daily *Federal Register* from the date of the latest *LSA* pamphlet to the current date. (The Reader Aids section of the *Federal Register* has this table in a cumulative list.) CFR Parts Affected is also available on the Internet. (www.gpoaccess.

gov/lsa/curlist.html). The *LSA* pamphlet and the CFR Parts Affected will tell you what pages of the *Federal Register* contain material that affects your regulation in the C.F.R. (You need to do this only until the next annual edition of the C.F.R. comes out, because anything affecting the regulation during the preceding year will be incorporated in the next edition of C.F.R.)

7. Check e-CFR (Electronic Code of Federal Regulations) for recent changes in the title of the C.F.R where your regulation is found (www.gpoaccess.gov/ecfr). The e-CFR is an unofficial update service of GPO Access.

8. Find out if there is an annotation on your regulation in the eight sets of A.L.R. (e.g., A.L.R.6th and A.L.R. Fed. 2d). There are several ways to do this. First, check the *ALR Table of Laws, Rules, and Regulations* that is part of the A.L.R. series. Look for the cite of your regulation in this table. Second, shepardize the regulation. As we saw in Exhibit 11.28, one of the citing materials when shepardizing a federal administrative regulation is citing annotations. Third, keycite the regulation in Westlaw to locate citing annotations.

9. The federal government has a valuable Web site that allows citizens to comment on proposed federal regulations (www.regulations.gov). The search features on this site can be useful in locating current as well as proposed C.F.R. regulations.

State Administrative Regulations

10. Most states have an administrative code and an administrative register that are comparable to the *Code of Federal Regulations* (C.F.R.) and the *Federal Register*. The exact title of the administrative code and register for every state can be found in the two main citation guides:

  ■ *The Bluebook: A Uniform System of Citation* (see the tables at the end of the *Bluebook*)

  ■ *AWLD Citation Manual* (see the appendix at the end of AWLD)

11. To find your state's administrative code online, try these searches in Google or any search engine:

  ■ Utah "administrative code" (use the name of your state)

  ■ Illinois "administrative register" (use the name of your state)

12. Other sites that help locate state administrative regulations online include:

  ■ www.law.cornell.edu/states/listing.html

  ■ findlaw.com/casecode/#state

13. State administrative law is also available on the fee-based online research services (e.g., Westlaw, LexisNexis, and Loislaw).

Federal and State Administrative Decisions

14. The best way to locate administrative decisions of federal and state agencies is to find out what is available online on the Web sites of individual agencies. Other sources include looseleaf services (see Exhibit 11.29) and the fee-based online services (e.g., Westlaw, LexisNexis, and Loislaw). Some large agencies also publish their administrative decisions in paper volumes. Unlike with court opinions, however, there is not an extensive system of publishing administrative decisions in paper volumes.

ASSIGNMENT 11.28

(a) What is the title of the administrative code of your state? Does your state have a register? If so, what is its title?

(b) Find and cite any state administrative regulation that covers when workers in your state are entitled to workers' compensation for injuries on the job.

(c) Select any regulation in the *Code of Federal Regulations* (C.F.R.). Give the citation of the regulation. Use the tables in the recent issues of the *Federal Register* to find out how that regulation has been affected within the last year. State how it has been affected, and give the citation to the page(s) in the *Federal Register* that tells you how it was affected. (If the tables in the *Federal Register* tell you that the regulation you selected has not been affected, pick a different regulation in C.F.R.)

(d) Find any five regulations in the *Code of Federal Regulations*, written by five different agencies, that mention attorneys. Quote one sentence from each regulation and give its citation.

(e) Give the cite for the enabling statute for each of the regulations you picked in part (d).

(f) Find any federal statute on taking a home office deduction on your federal income tax return. What is the citation of this statute? Find one regulation that carries out this statute. What is the citation of this regulation? How did you find it? List another way you could have used to find it.

[SECTION V]

FINDING LOCAL LAW

The local level of government consists of thousands of counties, cities, and towns throughout the country. They pass laws that deal with a wide variety of subjects, e.g., zoning, transportation, housing, sanitation. Among the most common kinds of local laws are charters and ordinances. (For their definitions, see Exhibit 6.1 in chapter 6.) The techniques for finding such laws are summarized in Exhibit 11.49.

EXHIBIT 11.49	Techniques for Finding Local Law

1. Begin by going to the Web site of the county, city, or town government whose local laws you are researching. They often have such laws online. Here are ways to obtain lists of and links to local governments in your state:
   - In Google or another search engine, type the name of your state and the words *cities* or *counties* (e.g., Vermont cities, or Texas counties)
   - National Association of Counties
     www.naco.org (In the "About Counties" pull-down menu, click "Find a County")
   - Cities Online (U.S. Conference of Mayors)
     usmayors.org/uscm/meet_mayors/cities_online
   - State and Local Governments on the Net
     www.statelocalgov.net
   - GovSpot Local Government
     www.govspot.com/categories/localgovernment.htm
2. In regular phone books, there is often a separate section covering government offices. Call the local offices or agencies that are relevant to your research and inquire about the laws they publish and where they can be read.
3. Call the central branch and the local branch of your public library. Ask each if it has county codes, municipal ordinances, and other local laws.
4. For charters and municipal codes online (sometimes called e-codes), see
   - www.spl.org/default.asp?pageID=collection_municodes
   - www.findlaw.com/11stategov/municipal.html
   - municipalcodes.lexisnexis.com
   - www.sterlingcodifiers.com/online.htm
   - www.municode.com
5. The sites for your state's statutory code (see Exhibit 11.42) may also link to charters, municipal codes, and other local laws of your state.
6. The key number digests have entire topics devoted to local law that will lead you to cases interpreting municipal codes, charters, etc. (On using digests, see Exhibit 11.23.) For example:
   - In the M volumes of these digests, check the topic "Municipal Corporations."
   - In the T volumes of these digests, check the topic "Towns."
7. Check discussions of local law in state and national legal encyclopedias (see Exhibit 11.32). For example:
   - In the M volumes of *American Jurisprudence 2d*, check the topic "Municipal Corporations, Counties, and Other Political Subdivisions."
   - In the M volumes of *California Jurisprudence*, check the topic "Municipalities."
8. Check discussions of local law in annotations found in the eight sets of A.L.R. (e.g., A.L.R.6th and A.L.R. Fed. 2d). In the *ALR Index*, check entries under "Charter," "City," and "Municipalities" to find annotations on local law. (See Exhibit 11.24.)

[SECTION W]

FINDING RULES OF COURT

You must always check the rules of court (also called *court rules* and *rules of procedure*) governing practice and procedure before a *particular* court. These rules govern the mechanics of litigation. They will tell you how to file a request for an extension of time, the number of days a defendant has to answer a complaint, the format of a complaint or appellate brief, etc. (See Exhibit 11.50.)

EXHIBIT 11.50	Techniques for Finding Rules of Court

Rules of Court for State Courts

1. Go to the Web site of the state court whose rules you are researching. The site often has links to online rules of court. Here are ways to find state court Web sites:
   - National Center for State Courts
     www.ncsconline.org/D_KIS/info_court_web_sites.html
   - Findlaw
     www.findlaw.com/11stategov (for your state, click "Courts")
   - In Google or another search engine, run a *courts* search that includes the name of your state (e.g., Wisconsin courts, or "North Carolina" courts)
2. Additional links to state rules of court:
   - www.llrx.com/courtrules
   - www.washlaw.edu
3. Your state statutory code may have the text of rules of court. For statutory codes online, see Exhibit 11.41.
4. Ask your law librarian if the library subscribes to a rules service (e.g., a looseleaf service) that publishes editions of rules of court that are regularly updated.
5. Fee-based online research services such as Westlaw, LexisNexis, and Loislaw contain rules of court for most state courts.

Rules of Court for Federal Courts

6. Go to the Web site of the federal court whose rules you are researching. The site often has links to online rules of court. Here are ways to find federal court Web sites:
   - www.uscourts.gov
   - www.law.emory.edu/cms/site/index.php?id=2997
   - www.findlaw.com/10fedgov/judicial/index.html
7. Official sites on federal rules of court:
   - www.uscourts.gov/rules/newrules8.html
   - www.uscourts.gov/rules

8. Major federal rules online:
   - Federal Rules of Civil Procedure
     www.law.cornell.edu/rules/frcp
     judiciary.house.gov/media/pdfs/printers/108th/civil2004.pdf
     en.wikipedia.org/wiki/Federal_Rules_of_Civil_Procedure
   - Federal Rules of Criminal Procedure
     www.law.cornell.edu/rules/frcrmp
     judiciary.house.gov/media/pdfs/printers/108th/crim2004.pdf
   - Federal Rules of Evidence
     www.law.cornell.edu/rules/fre
     judiciary.house.gov/media/pdfs/printers/108th/evid2004.pdf
     en.wikipedia.org/wiki/Federal_Rules_of_Evidence
   - Federal Rules of Appellate Procedure
     judiciary.house.gov/media/pdfs/printers/108th/appel2004.pdf
     www.law.cornell.edu/wex/index.php/Appellate_Procedure
   - Federal Rules of Bankruptcy Procedure
     www.law.cornell.edu/rules/frbp
9. Additional links to federal rules of court online:
   - www.llrx.com/courtrules (click "federal")
   - www.washlaw.edu (under the "Federal" column, click "Court Rules")
10. Many federal rules of court are also published in the U.S.C./ U.S.C.A./U.S.C.S. To find the U.S.C. online, see Exhibit 11.42.
11. Major multivolume legal treatises on federal rules include the following:
    - Wright & Miller, *Federal Practice and Procedure*
    - *Moore's Federal Practice*
    - *Weinstein's Federal Evidence*
12. Extensive leads to and discussions of federal rules of court can be found in ALR annotations (see Exhibit 11.24), legal encyclopedias (see Exhibit 11.32), looseleaf services (see Exhibit 11.29), and legal periodical literature (see Exhibit 11.30).
13. Fee-based online research services such as Westlaw, LexisNexis, and Loislaw contain rules of court for all federal courts.

ASSIGNMENT 11.29

Locate the rules of court governing the three courts listed below. For each court, find and quote from any rule that imposes a time limitation on one or more of the parties for litigation within that court (e.g., the time within which a party must file a particular motion or respond to a discovery request). Also give the name, address, fax number, and Internet address of each of the three courts you select:

(a) any state trial court of your state
(b) any U.S. District Court sitting in your state
(c) any U.S. Bankruptcy Court sitting in your state

[SECTION X]

FINDING INTERNATIONAL LAW

International law consists of legal principles and laws governing relations between nations. The primary kind of international law is the **treaty**, which is a formal agreement between two or

international law The legal principles and laws governing relations between nations. Also called *law of nations* and *public international law*.

treaty A formal agreement between two or more nations.

executive agreement An agreement between the United States and another country that does not require the approval of the Senate.

more nations. The president negotiates treaties with other nations, but the Senate must approve the treaty by at least a two-thirds vote. An **executive agreement**, in contrast, is an agreement between the United States and another country that does not require a vote of approval by the Senate. What can be covered in an executive agreement rather than a treaty is not clear and has always been the subject of considerable debate between the president and Congress.

The first step in researching international law is to read one or more legal periodical articles or sections of a legal treatise that cover the area of your research. Before you start reading the text of treaties, executive agreements, and case law interpreting them, you need an overview of the technical terms involved. Secondary sources such as legal periodicals and legal treatises will provide this. (For a summary of these and other techniques for finding international law, see Exhibit 11.51.)

EXHIBIT 11.51	Techniques for Finding International Law

1. Overviews of international law and terminology:
   - www.law.cornell.edu/wex/index.php/International_law
   - www.ll.georgetown.edu/tutorials/intl/2_overview.html
   - www.lexisnexis.com/infopro/zimmerman/disp.aspx?z=2027
   - www.law-lib.utoronto.ca/resguide/humrtsgu.htm
   - *Parry and Grant Encyclopedic Dictionary of International Law*
   - *Dictionary of International and Comparative Law* (James Fox)
2. Role of the U.S. Senate in the treaty-making process
   www.senate.gov/artandhistory/history/common/briefing/Treaties.htm
3. Guide to online resources for international law
   www.asil.org/resource/treaty1.htm
4. Executive agreements
   www.senate.gov/artandhistory/history/common/briefing/Treaties.htm#4
5. U.S. Treaties in force
   www.state.gov/s/l/treaties
6. Treaties: status and text (Thomas)
   thomas.loc.gov/home/treaties/treaties.htm
7. Other major sources of treaties:
   - *United States Treaties and Other International Agreements* (UST)
     www.wshein.com/Catalog/Product.aspx?sku=2072
   - *Treaties and Other International Acts Series* (TIAS)
     www.state.gov/s/l/treaty/tias
   - *United Nations Treaty Series*
     untreaty.un.org
   - *Treaties and International Agreements Online*
     www.oceanalaw.com/default.asp
   - *International Legal Materials*
     www.asil.org/resources/ilm.html
8. *Constitutions of the Countries of the World*
   www.oceanalaw.com/main_product_details.asp?ID=341
9. *Martindale-Hubbell Law Directory*—The Digest service contains brief summaries of the major laws of many countries.
10. Fee-based computer systems have extensive material on international law:
    - Westlaw (e.g., USTREATIES database)
    - LexisNexis (e.g., INTLAW library)
11. Discussions on international law can be found in legal periodicals (see Exhibit 11.30), legal treatises (see Exhibit 11.33), and looseleaf services (see Exhibit 11.29).

[SECTION Y]

THE THIRD LEVEL OF LEGAL RESEARCH: VALIDATION

INTRODUCTION

In Section N, we introduced the three levels of legal research:

- Background research
- Specific fact research
- Validation research

Exhibit 11.18 examined the steps for conducting *background research* on an area of law that is new to you. Section O to X examined the techniques of *specific fact research* through a series of extensive checklists. If you have done a comprehensive job on the first two stages of research, you may also have completed most of the third stage—**validation research**. At the validation stage, you use citators (e.g., Shepard's) and other legal materials to check the current validity of every primary authority (case, statute, etc.) you intend to rely on in the memorandum of law, appellate brief, or other document you are helping to prepare. This means making sure that the authority has not been affected by any later laws that you have not yet found.

validation research Using citators and other legal materials to check the current validity of every primary authority (case, statute, etc.) you intend to rely on in the memorandum of law, appellate brief, or other document you are helping to prepare.

WHY THERE IS A HIGH RISK THAT YOU WILL RELY ON INVALID LAW

The importance of validation research cannot be overestimated. You do not want to rely on a case that has been overruled or on a statute that has been amended, repealed, or declared unconstitutional. Surprisingly, however, it is relatively easy to make such mistakes. This is because some invalid laws are never removed from the shelves. Hence while you are reading such laws, you are given no indication that they are invalid and, therefore, are tempted—very tempted—to rely on them.

For example, a reporter volume may contain several hundred court opinions. Some of their holdings may have been overruled or declared unconstitutional years after the reporter volume was published. Yet no one goes back to this volume to insert corrections or warnings. An invalid case will be printed next to a valid case. You must perform validation research before you rely on any law. For cases, you must use paper or online citator services such as Shepard's and KeyCite.

The same danger exists with statutes. A code volume may contain several thousand statutory sections and subsections. Some of them may have been amended, repealed, or declared unconstitutional years after the code volume was published. Yet no one goes back to this volume to insert corrections or warnings. Eventually, however, statutory code volumes (unlike reporter volumes) *are* updated so that the code volumes containing invalid statutes are replaced by volumes containing valid statutes. But for some codes, this replacement may take more than ten years! Consequently, when you are reading a statute, there may be invalid statutes printed next to valid statutes without any indication of which were rendered invalid by subsequent action of the legislature or courts. To find out which statutes fall into this category, you must perform validation research. For statutes, you check available pocket parts, supplementation volumes or pamphlets, and paper or online citator services such as Shepard's and KeyCite.

In short, appearances are deceptive. Don't fall into the inviting trap of relying on invalid law simply because the law looks valid. Perform validation research on everything you want to use.

If you are lucky enough to be able to use fee-based research databases such as Westlaw and LexisNexis, you will be alerted by flags or other warning signs that a particular law is no longer valid or is of questionable validity. But these databases are very expensive to use. Most of your research will probably be done in the traditional paper formats of bound volumes, pamphlets, and looseleafs, where the danger of relying on invalid authority is very real.

Of course, you can also perform validation research on the free Internet. Sites run by legislatures, courts, and administrative agencies can be reliable, although they are not always kept current. If the site is not run by the government, be skeptical. Anyone can go on the Web and say just about anything on any topic.

PERSPECTIVE OF THE OTHER SIDE

A good way to approach validation research is to take the perspective of the other side. Suppose that you have helped do some of the research for an appellate brief. It has been filed in court and served on the attorney for the other side. Your brief is handed over to a researcher in the law office of your opponent. That person will do the following:

- Read the full text of all *primary authority* (see Exhibit 6.1 in chapter 6) on which the brief relies to see if it has interpreted the statutes, cases, regulations, etc., properly; to see whether it has taken quotations out of context, etc.
- *Shepardize* and/or KeyCite the statutes, cases, regulations, etc., that the brief cites to find out whether the law is still valid.
- Read the *secondary authority* (see Exhibit 11.10) that the brief cites to see whether it has interpreted the legal treatise, legal periodical article, etc., properly; to see whether it has taken quotations out of context, etc.
- Look for other applicable primary authority that the brief failed to mention.
- Look for other applicable secondary authority that the brief failed to mention.

Proper validation research means that you will be able to predict what this imaginary researcher will find when he or she checks your research through these steps. In short, at the validation stage of your research, you must ask yourself:

- Have I found everything I should have found?
- Is everything I found good law?
- Have I properly interpreted what I found?

The answer to the first two questions should be *no* if:

- You did an incomplete job of CARTWHEELing the indexes of all the sets of books mentioned in the checklists and techniques in this chapter (see Exhibit 11.16).
- You failed to shepardize and/or KeyCite cases, statutes, constitutional provisions, rules of court, ordinances, treaties, etc. (see Exhibit 11.28).
- You failed to take other standard validation steps, such as updating regulations in C.F.R. through the *LSA* pamphlet and the proper tables in the *Federal Register* (see Exhibit 11.48).

RESEARCH SELF-AUDIT

The checklist in Exhibit 11.52 is designed to help you achieve the comprehensiveness that is essential to all aspects of legal research, especially validation research. *Fill out a separate research self-audit for each issue you research.* Start by summarizing the issue in the box at the top of the form. The checklist serves as a reminder to make sure that you have covered all bases. Note that part IV tells you to keep a Research Log. You not only want to be comprehensive but also want to be able to tell others (and remind yourself) what steps you took along the way.

EXHIBIT 11.52   Research Self-Audit

ISSUE # _____ (briefly state issue researched)

I. What I Have Checked: Legal Materials
A. *Primary Authority*

☐ federal court opinions	☐ state court opinions	☐ ordinances
☐ federal statutes	☐ state statutes	☐ charter
☐ federal constitution	☐ state constitution	☐ local rules of court
☐ federal rules of court	☐ state rules of court	☐ local administrative regulations
☐ federal administrative regulations	☐ state administrative regulations	☐ local administrative decisions
☐ federal administrative decisions	☐ state administrative decisions	☐ international law

B. *Secondary Authority and Finding Aids*

☐ legal periodicals	☐ legal treatises	☐ looseleaf services
☐ ALR annotations	☐ legal encyclopedias	☐ legal newsletters
☐ *Words & Phrases* (legal dictionary)	☐ digests	

II. What I Have Checked: Nonlegal Materials
When relevant to the research problem, I have checked nonlegal literature in the areas of:

☐ medicine	☐ psychology	☐ psychiatry	☐ economics
☐ statistics	☐ accounting	☐ sociology	☐ other
☐ biology	☐ chemistry	☐ business management	

III. What I Intend to Rely On in My Research Memo
For every primary authority I intend to use, I have:
☐ used paper citators to determine whether it is still valid (e.g., Shepard's).
☐ used online citators to determine whether it is still valid (e.g., Shepard's, KeyCite, Auto-Cite)
☐ checked other standard updating features (e.g., pocket parts, supplement pamphlets, history tables)

IV. Research Log
For each paper volume, CD–ROM, or online resource (free or fee-based Internet) that I checked, I have made the following brief notations in my research notebook or log.
☐ the name of the resource
☐ the major words/phrases I have checked in the resource
☐ which library I used for this resource (if more than one)

V. People Consulted for Guidance/Leads before Completion
People with whom I have shared my research strategy to determine whether they think I have omitted something:

☐ supervisor	☐ experienced paralegal
☐ other attorney(s) in office	☐ experts (see Exhibit 11.34).
☐ law librarian	☐ other
☐ law clerk	

TIME TO STOP?

At the outset of your research, the difficulty you face is often phrased as "Where do I begin?" As you resolve this difficulty, another one emerges: "When do I stop?" Once the research starts flowing, you are sometimes faced with a mountain of material, and yet you do not feel comfortable saying to yourself that you have found everything there is to be found. Exhibit 11.53 presents some guidelines on handling this concern. With experience, you will begin to acquire a clearer sense of when it is time to stop, but it is rare for you to know this with certainty. You will always have the suspicion that if you pushed on just a little longer, you would find something new and more on point than what you have come up with to date. Also, there is no way around the reality that comprehensive research requires a substantial amount of time. It takes time to dig. It takes more time to dig comprehensively.

| **EXHIBIT 11.53** | **Guidelines for Determining When to End Your Legal Research** |

1. *Instructions from your supervisor.* You must, of course, live within time guidelines imposed by your supervisor. You cannot spend the rest of your career in the law library working on one problem! If your supervisor has not set specific time guidelines for the research project, ask him or her to do so as soon as you determine that the project is going to take a significant amount of time. This may be an opportunity for the supervisor to narrow the focus of the project or to redirect your energies entirely. It may also be an opportunity for the supervisor to let you know that you misunderstood the question to be researched.
2. *Repetition.* If you find that all the different avenues you are taking in the law library appear to be leading to the same primary and second-ary authority, it may be time to stop. This repetition is often a good indication that you have already found what there is to find. Many legal materials are designed to be finding aids to the same kind of law, as we saw in Section O on the nine major search resources. Digests and ALR annotations, for example, are both massive indexes to case law. Shepard's is also an excellent case finder. Always try to use more than one finding aid to locate any particular category of primary authority you are checking. (Also try to use finding aids published by different companies because the same publisher will often repeat the same material in different formats.) When multiple finding aids keep turning up the same cases, statutes, or other laws, it is a sign that you can stop.
3. *Comprehensive via checklists.* Work with checklists to be sure that you are covering all the bases in the law library. One indication of when it is time to stop is when you are able to check off everything on your checklists, particularly the research self-audit in Exhibit 11.52.

[SECTION Z]

ANNOTATED BIBLIOGRAPHY AND MORE RESEARCH PROBLEMS

An annotated bibliography is a report giving a list of library material on a particular topic, with a brief description of how the material relates to the topic. An annotated bibliography on contribu-tory negligence, for example, would list the major cases, statutes, periodical articles, etc., and would explain in a sentence or two what each says about contributory negligence. The same would be true of an annotated bibliography on a set of facts that you are researching. If the facts present more than one research issue, you would do an annotated bibliography for each issue, or you would subdivide a single annotated bibliography into sections so that it would be clear to the reader which issue you are covering at any given place in the bibliography. The annotated bibliography is, in effect, a progress report on your research. It will show your supervisor the status of your research to date. Exhibit 11.54 presents the instructions for preparing an annotated bibliography.

| **EXHIBIT 11.54** | **Instructions for Preparing an Annotated Bibliography** |

These instructions cover state and local law topics. All the instruc-tions can also apply to federal topics (with the exception of #9) by substituting the word *federal* for the word *state* in the instructions.

1. CARTWHEEL the topic of your annotated bibliography. (See Exhibit 11.16.)
2. *Annotated* here simply means that you provide some description of everything you list in the bibliography—not a long analysis, just a sentence or two explaining why you included it. If you find no relevant material in any of the fol-lowing sets of books, specifically say so in your report.
3. Hand in a report that will cover what you find on the topic in the sets of books mentioned in the following instructions.
4. Statutes. Go to your state code. Make a list of the statutes, if any, on the topic. For each statute, give its citation and a brief quotation from it to show that it deals with the topic. (See Exhibit 11.42.)
5. Constitutions. Go to your state constitution (usually found within your state code). Make a list of the constitutional provi-sions, if any, on the topic. For each provision, give its citation

and a brief quotation from it to show that it deals with the topic. (See Exhibit 11.47.)
6. Cases. If you found statutes or constitutional provisions on the topic, check to see if there are any cases summarized in the Notes of Decisions (see Exhibit 11.39) *after* these statutes or provisions. Select several cases that deal with the topic. For each case you select, give its citation and a brief quote from the case summary in the Notes of Decisions to show that it deals with the topic.
7. Digests. Go to the Descriptive Word Index of digests. Make a list of key numbers, if any, that deal with the topic. (See Exhibit 11.23.)
8. Rules of court. Go to the rules of court that cover courts in your state. Make a list of the rules, if any, that deal with the topic. For each rule, give its citation and a brief quotation from it to show that it deals with the topic. (See Exhibit 11.50.)
9. Ordinances. Go to the ordinances that cover your city or county. Make a list of the ordinances, if any, that deal with the topic. For each ordinance, give its citation and a brief quotation from it to show that it deals with the topic. (See Exhibit 11.49.)

(continues)

EXHIBIT 11.54	Instructions for Preparing an Annotated Bibliography—*continued*

10. Administrative regulations. Are there any state agencies that have jurisdiction over any aspect of the topic? If so, list the agencies. Make a list of the regulations, if any, that deal with the topic. For each regulation, give its citation and a brief quote from it to show that it deals with the topic. (See Exhibit 11.48.)

11. A.L.R. (A.L.R.1st), A.L.R.2d, A.L.R.3d, A.L.R.4th, A.L.R.5th, A.L.R.6th, A.L.R. Fed. and A.L.R. Fed. 2d. Go to these eight sets of books. Try to find one annotation in *each* set that deals with your topic. Give the citation of the annotation in each set. Give the citation of the annotation in each set. Flip through the pages of each annotation and try to find the citation of one case from a state court of your state, or from a federal court with jurisdiction over your state. Give the citation of the case. (See Exhibit 11.24.)

12. Legal periodical literature. Use the *Index to Legal Periodicals and Books* and the *Current Legal Index* to locate four legal periodical articles that deal with the topic. Try to find at least two relevant articles in each index. Give the citations of the articles. Put a check mark next to the citation if your library has the legal periodical in which the article is located. (See Exhibit 11.30.)

13. Legal treatises. Go to your card or computer catalog. Find any two legal treatises that cover your topic. Give the citation of the treatises. Sometimes you may not find entire books on the topic. The topic may be one of many subjects in a broader treatise. (See Exhibit 11.33.)

14. Looseleaf services. Are there any looseleaf services on this topic? Check the card or computer catalog and ask the librarian. For each looseleaf service, give its citation and explain how it covers the topic. (See Exhibit 11.29.)

15. *Words and Phrases.* Go to this multivolume legal dictionary. In this dictionary, locate definitions, if any, of the major words and phrases involved in your topic. Limit yourself to definitions from court opinions of your state, if any.

16. Shepardize and/or KeyCite every case, statute, or constitutional provision you find to make sure it is still valid. (See Exhibit 11.28.)

17. Other material. If you come across other relevant material not covered in the above instructions, include it in the bibliography as well.

18. When in doubt about whether to include something in the bibliography, include it.

19. There is no prescribed format for the bibliography. One possible outline format you can use is as follows:
    A. Statutes (instructions 4 and 16)
    B. Constitutions (instructions 5 and 16)
    C. Cases (instructions 6, 7, 11, and 16)
    D. Digests (instruction 7)
    E. Rules of court (instruction 8)
    F. Ordinances (instruction 9)
    G. Administrative regulations (instruction 10)
    H. Annotations (instruction 11)
    I. Legal periodical literature (instruction 12)
    J. Legal treatises (instruction 13)
    K. Looseleaf services (instruction 14)
    L. *Words and Phrases* (instruction 15)
    M. Other material (instruction 17)

RESEARCH PROBLEMS

ASSIGNMENT 11.30

Prepare an annotated bibliography (see Exhibit 11.54 for instructions) on one of the following topics:

(a) Common law marriage
(b) Negligence liability of a driver of a car to his or her guest passenger
(c) Negligence liability of paralegals
(d) Overtime compensation for paralegals
(e) Sex discrimination
(f) The felony-murder rule
(g) Default judgment
(h) Workers' compensation for injury on the way to work
(i) Fact situation assigned by your instructor

ASSIGNMENT 11.31

In the problems that follow, include citations that support every position you take in your responses. In analyzing and researching some of the problems below, you may find it difficult to proceed unless you know more facts about the problem. In such situations, clearly state the missing facts that you need to know. In order to proceed with the analysis and research, you can assume that certain facts exist as long as you state what your factual assumptions are *and* your assumptions are reasonable given the facts that you have.

(a) In your state, what entity (e.g., legislature, committee, court, or agency) has the authority to prescribe rules and regulations on who can and who cannot practice law?

(continues)

(b) List the kinds (or levels) of courts (local, state, or federal) that sit in your state, and identify the major powers of each court; i.e., indicate what kinds of cases each court can hear.

(c) In your state, find a statute or court opinion that defines the following words or phrases:

   (i) Summons
   (ii) In personam
   (iii) Mandamus
   (iv) Exhaustion of administrative remedies
   (v) Judgment
   (vi) Jurisdiction
   (vii) Warrant

(d) Using the statutory codes of five different states (one of which must be your own state), find out how old a male and female must be to marry without consent of parent or guardian in each of the states.

(e) Go to any statutory code that has a pocket part. Starting with the first few pages of the pocket part, identify any three statutes that have totally repealed or partially modified the corresponding three statutes in the body of the bound text. Describe what the repeal or modification was. (*Note:* You may have to compare the new section in the pocket part with the old section in the body of the text to describe the change.)

In the following problems, use the state law of your state whenever you determine from your research that state law governs the problem. Apply federal law as needed.

(f) John Jones was sent to a state mental hospital after being declared mentally ill. He has been institutionalized for the last five years. In his own view, he is not now mentally ill. The hospital disagrees. What can John do? What steps might he take to try to get out?

(g) Mrs. Peterson invites a neighbor to her house for dinner. Mrs. Peterson's dog bites the neighbor. Is Mrs. Peterson responsible for the injury?

(h) Sam, age fifteen, goes to a used car lot. He signs a purchase agreement on a used car: $500 down and $100 a month for the next ten months. One day after the purchase, Sam allows a friend to drive the car. The friend demolishes the car in an accident. When Sam tells the used car dealer about the accident, he is told that he must still make all payments until the purchase price has been paid. Is the dealer right?

(i) Dorothy Rhodes and John Samualson are the parents of Susan Samualson. (Dorothy married Robert Rhodes after divorcing John Samualson.) Dorothy died after separating from Robert Rhodes. Susan's father (John) has disappeared. Mr. and Mrs. Ford were neighbors of the Rhodes's. Susan lived with the Fords for a long period of time while her mother was having marital difficulties. A court granted the Fords custody and guardianship in 1988. The Social Security Administration sent Susan the social security benefits she was entitled to on the death of her mother. In 1990, the Fords formally adopted Susan but did not inform the Social Security office of this; they did not know that they had to. When the Social Security office learned of the adoption, they terminated the payments for Susan and informed the Fords that the money she had received since the adoption would have to be returned. The Fords and Susan want to know what substantive and procedural rights they have.

(j) The Henderson family owns a $140,000 home next door to a small grocery store. The store catches fire. The firefighters decide that to get at the fire from all angles, they must break through the Henderson home, which is not on fire. Damage to the Henderson home from the activity of the firefighters comes to $40,000. Who pays for this damage?

(k) After a series of serious accidents in which numerous riders are hurt, a bill is placed before the city council that would require all motorcyclists to wear protective helmets whenever riding. Is the bill constitutional?

(l) As a measure to enforce a standard of dental care, a bill is proposed that all the drinking water in the state be fluoridated and that every citizen be required to visit a dentist at least once a year. Is this bill constitutional?

(m) Tom Jones has terminal lung cancer. Modern technology, however, can keep him alive indefinitely. Tom requests that the hospital no longer use the technology on him. He wants to die. What are his rights?

(n) In 1992, James Fitzpatrick died, leaving an estate of $50,000. The executor tried to locate the heirs. In 1993, the probate court closed the estate and distributed the money to the heirs who were

(continues)

known at the time. In 2001, a hitherto unknown person comes forward and says he is an heir. He wants to go to court to reopen the estate and claim his share of the inheritance. Can he?

(o) Mary is the sole beneficiary of her father's will. Another sister is intentionally left out of the will by her father. There are no other heirs. Mary murders her father. Who gets his estate?

(p) Most kosher meat stores accept the United Kosher Butchers Association (UKBA) as the authoritative certifier that "all the religious requirements have been thoroughly observed." Associated Synagogues (AS) certifies caterers as authentic carriers of kosher food. AS refuses to certify caterers who buy meat from stores certified by the UKBA because the latter refuses to submit to supervision by the rabbinical committee of AS. Many caterers then withdraw their patronage from stores supervised by UKBA. What legal action, if any, can the UKBA take?

(q) Mary Perry belongs to a religion that believes that medical problems can be resolved through spiritual meditation. Her son Paul is ten years old. One day Paul is rushed to a hospital after collapsing at school. Mrs. Perry is called at home. When she arrives at the hospital, she is told that Paul will require emergency surgery. She refuses to give her consent. The doctor tells her that if the operation is not performed within the next twenty-four hours, Paul will die. Mrs. Perry responds by saying that "God will cure my son." What legal action, if any, can be taken to protect Paul's rights and to protect Mrs. Perry's rights?

Chapter Summary

The law is changing every day. The only dependable way to find out about all of these changes is through legal research. Research skills will take time and determination to develop. The major formats of legal research materials are paper (pamphlet, hardcover, and looseleaf), online (CALR), CD–ROM, and microforms (microfilm and ultrafiche). A useful first step is to compile a list of definitions or functions of the major research terms (such as citation, citator, cumulative, and headnote) and the major sets of research materials.

You need to know where to find law libraries in your community, particularly federal depository libraries. Within these libraries, you will find the following kinds of authority that courts consider in reaching a decision: primary authority, which consists of laws such as statutes and cases; secondary authority, which consists of nonlaws such as legal periodical articles and legal encyclopedias; mandatory authority, which a court *must* rely on; and persuasive authority, which a court has discretion to accept or reject.

A citation is an "address" where authority can be found in a library or online. Citation rules and manuals tell you what to abbreviate in the citation, where spaces and commas must be inserted, in what order the information in the citation must be provided, when to include a parallel cite, etc. When cite checking, you identify inaccuracies in citation form, shepardize or KeyCite the authorities cited, check the accuracy of any quotations used, etc.

Many law books have standard features. Each time you come across a new law book or set of law books, you should check features such as the copyright page, which contains the latest copyright date, and the foreword or preface, which may give a general description of how to use the book. The tables or lists at the beginning of the book will help you understand terms, symbols, or signals used in the book. Check also for updating features (such as pocket parts), various tables of contents, and index features that may be available.

The CARTWHEEL is a technique that helps you use the often poorly organized indexes (and tables of contents) of law books. The technique assumes that the entry you first check in the index (or table) leads you nowhere and that you must now think of some other entries that might be more productive. The CARTWHEEL is designed to help you identify these other entries.

There are three levels of legal research: background research, in which you start identifying the basic vocabulary and the major principles of an area of the law that is relatively new to you; specific fact research, in which you look for primary and secondary authority covering the facts of a client's case; and validation research, in which you check the current validity of whatever authority you initially believed was relevant to the problem you are researching. Occasionally, aspects of all three levels of research will be going on simultaneously.

A competent legal researcher knows how to use the major search tools or resources:

- Card or computer catalog to find what is available in the library you are using
- Digests to find court opinions
- Annotations to find court opinions
- Shepard's to shepardize court opinions, statutes, and regulations in order to validate cited material and to find citing material such as court opinions
- Looseleaf services to give you leads to, and explanations of, primary authority
- Legal periodical literature to give you leads to, and explanations of, primary authority
- Legal encyclopedias to give you leads to, and explanations of, primary authority
- Legal treatises to give you leads to, and explanations of, primary authority
- E-mail research to give you leads to primary authority

The major CALR (computer assisted legal research) tools are Westlaw and LexisNexis. (In chapter 13, we will cover them in greater detail.)

These major search tools or resources will often lead you to more than one kind of primary authority: court opinions, statutes (plus legislative history), constitutions, administrative law, local law, rules of court, and international law.

Key Terms

online
Internet
hypertext
primary authority
federal depository library
CALR
looseleaf service
public domain
CD–ROM
microform
abstract
digest
act
slip law
administrative code
advance sheet
reporter
legislative service
advance session law service
annotation
annotated reporter
legal encyclopedia
annotate
annotated statutory code
notes of decisions
Auto-Cite
bill
legislative history
bluebook
brief
appellate brief
amicus curiae brief
opinion
docket
official reporter
unofficial reporter
unpublished opinion
regional reporter
special edition state
    reporter
headnote
casebook
citation
parallel cite
citator

CLE materials
code
codify
cumulative
deskbook
key number
regional digest
form book
hornbook
World Wide Web
hypertext
intranet
interstate compact
KeyCite
legal dictionary
legal newsletter
legal newspaper
legal periodical
legal thesaurus
LegalTrac
legal treatise
legislation
public law
private law
LexisNexis
looseleaf service
law directory
nutshell
pattern jury instructions
pocket part
public domain citation
record
register
Restatement
rules of court
edition
series
session laws
shepardize
cited material
citing material
statutory code
slip opinion
star paging
official statutory code

unofficial statutory code
uniform laws
preliminary print
authority
primary authority
secondary authority
mandatory authority
persuasive authority
nonauthority
enacted law
legislative intent
analogous
overrule
stare decisis
precedent
conflicts of law
subject matter jurisdiction
personal jurisdiction
full faith and credit
Supremacy Clause
forum
diversity of citizenship
dictum
holding
plagiarism
first impression
bluebook it
short form citation
parallel cite
public domain citation
et al.
litigation status
In re
ex rel
docket number
writ of certiorari
overrule
nominative reporter
pinpoint cite
public domain citation
popular name
legislative history
legal treatise
legal periodical
legal encyclopedia

restatement
annotation
uniform resource locator
cite checking
table of authorities
supra
infra
id.
copyright
table of cases
table of statutes
pocket part
cumulative
errata page
term of art
CARTWHEEL
trace a key number
DWI
on point
shepardize
citator
cited material
citing material
docket number
reverse
overrule
session law cite
codified cite
enabling statute
case note
black letter law
construction
ejusdem generis
mandatory statute
discretionary statute
constitution
administrative regulation
administrative decision
Administrative Procedure
    Act
enabling statute
international law
treaty
executive agreement
validation research

Review Questions

1. Why can't legal research always provide definitive answers to legal problems?
2. What is the difference between what you learn in school and what you learn through legal research?
3. What are the major kinds of law libraries?
4. What are the four functions of research materials?
5. What are the four main categories of legal research media?
6. Explain the different uses of the word *advance* in legal research.

7. What are the main values of legal encyclopedias?

8. Explain the different uses of the word *bluebook* in legal research.

9. Explain the different uses of the word *brief* in legal research and writing.

10. Name eleven possible places where you may be able to read the same opinion.

11. What reporters print (1) opinions of the state courts in your state, (2) opinions of the U.S. district courts in your state, (3) opinions of the U.S. court of appeals for your state, and (4) opinions of the U.S. Supreme Court?

12. What are the major characteristics of West Group reporters?

13. What are the major functions of a citator?

14. What is the distinction between codes and session laws?

15. When is a law book cumulative?

16. What different kinds of digests exist?

17. What is a key number and what is its function?

18. What is the relationship between a key number in a West Group digest volume and a k number in Westlaw?

19. What are the functions of headnotes?

20. What is the distinction between public and private laws or statutes, and where are they published?

21. What is the distinction between cited and citing materials?

22. What is the distinction between edition and series?

23. What is meant by shepardizing?

24. What is the function of star paging?

25. What is the distinction between (1) primary and secondary authority and (2) mandatory and persuasive authority?

26. When is enacted law mandatory authority?

27. When is a court opinion mandatory authority?

28. What is the distinction between enacted law and common law?

29. When is a state court required to follow an opinion of another state court?

30. What is stare decisis?

31. What is the distinction between subject matter jurisdiction and personal jurisdiction?

32. When is a court opinion persuasive authority?

33. What is dictum?

34. When can secondary authority be persuasive authority?

35. What are the dangers of quoting secondary authority?

36. Explain what is meant by citation rules.

37. When are parallel cites required?

38. How can you find a parallel cite?

39. What is a public domain citation?

40. What is the distinction between the history and the treatment of a case?

41. What is a pinpoint cite?

42. What are the functions of cite checking?

43. What are some of the main features of many law books?

44. What kinds of law books always or often have pocket parts?

45. How does the CARTWHEEL work?

46. What are the three levels of legal research?

47. What are the main methods of doing background research?

48. What is a law-dash search?

49. What are the major categories of primary authority at the three levels of government?

50. How can the same key number help you find case law in different digests?

51. How do you trace a key number in the American Digest System?

52. What are the major ways of finding a key number?

53. What is the value of annotations and how do you update them in the eight sets of A.L.R.?

54. What kinds of information can you obtain when you shepardize (1) a court opinion, (2) a statute, and (3) an administrative regulation?

55. How do you determine whether you have a complete set of Shepard's?

56. What is the relationship between a session law cite and its codified cite?

57. What is the distinction between an asterisk and a delta symbol in Shepard's?

58. How are looseleaf services organized?

59. What are the main techniques of finding legal periodical literature?

60. Why are legal encyclopedias frequently used?

61. How can open stacks help you find legal treatises?

62. How can e-mail be a research tool?

63. What are the main techniques of finding case law (1) when you already have one case, (2) when you are looking for cases interpreting a statute, and (3) when you do not have a case or statute to begin with?

64. What are some of the features of an annotated code?

65. What are the main techniques of finding statutes?

66. What further research is needed once you have found a statute?

67. Why should you try to find legislative history?

68. What are the main techniques of finding the legislative history of a state statute?

69. What are the main techniques of finding the legislative history of a federal statute?

70. What are the main techniques of monitoring proposed legislation?

71. Why are constitutional provisions frequently interpreted by the courts?

72. What are the main techniques of finding constitutional law?

73. What is the Administrative Procedure Act?

74. What are the main techniques of finding state and federal administrative regulations and administrative decisions?

75. How do you update a federal regulation in the Code of Federal Regulations?

76. What are the main techniques of finding local law?

77. What are the main techniques of finding federal and state rules of court?

78. What are the main techniques of finding international law?

79. How do you conduct validation research?

80. What is a research self-audit?

Helpful Web Sites: More on Legal Research Guides and Tutorials

- www.ll.georgetown.edu/tutorials
- lawscout.uakron.edu
- lib.law.washington.edu/ref/guides.html
- tutorial.lib.uci.edu/index.php?page=legal_research_cases
- www.law.cornell.edu
- www.washlaw.edu
- www.catalaw.com
- www.virtualchase.com/topics/legal_research_index.shtml
- www.umuc.edu/library/tutorials/legal
- www.wvu.edu/~law/library/guides/internettutorial.htm
- www.law.umaryland.edu/Marshall/researchguides/
  TMLLguide/index.asp
- www.loc.gov/law/guide/usstates.html
- www.lectlaw.com
- www.llrx.com/category/1048

- www.west.net/~smith/research.htm
- www.hg.org

Google Searches (run the following searches for more sites)

- "New York" legal research (Insert your state)
- legal research techniques
- legal citation
- "finding court opinions"
- "finding statutes"
- "finding regulations"
- "finding court rules"
- "how to shepardize"
- "finding ordinances"
- "finding international law"

Student CD-ROM

For additional materials, please go to the CD in this book.

Online Companion™

For additional resources, please go to http://www.paralegal.delmar.cengage.com

Bibliography of Legal Research and Citation Guides on State Law

ALL STATES

- www.washlaw.edu
- www.loc.gov/law/guide/usstates.html
- www.romingerlegal.com
- www.ll.georgetown.edu/research/browse_jurisdictions.cfm

ALABAMA

- www.library.law.ua.edu/links/bama.htm
- www.loc.gov/law/guide/us-al.html
- Lynne Kitchens, *Alabama Practice Materials*, 82 Law Library Journal 703 (1990).

ALASKA

- www.state.ak.us/courts/aklegal.htm
- www.washlaw.edu/uslaw/states/Alaska/index.html

ARIZONA

- www.law.asu.edu/?id=141
- www.loc.gov/law/guide/us-az.html
- Kathy Shimpock-Vieweg, *Arizona Legal Research Guide* (Hein, 1992).
- Arturo Torres, *Arizona Practice Materials*, 80 Law Library Journal 577 (1988).

ARKANSAS

- www.loc.gov/law/guide/us-ar.html
- Coleen Barger, *Arkansas Legal Research* (Carolina Academic Press, 2007).
- Kathryn Fitzhugh, *Arkansas Practice Materials II*, 21 Univ. of Arkansas at Little Rock Law Review 363 (1999).

CALIFORNIA

- www.aallnet.org/chapter/scall/locating.htm
- www.washlaw.edu/uslaw/states/California/index.html
- www.calawnet.com
- Edward Jessen, *California Style Manual*, 4th ed. (West, 2000).
- Daniel Martin, *Henke's California Law Guide*, 8th ed. (LexisNexis, 2006).
- R. Formichi, *California Style Manual*, 3d ed. (1986).
- John Hanft, *Legal Research in California*, 5th ed. (West, 2004).

COLORADO

- www.loc.gov/law/guide/us-co.html
- Mitch Fontenot, *Colorado Practice Materials*, 88 Law Library Journal 427 (1996).

CONNECTICUT

- www.jud.state.ct.us/LawLib/state.htm
- www.washlaw.edu/uslaw/states/Connecticut/index.html
- Jonathan Saxon, *Connecticut Practice Materials*, 91 Law Library Journal 139 (1999).
- Lawrence Cheeseman & Arlene Bielefield, *Connecticut Legal Research Handbook* (Conn. Law Book Co., 1992).
- Shirley Bysiewicz, *Sources of Connecticut Law* (Lexis, 1987)

DELAWARE

- www.law.widener.edu/Law-Library/new/research/de.shtml
- www.loc.gov/law/guide/us-de.html
- Patrick Charles & David King, *Delaware Practice Materials*, 89 Law Library Journal 349 (1997).

DISTRICT OF COLUMBIA

- www.ll.georgetown.edu/states/dc.cfm
- Leah Chanin et al., *Legal Research in the District of Columbia, Maryland and Virginia*, 2d ed. (Hein, 2000).

FLORIDA

- www.law.ufl.edu/lic/guides
- www.washlaw.edu/uslaw/states/Florida/index.html
- Barbara Busharis & Suzanne Rowe, *Florida Legal Research*, 2d ed. (Carolina Academic Press, 2002).
- Betsy Stupski, *Guide to Florida Legal Research*, 6th ed. (Florida Bar, 2001).

GEORGIA

- www.law.uga.edu/library/research/internet/georgia.html
- www.loc.gov/law/guide/us-ga.html
- Nancy Johnson & Nancy Deel, *Researching Georgia Law*, 14 Georgia State University Law Review 545 (1998).
- Leah Chanin & Suzanne Cassidy, *Guide to Georgia Legal Research and Legal History* (Harrison, 1990).

HAWAII

- www.hsba.org/Legal_Research/index.htm
- www.washlaw.edu/uslaw/states/Hawaii/index.html

IDAHO

- www.law.uidaho.edu/default.aspx?pid=66157
- www.loc.gov/law/guide/us-id.html
- Leinaala Seeger, *Idaho Practice Materials*, 87 Law Library Journal 534 (1995).

ILLINOIS

- www.washlaw.edu/uslaw/states/Illinois/index.html
- Laurel Wendt, *Illinois Legal Research Manual*, 2d ed. (Hein, 2005).
- Mark Wojcik, *Illinois Legal Research* (Carolina Academic Press, 2003).

INDIANA

- www.loc.gov/law/guide/us-in.html
- www.romingerlegal.com/state/indiana.html

IOWA

- www.washlaw.edu/uslaw/states/Iowa/index.html
- John Edwards, ed., *Iowa Legal Research Guide* (Hein, 2003).

KANSAS

- www.loc.gov/law/guide/us-ks.html
- Joseph Custer, *Kansas Legal Research and Reference Guide*, 3d ed. (LexisNexis, 2003).

KENTUCKY

- www.louisvillelaw.com
- www.washlaw.edu/uslaw/states/Kentucky/index.html
- Kurt Metzmeier et al., *Kentucky Legal Research Manual*, 2d ed. (University of Kentucky, 2002).
- Arturo Torres, *Kentucky Practice Materials*, 84 Law Library Journal 509 (1992).

LOUISIANA

- www.megalaw.com/la/la.php
- www.loc.gov/law/guide/us-la.html
- Win-Shin Chiang, *Louisiana Legal Research*, 2d ed. (Butterworth, 1990).
- M. A. Cunningham, *Guide to Louisiana and Selected French Materials and Citation*, 67 Tulane Law Review 1305 (1993).

MAINE

- www.maine.gov/legis/lawlib
- www.washlaw.edu/uslaw/states/Maine/index.html
- William Wells, *Maine Legal Research Guide* (Tower Publishing, 1989).

MARYLAND

- www.loc.gov/law/guide/us-md.html
- www.ll.georgetown.edu/states/maryland-in-depth.cfm
- Leah Chanin et al., *Legal Research in the District of Columbia, Maryland and Virginia*, 2d ed. (Hein, 2000).

MASSACHUSETTS

- www.bu.edu/lawlibrary/research/mass/index.html
- www.washlaw.edu/uslaw/states/Massachusetts/index.html
- Mary Neary, *Massachusetts Legal Research* (Mass. Continuing Legal Education, 2001).

MICHIGAN

- www.lib.umich.edu/govdocs/michlaw.html
- www.loc.gov/law/guide/us-mi.html
- Pamela Lysaght, *Michigan Legal Research* (Carolina Academic Press, 2006)
- Richard Beer & Judith Field, *Michigan Legal Literature*, 2d ed. (Hein, 1991).

MINNESOTA

- www.law.umn.edu/library/tools/pathfinders/minnresearch.html
- www.washlaw.edu/uslaw/states/Michigan/index.html
- John Tessner, *Minnesota Legal Research Guide*, 2d ed. (Hein, 2002).

MISSISSIPPI

- www.megalaw.com/ms/ms.php
- www.loc.gov/law/guide/us-ms.html

MISSOURI

- www.loc.gov/law/guide/us-mo.html
- www.washlaw.edu/uslaw/states/Missouri/index.html

MONTANA

- www.umt.edu/lawinsider/library/lawbyjur/lawbyjur.htm
- www.washlaw.edu/uslaw/states/Montana/index.html
- Stephen Jordan, *A Guide to Montana Legal Research*, 6th ed. (State Law Library of Montana, 1999).

NEBRASKA

- law.unl.edu/inside.asp?d=nebraska-resources
- www.loc.gov/law/guide/us-ne.html
- Patrick Charles et al., *LexisNexis's Research Guide to Nebraska Law*, 2d ed. (LexisNexis, 1999).

NEVADA

- www.washlaw.edu/uslaw/states/Nevada/index.html
- Jennifer Gross et al., *Nevada Legal Research Guide* (Hein, 2005).
- LeGrande Fletcher, *Nevada Practice Materials*, 91 Law Library Journal 313 (1999).

NEW HAMPSHIRE

- www.loc.gov/law/guide/us-nh.html
- www.washlaw.edu/uslaw/states/NewHampshire/index.html

NEW JERSEY

- www.njstatelib.org/Research_Guides/Law/index.php
- www.loc.gov/law/guide/us-nj.html
- Paul Axel-Lute, *New Jersey Legal Research Handbook*, 4th ed. (N.J. Institute for Continuing Legal Education, 1998).

NEW MEXICO

- www.washlaw.edu/uslaw/states/NewMexico/index.html
- Mary Woodward, *New Mexico Practice Materials*, 84 Law Library Journal 93 (1992).

NEW YORK

- www.ll.georgetown.edu/states/newyork-in-depth.cfm
- www.loc.gov/law/guide/us-ny.html
- Ellen Gibson & William Manz, *New York Legal Research Guide*, 3d ed. (Hein, 2004).
- *New York Rules of Citation*, 5th ed. (St. John's Law Review, 2005).

NORTH CAROLINA

- library.law.unc.edu/research/nc_legal_databases.html
- www.washlaw.edu/uslaw/states/NorthCarolina/index.html
- Miriam Baer & James Ray, *Legal Research in North Carolina* (Carolina Academic Press, 2006)
- Constance Matzen, *A Selected Bibliography of North Carolina Practice Materials*, 24 Southeastern Law Librarian 25 (1999).

NORTH DAKOTA

- www.loc.gov/law/guide/us-nd.html
- www.washlaw.edu/uslaw/states/NorthDakota/index.html

OHIO

- www.uakron.edu/law/library/olrlinks.php
- www.washlaw.edu/uslaw/states/Ohio/index.html
- James Leonard, *A Select Annotated Bibliography of Ohio Practice Materials*, 17 Ohio Northern University Law Review 265 (1990).
- Melanie Putnam & Susan Schaefgen, *Ohio Legal Research Guide* (Hein, 1997).

OKLAHOMA

- oklegal.onenet.net
- www.loc.gov/law/guide/us-ok.html

OREGON

- www.washlaw.edu/uslaw/states/Oregon/index.html
- Suzanne Rowe, *Oregon Legal Research*, 2d ed. (Carolina Academic Press 2007)
- Karen Beck, *Oregon Practice Materials*, 88 Law Library Journal 288 (1996).

PENNSYLVANIA

- www.loc.gov/law/guide/us-pa.html
- Frank Liu et al., *Pennsylvania Legal Research Handbook* (America Lawyer Media, 2001).
- Mark Silverman, *A Short Guide to Pennsylvania Legal Research*, 12 Legal Reference Services Quarterly 107 (1992).

RHODE ISLAND

- www.washlaw.edu/uslaw/states/RhodeIsland/index.html
- www.loc.gov/law/guide/us-ri.html

SOUTH CAROLINA

- www.washlaw.edu/uslaw/states/SouthCarolina/index.html
- Karen Taylor, *Bibliography of South Carolina Practice Materials*, 24 Southeastern Law Librarian 18 (1999).

SOUTH DAKOTA

- www.loc.gov/law/guide/us-sd.html
- Delores Jorgensen, *South Dakota Legal Research Guide*, 2d ed. (Hein, 1999).

TENNESSEE

- www.romingerlegal.com/state/tennessee.html
- www.washlaw.edu/uslaw/states/Tennessee/index.html

TEXAS

- www.loc.gov/law/guide/us-tx.html
- Pamela Tepper and Peggy Kerley, *Texas Legal Research*, 2d ed. (Delmar 1997).
- Brandon Quarles & Matthew Cordon, *Legal Research for the Texas Practitioner* (Hein, 2003).
- *Texas Law Review Manual on Style*, 10th ed. (2005).
- Texas Law Review, *Texas Rules of Form*, 11th ed. (2006)

UTAH

- www.megalaw.com/ut/ut.php
- www.washlaw.edu/uslaw/states/Utah/index.html

VERMONT

- www.loc.gov/law/guide/us-vt.html
- www.lexisone.com/legalresearch/legalguide/states/vermont.htm

VIRGINIA

- www.washlaw.edu/uslaw/states/Virginia/index.html
- Leah Chanin et al., *Legal Research in the District of Columbia, Maryland and Virginia*, 2d ed. (Hein, 2000).
- John Eure, ed., *A Guide to Legal Research in Virginia*, 3d ed. (Virginia Law Foundation, 1999).

WASHINGTON

- lib.law.washington.edu/research/research.html
- www.loc.gov/law/guide/us-wa.html
- Julie Heintz, *Washington Legal Research* (Carolina Academic Press, 2005).

WEST VIRGINIA

- www.wvbar.org/technet
- www.washlaw.edu/uslaw/states/WestVirginia/index.html

WISCONSIN

- wsll.state.wi.us/legalresearch.html
- Ellen Platt & Mary Koshollek, *Wisconsin Practice Materials* (Hein, 1999).

WYOMING

- www.romingerlegal.com/state/wyoming.html
- www.loc.gov/law/guide/us-wy.html

Legal Writing

CHAPTER OUTLINE

[SECTION A]

INTRODUCTION

Legal writing is an important skill in the practice of law. To a large extent, the legal profession lives by the written word. Any important task of an attorney, judge, or legislator is often heavily documented in writing. Everyone is very reluctant to rely on oral communication alone. Consequently, a busy law office generates a vast quantity of paper—even in the computer age of digital communication. Once documents are prepared on a computer, they are often printed as **hard copy**, i.e., on paper.

Competent attorneys tend to be very particular about how something should be written. A paralegal who works for more than one attorney should not expect that they will all have the same style. This can sometimes be disconcerting. What pleases one attorney may upset another.

Before examining ways to cope in this environment, it is important to understand that the phrase *legal writing* can be used to describe different tasks:

- Preparing documents that require *legal analysis*
- Preparing documents that require *legal research*
- Making sure that legal documents conform to *special formats*
- Using clear and precise language to *communicate* effectively in any legal document

Although these four tasks are often interrelated, our primary focus in this chapter will be the latter two tasks: an introduction to the special formats used in some of the documents commonly prepared in a law office and an overview of important general communication techniques that can improve writing in any legal document. Legal analysis is covered in chapter 7. Legal research is covered in chapters 11 and 13.

hard copy A paper copy of what has been prepared on a computer. Also called a *printout*. A "soft" form of text is what exists on disk or on a computer screen.

587

We begin with suggestions that can be helpful in any writing assignment in a law office:

1. Obtain basic instructions on the assignment you are given:

   ■ What are you asked to write? (See "Kinds of Legal Writing," the next section.)
   ■ Who will be reading it? Who is the audience?
   ■ When is it due? Does it have priority over other assignments? (If you have assignments from different supervisors, consider asking the supervisors to establish the priorities.)
   ■ Is your time working on this assignment billable? If so, to what clients or accounts?
   ■ What format should you use in the document you will be preparing?
   ■ What resources can you use? For example, if your assignment requires legal research, can you use electronic research, e.g., Westlaw, LexisNexis, Loislaw (see chapters 11 and 13)?
   ■ Will the supervisor (or anyone else in the office) be available to provide feedback on a complete or partial draft of the assignment before the final draft is due?

2. Find out if the office has its own style manual. Someone in the office may have collected general **format** instructions for different kinds of writing the office often prepares. Everyone may be expected to follow these instructions. The style manual may also include sample documents that conform to these instructions. (If such a manual exists, it may be in a notebook or in a computer database.)

3. If the office does not have a style manual, ask your supervisor where in the office you can find copies of documents on other cases that you may be able to use as a model or guide for the document you are asked to prepare.

4. Find out if the office uses any commercial texts as guides for commonly prepared documents. Is there a bar practice manual or treatise that is considered the bible for the substantive area of law involved in the assignment? If so, it may contain sample documents.

5. Once you have a model, adapt it to the specific facts and instructions of the writing assignment you are given. See "How to Avoid Abusing a Standard Form" in Exhibit 10.4 in chapter 10.

6. Seek feedback before submitting the final draft. (See guideline 1.) For example, prepare an outline of the document and ask for feedback on the outline to make sure you are on the right track. (This will not be needed for relatively simple documents or ones that you often prepare.)

7. Carefully proofread to make sure there are no grammar and spelling errors in your final draft. Quietly reading your text out loud to yourself might turn up errors that were overlooked by silent reading and re-reading. Also, reading your text backward might help reveal glaring errors in spelling or punctuation. Spell checkers in word processing programs (see chapter 13) are sometimes helpful. Be careful, however, in using them. They will tell you if you misspelled the word *there*, but they will not tell you if you should have used the word *their*. If you asked your spell checker to check the sentence, "Due eye sense that you are a frayed?" you would be told that there are no spelling errors, although it should have read, "Do I sense that you are afraid?" Spell checkers cannot check the meaning or proper use of correctly spelled words.

[SECTION B]

KINDS OF LEGAL WRITING

Most of the legal writing in a law office falls into the following categories:

■ Letters
■ Memoranda
■ Appellate briefs
■ Instruments
■ Pleadings

We will discuss the first three in this chapter. Here is a brief overview of the other two:

Instruments: An **instrument** is a formal written document that gives expression to or embodies a legal act or agreement. Examples of instruments include contracts, deeds, wills, and leases.

Pleadings: A **pleading** is a formal document containing a statement of claims and responses to claims (such as defenses) exchanged between parties involved in litigation. The major pleadings are the complaint (see Exhibit 10.5 in chapter 10) and the answer to the complaint.

Instruments and pleadings are seldom drafted from scratch, particularly in law offices that have many clients with the same kind of case (e.g., a collections practice or a divorce practice). Form

---

format In word processing, the layout of the page when printed, e.g., the number of lines and margin settings.

instrument A formal written document that gives expression to or embodies a legal act or agreement.

pleadings A formal litigation document (e.g., complaint or answer) filed by a party that states or responds to claims or defenses of another party.

books and computer software often contain standard instruments or pleadings that the office can adapt to the facts of particular clients. Or the office can simply adapt instruments or pleadings already in its own computer files from prior client cases. Word processors can make needed adaptations with relative ease. If there are no instruments or pleadings already in the computer, the office can scan an old instrument or pleading into the computer for adaptation to a current client. (For more on scanning, see chapter 13.)

[SECTION C]

LETTER WRITING

A law office sends out different kinds of letters:

- Cover letter (transmittal letter)
- Demand letter
- Informational letter
- Status letter
- Confirmatory letter
- Opinion letter

There is overlap in these categories because a single letter may seek to accomplish more than one purpose. (Exhibit 12.1 presents the standard components of most letters.)

EXHIBIT 12.1 Standard Components of Most Letters

- **Heading** The heading at the top or beginning of the letter contains the firm's letterhead, which is often preprinted and centered. The letterhead identifies the law firm by full name, street address, and phone number. If available, a fax number, e-mail address, and World Wide Web homepage address may also be provided.
- **Date** Give the full date (month, day, and year) that the letter will be sent out. It is often placed at the left margin under the heading.
- **Recipient** This is the full name, title, and address of the person who will be receiving the letter. It is often placed at the left margin.
- **RE** A reference line is a brief statement that indicates the case to which the letter pertains, and occasionally the major theme of the letter (e.g., "RE: Henderson v. Jones, Civ. 03.179. Request for Extension of Time to File Responsive Declaration"). The notation *RE* goes at the beginning of the reference line. RE means *in the matter of* or *concerning*. The reference line is placed at the left margin after the address of the recipient and just before the salutation.
- **Salutation** Here, you address the recipient: "Dear . . . :". A colon (:) follows the last name of this person. If he or she is a doctor, professor, or important public official, use his or her title. The salutation often starts at the left margin on the line under the address.
- **Body** The body of the letter often includes:
  - *Identification line* In the first line of the letter, let the reader know who is sending the letter, unless this is already obvious to the recipient because of prior contact.
  - *Purpose line* Shortly after the identification line, briefly tell the reader the main purpose of the letter.
  - *Request line* If you are asking the recipient to do something, include a specific request line that makes this clear.
  - *Elaboration* As needed, explain why you are writing the letter.
- **Closing** Here, you conclude the letter. In a separate paragraph, you could say something like "If you have any questions about this matter, please do not hesitate to contact me" or "Thank you for your consideration in this matter." On the next line, write, "Sincerely" or "Very truly yours." Place the name and title of the signer of the letter below the space for his or her signature. As we saw in chapter 5 on ethics, when nonattorneys sign letters, their title should clearly indicate their nonattorney status. The titles *paralegal* and *legal assistant* comply with this ethical obligation; the titles *CLA, CP, RP, PACE,* and *PP* used alone do not because they give no clear indication that the signer is not an attorney. (On the meaning of these abbreviation, see Exhibit 4.7 in chapter 4.)
- **Copies Sent** If you are sending a copy of the letter to someone, indicate this by saying "cc:" followed by the name of the person(s) receiving the copy ("cc" stands for carbon copies; this abbreviation is still used even though carbon is seldom the method used today to make copies). Suppose you send out copies of the letter, but you do not want the recipient to know this. On the recipient's letter, you say nothing about copies. On the office copy of the letter, say "bcc:" (blind carbon copy) followed by the name of the person(s) receiving the copies. In this way, only your copy of the letter indicates who received copies. The main letter is silent ("blind") on this point. (This also works with e-mail messages. Beneath the cc box in your e-mail program, you will find (or you can add) a bcc box. The main recipients of the message will not know the names of anyone entered in the bcc box and vice versa.)
- **Enclosures** If you are enclosing anything with the letter, say "Encl." If enclosing more than one item, say "Encls."
- **Initials** If someone else typed the letter for you, place your initials in capital letters, followed by a colon (:) and the initials (in lowercase) of the person who did the typing.

A **cover letter** (also called a *transmittal letter*) tells the recipient what physical items (e.g., pleadings, photographs) are being sent in the envelope or package. The list of what is being sent should be detailed. If a response is expected, it should be clearly stated. For example:

cover letter A letter that tells the recipient what physical items are being sent in the envelope or package.

Enclosed for your records are:

- a copy of the defendant's answer (4 pages; dated May 3, 2008) filed with the court on May 5, 2008
- a copy of our response to the answer (5 pages; dated May 18, 2008)

Also enclosed is:

- a letter of authorization that allows us to obtain your confidential employment records from the personnel department.

Please read the letter of authorization, sign and date it, and return it to us. We will need it before May 30. If you have any questions, don't hesitate to call us.

demand letter An advocacy letter that asks the recipient to take or refrain from taking specific action affecting the client.

A **demand letter** is an advocacy letter that asks the recipient to take specific action (e.g., pay a debt owed to the client) or to refrain from taking specific action (e.g., not to terminate the client). The letter will often:

- Tell the recipient that the office represents the client,
- Specify what the recipient is being asked to do or to refrain from doing,
- Present essential facts and legal principles that support the demand.

Since the recipient is often a nonattorney, citations to authority are relatively rare except when a single statute or regulation is central to the demand.

Sending a demand letter is usually considered the practice of law. A paralegal can prepare a draft of the letter for an attorney's signature, but it would probably be the unauthorized practice of law (see chapters 4 and 5) for the paralegal to send the letter under his or her own name. If the demand letter seeks the collection of money that is owed, the letter must conform to the Fair Debt Collection Practices Act. For example, the letter must not use any "false, deceptive, or misleading representation or means in connection with the collection of any debt."[1]

informational letter A letter that provides or seeks information.

status letter A letter telling a client what has happened in the case thus far and what next steps are expected.

An **informational letter** provides information to the recipient, seeks information from the recipient, or both. See Exhibit 12.2 for a sample informational letter. An example of an informational letter is a **status letter** written to a client to inform him or her of what has happened in the case thus far and to indicate what next steps are expected.

EXHIBIT 12.2	Example of an Informational Letter

Heading (letterhead)	***Gordon, Davis & Kildare*** ***8268 Prestwick Drive*** ***Boston, MA 02127*** ***617-268-1899*** ***617-268-9203 (fax)*** ***www.gdk.com*** ***gdklaw@pacbell.net***

Mary Gordon, Esq.
John Davis, Esq.
Lance Kildare, Esq.

Date	March 13, 2009
Address of Recipient	Brenda A. Sarbanes Vice President Dennison Research Institute 74 Statler Road Belmont, MA 02177
Reference Line	RE: Massy Ford v. Cuttler 01-3456
Salutation	Dear Ms. Sarbanes:
Body of Letter (can include identification line, purpose line, and request line)	Our office represents a client in a stock distribution suit against a major automaker. I understand that your company provides marketing research that can be used in litigation. I want to obtain some information about your services. Do you have any literature you could send me on the kind of research you do? How are your fees determined? Finally, do you have any examples of reports you have prepared in the past that we could see? If you want to send me anything by e-mail attachment, you can reach me at swilliams_gdk@pacbell.net. To give you an idea of our practice, I am enclosing our firm brochure. You can also obtain an overview of our firm at www.gdk.com. Thank you for your consideration.

(continues)

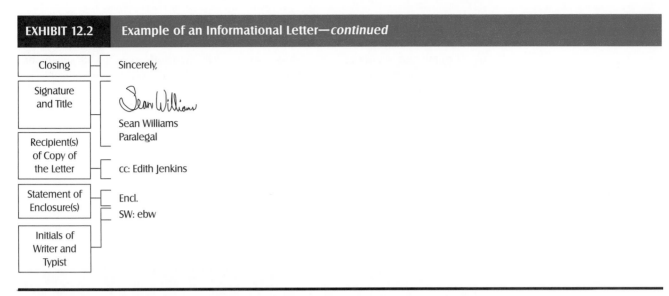

EXHIBIT 12.2   Example of an Informational Letter—*continued*

Closing — Sincerely,

Signature and Title — *Sean Williams*
Sean Williams
Paralegal

Recipient(s) of Copy of the Letter — cc: Edith Jenkins

Statement of Enclosure(s) — Encl.

Initials of Writer and Typist — SW: ebw

In a **confirmatory letter**, you confirm that something important has been done or said. Examples:

> This is to confirm that you have agreed to accept $5,000 in full settlement of the contract dispute between. . . .

> Thank you for coming to the office on Tuesday to discuss the extension of insurance coverage for the employees in the Southeast region of your company's operations. I want to state my understanding of what took place at the meeting. Please let me know if the following summary is consistent with your understanding. . . .

This kind of letter is important because it provides written confirmation of matters that might be subject to misunderstanding with the passage of time. It is also a good way to provide a record for the file. In this sense, a confirmatory letter is similar to a "memo to file," in which you communicate something about the case that has taken place, e.g., the substance of a recent telephone conversation or the result of some research in the law library. Confirmatory letters are different, of course, in that they are sent to specific individuals outside the office in an effort to remind them of something and to prompt them to voice any disagreements they may have with the contents of the letter.

In an **opinion letter**, the office writes to its client to explain the application of the law and advise the client what to do. Such letters try to clarify technical material. Unlike an appellate brief or memorandum, the opinion letter does not make extensive reference to court opinions or statutes. The client's need is for clear, concise, practical advice. Giving such advice constitutes the practice of law.

confirmatory letter A letter that verifies or confirms that something important has been done or said.

opinion letter A letter to a client explaining the application of the law and providing legal advice based on that explanation.

ASSIGNMENT 12.1

Prepare a letter for each of the following situations. You will need more facts to complete the letters (e.g., the address of the recipient, your address, and more details on the purpose of the letter). You can make up any of these facts as long as they are reasonably consistent with the facts provided. In each case, your supervisor is an attorney who wants you to draft the letter for his or her signature.

(a) The office represents Richard Clemens, who is a plaintiff in an automobile accident case against George Kiley. The latter's insurance company has offered to settle for $10,000. Draft a letter to Richard Clemens in which you tell him about the offer and ask him to call the office to schedule an appointment with your supervisor to discuss the offer. Point out that the supervisor is not pleased with the low amount of the offer but that the decision on whether to accept it will be entirely up to the client.

(b) Draft a letter to a client who failed to appear at two meetings last month with her attorney (your supervisor) at the office to discuss her case. The client is Diane Rolark. She is very wealthy. The office hopes to keep her as a client in the future on other cases. Hence the office does not want to antagonize her. The letter should remind her of the next appointment with her attorney (three weeks from today).

(continues)

(c) Write an opinion letter to a client, James Duband, in which you explain any legal concept that you have learned in another course. Assume that this concept is relevant to the case of this client and that the client has written the office asking your supervisor to explain the concept as it pertains to his case. The client is a construction worker who never finished high school.

[SECTION D]

MEMORANDUM OF LAW

memorandum of law A written explanation of how the law might apply to the facts of a client's case.

A **memorandum of law** is a written analysis of a legal problem. (The plural is *memoranda*; the shorthand is *memo*.) More specifically, it is a written explanation of how the law might apply to the facts of a client's case. There are two main kinds of memoranda: (1) an internal or office memorandum, sometimes called an *interoffice memorandum of law*; and (2) an external or advocacy memorandum. The differences are outlined in Exhibit 12.3.

EXHIBIT 12.3	Characteristics of Office and External Memoranda of Law

OFFICE MEMORANDUM OF LAW
- Emphasizes both the strengths and the weaknesses of the client's position on each issue (objective)
- Emphasizes both the weaknesses and the strengths of the opposing party's known or anticipated position on each issue (objective)
- Predicts the court's or the agency's probable decision on each issue
- Recommends the most favorable strategy for the client to follow

EXTERNAL MEMORANDUM OF LAW
- Emphasizes the strengths and minimizes or ignores the weaknesses of the client's position on each issue (advocacy)
- Emphasizes the weaknesses and minimizes or ignores the strengths of the opposing party's position on each issue (advocacy)
- Asks a court, agency, insurance company, or other recipient for a specific favorable decision or result based on the analysis in the memo

office memorandum of law A memorandum that objectively analyzes the law; the memo is written for your supervisor or for other individual(s) in your office.

1. *Office Memorandum of Law:* The main audience of your **office memorandum of law** is your supervisor or someone else in the office; this memo is an internal document. Your goal in the memo is to analyze the law in order to make a *prediction* of how a court or other tribunal will resolve the dispute in the client's case. It is extremely important that this memo present the strengths *and weaknesses* of the client's case. The supervisor must make strategy decisions based in part on what you say in the memo. Hence the supervisor must have a realistic picture of what the law is. Many students find it very difficult to present strengths and weaknesses in the same memo. They devote the vast majority of their memo to arguments that favor one side. This kind of writing is inappropriate in an office memorandum of law. Force yourself to find reasonable arguments that support both sides—no matter which side is the client of your office and no matter which side you think should win. A hallmark of the professional is the ability to step back and assess a problem objectively. This means being able to analyze strengths and weaknesses of both sides.

external memorandum of law A memorandum that analyzes the law in order to convince someone outside your office to take or to refrain from certain action.

2. *External or Advocacy Memorandum of Law:* The main audience of your **external memorandum of law** is someone outside the office, usually a judge or official in an administrative agency. An external memorandum might also be sent to an insurance company in support of a particular position (e.g., Memorandum in Support of the Life Insurance Claim of the Estate of George Samuelson). Your goal in this memo is to try to convince the reader to take or to refrain from certain action in the client's case. Hence the memo is an *advocacy* document. In it, you are highlighting the strengths of the client's case and the weaknesses of the opponent's case.

Different terminology is sometimes used for this kind of memo:

- **Points and authorities memorandum**: An external memorandum submitted to a trial judge or hearing officer.
- **Trial memorandum**: An external memorandum submitted to a trial judge. (A trial memorandum is sometimes referred to as a *trial brief*, although we will see later in the chapter that trial brief also has a very different meaning.)
- **Hearing memorandum**: An external memorandum submitted to a hearing officer within an administrative agency.

When the document is submitted to an appellate court, it is called an *appellate brief.* The structure of the appellate brief is discussed in Section E of the chapter.

Most of the discussion that follows is on the internal interoffice memo. The external advocacy memo is mentioned only when there are significant differences.

Be sure to obtain instructions on the format of the memo you are to prepare. For example, the standard format for office memos may be as follows:

- Double spaced
- 1" margin all around the page
- 8½" by 11" white bond paper (stapled in the top left corner)
- 12 **point** Times New Roman **font**
- Page numbers at the bottom center of each page (except for the first page, which will have no page number)
- A **footer** that states the name of the document, the client file name and number, etc.

Find out from your supervisor if you should follow format guidelines such as these. Also, try to locate examples of memos in the file that you can use as a guide.

> **points** A measure of the size of printed letters of the alphabet, punctuation marks, or other characters.
>
> **font** The design or style of printed letters of the alphabet, punctuation marks, or other characters.
>
> **footer** The same text that is printed at the bottom of every page.

STRUCTURE OF AN OFFICE MEMORANDUM OF LAW

Unless instructed otherwise by your supervisor, use the following organization for your office memorandum of law:

1. Heading
2. Introduction
3. Issues and summary conclusions
4. Facts
5. Discussion or analysis
6. Conclusion
7. Recommendations
8. Appendix

1. Heading

The heading of the memo contains basic information about you and the nature of the memo:

a. A **caption of memorandum** centered at the top of the page stating the kind of document it is (Office Memorandum of Law)
b. The name of the person to whom the memo is addressed (usually your supervisor)
c. Your name (the author of the memo)
d. The date the memo was completed and submitted
e. The name of the case (client's name and opponent, if any)
f. The office file number
g. The **docket number** (if the suit has already been filed and the clerk of the court has assigned a docket number)
h. A very brief summary of the subject matter of the memo following the notation **RE:**, meaning "in the matter of" or "concerning"

> **caption of memorandum** The beginning of a memorandum containing its title or name.
>
> **docket number** A consecutive number assigned to a case by the court and used on all documents filed with the court during the litigation of that case.
>
> **RE** In the matter of; concerning.

The example in Exhibit 12.4 illustrates how this information might be set forth in a memo written on behalf of client Brown, who is suing Miller.

EXHIBIT 12.4	**Heading of Office Memorandum**

Office Memorandum of Law

TO: Jane Patterson, Esq.
FROM: John Jackson, Paralegal
DATE: March 13, 2008
CASE: Brown v. Miller
OFFICE FILE NUMBER: 08-1168
DOCKET NUMBER: C-34552-08

RE: Substituted service under
Civil Code § 34–403(g)

Note that the subject matter description (RE) in this example briefly indicates the nature of the question you are treating in the memorandum. This information is needed for at least two reasons. First, the average law office case file contains a large number of documents, often including several legal memoranda. A heading that at least briefly indicates the subject of the memorandum makes it easier to locate the memorandum in the client's file. Second, your memo might be examined sometime in the future, long after the case is over. Many offices keep copies of old office memoranda in files or in computer databases. They are cataloged by subject matter for reference in future cases. The subject matter heading on the memo facilitates the cataloging, filing, and retrieving of such memos.

Including the date on which the memorandum was completed and submitted is also important. Although your analysis and conclusions may have been accurate at the time the memorandum was written, the law may have changed by the time the memorandum is examined again. Hence a later reader will need to verify the current validity of every case, statute, or other authority you cited in the memorandum and determine whether totally new laws have been written since the date you wrote it.

2. Introduction

After the heading, write a short introduction consisting of a roadmap paragraph and any limitations that have been imposed on your assignment. A **roadmap paragraph** is an overview or thesis paragraph that tells the reader what issues will be covered and briefly states the conclusions that will be reached. Example:

> **Introduction**
>
> This memorandum examines the question of whether cyanide sulfate falls within the category of "prohibited substances" under § 34.2 of the environmental code. It does.

Often your supervisor will place restrictions or limitations on what the memo should or should not cover. If so, they should be stated in the introduction. Examples:

- You have asked me not to examine the issue of damages.
- You have asked me to spend no more than four hours on the assignment.
- You have asked me not to use fee-based online research services at this time.

Also list any assumptions that you have been asked to make. Examples:

- You have asked me to assume that only New York law applies. (Or, you have asked me to discuss New York law only.)
- You have asked me to discuss the constitutionality of the client's statement to the police on the assumption that the state will be able to convince a trial judge that the statement was not privileged.

If you have any difficulty writing the statement of the assignment, consult with your supervisor immediately. The time to clarify what you are to do—and what you are not to do—is before you spend extensive time researching, analyzing, and writing. The value of clearly articulating the boundary lines of the memo cannot be overemphasized. Note that the introduction contains a more elaborate presentation of what was briefly summarized as the topic of the memo in the heading after the notation RE.

3. Issues and Summary Conclusions

The two critical components of an issue are as follows: (1) a brief quote from the element of the law in contention and (2) several of the important facts relevant to that contention. An **element** is a portion of a rule that is a precondition of the applicability of the entire rule. (See chapter 7.)

Assume, for example, that Mary Gallagher is suing Leo Grant, a store manager, for slander. While trying to buy a coat at his store with her credit card, Grant told Gallagher, "Your credit card is bogus." The merchant denies that his statement was defamatory. The law being applied here is the tort of slander. One of the requirements or elements of this tort is proof that the defendant uttered a "defamatory statement." This is the **element in contention**. The phrasing of the issue in this case might be:

> In an action for slander, has a merchant made a "defamatory statement" when he tells a customer seeking to make a credit purchase that her "credit card is bogus"?

roadmap paragraph An overview or thesis paragraph at the beginning of a memorandum of law that tells the reader what issues will be covered and briefly states the conclusions that will be reached.

element A portion of a rule that is a precondition of the applicability of the entire rule.

element in contention The portion of a rule about which the parties cannot agree. The disagreement may be over the definition of the element, whether the facts fit within the element, or both.

Note that the issue is made up of a quote from the element in contention and several of the important facts that are relevant to that element.

Let us look at another example. Assume that a taxpayer challenges a denial of a tax deduction under § 200.8 (a) of the state tax code. This statutory section says that an accelerated deduction can be taken for "equipment purchased for use primarily in areas of the state designated by the governor as economically blighted." Patricia Wallace has a restaurant in an area that the governor has designated as blighted. Wallace sought a § 200.8 (a) deduction for a refrigerator she leased for the restaurant with an option to buy after three years. The tax department has denied the deduction, asserting that a lease is not a purchase. Wallace claims that the lease with an option to buy within three years qualifies as a purchase, especially since she expects to exercise the option after three years of the lease. The law being applied here is § 200.8 (a) of the state tax code. The element of this law in contention is the requirement that the equipment be "purchased." The phrasing of the issue in this case might be:

> Has a taxpayer "purchased" a refrigerator, entitling her to a deduction under § 200.8 (a) of the tax code, when she leased the refrigerator with an option to buy after three years, which she expects to exercise?

Note again that the issue consists of a quote from the element in contention and several of the important facts that are relevant to that element.

For more on how to phrase issues, see the issue-statement skill in Section D of chapter 7 on legal analysis.

Often you must state and discuss certain issues *on the assumption* that the court or agency will decide against you on prior issues that you discuss early in the memorandum. Suppose that the client is a defendant in a negligence action. The first issue may concern the liability of the defendant: Was the defendant negligent? The memorandum will cover the liability question and will attempt to demonstrate in the discussion or analysis of this issue why the defendant is *not* liable. All the evidence and authority supporting nonliability will be examined under this issue. At the time the memorandum is written, of course, this issue will not have been resolved. Hence you must proceed *on the assumption* that the client will lose the first issue and be prepared for other issues that will then arise. For example, all issues concerning damages (how much money must be paid to a plaintiff who has successfully established liability) should be anticipated and analyzed in the event that the liability issue is lost. The statement of the damages issue in the memorandum should be prefaced by language such as:

> In the event that we lose the first issue, then we must discuss the issue of . . . .

or

> On the assumption that the court finds for [the other party] on the liability issue, the damages question then becomes whether. . . .

No matter how firmly you believe in your prediction of what a court or agency will do on an issue, be prepared for what will happen in the event that your prediction eventually proves to be erroneous. This must be done in an internal (office) memorandum, in an external memorandum (hearing or trial), and in an appellate brief.

After you have stated the issues, tell the reader what your answers are in the form of Summary Conclusions. Later in the memo, you will elaborate on the conclusions as needed. Here you provide brief answers to the issues raised. Example:

Summary Conclusions

I. Yes. The statute of frauds does not apply to the agreement because it can be performed within a year.

II. No. Section 745 of the Corporations Code does not require two confirmatory signatures from shareholders exercising the buy-back option.

4. Facts

Your statement of the facts of the client's case is one of the most important components of the memorandum. You should take great pains to see that it is concise, accurate, and well organized. The facts should be stated in the memo even if you and your supervisor are very familiar with the facts. Later, there may be other readers of the memo who are not as familiar with them.

The statement of facts should include the following:

- *All legally relevant facts* A fact is legally relevant if it will help prove or disprove one of the elements of a cause of action or of a defense. (See chapter 7 on identifying elements.)

- *Unknown facts* State facts that are unknown as of the date of the memo if they would be relevant to the dispute. (Example: We do not know if the substance seized by the police is a drug because the lab report has not yet been completed.)
- *Favorable and unfavorable facts* The reader of the memo needs to have an accurate picture of what happened in order to formulate an effective strategy on behalf of the client. This requires an honest and complete presentation of every relevant fact, regardless of which side it favors. (Example: The client insists that his sister paid for the service with cash. Thus far, however, we have not been able to locate a receipt or other indication that the payment was made.)
- *Procedural facts* If the client's case is already in litigation, include a summary of what has happened in court to date—the procedural facts. (Example: On March 26, 2009, we filed an action for medical malpractice against Sutter Hospital on behalf of Johnson and are now waiting for service of its answer.) Then proceed to the nonprocedural facts of the dispute.

Do not state legal conclusions in the statement of facts, and do not be argumentative. State the facts as objectively as you can.

If the statement of facts is fairly long, you might begin with a one- or two-sentence summary of the facts. For example:

Facts

During 12 years of employment at Sinclair Chemicals, Inc., Mary Kiley was subjected to numerous instances of sexual harassment. When she began work there in 1990, she . . . .

Then provide a *chronological* statement of the detailed facts. Occasional variations from strict chronological order can be justified as long as they do not interfere with the flow of the story. Sometimes it is useful to divide complicated facts into broad categories or topics. Suppose, for example, your firm represents three companies suing the same distributor for breach of contract. One way to present the facts would be to begin with those facts that pertain to all three. These facts would be stated chronologically. Then you would list each company individually and provide separate statements of facts—again, in chronological order—that pertain to each company.

5. Discussion or Analysis

Here, you state the law and explain its applicability to the facts. In the discussion or analysis portion of the memo, you will be giving a detailed answer to each issue through the *application* component of **IRAC**. As we saw in chapter 7, the principal structure used in legal analysis is summarized in the acronym **IRAC**: issue (I), rule (R), application of the rule to the facts (A), and conclusion (C). You have already stated the issues in the memo and referred to the rules within the issues. Next comes the application of the rule to the facts. Assume that the rule being applied is a statute. Here is a summary of the steps that would be taken:

IRAC An acronym that stands for the components of legal analysis: issue (I), rule (R), application of the rule to the facts (A), and conclusion (C). A structure for legal analysis.

- Quote the section or subsection of the statute you are analyzing. Include only what must be discussed in the memo. If the section or subsection is long, you may also want to place it in an appendix to the memo. If you are going to discuss more than one section or subsection, treat them separately in different parts of the memo unless they are so interrelated that they must be discussed together.
- Break the statute into its elements. List each element separately. (See "Organizing a Memorandum of Law" in Exhibit 7.2 in chapter 7.)
- Briefly tell the reader which elements will be in contention and why. In effect, you are telling him or her why you have phrased the issue(s) the way you did earlier in the memo.
- Go through each element you have identified, one at a time, spending most of your time on the elements that are most in contention.
- For the elements not in contention, simply tell the reader why you think there will not be any dispute about them. For example, you anticipate that both sides will probably agree that the facts clearly support the applicability or nonapplicability of the element.
- For the elements in contention, present your interpretation of each element; discuss court opinions that have interpreted the statute, if any; discuss administrative regulations and administrative decisions that have interpreted the statute, if any; discuss the legislative history of the statute, if any; discuss scholarly interpretation of the statute, if any, in legal periodicals and legal treatises (see chapter 11).
- Give opposing viewpoints for the elements in contention. Try to anticipate how the other side will interpret these elements. For example, what counterarguments will the other side probably make through court opinions or legislative history?

Counter arguments are particularly important. Too often student memos fail to provide a counter-analysis. They present only one side: either the side they think should, in fairness, win or the side their law office represents. To counteract this deficiency, use the **STOP** technique:

STOP

- after you write a **S**entence of your analysis
- **T**hink carefully
- about whether the **O**ther side
- would agree with the **P**osition you have just taken in that sentence

If you conclude (once you STOP yourself) that the other side would not agree with what you have written, a counteranalysis to your position will be needed somewhere in the memo. The counteranalysis does not have to occur immediately after the sentence you wrote. You may decide to present the counteranalysis in a separate paragraph or in a separate section of the memo. STOP is simply a technique to remind you that your analysis will not be complete until you have covered every position the other side will probably raise.

6. Conclusion

Give your personal opinion as to which side has the better arguments. Do not state any new arguments in the conclusion. Simply state your own perspective on the strengths and weaknesses of your arguments.

7. Recommendations

State recommendations you feel are appropriate in view of the analysis and conclusion you have provided. For example, further facts should be investigated (specify which ones), further research should be undertaken (identify each issue in need of further research), a letter should be written to the government agency involved in the dispute (summarize or submit a draft of the proposed letter), the case should be settled or litigated (summarize why you think so), etc.

8. Appendix

At the end of the memo, include special items, if any, that you referred to in the memo, such as photographs, statistical tables, and the full text of statutes or other rules.

Exhibit 12.5 presents an office memorandum of law that conforms with this structure. Assume that the supervisor wants this memorandum within a few hours after the assignment is given to you. You are asked to provide a preliminary analysis of a statute. Hence, at this point there has been no time to do any research on the statute, although the memo should indicate what research will be needed. As you will see at the end of the memo, the author recommends that a letter be drafted to the supervisor of the client. A draft of that letter for the signature of the supervisor is found in Exhibit 12.6.

STOP A writing technique alerting you to the need for a counteranalysis: after writing a Sentence, Think carefully about whether the Other side would take a Position that is different from the one you took in the sentence.

EXHIBIT 12.5	Sample Office Memorandum of Law on the Donaldson Case

OFFICE MEMORANDUM OF LAW

To: Isabelle F. Farrell, Esq.

FROM: Paul Vargas, Paralegal

DATE: March 23, 2008

CASE: Department of Sanitation v. Jim Donaldson

OFFICE FILE NUMBER: 08-114

DOCKET NUMBER: (none at this time; no action has been filed)

RE: Whether Donaldson has violated § 17

A. INTRODUCTION

You have asked me to do a preliminary analysis of 23 State Code Ann. § 17 (2007) to assess whether our client, Jim Donaldson, has violated this statute. The argument is strong that he did not. No research on the statute has been undertaken thus far, but I will indicate where such research might be helpful.

B. ISSUE AND SUMMARY CONCLUSION

Issue: When a government employee is asked to rent a car for his agency, but uses the car for personal business before he signs the lease, has this employee violated § 17, which prohibits the use of "property leased to the government" for nonofficial purposes?

Summary Conclusion: No. Until the lease is signed, § 17 does not prohibit personal use.

(continues)

EXHIBIT 12.5   Sample Office Memorandum of Law on the Donaldson Case—*continued*

C. FACTS

Jim Donaldson is a government employee who works for the State Department of Sanitation. On February 12, 2008, he is asked by his supervisor, Fred Jackson, to rent a car for the agency for a two-year period. At the ABC Car Rental Company, Donaldson is shown several cars available for rental. He asks the manager if he could test drive one of the cars before making a decision. The manager agrees. Donaldson then drives the car to his home in the area, picks up a TV, and takes it to his sister's home. When he returns, he tells the manager that he wants to rent the car for his agency. He signs the lease and takes the car to the agency. The supervisor, however, finds out about the trip that Donaldson made to his sister with the TV. He is charged with a violation of § 17. Because Donaldson is a new employee at the agency, he is fearful that he might lose his job.

D. ANALYSIS

Donaldson is charged with violating 23 State Code Ann. § 17 (2007), which provides as follows:

§ 17. Use of Government Property
An employee of any state agency shall not directly or indirectly use government property of any kind, including property leased to the government, for other than officially approved activities.

To establish a violation of this statute, the following elements must be proven:

(1) An employee of any state agency
(2) (a) shall not directly use government property of any kind including property leased to the government or
    (b) shall not indirectly use government property of any kind including property leased to the government.
(3) for other than officially approved activities.

The main problem in this case will be the second element.

(1) Employee of a state agency
Donaldson works for the State Department of Sanitation, which is clearly a "state agency" under the statute.

(2) Use of property leased to the government.
The central issue is whether Donaldson used property leased to the government. There should be no dispute that when Donaldson drove the car to his sister's, he directly used property. (He did not "indirectly" use property such as by causing someone else to drive the car.) The question is whether the car was "property leased to the government" within the meaning of § 17.

Donaldson's best argument is a strong one. When he made the trip to his sister, he had not yet signed the lease. He can argue that "leased" means contractually committed to rent. Under this definition, the car did not become property leased to the government until after he returned from his sister's house. No costs were incurred by the government because of the test drive. Rental payments would not begin until the car was rented through the signing of the lease.

The supervisor, on the other hand, will argue for a broader definition of "leased"—that it means the process of obtaining a contractual commitment to rent, including the integral steps leading up to that commitment. Under this definition, the car was "leased" to Donaldson when he made the unauthorized trip. The test drive was arguably an integral step in making the decision to sign a long-term leasing contract.

The supervisor will stress that the goal or purpose of the legislature in enacting § 17 should be kept in mind when trying to determine the meaning of any of the language of § 17. The legislature was trying to avoid the misuse of government resources. Public employees should not take advantage of their position for private gain. To do so would be a violation of the public trust. Yet this is what Donaldson did. While on the government payroll, he obtained access to a car and used it for a private trip. Common sense would lead to the conclusion that leasing in § 17 is not limited to the formal signing of a leasing contract. Anything that is an integral part of the process of signing that contract should be included. The legislature wanted to prevent the misuse of government resources in all necessary aspects of the leasing of property.

It is not clear from the facts whether the manager of the ABC Rental Company knew that Donaldson was considering the rental on behalf of a government agency when he received permission to take the test drive. The likelihood is that he did know it, although this should be checked. If the manager did know, then Donaldson probably used the fact that he was a government employee to obtain the permission. He held himself out as a reliable individual because of the nature of his employment. This reinforces the misuse argument under the broader definition of "leased" that the supervisor will present.

I have not yet checked whether there are any court opinions or agency regulations interpreting § 17 on this point. Nor have I researched the legislative history of the statute. All this should be done soon.

(3) Officially Approved Activities
Nothing in the facts indicates that Donaldson's supervisor gave him any authorization to make the TV trip. Even if the supervisor had authorized the trip, it would probably not be "officially" approved, since the trip was not for official (i.e., public) business.

E. CONCLUSION

Donaldson has the stronger argument based on the language of the statute. The property simply was not "leased" at the time he made the TV trip. I must admit, however, that the agency has some good points in its favor. Unlike Donaldson's technical argument, the agency's position is grounded in common sense. Yet on balance, Donaldson's argument should prevail.

F. RECOMMENDATIONS

Some further investigation is needed. We should find out whether the ABC Rental Company manager knew that Donaldson was a government employee at the time he asked for the test drive. In addition, legal research should be undertaken to find out if any court opinions and agency regulations exist on the statute. A check into the legislative history of § 17 is also needed.

(continues)

EXHIBIT 12.5	Sample Office Memorandum of Law on the Donaldson Case—*continued*

Finally, I recommend that we send a letter to Donaldson's supervisor, Fred Jackson, explaining our position. I have attached a draft of such a letter for your signature in the event you deem this action appropriate.

There is one matter that I have not addressed in this memo. Donaldson is concerned that he might lose his job over this incident. Assuming for the moment that he did violate § 17, it is not at all clear that termination would be an appropriate sanction. The statute is silent on this point. Let me know if you want me to research this issue.

EXHIBIT 12.6	Draft of Proposed Letter on the Donaldson Case

Farrell, Grote, & Schweitzer
Attorneys at Law
724 Central Plaza Place
West Union, Ohio 45693
513-363-7159

Isabelle F. Farrell, Esq.
Angela Grote, Esq.
Clara Schweitzer, Esq.

March 25, 2008

Frederick Jackson
Field Supervisor
Department of Sanitation
3416 34th St. NW
West Union, Ohio 45693

RE: James Donaldson
08-114

Dear Mr. Jackson:

Our firm represents Mr. James Donaldson. As you know, a question has arisen concerning Mr. Donaldson's use of a car prior to his renting it for your agency on February 12, 2008. Our understanding is that he was asked to go to the ABC Car Rental Company in order to rent a car that was needed by your agency, and that he did so satisfactorily.

Your agency became responsible for the car at the moment Mr. Donaldson signed the lease for the car rental on behalf of the agency. What happened prior to the time the lease was signed is not relevant. The governing statute (§ 17) is quite explicit. It forbids nonofficial use of property "leased" to the government. Such use did not occur in this case. No one has questioned Mr. Donaldson's performance of his duty once he "leased" the car.

If additional clarification is needed, we would be happy to discuss the matter with you further.

Sincerely,

Isabelle F. Farrell, Esq.
TF: ps

ASSIGNMENT 12.2

The Pepsi Cola Bottling Company is authorized to do business in Florida. It wishes to prevent another Florida company from calling itself the Pepsi Catsup Company because this name violates § 225.25. The Pepsi Catsup Company denies that its name is in violation of this statute. The secretary of state has the responsibility of enforcing this statute.

48 State Code Ann. § 225.25 (1999). The name of a company or corporation shall be such as will distinguish it from any other company or corporation doing business in Florida.

Your supervisor asks you to prepare a preliminary memorandum of law on the applicability of this statute. The office represents the Pepsi Catsup Company. You do not need to know trademark law or any other area of the law. Simply analyze the language of the statute (§ 225.25) in a manner similar to the analysis of the statute (§ 17) in the sample office memorandum of law in Exhibit 12.5. Do no legal research at this time, although you should point out what research might be helpful. After you complete the memo, draft a letter to the secretary of state giving the position of your office on the applicability of the statute. (You can make up the names and addresses of the people involved as well as any dates that you need.)

trial brief 1. An attorney's presentation to a trial court of the legal issues and positions of his or her client. Also called *trial memorandum*. 2. An attorney's personal notes on conducting a trial. Also called *trial manual* or *trial book*.

appellate brief A document submitted (filed) by a party to an appellate court (and served on an opposing party) in which arguments are presented on why the appellate court should affirm (approve), reverse, or otherwise modify what a lower court has done.

brief bank A collection of appellate briefs and related documents drafted in prior cases that might be used as models and adapted for current cases.

appellant The party bringing an appeal because of alleged errors made by a lower tribunal.

appellee The party against whom an appeal is brought. Also called respondent.

reply brief 1. An appellate brief of the appellant that responds to the appellate brief of the appellee. 2. Any appellate brief that responds to an opponent's appellate brief.

amicus curiae brief ("friend of the court" brief) An appellate brief submitted by a nonparty who obtains court permission to file the brief with its views on the case.

Front cover (title page) of an appellate brief submitted to the U.S. Supreme Court.

point heading A conclusion that a party wants a court to accept on one of the issues in the case.

[SECTION E]

APPELLATE BRIEF

The word *brief* has several meanings.

First, to *brief* a case is to summarize its major components, such as key facts, issues, reasoning, and disposition. (See Exhibit 7.3 in chapter 7.) Such a brief is your own summary of a court opinion for later use.

Second, a **trial brief** has several meanings: (1) an attorney's presentation to a trial court of the legal issues and positions of his or her client (also called *trial memorandum*), and (2) an attorney's personal notes on how he or she will conduct a particular trial (also called *trial manual* or *trial book*). The strategy notes will be on the opening statement, witnesses, exhibits, direct and cross-examination, closing argument, etc. The trial brief containing these notes is not submitted to the court or to the other side.

Third, the **appellate brief** is the formal written argument submitted (filed) by a party to an appellate court in which arguments are presented on why the appellate court should affirm (approve), reverse, or otherwise modify what a lower court has done. It is also served on the other side. The appellate brief is one of the most sophisticated kinds of legal writing. If the office prepares many appellate briefs, extra copies might be stored in its **brief bank**, where they can be easily accessed to determine whether they can be adapted for future similar cases.

The first appellate brief that is submitted is the *appellant's* brief. The **appellant** is the party initiating the appeal. Then the *appellee's* brief is filed in response. The appeal is taken against the **appellee** (sometimes called the *respondent*). Finally, the appellant is often allowed to submit a **reply brief** to counter the position taken in the appellee's brief.

Occasionally, a court will permit a nonparty to the litigation to submit an appellate brief. This is referred to as an **amicus curiae** (friend of the court) **brief**. The *amicus* brief presents the nonparty's view on whether the appellate court should affirm, reverse, or otherwise modify what the lower court has done.

Not all appellate briefs have the same structure. Rules of court often specify what structure or format the brief should take, the print (point) size, the maximum number of pages or words that can be used, the number of the copies to be submitted, the color of the paper that must be used for the title page, etc. The following are the major components of many appellate briefs:

a. *Caption:* The caption of an appellate brief states the names of the parties, the name of the court, the court file or docket number, and the kind of appellate brief it is. The caption goes on the title page (i.e., front cover) of the brief.

b. *The Statement of Jurisdiction:* In this section of the brief, there is a short statement explaining the subject matter jurisdiction of the appellate court. (Subject matter jurisdiction is the power of a court to resolve a particular category or kind of dispute. Subject matter jurisdiction is usually conferred by statute.) For example:

This Court has jurisdiction under 28 U.S.C. § 1291 (1997).

The jurisdiction statement may point out some of the essential facts that relate to the jurisdiction of the appellate court, such as how the case came up on appeal. For example:

On January 2, 1998, a judgment was entered by the U.S. Court of Appeals for the Second Circuit. The U.S. Supreme Court granted certiorari on February 6, 1998. 400 U.S. 302.

Later in the brief, there is a Statement of the Case that often includes more detailed jurisdictional information.

c. *Table of Contents:* The table of contents is an outline of the major components of the brief, including **point headings**, and the pages in the brief on which everything begins. (A point heading is the party's conclusion it wants the court to adopt for a particular issue. Every word in a point heading is capitalized or is printed in all capital letters. Point headings are printed in the table of contents and in the body of the appellate brief.) The function of the table of contents is to provide the reader with quick and easy access to each portion of the brief. Because the page numbers will not be known until the brief is completed, the table of contents is the last section of the brief to be written. Exhibit 12.7 is an excerpt from the respondent's brief. It illustrates the structure of a table of contents that includes the point headings as part of the "argument."

EXHIBIT 12.7	Table of Contents (with Point Headings) in an Appellate Brief

TABLE OF CONTENTS

d. *Table of Authorities:* The **table of authorities (TOA)** lists all the cases, statutes, regulations, administrative decisions, constitutional provisions, charter provisions, ordinances, rules of court, and secondary authority (e.g., legal periodical articles and legal treatises) cited in the brief. All the cases are listed in alphabetical order, all the statutes are listed in alphabetical and numerical order, etc. The page numbers on which each of these authorities is discussed in the brief are presented so that the table acts as an index to these authorities, as shown in Exhibit 12.8. The major word processing programs (e.g., Word and WordPerfect) include built-in assistance for creating tables of authorities. See the sites mentioned in "Helpful Web Sites" at the end of the chapter.)

table of authorities (TOA)
A list of primary authority (e.g., cases and statutes) and secondary authority (e.g., legal periodical articles and legal treatises) that a writer has cited in an appellate brief or other document. The list includes page numbers where each authority is cited in the document.

EXHIBIT 12.8	Table of Authorities in an Appellate Brief

TABLE OF AUTHORITIES

CASES: Page

    Smith v. Jones, 24 F.2d 445 (5th Cir, 1974) 2, 4, 12
    Thompson v. Richardson, 34 Miss. 650, 65 So. 109 (1930) 3, 9
    Etc.

CONSTITUTIONAL PROVISIONS
    Art. 5, Miss. Constitution 12, 17
    Art. 7, Miss. Constitution 20
    Etc.

STATUTES
    Miss. Code Ann. § 23(b) (1978) 2, 8, 23
    Miss. Code Ann. § 779 (1978)
    Etc.

LEGAL PERIODICAL ARTICLES
    Samuel Warren & Louis Brandeis, *The Right to Privacy*, 4 Harvard
    Law Review 193 (1890) 6, 18
    Thomas Cramer, *Government Controls Run Amok*, 84 American
    Bar Association Journal 449 (November 1990) 7
    Etc.

e. *Questions Presented:* The label used for the **questions presented** section of the brief varies. Other names for it include "Points Relied on for Reversal," "Points in Error," "Assignments of Error," and "Issues Presented." Regardless of the label, its substance is essentially the same: it is a statement of the legal issues that the party wishes the appellate court to consider and decide.

questions presented A statement of the legal issues in an appellate brief that a party wants the appellate court to resolve.

statement of the case The portion of an appellate brief that summarizes the procedural history of the case of date and presents the essential facts of the dispute. It may also state the appellate court's subject matter jurisdiction.

transcript A word-for-word account. A written copy of oral testimony.

f. *Statement of the Case:* The **statement of the case** has two main components: first, a summary of the procedural history of the dispute—what has happened in the lower courts and in the current court up to the time the brief is filed; and, second, the essential facts of the case. The statement of the case may also include the basis of the appellate court's subject matter jurisdiction to hear the appeal. The statement of the case should not contain legal analysis supported by authority. Such analysis comes later in the argument section of the brief. Exhibit 12.9 presents an example of a statement of the case. Note that the statement provides specific page references to the trial **transcript** (often abbreviated "Tr."). A transcript is a word-for-word account of something. Throughout the appellate brief, references to what occurred during the trial (e.g., the testimony of a particular witness, or a motion made by counsel) should be accompanied by cites to pages of the transcript on which those occurrences are recorded.

EXHIBIT 12.9	**Statement of the Case in an Appellate Brief**

Statement of the Case

These are actions based upon the Federal Tort Claims Act, 28 U.S.C. § 1346 (b), initiated by the appellants, Garrett Freightlines, Inc., and Charles R. Thomas in the United States District Court for the District of Idaho. The appellant alleged that appellee's employee, Randall W. Reynolds, while acting within the scope of his employment, negligently caused injury to appellants. The United States denied that the employee was acting within the scope of his employment.

On March 27, 2008, appellant Garrett made a motion for limited summary judgment on whether Reynolds was acting within the scope of his employment when the collision occurred. The actions of Garrett and Thomas were consolidated by order of the court, and appellee later moved for summary judgment (see trial transcript, page 204).

The District Court held, under the authority of *Berrettoni v. United States*, 436 F. 2d 1372 (9th Cir. 1970), that Reynolds was not within the scope of his employment when the accident occurred and granted appellee's motion for summary judgment. It is from that order and judgment that the injured now appeals.

Staff Sergeant Reynolds was a career soldier in the United States Military and, until November 9, 2005, stationed at Fort Rucker, Alabama. On or about July 30, 2005, official orders directed that Reynolds be reassigned to Japan. . . .

---

g. *Summary of Argument:* The major points to be made in the brief are summarized in this section.

h. *Argument:* Here, the attorney explains the legal positions of the client presented in the order of the point headings listed in the table of contents. The point headings are printed in the body of the argument exactly as they are printed in the table of content. All the primary and secondary authority relied on is analyzed.

i. *Conclusion:* The conclusion states what action the attorney is asking the appellate court to take.

j. *Appendixes:* The appendixes contain excerpts from statutes or other primary authority, excerpts from the trial transcript, charts, descriptions of exhibits entered into evidence at the trial, etc.

[SECTION F]

SOME WRITING GUIDELINES

I believe that [the legal profession does] not use plain language for two reasons: time and fear. Time is the enemy of brevity as evidenced by a quotation I am certain many of us remember: "Please excuse the length of this letter; I did not have time to be brief." Fear, however, is an unavoidable concern to lawyers—we tremble at the thought of saying it differently than it has been said for years. Thus, "in the event that" still prevails [over] "if." William Nussbaum, *Afraid to Change?*, 69 The Florida Bar Journal 6 (*December 1995*).

Lawyers like to throw around jargon and flowery language because it makes them feel self-important and prestigious. Debbie Laskey, *Legalese . . . Is It English?*, 20 At Issue 14 (San Francisco Ass'n of Legal Assistants, May 1993).

Review the self-improvement suggestions on grammar, spelling, and composition presented before chapter 1 in "How to Study Law in the Classroom and on the Job." Everything you write, including e-mail messages, should meet the high standards of communication that will be expected of you as a law office professional. Here are some additional guidelines:

1. *Do not use circumlocutions.*

A **circumlocution** is the use of more words than needed to express something. An example is the use of a pair of words that have the same effect. Here is a list of circumlocutions commonly found in the law. Avoid using them. Pick one of the words and discard the other.

circumlocution The use of more words than are needed to express something.

Do not say:	*Say:*	*Or say:*
alter and change	alter	change
any and all	any	all
by and with	by	with
each and every	each	every
final and conclusive	final	conclusive
full and complete	full	complete
made and entered into	made	entered
null and void	null	void
order and direct	order	direct
over and above	over	above
sole and exclusive	sole	exclusive
type and kind	type	kind
unless and until	unless	until

If language adds nothing to the sentence, don't use it. There is an easy test to find out if your phrase, clause, or sentence uses language that adds nothing. Remove it and ask yourself whether you have altered the meaning or emphasis desired. If not, keep it out.

Compare the sentences in these two columns:

Your maximum recovery is $100 under the provisions of the Warsaw Convention.	Your maximum recovery is $100 under the Warsaw Convention.

When we remove "the provisions of" from the first sentence, we lose neither meaning nor emphasis. Hence we don't need it.

Use the language in the second column unless you have a valid reason to use the language in the first column:

Do not say:	*Say:*
(1) all of the	(1) all the
(2) by means of	(2) by *or* with
(3) does not operate to	(3) does not
(4) despite the fact that	(4) because *or* since
(5) during the course of	(5) during
(6) in light of	(6) because *or* since
(7) in the event that	(7) if
(8) in the time of	(8) during
(9) in order to	(9) to
(10) or in the alternative	(10) or
(11) owing to the fact that	(11) because *or* since
(12) period of time	(12) period *or* time
(13) prior to	(13) before
(14) provision of law	(14) law
(15) State of New Jersey	(15) New Jersey
(16) subsequent to	(16) after
(17) until such time as	(17) until

2. *Use shorter words when longer ways of expressing the same idea add nothing.*

Use the language in the second column unless you have a valid reason to use the language in the first column:

Do not say:	*Say:*
(1) adequate number of	(1) enough
(2) prohibited from	(2) shall not
(3) at such time as	(3) when
(4) at the present time	(4) now

(5) during such time as	(5) while
(6) enter into a contact	(6) contract (verb)
(7) for the duration of	(7) during
(8) for the purpose of	(8) for
(9) for the purpose of entering	(9) to enter
(10) for the reason that	(10) because
(11) give consideration to	(11) consider
(12) give recognition to	(12) recognize
(13) have need of	(13) need
(14) in case	(14) if
(15) in a number of	(15) in some
(16) in cases in which	(16) when
(17) in connection with	(17) in *or* on
(18) in my considered opinion	(18) I think
(19) in regard to	(19) about
(20) in relation to	(20) about *or* toward
(21) in the case of	(21) if *or* in
(22) in the event of	(22) if
(23) in the matter of	(23) in *or* on
(24) in the majority of instances	(24) usually
(25) in view of	(25) because *or* since
(26) is able to	(26) can
(27) is applicable	(27) applies
(28) is binding on	(28) binds
(29) is dependent on	(29) depends on
(30) is entitled to	(30) may
(31) is permitted to	(31) may
(32) is required to	(32) shall
(33) is unable to	(33) cannot
(34) is directed to	(34) shall
(35) it is your duty to	(35) you shall
(36) make an appointment of	(36) appoint
(37) make a determination of	(37) determine
(38) make application	(38) apply
(39) make payment	(39) pay
(40) make provision for	(40) provide for
(41) on a few occasions	(41) occasionally
(42) on behalf of	(42) for
(43) on the part of	(43) by *or* among
(44) provided that	(44) if
(45) subsequent to	(45) after
(46) with reference to	(46) on
(47) with the exception that	(47) except

3. *Use a less complicated or less fancy way of expressing the same idea.*
   Use the language in the second column unless you have a valid reason to use the language in the first column:

Do not say:	*Say:*
(1) accorded	(1) given
(2) afforded	(2) given
(3) cause it to be done	(3) have it done *or* do it
(4) contiguous to	(4) touching
(5) deem	(5) consider
(6) endeavor (as a verb)	(6) try
(7) evince	(7) show
(8) expiration	(8) end
(9) expires	(9) ends

(10) have knowledge of	(10) know
(11) forthwith	(11) immediately
(12) in accordance with	(12) under
(13) in the event of	(13) if
(14) in the event that	(14) if
(15) in the interest of	(15) for
(16) is applicable	(16) applies
(17) is authorized to	(17) may
(18) is directed to	(18) shall
(19) is empowered to	(19) may
(20) is entitled (for a name)	(20) is called
(21) is hereby authorized	(21) may
(22) is not prohibited	(22) may
(23) per annum	(23) per year
(24) provided that	(24) if
(25) render service	(25) give service

ASSIGNMENT 12.3

Rewrite any of the following sentences that contain language that can be simplified without interfering with the meaning or effectiveness of the sentence.

(a) You are required to pay the fine.

(b) The period of time you have to render assistance is three months.

(c) For the duration of construction, it shall be unlawful for a person to enter or to attempt entry.

(d) If you are unable to enter into a contract with him for the materials, the oral commitment is still binding on you.

(e) She consulted with a lawyer with respect to possible litigation.

(f) She accepted the appointment due to the fact that she was qualified.

(g) It is green in color.

(h) Ask the witness questions about the bills.

(i) Judge Jones is currently on the bench.

4. *Use action verbs and adjectives.*

Avoid **nominalizations**, which are nouns formed from verbs or adjectives. Examples include the noun *consideration* from the verb *consider* and the noun *effectiveness* from the adjective *effective*. Nominalizations are not grammatically incorrect. In most cases, however, they weaken a sentence. Unfortunately, the legal profession is addicted to nominalizations. Avoid this addiction yourself.

nominalization A noun formed from a verb or adjective.

Compare the sentences in these two columns:

A	B
He came to the realization that the effort is futile.	He realizes the effort is futile.
She made the decision to retire.	She decided to retire.
A determination of who should pay was made by the court.	The court determined who should pay.

The nominalizations in column A are *realization, decision,* and *determination.* The sentences in column B using verbs (*realizes, decided,* and *determined*) are more forceful and direct. The sentences in column A using the nominalizations are more stilted and verbose. Using nominalizations often leads to longer words and longer sentences. It also encourages the use of the passive voice (in the third example), which should be avoided, as we will see.

Do not say:	*Say:*
(1) give consideration to	(1) consider
(2) give recognition to	(2) recognize
(3) have knowledge of	(3) know
(4) have need of	(4) need
(5) in the determination of	(5) determine

(6) is applicable	(6) applies
(7) is dependent on	(7) depends on
(8) is in attendance at	(8) attends
(9) make an appointment of	(9) appoint
(10) make application	(10) apply
(11) make payment	(11) pay
(12) make provision for	(12) provide for

5. *Use active voice.*

Use **active voice** rather than **passive voice** by making the doer of the action the subject and main focus of the sentence. Compare the sentences in the following two columns:

A (passive voice)

The decision was announced by the judge.
The report will be prepared.
The court was cleared.
By Friday, the bridge will have
been blown up by the workers.
The strike was ended by the injunction.

B (active voice)

The judge announced the decision.
I will prepare the report.
The clerk cleared the court.
By Friday, the workers will have
blown up the bridge.
The injunction ended the strike.

The verbs in the sentences in the "A" column are in the passive voice. The verbs in the sentences in the "B" column are in the active voice. What are the differences between these two kinds of sentences?

Sentences with verbs in the *passive voice* have the following characteristics:

- The doer of the action is either unknown or given less emphasis than what was done.
- The doer of the action, if referred to at all, is mentioned after the action itself.
- The subject of the sentence receives the action. The subject is acted upon.

If you do not mention the doer of the action in the sentence, the verb form is a **truncated passive**. In the following sentence, for example, you don't know who fired Jim:

Jim was fired at noon.

Sentences with verbs in the *active voice* have the following characteristics:

- The doer of the action is the important focus.
- The doer of the action is mentioned before the action itself.
- The subject of the sentence performs the action. The subject is the doer of the action.

The passive voice is often less effective because it is less direct and often less clear. It can dilute the forcefulness of a statement.

Weak: It is no longer allowed to take law library books overnight.
Better: The law library no longer allows you to take books overnight.
Or: The law library no longer allows borrowers to take books overnight.

The action in these sentences is the prohibition on taking books overnight. In the rewrite, we know who has performed this action—the law library. In the first sentence, we are not sure. The subject (and center of attention) in the rewrite is the law library; the subject (and center of attention) in the first sentence is the prohibition—the action.

---

active voice The grammatical verb form in which the subject or thing performing or causing the action is the main focus.

passive voice The grammatical verb form in which the object of the action is the main focus. The emphasis is on what is being done rather than on who or what is performing or causing the action.

truncated passive A form of passive voice in which the doer or subject of the action is not mentioned.

ASSIGNMENT 12.4

Rewrite any of the following sentences that use the passive voice. If you need to add any facts to the sentences to identify the doer of the action, you may make them up.

(a) As the semester came to a close, the students prepared for their exams.
(b) Examinations are not enjoyed.
(c) No drugs were prescribed after the operation.
(d) It has been determined that your license should be revoked.
(e) Consideration is being given this matter by the attorney.
(f) It is believed by district officials that the expense is legal.
(g) The fracture was discovered by the plaintiffs in 1998.

6. *Use positive statements.*

   Phrase something positively rather than negatively whenever possible.

Do not say:	*Say:*
It is not difficult to imagine.	It is easy to imagine.
The paper is not without flaws.	The paper has flaws.

   Whenever possible, replace a negative phrase with a single word that has the same meaning.

Do not say:	*Say:*
(1) not able	(1) unable
(2) not accept	(2) reject
(3) not certain	(3) uncertain
(4) not unlike	(4) similar *or* alike
(5) does not have	(5) lacks
(6) does not include	(6) excludes *or* omits
(7) not many	(7) few
(8) not often	(8) rarely
(9) not the same	(9) different
(10) not . . . unless	(10) only if
(11) not . . . except	(11) only if
(12) not . . . until	(12) only when

   When asked about the fundraising activities of a supporter, President Bill Clinton said,

   I had no reason to believe that he didn't know what the law was and wouldn't follow it.[2]

   Unless the president wanted to give a convoluted answer, he could have simply said, "I expected him to follow the law."

7. *Avoid verbosity.*

   Avoid unnecessary words.[3] Compare the following versions of the same sentence:

He consulted *with* a doctor *in regard* to his injuries.	He consulted a doctor *about* his injuries.
He drove to the left *due to the fact* that the lane was blocked.	He drove to the left *because* the lane was blocked.
This product is used for *hair-dyeing purposes.*	This product is used to *dye hair.*
The continuance was requested *in order to obtain the presence of a witness who was not then available.*	The continuance was requested *because a witness was unavailable.*

   Read the following sentences, with and without the italicized words.

   The court directed a verdict in favor of the defendant *and against the plaintiff.* (Verdicts for defendants are usually against the plaintiff.)
   The car was green *in color.* (This distinguishes it from the car that was green in size!)
   A delivery was made every Tuesday *on a regular weekly basis.* (What does *every Tuesday* mean if not weekly and regularly?)

8. *Use shorter sentences.*

   There is no rule on how long a sentence must be. Yet in general the longer a sentence is, the more difficult it is to follow. This is not to say that a reader cannot understand long sentences. It simply means that you are taxing the patience of readers when you subject them to long, involved sentences. As a general guideline, try to avoid sentences longer than twenty five words. Some authorities are even stricter. Judge Arthur Gilbert, for example, says, "If a sentence has more than twenty words, it usually needs to be redrafted."[4]

   Unfortunately, sentences are almost always too long in legal writing. Here is an example from a legal memorandum. In the rewrite, we have broken a fifty seven word sentence into four smaller, more readable sentences.

   Weak: Claims for child support were not fully and finally adjudicated pursuant to a North Carolina divorce judgment where the North Carolina court did not have personal jurisdiction over the husband and could not adjudicate any child support claims without this kind of jurisdiction and therefore Florida is not precluded from collecting monies from the husband toward arrearages.

Better: The North Carolina divorce judgment did not fully and finally adjudicate the claims for child support. The court in this state did not have personal jurisdiction over the husband. It could not adjudicate any child support claims without this kind of jurisdiction. Florida is therefore not precluded from collecting monies from the husband toward arrearages.

Other examples:

Weak: In May of 1999, a district personnel administrator informed Mary Miller that the district had decided to transfer her to a different school which was a decision that was based on information Miller provided, however the administrator had never talked to Miller in person prior to the decision.

Better: In May of 1999, a district personnel administrator informed Mary Miller that the district decided to transfer her to a different school. The district based its decision on information Miller provided. The administrator, however, never talked to Miller in person prior to the decision.

Weak: Her new job at the firm as the legal administrator in charge of personnel and finances was enjoyable, lucrative, educational, and challenging, but confusing and frightening at times.

Better: Her new job at the firm as legal administrator in charge of personnel and finances was enjoyable, lucrative, educational, and challenging. It was also confusing and frightening at times.

Weak: The final issue for discussion concerns the status of the national and international parties that has been the main stumbling block in the contract negotiations thus far.

Better: The final issue for discussion is the status of the national and international parties. This issue has been the main stumbling block in contract negotiations thus far.

Weak: There is no need for you to submit a revised report to the Board unless you wish to include new matter which should have been included in an earlier report provided that the new matter covers only procedural issues except for those procedural issues that have already been resolved by the commission.

Better: You do not need to submit a revised report to the Board. An exception is when you wish to include new matter on procedural issues that should have been included in an earlier report. These procedural issues must not be ones that the commission has already resolved.

ASSIGNMENT 12.5

Rewrite any of the following sentences that are too long.

(a) The board can, within sixty days of the receipt of a certification from the secretary, take action to return ownership of property to persons or corporations certified as owners from whom the property was acquired by expropriation or by purchase under threat of expropriation.

(b) A short time later, as George approached the intersection of Woodruff and Fuller, someone in the middle of the street started shooting, but George kept driving when he heard about fifteen shots that sounded like different guns firing, one of which hit his Pontiac, damaging the front windshield and dashboard.

(c) By way of illustration, presidential candidate Ross Perot and basketball player Michael Jordan arguably may have achieved such pervasive fame as to have become public figures for all purposes, while Dr. Jack Kevorkian may have voluntarily placed himself into the public controversy over euthanasia and physician-assisted suicide so as to have become a public figure for a limited range of issues.

9. *Be careful with pronoun references.*

Use pronouns only where the nouns to which the pronouns refer are unmistakably clear. Using pronouns with ambiguous referents can confuse the meaning of a sentence. If the pronoun could refer to more than one person or object in a sentence, repeat the name of the person or object to avoid ambiguity.

Do Not Say: After the administrator appoints a deputy assistant, he shall supervise the team. [Who does the supervising? The administrator or the deputy? If the latter is intended, then:]

Say: After the administrator appoints a deputy assistant, the deputy assistant shall supervise the team.

10. *Avoid sexism in language.*

Avoid gender-specific language when the intent is to refer to both sexes. If neutral language is not available, rewrite the sentence to avoid the problem.

Gender-Specific Language	*Gender-Neutral Alternatives*
(1) businessman	(1) executive, member of the business community
(2) chairman	(2) chairperson, chair, moderator, head, presiding officer
(3) draftsman	(3) drafter, writer
(4) man	(4) person, human, humankind
(5) man-hours	(5) worker hours
(6) mankind	(6) humanity, human race, people
(7) manpower	(7) work force, personnel
(8) fireman	(8) firefighter
(9) policeman	(9) officer, police officer
(10) mailman	(10) letter carrier, postal worker
(11) salesman	(11) seller, sales representative
(12) clergyman	(12) minister, priest, rabbi, member of the clergy
(13) actress	(13) actor
(14) foreman	(14) supervisor, manager
(15) reasonable man	(15) reasonable person
(16) waitress, waiter	(16) server

11. *Use plain English*

In the 1970s, the plain English movement began. The federal government and more than half the states passed laws requiring certain documents (e.g., insurance contracts, and securities disclosure statements) to be written in plain English. In general, the components of plain English are those that we have been discussing in this chapter:

- Avoid long sentences.
- Use the active voice rather than the passive voice.
- Use strong verbs rather than nominalizations.
- Avoid superfluous words.
- Phrase things positively; avoid multiple negatives.

The law might impose a *readability* level based in part on the number of words used in sentences. The lower the number of words a document uses in its sentences, on average, the better the overall readability score the document will have. (Readability refers to the ease with which someone can read a passage.) One way to force writers to use shorter sentences is to mandate that the document have a specified readability score.

Some states have enacted the Plain Language Consumer Contract Act, which states the guidelines that a court must consider when determining whether a contract is written in plain language. For example:

1. The contract should use short words, sentences, and paragraphs.
2. The contract should use active verbs.
3. The contract should not use technical legal terms, other than commonly understood legal terms, such as "mortgage," "warranty" and "security interest."
4. The contract should not use Latin and foreign words or any other word whenever its use requires reliance upon an obsolete meaning.
5. If the contract defines words, the words should be defined by using commonly understood meanings.
6. When the contract refers to the parties to the contract, the reference should use personal pronouns, the actual or shortened names of the parties, the terms "seller" and "buyer" or the terms "lender" and "borrower."
7. The contract should not use sentences that contain more than one condition.

8. The contract should not use cross references, except cross references that briefly and clearly describe the substances of the item to which reference is made.

9. The contract should not use sentences with double negatives or exceptions to exceptions. 73 Pennsylvania Statutes § 2205 (2007).

Plain English laws do not apply to the kind of writing prepared in a law office such as a memorandum of law or appellate brief. The laws are designed to help citizens understand written materials prepared by government and by businesses. Yet the writing principles proposed by the plain English movement can be applied to *any* writing. It would be a high compliment to say of any document prepared by an attorney or paralegal (particularly a document that covers complex legal material) that it was written in plain English.

Chapter Summary

Legal writing is critical in the practice of law. The phrase *legal writing* can refer to preparing documents that require legal analysis or legal research. It can also refer to special formats for legal documents and general communication techniques. When given a writing assignment, determine basics such as the audience, due date, models to use, and availability of feedback before the due date.

A law office prepares many different kinds of writing. Instruments such as deeds, contracts, and other agreements are formal written documents that give expression to a legal act or agreement. Pleadings such as complaints and answers state claims, defenses, and other positions of parties in litigation. Cover letters tell the recipient what is being sent in the letter or package. Demand letters are advocacy letters that ask the recipient to do or to refrain from doing something. Informational letters provide or seek information. A status letter is an informational letter that tells the client what has happened in the case thus far and what is expected next. Confirmatory letters seek verification that something important has been done or said. Opinion letters provide legal advice to a client. An office memorandum of law analyzes the law for other members of the office. An external memorandum of law (for example, a "points and authorities" memorandum) analyzes the law for someone

outside the office, such as a hearing officer. The major components of a memorandum of law are the heading, introduction, issues (based on the elements in contention), facts, discussion or analysis (including a counteranalysis), conclusion, recommendations, and appendix. A case brief is a summary of the major parts of a court opinion. A trial brief is an attorney's set of notes on how he or she intends to conduct a trial. An appellate brief is a written argument submitted to an appellate court on why the decision of a lower court should be affirmed, reversed, or otherwise modified.

The major components of an appellate brief are the caption, the statement of jurisdiction, the table of contents, the table of authorities, the questions presented, the statement of the case, the summary of the argument, the argument, the conclusion, and the appendixes.

Following a number of important guidelines will increase the clarity and effectiveness of any kind of writing. Avoid circumlocutions, omit excess language, use action verbs and adjectives, use active voice, express something positively whenever possible, use shorter sentences, make pronoun referents clear, and avoid sexist language. Following guidelines such as these will help produce a more readable document that might be classified as one written in plain English.

Key Terms

hard copy	external memorandum	roadmap paragraph	point heading
format	of law	element	table of authorities
instrument	points and authorities	element in contention	questions presented
pleading	memorandum	STOP	statement of the
cover letter	trial memorandum	trial brief	case
demand letter	hearing memorandum	appellate brief	transcript
informational letter	points	brief bank	circumlocution
status letter	font	appellant	nominalization
confirmatory letter	footer	appellee	active voice
opinion letter	caption of memorandum	reply brief	passive voice
memorandum of law	docket number	amicus curiae	truncated passive
office memorandum of law	RE	brief	

Review Questions

1. What are the different meanings of the phrase *legal writing*?
2. What general guidelines should be followed when receiving any writing assignment in a law office?
3. What are the major kinds of writing that exist in a law office?
4. What are instruments and pleadings?
5. How can computers be used to help draft instruments and pleadings?
6. What is the function of a cover letter?
7. What is the function of a demand letter?
8. What is the function of an informational letter, a status letter, and a confirmatory letter?
9. What is the function of an opinion letter?
10. What are the major guidelines for letter writing?
11. What is the function of the following components of a standard letter: heading, date, reference line (RE), salutation, body of letter (identification line, purpose line, request line, and elaboration), and closing?
12. How do you indicate that you are sending copies and are including enclosures?
13. What is a memorandum of law?
14. What is the distinction between an internal (office) memorandum of law and an external memorandum?
15. What are some of the names of external memoranda?
16. What is the function of the following components of an office memorandum of law: heading, introduction, issues, facts, discussion (analysis), conclusion, recommendations, and appendix?
17. What are the two main components of an issue?
18. What is an element in contention?
19. What guidelines should be followed when writing the statement of facts in a memorandum of law?
20. How could a memorandum of law be structured when applying a statute?
21. What is the function of STOP?
22. What are the following: (1) trial brief, (2) trial memorandum, (3) appellate brief, and (4) brief of a case?
23. What is the function of a reply brief?
24. What is a brief bank?
25. What is the function of an amicus curiae brief?
26. What are the major components of an appellate brief?
27. In an appellate brief, what is the function of the caption, statement of jurisdiction, table of contents, point headings, table of authorities, questions presented, and statement of the case?
28. What are circumlocutions and how can they be avoided?
29. What are nominalizations and how can they be avoided?
30. What is the distinction between the active voice and the passive voice, and why is the former preferred?
31. What is a truncated passive?
32. How can you avoid confusing pronoun references?
33. How can you avoid sexism in language?
34. What are the meaning and value of plain English? How is it achieved?

Helpful Web Sites: More on Legal Writing

Legal Writing Resources on the Web
- www.ualr.edu/cmbarger/otherpeople.html

Letter Writing
- www.4hb.com/letters
- esl.about.com/cs/onthejobenglish/a/a_basbletter.htm
- www.business-letters.com/business-letters.htm
- www.writinghelp-central.com/letter-writing.html
- writing.colostate.edu/guides/index.cfm?guides_active=business&category1=37

Sample Memorandum of Law
- www.alwd.org
  (click "ALWD Citation Manual" then "appendices" then "Appendix 6")

Copies of Appellate Briefs
- supreme.lp.findlaw.com/supreme_court/briefs/index.html
- www.usdoj.gov/osg/briefs/search.html
- www.abanet.org/jd/ajc/cal/briefs.html
- supremecourtus.gov/oral_arguments/briefsource.pdf

- www.briefserve.com/home.asp
- www.briefreports.com
  (type "paralegal" in the search box to find briefs that mention paralegals)

Online Appellate Brief Manual
- www.ca7.uscourts.gov/Rules/handbook.pdf
- www.ca8.uscourts.gov/newrules/coa/handbook.pdf

Preparing Tables of Authorities
- office.microsoft.com/en-us/word/CH063553391033.aspx
- www.corel.com/training/pdfs/AbsoluteBeginnersGuide_CH18_LegalTools.pdf
- library.law.olemiss.edu/library/students/authorities.shtml
- www.law.berkeley.edu/library/computing/toa.pdf

Style Manuals
- origin.www.gpoaccess.gov/stylemanual
- www.sec.gov/pdf/handbook.pdf
- www.nlrb.gov/nlrb/legal/manuals/stylemanual.pdf

Principles of Clear Writing

- www.archives.gov/federal-register/write/legal-docs/clear-writing.html
- owl.english.purdue.edu
- www.bartleby.com/usage
- www.rpi.edu/web/writingcenter/online.html
- grammar.ccc.commnet.edu/grammar
- www.efuse.com/Design/wa-more_better_writing.html

Plain English

- www.plainlanguage.gov
- plainlanguagenetwork.org
- www.blm.gov/nhp/NPR/pe_toc.html
- www.plainenglishcampaign.com/
- www.sec.gov/news/extra/handbook.htm

Plagiarism

- www.plagiarismtoday.com

Google Searches (run the following searches for more sites)

- legal writing drafting
- business letter writing
- "memorandum of law" writing drafting
- "appellate brief writing"
- "appellate brief writing"
- pleadings motions writing drafting
- plain english writing
- grammar tutorials

Endnotes

1. 15 U.S.C. § 1692e.
2. Mark Gladstone and Allan Miller, *Gore Called 38 Donors on White House Phone*, Los Angeles Times, August 8, 1997, at A.9.
3. L. Gray, *Writing a Good Appellate Brief*, 88 Case and Comment 44, 48–50 (No. 6, November/December 1983). Reprinted by special permission. Copyrighted © 1983 by the Lawyers Cooperative Publishing Co.
4. Bryan A. Garner, *Judges on Briefing: A National Survey*, 8 The Scribes Journal of Legal Writing 1, 9 (2001–2002).

Student CD-ROM

For additional materials, please go to the CD in this book.

Online Companion™

For additional resources, please go to http://www.paralegal.delmar.cengage.com

An Introduction to the Use of Computers in a Law Office

CHAPTER OUTLINE

A. Introduction
B. Terminology: A Review of Some of the Basics
C. Software in a Law Firm
D. Computer-Assisted Legal Research
E. Internet
F. Intranet and Extranet

[SECTION A]
INTRODUCTION

Computers dominate many aspects of the practice of law. Therefore, paralegals need to learn as much as they can about computers in general and how they are used in a law office. In your first job interview, don't be surprised if you are asked questions such as the following:

- What are your computer skills?
- What do you know about networks?
- Which operating systems have you used?
- What litigation support software have you studied or used?
- Are you familiar with Word or WordPerfect?[1]

Prospective employers often pay special attention to the computer experience you list on your résumé.

You can learn a great deal about computers on your own. Don't wait for someone to explain it all to you. Take the initiative by pursuing an aggressive program of self-education. Exhibit 13.1 presents an overview of steps you can begin now and continue after you graduate. Indeed, you will probably need to be a student of computers for the remainder of your career.

We have already covered different aspects of computers elsewhere in this book. At the end of every chapter, for example, there is a section called "Helpful Web Sites," which refers you to Internet sites that contain resources on topics covered in the chapter. In addition, a variety of computer-related materials can be found throughout the chapters. For example:

- Internet sites of the major national paralegal associations (chapter 1)
- Internet sites of major law firms in the country, of the state personnel office in every state, and of organizations relevant to finding paralegal employment (chapter 2)
- Internet sites of organizations relevant to the regulation of paralegals (chapter 4)

EXHIBIT 13.1	Developing Your Computer Skills: What to Do On Your Own Now

Courses, Meetings, and Groups

■ *Courses.* Take computer courses. Find out what is available at your school. Also check if free or low-cost computer courses exist in your community, e.g., adult education courses. Some may last no more than an afternoon. Call your local public library for leads. Once you know what is available, ask your instructor what courses would be most relevant to someone working in a law office. Anything on the basics of operating systems (e.g., Windows), word processing (e.g., Word), and the Internet will probably be valuable.

■ *Computer events at paralegal associations.* Contact your local paralegal association to find out what upcoming events will cover computer use. There may, for example, be a continuing legal education (CLE) session covering the Internet. (For a list of paralegal association Web sites in your state, see appendix B.) Ask if you can attend as a paralegal student. If there is a fee, ask if a reduced rate is available for students. Some of the meetings and sessions may be geared to experienced paralegals. Nevertheless, you should consider attending because the more exposure you have to computer topics, the more you will eventually absorb. It is worthwhile to take detailed notes, even if you will not fully understand all of them until later. Furthermore, any contact you have with a paralegal association can be an excellent networking opportunity.

■ *Computer events at bar associations.* Your state and local bar association may also have CLE sessions that cover computer basics for attorneys. Find out if you can attend at a reduced rate. Go to the Internet sites of these associations to find out what programs are scheduled. (For the Internet addresses of the bar associations in your state, see appendix C.)

Internet

■ *Law firm of the day.* Spend five minutes a day surfing Internet sites of law firms. (See appendix 2.A at the end of chapter 2 for a list of sites.) Conduct your own informal survey of the variety of features contained on the sites of different law firms.

■ *Search engine of the week.* Every week, pick one search engine to study. It can be a general search engine or a legal search engine. (See Exhibit 13.10 later in the chapter for a list of search engines.) During the week, spend ten minutes a day (1) reading the online tips often provided by the search engine on how to use it effectively and (2) trying out specific searches. For topics to search, open any of your paralegal textbooks at random and select topics. As you study different search engines, enter the same search terms in each search engine. Conduct your own informal survey on the effectiveness of each engine.

■ *Online tutorial of the week .* Every week, work on a tutorial. The Internet has many tutorials available. They cover topics such as understanding the Internet, using search engines, and learning word processors such as Word. To find these tutorials, type "computer tutorial" in the search box of any general search engine (e.g., www.google.com or www.yahoo.com). Also try specific searches (e.g., "shepards tutorial," "litigation tutorial," "westlaw tutorial," "google tutorial," and "search tutorial"). Keep clicking through the results of such searches until you find free tutorials on relevant topics. See also the sites of tutorials listed at the end of this chapter in the section called "Helpful Web Sites."

Miscellaneous

■ *Exchanging tutorials.* Most people know how to do something on a computer, e.g., insert footnotes in Word or Word Perfect, create a macro, edit a macro, find recent Supreme Court opinions on the Internet. As you meet your fellow students, find out what they know how to do on a computer. When they list a task that is new to you, ask them to teach it to you in exchange for your teaching them something you know that they do not. Once every two weeks, try to arrange a half hour of mutual hands-on teaching of this kind. Use your own computers or those available in public places such as neighborhood libraries.

■ *Read, read, read.* Every week, pick a major computer topic such as word processing, spreadsheets, databases, presentation graphics, litigation support, case management, Westlaw, LexisNexis, and any aspect of the Internet. During that week, devote some time reading about that topic. Don't wait to be assigned the topic for class. Begin reading on your own. To find the readings, start with your paralegal textbooks. Go to the index in all of them and check entries such as *computer* and *Internet.* In addition, type your topic in any general search engine to try to find online discussions and descriptions of your topic. Finally, ask your instructor and a librarian where you can find additional readings on the topic. Most public libraries have a large section of computer books. They will be very helpful for general computer topics. Find your topic in the index of books published within the last two years.

■ *Typing skills.* Brush up on your typing skills. In many law offices, there is a keyboard at every desk. At one time, legal professionals considered typing to be beneath their dignity. This is no longer true. Although you will not need the typing skill of a secretary, you should be able to type with moderate speed. There are online typing courses available (e.g., www.learn2type.com). To find such courses, enter "typing tutorial" in the search box of any general search engine.

■ Internet sites on ethics and software programs used to conduct conflicts-of-interest checks (chapter 5)
■ Fact investigation resources on commercial databases and on the Internet (chapter 9)
■ Software programs on timekeeping and filing systems (chapter 14)

In this chapter, our focus will be on some of the basics of computer use. This material will supplement what you will learn elsewhere. It will also serve as a review of the fundamentals.

[S E C T I O N B]

TERMINOLOGY: A REVIEW OF SOME OF THE BASICS

Before examining specific computer programs, we will briefly review some of the essential terminology that will be helpful in understanding these programs.

Hardware is the physical equipment (i.e., devices) of a computer system. Hardware is what you take out of the box and plug together when you buy a computer system. Examples include the keyboard, central processing unit (CPU), monitor, cables, mouse, and printer. **Software** is a computer program that tells or instructs the hardware what to do. There are two main categories of software: (1) operating or systems software and (2) applications software. The **operating system** software tells the computer how to operate. It is the master or central control program for the hardware and other software. When you turn on or restart the computer (called **booting up**), the operating system is the first program that is run or executed. The major operating system in use today is Windows, developed by Microsoft. Others include Macintosh, OS/2, UNIX, and a special version of UNIX called LINUX. (Software is written in programming language called *source code*. Most software manufacturers keep their source code secret. If, however, the software's source code is freely available to the public for use and modification, the software is called *open-source software*. LINUX is a prominent example of open-source software.) **Applications software** consists of programs that perform specific tasks that consumers (i.e., end users) ask computers to perform. Some of the major kinds of applications software are word processing, spreadsheets, and database management.

To place information into a computer, you need an input device. The most commonly used input device is the keyboard. When you type something on the keyboard, text is entered at the **cursor** on the screen of the monitor. (The cursor is the marker or pointer that indicates where the next letter or other character will be displayed on the screen.) Other input devices include the mouse, speech recognition programs, and scanners, all of which can be used along with the keyboard. A **mouse** is a handheld pointing device that is used to move the cursor by rolling, clicking, and dragging motions. For example, you can glide the mouse over a small picture (i.e., icon) of a printer, click on the mouse, and activate the printer connected to the computer. **Speech recognition** programs allow you to enter information by speaking rather than by typing on the keyboard. As you speak words and commands into a small microphone, the computer enters the words on the screen or executes the commands. A **scanner** is an input device that converts text and images into an electronic or digital format that a computer can recognize. The process by which a scanner digitizes text or images is called **imaging** (or *document imaging*). When a document is scanned into the computer, an exact image of the document appears on the screen, most commonly as a **PDF** (portable document format) file. The file can then be read on a free Adobe reader. PDF is an example of a fixed-layout format. (The main rival of Adobe PDF is Microsoft XPS.) If optical character recognition (OCR) software is used during the scanning, you can make changes in the language of the scanned document.

The **central processing unit (CPU)** is the "brain" of the computer that controls all of its parts. It performs operations and carries out software commands. In most computer systems, the CPU is the unit that contains the on/off switch and the slots for inserting and taking out disks.

Computers can hold a great deal of data. The internal storage capacity of a computer is called its **memory**. There are two main kinds of memory: read-only and random access. **Read-only memory (ROM)** is memory that stores data that cannot be altered, removed, or added to; the data can only be read. When you shut the computer off, the data in ROM are not erased. ROM contains critical data such as the code needed to boot the computer. **Random access memory (RAM)** is memory that stores temporary data. When you shut the computer off, these data vanish—unless you have properly saved the data. Data in RAM include whatever you have typed on the screen (e.g., a letter or your résumé). When you turn the computer back on, you can retrieve what had been in RAM if you properly saved it earlier. Newer applications require increasing amounts of RAM. At times, you may be running more than one application at the same time, e.g., a word processor, a spreadsheet, your Internet connection, and a game of solitaire. As more applications are created by manufacturers, the temptation is to run them simultaneously. This may create problems if you do not have enough RAM. (Inadequate RAM is such a common problem that RAM is humorously referred to as Rarely Adequate Memory.)

---

hardware The physical equipment of a computer system.

software A computer program that tells or instructs the hardware what to do.

operating system The software that tells the computer how to operate. It is the master or central software program that the hardware and all other software depend on to function.

booting up Turning on or restarting the computer and loading the operating system.

applications software A computer program that performs specific tasks directly for the consumer or end user.

cursor The marker or pointer on the screen that indicates where the next letter or other character will be displayed on the screen.

mouse A handheld input device that moves the cursor by rolling, clicking, and dragging motions.

speech recognition The ability of a computer to receive information from the user talking into a microphone.

scanner An input device that converts text and images into an electronic or digital format that a computer can recognize.

imaging The process by which a scanner digitizes text or images.

PDF (portable document format) A file format consisting of an electronic image of a document that preserves the features or elements of the document (e.g., its line spacing, photographs, and font size) that existed before it was converted into a digital document.

central processing unit (CPU) The part of the computer that controls all of its parts.

memory The internal storage capacity of a computer.

read-only memory (ROM) Memory that stores data that cannot be altered, removed, or added to. The data can be read only.

random access memory (RAM) Memory that stores temporary data that are erased (unless properly saved) whenever the computer's power is turned off.

byte The storage equivalent of one space or character of the alphabet typed into a computer.

The amount or quantity of memory is measured by units called **bytes**. A byte is the storage equivalent of one space or character of the alphabet typed into a computer. Bytes are expressed in the following quantities:

	Abbreviation	Approximate Number of Bytes
Kilobyte	K	one thousand
Megabyte	Mb	one million
Gigabyte	Gb	one billion
Terabyte	Tb	one trillion

One megabyte (1 Mb) can hold the equivalent of a 600-page novel. One gigabyte (1 Gb) can hold approximately 300,000 single-sided pages of text.

A number of different devices exist to store bytes of data. Most of these storage devices have read/write capability, while others are read-only. **Read/write** means that the computer can read the data on the device *and* you can write (i.e., insert) additional data onto the device. If a device is writable, you can save and store data on it. As we saw earlier, **read-only** means that the computer can read the data on the device but not alter, remove, or add to the data. If a storage device is read-only, it usually contains systems or applications software that the manufacturer does not want the user to be able to add to or otherwise modify.

read/write Able to read data on a device *and* write or insert additional data into it.

read-only Able to read data on a device but not to alter, remove, or add to the data.

When you create your own document (e.g., a letter, a memorandum of law), it first goes into RAM. If you shut the computer off without saving and storing the document, it is lost. To prevent the loss of documents that you create, you must send them to a storage device that has read/write capability.

Here is a brief overview of some of the major storage devices that exist:

hard disk A rigid magnetic disk that stores data.

- *Hard disk:* A rigid magnetic disk that stores data. The **hard disk** is located within a disk drive called a hard drive or hard disk drive. (A *drive* is hardware that holds disks.) If the drive is located inside the CPU, it is called an internal hard drive. If it sits outside the CPU, it is called an external hard drive or removable drive. (In many computer systems, the internal hard disk is the C drive. If the system also has an external drive, the latter might be the D drive.) Hard disks have read/write capability.
- *Floppy disk:* A floppy magnetic disk that stores data. It is inserted into and taken out of its own disk drive, called a floppy drive. (In many computer systems, the floppy drive is the A drive.) Floppy disks have a much smaller storage capacity than hard disks. Floppy disks have read/write capability. Because of their low storage capacity and the availability of effective alternatives, however, floppy disks are becoming increasingly unpopular. In fact, floppy drives are no longer standard equipment on most modern computers.
- *USB flash drive:* A portable memory drive that is inserted into and taken out of the computer's USB port. Also called a jump drive, pen drive, key drive, USB key, and USB stick. (*USB* means universal serial bus, which allows fast connections between a computer and external devices such as flash drives and cameras.) The high speed, low cost, and high storage capacity of flash drives have made them very popular, largely replacing floppy disks as the preferred method of external storage. Flash drives have read/write capability.
- *Magnetic tape system:* A device that stores data on tape reels or tape cartridges. Tape systems can store a great deal of data, but because they store data sequentially, they are often slower than disk systems. Magnetic tape systems have read/write capability.

CD–ROM (compact disk read-only memory). A compact disk that stores data in a digital format.

- *CD–ROM drive:* A device that can read data on a **CD–ROM**, which means compact disk read-only memory. A CD–ROM is a compact disk that uses optical technology or laser beams to store data. The disk looks similar to the disks that contain most popular music purchased today. Because of their large storage capacity, CD–ROMs are widely used. When you purchase software, it is usually contained on a CD–ROM. Most primary authority (e.g., court opinions, statutes, and administrative regulations) can also be purchased on CD–ROM. CD–ROM drives have read-only capability.
- *CD–R drive:* A device that permanently stores information on a compact disk. A CD–R (compact disk–recordable) drive has read/write capability. Whatever you write to it, however, cannot be erased. Phrased another way, you can read the data on a CD–R disk many times, but you can write new data on it only once.

- *CD–RW drive:* A device that can read and store data on a compact disk. The data you write to it can be changed. A CD–RW (compact disk–rewritable) drive has read/write capability. CD–RW disks are like floppy or hard disks in that the data on them can be read many times and you can write new data on them many times.
- *DVD–ROM drive:* A device that can read information on DVD–ROMs. DVD means digital versatile disk. DVD–ROM means digital versatile disk read-only memory. DVD–ROMs (like CD–ROMs) can be read but cannot be written to. A **DVD–ROM drive** is often used to play videos because of its large storage capacity. It has read-only capability. You can read data on it (e.g., watch movies) many times but you cannot write new data on it. With a **recordable DVD drive**, however, you can read and write data on DVD disks.[2]

The process of writing data to a CD or to a DVD is called *burning.*

The latest storage innovation allows you to store data on the Internet. Large companies like Google, Microsoft, and Yahoo are making it possible for users to store vast amounts of data in Internet data centers or "warehouses" so that the data can be accessed from any computer, or indeed, from a cell phone. Special software or applications programs that we will examine shortly can also be accessed from the Internet. Using the Internet for storage and for software programs in this way is sometimes referred to as *cloud computing.*

Computers are getting smaller and smaller. One of the smallest is the **PDA** (personal digital assistant). It is a handheld multifunctional digital organizer. It is capable of performing a variety of functions, e.g., send and receive e-mail, store address and contact information, display calendars, compose and edit short memos, act as a calculator, and, when combined with a cell phone, make and receive calls. The PDA can easily be linked (usually by wireless connection) to laptop and desktop computers for exchanging data.

If you want a **hard copy** of a document prepared on a computer, you need a printer to print that document. Printers use different technologies to produce characters and other images on a sheet of paper. Among the most popular are *ink-jet* printers, which use a spray of ionized ink, and *laser* printers, which use a laser beam.

Most printers allow you to print letters of the alphabet, punctuation marks, or other characters in different sizes (measured in **points**) and in different designs or styles (called **fonts**). Here are some examples:

This sentence is printed in a 10 point Arial font (regular).

This sentence is in a 15 point Arial font (bold).

This sentence is printed in a 10 point Serifa BT font (italics).

This sentence is printed in a 12 point Times New Roman font (regular).

Drafters of documents may occasionally want to print tables, headings, or titles in a point size or font that is different from what they use elsewhere in the document. See, for example, Exhibit 13.2 containing part of the front cover (title page) of an appellate brief filed in the U.S. Supreme Court. Note the different font styles and point sizes. If a court imposes page limitations on briefs and other documents, the limitations often include font and point instructions. For example, one court

DVD–ROM drive A drive that can read data on a DVD disk. DVD means digital versatile disk. DVD–ROM drives can read DVD disks and CD–ROM disks.

recordable DVD drive A drive that allows data to be recorded on DVD disks.

PDA (personal digital assistant) A handheld multifunctional digital organizer.

hard copy A paper copy of what has been prepared on a computer. Also called a printout. A "soft" form of text is what exists on disk or on a computer screen.

points A measure of the size of printed letters of the alphabet, punctuation marks, or other characters. (One point is approximately $1/72$ of an inch tall.)

font The design or style of printed letters of the alphabet, punctuation marks, or other characters.

EXHIBIT 13.2	Court Document Printed in Different Font Styles and Point Sizes

No. 05-11304

IN THE

Supreme Court of the United States

LAROYCE LATHAIR SMITH,
Petitioner,

v.

STATE OF TEXAS,
Respondent.

ON PETITION FOR A WRIT OF CERTIORARI
TO THE TEXAS COURT OF CRIMINAL APPEALS

BRIEF FOR THE CONSTITUTION PROJECT
AS AMICUS CURIAE IN SUPPORT OF PETITIONER

requires, "Computer-generated petitions, responses, and replies shall be submitted in either Times New Roman 14-point font or Courier New 12-point font."[3]

Computers at different locations can exchange data by using communications devices. A **modem** is a communications device that allows computers to use telephone lines to send and receive data to and from each other. Other communication devices include cable modems (that connect computers by coaxial cable) and digital phone lines such as ISDN (integrated services digital network) and DSL (digital subscriber line). These other communication devices can transmit text, voice, and video (e.g., for real-time videoconferencing) at high speeds.[4]

Real time means occurring now, as you are watching. Suppose, for example, you are on the Internet watching a witness answer questions in a deposition in another city. You would be watching in real time if the witness is talking in the room where the deposition is taking place at the same time you are watching this witness on your computer screen in another room or building. If, however, you are watching a deposition that was recorded earlier, you would not be experiencing the deposition in real time. Similarly, you are communicating in real time if what you type on your screen appears on the screen of others *as you type*. **Videoconferencing** is a meeting that occurs in more than one location between individuals who can hear and see each other on computer screens.

Computers in a busy law office need to be connected with each other for a variety of reasons. They may need to share the same data (e.g., a client file) or the same equipment (e.g., a laser printer). If the computers are relatively close to each other, such as within the same building, they can be connected by a **local area network (LAN)**. Once connected (i.e., networked), **groupware** allows the computer users to share calendars, have meetings, exchange e-mail, and work on files together. (Groupware is not the same as **shareware**; the latter is software that users pay for only after deciding to keep it after trying it out.) Examples of groupware include Lotus Notes and Microsoft Exchange. If the computers are not geographically close, they can still be networked on what is called a **wide area network (WAN)**. Large law firms with branches in different cities, for example, can be linked on a WAN. (Computers that are not connected to a network are called **stand-alone computers**.) As we will see later, another way to link offices so that they can share information is through an *intranet*, which is a private network that uses the technology of the Internet.

Before we begin a closer examination of software programs, a word about the critical importance of making **backup** copies of your work. You should assume that everything you type on a computer screen could be accidently erased in an instant. You must regularly save copies of your data to your hard drive and to devices such as flash drives and CD–ROMs that you can take to other rooms and preferably to other buildings (in the event of a fire where you work on your computer). Some extra-cautious computer users use e-mail as a storage option. They will make a copy of important work and send it to themselves as an attachment in an e-mail message. This option became realistic when e-mail providers such as Google, Yahoo, and AOL made available large quantities of free e-mail space that can be used for additional storage of this kind.

[SECTION C]

SOFTWARE IN A LAW FIRM

We turn now to an overview of some of the major software programs used in many law firms, particularly applications software. Later in the chapter, we cover software for legal research and the Internet. Here, we will examine programs that perform the following tasks:

Word processing
Spreadsheet calculation
Database management
Presentation graphics
Litigation support
Case management
Knowledge management

(Exhibit 13.3 presents an overview of these and other software programs used in a law office.) Some programs are suites or **integrated packages** that allow the user to perform multiple tasks such as word processing, spreadsheet calculations, and database management.

---

modem A communications device that allows computers at different locations to use telephone lines to exchange data.

real time Occurring now; happening as you are watching; able to respond immediately.

videoconference A meeting that occurs in more than one location between individuals who can hear and see each other on computer screens.

local area network (LAN) A multiuser system linking computers that are in close proximity to each other so that they can share data and resources.

groupware Software that allows computers on a network to work together.

shareware Software that users receive without cost and are expected to purchase if they want to keep it after trying it out.

wide area network (WAN) A multiuser system linking computers over a large geographical area so that they can share data and resources.

stand-alone computer A computer that is not connected to a network.

backup A copy of your data stored in a different location for safekeeping.

integrated package Software that contains more than one application (e.g., word processing, spreadsheet calculations, and database management) in a single program.

EXHIBIT 13.3	Software Used in Law Firms

Software	Function
Word processing	Enter and edit data in order to create and revise documents, e.g., letters, briefs, and memos.
Spreadsheet	Performs calculations on numbers and values entered by the user. Organizes, compiles, tracks, and calculates numerical data.
Database management	Organizes, searches, retrieves, and sorts information or data, e.g., conflict of interest records, client lists, and research materials in the office's law library.
Presentation graphics	Enhances the communication of data through the use of charts, graphs, video, clip art, and sound.
Litigation support	Stores, retrieves, and tracks documents, testimony, and other litigation materials.
Document control and case management	Helps maintain control over schedules, e.g., appointments and case deadlines.
Computer-assisted legal research (CALR)	Performs legal research in computer databases, e.g., Westlaw, LexisNexis, Loislaw, CD-ROM libraries, and Internet sites.
Web browser	Allows users to read pages on the World Wide Web.
Electronic mail (e-mail)	Sends and receives mail electronically, including complete documents that can be sent as e-mail attachments.
Timekeeping and billing	Tracks time and expenses; prepares client invoices.
Accounting	Tracks financial information needed for the operation of a law firm.
Project management	Helps manage large projects.
Groupware	Allows computer users on a network to work together, e.g., to share documents and work on the same information.
Operating system	Tells the computer how to operate. Manages the hardware and other software of the computer.
Custom-made software	Meets specialized needs. It is software that is written (programmed) for the needs of a particular office. If the software is prepackaged and usable by a wide variety of offices, it is called off-the-shelf software.

Source: Adapted from Brent Roper, *Using Computers in the Law*, 53 ff. (4th ed. 2004).

All of the major software vendors have Web sites that provide detailed information about their programs, including the ability to **download** new features and corrections to errors or "bugs" in previous versions of the software. The updates are often called **patches**.

WORD PROCESSING

A **word processor** is a software program that allows you to enter and edit data in order to create and revise documents. Word processors are enormous improvements over standard typewriters. When you make an error on a word processor, for example, you do not reach for a bottle of "white out" to take out the error. Instead, you simply press the backspace or delete key over the error and type your new text. If you left something out of a paragraph, you point the cursor to where the additional text should go and insert what you want to add. When you are in *insert mode*, the line can open up to make room for the new text. (See Exhibit 13.4 for the definition of insert mode and other features of word processors.) With relative ease, you can copy, save, and paginate (insert page numbers on) your text; insert footnotes or endnotes; underline or italicize text; and create tables or charts. Sophisticated word processors also allow you to spell check and grammar check your writing. (Be careful, however, when using spell checkers. They do not check for correct word usage. For example, if you wrote "Eye maid ate miss steaks," the spell checker would correctly tell you that none of the words in the sentence are misspelled even though you should have written "I made eight mistakes.") Similar cautions are needed when using grammar check programs. They can help point out difficulties you should address, but they are not comprehensive.

download To move data from a remote computer (e.g., a central computer or Web site) to your computer. Data is *uploaded* when you transfer it from your computer to the remote computer.

patch A software update that provides additional features and corrections to previous versions of the software.

word processor Application software that allows you to enter and edit data in order to create and revise documents.

EXHIBIT 13.4	Word Processing Terms and Functions

TERM	Function
Backspace	The key that allows you to delete the character to the left of the cursor.
Block move	To copy, delete, or change the position of text you highlight. The text you identify is called a *block*. You highlight it by giving it a black background.
Bold	Heavy or dark type. **This sentence is printed in bold.**
Character	A letter, number, or symbol.
Character enhancement	Altering the appearance of characters such as by underlining, **bolding**, or *italicizing* them.
Default setting	The value used by the word processor when it is not instructed to use any other value.
Editing	Adding to, subtracting from, or otherwise changing text.
Endnote	A numbered citation or explanatory text printed at the end of a document or chapter. If printed at the bottom of the page, the citation or text is called a footnote.
Footer	The same text that is printed at the bottom of each page of a document, usually identifying the name of the document and, sometimes, its author.
Format	The layout of a page when printed, e.g., the margin settings.
Global	Pertaining to the entire document.
Grammar checker	The identification of possible grammatical errors in a document, with suggested corrections.
Header	The same text that is printed at the top of each page of a document, usually identifying the name of the document and, sometimes, its author.
Insert mode	When new text is typed in a line that already has text, the line opens to receive the new text. Nothing is erased or overtyped. (The opposite of insert mode is typeover mode. See below.)
Justification	Every line is even (i.e., is aligned) at the left margin, at the right margin, or at both margins.
Macro	An automated way to insert frequently used text or to perform other repetitive tasks.
Paginate	To insert consecutive page numbers at the top or bottom of each page of a document.
Print preview	A screen that contains text (and graphics, if any) as it will appear once sent to the printer.
Scroll	To move a line of text onto or off the screen.
Spell checker	The identification of possible spelling errors in a document, with suggested corrections.
Status line	A message line (usually at the bottom of the screen) that can state the current position of the cursor (e.g., line 3, column 15) and provide other formatting information.
Subscript	A character that prints below the usual text baseline. For example, the number 7 in the following text is in subscript: Court$_7$.
Superscript	A character that prints above the usual text baseline. For example, the number 7 in the following text is in superscript: Court^7.
Table	A feature that allows the creation of a table of information using rows and columns.
Text file	A file containing text that you create. (A file containing a program—as opposed to text you create—is called a systems or applications file.)
Thesaurus	The identification of word alternatives that a user can substitute for words initially used or considered.
Tool bar	A list of shortcuts (often represented by icons) that can quickly execute commonly used functions such as saving a document or sending it to the printer.
Typeover mode	When new text is typed in a line that already has text, the old text is erased or overtyped with each keystroke.
Word wrap	When a word would extend beyond the right margin, the word is automatically sent to the beginning of the next line.
WYSIWYG	What You See (on the screen) Is What You will Get (when the screen is printed).

Source: Adapted from Steven Mandell, *Introduction to Computers*, 216 (3d ed. 1991).

If you want to justify your margins, the word processor will allow you to do so quickly. In the language of printers and typesetting, justification means alignment of each line of text along a margin. Lines are aligned if they come out even—as opposed to being ragged—at the margin. Left justified means that every line on the left margin is aligned (except for the first line of a paragraph if the first line is indented). **Right justified** means that every line on the right margin is aligned except for the last line if it ends before the margin. Full justification means that every line of the paragraph is aligned on both margins—with the possible exception of the first and last lines. (See Exhibit 13.5 for examples of justification and various indentation formats.)

right justified Every line of a paragraph on the right margin is aligned (except for the last line if it ends before the margin).

EXHIBIT 13.5	Arranging Text with a Word Processor

Here is an example of text created on a word processor that is *left justified* only. Note that the text is straight along the left margin but ragged along the right margin.

Left justification

Here is an example of text created on a word processor that is *right justified* only. Note that the text is ragged along the left margin, but straight along the right margin.

Right justification

Here is an example of text created on a word processor that has *full justification*. Note that the text is straight (not ragged) along both the left margin and the right margin (sometimes with the exception of the last line).

Full justification

Here is an example of text created on a word processor that uses the *left indent* feature. Note that the entire text is indented from the left margin. Such indentation is often used when presenting a numbered list or perhaps a bulleted list. (A bullet is a centered dot, e.g., ●.) The text is also left justified only.

Left indent

Here is an example of text created on a word processor that uses the *double indent* feature. Note that the entire text is indented the same amount from both the left margin and the right margin. Such indentation is often used when presenting a long quote. (The text is also left justified only.)

Double indent

Here is an example of text created on a word processor that uses the *hanging indent* feature. Note that the first line hangs or "sticks out" to the left.

Hanging indent

Here is an example of text created on a word processor that uses *first line indent*. Note that only the first line is indented in traditional paragraph format.

First line indent

One of the special features of word processors (and of other programs) is the ability to create **macros** that allow you to perform repetitive tasks without extensive retyping. Suppose, for example, that when you prepare a letter, you always type a heading at the top of the sheet containing your name, street address, city, state, zip code, phone number, and e-mail address. As you type the heading, you carefully center each line. Assume that this task consists of 100 keystrokes and takes about a minute to complete. An alternative is to create a macro to perform the task. Within the word processor's macro feature, you go through the steps of creating a macro. First, you name the macro—let's call our example *head*. Next, you type the repetitive text (all 100 strokes). You have now created a macro called *head*. From now on, every time you are preparing a new letter, you simply tell the word processor that you want to run the head macro. This is done by typing (or clicking) the word *head* within the macro feature of the word processor. In less than a second, all 100 keystrokes appear on the screen. If you type many letters, you can save a lot of time by using this macro.

macro An automated way to insert frequently used text or to perform other repetitive functions.

Let's look at another example. Suppose you are typing a memorandum of law that frequently uses the phrase *federal subject-matter jurisdiction*. To avoid constantly retyping this phrase, you could create a macro called *fsmj* (or you could call it *f*). Now every time you run the *fsmj* macro (or the *f* macro if you used the shorter name), the full phrase automatically goes into your memorandum wherever you want it to appear.[5]

The two main word processors on the market are Word by Microsoft and WordPerfect by Corel. Both have features or editions that are geared to specific needs of attorneys in the practice of law. For example, they assist you in creating a **table of authorities (TOA)**. (This is a list of primary and secondary authority referred to in a document with the page number of each reference to the authority.) As an extra service to attorneys, Microsoft has prepared an online guide on how law firms can effectively use Word in the practice of law. To find the latest version of this guide, type "Legal User's Guide" in any general search engine (e.g., www.google.com). To find comparable help for law offices that use WordPerfect, run a search for "wordperfect law office" in any search engine.

table of authorities (TOA) A list of primary authority (e.g., cases and statutes) and secondary authority (e.g., legal periodical articles and legal treatises) that a writer has cited in an appellate brief or other document. The list includes page numbers where each authority is cited in the document.

At one time, the most popular word processor in law firms was WordPerfect. Attorneys began to shift to Word, however, when many of their clients adopted Word. This made it easier to exchange electronic files between law firms and their clients. It is easier to read a document sent to you as an attachment to an e-mail message when your word processor is the same as the word processor on which the document was created. If you are using WordPerfect, it is not impossible to read a Word document, but communication is much simpler if the sender and recipient are using the same word processor. It's rather frustrating for a recipient to have to say to a sender, "I could not open your document."

A word of caution is needed about documents created by word processors and other software applications. As we saw in chapter 5, when you send someone a document online (e.g., a memo created by Word sent as an attachment to an e-mail message), you are sending more than the data that will be read on the screen when the document is opened. Digital documents also contain data about data, called **metadata**. This can include earlier drafts of the document that you thought you had erased before completing and sending the final draft! You obviously do not want recipients to be able to read this kind of data, and, therefore, you need to find out how your word processor can be used to remove the metadata. (Within Word's Help feature, for example, type "metadata" to obtain instructions on removal.)

metadata Data about data. Data about a computer document that is hidden within the document itself, e.g., earlier versions of the document.

SPREADSHEETS

Spreadsheets are programs that automatically perform calculations on numbers and values that you insert. A spreadsheet can perform many kinds of number-crunching tasks such as calculating future damages, tax liability, and mortgage payments. The spreadsheet lets you create many groups of interrelated numbers within a series of rows and columns. Once this is done, you can play "what if" by changing one of the numbers to see what happens to the other numbers. The spreadsheet will quickly recalculate all numbers that are dependent on the one that was changed. Suppose, for example, you are considering a loan to purchase a building and want to know what the monthly payments will be. Among the factors that will determine the amount of these payments are the interest rate, length of the mortgage, and amount of the loan. Entering these three numbers into a spreadsheet will give you the amount of the monthly payments. You can then change one or more of the numbers (e.g., enter a lower interest rate) to see what happens to the monthly payments.

spreadsheet Application software that automatically performs calculations on numbers and values that you enter.

What-if calculations can also be used in settlement negotiations. In a structured settlement, for example, the payment of damages will be spread over a period of time rather than paid in a lump sum. To calculate what these payments will be, the attorneys must make certain assumptions about the rate of inflation over this period. A spreadsheet will allow the attorneys to try different assumptions in order to see what impact they would have on the amounts to be paid over the period.

Commonly used spreadsheet programs such as Lotus/IBM 1–2–3 and Microsoft Excel can create charts (e.g., a pie chart) that graphically illustrate the results of these calculations.

DATABASE MANAGEMENT

Database management is software that allows you to organize, search, retrieve, and sort information or data. Such programs are sometimes called database management systems (DBMS). For example, a law firm can create a database containing a list of all of its past and present clients. Within this database, the categories of data could include:

database management Application software that allows you to organize, search, retrieve, and sort information or data.

- Client's name
- Street address
- Phone
- E-mail address
- Internet site
- Intranet site
- Type of case
- Case number

- Name of opponent
- Names of other parties
- Dates provided representation
- Attorney who brought the case to firm
- Fees and expenses billed
- Dates bills sent out
- Dates payments received

This database will allow the firm to accomplish a number of useful tasks. For example, it can be used to check for possible conflicts of interest. When the firm is considering a new client, it needs to find out if the firm has ever represented the opponent of the prospective client. One way to find out is to search that opponent's name in the firm's client database. (For a database used for conflicts checking, see Exhibit 5.10 in chapter 5.) In addition, the database in our example can:

- Generate a list of every probate and estate client in order to send them a mailing on a new tax law.
- Generate a list of every case that the firm closed in 2001.
- Generate a list of every client who has bills that have not been paid for more than sixty days since they were sent.
- Name the attorney who brought in clients with the largest billing totals in 2007.

Major database software used by law firms includes Microsoft's Access, Lotus/IBM's Approach, and Corel's Paradox.

PRESENTATION GRAPHICS

In many settings, a law firm must communicate a client's version of the facts. For example, during negotiations with opposing counsel or in a closing argument before a jury, an attorney may want to demonstrate:

- An injured plaintiff's loss of income for the months immediately after the accident
- The expenses of a parent seeking sole custody of a child in a divorce case
- The share of the market controlled by a company accused of antitrust violations
- The chemical components of a lake into which a manufacturing plant allegedly dumped pollutants over a ten-year period

The attorney can use **presentation graphics** (also called business graphics) to help communicate such facts forcefully by combining text with charts, graphs, video, clip art, and sound. In a courtroom, a trial judge might allow an attorney to use a laptop computer to project charts or graphs as a slide show on a large screen in front of the jury. To demonstrate the costs of caring for a particular child, for example, the attorney could prepare a pie chart that uses different colors and fonts to illustrate the percentage of the budget that each expense consumes. Visually appealing graphics of this kind can be very effective, particularly in cases where the facts are numerous and relatively complicated.

Presentation graphics programs are not limited to use in litigation. A law firm manager might use the software to report on expenses, billable hours, fee collection, cash flow, and other budget matters before a committee of senior partners. The software can also be effectively used by speakers at seminars or by instructors in office training programs. Examples of presentation graphics software used in law firms include Microsoft's PowerPoint and Corel's Presentations. (For examples of computer-generated charts and graphs, see Exhibits 14.4, 14.8, and 14.9 in chapter 14.)

> **presentation graphics** Application software used to combine text with charts, graphs, video, clip art, and sound in order to communicate data more effectively.

LITIGATION SUPPORT

Lawsuits often involve numerous documents, e.g., correspondence, memoranda, transcripts of depositions, interrogatories, answers to interrogatories, requests for admission, responses to requests for admission, medical reports, investigation reports, complaints, answers, motions, briefs, and business records. In complex litigation such as product liability, consumer fraud, and environmental law, the quantity of documents can be enormous. In a recent tobacco case, the attorney representing Lorillard Tobacco Company told the court:

> Lorillard has produced approximately 1.8 million pages of documents in this lawsuit. If you were to take those documents and stack them . . . one on top of the other, they would be 666 feet high. That's the equivalent of a 66-story office building.[6]

Litigation support software is designed to help a law firm manage the large number of facts and documents that can be involved in representing clients in litigation. The software can be used in large cases such as this tobacco case and in cases that are considerably less complex.

A major advantage of litigation support software is the time it can save when searching for information in documents, particularly when you need to search the full text (i.e., every word) of those documents. In a medical malpractice case, for example, suppose you wanted to locate every document in the litigation that mentions Dr. Daniel Summers, one of the primary witnesses in the case. If the full text of every document was in the computer database, you would conduct a **full-text search** of these documents. The software would search every word in every

> **litigation support** Application software used to help a law office store, retrieve, and track facts and documents that pertain to a lawsuit.

> **full-text search** A search of every word in every document in a database.

document to find those that mention Dr. Daniel Summers. Of course, to be able to conduct such searches, the complete text of every document must be in the database. (The primary method of entering complete documents is *scanning*.) If entering the full text of every document is not practical, the office may be able to create summaries or abstracts of every document and then conduct a search of these abstracts. (In large cases, a law office might hire *document coders* to create and enter these abstracts.) The search would find every document whose abstract mentioned Dr. Daniel Summers.

If computers were not available, the searches would have to be done manually. A recent study by a bar association found that a manual search of 10,000 documents took sixty-seven paralegal hours and produced fifteen relevant documents, while the same search conducted with litigation support software took a few seconds and produced twenty relevant documents.[7]

Numerous litigation support programs exist. Examples include Summation, CaseSoft, and Zylab.

CASE MANAGEMENT

A law office cannot practice law without managing the clock. Representing clients often involves numerous appointments and deadlines. The calendar is filled with scheduled interviews, strategy meetings, negotiating sessions, hearing dates, and filing deadlines. For example:

- The date of a client meeting
- The date of a meeting with opposing counsel to discuss settlement options
- The date a lease must be renewed
- The date a stock option must be exercised
- The date a complaint must be filed
- The number of days within which the answer to the complaint must be filed
- The number of days within which answers to interrogatories must be served
- The date of a deposition
- The date of the trial
- The number of days within which an appeal of a judgment must be filed
- The date client bills are due

case management Application software used to help a law office maintain control over its appointments and deadlines.

tickler A system designed to provide reminders of important dates.

statute of limitations A law stating that civil or criminal actions are barred if not brought within a specified period of time.

default judgment A judgment against a party because of a failure to file a required pleading or otherwise to respond to an opponent's claim.

Case management software (also called *docket control* software) is designed to help a law office meet these time commitments. Another name for such programs is *personal information manager* (PIM). In addition to calendar control, PIMs also store related information such as e-mail addresses and "snail mail" (street) addresses. Any system that reminds the office of important dates is called a **tickler**—it prods or tickles the memory about what must be done by certain dates. The consequences of missed deadlines can be devastating. A nightmare of every plaintiff's attorney, for example, is the dismissal of an action because of the failure to file a complaint before the **statute of limitations** barred the action; a nightmare of every defendant's attorney is the entry of a **default judgment** because of a failure to file an answer to the complaint within the time allotted by law. Surprisingly, such devastating lapses are not uncommon. When an insurance company is considering an application for malpractice insurance by a law firm, one of the primary concerns of the company is whether the firm has effective case management systems in place for calendar control.

Commonly used case management/PIM software includes Abacus by Abacus Data Systems and Outlook by Microsoft.

KNOWLEDGE MANAGEMENT (KM)

As you can see, law offices generate a vast quantity of documents. All of these documents contain what attorneys sell: knowledge. The intellectual property of a law firm is its vast collection of briefs, memoranda, pleadings, deposition and trial transcripts, contracts, corporation and banking instruments, wills, trusts, estate plans, government applications, checklists, form files, manuals, e-mail messages, regular correspondence, and reports. To a large extent, however, once these documents are generated and used, they become an untapped resource. When the office completes work on a client's case, the file gets stored away and everyone moves on to the next client. There is no systematic way to tap into and reuse prior case work in current cases. For example, a document created for a real estate case in 2001 might be relevant to the case of a corporate client in 2008. Yet the attorneys and paralegals working on the 2008 case may never find out about the 2001 document. This is all the more true if they are working in a branch office that is hundreds of miles away from the office that generated the 2001 document. Consequently, a lot of wasteful reinvention of the wheel occurs on a regular basis.

 Brief banks are somewhat helpful. They contain copies of old appellate briefs and other documents that can be used as models and adapted for current cases. But not all law firm documents are in brief banks, and the banks are not smoothly integrated into the everyday operation of the office. More effective systems are needed to tap into the vast knowledge pool generated in hundreds of thousands of documents over the years. Slowly these systems are being created as computers become more sophisticated. The systems are called **knowledge management (KM)**. KM is a system for linking into the knowledge base of a law firm that is embodied in the documents generated by all of the cases handled by the office. The goal is to be able to use this knowledge so that the office can better meet the needs of current and prospective clients. KM is a way to avoid starting every case from scratch. The makers of Westlaw and LexisNexis are both designing KM software that can be used in conjunction with their legal research systems. Other vendors are also creating products. KM is a relatively new concept in the law. Many are excited by its potential to increase efficiency.

brief bank A collection of appellate briefs and related documents drafted in prior cases that might be used as models and adapted for current cases.

knowledge management (KM) A system of linking into the knowledge base of a law office embodied in the documents generated by all of the cases it has handled so that it can better meet the needs of current and prospective clients. KM is a productivity tool for capturing and reusing knowledge.

[S E C T I O N D]
COMPUTER-ASSISTED LEGAL RESEARCH

INTRODUCTION

 Computer-assisted legal research (CALR) is one of the great inventions in the practice of law. What once took hours poring through library volumes can now be accomplished in seconds by CALR. A vast amount of legal material is available **online** twenty-four hours a day. (One of the meanings of *online* is being connected to other computers, often through the Internet. The major commercial fee-based online legal research services are Westlaw, LexisNexis, Loislaw, and Versuslaw, all available on the Internet. The giants of the field are Westlaw and LexisNexis, two fierce competitors. [The legal community jokingly refers to them together as Wexis.]) In addition, as we will see in the next section, there are numerous free legal resources on the Internet.

 We begin our study of CALR with the fee-based online services.

 Westlaw is a product of West Group (www.westlaw.com). LexisNexis is a product of Reed Elsevier (www.lexis.com). See Exhibits 13.6 and 13.7 for the opening pages of these

computer-assisted legal research (CALR) Performing legal research in computer databases.

online 1. Connected to another computer or computer network, often through the Internet. 2. Residing on a computer and available for use; activated and ready for use on a computer.

Westlaw A fee-based system of computer-assisted legal research owned by West Group.

EXHIBIT 13.6 **Search Page of Westlaw (www.westlaw.com)**

EXHIBIT 13.7 **Search Page of LexisNexis (www.lexis.com)**

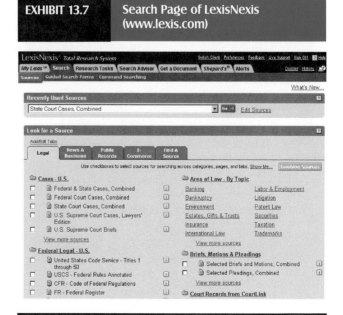

services. To use either service, you set up a billing account, enter your password, select the part of the service you want to search, and type your search terms. Westlaw calls its parts *databases*; LexisNexis calls its parts *libraries*. For example, there is a database in Westlaw and a library in LexisNexis that contain all the court opinions of Pennsylvania. Similarly, there is a database in Westlaw and a library in LexisNexis that contain all the federal statutes passed by Congress. (For convenience, the following discussion will refer to the resources in both services as databases.)

SCOPE OF WESTLAW AND LEXISNEXIS

Westlaw and **LexisNexis** allow you to search the full text of **primary authority** such as the following:

- Federal and state constitutions
- Federal and state statutes
- Federal and state court opinions
- Federal, state, and local administrative regulations
- Federal, state, and local administrative decisions
- Federal, state, and local rules of court
- Federal treaties and executive agreements
- Local charters and municipal codes

You can also conduct full-text searches of **secondary authority** such as the following:

- Legal periodicals
- Legal treatises
- Legal newsletters

In addition, Westlaw and LexisNexis give you access to a large variety of factual information such as the following:

- The status of pending lawsuits in federal, state, and local courts
- Records of judgments in bankruptcy courts, federal district courts, other federal courts, state courts, county courts, and other local courts
- Statistics on jury awards for specific kinds of injuries
- Mechanic's lien filings
- Uniform Commercial Code (UCC) filings
- Business and personal addresses
- Names of key personnel in particular companies (e.g., officers, members of the board of directors)
- Major properties (e.g., land, stock, commercial equipment) owned by particular individuals and businesses
- Financial status of companies based on sales data, stock market prices, and property holdings
- Financial details and status of proposed mergers and acquisitions
- Chain of title records on specific property
- Medical research (e.g., side effects of particular drugs)
- News stories on particular topics, companies, or individuals in newspapers and other media throughout the world
- Birth and death records
- Social science studies

This overview is not meant to suggest that the contents of Westlaw and LexisNexis are identical. Each claims to outdo the other in special features, ease of use, comprehensiveness, and diversity of coverage. Yet as demonstrated by the above overview, the coverage in both systems is substantially similar.

SEARCH QUERIES

Every computer database will have a search box in which you enter your search terms. This is true in Westlaw and LexisNexis as well as in free research sites on the Internet. (Later in the chapter we will discuss Internet research sites called search engines.) Any search term you enter

LexisNexis A fee-based system of computer-assisted legal research owned by Reed Elsevier.

primary authority Any law that a court could rely on in reaching its decision.

secondary authority Any nonlaw that a court could rely on in reaching its decision.

in a search box will be interpreted by the computer as a **query**, which is simply a question or set of instructions on what you want to find in the database.

There are two methods of phrasing queries on Westlaw and LexisNexis: (1) natural language and (2) terms and connectors. These two methods also exist on many of the free research sites on the Internet. Keep in mind, however, that each research site can establish its own way of phrasing queries. You will note similarities, but watch for differences among the various sites.

Natural-Language Searching

Natural-language searching uses everyday speech to phrase questions. LexisNexis calls its natural-language method *Freestyle;* Westlaw calls its natural-language method *Natural Language.* Here are some examples of natural-language questions:

What is the statute of limitations for embezzlement?
When can a minor enter a contract?
Can strict liability be imposed for harm caused by smoking?

You type the query in the same way that you would ask a question in plain English to a friend or colleague.

Terms-and-Connectors Searching

A more commonly used and more precise method of phrasing queries on Westlaw and LexisNexis uses **terms and connectors**. (This method is based on rules of search logic referred to as Boolean logic.) In a terms-and-connectors search, you specify relationships between terms in a search query in order to identify the documents you want included in or excluded from the search. The relationships are indicated by powerful connectors such as *and*, &, *or*, and *not*.

Here is an example of a terms-and-connectors search in Westlaw:

marijuana & arrest

Let us assume you want to use this query to search for opinions in a database that contains opinions of your state courts. The query tells the computer to find every opinion in the database that contains the term *marijuana* anywhere in the opinion and that also contains the term *arrest* anywhere in the opinion. The terms being searched are marijuana and arrest. The AND connector (phrased in Westlaw by using the word AND or an ampersand, &) tells the computer that you want to be given every opinion in the database that contains both terms.

Of course, if your search query consists of a single term, you do not need connectors. You are simply telling the computer to find every document that contains that term. Single-term searches, however, are usually unproductive because they produce too many documents. Suppose, for example, you entered the following search query:

law

This query would probably identify hundreds of thousands of documents because of the large number of documents that contain this term. In fact, Westlaw will quickly flash a message on the screen telling you to change your query because the one you are using is likely to generate too many documents. Hence, unless your single term is a unique legal term (e.g., asportation) or an unusual surname (e.g., Wyzinski), your query should include more than one term. When it does, connectors are needed to state the relationship between the terms. Although in the following discussion we will use some single-term queries for purposes of highlighting a particular search technique, keep in mind that multiple-term searches are usually more effective than single-term searches.

We turn now to a closer examination of terms-and-connectors searching in Westlaw and LexisNexis. Here are the topics we will be covering:

Universal character (*) in Westlaw and LexisNexis
Root expander (!) in Westlaw and LexisNexis
Plurals in Westlaw and LexisNexis
Formulating queries in Westlaw
Formulating queries in LexisNexis

---

query A question that is used to try to find something in a computer database.

natural language Plain English as spoken or written every day as opposed to language that is specially designed for computer communication.

terms and connectors Relationships between terms in a search query that specify documents that should be included in or excluded from the search.

universal character An asterisk (*) that stands for one character within a term you are searching in Westlaw or LexisNexis. (*Caution:* The asterisk might have a different meaning in other search systems such as Google or Findlaw.)

Universal Character (*) in Westlaw and LexisNexis   Both Westlaw and LexisNexis use the asterisk (*) as a **universal character** that stands for any single character such as a letter of the alphabet. A universal character is useful when you are not sure of the spelling of a term you want to search. For example, in the drug arrest example we just examined, suppose you were not sure whether the drug was spelled marijuana or marihuana. You could enter the search as:

mari*uana & arrest

This query will find any document that spells the term as marijuana, marihuana, mariiuana, marizuana, etc. Because the asterisk stands for *any* single letter or character, it is called the universal character. You are not limited to one universal character per term. The following query:

int**state

will find every document that contains the term *interstate* anywhere in the document and every document that contains the term *intrastate* anywhere in the document.

Similarly, the query:

s****holder

will find:

- Every document that contains the term *shareholder* anywhere in the document, and
- Every document that contains the term *stockholder* anywhere in the document, and
- Every document that contains the term *stakeholder* anywhere in the document.

The query:

w**nst**n

will find any document that contains words with the following spellings (or misspellings) anywhere in the document: *Weinstein, Weinstien, Weinsteen, Wienstein, Wienstien,* and *Wiensteen.*

root expander An exclamation mark (!) that stands for one or more characters added to the root of a term you are searching in Westlaw or LexisNexis. (*Caution:* The exclamation point might have a different meaning in other search systems such as Google or Findlaw.)

wildcard A special character (e.g., *, !, ?) that can be used to represent one or more characters in a search query. The main wildcards in Westlaw and LexisNexis are * and !.

Root Expander (!) in Westlaw and LexisNexis   Both Westlaw and LexisNexis use the exclamation point (!) as a **root expander**. When added to the root of any term, the ! acts as a substitute for one or more characters. (The root expander and the universal character are examples of **wildcards**, special characters that can be used to represent one or more characters in a search query.) The root expander in Westlaw and LexisNexis is inserted at the end of a term (or at the end of a fragment of a term) in order to broaden the scope of the search. If your query is:

litig!

you will find every document that contains any of the following terms anywhere in the document: *litigable, litigate, litigated, litigating, litigation, litigator, litigious,* and *litigiousness.* The root expander is quite powerful and can be overused. The query:

tax!

will find every document that contains any of the following terms anywhere in the document: *tax, taxability, taxable, taxation, taxational, taxer, Taxco, taxeme, taxes, tax-deductible, tax-exempt, tax-free, taxi, taxicab, taxidermy, taxidermist, taxied, taximeter, taximetrics, taxing, taxis, taxiway, taxman, taxol, taxon, taxonomist, taxonomy, taxpayer, tax-shelter, taxy,* and *taxying.* Hence, if you use *tax!* as a search query in a large database, you are likely to find documents that are far beyond the scope of your research problem.

Plurals in Westlaw and LexisNexis   In Westlaw and LexisNexis searches, it is not necessary to use the universal character or the root expander to search for the plural of a term. The query:

prosecutor

will give you every document that contains the term *prosecutor* or the term *prosecutors* anywhere in the document. The same is true of irregular plurals:

- The query *child* will give you every document that contains the term *child* or the term *children* anywhere in the document.
- The query *memorandum* will give you every document that contains the term *memoranda* or the term *memorandums* anywhere in the document.

Entering the singular form of a term will automatically result in a search for the plural form of that term also.

Thus far we have examined the universal character (*) and root expander (!). Again keep in mind that this discussion applies only to Westlaw and LexisNexis. When you are searching in other search resources (e.g., on Internet search engines), you may find that these notations (* and !) serve related but different functions.

Formulating Queries in Westlaw To understand terms-and-connectors searches in Westlaw, we need to examine:

- The OR connector
- The AND connector
- The sentence connector (/s) (+s)
- The paragraph connector (/p) (+p)
- The BUT NOT connector (%)
- The numerical connector (/n) (+n)
- Phrase searching (" ")

OR connector The simplest connector in Westlaw is OR, which is expressed by leaving a blank space between search terms. Westlaw interprets the blank space in the query to mean OR. This connector tells Westlaw to treat the terms as alternatives and to find every document that contains either term or both terms anywhere in the document. Hence the query:

doctor physician

will find:

- Every document that contains the term *doctor* and the term *physician* anywhere in the document
- Every document that contains the term *doctor* anywhere in the document even if it does not contain the term *physician*
- Every document that contains the term *physician* anywhere in the document even if it does not contain the term *doctor*

AND connector (&) As we have seen, the AND connector in Westlaw is expressed by typing the word AND or an ampersand (&) between terms. The query:

paralegal & fee

will find every document that contains the term *paralegal* and the term *fee* anywhere in the document. (The same result would be obtained by phrasing this query as paralegal AND fee.) If a particular document mentions *paralegals* 100 times but never mentions *fee*, the document will not be found by this query. The query requires both terms to be in the document. If you want documents that mention either term, the query would have to use Westlaw's OR connector (a blank space):

paralegal fee

Sentence connector (/s) (+s) The sentence connector in Westlaw is expressed by typing /s or +s between terms. When you type /s between terms, you want the terms to appear anywhere (in any order) in the same sentence in the document. The query:

child /s support

will find every document in which the terms *child* and *support* appear together in any sentence in the document. The query would find:

- A document containing the sentence "The payment of *child support* is a state function."
- A document containing the sentence "*Children* are entitled to the *support* of their school teachers."
- A document containing the sentence "Objections to the petitioner's attempt to *support* his first wife cannot be made by the attorney appointed to represent the *child*."
- A document containing the sentence "He would not *support* the decision to send the *child* to jail."

All of these sentences fit the query even though the meaning of the term *support* is hardly the same in each. Your research problem probably does not involve all of these meanings. Later we will see how to use other connectors that narrow the focus of your search in order to avoid this problem.

In the first and second documents, note that the term *child* (and its plural *children*) appear before the term *support* in the sentence. In the third and fourth documents, however, the order of the terms is reversed. The /s connector does not require that the terms appear in the sentence in the order in which you type them in the query. All that is required is that all the terms separated by /s appear anywhere in the same sentence.

If you want the terms to appear in the sentence in the order you type them in the query, use the +s version of the sentence connector. Hence the query:

child +s support

will find only those documents in which the term *child* appears before the term *support* in any sentence in the document. This query would find the first and second documents above. It would not find the third and fourth documents because *child* does not appear before *support* in the sentences of these documents.

Paragraph connector (/p) (+p)   The paragraph connector in Westlaw is expressed by typing /p or +p between terms. When you type /p between terms, you want the terms to appear anywhere (in any order) in the same paragraph in the document. When you type +p between terms, you want the terms to appear in the paragraph in the same order that you type the terms in the query. The query:

paralegal /p certif!

would find a document in which the term *paralegal* appears anywhere in a paragraph and one of the following terms also appears anywhere in the same paragraph: *certify, certified, certifying,* or *certification*. The query does not require that the term *paralegal* appear first. If you want to limit your search to documents in which the term *paralegal* appears first in the paragraph, the query would be:

paralegal +p certif!

BUT NOT connector (%)   The BUT NOT connector in Westlaw is expressed by typing the percent symbol (%) between terms. When you type % after a term, everything after % is excluded from your search. The BUT NOT connector is helpful to narrow your search. Assume, for example, that you are looking for opinions involving robbery with a gun. You try this query:

gun & robbery

You find that most of the documents found by this query involve bank robberies. If your research problem has nothing to do with banks, you could try the query:

gun & robbery % bank

This query will find every document in which the terms *gun* and *robbery* appear anywhere in the document so long as the term *bank* does not also appear anywhere in the document. For example, the query will not lead you to a document that mentions *gun* ten times, *robbery* twenty times, and *bank* once. Any mention of *bank* disqualifies the document from fitting within the query.

Numerical connector (/n) (+n)   The numerical connector in Westlaw is expressed by typing /n or +n between terms. You use this connector when you want to specify how close you want the terms to appear to each other in the document. Closeness is measured by a specified number (n) of words. The query:

paralegal /5 license

would find every document in which the term *paralegal* appears within five words of the term *license*. Here is an example of text in a document that this query would find:

"... the *paralegal* had no *license* from the state."

This document fits the query because our search terms are two words apart, well within the five-word limit (/5) set by the query. Here is an example of text in a document that this query would not find because the terms are more than five words apart:

"... *paralegals* as well as notaries and process servers are not required to have a *license.*"

The /n connector does not require that the terms in the document appear in the order in which you type them in the query. Hence our query would find a document containing the following text:

"The driver's *license* was found on the *paralegal.*"

If you want to restrict your search to those documents in which the terms appear in the order you type them in the query, use the +n version of the numerical connector in the same manner that +s and +p are used in the sentence and paragraph connectors. Hence a document containing the sentence in the above example would not be found by the following query:

paralegal +5 license

Phrase searching (" ")   There are many technical phrases in the law, e.g., habeas corpus, due process of law, search and seizure, and beyond a reasonable doubt. You need to be careful when entering phrases in Westlaw queries. If, for example, your query was the phrase:

medical malpractice

the space between the terms would be interpreted by Westlaw as an OR connector, so that the query would find:

- Every document that contains the term *medical* and the term *malpractice* anywhere in the document
- Every document that contains the term *medical* anywhere in the document even if it does not contain the term *malpractice*
- Every document that contains the term *malpractice* anywhere in the document even if it does not contain the term *medical*

This query could lead to an enormous number of documents, many of which having nothing to do with medical malpractice. When searching for phrases, therefore, you need to tell Westlaw not to interpret a space as an OR connector. This is done by placing the phrase within quotation marks. Hence our query should read:

"medical malpractice"

Later we will see that LexisNexis does not require quotation marks when conducting a phrase search because LexisNexis does not interpret every space as an OR connector.

Formulating Queries in LexisNexis   To understand terms-and-connectors searches in Lexis, we need to examine:

- The OR connector
- The AND connector
- The sentence connector (w/s)
- The paragraph connector (w/p)
- The AND NOT connector
- The numerical connector (w/n)
- Phrase searching

As we examine each of these topics, we will see that there are similarities and differences between LexisNexis and Westlaw search queries.

OR connector   In LexisNexis, the OR connector is expressed by typing the word OR between search terms. The query:

doctor OR physician

will find:

- Every document that contains the term *doctor* and the term *physician* anywhere in the document

- Every document that contains the term *doctor* anywhere in the document even if it does not contain the term *physician*
- Every document that contains the term *physician* anywhere in the document even if it does not contain the term *doctor*

Note that the phrasing of the OR connector is substantially different in LexisNexis and Westlaw. In LexisNexis, you use the word OR, whereas in Westlaw, you simply leave a space between the search terms. The use of OR in LexisNexis (doctor OR physician) serves the same function as a space in Westlaw (doctor physician).

AND connector   In LexisNexis, the AND connector is phrased by typing AND between search terms. The query:

paralegal AND fee

will find every document that contains the term *paralegal* and the term *fee* anywhere in the document. The query will not find any document that mentions only one of these terms. This is also true in Westlaw; both LexisNexis and Westlaw use the AND connector in the same way. As we have seen, however, you can also phrase the AND connector in Westlaw by typing the ampersand (&) between search terms.

Sentence connector (w/s)   The sentence connector in LexisNexis is expressed by typing w/s between terms. When you type w/s between terms, you want the terms to appear in the same sentence in the document. The query:

overdose w/s drug

will find every document in which the terms *overdose* and *drug* appear in any sentence in the document. The sentence connector (w/s) in LexisNexis works the same as the sentence connector (/s) in Westlaw. (Unlike Westlaw, however, LexisNexis does not have the +s option described earlier.)

Paragraph connector (w/p)   The paragraph connector in LexisNexis is expressed by typing w/p between terms. When you type w/p between terms, you want the terms to appear in the same paragraph in the document. The query:

international w/p ship!

will find every document in which the term *international* appears anywhere in a paragraph and one of the following terms also appears anywhere in the same paragraph: *ship, shipbuilding, shipload, shipmate, shipment, shipper, shipworm, shipwreck,* and *shipyard.*

The paragraph connector (w/p) in LexisNexis works the same as the paragraph connector (/p) in Westlaw. (Unlike Westlaw, however, LexisNexis does not have the +p option described earlier.)

AND NOT connector   The AND NOT connector in LexisNexis is expressed by typing AND NOT between terms. Every term after AND NOT is excluded from your search. The query:

cruelty AND NOT divorce

will find every document in which the term *cruelty* appears anywhere in the document so long as the term *divorce* does not also appear anywhere in the document. The query will not lead you to a document that mentions *cruelty* ten times and *divorce* once. Any mention of *divorce* disqualifies the document from fitting within the query. The AND NOT connector in LexisNexis works the same as the BUT NOT (%) connector in Westlaw.

Numerical connector (w/n) (PRE/n)   The numerical connector in LexisNexis is expressed by typing either w/n or PRE/n between terms. You use this connector when you want to specify how close you want the terms to appear to each other in the document. Closeness is measured by a specified number (n) of words. Assume you wanted to find documents on the appointment of Chief Justice Rehnquist to the United States Supreme Court. The query

Rehnquist w/4 appointment

would find every document in which the term *Rehnquist* appears within four words of the term *appointment*. The words can appear in any order when you use a w/n connector. If you want the terms to appear in the document in the order you type them in the query, use the PRE/n version of the numerical connector. The query

Rehnquist PRE/4 appointment

- Will find a document containing the sentence "Justice *Rehnquist* received his *appointment* during the session."
- Will not find a document containing the sentence "The *appointment* of Justice *Rehnquist* had not been anticipated."

The second sentence is disqualified because *Rehnquist* does not appear before *appointment* as required by the PRE/n numerical connector.

The numerical connector (w/n) (PRE/n) in LexisNexis works the same as the numerical connector (/n) (+n) in Westlaw.

Phrase searching   Recall that phrase searching in Westlaw requires the use of quotation marks because Westlaw interprets a space between terms to mean OR. This is not so in LexisNexis. To search for a phrase in LexisNexis, you simply type that phrase. The query:

equal employment opportunity commission

would find any document in which the phrase *equal employment opportunity commission* appears anywhere in the document. The same search in Westlaw would have to be phrased:

"equal employment opportunity commission"

Combination Queries   Most of the examples of queries we have examined thus far have involved one of the connectors. The exception was the example of the Westlaw query that combined the AND and the BUT NOT connectors in one query (gun & robbery % bank). You can use many connectors in a query in order to narrow your search. Here is another example of a Westlaw query that contains multiple connectors:

bankruptcy /25 discharg! & student college education % foreign international

In LexisNexis, this same query would be written:

bankruptcy w/25 discharg! AND student OR college OR education AND NOT foreign OR international

For a document to fit either of these queries, it would have to meet all of the following criteria:

- The document must contain the term *bankruptcy*.
- This term *bankruptcy* must be found within twenty-five words of any of the following terms: *discharge, discharged, dischargeable, dischargeability*.
- The document must also contain one or more of the following terms: *student, college, education*.
- The terms *foreign* and *international* must not appear anywhere in the document.

You might use this query if you were looking for documents on whether domestic student loans can be discharged in bankruptcy.

ASSIGNMENT 13.1

(a) Here are five separate queries. If they were run in either Westlaw or LexisNexis, what terms in documents would they find?
   1. para!
   2. assign!
   3. crim!
   4. legis!
   5. e****e

(continues)

(b) You are looking for cases in which a paralegal is charged with unauthorized practice of law.
1. Write a query for Westlaw.
2. Write a query for LexisNexis.

(c) You are looking for cases in which a law firm illegally failed to pay overtime compensation to its paralegals.
1. Write a query for Westlaw.
2. Write a query for LexisNexis.

(d) You would like to know what your state courts have said about paralegals.
1. Write a query for Westlaw.
2. Write a query for LexisNexis.

(e) Here is a query to be entered in Westlaw:

cigar! tobacco smok! /p product strict! /5 liab!

Explain this query. State what the symbols and spaces mean. State what the query is designed to find.

FIELD AND SEGMENT SEARCHING

When searching for documents such as court opinions in Westlaw and LexisNexis, you probably want to find your search terms anywhere in documents. As we saw earlier, such searches are called full-text searches. Yet it is also possible to limit your search to part of each document. Westlaw calls these parts **fields**; LexisNexis calls them **segments**. For example, one of the fields in the court opinion databases of Westlaw is title (ti), which covers the names of the parties. Assume that you wanted to obtain the name of every opinion in which General Motors was a party. Instead of doing a full-text search of the entire opinion in Westlaw, you could restrict your search to the title of every opinion. The field query would be:

> ti ("General Motors")

This query would ask for a list of every opinion in which General Motors was a party (e.g., a plaintiff or defendant). The comparable segment in LexisNexis is called *name*. The segment query would be:

> name (General Motors)

Here is a summary of the major field searches in Westlaw and segment searches in LexisNexis when the documents you are searching are court opinions:

Westlaw

> *title* (ti): The names of the parties in the opinion.
> Example: ti(Miranda)
> *attorney* (at): The names of the attorneys litigating the case.
> Example: at("Clarence Darrow")
> *synopsis* (sy): The short summary of the entire opinion.
> Example: sy("double jeopardy")
> *author* (au): Opinions written (authored) by a particular judge.
> Example: au(scalia)

LexisNexis

> *name:* The name of the parties in the opinion.
> Example: name(Miranda)
> *counsel:* The names of the attorneys litigating the case.
> Example: counsel(Clarence Darrow)
> *syllabus:* The short summary of the entire opinion.
> Example: syllabus(double jeopardy)
> *writtenby:* Opinions written (authored) by a particular judge.
> Example: writtenby(scalia)

CITATORS IN WESTLAW AND LEXISNEXIS

A **citator** helps you assess the current validity of a law (e.g., opinion, statute) and gives you leads to other relevant materials. The online citator in Westlaw is called *KeyCite*. The

---

field A portion of a document in Westlaw that can be separately searched.

segment A portion of a document in LexisNexis that can be separately searched.

citator A book, CD–ROM, or online service containing lists of citations that can (1) help you assess the current validity of an opinion, statute, or other item and (2) give you leads to other relevant materials.

online citator in LexisNexis is called *Shepards*. (The latter is the electronic version of the paper volumes called *Shepard's Citations*.) Suppose, for example, you want to know whether a particular court opinion is still good law. Has the opinion been reversed on appeal? Have any other courts followed it or criticized it? Has the opinion been overruled? One of the ways to answer such questions is by using the online citators of Westlaw and LexisNexis. Both systems use colored flags or other alert signals to tell the reader about changes in the court opinion, statute, or other authority they are checking in the citator. Another online citator offered by LexisNexis is Auto-Cite, which we briefly examined in chapter 11 (see also the glossary). (For the use of traditional *Shepard's Citations* in paper volumes on the shelves of libraries, see Exhibit 11.28 in chapter 11.)

LOCATING A DOCUMENT ONLINE WHEN YOU HAVE ITS CITATION

The most common reason you use Westlaw and LexisNexis is to search for documents that you do not have. Suppose, however, that you already have the citation to a document and you simply want to read that document. You could take the citation to a law library and read the document in a traditional volume from the shelf. Alternatively, you could take your citation to Westlaw or LexisNexis and read the document online.

To retrieve the document on Westlaw, type the citation in a box called "Enter Citation" or "Find by citation" and click "GO." (See Exhibit 13.6.) Westlaw also allows you to retrieve the document by using a find (fi) command with the citation. Here, for example, are find commands for a court opinion and a statute:

> fi 5 F3d 1412
> fi 42 usca 12101

To retrieve a court opinion on LexisNexis, type the citation in a box on its homepage called "Enter a Citation" and click "Go." LexisNexis also allows you to:

- Retrieve a court opinion by typing the citation of the court opinion in the *lexsee* feature of LexisNexis and
- Retrieve a statute by typing the citation of the statute in the *lexstat* feature of LexisNexis.

ONLINE ASSISTANCE/TUTORIALS ON WESTLAW AND LEXISNEXIS

There are several sites you can use to obtain online assistance and tutorials on the effective use of Westlaw and LexisNexis:

Westlaw

- lawschool.westlaw.com/shared/marketinfodisplay.asp?code=re&id=2&subpage=1
- west.thomson.com/documentation/westlaw/wlawdoc/web/rswlcm04.pdf
- www.law.harvard.edu/library/services/research/tutorials
- www.ll.georgetown.edu/tutorials/calr/Westlaw/wl-start/html

LexisNexis

- support.lexisnexis.com/academic/default.asp
- w3.lexis.com/lawschoolreg/tutorials/case_val
- web.lexis.com/help/multimedia/detect.asp?sPage=shepards
- www.ll.georgetown.edu/tutorials/calr/Lexis/lx-start.html
- parklibrary.jomc.unc.edu/lexis.html

[SECTION E]

INTERNET

INTRODUCTION

Hundreds of millions of people around the world use the **Internet**, a self-governing network of networks, popularly known as the information superhighway, on which users can share information. A network is two or more computers (or other devices) that are connected by telephone lines, fiber-optic cables, satellites, or other systems in order to share hardware, software, messages, and other data. These different networks can communicate

Internet A worldwide electronic network of networks on which millions of computer users can share information.

with each other because they all follow a set of specifications called *protocols* that make the communication possible.

The Internet was developed in the 1960s by the U.S. Department of Defense to link a handful of computers in the event of a nuclear attack.[8] The idea was to design a system that would allow communication over a number of routes between linked computers. Thus, a message sent from a computer in Boston to a computer in Seattle might first be sent to a computer in Philadelphia, and then be forwarded to a computer in Pittsburgh, and then to Chicago, Denver, and Salt Lake City, before finally reaching Seattle. If the message could not travel along that path (because of military attack, technical malfunction, or other reason), the message would automatically be rerouted, perhaps, from Boston to Richmond, and then to Atlanta, New Orleans, Dallas, Albuquerque, and Los Angeles, and finally to Seattle. This type of transmission, and rerouting, could occur in a matter of seconds without human intervention or knowledge.

When the government no longer needed this link, it turned the system over to the public. Hence no single governmental, corporate, or academic entity owns or administers the Internet. It exists and functions because hundreds of thousands of separate operators of computers and computer networks independently decided to use common data transfer protocols to exchange communications and information with other computers (which in turn exchange communications and information with still other computers). There is no centralized storage location, control point, or communications channel for the Internet. Indeed, it would not be technically feasible for a single entity to control everything that is conveyed on the Internet.

To connect to the Internet, you need a company or organization that provides access, called an **Internet service provider (ISP)**, also called an Internet Access Provider (IAP), e.g., America Online, AT&T, and EarthLink. Once connected, most of your online time will be spent on the "Web"—the **World Wide Web (WWW)**. The Web is a system of sites using **hypertext** to enable you to display and link information in different locations on the same site or on different sites. When you are on a Web page, you will see words, pictures, or buttons that are highlighted in some way, often with the use of color. If the words, pictures, or buttons on a site are highlighted (i.e., hypertexted), you can click on them and you will be taken to another section of the site or to another site. Suppose, for example, you are on the Legal Resources page of the Internet site of the National Federation of Paralegal Associations (see Exhibit 13.8).

Internet service provider (ISP) A company that provides access to the Internet, usually for a monthly fee.

World Wide Web (WWW) A system of sites on the Internet that can be accessed through hypertext links.

hypertext A method of displaying and linking information found in different locations on the same site or on different sites of the World Wide Web.

EXHIBIT 13.8   **Legal Resources Site of the National Federation of Paralegal Associations (NFPA)**

National Federation of Paralegal Associations www.paralegals.org (click "Legal Resources")

Note the fifteen resource buttons on this page. By clicking on any of these buttons, you will be led to thousands of other Web sites on the Internet that will help you do factual and legal research. Do you want to find federal statutes? Click the option called "Federal Laws, Codes, Statutes" at the top of the second column of buttons. Do you want information on the Federal Trade Commission? Click the option called "Federal Agencies and Departments" at the top of the first column.

A great deal of legal and factual information is available on the Internet for free. Much of this information is also available for a fee from the major commercial online services, Westlaw and LexisNexis. (See Exhibits 13.6 and 13.7.) Neither of these giants, however, is likely to go out of business because of competition from the free resources on the Internet. Westlaw and LexisNexis spend a great deal of editorial time ensuring the accuracy and currentness of the information they make available. No comparable control mechanisms exist for much of the even larger quantity of free information found on the Internet. The reliability of free information is increasing (particularly at government-run sites that provide access to the government's own statutes, cases, and administrative regulations), but these free sites are not yet able on their own to satisfy the legal community's need for accurate and current online legal information. Westlaw and LexisNexis (and some smaller fee-based services such as www.loislaw.com and www.versuslaw.com) will continue to play major roles in online research.

INTERNET ADDRESSES

The address of a resource (or any page) on the World Wide Web (e.g., a document or an image) is called the **uniform resource locator (URL)**. Here is an example of a URL:

http://www.loc.gov

Http means hypertext transfer protocol. As we saw earlier, the protocol is the set of specifications or standards that allow computers to communicate with each other. Because most **web browsers** assume you are using the http protocol, you do not need to type http://. (A web browser is simply a program that allows you to read pages on the World Wide Web. The most popular browsers are Microsoft's Internet Explorer and Mozilla's Firefox.) After the protocol in our URL example comes the address of the **server** (www.loc.gov) on which the resource is located. A server is a computer program that provides resources or services (e.g., access to data) to other computers. Typing the address of the server will usually lead you to its opening or homepage. The last three digits of the server address (.gov) are the domain name or identifier, which indicates the category or type of server. Our example *(www.loc.gov)* will lead you to a government agency, the Library of Congress (loc). Here are the main categories of domain names:

.com (commercial entity)
.gov (government office)
.org (organization, often nonprofit)
.edu (educational institution)
.mil (military institution)
.net (network provider)

Other categories have been approved or are being planned, such as .info, .biz, and .travel.
After the URL's server name, you may find additional characters. For example:

www.loc.gov/law/public/law.html

The additional characters (/law/public/law.html) bypass the homepage and take you directly to specific documents, images, or links available on the site.

When you type in a long address such as this, you will occasionally find that no results (or "hits") are produced. You may get a message telling you that "your search did not match any documents." You may be trying to access a site that no longer exists or that no longer exists at the address you are using. Before giving up, check the exact spelling of the address you typed. Make sure that the slashes were correctly typed (\ should not be typed as /) and that you have not added any spaces in the address. If your address is still unproductive, start removing segments from the end of the address—one at a time:

www.loc.gov/law/public/law.html
www.loc.gov/law/public/law

---

uniform resource locator (URL) The address of a resource (or any page) on the Internet.

web browser The program that allows you to read pages on the World Wide Web.

server A computer program that provides resources or services to other computers.

www.loc.gov/law/public
www.loc.gov/law
www.loc.gov

Keep removing segments until you get back to the homepage. Try each new address (there are four in our example) to see if it yields what you want. At the last address—the homepage—you may find links that will lead you to what you are looking for. Or you may find a search box on the homepage in which you can try some new search terms.

INTRODUCTION TO SEARCHING THE INTERNET

According to some estimates, over 8.1 billion World Wide Web pages are on the Internet. Every second, twenty-five new Web pages are added. In light of this extraordinary volume of material, finding what you need can sometimes be a challenge. Exhibit 13.9 presents guidelines for using search engines, the major Internet finding tool.

EXHIBIT 13.9	**Internet Search Techniques and Assessing the Reliability of What You Find**

1. Select the search engine you want to use. (See the choices in Exhibit 13.10.) Be prepared, however, to try your search on more than one search engine.

2. Every search engine has its own help section that gives instructions and suggestions on how to search effectively within it. The section may be called Help, How to Search, Advanced Search, etc. Read this section carefully for every search engine you try. The section may have suggestions on how to rephrase an unproductive query by narrowing it (e.g., use more specific search terms in the query) or by broadening it (e.g., add synonyms to the query). Unfortunately, many researchers do not check this help section. They type in their search terms and quickly abandon the search site if the first page of results is not productive. Unproductive results, however, may be due to a failure of the researcher to take the time to learn how to use the search engine effectively. "What's the best search engine? The one you learn to use well" (powerreporting.com/altavista.html).

3. Here are six of the most important questions you want answered about every search engine you use. Try to answer these questions by checking its help section. The questions are as follows:

   ■ How do you search for phrases? Do you need to add quotation marks around the phrase, e.g., "capital punishment"?

   ■ How do you search for plurals (e.g., *vehicles* or *children*)? Does the engine automatically search for plurals when you enter the singular form of a search term?

   ■ Does the engine have an AND connector? When your search query has more than one term (e.g., battery woman), how do you indicate that you want to limit your search to sites that contain all of your terms? Do you add AND between the terms (*battery AND woman*)? Do you place a plus sign (+) immediately in front of each term (*+battery +woman*) that must appear in the site? Other method?

   ■ Does the engine have an OR connector? How do you express alternative terms in your search query? Do you add OR between the terms (e.g., *zoning OR easement*) or does the engine automatically treat every space between search terms as an OR so that OR does not have to be typed?

   ■ Does the engine have a BUT NOT or AND NOT connector? How do you tell the engine to avoid specific categories of sites? For example, how do you tell it that you want sites on penicillin for adults only? Do you use the BUT NOT connector (*penicillin BUT NOT child*), the AND NOT connector (e.g., *penicillin AND NOT child*), or do you place a minus sign (–) immediately in front of any term that must not appear (*+penicillin +adult –child*)?

   ■ If you are not sure how to spell a term (e.g., Gieco? Geico?), can you use any universal characters or wildcards such as * (G**co) or ! (G!!co)? When we studied Westlaw and LexisNexis earlier, we saw how they use the asterisk and exclamation in search queries, but other search resources may use these symbols differently.

   ■ How does the engine treat common words, e.g., *a, an, the, that* (sometimes called *stop words*)? If you type them as part of your query, does the search engine ignore them? If you want them included (and searched for) along with the other words in your query, how is this done? Some search engines require the use of quotation marks around the language that includes the common words.

   ■ Are searches *case sensitive*? Will the search engine give you the same results if all your search words are in capital letters (GUN AND THEFT), in all lowercase letters (gun and theft), or in a combination of capital and lowercase letters (gun AND theft)? A search is *not* case sensitive if the use of capital letters has no effect on the search results. The search is case sensitive if the results would differ when capital letters are used. The help section of the site will tell you if searches are case sensitive.

4. Be specific in your use of search terms. For example, if you are looking for attorney fee cases in litigation involving the Ojibwa tribe in Maine, type *+attorney +fee +Ojibwa +Maine* (or *attorney AND fee AND Ojibwa AND Maine*); do not simply type *+attorney +fee* (or *attorney AND fee*).

5. Use synonyms in your search (e.g., *divorce* OR *dissolution*). The help section of the search engine will tell you more about using synonyms. In Google, you will learn that the tilde (~) in front of a word will automatically search for synonyms of that word. If, for example, the search consists of one word (gun) with a tilde in front of it (~gun), your search will give you sites that contain the following words: gun, rifle, firearm, pistol, revolver, shooter, etc.

6. Refine your search terms as you continue to search. Some of the early sites you come across may not be what you need, but these sites may suggest new search terms to try. Also, watch for hyperlinks in every site you visit. A less-than-productive site may allow you to "jump" to a productive one.

7. If you have more than one search term, type the most important terms first. For example, if you are looking for sites on the incompatibility grounds of divorce, your query might be *+divorce +incompatibility +grounds* (or *divorce AND incompatibility AND grounds*).

8. Search the invisible Web to try to find materials that are not picked up by regular search engines or directories. For sites that help you search the invisible Web, see Exhibit 13.10.

(continues)

EXHIBIT 13.9	Internet Search Techniques and Assessing the Reliability of What You Find—*continued*

9. Once you are in a site, you can sometimes use the find command (e.g., ctrl-F) to try to find your search terms within the pages of the site.

10. Need the definition of a legal term? Use the powerful definition search feature available on many search engines. For example, run the following search on Google: define:habeas corpus.

11. Once you have found something on the Internet through these techniques, you need to assess its reliability. The old saying "You can't believe everything you read in the newspaper" applies with greater force to what you read on the Internet. Because the Internet is essentially unregulated, anyone can post whatever they want on the information superhighway. The expensive fee-based sites we examined earlier (Westlaw and LexisNexis) are very reliable because of the large editorial staffs they employ. This is rarely so with free Internet sites. For the latter, keep the following guidelines in mind:

   ■ In general, the most reliable free sites are those with government domains (.gov) and with educational institution domains (.edu). Many sites with business domains (.com) can also be reliable, although their need to sell you something can color what they say. The reliability of association sites (.org) depends on the quality and reputation of the association.

   ■ At the bottom of any page on a site, particularly its homepage, look for the "Updated On" or "Last Updated" date as an indication of how current the material is. Be extra cautious of sites that do not provide such dates.

   ■ Find out who owns the site (e.g., enter the address of the site at www.whois.net).

   ■ The most reliable sites have "About Me" or "About Us" links that will provide background information about the authors of the site. This can help you assess reliability.

   ■ Approach Wiki sites with added care. These are sites that allow anyone to add content; they have a collaborative authorship. (Interactive sites of this kind are said to be part of *Web 2.0*, the so-called next generation of the Internet, in which end users participate in the creation of Web sites by adding to, editing, or modifying the content of the sites. Other examples of interactive Web 2.0 sites include YouTube, MySpace, and *tagging* sites such as del.icio.us and Flickr, in which users add labels to sites and images that others use to help them find and assess what is available. Web 2.0 is essentially a collection of add-your-own-content sites.) The most widely used example of a Wiki site is the online encyclopedia, Wikipedia (wikipedia.org). Hundreds of thousands of people with varying degrees of expertise have written the sections of this encyclopedia. The final guideline on the reliability of data in Web sites applies to all sites, including Wiki sites:

   ■ Don't rely on the data in a site unless you can verify it on at least one other site or in a non-Internet source.

   For more information on determining the reliability of Internet sites, see:

   ▪ www.marquette.edu/library/search/evaluatingweb.html

   ▪ www.library.jhu.edu/researchhelp/general/evaluating/index.html

   ▪ www.lib.vt.edu/help/instruct/evaluate/evaluating.html

   ▪ www.hopetillman.com/findqual.html

A **search engine** is a search tool that will find sites on the Internet that contain terms you enter on any subject. The terms you enter are sometimes called key words. Another major search tool is the **directory**, which allows for a more focused search. When you use a directory, you first select a broad subject from a short list that you think fits the category of information you want. Here are some of the commonly used subject categories in directories:

Art	Entertainment	International	Shopping
Business	Fitness	Lifestyle	Sports
Careers	Games	News	Travel
Computers	Government	Reference	Weather
Education	Health	Science	

Once you select the subject, you click through numerous subcategories of that subject until you find what you want. Examples of good directories are Yahoo (dir.yahoo.com), Open Directory (dmoz.org) and the Librarians' Internet Index (www.lii.org).

There are a large number of search engines and directories on the Internet. Here are some of the variations that exist among them:

   ■ Some search sites are a combination of search engine and directory.

   ■ Some search sites allow you to conduct **metasearches**, which search for your terms in more than one search engine simultaneously.

   ■ Some search engines allow you to search in natural language; in these sites, you type your queries in everyday sentences (e.g., *Where can I find the address of the IRS?*).

   ■ Some search sites allow you to search the **invisible Web**, which consists of sites that contain specialized databases or formats that are not reached by traditional search engines.

Exhibit 13.10 contains a list of some of the most important search engines, directories, and their variations.

search engine A search tool that will find sites on the Internet that contain terms you enter on any subject.

directory A search tool in which you select from a list of broad subject categories and then keep clicking through subcategories of that subject until you find what you want.

metasearch A search for terms in more than one search engine simultaneously.

invisible Web That part of the Internet that is not found by traditional search engines.

| **EXHIBIT 13.10** | **Search Engines and Directories** |

MAJOR SITES

Lists of Available Search Engines and Directories
searchenginewatch.com/showPage.html?page=links
www.searchenginecolossus.com
www.top100-search.com
www.refdesk.com/newsrch.html

Search Engine Comparison Charts
www.llrx.com/features/searchenginechart.htm
www.infopeople.org/search/chart.html
www.searchengineshowdown.com/features
www.mlb.ilstu.edu/ressubj/subject/intrnt/srcheng.htm
www.lib.berkeley.edu/TeachingLib/Guides/Internet/SearchEngines.html

Glossary of Search Engine Terms
searchenginewatch.com/showPage.html?page=2156001
www.searchenginedictionary.com

General Search Engines
www.google.com
www.yahoo.com
www.ask.com
www.altavista.com
www.live.com
www.alltheweb.com
www.excite.com
www.lycos.com
www.webcrawler.com

Metasearch Engines
(searches more than one search engine simultaneously)
www.dogpile.com
vivisimo.com
www.kartoo.com
www.mamma.com
www.surfwax.com
www.ixquick.com
clusty.com

Directories: Browsing by Subjects or Topics
dir.yahoo.com
directory.google.com
search.looksmart.com
dmoz.org
about.com
www.lii.org
www.refdesk.com

Natural Language Searching
www.ask.com
www.webcrawler.com

Searching the Invisible Web
en.wikipedia.org/wiki/Deep_web
www.powerhomebiz.com/vol25/invisible.htm
aip.completeplanet.com
www.lib.berkeley.edu/TeachingLib/Guides/Internet/InvisibleWeb.html

LEGAL RESEARCH ON THE INTERNET

There are numerous free online resources that provide access to primary authority such as constitutions, statutes, cases, court rules, ordinances, charters, and international law. Many of them are operated or sponsored by government entities. Hence, they are among the most reliable sites on the Internet. They may not always be as current as paid services such as Westlaw, LexisNexis, and Loislaw, but they are improving in this regard.

Exhibit 13.11 presents an overview of some of the major online legal resources. Although these sites can be very helpful in doing legal research, you should not neglect the general search sites in Exhibit 13.10 when trying to do online legal research. On Google, Alltheweb, and Altavista, for example, entering the search terms "search and seizure" or "adverse possession" can be very productive.

| **EXHIBIT 13.11** | **Legal Research on the Internet** |

The Law of Your State
govengine.com
www.statelocalgov.net
www.prairienet.org/~scruffy/f.htm
www.romingerlegal.com
www.washlaw.edu/uslaw/states/allstates
www.loc.gov/rr/news/stategov/stategov.html
www.legalengine.com

Federal Law
www.washlaw.edu/reflaw/reflawfed.html
www.fedworld.gov
www.fedworld.gov/govlinks.html

Legal Forms
forms.lp.findlaw.com
www.ilrg.com/forms.html
www.lectlaw.com//form.html
www.formsguru.com

Court Rules (Rules of Court)
www.llrx.com/courtrules

Public Records Search
www.brbpub.com/pubrecsitesStates.asp
www.brbpub.com
www.publicrecordfinder.com
www.50states.com/publicrecords

(continues)

EXHIBIT 13.11	Legal Research on the Internet—*continued*

Comprehensive General Legal Sites

www.findlaw.com
www.plol.org
www.hg.org
www.law.cornell.edu
www.catalaw.com
www.law.indiana.edu/v-lib
www.alllaw.com
www.ilrg.com
www.washlaw.edu/reflaw/reflaw.html
www.legalengine.com

Legal Research Guides

www.washlaw.edu/reflaw/researchguides.html
www.ll.georgetown.edu/research/index.cfm
lib.law.washington.edu/ref/guides.html
www.law.harvard.edu/library/services/research/guides
www.wm.edu/law/lawlibrary/research/researchguides
lawscout.uakron.edu
www.law.gwu.edu/Burns/Research/Library+Publications.htm

Legal Research by Subject Matter

(e.g., bankruptcy, women's rights, etc.)
lib.law.washington.edu/ref/guides.html
jurist.law.pitt.edu/subj_gd.htm
www.lexisnexis.com/infopro/zimmerman
search.lii.org/index.jsp?more=SubTopic6
www.ilrg.com/subject_ref.html
dir.yahoo.com/Government/Law/Web_Directories

www.netronline.com/frameset.asp?StateID=37
www.searchsystems.net
www.virtualchase.com/topics/introduction_public_records.shtml
www.oatis.com/publicrecords.htm
www.pretrieve.com
www.knowx.com
www.dr-rec-fac.com
www.ancestry.com/search/rectype/military/main/main.htm
www2.genealogy.com/ssdi_cgi/gen_foot4.html
www.cdc.gov/nchs/howto/w2w/w2welcom.htm
www.vitalrec.com
www.vitalchek.com

Legal News

www.washlaw.edu/reflaw/reflegalnews.html
news.findlaw.com
www.law.com

International Law

www.un.org/law
www.law.cornell.edu/wex/index.php/International_law
www.findlaw.com/01topics/24international
en.wikipedia.org/wiki/International_law

Factual Research

(background investigations, finding people, locating assets, business directories, government statistics, maps, etc.)
(See "Helpful Web Sites" at the end of chapter 9.)

FACTUAL RESEARCH ON THE INTERNET

For leads to factual research on the Internet, see chapter 9, particularly the "Helpful Web Sites" at the end of chapter 9.

ASSIGNMENT 13.2

For each of the following questions, use general search engines, directories, or legal search sites. (You can check the sites listed in Exhibits 13.10 and 13.11, although you are not limited to these sites. You can also use the sites in the section called "Helpful Web Sites" at the end of the chapter.) For each answer, give the complete uniform resource locator (URL) you used, the name of the site, and the date you visited it.

(a) List any three civil rights organizations. What is the cost of an annual membership in each?

(b) In any three states, find an attorney or law firm with experience in bank mergers.

(c) In any three states, find an independent paralegal who represents clients at social security hearings. Describe the services offered by each.

(d) How many legal abortions were performed in the United States in 1980, 1990, and 2000?

(e) In your state and in any two others, what is the minimum age someone must be to enter a valid marriage without the consent of his or her parents or guardians?

(f) Where can you obtain copies of appellate briefs filed with any state court in your state and with the U.S. Court of Appeals that covers your state? (See Exhibit 6.3 in chapter 6.)

(g) Identify every paralegal listserv on the Internet and give instructions on how to subscribe to each one. (See the next section on listservs.)

LISTSERVS

A **listserv** is a program that manages computer mailing lists automatically. These lists consist of individuals interested in receiving and sending **e-mail** (electronic mail) to each other on a topic of mutual interest. Thousands of topics are covered on listservs, e.g., travel, hobbies, job

listserv A program that manages computer mailing lists automatically, including the receipt and distribution of messages from and to members of the list.

e-mail A message sent electronically.

searching, and cancer. Numerous *legal listservs* cover a large variety of law and law-related topics, e.g., bankruptcy, law office management, job hunting, and the law of a particular state. (For sites that will tell you how to subscribe to listservs on legal topics, including those devoted to paralegal issues, see "Helpful Web Sites" at the end of the chapter.) Once you have subscribed to a list, you can read the comments, questions, and replies sent by everyone else on the list. By reading these messages, you can keep abreast of developments in the subject matter of the group.

Here are examples of the kinds of questions that might be posed on different listservs. On a paralegal listserv, a paralegal asks:

> I'm thinking about taking either NALA's certification exam (CLA) or NFPA's certification exam (PACE). Have any of you taken both so that you can give me some comparison?

A California paralegal member of a real estate listserv asks:

> We have a client who bought and sold land in Georgia in 1985, I'm trying to find a copy of the standard purchase agreement used by the Georgia Association of Real Estate Agents in the 1970s before they substantially changed the format of the contract. Anyone in Georgia who can help me? If you can fax me a copy, I'd appreciate it. Help!

At the beginning of the week, a New York attorney, in immediate need of locating Mississippi regulations on nursing homes, sends out the following urgent e-mail to the members of his listserv:

> I'm looking for the Mississippi Department of Health regulations on nursing homes. I didn't find them on Westlaw or Lexis. The Department tells me it can't supply them until Friday. Anyone willing to FedEx the sections I need using my firm's account number?

Someone who uses a Word word processor sends this e-mail to members of a Word users listserv:

> I just got the upgrade and I can't get it to hook up with my HP 6620 printer. Are any of you out there using the upgrade with this printer? Were you able to get the two to work together?

Depending on the number of members in the listserv, you could receive scores of replies. Many members who have had their questions answered send "thanks-for-saving-my-life" messages to the group. Even if you do not send any questions yourself, you will probably find it instructive—and fun—to read the questions and answers others are sending to each other on topics that are relevant to your work. (Reading online messages of others without sending any of your own is called *lurking*.)

It is possible to attach documents, pictures, and programs to e-mail messages. Unfortunately, these attachments can be extremely dangerous. There are individuals around the world who send out millions of e-mail messages with attachments that contain **viruses**. By reproducing themselves, the viruses can damage or destroy data on the computers of recipients who unwittingly open the infected attachments. A virus can go into your online address book, capture all the addresses you have there, and send each of them a message that appears to be coming from you. This lulls the recipients into thinking that the attachment in the e-mail message is probably safe to open since it comes from someone they know—you. Once they open the attachment, however, their computers become infected with the virus. To try to protect yourself, you need to install **firewalls** and other security systems covering all aspects of Internet use. Many cautious computer users refuse to open any attachment unless they have been told *in advance* by the sender that a message will be coming with an attachment.

The danger posed by e-mail is not limited to participation in listservs. Every e-mail message you send out or receive can potentially be read by others. When confidentiality is needed, cautious e-mail users have their messages **encrypted**. This converts the message into a code that renders it unreadable until an authorized recipient can unscramble it (i.e., decrypt it) with special software. Another danger posed by e-mail messages is **phishing**, the fraudulent attempt to obtain your bank identification numbers or passwords and other personal information by sending you a message that has the design or appearance of a legitimate institution. Encryption won't help with this problem. You simply must resist the inclination to click open any attachment that is suspicious. Phishing is a form of **identity theft**.

Listservs are not the only way for computer users to communicate on the Internet. *Usenet* is a network of computers that offers news and discussion groups (also called newsgroups). *Internet relay chats* allow users to communicate in real time. One user types a message on the screen, and the other users can see the message on their screens as it is typed.

One of the newest features of the Internet is the web log, called a **blog** (or weblog). It is an online journal or diary in which you give your personal thoughts on any topic. You could simply chronicle what you do during the day, talk about your hobbies, or comment on important issues in society. You can also include links to your favorite Web sites. Thousands of blogs exist. Legal

---

virus A program that can reproduce itself and damage or destroy data on computers.

firewall Security hardware or software that limits access to your computer when you are on a network by attempting to filter out viruses and other unauthorized or potentially dangerous material.

encrypted Converted into a code that renders the data incomprehensible until they are reconverted to a readable format by an authorized recipient.

phishing The fraudulent attempt to obtain personal information by tricking the recipient of an e-mail message into believing that the sender seeking the information is legitimate.

identity theft Knowingly using a means of identification of another person with the intent to commit any unlawful activity.

blog A journal or diary available on the World Wide Web.

blogs (sometimes called *blawgs*) are often written by attorneys who provide daily commentaries about their particular areas of practice. To find blogs run by paralegals, type "paralegal blog" in any general search engine such as www.google.com. For more information on blogs, see "Helpful Web Sites" at the end of the chapter.

It is also possible to broadcast a blog as an audio file so that it can be listened to rather than read on a screen. A **podcast** (sometimes called an *audioblog*) is an Internet radio-type audio file that the public can download and listen to through a browser or on audio devices such as iPods and MP3 players. Many legal podcasts are available (e.g., "The Supreme Court Watch Podcast," "Legal Talk Network," and "The Legal Underground"). Law-related podcasts are called *plawdcasts* (www.blawg.com/Listing. aspx?CategoriesID=160).

Almost all Internet users have their list of Web sites that they visit frequently. **Bookmarking** acts as a convenient online address book for such *favorite* sites. Some Internet services (e.g., del.icio. us) allow users to tag and share favorite sites with each other. The problem is that lists of favorites can become very long. It can be time-consuming to check every favorite site to find out if anything new has been added since your last visit. Some sites let you sign up for e-mail alerts that notify you of new content. A more convenient notification system is **really simple syndication (RSS)**. Assume that you have twenty must-visit sites that contain important material (e.g., new cases on a court site, and a job opening for a paralegal on a job placement site). If these twenty sites offer RSS feeds, you can subscribe to them and receive notification whenever anything new exists on any of the sites. (When a site allows RSS feeds, it is called *syndicating its content*.) The notification is not through e-mail but through an RSS list that can be placed on your browser. You go to this list to find out which of your sites, if any, are listed. If, for example, only two of your favorite sites are on the list, you simply click on them to find out what is new. You can ignore the other eighteen. Their absence on the RSS list means there is nothing new for you to check on them.

> **podcast** An Internet audio file that the public can download and listen to through a browser or on audio devices such as iPods and MP3 players. Also called an *audioblog*.
>
> **bookmarking** Inserting the address of a *favorite* Internet site on a list in your browser so that you can easily return to the site in the future.
>
> **really simple syndication (RSS)** A method of notifying subscribers of new content (e.g., news stories or product updates) on an Internet site by syndicating (feeding) notice of the new content to subscribers.

[SECTION F]

INTRANET AND EXTRANET

Some organizations such as businesses and associations are able to set up the equivalent of a mini-Internet for internal use. It is called an **intranet**. Surfers around the globe would not have access to it. A law firm's intranet, for example, could give its employees access to:

- Vacation schedules
- Court dates of current cases
- Client databases, including current litigation documents
- Brief banks and legal forms
- A staff directory (with pictures)
- The personnel manual of the firm
- Lists of law library purchases
- Training manuals and continuing legal education (CLE) programs available at the firm

> **intranet** A private network of computers within a particular firm, company, or other organization, established so that the computers can share information online, often using features similar to those of the World Wide Web.

The employees can be in the same office or in branch offices around the world. (There are many similarities between an intranet and the local area network [LAN] and wide area network [WAN] discussed earlier.) An organization can allow selected outsiders to have online access to its intranet. (Such access converts the intranet to an **extranet**.) A law firm, for example, could permit a client to read the documents being prepared for the client on the firm's intranet.

> **extranet** That part of an intranet to which selected outsiders have been given access.

ASSIGNMENT 13.3

Each student will make a presentation in front of the class on a computer product used in a law office. You can select your own product. (The instructor must approve the product in advance to ensure that it is suitable for a presentation and that no other student has selected that product.) You can select any product mentioned in this chapter, although you are not limited to the products discussed in the chapter. The product must meet the following characteristics:

- It is a hardware or software product that is offered for sale, lease, or subscription.
- It is extensively (although not necessarily exclusively) used by law offices.
- You can find at least two vendors on the Internet that sell their own version of the product, each with its own features.

(continues)

The setting for your presentation will be a mock staff meeting of the law office where you work. You have been asked to research the product and give a presentation at the meeting. Your presentation will cover:

- A description of the function of the product, including how it is used
- The pros and cons of the two versions offered by the two vendors you have found
- Your recommendation of which vendor to select

If you can, download and print photographs or drawings of the two versions of the product in order to pass them around the room while you are making your presentation. If needed, you can make any reasonable assumptions about the office where you work such as what equipment it already has.

While you are making your presentation, the staff members in the room (i.e., your fellow students) will be asking you questions about the product. To be able to answer such questions, your research on the product must be substantial. Try to find product reviews by consumers that are posted on the Internet (e.g., www.epinions.com).

In addition to your presentation, prepare a written report on the two versions of the product. This will be for staff members who could not be present at your presentation but who will need the same information.

Chapter Summary

The computer plays a major role in the practice of law. You need to take every opportunity to learn as much as you can about computers. Take short-term computer courses available in the community, attend computer events at paralegal and bar associations, peruse the Internet sites of law firms, try out different search engines, take online tutorials, etc.

Hardware is the physical equipment of a computer system. Software is a computer program that tells the hardware what to do. The two main categories of software are operating or systems software (programs that tell the computer how to operate all its parts) and applications software (programs that perform specific tasks for end users). Input devices that place information in a computer include the keyboard, the mouse, speech recognition programs, and scanners. The central processing unit (CPU) is the hardware that controls all of the computer's parts. The two main kinds of memory are read-only memory (ROM) and random access memory (RAM). Data in memory are measured in bytes. Storage devices with read/write capability allow users to read the data on the device and write additional data on the device. You cannot write data on a read-only device. Major storage devices include hard drives, floppy drives, flash drives, magnetic tape systems, CD–ROM drives, CD–R drives, CD–RW drives, and DVD–ROM drives. A paper or hard copy of a computer-created document is made on a printer that can print text in different point sizes and fonts. Computers at different locations can exchange data by using communications devices such as modems. Computers can be connected by a local area network (LAN) (if they are relatively close to each other) or by a wide area network (WAN) (if they are not close). Backup strategies are essential in view of how easy it is to erase digital data.

A word processor is a software program that allows you to enter and edit data in documents. Special formatting features and shortcuts using macros make the creation of documents relatively easy. When sending documents created on word-processing and other software programs, care is needed to avoid sending inappropriate metadata. A spreadsheet is a software program that automatically performs calculations on numbers and values that you enter. Database management software allows you to organize, search, retrieve, and sort information or data. Presentation graphics software is used to present text data with charts, graphs, video, and sound in order to communicate the data most effectively. Litigation support software helps a law office store, retrieve, and track the potentially large volume of data involved in litigation. Case management or docket control software helps a law office maintain control over its appointments and deadlines. KM (knowledge management) software helps a law office capture and reuse its knowledge base.

The main fee-based sources of computer-assisted legal research (CALR) for primary and secondary authority are Westlaw and LexisNexis. Numerous business, medical, and social data are also available on both systems. There are two methods of phrasing search queries: natural language (using everyday sentences) and terms and connectors (stating relationships between the terms of the search). The universal character (*) stands for any character in a search term. The root expander (!) stands for any one or more characters added to the root of a word. Typing the singular form of a word in Westlaw and LexisNexis will also find its plural. The connectors include the OR connector (space in Westlaw, OR in LexisNexis); the AND connector; the sentence connector; the paragraph connector; the BUT NOT or AND NOT connector; and the numerical connector. To search for a phrase in Westlaw, use quotation marks; in LexisNexis, simply type the phrase. It is possible to limit a search to a portion of a document (fields in Westlaw, segments in LexisNexis). Both Westlaw and LexisNexis have online citators and allow you to retrieve a document if you already know its citation.

The Internet is a self-governing network of networks on which millions of computer users share information all over the world. The hypertext features of the World Wide Web allow relatively easy access to a vast quantity of data. The major search tool is the search engine. Check its help feature to identify its unique search techniques. Once you have found something on the Internet, you must assess its reliability. A listserv (a program that manages computer mailing lists automatically) can be a useful way to keep current on specialty topics. A blog (an online journal or diary) on legal topics can also be useful. (Legal blogs are called *blawgs*.) Podcasts are Internet audio files. (Those on legal topics are called *plawdcasts*.) RSS feeds simplify the task of checking new content on favorite sites. Virus protection strategies (e.g., firewalls) are essential. Cautious computer users encrypt confidential e-mail messages. Intranets use Internet technology to allow members of a single company or organization to communicate with each other. When selected outsiders are allowed to have access to an intranet, it becomes an extranet.

Key Terms

hardware	point	case management	Internet service provider
software	font	tickler	World Wide Web (WWW)
operating system	modem	statute of limitations	hypertext
booting up	real time	default judgment	uniform resource locator
applications software	videoconference	brief bank	(URL)
cursor	local area network (LAN)	knowledge management	Web browser
mouse	groupware	(KM)	server
speech recognition	shareware	computer-assisted legal	search engine
scanner	wide area network	research (CALR)	directory
imaging	(WAN)	online	metasearch
central processing unit	stand-alone computer	Westlaw	invisible Web
(CPU)	integrated package	LexisNexis	listserv
memory	download	primary authority	e-mail
read-only memory	patch	secondary authority	virus
(ROM)	word processor	query	firewall
random access memory	right justified	natural language	encrypted
(RAM)	macro	terms and connectors	phishing
byte	table of authorities	universal character	identity theft
read/write	metadata	root expander	blog
read-only	spreadsheet	wildcard	podcast
hard disk	database management	field	bookmarking
CD–ROM	presentation graphics	segment	really simple syndication (RSS)
PDA	litigation support	citator	intranet
hard copy	full-text search	Internet	extranet

Review Questions

1. What are some of the computer questions you may be asked during an employment interview?
2. What self-help steps can you take to further your training about computers?
3. Distinguish between hardware and software.
4. Distinguish between operating system software and applications software.
5. What are the major operating systems in use today?
6. What is open-source software?
7. Briefly describe the major input devices.
8. What are PDF and XPS?
9. What is the function of the CPU?
10. What is the distinction between read/write and read-only?
11. Briefly describe the major storage devices.
12. Distinguish between ink-jet and laser printers.
13. Distinguish between points and fonts.
14. What is the function of a modem?
15. What is videoconferencing?
16. Distinguish between a LAN and a WAN.
17. Distinguish between groupware and shareware.
18. What backup steps should be regularly taken?
19. What is integrated software?
20. Distinguish between custom-made and off-the-shelf software.
21. What is the function of word-processing software?
22. What is a macro?
23. Why have many law offices switched from WordPerfect to Word?
24. What are metadata?
25. What is the function of spreadsheet software?

26. Give an example of a what-if calculation a spreadsheet can perform.
27. What is the function of database management software?
28. What is the function of presentation graphics software?
29. Distinguish between searching databases by full text and searching by summaries or abstracts.
30. What is the function of case management software?
31. What is the function of knowledge management (KM)?
32. What is CALR?
33. How are Westlaw and LexisNexis accessed?
34. What are some of the major categories of primary and secondary authority found on Westlaw and LexisNexis?
35. Distinguish between a natural-language search and a terms-and-connectors search.
36. What is the function of the following wildcards in Westlaw and LexisNexis: a universal character (*) and a root expander (!)?
37. How do you search for plural terms in Westlaw and LexisNexis?
38. In Westlaw and in LexisNexis, explain how to use the following connectors: OR, AND, sentence, paragraph, BUT NOT/AND NOT, and numerical.

39. Distinguish between a field search on Westlaw and a segment search on LexisNexis.
40. What are the names and functions of the online citators of Westlaw and LexisNexis?
41. What is the Internet, and how was it created?
42. What is the function of hypertext?
43. What are the components of a URL address?
44. What are some of the major techniques for searching the Internet?
45. What is the distinction between a search engine and a directory?
46. What is a metasearch?
47. What is the invisible Web?
48. How can you assess the reliability of data found on the Internet?
49. What are listservs, blogs, blawgs, podcasts, plawdcasts, and RSS feeds? How can they be helpful?
50. What steps should be taken to protect your computer against viruses and other potentially dangerous material?
51. What is the distinction between an intranet and an extranet?

Helpful Web Sites: More on the Use of Computers in the Law

Online Dictionary of Computer Terms
- www.webopedia.com
- foldoc.org
- www.csgnetwork.com/glossary.html
- www.computeruser.com/resources/dictionary
- www.learnthenet.com/english/glossary/glossary.htm

Law Office Technology Resources
- www.abanet.org/tech/ltrc
- marketcenter.findlaw.com/software.html
- spellex.com/legalblog
- www.lexisone.com/legalresearch/legalguide/ legal_guide_index.html (click "Law Office Software Center")
- www.lawofficecomputing.com

Tutorials
- www.sc.edu/beaufort/library/pages/bones/bones.shtml
- www.livinginternet.com
- www.legalspreadsheets.com
- www.searchenginewatch.com/resources/tutorials.html
- www.lib.berkeley.edu/TeachingLib/Guides/Internet/ FindInfo.html
- www.anniston.lib.al.us/computerinternettutorial.htm
- www.comptechdoc.org/basic/basictut

Software Manufacturers
- www.microsoft.com
- www.corel.com
- www.abacuslaw.com
- www.compulaw.com

- www.amicusattorney.com
- www.casesoft.com
- www.summation.com

Metadata
- en.wikipedia.org/wiki/Metadata
- www.library.uq.edu.au/iad/ctmeta4.html

Intranets
- www.hotoffice.com
- www.intranetjournal.com
- en.wikipedia.org/wiki/Intranet

Legal Listservs
- www.washlaw.edu/listserv
- www.washlaw.edu/discussion
- www.lsoft.com/lists/listref.html
- tile.net/lists
- groups.yahoo.com
- groups.google.com

Paralegal Listservs
- www.legalassistanttoday.com/lat-forum
- legalminds.lp.findlaw.com/list/law-lib/msg09536.html

Legal Blogs
- www.blawg.com
- blawgsearch.justia.com
- law-library.rutgers.edu/resources/lawblogs.php
- legalblogwatch.typepad.com
- 3lepiphany.typepad.com/3l_epiphany/2006/03/ a_taxonomy_of_l.html

Paralegal Blogs

- paralegalgateway.typepad.com/my_weblog
- texasparalegal.typepad.com
- estrinlegaled.typepad.com
- indianaparalegals.blogspot.com
- paralegalonline.blogspot.com
- www.blawg.com/Listing.aspx?CategoriesID=34
- www.niqabiparalegal.com

Computer Security

- www.microsoft.com/protect/computer/basics/virus.mspx
- en.wikipedia.org/wiki/Computer_security
- computersecuritynews.us
- www.tulane.edu/~dmsander/Big_Virology/BVHomePage.html

Google Searches (run the following searches for more sites)

- introduction to computers
- computer tutorials
- legal software
- westlaw tutorial
- lexis tutorial
- "law on the internet"
- internet search techniques
- blawg
- legal listserv
- intranet

Endnotes

1. C. Estrin & S. Hunt, *The Successful Paralegal Job Search Guide* 71, 236 (2001).
2. Brent Roper, *Using Computers in the Law* 27 (4th ed. 2004).
3. Florida Rules of Appellate Procedure, Rule 9.100(l). See also www.1dca.org/notice.pdf.
4. Roper, supra note 2 at 33.
5. Within a macro, you can also insert certain commands such as saving the document or inserting a number from another software application.
6. *State of Minnesota and Blue Cross and Blue Shield of Minnesota v. Philip Morris, Inc.*, Trial Transcript, Closing Argument, 1998 WL 242426 (D. Minn. May 7, 1998).
7. Roper, supra note 2, at 333.
8. See the historical overview in *American Civil Liberties Union v. Reno*, 929 F. Supp. 824, 832–34 (E.D. Pa. 1996).

Student CD-ROM
For additional materials, please go to the CD in this book.

Online Companion™
For additional resources, please go to http://www.paralegal.delmar.cengage.com

Introduction to Law Office Administration*

CHAPTER OUTLINE

[SECTION A]

THE PRACTICE OF LAW IN THE PRIVATE SECTOR

Our study of law practice management begins with some statistics:

- In 1983, there were 612,000 attorneys in the United States. In 2006, the number was 1,116,967. Approximately 33 percent are women, 5 percent are African American, and 8 percent are Asian, Hispanic, or Latino.[1]
- In 2007, there were 141,031 students enrolled in the 195 law schools in the country; just under half were women. In this year 43,920 graduates were awarded juris doctor (J.D.) or bachelor of laws (LL.B.) degrees.[2] (The J.D. and LL.B. degrees are equivalent.)
- In 2006 there were 88,991 persons who took a bar examination; 55,401 of them passed (a pass rate of approximately 67 percent).[3] (For the pass rate in your state, click "Bar Admission Statistics" at www.ncbex.org.)
- In 2004, the median earnings of attorneys were:
  - $55,000 for attorneys nine months after law school
  - $94,930 for all attorneys[4]

About 70 percent of attorneys practice in private law firms. Another 10 percent work in the legal department of corporations. The remainder practice in the public sector for government, for legal aid and legal service offices, or for organizations such as unions, trade associations, and

---

*Portions of this chapter were originally written with Robert G. Baylor, business manager at Manatt, Phelps, Rothenberg, and Tunney, Los Angeles. Others who have reviewed this chapter and provided valuable commentary include Dorothy B. Moore, Kathleen M. Reed, Michele A. Coyne, Patsy R. Pressley, Deborah L. Thompson, and Shawn A. Jones.

public interest groups, or they do not practice law at all. In this chapter, our primary focus will be on attorneys who practice law in relatively large private offices, although we will also look at other kinds of practice as well.

In the private sector, law is practiced in a variety of settings:

- Sole proprietorship
- Office-sharing arrangement
- Partnership
- Professional corporation
- Limited liability entity
- Corporate law department

SOLE PROPRIETORSHIP

Any business can be operated as a **sole proprietorship**, which means that one person—the sole proprietor—owns all the assets of the business (including all profits) and assumes all of its debts or liabilities. (The business does not have a separate legal identity.) Because this person has **personal liability**, debtors can reach his or her personal assets (e.g., a family checking account, a vacation home) *in addition to* his or her business assets (e.g., a business bank account, office furniture). If sole proprietors had **limited liability**, a debtor would be limited to their business assets when collecting business debts. The liability of sole proprietors, however, is not limited; it is personal.

Many attorneys begin their practice of law as sole proprietorships. If they practice alone, they are **sole practitioners**, also called solo practitioners. (They are said to be "going solo.") Some owner-attorneys, however, employ other attorneys. If so, the latter receive a salary rather than a share of the profits. Furthermore, these employee-attorneys do not assume the debts or liabilities of the office.

An attorney in a sole proprietorship can be a generalist or a specialist. A generalist is the equivalent of a doctor in general practice. An attorney who is a **general practitioner** often handles all kinds of cases. If, however, the case is unusually complex or if the attorney is very busy with other cases, he or she might consult with an attorney in another firm or refer the case to another attorney. Other sole practitioners specialize in one main area of the law. Their practice might be limited, for example, to tax, criminal, or patent and trademark cases, or—more commonly—to personal injury cases. (Specialty offices are sometimes called **boutique law firms** no matter how many attorneys work in them.)

Most sole proprietorships have very few employees. There is a secretary, who often performs many paralegal functions along with the traditional clerical responsibilities of typing, filing, and reception work. He or she may also perform bookkeeping chores. The most common job title of this individual is *legal secretary*, although he or she might be called a *legal assistant* or a *paralegal/secretary*. You will sometimes find job ads for small offices seeking paralegals with clerical skills. These skills are often phrased more positively as administrative or word processing skills, but they are, in essence, clerical. In recent years, however, more small offices have begun to hire one or more paralegals who are given minimal or no clerical duties. The office may also have a **law clerk**. This is a full- or part-time law office employee who is studying to be an attorney or who has graduated from law school and is waiting to pass the bar examination. (*Law clerk* is also the title of someone who provides research and writing assistance to a judge.) Another name for a worker in the office who is still a student is **legal intern**. Often unpaid, the primary goal of interns is to obtain practical experience in the law.

OFFICE-SHARING ARRANGEMENT

It can be very expensive to start a practice, particularly in high-rent areas of the country. One cost-saving alternative is **office sharing**, in which two or more attorneys with independent practices share the use and **overhead** costs of an office. For example, each pays a portion of the monthly office rent and also shares the cost of buying or leasing computers or other equipment. If the office has a secretary/receptionist, each attorney pays a part of this person's salary. The attorneys do not practice together as a partnership or corporation; in most office-sharing arrangements, each attorney practices alone in a sole proprietorship. To avoid the conflict-of-interest and confidentiality problems discussed in chapter 5, the attorneys (and their employees) must be careful in selecting clients and discussing their cases with each other.

Occasionally, a law firm will allow a newly admitted attorney to use the facilities of the firm to work on his or her own cases. Rather than charge the new attorney for this use, the law firm will ask the attorney to do some work on one or more of the firm's cases. This is another kind of office-sharing arrangement.

---

sole proprietorship A form of business that does not have a separate legal identity apart from the one person who owns all assets and assumes all debts and liabilities.

personal liability Liability that can be satisfied out of an individual's personal assets.

limited liability Restricted liability; liability that can be satisfied out of business assets, not out of personal assets.

sole practitioner An attorney who practices alone—without partners or associates in the office.

general practitioner A professional who handles any kind of case.

boutique law firm A firm that specializes primarily in one area of the law.

law clerk (1) An employee who is still in law school or who has completed law school and is waiting to pass the bar examination. (2) One who provides research and writing assistance to a judge.

legal intern A student in a law office seeking practical experience.

office sharing Attorneys who are sole practitioners share the use and overhead costs of an office.

overhead The operating expenses of a business (e.g., office rent, furniture, insurance, clerical staff) for which customers or clients are not charged a separate fee.

PARTNERSHIP

partnership A voluntary association of two or more persons to place their resources in a jointly owned business or enterprise, with a proportional sharing of profits and losses. Partners make the ultimate decisions on how the business or enterprise (e.g., law firm) should be managed.

A **partnership** is an association of two or more individuals who jointly own a business. Each partner has personal liability for the debts of the partnership. (In this respect, a partnership is similar to a sole proprietorship.) Furthermore, one partner is liable for the torts or other wrongdoing committed by another partner.

In a law partnership, the attorneys share the profits and losses of the law practice that they jointly own. If their partnership is relatively large, it will probably be organized into a series of departments (such as an antitrust department and a litigation department) based on client needs and will be managed through a series of committees (such as a recruitment committee, a library committee, and a records committee) based on the variety of support services available to the attorneys. See Exhibit 14.1 for an example of the organization structure of a large law firm.

A large partnership can include a number of different categories of attorneys, the most common of which are:

- Partners
- Associates
- Staff attorneys
- Of counsel
- Contract attorneys

EXHIBIT 14.1	Large Law Firm Organization Chart: An Example

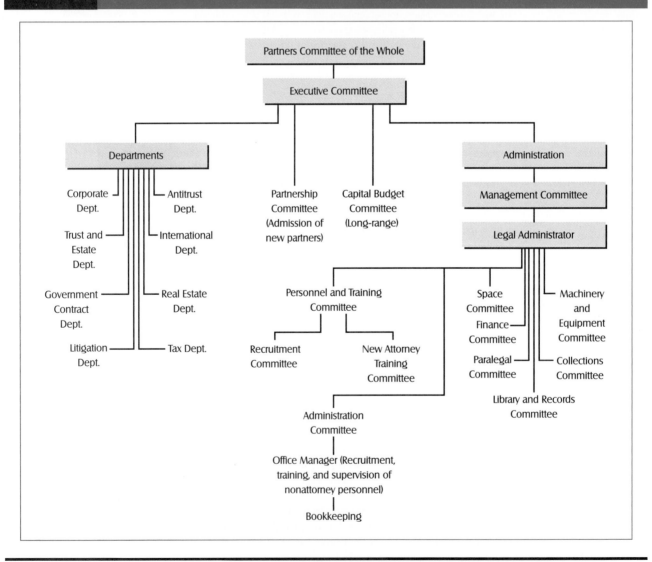

1. Partners

The founding partners contribute the capital that is needed to create the firm and to expand it as needed. They share the profits and losses of the firm pursuant to an elaborate partnership agreement. In a system referred to as "eat what you kill," the amount paid to partners often depends in large part on how much new business they generate for the firm. (Any attorney who attracts business due to contacts and/or reputation as a skilled attorney is called a **rainmaker**.) Partners decide how the firm should be managed; when to take on new partners; whether to merge with another firm; what attorneys, paralegals, and other employees to hire; etc. Most of this is done through a variety of administrative staff. In short, the partners own the firm. A firm may have different categories of partners (for example, senior partner and junior partner) depending on such factors as the amount of capital the attorney contributed to the firm and how involved he or she is in the firm's management. As we will see, a distinction also exists between equity and nonequity partners.

Generally, partners are not on salary in the traditional sense, although they do receive a periodic **draw**, which is an advance against profits (or net income) in some firms and an overhead expense in others.

> **rainmaker** An attorney who brings fee-generating cases into the office due to his or her extensive contacts and/or reputation as a skilled attorney.

> **draw** A partner's advance against profits or net income.

2. Associates

Associates are attorney employees of the firm who are hoping for a promotion to become partners. Often they are hired right out of law school while studying for the bar examination. As students, they may have worked for the firm as a law clerk. Other associates, however, are hired from other law firms. They are known as **lateral hires**. (When partners and paralegals switch law firms, they also are referred to as lateral hires.) After a certain number of years at the firm, e.g., seven, associates are usually considered for partnership. If they are *passed over* for partner, they often leave the firm to practice elsewhere, although a few may be invited to stay as a **senior associate**. This person, in effect, becomes a permanent associate.

Some firms are moving away from the "up-or-out" system because it adds great tension to the ranks of associates. To encourage good people to stay, the firms have created different tiers of partners. For example, a firm might create the category of **nonequity partner** (also called an income partner), to be distinguished from an **equity partner** (also called a capital partner). An equity partner is a full partner in the sense of owning the firm and sharing in its profits and losses. At the other end of the partner spectrum is the nonequity or income partner who has not made, or who does not aspire to become, a full partner. In effect, he or she is a permanent associate with a more inviting title.

> **associate** An attorney employee of a partnership who hopes to eventually be promoted to partner.

> **lateral hire** Anyone hired from another law office.

> **senior associate** An attorney who has been passed over for partner status but who remains at the firm.

> **nonequity partner** A special category of partner who does not own the firm in the sense of an equity or capital partner.

> **equity partner** A full owner-partner of a law firm.

3. Staff Attorneys

Staff attorneys (sometimes called second-tier attorneys) are employees hired with the understanding that they will never be considered for partnership. This is what distinguishes them from associates.

> **staff attorney** A full-time attorney employee who has no expectation of becoming a full partner.

4. Of Counsel

There is no fixed definition of this category of attorney. He or she is not a full partner or associate but has a special relationship at the firm. An attorney who is **of counsel** may be a semiretired partner or may work on a mixture of firm cases and his or her own cases. Not all firms use the title "of counsel." Some prefer "special counsel" or simply "counsel."

> **of counsel** An attorney who is semiretired or has some other special status in the law firm.

5. Contract Attorneys

Contract attorneys (sometimes called project attorneys) are hired when the firm has a temporary shortage of attorneys or needs expertise in a certain area for a limited period. Often paid on an hourly basis, the contract attorney is not a full-time employee.

> **contract attorney** An attorney hired to work for a relatively short period of time, usually on specific cases or projects.

PROFESSIONAL CORPORATION

In most states, it is possible for persons with professional licenses (e.g., attorneys) to incorporate their business as a **professional corporation** (P.C.) through which they can provide professional services. A law office that incorporates its practice uses the P.C. designation after its name, e.g., Jamison & Jamison, P.C. From a liability and estate-planning perspective, it may be more advantageous to organize as a corporation than as a partnership. An important feature of a corporation is limited liability. As we saw earlier, if the owner of a business has limited liability, his or her business debts are satisfied out of business assets, not out of personal assets. (If the owner

> **professional corporation (P.C.)** A corporation of persons performing services that require a professional license, e.g., attorneys.

has personal liability, his or her personal as well as business assets can be reached to satisfy business debts.) A disadvantage of a corporation is *double taxation:* the same income is taxed twice. First, the corporation pays corporate taxes on its income. Second, shareholders pay individual taxes on the dividends they receive from the corporation. This means that corporate earnings are taxed at the corporate level and at the shareholder level.

Like any corporation, the owners of a professional corporation are its shareholders. They elect the board of directors, who in turn appoint officers. Shareholders, directors, and officers of a professional corporation must be attorneys in order to avoid ethical violations such as nonattorney control or interference with the professional judgment of an attorney. The day-to-day operation of a professional corporation is practically identical to the operation of a traditional partnership. A client would hardly notice the difference.

LIMITED LIABILITY ENTITY

limited liability entity A company or partnership whose owners are taxed like a partnership and have the limited liability of a corporation.

Recently, a new form of organization has been developed—the **limited liability entity**. It can be a limited liability company (LLC) or a limited liability partnership (LLP). These entities are hybrid structures in that they combine features of a corporation and a partnership. The owners are taxed like a partnership (hence eliminating double taxation) and have the limited liability of a corporation.

CORPORATE LEGAL DEPARTMENT

corporate legal department A law office within a corporation containing salaried attorneys (called in-house attorneys) who advise and represent the corporation.

general counsel The chief attorney in a corporate law department.

Many large corporations have a **corporate legal department** (sometimes called the *law department*) headed by a **general counsel** (sometimes called *corporate counsel*) who may also be a vice-president of the company. Other attorneys in this office can include deputy or associate general counsel, senior attorneys, staff attorneys, etc. They are the in-house attorneys who handle the day-to-day tasks of advising the company on legal matters. They have one client—the corporation that hires them and that pays them a salary. Frequently, paralegals work with these attorneys. Other personnel may include legal administrators, legal secretaries, word processing and data processing operators, clerks, librarians, and record managers. There are, of course, no client fees. Funds to operate the department come directly from the corporate treasury. When expertise is not available "in-house," such as trial experience in a certain specialty, the general counsel will hire "outside" attorneys from other law firms.

[SECTION B]
THE LEGAL ADMINISTRATOR AND
THE PARALEGAL MANAGER

The practice of law is a profession, but it is also a business. The larger the practice, the more likely its business component will be managed by individuals whose main or sole responsibility is administration. Although the owners of a law firm have ultimate responsibility for administration, they often delegate this responsibility to others. For example, there may be a **managing partner**, often an attorney with a small case load or none at all. More and more firms are hiring new categories of management personnel who are not attorneys. We will focus on two such individuals: the **legal administrator** and the **paralegal manager**. Each has a national association: the Association of Legal Administrators (www.alanet.org) and the International Paralegal Management Association (www.paralegalmanagement.org). One way to obtain an overview of law office management is to examine the job description of the legal administrator and the paralegal manager.

managing partner A partner whose primary responsibility is management of the law firm.

legal administrator An individual, usually a nonattorney, who has responsibility for the day-to-day administration of a law office.

paralegal manager A paralegal who helps recruit, train, and supervise all paralegals in a law office.

The legal administrator works under the supervision of the managing partner or of an executive or management committee of the firm. The range of this person's responsibility, and of the business component of the practice of law, can be seen in the job description in Exhibit 14.2.

EXHIBIT 14.2	Legal Administrator: Job Description

Summary of Responsibilities

The legal administrator manages the planning, marketing, and business functions, as well as the overall operations, of a law office. He or she reports to the managing partner or the executive committee and participates in management meetings. In addition to having general responsibility for financial planning and controls, personnel administration (including compensation), systems, and physical facilities, the legal administrator also identifies and plans for the changing needs of the organization, shares responsibility with the appropriate partners for strategic planning, practice management, and marketing, and contributes to cost-effective management throughout the organization.

(continues)

EXHIBIT 14.2	Legal Administrator: Job Description—*continued*

DIRECTLY OR THROUGH A MANAGEMENT TEAM, THE LEGAL ADMINISTRATOR IS RESPONSIBLE FOR MOST OR ALL OF THE FOLLOWING:

Financial Management:
- Planning
- Forecasting
- Budgeting
- Variance analysis
- Profitability analysis
- Financial reporting
- Operations analysis
- General ledger accounting
- Rate analysis
- Billing and collections
- Cash flow control
- Banking relationships
- Investment
- Tax planning and reporting
- Trust accounting
- Payroll and pension plans
- Other related functions

Systems Management:
- Systems analysis
- Operational audits
- Procedures manual
- Cost-benefit analysis
- Computer systems design
- Programming and systems development
- Information services
- Records and library management
- Office automation
- Document construction systems
- Information storage and retrieval

- Telecommunications
- Litigation support
- Conflict-of-interest docket systems
- Legal practice systems
- Other related services

Facilities Management:
- Lease negotiations
- Space planning and design
- Office renovation
- Purchasing and inventory control
- Reprographics
- Reception/switchboard services
- Telecommunications
- Mail messenger services
- Other related functions

Human Resource Management:
- Recruitment, selection, and placement
- Orientation, training, and development
- Performance evaluation
- Salary and benefits administration
- Employee relations
- Motivation and counseling
- Discipline
- Termination
- Workers' compensation
- Personnel data systems
- Organization analysis
- Job design, development of job descriptions
- Resource allocation
- Other human resource management functions for the legal and support staff

AS A MEMBER OF THE LEGAL ORGANIZATION'S MANAGEMENT TEAM, THE LEGAL ADMINISTRATOR MANAGES AND/OR CONTRIBUTES SIGNIFICANTLY TO THE FOLLOWING:

General Management:
- Policymaking
- Strategic and tactical planning
- Business development
- Risk management
- Quality control
- Organizational development
- Other general management functions

Practice Management:
- Attorney recruiting
- Attorney training and development
- Paralegal supervision
- Work-product quality control
- Professional standards
- Substantive practice systems
- Other related functions

Marketing:
- Management of client-profitability analysis
- Forecasting of business opportunities
- Planning client development
- Marketing legal services: enhancement of the firm's visibility and image in the desired markets

Job Requirements

Knowledge: Has familiarity with legal or other professional service organizations, and experience in managing business operations, including planning, marketing, financial and personnel administration, and management of professionals.

Skills and Abilities: Able to identify and analyze complex issues and problems in management, finance, and human relations, and to recommend and implement solutions. Able to manage office functions economically and efficiently, and to organize work, establish priorities, and maintain good interpersonal relations and communications with attorneys and support staff. Excellent supervisory and leadership skills, as well as skills in written and oral communication. Demonstrated willingness and ability to delegate.

Education: Graduation from a recognized college or university with major coursework in business administration, finance, data processing, or personnel management, or comparable work experience.

Source: Reprinted with permission of the Association of Legal Administrators (www.alanet.org)

The job description of the legal administrator in Exhibit 14.2 fits an individual who works for a law office that is fairly large. The support staff for such an office can also be quite extensive. Here are some examples:[5]

Administrative Support Staff in a Large Law Office

Legal administrator	Secretaries
Paralegal manager	Data processing operators

Personnel manager	Word processing supervisor
Records information manager	Word processors
Employee benefits manager	Proofreaders
Recruiter	Docket clerks
Director of marketing	Computer specialists
Facilities manager	Equipment managers
Risk manager	File room clerks
Office manager	Librarian
Financial manager	Library aides
Credit/collections manager	Messengers/pages
Chief financial officer/comptroller	Copy room clerks
Bookkeepers	Mail clerks
Analysts	Purchasing clerks
Payroll specialists	Receptionists
Accounts payable clerk	Telephone operators
Accounts receivable clerk	Reservation clerks
Time and billing assistants	

Prominent on this list is the paralegal manager, whose job description is presented in Exhibit 14.3.

EXHIBIT 14.3   Paralegal Manager: Job Description

POSITION DESCRIPTION

POSITION TITLE: Paralegal Manager

DEPARTMENT: Paralegal Administration

A. Summary

Responsible for supervision of the paralegal staff, including recruiting, coordinating work assignments, and administering all firm policies regarding the paralegal staff.

B. Primary Duties and Responsibilities

■ Recruits, hires, and orients new and temporary paralegals. When appropriate, assists in disciplinary actions and terminations.
■ Provides continuing legal education (CLE) by presenting in-house training programs and suggesting attendance at outside seminars.
■ Assigns projects to paralegals, coordinates work flow, and monitors billable and nonbillable hours.
■ Prepares financial and statistical reports including a yearly budget for the Paralegal Program, periodic employee status reports, work assignment statistics, and profitability analyses.
■ Participates in periodic and yearly salary reviews and evaluations of paralegals.
■ Participates in long-range planning of the firm, with a focus on paralegal staffing.

C. Secondary Duties and Responsibilities

■ Performs other administrative duties, including solving personnel problems; proposing new paralegal policies and administering existing firm policies; complying with labor laws; and acting as a liaison between the paralegals, attorneys, and the firm's Paralegal Committee to promote effective utilization of paralegals.

D. Reporting Relationship

    1. Reports directly to: Paralegal Committee [or to Personnel Director, Executive Director of Administration, etc.].
    2. Also works with: Internal—Litigation Support Staff; Personnel Manager, various personnel at all levels.
                                    External—Consultants, placement offices, vendors.
    3. Supervises: Directly—All paralegals, secretary.
                            Indirectly—Project clerks, other nonattorney personnel on a project-oriented basis.

E. Minimum Qualifications

    1. Education: College Degree, Post-graduate degree or paralegal certificate preferred.
    2. Experience: At least 3–5 years' experience as paralegal. Previous management background preferred.
    3. Special Skills: Computer skills, public speaking skills, financial reporting skills.

Source: Reprinted with permission of International Paralegal Management Association (IPMA) (www.paralegalmanagement.org).

The vast majority of support staff are full-time employees of the law office. Increasingly, however, law offices are considering the option of **outsourcing,** in which the office pays outside companies or services to perform tasks that would otherwise be performed by one of its own employees. Outsourcing is not new. Some tasks are regularly outsourced, e.g., printing companies (referred to as *third-party providers*) are often hired to photocopy, print, and bind the office's appellate briefs. What is new is the technology that allows easy communication with English-speaking, technically proficient, low-wage workers in foreign countries. Such workers have been able to take over some accounting and word-processing tasks. Not all outsourcing, however, involves administrative or clerical tasks. Using e-mail messages and attachments, it is relatively easy:

- to send a transcript of a deposition to an Indian service company and ask that the deposition be digested; or
- to send a statement of facts from a client case to a Pakistani service company and ask it to prepare a legal research memorandum that uses U.S. laws posted online, which are as readily accessible abroad as they are in this country.

> **outsourcing** Paying an outside company or service to perform tasks usually performed by one's own employees.

The U.S. Bureau of Labor Statistics has estimated that 12,000 legal jobs were sent offshore in 2004; the number is expected to rise to 79,000 by 2015.[5a]

Some paralegals are concerned. The National Federation of Paralegal Associations (NFPA) has issued a policy statement on the issue. It asserts that "since paralegals are highly trained and qualified professionals who provide efficient, cost-effective, and timely service to attorneys and clients, they should be utilized first and foremost for all non-attorney legal work."[5b] The concern of NFPA is not limited to job protection. When client facts and documents are sent outside the office, client confidentiality could be at risk. Recently a woman in Pakistan threatened an online posting of the medical records she was asked to transcribe unless a payment dispute was resolved to her satisfaction.[5c] As we saw in chapter 5, there could also be conflict-of-interest problems if the same foreign company provides services to persons who have adverse interests. It is difficult to predict the impact that outsourcing will have in the legal community. Thus far it has been relatively minor, but many are watching developments closely—and warily.

[SECTION C]
EXPENSES

How does a large law firm spend the fee income that it receives? A number of organizations conduct surveys to answer this question. One of the largest is the Altman Weil Survey of Law Firm Economics. Its recent survey of 360 law firms covered 17,452 attorneys and over 4,000 paralegals.[6] The average gross receipts of the law firms for the year were $371,607. To obtain these receipts, here are the billing rates and hours worked for the major fee earners in the firms:

Standard hourly billing rates

- $261 billed by equity partners/shareholders
- $178 billed by associates
- $83 billed by paralegals
- $104 billed by paralegal supervisors

Average annual billable hours worked

- 1,744 by equity partners/shareholders
- 1,842 by associates
- 1,400 by paralegals
- 1,486 by paralegal supervisors

How did the firms spend the $371,607 that they received? On average, the law firms spent:

- $8,601 per attorney for equipment. (This constituted 2.3 percent of gross receipts.)
- $25,909 per attorney for occupancy expenses. (This constituted 7 percent of gross receipts.)
- $6,002 per attorney for promotional expenses. (This constituted 1.6 percent of gross receipts.)
- $4,171 per attorney for library/reference expenses. (This constituted 1.1 percent of gross receipts.)
- $15,014 per attorney for paralegal expenses. (This constituted 4.0 percent of gross receipts.)
- $54,932 per attorney for support staff expenses. (This constituted 14.8 percent of gross receipts.)
- $37,933 per attorney for other expenses including malpractice insurance and settlement of malpractice claims. (This constituted 10.2 percent of gross receipts.)

These and other expenses totaled $152,562 per firm. The income available to the attorneys in the firm after paying these expenses was $219,045 (calculated by subtracting $152,562 from gross receipts of $371,607). Attorney income constituted 59 percent of gross receipts. (See Exhibit 14.4.)

| **EXHIBIT 14.4** | **Average Income and Expenses Per Attorney as a Percentage of Receipts** |

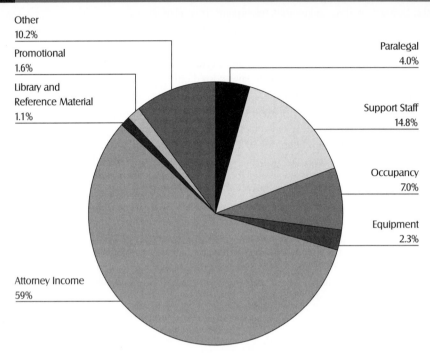

Other
10.2%

Promotional
1.6%

Library and
Reference Material
1.1%

Paralegal
4.0%

Support Staff
14.8%

Occupancy
7.0%

Equipment
2.3%

Attorney Income
59%

Source: Survey of Law Firm Economics. Reprinted with permission of Altman Weil, Inc. (www.altmanweil.com)

[SECTION D]
TIMEKEEPING

timekeeping Recording time spent on a client matter for purposes of billing and productivity assessment. Individuals who must record their time (e.g., attorneys and paralegals) are called timekeepers.

Abraham Lincoln's famous statement that a "lawyer's time is his stock in trade" is still true today. Effective **timekeeping** is critical to the success of a law firm. In some firms, it is an obsession, as typified by the following story. A senior partner in a very prestigious Wall Street law firm walked down the corridor to visit Howard, another senior partner at the firm. Upon entering the room, he was startled to find his colleague on the floor writhing in pain, apparently due to a heart attack. Standing there, he could think of only one thing to say to him: "Howard, are your time sheets in?"[7]

In some firms, the pressures of the clock on timekeepers (e.g., attorneys and paralegals) can be enormous:

[Y]oung lawyers often are shocked to discover their new employer's time expectations. Many firms in major cities require as many as 2,400 billable hours per year. When one considers that many full-time employees outside of the law only work 2,000 hours per year, the time commitment required by these firms is staggering.[8]

The cry for billable hours is thought by many to be at the heart of much of the problem. Many legal assistants as well as attorneys have quotas of billable hours. Zlaket [the president of the State Bar of Arizona] stated that some firms require 2,200 hours a year and he deems this to be outrageous. He suggested that this only leads to padding of bills and time sheets, and it leads to unnecessary work that will be paid by somebody.[9]

The ethical dimensions of this problem are considered in chapter 5. Here, our concern is the administration of the timekeeping and billing system.

To gain an understanding of how a timekeeping and billing system might work in many large law firms, we will now trace the accounting route taken by a client's *case* (sometimes called a *matter*) within a law firm. After the initial client interview, the accounting starting point can be a **new file worksheet** (see Exhibit 14.5). It is also sometimes referred to as a *new matter sheet* or a *new business sheet*. The new file worksheet becomes the source document for the creation of all the necessary accounting records involved in working on a new client case or matter. As the example in Exhibit 14.5 demonstrates, the new file worksheet can also be used to record data that will help identify possible conflicts of interest. (See chapter 5 for the ethical rules on conflicts of interest.)

new file worksheet A form used by some law firms that is the source document for the creation of all necessary accounting records that are needed when a law firm begins working on a new client case or matter.

EXHIBIT 14.5	New File Worksheet

NEW CLIENT/MATTER/CONFLICT FORM

Client Number: **Matter Number:**   **Client Phone:**
                                                        Client Fax:
                                              Client E-Mail Address:

Client Name and Address: Billing Name and Address:

Attn: **Attn:**

Biller			Originator			Responsible		
Name	Net ID	Pct	Name	Net ID	Pct	Name	Net ID	Pct
		%			%			%
		%			%			%
		%			%			%
		%			%			%
(Percent must = 100%)		100%			100%			100%

MATTER NAME:
CASE SYNOPSIS/COMMENTS:

PARENT/RELATED CLIENT:
CLIENT'S REF. NUMBER:
BUSINESS TYPE:
PRACTICE GROUP CODE:
INVOICE STYLE CODE:
COUNTRY CODE:
SIC CODE:
CASE CODE:

[NONSTANDARD FEE ARRANGEMENTS (OTHER THAN CONTINGENT) REQUIRE THE WRITTEN APPROVAL OF THE PRACTICE GROUP CHAIR. CONTINGENT FEE ARRANGEMENTS REQUIRE THE COMPLETION OF A CONTINGENT FEE INTAKE INFORMATION FORM AND WRITTEN APPROVAL OF THE CONTINGENT FEE COMMITTEE.]

FEE ARRANGEMENT	BILLING CYCLE

Billing Attorney:_____   Practice Group Chair:_____

September 17, 2008   Completed by :   /

CONFLICT CHECK

Billing Attorney:

Client Name:

Client Number, if not new:

Matter Name:

Matter Address (if matter name is a company different from client):

Standard Industrial Code (SIC), if known:

Case Synopsis/Comments: _____

These questions are designed to identify potential conflicts of interest. Examples given are for illustration only. Please be complete in responding to the questions. Additional Name/Relationship information may be added after the form is assembled by adding rows to the existing table.

CLIENT IDENTIFICATION (new clients only):

 If the client is a corporation, please provide, to the extent possible, the name(s) of all corporate parents and subsidiaries (including sister subsidiaries): If there is a different "real party in interest," *e.g.,* the beneficiary of our trustee or other fiduciary client, or the client of the law firm or accounting firm for whom we provide local or special representation, please provide, to the extent possible, the name of each such person or entity.

POTENTIALLY ADVERSE PARTIES:

 In *litigation*, please identify, to the extent possible, all other parties, including co-defendants, co-plaintiffs, intervenors and third parties. In *enforcement of remedies cases*, please identify, to the extent possible, all other lien claimants, etc. In *commercial or corporate transactions*, please identify, to the extent possible, all potentially adverse individuals or entities, such as the purchaser when we represent the seller; the lessee when we draft a lease for the lessor, etc. Please identify, to the extent possible, all other potentially adverse individuals or entities.

****

FOR ADMINISTRATIVE USE

New Business Department:

 Conflict check performed and report attached — no potential conflicts found.

 Signature _____

 Date _____

                    OR

Potential conflicts found and report sent to Billing Attorney.

 Signature _____

 Date _____

Billing Attorney:

 Sign only <u>after</u> resolving potential conflicts and forward to New Business Department.

 Billing Attorney's Signature _____

 Printed Name _____

 Date _____

As timekeepers, attorneys and paralegals must keep an account of the time they spend on behalf of a client. Time records are needed for accurate billing of every client who is charged by the hour. Of course, all clients do not pay by the hour. A firm may be charging its client a flat fee under arrangements we will examine later in the chapter. Yet even in flat-fee cases, there are management reasons for keeping accurate time records. One of the ways to determine whether a particular case or client is profitable is to know how much time was needed to complete the work involved. Without time records, however, this is not always easy to determine when every individual in the office is probably working on more than one case simultaneously. Accurate time records are valuable management tools even in corporations where the corporate law office is financed out of the corporate treasury rather than out of fees. Decisions on whether to hire additional staff or to lay off present staff depend, in part, on knowing how much time is needed to complete certain tasks and who is and is not meeting those expectations.

Many paralegals keep their own timesheets, even if they are not required to do so by their employer. In fact, some paralegals have two sets: the timesheets required by their employer and the even more meticulous timesheets that they keep as part of their personal files. Detailed timesheets allow the paralegal to track time spent on billable and nonbillable tasks and can be invaluable when making an argument for a raise or when someone raises questions about events that occurred weeks or months ago.

statutory fee case A case applying a special statute that gives a judge authority to order the losing party to pay the winning party's attorney and paralegal fees.

As we saw in chapter 1, a losing party can be forced to pay the attorney and paralegal fees of the winning party in special **statutory fee cases** such as those alleging civil rights or environmental violations. To claim such fees, the winning side must be prepared to give the court detailed records of the time spent on these cases. Judges sometimes reject requests for paralegal fees because the requests fail to provide adequate documentation that shows (1) that the time spent by the paralegal was on substantive (as opposed to clerical) tasks and (2) that the work was not duplicative of the work of others in the office. In the main, the documentation consists of timesheets, which are offered into evidence at the time of the fee request.

There are two main ways that time is recorded: by using paper forms or by using the computer. Some firms initially ask their timekeepers to record their time on paper forms, which are then coded into (i.e., transferred to) the computer for assessment and billing.

daily time sheet A paper form on which timekeepers record how much time they spend on particular client matters.

A commonly used paper form is the **daily time sheet** (see Exhibit 14.6). This form becomes the journal from which all time entries are posted to individual clients. Suppose, for example, that a paralegal spends some time summarizing or digesting a deposition. Using the abbreviations at the top of the daily time sheet, the "Description of Work" in the third column of Exhibit 14.6 might be "digesting DEPO."

Note that the last column of Exhibit 14.6 asks for the amount of time taken for each task. Law firms often use tenths of an hour (increments of six minutes) as the base unit for the measurement

---

EXHIBIT 14.6	Daily Time Sheet

DAILY SERVICE REPORT OF: James O'Brien   DATE: 1/28/08

ANS –Answer	DEPO –Deposition	K –Contract	O –Order	RES –Research
APP –Appearance or Attending	DIC –Dictation	L –Legal	OP –Opinion	REV –Revision
ARG –Argue or Argument	DOC –Document	LT –Letter to	P –Preparation	S –Settlement
BR –Brief	DR –Drafting	LF –Letter from	PL –Plaintiff	TF –Telephone from
COMP –Complaint	F –Facts	MT –Memorandum to	PR –Praecipe	TT –Telephone to
CW –Conference–Office	FL –File	MF –Memorandum from	PRT –Pretrial	TR –Trial
CWO –Conference–Outside Office	H –Hearing	MOT –Motion	R –Reading and Review	TRV –Travel
DEF –Defendant	INV –Investigation	NEG –Negotiation	REL –Release	W –Witness
DEM –Demurrer	INT –Interview			

CLIENT (State billing division or department)	MATTER	DESCRIPTION OF WORK (Use abbreviations above)	TIME Minutes	10ths
AJAX, INC. (LITIGATION)	AJAX vs. SMITH	digesting DEPO	30	.50
AJAX, INC. (LITIGATION)	AJAX vs. SMITH	DR COMP	104	1.40

of time, although a few firms use one-fourth of an hour as their base. Time is recorded in fractions of an hour as follows:

Tenths of an Hour as Base	One-Fourth of an Hour as Base
6 minutes = .10 of an hour	15 minutes = .25 of an hour
12 minutes = .20 of an hour	30 minutes = .50 of an hour
18 minutes = .30 of an hour	45 minutes = .75 of an hour
24 minutes = .40 of an hour	60 minutes = 1.0 hour
30 minutes = .50 of an hour	
36 minutes = .60 of an hour	
42 minutes = .70 of an hour	
48 minutes = .80 of an hour	
54 minutes = .90 of an hour	
60 minutes = 1.0 hour	

If, for example, the paralegal spends an hour and thirty minutes digesting the deposition in an office that records time in tenths of an hour, his or her time for this task would be entered as 1.50. Suppose the paralegal spent an hour and forty-four minutes on the project. Forty-four minutes does not evenly divide into tenths of an hour. In most offices, timekeepers are instructed to round up or down to the nearest increment. The nearest six-minute increment is forty-two minutes. Hence an hour and forty-four minutes would be recorded as 1.70. Other office policies may also exist on how to record travel time or short telephone conversations.

If computers are used for this task, time and billing software automatically records time once the timekeeper clicks the start-and-stop buttons on the screen. Menus on the screen allow the timekeeper to tell the computer what client or matter is being worked on, whether the time is billable, and the nature of the work being performed. For an example of such a screen, see Exhibit 14.7. Time and billing software also helps the office generate the bills and administrative reports that we will examine later in the chapter.

EXHIBIT 14.7	Computer–Assisted Timekeeping

Source: Courtesy PCLaw by Alumni Computer Group, Inc. (www.pclaw.com)

If you have never kept close track of your time, you will find that the task requires a great deal of effort and discipline; it does not come naturally to most of us. The key to performing the task effectively is to do it consistently and comprehensively until it becomes second nature. A key recommendation of timekeepers is to record time **contemporaneously** rather than hours, days, or weeks after performing the task that must be timed. (Contemporaneous means happening or beginning at the same time or shortly thereafter.)

contemporaneous Existing or occurring in the same period of time; pertaining to records that are prepared on events as the events are occurring or shortly thereafter.

Here is how Tory Barcott, a paralegal in Anchorage, describes the process:

It "sometimes scares me a little to contemplate clients paying" $10.00 or more "for every six minutes of our time." To survive in this world, the paralegal must possess the accuracy and efficiency of a Swiss watch. "I keep one of those small, cheap, adhesive digital clocks where it can't be missed or covered with paperwork. Sticking it to my phone, in the middle of my desk, works best for me. The first step in performing any task is to record the time on my time sheet. I do this before retrieving the file, making a phone call," or going to meet a supervising attorney. The clock is also helpful in recording the time when a task is interrupted by anything unrelated to the current client matter. "I take notes on the start and stop times exactly as displayed on my digital clock." Some Saturdays, while absently attending to household chores, I'll glance at the clock and catch myself thinking, "that floor took only 0.4 to clean." This is a sure sign that the discipline of timekeeping has been internalized![10]

nonbillable time Time spent on tasks for which clients cannot be asked to pay.

pro bono Concerning or involving legal services that are provided for the public good (*pro bono publico*) without fee or compensation. Sometimes also applied to services given at a reduced rate.

indigent Impoverished; without funds to hire a private attorney.

Time spent by paralegals and attorneys on tasks for which clients cannot be asked to pay is called **nonbillable time**. Examples of such tasks include general file maintenance, learning to operate a new data processing program that the firm is implementing throughout the office, helping to develop standard forms, and taking lunch breaks. **Pro bono** work is also nonbillable. This consists of legal services provided without cost, usually for an **indigent** individual or for a public interest organization such as the Red Cross or a local group of community artists. (Someone is indigent if he or she does not have sufficient funds to hire a private attorney.) A firm's regular clients cannot be asked to pay for pro bono work the office does for others.

The firm needs to know how many billable and nonbillable hours paralegals and attorneys have accumulated over a particular period of time. Computer programs are very helpful in allowing timekeepers such as paralegals and attorneys to indicate which tasks fall into which category. They can also produce clear graphs that present this information in summary form. An example is the chart in Exhibit 14.8.

Law firms also set *targets* on how many billable hours they hope to obtain from partners, associates, and paralegals. Exhibit 14.9 shows different formats that computers can help generate to provide a graphic presentation of these expectations.

EXHIBIT 14.8	**Chart Showing Billable versus Unbillable Hours for Each Timekeeper**

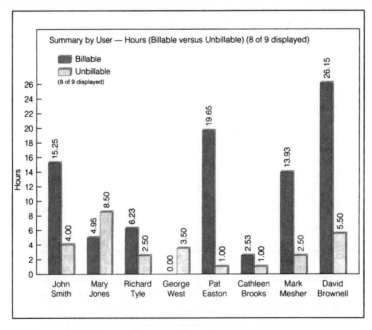

Source: Courtesy Timeslips Corporation (www.timeslips.com)

EXHIBIT 14.9	Billable Hour Expectations: Timekeeper Productivity Report					
AVERAGE BILLABLE HOURS BY TIMEKEEPER						
	Jan	Feb	Mar	Apr	May	Jun
Partners	128	132	127	134	144	141
Associates	170	163	175	170	159	179
Paralegals	118	111	120	119	121	108

YEAR-TO-DATE SUMMARY			
	Target	Average Year-to-Date	Variance
Partners	140	134	–4%
Associates	165	169	+2%
Paralegals	125	116	–7%

Source: Jeff Coburn, *Creating Financial Reports That Partners Will Read,* 14 Legal Management 40 (November/December, 1995), reprinted with permission from the Association of Legal Administrators, Vernon Hills, Illinois (www.alanet.org).

[SECTION E]

KINDS OF FEES

Most fees are based on the amount of time spent in providing legal services. Yet there are alternatives. Here is an overview of fee arrangements.

CLOCK-BASED FEES

1. Hourly Rate

An hourly rate fee is based on the number of attorney hours worked. Paralegals have a separate hourly rate covering their time.

2. Blended Hourly Rate

A partner and an associate who have different hourly rates may work on the same case. The bill to the client could break the fee down by rates. For example: $600 for two hours spent by Smith (a partner who bills at $300 an hour) and $450 for three hours spent by Jacob (an associate who bills at $150 an hour). An alternative is to charge a **blended hourly rate**. This is a single hourly rate that is based on a blend or mix of partner and associate rates. For example, to calculate the blended hourly rate, the firm might take the average of the normal rates charged by the partner and associate working on the case. In some states, the firm is allowed to add a paralegal's time into this blended hourly rate.

blended hourly rate A single hourly rate based on a blend or mix of the rates normally charged by different individuals, e.g., a partner, a senior associate, a junior associate, and sometimes a paralegal.

ALTERNATIVES

Many individuals are not happy with billing that is controlled by the clock, as reflected in the following comments made by a business client who often hires attorneys:

[We] have to look not only at the service and quality of law firms with which we do business but also at the linkage between price and performance. Hourly billing provides no such linkage. It is an accounting device. There is no credible economic theory underlying the hourly billing method, and for that reason, we no longer accept it as the sole, or even predominant, method of pricing legal services. In fact, hourly billing pushes the economic incentives in the wrong direction— weakening rather than strengthening the bonds between performance and pay. It also pushes law firms to near-obsession with billable hours. And this in turn supports the great unwritten rule of all law practices: those who want to get ahead must tally up the hours. This is first and foremost dubious economics. The number of hours spent on a matter is no measure of productivity. Productivity is better measured by results, including both outcome and time-frame. Linking the economic structure . . . to true measures of productivity—or value—will benefit both the firms and the client.[11]

Although billing by the hour is likely to remain an important method of financing legal services in most kinds of cases, there are alternatives, as suggested by this client. These alternatives are either to abandon the clock or to use it as only one factor in determining the fee.

A great deal of discussion centers on what is called **value billing**. This means that the fee is not based solely on the time required to perform the work but also takes into account factors such as the following.[12]

- The results achieved
- The nature of the services provided
- The complexity, novelty, and difficulty of the question
- The time pressure under which the services were provided
- The time limitations imposed by the client
- The amount of responsibility assumed by the firm
- The extent to which the services provided precluded the firm from taking other clients
- The amount of money involved in the matter
- The nature and length of the firm's relationship with the client
- The efficiency with which the services were performed

Using factors such as these, a number of different fee arrangements have been devised. Here is an overview of these arrangements, some of which overlap.

1. Fixed Fee

A **fixed fee** is a flat fee for the service—a set figure regardless of the amount of time needed to complete the service. The fixed fee can be a specific sum or a percentage of the recovery.

2. Capped Fee

Under a **capped fee**, the firm bills an hourly rate, but the total bill will not exceed a predetermined budgeted amount.

3. Task-Based Billing

Most attorney services consist of a mix or bundle of tasks such as legal advice, investigation, document preparation, document review, document filing, legal research, negotiation, and court representation. Collectively, these tasks are called **bundled legal services**. Suppose, however, that a client does not want the full range of attorney services. The client might be representing him or herself **(pro se)** but would like the attorney to perform specific tasks such as reviewing a document the client has prepared or making a phone call on the client's behalf. Attorneys who agree to provide discrete task representation of this kind are providing **unbundled legal services**. Charging for such services is called **task-based billing**. (It is also referred to as *unit billing* or *project billing*.) There are different ways the attorneys can charge clients for such services:

- A set or fixed fee per task, regardless of how long it takes to perform the task,
- The same hourly rate the attorney charges for full (bundled) legal services, or
- A special hourly rate referred to as an unbundled rate.

Task-based billing for legal services is becoming increasingly popular as more consumers use the Internet to locate attorneys willing to provide such services. To find out more, run a search for "unbundled legal services" in Google or another search engine that includes the name of your state (example: "unbundled legal services" Texas). See also www.unbundledlaw.org.

4. Hourly Plus Fixed Fee

With an **hourly plus fixed fee**, the firm charges an hourly rate until the nature and scope of the legal problem are identified; thereafter, a fixed fee is charged for services provided.

5. Volume Discounts

The hourly or fixed fee might be reduced if the client gives the office a large amount of business, particularly when the office is able to reduce its own costs by standardization of work. A bill reduced for such reasons is called a **discounted hourly fee** or a volume discount.

---

*Margin glossary:*

value billing A method of charging for legal services based on factors such as the complexity of the case or the results achieved rather than solely on the number of hours spent on the client's case.

fixed fee A flat fee for services regardless of the amount of time needed to complete the task.

capped fee An hourly rate leading to a final bill that will not exceed a predetermined amount.

bundled legal services All tasks needed to represent a client; all-inclusive legal services.

pro se (on one's own behalf) Appearing for or representing oneself. Also called *in propria persona* and *pro per*.

unbundled legal services Discrete task representation.

task-based billing Charging a specific amount for each legal task performed.

hourly plus fixed fee An hourly rate charged until the nature and scope of the legal problem are known, at which time fixed fees are charged for services provided thereafter.

discounted hourly fee An hourly or fixed fee that is reduced because of the volume of business the client gives the office.

6. Contingency Billing

The traditional **contingent fee** is a fee that is dependent—contingent—on the outcome of the case. The fee could be a fixed amount (e.g., $25,000) or a percentage of the amount the plaintiff wins in the litigation or settlement. (The percentage could be 33 percent if the case is settled before trial, 40 percent if the case goes to trial, and 50 percent if the case is appealed.) No fee is owed if the plaintiff loses, although he or she may still be responsible for the payment of expenses and court costs (discussed below) incurred by the office in the losing effort. Contingent fees are most often used in personal injury (PI) cases. Such fees, however, can also be used in other kinds of cases. Suppose, for example, an attorney is hired to handle a transaction case such as a contract dispute the client is having with one of its suppliers. Under a contingent billing arrangement with the attorney, "the law firm takes on part of the risk of the transaction. If the transaction (in this case, the contract) fails to go through, the law firm bills the client either a pre-negotiated sum or a small portion of the actual billable hours. Conversely, if the deal is successful, the firm bills the client either a higher pre-negotiated sum or a premium."[13] A premium is sometimes referred to as **incentive billing** (or a *performance bonus*). The attorney receives an increased fee for achieving an exceptional result such as settling a case for an amount that exceeds a target set by the plaintiff-client and attorney.

Most contingent fees are earned by the plaintiff's attorney. A **defense contingent fee** (also called a *negative contingency*) is a fee for the defendant's attorney that is dependent on the outcome of the case. Most often the fee is a fixed amount.

Contingent fees are not allowed in every case. See chapter 5 for a discussion of when such fees are unethical in criminal and divorce cases.

7. Retroactive Negotiated Fee

Occasionally, a client and attorney might agree to finalize the fee *after* the services are provided. This is called a **retroactive negotiated fee**. When the case is over, the attorney and client agree on the value of the services provided and set the fee accordingly.

[SECTION F]

BILLING

In addition to fees for services, a law firm usually recovers out-of-pocket expenses that the firm incurs while working on the case. Examples include witness fees, long-distance phone calls, and out-of-town travel for the attorney or paralegal. The client also pays **court costs** imposed by the court. They include filing fees, jury fees, and special court taxes. Each time attorneys or paralegals incur such expenses, they often fill out an **expense slip** (see Exhibit 14.10), which goes into the office's accounting system. In some cases, a court might order a party to pay court costs incurred by an *opposing* party. For example, if a defendant is forced to litigate what the court determines to be a **frivolous position** of the plaintiff, the court might order the plaintiff to pay all court costs associated with the litigation of that position.

contingent fee A fee that is paid only if the case is successfully resolved by litigation or settlement. (The fee is also referred to as a *contingency*.)

incentive billing A fee that is increased if a designated target is met; an increased fee for achieving an exceptional result.

defense contingent fee A fee received by the defendant's attorney that is dependent on the outcome of the case.

retroactive negotiated fee A client bill that is finalized *after* the services are rendered.

court costs Charges or fees imposed by the court directly related to litigation in that court.

expense slip A form used by an office to indicate that an expense has been incurred for which the client may or may not be billed.

frivolous position A position taken on behalf of a client that the attorney cannot support by a good faith argument based on existing law or on the need for a change in the law.

retainer (1) The act of hiring or engaging the services of someone, usually a professional. (The verb is *retain*.) (2) An amount of money (or other property) paid by a client as a deposit or advance against future fees, costs, and expenses of providing services.

EXHIBIT 14.10	**Example of an Expense Slip**

Client name _____ File number _____

Nature of expense incurred _____

_____

Billable or nonbillable _____

Expense code _____ Date incurred _____ Amount paid or due _____

Name/address of vendor _____

Person incurring the expense _____

Approved by _____

The fees, expenses, and costs to be paid by the client should be spelled out in the attorney-client fee agreement. (For an example of such an agreement, see Exhibit 8.1 in chapter 8.) If a **retainer** is involved, the agreement should describe how it will work. The word *retainer* can mean the act of hiring or engaging the services of someone, usually a professional. ("Fred retained the firm of Hailey and Ava.") More specifically, a retainer is an amount of money (or other property) paid by a client as a deposit or advance against future fees, costs, and expenses of providing services. Additional money is paid only when the deposit or advance runs out. The agreement should specify whether such money or other property from the client are refundable if the client terminates the relationship because he or she fires the attorney or simply decides not to pursue the matter.

The actual billing process differs from firm to firm, and occasionally differs from case to case within the same firm. Client billing sometimes occurs only after the matter is completed. More commonly, a client is billed monthly, quarterly, or semiannually. An administrator in the firm usually works with the billing attorney to prepare the bill. When a matter is called for billing, the administrator may prepare a billing memorandum (the **draft bill**), which specifies the out-of-pocket expenses and costs incurred by the firm in connection with the matter, plus the amount of time each attorney and paralegal has spent on the matter (along with the billing rate of each). For example:[14]

> **draft bill** A billing memorandum prepared by a law office on a particular client case stating expenses, costs, time spent, and billing rates of attorneys and paralegals working on the case.

- *Attorney Jones: $1,000.* This attorney, who has a billing rate of $200 an hour, spent 5 hours on the matter (5 × $200 = $1,000).
- *Attorney Sampson: $1,200.* This attorney, who has a billing rate of $150 an hour, spent 8 hours on the matter (8 × $150 = $1,200).
- *Paralegal Kelly: $900.* This paralegal, who has a billing rate of $75 an hour, spent 12 hours on the matter (12 × $75 = $900).

The billing attorney has three choices: (1) Bill the total of the actual amounts. In our example, this would produce a bill of $3,100 ($1,000 + $1,200 + $900). (2) **Write down** the matter by subtracting a certain amount, e.g., $300. This would produce a bill of $2,800. (3) **Write up** the matter by adding an amount, e.g., $600. This would produce a bill of $3,700. This adjustment downward or upward is known as **valuing the bill**. An increase is sometimes called a *premium adjustment;* a decrease, a *discount adjustment.* The decision to adjust is based on factors such as the potential liability exposure of the firm (leading to a write-up) and the relative inexperience of an attorney or paralegal working on the matter (leading to a write-down). If, for example, recently hired attorneys or paralegals take an unusually long time to complete a task they have not performed before, a write-down may be appropriate so that the client does not have to bear the full cost of their on-the-job training.

> **write down** Deduct an amount from the bill.
>
> **write up** Add an amount to the bill.
>
> **valuing the bill** Determining whether there should be a write-down or a write-up of a bill to be sent to the client.

See Exhibit 14.11 for an example of a bill sent to a client covering work of attorneys and paralegals on a matter. The bill in Exhibit 14.11 is a traditional letter sent by regular mail. Increasingly, law firms are sending out bills as e-mail attachments, particularly to corporate clients. The practice is referred to as *e-billing*.

EXHIBIT 14.11	Bill Sent to Client for Attorney and Parlegal Services

Rubin, Rinke, Pyeumac & Craigmoyle
1615 Broadway, Suite 1400
Oakland, California 94612–2115
(415) 444–5316
Tax ID 94–2169491

April 10, 2008

IBM Corporation
Norm Savage
3133 Northside Parkway
Atlanta GA 33033

Statement for Professional Services Rendered

Re: Chapter 11   (IBM-1)
       Reorganization

Description of services

04/17/08	Receipt and review of contracts regarding Armonk home office liquidation.
04/18/08	Meeting with opposing attorney regarding court appearance in Atlanta.
04/21/08	Receipt and preliminary review of depositions from seven hundred forty-three (743)
04/22/08	claimants to Austin plant parking facilities.
	Meeting with officers of the corporation to discuss liquidation of office furniture in all branch offices. Scheduling of 2,000 simultaneous garage sales in marketing managers' driveways to be advertised during next year's Varsity Bowl.

		Total for legal services rendered	$1,797.50
	Hours	Rate	
Partners	6.00	$250	1,500.00
Paralegals	3.50	$85	297.50

(continues)

EXHIBIT 14.11	Bill Sent to Client for Attorney and Parlegal Services

Reimbursable expenses and costs

04/17/08	Lunch meeting with three opposing attorneys.	185.17
04/27/08	Atlanta Bankruptcy Court filing fee due September 1, 2008	55.00
04/29/08	Photocopies	5.69
04/29/08	Long-distance telephone charges	36.90
	Total expenses	$282.76
	Total current charges.	$2,080.26

Source: Computer Software for Professionals, Inc., Legalmaster (www.legalmaster.com)

Of course, not all client bills are paid immediately upon receipt. Collection problems can sometimes be substantial, as we will see later when we discuss the aged accounts receivable report.

Furthermore, more and more clients are carefully scrutinizing the bills that they receive. Business clients that frequently hire attorneys may use outside auditors to review attorney bills before paying them. The auditor will look for potential problems that should be brought to the attention of the client. Law Audit Services, for example, reviews an average of $60,000 in bills a day from over 5,100 law firms hired by different insurance companies. Here are some of the more egregious irregularities flagged by this auditor:[15]

- An attorney bills for a thirty-eight-hour workday
- An attorney charges 31¢ a mile for a rental car with unlimited mileage
- An attorney bills 4.5 hours to look up addresses at a library

When the law firm employs paralegals, clients sometimes have asked the law firm to explain:

- Why a particular task performed by an attorney (and billed at attorney rates) was not delegated to a paralegal
- Why paralegal fees are sought for clerical tasks performed by the paralegal

Questions such as these are also asked in statutory fee cases in which the court has authority to order the losing side to pay the attorney fees (including paralegal fees) of the winning side.

Even if a client does not use an outside auditor, it is wise to assume that someone in the client's office will be scrutinizing law firm bills for potential problems. Furthermore, the rules of ethics must always be kept in mind. For an overview of the major fee and billing ethical violations involving paralegals (e.g., padding, block billing), see chapter 5 (page 222).

[SECTION G]
CLIENT TRUST ACCOUNTS

Law firms must keep at least two separate checking accounts. One is the office account from which the office pays general operating expenses such as salaries, utility bills, and other overhead items. The second is the **client trust account** (also called a client account or escrow account), which contains client funds that may not be used to cover office expenses or the attorney's personal expenses. Each client does not need its own client trust account. There can be one client trust account into which the funds of all office clients are deposited. When deposits and withdrawals are made, careful records must indicate the client for which a particular deposit and withdrawal is made. Occasionally, however, an office may have separate client trust accounts for those clients whose cases involve large amounts of money. (The trust accounts earn bank interest. In most states, law firms must send this interest to a public fund that makes grants to organizations that provide legal services to low-income clients. The use of these funds in this way is called the **IOLTA** (Interest on Lawyers' Trust Account) **program**.)

There must be no **commingling** or mixing of office funds and client funds. It is unethical for the office to place everything in one account, no matter how meticulous the office may be about recording which funds in the single account belong to the office and which belong to clients. Furthermore, it is equally unethical for the attorney to use any client funds for a personal purpose (e.g., paying the attorney's home mortgage bill) or for an office purpose (e.g., paying the office rent) during a time when the attorney is experiencing a temporary cash flow problem. This is unethical even if the attorney returns the client funds with interest. When attorneys are audited by the bar association, the auditor (or monitor) often gives careful attention to the accounting records in the office to determine whether these rules on separate accounts are being followed.

client trust account A bank account controlled by an attorney that contains client funds that may not be used for office operating expenses or for any personal purpose of the attorney.

IOLTA program (Interest on Lawyers' Trust Accounts) A program that helps fund legal services for the poor with funds that attorneys are required to turn over from interest earned in client trust accounts containing client funds.

commingling Mixing what should be kept separate, e.g., depositing client funds in a single account with general law firm funds or with an attorney's personal funds.

What funds must go into a client trust account? Here are some examples:

- A settlement check from an opposing party (or from its insurance company) when a case is settled
- A court award of damages paid by an opposing party (or its insurance company)
- Escrow funds from the sale of real property
- Prepayment of costs
- Unearned attorney fees

The last category is particularly important. Where attorney fees must be deposited depends on what the fees are for and whether they have been earned. Suppose, for example, an attorney agrees to take a divorce case for a fee of $200 an hour upon the client's payment of an advance of $25,000. If this advance is a deposit against future fees (which is often the case), it must be deposited in the client trust account because it has not yet been earned by the attorney. It is still the client's money; the attorney is holding it "in trust" for the client. Once the attorney earns the right to be paid by working on the case, funds can be transferred from the client trust account to the office account. For example, if the attorney spends twenty hours on the divorce case, he or she can bill the client for $4,000 (20 × $200) and instruct the bank to transfer this amount from the client trust account into the office account. This leaves $21,000 in the client trust account. If the client decides to discharge the attorney or wants to drop the case, the attorney must refund all unearned cash remaining in the client fund.

Some attorney fees, however, are not advances against future legal services. They may constitute a nonrefundable sign-up bonus that commits the attorney to be available to the client as needed over a designated period of time. Such fees can be deposited directly into the attorney's office account because they are considered earned when received.

To avoid disputes, the contract of employment (the fee agreement) between an attorney and client should clarify the purpose and nature of fees to be paid. Are they advances? Are they refundable or nonrefundable? When are they considered earned? Such questions should be answered and the answers understood by the client before the attorney-client relationship begins. The ethical rules of each state must also be carefully checked in this area of practice. Some states, for example, place restrictions on an attorney's right to nonrefundable fees, even if the client agrees to pay them.

[SECTION H]
ADMINISTRATIVE REPORTS

The managers of a law firm need to know what everyone in the firm is doing. Many attorneys routinely complete a form similar to that illustrated in Exhibit 14.12, the work summary. It can be filled out by computer or on a paper form provided by the office. Paralegals also fill out work

EXHIBIT 14.12	Work Summary

```
[  ] Can Handle More Work                        C    (Work Completed
[  ] Have All the Work                                 since Last Report)
     I Can Handle                              WP    (Work in Progress)
[  ] Need Help                                  IA    (Matter Is Inactive)
Report of:                                      Date:
```

Client	Matter	Description of Work [Designate Specialty Work by Symbol (S)]	Date Assgnd	Part-ner	Sta-tus

summary reports, depending on the nature of the work they're doing. If they are working for many attorneys in one department, the department head and the paralegal supervisor, if any, often require copies of the work summary report in order to keep track of the work being done.

Administrative reports of this kind are common in law offices. For other examples of administrative reports, see Exhibit 14.13.

Of particular interest to paralegals are reports generated from timekeeping records that analyze how much time paralegals are investing in client matters. This analysis is similar to the analysis the firm performs on the time invested by attorneys. Managers use these data to

EXHIBIT 14.13	Administrative Reports in a Law Office

- *Aged Accounts Receivable Report.* A report showing all cases that have outstanding balances due and how long these balances are past due. For example, the report may state how many of the total receivables (i.e., accounts due and payable) are less than thirty days old, how many are 30–59 days old, how many are 60–90 days old, and how many are more than ninety days old. (Also called a firm utilization report.) (See Exhibit 14.14.)
- *Timekeeper Productivity Report.* A report showing how much billable and nonbillable time is being spent by each timekeeper. (See Exhibits 14.8 and 14.9.)
- *Case-Type Productivity Report.* A report showing which types of cases in the firm (e.g., bankruptcy, personal injury, and criminal) are most profitable. (Also called a practice analysis report.)
- *Fee Analysis Report.* A report on the fees generated by client, by area of law, by law firm branch office, by individual attorney, and by individual paralegal. The report helps the firm identify which cases, offices, attorneys, and paralegals are profitable and which are not.
- *Work-in-Progress Report.* A report that provides the details of unbilled hours and costs per timekeeper, including client totals.
- *Cash Receipts Report.* A report that describes the income received in a day, week, month, quarter, or year. The cash receipts can be compared with the amount of projected income for a specific time period.
- *Client Investment Summary Report.* A report of the total amount billed and unbilled, with a calculation of the actual costs of providing legal services for a particular client.
- *Budget Performance Report.* A report that compares a firm's actual income and expenditures with budgeted or projected income and expenditures.

Sources: Brent Roper, *Practical Law Office Management* (3d ed. Delmar Cengage Learning 2002); Pamela Everett Nollkamper, *Fundamentals of Law Office Management* (3d ed. Delmar Cengage Learning 2003)

EXHIBIT 14.14	Accounts Receivable (AR)—Bills Not Yet Collected

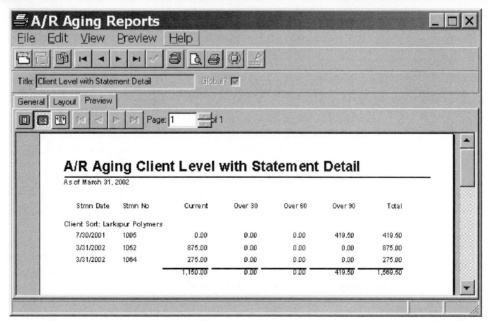

Source: Reprinted with permission of ProLaw Software (www.prolaw.com)

evaluate where the profit centers are, whether costs need to be contained, whether work is properly allocated among attorneys and among paralegals, which attorneys and paralegals are in line for salary increases and bonuses, etc.

[SECTION I]

CLIENT FILE MANAGEMENT

When you begin work in a law office, one of your early tasks will be to learn the office's system for organizing, locating, and storing client files. In some offices, particularly small ones, paralegals are given considerable responsibility for maintaining this system. Efficient file management is of critical importance. "Files are the nerve center of any office. Therefore, the proper storage, safe-keeping, and expeditious retrieval of information from the files is the key to . . . efficient operation."[16] Attorneys and paralegals will tell you that few experiences are more frustrating than coping with a lost document or a missing file. "But the damage can run even deeper." Lost and misplaced files can cause deadlines to be missed, "leading to one of the most common causes of malpractice claims against attorneys."[17]

Once an office accepts a client, its file soon begins to collect many documents. They are often placed in separate folders within the file. On the right side of one of the folders, you may find all incoming correspondence and copies of all outgoing correspondence. They will be in reverse chronological order, with the most recent correspondence always placed on top. To keep them all together, they will probably be two-hole punched and clipped to the right side of the folder. All other documents (e.g., copies of pleadings) might be similarly clipped to the left side of the folder. Large documents such as transcripts of depositions are often kept in separate folders.

Almost every law office has multiple clients. The location of the files of these clients will depend on factors such as the kind and size of cases the office handles, the number of attorneys in the office, the use of computers, and the availability of storage space. Large law firms often have a centralized filing area where all or most files are located. File clerks (under the direction of a **record information manager**) file, check out, and keep track of every file. Smaller offices tend to be more decentralized, allowing files to be located in or near the office of the attorney working on those files.

There are two major kinds of filing systems: alphabetical and numerical.

In an **alphabetical filing system**, files are arranged in alphabetical order by client surname or by organization name. For example, the file of George Bellman would go in front of the file of Kelly Motor Corp., which would go in front of the file of Mrs. John Thompson, etc. This system works relatively well if the office does not have a large number of clients. The more clients in the office, however, the more likely their names will be confusingly similar. Suppose, for example, that an office has the following clients, each with separate cases (or matters) handled by different attorneys in the office:

> A-1 North's Appliance Center (a tax case)
> North Central Bank (a securities case)
> Jason North (a divorce case)
> Sam North (Jason's father) (a landlord-tenant case)
> Northern Light, Inc. (a trademark case)

In an alphabetical filing system, there are rules that determine the order in which the files of these five clients would be kept in the file cabinet. Yet filing mistakes are fairly common in spite of the rules. Busy office workers do not always take the time to find out what the rules are. As documents in these files are used, returned, and reused throughout the day, the danger of misfiling is increased because of the similarity of some file names. A bank statement in Jason North's divorce case, for example, might end up in his father's landlord-tenant case or as one of the financial records in the unrelated North Central Bank's securities case.

Color coding can help. To speed up the retrieval and return of files, the office can use colored file folders, colored file labels, or colored stickers. If, for example, colors are assigned to a particular area of the law, the folders and labels for all corporate law cases might be blue; those for all tax cases, orange; those for all family law cases, white; etc.[18] Alternatively, an office may use one color for every folder and file opened in a particular year regardless of the kind of case it is. When a new year arrives, new client cases go into folders and files of a different color.

A **numerical filing system** is substantially different from an alphabetical filing system. Numerical filing systems use numbers or letter-number combinations (rather than surnames) to

record information manager
Someone in charge of files in a large office.

alphabetical filing system
A method of storing client files in alphabetical order by the client's surname or organization name.

numerical filing system
A method of storing client files by numbers or letter-number combinations.

identify files. Many varieties of numerical filing systems are in use. Here are five examples of how files might be identified in five different law offices:

- 02–778. The first two characters indicate the year the case was opened (02 = the year 2002) (778 is the number assigned to a particular client).
- LA01–55113. The first two letters indicate which branch office is handling the case (LA = the Los Angeles branch; 01 = the year 2001).
- PB–552. The first two letters indicate the type of case (PB = a probate case) (other examples: TX = a tax case; WC = a workers' compensation case).
- JH.02.111. The first two letters indicate the particular attorney in charge of the case (JH = Jane Harrison, Esq.).
- 37.007. The initial numbers indicate particular clients (37 = Avon Electronics, Inc.), and the following numbers indicate how many matters are being handled for those clients (007 = the seventh matter the office has handled for Avon).[19]

Some offices will assign a range of numbers to a particular type of case or matter, e.g., all estate and trust cases will use the numbers 001–999; all tax cases will use the numbers 1,000–1,999; and all criminal cases will use the numbers 2,000–2,999. Other variations are also possible.

Index cards can be used to help locate particular files organized under a numerical filing system. For example, Avon Electronics, Inc., would have its own card on which every file number assigned to it would be placed (37.007, 37.008, 37.009, etc.). These index cards would be kept in alphabetical order. If you want to read the file of a particular client, you would go to the index cards, find that client's name, jot down the numbers of the files that pertain to that client, and go to the file cabinets to locate those numbers. Additional cards allow for cross-indexing. For example, individual attorneys could have their own cards that contain all the case numbers they are handling or have handled. Also, cards for specific topics could be created (e.g., medical malpractice interrogatories and patent applications) on which the numbers for every case file containing documents on those topics would be written. If you want to look at medical malpractice interrogatories that the office has used in the past, go to the "m" cards, find the card on medical malpractice interrogatories, and jot down the number of every case containing such interrogatories.

Of course, a system of index cards can become cumbersome as the caseload of an office grows in volume and diversity. In many offices, special computer software is used to do the work of the index cards faster and more efficiently.

Some large offices use bar coding to facilitate file management. Every file is assigned a **bar code**, which is a sequence of numbers and vertical lines that can be read by an optical scanner. Most supermarkets use this technology at checkout to record prices and provide inventory data to managers. Similarly, whenever you want to use a file that has been bar coded, you simply scan the bar code and take the file to your office. This is also done when you return the file to the file cabinet or storage room. The office thereby obtains an efficient computer record of who has which files, how long they have had them, and when they were returned.

In a bar code system, you scan the bar code into a computer. Suppose you are also able to scan the contents of *every document in every file* into the computer. This amounts to a fully automated file management system. Every attorney, paralegal, and secretary in the office can then be given instant computer access to any document in the files. Finding documents becomes substantially easier than combing through file drawers or boxes and carrying what you need to your desk. Search software allows you to define what you are looking for (e.g., the Ellerson deposition or all personal injury complaints filed in Suffolk Superior Court after 1997). Not many law offices are sophisticated enough to have every document on computer. We have not yet reached the paperless office, although we are clearly moving in this direction.

Once the office completes its work on a case, the file becomes a **closed file**, also called a dead file or a retired file. Some offices give the file a new number (e.g., a CF, or closed file, number) to differentiate it from active files.[20] The file might be placed in storage boxes or transferred to microfilm or ultrafiche. Important original documents (e.g., wills, estate plans, deeds, and tax returns) are usually returned to the client. The office keeps a copy.

The cost of storing client files can be substantial, particularly for law firms with many clients. Firms do not want the burden of keeping old files forever. Ethical rules in the state may impose an obligation to keep specified files for designated periods of time. "Firms should have policies on retention of files, turning files over to clients, destroying files, and security for files maintained in off-site storage. Since the client file is the property of the client, the attorney cannot destroy old files without informing the client and getting permission and/or giving the client the chance to keep the file."[21]

bar code A sequence of numbers and vertical lines of different shapes that can be read by an optical scanner.

closed file The file of a client whose case is no longer active in the firm.

Finally, closed case files can often be of help to an office in future cases. To avoid reinventing the wheel, offices like to have closed case files accessible. Whenever work on a current case involves the drafting of a document, for example, examining the same or a similar document prepared for a prior case can often be a good starting point. As we saw in chapter 13, *knowledge management* (KM) systems are being used by large law offices to enable them to locate, adapt, and reuse documents generated in prior cases.

ASSIGNMENT 14.1

(a) In the practice of law, time is money. Hence you must develop the discipline of recording your time. Supervisors will later decide what portions of your time are billable—and to what clients. Step one is to compile a record of your time.

To practice this discipline, fill out a daily time sheet for a day that you select. On *one* sheet of paper, record (in a chart form that you design) everything (approximately) that you do *in six-minute* intervals over a continuous eight-hour period. Once you design your chart, *it should take you no more than about fifteen minutes to fill it out* during the eight-hour period. You do not, however, fill it out at one time; you fill it out contemporaneously as you go through the tasks you are keeping track of throughout the eight hours.

Select an eight-hour period in which you are engaged in a fairly wide variety of activities. If possible, avoid an eight-hour period that contains any single activity lasting over two hours. Draw a chart covering the eight-hour period. At the top of the chart, place your name, the date of the eight-hour period that you used, and the starting/ending times of the eight-hour period. The period can be within a school day, a workday, a day of leisure, etc.

Using abbreviations, make specific entries on your activities within the eight hours—in six-minute intervals. For example, "Reading a chapter in a real estate school text" might be abbreviated as RE-R. "Driving to school" might be abbreviated as D-Sch. "Purely personal matters" (such as taking a shower) might be abbreviated as PPM. You decide what the abbreviations are. On the back of the sheet of paper containing the chart, explain what the abbreviations mean. When an activity is repeated in more than one six-minute interval, simply repeat the abbreviation.

One format for the chart might be a series of vertical and horizontal lines on the sheet of paper. This will give you a small amount of space on which to insert your abbreviations for each six-minute interval. Design the chart any way that you want, keeping in mind the goal of the exercise: to enable someone else to know what you did within the eight-hour period.

In Exhibit 14.6, there is an example of a daily time sheet used in a law office. *Do not* follow the format in Exhibit 14.6. Use the guidelines listed here, e.g., place your abbreviations on the other side of the sheet of paper that you submit.

(b) Repeat this assignment for a period of a week. Your instructor will tell you which week to select. For each of the seven days of that week, fill out a daily time sheet.

ASSIGNMENT 14.2

Call a private law firm in the area that is large enough to have an office manager or legal administrator. Ask this person if you can interview him or her on the phone or in person for several minutes. Explain that you are taking a paralegal course that requires you to interview a manager. Ask this person about the following topics:

- How the office is organized (partnership, sole proprietorship, or other)
- Major duties of the manager or administrator (use Exhibit 14.2 as a guide to some of the areas to cover)
- Categories of attorneys and other staff in the office, their duties, and the chain of command among them
- Kinds of fees
- Timekeeping methods
- How work is delegated and evaluated
- Filing system
- Law library size

Prepare a report on what you learned from this interview.

Chapter Summary

Our examination of law office administration began with an overview of the different settings in which attorneys practice law in the private sector and of the different kinds of attorneys found in each setting.

A sole practitioner may operate a sole proprietorship, in which a single attorney owns the practice even if he or she employs other attorneys. The latter do not share in the profits and losses of the firm. To save on expenses, several sole practitioners may enter into an office-sharing arrangement under which the attorneys share expenses for office space, secretarial help, etc.

In a partnership, the equity or capital partners share in the profits and losses of the firm and control its management, often through a committee or department structure. Associates are attorneys in the firm who hope one day to be invited to become partners. There are, however, special categories of associates created for those who do not become partners, such as senior associate.

Other categories of attorneys who might be hired by a law firm include staff attorneys, of-counsel attorneys, and contract attorneys. For tax and estate-planning purposes, many states allow attorneys to practice law as a professional corporation. There is little practical difference, however, between the administration of a partnership and a professional corporation. The newest formats for law firms are the limited liability company (LLC) and the limited liability partnership (LLP). They combine features of a corporation and a partnership.

Finally, some attorneys practice law in the legal departments of corporations. They are employees of the corporation, which is their sole client.

Large law offices may have many nonattorney employees to help manage the office. Among the most prominent is the legal administrator. Also, if there are more than a few paralegals in the office, a paralegal manager is often hired to help administer the office's system for recruiting, hiring, training, and monitoring the progress of paralegals. Technology and a low-wage, skilled labor force abroad have encouraged some law firms to consider outsourcing law office tasks, although there are ethical problems that need to be considered.

The accounting foundation for new clients or matters is the new matter worksheet. There is considerable pressure on attorneys and paralegals to keep precise track of their time. The accounting records and financial health of the law firm depend on it. Time is recorded by using handwritten paper forms and/or by using the computer. A number of different fee arrangements exist: clock-based (e.g., hourly rate, blended hourly rate), and alternatives that stress value billing (e.g., fixed fee, capped fee, task-based billing, hourly plus fixed fee, discounted hourly fee, contingent fee, and retroactive negotiated fee). The method of paying the bill (including expenses and court costs) should be spelled out in the attorney-client fee agreement. The amount actually paid by a client is not determined until there has been a valuing of the bill, which might result in a write-up, a write-down, or no change. Some business clients use an outside auditor to help them monitor law firm bills, particularly to identify irregularities.

Law firms must keep at least two separate bank accounts: the office account and the client trust account. The latter contains funds that belong to the clients such as settlement checks and unearned attorney fees. There must be no commingling (mixing) of office and client funds.

An efficient law firm uses administrative reports to help it keep track of and manage the practice. Examples include the aged accounts receivable report and the timekeeper productivity report.

Correspondence in client folders is often filed in reverse chronological order, with the most recent item placed on top. Correspondence is clipped to the right of the folder and all other documents are clipped on the left.

The location of client files in an office will be either centralized (often with the use of special filing personnel) or decentralized. The two major kinds of filing systems are the alphabetical system and the numerical system accompanied by a card index. An alphabetical system arranges files in alphabetical order by client surname or by organization name. A numerical system uses numbers or letter-number combinations (rather than surnames) to identify files. Offices can have the numbers and letters mean different things. Index cards help locate particular files and allow for cross-indexing. Some large offices use bar coding to facilitate file management. Once the office completes its work on a case, the file becomes a closed file. Practical considerations and the rules of ethics determine how long a firm must keep closed files. Important documents are returned to the client.

Key Terms

sole proprietorship	partnership	contract attorney	new file worksheet
personal liability	rainmaker	professional corporation	statutory fee case
limited liability	draw	limited liability entity	daily time sheet
sole practitioner	associate	corporate legal department	contemporaneous
general practitioner	lateral hire	general counsel	nonbillable time
boutique law firm	senior associate	managing partner	pro bono
law clerk	nonequity partner	legal administrator	indigent
legal intern	equity partner	paralegal manager	blended hourly rate
office sharing	staff attorney	outsourcing	value billing
overhead	of counsel	timekeeping	fixed fee

capped fee	incentive billing	write down	record information
bundled legal services	defense contingent fee	write up	manager
pro se	retroactive negotiated fee	valuing the bill	alphabetical filing
unbundled legal services	court costs	client trust account	system
task-based billing	expense slip	Interest on Lawyers' Trust	numerical filing system
hourly plus fixed fee	frivolous position	Accounts (IOLTA)	bar code
discounted hourly fee	retainer	commingling	closed file
contingent fee	draft bill		

Review Questions

1. Approximately how many attorneys practice in the private sector?
2. Name six major forms of private practice.
3. What is a sole proprietorship?
4. What is the distinction between limited liability and personal liability?
5. What is a sole practitioner?
6. What is the distinction between a general practitioner and a specialist?
7. What are law clerks and legal interns?
8. What is meant by an office-sharing arrangement?
9. What is overhead?
10. Distinguish between a sole proprietorship and a partnership.
11. What is a rainmaker?
12. What are the different kinds of partners that can exist?
13. What is a partner's draw?
14. What are the different kinds of associates that can exist?
15. What is a lateral hire?
16. What is meant by being passed over?
17. Define the following categories of attorneys: staff attorney, of counsel, and contract attorney.
18. What is a professional corporation?
19. What is a limited liability entity?
20. Describe the function of a corporate legal department.
21. What categories of attorneys and nonattorneys work in a corporate legal department?
22. What are some of the major responsibilities of the legal administrator?
23. List some of the main categories of administrative support staff in a large law office.
24. What are some of the major responsibilities of a paralegal manager?
25. What is outsourcing and what ethical dangers does it pose?

26. What is a new file worksheet?
27. Why are accurate time records important even in law offices that do not charge hourly fees?
28. What is the function of a daily time sheet?
29. What is nonbillable time? Give some examples.
30. Describe the following kinds of fees and billing arrangements: hourly rate, blended hourly rate, fixed fee, task-based billing (unbundled legal services), hourly plus fixed fee, discounted hourly fee, contingent fee, incentive billing, defense contingent fee, and retroactive negotiated fee.
31. What is value billing?
32. What are expenses and court costs?
33. Give two meanings of retainer.
34. What is the function of a draft bill?
35. What is meant by valuing the bill?
36. What is the distinction between a write-down and a write-up?
37. What is the function of law audit services?
38. What is e-billing?
39. What is a client trust account and why is it required?
40. What is the IOLTA program?
41. When can attorney fees be deposited in the attorney's personal account?
42. What is the function of the following administrative reports: work summary report, aged accounts receivable report, timekeeper productivity report, case-type productivity report, fee analysis report, work-in-progress report, cash receipts report, client investment summary report, and budget performance report?
43. What is the role of a records information manager?
44. Describe an alphabetical and a numerical filing system.
45. How can bar codes be used in file management?
46. How should offices handle closed case files?

Helpful Web Sites: More on Law Office Management

Occupational Outlook Handbook: Attorneys and Law Practice

- www.bls.gov/oco/home.htm

Law Office Management Resources

- www.ioma.com

- www.abanet.org/lpm/home.shtml
- www.abanet.org/genpractice
- www.texasbar.com/lomp/resource.htm
- www.myshingle.com
- www.weilandco.com/manage.html

American Bar Association Market Research and Statistics

- www.abanet.org/marketresearch/resource.html

American Bar Association Commission on Billable Hours Report

- www.abanet.org/careercounsel/billable/toolkit/bhcomplete.pdf

International Legal Technology Association

- www.peertopeer.org

Time and Billing Software

- www.timeslips.com
- www.pclaw.com
- www.prolaw.com
- www.legalmaster.com

Marketing

- www.lfmi.com
- www.abanet.org/lpm/resources/marketing.shtml
- www.lawyermarketing.com

Outsourcing

- www.lexadigm.com
- www.outsourcing.org/Directory/Legal
- www.rediff.com/money/2005/may/18bpo.htm
- www.legalaffairs.org/issues/May-June-2005/scene_brook_mayjun05.msp

Legal Consulting Firms

- Altman Weil
  www.altmanweil.com

- Baker Robbins & Co.
  www.brco.com
- Hildebrandt International
  www.hildebrandt.com
- Jaffe Associates
  www.jaffeassociates.com
- John P. Weil & Company
  weilandco.com
- LawBiz Management Company, Edward Poll & Associates
  www.lawbiz.com
- Robert Denney Associates
  www.robertdenney.com

"Greedy" Associates

- www.infirmation.com/bboard/clubs-top.tcl

Google Searches (run the following searches for more sites)

- law office management
- law office administration
- "legal administrator" role
- "paralegal manager"
- outsourcing legal
- timekeeping in a law office
- "billable hour"
- billing software law
- client trust account

Endnotes

1. American Bar Association, *National Lawyer Population by State* (2006) (www.abanet.org/marketresearch/resource.html) See also Bureau of Census (www.bls.gov/cps/cpsaat11.pdf).

2. American Bar Association Section on Legal Education and Admission to the Bar, *Enrollment and Degrees Awarded* (2007) (www.abanet.org/legaled/statistics/charts/stats%20-%201.pdf)

3. National Conference of Bar Examiners, *2006 Statistics* (www.ncbex.org/fileadmin/mediafiles/downloads/Bar_Admissions/2006stats.pdf).

4. U.S. Department of Labor, Bureau of Labor Statistics, *Occupational Outlook Handbook*, "Lawyers" (2006–2007) (www.bls.gov/oco/ocos053.htm#earnings).

5. R. Green, ed., *The Quality Pursuit* 69 (American Bar Association, 1989).

5a. Ann Sherman, *Should Small Firms Get on Board with Outsourcing?* Small Firm Business (September 12, 2005) (www.law.com/jsp/law/sfb/lawArticleSFB.jsp?id=1126256712489).

5b. National Federation of Paralegal Associations, Position Statement on the Outsourcing of Paralegal Duties to Foreign Countries (www.paralegals.org/associations/2270/files/paralegal_outsourcing.pdf).

5c. Eileen B. Libby, *Offshore Ripples Make Waves for US Paralegals*, 34 Facts and Findings 20 (May, 2007).

6. Altman Weil, Inc., *2003 Survey of Law Firm Economics*, at (www.altmanweil.com/products/surveys/slfe/annual.cfm).

7. J. Margolis, *At the Bar*, N. Y. Times, September 7, 1990, at B13.

8. A. Walljasper, *I Quit!*, Wisconsin Lawyer 16 (March 1990).

9. Morris, *Join the Effort to Restore Respect to the Legal Profession*, The Digest 3 (Arizona Paralegal Ass'n, April 1989).

10. T. Barcott, *Time Is Money*, AALA News (Alaska Ass'n of Legal Assistants, April 1990).

11. S. Matteucci, *What the Heck Is "Value Billing" Anyway?*, 18 The Montana Lawyer 2 (November 1992). See also D. Ricker, *The Vanishing Hourly Fee*, 80 American Bar Ass'n Journal 66 (March 1994); F. Marcotte, *Billing Choices*, 75 American Bar Ass'n Journal 38 (November 1989).

12. G. Emmett Raitt, *What if Your Client Used Value Billing?*, Orange County Lawyer 37 (April 1992).

13. Michele Coyne, *Alternatives to Customary Billing Practices*, The LAMA Manager 19 (Legal Assistant Management Ass'n, Summer 1991).

14. Darby, *Of Firms and Fees: The Administrator's Role*, 8 Legal Management 34, 39 (March/April 1989).

15. M. Geyelin, *If You Think Insurers Are Tight, Try Being One of Their Lawyers*, Wall Street Journal, February 9, 1999, at Al.

16. P. Hoffman, *Law Office Economics and Management Manual* § 41:04, at 4 (1986).

17. T. Light, *The Procedure Manual*, 26 The Practical Lawyer 71 (January 1980).

18. P. Everett, *Fundamentals of Law Office Management* 445 (2d ed. 2000).

19. B. Roper, *Practical Law Office Management* 387 (1995).

20. Id. at 393.

21. T. Cannon, *Ethics and Professional Responsibility for Legal Assistants* 258 (3d ed. 1999).

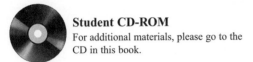

Student CD-ROM

For additional materials, please go to the CD in this book.

Online Companion™

For additional resources, please go to http://www.paralegal.delmar.cengage.com

Informal and Formal Administrative Advocacy

CHAPTER OUTLINE

A. The Nature of Advocacy
B. The Techniques of Informal Advocacy
C. Procedural Due Process
D. Formal Administrative Advocacy

[SECTION A]

THE NATURE OF ADVOCACY

Advocacy is the process by which an individual attempts to influence the behavior of others, often according to predetermined goals. Advocacy is a basic component of everyday life; we are frequently advocates for ourselves and for others. Note, for example, the advocacy involved, or potentially involved, in the following circumstances:

1. At a supermarket checkout counter, a clerk tells a customer that the price of tomatoes is 99¢ a pound. The customer replies, "But the sign back there said 89¢ a pound." The clerk says, "I'm sorry, but the price is 99¢."
2. A student goes to the teacher to say that a term paper should have been graded "A" rather than "B."
3. A tenant tells the landlord that a $500 a month rent increase is ridiculous because the building has been steadily deteriorating.
4. A homeowner has been away on a vacation. Upon his return, he finds that his house has been burglarized. When he goes to the police station to report the crime, he asks the desk sergeant why his neighborhood has not been receiving better protection in view of all the burglaries that have been occurring in the area lately. The sergeant replies that there are not enough police available to patrol the neighborhood adequately. The homeowner is not satisfied with this response and asks to see the precinct captain.

The customer, student, tenant, and homeowner all have complaints. They are *complainants*. They are not satisfied with something. Their natural response is to make an argument for better service. In so doing, they become advocates for the goals or objectives that they are seeking. Advocacy does not always require courtrooms, judges, and attorneys; all that is needed is a complaint, a complainant, and someone who should be able to act on the complaint.

The distinction between *formal* and *informal advocacy* is primarily one of degree. Generally, the more the setting looks like a court procedure (for example, with a hearing officer present, evidence or testimony taken, or written decisions issued), the more formal it is. As we saw in chapter 6, an administrative agency's quasi-judicial powers are often exercised through hearings that have

> advocacy The process by which you attempt to influence the behavior of others, often according to predetermined goals.

675

quasi-judicial proceeding
A proceeding within an administrative agency that seeks to resolve a dispute in a manner that is similar to a court (i.e., judicial) proceeding to resolve a dispute.

many similarities to courtroom proceedings. A **quasi-judicial proceeding** is one in which the agency acts much like a court when resolving a dispute between a citizen and the agency (such as between a social security recipient and the Social Security Administration) or between two or more citizens under the control of the agency (e.g., two students in the same school or two inmates in the same prison who are having a dispute). If you are representing yourself or someone else at such a hearing, you are engaged in formal advocacy, even if all of the formal procedures of a court proceeding are not followed.

Our first concern in this chapter is *in*formal advocacy that occurs (1) in connection with administrative agencies not involving formal hearings or (2) outside the realm of administrative agencies altogether, as in the supermarket example. Our primary focus will be the informal advocacy techniques that can be used when confronting employees of *any* organization—for example, a public agency such as a workers' compensation office or a private business such as an insurance company.

Paralegals often have contact with organizations that require the application of informal advocacy techniques. Here are several examples:

- Determining the names and addresses of the principal shareholders of a corporation
- Gaining access to the records of an agency or of a company
- Obtaining copies of forms from the Securities and Exchange Commission on the disclosure and reporting requirements of a corporation
- Writing to or visiting an agency or company to obtain its position on a matter involving a client
- Trying to convince a caseworker or a social worker that the action the agency has taken (or that it proposes to take) is illegal or ill-advised

A paralegal can meet resistance in any and all of these situations. The basic techniques of informal advocacy should help in handling this resistance.

[SECTION B]
THE TECHNIQUES OF INFORMAL ADVOCACY

Exhibit 15.1 presents a summary of nineteen techniques of informal advocacy that are sometimes useful when trying to obtain action from an administrative agency or from any large organization. The techniques are listed in the approximate order of effectiveness. Of course, whether a particular technique will be effective depends on what you are trying to accomplish, whom the technique is directed against, and how well you execute the technique. In general, though, the techniques at the beginning of Exhibit 15.1 are more likely to be effective than those at the end. Do you agree?

EXHIBIT 15.1	**Techniques of Informal Advocacy**

1. *Put your cards on the table.* Be direct and completely above-board in telling the agency official what your position is and what you want.
2. *Insist on adequate service.* Point out to the agency official that the purpose of the agency is service and that this principle should guide the official's actions.
3. *Ask for authorization.* Insist that the agency official show you the regulation, law, or other authority that supports the action taken or proposed by the agency.
4. *Climb the chain of command.* Normally, everyone has a boss who can overrule decisions made by those beneath him or her. When you are dissatisfied with the decision or action of an employee, "appeal," or complain, "up the chain of command" to the employee's supervisor and to the supervisor's supervisor, if needed.
5. *Insist on common sense.* Convey to the agency official the impression that common sense supports your position—in

addition to or despite regulations or technicalities that might be cited against you.
6. *Take the role of the tired, battered, helpless citizen.* Do not insist on anything. Play dumb; act exhausted; act in such a way that the agency official will think, "This person needs help"; act as if everyone else has given you the runaround and you are praying that this official (whom you have not dealt with before) will finally give you a sympathetic ear—and some help.
7. *Cite a precedent.* Point out to the agency official (if it is true) that your case is not unusual because the agency has granted what you want to others under the same or similar circumstances in the past.
8. *Find the points of compromise.* Ferret out the negotiable points in the dispute, and determine whether you can bargain your way to a favorable result.
9. *Uncover the realm of discretion.* Those in authority often want you to believe that their hands are tied, that there is

(continues)

EXHIBIT 15.1   Techniques of Informal Advocacy—*continued*

only one way to apply the rule. In fact, some discretion is often involved in the application of rules. You need to find the realm of discretion and try to fit your case within it. The goal is to show that the discretion provides the agency official enough flexibility to give you what you are seeking.

10. *Demonstrate the exception.* Insist on the uniqueness of your client's situation. Show agency officials that the general rule they are using to deny your client a benefit is inapplicable.

11. *Cite the law.* Show the agency official that you know what administrative regulations apply to the case. Also cite statutes and other laws to demonstrate your point.

12. *Be a buddy.* Show agency officials that you are not an enemy, that you respect and like them, and that you are aware of how difficult their job is.

13. *Make clear that you and your office are going to fight this case all the way up.* Make the agency official aware of how important the case is. Point out that you are thinking about taking the case to a formal agency hearing and that your office may go to court, if necessary.

14. *Redefine the problem.* If you can't solve a problem, redefine it—as long as you can still achieve the essentials of what

the client seeks. For example, stop trying to qualify the client for program "Z" if program "Y" will serve the client equally well (or almost so), and the problems of qualifying the client for "Y" are not as great as you'll face by continuing to insist on "Z."

15. *Do a favor to get a favor.* Be willing to do something (within reason) for the person from whom you are seeking something.

16. *Seek the support of third persons.* Before you make your position known, gather the support of individuals or groups within and outside the agency so you can demonstrate that you are not alone.

17. *Preach.* Lecture the agency official about his or her responsibilities within the agency. Elaborate on the mission of the agency, making clear that the denial of what you want violates or is inconsistent with that mission.

18. *Embarrass the official.* Show the agency official that you do not respect him or her. Do it in such a way that the official is made to look silly.

19. *Demonstrate anger.* Be completely open about the hostility you feel concerning what is being done or proposed.

Effective advocacy involves other concerns as well:

Advocacy

I. *Threshold Concerns*
   1. Define your goals in order of priority.
   2. Decide when to intervene.

II. *Self-Evaluation of Techniques Used*
   1. Are you making yourself clear?
   2. Are you creating more problems than you are solving?
   3. Are you accomplishing your goal?

III. *Adaptation.* Are you flexible enough to shift your techniques as needed?

IV. *Recording/Record Keeping*
   1. Describe what you saw.
   2. Describe what you did.

The focus of the first threshold concern is the priority of goals. This concern, of course, would not be applicable if the assignment you are given contains only one goal, such as obtaining a copy of a record at the agency or organization. Sometimes, however, an assignment contains a variety of objectives at the outset, or a single-objective assignment subsequently blossoms into tasks involving more than one goal. In that case, priorities must be set. If you try to do everything, you may end up accomplishing nothing. Every technique of informal advocacy will probably fail if you have unrealistic expectations of what can be accomplished.

The second threshold issue is to decide when to intervene with the advocacy techniques. The decision to intervene involves a strategic judgment about when it would be most appropriate to seek what you are after at the agency or organization. In most situations, a sense of timing is very important. For example, suppose that you must contact the complaint bureau of an agency that is relatively new to you. One approach would be simply to walk up to the complaint bureau and delve right into the matter that brought you there. Another approach would be to try to find out something about the bureau *before* going to it. There may be some literature available on the structure of the agency that will provide you with at least a general idea of what to expect. You may be able to talk to attorneys or other paralegals who have had prior contact with the bureau. Suppose you learn that two agency employees rotate their work at the bureau and that one employee has a reputation of being more cooperative than the other. You may decide not to go to the bureau until this employee is on duty. In short, you decide to postpone your contact with the bureau until circumstances are most favorable to the objective you are seeking.

As you use any of the techniques in Exhibit 15.1, you must simultaneously judge the *effectiveness* of the technique in light of what you are trying to accomplish. Are you making yourself clear? Are you complicating rather than resolving the problem? Are you getting through? Are you comfortable with the technique you are using? Does it clash with your personality? Are you pacing yourself properly? Is your insistence on immediate success encouraging a negative response?

One of the major signs of ineffective advocacy is becoming so involved in the case that you begin to take roadblocks and defeat *personally*. Everyone agrees that objectivity is a good quality—and most of us claim to possess this quality in abundance. The unfortunate fact, however, is that *we tend to lose objectivity as friction increases*. We allow our careers and our lifestyles to be threatened when someone says to us, "You can't do that." We rarely admit that we can be so threatened. We justify our response by blaming someone else for insensitivity, unfairness, or stupidity.

Once you have disciplined yourself to identify the techniques you are using and to evaluate their effectiveness, you must be flexible enough to *adapt* your techniques and shift to more effective ones when needed.

Finally, the paralegal usually will have a recording/record keeping responsibility. Almost every case you work on must be heavily documented in the office files. Your efforts at informal advocacy should be included in those files.

CLASS EXERCISE 15.A

In each role-playing exercise, there are two characters: C (the complainant) and E (the agency employee). Students from the class will be assigned one or the other role. In each setting, C is seeking something from E. E is uncooperative. The objective of E is to antagonize C (within reason) to the point where C loses objectivity. The objective of C is to use effective advocacy techniques without losing objectivity.

(a) At 4:30 P.M., C goes to the Department of Motor Vehicles to apply for a license. E tells C that the office closes at 5:00 P.M. and the application procedure takes forty-five minutes. E refuses to let C apply.

(b) C is filing a document at the clerk's office. The filing fee is $6. E tells C that the fee must be paid by check or the exact amount in cash. All C has is a $100 bill and must use some of it to take a long cab ride back to the office.

(c) C goes to the Bureau of Vital Statistics and requests a copy of his mother's birth certificate. E tells C that no citizen can obtain the birth certificate of another person without the written permission of the person. C's mother is ill in a hospital a thousand miles away. C wants the record without going through the bother of obtaining this permission.

Those members of the class who are not participating in the role-playing exercises should identify and evaluate the techniques of informal advocacy that C uses.

We now examine informal advocacy techniques in the context of the following fact situation:

You are in your own home or apartment. You receive a letter from the gas company stating that your gas will be shut off in ten days if you do not pay your bill. Your spouse tells you that all the bills have already been paid. You call the gas company, and when you question the clerk, she says to you, "I'm sorry sir; our records reflect an unpaid bill. You must pay the bill immediately." To try to straighten matters out, you take a trip to the utilities office.

In the dialogue that follows, the complainant is his own advocate. "C" is the complainant and "E" is a gas company employee. As you read the dialog, ask yourself how effective is C's informal advocacy.

E: Can I help you?
C: Yes, I want to see someone about a problem with my bill.
E: I'm sorry, sir, but the customer complaint division closed at 2 P.M. You'll have to come back or call tomorrow.
C: Closed! Well, let me see someone about terminating the gas service altogether.
E: All right, would you step over to that desk?

TECHNIQUE: *If you can't solve a problem, redefine the problem* to manageable proportions if, on balance, it is consistent with your objectives. (See Exhibit 15.1.) The client is taking a risk. He cannot get to the complaint division, so he is going to try to achieve his objective through the termination division. He has substituted one problem (getting to the termination division) for another problem (getting to the complaint division) in the hope of expressing his grievance.

> E: Can I help you?
> C: Yes, I want to terminate my gas if I can't get this problem straightened out.
> E: You'll have to go over to the bill complaint division, sir.
> C: Look, stop sending me somewhere else! This has got to be straightened out immediately!

TECHNIQUE: *Demonstrate anger.* This is a dangerous tactic to employ. It is a fact of life, however, that some people respond to this kind of pressure.

> C: Aren't you here to serve the public?

TECHNIQUE: *Insist on adequate service.* Point out that the organization exists to serve and that you need better service.

> E: There are rules and procedures that we all must abide by and . . .
> C: Your responsibility is to take care of the public!

TECHNIQUE: *Preach.* Perhaps the most common way people try to change other people is to lecture them, to tell them what they should or should not be doing.

TECHNIQUE: *Embarrass the official.* Make the agency official look silly and unworthy of respect. At this point, has the complainant lost all objectivity? What risks are being taken? Do you think the complainant is aware of what he is doing? If you asked him whether he's being effective, what do you think his response would be? Is he more involved with the "justice" of his case than with the effectiveness of his approach?

> C: I'd like to speak to your supervisor. Who is in charge of this office?
> E: Well, Mr. Adams is the unit director. His office is in Room 307.
> C: Fine.

TECHNIQUE: *Climb the chain of command.* Everyone has a boss who can overrule his or her subordinate's decisions. If you're unhappy about a decision, complain "up the chain of command," to the top if necessary.

> E: Can I help you?
> C: I want to speak to Mr. Adams about a complaint. Tell him that it is very important.
> E: Just a moment. [*She goes into Mr. Adams's office for a few moments and then returns.*] You can go in, sir.
> C: Mr. Adams?
> E: Yes, what can I do for you? I understand you are having a little problem.
> C: It's about this bill. I have been talking to person after person in this office without getting any response. I'm going in circles. I need to talk to someone who is not going to send me to someone else!

TECHNIQUE: *Take the role of the tired, battered, helpless citizen.*

> E: Well, let me see what I can do. I've asked the secretary to get your file. . . . Here it is. The records say that you haven't paid several months' bills. Our policy here is to terminate utility service if payment is delinquent sixty days or more.
> C: What policy is that? Could I see a copy of this policy and what law it is based on?

TECHNIQUE: *Ask for authorization.* Make the agency show you the regulation, law, or authority that allegedly backs up the action it has taken or says it will take. What risk is the complainant taking by resorting to this technique? Is the complainant suggesting to Mr. Adams that he does not trust him? How would you have asked for authorization in this situation? Does the request for authorization always have to be made in a hostile manner?

> E: Well, I'll be glad to show you the brochure.
> C: I would like to see it and also the law it is based on. My position, Mr. Adams, is that my wife has paid the bills.

E: Well, our records don't reflect it.

C: The canceled checks have not all come back from the bank yet. I would like a photocopy of your file on me. Under the law, I am entitled to it.

TECHNIQUE: *Cite the law.* Demonstrate that you know what regulations and other laws apply to the case.

E: You do have this right, but only if you make the request in writing.

C: Let's be reasonable. I'm making the request in person. That should be sufficient.

TECHNIQUE: *Insist on common sense.* Show the agency official that your position makes good common sense, even if regulations or technicalities go against you.

C: Surely, your rule calling for a written request can't apply when the person making the request is right in front of you.

TECHNIQUE: *Interpret the law.* Regulations, statutes, and cases often are susceptible to more than one meaning; identify and argue for the meaning most favorable to your cause.

TECHNIQUE: *Demonstrate the exception.* Insist that your situation is unique, not governed by the general rule.

C: Don't you have the power to waive this rule in such a case?

TECHNIQUE: *Uncover the realm of discretion.* Argue that rules do not exist until they are applied and that in the application of rules, agency officials often have some latitude in interpreting them in spite of their claim that their hands are tied by the rules.

E: Well, all right, I'll see if I can get a copy run off for you while you are here, but it will take a little time, and I must point out that it's highly irregular.

C: Now, Mr. Adams, I understand that you are a very busy man and that you have responsibilities more demanding than listening to people like me all day.

TECHNIQUE: *Be a buddy.* Show the agency official that you are not his enemy and that you respect and like him and that you are aware of how difficult his job is. Here the complainant has obviously shifted his tactic; he is no longer antagonistic. Consciously or unconsciously, he has made an evaluation of how successful his techniques have been thus far and has decided on a different course of action. What risk is he running in making this shift?

C: All I want is a two-week extension of time so that I can collect the proof needed to show you that the bill has been paid.

TECHNIQUE: *Put your cards on the table.* Tell the agency official, directly and openly, what your position is and what you want.

E: Well, we seldom give extensions. The situation must be extreme. I don't know . . .

C: Mr. Adams, suppose we forget my request for a copy of the records for the time being. All I want is two weeks.

TECHNIQUE: *Find the points of compromise.* Look for the negotiable points and figure out whether you can bargain your way to a good result.

E: I don't think so.

C: Well, Mr. Adams, it's either that or I'm going to go to court. All I'm asking for is some fair treatment. There's a principle involved and I intend to fight for it.

TECHNIQUE: *Make clear that you are going to fight this case "all the way up."* Make the agency official aware of how important this case is. When you have grounds to back you, point out that you are thinking about taking the case to a formal hearing and, if necessary, to court.

E: I'm sorry you feel that way, but we have our rules here. It would be chaos if we broke them every time someone asked for it.

C: Good day, Mr. Adams. [*You leave the office, resolved not to come back alone.*]

TECHNIQUE: *Seek the support of third persons.* Gather the support of individuals or groups within and outside the agency so that you can demonstrate that you are not alone.

Has the complainant failed? Was he a "bad" advocate? Has he accomplished anything? Should he give up? Do you think he will? If he does not, do you think he has learned (or that he should have learned) enough about the utility company to come back next time better equipped to handle his problem? If he comes back, what approach should he take and whom should he see? Should he see the supervisor of Mr. Adams, for example?

[S E C T I O N   C]

PROCEDURAL DUE PROCESS

Where paralegals are authorized by law to engage in *formal advocacy* by representing clients at administrative hearings (see chapter 4), it is one of the great challenges that they enjoy. In the remainder of the chapter, we will explore some of the skills required to perform this task effectively.

The subject matter of a hearing, as well as its procedure, can range from the very simple to the very complex. Our approach will be to examine a relatively simple hearing, after identifying the components of procedural due process.

When a government agency and a citizen have a serious dispute, basic fairness may require a number of procedural safeguards for the citizen. These safeguards are known as **procedural due process.** Let's look at an example:

> Tom is a civilian employee of the army. One day he receives a call from the manager of the division, who says, "I have just finished reading the report of the assistant manager. Based on my own observations and on this report, it is clear to me that you have been using the agency car for your own personal use. I have decided to fire you."

As a matter of fairness and common sense, what is wrong with the manager's approach? Assume that Tom denies the charge and that this is the first time he has heard anything about an alleged improper use of an agency car. The *substantive* question is whether Tom used the car improperly. The *procedural* question is whether the agency's method of resolving this problem is fair. The latter is a question of procedural due process.

In Exhibit 15.2, you will find some of the visceral responses that Tom or any citizen might make, plus their legal translation in terms of procedural safeguards.

procedural due process
Procedural protections that are required before the government can take away or refuse to grant liberty or a public benefit.

EXHIBIT 15.2	Procedural Safeguards (Procedural Due Process)

VISCERAL RESPONSE	LEGAL TRANSLATION
"Before I was fired, I should have been told the agency thinks I used the car illegally."	1. *Notice.* To enable you to prepare a response, you should be given adequate advance **notice** of the charge against you.
"Show me the report the assistant manager wrote on me so that I can see what he's talking about. And tell me what made you [the manager] arrive at this conclusion."	2. *Examination of evidence.* In order to respond to the evidence against you, you should be able to see what that evidence is.
"Before you fire me, give me a chance to explain myself."	3. *Hearing.* You should be given a formal meeting or **hearing**, where you can present your case.
"I want to present my case before someone other than the assistant manager or the manager."	4. *Hearing officer free of bias.* The hearing officer should be uninvolved—free of **bias**. The person making the charge against you, or giving any evidence against you, should not be making the final decision as to whether the charge is true. (The accuser should not be the executioner.)

notice Information about a fact; knowledge of something.

hearing A proceeding convened to resolve a dispute during which parties in the dispute can present their case.

bias Prejudice for or against something or someone. An inclination or tendency to think and to act in a certain way. A danger of prejudgment. (A person without a bias is objective, dispassionate, or disinterested.)

(continues)

EXHIBIT 15.2	Procedural Safeguards (Procedural Due Process)—*continued*

VISCERAL RESPONSE	LEGAL TRANSLATION
"If someone has something to say against me, I want to hear it from his own mouth, and I want to be able to ask him questions myself."	5. *Confrontation and cross-examination.* Whoever is accusing you or giving any evidence against you should be required to do so in your presence (**confrontation**). You should be able to ask this person questions about his or her allegations (**cross-examination**).
"I want to be able to bring my own counsel to help me."	6. *Legal representation.* You should have the right to representation by an attorney or an attorney substitute of your own choosing.
"I've had some unrelated troubles on the job in the past, plus some personal problems at home, but they have nothing to do with my use of the car."	7. *Relevancy of evidence.* The hearing officer should consider only **relevant** evidence. Relevancy refers to anything that logically tends to establish or disprove a fact.
"My coworker knows everything about my use of agency cars. I want to bring him to the hearing."	8. *Presentation of own witnesses.* You should be given the opportunity to present your own witnesses and any other evidence that supports your position.
"I want to see the decision in writing."	9. *Written decision with reasons.* To enable you to prepare an appeal, you should be given the decision in writing as well as the reasons for the decision.
"I want to be able to appeal."	10. *Appeal.* You should be given the right to **appeal** the decision to another individual or body.

confrontation Being present when others give evidence against you and having the opportunity to question them.

cross-examination Questioning of a witness at a hearing by an opponent after the other side has conducted a direct examination of that witness.

relevant Logically tending to establish or disprove a fact. Pertinent. Relevant evidence is evidence having any tendency to make the existence of a fact more probable or less probable than it would be without the evidence.

appeal Asking a higher tribunal to review or reconsider the decision of an inferior tribunal.

As a matter of constitutional law, a citizen is not entitled to all ten components of procedural due process outlined in Exhibit 15.2 in every dispute with a government agency. What procedural safeguards are required? The answer depends primarily on the seriousness of the dispute. In a hearing on terminating public assistance, for example, all ten safeguards are required when the recipient is challenging the termination. This is so because of the extreme consequences that could result from termination. The more extreme the possible consequences, the more procedural safeguards the law imposes on the conduct of hearings to determine whether those consequences should be imposed.

[SECTION D]
FORMAL ADMINISTRATIVE ADVOCACY

"What would it be like to stand before a judge, and it would be you—yes, you—standing (without a law degree) before a judge representing a client? A person in need would be depending on your ability as a representative to help win the case. What would it be like?" Jeffrey S. Wolfe, United States Administrative Law Judge[1]

We turn now to a paralegal's role in formal administrative advocacy. As we saw in chapter 4, there are a number of state and federal administrative agencies that allow paralegals to provide a full range of legal services, including representation of their own clients at administrative hearings.

One of the largest agencies where this occurs is the Social Security Administration (SSA). Although formal administrative advocacy differs from agency to agency, an examination of a paralegal's role at SSA can help us understand what is possible at many agencies.

One of SSA's largest programs provides disability benefits to individuals who suffer from an "inability to engage in any substantial gainful activity by reason of any medically determinable physical or mental impairment."[2] Every year 2.5 million people apply for Social Security disability benefits under one of two programs:

- Disability Insurance Benefits (DIB) for individuals who have a qualifying work history
- Supplemental Security Income (SSI) for individuals who may have never worked

Approximately 1.7 million of these applications are denied. The denials lead to a staggering 600,000 annual appeals handled by federal **administrative law judges (ALJ)** throughout the country. "The Social Security Administration . . . adjudicates more cases than all federal courts combined."[3] Social Security law, as many citizens know from first-hand experience, can be complicated. This is particularly true of disability law. Consequently, the need for legal assistance in the 600,000 annual disability hearings is enormous.

> **administrative law judge (ALJ)** A government officer who presides over a hearing at an administrative agency.

Unfortunately, not enough attorneys practice Social Security law, although a growing number take Social Security cases under the broader practice of elder law. Part of the reason many attorneys stay away from disability cases is that they do not generate enough revenue. In most cases, a representative can collect $5,300 or 25 percent of back-due disability benefits, whichever is less. The fee cannot be higher even if the client agrees to pay more. Nationally, the average fee collected is $2,500.[4] This is not enough to interest many attorneys. Fortunately, claimants seeking legal representation have an alternative. Congress has specifically provided that persons:

"other than attorneys" may represent "claimants before the Commissioner of Social Security."[5]

Hence paralegals have a federal mandate to practice law before SSA, including the right to charge fees for their services. One of the ALJs makes the following comment about the effectiveness of paralegal advocates and whether having a law degree is important: "It's not being a lawyer that makes a difference, but knowing what is a disability. Advocates who know what they are doing do a better job than an attorney who doesn't know disability."[6]

Some attorneys may not want to refer to paralegal representation as practicing law, but that's what it is. This is not to say, however, that attorneys and paralegals are treated alike in Social Security cases. They both have the same responsibilities as representatives, but they are treated differently in the crucial area of fees. When attorneys win a disability case, their fee is deducted from the claimant's award by SSA and sent directly to the attorneys. When nonattorney representatives win a case, however, they must collect their fee on their own from the client. As pointed out in chapter 4, however, SSA recently began a demonstration project that authorizes direct payment of fees to nonattorney representatives who have experience representing clients before SSA, pass an examination on Social Security law, and carry liability insurance to protect clients against malpractice.[7] Paralegals who do not meet these qualifications must collect their fees directly from their clients.

The first step in being a representative is to be appointed by the client. (See Exhibit 4.3 in chapter 4 for the form that a Social Security applicant must use to appoint a representative.) There is no examination, license, or registration requirement imposed by SSA to be a representative. Yet there is a requirement that a representative know the "significant issue(s) in a claim" and have a "working knowledge" of Social Security statutes, regulations, and rulings.[8]

SAMPLE CASE

To gain a greater appreciation of paralegal representation at SSA disability hearings, we will examine a sample case. It involves a dispute over an overpayment to a recipient of disability payments under the Supplemental Security Income (SSI) program. Here are the major participants in the case:

Mary O'Brien: SSI recipient and claimant
George O'Brien: Mary's husband
John Powell: paralegal representative of Mary
Helen Davis: witness for Mary
Alex Bolton: administrative law judge at SSA

Background

Mary O'Brien is disabled. She suffers from depression, an affective disorder, and receives $531 a month in SSI. This amount assumes a total income of $3,600 a year in the O'Brien household. Benefits under SSI are, in part, dependent on available income in the recipient's home. When Mary applied for SSI benefits, she told SSA that her husband, George O'Brien, earns $3,600 a year from a part-time job as a night watchman.

Mary and George have a strained relationship, although they continue to live together. She is not aware of what he does during the day. Indeed, when she questions him about his activities, he becomes hostile. He can be violent. On June 1, 2005, she called the police when he went into a rage. The police referred Mary to the County Domestic Violence Center. She went there and met with a counselor, Helen Davis. After describing what happened, Davis advised Mary to obtain a restraining order against her husband. Mary, however, did not want to involve the courts, since she felt this would enrage her husband all the more. Hence she did not file for a restraining order, although she continued to come to the center to attend counseling sessions for abused women.

On September 1, 2006, SSA sends Mary a Notice of Overpayment. It states that according to information received from the Internal Revenue Service, George O'Brien reported taxable earnings of $12,000 during the year 2005. Her payment of $531 a month was based on a household income of $3,600. Since her husband was in fact earning considerably more, her 2005 entitlement has been recalculated. The SSA has concluded that Mary received an overpayment of $3,250 during 2005. To recoup this amount, SSA will deduct $53.10 a month from her disability check until the overpayment of $3,250 has been repaid.

This notice is quite distressing for Mary. She calls the local Neighborhood Legal Services Office for help. On the phone, a receptionist determines that she is eligible for free legal services because of her low income. The receptionist tells Mary to come in the next day for an appointment with John Powell, a paralegal in the office who handles social security cases.

John conducts an extensive interview of Mary. She tells John that her husband admits that he earned the extra money in 2005 but that it was "none of your business." He works as a night guard for a security firm that is managed by his cousin. She also describes his anger and violence over anything that questions or challenges his authority or that is considered an interference in his affairs.

Prehearing Advocacy

John points out to Mary that if the extra money was earned, the only way she can avoid making the repayment is to file a Request for Waiver of Overpayment on the ground that she is without fault in causing the overpayment or in failing to report it and that requiring repayment will be a hardship and is against equity and good conscience. Furthermore, if they act quickly, they might prevent SSA from starting the deductions from her monthly disability check. Mary begins to feel relieved. She signs the SSA form appointing John as her representative (see Exhibit 4.3 in chapter 4) and asks him to take whatever steps are necessary to try to avoid the repayment. He explains that if the request for waiver is denied, they can ask for a conference to explain their side and ultimately they can ask for a hearing before an administrative law judge.

In the weeks following the meeting between John and his client, a number of events occur:

- John helps Mary fill out the Request for Waiver of Overpayment. The basis of the request is that Mary is without fault because she knew nothing about her husband's side job, he is secretive about his finances, and he is abusive, particularly when she questions him about anything he does outside the home.
- John sends this request to SSA along with a cover letter asking SSA not to begin deductions from Mary's monthly payment until the appeal process is complete. He makes this request as a precaution even though SSA's policy is not to begin "adjustment action" until the waiver issue is resolved.
- A month later SSA sends Mary and John its response. The request for waiver is denied.
- John then asks the SSA field office for a personal conference during which he and Mary will explain their case before an SSA official who has not been involved in the initial decision to require the repayment of the overpayment. This request is granted.
- Five days before the personal conference, John exercises Mary's right to go to the SSA office in order to examine the file that contains the records used by SSA to demand the return of the overpayment. He photocopies the records that he does not already have.
- By studying the SSA records in Mary's file, John identifies further evidence he will pursue to be better prepared to respond to the SSA's case against Mary.
- The personal conference takes place at the SSA office. It lasts about an hour. John goes over the details of what happened during 2005 and why Mary knew nothing about her husband's extra

income. One of the reasons the conference is valuable (even if it does not result in a decision in Mary's favor) is that it gives John a clearer understanding of the SSA's case against her.

- A month later Mary and John receive a notice from SSA reaffirming the decision not to grant her the waiver.
- Further efforts to resolve the case (including use of reconsideration procedures) are unsuccessful. John then files a Request for Hearing before an administrative law judge.
- Several weeks later, John receives a call from the Office of Hearings and Appeals to arrange a date for the hearing. After consulting with Mary, a date for the hearing is set. John and Mary receive a formal Notice of Hearing indicating that the hearing will be held before U.S. Administrative Law Judge Alex Bolton on the agreed-upon date.

Characteristics of Disability Hearings

A disability hearing in SSA's Office of Hearings and Appeals is **nonadversarial** because it is a one-party proceeding. At a hearing, the following participants might be present:

- The claimant
- His or her representative (e.g., a paralegal)
- One or more witnesses (e.g., a vocational counselor, a relative)
- A reporter (often an SSA secretary) who makes a voice recording of the hearing
- The presiding administrative law judge (ALJ)

(See Exhibit 15.3 for a typical arrangement of a SSA hearing room.) An official representing the SSA is not present. The only party at the hearing is the claimant.

nonadversarial Pertaining to a conflict-resolution proceeding in which all opposing parties to the conflict or dispute are not present.

EXHIBIT 15.3	Typical Social Security Hearing Room

An administrative law judge presides over a Social Security hearing. Present are the paralegal representative, the claimant, a witness, and a court reporter. Before the paralegal begins asking questions of the witness, the judge swears in the witness as the reporter makes a voice recording of the proceeding.

This does not mean, however, that the claimant's representative will have an easy time establishing the position of the claimant. The ALJ is not an advocate, but he or she has an obligation to "develop the record." To fulfill this duty, the ALJ might take an affirmative role at the hearing such as by actively questioning the claimant and arranging for a vocational expert to be present to give testimony. The representative must convince the ALJ that the claimant's case fits within the guidelines of eligibility for disability benefits. This is done primarily through the testimony of the claimant and the introduction of documentary evidence such as medical and vocational records. Medical records can be lengthy, complicated, incomplete, confusing, and, at times, contradictory. Nevertheless, most ALJs will not tolerate a sloppy presentation; they will hold a representative's feet to the fire by insisting on a coherent presentation of the claimant's case. The representative must be able to anticipate possible questions from the ALJ and provide answers by citing information on specific pages of exhibits in the record. Competent representation can be a challenge even though the other side is technically absent and unrepresented.

A disability hearing is similar to a court trial in that both are **on-the-record** proceedings in which testimony is given under oath. A recorder is present at the disability hearing to tape-record everything that is said. Yet unlike court trials, the rules of evidence do not fully apply to disability hearings. The ALJ will consider any evidence that is relevant (broadly defined) to the issues in the case.

To a large extent, the conduct of a hearing depends on the style and personality of the presiding ALJ. Some ALJs will let the representative take the lead by making an opening statement, introducing documentary evidence, and questioning witnesses. The ALJ might ask his or her own questions after the representative has finished. Other ALJs take a more aggressive role. They might not allow the representative to take over until they ask questions of the claimant or other witnesses.

Preparation for the Hearing

To prepare for Mary's hearing, John does the following:

- Asks Helen Davis to come to the hearing as a witness for Mary. Davis is the counselor at the County Domestic Violence Center where Mary went for assistance during 2005. (In the event Davis cannot come to the hearing, John will obtain her **affidavit** that states the circumstances of Mary's involvement with the center.)
- Obtains a letter from Mary's doctor, David Stepps, M.D., that describes the medication he prescribed for her due to the tension she was under at home.
- Researches this medication on the Internet and finds a report from the National Institute of Mental Health on the reasons the medication is prescribed and its side effects of lethargy and extreme sensitivity to conflict. John downloads this report and prints the pertinent section for use at the hearing.
- Researches battered women syndrome on the Internet and finds a medical study on the helplessness experienced by women faced with severe abuse from their husbands and boyfriends. He downloads and prints the study for use at the hearing.
- Researches SSA's policy manual on the Internet (*policy.ssa.gov/poms.nsf/aboutpoms*) to make sure he has a full grasp of all of the procedures that SSA should be following in Mary's case.
- Prepares a complete summary of all Mary's assets and liabilities, showing monthly household income and expenses.
- Obtains copies of the O'Briens' federal and state tax returns for 2005.
- Compiles Mary's medical history, which will be relevant to the hardship issue (particularly the amounts she must pay for drugs and other medical care) and to her ability to handle stress and understand household finances.
- Prepares a set of notes in which he identifies Mary's theory of the case, together with citations to applicable regulations and supporting facts in the exhibits.
- Meets with Mary in his office to go over what is likely to happen at the hearing and to roleplay her responses to the questions that he plans to ask her and that the ALJ might ask her. John comments on each of her responses, pointing out the importance of telling the truth and of giving detailed answers. He tells her that the hearing will be tape-recorded so she should speak clearly and answer questions verbally. The tape recorder will not know if she answers a question with a nod of her head.

on the record Noted or recorded in an official record of the proceeding.

affidavit A written or printed statement of facts made by a person (called the *affiant*) before a person with authority to administer the oath.

The O'Brien Hearing

Judge Bolton begins the hearing by introducing himself and letting everyone know that a reporter will be recording the proceeding. He then asks everyone to identify themselves for the record:

Mary O'Brien: SSI recipient and claimant
John Powell: paralegal representative of Mary
Helen Davis: witness for Mary

Judge Bolton turns his attention to the reports and other exhibits already in the file and those that anyone wants considered. They are all identified with an exhibit number. He asks John if he has any objections to any of the exhibits. John responds that he does not but that he hopes to have the chance during the hearing to comment on some of the SSA reports in the file.

Judge Bolton administers the oath to tell the truth to all witnesses who will be giving testimony (Mary O'Brien and Helen Davis) and tells John to present his case.

John begins by summarizing the position of his client that she is without fault in receiving the overpayment because she had no knowledge of the extra earnings of her husband and that he has been physically abusive to her whenever she tries to question him about any financial matters. He also says that forcing a repayment will be a severe hardship on Mary.

John then asks Mary a series of questions to elaborate on these and other relevant points. For example:

Who takes care of the finances in the household?
Is your name on any bank accounts with your husband?
Describe the living expenses you and your husband have in the home.
Explain whether it will be a hardship to have to repay the overpayment.
Has your husband told you what he does during the day?
When do you see him during the course of the day?
Did your husband hit you during 2005?
Did you call the police?
Why have you stayed living with a husband who is abusive?
Are any other living arrangements available to you if you leave your husband?
Describe your health during 2005.
Were you taking any medication?
What effect did the medication have on you?

While asking such questions, John refers to specific exhibits such as the letter of Dr. David Stepps on why he prescribed the medication, the report on the side effects of the medication, and the study on battered women syndrome.

When John finishes questioning Mary, Judge Bolton asks her several questions about her educational background and about the times at home when she is able to get along with her husband. After Mary answers, John asks her some follow-up questions designed to reinforce her inability to understand financial matters and her fear of her husband.

Finally, John begins questioning Helen Davis, the counselor at the County Domestic Violence Center. John asks her to explain the services of the center and the level of agitation and fear Mary expressed when she came there for help. He asks her whether it is common for abused women to remain with their abusers. Finally, he asks her to explain why she recommended that Mary obtain a restraining order against her husband and whether it is unusual for an abused woman to be afraid to do so.

At the conclusion of all the testimony, Judge Bolton thanks everyone and says that he will render a decision as soon as possible.

Before leaving, John has one final request of Judge Bolton. He asks if he can submit a memorandum to the judge in which he presents the facts in the light of the applicable law. Judge Bolton says he will be glad to receive such a memorandum. John knows that ALJs hold many hearings and a memorandum of this kind might help influence the outcome of his case. Preparing it after the hearing gives John the opportunity to highlight those facts and legal matters that appeared to be of concern to the ALJ at the hearing.

Seven months after submitting the memorandum, John and Mary receive the decision of Judge Bolton. Mary is found to have been without fault in causing the overpayment and it would be an undue hardship to require repayment. Victory!

Further Appeals

If the decision had gone against Mary, the next step would have been a Request for Review by the Appeals Council. This is an appeal within the SSA. The claimant submits a brief to the Appeals Council indicating why the decision of the administrative law judge should be reversed. John would prepare the brief for Mary. A paralegal representative can write and sign these briefs. In the vast majority of cases, neither the party nor his or her representative makes a personal appearance before the Appeals Council. A decision is rendered on the record.

exhaust administrative remedies To go through all dispute-solving avenues that are available in an administrative agency before asking a court to review what the agency did.

If a claimant was dissatisfied by the decision of the Appeals Council, the next step would be an appeal to a U.S. District Court. The case could be taken to court because the party had **exhausted administrative remedies**. At this point, an attorney would have to take over the case, although a paralegal could assist the attorney, as in any court case. The attorney could ask a competent paralegal to help prepare the pleadings and briefs that would be submitted to the court, but only an attorney could sign them. The federal authorization for paralegals to represent claimants within SSA does not include court representation.

Conclusion

pro bono Concerning or involving legal services that are provided for the public good (*pro bono publico*) without fee or compensation. Sometimes also applied to services given at a reduced rate.

As you can see from John Powell's role as a representative before the SSA, formal administrative advocacy by paralegals, where it is allowed, can be a major undertaking. Although most paralegals do not have the opportunity to engage in such advocacy in their everyday work, you might consider **pro bono** work where such advocacy is needed. (See the list of pro bono work in Section C of chapter 2.) There are neighborhood legal service offices, legal aid societies, and homeless projects in many cities that would welcome part-time volunteer work on Social Security cases. Perhaps you could inquire about teaming with an experienced paralegal whom you could assist until you felt comfortable enough to venture out on your own cases. The need for legal help in this area is enormous.

Chapter Summary

Advocacy takes place all the time. It is an everyday process by which all citizens—not just attorneys—attempt to influence or change the actions of others. Informal advocacy occurs outside of courts or other tribunals where hearings are held to resolve controversies that the participants have not been able to resolve informally.

Advocates try many techniques of informal advocacy, with varying degrees of success. Among the most common are the following:

1. Placing your cards on the table
2. Insisting on adequate service
3. Asking for authorization
4. Climbing the chain of command
5. Insisting on common sense
6. Taking the role of the tired, battered, helpless citizen
7. Citing a precedent
8. Finding the points of compromise
9. Uncovering the realm of discretion
10. Demonstrating the exception
11. Citing the law
12. Being a buddy
13. Making clear that you will fight the case all the way up
14. Redefining the problem
15. Doing a favor to get a favor

16. Seeking the support of third parties
17. Preaching
18. Embarrassing the official
19. Showing anger

While using any of these techniques, you need to evaluate your effectiveness and modify the techniques based on this evaluation.

Whenever the government takes an action that seriously affects a citizen, such as denying or removing a benefit, basic fairness may require a number of procedural safeguards. These requirements are referred to as *procedural due process*. While not applicable to every situation, the safeguards can include notice, a hearing, a personal appearance at the hearing, the absence of bias, representation, relevance of the evidence, an opportunity to examine the evidence, an opportunity to present your own witnesses, a decision in writing, and an opportunity to appeal.

At some state and federal administrative agencies, paralegals are authorized to provide a full range of legal services, including representation of their own clients at administrative hearings. A major example of such an agency is the Social Security Administration, particularly in the representation of applicants at disability hearings. Competent representation at such hearings requires extensive preparation and skill in marshalling facts and coherently presenting them at the hearing in light of the applicable law.

Key Terms

advocacy
quasi-judicial proceeding
procedural due process
notice
hearing
bias

confrontation
cross-examination
relevant
appeal
administrative law judge
   (ALJ)

nonadversarial
on the record
affidavit
exhaust administrative
   remedies
pro bono

Review Questions

1. What is advocacy?
2. What is the distinction between formal advocacy and informal advocacy?
3. What is a quasi-judicial proceeding?
4. What are the major techniques of informal advocacy?
5. What are the roles of goal setting, timing, self-assessment, and flexibility in informal advocacy?
6. What is procedural due process?
7. What are the definitions of *notice, hearing, bias, confrontation, cross-examination, relevancy,* and *appeal*?

8. What is the function of an ALJ?
9. What roles can paralegals play in Social Security hearings?
10. When is a hearing nonadversarial?
11. When is a proceeding on the record?
12. What are some of the major steps an effective paralegal will take when representing a client in a Social Security hearing?
13. How does a client exhaust administrative remedies?
14. What is meant by pro bono?

Helpful Web Sites: More on Administrative Advocacy

Social Security Representation
- www.ssa.gov/representation
- www.ssa.gov/pubs/10075.html

National Organization of Social Security Claimants' Representatives
- www.nosscr.org

National Association of Disability Representatives
- www.nadr.org

Social Security Disability Certification
- www.nbtanet.org

Google Searches (run the following searches for more sites)
- administrative advocacy
- procedural due process
- "informal advocacy"
- Social Security Hearings

Endnotes

1. Jeffrey S. Wolfe, *Professional Service to the Beat of a Different Drum: Non-Lawyer Representation before Social Security's Office of Hearings and Appeals,* Facts & Findings 37 (May 2000). The assistance of Judge Wolfe and of Christopher J. Holly, RP (an Indiana independent paralegal), in the preparation of the social security materials in this chapter is gratefully acknowledged. See Judge Wolfe's book *Social Security and the Legal Professional* (Delmar, 2003) and Christopher Holly's Internet site (www.medicaidguide.com.)
2. 42 U.S.C. § 416(i)(1)(A).
3. Milton Carrow, *A Tortuous Road to Bureaucratic Fairness,* 46 Administrative Law Review 297 (Summer 1994).
4. Wolfe, *supra* note 1, at 39.
5. 42 U.S.C. § 406(a)(1).
6. Herbert M. Kritzer, *Legal Advocacy* 133 (1998).
7. Federal Register 2447–50 (January 13, 2005) (www.ssa.gov/representation/FR108_01_13_2005.txt) (www.ssa.gov/representation/overview.htm). See also 42 U.S.C. § 406(b)(1)(A) (2001).
8. 20 C.F.R. § 404.1740(b)(3)(I).

Student CD-ROM
For additional materials, please go to the CD in this book.

Online Companion™
For additional resources, please go to
http://www.paralegal.delmar.cengage.com

Bibliography

A

AARP's Legal Services Network: Expanding Legal Services to the Middle Class by W. Moore, 32 Wake Forest Law Review 503 (1997).

ABA Formal Opinion 93–379: Double Billing, Padding and Other Forms of Overbilling by S. Chan, 9 Georgetown Journal of Legal Ethics 611 (1996).

ABA Model Guidelines for the Utilization of Paralegal Services (American Bar Association 2004) (www.abanet.org/legalservices/paralegals/downloads/modelguidelines.pdf).

ABA Report Debates Nonlawyers' Role in Providing Legal Services, 23 Montana Lawyer 11 (May 1998).

Accounting Firms and the Unauthorized Practice of Law: Who Is the Bar Really Trying to Protect? by E. Farrell, 33 Indiana Law Review 599 (2000).

Activities of Insurance Adjusters as Unauthorized Practice of Law, 29 A.L.R.4th 1156 (1984).

Activities of Law Clerks as Illegal Practice of Law, 13 A.L.R.3d 1137 (1967).

Activities of Stock or Securities Broker Constitute Unauthorized Practice of Law, 34 A.L.R.3d 1305 (1970).

[Alabama] *Imputed Disqualification of Law Firms When Non-lawyer Employees Change Firms* by J. McClain, 63 Alabama Lawyer 94 (March 2002).

[Alabama] *Legal Assistants: A Growing Role in the Practice of Law in Alabama* by K. Rasmussen, 52 The Alabama Lawyer 214 (1991).

[Alabama] *Legal Assistants: An Evolving Role in the Practice of Law in Alabama* by G. McPherson, 63 The Alabama Lawyer 178 (May 2002).

Alternative Staffing Option: Freelance Paralegals by E. Siemek, 27 Colorado Lawyer 49 (April 1998).

Approaches for Continuing Legal Education for Paralegals, 7 Journal of Paralegal Education and Practice 43 (1990).

Are Organizations That Provide Free Legal Services Engaged in the Unauthorized Practice of Law? by W. Moore, 67 Fordham Law Review 2397 (1999).

[Arizona] *Bar Seeks to Protect Public with Non-lawyer Practice Rules*, 30 Arizona Attorney 10 (March 1994).

[Arizona] *How to Evaluate the Qualifications of Legal Assistants* by T. Clarke, 30 Arizona Attorney 28 (May 1994).

[Arizona] *Legal Document Preparer*, Arizona Code of Judicial Administration, § 7–208 (www.supreme.state.az.us/orders/admcode/curcode.htm).

[Arizona] *Self-Presented Litigants and the Unauthorized Practice of Law* by B. James, 35 Arizona Attorney 18 (May 1999).

[Arizona] *We Can't All Be Lawyers . . . or Can We? Regulating the Unauthorized Practice Of Law in Arizona* by R. Talamante, 34 Arizona Law Review 873 (1992).

[Arizona] *Where We are Today: Non-lawyer Practice in Arizona* by L. Shely, 30 Arizona Attorney 11 (February 1994).

The Art of Managing Your Support Staff (American Bar Association Section of Economics of Law Practice, 1986).

Asserting Confidentiality: The Need for a Lay Representative-Claimant Privilege by J. Kaufman, 15 Pacific Law Journal 245 (1984) (administrative hearings).

Attorney Robert Shapiro Launches On-Demand Paralegal Service, 20 Lawyer's PC 6 (September 1, 2003) (www.proxilaw.com).

Attorneys' Fees: Cost of Services Provided by Paralegals, 73 A.L.R.4th 938 (1987).

Attorney's Guide to Practicing with Legal Assistants, 2d ed. (State Bar of Texas, 1992).

Attorney's Splitting Fees with ... Laymen as Grounds for Disciplinary Proceeding, 6 A.L.R.3d 1446 (1966).

The Authorized Practice of Legal Reference Service, 87 Law Library Journal 203 (1995).

B

Bankruptcy Paralegal Regulation by M. Testerman, 23 California Bankruptcy Journal 37 (1996).

The Beginning of Wisdom: Why Paralegal Educators Should Address Domestic Violence in Family Law Courses by M. Flaherty, 16 Journal of Paralegal Education and Practice 49 (2000).

Better Resumes for Attorneys and Paralegals by A. Lewis (Barron's, 1986).

Between Law and Society: Paralegals and the Provision of Justice Services in Sierra Leone and Worldwide by V. Maru, 31 Yale Journal of International Law 427 (Summer 2006).

Building a Strong Attorney-Paralegal Team by N. Cattie, 27 Trial 24 (January 1991).

C

California Paralegal's Guide, 5th ed. by Z. Mack (LEXIS Publishing, 1998).

[California] *Call the ~~Doctor~~ Nurse! The Role of the Legal Nurse Consultant*, 19 San Francisco Attorney Magazine 20 (December 1993/January 1994).

[California] *Handbook on Paralegal Utilization* by the California Alliance of Paralegal Associations (2004).

[California] *Laws Affecting the Paralegal* by M. Laurado 29 Los Angeles Lawyer 16 (February 2007).

[California] *Looking Closely at the Role Of Paralegals: The California, New Jersey, and Wisconsin Experiences*, 80 Michigan Bar Journal 56 (March 2001).

The California Paralegal: Essential Rules, Documents, and Resources by W. Statsky & S. Sandberg (Delmar Cengage Learning 2008).

[California] *Paralegal Requirements Tighten in 2004* by K. Simonson, 45 Orange County Lawyer 8 (November 2003).

[California] *Poverty Law for the '90s: Business Is Booming for Storefront Paralegals on the Poor Side of Town* by T. Sisco, 15 California Lawyer 31 (June 1995).

[California] *There Goes the Monopoly: The California Proposal to Allow Nonlawyers to Practice Law* by K. Justice, 44 Vanderbilt Law Review 179 (1991).

Career Opportunities in the Paralegal Profession by R. Berkey (Arco, 1983).

Catering to Our Clients: How In Re Cater Exposes the Flaws in Model Rule 5.3—and How They Can Be Solved by J. Putnam, 19 Georgetown Journal of Legal Ethics 925 (Summer 2006).

Chinese Walls by M. Moser, 3 Georgetown Journal of Legal Ethics 399 (1990) (conflict of interest).

Code Crackdown: Bankruptcy Trustees Use Law to Police (Nonlawyer) Petition Preparers by H. Samborn, 82 American Bar Association Journal 18 (May 1996).

Code of Ethics and Professional Responsibility by the National Association of Legal Assistants (1995) (www.nala.org/benefits-code.htm).

Collection Agencies and the Unauthorized Practice of Law by K. Folts, 77 Nebraska Law Review 365 (1998).

Colloquium on Nonlawyer Practice before Administrative Agencies, 37 Administrative Law Review 359 (1985).

[Colorado] *The Adventures of a Paralegal* by G. Stephens, 28 Colorado Lawyer 33 (April 1999).

[Colorado] *Avoiding the Unauthorized Practice of Law by Non-Lawyer Assistants* by D. Kueck, 32 Colorado Lawyer 27 (March 2003).

[Colorado] *Increasing Access to Justice: Expanding the Role of Nonlawyers…*, by M. Lock, 72 University of Colorado Law Review 459 (2001).

[Colorado] *Overtime for Law Firm Employees: the Fair Labor Standards Act* by B. Benrud, 28 Colorado Lawyer 99 (September 1999).

[Colorado] *Paralegals: Powerful Performers in a Changing World* by J. Bourgoin, 24 Colorado Lawyer 2193 (September 1995).

Colorado Paralegals: Proposed Guidelines by S. Davis, 25 The Colorado Lawyer 63 (October 1996) (see also 25 The Colorado Lawyer 33 [November 1996]).

[Colorado] *Probono and Paralegals: Making a Difference* by J. Price, 30 Colorado Lawyer 55 (September 2001).

[Colorado] *Use of Legal Assistants in Client Representation at Hearings, Depositions or Administrative Proceedings*, 18 The Colorado Lawyer 1149 (February 18, 1989).

Community Courts by W. Statsky, 3 Capital University Law Review 2 (1974).

Computer Programs and Systems Optimize Legal Assistant Productivity by M. Bjorkman, 70 Michigan Bar Journal 1154 (November 1991).

Conflicts and Confidences: Codes Address Ethics for Paralegals by H. Samborn, 82 American Bar Association Journal 24 (June 1996).

[Connecticut] *Guidelines for Lawyers Who Employ or Retain Legal Assistants*, Connecticut Bar Association (www.ctbar.org/article/articleview/197).

[Connecticut] *Guidelines for Legal Assistants*, Connecticut Bar Association (www.ctbar.org/article/view/198/1/57).

[Connecticut] *What's in a Name? Should Paralegals Be Liable for Malpractice?* by C. Lissitzyn, 77 Connecticut Bar Journal 86 (2003). Also printed in 15 Professional Lawyer 2 (No. 4, 2005).

Contesting Professionalism: Legal Aid and Nonlawyers in England and Wales by R. Moorhead et al., 37 Law and Society Review 765 (December 2003).

Criminal Defendant's Representation by Person Not Licensed to Practice Law as Violation of Right to Counsel, 19 A.L.R.5th 351 (1994).

D

Dances with Nonlawyers: A New Perspective on Law Firm Diversification by G. Munneke, 61 Fordham Law Review 559 (1992).

Defining Mediation and Its Use for Paralegals by A. Chasen, 9 Journal of Paralegal Education and Practice 61 (1993).

Defining the Unauthorized Practice of Law, 4 Nova Law Journal 363 (1980).

Definition, Regulation, and Licensure of Paralegals in the United States by Lou Dawn Bishop, Ph.D. dissertation, Virginia Polytechnic Institute and State University (December 2002) (scholar.lib.vt.edu/theses/available/etd-12192002-132757/unrestricted/Dissertation.pdf#search=%22212-330-8213%22).

Delawyerizing Labor Arbitration by R. Alleyne, 50 Ohio State Law Journal 93 (1989).

The Delivery of Legal Services by Non-Lawyers by D. Rhode, 4 Georgetown Journal of Legal Ethics 209 (1990).

Deregulation of the Practice of Law by M. Munro, 42 Hastings Law Journal 203 (1990).

Disciplinary Action against Attorney for Aiding or Assisting Another Person in Unauthorized Practice of Law, 41 A.L.R.4th 361 (1985).

Disqualified: Switching Sides by Legal Assistants in Litigation, 77 American Bar Association Journal 88 (October 1991).

[District of Columbia] *Independent Paralegals Can Fill the Gap in Unmet Legal Services for the Low-Income Community* by T. Mootz, 5 University of the District of Columbia Law Review 189 (Fall 2000).

Divorce Litigants without Lawyers by R. Yegge, 28 Family Law Quarterly 407 (1994).

DOJ [Department of Justice] Probes Law Firms: Paralegal Who Copied Tobacco Company Documents Subpoenaed, 80 American Bar Association Journal 14 (June 1994).

Dollars and $ense of Paralegal Utilization, DuPont Legal (2002).

Domestic Violence Advocates' Exposure to Liability for Engaging in the Unauthorized Practice of Law by M. Brown, 34 Columbia Journal of Law and Social Problems 279 (2001).

Don't Let Your Staff Do Wrong by D. Walther, 13 Family Advocate 40 (American Bar Association, Spring 1991).

Does Your Confidences Go Out the Window When Your Employees Go Out the Door? by K. Rendall, 42 Hastings Law Journal 1667 (1991).

Drafting of Will or Other Estate Planning Activities as Illegal Practice of Law, 22 A.L.R.3d 1112 (1968).

The Duty to Supervise … Model Rules … 5.3 by R. Reiland, 14 Georgetown Journal of Legal Ethics 1151 (2002).

E

The Education and Utilization of Paralegals in … Immigration by A. Wernick, 7 Journal of Paralegal Education and Practice 23 (1990).

Education for the Practice of Law: The Times They Are A-Changin' by R. Stuckey, 75 Nebraska Law Review 648 (1996).

The Education of Legal Paraprofessionals: Myths, Realities, and Opportunities by W. Statsky, 24 Vanderbilt Law Review 1083 (1971).

Education towards a Rights Culture in Uganda: A Paralegal Reference Handbook (Kampala, Uganda: Foundation for Human Rights Initiative, 2002).

Effective Use of Legal Assistants Equates to Greater Profit by K. Libman, 23 Law Practice Management 40 (July/August 1997).

Emotional Labor Among Paralegals by Jennifer Pierce, 561 Annals of the American Academy of Political and Social Science 127 (January 1999) (www.jstor.org/pss/1049286).

Ensuring Meaningful Jailhouse Legal

Assistance: The Need for a Jailhouse Lawyer–Inmate Privilege by J. Nobel, 18 Cardozo Law Review 1569 (January 1997).

Essentials of Paralegalism, 4th ed. by W. Statsky (Delmar Cengage Learning, 2006).

Ethical Considerations for Law Clerks and Paralegals, by E. Peterson, 23 Journal of the Legal Profession 235 (1999).

Ethical Responsibility of Lawyers for Deception by Undercover Investigators by D. Isbell, 8 Georgetown Journal of Legal Ethics 791 (1995).

Ethical Standards for Legal Assistants by V. Voisin, 70 Michigan Bar Journal 1178 (November 1991).

The Ethical Utilization of Paralegals in Ohio by W. Wills, 45 Cleveland State Law Review 711 (1997).

Ethics and Professional Responsibility for Legal Assistants, 4th ed. by T. Cannon (Aspen, 2004).

Ethics for the Legal Professional, 6th ed. by D. Orlik (Prentice Hall, 2007).

The Ethics of Giving Legal Advice: Legal Assistants Must Be Wary of Crossing the Line with Clients by E. Lockwood, 27 Montana Lawyer 22 (September 2001).

Ethics: Top Ten Rules for Paralegals by D. Orlik (Pearson Prentice Hall, 2005).

Everything You Need to Know about Being a Legal Assistant by C. Estrin (Delmar Cengage Learning, 1995).

Evolving Standards of Nonlawyer Liability by C. Honchar, 6 Professional Lawyer 14 (May 1995).

Exempt from Overtime Pay by D. Ridgway, 8 West Virginia Lawyer 16 (February 1995).

F

Facts & Findings (periodical of National Association of Legal Assistants) (www.nala.org).

To Fee or Not to Fee: The Tenth Anniversary of Missouri v. Jenkins by K. Rute, 16 Journal of Paralegal Education and Practice 85 (2000).

Fixed Salary for Paralegal Indicated Employee Status, 80 Journal of Taxation 183 (March 1994).

The Florida Bar v. American Senior Citizens Alliance: Is "Gathering the Necessary Information" the Unlicensed Practice of Law? by A. Bromfield, 12 Quinnipiac Probate Law Journal 523 (1998).

The Florida Bar Advisory Opinion on Nonlawyer Representation in Securities Arbitration Adopted by Florida Supreme Court, 696 Southern Reporter 2d 1178 (Florida Supreme Court 1997).

Florida Paralegal: Essential Rules, Documents, and Resources by W. Statsky, B. Diotalevi, & P. Linquist (Delmar Cengage Learning, 2009).

FLSA: Exempting Paralegals from Overtime Pay by A. Engel, 74 Washington University Law Quarterly 253 (1996).

Focus on Corporate Practice: Legal Assistants and Legal Opinion Due Diligence by C. Drozd, 7 Journal of Paralegal Education and Practice 63 (1990).

Folly by Fiat: Pretending That Death Row Inmates Can Represent Themselves in State Capital Post-Conviction Proceedings by C. Smith, 45 Loyola Law Review 55 (Spring 1999).

Foreword to Colloquium on Nonlawyer Practice before Federal Administrative Agencies, by W. Robie, 37 Administrative Law Review 359 (1985).

The Freelance Legal Assistant by P. Davidson, 70 Michigan Bar Journal 1184 (November 1991).

From the Reference Desk to the Jailhouse: Unauthorized Practice of Law and Librarians by Y. Brown, 13 Legal Reference Services Quarterly 31 (1994).

Functional Division of the American Legal Profession: The Legal Paraprofessional by C. Selinger, 22 Journal of Legal Education 22 (1969).

Functional Overlap between the Lawyer and Other Professionals: Its Implications for the Privileged Communications Doctrine, 71 Yale Law Journal 1226 (1962).

Fundamentals of Law Office Management, 3d ed. by P. Everett (Delmar Cengage Learning, 2003).

G

Gender and Emotional Labor in the Contemporary Law Firm by C. Franklin, 7 UCLA Women's Law Journal 131 (1996) (paralegal roles and gender).

A Guide for Legal Assistants: Roles, Responsibilities, Specializations, 2d ed. (Practicing Law Institute, 1991).

Guidelines for the Approval of Paralegal Education Programs, American Bar Association Standing Committee on Paralegals (2003) (www.abanet.org/legalservices/paralegals).

H

Handling, Preparing, Presenting, or Trying Workmen's Compensation Claims or Cases as Practice of Law, 2 A.L.R.3d 724 (1966).

[Hawaii] *Mandatory Supervised Paralegal Regulation Is in the Public Interest* by R. Johnson, 8 Hawaii Bar Journal 32 (July 2004).

Hawaii Paralegals Head toward Certification through Federal Court by V. Nakaahiki, 2 Hawaii Bar Journal 22 (August 1998).

Hawaii Paralegals to Make History by V. Nakaahiki, 46 Federal Lawyer 24 (June 1999).

The Hawaii Supreme Court Considers Adopting a Comprehensive System of Paralegal Certification by R. LeClair, 5 Hawaii Bar Journal 23 (January 2001).

How Should We Determine Who Should Regulate Lawyers? by D. Wilkins, 65 Fordham Law Review 465 (1996).

How to Find a Job as a Paralegal, 3d ed. by M. Kisiel (Delmar Cengage Learning, 1996).

How to Find and Groom the Practical—and Practiced—Paralegal by L. Tripoli, 3 Of Counsel 12 (March 2007).

How to Land Your Find Paralegal Job, 4th ed. by A. Wagner (Prentice Hall, 2005).

How to Use Legal Assistants to Enforce Commercial Secured Claims by J. Verellen, 33 Practical Lawyer 9 (December 1987).

I

[Idaho] *Could Your Office Use a Paralegal?* by R. Blount, 44 Advocate 23 (January 2001).

[Idaho] *Model Guidelines for the Utilization of Legal Assistant Services,* Utah Bar Association (1992) (www2.state.id.us/isb/PDF/Legasst.pdf).

[Idaho] *To the Rescue: Paralegals/Legal Assistants* by R. Kerl, 35 Advocate 7 (March 1992).

[Idaho] *What Is a Paralegal, Anyway?* by D. Taylor, 37 Advocate 22 (July 1994).

[Illinois] *Can a Disbarred Lawyer Be a Paralegal?* 95 Illinois Bar Journal 266 (May 2006).

[Illinois] *Law Clerks as Independent Contractors: A Cost-Saver You Can't Afford* by J. Ellis, 85 Illinois Bar Journal 436 (September 1997).

[Illinois] *Restrictions on Attorney Contacts with Adversaries' Former Employees* by C. Lewis, 83 Illinois Bar Journal 242 (May 1995).

[Illinois] *The Supreme Court Latest UPL Case…Allows Nonlawyer Lenders to Charge for Preparing Mortgages but Reaffirms That Drafting and Filling Out Real Estate Documents Is the Practice of Law* by H. Gunnarsson, 93 Illinois Bar Journal 276 (June 2005).

Immigration Law for Paralegals by M. Casablanca & G. Bodin (Carolina Academic Press, 2005).

Income Tax Practice and Certified Public Accountants: The Case for a Status Based Exemption from State Unauthorized Practice of Law Rules by M. Melone, 11 Akron Tax Journal 47 (1995).

Independent Paralegals: Friends in Need or Foes at the Gate? by J. Middlemiss, 17 Canadian Lawyer 26 (February 1993).

The Independent Paralegal's Handbook: How to Provide Legal Services without Becoming a Lawyer, 6th ed. by R. Warner et al.

(Nolo Press, 2004).

[Indiana] *Developments in the Law of Professional Responsibility*, "Use of Legal Assistants" by C. Kidd, 28 Indiana Law Review 1013, 1015 (1995).

[Indiana] *Providing Cost-Effective Legal Services: Paralegal Utilization* by L. Cox, 47 Res Gestae 41 (April 2004).

[Indiana] *Who's on First? Paralegals with an ISBA Membership* by E. Wallace, 49 Res Gestae 26 (January/February 2006).

Inmate Access to Prison Computers for Legal Work and the Right of Access to the Courts by J. Snyder, 72 North Carolina Law Review 1697 (1994).

Introduction to Legal Nurse Consulting by C. Weishapple (Delmar Cengage Learning, 2001).

[Iowa] *Paralegals, Clients, Fees* by J. Honohan, 51 The Iowa Lawyer 23 (August 1991).

Issues in Paralegalism: Education, Certification, Licensing, Unauthorized Practice by P. Haskell, 15 Georgia Law Review 631 (1981).

J

The Jailhouse Lawyer as a Paraprofessional: Problems and Prospects by Wexler, 7 Criminal Law Bulletin 139 (1971).

Jailhouse Lawyer's Handbook, 4th ed. by the Center for Constitutional Rights & National Lawyers Guild (2006) (www.jailhouselaw.org/download.html).

A Jailhouse Lawyer's Manual, 5th ed. (Columbia Human Rights Law Review, 2000) (www.columbia.edu/cu/hrlr/JLMOnline.html).

Jailhouse Lawyer: Nuisance or Necessity? by A. Love, The Philadelphia Lawyer 31 (September 1993).

Judging Credentials: Nonlawyer Judges and the Politics of Professionalism by D. Provine (University of Chicago Press, 1986).

Job Placement Strategies for Paralegals by Margaret E. Pickard (Delmar Cengage Learning, 2008).

K

[Kansas] *Calculating Profit from Associates and Paralegals*, 58 Journal of the Kansas Bar Association 5 (April 1989).

[Kansas] *How Legal Assistants Can Aid You with Real Estate Foreclosures* by C. Burns, 63 Journal of the Kansas Bar Association 18 (May 1994).

[Kansas] *The Legal Assistant in a Small Law Firm* by D. Holliday, 63 Journal of the Kansas Bar Association 7 (June/July 1994).

[Kansas] *Legal Assistants as Law Office Managers*, by L. Kreipe 59 Journal of the Kansas Bar Association 19 (July 1990).

[Kansas] *Legal Assistants Listed on Letterheads?* by B. Kent, 60 Journal of the Kansas Bar Association 15 (February/March 1991).

[Kansas] *Official Standards and Guidelines for the Utilization of Legal Assistants/Paralegals in Kansas*, Kansas Bar Association (2004) (www.ksbar.org/pdf/laguidelines.pdf).

[Kansas] *Questions Concerning the Utilization Of Legal Assistants/Paralegals Answered*, 69 Journal of the Kansas Bar Association 3 (August 2000).

[Kansas] *Why Paralegal Certification Counts* by D. Monke, 75 Journal of the Kansas Bar Association 16 (March 2006).

[Kentucky] *What Your Paralegals Always Wanted to Tell You but Didn't Dare Because They Needed a Job* by F. Dowell, 54 Kentucky Bench and Bar 40 (Fall 1993).

[Kentucky] *What Your Office Support Staff and You Need to Know about Professional Responsibility for Nonlawyer Assistants* by D. O'Roark, 54 Kentucky Bench and Bar 40 (Fall 1993).

L

Law Clerks and the Unauthorized Practice of Law, 46 Chicago-Kent Law Review 214 (1969).

Law Firm Diversification and Affiliation between Lawyers and Nonlawyer Professionals by D. Pitofsky, 3 Georgetown Journal of Legal Ethics 885 (1995).

Law Firm Life for the Legal Assistant: Practical Guidance from a Veteran by J. Dwight (Professional Education Systems, 2001).

Law Firms on the Big Board? A Proposal for Nonlawyer Investment in Law Firms by E. Adams, 86 California Law Review 1 (1998).

The Lawyer from Antiquity to Modern Times by R. Pound (West, 1953).

Lawyers, Accountants, and the Battle to Own Professional Services by G. Munneke, 20 Pace Law Review 73 (1999).

Lawyers as Monopolists, Aristocrats, and Entrepreneurs by M. Osiel, 103 Harvard Law Review 2009 (1989).

Lawyers, Foreign Lawyers, and Lawyer-Substitutes: The Market for Regulation in Japan by J. Ramseyer, 27 Harvard International Law Journal 499 (1986).

The Lay Advocate by E. Sparer, 43 University of Detroit Law Journal 493 (1966).

Layman's Assistance to Party in Divorce Proceeding as Unauthorized Practice of Law, 12 A.L.R.4th 656 (1982).

Laymen Cannot Lawyer, but Is Mediation the Practice of Law? by J. Schwartz, 20 Cardozo Law Review 1715 (1999).

Learning Styles and Paralegal Studies by B. Nagle & P. Lechman-Woznick, 11 Journal of Paralegal Education and Practice 67 (1995).

The Least Best Hope of Legal Services for the Poor in the Eighties: The Need for Public Sector Lay Advocates with Confidential

Communications by T. Siporin, 10 San Fernando Valley Law Review 21 (1982).

Legal Advocacy: Lawyers and Nonlawyers at Work by H. Kritzer (University of Michigan Press, 1998) (reviewed at 73 Wisconsin Lawyer 26 [February 2000]).

Legal Aid Community Law Centre: Empowering Rural South African Communities by C. Baekey, 5 Maryland Journal of Contemporary Legal Issues 399 (1994) (paralegals in South Africa).

Legal and Paralegal Services on Your Home-Based PC by K. Hussey (Windcrest/McGraw-Hill, 1994).

Legal Assistant's Guide to Alternative Dispute Resolution by J. Quan (Clark Boardman, 1994).

Legal Assistant's Handbook, 2d ed. by T. Brunner et al. (Bureau of National Affairs, 1988).

The Legal Assistant's Letter Book by S. von Matt Stoddard (Prentice Hall, 1996).

The Legal Assistants' Practical Guide to Professional Responsibility, 2d ed. by the American Bar Association (2004).

Legal Assistant Professional, Educational and Career-Related Organizations by G. Schrader, 8 Journal of Paralegal Education and Practice 63 (1991).

Legal Assistants: Has the Time Arrived for State-by-State Licensing? by H. Samborn, 78 American Bar Association Journal 42 (December 1992).

The Legal Assistant's Role in Automated Litigation Support by A. Huffman, 44 Am. Jur. Trials 79 (1992).

Legal Assistant Today (periodical) (www.legalassistanttoday.com).

Legal Ethics for Paralegals and the Law Office by L. Morrison (Delmar Cengage Learning, 1995).

Legal Nurse Consultants by B. Faherty, 41 Medical Trial Technique Quarterly 228 (1994).

Legal Nurse Consulting: Principles and Practice (America Association of Legal Nurse Consultants, 1998).

Legal Paraprofessionals and Unauthorized Practice, 8 Harvard Civil Rights–Civil Liberties Law Review 104 (1973).

Legal Profession Faces Rising Tide of Nonlawyer Practice by J. Podgers, 79 American Bar Association Journal 24 (March 1994).

Legal Services for Inmates: Co-opting the Jailhouse Lawyer by W. Bluth, 1 Capital University Law Review 59 (1972).

Leveraging with Legal Assistants, A. Greene, editor (American Bar Association, 1993).

Life outside the Law Firm: Non-traditional Careers for Paralegals by K. Treffinger (West, 1995).

The Litigation Paralegal, 5th ed. by J. McCord (Delmar Cengage Learning, 2007).

Living Trusts in the Unauthorized Practice of

Law by A. Vallario, 59 Maryland Law Review 595 (2000).

[Louisiana] *Paralegals: Getting Everything in Order* by E. Coari, 39 Louisiana Bar Journal 265 (November 1991).

M

[Maine] *An Attorney's Professional Responsibility for Non-lawyer Staff…* by J. Thaler, 17 Maine Bar Journal 106 (Spring 2002).

[Maine] *The Certified Legal Assistant Credential*, 11 Maine Bar Journal 376 (November 1996).

[Maine] *Delegate to Your Legal Assistant* by M. Gaige, 5 Maine Bar Journal 98 (March 1990).

[Maine] *The Practice of Law with Non-lawyer Colleagues in Maine* by T. Shaffer, 14 Maine Bar Journal 202 (July 1999).

[Maine] *Stemming the Tide Of Unauthorized Practice* by S. Kimmel, 13 Maine Bar Journal 164 (July 1998).

[Maine] *Taking Note of Notary Employees: Employer Liability for Notary Employee Misconduct* by N. Spyke, 50 Maine Law Review 23 (1998).

Managing Associates and Legal Assistants by M. Magness, 40 Practical Lawyer 25 (June 1994).

Manual for Legal Assistants, 4th ed. by the National Association of Legal Assistants (Delmar Cengage Learning, 2005).

[Maryland] *Lawyers Practicing Law with Non-lawyers?* by J. Eveleth, 34 Maryland Bar Journal 40 (January/February 2001).

[Maryland] *Should Nonlawyers Provide Legal Services?* by M. Brockmeyer, 27 Maryland Bar Journal 12 (July/August 1994).

[Massachusetts] *The New Massachusetts Rules of Professional Conduct: Ethical Responsibilities in Supervising Others* by J. Whitlock, 82 Massachusetts Law Review 289 (1997).

Massachusetts Paralegal Practice Manual (Massachusetts Continuing Legal Education, 1999).

[Massachusetts] *Successful Paralegal Utilization* by R. Simkins, 21 Massachusetts Lawyers Weekly 2409 (April 26, 1993).

Medical Advocates: A Call for a New Profession by M. Mehlman, 1 Widener Law Symposium Journal 299 (Spring 1996).

Meet Legal Needs with Nonlawyers: It Is Time to Accept Law Practitioners—and Regulate Them by D. Rhode, 82 American Bar Association Journal 104 (January 1996).

[Michigan] *Assisting Clients in Achieving the American Dream* by M. Burgner, 75 Michigan Bar Journal 44 (January 1996) (paralegals in real estate).

[Michigan] *Computer Programs and Systems Optimize Legal Assistant Productivity* by M. Bjorkman, 70 Michigan Bar Journal

1154 (November 1991).

[Michigan] *A Day with a Legal Assistant* by N. Stecker, 80 Michigan Bar Journal 58 (March 2001).

[Michigan] *Directions in Legal Assistant Training and Education* by L. Jevahirian, 75 Michigan Bar Journal 38 (January 1996).

[Michigan] *Ethical Standards for Legal Assistants* by V. Voisin, 70 Michigan Bar Journal 1178 (November 1991).

[Michigan] *Examining the Issue of Paralegal Regulation* by R. Sova, 75 Michigan Bar Journal 34 (January 1996).

[Michigan] *The Freelance Legal Assistant* by P. Davidson, 70 Michigan Bar Journal 1184 (November 1991).

[Michigan] *Going Global* by G. Avramov, 80 Michigan Bar Journal 46 (March 2001) (paralegals in immigration law).

[Michigan] *Guidelines for the Utilization of Legal Assistant Services*, State Bar of Michigan (1993) (www.michbar.org/ legalassistants/pdfs/labrochure.pdf).

[Michigan] *Lay Practice before Administrative Tribunals: Clarification Needed*, 66 Michigan Bar Journal 675 (1987).

[Michigan] *The Litigation Legal Assistant: From Case Inception to Pretrial*, 75 Michigan Bar Journal 50 (January 1996).

[Michigan] *Looking Closely at the Role of Paralegals: The California, New Jersey, and Wisconsin Experiences*, 80 Michigan Bar Journal 56 (March 2001).

[Michigan] *Not Just for Lawyers* by M. Agius, 80 Michigan Bar Journal 30 (March 2001) (ethics and paralegals).

[Michigan] *Permanent Injunctions: Unauthorized Practice of Law* by T. Byerley, 78 Michigan Bar Journal 458 (May 1999).

[Michigan] *Plain Language for the Legal Assistant: Preparing Enclosure Letters* by S. McIntyre, 75 Michigan Bar Journal 73 (January 1996).

[Michigan] *The Role of a Legal Assistant in Real Estate Practice* by E. Mahoney, 70 Michigan Bar Journal 1160 (November 1991).

[Michigan] *The Role of the Legal Assistant in Family Law Matters* by B. Miller, 75 Michigan Bar Journal 54 (January 1996).

[Michigan] *Should More Be Done to Credential Paralegals?* by T. Flynn, 80 Michigan Bar Journal 52 (March 2001).

[Michigan] *When Legal Assistants Change Jobs: Ethical Issues and Solutions* by D. Kowalski, 75 Michigan Bar Journal 42 (January 1996).

Midwifery Is Not the Practice of Medicine by S. Suarez, 5 Yale Journal of Law and Feminism 315 (Spring 1993).

[Mississippi] *Paralegal Education* by R. Marquardt, 40 Mississippi Lawyer 13 (November/December 1993).

[Mississippi] *Paralegalism: A Still Evolving Profession* by W. Peters, 40 Mississippi Lawyer 18 (November/December 1993).

[Missouri] *How Paralegals Make Money for Law Firms* by M. McClane, 46 St. Louis Bar Journal 28 (Summer 1999).

[Missouri] *Litigation, Law Firms, and Legal Assistants* by Sandra A. Naro & Monica McCarthy, 46 St. Louis Bar Journal 20 (Summer 1999).

[Missouri] *Practicing with Paralegals*, Missouri Bar (1987) (type "paralegal" in the search box at www.mobar.org).

[Missouri] *Still Paralegals after All These Years* by C. Gilsinan, 46 St. Louis Bar Journal 10 (Summer 1999).

[Missouri] *Trouble for Nonlawyers Who Furnish Estate Planning Services and for the Lawyers Who Help Them and Other Recent Developments* by D. Doerhoff, 52 Journal of the Missouri Bar 269 (September/October 1996).

[Missouri] *Sole Practitioner Penalized for Treating Legal Assistants as Independent Contractors* by S. Vincent, 59 Journal of the Missouri Bar 234 (September/ October 2003).

Model Code of Ethics and Professional Responsibility by the National Federation of Paralegal Associations (1993) (www.paralegals.org).

Model Standards and Guidelines for the Utilization of Legal Assistants/Paralegals by National Association of Legal Assistants (1991) (www.nala.org/ 98model.htm).

Modifying Model Rule 5.4 to Allow for Minority Ownership of Law Firms by Nonlawyers by B. Sharfman, 13 Georgetown Journal of Legal Ethics 477 (2000).

[Montana] *ABA Report Debates Nonlawyers' Role in Providing Legal Services*, 11 Montana Lawyer 23 (May 1998).

[Montana] *The Changing Role of Legal Secretaries* by J. Mitchell, 25 Montana Lawyer 15 (December 1999).

[Montana] *The Ethics of Giving Legal Advice: Legal Assistants Must Be Wary of Crossing the Line with Clients* by E. Lockwood, 27 Montana Lawyer 22 (September 2001).

[Montana] *Fake Lawyers: Unauthorized Practice Issue Is Coming to a Head* by S. Hilander, 22 Montana Lawyer 3 (May 1997).

[Montana] *It's a Good Idea to Let Paralegals Join the State Bar*, 23 Montana Lawyer 4 (May 1998).

[Montana] *Paralegals Can Apply to Join the State Bar* by C. Bronson, 24 Montana Lawyer 28 (March 1999).

[Montana] *Paralegals Can Be More Profitable than Associates* by A. Jones, 16 Montana Lawyer 7 (December 1990).

[Montana] *Paralegals' Image and How to Improve It* by B. Kautz, 25 Montana Lawyer 16 (January 2000).

[Montana] *Unauthorized Practice Linked to Unmet Pro Bono Need* by S. Hilander, 23 Montana Lawyer 1 (December 1997).

[Montana] *Paralegal Adventures in the Non-profit Corporation* by A. Brown, 26 Montana Lawyer 30 (February 2001).

N

Nature of Legal Services . . . Which May Be Performed by Disbarred or Suspended Attorney, 7 A.L.R.3d 279 (1978).

The Nebraska "Bright Line" Rule: The Automatic Disqualification of a Law Firm Due to a New Lawyer's or Nonlawyer's Prior Affiliations by A. Romshe, 28 Creighton Law Review 213 (1994).

[Nebraska] *Collection Agencies and the Unauthorized Practice of Law* by K. Folts, 77 Nebraska Law Review 365 (1998).

[Nebraska] *Education for the Practice of Law: The Times They Are A-Changin'* by R. Stuckey, 75 Nebraska Law Review 648 (1996).

[Nebraska] *Systemization and the Legal Assistant in the Law Office* by Endacott, 54 Nebraska Law Review 46 (1975).

[Nevada] *The Attorney Timesaver: Records Requests and the Legal Assistant* by E. Moulton, 6 Nevada Lawyer 20 (April 1998).

[Nevada] *Criteria for Recovering Legal Assistant Fees* by C. Embry, 5 Nevada Lawyer 30 (February 1997).

[Nevada] *Ethics and the Legal Assistant* by Candace Jones, 6 Nevada Lawyer 13 (July 1998).

[Nevada] *Is Regulation Necessary for the Legal Assistant?* by M. Marsh, 5 Nevada Lawyer 28 (August 1997).

[Nevada] *Legal Assistants Provide Responsible Services For Nevada Government* by K. Swain, 6 Nevada Lawyer 27 (March 1998).

[Nevada] *Legal Assistants Well-Suited for Malpractice Cases* by E. Moulton, 5 Nevada Lawyer 36 (December 1997).

[Nevada] *Litigation Legal Assistants: Saving Time and Money for the Litigator!* by L. Sifuentes, 4 Nevada Lawyer 24 (June 1996).

[Nevada] *Paralegals Can Play Major Role in Preparation of Criminal Case* by C. Embry, 6 Nevada Lawyer 26 (June 1998).

[Nevada] *Professional Paralegal Organizations in Nevada and Their Benefits to You* by H. Heck, 5 Nevada Lawyer 29 (March 1997).

[Nevada] *Should Legal Assistants Be Exempt or Non-exempt from Overtime Pay?* 5 Nevada Lawyer 29 (January 1997).

[Nevada] *We Are Going to Build a Chinese Wall* by E. Moulton, 5 Nevada Lawyer 28 (September 1997) (conflict of interest).

[Nevada] *When Attorneys and Paralegals Change Firms* by M. Suglia, 8 Nevada Lawyer 18 (August 2000).

[New Hampshire] *Guidelines for the Utilization by Lawyers of the Services of Legal Assistants under the New Hampshire Rules of Professional Conduct*, New Hampshire Supreme Court (1987) (www.nh.gov/judiciary/rules/scr/scr-35.htm).

[New Jersey] *The Essential Role of the Paralegal* (New Jersey State Bar Association, 2001).

[New Jersey] *Looking Closely at the Role of Paralegals: The California, New Jersey, and Wisconsin Experiences*, 80 Michigan Bar Journal 56 (March 2001).

[New Jersey] *Paralegals Taking a Bite Out of Associates' Work* by H. Rosen, 134 New Jersey Law Journal 195 (May 17, 1993).

[New Jersey] *Sign of Tough Times: Out-of-Work Lawyers Taking Paralegal Jobs* by R. Cammarere, The New Jersey Lawyer, September 11, 1995, at 1.

[New Mexico] *Code of Ethics and Professional Responsibility* by the State Bar of New Mexico, Paralegal Division (click "divisions" at www.nmbar.org).

[New Mexico] *Disorder in the People's Court: Rethinking the Role Of Non-lawyer Judges* by C. Mansfield, 29 New Mexico Law Review 119 (Winter 1999).

[New Mexico] *Rules Governing Paralegal Services* (Rules 20–101 et seq.) by the New Mexico Supreme Court (click "rules" at www.supremecourt.nm.org).

[New York] *Do Nonlawyer Justices Dispense Justice?* by C. Fieman, 69 New York State Bar Journal 20 (January 1997).

New York Paralegal: Essential Rules, Documents, and Resources by W. Statsky & R. Sarachan (Delmar Cengage Learning, 2009).

[New York] *Paralegals in New York* by E. Gansberg (Delmar Cengage Learning, 1994).

No, a Paralegal Is Not a Lawyer by F. Kao, 16 Business Law Today 11 (January/February 2007).

Nonlawyer Activities in Law-Related Situations (American Bar Association Commission on Nonlawyer Practice, 1995).

Nonlawyer Assistance to Individuals in Federal Mass Justice Agencies by Z. Hostetler, 2 Administrative Law Journal 85 (1988).

Nonlawyer Legal Assistance and Access to Justice by A. Hurder, 67 Fordham Law Review 2241 (1999).

The Nonlawyer Partner: Moderate Proposals Deserve a Chance by S. Gilbert, 2 Georgetown Journal of Legal Ethics 383 (1988).

Nonlawyer Practice before Administrative Agencies Should Be Discouraged by Heiserman, 37 Administrative Law Review 375 (1985).

Nonlawyer Practice before Administrative Agencies Should Be Encouraged by J. Rose, 37 Administrative Law Review 363 (1985).

Nonlawyer Practice before Immigration Agencies by Holmes, 37 Administrative Law Review 417 (1985).

Nonlawyer Practice: Will GP's [General Practitioners] Survive the Onslaught? by A. Garwin, 10 The Compleat Lawyer 31 (Fall 1993).

The Nonlawyer Provider of Bankruptcy Legal Services: Angel or Vulture by A. Cristol, 2 American Bankruptcy Institute Law Review 353 (1994).

Nonlawyers and the Unauthorized Practice of Law: An Overview of the Legal and Ethical Parameters by D. Denckla, 67 Fordham Law Review 2581 (1999).

Nonlawyers Are Not the Answer by T. Curtin, 80 American Bar Association Journal 128 (April 1994).

Nonlawyers as Legal Practitioners by C. Jones, 17 Journal of the Legal Profession 287 (1992).

Nonlawyers in the Business of Law by T. Andrews, 40 Hastings Law Journal 577 (1989).

Nonlawyers Should Not Practice Law by R. Ostertag, 82 American Bar Association Journal 116 (May 1996).

[North Carolina] *Ensuring Attorney/Paralegal Team Excellence* by G. Green, 38 The North Carolina State Bar Quarterly 33 (Winter 1991).

[North Carolina] *Guidelines for Use of Non-lawyers in Rendering Legal Services*, North Carolina State Bar (1998) (www.ncbar.com/home/non_lawyer_guidelines.asp).

[North Carolina] *Paralegals: Untapped Potential for Performance and Profit* by P. Potter, 40 North Carolina State Bar Quarterly 16 (Summer 1993).

[North Dakota] *Paralegals: Changing the Practice of Law* by J. Rasmussen, 44 South Dakota Law Review 319 (1999).

No Substitutions: Legal Aides Are Crucial, but Some Tasks Lawyers Should Not Delegate by K. Maher, 86 American Bar Association Journal 66 (October 2001).

The Nursing Profession in the 1990's: Negligence and Malpractice Liability by F. Cavico, 43 Cleveland State Law Review 557 (1995).

O

The Obligation of Legal Aid Lawyers to Champion Practice by Nonlawyers by D. Cantrell, 73 Fordham Law Review 883 (December 2004)

Occupational Claims to Professionalism: The Case of Paralegals by K. Lively (2001) (caliber.ucpress.net/doi/abs/10.1525/si.2001.24.3.343).

[Ohio] *Delawyerizing Labor Arbitration* by R. Alleyne, 50 Ohio State Law Journal 93 (1989).

[Ohio] *The Ethical Utilization of Paralegals in Ohio* by W. Wills, 45 Cleveland State Law Review 711 (1997).

The Ohio Paralegal: Essential Rules, Documents, and Resources by W. Statsky, K. Myers, & B. Moore (Delmar Cengage Learning, 2008).

$100,000 a Year for Paralegals? by P. Marcotte, 73 American Bar Association Journal 19 (October 1987).

On the Question of Negligence: The Paraprofessional by B. Davis, 4 University of Toledo Law Review 553 (1973).

Operations of Collection Agency as Unauthorized Practice of Law, 27 A.L.R.3d 1152 (1969).

Opportunities in Paralegal Careers by A. Fins (VGM Career Horizons, 1985).

[Oregon] *Choice for Legal Services: Consumer Need for Legal Technicians Increasing* by R. Smith, 52 Oregon State Bar Bulletin 26 (June 1992).

[Oregon] *Let the Consumer Choose: Does Government Protect or Harm Consumers by Allowing Them to Choose a Non-lawyer?* by J. Stubenvoll, 52 Oregon State Bar Bulletin 21 (June 1992).

[Oregon] *Supervise Paralegals: The Watchwords Are: "Train" and "Supervise"*, 65 Oregon State Bar Bulletin 27 (November 2004).

[Oregon] *Suspended Life: A Lawyer's Life as a Legal Assistant* by D. Elkanich et al., 66 Oregon State Bar Bulletin 27 (January 2006).

[Oregon] *Too Many Hands in the Cookie Jar: The Unauthorized Practice of Law by Real Estate Brokers* by S. Goudey, 75 Oregon Law Review 889 (1996).

Overtime for Law Firm Employees: The Fair Labor Standards Act by B. Benrud, 28 Colorado Lawyer 99 (September 1999).

P

Parajudges and the Administration of Justice by T. Clark, 24 Vanderbilt Law Review 1167 (1971).

Paralegal Advocacy before Administrative Agencies by W. Statsky, 4 University of Toledo Law Review 439 (1973).

(Para) Legal Aid: What [Sort] of Assignments Can You Delegate to Nonlawyer Assistants? by A. Garwin, 79 American Bar Association Journal 101 (July 1993).

Paralegal: An Insider's Guide to the Fastest-Growing Occupation in the 1990s, 3d ed. by B. Bernardo (Peterson's Guides, 1997).

The Paralegal as [Law Library] Patron by K. Carlson, 84 Law Library Journal 567 (1992).

The Paralegal Book of Letters (Aspen/Wiley, 1995).

Paralegal Career Guide, 3d ed. by C. Estrin (Prentice Hall, 2001).

Paralegal Career for Dummies by S. Hatch & L. Hatch (Wiley, 2006).

Paralegal Careers by A. Schneeman (Delmar Cengage Learning, 2000).

Paralegal Careers by W. Fry & R. Hoopes (Enslow, 1986).

Paralegal Career Starter, 3d ed. by J. Southard (Learning Express, 2006).

Paralegal Discovery: Organization and Management by D. Dupre Zalewski & J. Walden (Wiley, 1987–).

Paralegal Discovery: Procedures and Forms, 3d ed. by P. Medina (Aspen, 2001).

Paralegal Drafting Guide by D. McClellan (Wiley, 1993).

The Paralegal Educator (periodical of American Association for Paralegal Education) (www.aafpe.org).

Paralegal Employment, 2d ed. by W. Statsky (Delmar Cengage Learning, 1993).

Paralegal Ethics by A. Schneeman (Delmar Cengage Learning, 2000).

Paralegal Ethics Handbook by the Paralegal Division of the State Bar of Texas (West, 2007).

Paralegal Ethics and Regulation, 2d ed. by W. Statsky (Delmar Cengage Learning, 1993).

Paralegal Guide to Automobile Accident Cases by J. Murvin (Wiley, 1995).

Paralegal Guide to Child Support by G. Brownstein (Wiley, 1997).

Paralegal Guide to Intellectual Property by V. Atkinson (Wiley, 1994).

Paralegal Guide to Qualified Pension Plans by G. Lee (Wiley, 1997).

Paralegal Guide to UCC Filing by M. Glancey (Wiley, 1997).

Paralegal Handbook by C. Nemeth (Prentice Hall, 1986).

Paralegal Handbook by V. Brittain & T. Hull (Delmar Cengage Learning, 2003).

The Paralegal in Army Legal Practice by R. Black, Army Lawyer 70 (November 1990).

Paralegal Internships by R. Post (Delmar Cengage Learning, 1999).

Paralegalism: The United Profession by J. Farinacci, 8 Journal of Paralegal Education and Practice 148 (1991).

Paralegal Litigation Forms and Procedures, 3d ed. by M. Fawcett-Delesandri (Wiley, 2001).

Paralegal Management Handbook by M. Brophy & P. Pressley (Wiley, 1993).

Paralegal Medical Records Review by K. Appleby & J. Tarver (Wiley, 1989).

Paralegal Personnel for Attorneys General's Offices (National Association of Attorneys General, 1976) (www.naag.org).

Paralegal Practice and Procedure, 3d ed. by

D. Larbalestrier (Prentice-Hall, 1994).

A Paralegal Primer by S. Hatch & L. Hatch (Center for Legal Studies, 1993).

Paralegal Procedures and Practices by S. Hatch & L. Hatch (Delmar Cengage Learning, 1993).

The Paralegal Profession by H. Brown, 19 Howard Law Journal 117 (1976).

The Paralegal Profession by N. Shayne (Oceana, 1977).

The Paralegal Reporter (periodical of National Federation of Paralegal Associations) (www.paralegals.org).

Paralegal Representation of Social Security Claimants by E. Tackett, 16 Journal of Paralegal Education and Practice 67 (2000).

The Paralegal Resource Manual by C. Nemeth (McGraw-Hill, 2008).

Paralegals and Lawyers: A Team Approach by K. Dulin, 32 Trial 62 (January 1996).

Paralegals and Sublegals: Aids to the Legal Profession by H. Holme, 46 Denver Law Journal 392 (1969).

Paralegals and Successful Law Practice by R. Kurzman & R. Gilbert (Institute for Business Planning, 1981).

Paralegals and the Imputed Disqualification Rule by M. Schairer, 7 Journal of Paralegal Education and Practice 1 (1990).

Paralegals: A Resource for Public Defenders and Correctional Services by J. Stein (National Institute of Law Enforcement and Criminal Justice, 1976).

The Paralegal's Desk Reference by S. Albrecht (Arco, 1993).

Paralegal's Encyclopedic Dictionary by V. Grapp (Prentice Hall, 1979).

Paralegal Services: How to Manage Your Own Firm by C. Heath (Rimrock, 2000).

The Paralegal's Guide to Administrative Law by W. Haders (Anderson, 1994).

The Paralegal's Guide to Family Law and Practice by G. Luppino & J. Miller (Prentice Hall, 2002).

The Paralegal's Guide to U.S. Government Jobs, 7th ed. (Federal Reports, 1996).

Paralegals in Rural Africa, A. Dieng, ed. (International Commission of Jurists, Switzerland, February 1990).

The Paralegal's Litigation Handbook, 2d ed. by C. Bruno (West, 1993).

A Paralegal's Primer on Contract and Corporate Law by R. Bohner (Gemini, 1990).

Paralegals, Profitability, and the Future of Your Law Practice by A. Greene & T. Cannon (American Bar Association, 2003).

Paralegals: Progress and Prospects of a Satellite Occupation by Q. Johnstone (Greenwood Press, 1985).

The Paralegal's Role at Trial by K. Feeney (Wiley, 1993).

Paralegals: Should Legal Technicians Be Allowed to Practice Independently? by

D. Chalfie, 77 American Bar Association Journal 40 (March 1991).

Paralegals: The Good, the Bad, and the Ugly by G. Mund, 2 American Bankruptcy Institute Law Review 337 (1994).

Paralegal Success: Going from Good to Great in the New Century by D. Bogen (Prentice Hall, 2000).

A Paralegal Trainer's Manual for Africa by A. Tsanga (Geneva: International Commission of Jurists, 1994).

Paralegal Trial Handbook, 2d ed. by B. Hudson (Wiley, 1995).

Paraprofessionals: Expanding the Legal Service Delivery Team by W. Statsky, 24 Journal of Legal Education 397 (1972).

[Pennsylvania] *Another Perspective on Employing Disbarred or Suspended Attorneys* by C. Simpson, 2 The Lawyers Journal 5 (October 2000).

[Pennsylvania] *How Many Non-lawyers Does It Take to Run a Law Firm?* by E. Freedman, 23 Pennsylvania Lawyer 32 (March/April 2001).

[Pennsylvania] *How to Get the Most Out of Your Support Staff* by S. Meyerowitz, 23 Pennsylvania Lawyer 40 (March/April 2001).

[Pennsylvania] *A Piece of Your Business: Competition from Nonlawyer "Technicians": Cause for Alarm?* by G. Yuda, 15 The Pennsylvania Lawyer 6 (May 1993).

Pennsylvania Paralegal: Essential Rules, Documents, and Resources by W. Statsky, J. DeLeo, & J. Geis (Delmar Cengage Learning, 2009).

Policing the Professional Monopoly: A Constitutional and Empirical Analysis of Unauthorized Practice Prohibitions by D. Rhode, 34 Stanford Law Review 1 (1981).

Post-law School Job (of Attorney) May Be as Paralegal by H. Samborn, 81 American Bar Association Journal 14 (May 1995).

Practical Law Office Management, 3d ed. by B. Roper (Delmar Cengage Learning, 2007).

Practice before Administrative Agencies and the Unauthorized Practice of Law by V. Baur, 15 Federal Bar Journal 103 (1955).

Practice by Non-lawyers before the National Labor Relations Board by Gall, 15 Federal Bar Journal 222 (1955).

Practice by Non-lawyers before the U.S. Patent Office by Bailey, 15 Federal Bar Journal 211 (1955).

The Practice of Law by Laymen and Lay Agencies, 41 Yale Law Journal 69 (1931).

Practicing Law at the Margins: Surveying Ethics Rules for Legal Assistants and Lawyers Who Mediate by J. Beyer, 11 Georgetown Journal of Legal Ethics 411 (1998).

Practicing Law without a License by F. Apicella, 81 American Bar Association Journal 36 (January 1995).

Preventing Misconduct by Promoting the Ethics

of Attorneys' Supervisory Duties by I. Miller, 70 Notre Dame L. Rev. 259 (1994).

Preventive Law and the Paralegal by L. Brown, 24 Vanderbilt Law Review 1181 (1971).

Professionalism in Perspective: Alternative Approaches to Nonlawyer Practice by D. Rhode, 22 New York University Review of Law and Social Change 701 (1996).

Professional Negligence, Paralegals and Modern Ethics by H. Cohen, 11 Journal of the Legal Profession 143 (1986).

The Professional Paralegal, 2d ed. by H. Cheeseman & T. Goldman (Prentice Hall, 2008).

The Professional Paralegal Job Search by C. French (Aspen, 1995).

Paralegal Professional's Guidebook by Cindy Lopez (njparalegal.com) (2007).

Proper Scope of Nonlawyer Representation in State Administrative Proceedings by G. Stevens, 43 Vanderbilt Law Review 245 (1990).

Propriety and Effect of Corporation's Appearance Pro Se through Agent Who Is Not Attorney, 8 A.L.R.5th 653 (1992).

Pro Se Users, Reference Liability, and the Unauthorized Practice of Law by Paul Healey, 93 Law Library Journal 133 (2002).

Protecting the Public, Not Anyone's Turf: The Unlicensed Practice of Law in Securities Arbitration by J. Cleary, 26 Pepperdine Law Review 543 (1999).

Public Benefits Issues in Divorce Cases: A Manual for Lawyers and Paralegals (Center for Law and Social Policy, 1994).

R

Recoverability of Legal Assistant Time in Attorney Fee Applications by S. Koran, 9 Journal of Paralegal Education and Practice 1 (1993).

Recovery of Legal Assistant Fees in Litigation by C. Smith, 30 Trial 59 (September 1994).

Regulating Legal Assistant Practice: A Proposal That Offers Something for Everyone by Daniel R. Ray, 11 Washington University Journal of Law and Policy 249 (2003).

Report of the Working Group on the Use Of Nonlawyers, 67 Fordham Law Review 1813 (1999) (paralegals and legal services to the poor).

Representation of Clients before Administrative Agencies: Authorized or Unauthorized Practice of Law? 15 Valparaiso University Law Review 567 (1981).

Representation of Claimants at Unemployment Compensation Proceedings: Identifying Models and Proposed Solutions by M. Emsellem, 29 University of Michigan Journal of Law Reform 289 (1995).

The Retention of Limitations on the Out-

of-Court Practice of Law by Independent Paralegals by C. Selinger, 9 Georgetown Journal of Legal Ethics 879 (1996).

Rethinking Barriers to Legal Practice by H. Kritzer, 80 Judicature 100 (November/December 1997).

Revitalization of the Legal Profession through Paralegalism by J. Wells, 30 Baylor Law Review 841 (1978).

[Rhode Island] *Guidelines for Use of Legal Assistants*, Provincial Order No. 18, Rhode Island Supreme Court (1983). (See Rule 5.5 at www.law.cornell.edu/ ethics/ri/code/RI_CODE.HTM.)

[Rhode Island] *Separate Fee Awards for Paralegals* by T. Wright, 44 Rhode Island Bar Journal 23 (May 1996).

Right of Juvenile Court Defendant to Be Represented during Court Proceedings by Parent, 11 A.L.R.4th 719 (1982).

The Role of the Paralegal in the Civil Commitment Process by R. Lockwood, 10 Capital University Law Review 721 (1981).

S

Sale of Books or Forms … as Unauthorized Practice of Law, 71 A.L.R.3d 1000 (1976).

The Secretarial Advantage, Law Students, Paralegal Tasks by B. Morgenstern, 81 American Bar Association Journal 75 (January 1995).

Shades of Regulation: State Bills Apply Sundry Standards to Independent Paralegals, 83 American Bar Association Journal 26 (1997).

Should Law Societies "Prosecute the Hell" out of Independent Paralegal Firms? by P. Pevato, 7 Journal of Law & Social Policy 215 (Fall 1991).

Should Social Workers Engage in the Unauthorized Practice Of Law? by A. Bertelli, 8 Boston University Public Interest Law Journal 15 (Fall 1998).

The Side-Switching Staff Person in a Law Firm by S. Kalish, 15 Hamline Law Review 35 (1991).

Software and Hard Choices: Interactive Software Should Be Considered before Independent Paralegals Are Licensed by C. James, 52 Oregon State Bar Bulletin 15 (July 1992).

[South Carolina] *Avoiding the Unauthorized Practice of Law: Proposed Regulations for Paralegals in South Carolina*, by Julie Fleming, 53 South Carolina Law Review 487 (Winter 2002).

[South Carolina] *In re Unauthorized Practice of Law Rules Proposed by the South Carolina Bar*, 309 S.C. 304, 422 S.E.2d 123 (1992).

[South Dakota] *Paralegals: Changing the Practice of Law* by J. Rasmussen & P. Sedlacek, 44 South Dakota Law Review 319 (1999).

[South Dakota] *Utilization of Legal Assistants*, South Dakota Codified Laws

(§ 16-18-34.2) (in text search for statutes, type "legal assistant" at legis.state.sd.us/statutes).

The Successful Paralegal Job Search Guide by C. Estrin & S. Hunt (Delmar Cengage Learning, 2001).

A Survival Guide for Paralegals: Tips from the Trenches by A. Gelb & K. Levine (Delmar Cengage Learning, 2003).

T

Teaching Corrections Law to Corrections Personnel by W. Statsky, 37 Federal Probation 42 (June 1972).

Techniques for Supervising Paralegals by W. Statsky, 22 Practical Lawyer 81 (November 1976).

[Tennessee] *What to Know before Your Firm Hires a Legal Assistant …* by D. Monke, 41 Tennessee Bar Journal 22 (August 2005).

Ten Steps to Finding the Perfect Legal Assistant by S. Aronfeld, 42 Trial 43 (March 2006).

[Texas] *Another First for State Bar of Texas: Specialty Certification of Legal Assistants*, 57 Texas Bar Journal 58 (January 1994).

[Texas] *Are We Our Brother's Keepers? A Discussion of Nonlawyer Representation before Texas Administrative Agencies and Recommendations for the Future* by B. Clayton, 8 Texas Tech. Administrative Law Review 115 (Spring 2007).

[Texas] *Attorney's Guide to Practicing with Legal Assistants*, 2d ed. (State Bar of Texas, 1992).

[Texas] *Code of Ethics for Legal Assistants* by the Legal Assistants Division of the State Bar of Texas (www.txethics.org/reference_ethics.asp).

[Texas] *Common Questions RE: Legal Assistants* by S. Keaton-Hardin, 63 Texas Bar Journal 272 (March 2000).

[Texas] *Evidence Required to Prove Validity of Legal Assistant Fees …* by V. Brittain, 63 Texas Bar Journal 261 (March 2000).

[Texas] *Filing, Handling, Perfecting and Foreclosing Oil and Gas Liens, Oil and Gas Law: For Legal Assistants and Attorneys* by Stinnett (State Bar of Texas, 1984).

[Texas] *Finding, Interviewing, Hiring, and Retaining the Best Paralegal for Your Practice* by A. Dunkin, 63 Texas Bar Journal 276 (March 2000).

[Texas] *General Guidelines for the Utilization of the Services of Legal Assistants by Attorneys*, 63 Texas Bar Journal 280 (March 2000).

[Texas] *Help! … Can My Office Use a Legal Assistant?* by J. Work, 57 Texas Bar Journal 42 (January 1994).

[Texas] *Legal Assistant Ethics for Attorney* by E. Lockwood, 63 Texas Bar Journal 270 (March 2000).

[Texas] *Legal Assistants: Saving Time and Resources for Lawyers and Clients*, 57 Texas Bar Journal 28 (January 1994).

Texas Makes Solicitation a Felony by M. Hansen, 79 American Bar Association Journal 32 (September 1993).

[Texas] *National Regulation of Nonlawyer Practice* by P. Young, 57 Texas Bar Journal 28 (January 1994).

[Texas] *New Health Professionals: The Physician Assistant and Advanced Nurse Practitioner in Texas*, 22 South Texas Law Journal 132 (1982).

Texas Paralegal: Essential Rules, Documents, and Resources by W. Statsky & L. Crossett (Delmar Cengage Learning, 2009).

[Texas] *Paralegal Ethics for Attorneys* by E. Lockwood, 69 Texas Bar Journal 880 (October 2006).

[Texas] *Paralegal Overtime: Yes, No, or Maybe* by X. Rodriguez, 63 Texas Bar Journal 266 (March 2000).

[Texas] *Recruiting, Interviewing, and Hiring Legal Assistants* by A. Dodds, 57 Texas Bar Journal 40 (January 1994).

[Texas] *State Bar Adopts New Paralegal Standards* by X. Rodriguez, 69 Texas Bar Journal 876 (October 2006).

Texas] *Staying Out of the Briar Patch: Ethical Considerations and the Legal Assistant* by M. Wise, 57 Texas Bar Journal 30 (January 1994).

[Texas] *Supervising Lawyers, Supervised … Nonlawyer Assistants: Ethical Responsibilities* by E. Wilkinson, 64 Texas Bar Journal 452 (May 2001).

[Texas] *Supervision of Non-lawyer Employees* by W. Steele, 58 Texas Bar Journal 798 (September 1995).

[Texas] *A Timeline of the Paralegal Division* by J. Johnson, 69 Texas Bar Journal 884 (October 2006).

The Thin Red Line: An Analysis of the Role of Legal Assistants in the Chapter 13 Bankruptcy Process by G. Sullivan, 23 Journal of the Legal Profession 15 (1998–1999).

Title Examination Activities by Lending Institution, Insurance Company, or Title and Abstract Company, as Illegal Practice of Law by C. Marvel, 85 A.L.R. 2d 184 (2004).

Tort Liability of Paralegals and Lawyers Who Use Their Services by J. Wade, 24 Vanderbilt Law Review 1133 (1971).

Trademark Administration: A Guide for Paralegals and Trademark Administrators, 3d ed. by the International Trademark Association (2005).

The Training of Community Judges by W. Statsky, 4 Columbia Human Rights Law Review 401 (1972).

U

Unauthorized Practice of Law/Nonlawyer Practice Bibliography (American Bar Association, Standing Committee on Client Protection 2007) (www.abanet.org/cpr/clientpro/nlp_biblio.pdf).

Unauthorized Practice and Pro Se Divorce, 86 Yale Law Journal 104 (1976).

Unauthorized Practice of Law: Does Anyone Know What It Is? by K. Currier, 8 Journal of Paralegal Education and Practice 21 (1991).

The Unauthorized Practice of Law in Immigration by A. Ashbrook, 5 Georgetown Journal of Legal Ethics 237 (1991).

Unauthorized Practice of Law—Real Estate Closings by M. Shields, 119 A.L.R. 5th 191 (2004)

Under New Mismanagement: The Problem of Nonlawyer Equity Partnership in Law Firms by C. Carson, 7 Georgetown Journal of Legal Ethics 593 (1994).

Use of Lay Representatives, 58 Michigan Law Review 456 (1960).

Use of Paralegal Assistants in Divorce Practice by P. Grove, 4 American Journal of Family Law 41 (Spring 1990).

Using Computers in the Law Office, 3d ed. by B. Roper (Delmar Cengage Learning, 2000).

[Utah] *Beyond Civility for Paralegals* by A. Whitby, 20 Utah Bar Journal 57 (May/June 2006).

[Utah] *Civility for Paralegals* by G. Wayment, 19 Utah Bar Journal 40 (No. 7, 2006).

[Utah] *Canon of Ethics for Legal Assistants*, Utah State Bar Legal Assistant Division (click "About LAD" at www.utahbar.org/sites/lad).

[Utah] *Guidelines for the Utilization of Legal Assistants*, Utah State Bar Legal Assistant Division (click "About LAD" at www.utahbar.org/sites/lad).

[Utah] *How to Effectively Use a Paralegal in a Probate Matter* by S. Faulkner, 17 Utah Bar Journal 42 (January/February 2004).

[Utah] *Legal Assistant Utilization May Optimize Client Service in Litigation Practice* by P. Lowden, 16 Utah Bar Journal 44 (June/July 2003).

[Utah] *Nonlawyers Help Keep Lawyers Out of the "Discipline Corner"* by P. Lowden, 20 Utah Bar Journal 57 (January/February 2007)

[Utah] *Non-lawyer Legal Technicians* by D. Nuffer, 7 Utah Bar Journal 6 (October 1994).

[Utah] *Practice Pointer: Training and Supervising Non-lawyer Assistants* by K. Toomey, Utah Bar Journal 16 (April 2004).

[Utah] *What Is Paralegal Work? The Utah Supreme Court Offers a Three-Pronged Test* by P. Lowden, 20 Utah Bar Journal 54 (April 2007).

V

Validity of Will Drawn by Layman, 18 A.L.R.2d 918 (1951).

W

The War between Attorneys and Lay Conveyancers: Empirical Evidence Says "Cease Fire!" by J. Palomar, 31 Connecticut Law Review 423 (1999).

[Washington State] *It's Time to Open the Legal Profession* by J. Scalone, 49 Washington State Bar News 41 (March 1995).

[West Virginia] *The Client's Viewpoint on Paralegals* by W. Redd, 8 West Virginia Lawyer 19 (April 1995).

[West Virginia] *Exempt from Overtime Pay* by D. Ridgway, 8 West Virginia Lawyer 16 (February 1995).

[West Virginia] *The Golden Age of Paralegals and Risk Managers* by R. Martin, 9 West Virginia Lawyer 18 (November 1995).

[West Virginia] *Legal Assistants: Look What They Can Do for You* by C. Given, 9 West Virginia Lawyer 22 (March 1996).

[West Virginia] *Paralegals: Entitled to Overtime Rate* by C. Quasebarth, 5 West Virginia Lawyer 21 (February 1992).

[West Virginia] *Tips for the Paralegal …*

Out-of-Town Trial by T. Welch, 2007 West Virginia Lawyer 18 (January/February 2007).

What Activities of Stock or Securities Broker Constitute Unauthorized Practice of Law, 34 A.L.R.3d 1305 (1970).

What Constitutes Unauthorized Practice of Law by Paralegal by Jay M. Zitter, 109 A.L.R.5th 275 (2003).

What Is the Unauthorized Practice of Law and How Is It Regulated by E. Holmes, 76 Michigan Bar Journal 580 (June 1997).

What's in a Name? Should Paralegals Be Liable for Malpractice? by C. Lissitzyn, 77 Connecticut Bar Journal 86 (2003). Also printed in 15 Professional Lawyer 2 (No. 4, 2005).

Who Should Regulate Lawyers? by D. Wilkins, 105 Harvard Law Review 799 (1992).

[Wisconsin] *Looking Closely at the Role of Paralegals: The California, New Jersey, and Wisconsin Experiences*, 80 Michigan Bar Journal 56 (March 2001).

Wisconsin's Elderlinks Initiative: Using Technology to Provide Legal Services to Older Persons by M. Doremus, 32 Wake Forest Law Review 545 (1997) (paralegal benefit specialists, administrative advocacy).

[Wisconsin] *Nonlawyer Practice: An Expanding Role* by D. Tenenbaum, 67 Wisconsin Lawyer 12 (November 1994).

[Wisconsin] *Unauthorized Practice of Law: Protection or Protectionism?* by D. Tenenbaum, 67 Wisconsin Lawyer 14 (September 1994).

Women's Rights in Russia: Training Nonlawyers to Represent Victims of Domestic Violence by D. Post, 4 Yale Human Rights and Development Law Journal 135 (2001).

Working with Legal Assistants, P. Ulrch, ed. (American Bar Association, 1980).

The Writ-Writers: Jailhouse Lawyers Right of Meaningful Access to the Courts by J. Myers, 18 Akron Law Review 649 (1984).

[Wyoming] *Support Staff Conflicts of Interest* by J. Burman, 20 Wyoming Lawyer 12 (October 1997).

[Wyoming] *Why Paralegal Certification Counts* by D. Monke, 29 Wyoming Lawyer 27 (August 2006).

Y

You Are Not a Lawyer: Does Representation of Carriers by Non-lawyers in Federal Motor Carrier Safety Administration Enforcement Cases Constitute the Unauthorized Practice of Law? by O. Nawaz, 32 Transportation Law Journal 21 (Fall 2004).

Paralegal Associations, Bar Associations That Allow Paralegal Membership, and Related Organizations

A. Paralegal Associations (National)
B. Paralegal Associations (State and Local)
C. Other Associations (America)
D. Other Associations (International)

A. PARALEGAL ASSOCIATIONS (NATIONAL)

There are four major national paralegal associations. The first three listed below (NALA, NFPA, and NALS) are the largest.

National Association of Legal Assistants (NALA)

Web: www.nala.org
E-mail: nalanet@nala.org
Phone: 918-587-6828 (Tulsa, OK)
Certification Awarded: certified legal assistant (CLA); certified paralegal (CP); advanced certified paralegal (ACP)
Certification Requirements: (www.nala .org/cert.htm) (www.nala.org/apcweb/ index.html)
Ethics Code: (www.nala.org/code.htm) (www.nala.org/benefits-code.htm) (www.nala.org/98model.htm)
Newsletter: *Facts and Findings* (www.nala .org/Facts_Findings.htm)
Continuing Legal Education Offered: www.nalacampus.com
Affiliated Associations: www.nala.org/ Affiliated_Associations_Info.HTM

National Federation of Paralegal Associations (NFPA)

Web: www.paralegals.org
E-mail: info@paralegals.org
Phone: 425-967-0045 (Edmonds, WA)
Certification Awarded: PACE registered paralegal (RP)
Certification Requirements: www .paralegals.org (click "PACE/RP")
Ethics Code: www.paralegals.org (click "Positions & Issues")

Newsletter: *National Paralegal Reporter* (www.paralegals.org)
Continuing Legal Education Offered: www.paralegals.org (click "CLE")
Career Center: www.paralegals.org (click "NFPA Career Center")
Affiliated Associations: www.paralegals. org (click "About NFPA," then "Local Member Associations")

NALS the Association of Legal Professionals (NALS)

Web: www.nals.org
E-mail: info@nals.org
Phone: 918-582-5188 (Tulsa, OK)
Certification Awarded: professional paralegal (PP)
Certification Requirements: www.nals .org/certification
Ethics Code: www.nals.org/aboutnals/ Code
Newsletter: *@Law* (www.nals.org/ newsletters/index.html)
Continuing Legal Education Offered: www.nals.org/onlinelearning/index .html
Career Center: www.nals.org/ careercenter/index.html
Affiliated Associations: www.nals.org/ membership/states/index.html

American Alliance of Paralegals (AAPI)

Web: www.aapipara.org
E-mail: info@aapipara.org
Certification Awarded: American Alliance certified paralegal (AACP)
Certification Requirements: www .aapipara.org/Certification.htm
Ethics Code: www.aapipara.org/ Ethicalstandards.htm
Newsletter: *Alliance Echo* (www.aapipara .org/Newsletter. htm)
Job Bank: www.aapipara.org/Jobbank.htm

B. PARALEGAL ASSOCIATIONS (STATE AND LOCAL)

The street (or "snail mail") addresses of many local paralegal associations change often. Very few have business offices. Most rent a P.O. box number and keep all association files in the home of an active paralegal member (often the current president) or in an available file cabinet of the law office where he or she works. If one of the addresses below turns out to be unproductive, (1) check the Internet by typing the name of the association in any search engine, (2) check with your program director, (3) ask your classmates if they have a different address, (4) ask a working paralegal in your area, (5) contact the national office of NALA or the NFPA if the association is affiliated with either, and (6) contact the association that is geographically closest to the one you are trying to contact and ask if it knows the current address. Periodically, run Google (or another search engine) searches for your city, county, or state to find out if any new associations have recently come into existence (e.g., Boston paralegal association; Utah paralegal association).

In the following paralegal associations you will also find information about job banks, where available. For more leads to employment, see your state in appendix E.

Sites for legal administrators and legal secretaries are included for potential networking opportunities. Such sites might also become direct or indirect links for finding out about paralegal job openings.

Alabama

Alabama Association of Paralegals (Birmingham)
www.aaopi.com
Membership: $65 (active); $40 (student)
Job Bank: www.aaopi.com/ employmentopportunties.htm

Northeast Alabama Litigation Support Association
www.nealsa.net

AALS (Alabama Association of Legal Secretaries)
www.alabama-als.org
www.nals.org/membership/regions/alabama.html

Baldwin County Association of Legal Professionals
www.nals.org/membership/regions/alabama.html

BLSA (Birmingham)
www.nals.org/membership/regions/alabama.html

Dallas County Legal Secretaries Association
www.nals.org/membership/regions/alabama.html

Mobile Legal Secretaries Association
www.nals.org/membership/regions/alabama.html

Montgomery Legal Secretaries Association
www.nals.org/membership/regions/alabama.html

Tuscaloosa County Legal Professionals Association
www.nals.org/membership/regions/alabama.html

NALS of Shelby County
www.nals.org/membership/regions/alabama.html

American Association of Legal Nurse Consultants, Birmingham Chapter
www.bhamchapteraalnc.org

Alaska

Alaska Association of Paralegals (Anchorage)
www.alaskaparalegals.org
E-mail: info@alaskaparalegal.org
Phone: 907-646-8018
Membership: $85 (full); $40 (student)
Job Bank: Available for members only

NALS (Association of Legal Professionals) of Anchorage
www.nalsofanchorage.org
E-mail: info@nalsotanchorage.org
Phone: 907-566-2572
Membership: $115 (regular/active/Full); $35 (student)
Handbook for Legal Professionals: www.nalsofanchorage.org/handbk.htm

Fairbanks Association of Legal Assistants
P.O. Box 74771
Fairbanks, AK 99707

Alaska Association of Legal Administrators
www.alaskaala.org

Arizona

Arizona Paralegal Association (Phoenix)
www.azparalegal.org
Phone: 602-258-0121
Membership: $65 (voting); $25 (student)
Job Bank: www.azparalegal.org/jobbank.html

Legal Assistants of Metropolitan Phoenix
www.geocities.com/azlamp
E-mail: azlamp@lawyer.com
Membership: $25 (active); $10 (student)

Tucson Paralegal Association
www.tucsonparalegals.org
Membership: $45 (active); $30 (student)
Job Bank: www.tucsonparalegals.org/html/jobbank.html

NALS (Association for Legal Professionals) of Arizona
www.nalsofarizona.org
www.nals.org/membership/regions/arizona.html
E-mail: assistance
Phone: 918-582-5188
Membership: $135 (active); $19 (student)

NALS (Association for Legal Professionals) of Tucson and Southern Arizona
www.tucsonlegalsupport.com
www.nals.org/membership/regions/arizona.html
Employment Information: www.tucsonlegalsupport.com

NALS (Association for Legal Professionals) of Phoenix
www.nals.org/membership/regions/arizona.html

NALS (Association for Legal Professionals) of Yavapai
www.nalsofarizona.org/Membership.htm
www.nals.org/membership/regions/arizona.html

Arizona Legal Support
www.arizonalegalsupport.com

Maricopa County Bar Association Paralegal Division Membership: $95
www.maricopaparalegals.org
E-mail: president@maricopaparalegals.org
Phone: 602-257-4200

Job Bank: www.maricopaparalegals.org/Paralegals.htm

Pima County Bar Association Associate Non-Attorney Membership: $100
www.pimacountybar.org

Arizona Association of Independent Paralegals
(Certified Legal Document Preparers)
www.azaip.com
Phone: 602-864-7291
Membership: $150

American Association of Legal Nurse Consultants, Phoenix Chapter
www.aalnc-az.org

Association of Legal Administrators, Valley of the Sun Chapter
www.alaphoenix.org

Arkansas

Paralegal Association of Arkansas (Little Rock)
www.aala-legal.org
E-mail: info@aala-legal.org
Membership: $35 (active); $15 (student)
Job Bank: Available for members

Association for Arkansas Legal Support Professionals
www.arkansasals.org
www.nals.org/membership/regions/arkansas.html
Membership: $135 (active); $19 (student)
Job Bank: Available for members

Saline County Legal Support Professionals
www.salinecountylsp.com-1.net
www.nals.org/membership/regions/arkansas.html
E-mail: salinecountylsp@msn.com

Garland County Legal Support Professionals
www.gclsp.com
www.nals.org/membership/regions/arkansas.html

Greater Little Rock Legal Support Professionals
www.greaterlittlerocklsp.com
www.nals.org/membership/regions/arkansas.html

Jefferson County Association of Legal Support Professionals
www.nals.org/membership/regions/arkansas.html

Northeast Arkansas Legal Support Professionals
www.nealsp.org
www.nals.org/membership/regions/arkansas.html

White County Association of Legal Support Professionals
www.nals.org/membership/regions/arkansas.html

Advanced Paralegal Education Group
www.apeglegal.com

Association of Legal Administrators, Arkansas Chapter
www.arkansasala.com

California

California Alliance of Paralegal Associations
www.caparalegal.org

Central Coast Paralegal Association
www.ccpaslo.org
Phone: 805-438-3762
Membership: $50 (active); $35 (student)

Fresno Paralegal Association
www.fresnoparalegal.org
Membership: $40 (voting); $20 (student)
Job Bank: www.fresnoparalegal.org/job_bank/index.html

Inland Counties Association of Paralegals (Riverside)
www.icaponline.org
E-mail: info@icapoline.org
Phone: 951-750-1071
Membership: $60 (regular); $40 (student)

Kern County Paralegal Association (Bakersfield)
www.kcpaonline.org
Job Bank: www.kcpaonline.org/jobbank

Los Angeles Paralegal Association
www.lapa.org
E-mail: info@lapa.org
Phone: 866-626-LAPA
Membership: $77 (voting); $62 (student)
Job Bank (career center): lapa.legalstaff.com/Common/HomePage.aspx?abbr=LAPA

NALS (Association for Legal Professionals) of Orange County
www.nalsoc.org
Membership: $115 (active); $27 (student)
Job Bank: "We work with several legal placement agencies, which are advertised on our website."

Orange County Paralegal Association (Newport Beach)
www.ocparalegal.org
Phone: 714-744-7747
Membership: $60 (voting); $40 (student)
Job Bank (career center):
ocparal.legalstaff.com/Common/HomePage.aspx?abbr=OCPARAL

Paralegal Association of Santa Clara County
www.sccparalegal.org

Phone: 408-235-0301
Membership: $55 (voting); $40 (student)
Job Bank: www.sccparalegal.org/lawfirms.php

Redwood Empire Legal Assistants (Santa Rosa)
redwoodempirelegalassistants.com
Membership: $40 (voting); $20 (student)
Job Bank: redwoodempirelegalassistants.com

Sacramento Valley Paralegal Association
www.svpa.org
Phone: 925-941-2138
Membership: $65 (voting); $25 (student)
Job Bank: www.svpa.org

Sacramento County Bar Association Associate Membership for Non-Lawyers: $110
www.sacbar.org

San Diego Paralegal Association
www.sdparalegals.org
E-mail: president@sdparalegals.org
Membership: $75 (voting); $30 (student)
Job Bank: www.sdparalegals.org/users-only.php

San Diego County Bar Association Associate Membership for Paralegals: $80
www.sdcba.org

San Francisco Paralegal Association
www.sfpa.com
E-mail: info@sfpa.com
Phone: 415-777-2390
Membership: $80 (voting); $50 (student)
Job Bank (career center): www.sfpa.com/a-cc.htm

San Francisco, Bar Association of Membership for paralegals ("legal professionals"): $95
www.sfbar.org

Santa Barbara Paralegal Association
www.sbparalegals.org
Membership: $50 (active); $30 (student)
Job Bank: www.sbparalegals.org/Job%20Bank.htm

Sequoia Paralegal Association (Visalia)
www.sequoiaparalegals.com
Phone: 559-733-1065
Membership: $40 (voting); $17 (student)
Job Board: www.sequoiaparalegals.com/jobs.asp

Ventura County Paralegal Association
www.vcparalegal.org
Membership: $40 (active); $30 (student)
Job Bank: "Yes, we do have a job bank for members only. In addition, as a new position is advertised, our Employment Liaison sends out an e-mail to each

member to let them know of the available position."

Ventura County Bar Association Non-Attorney Membership: $120
www.vcba.org/Intus/memberapp/FirstPage.asp

Ventura County Asian American Bar Association
("Membership is open to everyone: $25 for attorneys and $25 for nonattorneys.")
www.vcba.org/about/affiliates.shtml

Commission for Advanced Paralegal Specialization (San Leandro)
The commission administers California's certification program (now under revision).
www.cla-cas.org

California Association of Legal Document Assistants (Fremont)
www.calda.org
Membership: $200 (voting); $100 (student)

Alliance of Legal Document Assistant Professionals (Anaheim)
www.aldap.com
E-mail: president@ALDAP.com

Bay Area Legal Secretaries Forum
www.balsf.org

Beverly Hills/Century City Legal Secretaries Association
www.bhcclsa.org

California Association of Photocopiers and Process Servers
www.capps.org

California Lawyers' Assistants Secretaries & Students
www.lawguru.com/users/law/class/class.html

California Society of Enrolled Agents
www.csea.org

CAMAL Association of Legal Professionals
www.nals.org/membership/regions/california.html

Capitol City Legal Professionals Association
www.capitolcitylpa.org

Mt. Diablo Legal Professionals Association
www.mtdiablolpa.info/home

NALS of Orange County
www.nals.org/membership/regions/california.html

NALS of San Diego
www.nals.org/membership/regions/california.html

Orange County Legal Secretaries Association
www.oclsa.org

Palo Alto Legal Secretaries Association
www.palsa.net

Pomona Valley–Citrus LSA
www.nals.org/membership/regions/
california.html

Port Stockton LSA
www.nals.org/membership/regions/
california.html

Sacramento Legal Secretaries Association
www.slsa.org

San Diego Legal Secretaries Association
www.sdlsa.org

San Fernando Valley Legal Secretaries Association
www.sfvlsa.com

San Mateo County Legal Secretaries Association
www.smclsa.com

Santa Clara County Legal Secretaries Association
www.santaclaralegalsecrty.org

American Association of Legal Nurse Consultants, Bay Area Chapter
www.bacnc.org

American Association of Legal Nurse Consultants, Northern California Chapter
www.bacnc.org

American Association of Legal Nurse Consultants, Sacramento Chapter
www.gsac-aalnc.org

American Association of Legal Nurse Consultants, Los Angeles Chapter
www.aalncla.org

American Association of Legal Nurse Consultants, Orange County Chapter
www.aalnc-orangecounty.org

American Association of Legal Nurse Consultants, San Diego Chapter
www.aalncsandiego.org

Association of Legal Administrators, East Bay Chapter
www.ebala.org

Association of Legal Administrators, Golden Gate Chapter
www.alasf.org

Association of Legal Administrators, Greater Los Angeles Chapter
www.glaala.org

Association of Legal Administrators, Orange County Chapter
www.orangecountyala.org

Association of Legal Administrators, Sacramento Valley Chapter
www.ala-sacramentovalley.org

Association of Legal Administrators, San Diego Chapter
www.alasandiego.org

Association of Legal Administrators, Silicon Valley Chapter
www.alasvc.org

Southern California Background Investigators Association
www.scbia.com

Colorado

Rocky Mountain Paralegal Association (Denver)
www.rockymtnparalegal.org
E-mail: webmaster@rockymtnparalegal.com
Membership: $60 (voting); $35 (student)
Job Bank: www.rockymtnparalegal.
org/jobs

NALS (Association for Legal Professionals) of Colorado
www.nalscolorado.org
Membership: $120 (regular); $19 (student)
Job Bank: www.nalscolorado.org/jobs.htm

Colorado Association of Professional Paralegals and Legal Assistants
www.capplaweb.org
E-mail: mail@capplaweb.org
Membership: $40 (active); $20 (student)
Job Bank: www.capplaweb.org/5.html

Pikes Peak Paralegals
pikespeakparalegals.org
Membership: $30 (voting); $10 (student)
Job Bank: pikespeakparalegals.org/
jobbank.html

Pikes Peak Association of Legal Support Staff (Colorado Springs)
www.elpasocountybar.org/organizations_
detail.cfm?areaid=48
sfs.colostate.edu/J211011.cfm?ID=385

Colorado Association of Legal Support Staff
www.CALSS.org

Legal Assistants of the Western Slope
www.nala.org/aff-roster-LINKS.htm

Colorado Bar Association
Associate Membership for Paralegals: $100
www.cobar.org/group/index.cfm?category=
767&EntityID=dpmem
www.cobar.org/group/index.
cfm?EntityID=CLAS

American Association of Legal Nurse Consultants, Denver Chapter
www.coaalnc.com

Association of Legal Administrators, Mile High Chapter
www.milehighala.org

Connecticut

Central Connecticut Paralegal Association (Hartford)
www.ctparalegals.org
E-mail: info@ctparalegals.com
Membership: $75 (voting); $48 (student)
Job Bank: www.ctparalegals.org

Connecticut Association of Paralegals (Bridgeport)
www.paralegals.org/displaycommon.
cfm?an=1&subarticlenbr=747
E-mail: Connecticut@paralegals.org
Membership: $60 (voting); $35 (student)

New Haven County Association of Paralegals
www.paralegals.org/displaycommon
.cfm?an=1&subarticlenbr=751
E-mail: Newhaven@paralegals.org
Membership: $65 (voting); $30 (student)
Job Bank: "We forward incoming job postings via e-mail to all of our members."

Connecticut Bar Association
Associate Membership for Paralegals: $80
www.ctbar.org

New Haven County Bar Association
Associate Membership for Paralegals: $60
www.newhavenbar.org

Association of Legal Administrators, Nutmeg Chapter
www.alanutmeg.org

Delaware

Delaware Paralegal Association (Dover)
www.deparalegals.org
E-mail: info@deparalegals.org;
downstate@deparalegals.org
Phone: 302-426-1362
Membership: $60 (full); $35 (student)
Job Bank: www.deparalegals.org/
jobbank.htm

American Association of Legal Nurse Consultants, Delaware Chapter
www.deaalnc.org

Association of Legal Administrators, Delaware Chapter
www.firststateala.org

District of Columbia

National Capital Area Paralegal Association (Wash. D.C.)
www.ncapa.com
E-mail: info@ncapa.com
Membership: $80 (voting); $60 (student)
Job Bank: www.ncapa.com

Navy Legalmen Association
www.jag.navy.mil/JAGMAG/May–
JunLegalmen.pdf
www.mnparalegals.org/
LegalmenProject3516.php
www.wnyparalegals.org/navy.htm

District of Columbia Legal Secretaries Association
www.nals.org/membership/regions/DC.html

Association of Legal Administrators, District of Columbia Chapter
www.alacapchap.org

Florida

Central Florida Paralegal Association (Orlando)
www.cfpainc.com
Phone: 407-672-6372
Membership: $45 (active); $25 (student)
Job Bank: "We place the advertisements for the job bank in our quarterly issue of the *FOCUS*; and send them through the membership on our Yahoo! Group."

Gainesville Association of Legal Assistants
www.afn.org/~gala
E-mail: gala@afn.org
Phone: 904-462-2249

Gulf Coast Paralegal Association (Naples)
www.gcpa.info
Membership: $50 (active); $20 (student)
Job Bank: www.gcpa.info/about_us

NALS the Association for Legal Professionals of Central Florida
www.nals.org/membership/regions/Florida.html

Northeast Florida Paralegal Association (Jacksonville)
www.nefpa.org
Membership: $55 (active); $35 (student)
Job Bank: "We have a members-only Job Bank."

Northwest Florida Paralegal Association (Pensacola)
www.nwfpa.com
Membership: $40 (active); $20 (student)
Job Postings: www.nwfpa.com/jobs.htm

Paralegal Association of Florida (West Palm Beach)
www.pafinc.org
E-mail: execdirector@pafinc.org
Phone: 561-833-1408
Membership: $65 (active); $35 (student)
Job Bank: "We have a job bank within each chapter that members can access."

South Florida Paralegal Association (Miami)
www.sfpa.info
E-mail: sfpaadmin@sfpa.info
Phone: 305-944-0204
Membership: $70 (active); $60 (student)

Southwest Florida Paralegal Association (Sarasota)
www.swfloridaparalegals.com
E-mail: info@swfloridaparalegals.com

Phone:
Membership: $45 (active); $15 (student)
Job Bank: www.swfloridaparalegals.com/employment/opps.html

Tampa Bay Paralegal Association
www.tbpa.org
E-mail: membership@tbpa.org
Membership: $50 (active); $20 (student)
Job Bank: www.tbpa.org/Jobs.htm

Volusia Association of Paralegals (Daytona Beach)
volusiaparalegals.org
Membership: $65 (general); $40 (student)
Job Bank: volusiaparalegals.org/careers.htm

Caribbean Bar Association, South Florida Chapter
Associate Membership for Nonlawyers: $30
www.caribbeanbar.org/members/register

Central Florida Bankruptcy Law Association
Paralegal Associate Membership: $40
www.cfbla.org

Collier County Bar Association
Associate Membership for Certified Legal Assistants: $75
colliercountybar.org
Job Bank: colliercountybar.org/jobs.htm

Florida Association of Criminal Defense Lawyers
Affiliate Membership: $190
www.facdl.org/MemberCenter/Member_Center.html

Florida Justice Association
Paralegal Membership: $165
www.aftl.org/join.asp

National Employment Lawyers Association, Florida Chapter
Paraprofessional Membership: $50
www.floridanela.org/pdf/application.pdf

South Palm Beach County Bar Association
Membership for Associates: $100
www.southpalmbeachbar.org

Hillsborough County Bar Association
Affiliate Membership for Non-Lawyers: $245
www.hillsbar.com

Orange County Bar Association
Affiliate Membership for Paralegals: $50
www.orangecountybar.org

Florida Association of Legal Support Specialists
www.falss.org (click "Chartered Chapters" to find links to chapters in Broward County, Collier, Jacksonville, Lee County, Marion County, Miami-Dade, North Pinellas, Okaloosa-Walton, Orange County, Pensacola, St. Augustine, St. Petersburg, Sarasota-Manatee, Space Coast, Tallahassee, and West Pasco)

Miami-Dade Legal Support Association
www.falss.org

Pensacola Legal Support Specialists Association
www.falss.org

Sarasota-Manatee Association of Legal Support Specialists
www.smalss.com

Tallahassee Association of Legal Support Specialists
www.falss.org

Tampa Independent Paralegals
www.tampaindependentparalegals.com

American Association of Legal Nurse Consultants, Jacksonville Chapter
www.aalnc.org/about/chapter_directory.cfm

American Association of Legal Nurse Consultants, Orlando Chapter
www.orlandoaalnc.org

American Association of Legal Nurse Consultants, Tampa Bay Chapter
www.tbaalnc.org

American Association of Legal Nurse Consultants, South Florida Chapter
www.sflaalnc.org

Association of Legal Administrators, Capital Chapter
www.alatally.org

Association of Legal Administrators, Central Florida Chapter
www.cfcala.org

Association of Legal Administrators, Jacksonville Chapter
www.alajax.org

Association of Legal Administrators, Palm Beach County Chapter
www.pbcala.org

Association of Legal Administrators, Sarasota-Manatee Chapter
www.smcala.org

Association of Legal Administrators, South Florida Chapter
www.alasofla.org

Association of Legal Administrators, Sunset Coast (Tampa) Chapter
www.alasuncoast.org

Georgia

Georgia Association of Paralegals (Atlanta)
www.gaparalegal.org
E-mail: gaparalegal@comcast.net
Phone: 404-229-8632
Membership: $125 (active); $65 (student)
Job Board: gap.legalstaff.com/Common/HomePage.aspx?abbr=GAP

Southeastern Association of Legal Assistants (Savannah)
seala.org
Membership: $100 (active); $50 (associate) $50 (student)
Job Networking: seala.org/about.html

NALS (Association for Legal Professionals) of Georgia
www.nals.org/membership/regions/Georgia.html

NALS (Association for Legal Professionals) of Atlanta
www.nalsofatlanta.org
www.nals.org/membership/regions/Georgia.html
Membership: $100 (full); $19 (student)

American Association of Legal Nurse Consultants, Atlanta Chapter
www.atlantaaalnc.org

American Association of Legal Nurse Consultants, Augusta Chapter
www.aalnc.org/about/chapter_directory.cfm

Association of Legal Administrators, Atlanta Chapter
www.atlanta-ala.org

Cobb County Legal Secretaries Association
www.cobblsa.org
www.nals.org/membership/regions/Georgia.html

International Paralegal Management Association (Avendale Estates)
www.paralegalmanagement.com

Atlanta Bar Association
Affiliate Membership for Legal Assistants: $50
www.atlantabar.org

Hawaii

Hawaii Paralegal Association(Honolulu)
www.hawaiiparalegal.org
E-mail: membership@hawaiiparalegal.org
Membership: $70 (voting); $50 (student)
Job Bank: Click "Get a Job"

Hawaii Legal Support Professionals (Honolulu)
hawaiilsp.org
www.nals.org/membership/regions/Hawaii.html
Membership: $110 (active); $29 (student)

Association of Legal Administrators, Hawaii Chapter
www.alahawaii.org

Idaho

Idaho Association of Paralegals (Boise)
idahoparalegals.org
Membership: $50 (active); $35 (student)
Job Bank: Available for members only

BLSA—the Association for Legal Professionals
www.blsa.net
www.nals.org/membership/regions/Idaho.html

Intermountain Paralegal Association
P.O. Box 817
Pocatello, ID 83204

Association of Legal Professionals (Boise)
www.idals.net (www.idals.org)
www.nals.org/membership/regions/Idaho.html

North Idaho Legal Secretaries Association
www.nals.org/membership/regions/Idaho.html

LLSA (Lewiston)
www.nals.org/membership/regions/Idaho.html

Illinois

Central Illinois Paralegal Association (Bloomington)
www.ciparalegal.org
E-mail: cipa@ciparalegal.org
Membership: $50 (active); $35 (student)
Job Bank: Available for members only

Illinois Paralegal Association (New Lenox)
www.ipaonline.org
E-mail: ipa@ipaonline.org
Phone: 815-462-4620
Membership: $65 (regular); $40 (student)
Employment Opportunities: www.ipaonline.org/displaycommon.cfm?an=12

NALS (Association for Legal Professionals) of Illinois
www.nalsofillinois.org
www.nals.org/membership/regions/Illinois.html
E-mail: info@nalsofillinois.org

Illinois State Bar Association
Associate Membership for Legal Assistants: $48
www.isba.org/Association/join.asp

DuPage County Bar Association
Associate Membership for Paralegals: $80
www.dcba.org

Chicago Association of Litigation Support Managers
www.calsm.org/calsm/calsm.asp

American Association of Legal Nurse Consultants, Chicago Chapter
www.aalncchicago.org

Association of Legal Administrators, Greater Chicago Chapter
www.alachicago.org

Justice Weighed Here (Blog)
icclaw.blogspot.com/index.html

Indiana

Indiana Paralegal Association (Indianapolis)
www.indianaparalegals.org
E-mail: Information@indianaparalegals.org
Membership: $70 (voting); $40 (student)
Job Bank: www.indianaparalegals.org/Job_Bank.htm
IPA Blog: www.indianaparalegals.org/IPA_Blawg.htm

Michiana Paralegal Association (South Bend)
www.paralegals.org/displaypersonalwebpage.cfm?id=952218
E-mail: michiana@paralegals.org
Membership: $60 (voting); $30 (student)

Northeast Indiana Paralegal Association (Fort Wayne)
www.paralegals.org/displaypersonalwebpage.cfm?id=952218
Membership: $60 (voting); $30 (student)

Indiana State Bar Association
Paralegal Associate Membership: $50
www.inbar.org/content/news/article.asp?art=87

Evansville Bar Association
Paralegal Membership: $0
www.evvbar.org/Benefits.asp

American Association of Legal Nurse Consultants, Indianapolis Chapter
www.indyaalnc.org

Association of Legal Administrators, Indiana Chapter
www.alaindiana.org

Iowa

Iowa Association of Legal Assistants (Des Moines)
www.ialanet.org
E-mail: info@iala.et.org; membership@ialanet.org
Membership: $90 (active); $25 (student)
Job Openings: www.ialanet.org/job_opportunities.asp

Kansas

Heartland Association of Legal Assistants (Overland Park)
www.accesskansas.org/hala
www.kansas.gov/hala
Phone: 816-421-7100
Membership: $40 (voting); $20 (student)
Job Bank: "We have a job bank chairman who distributes job notices to our membership."

Kansas Association of Legal Assistants (Wichita)
www.accesskansas.org/kala

www.kansas.gov/kala/about_kala.htm
Membership: $35 (voting); $15 (student)
Job Bank: "We have a job registry that firms or companies can e-mail us to post paralegal job postings."

Kansas Paralegal Association (Topeka)
www.ksparalegals.org
www.accesskansas.org/ksparalegals
E-mail: info@ksparalegals.org
Membership: $65 (voting); $30 (student)
Employment Opportunities: www.ksparalegals.org

Kansas Bar Association
Paralegal Associate Membership: $75
www.ksbar.org/prospective/categories.shtml

Association of Legal Administrators, Wichita Chapter
www.walanet.org

Kansas Legal Professionals
www.klpi.org

Topeka Legal Professionals
www.klpi.org/tlp/tlp.html

Wichita Legal Professionals
www.klpi.org/wlp/Pager.html

Kentucky

Greater Appalachian Paralegal Association (Meally)
www.kypa.org/gapaapp.html

Greater Lexington Paralegal Association
www.lexingtonparalegals.com
Membership: $70 (active); $30 (student)
Job Bank: www.lexingtonparalegals.com/jobs

Kentucky Paralegal Association (Louisville)
www.kypa.org
Membership: $50 (active); $10 (student)
Job Bank: www.kypa.org/jobbank.html

Louisville Association of Paralegals
www.loupara.com
Membership: $45 (voting); free (student)
Job Bank: www.loupara.com/JOBBANK.html

Northern Kentucky Association of Paralegals
www.kypa.org/NKAP.htm
Membership: $25 (active); $20 (student)

Western Kentucky Paralegals (Paducah)
www.kypa.org/WKP.html
Membership: $35 (active); $5 (student)

Louisville Bar Association
Paralegal Membership: $55
loubar.org/signup.Cfm

American Association of Legal Nurse Consultants, Lexington Chapter
www.aalnc.org/about/chapter_directory.cfm

Association of Legal Administrators, Kentucky Chapter
www.ky-ala.org

Louisiana

Louisiana State Paralegal Association (Baton Rouge)
www.la-paralegals.org
Membership: $40 (active); $25 (student)
Job Bank: www.la-paralegals.org/jobbank.htm

New Orleans Paralegal Association
www.paralegals.org/displaypersonal webpage.cfm?id=952245
E-mail: neworleans@paralegals.org
Phone: 504-467-3136
Membership: $60 (voting); $40 (student)
Job Bank: Available for members only.

Baton Rouge Paralegal Association
brparalegals.org
Membership: $35 (voting); $20 (student)

Lafayette Paralegal Association (La)
www.lpa-la.org
E-mail: lpa@lpa.org
Membership: $25 (voting); $25 (student)
Job Bank: www.lpa-la.org/images/Job_Bank_Web_Page.doc

Southwest Louisiana Paralegal Association (Lake Charles)
swlap.tripod.com
E-mail: SWLAP_Paralegals@msn.com
Membership: $35 (voting); $15 (student)

Northwest Louisiana Paralegal Association (Shreveport)
www.nala.org/aff-roster-LINKS.htm

American Association of Legal Nurse Consultants, Greater Jackson/New Orleans Area Chapter
www.aalnc.org/about/chapter_directory.cfm

American Association of Legal Nurse Consultants, Shreveport-Bossier Chapter
www.aalnc.org/about/chapter_directory.cfm

Association of Legal Administrators, New Orleans Chapter
www.alanola.org

Maine

NALS (Association of Legal Professionals) of Maine
www.nalsofmaine.org
www.nals.org/membership/regions/Maine.html

NALS (Association of Legal Professionals) of Southern Maine
www.nalsofmaine.org/WHO.html

www.nals.org/membership/regions/Maine.html

NALS (Association of Legal Professionals) of Midcoast Maine
www.nalsofmaine.org/WHO.html
www.nals.org/membership/regions/Maine.html

NALS (Association of Legal Professionals) of Central Maine
www.nalsofmaine.org/WHO.html
www.nals.org/membership/regions/Maine.html

NALS (Association of Legal Professionals) of Northeast Maine
www.nalsofmaine.org/WHO.html
www.nals.org/membership/regions/Maine.html

Maryland

Maryland Association of Paralegals (Severna Park)
www.mdparalegals.org
E-mail: info@MDparalegals.org; maryland@MDparalegals.org
Membership: $200 (active); $100 (student)

Maryland Bar Association
Paralegal Membership: $50
www.msba.org

American Association of Legal Nurse Consultants, Baltimore Chapter
www.lnc-balt.org

Association of Legal Administrators, Maryland Chapter
www.marylandala.org

Maryland State Bar Association
Associate Membership for Paralegals: $50
www.msba.org/departments/membership/join.htm

Massachusetts

Massachusetts Paralegal Association
www.massparalegal.org
E-mail: massachusetts@paralegal.org
Membership: $75 (voting); $40 (student)
Job Bank: "Job postings are frequently posted on the MPA website specifically for members; many of these jobs are not advertised elsewhere."
Yahoo Group: groups.yahoo.com/group/MassachusettsParalegals

Western Massachusetts Paralegal Association (Springfield)
www.wmassparalegal.org
E-mail: WesternMassachusetts@paralegals.org

Central Massachusetts Paralegal Association (Worcester)
centralMassachusetts@paralegals.org

Massachusetts Bar Association
Associate Membership for Paralegals:
$150
www.massbar.org

Real Estate Bar Association for Massachusetts
Associate Membership for Paraprofessionals
www.reba.net/page/join

American Association of Legal Nurse Consultants, Southern New England Chapter
www.aalnc.org/about/chapter_directory.cfm

Michigan

Michiana Paralegal Association (Southwestern Michigan)
www.paralegals.org/
displaypersonalwebpage.cfm?id=952218
E-mail: michiana@paralegals.org
Membership: $60 (voting); $30 (student)

State Bar of Michigan
Affiliate Paralegal/Legal Assistants Membership: $75
www.michbar.org/legalassistants
Phone: 800-968-1442
Listserv: www.michbar.org/
legalassistants/listserv.cfm

Detroit Metropolitan Bar Association
Paralegal Section Membership: $50
www.detroitlawyer.org/topic.
jsp?topicId=665

Grand Rapids Bar Association
Affiliate Legal Assistant Membership: $85
www.grbar.org/sections.htm

Macomb County Bar Association
Legal Assistant Membership: $35
www.macombbar.org/registernewmembers
.cfm

Oakland County Bar Association
Legal Assistant Membership: $45
www.ocba.org/ocbamembers.id.8.htm

Grand Traverse Area Legal Professionals
www.nalsofmichigan.org/GrandTraverseArea
.html
www.nalsofmichigan.org/ChaptersPage2.htm

Genessee Association of Legal Support Professionals
www.nals.org/membership/regions/
Michigan.html

Jackson County Legal Support professionals
www.geocities.com/pamfeb55_511/JCLSP
.htm
www.nalsofmichigan.org/ChaptersPage3
.htm

Mid-Michigan Association of Legal Support Professionals
www.nalsofmichigan.org/mid-michigan
www.nalsofmichigan.org/ChaptersPage4.
htm
www.nals.org/membership/regions/
Michigan.html

NALS (Association of Legal Professionals) of Michigan
www.nalsofmichigan.org
www.nals.org/membership/regions/
Michigan.html

NALS (Association of Legal Professionals) of Berrien-Cass
www.nalsofmichigan.org/berrien-cass
www.nals.org/membership/regions/
Michigan.html

NALS (Association of Legal Professionals) of Calhoun County
www.nalsofmichigan.org/ChaptersPage1
.htm
www.nals.org/membership/regions/
Michigan.html

NALS (Association of Legal Professionals) of Detroit
www.nalsofdetroit.org
www.nals.org/membership/regions/
Michigan.html

NALS (Association of Legal Professionals) of Kalamazoo
www.nalsofgreaterkalamazoo.org
www.nalsofmichigan.org/ChaptersPage2
.htm

NALS (Association of Legal Professionals) of Lansing
www.nalsoflansing.org
www.nals.org/membership/regions/
Michigan.html

NALS (Association of Legal Professionals) of Livingston County
www.nalsofmichigan.org/ChaptersPage3.
htm
www.nals.org/membership/regions/
Michigan.html

NALS (Association of Legal Professionals) of Northern Michigan
www.nalsofmichigan.org/NorthernMI/
index.html
www.nalsofmichigan.org/ChaptersPage4.
htm
www.nals.org/membership/regions/
Michigan.html

NALS (Association of Legal Professionals) of Oakland County
www.nalsofmichigan.org/oakland
www.nals.org/membership/regions/
Michigan.html

NALS (Association of Legal Professionals) of Washtenaw
www.absims.com/wcalsp
www.nalsofmichigan.org/ChaptersPage5
.htm
www.nals.org/membership/regions/
Michigan.html

NALS (Association of Legal Professionals) of West Michigan
www.nalsofwmi.org
www.nalsofmichigan.org/ChaptersPage5
.htm
www.nals.org/membership/regions/
Michigan.html

American Association of Legal Nurse Consultants, Detroit Chapter
www.aalnc.org/about/chapter_directory.cfm

Association of Legal Administrators, Detroit Chapter
www.aladetroit.org

Minnesota

Minnesota Paralegal Association
mnparalegals.org
E-mail: info@mnparalegals.org
Phone: 651-633-2778
Membership: $100 (voting); $45 (student)
Job Bank: mnparalegals.org/
JobBankInfoforEmployers3836.php

Duluth Chapter, Minnesota Paralegal Association
mnparalegals.org/Duluth3416.php

Rochester Chapter, Minnesota Paralegal Association
mnparalegals.org/Rochester3417.php

Southern Minnesota/Mankato Chapter, Minnesota Paralegal Association
mnparalegals.org/SouthMNMankato3418
.php
E-mail: info@mnparalegals.org

Minnesota Bar Association
Paralegal Membership: $127
www2.mnbar.org/committees/paralegal/
index.htm

NALS (Association of Legal Professionals) of Greater Minnesota
www.nals.org/membership/regions/Minn.
html

NALS (Association of Legal Professionals) of the Twin Cities
www.nals.org/membership/regions/Minn
.html

Minnesota Association of Litigation Support Managers
www.malsm.org

American Association of Legal Nurse Consultants, Minneapolis Chapter
www.minneapolischapterofaalnc.org

Association of Legal Administrators, Minnesota Chapter
www.mlaa-ala.org

Mississippi

Mississippi Division of NALS (Association for Legal Professionals)
www.msnals.org
www.nals.org/membership/regions/ Mississippi.html
Membership: $100 (full); $19 (student)
Chat: www.msnals.org/page13.html

Mississippi Association of Legal Assistants (Jackson)
www.nala.org/aff-roster-LINKS.htm
www.msmala.com

Mississippi Paralegal Association
www.msparalegals.org
E-mail: ContactUs@MSParalegals.com
Phone: 601-292-1016
Membership: $45 (active); $20 (student)
Job Bank: www.msparalegals.org/jobs

Columbus Legal Professionals Association
www.msnals.org/page4.html
www.nals.org/membership/regions/ Mississippi.html

Greenwood Legal Professionals Association
www.msnals.org/page4.html
www.nals.org/membership/regions/ Mississippi.html

Gulf Coast Association of Legal Support Professionals
www.gcalsp.org
www.nals.org/membership/regions/ Mississippi.html

Jackson Legal Professionals Association
www.msnals.org/page4.html
www.nals.org/membership/regions/ Mississippi.html

Metro Legal Professionals Association
www.msnals.org/page4.html
www.nals.org/membership/regions/ Mississippi.html

Pinebelt Legal Professionals Association
www.msnals.org/page4.html
www.nals.org/membership/regions/ Mississippi.html

Tri-County Legal Support Professionals Association
www.tclspa.org
www.nals.org/membership/regions/ Mississippi.html

American Association of Legal Nurse Consultants, Jackson/New Orleans Chapter
www.aalnc.org/about/chapter_directory.cfm

Mississippi Association of Legal Assistants (Jackson)
www.nala.org/aff-roster-LINKS.htm
www.msmala.com

Missouri

Kansas City Paralegal Association (Lee's Summit)
www.kcparalegals.org
E-mail: info@kcparalegals.org
Phone: 816-421-0302
Membership: $45 (voting); $20 (student)
Job Bank: www.kcparalegals.org/jobBank .php

Missouri Paralegal Association (Jefferson City)
www.missouriparalegalassoc.org
Membership: $44 (voting); $22 (student)
Job Bank: Click "Job Bank" on the home page.

St. Louis Association of Legal Assistants
www.slala.org
Membership: $50 (voting); $35 (student)
Job Bank: slala.org/JobBank/index.php

Springfield Paralegal Association
www.paralegals.org/displaycommon. cfm?an=1&subarticlenbr=488

Missouri Bar Association Paralegal Membership on Committee on Paralegals: Free
www.mobar.org/forms/paralegal-form.htm
www.mobar.org/ece8dc5c-0293-4990-8f54-be7193f99abe.aspx

Practicing with Paralegals: www. mobar.org/bc1c9200-2123-46fb-9727-8bc6a83f2cf7.aspx

NALS (Association for Legal Professionals) of Missouri
www.nalsofMissouri.org
www.nals.org/membership/regions/ Missouri.html

NALS (Association for Legal Professionals) of Greater St. Louis
www.nalsofmissouri.org/affiliations.htm
www.nals.org/membership/regions/ Missouri.html

Central Ozarks Legal Secretaries Association
www.nalsofmissouri.org/affiliations.htm
www.nals.org/membership/regions/ Missouri.html

Franklin County Association of Legal Support Professionals
www.nalsofmissouri.org/affiliations.htm
www.nals.org/membership/regions/ Missouri.html

Heart of America Legal Professionals Association
www.nalsofmissouri.org/affiliations.htm

www.nals.org/membership/regions/ Missouri.html

Kansas City Legal Secretaries Association
www.kclsa.net
www.nals.org/membership/regions/ Missouri.html

Lakes Area Legal Support Association
www.nalsofmissouri.org/affiliations.htm
www.nals.org/membership/regions/ Missouri.html

St. Louis County Association of Legal Professionals
www.nalsofmissouri.org/affiliations.htm

Springfield Area Legal Support Professionals
www.nalsofmissouri.org/affiliations.htm
www.nals.org/membership/regions/ Missouri.html

Tri-County Association of Legal Support Professionals
www.nals.org/membership/regions/ Missouri.html

Kansas City Legal Secretaries Association
www.kclsa.net

American Association of Legal Nurse Consultants, St. Louis Chapter
www.aalncstlouis.org

Association of Legal Administrators, Kansas City Chapter
www.kcala.org

Association of Legal Administrators, St. Louis Chapter
www.ala-gateway.org

Montana

Montana Association of Legal Assistants (Missoula)
www.malanet.org
E-mail: mala@montana.com
Membership: $25 (active); $25 (student)
Job Bank: www.malanet.org/#Jobs

NALS (Association of Legal Professionals) of Montana
www.nals.org/membership/regions/ Montana.html

Montana State Bar Association Paralegal Section Membership: $60
www.montanabar.org/groups/ paralegalsection/paralegalsectionhome .html

American Association of Legal Nurse Consultants, Big Sky Chapter
www.aalnc.org/about/chapter_directory .cfm

Nebraska

Nebraska Association of Legal Assistants (Omaha)
www.neala.org
E-mail: info@neala.org
Membership: $65 (active); $30 (student)
Job Bank: www.neala.org/Careers.aspx

Rocky Mountain Paralegal Association (Nebraska Chapter)
www.rockymtnparalegal.org

Lincoln Legal Professionals Association
lincolnlegalprofessionalsassociation.com

Nevada

Nevada Paralegal Association (Las Vegas)
www.nevadaparalegal.org
E-mail: jwiley@nevadafirm.com; ltreadway@sheacarlyon.com
Membership: $60 (regular); $45 (student)
Employment: "We have a job board on our Web site for members only and we recruit employers to list employment opportunities."

Sierra Nevada Association of Paralegals (Reno)
www.snapreno.com
E-mail: membership@snapreno.com
Membership: $50 (active); $15 (student)
Job Bank: Available for members

Paralegal Association of Southern Nevada (Las Vegas)
www.paralegals.org/displaycommon .cfm?an=1&subarticlenbr=488

NALS (Association for Legal Professionals) of Las Vegas
www.nalsoflasvegas.org
www.nals.org/membership/regions/ Nevada.html

NALS (Association for Legal Professionals) of Washoe County (Reno)
www.nalsofwashoecounty.com
www.nals.org/membership/regions/ Nevada.html

Douglas-Carson Legal Professionals
www.nals.org/membership/regions/ Nevada.html

State Bar of Nevada
Legal Assistant Division Membership: $65
www.nvbar.org/sections/Sections_ Legal_Assistants_Division.htm

Clark County Bar Association
Associate Membership for Paralegals: $50
www.clarkcountybar.org

Association of Legal Administrators, Las Vegas Chapter
alalasvegas.org

New Hampshire

Paralegal Association of New Hampshire (Manchester)
www.panh.org
E-mail: contactus@panh.org
Membership: $65 (voting); $40 (student)

New Jersey

Paralegal Association of New Jersey (Caldwell)
www.laanj.org
E-mail: info@laanj.org
Membership: $50 (regular); $30 (student—associate)
Job Bank: "E-mail us at jobbank@laanj. org and we'll provide you with the most recent listings."

South Jersey Paralegal Association (Haddonfield)
www.sjpaparalegals.org
E-mail: SJPAParalegals@yahoo.com
Membership: $60 (voting); $40 (student)
Job Bank: "We notify our membership [of available jobs] via e-mail and through our bimonthly newsletter."

NALS (Association for Legal Professionals) of New Jersey
www.njals.org
www.nals.org/membership/regions/ NewJersey.html
Job Bank: Click "Job Bank" on the home page.

Union Essex Legal Professional Association
www.njals.org (click "Chapters")
www.nals.org/membership/regions/ NewJersey.html

New Jersey State Bar Association
Paralegal Associate Membership: $75
www.njsba.com/membership_info/index. cfm?fuseaction=membership_info

Association of Trial Lawyers of America—New Jersey
Allied Membership for Paralegals: $185
www.atlanj.org/nj

New Jersey Paralegal
(resources for paralegals)
www.njparalegal.com
www.njparalegal.com/jobs.htm

Hunterdon County Legal Secretaries Association
www.nals.org/membership/regions/ NewJersey.html

Monmouth Legal Secretaries Association
www.nals.org/membership/regions/ NewJersey.html

Morris County Legal Secretaries Association
www.nals.org/membership/regions/ NewJersey.html

Somerset County Legal Secretaries Association
www.nals.org/membership/regions/ NewJersey.html

UCLSA (Union County) the Association for Legal Professionals
www.nals.org/membership/regions/ NewJersey.html

American Association of Legal Nurse Consultants, Morristown Chapter
www.aalnc.org/about/chapter_directory .cfm

Association of Legal Administrators, New Jersey Chapter
www.njala.net

New Mexico

State Bar of New Mexico
Paralegal Membership: $75
www.nmbar.org (type "paralegal" in the search box)
E-mail: PD@nmbar.org
Phone: 505-797-6000

Albuquerque Association of Legal Professionals
www.nmbar.org/Template .cfm?Section=State_Local_ Organizations
www.nals.org/membership/regions/ NewMexico.html

American Association of Legal Nurse Consultants, Albuquerque Chapter
www.aalnc.org/about/chapter_directory .cfm

Association of Legal Administrators, New Mexico Chapter
www.nmala.org

New York

Capital District Paralegal Association (Albany)
www.cdpa.info
E-mail: info@cdpa.info
Membership: $55 (active); $35 (student—associate)

Long Island Paralegal Association (East Meadow)
www.liparalegals.org
Phone: 516-357-9820
Membership: $70 (voting); $55 (student)
Job Bank: www.liparalegals.org/main_ web/mjobbank_main.htm

New York City Paralegal Association
www.nyc-pa.org
Membership: $65 (voting); $40 (student)

Paralegal Association Of Rochester
www.par.itgo.com
Membership: $60 (voting); $30 (student)
Job Bank: www.par.itgo.com/custom3.html

Southern Tier Paralegal Association (Binghamton)
www.nysba.org (type "Southern Tier" in the search box)

Western New York Paralegal Association (Buffalo)
www.wnyparalegals.org
E-mail: contact@wnyparalegals.org
Membership: $60 (voting); $40 (student)
Job Bank: "We have a members-only job bank."
Discussion Forum: www.wnyparalegals.org/vbbs

Empire State Alliance of Paralegal Associations
www.geocities.com/empirestateparalegals

NALS (the Association for Legal Professionals) of the Lower Hudson Valley
www.nalsofnewyorkinc.org/lowerhudsonvalley.html

NALS (the Association for Legal Professionals) of Nassau County
www.nalsofnewyorkinc.org/nassau.html
www.nals.org/membership/regions/NewYork.html

NALS (the Association for Legal Professionals) of New York
www.nalsofnewyorkinc.org
www.nals.org/membership/regions/NewYork.html

NALS (the Association for Legal Professionals) of New York City
www.nalsofnewyorkinc.org/newyorkcity.html
www.nals.org/membership/regions/NewYork.html

NALS (the Association for Legal Professionals) of Suffolk County
www.nalsofnewyorkinc.org/suffolk.html
www.nals.org/membership/regions/NewYork.html

NALS (the Association for Legal Professionals) Central New York (Syracuse)
www.nalsofnewyorkinc.org/onondaga.html
www.nals.org/membership/regions/NewYork.html

Onondaga County Bar Association Affiliate Membership for Paralegals: $60
www.onbar2.org/sect-comms/paralegals/index.htm
Phone: 315-471-2667

Oswego County Bar Association Affiliate Membership for Paralegals: $50
www.oswego-bar.org/members.htm

New York State Society of Enrolled Agents
www.nyssea.org

East Coast Association of Litigation Support Managers
www.ecalsm.com

American Association of Legal Nurse Consultants, New York City Chapter
www.nyccaalnc.org
www.aalnc.org/about/chapter_directory.cfm

American Association of Legal Nurse Consultants, Rochester Chapter
www.rochesterlnn.com
www.aalnc.org/about/chapter_directory.cfm

Association of Legal Administrators, Buffalo Chapter
www.alabuffalo.org

Association of Legal Administrators, Hudson Valley Chapter
www.hudsonvalleyala.org

Association of Legal Administrators, New York City Chapter
www.alanyc.org

North Carolina

North Carolina Paralegal Association (Charlotte)
www.ncparalegal.org
E-mail: info@ncparalegal.org
Phone: 704-535-3363
Membership: $85 (general); $30 (student)
Jobs (Career Center): www.ncparalegal.org/mc/page.do?sitePageId=35034&orgId=ncpa

North Carolina Bar Association
Legal Assistant Division Membership: $50
legalassistantsdivision.ncbar.org
Phone: 800-662-7407
Listserv: legalassistantsdivision.ncbar.org (click "LISTSERV")

Asheville Paralegal Association
www.aapaonline.net
Membership: $30 (general); $10 (student)
Job Bank: www.aapaonline.net/jobbank.htm

Guilford Paralegal Association (Greensboro)
www.guilfordparalegalassociation.org
E-mail: president@guilfordparalegalassociation.org
Membership: $50 (full); $30 (student-associate)
Job Bank: Click "GPA Job Bank"

Metrolina Paralegal Association (Charlotte)
www.charlotteareaparalegals.com
E-mail: info@charlotteareaparalegals.com
Membership: $45 (general); $30 (student-associate)

Job Bank: www.charlotteareaparalegals.com/job_bank.html

NALS (Association for Legal Professionals) of Charlotte
www.nals.org/membership/regions/NorthCaro.html

Raleigh-Wake Paralegal Association
www.rwpa.net
E-mail: rwpa@yahoo.com
Membership: $55 (general); $35 (student-associate)

Research Triangle Paralegal Association
www.rtpanc.org
E-mail: info@rtpanc.org
Membership: $20 (general); $10 (student-associate)

Alamance County Paralegal Association
www.ncparalegal.org/mc/page.do?sitePageId=34565

Cumberland County Paralegal Association
www.ncparalegal.org/mc/page.do?sitePageId=34565

Pitt County Paralegal Association
www.nccertifiedparalegal.gov/links.asp

Sandhills Paralegal Association (Southern Pines)
www.nccertifiedparalegal.gov/links.asp

North Carolina Academy of Trial Lawyers
Legal Assistant Membership: $125 (first year free)
www.ncatl.org/page/22453/index.v3page;jsessionid=3254vr6hersg8#B
Phone: 800-688-1413

Alliance for Paralegal Professional Standards
www.apps-nc.org

American Association of Legal Nurse Consultants, Charlotte Chapter
www.aalnc.org/about/chapter_directory.cfm

American Association of Legal Nurse Consultants, Eastern North Carolina Chapter
www.aalnc.org/about/chapter_directory.cfm

American Association of Legal Nurse Consultants, Western North Carolina Chapter
www.aalnc.org/about/chapter_directory.cfm

Association of Legal Administrators, Charlotte Chapter
www.alacarolinas.org

Association of Legal Administrators, North Carolina Chapter
www.alacarolinas.org

Association of Legal Administrators, Raleigh-Durham Chapter
www.alacarolinas.org/pages/raldur_home .html

Association of Legal Administrators, Triad Chapter
www.alacarolinas.org/pages/triad_home .html

North Dakota

Red River Valley Legal Assistants (Fargo)
www.rrvpa.org
Membership: $45 (voting); $15 (student)

Western Dakota Association of Legal Assistants (Bismarck)
www.wdala.org
Membership: $50 (active); $25 (student)

NALS (Association for Legal Professionals) of Fargo-Moorhead
www.nals.org/membership/regions/ NorthDakota.html

Minot Legal Secretaries Association
www.nals.org/membership/regions/ NorthDakota.html

Ohio

Cincinnati Paralegal Association
www.cincinnatiparalegals.org
E-mail: Cincinnati@cincinnatiparalegals .org
Phone: 513-244-1266
Membership: $60 (active); $35 (student)

Cleveland Association of Paralegals
www.capohio.org
Phone: 216-556-5437
Membership: $105 (voting); $50 (student)

Greater Dayton Paralegal Association
www.gdpa.org
E-mail: info@gdpa.org
Membership: $60 (active); $40 (student)
Job Bank: www.gdpa.org/login.asp

Paralegal Association of Central Ohio (Columbus)
www.pacoparalegals.org
E-mail: info@pacoparalegals.org
Phone: 614-470-2000
Membership: $130 (active); $70 (student)
Job Bank: www.pacoparalegals.org/job_ bank.htm

Paralegal Association of Northwest Ohio (Toledo)
www.panonet.org
E-mail: president@panonet.org
Membership: $50 (active); $20 (student)
Job Bank: www.panonet.org/ enterpassword.htm

Akron Bar Association
Associate Membership for Paralegals: $90
www.akronbar.org
Job Leads: akronbar.legalstaff.com

Cincinnati Bar Association
Affiliate Membership for Paralegals: $50
www.cincybar.org/pdfs/cbaInformationKit .pdf
Job Leads: www.cincybar.org/member/ jobs.asp

Cleveland Bar Association
Affiliate Membership for Paralegals: $75
www.clevelandbar.org/join.asp
Job Leads: clevelandbar.legalstaff.com

Columbus Bar Association
Non-Lawyer Associate Membership: $65
www.cbalaw.org/members

Cuyahoga County Bar Association
Paralegal Membership: $45
www.cuybar.org/membership-application. shtml

Dayton Bar Association
Associate Non-Attorney Membership: $130
www.daybar.org/html/join/join.htm

Ohio State Bar Association
Paralegal Membership: $70
www.ohiobar.org/join/?articleid=273
Phone: 800-232-7124
Certification Program: www.ohiobar. org/pub/?articleid=785

Stark County Bar Association
Associate Membership for Paralegals: $25
Phone: 330-453-0685
starkctybar.com/membership.htm

Toledo Bar Association
Associate Membership for Paralegals: $55
www.toledobar.org

NALS (Association for Legal Professionals) of Ohio
www.nals.org/membership/regions/Ohio .html

NALS (Association for Legal Professionals) of Central Ohio
www.nals.org/membership/regions/Ohio .html

Medina County Association of Legal Support Professionals
www.medinalegalprofessionals.org
nalsofohio.org

Stark County Association for Legal Professionals
www.nals.org/membership/regions/Ohio .html

Summit County Legal Professionals
www.nals.org/membership/regions/Ohio .html

American Association of Legal Nurse Consultants, Cleveland Chapter
www.aalnc.org/about/chapter_directory.cfm

Association of Legal Administrators, Cleveland Chapter
www.alacleveland.org/ws

Association of Legal Administrators, Columbus Chapter
www.alacolumbus.org

Association of Legal Administrators, Cincinnati Chapter
www.alacincinnati.org

Association of Legal Administrators, Northwest Ohio Chapter
www.alanwohio.org

Oklahoma

Central Oklahoma Association of Legal Assistants (Oklahoma City)
www.coala.cc
Membership: $50 (active); $25 (student)

Oklahoma Paralegal Association (Weatherford)
www.okparalegal.org
Membership: $50 (active); $25 (student)

Tulsa Association of Legal Assistants
www.tulsatala.org
Membership: $55 (active); $25 (student)
Job Bank: Click "Job Bank Form"

NALS (the Association for Legal Professionals) of Oklahoma
www.nalsofok.org
www.nals.org/membership/regions/ Oklahoma.html

American Association of Legal Nurse Consultants, Oklahoma Chapter
www.aalnc.org/about/chapter_directory .cfm

Association of Legal Administrators, Oklahoma City Chapter
www.alaokc.org

Association of Legal Administrators, Tulsa Chapter
www.alatulsa.org

Oregon

Oregon Paralegal Association (Portland)
www.oregonparalegals.org
E-mail: Info@oregonparalegals.org
Phone: 503-796-1671
Oregon Paralegal Association (Portland)
Revise the membership line to read:
Membership: $85 (regular); $40 (student)

Job Bank: www.oregonparalegals.org/
news.php?cat.5

**Pacific Northwest Paralegal Association
(Eugene)**
pnpa.org
www.pnwpa.org
E-mail: pnwpa@version.net
Membership: $50 (regular); $25 (student)
Job Bank: "Yes, we have a job bank."

**NALS (Association of Legal
Professionals) of Oregon**
www.nalsor.org
www.nals.org/membership/regions/
Oregon.html
E-mail: nalsoforegon@netzero.com
Membership: $115 (full); $19 (student)
Job Search: nals.legalstaff.com/Common/
HomePage.aspx?abbr=NALS

Central Oregon Legal Professionals
nalsor.org/COLP/index.htm
www.nals.org/membership/regions/
Oregon.html

Legal Professionals of Douglas County
nalsor.org/LPDC/index.htm
www.nals.org/membership/regions/
Oregon.html

Mt. Hood Legal Professionals
nalsor.org/Mt_Hood/index.htm
www.nals.org/membership/regions/
Oregon.html

**NALS (Association of Legal
Professionals) of Lane County**
nalsor.org/Lane/index.htm
www.nals.org/membership/regions/
Oregon.html

**NALS (Association of Legal
Professionals) of Mid-
Willamette Valley**
nalsor.org/MWValley/index.htm
www.nals.org/membership/regions/
Oregon.html

**NALS (Association of Legal
Professionals) of Portland**
www.nalsor.org/Portland/index.htm
www.nals.org/membership/regions/
Oregon.html

**NALS (Association of Legal
Professionals) of Southern
Oregon Coast**
www.nalsor.org/SOC/index.htm
www.nals.org/membership/regions/
Oregon.html

**Oregon Trial Lawyers Association
Legal Staff Membership:** $75
www.oregontriallawyers.org

**American Association of Legal Nurse
Consultants, Portland Chapter**
www.aalnc.org/about/chapter_directory.cfm

**Association of Legal Administrators,
Oregon Chapter**
www.oregonlegal.org

Pennsylvania

**Central Pennsylvania Paralegal
Association (Harrisburg)**
home.comcast.net/~cppageneral
E-mail: cppageneral@comcast.net
Membership: $60 (voting); $30
(student)

**Chester County Paralegal Association
(West Chester)**
www.chescoparalegal.org
Membership: $50 (full); $35 (student)
Job Bank: www.chescoparalegal.org/jobs.
html

Lancaster Area Paralegal Association
www.lapaparalegals.com
E-mail: LAPAParalegals@aol.com
Membership: $45 (voting); $20 (student)
Job Bank: www.lapaparalegals.com/
memonly.html

**Lycoming County Paralegal
Association**
www.lycolaw.org/lcpa/main.htm
Membership: $65 (voting); $40
(student—associate)
Job Bank: "The Job Bank retains résumés
of our members who are seeking
employment as well as accepts employment postings for positions currently
available."

**Montgomery County Paralegal
Association**
www.paralegals.org/displaycommon.
cfm?an=1&subarticlenbr=572
E-mail: Montgomery@Paralegals.org
Membership: $70 (voting); $25 (student)
Job Bank (Career Center): mcpa
.legalstaff.com
Listserv: montocoparalegals (Yahoo! groups)

Philadelphia Association of Paralegals
philaparalegals.com
E-mail: philaparalegals@aol.com
Phone: 215-255-8405
Membership: $75 (voting); $35 (student)
Job Bank: philaparalegals.com/job_bank
.php
Association Blog: philaparalegals.com/
blog/index.php

Pittsburgh Paralegal Association
www.pghparalegals.org
Membership: $75 (voting); $25 (student)
Job Bank: www.pghparalegals.org/login
.php?msg=login

York County Paralegal Association
E-mail: webmaster@ycpaonline.com
Membership: $60 (voting); $20 (student)
www.ycpaonline.com

**NALS (Association for Legal
Professionals) of Pennsylvania**
www.palegal.org
www.nals.org/membership/regions/Penn
.html

**Capital Area Association of Legal
Professionals**
www.nals.org/membership/regions/Penn
.html
www.palegal.org/Chapters_Page.htm

**Lehigh-Northampton Counties Legal
Secretaries Association**
www.nals.org/membership/regions/Penn
.html
www.palegal.org/Chapters_Page.htm

**Pennsylvania Legal Secretaries
Association**
www.philalsa.org
www.nals.org/membership/regions/Penn
.html

Pittsburgh Legal Secretaries Association
www.nals.org/membership/regions/Penn
.html
www.palegal.org/Chapters_Page.htm

**Schuylkill County Legal Secretaries
Association**
www.nals.org/membership/regions/Penn
.html
www.palegal.org/Chapters_Page.htm

Pennsylvania Society of Enrolled Agents
paenrolledagents.com

**Association of Legal Administrators,
Independence Chapter**
www.ala-independence.org

**Association of Legal Administrators,
Philadelphia Chapter**
www.phila-ala.org

**Pittsburgh Legal Administrators
Association**
www.plaa.com

**American Association of Legal Nurse
Consultants, Philadelphia Chapter**
www.aalnc.org/about/chapter_directory.cfm

**American Association of Legal Nurse
Consultants, Pittsburgh Chapter**
www.pittsburghchapteraalnc.org
www.aalnc.org/about/chapter_directory
.cfm

**Association of Legal Administrators,
Independence Chapter**
www.ala-independence.org

**Association of Legal Administrators,
Philadelphia Chapter**
www.phila-ala.org

**Association of Legal Administrators,
Pittsburgh Chapter**
www.plaa.com

Rhode Island

Rhode Island Paralegal Association (Providence)
www.paralegals.org/associations/2270/files/home149.html
E-mail: RhodeIsland@paralegals.org
Membership: $50 (voting); $35 (student)

South Carolina

Charleston Association of Legal Assistants
www.charlestonlegalassistants.org
Membership: $60 (full); $30 (student)
Job Bank: www.charlestonlegalassistants.org/job.html

Palmetto Paralegal Association (Columbia)
www.ppasc.org
backup.paralegals.org/Palmetto/home.html
E-mail: Palmetto@paralegals.org
Phone: 803-252-0460
Membership: $75 (voting); $25 (student)

South Carolina Upstate Paralegal Association
www.scupa.org
E-mail: info@scupa.org
Membership: $75 (active); $15 (student)
Job Bank: scupa.org/?page_id=15

Legal Staff Professionals of South Carolina
www.lspsc.org
www.nals.org/membership/regions/SouthCaro.html

Hilton Head Legal Staff Professionals
www.lspsc.org/LocalChapters.html
www.nals.org/membership/regions/SouthCaro.html

Legal Staff Professionals of Greenville
www.lspg.org
www.nals.org/membership/regions/SouthCaro.html

Legal Staff Professionals of the Low Country
www.lspsc.org/LocalChapters.html
www.nals.org/membership/regions/SouthCaro.html

Legal Staff Professionals of the Midlands
www.lspsc.org/LocalChapters.html
www.nals.org/membership/regions/SouthCaro.html

Legal Staff Professionals of Orangeburg
www.lspsc.org/LocalChapters.html
www.nals.org/membership/regions/SouthCaro.html

Spartanburg County Legal Staff Professionals
www.lspsc.org/LocalChapters.html

www.nals.org/membership/regions/SouthCaro.html

American Association of Legal Nurse Consultants, Columbia Chapter
www.aalnc.org/about/chapter_directory.cfm

Association of Legal Administrators, South Carolina Chapter
www.scalanet.org

South Carolina Association of Legal Investigators
www.scalinv.com

South Dakota

South Dakota Paralegal Association (Rapid City)
www.sdparalegals.com
Membership: $50 (active); $10 (student)
Job Bank: www.sdparalegals.com/Membership/Job_Bank/job_bank.html

Rocky Mountain Paralegal Association (South Dakota Chapter)
www.rockymtnparalegal.org

Black Hills Legal Professionals Association
www.bhlpa.org
www.nals.org/membership/regions/SouthDakota.html

South Dakota Trial Lawyers Association
Legal Support Staff Membership: $50
www.sdtla.com/mem.cat.htm

Tennessee

Greater Memphis Paralegal Alliance
www.memphisparalegals.org
Phone: 901-527-6254

Memphis Paralegal Association
www.memphisparalegalassociation.org
Membership: $75 (regular); $25 (student)
Job Posting: www.memphisparalegalassociation.org/jobs.htm

Middle Tennessee Paralegal Association (Nashville)
www.mtpaonline.com
Membership: $85 (full); $35 (student)
Job Bank: Available to members only.

Smokey Mountain Paralegal Association (Knoxville)
www.smparalegal.org
E-mail: president@smparalegal.org
Membership: $60 (active); $25 (student)
Job Bank: "Notice of job openings are immediately e-mailed to our entire membership."

Tennessee Paralegal Association (Chattanooga)
www.tnparalegal.org
Membership: $55 (active); $25 (student)
Job Bank: www.tnparalegal.org/job.html

Tennessee Paralegal Association, East Tennessee Chapter
www.tnparalegal.org/east.html

Tennessee Paralegal Association, Southeast Tennessee Chapter
www.tnparalegal.org/southeast.html

Tennessee Paralegal Association, West Tennessee Chapter
www.tnparalegal.org/west.html

Chattanooga Bar Association
Paralegal Associate Membership: $75
www.chattbar.org

Nashville Bar Association
Paralegal Associate Membership: $75
www.nashvillebar.org

TALS—Legal Professionals of Tennessee
www.talstn.org
www.nals.org/membership/regions/Tenn.html

Legal Professionals of Memphis
www.memphislsa.org
www.nals.org/membership/regions/Tenn.html

Chattanooga Legal Professionals
www.chattbar.org/www/docs/141
www.nals.org/membership/regions/Tenn.html

NALS of Nashville
www.nals.org/membership/regions/Tenn.html

Rutherford/Canon County LP
www.nals.org/membership/regions/Tenn.html

Williamson County LP
www.nals.org/membership/regions/Tenn.html

American Association of Legal Nurse Consultants, Nashville Chapter
www.aalnc.org/about/chapter_directory.cfm

Association of Legal Administrators, Knoxville Chapter
www.knoxala.org

Texas

Texas Alliance of Paralegal Associations
www.capatx.org/tapa.html

State Bar of Texas, Paralegal Division
txpd.org
E-mail: txpd.org/feedback.asp
Phone: 512-280-1776
Membership: $70 (active); $35 (student)

Alamo Area Paralegal Association (San Antonio)
www.alamoparalegals.org
E-mail: membership@alamoparalegals.org

Phone: 210-231-5791
Membership: $45 (voting); $25 (student)
Job Bank: www.alamoparalegals.org/mc/
    page.do?sitePageId=5482&orgId=
    aaplai

**Capitol Area Paralegal Association
    (Austin)**
www.capatx.org
E-mail: email@capatx.org
Phone: 512-505-6822
Membership: $50 (voting); $25 (student)
Job Bank: www.capatx.org/job.html

Dallas Area Paralegal Association
www.dallasparalegals.org
E-mail: executivedirector@dallasparalegals
    .org
Membership: $70 (voting); $60 (student)
Job Bank: dallasparalegals.org/page.
    asp?p=Job%20Bank%20Posting

El Paso Association of Legal Assistants
www.elppa.org
Membership: $40 (active); $15 (student)

El Paso Bar Association
Associate Membership for Paralegals:
    $30
www.elpasobar.com/join.asp

Fort Worth Paralegal Association
fwpa.org
Membership: $55 (voting); $30 (student)
Job Bank: fwpa.org/jobbank.asp

**Houston Corporate Paralegal
    Association**
www.hcpa.cc
www.nala.org/aff-roster-LINKS.htm

**Houston Metropolitan Legal Assistants
    Association**
hmpa-hlaa.com
E-mail: hlaa@hmpa-hlaa.com
Phone: 713-236-7724
Membership: $75 (voting); $35 (student)
Job Bank: Available to members only

Houston Paralegal Association
www.houstonparalegalassociation.org
E-mail: texasparalegal@hotmail.com
Membership: $25 (active); $20
    (student-associate)

**Metroplex Association of Corporate
    Paralegals (Arlington)**
www.macp.net

**North Texas Paralegal Association
    (Dallas)**
www.ntparalegals.org
E-mail: www.ntparalegals.org/officers.html
Membership: $50 (active); $10 (student)
Job Bank: www.ntparalegals.org/
    committees.html

Paralegal Association of Collin County
www.paralegalcc.org

E-mail: info@paralegalcc.org
Membership: $25 (active); $15 (student)
Job Bank: www.paralegalcc.org/jobs

**Paralegal Association/Permian Basin
    (Midland)**
www.paralegalspb.org
E-mail: info@papd.org
Membership: $35 (active); $20
    (student-associate)

**Southeast Texas Association of Legal
    Assistants (Beaumont)**
www.capatx.org/tapa.html

**South Texas Organization of Paralegals
    (San Antonio)**
www.southtexasparalegals.org
E-mail: info@southtexasparalegals.org
Membership: $45 (voting); $20 (student)

**Texarkana Association of Legal
    Assistants**
www.capatx.org/tapa.html

**Texas Panhandle Association of Legal
    Assistants (Amarillo)**
www.capatx.org/tapa.html

Tyler Area Association of Legal Assistants
www.nala.org/aff-roster-LINKS.htm

**West Texas Association of Legal
    Assistants (Laredo)**
www.capatx.org/tapa.html
www.nala.org/aff-roster-LINKS.htm

Arlington Legal Secretaries Association
www.nals.org/membership/regions/Texas
    .html

Austin Association for Legal Professionals
www.austinlsa.org
www.nals.org/membership/regions/Texas
    .html
Membership: $127 (active); $46 (student)
Job Bank: www.austinlsa.org/careers

Beaumont Legal Secretaries Association
www.nals.org/membership/regions/Texas
    .html

**Corpus Christi Association of Legal
    Professionals**
www.ccalp.com
www.nals.org/membership/regions/Texas
    .html

**Dallam-Hartley-Moore Counties Legal
    Secretaries Association**
www.nals.org/membership/regions/Texas
    .html

Dallas Association of Legal Secretaries
www.nals.org/membership/regions/Texas
    .html

**East Texas Area Legal Professionals
    Association**
www.nals.org/membership/regions/Texas
    .html

**El Paso County Legal Support
    Professionals**
www.nals.org/membership/regions/Texas
    .html

Fort Worth Legal Secretaries Association
www.nals.org/membership/regions/Texas
    .html

**Greater Dallas Association of Legal
    Professionals**
www.gdalp.org
www.nals.org/membership/regions/Texas
    .html

**Houston Association of Legal
    Professionals**
www.houstonalp.org
www.nals.org/membership/regions/Texas
    .html

Lubbock Legal Secretaries Association
www.nals.org/membership/regions/Texas
    .html

Midland Legal Secretaries Association
www.nals.org/membership/regions/Texas
    .html

**NALS (the Association for Legal
    Professionals) of Amarillo**
www.nals.org/membership/regions/Texas.
    html

**Rio Grande Valley Legal Support
    Professionals**
www.nals.org/membership/regions/Texas
    .html

**San Antonio Legal Secretaries
    Association**
www.sanantoniolsa.org
www.nals.org/membership/regions/Texas
    .html

Texas Association of Legal Professionals
www.texasalp.org
Membership: $100 (active); $46 (student)

**Tyler Area Association of Legal
    Professionals**
taalp.com
Membership: $40 (active); $30
    (associate); $15 (government)
Job Bank: taalp.com/jobbank.aspx

Waco Legal Professionals Association
www.wacolpa.com
www.nals.org/membership/regions/Texas
    .html

**Wichita County Legal Secretaries
    Association**
www.nals.org/membership/regions/Texas
    .html

**Association of Legal Administrators,
    Alamo Chapter**
www.alamoala.org

Association of Legal Administrators, Austin Chapter
austinala.org

American Association of Legal Nurse Consultants, Houston Chapter
www.aalnc-houston.com

Dallas/Ft. Worth Association of Litigation Support Managers
www.dfwalsm.com

American Association of Legal Nurse Consultants, Capital Area Chapter
www.aalnc.org/about/chapter_directory.cfm

American Association of Legal Nurse Consultants, Dallas Chapter
www.aalncdallas.org
www.aalnc.org/about/chapter_directory.cfm

American Association of Legal Nurse Consultants, Fort Worth Chapter
www.aalnc.org/about/chapter_directory.cfm

American Association of Legal Nurse Consultants, Houston Chapter
www.aalnc-houston.com
www.aalnc.org/about/chapter_directory.cfm

Association of Legal Administrators, Alamo Chapter
www.alamoala.org

Association of Legal Administrators, Austin Chapter
www.austinala.org

Association of Legal Administrators, Dallas Chapter
www.dallasala.org

Association of Legal Administrators, Fort Worth Chapter
www.alafw.org

Association of Legal Administrators, Houston Chapter
www.alahou.org

Utah

Legal Assistants Association of Utah (Salt Lake City)
www.laau.info
Membership: $50 (active); $15 (student)

Utah State Bar
Legal Assistant Division Membership: $75
www.utahbar.org/sections/paralegals/info.html
Blog: www.utahbar.org/sections/paralegals/blog

Rocky Mountain Paralegal Association (Utah Chapter)
www.rockymtnparalegal.org

Utah Legal Professionals Association
www.nals.org/membership/regions/Utah.html

Vermont

Vermont Paralegal Organization (Burlington)
www.paralegals.org/associations/2270/files/home204.html
E-mail: Vermont@paralegals.org
Membership: $60 (full); $35 (student)
Job Bank: Available online and in quarterly newsletter.

Vermont Bar Association
Associate Membership for Paralegals: $90
www.vtbar.org

Virginia

Virginia Alliance of Paralegal Associations
www.vaparalegalalliance.org

Appalachian Paralegal Association
richmondparalegals.org/contact.html

Central Virginia Paralegal Association
richmondparalegals.org/contact.html

Charlottesville Association of Legal Assistants
richmondparalegals.org/contact.html

Fredericksburg Paralegal Association
www.paralegals.org/associations/2270/files/home209.html
E-mail: fredericksburg@paralegals.org
Membership: $60 (active); $25 (student)

Local Government Paralegal Association of Virginia
www.lgpa-va.org
E-mail: info
Membership: $25 (active)

Richmond Paralegal Association
rpa@richmondparalegals.org; richmondparalegals.org
Membership: $75 (active); $25 (student)
Job Bank: richmondparalegals.org/job_bank.pdf

Roanoke Valley Paralegal Association
www.rvpa.org
Membership: $45 (general); $15 (student)

Shenandoah Valley Paralegal Association (Harrisonburg)
www.geocities.com/svparalegal
E-mail: svparalegal@yahoo.com
Membership: $30 (regular); $15 (student)

Southside Paralegal Association
richmondparalegals.org/contact.html

Tidewater Paralegal Association
www.tidewaterparalegals.org
Membership: $45 (active); $25 (student)

Virginia Peninsula Paralegal Association (Newport News)
www.vappa.org
Membership: $35 (active); $25 (student)

Fairfax Bar Association
Affiliate Membership for Paralegals: $35
fba.affiniscape.com/index.cfm

Virginia Trial Lawyers Association
Paralegal Membership: $90
www.vtla.com/va/index.cfm?event=showPage&pg=ParaApp

VALS–Association of Legal Professionals
www.v-a-l-s.org
www.nals.org/membership/regions/Virginia.html

Charlottesville-Albemarle Legal Staff Association
monticello.avenue.org/calsa
www.nals.org/membership/regions/Virginia.html

Fredericksburg Area Legal Secretaries Association
www.nals.org/membership/regions/Virginia.html

New Red River Valley Legal Secretaries Association
www.nals.org/membership/regions/Virginia.html

Norfolk-Portsmouth Area Legal Secretaries Association
www.nals.org/membership/regions/Virginia.html

NVLSA (Association for Legal Professionals in Northern Virginia)
www.nvlsa.org
www.nals.org/membership/regions/Virginia.html

Peninsula Legal Secretaries Association
www.nals.org/membership/regions/Virginia.html

Prince William County Association for Legal Professionals
www.nals.org/membership/regions/Virginia.html

Richmond Legal Secretaries Association
www.nals.org/membership/regions/Virginia.html

Roanoke Valley Legal Secretaries Association
www.nals.org/membership/regions/Virginia.html

RLSA . . . the Association for Legal Professionals (Richmond)
www.rlsa.org

Virginia Beach Legal Staff Association
www.vblsa.org
www.nals.org/membership/regions/Virginia.html

Virginia Highlands Legal Secretaries Association
www.nals.org/membership/regions/Virginia.html

American Association of Legal Nurse
Consultants, Virginia Chapter
www.cvc-aalnc.org
www.aalnc.org/about/chapter_directory
.cfm

Association of Legal Administrators,
Hampton Roads Chapter
www.hrala.org

Association of Legal Administrators,
Northern Virginia Chapter
alanova.org

Association of Legal Administrators,
Richmond Chapter
www.richmondala.org

Virgin Islands
Virgin Islands Association of Legal
Assistants
www.nala.org/aff-roster-LINKS.htm

Washington State
Washington State Paralegal Association
www.wspaonline.org
E-mail: membership@wspaonline.org
Phone: 866-257-9772
Membership: $150 (voting); $75 (student)
Job Bank: www.wspaonline.org/jobbank
.htm

Listserv: www.wspaonline.org/Listservs
.htm

Washington State Paralegal
Association, East King
County Chapter
www.wspaonline.org/chapters/EastKing
.htm

Washington State Paralegal
Association, Spokane Chapter
www.wspaonline.org/chapters/Spokane
.htm

Washington State Paralegal
Association, South Puget
Sound Chapter
www.wspaonline.org/chapters/Tacoma.htm

Washington State Paralegal
Association, Snohomish
County Chapter
www.wspaonline.org/chapters/snohomish
.htm

NALS (Association for Legal
Professionals) of Greater
Wenatchee
www.nals.org/membership/regions/
Washington.html

NALS (Association of Legal
Professionals) of Washington
www.nalsofwashington.org
www.nals.org/membership/regions/
Washington.html

NALS (Association for Legal
Professionals) of Seattle
www.nalsofwashington.org/nals/
chapter_pages/greater_seattle.htm
www.nals.org/membership/regions/
Washington.html

NALS (Association for Legal
Professionals) of Kitsap County
www.nalsofkitsap.org
www.nals.org/membership/regions/
Washington.html

NALS (Association for Legal
Professionals) of Snohomish County
www.nals.org/membership/regions/
Washington.html

NALS (Association for Legal
Professionals) of Pierce County
www.nals.org/membership/regions/
Washington.html

NALS (Association for Legal
Professionals) of Thurston County
www.nals.org/membership/regions/
Washington.html

NALS (Association for Legal
Professionals) of Spokane County
www.nals.org/membership/regions/
Washington.html

NALS (Association for Legal
Professionals) of Yakima County
www.nals.org/membership/regions/
Washington.html

East King County Legal Support
Professionals
www.nals.org/membership/regions/
Washington.html

Washington Association of Legal
Investigators
www.wali.org

American Association of Legal Nurse
Consultants, Puget Sound Chapter
www.aalncseattle.org
www.aalnc.org/about/chapter_directory.cfm

Association of Legal Administrators,
Puget Sound Chapter
www.psala.org

West Virginia
Association of West Virginia Paralegals
www.awvp.org
Membership: $40 (general); $25 (student)

Legal Assistants/Paralegals of Southern
West Virginia
www.lapswv.org
Membership: $30 (general); $20 (student)
E-mail: info@lapswv.org

Ohio Valley Paralegal Organization
www.nala.org/aff-roster-LINKS.htm

West Virginia Bar Association
Legal Assistant Division Membership:
$45
www.wvbarassociation.org/laad.asp
Phone: 800-944-9822

American Association of Legal Nurse
Consultants, Ohio Valley Chapter
www.aalnc.org/about/chapter_directory.cfm

American Association of Legal Nurse
Consultants, Southern West Virginia
Chapter
www.wvbarassociation.org/lnc
www.aalnc.org/about/chapter_directory.cfm

Wisconsin
Madison Area Paralegal Association
www.madisonparalegal.org
E-mail: info@madisonparalegal.org
Membership: $70 (active); $25 (student)
Job Bank: www.madisonparalegal.org/
job_post_form.html

Paralegal Association of Wisconsin
www.wisconsinparalegal.org
E-mail: info@WisconsinParalegal.org
Membership: $75 (active); $25 (student)
Job Bank: "Current members have access
to a résumé bank and a job bank."

Paralegal Association of Wisconsin, La
Crosse Chapter
www.wisconsinparalegal.org/chapters/
index.html

Paralegal Association of Wisconsin,
Madison Chapter
www.wisconsinparalegal.org/chapters/
index.html

Paralegal Association of Wisconsin,
Milwaukee Chapter
www.wisconsinparalegal.org/chapters/
index.html

Wisconsin Association for Legal
Professionals
www.wisconsinalp.org
www.nals.org/membership/regions/
Wisconsin.html

Brown County Association for Legal
Professionals
www.nals.org/membership/regions/
Wisconsin.html

Fox Valley Association for Legal
Professionals
www.orgsites.com/wi/fvalp
www.nals.org/membership/regions/
Wisconsin.html

Greater Milwaukee Association for
Legal Professionals
www.gmalp.org
www.nals.org/membership/regions/
Wisconsin.html

Lakeshore Area Association for Legal Professionals
www.nals.org/membership/regions/
Wisconsin.html

Legal Personnel of South Central Wisconsin
www.lpscw.org
www.nals.org/membership/regions/
Wisconsin.html

Northcentral Association of Legal Professionals
www.nals.org/membership/regions/
Wisconsin.html

Racine-Kenosha Legal Professionals
www.nals.org/membership/regions/
Wisconsin.html

St. Croix Valley Legal Professionals
www.nals.org/membership/regions/
Wisconsin.html

Wisconsin Association of Legal Administrators
www.wi-ala.org/ClubPortal/wala

Wyoming

Legal Assistants of Wyoming (Casper)
www.lawyo.com
Membership: $45 (active); $25 (student)
Job Bank: www.lawyo.com/LAW/
Job Openings.htm

Rocky Mountain Paralegal Association (Wyoming Chapter)
www.rockymtnparalegal.org

American Association of Legal Nurse Consultants, Casper Chapter
www.aalnc.org/about/chapter_directory
.cfm

C. OTHER ASSOCIATIONS (UNITED STATES)

ABA Standing Committee on Paralegals
www.abanet.org/legalservices/paralegals

American Alliance of Paralegals
www.aapipara.org

American Association for Justice
Affiliate Membership for Paralegals:
$75
www.atlanet.org

American Association for Paralegal Education
www.aafpe.org
Phone: 856-423-2829

American Association for Justice Paralegal Affiliate Program
www.atlanet.org/Networking/Tier3/
ParalegalAffiliates.aspx

American Association of Law Librarians
www.aallnet.org

American Association of Legal Nurse Consultants
www.aalnc.org

American Disability Representation Specialist Association
www.adrsa.com

American Freelance Paralegal Association
www.freelanceparalegal.org

American Health Lawyers Association
Paralegal Membership: $75
www.healthlawyers.org

American Institute of Certified Public Accountants
www.aicpa.org

American Pro Se Association
www.legalhelp.org

Association of Bankruptcy Judicial Assistants
www.abja.org

Association of Legal Administrators
www.alanet.org

Center for Legal Studies, Clearinghouse for Pro Bono Internships
www.legalstudies.com; hatcheducation.com
800-522-7737

National Association of Freelance Legal Professionals
freelancelegalprofessionals.blogspot.com

HALT: An Organization of Americans for Legal Reform
www.halt.org
888-FOR-HALT

International Paralegal Management Association
www.paralegalmanagement.org
404-292-4762

Legal Assistant Today (magazine)
www.legalassistanttoday.com
800-394-2626

Legal Marketing Association
www.legalmarketing.org

NALS the Association of Legal Professionals (formerly National Association of Legal Secretaries)
www.nals.org

National Association for Law Placement
www.nalp.org

National Association of Document Examiners
www.documentexaminers.org

National Association of Enrolled Agents
www.naea.org

National Association of Legal Assistants
www.nala.org
918-587-6828

National Association of Legal Document Preparers
www.naldp.org

National Association of Legal Investigators
www.nalionline.org

National Association of Patent Practitioners
www.napp.org

National Association of Professional Process Servers
www.napps.org

National Association of Tax Professionals
www.natptax.com

National Conference of Bar Examiners
www.ncbex.org

National Court Appointed Special Advocate Association
www.casanet.org

National Court Reporters Association
www.ncraonline.org

National Federation of Paralegal Associations
www.paralegals.org
425-967-0045

National Independent Paralegal Association
www.paralegalgateway.com/Foster5.html
scottfo2@yahoo.com

National Notary Association
www.nationalnotary.org

National Organization of Legal Services Workers
www.geocities.com/~uaw2320

National Organization of Social Security Claimants' Representatives
www.nosscr.org

National Paralegal Association
www.nationalparalegal.org

Navy Legalmen Association
www.jag.navy.mil/JAGMAG/
May-JunLegalmen.pdf
www.mnparalegals.org/
LegalmenProject3516.php
www.wnyparalegals.org/navy.htm

NOLO Press (self-help legal materials)
www.nolo.com

D. OTHER ASSOCIATIONS (INTERNATIONAL)

Alberta Association of Professional Paralegals (Canada)
Alberta-paralegal.com

British Columbia Paralegal Association (Canada)
www.bcala.com

Canadian Association of Paralegals
www.caplegal.ca

Institute of Law Clerks of Ontario (Canada)
www.ilco.on.ca

Institute of Legal Executives (England)
www.ilex.org.uk

Institute of Legal Executives, Paralegals (England)
www.ilexpp.co.uk

Institute of Legal Executives (Australia)
www.liv.asn.au/legalexecutives

International Association of Administrative Professionals
www.iaap-hq.org

International Process Servers Association
www.iprocessservers.com

Irish Institute of Legal Executives (Ireland)
www.irishinstituteoflegalexecutives.com

Legal Secretaries International
www.legalsecretaries.org

National Community-Based Paralegal Association (South Africa)
www.paralegaladvice.org.za/docs/chap15/06.html

New Zealand Institute of Legal Executives
www.nzile.org.nz

Paralegal Society of Ontario (Canada)
www.paralegalsociety.on.ca

Scottish Paralegal Association (Scotland)
www.scottish-paralegal.org.uk

Bar Associations and Related Attorney Organizations

A. STATE AND LOCAL BAR ASSOCIATIONS

There are several reasons you should check Internet sites of state and local bar associations:

1. You need to become familiar with bar associations in your state as soon as possible. They will continue to have a major impact on your paralegal career. At each bar site, try to find out which committees or sections are involved with paralegals. (Also take a look at those on law office management and the practice of law.) If there is a search feature on the site, type in *paralegal* or *legal assistant*.
2. Check any information or links on ethics, professional responsibility, and unauthorized practice of law.
3. Explore different areas of the law. Almost all of the sites (either directly or through links) will provide information about what attorneys do in different areas of the law. This information will be valuable in helping you decide what areas of the law you might want to pursue.
4. When you have your first job interview, part of your preparation should be to find out what state and national organizations are relevant to the kind of law practiced where you will be interviewing. There is probably a bar association committee or section and a national organization that are relevant to every employment setting.

The Internet sites listed below will lead you to street addresses, online addresses, and program information for every state and local bar association in the country:

www.abanet.org/barserv/stlobar.html
www.lpig.org/assoc.html
www.alllaw.com/legal_organizations
www.washlaw.edu/bar
www.ilrg.com/non-profit.html
findlaw.com/06associations
www.kautzlaw.com/links1.htm
www.citylegalguide.com/bar.cfm
www.hg.org/bar-associations-usa.html

B. SPECIALTY BAR ASSOCIATIONS AND RELATED ORGANIZATIONS

The following sites will give you information about specific areas of law and possible links to employment opportunities in those areas.

Academy of Legal Studies in Business
www.alsb.org

Alliance for Justice
www.afj.org

American Academy of Estate Planning Attorneys
www.aaepa.com

American Academy of Forensic Sciences
www.aafs.org

American Academy of Matrimonial Lawyers
www.aaml.org

American Agricultural Law Association
www.aglaw-assn.org

American Arbitration Association
www.adr.org

American Association for Justice (formerly Association of Trial Lawyers of America)
www.atlanet.org

American Association of Attorney-Certified Public Accountants
www.attorney-cpa.com

American Association of Law Libraries
www.aallnet.org

American Association of Nurse Attorneys
www.taana.org

American Bar Association
www.abanet.org

American Civil Liberties Union
www.aclu.org

American College of Family Trial Lawyers
www.acftl.com

American College of Real Estate Lawyers
www.acrel.org

American College of Trust and Estate Counsel
www.actec.org

American Constitution Society
www.americanconstitutionsociety.org

American Health Lawyers Association
www.healthlawyers.org

American Immigration Lawyers Association
www.aila.org

American Inns of Court
www.innsofcourt.org

American Intellectual Property Law Association
www.aipla.org

American Judges Association
aja.ncsc.dni.us

American Judicature Society
www.ajs.org

American Law and Economics Association
www.amlecon.org

American Law Institute
www.ali.org

American Masters of Laws Association
www.amola.org

American Prepaid Legal Services Institute
www.aplsi.org

American Pro Se Association
www.legalhelp.org

719

American Society for Pharmacy Law
www.aspl.org

American Society of Comparative Law
www.comparativelaw.org

American Society of International Law
www.asil.org

American Society of Law, Medicine & Ethics
www.aslme.org

Animal Legal Defense Fund
www.nawj.org

Association for Conflict Resolution
www.acrnet.org

Association for Continuing Legal Education (CLE)
www.aclea.org

Association of Attorney-Mediators
www.attorney-mediators.org

Association of Collaborative Family Law Attorneys
nycollaborativelaw.com

Association of Corporate Counsel
www.acc.com

Association of Family and Conciliation Courts
www.afccnet.org

Association of Professional Responsibility Lawyers (ethics)
www.aprl.net

Black Entertainment and Sports Lawyers Association
www.besla.org

Canadian Bar Association
www.cba.org

Center for American and International Law
www.swlegal.org

Center for Law and Social Policy
www.clasp.org

Christian Legal Society
www.clsnet.org

Commercial Law League of America
www.clla.org

Council on Law in Higher Education
www.clhe.org

Court Appointed Special Advocates
www.casanet.org

Criminal Justice Legal Foundation
www.cjlf.org

Customs and International Trade Bar Association
www.citba.org

Cyber Law Association
www.cyberlawassociation.com

Cyberspace Bar Association
www.cyberbar.net

Decalogue Society of Lawyers (bar association for Jewish attorneys)
decaloguesociety.org

Defense Research Institute
www.dri.org

Dominican Bar Association
www.dominicanbarassociation.org

Education Law Association
www.educationlaw.org

Environmental Law Institute
www2.eli.org

Federal Communications Bar Association
www.fcba.org

Federal Bar Association
www.fedbar.org

Federal Circuit Bar Association
www.fedcirbar.org

Federal Magistrate Judges Association
www.fedjudge.org

Federation of Insurance & Corporate Counsel
www.thefederation.org

Fully Informed Jury Association
www.fija.org

Hellenic Bar Association
www.hellenicbarassociation.com

Hispanic National Bar Association
www.hnba.com

Home School Legal Defense Association
www.hslda.org

Human Rights First
www.humanrightsfirst.org

Inner Circle of Advocates
www.innercircle.org

International Academy of Matrimonial Lawyers
www.iaml-usa.com

International Center for Not-for-Profit Law
www.icnl.org

International Law Association
www.ila-hq.org

International Masters of Gaming Law
www.gaminglawmasters.com

International Technology Law Association
www.itechlaw.org

Internet Bar Association
lawyers.org

Italian–American Lawyers Association
www.iala.lawzone.com

Judge Advocates Association (military and veterans law)
www.jaa.org

Justinian Society (Italian American attorneys)
www.justinian.org

Lambda Legal Defense and Education Fund (gay, lesbian, bisexual, and transgender issues)
www.lambdalegal.org

Lawyer Pilots Bar Association
www.lpba.org

Lawyers Without Borders
www.lawyerswithoutborders.org

Legal Marketing Association
www.legalmarketing.org

Licensing Executives Society
les-europe.org

Lithuanian-American Bar Association
javadvokatai.org

Million Dollar Advocates Forum (attorneys who have won $1,000,000+ in damages)
www.milliondollaradvocates.com

Multilaw (Global Law Network)
www.multilaw.com

National Asian Pacific American Bar Association
www.napaba.org

NAACP Legal Defense and Education Fund
www.naacpldf.org

National Academy of Elder Law Attorneys
www.naela.com

National American Indian Court Judges Association
www.naicja.org

National Association for Law Placement
www.nalp.org

National Association for Rights Protection and Advocacy
www.narpa.org

National Association of Assistant United States Attorneys
www.naausa.org

National Association of Attorneys General
www.naag.org

National Association of Bond Attorneys
www.nabl.org

National Association of College and University Attorneys
www.nacua.org

National Association of Consumer Bankruptcy Attorneys
nacba.com

National Association of Criminal Defense Lawyers
www.criminaljustice.org

National Association of Legal Search Consultants
www.nalsc.org

National Association of Patent Practitioners
www.napp.org

National Association of Retail Collection Attorneys
www.narca.org

National Association of Secretaries of State
www.nass.org

National Board of Trial Advocacy
www.nbtanet.org

National Association of Women Judges
www.nawj.org

National Association of Women Lawyers
www.abanet.org/nawl

National Bar Association (African American attorneys)
www.nationalbar.org

National Center for Lesbian Rights
www.nclrights.org

National Center for Poverty Law
www.povertylaw.org

National Center for State Courts
www.ncsconline.org

National Crime Victim Bar Association
www.victimbar.org

National District Attorneys Association
www.ndaa.org

National Employment Lawyers Association
www.nela.org

National Lawyers Association (alternative to the American Bar Association)
www.nla.org

National Lawyers Guild (civil rights group of lawyers, "jailhouse lawyers and legal workers")
www.nlg.org

National Legal Aid and Defender Association
www.nlada.org

National Lesbian and Gay Rights Association
www.nlgla.org

National Legal Center for the Public Interest
www.nlcpi.org

National Native American Bar Association
www.nativeamericanbar.org

National Organization of Bar Counsel
www.nobc.org

National Right to Work Legal Defense Foundation
www.nrtw.org

National Transportation Safety Board Bar Association
www.ntsbbar.org

National Whistleblower Center
www.whistleblowers.org

Network of Trial Law Firms
www.trial.com

Phi Alpha Delta Law Fraternity
www.pad.org

Philippine American Bar Association
www.philconnect.com/paba

Professional Mediation Association
www.promediation.com

Prosecutors Bar Association
www.ipba.net

Public Justice
www.tlpj.org

Public Law Research Institute
www.uchastings.edu/?pid=134

Renaissance Lawyer Society
www.renaissancelawyer.com

Rocky Mountain Mineral Law Foundation
www.rmmlf.org

Rutherford Institute (civil and human rights)
www.rutherford.org

Societies of Corporate Secretaries and Governance Professionals
www.governanceprofessionals.org

Sport and Recreation Law Association
srlaweb.org

Sports Lawyers Association
www.sportslaw.org

Ukrainian American Bar Association
www.uaba.net

United Citizens for Legal Reform
www.atps.com/uclr

Federal Government Organization Chart

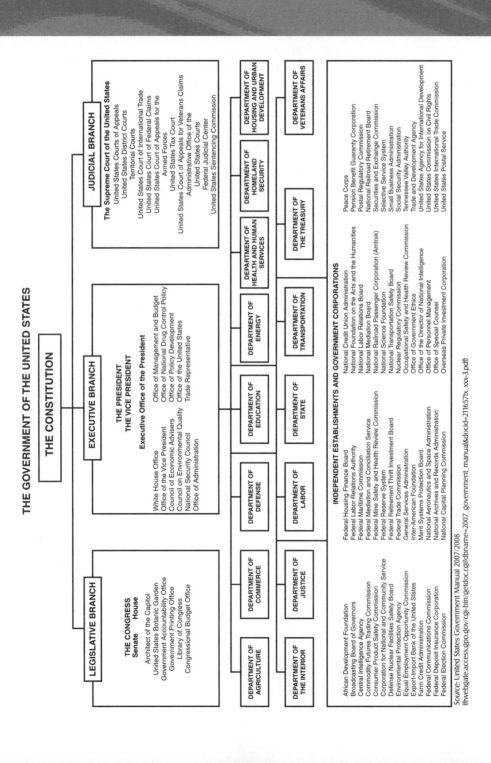

THE GOVERNMENT OF THE UNITED STATES

THE CONSTITUTION

LEGISLATIVE BRANCH

THE CONGRESS
Senate   House

Architect of the Capitol
United States Botanic Garden
Government Accountability Office
Government Printing Office
Library of Congress
Congressional Budget Office

EXECUTIVE BRANCH

THE PRESIDENT
THE VICE PRESIDENT

Executive Office of the President

White House Office
Office of the Vice President
Council of Economic Advisers
Council on Environmental Quality
National Security Council
Office of Administration

Office of Management and Budget
Office of National Drug Control Policy
Office of Policy Development
Office of the United States
Trade Representative

JUDICIAL BRANCH

The Supreme Court of the United States
United States Courts of Appeals
United States District Courts
Territorial Courts
United States Court of International Trade
United States Court of Federal Claims
United States Court of Appeals for the
Armed Forces
United States Tax Court
United States Court of Appeals for Veterans Claims
Administrative Office of the
United States Courts
Federal Judicial Center
United States Sentencing Commission

DEPARTMENT OF AGRICULTURE
DEPARTMENT OF COMMERCE
DEPARTMENT OF DEFENSE
DEPARTMENT OF EDUCATION
DEPARTMENT OF ENERGY
DEPARTMENT OF HEALTH AND HUMAN SERVICES
DEPARTMENT OF HOMELAND SECURITY
DEPARTMENT OF HOUSING AND URBAN DEVELOPMENT

DEPARTMENT OF THE INTERIOR
DEPARTMENT OF JUSTICE
DEPARTMENT OF LABOR
DEPARTMENT OF STATE
DEPARTMENT OF TRANSPORTATION
DEPARTMENT OF THE TREASURY
DEPARTMENT OF VETERANS AFFAIRS

INDEPENDENT ESTABLISHMENTS AND GOVERNMENT CORPORATIONS

African Development Foundation
Broadcasting Board of Governors
Central Intelligence Agency
Commodity Futures Trading Commission
Consumer Product Safety Commission
Corporation for National and Community Service
Defense Nuclear Facilities Safety Board
Environmental Protection Agency
Equal Employment Opportunity Commission
Export-Import Bank of the United States
Farm Credit Administration
Federal Communications Commission
Federal Deposit Insurance Corporation
Federal Election Commission

Federal Housing Finance Board
Federal Labor Relations Authority
Federal Maritime Commission
Federal Mediation and Conciliation Service
Federal Mine Safety and Health Review Commission
Federal Reserve System
Federal Retirement Thrift Investment Board
Federal Trade Commission
General Services Administration
Inter-American Foundation
Merit Systems Protection Board
National Aeronautics and Space Administration
National Archives and Records Administration
National Capital Planning Commission

National Credit Union Administration
National Foundation on the Arts and the Humanities
National Labor Relations Board
National Mediation Board
National Railroad Passenger Corporation (Amtrak)
National Science Foundation
National Transportation Safety Board
Nuclear Regulatory Commission
Occupational Safety and Health Review Commission
Office of Government Ethics
Office of the Director of National Intelligence
Office of Personnel Management
Office of Special Counsel
Overseas Private Investment Corporation

Peace Corps
Pension Benefit Guaranty Corporation
Postal Regulatory Commission
National Railroad Retirement Board
Securities and Exchange Commission
Selective Service System
Small Business Administration
Social Security Administration
Tennessee Valley Authority
Trade and Development Agency
United States Agency for International Development
United States Commission on Civil Rights
United States International Trade Commission
United States Postal Service

Source: United States Government Manual 2007/2008
(frwebgate.access.gpo.gov/cgi-bin/getdoc.cgi?dbname=2007_government_manual&docid=211657bx_xxx-3.pdf)

State Survey: Opinions, Rules, Statutes, and Reports on Paralegal Ethics and Related Topics

The following summary of the fifty states and the District of Columbia covers paralegals and other nonattorneys. The purpose of the summary is to give an overview of the kinds of issues that have arisen. It is *not* meant to describe the current state of the law or provide the current ethics regulations of any particular state. Keep in mind that the rules governing paralegals are undergoing considerable change. See Section F of chapter 5 on how to do legal research to determine the current ethics rules that apply to your state. You will occasionally see the abbreviation WL in this appendix. This abbreviation means Westlaw, the commercial online research service discussed in chapters 11 and 13. If you do not have access to Westlaw, check the Internet sources that are given for your state to determine whether the item is available to you on the free Internet.

ALABAMA

ETHICAL RULES AND GUIDELINES IN ALABAMA

- For a discussion of the state's ethical Rule 5.3 ("Responsibilities Regarding Nonlawyer Assistants") in the *Alabama Rules of Professional Conduct*, see the end of Section C in chapter 5. For the text of 5.3 in Alabama, see also www.law.cornell.edu/ethics/al/narr.
- Under Rule 7.6 of the Rules of Professional Conduct, the title "Legal Assistant" is acceptable on a business card that also contains an attorney's or a law firm's name. The title of the nonattorney employee should be legibly and prominently displayed in close proximity to the employee's name. A casual observer of the card should not be misled into thinking that it is the card of an attorney (www.alabar.org/public/ropc/rule7-6.htm). An earlier ethics opinion preferred the title *nonlawyer assistant*, since *paralegal* could be a misleading title. Alabama State Bar, *Opinion 86–04* (3/17/86). See also *Opinion 86–120* (12/2/86).
- When a paralegal signs a letter to a nonattorney, the paralegal's name should be followed by one of these titles: *nonlawyer assistant*, *nonlawyer paralegal*, or *nonlawyer investigator*. Alabama State Bar, *Opinion 87–77* (6/16/87).
- It is improper to include the name of a nonattorney assistant on the letterhead of law firm stationery. Alabama State Bar, *Opinion 83–87* (5/23/83).
- The business card of a legal secretary can list the fact that she has been certified by passing an examination of the National Association of Legal Secretaries. Alabama State Bar, *Opinion 90–01* (1/17/90).

- A nonlawyer employee who changes law firms must be held to the same standards as a lawyer in determining whether a conflict of interest exists. A firm that hires a nonlawyer employee previously employed by opposing counsel in pending litigation would have a conflict of interest and must therefore be disqualified if, during the course of the previous employment, the employee acquired confidential information concerning the case. A firm may avoid disqualification if (1) the nonlawyer employee has not acquired material and confidential information regarding the litigation or (2) if the client of the former firm waives disqualification and approves the use of a screening device or Chinese wall. Alabama State Bar, *Opinion 2002–01*.
- An attorney cannot allow his paralegal to ask questions of debtors at meetings of creditors in bankruptcy cases. Alabama State Bar, *Opinion 89–76* (9/20/90).
- Paralegals may draft documents if supervised by an attorney, but they cannot make court appearances or give legal advice. Alabama State Bar, *Opinion 86–120* (12/2/86).
- An attorney engaged in collection work may not pay his lay employees on a commission basis. *Opinion of the General Counsel* (2/3/88, revised 2/14/90).
- Nonattorney independent contractors who sell legal research services to attorneys are not engaged in the unauthorized practice of law. Alabama State Bar, *Opinion 90–04* (1/18/90).
- A law firm may not employ, retain, contract with, or hire a disbarred lawyer to provide legal services. This specifically includes paralegal services. A suspended lawyer may seek permission from the Disciplinary Commission to seek employment in the legal profession. In the event that permission is granted, the lawyer shall not have any contact with clients. Alabama Rules of Disciplinary Procedure, Rule 26. (See also Alabama State Bar, *Opinion 1996–08*.)
- Members of the bar, paralegals, or other personal assistants to members of the bar when accompanied by an attorney are permitted to bring laptops and personal digital assistants into the courthouse after such devices have been properly screened. Local Rules of the U.S. District Court, S.D. Alabama, Order 31.

DEFINING THE PRACTICE OF LAW IN ALABAMA

- § 34–3–6 (*Michie's Alabama Code*): . . . (b) For the purposes of this chapter, the practice of law is defined as follows: Whoever,

(1) in a representative capacity appears as an advocate or draws papers, pleadings or documents, or performs any act in connection with proceedings pending or prospective before a court or a body, board, committee, commission or officer constituted by law or having authority to take evidence in or settle or determine controversies in the exercise of the judicial power of the state or any subdivision thereof; or (2) For a consideration, reward or pecuniary benefit, present or anticipated, direct or indirect, advises or counsels another as to secular law, or draws or procures or assists in the drawing of a paper, document or instrument affecting or relating to secular rights; or (3) For a consideration, reward or pecuniary benefit, present or anticipated, direct or indirect, does any act in a representative capacity in behalf of another tending to obtain or secure for such other the prevention or the redress of a wrong or the enforcement or establishment of a right; or (4) As a vocation, enforces, secures, settles, adjusts or compromises defaulted, controverted or disputed accounts, claims or demands between persons with neither of whom he is in privity or in the relation of employer and employee in the ordinary sense; is practicing law.

- § 6–5–572 (*Michie's Alabama Code*): Paralegals and legal assistants as legal service providers. Under the Alabama Legal Services Liability Act, the term "legal service provider" is defined as follows: Anyone licensed to practice law by the State of Alabama or engaged in the practice of law in the State of Alabama. The term legal service provider includes professional corporations, associations, and partnerships and the members of such professional corporations, associations, and partnerships and the persons, firms, or corporations either employed by or performing work or services for the benefit of such professional corporations, associations, and partnerships including, without limitation, law clerks, legal assistants, legal secretaries, investigators, paralegals, and couriers.

ALABAMA ETHICS AND PRACTICE RULES ON THE INTERNET

- www.law.cornell.edu/ethics/alabama.html
- www.law.cornell.edu/ethics/al/narr
- www.legalethics.com/ethics.law?state=Alabama

PARALEGALS (AND OTHER NONATTORNEYS) IN ALABAMA STATE AND FEDERAL COURTS

- *Metropolitan Life Insurance Co. v. Akins*, 388 So. 2d 999 (Court of Civil Appeals of Alabama, 1980) (the failure of a "paralegal" to inform an attorney of a matter is not a sufficient excuse for the attorney's neglect of that matter).
- *Browder v. General Motors Corp.*, 5 F. Supp. 2d 1267, 1275 (U.S. District Court, M.D. Alabama, 1998) (the attorney's carelessness included the failure to review a proposed pretrial order drafted by a paralegal).
- *Ex Parte Moody*, 684 So. 2d 114 (Supreme Court of Alabama) (an indigent defendant in a criminal case is not entitled to a court-appointed paralegal who is paid by the state or a court-appointed paralegal who works on a volunteer basis).
- *Serra Chevrolet, Inc. v. General Motors*, 446 F.3d 1137 (U.S. Court of Appeals for the 11th Circuit) (General Motors hired fourteen paralegals to conduct a manual review of documents in 4,100 contract files).
- *Allen v. Fountain*, 861 So. 2d 1104 (Court of Civil Appeals of Alabama, 2002) (constitutional and statutory provisions

allowing self-representation in civil court actions protect only natural persons, and do not allow for representation of separate legal entities, such as estates and corporations, by nonlawyers).

- *Surge v. Massanari*, 155 F. Supp. 2d 1301 (U.S. District Court, M.D. Alabama, 2001) (hours claimed for paralegal time are reduced; there was duplication of effort between attorney and paralegal in working on a brief; also, the plaintiff has failed to submit any information regarding the paralegal's education, experience, or qualifications).
- *Allen v. McClain EZ Pack of Alabama*, 2005 WL 1926636 (U.S. District Court, S.D. Alabama 2005) (plaintiff has provided no information concerning prevailing paralegal rates; because there is no evidence regarding the paralegals' expertise in a civil rights case, the court finds that compensation at the lowest rate for paralegals is an appropriate fee).
- *Hall v. Lowder Realty Co.*, 263 F. Supp. 2d 1352 (U.S. District Court, M.D. Alabama, 2003) (paralegal work is compensable when it involves, for example, factual investigation, including locating and interviewing witnesses, assistance with depositions, interrogatories, and document production, compilation of statistical and financial data, checking legal citations, and drafting correspondence; but paralegal's hours spent reviewing documents and helping to prepare chart exhibits were clerical in nature and thus would be reduced).

DOING LEGAL RESEARCH IN ALABAMA LAW

Statutes: www.legislature.state.al.us
Cases: www.loc.gov/law/guide/us-al.html
Court Rules: www.judicial.state.al.us/rules.cfm
General: www.alllaw.com/state_resources/alabama

FINDING EMPLOYMENT IN ALABAMA

- legal.jobs.net/Alabama.htm
- www.indeed.com/q-Litigation-Paralegal-l-Alabama-jobs.html
- jobs.careerbuilder.com/al.ic/Alabama_Legal.htm
- www.lawcrossing.com (select Legal Staff positions in Alabama)

ALASKA

ETHICAL RULES AND GUIDELINES IN ALASKA

- For a discussion of the state's ethical Rule 5.3 ("Responsibilities Regarding Nonlawyer Assistants") in the *Alaska Rules of Professional Conduct*, see the end of Section C in chapter 5. For the text of 5.3 in Alaska, see also www.law.cornell.edu/ethics/ak/code/AK_CODE.HTM.
- A law firm may ethically employ an accountant to advise and assist attorneys in the performance of legal services and to provide accounting services relating to or arising from legal services provided by the firm. An accountant so employed may not be a partner and shall be compensated by salary so as to avoid the prohibitions of Disciplinary Rules 3–102 and 3–103. Further, the letterhead, office sign and professional cards of the law firm shall not indicate the availability of the accounting services to clients of the firm. Alaska Bar Ass'n, *Ethics Opinion 79–3* (10/26/79).
- A suspended attorney may work as a paralegal but only under the supervision of an attorney in good standing. He or she

may not have a direct relationship with a client. Alaska Bar Ass'n, *Ethics Opinion 84–6* (8/25/84).

- Under the supervision or review of an attorney, a legal assistant can investigate claims and have contact with insurance agents regarding the settlement of claims in worker's compensation cases. Alaska Bar Ass'n, *Ethics Opinion 73–1* (10/6/73).
- Paralegal employees of attorneys may not conduct worker's compensation hearings. Alaska Bar Ass'n, *Ethics Opinion 84–7* (8/25/84). Note: this Opinion was *reversed* on 11/9/84.

DEFINING THE PRACTICE OF LAW IN ALASKA

- § 08.08.230 (*Alaska Statutes*): Unlawful practice a misdemeanor. (a) A person not an active member of the Alaska Bar and not licensed to practice law in Alaska who engages in the practice of law or holds out as entitled to engage in the practice of law as that term is defined in the Alaska Bar Rules, or an active member of the Alaska Bar who willfully employs such a person knowing that the person is engaging in the practice of law or holding out as entitled to so engage is guilty of a class A misdemeanor. (b) This section does not prohibit the use of paralegal personnel as defined by rules of the Alaska Supreme Court.
- Rule 63. *Rules of the Alaska Bar Association*: For purposes of Alaska Statutes § 08.08.230 [making unauthorized practice of law a misdemeanor], "practice of law" is defined as: (a) representing oneself by words or conduct to be an attorney, and, if the person is authorized to practice law in another jurisdiction but is not a member of the Alaska Bar Association, representing oneself to be a member of the Alaska Bar Association; and (b) either (i) representing another before a court or governmental body which is operating in its adjudicative capacity, including the submission of pleadings, or (ii), for compensation, providing advice or preparing documents for another which effect legal rights or duties.

RULES ON PARALEGAL FEES IN ALASKA

- *Alaska Rules of Civil Procedure*: Rule 82 provides:

    (a) Except as otherwise agreed to by the parties, the prevailing party in a civil case shall be awarded attorney's fees calculated under this rule . . . .

    (b) (2) In cases in which the prevailing party recovers no money judgment, the court shall award the prevailing party in a case which goes to trial 30 percent of the prevailing party's reasonable actual attorney's fees which were necessarily incurred, and shall award the prevailing party in a case resolved without trial 20 percent of its actual attorney's fees which were necessarily incurred. The actual fees shall include fees for legal work customarily performed by an attorney but which was delegated to and performed by an investigator, paralegal or law clerk.

- Title 8, § 45.180 *Alaska Administrative Code*: Costs and Attorney's Fees in Workers' Compensation Cases.

    (f) The board will award an applicant the necessary and reasonable costs relating to the preparation and presentation of the issues upon which the applicant prevailed at the hearing on the claim. The applicant must file a statement listing each cost claimed, and must file an affidavit stating that the costs are correct and that the costs were incurred in connection with the claim. The following costs will, in the board's discretion, be awarded to an applicant: . . .

(14) fees for the services of a paralegal or law clerk, but only if the paralegal or law clerk

    (A) is employed by an attorney licensed in this or another state;

    (B) performed the work under the supervision of a licensed attorney;

    (C) performed work that is not clerical in nature;

    (D) files an affidavit itemizing the services performed and the time spent in performing each service; and

    (E) does not duplicate work for which an attorney's fee was awarded.

ALASKA ETHICS AND PRACTICE RULES ON THE INTERNET

- www.law.cornell.edu/ethics/alaska.html
- touchngo.com/lglcntr/ctrules/profcon/htframe.htm
- www.alaskabar.org/index.cfm?id=5258

PARALEGALS (AND OTHER NONATTORNEYS) IN ALASKA STATE AND FEDERAL COURTS

- *Morgan v. State*, 162 P.2d 636 (Court of Appeals of Alaska, 2007) (paralegal given the task of watching vehicles in front of a restaurant parking lot to count the number of vehicles using their turn signals).
- *Marsingill v. O'Malley*, 58 P.3d 495 (Supreme Court of Alaska, 2002) (paralegal was prohibited from asking jurors, during posttrial interview in medical malpractice action, about jury's alleged confusion regarding an aspect of the jury instructions).
- *Nielson v. Benton*, 903 P.2d 1049 (Supreme Court of Alaska, 1995) (paralegal fees and Alaska Rule of Civil Procedure 82(b)(2)).
- *Frontier Companies of Alaska v. Jack White Co.*, 818 P.2d 645 (Alaska Supreme Court, 1991) (paralegal fees).
- *Carlson v. United Academics-AAUP/AFT/APEA/AFT-CIO*, 2002 WL 487179 (U.S. District Court, Alaska, 2002) (in this day and age of computerized records, accounting programs, and computer databases storing briefing records, much of the preparation of a fee application should usually be delegated to a secretary or paralegal).
- *Government Employees Ins. Co. v. Dunst*, 2006 WL 1663844 (U.S. District Court, Alaska, 2006) (157.15 paralegal hours at $85 per hour totaling $13,357).
- *Lebiedzinski v. Crane*, 2005 WL 906368 (U.S. District Court, Alaska 2005) (the question of whether fees and costs award should include work done by paralegals and clerks is a very close one; on balance, the court concludes that it is wiser to include the cost of work done by paralegals and clerks).

DOING LEGAL RESEARCH IN ALASKAN LAW

Statutes: www.legis.state.ak.us/folhome.htm
Cases: www.state.ak.us/courts
Court Rules: www.state.ak.us/courts/rules.htm
General: www.alllaw.com/state_resources

FINDING EMPLOYMENT IN ALASKA

- www.alaskabar.org/index.cfm?id=5812
- www.indeed.com/q-Paralegal-l-Alaska-jobs.html
- www.simplyhired.com/a/jobs/list/l-Alaska-t-Paralegal
- anchorage.craigslist.org/lgl

ARIZONA

ETHICAL RULES AND GUIDELINES IN ARIZONA

- For a discussion of the state's ethical Rule 5.3 ("Responsibilities Regarding Nonlawyer Assistants") in the *Arizona Rules of Professional Conduct*, see the end of Section C in chapter 5. For the text of 5.3 in Arizona, see also www.myazbar.org/Ethics/rules.cfm.

- The letterhead of an attorney or law firm can list nonattorney support personnel if their nonattorney status is made clear. State Bar of Arizona, *Ethics Opinion 90–03* (3/16/90). This overrules *Opinion 84–14* (10/5/84), which held to the contrary. The latter opinion also said that a separate letterhead for paralegals is not allowed).

- A corporation consisting of independent contractor paralegals and a salaried attorney employee is impermissible. State Bar of Arizona, *Opinion 82–18* (12/1/82). It is unethical for an attorney to associate with a nonattorney-operated eviction service; there would be inadequate attorney supervision of the nonattorneys and improper sharing of fees with nonattorneys. State Bar of Arizona, *Ethics Opinion 93–01* (2/18/93).

- An attorney ethically may contract with a paralegal to have the paralegal assist with conducting initial interviews of and signing of documents by estate planning clients, as long as: 1) the attorney supervises and controls the paralegal's activities to assure that the paralegal does not engage in the unauthorized practice of law; 2) there is no fee sharing; 3) the initial interviews are only with existing clients; and 4) there is no solicitation of new business by the paralegal. State Bar of Arizona, *Ethics Opinion 98–08* (10/98).

- An Arizona attorney may permit his non-lawyer paralegal, who is a licensed tribal advocate, to represent clients in tribal court if that court's rules so permit, because that court's rules govern the conduct. Such representations will not run afoul of the Arizona lawyer's duty to not assist unauthorized practice of law as long as the paralegal representation is limited to tribal court. State Bar of Arizona, *Ethics Opinion 99–13* (12/99).

- An Arizona lawyer cannot assist an independent paralegal in collecting a fee for services by the paralegal that the lawyer believes constitute the unauthorized practice of law. State Bar of Arizona, *Ethics Opinion 03–03* (4/2003).

- Lawyers ethically may not negotiate with an opposing party's nonlawyer public adjuster if the adjuster is not supervised by a lawyer. A lawyer may communicate directly with an opposing party who is "represented" by a public adjuster if the adjuster is not supervised by a lawyer or authorized to practice law. State Bar of Arizona, *Ethics Opinion 99–07* (6/1999).

- A law firm can ethically compensate one of its nonattorney employees by a base monthly fee plus quarterly bonuses measured by a percentage of the firm's increased revenues derived from areas the nonattorney employee was hired to develop. State Bar of Arizona, *Ethics Opinion 90–14* (10/17/90).

- A judge did not have to recuse himself where his daughter was employed as a paralegal in a law firm appearing in a case before him unless his daughter's work on the case was so extensive that a question might arise. Arizona Supreme Court Judicial Ethics Advisory Committee, *Opinion 77–1* (4/29/77).

- Other State Bar of Arizona Opinions involving nonattorneys: *Ethics Opinion 86–7* (2/26/86) (it is ethically improper for an attorney to cooperate with a nonattorney "consulting service" that provided expert testimony to its customers for a contingent fee); *Ethics Opinion 82–18* (12/1/82) (it is ethically improper for an attorney to be a salaried employee—not an owner—of a paralegal-run corporation that contracted with attorneys to provide legal services on an as-needed basis).

DEFINING LEGAL ASSISTANTS/PARALEGALS IN ARIZONA

- Rule 31(a) (C) (*Arizona Supreme Court Rules*): "Legal assistant/paralegal" means a person qualified by education and training who performs substantive legal work requiring a sufficient knowledge of and expertise in legal concepts and procedures, who is supervised by an active member of the State Bar of Arizona, and for whom an active member of the state bar is responsible, unless otherwise authorized by supreme court rule. 17A Arizona Revised Statutes.

DEFINING THE PRACTICE OF LAW IN ARIZONA

- Rule 31(a) (A) (*Arizona Supreme Court Rules*) "Practice of law" means providing legal advice or services to or for another by:
  (1) preparing any document in any medium intended to affect or secure legal rights for a specific person or entity;
  (2) preparing or expressing legal opinions;
  (3) representing another in a judicial, quasi-judicial, or administrative proceeding, or other formal dispute resolution process such as arbitration and mediation;
  (4) preparing any document through any medium for filing in any court, administrative agency or tribunal for a specific person or entity; or
  (5) negotiating legal rights or responsibilities for a specific person or entity. 17A Arizona Revised Statutes.

LEGAL DOCUMENT PREPARERS IN ARIZONA

- In 2003, the Supreme Court of Arizona adopted a new section to the Code of Judicial Administration, Section 7–208, and established the Legal Document Preparer Program ("the Program"). The Supreme Court Administrative Order 2003–14, defines legal document preparers as non-lawyers who "prepare or provide legal documents, without the supervision of an attorney, for an entity or a member of the public who is engaging in self representation in any legal matter." Under Section 7–208 (F) (1) (b), certified legal document preparers may provide general legal information but may not give legal advice. Section 7–208 (D) (4) established the Board of Legal Document Preparers ("the Board"), which, in part, hears and adjudicates complaints against certified legal document preparers. *Sobol v. Alarcon*, 131 P. 3d 487 (Court of Appeals of Arizona, 2006) (www.supreme.state.az.us/cld/ldp.htm).

- Regulation of nonlawyers (www.azbar.org/workingwithlawyers/upl.cfm).

OTHER IMPORTANT ARIZONA LAWS ON PARALEGALS

- § 12–2234 (A) (*Arizona Revised Statutes Annotated*): In a civil action an attorney shall not, without the consent of his client, be examined as to any communication made by the client to him, or his advice given thereon in the course of professional employment. An attorney's paralegal, assistant, secretary, stenographer or clerk shall not, without the consent of his employer, be examined concerning any fact the knowledge of which was acquired in such capacity. . . .

- R9–21–209 (B)(3) (*Arizona Administrative Code*): Mental Illness Records. An attorney, paralegal working under the supervision of an attorney, or other designated representative of the client shall be permitted to inspect and copy the record, if such attorney or representative furnishes written authorization from the client or guardian.

ARIZONA ETHICS AND PRACTICE RULES ON THE INTERNET

- www.law.cornell.edu/ethics/arizona.html
- www.law.cornell.edu/ethics/az/narr/AZ_NARR_1_14.HTM
- www.myazbar.org/Ethics

PARALEGALS (AND OTHER NONATTORNEYS) IN ARIZONA STATE AND FEDERAL COURTS

- *Styles v. Ceranski*, 916 P.2d 1164 (Court of Appeals of Arizona, 1996) (propriety of communication by a defense paralegal with an employee of the plaintiff without consent of the plaintiff's attorney).
- *In the Matter of Miller*, 872 P.2d 661 (Supreme Court of Arizona, 1994) (discipline of attorney for failure to supervise paralegals).
- *Smart Industries Corp. v. Superior Court*, 876 P.2d 1176 (Court of Appeals of Arizona, 1994) (disqualification of a plaintiff's attorney when he hired a legal assistant who once worked for the defendant's attorney).
- *Samaritan Foundation v. Goodfarb*, 862 P.2d 870 (Supreme Court of Arizona, 1993) (defendant's attorney hires a nurse paralegal who interviews hospital employees in a medical malpractice case; the statements of the employees are not within the hospital's attorney-client privilege). See, however, § 12-2234(A) above.
- *Sobol v. Alarcon*, 131 P.3d 487 (Court of Appeals of Arizona, 2006) (a certified legal document preparer sued an attorney for defamation, after the attorney sent a letter to the state bar accusing the document preparer of unauthorized practice of law and other improper conduct; the court ruled that the attorney's complaint was privileged).
- *Agster v. Maricopa County*, 486 F. Supp. 2d 1005 (U.S. District Court, Arizona, 2007) (80 percent of the reasonable hours expended by plaintiffs' paralegals and legal assistants should be billed at a rate of $110, and the other 20 percent at $70; these rates more closely approximate the prevailing rates in this community; the court will deduct 933.82 hours from the time total for the fifteen paralegals/legal assistants because of duplication of effort, turnover of staff, and inefficiencies).
- *Oliver v. Long*, 2007 WL 623783 (U.S. District Court, Arizona 2007) (judges have no obligation to act as counsel or paralegal to pro se litigants because requiring trial judges to explain the details of federal procedure or act as the pro se's counsel would undermine the judges' role as impartial decision makers).
- *Miller v. Schriro*, 2007 WL 63613 (U.S. District Court, Arizona, 2007) (an Arizona inmate's legal access to the courts system relies on designated staff, paralegals, legal access monitors, attorneys, and inmates).
- *Gametech Intern., Inc. v. Trend Gaming Systems*, 380 F. Supp. 2d 1084 (U.S. District Court, Arizona, 2005) (Gametech specifically challenges billing entries for a paralegal, who had several multiple entries per day without segregating time; many of those entries were data entries or exhibit entries preparing the database for this action; this was a complex matter that involved thousands of pages of documents, dozens of depositions, and a four-week jury trial; the hours billed by the paralegal were reasonable.)

DOING LEGAL RESEARCH IN ARIZONA LAW

Statutes: www.azleg.state.az.us/ArizonaRevisedStatutes.asp
Cases: www.supreme.state.az.us/welcome.htm
Court Rules: www.supreme.state.az.us/rules
General: www.law.asu.edu/Library/azlegalmaterials

FINDING EMPLOYMENT IN ARIZONA

- azbar.legalstaff.com
- www.azparalegal.org/jobbank.html
- www.indeed.com/q-Litigation-Paralegal-l-Arizona-jobs.html
- phoenix.craigslist.org/lgl

ARKANSAS

ETHICAL RULES AND GUIDELINES IN ARKANSAS

- For a discussion of the state's ethical Rule 5.3 ("Responsibilities Regarding Nonlawyer Assistants") in the *Arkansas Rules of Professional Conduct*, see the end of Section C in chapter 5. For the text of 5.3 in Arkansas, see also courts.state.ar.us/professional_conduct/index.cfm.
- "The paralegal should never be placed in a position to decide what information takes priority over other information or to make decisions which affect the client." This function should never be delegated to a paralegal, even though "sometimes a fine line exists in the area of professional judgment." Paralegals need "specific guidelines," preferably in writing, in carrying out responsibilities. *The Paralegal in Practice* by A. Clinton, chairperson of the Paralegal Committee of the Arkansas Bar Ass'n, 23 Arkansas Lawyer 22 (January 1989).

DEFINING THE PRACTICE OF LAW IN ARKANSAS

- § 2.02 (*Arkansas Code Annotated*): Defining the Practice of Law, Court Rules Regulations of the Arkansas Continuing Legal Education Board. Inactive Status.

  (2) Definition: Practice of Law.—The practice of law shall be defined as any service rendered, regardless of whether compensation is received therefor, involving legal knowledge or legal advice. It shall include representation, provision of counsel, advocacy, whether in or out of court, rendered with respect to the rights, duties, regulations, liabilities, or business relations of one requiring the legal services.

- § 16–22–501 (*Arkansas Code of 1987 Annotated*): Unauthorized Practice of Law.

  (a) A person commits an offense if, with intent to obtain a direct economic benefit for himself or herself, the person:

  (1) Contracts with any person to represent that person with regard to personal causes of action for property damages or personal injury;

  (2) Advises any person as to the person's rights and the advisability of making claims for personal injuries or property damages;

  (3) Advises any person as to whether or not to accept an offered sum of money in settlement of claims for personal injuries or property damages;

(4) Enters into any contract with another person to represent that person in personal injury or property damage matters on a contingent fee basis with an attempted assignment of a portion of the person's cause of action;

(5) Enters into any contract, except a contract of insurance, with a third person which purports to grant the exclusive right to select and retain legal counsel to represent the individual in any legal proceeding; or

(6) Contacts any person by telephone or in person for the purpose of soliciting business which is legal in nature, as set forth above . . . .

(e) This section shall not apply to a person who is licensed as an adjuster or employed as an adjuster by an insurer as authorized by § 23–64–101.

- § 4–109–101(3) (*Arkansas Code Annotated*): "Practice of law" means:
(A) Holding oneself out to the public as being entitled to practice law; (B) Tendering or furnishing legal services or advice; (C) Furnishing attorneys or counsel; (D) Rendering legal services of any kind in actions or proceedings of any nature or in any other way or manner; (E) Acting as if or in any other manner assuming to be entitled to practice law; or (F) Advertising or assuming the title of lawyer or attorney, attorney at law, or equivalent terms in any language in such a manner as to convey the impression that one is entitled to practice law or to furnish legal advice, service, or counsel.

ARKANSAS ETHICS AND PRACTICE RULES ON THE INTERNET

- www.courts.state.ar.us/rules/index2.html#Rules
- courts.state.ar.us/courts/cpc.html
- www.arkbar.com/resources/resources_eth_disc.html
- www.law.cornell.edu/ethics/ar/narr/AR_NARR_1_01.HTM

PARALEGALS (AND OTHER NONATTORNEYS) IN ARKANSAS STATE AND FEDERAL COURTS

- *Fink v. Neal*, 328 Ark. 646, 945 S.W.2d 916 (Supreme Court of Arkansas, 1997) (the mistakes made by an attorney's paralegal do not constitute an excuse for the attorney's own negligence).
- *Brooks v. Central Arkansas Nursing Center*, 31 F. Supp. 2d 1151, 1154 (U.S. District Court, E.D. Arkansas, 1999) (award of attorney fees is reduced because "the Court is of the view these tasks could have been performed by a clerk or paralegal").
- *Duvall v. City of Rogers, Arkansas*, 2006 WL 931908 (U.S. District Court, W.D. Arkansas, 2006) (one and one half hours charged for "Court Appearance to file Motions" will be disallowed because all filings in this court are handled electronically, and this task could have been accomplished in a few minutes by a secretary or paralegal).
- *In re Seay*, 2007 WL 1623156 (U.S. Bankruptcy Court, E.D. Arkansas, 2007) (work done by paralegals is compensable if it is work that would have been done by an attorney; if such hours were not compensable, then attorneys may be compelled to perform the duties that could otherwise be fulfilled by paralegals, thereby increasing the overall cost of legal services; paralegal work that is purely clerical in nature is not reimbursable).
- *Crump-Donahue v. U.S. Dept. of Agriculture*, 2007 WL 1702567 (U.S. District Court, E.D. Arkansas, 2007) (when a nonlawyer attempts to represent the interests of other persons, the practice constitutes the unauthorized practice of law and results in a nullity).

- *Herron v. Jones*, 637 S.W.2d 569 (Supreme Court of Arkansas, 1982) (conflict of interest allegation; an employee—a legal secretary—switches law firms in the same case; court refuses to disqualify current employer because confidentiality was not breached).
- *In re Anderson*, 851 S.W.2d 408 (Supreme Court of Arkansas, 1993) (attorney surrenders his license to practice law after a drug conviction and then goes to work as a paralegal in his father's law firm; readmission denied).

DOING LEGAL RESEARCH IN ARKANSAS LAW

Statutes: www.arkleg.state.ar.us/data/ar_code.asp
Cases: courts.state.ar.us
Court Rules: courts.state.ar.us/rules/index.cfm
General: www.lawguru.com/search/states/arkansas.html

FINDING EMPLOYMENT IN ARKANSAS

- arkbar.legalstaff.com
- www.indeed.com/q-Paralegal-l-Arkansas-jobs.html
- www.simplyhired.com/job-search/l-Arkansas/o-232000/t-Paralegal

CALIFORNIA

DEFINING LEGAL ASSISTANTS/ PARALEGALS IN CALIFORNIA

- § 6450(a) (*West's California Business & Professions Code*): "Paralegal" means a person who holds himself or herself out to be a paralegal, who is qualified by education, training, or work experience, who either contracts with or is employed by an attorney, law firm, corporation, governmental agency, or other entity, and who performs substantial legal work under the direction and supervision of an active member of the State Bar of California, as defined in Section 6060, or an attorney practicing law in the federal courts of this state, that has been specifically delegated by the attorney to him or her. Tasks performed by a paralegal include, but are not limited to, case planning, development, and management; legal research; interviewing clients; fact gathering and retrieving information; drafting and analyzing legal documents; collecting, compiling, and utilizing technical information to make an independent decision and recommendation to the supervising attorney; and representing clients before a state or federal administrative agency if that representation is permitted by statute, court rule, or administrative rule or regulation. (caselaw.lp.findlaw.com/cacodes/bpc/6450–6456.html)

ETHICAL RULES AND GUIDELINES IN CALIFORNIA

- See appendix G and chapter 4 for the new law stating that the titles *paralegal* and *legal assistant* are restricted to those who work under attorney supervision. The law also imposes education and continuing legal education requirements. Appendix G and chapter 4 also cover the position of legal document assistant for individuals formerly known as independent paralegals.
- Attorneys not in practice together who share office space and paralegal services must take reasonable steps to protect each client's confidence and secrets. State Bar of California, *Opinion 1997–150* (1997) (1997 WL 240818).

- When a paralegal is authorized to represent a client before the Workers' Compensation Appeals Board, a law firm can use its paralegal to represent a client of the firm before this Board if the client consents and the firm supervises the paralegal. State Bar of California, *Opinion 1988–103*.

- Attorneys must take steps to ensure that nonattorney employees understand their obligation not to disclose client confidences and secrets. State Bar of California, *Opinion 1979–50*.

- A nonattorney can use a business card if it is used for identification rather than for solicitation of business. Los Angeles County Bar Ass'n, *Opinion 381*.

- A law firm can pay a bonus to its paralegal as long as the bonus does not involve a sharing of legal fees. Los Angeles Count Bar Ass'n, *Opinion 457* (11/20/89).

- A nonprofit legal services center for the elderly cannot advertise in a local newspaper the availability of "legal help" from "para-legal aides" trained by a local attorney. Legal help implies legal services. San Diego Bar Ass'n, *Opinion 1976–9* (7/1/76).

- A business that provides paralegal services to the public should have attorney supervision except for some purely ministerial tasks. San Diego Bar Ass'n, *Opinion 1983–7*.

- It is not the unauthorized practice of law for a paralegal to visit the homes of prospective clients for an attorney's estate and trust practice. She answers only those questions the attorney has trained her to answer; the attorney drafts the documents. Orange County Bar Association, *Opinion 94–002* (www.ocbar.org/pdf/OCBA94002.pdf).

DEFINING THE PRACTICE OF LAW IN CALIFORNIA

- *California v. Landlords Professional Services*, 264 Cal. Rptr. 548, 550 (Court of Appeals, 4th District, 1990): Business and Professions Code section 6125 states: "No person shall practice law in this State unless he is an active member of the State Bar." Business and Professions Code section 6126, subdivision (a), provides: "Any person advertising or holding himself or herself out as practicing or entitled to practice law or otherwise practicing law who is not an active member of the State Bar, is guilty of a misdemeanor." The code provides no definition for the term "practicing law." . . . "[A]s the term is generally understood, the practice of law is the doing and performing services in a court of justice in any manner depending therein throughout its various stages and in conformity with the adopted rules of procedure. But in a larger sense it includes legal advice and counsel and the preparation of legal instruments and contracts by which legal rights are secured although such matter may or may not be [pending] in court." . . . [N]onetheless . . . "ascertaining whether a particular activity falls within this general definition may be a formidable endeavor." . . . In close cases, the courts have determined that the resolution of legal questions for another by advice and action is practicing law "if difficult or doubtful legal questions are involved which, to safeguard the public, reasonably demand the application of a trained legal mind."

OTHER IMPORTANT CALIFORNIA LAWS ON PARALEGALS

- § 6400, *West's Annotated California Business & Professions Code* (legal document assistants and unlawful detailer assistants) (for the text of this law, see appendix G).

- Rule 10.140, *Los Angeles County Superior Court Rules, Probate Department*. The use of paralegals to perform services of an extraordinary nature is permitted. The court will require an itemized statement of services rendered by each paralegal, accompanied by allegations relating to the qualifications of the paralegal, as to both experience and training.

CALIFORNIA ETHICS AND PRACTICE RULES ON THE INTERNET

- www.law.cornell.edu/ethics/california.html
- www.calbar.org/2pub/3eth/3ethndx.htm
- www.calbar.org/pub250/index.htm
- www.calbar.org/pub250/crpc.htm

PARALEGALS (AND OTHER NONATTORNEYS) IN CALIFORNIA STATE AND FEDERAL COURTS

- *In re Complex Asbestos Litigation*, 283 Cal. Rptr. 732 (California Court of Appeals, 1991) (a paralegal who switches jobs might cause the disqualification of his or her new employer to represent clients about whom the paralegal obtained confidential information while working at a prior (opposing) law firm; a rebuttable presumption exists that the paralegal shared this information with the new employer; the most likely way for the new employer to rebut this presumption, and hence to avoid disqualification, is to show that when the paralegal was hired, a Chinese Wall was built around the paralegal with respect to any cases the paralegal worked on while at the prior employment). (See chapter 5.)

- *Devereux v. Latham & Watkins*, 38 Cal. Rptr. 2d 849 (California Court of Appeals, 1995) (litigation paralegal sues her former law firm employer after the paralegal testified against the law firm in an overbilling case).

- *Saret-Cook v. Gilbert, Kelly, Crowley & Jennett*, 88 Cal. Rptr. 2d 732 (California Court of Appeals, 1999) ("fatal attraction" case: paralegal loses sex harassment case against office attorney with whom she had an affair).

- *People v. Gaines*, 2004 WL 2386748 (California Court of Appeals, 2004) (it was not error for the prosecutor to reject a paralegal as a juror; the paralegal had taken classes in criminal law and felt capable of informing people about criminal cases; the prosecutor may have reasonably believed there was a possibility this juror would resist following the court's instructions in favor of his own conception of the law).

- *In re White*, 18 Cal. Rptr 3d 444 (California Court of appeals, 2004) (attorney discipline upheld; his health problems provide no excuse for his authorizing a paralegal to sign his name on habeas corpus petitions that the attorney did not read).

- *Rico v. Mitsubishi*, 10 Cal. Rptr. 3d 601 (California Court of Appeals 2004) (the attorney's work-product doctrine covers documents created not only by an attorney, but also by his agents or employees, including his paralegal).

- *In re Hessinger & Associates*, 192 Bankruptcy Reporter 211 (U.S. Bankruptcy Court, N.D. California, 1996) (law firm unethically allowed paralegals to complete bankruptcy petitions and to perform other work of legal character without adequate attorney supervision; the firm was organized much like a production line, with little or no review by attorneys; a persistent theme in appellant's position on the role of paralegals in its practice is the argument that "everybody does it"; that is, all large consumer bankruptcy firms rely on paralegals to perform a large amount of the work required for filing a bankruptcy petition, and in all such firms the paralegals do so with only minimal attorney supervision; while this may well be true, the court will not condone an unethical practice merely because most consumer bankruptcy firms are engaging in it).

- *Oakland v. McCullough*; 53 Cal. Rptr. 2d 531 (California Court of Appeals, 1st District, 1996 (a claim for paralegal fees is rejected because of a failure to provide documentation in support of the claim).

- *Sanford v. GMRI, Inc.*, 2005 WL 4782697 (U.S. District Court E.D. California, 2005) (paralegal fees are challenged in part because of doubts on whether the paralegal complied with the new California law on education and CLE requirements of paralegals; see chapter 4 and appendix G on these requirements).

- *In re Stebbins*, 2007 WL 1877894 (U.S. Bankruptcy Court, E.D. California, 2007) (paralegal fees are denied for basic services, such as entering data in the computer, preparing a transmittal letter, or faxing a letter; such tasks are included in general office overhead and are not appropriately charged as paralegal or attorney time).

- *Robinson v. Chand*, 2007 WL 1300450 (U.S. District Court, E.D. California, 2007) (counsel seeks to bill at attorney rates work more appropriately handled by paralegals or secretaries; this work includes preparing cover sheets, converting files to PDFs, e-filing documents, mailing documents, arranging for service of documents, scheduling matters, researching nonlegal issues such as business ownership, preparing boilerplate documents, and organizing case files).

DOING LEGAL RESEARCH IN CALIFORNIA LAW

Statutes: www.leginfo.ca.gov/calaw.html
Cases: www.courtinfo.ca.gov/opinions/continue.htm
Court Rules: www.courtinfo.ca.gov/rules
General: www.ll.georgetown.edu/states/california.cfm

FINDING EMPLOYMENT IN CALIFORNIA

- www.caparalegal.org/capacc.html
- www.calawjobs.com
- legal.jobs.net/California.htm
- losangeles.craigslist.org/lgl
- www.indeed.com/q-Paralegal-l-California-jobs.html

COLORADO

DEFINING LEGAL ASSISTANTS/ PARALEGALS IN COLORADO

Legal assistants (also known as paralegals) are a distinguishable group of persons who assist attorneys in the delivery of legal services. Through formal education, training and experience, legal assistants have knowledge and expertise regarding the legal system and substantive and procedural law which will qualify them to do work of a legal nature under the direct supervisions of a licensed attorney. Colorado Bar Association, *Colorado Paralegals-Proposed Guidelines to the Next Century and Beyond: Part I*, 63 (1996).

ETHICAL RULES AND GUIDELINES IN COLORADO

- For a discussion of the state's ethical Rule 5.3 ("Responsibilities Regarding Nonlawyer Assistants") in the *Colorado Disciplinary Rules of Professional Conduct*, see the end of Section C in chapter 5. For the text of 5.3 in Colorado, see also www.law.cornell.edu/ethics/co/code.

- The names of support personnel can be printed on law firm letterhead, and they can be given their own business card as long as they reveal clearly that they are not attorneys. Colorado Bar Ass'n, *Formal Ethics Opinion 84* (4/1990).

- Paralegals must disclose their nonattorney status to everyone at the outset of any professional relationship. They should be given no task that requires the exercise of unsupervised legal judgment. They can write letters and sign correspondence on attorney letterhead as long as their nonattorney status is clear and the correspondence does not contain legal opinions or give legal advice. They can have their own business cards with the name of the law firm on them if their nonattorney status is made clear. The services performed by the paralegal must supplement, merge with, and become part of the attorney's work product. Colorado Bar Ass'n, *Guidelines for the Utilization of Legal Assistants* (1986).

- The Colorado Bar Association has also approved *Guidelines for Utilization of Paralegals* in eighteen specialty areas of the law:

Civil litigation paralegal	Estate planning paralegal
Collections law paralegal	Family law paralegal
Commercial law paralegal	Immigration law paralegal
Corporate law paralegal	Intellectual property paralegal
Corporate securities paralegal	Natural resource paralegal
Criminal litigation paralegal	Real estate paralegal
Elder law paralegal	Special district law paralegal
Employment law paralegal	Water law paralegal
Environmental paralegal	Workers' compensation paralegal

(www.cobar.org/group/index.cfm?category=106&Entity ID=CLAS)

- Attorneys not in the same law firm sometimes share offices. To ensure confidentiality in such situations, the attorneys should avoid the sharing of staff to the extent possible, particularly secretaries and paralegals. Colorado Bar Assn, *Formal Ethics Opinion 89* (1999).

- A law firm can use a paralegal to represent clients at administrative proceedings when authorized by statute and when the practice of law is not involved. To ensure competent representation, the attorney must train and supervise the paralegal. Colorado Bar Ass'n, *Opinion 79* (2/18/89).

- An attorney shall continually monitor and supervise the work of assistants to assure that the services they render are performed competently and efficiently. Colorado Bar Ass'n, *Ethics Opinion 61* (10/23/82).

- An attorney may not participate with nonattorneys in preparing and marketing estate planning documents when the venture consists of the unauthorized practice of law. Colorado Bar Ass'n, *Opinion 87* (7/14/90).

- It is also generally improper for an attorney to direct or even authorize another, such as an investigator or legal assistant, to record conversations surreptitiously. Colorado Bar Ass'n, *Formal Ethics Opinion 112* (2003).

- Comment [3], Rule 5.5 (*Rules of Professional Conduct*): A lawyer may employ or contract with a disbarred, suspended lawyer or a lawyer on disability inactive status, to perform services that a law clerk, paralegal or other administrative staff may perform so long as the lawyer directly supervises the work. Lawyers who are suspended but whose entire suspension has been stayed may engage in the practice of law, and the portion of the Rule limiting what suspended lawyers may do does not apply.

DEFINING THE PRACTICE OF LAW IN COLORADO

- *Unauthorized Practice of Law Committee of the Supreme Court of Colorado v. Prog*, 761 P.2d 1111, 1115 (Supreme Court of Colorado, 1988): The determination of what acts do or do not constitute the practice of law is a judicial function . . . .While recognizing the difficulty of formulating and applying an all-inclusive definition of the practice of law, we have stated that "generally one who acts in a representative capacity in protecting, enforcing, or defending the legal rights and duties of another and in counseling, advising and assisting him in connection with these rights and duties is engaged in the practice of law."

- Rule 201.3. *Court Rules Annotated* (*West's Colorado Revised Statutes Annotated*): Rules Governing Admission to the Bar . . . .

    (2) For purposes of this rule, "practice of law" means:

    (a) the private practice of law . . . ; or

    (b) employment as a lawyer for a corporation . . . or other entity with the primary duties of:

    (i) furnishing legal counsel, drafting documents and pleadings, and interpreting and giving advice with respect to the law, and/or

    (ii) preparing, trying or presenting cases before courts, executive departments, administrative bureaus or agencies . . . .

IMPORTANT COLORADO LAWS OR RULES ON PARALEGALS

- § 13–90–107 (*West's Colorado Revised Statutes Annotated*):

    (1) There are particular relations in which it is the policy of the law to encourage confidence and to preserve it inviolate; therefore, a person shall not be examined as a witness in the following cases: . . .

    (b) An attorney shall not be examined without the consent of his client as to any communication made by the client to him or his advice given thereon in the course of professional employment; nor shall an attorney's secretary, paralegal, legal assistant, stenographer, or clerk be examined without the consent of his employer concerning any fact, the knowledge of which he has acquired in such capacity.

- Rule 33.1. (*West's Colorado Revised Statutes Annotated*): Colorado Rules of Probate Procedure. Personal representatives and attorneys representing an estate are entitled to reasonable compensation. In setting attorneys' fees, the time expended by personnel performing paralegal functions under the direction and supervision of the attorney may be considered as an item separate from and in addition to the time spent by the attorney. In setting other fees, the time expended by personnel performing paraprofessional functions may be considered as a separate item.

- Rule 6.1 (*Rules of Professional Conduct*): G. Paralegal Pro Bono Opportunities. Approved pro bono legal work for paralegals includes: (1) work taken on in conjunction with and under the supervision of an attorney working on a specific pro bono legal matter, or (2) work handled independently for an organization that provides pro bono legal opportunities, provided, however, that such participation does not create an attorney-client relationship and/or involve the paralegal's provision of legal advice.

COLORADO ETHICS AND PRACTICE RULES ON THE INTERNET

- www.law.cornell.edu/ethics/colorado.html
- www.law.cornell.edu/ethics/co/code
- www.cobar.org/group/index.cfm?EntityID=CETH

PARALEGALS (AND OTHER NONATTORNEYS) IN COLORADO STATE AND FEDERAL COURTS

- *Robinson v. Colorado State Lottery Div.*, 155 P. 3d 409 (Colorado Court of Appeals, 2006) (To the extent plaintiff objects to the award of fees for work performed by paralegals, we note that the supreme court has also allowed for the recovery of time charged for paralegal services. *Am. Water Dev., Inc. v. City of Alamosa*, 874 P. 2d 352 [Colo. 1994].)

- *Carr v. Fort Morgan School District*, 4 F. Supp. 2d 998 (U.S. District Court, Colorado, 1998) (fees involving paralegal time are reduced by 15 percent due to lack of detail as to the work done and apparent duplication of effort).

- *In re Estate of Myers*, 130 P.3d 1023 (Supreme Court of Colorado, 2006) (a paralegal obtained a copy of a credit report through a ruse; the law firm denied allegations that the actions of the paralegal reflected the firm's normal practice).

- *Carbajal v. American Family*, 2006 WL 2988955 (U.S. District Court, Colorado 2006) (the court denied the defendant's motion to disqualify the law firm of the plaintiff on the basis of a brief social relationship between one of the plaintiff's attorneys and a paralegal for the defendant; although the relationship was not wise, it was limited and no disclosure of information about the litigation occurred).

- *People v. Smith*, 74 P.3d 566 (The Office of the Presiding Disciplinary Judge, 2003) (a lawyer failed to adequately supervise his paralegal, in violation of disciplinary rule requiring a lawyer with direct supervisory authority over a nonlawyer employee to make reasonable efforts to ensure that the employee's conduct is compatible with the lawyer's professional obligations; the attorney failed to review the client's marriage dissolution file to determine if the paralegal was attending to the case as she described to the attorney, and such inadequate supervision allowed the paralegal to conceal problems developing in the case, including failure to comply with court orders, and allowed the paralegal to engage in the unauthorized practice of law; the measures that should have been taken, such as an informal program of instructing or monitoring the paralegal, must often assume the likelihood that a particular nonlawyer employee may not yet have received adequate preparation for carrying out that person's own responsibilities).

- *People v. Milner*, 35 P.3d 670 (The Office of the Presiding Disciplinary Judge, Colorado, 2001) (although lacking in tact, a paralegal's single impolite outburst toward a client, to "stop calling and bitching," would not be a separate basis for attorney discipline).

- *In re Gomez*, 259 Bankruptcy Reporter 379 (U.S. Bankruptcy Court, Colorado, 2001) (bankruptcy petition preparer, by its use of trade name that included the word *paralegals* on its letterhead and brochures, in answering telephone, and in its communications with prospective customers, violated Bankruptcy Code provision barring any petition preparer from using the word *legal* or "any similar term" in its advertisements).

- *People v. Felker*, 770 P.2d 402 (Supreme Court of Colorado, 1989) (attorney disciplined for allowing nonattorney employee to give a client legal advice).

DOING LEGAL RESEARCH IN COLORADO LAW

Statutes: www.state.co.us/gov_dir/leg_dir/olls/colorado_revised_statutes.htm
Cases: www.cobar.org/opinions/index.cfm?CourtID=2
Court Rules: 198.187.128.12/colorado/lpext.dll?f=templates&fn=fs-main.htm&2.0
General: www.state.co.us/courts/sctlib/links.html

FINDING EMPLOYMENT IN COLORADO

- cobar.legalstaff.com
- www.indeed.com/q-Paralegal-l-Colorado-jobs.html
- www.cobar.org/group/index.cfm?entityid=dpmem&category=678
- legal.jobs.net/Colorado.htm
- denver.craigslist.org/lgl

CONNECTICUT

DEFINING LEGAL ASSISTANTS/ PARALEGALS IN CONNECTICUT

A legal assistant is a person, qualified through education, training, or work experience, who is employed or retained by a lawyer, law office, governmental agency, or other entity in a capacity or function which involves the performance under the ultimate direction and supervision of an attorney, of specifically delegated substantive legal work, which work, for the most part, requires a sufficient knowledge of legal concepts that, absent such assistant, the attorney would perform the task. Connecticut Bar Association, *Guidelines for Lawyers Who Employ or Retain Legal Assistants*, 1 (1997) (www.ctbar.org/article/articleview/197).

ETHICAL RULES AND GUIDELINES IN CONNECTICUT

- For a discussion of the state's ethical Rule 5.3 ("Responsibilities Regarding Nonlawyer Assistants") in the *Connecticut Rules of Professional Conduct*, see the end of Section C in chapter 5. For the text of 5.3 in Connecticut, see also www.law.cornell.edu/ethics/ct/narr/index.htm.
- A lawyer should take all reasonable supervisory measures to make sure the legal assistant acts in accordance with the lawyer's ethical obligations. (Guideline 1) Legal assistants can perform many tasks with lawyer supervision and review. They cannot give legal advice, accept cases, reject cases, or set legal fees. They may appear before adjudicatory bodies if authorized to do so. They may act as a witness at will executions. They may attend real estate closings alone but can act only as a messenger to deliver and pick up documents and funds. They cannot express any independent opinion or judgment about execution of the documents, changes in adjustments or price, or other matters involving documents or funds. (Guideline 2) The lawyer should take reasonable measures to ensure that all client confidences are protected by the legal assistant (Guideline 3) and that third persons are aware upon first contact with a legal assistant that the latter is not licensed to practice law (Guideline 4). The name and title of a legal assistant may appear on the lawyer's letterhead and on business cards identifying the lawyer's firm. (Guideline 5) A lawyer must take reasonable measures to ensure that the legal assistant does not create a conflict of interest due to current or prior employment, or to other business or personal interests. (Guideline 6) A lawyer shall not split legal fees with a legal assistant or pay a legal assistant for the referral of legal work. (Guideline 7) If a client consents, the lawyer can charge a reasonable and separate charge for legal assistant work. (Guideline 8) A lawyer shall not form a partnership with a legal assistant if any of the partnership's activities consist of the practice of law. (Guideline 9) A lawyer should encourage the legal assistant's participation in continuing education and pro bono publico activities. (Guideline 10) Connecticut Bar Association, *Guidelines for Lawyers Who Employ or Retain Legal Assistants* (1997) (www.ctbar.org/article/articleview/197, www.ctbar.org/article/articleview/198). See also *Lawyers'*

Professional Responsibility Obligations Concerning Paralegals, 59 Connecticut Bar Journal 425 (1985).

- Section 51–86 of *Connecticut General Statutes Annotated* covers solicitation by nonattorneys: "(a) A person who has not been admitted as an attorney in this state under the provisions of section 51–80 shall not solicit, advise, request or induce another person to cause an action for damages to be instituted, from which action or from which person the person soliciting, advising, requesting or inducing the action may, by agreement or otherwise, directly or indirectly, receive compensation from such other person or such person's attorney, or in which action the compensation of the attorney instituting or prosecuting the action, directly or indirectly, depends upon the amount of the recovery therein. (b) Any person who violates any provision of this section shall be fined not more than one hundred dollars or imprisoned not more than six months or both."
- An attorney may use a paralegal as a messenger to deliver and pick up already prepared documents and funds required for a real estate closing. The supervising attorney does not have to be present. The paralegal can communicate information or questions from an attorney in the firm to the buyer's attorney. The paralegal, however, must not provide information or give an independent opinion regarding the legal implications or sufficiency of any of the documents. Connecticut Bar Ass'n, *Informal Opinion 96–16* (7/3/96) (1996 WL 405034).
- A government attorney is not relieved of the obligation to exercise independent professional judgment simply because the attorney is under the supervision and direction of a government paralegal (a "supervisory paralegal specialist"). Connecticut Bar Ass'n, *Informal Opinion 00–9* (4/27/00) (2000 WL 1370788).
- A law firm can take a new case even though one of its nonlawyer assistants worked on the other side of the same case while employed at a different firm so long as the employee has not already disclosed confidential information about the case learned while at the other firm and is screened from the case at the current firm. It is important that the paralegal not disclose, intentionally or inadvertently, information relating to representation of the former client and not otherwise work against the interest of the former client on the same or a substantially related matter. Connecticut Bar Ass'n, *Informal Opinion 00–23* (12/27/00) (2000 WL 33157218).
- Other ethics opinions: Paralegals can have their own business card if their nonattorney status is clear, *Opinion 85–17* (11/20/85); it is unethical for an attorney to instruct a nonattorney to make misrepresentations to the public, *Informal Opinion 95–4* (1/6/95) (1995 WL 170147).

DEFINING THE PRACTICE OF LAW IN CONNECTICUT

- *In re Darlene C*, 717 A. 2d 1242, 1246 (Supreme Court of Connecticut, 1998): [while acknowledging that a]ttempts to define the practice of law have not been particularly successful, [the court nonetheless observed that] determining the legal theory of a case, drafting the papers necessary to commence a legal action, checking the various possible legal grounds, signing the pleadings and submitting them to the court [are] acts that are commonly understood to [constitute] the practice of law.
- *State Bar Ass'n of Connecticut v. the Connecticut Bank and Trust Co.*, 140 A.2d 863, 870, 69 A.L.R.2d 394 (Supreme Court of Errors of Connecticut, 1958): The practice of law consists in no small part of work performed outside of any court and having no immediate relation to proceedings in court. It embraces the giving of legal advice on a large variety of

subjects and the preparation of legal instruments covering an extensive field. Although such transactions may have no direct connection with court proceedings, they are always subject to subsequent involvement in litigation. They require in many aspects a high degree of legal skill and great capacity for adaptation to difficult and complex situations. No valid distinction can be drawn between the part of the work of the lawyer which involves appearance in court and the part which involves advice and the drafting of instruments.

CONNECTICUT ETHICS AND PRACTICE RULES ON THE INTERNET

- www.jud.ct.gov/pb.htm
- www.law.cornell.edu/ethics/connecticut.html
- www1.ctbar.org/sectionsandcommittees/committees/Paralegals.aspx
- www1.ctbar.org/sectionsandcommittees/committees/ProfessionalEthics.aspx

PARALEGALS (AND OTHER NONATTORNEYS) IN CONNECTICUT STATE AND FEDERAL COURTS

- *Conn. State Dept. of Social Services v. Thompson*, 289 F. Supp. 2d 198 (U.S. District Court for Connecticut, 2003) (the better practice would have been for the paralegals to keep contemporaneous time records, and had they done so the fees awarded in this case would be larger).
- *Powell v. Harriott*, 2006 WL 2349450 (U.S. District Court for Connecticut, 2006) (the request for paralegal fees contains no information about the skills or experience of the firm's paralegals, rendering it difficult for the court to discern why they should be awarded above an average hourly rate).
- *Haye v. Ashcroft*, 2004 WL 1936204 (U.S. District Court for Connecticut, 2004) (a suspended attorney may assist a licensed attorney [as a paralegal] so long as the attorney exercises close supervision and retains responsibility for the work of the suspended attorney).
- *Statewide Grievance Committee v. Harris*, 239 Conn. 256, 683 A. 2d 1362 (Supreme Court of Connecticut, 1996) (injunction against a paralegal charged with unauthorized practice of law in violation of General Statutes § 51–88; he ran an advertisement in the *Hartford Courant*, titled "Uncontested Pro se Divorce," in which he represented that "Paralegals prepare all papers for your signing and step you through the self-help divorce").
- *In re Darlene C*, 717 A.2d 1242 (Supreme Court of Connecticut, 1998) (nonlawyer representatives, who work for the state, prepare, sign, and file petitions for termination of parental rights; because a Connecticut statute authorizes these activities, they do not constitute the unauthorized practice of law).
- *Rivera v. Chicago Pneumatic Tool Co.*, 1991 WL 151892 (Connecticut Superior Court, 8/5/91) (trial court denies a motion to disqualify the plaintiff's attorney who hired a paralegal formerly employed by defendant's attorney even though the paralegal had been extensively involved in litigation concerning the defendant; there must be a sufficient Chinese wall built around such a paralegal to ensure that confidences are not divulged).
- *Gazda v. Olin Corp.*, 5 CSCR 227 (1/18/90) (legal secretary switches firms; disqualification denied where reasonable efforts were taken to ensure that the nonattorney employee would not divulge any confidences she might have acquired).

DOING LEGAL RESEARCH IN CONNECTICUT LAW

Statutes: www.cga.ct.gov/2007/pub/titles.htm
Cases: www.jud.state.ct.us/LawLib/state.htm#cases
Court Rules: www.megalaw.com/ct/ctrules.php
General: www.washlaw.edu/uslaw/states/Connecticut/index.html

FINDING EMPLOYMENT IN CONNECTICUT

- www.ctbar.org/sectionsandcommittees/committees/Paralegals.aspx
- www.ctbar.org/article/articleview/29
- www.themillardgroup.com
- newhaven.craigslist.org/lgl

DELAWARE

DEFINING LEGAL ASSISTANTS/PARALEGALS IN DELAWARE

McMackin v. McMackin, 651 A.2d 778 (Delaware Family Court, 1993): Persons who, although not members of the legal profession, are qualified through education, training, or work experience, are employed or retained by a lawyer, law office, governmental agency, or other entity in a capacity or function which involves the performance, under the direction and supervision of an attorney, of specifically delegated substantive legal work, which work, for the most part, requires a sufficient knowledge of legal concepts such that, absent that legal assistant, the attorney would perform the task. (Citing the American Bar Association).

ETHICAL RULES AND GUIDELINES IN DELAWARE

- For a discussion of the state's ethical Rule 5.3 ("Responsibilities Regarding Nonlawyer Assistants") in the *Delaware Rules of Professional Conduct*, see the end of Section C in chapter 5. For the text of 5.3 in Delaware, see also courts.delaware.gov/odc/DLRPC101905.pdf.
- A law firm cannot allow its paralegal to represent a client before the Industrial Accident Board on a worker's compensation case. Delaware State Bar Ass'n, *Opinion 1985–3*.
- A nonattorney law clerk cannot work on a case where the other side is represented by the clerk's former employer. The clerk must be screened from involvement in the case. Delaware State Bar Ass'n, *Opinion 1986–1*.

DEFINING THE PRACTICE OF LAW IN DELAWARE

- *Delaware State Bar Ass'n v. Alexander*, 386 A.2d 652, 661, 12 A.L.R.4th 637 (Supreme Court of Delaware, 1978): In general, one is deemed to be practicing law whenever he furnishes to another advice or service under circumstances which imply the possession and use of legal knowledge and skill. The practice of law includes "all advice to clients, and all actions taken for them in matters connected with the law.... Practice of law includes the giving of legal advice and counsel, and the preparation of legal instruments and contracts [by] which legal rights are secured....Where the rendering of services for another involves the use of legal knowledge or skill on his behalf where legal advice is required and is availed of or rendered in connection with such services these services necessarily constitute or include the practice of law." ... "In determining what is the practice of law, it is well settled that it is the character of the acts performed and not the place where they are done that is decisive. The practice of law is not, therefore, necessarily limited to the conduct of cases in court but is engaged in whenever and wherever legal knowledge, training, skill and ability are required."

- Delaware Rules of Court, Rules of the Board on the Unauthorized Practice of Law, Rule 4: In evaluating possible unauthorized practice of law, the following types of conduct shall be examined: (i) giving legal advice on matters relating to Delaware law, (ii) drafting legal documents or pleadings for a person or entity (other than one's self) reflecting upon Delaware law, for use in a Delaware legal tribunal or governmental agency, unless the drafting of such documents or pleadings has been supervised by a person authorized to practice law in the State of Delaware, (iii) appearing as legal counsel for, or otherwise representing, a person or entity (other than one's self) in a Delaware legal tribunal or governmental agency, (iv) holding one's self out as being authorized to practice law in the State of Delaware, (v) engaging in an activity which has traditionally been performed exclusively by persons authorized to practice law.

DELAWARE ETHICS AND PRACTICE RULES ON THE INTERNET

- www.law.cornell.edu/ethics/delaware.html
- www.dsba.org/AssocPubs/ethics.htm

PARALEGALS (AND OTHER NONATTORNEYS) IN DELAWARE STATE AND FEDERAL COURTS

- *In re Worldwide Direct*, 316 Bankruptcy Reporter 637 (U.S. Bankruptcy Court, Delaware, 2004) ("The past two decades have witnessed a remarkable transformation of the legal market .... A critical component of this transformed legal market is the incorporation of paralegals providing a wide range of legal services into the law firm tapestry, a component brought about by the cost-effectiveness of employing an intermediate level of professional to handle matters beyond the ken of the average legal secretary but not demanding the full education, experience, or skill of a licensed attorney.") (quoting *Busy Beaver*, 19 F.3d 849 (3d Cir. 1994).

- *In the Matter of the Estate of Ross*, 1996 WL 74731 (Court of Chancery of Delaware, 1996) ("In an age in which attorney fees are high, it is always welcome to see that good use is made of paralegals, with a resulting benefit to the client").

- *Ciappa Const., Inc. v. Innovative Property Resources*, 2007 WL 1705632 (Delaware Superior Court, 2007) (Delaware courts have routinely included fees charged for a legal assistant's time when granting attorney's fees).

- *Spark v. MBNA*, 289 F. Supp. 2d 510 (U.S. District Court, Delaware, 2003) (counsel has submitted no evidence of the reasonable hourly rate for paralegal time to justify a charge of $175 per hour).

- *Spark v. MBNA Corp.*, 157 F. Supp. 2d 330 (U.S. District Court, Connecticut, 2001) (the request for paralegal fees did not set out information on the education and experience of the paralegals or on comparable billing rates for this professional in the market).

- *In re Hull*, 767 A.2d 197 (Supreme Court of Delaware, 2001) (attorney disciplined for failure to supervise her legal assistant and for paying the latter an improper commission).

- *In re Arons*, 756 A.2d 867 (Supreme Court of Delaware, 2000) (it is the unauthorized practice of law for nonattorney lay advocates to represent families of children with disabilities in "due process" hearings held by Delaware Department of

Public Instruction on federal disability issues; Congress did not authorize such lay representation).

- *In the Matter of Mekler*, 672 A.2d 23 (Supreme Court of Delaware, 1995) (suspended attorney can act as a paralegal but cannot have any contact with clients, prospective clients, or witnesses).

- *Dickens v. Taylor*, 464 F. Supp. 2d 341 (U.S. District Court, Delaware 2006) (prison authorities are required to assist inmates in the preparation and filing of meaningful legal papers by providing prisoners with adequate law libraries or adequate assistance from persons trained in the law—at least access to a prison paralegal or paging system by which to obtain legal materials).

DOING LEGAL RESEARCH IN DELAWARE LAW

Statutes: delcode.delaware.gov
Cases: courts.state.de.us
Court Rules: www.megalaw.com/de/derules.php
General: www.washlaw.edu/uslaw/states/Delaware/index.html

FINDING EMPLOYMENT IN DELAWARE

- delaware.craigslist.org/lgl
- www.indeed.com/q-Litigation-Paralegal-l-Delaware-jobs.html
- www.lawcrossing.com (select Delaware)

DISTRICT OF COLUMBIA

ETHICAL RULES AND GUIDELINES IN THE DISTRICT OF COLUMBIA

- For a discussion of the state's ethical Rule 5.3 ("Responsibilities Regarding Nonlawyer Assistants") in the *D.C. Rules of Professional Conduct*, see the end of Section C in chapter 5. For the text of 5.3 in the District of Columbia, see also www.dcbar.org/new_rules/rules.cfm.

- A paralegal who switches firms must be screened from any cases involving clients represented by both firms. This will protect confidences and avoid imputed disqualification. D.C. Bar, *Opinion 227*, 21 Bar Report 2 (August/September 1992).

- A lawyer who employs a nonlawyer former government employee must screen that person from matters that are the same as, or substantially related to, matters on which the nonlawyer assisted government lawyers in representing a government client. D.C. Bar, *Opinion 285* (November 1998).

- Nonattorneys can have a business card that prints the name of the law firm where they work as long as their nonattorney status is clear. D.C. Bar, *Opinion 19*. See also *Speaking of Ethics*, Bar Report 2 (February/March 1988).

- A law firm can share a "success fee" with nonattorney experts on a case. *Opinion 233*, Bar Report 2 (June/July 1993).

- A law firm may not compensate a nonlawyer employee, hired to work on designated class action claims against defendants who are members of a particular industry, based on a percentage of the profits earned from those cases. D.C. Bar, *Opinion 332* (February 2004).

- A nonattorney *can* be a partner in a law firm. Hence a District of Columbia law firm *can* share fees with nonattorneys under the guidelines of Rule 5.4. For example, a lobbyist or an economist could form a partnership with an attorney. The nonattorney must agree to abide by the Rules of Professional Conduct. Rule 5.4, *Model Rules of Professional Conduct*.

■ A nonattorney who is an officer, director, or employee of a corporation can appear for that corporation in the settlement of any landlord-and-tenant case. If, however, the corporation files an answer, cross-claim, or counterclaim, the corporation must be represented by an attorney. D.C. Court of Appeals, Rule 49(c)(8), *Rules of the District of Columbia Court of Appeals*.

■ Law clerks, paralegals and summer associates are not practicing law where they do not engage in providing advice to clients or otherwise hold themselves out to the public as having authority or competence to practice law. D.C. Court of Appeals, Commentary to Rule 49, *Rules of the District of Columbia Court of Appeals*.

DEFINING THE PRACTICE OF LAW IN THE DISTRICT OF COLUMBIA

■ Rule 49 (*Court Rules of the District of Columbia Court of Appeals*): (a) General Rule. No person shall engage in the practice of law in the District of Columbia or in any manner hold out as authorized or competent to practice law in the District of Columbia unless enrolled as an active member of the District of Columbia Bar . . . .

(b) (2) "Practice of Law" means the provision of professional legal advice or services where there is a client relationship of trust or reliance. One is presumed to be practicing law when engaging in any of the following conduct on behalf of another: (A) Preparing any legal document, including any deeds, mortgages, assignments, discharges, leases, trust instruments or any other instruments intended to affect interests in real or personal property, wills, codicils, instruments intended to affect the disposition of property of decedents' estates, other instruments intended to affect or secure legal rights, and contracts except routine agreements incidental to a regular course of business; (B) Preparing or expressing legal opinions; (C) Appearing or acting as an attorney in any tribunal; (D) Preparing any claims, demands or pleadings of any kind, or any written documents containing legal argument or interpretation of law, for filing in any court, administrative agency or other tribunal; (E) Providing advice or counsel as to how any of the activities described in sub-paragraph (A) through (D) might be done or whether they were done, in accordance with applicable law; . . . .

DISTRICT OF COLUMBIA ETHICS AND PRACTICE RULES ON THE INTERNET

● www.law.cornell.edu/ethics/dc.html
● www.dcbar.org/for_lawyers/ethics/legal_ethics

PARALEGALS (AND OTHER NONATTORNEYS) IN DISTRICT OF COLUMBIA COURTS

■ *Minebea Co., Ltd. v. Papsti*, 374 F. Supp. 2d 231 (U.S. District Court, District of Columbia, 2005) (the party's counsel of record, their legal assistants, interpreters, and technical personnel were "essential" to the presentation of the party's case, and therefore could not be excluded from courtroom pursuant to sequestration rule).

■ *Role Models America, Inc. v. Brownlee*, 353 F.3d 962 (U.S. Court of Appeals, D.C. Circuit, 2004) (requested rates for the services of law clerks and legal assistants would be reduced by

25 percent, where prevailing party did not submit information about the prevailing market rate in the Washington area, refer to either of two matrices upon which court had allowed reliance in past, or submit an affidavit dealing with the non-attorneys' experience and education).

■ *Palmer v. Rice*, 2005 WL 1662130 (U.S. District Court, District of Columbia, 2005) ("A paralegal, having performed classic paralegal duties such as drafting a letter to a client or cite checking a motion for summary judgment, may also make copies of those documents or send them in the mail once they have been approved by the supervising lawyer. In other words, it is impossible for a reviewing court to draw distinctions this fine and require that every task be delegated to the lowest competent level, no matter how small the task and no matter the time that may be wasted in accomplishing such delegation.")

■ *In re Meese*, 907 F.2d 1192, 1202 (U.S. Court of Appeals, D.C. Circuit, 1990) (the rates billed for paralegals are reasonable; however, we deduct $4,253 for services billed at these rates that were of a purely clerical nature).

■ *Hampton Courts Tenants Ass'n v. DC Rental Housing Commission*, 599 A.2d 1113 (District of Columbia Court of Appeals, 1991) (attorneys should not be performing tasks normally performed by paralegals).

■ *Fonville v. District of Columbia*, 230 Federal Rules Decisions 38 (U.S. District Court, District of Columbia, 2005) (it is improper for a paralegal to sign answers to interrogatories, rather than the party to whom interrogatories are directed).

■ *In Re Ryan*, 670 A.2d 375 (District of Columbia Court of Appeals, 1996) (attorney disciplined in part because of her overreliance on paralegals who had no paralegal training).

■ *In Re Davis*, 650 A.2d 1319 (District of Columbia Court of Appeals, 1994) (disbarred attorney ordered to perform 250 hours of community service as a paralegal).

DOING LEGAL RESEARCH IN DISTRICT OF COLUMBIA LAW

Statutes: government.westlaw.com/linkedslice/default.asp?rs=gvt1.0&vr=2.0&sp=dcc-1000
Cases: www.dcappeals.gov/dccourts/appeals/opinions_mojs.jsp
Court Rules: www.llrx.com/courtrules-gen/state-District-of-Columbia.html
General: www.ll.georgetown.edu/states/dc-in-depth.cfm

FINDING EMPLOYMENT IN THE DISTRICT OF COLUMBIA

● dcbar.legalstaff.com
● www.hg.org/legal_jobs_district-of-columbia.asp
● www.lawcrossing.com (select District of Columbia location)

FLORIDA

DEFINING LEGAL ASSISTANTS/ PARALEGALS IN FLORIDA

■ Rule 10–2.1(b) (Rules Regulating the Florida Bar): A paralegal or legal assistant is a person qualified by education, training, or work experience, who works under the supervision of a member of The Florida Bar and who performs specifically delegated substantive legal work for which a member of The Florida Bar is responsible.

- § 57.104 (Florida Statutes Annotated): In any action in which attorneys' fees are to be determined or awarded by the court, the court shall consider, among other things, time and labor of any legal assistants who contributed nonclerical, meaningful legal support to the matter involved and who are working under the supervision of an attorney. For purposes of this section "legal assistant" means a person, who under the supervision and direction of a licensed attorney engages in legal research, and case development or planning in relation to modifications or initial proceedings, services, processes, or applications; or who prepares or interprets legal documents or selects, compiles, and uses technical information from references such as digests, encyclopedias, or practice manuals and analyzes and follows procedural problems that involve independent decisions (www.leg. state.fl.us/statutes).

REGISTRATION OF PARALEGALS IN FLORIDA

- www.floridasupremecourt.org/decisions/2007/sc06–1622.pdf
- www.flabar.org
  (click "Search" then type "registered paralegal")

CERTIFICATION OF PARALEGALS IN FLORIDA

- www.pafinc.org/certification.php
- www.nala.org/cert-FL_certif.htm

ETHICAL RULES AND GUIDELINES IN FLORIDA

- For a discussion of the state's ethical Rule 4–5.3 ("Responsibilities Regarding Nonlawyer Assistants") in the *Florida Rules of Professional Conduct*, see the end of Section C in chapter 5. For the text of 4–5.3 in Florida, see also www.floridabar.org (click "Lawyer Regulation").
- Rule 10–2.1(a)(2) (Rules Regulating the Florida Bar): It shall constitute the unlicensed practice of law for a person who does not meet the definition of paralegal or legal assistant as set forth elsewhere in these rules to offer or provide legal services directly to the public or for a person who does not meet the definition of paralegal or legal assistant as set forth elsewhere in these rules to use the title paralegal, legal assistant, or other similar term in providing legal services or legal forms preparation services directly to the public (www3.flabar.org/divexe/rrtfb.nsf/WContents?OpenView).
- Paralegals can have their own business cards. They may also be listed on a law firm's letterhead, but a title indicating their nonattorney status should appear beneath their name. Attorneys should not hold their paralegals out as "certified" if they are not. Florida Bar, *Opinion 86–4* (8/1/86). See also Florida Bar, *Opinion 71–39* (10/20/71) (nonattorney employee can use the law firm's name on his business card).
- Law firms can outsource paralegal functions to nonattorneys in India if adequate supervision is maintained, conflicts of interest are avoided, confidentiality is preserved, client consent is obtained, and billing arrangements are proper. *Proposed Advisory Opinion 07-2* (9/7/07).
- When a nonattorney changes jobs to an opposing law firm, the old and new employers must admonish him or her not to reveal any confidences or secrets obtained during prior employment, and the new employer must take steps to ensure there is no breach of confidentiality by this employee. Florida Bar, *Opinion 86–5* (8/1/86).
- A law firm can allow a nonattorney to conduct a real estate closing if certain conditions are met, e.g., an attorney is available (in person or by telephone) to answer legal questions, the nonattorney performs only ministerial acts (he or she must not give legal advice or make any legal decisions), and the client consents to having the closing handled by a nonattorney. Florida Bar, *Opinion 89–5* (11/1989) (overruling *Opinion 73–43*).
- Attorneys cannot delegate to lay persons the handling of negotiations with insurance company adjustors regarding claims of the attorney's clients. Florida Bar, *Opinion 74–35* (9/23/74).
- Preparing living trust documents constitutes the practice of law. It is the unauthorized practice of law for a nonattorney to decide whether a living trust is appropriate, and to prepare and execute the documents involved. *Florida Bar Re: Advisory Opinion on Nonlawyer Preparation of Living Trusts*, 613 So. 2d 426 (Supreme Court of Florida, 1992). See also *Florida Bar Re: Advisory Opinion on Nonlawyer Preparation of Residential Leases Up to One Year in Duration*, 602 So. 2d 914 (Supreme Court of Florida, 1992), and *Florida Bar Re: Nonlawyer Preparation of and Representation of Landlord in Uncontested Residential Evictions*, 605 So. 2d 868 (Supreme Court of Florida, 1992).
- It is ethically improper for a law firm to delegate to nonattorneys the handling of negotiations with adjusters on claims of the firm's clients. Florida Bar, *Ethics Opinion 74–35* (9/23/74). But the nonlawyer employee can transmit information from the attorney. "For example, the nonlawyer employee may call the adjuster and inform the adjuster that the attorney will settle the matter for X. If the adjuster comes back with a counteroffer, the nonlawyer employee must inform the attorney. The employee cannot be given a range in which to settle." *Ethically Speaking*. The Florida Bar News, September, 15, 1991, at 15.
- An attorney can allow a supervised nonattorney to conduct an initial interview of a prospective client if his or her nonattorney status is disclosed to the client and only factual information is obtained. Florida Bar, *Opinion 88–6* (4/15/88).
- Other Florida Bar Opinions involving nonattorneys: *Opinion 88–15* (10/1/88) (sharing office space with nonattorneys); *Opinion 87–11* (4/15/88) (nonattorney signing pleadings); *Opinion 70–62* (2/12/71) (a law firm cannot delegate anything that requires personal judgment to a nonattorney employee); *Opinion 68–58* (1/17/69) (nonattorney employees of a law firm can be part of a retirement plan funded from firm profits); *Opinion 73–41* (3/11/74) (nonattorneys cannot take depositions); *Opinion 76–33* (3/15/77) (an attorney must not overbill for paralegal time). *Opinion 02–1* (1/11/02) (attorney may not give a bonus to a nonlawyer employee solely based on the number of hours worked by the employee); *Opinion 02–8* (1/18/04) (attorney may not enter into a referral arrangement with a nonlawyer who is a securities dealer to refer the attorney's clients to the securities dealer, who would then pay the attorney a portion of the advisory fee for the clients referred).

DEFINING THE PRACTICE OF LAW IN FLORIDA

- *State ex rel. Florida Bar v. Sperry*, 140 So. 2d 587 (Supreme Court of Florida 1962) (vacated on other grounds 373 U.S. 379 (1963)). It is generally understood that the performance of services in representing another before the courts is the practice of law. But the practice of law also includes the giving of legal advice and counsel to others as to their rights and obligations under the law and the preparation of legal instruments, including contracts, by which legal rights are either obtained, secured or given away, although such matters may not then or ever be the subject of proceedings in a court . . . . In determining whether the giving of advice and counsel and the performance of services in legal matters for compensation constitute the practice of law it is safe to follow the rule that if the giving of such advice and performance of such services affect important rights of a person under the law, and if the reasonable protection of the rights and property of those advised and served requires that the persons giving such advice possess legal skill and a knowledge of the law greater than that possessed by the average citizen, then the giving of such advice and the performance of such services by one for another as a course of conduct constitute the practice of law.

■ Rule 10–2. 1, *Rules Regulating The Florida Bar* (West's Florida Statutes Annotated): (a) Unlicensed Practice of Law. The unlicensed practice of law shall mean the practice of law, as prohibited by statute, court rule, and case law of the State of Florida. For purposes of this chapter, it shall not constitute the unlicensed practice of law for a nonlawyer to engage in limited oral communications to assist a person in the completion of blanks on a legal form approved by the Supreme Court of Florida. Oral communications by nonlawyers are restricted to those communications reasonably necessary to elicit factual information to complete the blanks on the form and inform the person how to file the form.

FLORIDA ETHICS AND PRACTICE RULES ON THE INTERNET

- www.law.cornell.edu/ethics/florida.html
- www.sunethics.com
- www.floridabar.org (click "Lawyer Regulation")
- www.floridabar.org/tfb/TFBETOpin.nsf/ EthicsIndex?OpenForm

PARALEGALS (AND OTHER NONATTORNEYS) IN FLORIDA STATE AND FEDERAL COURTS

■ *Stewart v. Bee-Dee Neon & Signs, Inc.*, 751 So. 2d 196 (Florida District Court of Appeal, 2000) (disqualification of law firm that hired paralegal of opposing firm was improper where no evidence was presented that the paralegal actually disclosed material confidential information to hiring firm, that the paralegal would necessarily work on case, or that screening measures would be ineffective) (compare *Koulisis v. Rivers*, 730 So. 2d 289 (Florida District Court of Appeal, 1999).

■ *Eastrich No. 157 Corp. v. Gatto*, 868 So. 2d 1266 (Florida District Court of Appeals, 2004) (The fact that an individual, who had formerly worked as a legal secretary for plaintiff's counsel, was briefly used by defendant's counsel as an independent contractor in nonlegal capacity did not require disqualification of defendant's counsel in this premise's liability action. The individual worked for defendant's firm for only ten hours, over two days, entering billing data into computer, and the billing records did not concern the underlying case).

■ *Miami-Dade County v. Walker*, 948 So. 2d 68 (Florida District Court of Appeals, 2007) (Plaintiff's counsel hired a paralegal who had previously worked for defendant's counsel. While employed by defendant's counsel, this paralegal worked on the plaintiff's lawsuit. The trial court granted defendant's motion to disqualify plaintiff's counsel.)

■ *Wells Fargo Credit Corp. v. Martin*, 605 So. 2d 531 (Florida District Court of Appeal, 1992) (paralegal misreads her instructions and causes a $100,000 mistake).

■ *The Florida Bar v. Florida Service Bureau*, 581 So. 2d 900 (Supreme Court of Florida, 1991) (it is not the unauthorized practice of law for nonattorneys to give assistance to landlords by explaining what the eviction procedure entails as long a they do not give legal advice; the "information given was no greater than that which anyone could glean from reading the eviction statute").

■ *The Florida Bar v. We The People Forms and Service Center of Sarasota*, 883 So. 2d 1280 (Supreme Court of Florida, 2004) (providers of legal form preparation services engaged in the unlicensed practice of law when they provided customers with legal assistance in the selection, preparation, and completion of legal forms; corrected customers' errors or omissions; and prepared or assisted in the preparation of pleadings).

■ *In re Amendments to the Florida Rules of Judicial Admin.* 939 So. 2d 966 (Supreme Court of Florida, 2006) (the words "other person" in Rule 2.515(2) of the Florida Rules of Judicial Administration do not authorize nonattorneys to sign and file pleadings on behalf of another).

■ *The Florida Bar v. Shankman*, 908 So. 2d 379 (Supreme Court of Florida, 2005) (it is an improper sharing of fees with a nonattorney for an attorney to pay his paralegal a bonus of 7 percent of the fees generated in excess of overhead).

■ *In re Carter*, 326 Bankruptcy Reporter 892 (U.S. Bankruptcy Court, Southern District Florida, 2005) (A paralegal should be engaged in matters, under the supervision of an attorney, that require some independent judgment or are matters that an attorney would be expected to perform but can, under an attorney's supervision, be performed by an individual with specialized training or experience. Clerical functions such as typing, filing, photocopying, faxing, scanning, or filing documents either electronically or traditionally, are not such functions. Secretarial tasks are overhead expenses of the attorney and are not additionally compensable.)

■ *Watson v. Wal-Mart Stores, Inc.*, 2005 WL 1266686 (U.S. District Court, Northern District Florida, 2005) (Plaintiff alleges that the paralegal time claimed by defendant for summarizing deposition transcripts was excessive. Plaintiff specifically complains of 9.1 hours for summarizing the 110-page deposition of the plaintiff. Defendant's attorneys say their paralegals usually summarize 14 to 18 pages per hour. At that rate, a paralegal should have completed plaintiff's 110-page deposition in 6.1 to 7.9 hours. Some attorneys still have paralegals summarize depositions (a practice that developed when transcripts came without indexes, and searchable text was unheard of), and the market still sometimes pays the charge. One might reasonably question why that is so. Searchable transcripts are now readily available, and laptop computers on counsel table are commonplace. Moreover, in a slip and fall case, one wonders how hard it could be to have a command of the depositions, perhaps with Post-It notes marking key passages, without the need for separate detailed summaries. It is perhaps no coincidence that some personal injury defense attorneys and commercial litigators [who typically charge by the hour, not only for their own time, but for paralegals] choose to have detailed summaries prepared, while most personal injury plaintiff's lawyers [who are paid based only on the result] do not. With the exception of a duplicative time entry, however, the time devoted to summarizing depositions in this case was a reasonable amount of time for completing the task.)

■ *United States v. Pepper's Steel*, 742 F. Supp. 641 (U.S. District Court, S.D. Florida, 1990) (although a paralegal accidentally delivered documents to the opposing party[!], the documents are still protected by the attorney-client privilege).

■ *The Florida Bar v. Neiman*, 816 So. 2d 587 (Florida Supreme Court, 2002) (Under Rule 3–6.1 of the Rules Regulating the Florida Bar, a suspended or disbarred attorney can be an employee of a law firm with the following restriction: "No employee shall have direct contact with any client.")

■ *Florida Bar v. Furman*, 376 So. 2d 378 (Florida Supreme Court, 1979) (see discussion of this UPL case in chapter 4).

DOING LEGAL RESEARCH IN FLORIDA LAW

Statutes: www.leg.state.fl.us/Welcome/index.cfm
Cases: www.flcourts.org
Court Rules: www.llrx.com/courtrules-gen/state-Florida.html
General: www.washlaw.edu/uslaw/states/Florida/index.html

FINDING EMPLOYMENT IN FLORIDA

- legal.jobs.net/Florida.htm
- miami.craigslist.org/lgl
- hotjobs.yahoo.com/jobs/FL/legal-jobs
- www.simplyhired.com/job-search/l-Florida/o-232000/t-Paralegal

GEORGIA

DEFINING LEGAL ASSISTANTS/PARALEGALS IN GEORGIA

- [T]he terms "legal assistant", "paraprofessional" and "paralegal" are defined as any lay person, not admitted to the practice of law in this State, who is an employee of, or an assistant to, an active member of the State, who is an employee of, or an assistant to, an active member of the State Bar of Georgia or to a partnership or professional corporation comprised of active members of the State Bar of Georgia and who renders services relating to the law to such member, partnership or professional corporation under the direct control, supervision and compensation of a member of the State Bar of Georgia. State Bar of Georgia, State Disciplinary Board, *Advisory Opinion 19* (7/18/75) (www.gabar.org/public/pdf/06-07_handbook_web.pdf).

ETHICAL RULES AND GUIDELINES IN GEORGIA

- For a discussion of the state's ethical Rule 5.3 ("Responsibilities Regarding Nonlawyer Assistants") in the *Georgia Rules of Professional Conduct*, see the end of Section C in chapter 5. For the text of 5.3 in Georgia, see also www.gabar.org/handbook.
- It is the unauthorized practice of law for a law firm to allow a nonattorney to conduct a real estate closing. State Bar of Georgia, *Opinion 86–5* (5/12/89). It is not sufficient for the attorney to be available on the telephone during the course of the closing to respond to questions or to review documents. The lawyer's physical presence at a closing will assure that there is supervision of the work of the paralegal that is direct and constant. Supreme Court of Georgia, *Formal Advisory Opinion 00–3* (2/11/00).
- An attorney aids a nonlawyer in the unauthorized practice of law when the attorney allows his or her paralegal to prepare and sign correspondence that threatens legal action or provides legal advice or both. Supreme Court of Georgia, *Formal Advisory Opinion 00–2* (2/11/00).
- The payment of a monthly bonus by a lawyer to nonlawyer employees based on the gross receipts of his or her law office in addition to the nonlawyer employees' regular monthly salary is permissible. Also, nonattorney employees can be compensated pursuant to a plan that is based in whole or in part on a profit-sharing arrangement. *Formal Advisory Opinion 05–4*, 642 S.E.2d 686 (Supreme Court of Georgia, 2007).
- An attorney should not allow a paralegal to correspond with an adverse party (or the latter's agents) on the attorney's letterhead if the letter discusses legal matters that suggest or assert claims. (Routine contacts with opposing counsel not involving the merits of the case are, however, permitted.) *Advisory Opinion 19* (7/18/75).
- An attorney may delegate tasks to a paralegal that ordinarily comprise the practice of law, but only if the attorney has direct contact with the client and maintains "constant supervision" of the paralegal. The paralegal can render specialized advice on scientific or technical topics. The paralegal cannot negotiate with parties or opposing counsel on substantive issues. The paralegal's name may not appear on the letterhead or office door. The paralegal must not sign any pleadings, briefs, or other legal documents to be presented to a court. The paralegal can have a business card with the name of the firm on it if the word *paralegal* is clearly used to indicate nonattorney status. Unless previous contacts would justify the paralegal in believing that his or her nonattorney status is already known, the paralegal should begin oral communications, either face to face or on the telephone, with a clear statement that he or she is a paralegal employee of the law firm. Georgia, *Advisory Opinion 21* (9/16/77, revised 1983). (www.gabar.org/handbook/state_disciplinary_board_opinions/adv_op_21)
- Nonlawyers who represent debtors in negotiations with creditors engage in unauthorized practice of law. *In re UPL Advisory Opinion 2003–1*, 623 S.E.2d 464 (Supreme Court of Georgia, 2006).
- After a final judgment of disbarment or suspension under Part IV of these Rules . . . the respondent shall take such action necessary to cause the removal of any indicia of the respondent as a lawyer, legal assistant, legal clerk or person with similar status. In the event the respondent should maintain a presence in an office where the practice of law is conducted, the respondent shall not: (i) have any contact with the clients of the office either in person, by telephone, or in writing; or (ii) have any contact with persons who have legal dealings with the office either in person, by telephone, or in writing. *State Bar Rules and Regulations*, Rule 4–219(c)(2).

DEFINING THE PRACTICE OF LAW IN GEORGIA

- § 15–19–50 (*Code of Georgia*): The practice of law in this state is defined as: (1) Representing litigants in court and preparing pleadings and other papers incident to any action or special proceedings in any court or other judicial body; (2) Conveyancing; (3) The preparation of legal instruments of all kinds whereby a legal right is secured; (4) The rendering of opinions as to the validity or invalidity of titles to real or personal property; (5) The giving of any legal advice; and (6) Any action taken for others in any matter connected with the law.
- § 15–19–51 (*Code of Georgia*): Unauthorized practice of law forbidden.

    (a) It shall be unlawful for any person other than a duly licensed attorney at law: . . .

    (4) To render or furnish legal services or advice; . . .

    (6) To render legal services of any kind in actions or proceedings of any nature; . . .

    (8) To advertise that . . . he has, owns, conducts, or maintains an office for the practice of law or for furnishing legal advice, services, or counsel.

GEORGIA ETHICS AND PRACTICE RULES ON THE INTERNET

- www.gabar.org/ethics
- www.law.mercer.edu/library/Research/Legal%20Ethic%20Final%20Web.htm
- www.abanet.org/cpr/links.html#States

PARALEGALS (AND OTHER NONATTORNEYS) IN GEORGIA STATE AND FEDERAL COURTS

- *In re Arp*, 546 S.E.2d 486 (Supreme Court of Georgia, 2001) (attorney unethically pays a paralegal for the referral of cases and clients in violation of Standard 13 of Bar Rule 4–102, which prohibits an attorney from compensating a person or organization to recommend or secure employment by a client or as a reward for a recommendation).
- *In re Eichholz*, 2007 WL 1223613 (U.S. Court of Appeals, 11th Circuit (Georgia), 2007) (the attorney failed to supervise his employees, allowing them to engage in activities that required legal knowledge such as explaining legal documents to clients).
- *In re Gaff*, 524 S.E.2d 728 (Supreme Court of Georgia, 2000) (attorney hires a disbarred attorney but fails to take any action to ensure that disbarred attorney, working as paralegal, had no contact with his clients after the state bar had warned him of potential ethical problems that his employment of disbarred attorney might engender; one-year suspension was warranted).
- *Peters v. Hyatt Legal Services*, 469 S.E.2d 481 (Court of Appeals of Georgia, 1996) (a paralegal is sued for legal malpractice along with the law firm).
- *Cullins v. Georgia Dept. of Transportation*, 827 F. Supp. 756, 762 (U.S. District Court, M.D. Georgia, 1993) ("paralegal costs are recoverable as a part of . . . attorney's fees and expenses but only to the extent such work is the type traditionally performed by an attorney. Otherwise, paralegal expenses are separately unrecoverable overhead expenses").
- *U.S. v. Patrol Services, Inc.*, 202 Federal Appendix 357, 2006 WL 2990211 (U.S. Court of Appeals, 11th Circuit (Georgia), 2006) (paralegal fees were denied because no details were provided about the paralegal's experience).
- *In re Golf Augusta Pro Shops, Inc.*, 2004 WL 768576 (U.S. Bankruptcy Court, S.D. Georgia, 2004) (I reviewed each entry of legal assistant time to determine which tasks required the use of independent paraprofessional judgment and therefore warranted inclusion in the Applicant's Fee Application. I hold that tasks such as preparing certificates of service and preparing affidavits of service require the use of independent paraprofessional judgment. However, proof reading labels, proof reading service lists, processing notices of hearing, and processing the mail do not require that judgment. Labeling these tasks as paralegal time doesn't change the true nature of the task as secretarial and part of counsel's overhead expense included in the approved hourly rate.)
- *Morganactive Songs, Inc. v. Padgett*, 2007 WL 934609 (U.S. District Court, M.D. Georgia, 2007) Employing *six* legal professionals (four attorneys and two paralegals) on what was, in this Court's view, a rather simple copyright infringement case, lead to an unreasonable accumulation of billed hours per task. Examples of overstaffing: the lead attorney and a paralegal spent 15.3 hours drafting a boilerplate complaint, preparing the scheduling order, and engaging in other preliminary matters; two attorneys and one paralegal spent 64.58 hours researching and writing a relatively simple motion for summary judgment. Finally, the Court notes that the amount of plaintiffs' request for attorneys' fees ($58,544) is wholly disproportionate to the final $14,000 judgment plaintiffs received as the result of counsel's efforts.)

DOING LEGAL RESEARCH IN IDAHO LAW

Statutes: law.justia.com/georgia/codes
Cases: www.appeals.courts.state.ga.us/opinions/index.cgi

Court Rules: www.georgiacourts.org/courts/superior/uniform_rules.html
General: www.romingerlegal.com/state/georgia.html

FINDING EMPLOYMENT IN GEORGIA

- gap.legalstaff.com/Common/HomePage.aspx?abbr=GAP
- www.indeed.com/q-Paralegal-l-Georgia-jobs.html
- legal.jobs.net/Georgia.htm
- atlanta.craigslist.org/lgl

HAWAII

ETHICAL RULES AND GUIDELINES IN HAWAII

- For a discussion of the state's ethical Rule 5.3 ("Responsibilities Regarding Nonlawyer Assistants") in the *Hawaii Rules of Professional Conduct*, see the end of Section C in chapter 5. For the text of 5.3 in Hawaii, see also www.state.hi.us/jud/ctrules/hrpcond.htm.
- An attorney may list a paralegal on professional cards, letterhead, and professional notices or announcement cards as long as the employee is identified as a paralegal or legal assistant. A paralegal can use a business card identifying him or her as an employee of the law firm. A paralegal can sign correspondence as a paralegal. Hawaii Supreme Court Disciplinary Board, *Formal Opinion 78–8–19* (6/28/84). See also *Opinion 78–8–19–Supp.*
- The phrase "& Associates" cannot refer to nonlawyers, such as paralegals. Carole Richelieu, *Disciplinary Counsel's Report*, 1997 Hawaii Bar Journal 16 (March 1997).
- A lawyer shall not allow any person who has been suspended or disbarred and who maintains a presence in an office where the practice of law is conducted by the lawyer to have any contact with the clients of the lawyer either in person, by telephone, or in writing or to have any contact with persons who have legal dealings with the office either in person, by telephone, or in writing. *Rules of Professional Conduct*, Rule 5.5(c). Comment to the Rule: In order to protect the public, strict prohibitions are essential to prevent permissible paralegal activities from crossing the line to giving legal advice, taking fees, or misleading clients and others who deal with the attorney's office.

DEFINING THE PRACTICE OF LAW IN HAWAII

Fought & Co., Inc. v. Steel Engineering and Erection, Inc., 951 P.2d 487, 496 (Supreme Court of Hawaii, 1998): The legislature has "expressly declined to adopt a formal definition of the term "practice of law," noting that "[a]ttempts to define the practice of law in terms of enumerating the specific types of services that come within the phrase are fruitless because new developments in society, whether legislative, social, or scientific in nature, continually create new concepts and new legal problems. . . . The legislature recognized that the practice of law is not limited to appearing before the courts. It consists, among other things of the giving of advice, the preparation of any document or the rendition of any service to a third party affecting the legal rights . . . of such party, where such advice, drafting or rendition of service requires the use of any degree of legal knowledge, skill or advocacy. Similarly, . . . this court has never formally defined the term 'practice of law'."

BAR ASSOCIATION PROPOSAL FOR A NEW DEFINITION OF THE PRACTICE OF LAW SUBMITTEED TO THE SUPREME COURT OF HAWAII

(b) Definition. The "practice of law" is defined as giving legal advice or legal assistance to another person. The term "person" as used in this section refers to individuals and entities. The practice of law includes, but is not limited to:

1. Giving advice or counsel to another person as to their legal rights and obligations or the legal rights and obligations of others, in person, in writing, by telephone or any other medium.
2. Performing legal research for another person.
3. Selecting, drafting or completing documents which affect the legal rights of another person.
4. Except as otherwise allowed by statute or rule, representing another person in court, an administrative proceeding, an arbitration proceeding, hearing, deposition, or other formal or informal dispute resolution process in which legal documents are submitted and a record established as a basis for review.
5. Negotiating legal rights or obligations with others on behalf of another person,
6. Providing oral or written legal opinions.

(c) Exceptions and Exclusions: The following are not prohibited under Section (a):

1. Appearing pro se (as a party representing oneself in a matter before a tribunal).
2. Acting as a representative when authorized by law or governmental agency.
3. Serving as a neutral mediator, arbitrator, conciliator or facilitator when such service does not include rendering advice or counsel as set forth under Section (b) (1) above.
4. Acting as a legislative lobbyist.
5. The sale of legal forms by a retail commercial business.

HAWAII ETHICS AND PRACTICE RULES ON THE INTERNET

- www.law.cornell.edu/ethics/listing.html
- www.state.hi.us/jud/ctrules/hrpcond.htm
- www.law.cornell.edu/ethics/hawaii.html

PARALEGALS (AND OTHER NONATTORNEYS) IN HAWAII STATE AND FEDERAL COURTS

- *Schefke v. Reliable Collection Agency, Ltd.*, 32 P.3d 52 (Hawaii Supreme Court, 2001) (courts should reduce an award of attorney's fees for excessive preparation time by a paralegal, duplicative efforts by the attorney and paralegal, and performance of clerical functions; where there is no documentation for paralegal time, courts can decline to make award for fees).
- *Blair v. Ing*, 31 P.3d 184 (Hawaii Supreme Court, 2001) (an award of paralegal fees is limited to charges for work performed that would otherwise have been required to be performed by a licensed attorney at a higher rate; this encourages cost-effective delivery of legal services; the fees will be for legal work, not for secretarial work the paralegal may perform).
- *Tirona v. State Farm Mutual Insurance Co.*, 821 F. Supp. 632 (U.S. District Court, Hawaii, 1993) (paralegal fees denied when most of the services performed by paralegals were clerical in nature).
- *Doe ex rel. Doe v. Keala*, 361 F. Supp. 2d 1171 (U.S. District Court, Hawaii, 2005) (excessive fees: it is unreasonable to charge for a paralegal's time spent traveling to and attending a status conference when two attorneys are present).
- *Office of Disciplinary Counsel v. Au*, 113 P.3d 203 (Hawaii Supreme Court, 2005) (attorney disciplined for paying a nonattorney "runner" a fee in exchange for client referrals).
- *Hawaii v. Liuafi*, 623 P.2d 1271 (Intermediate Court of Appeals of Hawaii, 1981) (paralegal assistance to prisoners).

DOING LEGAL RESEARCH IN HAWAII LAW

Statutes: www.capitol.hawaii.gov/site1/docs/docs.asp
Cases: www.hsba.org/Legal_Research/Hawaii/cases.htm
Court Rules: www.llrx.com/courtrules-gen/state-Hawaii.html
General: www.hsba.org/Legal_Research/index.htm

FINDING EMPLOYMENT IN HAWAII

- www.indeed.com/q-Attorney-l-Hawaii-jobs.html
- jobs.careerbuilder.com/al.ic/Hawaii_Legal.htm
- www.lawcrossing.com (select Hawaii location for Legal Staff positions)
- honolulu.craigslist.org/lgl

IDAHO

ETHICAL RULES AND GUIDELINES IN IDAHO

- For a discussion of the state's ethical Rule 5.3 ("Responsibilities Regarding Nonlawyer Assistants") in the *Idaho Rules of Professional Conduct*, see the end of Section C in chapter 5. For the text of 5.3 in Idaho, see also www2.state.id.us/isb/PDF/IRPC.pdf.
- A lawyer is responsible for the professional actions of legal assistants and must take reasonable steps to ensure that they follow ethics rules governing attorneys. (Guideline 1) A lawyer can delegate tasks normally performed by lawyers unless the tasks are proscribed to one not licensed. (Guideline 2) Legal assistants cannot establish an attorney-client relationship, establish fees, or be responsible for giving a legal opinion to a client. (Guideline 3) The layer must take reasonable measures to disclose their nonattorney status. (Guideline 4) Their name and title can be on lawyer letterhead and on business cards that identify the lawyer's firm. (Guideline 5) The lawyer must take reasonable measures to ensure that legal assistants preserve confidentiality (Guideline 6) and do not create conflicts of interest based on other employment or interests. (Guideline 7) The lawyer can charge clients for the work legal assistants perform. (Guideline 8) A lawyer may not split fees with legal assistants nor pay them for referrals. Their pay cannot be contingent, by advance agreement, upon the profitability of the lawyer's practice. (Guideline 9) The lawyer should facilitate a legal assistant's participation in continuing legal education and pro bono work. (Guideline 10) *Model Guidelines for the Utilization of Legal Assistant Services* (www2.state.id.us/isb/PDF/Legasst.pdf)
- An attorney must not share fees with nonattorneys. The attorney can request compensation for the work of a paralegal or other laypersons acting under his or her supervision as long as the request specifies that laypersons performed the work. Idaho State Bar, *Formal Ethics Opinion 125.*
- A law firm cannot list legal assistants on its letterhead. Idaho State Bar, *Formal Opinion 109* (11/30/81).
- Attorneys must not split fees with nonattorneys. Idaho State Bar Committee on Ethics, *Opinion 117* (3/14/86).

DEFINING THE PRACTICE OF LAW IN IDAHO

- *Idaho State Bar v. Meservy*, 335 P.2d 62, 64 (Idaho Supreme Court, 1959): The practice of law as generally understood, is the doing or performing services in a court of justice, in any matter depending [sic] therein, throughout its various stages, and in conformity with the adopted rules of procedure. But in a larger sense, it includes legal advice and counsel, and the preparation of instruments and contracts by which legal rights are secured, although such matter may or may not be [pending] in a court. . . . The drafting of . . . documents . . . or the giving of advice and counsel with respect thereto, by one not a licensed attorney at law, would constitute an unlawful practice of law, whether or not a charge was made therefor, and even though the documents or advice are not actually employed in an action or proceeding pending in a court. I.C. § 3–104.

IMPORTANT IDAHO RULES ON PARALEGALS

- Rule 54(e)(1), *Rules of Civil Procedure*, (*West's Idaho Rules of Court*): Attorney Fees. In any civil action the court may award reasonable attorney fees, which at the discretion of the court may include paralegal fees, to the prevailing party or parties as defined in Rule 54(d)(1)(B), when provided for by any statute or contract.
- § 19–2705 (*Idaho Code*): A paralegal, as an agent of the attorney of record, is allowed to visit a defendant who has been sentenced to death. (Historical note: "The Legislature further recognizes that under American jurisprudence an adequate defense of a death penalty inmate is an interdisciplinary endeavor requiring the skills of counsel, experts, investigators and paralegals working together on the convict's behalf.")
- *Medical Recovery Services, LLC, v. Jones*, 175 P.3d 795, 800 (Court of Appeals of Idaho, 2007) Case remanded for failure to consider a request for an award of paralegal fees under I.R.C.P. 54(e) (1).

IDAHO ETHICS AND PRACTICE RULES ON THE INTERNET

- www.law.cornell.edu/ethics/idaho.html
- www2.state.id.us/isb/PDF/E2K%20Recommended%20Rules.pdf
- www2.state.id.us/isb/rules/irpc.htm

PARALEGALS (AND OTHER NONATTORNEYS) IN IDAHO STATE AND FEDERAL COURTS

- *Defendant A v. Idaho State Bar*, 25 P.3d 846 (Idaho Supreme Court, 2001) (attorney disciplined for overcharging for paralegal's work on a case).
- *In re Castorena*, 270 Bankruptcy Reporter 504 (U.S. Bankruptcy Court, Idaho, 2001) (bankruptcy attorneys may utilize paraprofessionals to assist them in rendering legal service to their clients but only if certain conditions are met: paralegals must be qualified, through training and experience, and capable of performing such services; must be adequately supervised; may not independently provide any legal advice; and may legitimately be delegated work only after attorney has first met with clients, determined what tasks need to be performed, and determined who may competently perform those tasks; also, neither attorneys nor paralegals may charge professional rates for clerical functions).
- *In re Doser*, 281 Bankruptcy Reporter 292 (U.S. Bankruptcy Court, 2002) (bankruptcy petition preparer charged with unauthorized practice of law). *In re Bush*, 275 Bankruptcy Reporter 69 (U.S. Bankruptcy Court, 2002) (Bankruptcy petition preparer improperly calls himself a "certified" independent paralegal).
- *P.O. Ventures, Inc. v. Loucks Family Irrevocable Trust*, 159 P.3d 870 (Idaho Supreme Court, 2007) (In this case, the trial judge applied Rule 54(e)(1)'s restriction that fees may only be awarded for costs associated with attorney and paralegal work, distinguishing such costs from those incurred for clerical work. The trial judge struck those items that were not properly paralegal work.)
- *Idaho State Bar v. Jenkins*, 816 P.2d 335 (Idaho Supreme Court, 1991) (an attorney was not sanctioned when his paralegal unethically solicited clients for the law firm, but without the knowledge or ratification of her attorney employer; hence there was no violation of Rule 5.3 of the code of ethics).
- *Kyle v. Beco Corp.*, 707 P.2d 378 (Idaho Supreme Court, 1985) (a party before the Industrial Commission must be represented by an attorney, if represented at all).
- *Coleman v. Idaho*, 762 P.2d 814, 817 (Idaho Supreme Court, 1988) (prison officials may not constitutionally prevent inmate paralegals from assisting illiterate inmates).
- *Idaho State Bar v. Williams*, 893 P.2d 202 (Idaho Supreme Court, 1995) (disbarred attorney as paralegal).

DOING LEGAL RESEARCH IN IDAHO LAW

Statutes: www3.state.id.us/idstat/TOC/idstTOC.html
Cases: www.isc.idaho.gov/opinions/scopins.htm
Court Rules: www.isc.idaho.gov/rulestxt.htm
General: www2.state.id.us/isb/gen/links.htm

FINDING EMPLOYMENT IN IDAHO

- www2.state.id.us/isb/job_announce/announcements.cfm
- www.indeed.com/q-Litigation-Paralegal-l-Idaho-jobs.html
- www.simplyhired.com/job-search/l-Idaho/o-232000/t-Paralegal
- boise.craigslist.org/lgl

ILLINOIS

DEFINING LEGAL ASSISTANTS/ PARALEGALS IN ILLINOIS

"Paralegal" means a person who is qualified through education, training, or work experience and is employed by a lawyer, law office, governmental agency, or other entity to work under the direction of an attorney in a capacity that involves the performance of substantive legal work that usually requires a sufficient knowledge of legal concepts and would be performed by the attorney in the absence of the paralegal. A reference in an Act to attorney fees includes paralegal fees, recoverable at market rates. 5 *Illinois Compiled Statutes Annotated* 70/1.35.

ETHICAL RULES AND GUIDELINES IN ILLINOIS

- For a discussion of the state's ethical Rule 5.3 ("Responsibilities Regarding Nonlawyer Assistants") in the *Illinois Rules of Professional Conduct*, see the end of Section C in chapter 5. For the text of 5.3 in Illinois, see also www.state.il.us/court/SupremeCourt/Rules/Art_VIII/default.asp.
- Paralegal names can be printed on a firm's letterhead. The nonattorney status of the employee must be indicated. Illinois

State Bar Ass'n, *Opinion 87–1* (9/8/87). This apparently over-rules an earlier opinion that prohibited placing a nonattorney name on letterhead. *Opinion 350.*

- Supervising attorneys must be sure their paralegals understand the rules of ethics governing attorneys. Paralegals can have contact with clients, but a direct attorney-client relationship remains primary. Paralegals must preserve confidentiality and make sure the paralegal's work does not benefit the client's adversaries. Attorneys may charge clients for paralegal services, but they may not form partnerships with paralegals. Illinois State Bar Ass'n, *Recommendations to Lawyers for the Use of Legal Assistants* (1988).

- It is professionally improper to charge an hourly rate for a salaried paralegal as an expense in addition to a percentage of recovery on a contingent fee contract. Illinois State Bar Ass'n, *Opinion 86–1* (7/7/86).

- A paralegal cannot handle phone calls involving legal matters of her law firm while at a collection agency that is one of the clients of the law firm. The law firm would not be able to supervise the paralegal. Illinois State Bar Ass'n, *Opinion 88–8* (3/15/89).

- Attorney assistants can prepare standardized deeds and other real estate documents; correspond with any party, but only to obtain factual information; and assist at real estate closings, but only in the company of a supervising attorney. Illinois State Bar Ass'n, *Position Paper on Use of Attorney Assistants in Real Estate Transactions* (approved by Board of Governors, 5/16/84).

- It is the unauthorized practice of law for a nonattorney to represent an employer before the Illinois Department of Employment Security in an unemployment compensation case in which the nonattorney prepares and presents evidence. The employer must be represented by an attorney. An attorney does not aid in the unauthorized practice of law by continuing to represent his client when the other side is represented by a nonattorney. Illinois State Bar Ass'n, *Advisory Opinion 93–15* (3/94).

- Sharing fees with a nonattorney via profit-sharing is proper provided the sharing is based on a percentage of overall firm profit and is not tied to fees in a particular case. Illinois State Bar Ass'n, *Opinion 89–5* (7/17/89).

- An attorney may not, pursuant to an arrangement with an organization that refers work to the attorney, employ the clerical or paralegal services of that organization. Illinois State Bar Ass'n, *Opinion 827* (4/1983). Also, it is professionally improper for a lawyer to participate in an arrangement with a nonlawyer whereby the lawyer obtains referrals in return for the payment of fees by the lawyer to the nonlawyer. Illinois State Bar Ass'n, *Advisory Opinion 99–02* (9/1999).

- In taking a salary from the insurance company, the lawyer must take steps to avoid the company regulating or directing his professional judgment in representing the client. The lawyer must use his independent judgment in determining the level of clerical or paralegal support and all other aspects of representation must be determined by the attorney as is necessary to properly represent the insured. Illinois State Bar Association, *Opinion 89–17* (1990).

- Upon entry of the final order of discipline, the disciplined attorney shall not maintain a presence or occupy an office where the practice of law is conducted. The disciplined attorney shall take such action necessary to cause the removal of any indicia of the disciplined attorney as lawyer, counsellor at law, legal assistant, legal clerk, or similar title. Illinois Supreme Court Rules, Rule 764.

- A paralegal can conduct a real estate closing without his or her attorney-supervisor present if no legal advice is given, if all the documents have been prepared in advance, if the attorney-supervisor is available by telephone to provide help, and if the other attorney consents. Chicago Bar Ass'n (1983).

- Legal assistants can be listed on law firm letterhead or on the door as long as their nonattorney status is clear. Chicago Bar Ass'n, *Opinion 81–4.*

DEFINING THE PRACTICE OF LAW IN ILLINOIS

- *Continental Cas. Co. v. Cuda*, 715 N.E.2d 663 (Appellate Court of Illinois, 1999): Our supreme court has described the practice of law as: "[T]he giving of advice or rendition of any sort of service by any person, firm or corporation when the giving of such advice or rendition of such service requires the use of any degree of legal knowledge or skill." *People ex rel. Illinois State Bar Ass'n v. Schafer*, 87 N.E.2d 773 (Supreme Court of Illinois, 1949).

- *In re Howard*, 721 N.E.2d 1126, 1134 (Illinois Supreme Court, 1999): determining what conduct constitutes practicing law defies mechanistic formulation. It encompasses not only court appearances, but also services rendered out of court and includes the giving of any advice or rendering of any service requiring the use of legal knowledge.

- § 205/1, chapter 705 (*Illinois Compiled Statutes Annotated*): Nothing in this Act [which restricts the practice of law to licensed attorneys] shall be construed to prohibit representation of a party by a person who is not an attorney in a proceeding before . . . the Illinois Labor Relations Board, . . . the Illinois Educational Labor Relations Board, . . . the State Civil Service Commission, . . . the University Civil Service Merit Board, to the extent allowed pursuant to rules and regulations promulgated by those Boards and Commissions.

ILLINOIS ETHICS AND PRACTICE RULES ON THE INTERNET

- www.law.cornell.edu/ethics/illinois.html
- www.law.cornell.edu/ethics/il/code
- www.isba.org/EthicsOpinions

PARALEGALS (AND OTHER NONATTORNEYS) IN ILLINOIS STATE AND FEDERAL COURTS

- *Becker v. Zellner*, 684 N.E.2d 1378 (Appellate Court of Illinois, 1997) (independent paralegals sue attorney for defamation for asserting that their work was worthless).

- *In re Estate of Divine*, 635 N.E.2d 581 (Appellate Court of Illinois, 1994) (attorney supervisors are liable for the actions of their paralegals, but the latter should not be liable for the actions of their supervisors; a paralegal does not have an independent fiduciary duty to a law firm client).

- *Kapco Mfg. Co., Inc. v. C&O Enterprises, Inc.*, 637 F. Supp. 1231 (U.S. District Court, N. D. Illinois, 1985) (disqualification of a law firm is not required simply because it hired a law office manager-secretary who had worked for opposing party at another law firm).

- *Johnson v. Thomas*, 794 N.E.2d 919 (Appellate Court of Illinois, 2003) (generally overhead office expenses, namely expenses that an attorney regularly incurs regardless of specific litigation, including telephone charges, in-house delivery charges, in-house photocopying, check processing, newspaper subscriptions, and in-house paralegal and secretarial assistance, are not recoverable as costs of litigation.)

- *Delgado v. Village of Rosemont*, 2006 WL 3147695 (U.S. District Court, 2006) (defendants argue that this court should not award fees for certain tasks that were not sufficiently complex to justify their completion by a paralegal. To award paralegal fees, a court must determine "the work was sufficiently complex to justify the efforts of a paralegal, as opposed to an employee at the next rung lower on the pay-scale ladder." A court should disallow time spent on "clerical" or "secretarial" tasks. Courts have found organizing file folders, preparing document, copying documents, assembling filings, electronically filing documents, sending materials, docketing or "logging" case events into an internal case tracking system, and telephoning court reporters to be clerical. In contrast, factual investigation, conducting legal research, summarizing depositions, checking citations, compiling statistical and financial data, preparing court documents, serving process, and discussing the case with attorneys are sufficiently complex.)

- *Shortino v. Illinois Telephone Co.*, 665 N.E.2d 414, 419 (Appellate Court of Illinois, 1996) (just because an experienced attorney is paid $350 an hour while appearing in court, he or she should not also be paid $350 per hour for tasks that could easily be done by . . . paralegals . . . at a lower hourly rate).

- *Boettcher v. Fournie Farms, Inc.*, 612 N.E.2d 969 (Appellate Court of Illinois, 1993) (confidential communications made by a client to the paralegal of the client's attorney are protected by the attorney-client privilege).

- *Voris v. Creditor's Alliance*, 2007 WL 317033 (U.S. District Court, 2007) (waiver of attorney-client privilege asserted when paralegal mistakenly faxes confidential client material).

- *Harrington v. City of Chicago*, 433 F.3d 542 (U.S. Court of Appeals, 7th Circuit, 2002) (plaintiff attorney's paralegal could not participate in the on-the-record status conference; to the extent that the paralegal was carrying a message that the attorney was in trial and unable to attend, that message was too late and should have been provided to the court and opposing counsel before the hearing; the paralegal was not licensed to practice law and could not make an appearance in court.)

- *People v. Alexander*, 202 N.E.2d 841 (Appellate Court of Illinois, 1964) (a nonattorney can appear in court for purposes of handling ministerial acts such as submitting agreed or stipulated matters) (see discussion of this case in chapter 4).

DOING LEGAL RESEARCH IN ILLINOIS LAW

Statutes: www.ilga.gov/legislation/ilcs/ilcs.asp
Cases: www.isba.org/illinoiscourts
Court Rules: www.llrx.com/courtrules-gen/state-Illinois.html
General: www.romingerlegal.com/state/illinois.html

FINDING EMPLOYMENT IN ILLINOIS

- legal.jobs.net/Illinois.htm
- www.indeed.com/q-Paralegal-l-Illinois-jobs.html
- hotjobs.yahoo.com/job-search-l-All-IL-c-Legal
- chicago.craigslist.org/lgl

INDIANA

DEFINING LEGAL ASSISTANTS/ PARALEGALS IN INDIANA

- § 6(a). As used in this section, "paralegal" means a person who is: (1) qualified through education, training, or work experience; and (2) employed by a lawyer, law office, governmental agency, or other entity; to work under the direction of an attorney in a capacity that involves the performance of substantive legal work that usually requires a sufficient knowledge of legal concepts and would be performed by the attorney in the absence of the paralegal. (b) A reference in the Indiana Code to attorney's fees includes paralegal's fees. *Indiana Code* 1–1–4–6.

ETHICAL RULES AND GUIDELINES IN INDIANA

- For a discussion of the state's ethical Rule 5.3 ("Responsibilities Regarding Nonlawyer Assistants") in the *Indiana Rules of Professional Conduct*, see the end of Section C in chapter 5. For the text of 5.3 in Indiana, see also www.in.gov/judiciary/rules/prof_conduct.

- *Rules of Professional Conduct, Use of Legal Assistants* (1993). *Guideline 9.1*: An attorney must supervise the work of the legal assistant. Independent legal assistants, to wit, those not employed by a specific firm or by specific attorney are prohibited. *Guideline 9.2*: An attorney may delegate any task to a legal assistant so long as that task is not prohibited by law. The attorney must be responsible for the work product of the legal assistant. *Guideline 9.3*: An attorney cannot delegate to a legal assistant the tasks of establishing the attorney-client relationship, setting fees, or giving legal opinions to a client. *Guideline 9.4*: The attorney has the duty to make sure the client, the courts, and other attorneys know the legal assistant is not an attorney. *Guideline 9.5*: The legal assistant's name and title can appear on the attorney's letterhead and business card that also identifies the attorney's firm. *Guideline 9.6*: The attorney must take reasonable measures to ensure the legal assistant preserves client confidences. *Guideline 9.7*: The attorney can charge for the work performed by the legal assistant. *Guideline 9.8*: An attorney may not split fees with a legal assistant or pay legal assistants for referring legal business. An attorney may compensate a legal assistant based on the quantity and quality of the legal assistant's work and the value of that work to a law practice, but the legal assistant's compensation may not be contingent, by advance agreement, upon the profitability of the attorney's practice. *Guideline 9.9*: An attorney who employs a legal assistant should facilitate the legal assistant's participation in appropriate continuing legal education and pro bono publico activities. *Guideline 9.10*: All attorneys who employ legal assistants in the State of Indiana shall assure that such legal assistants conform their conduct to be consistent with the following ethical standards: (a) A legal assistant may perform any task delegated and supervised by an attorney so long as the attorney is responsible to the client, maintains a direct relationship with the client, and assumes full professional responsibility for the work product. (b) A legal assistant shall not engage in the unauthorized practice of law. (c) A legal assistant shall serve the public interest by the improvement of the legal system. (d) A legal assistant shall achieve and maintain a high level of competence, as well as a high level of personal and professional integrity and conduct. (e) A legal assistant's title shall be fully disclosed in all business and professional communications. (f) A legal assistant shall preserve all confidential information provided by the client or acquired from other sources before, during, and after the course of the professional relationship. (g) A legal assistant shall avoid conflicts of interest and shall disclose any possible conflict to the employer or client, as well as to the prospective employers or clients. (h) A legal assistant shall act within the bounds of the law, uncompromisingly for the benefit of the client. (i) A legal assistant shall do all things incidental, necessary, or expedient for the attainment of the ethics and responsibilities imposed by statute or rule of court. (j) A legal assistant shall be governed by the American Bar Association *Model Code of Professional Responsibility* and the American Bar Association *Model Rules of Professional Conduct*.

- The above rules (particularly Guideline 9.1) on the *Use of Legal Assistants* do not prohibit the use of paralegals through temporary services, contract services, and leasing firms so long as the work on a given project is under the direct supervision of the lawyer. Indiana Bar Ass'n, *Opinion 4* (1994).

- An attorney may properly engage a contract paralegal to assist with client matters provided that such attorney (a) maintains proper supervision and control over the paralegal's work and (b) takes such action as may be necessary to satisfy the requirements of Guidelines 9.1 through 9.10. Such steps should certainly address specifically the issues of client confidentiality and conflicts of interest. Indiana Bar Association, *Opinion 3* (2000).

- An attorney can utilize a paralegal to conduct a negotiation session where no lawsuit has been filed so long as the paralegal is not responsible for rendering any legal opinions to the client. The attorney cannot however, delegate to a paralegal the representation of the client in mediation. Legal Ethics Committee of the Indiana State Bar Ass'n, *Opinion 1* (1997) (40 Res Gestae 22 (April 1997)).

- Paralegal names can be printed on a firm's letterhead if their nonattorney status is clear. The attorneys and nonattorneys must be distinguished clearly. Indiana Bar Ass'n, *Opinion 9* (1985) (overruling *Opinion 5*).

- Paralegals may have a business card as long as their capacity is stated and the identity of their employing attorney is disclosed. Indiana Bar Ass'n, *Opinion 8* (1984).

- An attorney aids an accountant in the unauthorized practice of law if the attorney prepares blank legal forms for the accountant who will help his clients fill them out without any attorney supervision. Indiana Bar Ass'n, *Opinion 2* (1995).

- Upon receiving notice of the order of suspension or disbarment, [an attorney] shall not maintain a presence or occupy an office where the practice of law is conducted. A respondent suspended for more than six (6) months or disbarred shall take such action as is necessary to cause the removal of any indicia of lawyer, counselor at law, legal assistant, law clerk or similar title. Rule 23 (*Indiana Rules for . . . the Discipline of Attorneys*): § 26(b).

DEFINING THE PRACTICE OF LAW IN INDIANA

- *Matter of Thonert*, 693 N.E.2d 559 (Supreme Court of Indiana, 1998): The core element of practicing law is the giving of legal advice to a client. Also, to practice law is to carry on the business of an attorney at law, and to make it one's business to act for, and by the warrant of, others in legal formalities, negotiations, or proceedings. A person who gives legal advice to clients and transacts business for them in matters connected with the law is engaged in the practice of law.

- *In the Matter of Fletcher*, 655 N.E.2d 58, 60 (Supreme Court of Indiana, 1995): It is the province of this Court to determine what acts constitute the practice of law. . . . The practice of law includes "the doing or performing services in a court of justice, in any matter depending therein, throughout its various stages . . . [b]ut in a larger sense it includes legal advice and counsel . . . ." The core element of practicing law is the giving of legal advice to a client and placing oneself in the very sensitive relationship wherein the confidence of the client, and the management of his affairs, is left totally in the hands of the attorney. . . . The practice of law includes the appearance in court representing another.

INDIANA ETHICS AND PRACTICE RULES ON THE INTERNET

- www.law.cornell.edu/ethics/indiana.html
- www.inbar.org/content/legalethics/legalethics2.asp
- www.inbar.org/content/commitees/standing/legalEthics.asp
- www.inbar.org/content/legalethics/legalethics.asp

PARALEGALS (AND OTHER NONATTORNEYS) IN INDIANA STATE AND FEDERAL COURTS

- *Shell Oil Co. v. Meyer*, 684 N.E.2d 504, 525 (Court of Appeals of Indiana, 1997) ("When one considers that attorneys utilize paralegals to perform tasks which might otherwise have to be accomplished by a lawyer with a higher billing rate, recovery for a paralegal's fees is hardly unreasonable").

- *Daimler Chrysler Corp. v. Franklin*, 814 N.E.2d 281 (Court of Appeals of Indiana, 2004) (In this case, the paralegal's hourly rate was $100. We find that the trial court abused its discretion in including her fees for copying and mailing documents, which is work that requires no particular knowledge of legal concepts and is more in the nature of clerical or support staff work.)

- *Eli Lilly & Co. v. Zenith*, 264 F. Supp. 2d 753 (U.S. District Court, S.D. Indiana, 2003) (defendant questions substantial amounts of time plaintiff's legal assistants spent shopping and coordinating travel arrangements and trial logistics, such as setting up the "war rooms." Defendant's criticisms are valid. Plaintiff's time records include a great deal of excessive time by legal assistants, including time devoted to clerical or other tasks for which a $100 rate is not remotely justifiable.)

- *Mayberry v. State*, 670 N.E.2d 1262 (Supreme Court of Indiana, 1996) (statement to paralegal is protected by attorney-client privilege).

- *Whitehead v. Indiana*, 511 N.E.2d 284 (Supreme Court of Indiana, 1987) (paralegal allowed to sit at counsel's table during trial).

- *In re Blumenthal*, 825 N.E.2d 374 (Supreme Court of Indiana, 2005) (attorney instructed her paralegal to alter one of the release forms plaintiff had signed by adding the name of an unnamed physician, and to alter the execution date of the document, which had expired some months before).

- *Exterior Systems v. Noble Composites*, 210 F. Supp. 2d 1062 (U.S. District Court, N.D. Indiana, 2002) (under Indiana law, conflict of interest rules do not apply to paralegals who are assisting lawyers in a law firm. Ind. Rules of Prof. Conduct, Rules 1.9, 1.10. Mills is not a lawyer; she is a paralegal. Strictly speaking, the conflict of interest rules do not apply to paralegals who are assisting the lawyers in a law firm. Instead, paralegals are governed indirectly by Rule 5.3, which imposes on the supervising lawyers the duty to ensure that their nonlawyer assistants' conduct is "compatible with the professional obligations of the lawyer.")

DOING LEGAL RESEARCH IN INDIANA LAW

Statutes: www.in.gov/legislative/ic/code
Cases: www.state.in.us/judiciary/opinions
Court Rules: www.in.gov/judiciary/rules
General: www.megalaw.com/in/in.php

FINDING EMPLOYMENT IN INDIANA

- inbar.legalstaff.com/Common/HomePage.aspx?abbr=INBAR
- legal.jobs.net/Indiana.htm
- www.indeed.com/q-Litigation-Paralegal-l-Indiana-jobs.html
- www.lawfirmstaff.com/joblistings.php?job_type_id=1

IOWA

DEFINING LEGAL ASSISTANTS/PARALEGALS IN IOWA

- *Iowa Code of Professional Responsibility*:
  - EC 3–6(4). A nonlawyer employed by a lawyer, law firm, agency or other employer may be referred to as a legal assistant if the majority of the nonlawyer's job responsibilities include duties as defined in EC 3–6(1).
  - EC 3–6(1). [Delegation is proper if for the purpose of] (a) investigation of a factual situation or consultation with a lawyer's client for the purpose, only, of obtaining factual information; or (b) legal research; or (c) preparation or selection of legal instruments and documents, provided, however, that in each such situation the delegated work will assist the employer–lawyer in carrying the matter to a completed service either through the lawyer's personal examination and approval thereof or by other additional participation by the lawyer. However, the delegated work must be such as loses its separate identity and becomes the service or is merged in the service of the lawyer.

  Note: the *Iowa Code* has been replaced by the *Iowa Rules of Professional Conduct*.

ETHICAL RULES AND GUIDELINES IN IOWA

- For a discussion of the state's ethical Rule 5.3 ("Responsibilities Regarding Nonlawyer Assistants") in the *Iowa Rules of Professional Conduct*, see the end of Section C in chapter 5. For the text of 5.3 in Iowa, see also www.judicial.state.ia.us/Professional_Regulation/Rules_of_Professional_Conduct.
- The following six guidelines are based on the *Iowa Code of Professional Responsibility*, which has been replaced by the *Iowa Rules of Professional Conduct*. A lawyer often delegates tasks required in performance of the client's legal services to clerks, secretaries and other nonlawyer personnel employed by the lawyer. Such delegation which extends beyond duties merely ministerial in nature is proper under the following circumstances:
  (1) If it is for the purposes of (a) investigation of a factual situation or consultation with a lawyer's client for the purpose, only, of obtaining factual information; or (b) legal research; or (c) preparation or selection of legal instruments and documents, provided, however, that in each such situation the delegated work will assist the employer-lawyer in carrying the matter to a completed service either through the lawyer's personal examination and approval thereof or by other additional participation by the lawyer. However, the delegated work must be such as loses its separate identity and becomes the service or is merged in the service of the lawyer.
  (2) The lawyer must maintain an initial, continuing and direct relationship with the client, directly supervise the delegated work, and assume complete professional responsibility for

the work product. This requirement must not be ignored by a lawyer or given superficial recognition.
  (3) The lawyer shall not permit employed laypersons to counsel the lawyer's clients about legal matters, appear in any court or administrative proceeding except to the extent authorized by court rule or administrative rule or regulation, or otherwise engage in the unauthorized practice of law. A lawyer should recognize the importance of being present, if practicable, when a client executes a will, contract, deed or other legal document, to insure that it is executed in compliance with the law and to answer the client's questions. A lawyer has a continuing affirmative duty to preserve and enhance the public's confidence in the legal profession. This is best accomplished when the client has direct access to a lawyer for the purpose of asking for and receiving legal advice prior to or at the time the client takes any contemplated legal action.
  (4) A nonlawyer employed by a lawyer, law firm, agency or other employer may be referred to as a legal assistant if the majority of his or her job responsibilities include duties as defined in EC 3–6 (1). Such a legal assistant and the responsible supervising lawyer are at all times subject to all the provisions of EC 3–6. Such a legal assistant may be furnished with, and use, a professional card. The card must contain the following information on its face: Name; "Legal Assistant" centered immediately below the name; the name of the lawyer, law firm, agency or other employer whose lawyer is authorizing the issuance of the card; name of the employer or agency, if applicable; address and telephone number of the attorney, law firm, agency or other employer.
  (5) When communicating with persons outside the law office, including other lawyers, a nonlawyer employed by a lawyer must disclose the nonlawyer's status. The disclosure must be made in a way that avoids confusion. With respect to oral communications, disclosure must be made at the outset of the conversation. It is permissible for layperson office personnel to sign letters on the firm's stationery as long as the nonlawyer status is clearly indicated.
  (6) The supervising lawyer must exercise care to insure nonlawyer personnel comply with all applicable provisions of the Code of Professional Responsibility. This includes the obligation referred to in DR 4–101 (D) and EC 4–2 to see that such employees preserve and refrain from using the confidence and secrets of the lawyer's clients. Ethical Consideration 3–6, *Code of Professional Responsibility*. Rule 32. EC 3–6, *Iowa Code Annotated*.

- A legal assistant to an Iowa lawyer or law firm who has met the certification requirements of the National Association of Legal Assistants may add "Certified Legal Assistant" where his or her name properly appears, but not "CLA." Using CLA alone could mislead the public, even to the point of believing it to be a legal degree. Iowa Supreme Court Board of Professional Ethics and Conduct, *Opinion 04–01* (9/11/03). This opinion changes *Opinion 88–05*.
- It is proper to sign letters with the titles *legal assistant* or *paralegal*. Iowa Supreme Court Board of Professional Ethics and Conduct, *Opinion 88–22* (12/8/89).
- Paralegals and other nonattorney employees may not be listed on the law firm letterhead. Iowa Supreme Court Board of Professional Ethics and Conduct, *Opinion 87–18* (2/2/88). The office of the county public defender may not list the names of nonattorney personnel on its letterhead. *Opinion 89–35* (12/14/89).

- A sign outside the door of a law firm may not list the name of nonattorney employees even though they are called *legal assistants*. Iowa Supreme Court Board of Professional Ethics and Conduct, *Opinion 89–23* (12/26/88). A law firm may not list its paralegals or other nonattorney employees in law directories such as *Martindale-Hubbell*. Iowa Supreme Court Board of Professional Ethics and Conduct, *Opinion 92–33* (5/27/93).

- As an incentive, a law firm can pay a paralegal a percentage of the total income it earns as long as the compensation relates to the firm's profits and not the receipt of specific legal fees. Iowa Supreme Court Board of Professional Ethics and Conduct, *Opinion 90–9* (8/23/90).

- A law firm and a departing lawyer taking a contingency fee file with him that originated with the law firm can enter into an agreement for a blanket formula to govern the value of services rendered by both attorney and legal assistants before and after the departure if the legal assistant services are computed in the formula at the usual rate charged to clients for legal assistant services and the legal assistants do not share in the allocations between the lawyers and the law firm under the formula agreement. Iowa Supreme Court Board of Professional Ethics and Conduct, *Opinion 96–11* (12/12/96).

- It would be the unauthorized practice of law for a paralegal to represent a client in Small Claims Court. Iowa Supreme Court Board of Professional Ethics and Conduct, *Opinion 89–30* (12/8/89), and *Opinion 88–18* (2/20/89). Nor can a nonattorney represent someone before the city Civil Service Commission. *Opinion 92–18* (12/3/92).

- It is unethical for an attorney to allow his or her paralegal to ask questions at a deposition even though the paralegal is supervised. Iowa Supreme Court Board of Professional Ethics and Conduct, *Opinion 96–03* (8/29/96).

- In a Section 341 bankruptcy proceeding, a paralegal cannot sit with a debtor at the counsel table in the absence of the paralegal's supervising attorney. The paralegal can help the debtor find things in the schedule but cannot counsel the debtor. Iowa Supreme Court Board of Professional Ethics and Conduct, *Opinion 92–24* (2/28/93).

- A retired attorney who is still licensed cannot function as a paralegal in a law office. Iowa Supreme Court Board of Professional Ethics and Conduct, *Opinion 94–1* (9/13/94).

DEFINING THE PRACTICE OF LAW IN IOWA

- *Iowa Supreme Court Com'n on Unauthorized Practice of Law v. Sturgeon*, 635 N.W.2d 679 (Supreme Court of Iowa, 2001). Ethical Consideration 3–5, *Code of Professional Responsibility* (*Iowa Code Annotated*): It is neither necessary nor desirable to attempt the formulation of a single, specific definition of what constitutes the practice of law. However, the practice of law includes, but is not limited to, representing another before the courts; giving of legal advice and counsel to others relating to their rights and obligations under the law; and preparation or approval of the use of legal instruments by which legal rights of others are either obtained, secured or transferred even if such matters never become the subject of a court proceeding. Functionally, the practice of law relates to the rendition of services for others that call for the professional judgment of a lawyer. The essence of professional judgment of the lawyer is the educated ability to relate the general body and philosophy of law to a specific legal problem of a client.

- Iowa Court Rules, Rule 39.7: The practice of law as that term is employed in this chapter includes the examination of abstracts, consummation of real estate transactions, preparation of legal briefs, deeds, buy and sell agreements, contracts, wills and tax returns as well as the representation of others in any Iowa courts, the right to represent others in any Iowa courts, or to regularly prepare legal instruments, secure legal rights, advise others as to their legal rights or the effect of contemplated actions upon their legal rights, or to hold oneself out to so do; or to be one who instructs others in legal rights; or to be a judge or one who rules upon the legal rights of others unless neither the state nor federal law requires the person so judging or ruling to hold a license to practice law.

IOWA ETHICS AND PRACTICE RULES ON THE INTERNET

- www.law.cornell.edu/ethics/iowa.html
- www.iowabar.org/ethics.nsf/e61beed77a215f668625649 7004ce492?OpenView

PARALEGALS (AND OTHER NONATTORNEYS) IN IOWA STATE AND FEDERAL COURTS

- *Baker v. John Morrell & Co.*, 263 F. Supp. 2d 1161 (U.S. District Court, 2003) ("counsel's efficient delegation of work to their experienced paralegal, Ms. Collins, is in part responsible for keeping costs down in this case").

- *Northeast Iowa Citizens For Clean Water v. Agriprocessors*, 489 F. Supp. 2d 881 (U.S. District Court, N.D. Iowa, 2007) (The court approves $80 an hour for legal assistants. "Although the court is not familiar with any of the legal assistants, the requested rates do not exceed prevailing market rates for such professionals.")

- *Foxley Cattle Co. v. Grain Dealers*, 142 Federal Rules Decisions 677, 681 (U.S. District Court, S.D. Iowa, 1992) (attorney's claim for 8.8 hours to prepare a motion is excessive; this document "easily could have been prepared by a legal assistant in two to three hours.").

- *Knudsen v. Barnhart*, 360 F. Supp. 2d 963 (U.S. District Court, Iowa, 2004) (the tasks of filing, serving summons, calendaring, and receiving and retrieving documents were administrative tasks, and therefore, could not be billed as paralegal time; such tasks are clerical in nature and are considered part of overhead).

- *GreatAmerica Leasing Corp. v. Cool Comfort Air Conditioning and Refrigeration*, 691 N.W.2d 730 (Supreme Court of Iowa, 2005) (the district court abused its discretion insofar as it adopted a policy capping fees for all paralegals in civil cases; Iowa Code § 625.22 contains no such requirement.)

- *The CBE Group v. Anderson*, 2007 WL 2120278 (Court of Appeals of Iowa, 2007) (We "note with concern the notion of a legal assistant representing a client at a pretrial conference.")

- *Doyle v. First Federal Credit Union*, 2007 WL 1231809 (U.S. District Court, N.D. Iowa, 2007) (the notes taken by the legal assistant constitute attorney work product and are generally not discoverable).

- *Mlynarik v. Bergantzel*, 675 N.W.2d 584 (Supreme Court of Iowa, 2004) (a contingency fee agreement between former client and a nonlawyer, under which the nonlawyer agreed to negotiate the settlement of a personal injury case, was unenforceable as against public policy; accordingly, the former client was entitled to recover the fees paid pursuant to the illegal contract).

- *Committee on Professional Ethics . . . v. Lawler*, 342 N.W.2d 486 (Supreme Court of Iowa, 1984) (attorney disciplined for fee splitting with a nonattorney and failing to supervise his paralegal).

DOING LEGAL RESEARCH IN IOWA LAW

Statutes: www.legis.state.ia.us
Cases: http: www.judicial.state.ia.us
Court Rules: www.legis.state.ia.us/Rules2.html
General: www.lexisone.com/legalresearch/legalguide/states/iowa.htm

FINDING EMPLOYMENT IN IOWA

- legal.jobs.net/Iowa.htm
- www.simplyhired.com/job-search/l-Iowa/o-232000/t-Paralegal
- www.indeed.com/q-Paralegal-l-Iowa-jobs.html
- hotjobs.yahoo.com/job-JT6EGUFR1SV-l-Iowa_City-IA-c-Legal

KANSAS

DEFINING LEGAL ASSISTANTS/PARALEGALS IN KANSAS

A legal assistant or paralegal is a person, qualified by education, training, or work experience who is employed or retained by a lawyer, law office, corporation, governmental agency or other entity and who performs specifically delegated substantive legal work for which a lawyer is responsible. Kansas Bar Association, *Official Standards and Guidelines for the Utilization of Legal Assistants/Paralegals in Kansas* (2004) (www.ksbar.org/pdf/laguidelines.pdf).

ETHICAL RULES AND GUIDELINES IN KANSAS

- For a discussion of the state's ethical Rule 5.3 ("Responsibilities Regarding Nonlawyer Assistants") in the *Kansas Rules of Professional Conduct*, see the end of Section C in chapter 5. For the text of 5.3 in Kansas, see also www.kscourts.org/ctruls/atrul.htm.

- Kansas Bar Association, *Official Standards and Guidelines for the Utilization of Legal Assistants/Paralegals in Kansas* (2004) (www.ksbar.org/pdf/laguidelines.pdf). *Guideline I*: An attorney shall not permit a legal assistant/paralegal to give legal advice or to engage in the practice of law except as provided for herein. *Guideline II*: An attorney shall not permit a legal assistant/paralegal to represent a client before any court or administrative agency, nor shall a legal assistant/paralegal sign any pleading, paper, or document filed on behalf of a client with any court or agency unless expressly permitted by statute or administrative regulation. *Guideline III*: An attorney should exercise care to prevent a legal assistant/paralegal from engaging in conduct which would involve the attorney in a violation of the Kansas Rules of Professional Conduct (Rules) or which would result in the loss of designation for the legal assistant/paralegal. *Guideline IV*: Except as otherwise prohibited by statute, court rule or decision, administrative rule or regulation, or by the Rules or these guidelines, an attorney may permit a legal assistant/paralegal to perform services in representation of a client provided: A. the client is fully informed and understands that the legal assistant/paralegal is not an attorney; B. the attorney remains fully responsible for such representation, including all actions taken or not taken by the legal assistant/paralegal; C. the attorney maintains a direct relationship with the client; and D. the attorney supervises the performance of the legal assistant/paralegal. *Guideline V*: An attorney shall instruct the legal assistant/paralegal to preserve the confidences and secrets of a client. *Guideline VI*: An attorney shall not share fees with a legal assistant/paralegal. Comment: This guideline is not intended to deny legal assistants/paralegals salaries, bonuses, or benefits, even though they may be tied to the profitability of the firm. It prohibits any form of compensation directly tied to the existence or amount of a particular legal fee. The legal assistant/paralegal should not be compensated for the recommendation of the attorney's services or be deprived of compensation because of the lack of such referrals. *Guideline VII*: An attorney shall not form a partnership with a legal assistant/paralegal if any of the activities of such partnership consist of the practice of law. *Guideline VIII*: A legal assistant/paralegal may have business cards and may be included on the letterhead of an attorney or law firm with their nonattorney status designated. *Guideline IX*: An attorney shall instruct the legal assistant/paralegal to disclose at the beginning of any professional contact that the legal assistant/paralegal is not an attorney. *Guideline X*: An attorney is responsible to ensure that no personal, social, or business interest or relationship of the legal assistant/paralegal conflicts with the services rendered to the client.

- Legal assistants may be listed on law firm letterhead if their nonattorney status is clear and they have achieved some minimal training as a legal assistant over and above that customarily given legal secretaries. Supervised nonattorney employees may also have their own business cards. Kansas Bar Ass'n, *Opinion 92–15* (12/2/92). This overrules *Opinion 88–02* (7/15/88), which did *not* allow legal assistant names on attorney letterhead. See also *Opinion 82–38* (11/4/82).

- A legal assistant can use a business card that prints the name of his or her law firm if the legal assistant is identified as such. Kansas Bar Ass'n, *Opinion 85–4*. This overrules *Opinion 84–18*.

- A disbarred or suspended attorney can work as a paralegal if his or her functions are limited exclusively to work of a preparatory nature under the supervision of a licensed attorney-employer and does not involve client contact. *In re Juhnke*, 41 P.3d 855 (Supreme Court of Kansas, 2002).

DEFINING THE PRACTICE OF LAW IN KANSAS

- *State ex rel. Stephan v. Williams*, 793 P.2d 234, 240 (Supreme Court of Kansas, 1990): In determining what constitutes the "practice of law" no precise, all-encompassing definition is advisable, even if it were possible. Every matter asserting the unauthorized practice of law must be considered on its own facts on a case-by-case basis. . . . "As the term is generally understood, the practice of law is the doing or performing of services in a court of justice, in any matter depending therein, throughout its various stages, and in conformity to the adopted rules of procedure. But in a larger sense it includes legal advice and counsel, and the preparation of legal instruments and contracts by which legal rights are secured, although such matters may or may not be depending in a court." . . . [T]he practice of law [is] "the rendition of services requiring the knowledge and application of legal principles and technique to serve the interests of another with his consent."

KANSAS ETHICS AND PRACTICE RULES ON THE INTERNET

- www.law.cornell.edu/ethics/kansas.html
- www.kscourts.org/ctruls/atrul226.htm
- www.ksbar.org/public/legislative/ethics_request.shtml

PARALEGALS (AND OTHER NONATTORNEYS) IN KANSAS STATE AND FEDERAL COURTS

- *Zimmerman v. Mahaska Bottling Co.*, 19 P.3d 784 (Supreme Court of Kansas, 2001) (when a nonlawyer moves from one private firm to another where the two firms are involved in pending litigation and represent adverse parties, a firm may avoid disqualification if (1) the nonlawyer employee has not acquired material and confidential information regarding the litigation or (2) if the client of the former firm waives disqualification and approves of the use of a screening device or Chinese wall).
- *In re Arabia*, 19 P.3d 113 (Supreme Court of Kansas, 2001) (attorney gave his paralegals too little direction and supervision regarding the quantity of research they performed).
- *Satterlee v. Allen Press*, 455 F. Supp. 2d 1236 (U.S. District Court, Kansas, 2006) (although counsel contends that the documents were not filed because their large size exceeded the maximum amount allowed by the electronic filing system and this was the fault of his legal assistant, counsel bears responsibility for this oversight).
- *MomsWin, LLC v. Lutes*, 2003 WL 21077437 (U.S. District Court, Kansas, 2003) (the legal assistant notarized a signature that she apparently knew was not genuine. "This is a serious violation of a notary's duties which the Court must report" to the state.)
- *In re Lady Baltimore Foods*, 2004 WL 2192368 (U.S. Bankruptcy Court, Kansas 2004) (the use of paralegals can be especially valuable when they render legal services, such as the research of legal issues or drafting legal pleadings, at less cost than if those same services were performed by an attorney. Yet counsel should explain why certain tasks in this case were delegated to a highly paid paralegal, instead of being absorbed in the firm's overhead by a competent legal secretary.)
- *Erickson v. City of Topeka*, 239 F. Supp. 2d 1202 (U.S. District Court, Kansas, 2002) (the prevailing party in this civil rights action was not entitled to recover fees for time spent by paralegal, where the paralegal did not itemize his billings, but instead lumped all his tasks together in a generalized description, and the tasks described were largely clerical in nature).

DOING LEGAL RESEARCH IN KANSAS LAW

Statutes: www.kslegislature.org/legsrv-statutes/index.do
Cases: www.kscourts.org/kscases
Court Rules: www.kscourts.org/ctruls
General: www.washlaw.edu/uslaw/states/Kansas

FINDING EMPLOYMENT IN KANSAS

- ksbar.legalstaff.com/Common/HomePage. aspx?abbr=KSBAR
- www.indeed.com/q-Paralegal-l-Kansas-jobs.html
- www.simplyhired.com/job-search/l-Kansas/o-232000/ t-Paralegal
- jobs.careerbuilder.com/al.ic/Kansas_Legal.htm

KENTUCKY

DEFINING LEGAL ASSISTANTS/ PARALEGALS IN KENTUCKY

A paralegal is a person under the supervision and direction of a licensed lawyer, who may apply knowledge of law and legal procedures in rendering direct assistance to lawyers engaged in legal research; design, develop or plan modifications or new procedures, techniques, services, processes or applications; prepare or interpret legal documents and write detailed procedures for practicing in certain fields of law; select, compile and use technical information from such references as digests, encyclopedias or practice manuals; and analyze and follow procedural problems that involve independent decisions. Kentucky Paralegal Code, *Supreme Court Rule 3.700* (www.kybar.org/documents/scr/scr3/ scr_3.700.pdf).

ETHICAL RULES AND GUIDELINES IN KENTUCKY

- For a discussion of the state's ethical Rule 5.3 ("Responsibilities Regarding Nonlawyer Assistants") in the *Kentucky Rules of Professional Conduct*, see the end of Section C in chapter 5. For the text of 5.3 in Kentucky, see also www.kybar.org/ Default.aspx?tabid=237.
- The letterhead of an attorney can include the name of a paralegal. An attorney's name can appear on the business card of a paralegal if the latter's nonattorney status is clear. An attorney shall not share, on a proportionate basis, legal fees with a paralegal. When dealing with a client, a paralegal must disclose at the outset that he or she is not an attorney. This disclosure must be made to anyone who may have reason to believe that the paralegal is an attorney or is associated with an attorney. Kentucky Paralegal Code, *Supreme Court Rule 3.700.*
- A paralegal can be outside the office alone talking with clients if: (1) it is made clear that the paralegal is not a lawyer; (2) the lawyer discusses the specific issues with the paralegal both before the paralegal-client discussions and afterwards; and (3) the attorney accepts full responsibility for the paralegal's actions and advice. Kentucky Bar Association, *KBA U-47* (1994).
- Without client consent, it is unethical for an attorney to charge a client for paralegal services when the attorney's contract with the client calls for a statutory-set fee, a lump sum fee, or a contingent fee. The attorney who charges an hourly rate *can* charge for paralegal services, which may be separately stated. Kentucky Bar Ass'n, *Opinion E-303* (5/1985).
- To avoid disqualification, a law firm that hires a paralegal who brings a conflict of interest because of prior employment must screen the paralegal from the case in which the conflict arises and take other steps to avoid a breach of confidentiality. Kentucky Bar Ass'n, *Opinion E-308* (1985).
- A paralegal cannot appear in court on motion day or for the motion docket. Kentucky Bar Ass'n, *Opinion E-227* (1/80).
- A lay assistant cannot take (i.e., conduct) a deposition. Kentucky Bar Ass'n, *Opinion E-341* (1990).
- Independent paralegals cannot provide legal services to the public without attorney supervision. Kentucky Bar Ass'n, *Opinion U-45* (1992).
- A nonattorney cannot represent a corporation except in small claims court. Kentucky Bar Ass'n, *Opinion E-344* (1991).
- A nonattorney nurse ombudsman cannot represent a nursing home patient before an administrative agency unless federal law allows it. Kentucky Bar Ass'n, *Opinion U-46* (1994).
- An attorney may agree to insurance company guidelines establishing an appropriate allocation of lawyer and nonlawyer/paralegal tasks, but not agree that all investigative work or all records review will be performed only by the insurer's employees or, if performed by the lawyer's firm, to be billed only at a paralegal rate. Kentucky Bar Ass'n, *Opinion E-416* (3/2001).

- A suspended attorney may work in a law firm as a paralegal after the period of his suspension has expired, even if he has not been reinstated. Kentucky Bar Ass'n, *Opinion E-336* (9/1989).

DEFINING THE PRACTICE OF LAW IN KENTUCKY

§ 3.020 (*Rules of the Kentucky Supreme Court*): The practice of law is any service rendered involving legal knowledge or legal advice, whether of representation, counsel or advocacy in or out of court, rendered in respect to the rights, duties, obligations, liabilities, or business relations of one requiring the services. But nothing herein shall prevent any natural person not holding himself out as a practicing attorney from drawing any instrument to which he is a party without consideration unto himself therefor. An appearance in the small claims division of the district court by a person who is an officer of or who is regularly employed in a managerial capacity by a corporation or partnership which is a party to the litigation in which the appearance is made shall not be considered an unauthorized practice of law.

ADDITIONAL KENTUCKY LAWS ON PARALEGALS

- Rule 6.24, *Kentucky Rules of Criminal Procedure* (*Kentucky Revised Statutes Annotated*): (Prior judicial approval for grand jury subpoena of an attorney or attorney's agent to obtain evidence concerning attorney's client.) A prosecutor shall not in comparable circumstances subpoena an agent of the attorney, such as an investigator or a paralegal, without prior judicial approval.
- Rule 18, *Rules of Court* (*Kentucky Revised Statutes Annotated*): Uniform Local Rules of the Circuit and District Courts of Boone, Campbell, Gallatin and Kenton Counties. *B.* Persons Permitted Inside the Bar of the Courtroom. Unless otherwise ordered by the Court, in all proceedings held in open Court, only the parties, the witnesses when actually testifying, the jury, if any, attorneys duly admitted to practice before the Court and paralegals or legal assistants working under their direction, the sheriff and/or deputies, the clerk and/or deputies, bailiffs; and other officers and employees with the Court's permission shall be permitted inside the bar of the courtroom.

KENTUCKY ETHICS AND PRACTICE RULES ON THE INTERNET

- www.law.cornell.edu/ethics/kentucky.html
- www.law.cornell.edu/ethics/ky/code
- www.kybar.org/Default.aspx?tabid=463
- www.uky.edu/Law/Library/ky_ethics_opinions.html

PARALEGALS (AND OTHER NONATTORNEYS) IN KENTUCKY STATE AND FEDERAL COURTS

- *Turner v. Kentucky Bar Ass'n*, 980 S.W. 2d 560 (Supreme Court of Kentucky, 1998) (a statute authorizing nonlawyers to represent parties in worker's compensation proceedings violated constitutional principle of separation of powers; nonlawyer worker's compensation specialists did not engage in unauthorized practice of law when processing claims while supervised by an attorney; nonlawyers could not represent parties before any adjudicative tribunal).
- *Wal-Mart Stores, Inc. v. Dickinson*, 29 S.W.3d 796 (Supreme Court of Kentucky, 2000) (work product prepared by a paralegal is protected with equal force by attorney work product rule as is any trial preparation material prepared by an attorney in anticipation of litigation; the attorney-client privilege applies with equal force to paralegals).

- *Wyatt, Tarrant & Combs v. Williams*, 892 S.W.2d 584 (Supreme Court of Kentucky, 1995) (paralegal works on tobacco litigation at law firm; when the paralegal stopped working at the firm, he took copies of some of the tobacco litigation documents with him; law firm seeks injunction against the paralegal to prevent disclosure of the contents of these "stolen" documents). (See discussion of this case in chapter 5.)
- *Kentucky Bar Ass'n v. Legal Alternatives, Inc.*, 792 S.W.2d 368 (Supreme Court of Kentucky, 1990) (independent paralegals sued for unauthorized practice of law).
- *In re Belknap, Inc.*, 103 Bankruptcy Reporter 842, 844 (U.S. Bankruptcy Court, W.D. Kentucky, 1989) (in the award of fees: "Senior partners should not perform services which could be as competently performed by associates or paralegals; paralegals should not be used to perform tasks which are clerical in nature").
- *Sawyer v. Mills*, 2007 WL 1113038 (Court of Appeals of Kentucky, 2007) (a paralegal's secret tape-recording of the conversation with an attorney in which the attorney promised to pay her a bonus of $1 million for her help on class action lawsuits did not satisfy the writing requirement of the statute of frauds).
- *Countrywide Home Loans, Inc. v. Kentucky Bar Ass'n*, 113 S.W.3d 105 (Supreme Court of Kentucky, 2003) (a "real estate closing" is at best ministerial in nature. Some lawyers allow secretaries and paralegals to participate in closings. The closing, which consists mainly of financial matters, payments, schedules of payment, and insurance, is basically a nonlegal function. So long as the layperson avoids the giving of legal advice, there is no problem with a lay employee closing a real estate transaction. The rub that frequently arises in a real estate closing situation is that often questions of a legal nature are posed to the layman who is closing the transaction. Any response would constitute legal advice and would be the unauthorized practice of law by the person answering the questions. In such an instance, the layperson should discontinue the closing and seek proper legal advice. It should be observed that many federal loans involve significant knowledge of the law, and questions as to what is meant in the documents would certainly involve the unauthorized practice of law.)

DOING LEGAL RESEARCH IN KENTUCKY LAW

Statutes: www.lrc.ky.gov/krs/titles.htm
Cases: courts.ky.gov/courts
Court Rules: kyrules.west.thomson.com/home/kyrules/default.wl
General: www.washlaw.edu/uslaw/states/Kentucky/index.html

FINDING EMPLOYMENT IN KENTUCKY

- loubar.org/placement_overview.cfm
- legal.jobs.net/Kentucky.htm
- www.simplyhired.com/job-search/l-Kentucky/o-232000/t-Paralegal
- lexington.craigslist.org/lgl

LOUISIANA

ETHICAL RULES AND GUIDELINES IN LOUISIANA

- For a discussion of the state's ethical Rule 5.3 ("Responsibilities Regarding Nonlawyer Assistants") in the *Louisiana Rules of Professional Conduct*, see the end of Section C in chapter 5. For the text of 5.3 in Louisiana, see also www.law.cornell. edu/ethics/la/code.

- An attorney may pay a paralegal or legal assistant a salary and charge clients for their services at a rate greater than their actual salary. *Docket: 96–00068.*
- An attorney engaged in debt collection may not pay a non-lawyer a salary plus a bonus that is linked to increased revenues in the collections area. *Docket: 95–00098.*
- A lawyer shall not . . . employ, contract with as a consultant, engage as an independent contractor, or otherwise join in any other capacity, in connection with the practice of law, any person the attorney knows or reasonably should know is a suspended attorney, during the period of suspension, unless first preceded by the submission of a fully executed employment registration statement to the Office of Disciplinary Counsel, on a registration form provided by the Louisiana Attorney Disciplinary Board, and approved by the Louisiana Supreme Court. *Rules of Professional Conduct*, Rule 5.5(e)(1)(ii).

DEFINING THE PRACTICE OF LAW IN LOUISIANA

§ 37:212 (*West's Louisiana Statutes Annotated*): A. The practice of law means and includes: (1) In a representative capacity, the appearance as an advocate, or the drawing of papers, pleadings or documents, or the performance of any act in connection with pending or prospective proceedings before any court of record in this state; or (2) For a consideration, reward, or pecuniary benefit, present or anticipated, direct or indirect; (a) The advising or counseling of another as to secular law; (b) In behalf of another, the drawing or procuring, or the assisting in the drawing or procuring of a paper, document, or instrument affecting or relating to secular rights; (c) The doing of any act, in behalf of another, tending to obtain or secure for the other the prevention or the redress of a wrong or the enforcement or establishment of a right; or (d) Certifying or giving opinions as to title to immovable property or any interest therein or as to the rank or priority or validity of a lien, privilege or mortgage as well as the preparation of acts of sale, mortgages, credit sales or any acts or other documents passing titles to or encumbering immovable property.

B. Nothing in this Section prohibits any person from attending to and caring for his own business, claims, or demands; or from preparing abstracts of title; or from insuring titles to property, movable or immovable, or an interest therein, or a privilege and encumbrance thereon, but every title insurance contract relating to immovable property must be based upon the certification or opinion of a licensed Louisiana attorney authorized to engage in the practice of law. Nothing in this Section prohibits any person from performing, as a notary public, any act necessary or incidental to the exercise of the powers and functions of the office of notary public, as those powers are delineated in Louisiana Revised Statutes of 1950, Title 35, Section 1, et seq.

C. Nothing in this Section shall prohibit any partnership, corporation, or other legal entity from asserting any claim, not exceeding five thousand dollars, or defense pertaining to an open account or promissory note, or suit for eviction of tenants on its own behalf in the courts of limited jurisdiction on its own behalf through a duly authorized partner, shareholder, office, employee, or duly authorized agent or representative. No partnership, corporation, or other entity may assert any claim on behalf of another entity or any claim assigned to it.

LOUISIANA ETHICS AND PRACTICE RULES ON THE INTERNET

- www.law.cornell.edu/ethics/louisiana.html
- www.lsba.org/committees/ethics_advisory_service_commit.asp
- www.ladb.org

PARALEGALS (AND OTHER NONATTORNEYS) IN LOUISIANA STATE AND FEDERAL COURTS

- *T.S.L. v. G.L.*, 976 So. 2d 793 (Court of Appeals of Louisiana, 2008) (here, a paralegal employed by the attorney for respondent had prior access to relator's privileged information while working for relator's former counsel. Therefore, because respondent's counsel is responsible for the conduct of her employees and because her paralegal has a direct conflict of interest in this case, this conflict disqualifies her from representing respondent.)
- *In re Watley*, 802 So. 2d 593 (Supreme Court of Louisiana, 2001) (an attorney's entry into a contract calling for fee splitting with an agency providing secretarial and paralegal support violated disciplinary rule prohibiting fee sharing with nonlawyers (see also *"We the People" Paralegal' Services v. Watley* 766 So. 2d 744 (Court of Appeals of Louisiana, 2000)).
- *State v. Diaz*, 708 So. 2d 1192 (Court of Appeal of Louisiana, 1998) (paralegal tells authorities of possible fraud committed by her attorney supervisor).
- *Louisiana State Bar v. Edwins*, 540 So. 2d 294 (Supreme Court of Louisiana, 1989) (an attorney can be disbarred for delegating too much to a paralegal and for failing to supervise the paralegal).
- *Louisiana State Bar v. Lindsay*, 553 So. 2d 807 (Supreme Court of Louisiana, 1989) (an attorney charged with professional misconduct tries to shift the blame to his paralegal).
- *United States v. Cabra*, 622 F. 2d 182 (U.S. Circuit Court, 5th Circuit, 1980) (it is improper to impound a paralegal's trial notes taken during a federal trial).
- *In re Coney*, 891 So. 2d 658 (Supreme Court of Louisiana, 2005) (attorney tries to convince his legal assistant to lie to a federal grand jury that was investigating the attorney's activities).
- *Kelly v. Housing Authority of New Orleans*, 826 So. 2d 571 (Court of Appeals of Louisiana, 2002) (A paralegal was allowed to testify for the sole purpose of introducing photographs he took of the alleged accident site. The only proof offered that these photographs were of the accident site was the paralegal's testimony that Ms. Kelly told him where she had fallen. What Ms. Kelly told the paralegal is clearly inadmissible hearsay.)
- *Stagner v. Western Kentucky Navigation*, 2004 WL 253453 (U.S. District Court, 2004) (The cost of paralegal services are to be included in the assessment and award of attorney's fees if the following criteria are met: (1) The services performed must be legal in nature. (2) The performance of such services by the paralegal must be supervised by an attorney. (3) The qualifications of the paralegal performing the services must be specified in the application or motion requesting an award of fees in order to demonstrate that the paralegal is qualified by virtue of education, training, or work experience to perform substantive work. (4) The nature of the services performed by the paralegal must be specified in the application/motion requesting an award of fees in order to permit a

determination that the services performed were legal rather than clerical in nature. (5) The amount of time expended by the paralegal in performing the services must be reasonable and must be set out in the motion. (6) The amount charged for the time spent by the paralegal must reflect reasonable community standards of remuneration.)

- *Hanley v. Doctors Hosp. of Shreveport*, 821 So. 2d 508 (Court of Appeals of Louisiana, 2002) (In reviewing the time sheets for the paralegal services, we note numerous entries labeled as "summarize depositions," "preparation for trial" and "work on exhibit books." Such general labels do not give the court sufficient information to determine the specific service performed or whether the work was reasonably necessary.)

DOING LEGAL RESEARCH IN LOUISIANA LAW

Statutes: www.legis.state.la.us
Cases: www.megalaw.com/la/lacases.php
Court Rules: www.megalaw.com/la/larules.php
General: www.romingerlegal.com/state/louisiana.html

FINDING EMPLOYMENT IN LOUISIANA

- www.shuart.com
- legal.jobs.net/Louisiana.htm
- neworleans.craigslist.org/lgl
- www.simplyhired.com/job-search/l-Louisiana/ o-232000/t-Paralegal

MAINE

DEFINING LEGAL ASSISTANTS/ PARALEGALS IN MAINE

- "Paralegal" and "legal assistant" mean a person, qualified by education, training or work experience, who is employed or retained by an attorney, law office, corporation, governmental agency or other entity and who performs specifically delegated substantive legal work for which an attorney is responsible. 4 *Maine Revised Statutes Annotated* § 921(1).
- (1) A person may not use the title "paralegal" or "legal assistant" unless the person meets the definition in section 921, subsection 1. (2) A person who violates subsection 1 commits a civil violation for which a forfeiture of not more than $1000 may be adjudged. 4 *Maine Revised Statutes Annotated* §§ 922.

ETHICAL RULES AND GUIDELINES IN MAINE

- The names of paralegals can be printed on a firm's letterhead as long as it is not misleading. Maine Board of Overseers of the Bar, *Opinion 34* (1/17/83).
- An attorney cannot form a partnership or professional corporation with a nonattorney to provide legal and nonlegal services to clients. Maine Board of Overseers of the Bar, *Opinion 79* (5/6/87).
- Attorneys have a responsibility to adequately train, monitor and discipline nonattorney staff on ethics. Here a secretary revealed confidential information. Yet there is no indication that this was due to the attorney's failure to use reasonable care to prevent such disclosure. Maine Board of Overseers of the Bar, *Opinion 134* (9/21/93).
- Secretaries, paralegals and other non-legal staff members frequently leave one law firm and later work for another. A law firm must be sensitive to potential conflicts of interest when hiring non-legal staff members. Accordingly, the lawyer or

law firm during the hiring process should make reasonable efforts to obtain information to determine whether there is a potential for conflicts and have systems and procedures in place to detect and manage conflicts after a new employee joins the firm. Assume that Law Firm A hires a new secretary. The secretary previously worked for Law Firm B. While at Law Firm B, the secretary worked on matters for Client X. After the secretary joins Law Firm A, the firm is retained to represent Client Y in litigation against Client X. The secretary was privy to confidential information pertaining to Client X that is relevant to the pending litigation and that was acquired through the prior employment with Law Firm B. We believe that screening of non-lawyer staff employed by a law firm is generally permissible to avoid conflicts of interest presented by that staff. The exceptions are when the confidential information has already been revealed by the non-legal staff member or when screening would be ineffective. Assume that a law firm paralegal is a member of the Board of a non-profit entity against which the paralegal's law firm is now involved in litigation. The paralegal should be shielded from any involvement in or knowledge about the case, and should be instructed to abstain from any involvement in discussion or decision making in his or her capacity as a Board member of the non-profit entity with respect to issues related to the case. Other precautionary measures may also be necessary to avoid the risk that the personal interests of the paralegal or the paralegal's obligations to the non-profit entity might in some way adversely affect the representation provided by the lawyer or firm or might otherwise cause harm to the client. We also suggest that the Maine lawyer consider whether disclosure of conflict-like nonlawyer assistant relationships should be made to the lawyer's client. Maine Board of Overseers of the Bar, *Opinion 186* (7/22/04).

- A law firm can set up a profit-sharing compensation arrangement under which the firm will make quarterly distributions out of the profits of the partnership directly to nonattorneys employed by the firm in addition to their regular pay provided that the amounts paid to lay employees in addition to fixed salary (1) are not based upon business brought to the law firm by such employees; (2) are not based upon services performed by such employees in a particular case; and (3) do not constitute the greater part of the total remuneration of such employees. Maine Board of Overseers of the Bar, *Opinion 31* (9/22/82).

DEFINING THE PRACTICE OF LAW IN MAINE

- *Board of Overseers of the Bar v. Mangan*, 763 A. 2d 1189 (Supreme Judicial Court of Maine, 2001): The term "practice of law" is a term of art connoting much more than merely working with legally-related matters. The focus of the inquiry is, in fact, whether the activity in question required legal knowledge and skill in order to apply legal principles and precedent. Even where trial work is not involved but the preparation of legal documents, their interpretation, the giving of legal advice, or the application of legal principles to problems of any complexity, is involved, these activities are still the practice of law. The practice of law includes utilizing legal education, training, and experience to apply the special analysis of the profession to a client's problem. The hallmark of the practicing lawyer is responsibility to clients regarding their affairs, whether as advisor, advocate, negotiator, as intermediary between clients, or as evaluator by examining a client's legal affairs. As attorneys' roles increase in complexity and overlap with other professions, the answer to [the question of what constitutes the practice of law] will continue to evolve. Ultimately, the question will turn on the specific facts of the work undertaken and the understanding of the parties. (Internal cites omitted).

- 4 *Maine Revised Statutes Annotated* § 807(1)&(3) No person may practice law unless that person has been admitted to the bar of this State. This section shall not apply to:
  - a nonattorney employee of designated companies who appears for the company in a small claims action;
  - a nonattorney who is represents a party in any hearing before the Workers' Compensation Board.

MAINE ETHICS AND PRACTICE RULES ON THE INTERNET

- www.law.cornell.edu/ethics/maine.html
- www.mebaroverseers.org/Ethics%20Opinions/Index-A-Z.htm

PARALEGALS (AND OTHER NONATTORNEYS) IN MAINE STATE AND FEDERAL COURTS

- *Maine v. DeMotte*, 669 A.2d 1331 (Supreme Judicial Court of Maine, 1996) (Chinese wall built around paralegal to prevent disclosure of privileged communications and a conflict of interest).
- *First NH Banks Granite State v. Scarborough*, 615 A.2d 248, 251 (Supreme Judicial Court of Maine, 1992) (allows paralegal fees; we "adopt no talismanic formula with regard to the inclusion of paralegal fees").
- *Brennan v. Barnhart*, 2007 WL 586794 (U.S. District Court, Maine, 2007) (While counsel may have preferred to organize the files himself, the work could have been performed by a paralegal. Fee reduction ordered.)
- *St. Hilaire v. Industrial Roofing Corp.*, 416 F. Supp. 2d 137 (U.S. District Court, 2006) (Plaintiff requests $7,826.50 relating to work on discovery issues. Of this, $1,310 is attributed to paralegal work. As this court has previously held, such work is not recoverable as attorneys' fees).
- *Okot ex rel. Carlo v. Conicelli*, 180 F. Supp. 2d 238 (U.S. District Court, Maine, 2002) (This Court has previously expressed its view that charges for the work of paralegals "are properly included in firm overhead" and that, "[t]o the extent that paralegals are allowed to perform work that constitutes 'the practice of law' under Maine law, such practice is inconsistent with Maine law." *Weinberger*, 801 F. Supp. at 823. The Court continues to regard 4 M.R.S.A. § 807(1) as prohibiting the recovery of attorneys' fees for work done by paralegals that involves the legal judgment and analysis constituting the practice of law. Although the Court of Appeals for the First Circuit did affirm a district court's decision to grant fees for paralegal times in *Lipsett*, it did not hold that such fees were not required, and it did not address the unauthorized practice of law issue and the overhead inclusion rationale that have consistently motivated this Court's decisions to deny compensation for paralegal fees. The documentation submitted by Plaintiffs fails to distill tasks performed by Paralegal Tracy that do not involve the type of legal judgment properly performed by lawyers or that are not properly accounted for in firm overhead. The Court, therefore, will not award any attorneys' fees for the work that she performed.)
- *Currier v. United Technologies Corp.*, 2005 WL 1217278 (U.S. District Court, Maine, 2005) (My review of the entries on the challenged dates quickly reveals many entries which are the essence of paralegal work, *e.g.*, compile and redact exhibits, attention to exhibits for trial, preparation of trial and witness notebooks. I conclude that even the entries for preparation of a certificate of service and correspondence to the clerk of court fall into the gray area between purely clerical tasks and those properly entrusted to a paralegal, and recommend that they not be disallowed.)

DOING LEGAL RESEARCH IN MAINE LAW

Statutes: janus.state.me.us/legis/statutes
Cases: www.courts.state.me.us
Court Rules: www.courts.state.me.us/rules_forms_fees/rules
General: www.ll.georgetown.edu/states/maine.cfm

FINDING EMPLOYMENT IN MAINE

- www.indeed.com/q-Paralegal-l-Maine-jobs.html
- www.simplyhired.com/job-search/l-Maine/o-232000/t-Paralegal
- maine.craigslist.org/lgl

MARYLAND

DEFINING LEGAL ASSISTANTS/ PARALEGALS IN MARYLAND

A Legal Assistant is a person, qualified through education, training or work experience, who is employed or retained by a lawyer, law office, corporation, governmental agency, or other entity in a capacity or function which involves the performance, *under the ultimate direction and supervision of an attorney*, of specifically-delegated substantive legal work, which work, for the most part, requires a sufficient knowledge of legal concepts that, absent such assistant, the attorney would perform the task. *Attorney Grievance Comm'n v. Hallmon*, 681 A.2d 510 (Court of Appeals of Maryland, 1996) (quoting the ABA definition).

ETHICAL RULES AND GUIDELINES IN MARYLAND

- For a discussion of the state's ethical Rule 5.3 ("Responsibilities Regarding Nonlawyer Assistants") in the *Maryland Lawyer's Rules of Professional Conduct*, see the end of Section C in chapter 5. For the text of 5.3 in Maryland, see also www.law.cornell.edu/ethics/md/code.
- Legal assistants can have business cards as long as their legal assistant status is designated. Maryland Bar Ass'n, *Ethics Opinion 77–28* (10/18/76).
- An attorney can list the names of paralegals on office letterhead or on the office door as long as their nonattorney status is designated. Maryland Bar Ass'n, *Ethics Opinion 81–69* (5/29/81).
- A nonattorney once worked for attorney #A. She now works for attorney #B. These attorneys are opponents on a case in litigation. This case was underway when the nonattorney worked for attorney #A. If effective screening (i.e., a "Chinese Wall") is used to insulate the nonattorney from the case, attorney #B does not have to withdraw from the litigation. Maryland Bar Ass'n, *Ethics Docket 90–17* (1990).
- An attorney can hire a freelance paralegal as long as the latter is supervised at all times by the attorney who takes steps to ensure there is no disclosure of client confidences. Maryland Bar Ass'n, *Opinion 86–83* (7/23/86).
- It is unethical to pay a bonus to a paralegal for bringing business to the office. Maryland State Bar Ass'n, *Ethics Docket 86–57* (2/12/86).

- An attorney cannot divide a fee with a nonattorney. Maryland Bar Ass'n, *Opinion 86–59* (2/12/86).
- A legal assistant cannot be paid a percentage of the recovery in a case on which the assistant works. Maryland Bar Ass'n, *Ethics Opinion 84–103* (1984).
- An attorney can rent office space to a nonattorney as long as confidentiality of the attorney's clients is not compromised. Maryland Bar Ass'n, *Ethics Opinion 89–45* (6/12/89).
- It is unethical for a sole practitioner to hire as a paralegal his disbarred former associate. The public would think the paralegal is an attorney. Maryland State Bar Ass'n, *Ethics 79–41*. On the same issue, see *Attorney Grievance Commission of Maryland v. James*, 666 A.2d 1246 (Court of Appeals of Maryland, 1995).

DEFINING THE PRACTICE OF LAW IN MARYLAND

- § 10–101 (*Annotated Code of Maryland, Business Occupations & Professions Code*): Lawyers.

  (h) (1) "Practice law" means to engage in any of the following activities:
  (i) giving legal advice;
  (ii) representing another person before a unit of the State government or of a political subdivision; or
  (iii) performing any other service that the Court of Appeals defines as practicing law.
  (2) "Practice law" includes:
  (i) advising in the administration of probate of estates of decedents in an orphans' court of the State;
  (ii) preparing an instrument that affects title to real estate;
  (iii) preparing or helping in the preparation of any form or document that is filed in a court or affects a case that is or may be filed in a court; or
  (iv) giving advice about a case that is or may be filed in a court.

- When defining the practice of law, the focus of the inquiry is whether the activity in question required legal knowledge and skill in order to apply legal principles and precedent. *Attorney Grievance Com'n of Maryland v. Shaw*, 732 A.2d 876 (Court of Appeals of Maryland, 1999).
- On the distinction between legal information and legal advice, see the chapter 4 discussion of *Opinion 95–056*, Opinion of the Attorney General of Maryland.

MARYLAND ETHICS AND PRACTICE RULES ON THE INTERNET

- www.law.cornell.edu/ethics/maryland.html
- www.msba.org/members/ethics.asp
- www.law.cornell.edu/ethics/md/code

PARALEGALS (AND OTHER NONATTORNEYS) IN MARYLAND STATE AND FEDERAL COURTS

- *Attorney Grievance Commission v. Brennan*, 714 A.2d 157 (Court of Appeals of Maryland, 1998) (it is permissible for a disbarred or suspended lawyer to work as a paralegal, provided that proper procedures and constraints are in place to assure that no one is confused as to the person's status as a paralegal) (work performed by a paralegal does constitute the practice of law; whether it is the unauthorized practice of law depends on the extent to which it is supervised by the lawyer).
- *Friolo v. Frankel*, 819 A.2d 354 (Court of Appeals of Maryland, 2003) (Because the fee shifting statutes under the Wage and Hour Law and the Payment Law allow only reasonable "counsel fees," a court when awarding attorney fees to a successful employee must exclude any fees of non-lawyers; charges for paralegals and legal interns are subsumed within the attorney's fees. West's Ann.Md.Code, Labor and Employment, §§ 3–427(d), 3–507.1(b).)
- *Sterling v. Atlantic Automotive Corp.*, 2005 WL 914348 (Circuit Court of Maryland, 2005) (Because there was no evidence that any of these "legal assistants" had paralegal degrees, the charge of $115 was too high. Tasks not requiring legal training should not be billed to a client because a "legal assistant" performs them. The court has conducted an independent review of the charges and disallowed those which in its view did not require legal training or experience—assuming that paralegal fees are recoverable under Article 49B, § 42 of the Maryland Annotated Code.)
- *In re Boyds Collection Ltd.*, 2006 WL 4671849 (U.S. Bankruptcy Court, Maryland, 2006) (A small amount of the time logged by paralegals is for clearly clerical work for which separate compensation will not be allowed. This includes time logged to print pleadings and prepare sets of orders.)
- *DiBuo v. Board of Educ. of Worcester County*, 2002 WL 32909389 (U.S. District Court, Maryland, 2002) (the plaintiffs may properly recover paralegal fees as an expense, given the relatively small amount of work done by the paralegal, which eliminated what would undoubtedly have been an even larger lawyer bill for the same work).
- *In re Ward*, 190 Bankruptcy Reporter 242, 248 (U.S. Bankruptcy Court, Maryland, 1995) ("[w]hen seeking compensation for clerical services performed by an attorney or a paralegal, an applicant must provide sufficient information enabling the court to make a determination as to why such services were performed by an attorney or paralegal as opposed to a paralegal or secretary, respectively").
- *Attorney Grievance Com'n of Maryland v. Ward*, 904 A.2d 477 (Court of Appeals of Maryland, 2006) (a legal assistant illegally notarized a signature of a person who was not actually present at the moment of notarization).
- *Attorney Grievance Com'n of Maryland v. Zakroff*, 876 A.2d 664 (Court of Appeals of Maryland, 2005) (an attorney is disciplined for instructing his paralegal to mislead clients' medical providers concerning the status of settled cases).

DOING LEGAL RESEARCH IN MARYLAND LAW

Statutes: mlis.state.md.us/#stat
Cases: www.courts.state.md.us/opinions.html
Court Rules: www.megalaw.com/md/mdrules.php
General: www.romingerlegal.com/state/maryland.html

FINDING EMPLOYMENT IN MARYLAND

- msba.legalstaff.com/Common/HomePage.aspx?abbr=MSBA
- www.simplyhired.com/job-search/l-Maryland/o-232000/t-Paralegal
- hotjobs.yahoo.com/job-search-l-All-MD-c-Legal
- baltimore.craigslist.org/lgl

MASSACHUSETTS

ETHICAL RULES AND GUIDELINES IN MASSACHUSETTS

- For a discussion of the state's ethical Rule 5.3 ("Responsibilities Regarding Nonlawyer Assistants") in the *Massachusetts Rules of Professional Conduct*, see the end of Section C in chapter 5. For the text of 5.3 in Massachusetts, see also www.mass.gov/obcbbo/rpcnet.htm.

- It is unethical for an attorney who represents insurance company to delegate tasks to paralegals without first determining that they are competent to perform those tasks even if the insurer requires such delegation. An insurer's guidelines on paralegal use cannot supplant the attorney's judgment on when such use is appropriate. Massachusetts Bar Ass'n, *Opinion 00–4* (9/29/00).
- Paralegal names can be printed on a firm's letterhead if their nonattorney status is clear. Massachusetts Bar Ass'n, *Ethics Opinion 83–10* (11/29/83).
- A paralegal can sign his or her name on law firm letterhead. Massachusetts Bar Ass'n, *Ethics Opinion 73–2.*
- A law firm cannot pay its office administrator (a nonattorney) a percentage of the firm's profits in addition to his fixed salary. Massachusetts Bar Ass'n, *Opinion 84–2* (1984).
- [N]o lawyer who is disbarred or suspended . . . shall engage in paralegal work, and no lawyer or law firm shall knowingly employ or otherwise engage, directly or indirectly, in any capacity, a person who is suspended or disbarred. Clerks' Committee on Ethical Opinions, Rule 4:01.

DEFINING THE PRACTICE OF LAW IN MASSACHUSETTS

- *Massachusetts Conveyancers Ass'n, Inc. v. Colonial Title & Escrow, Inc.*, 2001 WL 669280 (Massachusetts Superior Court, 2001) (Whether a particular activity constitutes the practice of law is fact specific. While a comprehensive definition would be impossible to frame, what constitutes "the practice of law", in general, consists of: "[D]irecting and managing the enforcement of legal claims and the establishment of the legal rights of others, where it is necessary to form and to act upon opinions as to what those rights are and as to the legal methods which must be adopted to enforce them, the practice of giving or furnishing legal advice as to such rights and methods and the practice, as an occupation, of drafting documents by which such rights are created, modified, surrendered or secured. . . .")
- *In re Bonarrigo*, 282 Bankruptcy Reporter 101 (U.S. District Court, 2002) (The "unauthorized practice of law" is prohibited, but not defined, by Massachusetts law. Massachusetts courts and courts in other jurisdictions have concluded that trying to express a comprehensive "definition of what constitutes the practice of law" is an impossibility and that "each case must be decided upon its own particular facts." *In re Shoe Mfrs. Protective Ass'n*, 295 Mass. 369 (1936). Generally speaking, the practice of law can include, "the examination of statutes, judicial decisions, and departmental rulings, for the purpose of advising upon a question of law . . . and the rendering to a client of an opinion thereon.")
- *In re Chimko*, 831 N.E.2d 316 (Supreme Judicial Court of Massachusetts, 2005) (We have rejected the proposition "that whenever, for compensation, one person . . . performs for another some service that requires some knowledge of law, or drafts for another some document that has legal effect, he is practicing law." Architects prepare building contracts, insurance agents prepare riders to policies, auctioneers prepare sale notes, and custom house brokers prepare important documents, all without practicing law.)

MASSACHUSETTS ETHICS AND PRACTICE RULES ON THE INTERNET

- www.law.cornell.edu/ethics/massachusetts.html
- www.massbar.org/for-attorneys/publications/ethics-opinions
- www.law.cornell.edu/ethics/ma/code/MA_CODE.HTM
- www.mass.gov/obcbbo/rpcnet.htm

PARALEGALS (AND OTHER NONATTORNEYS) IN MASSACHUSETTS STATE AND FEDERAL COURTS

- *Matter of Eisenhauer*, 689 N.E.2d 783 (Supreme Judicial Court of Massachusetts, 1998) (attorney disciplined for charging attorney rates for paralegal time).
- *Cerqueira v. American Airlines*, 484 F. Supp. 2d 241 (U.S. District Court, Massachusetts, 2007) (fee-shifting statutes are designed to ensure effective access to the judicial process for persons with civil rights grievances, and are not to serve as full employment or continuing education programs for lawyers and paralegals).
- *Mogilevsky v. Bally Total Fitness Corp.*, 311 F. Supp. 2d 212 (U.S. District Court, Massachusetts, 4004) (a court must not permit an attorney to recover his standard hourly rate for work appropriate for a less experienced lawyer or a paralegal or secretary).
- *Dixon v. International Broth. of Police Officers*, 434 F. Supp. 2d 73 (U.S. District Court, Massachusetts, 2006) (for purposes of calculating award of attorney fees under Title VII and the Massachusetts discrimination statute, undetailed and general billing entries and duplicative work warranted a significant reduction of hours billed by the paralegal).
- *Crance v. Commissioner of Public Welfare*, 507 N.E.2d 751 (Supreme Judicial Court of Massachusetts, 1987) (paralegal fees awarded where the paralegal's work was not merely ministerial but required the exercise of judgment).
- *DeVaux v. American Home Assurance Co.*, 444 N.E.2d 355 (Supreme Judicial Court of Massachusetts, 1983) (nonattorney employee negligently misfiles a letter seeking legal assistance; client sues attorney for legal malpractice after the statute of limitations runs out on her claim).
- *Deo-Agbasi v. The Parthenon Group*, 229 Federal Rules Decisions 348 (U.S. District Court, Massachusetts, 2005) (the neglect of a civil rights action by plaintiff's paralegal, leading to the failure to timely respond to defendant's motion to dismiss, and attributed to paralegal's heavy caseload, did not constitute "excusable neglect" so as to warrant setting aside the dismissal).
- *In re LaFrance*, 311 Bankruptcy Reporter 1 (U.S. Bankruptcy Court, Massachusetts, 2004) (As for paralegals, they do from time to time get sick, or take vacation, or sever their relationship with attorneys. When that happens, an attorney must timely replace those services with those of another paralegal of sufficient skill or step in to do that work him or herself.)
- *Rodriguez v. Montalvo*, 337 F. Supp. 2d 212 (U.S. District Court, Massachusetts, 2004) (if a nonlawyer paralegal established a confidential relationship with a client, that relationship may be imputed to the attorney supervisor and consequently to the firm as a whole, for the purpose of a motion under Massachusetts law to disqualify an attorney based on a former representation).

DOING LEGAL RESEARCH IN MASSACHUSETTS LAW

Statutes: www.mass.gov/legis/laws/mgl
Cases: www.findlaw.com/11stategov/ma/laws.html
Court Rules: www.lawlib.state.ma.us/rules.html
General: www.ll.georgetown.edu/states/massachusetts.cfm

FINDING EMPLOYMENT IN MASSACHUSETTS

- legal.jobs.net/Massachusetts.htm
- www.indeed.com/q-Paralegal-l-Massachusetts-jobs.html
- boston.craigslist.org/lgl

MICHIGAN

DEFINING LEGAL ASSISTANTS/ PARALEGALS IN MICHIGAN

- Any person currently employed or retained by a lawyer, law office, governmental agency or other entity engaged in the practice of law, in a capacity or function which involves the performance under the direction and supervision of an attorney of specifically delegated substantive legal work, which work, for the most part, requires a sufficient knowledge of legal concepts such that, absent that legal assistant, the attorney would perform the task and which is not primarily clerical or secretarial in nature. Article 1, Sec 6, of the *Bylaws of the State Bar of Michigan* Article 1, § 6 (www.michbar.org/generalinfo/bylaws.cfm).

- To be eligible for membership in the Legal Assistant Division of the State Bar of Michigan, you must meet the above definition and you must be a person (1) who has graduated from an ABA approved program of study for legal assistants and has a baccalaureate degree; or (2) who has received a baccalaureate degree in any field, plus not less than two years of in-house training as a legal assistant; or (3) who has received an associate degree in the legal assistant field, plus not less than two years of in-house training as a legal assistant; or (4) who has received an associate degree in any field and who has graduated from an ABA approved program of study for legal assistants, plus not less than two years of in-house training as a legal assistant; or (5) who has a minimum of four years of in-house training as a legal assistant. (www.michbar.org/legalassistants/pdfs/labrochure.pdf).

ETHICAL RULES AND GUIDELINES IN MICHIGAN

- For a discussion of the state's ethical Rule 5.3 ("Responsibilities Regarding Nonlawyer Assistants") in the *Michigan Rules of Professional Conduct*, see the end of Section C in chapter 5. For the text of 5.3 in Michigan, see also www.michbar.org/professional/pdfs/mrpc.pdf.

- State Bar Board of Commissioners, *Michigan Guidelines for the Utilization of Legal Assistant Services* (1993) (www.michbar.org/legalassistants/pdfs/labrochure.pdf). *Guideline 1*: An attorney must take reasonable steps to ensure that his or her legal assistant complies with the ethical rules governing Michigan attorneys. *Guideline 2:* The attorney must directly supervise and evaluate assigned tasks. A legal assistant may not convey to persons outside the law firm the legal assistant's opinion on the applicability of laws to particular cases. Legal documents on which a legal assistant works must be signed by an attorney. *Guideline 3:* An attorney cannot delegate to legal assistants the task of establishing an attorney-client relationship or the fee to be paid. *Guideline 4:* A legal assistant may be identified on attorney letterhead and on business cards that mention the law firm's name. *Guideline 5:* The attorney should take reasonable measures to ensure that no conflict of interest is presented arising out of the legal assistant's current or prior employment, or from the legal assistant's other business or personal interests. *Guideline 6:* An attorney can charge a client for legal assistant time if the client consents. *Guideline 7:* An attorney must not split fees with a legal assistant nor pay a legal assistant for referring legal business. A legal assistant can be included in a firm's retirement plan even if based on a profit-sharing arrangement. *Guideline 8:* The attorney should facilitate the legal assistant's participation in continuing legal education and public service activities.

- Where a paralegal has had access during prior employment to confidential or secret information concerning a legal matter substantially related and materially adverse to a matter in which the new law firm employer is representing a client, the law firm must promptly and adequately screen the nonlawyer from the matter in order to avoid disqualification. State Bar of Michigan, *Opinion RI-285* (12/11/96). See also *Opinion CI-1168* (12/10/86) and *Opinion RI-115* (1/31/92).

- When nonattorney employees with access to the files move to another law firm, a Chinese Wall may have to be built around them to prevent the imputed disqualification of the new firm. State Bar of Michigan, *Opinion R-4* (9/22/89).

- Business cards and law firm letterhead can list the name of nonattorney employees with titles such as *legal assistant* or *paralegal*. The public must not be confused as to their nonattorney status. State Bar of Michigan, *Opinion RI-34* (10/25/89).

- A law firm may not list a non-lawyer on its letterhead, identifying the non-lawyer with the job title "Estate Administrator," indicating that the non-lawyer holds a MBA degree and interposing a horizontal line and a space between the last-listed lawyer's name and the non-lawyer's name, without doing more to indicate that the non-lawyer is not a lawyer. State Bar of Michigan, *Opinion RI-323* (6/5/01).

- A law firm may pay a legal assistant compensation based on a set salary and a percentage of the net profits of the practice area in which the legal assistant is involved as long as no payments are made based on fees generated from particular clients. State Bar of Michigan, *Opinion RI-143* (8/25/92).

- It is not possible for an attorney to give quality supervision to 24 paralegals located at six separate sites in the state. State Bar of Michigan, *Opinion R-1* (12/16/88).

- An attorney's paralegal can represent clients in administrative hearings where authorized by law. The attorney must make sure that this paralegal acts ethically in providing this representation. State Bar of Michigan, *Opinion RI-125* (4/17/92). See also *Opinion RI-103* (10/9/91).

- An attorney may not establish a business employing a paralegal who will sell will and trust forms where the paralegal will probably provide consultation and advice to clients. State Bar of Michigan, *Opinion RI-191* (2/14/94).

- An attorney cannot avoid all direct client contact by obtaining all information about and from the client through the attorney's paralegal. State Bar of Michigan, *Opinion RI-128* (4/21/92).

- An attorney is prohibited from representing a client if one of his nonattorney employees will become a witness who will give testimony that is not consistent with the interests of the attorney's client. State Bar of Michigan, *Opinion RI-26* (7/19/89).

- Information collected by a legal assistant during an interview is protected against disclosure by the attorney-client privilege. State Bar of Michigan, *Opinion RI-123* (3/13/92).

- A disbarred or suspended lawyer may not be employed as a "paralegal assistant" by a lawyer or law firm. State Bar of Michigan, *Opinion C-211* (7/72).

DEFINING THE PRACTICE OF LAW IN MICHIGAN

- *Dressel v. Ameribank*, 664 N.W.2d 151 (Supreme Court of Michigan, 2003) A person engages in the practice of law when he or she counsels or assists another in matters that require the use of legal discretion and profound legal knowledge:

  (1) Conducting cases in courts, preparing pleadings and other papers incident to actions, and managing such actions and proceedings on behalf of clients before judges and courts (these tasks demand the unique training and skills of an attorney);

  (2) Giving legal advice in any action taken for others in any matter connected with the law even though unrelated to any action in court (this task requires a lawyer's training and skill);

  (3) Drafting legal documents, such as wills, that require the determination of the legal effect of special facts and conditions (this task requires legal training and profound legal knowledge) (note, however, that the practice of law does *not* include drafting simple standardized legal documents, such as ordinary leases, mortgages, and deeds, that do not require legal training and knowledge—so long as the drafting does not entail giving advice or counsel as to their legal effect and validity).

IMPORTANT MICHIGAN RULES ON PARALEGAL FEES

- Rule 2.626 (*West's Michigan Rules of Court*): An award of attorney fees may include an award for the time and labor of any legal assistant who contributed nonclerical, legal support under the supervision of an attorney, provided the legal assistant meets the criteria set forth in Article 1, § 6 of the Bylaws of the State Bar of Michigan [governing eligibility to become an affiliate member of the State Bar of Michigan].

- Rates charged must be commensurate with the level of skill required for a particular task . . . . [P]aralegal rates may not be charged for nonlegal work, such as copying or delivering documents, preparing or filing proofs of service . . . . When paralegals are utilized to perform legal services for an estate, they may be compensated as paraprofessionals rather than treated as an overhead expense. *Local Bankruptcy Rules of the U.S. Bankruptcy Court for the Western District of Michigan*, LBR 9013–1.

MICHIGAN ETHICS AND PRACTICE RULES ON THE INTERNET

- www.law.cornell.edu/ethics/michigan.html
- www.michbar.org/opinions/ethicsopinions.cfm

PARALEGALS (AND OTHER NONATTORNEYS) IN MICHIGAN STATE AND FEDERAL COURTS

- *Michigan v. Hurst*, 517 N.W.2d 858, 862–63 (Court of Appeals of Michigan, 1994) (the "defendant's supplemental appellate brief . . . prepared by an apparently competent legal assistant, sufficiently apprised this court of the finer points of defendant's arguments").

- *In the Matter of Bright*, 171 Bankruptcy Reporter 799, 802 (U.S. Bankruptcy Court, E.D. Michigan, 1994) (bankruptcy trustee charges paralegal with the unauthorized practice of law in helping the debtor; a disclaimer that one is "only providing 'scrivener' or 'paralegal' services is irrelevant if the nonlawyer in fact engages in the unauthorized practice of law.")

- *Cobb Publishing Co. v. Hearst Corp.*, 907 F. Supp. 1038 (U.S. District Court, E. D. Michigan, 1995) (Chinese wall set up to prevent disqualification of law firm due to conflict of interest; memo sent to all attorneys, paralegals, and other staff to stay away from the contaminated employee).

- *Kearns v. Ford Motor Co.*, 114 Federal Rules Decisions 57 (U.S. District Court, E.D. Michigan, 1987) (paralegal gives copy of privileged litigation documents to someone with whom she was having a romantic relationship).

- *RVP Development Corp. v. Furness Golf Const.*, 2004 WL 1737589 (Court of Appeals of Michigan, 2004) (7 MCR 2.626 provides: An award of attorney fees may include an award for the time and labor of any legal assistant who contributed nonclerical, legal support under the supervision of an attorney, provided the legal assistant meets the criteria set forth in Article 1, § 6 of the Bylaws of the State Bar of Michigan. However, an award for the time and labor of legal assistants under MCR 2.626 allows only for "the time and labor" of a legal assistant. MCR 2.626 does not express that the award for time and labor of legal assistants be based upon [a] "reasonable hourly or daily rate." Legal assistants' wages are considered fixed overhead costs. Because wages of legal assistants are considered fixed and MCR 2.626 does not indicate otherwise, an award for the time and labor of legal assistants cannot exceed the actual charge.)

- *Auto Alliance Intern., Inc. v. U.S. Customs Service*, 155 Federal Appendix 226 (U.S. Court of Appeals, 6th Cir. Michigan, 2005) (The billing records reflect that the vast majority of the paralegal work consisted of picking up and indexing documents. This is nonrecoverable clerical work, as contrasted with paralegal work that would be otherwise have to be done by an attorney.)

- *PML North America, LLC v. ACG Enterprises of NC*, 2007 WL 925627 (U.S. District Court, E.D. Michigan, 2007) (The 2003 State Bar of Michigan survey demonstrates that, during 2003, the average billing rate for paralegals with at least five years of experience in large firms (over 20 attorneys) was $100 per hour. For paralegals with at least five years of experience, the rate was $90 in Southeast Michigan. Because the paralegals and clerk in this case are in a large firm working on a complex case, the court finds that an hourly rate higher than the average rate of $100 is appropriate.)

DOING LEGAL RESEARCH IN MICHIGAN LAW

Statutes: www.legislature.mi.gov
Cases: www.michbar.org/opinions/content.cfm
Court Rules: www.megalaw.com/mi/mirules.php
General: www.lib.umich.edu/govdocs/michlaw.html

FINDING EMPLOYMENT IN MICHIGAN

- legal.jobs.net/Michigan.htm
- www.indeed.com/q-Litigation-Paralegal-l-Michigan-jobs.html
- www.simplyhired.com/job-search/l-Michigan/o-232000/t-Paralegal detroit.craigslist.org/lgl

MINNESOTA

ETHICAL RULES AND GUIDELINES IN MINNESOTA

- For a discussion of the state's ethical Rule 5.3 ("Responsibilities Regarding Nonlawyer Assistants") in the *Minnesota Rules of Professional Conduct*, see the end of Section C in chapter 5.

For the text of 5.3 in Minnesota, see also www.law.cornell.edu/ethics/mn/code.

- Paralegal names can be printed on a firm's letterhead, business cards, professional announcement cards, office signs, telephone directory listings, law lists, and legal directory listings if their nonattorney status is clear. Paralegals, so identified, may sign correspondence on behalf of the law firm if acting under an attorney's direction. But they cannot be named on pleadings under any identification. Minnesota Bar Ass'n, *Ethics Opinion 8* (6/26/74; amended 6/18/80 and 12/4/87). On letterheads, see also *Opinion 93* (6/7/84).

- It is improper for a lawyer to permit any nonattorney employee to accept a gratuity offered by a court reporting service or other service for which the client is expected to pay unless the client consents. Minnesota Lawyers Professional Responsibility Board, *Opinion 17* (6/18/93).

DEFINING THE PRACTICE OF LAW IN MINNESOTA

- § 481.02 (*Minnesota Statutes Annotated*): Subdivision 1. Prohibitions. It shall be unlawful for any person or association of persons, except members of the bar of Minnesota admitted and licensed to practice as attorneys at law, to appear as attorney or counselor at law in any action or proceeding in any court in this state to maintain, conduct, or defend the same, except personally as a party thereto in other than a representative capacity, or, by word, sign, letter, or advertisement, to hold out as competent or qualified to give legal advice or counsel, or to prepare legal documents, or as being engaged in advising or counseling in law or acting as attorney or counselor at law, or in furnishing to others the services of a lawyer, or lawyers, or, for a fee or any consideration, to give legal advice or counsel, perform for or furnish to another legal services, or, for or without a fee or any consideration, to prepare, directly or through another, for another person, firm, or corporation, any will or testamentary disposition or instrument of trust serving purposes similar to those of a will, or, for a fee or any consideration, to prepare for another person, firm, or corporation, any other legal document, except as provided in subdivision 3. . . .

- Subdivision 3. Permitted actions. The provisions of this section shall not prohibit: . . . (2) a person from drawing a will for another in an emergency if the imminence of death leaves insufficient time to have it drawn and its execution supervised by a licensed attorney-at-law . . . . (5) any bona fide labor organization from giving legal advice to its members in matters arising out of their employment . . . . (14) the delivery of legal services by a specialized legal assistant in accordance with a specialty license issued by the supreme court before July 1, 1995. . . .

- Subdivision 3a. Real estate closing services. Nothing in this section shall be construed to prevent a real estate broker, a real estate salesperson, or a real estate closing agent, as defined in section 82.17, from drawing or assisting in drawing papers incident to the sale, trade, lease, or loan of property, or from charging for drawing or assisting in drawing them, except as hereafter provided by the supreme court. . . .

- Subdivision 7. Lay assistance to attorneys. Nothing herein contained shall be construed to prevent a corporation from furnishing to any person lawfully engaged in the practice of law, such information or such clerical service in and about the attorney's professional work as, except for the provisions of this section, may be lawful, provided, that at all times the lawyer receiving such information or such services shall maintain full, professional and direct responsibility to the attorney's clients for the information and services so received . . . .

MINNESOTA ETHICS AND PRACTICE RULES ON THE INTERNET

- www.law.cornell.edu/ethics/minnesota.html
- www.courts.state.mn.us/lprb/index.asp
- www.courts.state.mn.us/lprb/opinions.html

PARALEGALS (AND OTHER NONATTORNEYS) IN MINNESOTA STATE AND FEDERAL COURTS

- *In Re Rubin*, 484 N.W.2d 786 (Supreme Court of Minnesota, 1992) (attorney disciplined for permitting a legal assistant to back-date a signature on a deed).
- *In re Petition for Disciplinary Action against Jeff D. Bagniefski*, 690 N.W.2d 558 (Supreme Court of Minnesota, 2005) (attorney has his client sign a blank signature page and then has his paralegal notarize the signature).
- *Minnesota v. Richards*, 456 N.W.2d 260 (Supreme Court of Minnesota, 1990) (a county attorney's office is not disqualified from prosecuting the defendant merely because the office hired a paralegal who had previously interviewed for a job with defense counsel).
- *In re Disciplinary Action against Garcia*, 709 N.W.2d 237 (Supreme Court of Minnesota, 2006) (attorney cannot be reinstated to the practice of law until he demonstrates to the director of the Office of Lawyers Professional Responsibility that he has established written office procedures designed to ensure that he is properly training and supervising nonlawyer employees).
- *Silverman v. Silverman*, 2004 WL 2066778 (U.S. District Court, Minnesota, 2004) (15 percent would be excised to reflect the underutilization of paralegals and less senior associates to research issues, prepare correspondence, draft simple motions, and other matters more properly billed at a lower rate).
- *Macgregor v. Mallinckrodt*, 2003 WL 23335194 (U.S. District Court, Minnesota, 2003) (It is appropriate to bill for paralegal work at reasonable paralegal rates, but clerical duties do not justify attorney and paralegal rates. A few examples of clerical or nonlegal work performed by counsel or the paralegal and charged at those rates include: update witness addresses, file complaint in federal court for client, serve CT corporation for Mallinckrodt, schedule conference with defendant, serve subpoena, edit and type summary judgment brief.)
- *In re Reinstatement of Jellinger*, 728 N.W.2d 917 (Supreme Court of Minnesota, 2007) (suspended attorney works as a paralegal during the suspension).

DOING LEGAL RESEARCH IN MINNESOTA LAW

Statutes: www.leg.state.mn.us/leg/statutes.asp
Cases: hclaw.co.hennepin.mn.us/screens/ll_mn_cases.html
Court Rules: www.courts.state.mn.us/?page=511
General: www.lawmoose.com

FINDING EMPLOYMENT IN MINNESOTA

- www2.mnbar.org/committees/paralegal/Employment Opportunities.htm
- www.indeed.com/q-Paralegal-l-Minnesota-jobs.html
- legal.jobs.net/Minnesota-Minneapolis.htm
- minneapolis.craigslist.org/lgl

MISSISSIPPI

ETHICAL RULES AND GUIDELINES IN MISSISSIPPI

- For a discussion of the state's ethical Rule 5.3 ("Responsibilities Regarding Nonlawyer Assistants") in the *Mississippi Rules of Professional Conduct*, see the end of Section C in chapter 5. For the text of 5.3 in Mississippi, see also www.mssc.state.ms.us/rules.

- Paralegal names can be printed on a firm's letterhead if their nonattorney status is clear. The paralegal should not be called a *paralegal associate*, since in common usage the term *associate* carries a connotation of being an attorney in a law firm. Mississippi Bar Ass'n, *Opinion 93* (6/7/84).

- An attorney can pay a paralegal a bonus based on the number of her hours billed and collected in excess of a designated minimum. A nonattorney compensation or retirement plan can be based in whole or in part on a profit-sharing arrangement. Mississippi State Bar, *Opinion 154* (9/12/89).

- Legal assistants can use the initials *CLA* (Certified Legal Assistant) or *CLAS* (Certified Legal Assistant Specialist) after their names on law firm letterhead as long as the designation is accompanied by language indicating that the legal assistant is not an attorney. These initials indicate the legal assistant has passed the test and met the other requirements of the National Association of Legal Assistants. Mississippi State Bar, *Opinion 223* (1/19/95).

- A disbarred attorney can be a paralegal under the supervision of an attorney in good standing, but must have no direct or indirect contact with clients and must be totally separated from his or her prior law practice. *In re Reinstatement of Parsons*, 890 So. 2d 40 (Supreme Court of Mississippi, 2003).

- A notary public who is not an attorney licensed to practice law is prohibited from representing or advertising that the notary public is an immigration consultant, immigration paralegal or expert on immigration matters unless the notary public is an accredited representative of an organization recognized by the board of immigration appeals pursuant to 8 CFR Section 292.2(a-e) or any subsequent federal law. *Mississippi Code Annotated* § 25–33–27.

- A request for a hearing [on eligibility for Medicaid], either state or local, must be made in writing by the claimant or claimant's legal representative. "Legal representative" includes the claimant's authorized representative, an attorney retained by the claimant or claimant's family to represent the claimant, a paralegal representative with a legal aid services. . . . *Mississippi Code Annotated*, § 43–13–116(3)(b).

DEFINING THE PRACTICE OF LAW IN MISSISSIPPI

- *Mississippi Commission on Judicial Performance v. Jenkins*, 725 So. 2d 162 (Supreme Court of Mississippi, 1998): This Court defined the practice of law to include the drafting or selection of documents, the giving of advice in regard to them, and the using of an informed or trained discretion in the drafting of documents to meet the needs of the person being served. So any exercise of intelligent choice in advising another of his legal rights and duties brings the activity within the practice of the legal profession.

- *Mississippi Code Annotated*, § 73–3–55: It shall be unlawful for any person to engage in the practice of law in this state who has not been licensed according to law. Any person violating the provisions of this section shall be deemed guilty of a misdemeanor, and, upon conviction, shall be punished in accordance with the provisions of section 97–23–43. Any person who shall for fee or reward or promise, directly or indirectly, write or dictate any paper or instrument of writing, to be filed in any cause or proceeding pending, or to be instituted in any court in this state, or give any counsel or advice therein, or who shall write or dictate any bill of sale, deed of conveyance, deed of trust, mortgage, contract, or last will and testament, or shall make or certify to any abstract of title or real estate other than his own or in which he may own an interest, shall be held to be engaged in the practice of law. This section shall not, however, prevent title or abstract of title guaranty companies incorporated under the laws of this state from making abstract or certifying titles to real estate where it acts through some person as agent, authorized under the laws of the State of Mississippi to practice law; nor shall this section prevent any abstract company chartered under the laws of the State of Mississippi with a paid up capital of fifty thousand dollars ($50,000.00) or more from making or certifying to abstracts of title to real estate through the president, secretary or other principal officer of such company.

- *Darby v. Mississippi State Board of Bar Admissions*, 185 So. 2d 684, 687 (Supreme Court of Mississippi, 1966):

MISSISSIPPI ETHICS AND PRACTICE RULES ON THE INTERNET

- www.law.cornell.edu/ethics/mississippi.html
- www.msbar.org/ethic_opinions.php
- www.msbar.org/professional_responsibility.php
- www.law.cornell.edu/ethics/ms/code/MS_CODE.HTM

PARALEGALS (AND OTHER NONATTORNEYS) IN MISSISSIPPI STATE AND FEDERAL COURTS

- *Owens v. First Family Financial Services*, 379 F. Supp. 2d 840 (U.S. District Court, S.D. Mississippi, 2005) (Defendants moved to disqualify attorneys for plaintiffs. Under Mississippi's rules of professional conduct, a conflict of interest arising from a paralegal's prior work for the law firm that formerly represented defendants and subsequent work for the law firm during its representation of plaintiffs in their consumer fraud action against defendants had to be imputed to law firm representing plaintiffs for purposes of the defendants' motion to disqualify plaintiffs' counsel. Even if the device of a "Chinese wall" was available to shield the plaintiffs' law firm from imputed disqualification, that device did not apply, notwithstanding that the paralegal was no longer with the firm when disqualification was sought, given that the paralegal was involved in work on the plaintiffs' action against defendants for several months before the "Chinese wall" was erected.)

- *Ivy v. K.D. Merchant*, 666 So. 2d 445 (Supreme Court of Mississippi, 1995) (inmate paralegal assistance; paralegal fined $25 for assisting an inmate who filed a frivolous lawsuit).

- *Minnick v. Mississippi*, 551 So. 2d 77, 101 (Supreme Court of Mississippi, 1988) (lawyer should not use a paralegal "to do his dirty work" in communicating with the other side).

- *Mississippi State Chapter Operation Push v. Mabus*, 788 F. Supp. 1406, 1421 (U.S. District Court, N.D. Mississippi, 1992) (award of paralegal fees criticized: it "is unnecessary to have three paralegals assisting at trial"; "using three paralegals when one would be sufficient").

- *In re White*, 171 Bankruptcy Reporter 554 (U.S. Bankruptcy Court, S.D. Mississippi, 1994) (attorney fees reduced; "too many lawyers are spending too much time on this case"; they "used paralegals to perform secretarial tasks").

- *Williams v. Mississippi State Bar Ass'n*, 492 So. 2d 578 (Supreme Court of Mississippi, 1986) (a disbarred attorney should not act as a paralegal).

DOING LEGAL RESEARCH IN MISSISSIPPI LAW

Statutes: www.sos.state.ms.us/ed_pubs/MSCode
Cases: www.mssc.state.ms.us/decisions/search/default.asp
Court Rules: www.mssc.state.ms.us/rules/default.asp
General: www.washlaw.edu/uslaw/states/Mississippi

FINDING EMPLOYMENT IN MISSISSIPPI

- msbar.legalstaff.com/Common/HomePage. aspx?abbr=MSBAR
- www.simplyhired.com/job-search/l-Mississippi/ o-232000/t-Paralegal
- www.indeed.com/q-Litigation-Paralegal-l-Mississippi- jobs.html
- jackson.craigslist.org/lgl

MISSOURI

DEFINING LEGAL ASSISTANTS/ PARALEGALS IN MISSOURI

A paralegal, qualified through education, training or work experience, is employed or retained by an attorney, law firm, government agency, corporation, or other entity to perform substantive and procedural legal work under the ultimate direction and supervision of an attorney or as authorized by administrative, statutory, or court authority. "Paralegal Experience" shall mean the performance of substantive legal work, non-clerical or non-administrative in nature, that absent a paralegal, an attorney would perform. (Missouri Bar Association, *Practicing with Paralegals* (www.mobar.org/bc1c9200–2123–46fb-9727– 8bc6a83f2cf7.aspx).

ETHICAL RULES AND GUIDELINES IN MISSOURI

- For a discussion of the state's ethical Rule 4–5.3 ("Responsibilities Regarding Nonlawyer Assistants") in the *Missouri Rules of Professional Conduct*, see the end of Section C in chapter 5. For the text of 4–5.3 in Missouri, see also www.courts .mo.gov/page.asp?id=707.
- *Missouri Bar Guidelines for Practicing with Paralegals* (www .mobar.org/bc1c9200–2123–46fb-9727–8bc6a83f2cf7.aspx).
- *Guideline I:* A lawyer is responsible for the professional and ethical conduct of a paralegal under his or her supervision. *Guideline II:* A lawyer shall not assist a paralegal in the performance of an activity that constitutes the unauthorized practice of law (UPL). A lawyer must supervise nonlawyer employees and ensure that their conduct is compatible with the professional obligations of the lawyer. Case law does not provide much guidance in defining where the actions of a paralegal cross the line from assisting a lawyer in the practice of law to actually performing acts that would violate the unauthorized practice of law statute. A paralegal is not practicing law if, under the ultimate direction and supervision of a licensed lawyer, the paralegal is applying knowledge of law and legal procedures in rendering direct assistance to a licensed lawyer. This assistance may include but is not limited to: (a) researching legal matters; (b) developing an action, procedure, technique, service or

application; (c) preparing and interpreting legal documents; (d) selecting, compiling and using technical information; (e) assisting the lawyer in court; (f) handling administrative matters with the tribunal; (g) handling will attestations and real estate closings; and (h) analyzing and following procedural problems that involve independent decision. *Guideline III:* A lawyer shall not share legal fees with a paralegal, but may include paralegals in a compensation or retirement plan that is based on profit-sharing. The prohibition against "fee splitting" is not intended to deny salary or bonuses to paralegals even though it is tied to the profitability of the firm. Rather, the prohibition is to any form of compensation directly tied to the existence or amount of a particular legal fee, where such fee-splitting would influence the lawyer's professional independent judgment. To preserve a lawyer's independence, a lawyer and a paralegal cannot form a partnership that practices law. Nor can a lawyer practice law with a company or corporation in which a paralegal has an ownership interest or is a director or officer. *Guideline IV:* A lawyer must (a) develop policies that clearly define tasks paralegals can perform, (b) directly supervise the paralegal, (c) be responsible for the paralegal's work product, (d) give the paralegal copies of governing ethical rules and policies, (e) instruct the paralegal on ethical conduct, particularly the need to preserve client confidentiality, (f) check that the paralegal does not create a conflict of interest, and (g) check that the paralegal is qualified by education, training, or experience to act as a paralegal. *Guideline V:* A lawyer must (a) instruct the paralegal to disclose his or her paralegal status in all dealings with any other persons, (b) use the paralegal's title on all communications such as business cards and letterheads, and (c) instruct the paralegal to identify his/her title on written communications to others. A paralegal may sign correspondence on the law firm letterhead provided the signature is followed by an appropriate identifying designation as a paralegal. A paralegal's name can also appear on the letterhead of an office if clearly identified as a paralegal.

- *Practicing with Paralegals*, The Missouri Bar (www.mobar. org/bc1c9200–2123–46fb-9727–8bc6a83f2cf7.aspx)

  - Generally paralegals may not appear as an advocate. However, specific exceptions to the unauthorized practice of law statute have been created through statutes and regulations that permit paralegals to represent clients in court.
  - Paralegals can answer clients' questions by giving factual and procedural information. The paralegal cannot give legal opinions in response to client questions. When asked legal questions, paralegals must inform clients that they cannot give legal advice. Paralegals may relay advice specifically given to them by their supervising attorney.
  - Paralegals can prepare and draft legal documents, but the lawyer is responsible for reviewing and approving the contents of the documents.
  - Paralegals can engage in legal research.
  - Paralegals cannot take a deposition, but they attend a deposition and assist the lawyer by taking notes and coordinating documents and exhibits.
  - Paralegals can sit at the counsel table in court if permitted by local court rules. (Paralegals can be of great assistance to lawyers at trial and often sit at counsel tables if court rules do not restrict their presence.)
  - Paralegals can have business cards on which they are clearly identified as paralegals.
  - A paralegal's name can be included on law office letterhead if he or she is clearly identified as a paralegal.

- Paralegals can sign correspondence from a law firm as long as the paralegal's status is clearly identified. (Example: Very truly yours, TAYLOR & JONES By ———————— John J. Smith, Paralegal)
- Paralegals can be paid based upon the profitability of the firm. Law firms may give paralegals pensions, profit sharing plans and salary increases based upon the firm's profitability. These benefits can be given based upon individual performance and/or the firm's profitability. However, a firm may not base compensation upon the outcome of a case.
- The substantive legal work of a paralegal (work normally performed by an attorney in the absence of a paralegal) may be billed directly to the client in the same way an attorney's work is billed. To be billable, the work paralegals perform must not be clerical or ministerial. In circumstances where "attorneys fees" are reviewed or awarded by a court, the paralegal hours may be recovered as part of the attorney fee that is reviewed or awarded.
- A paralegal may not be a partner or shareholder in a law firm. Nonlawyers cannot have ownership or controlling interests in an entity where the lawyer practices law.
- The Rules of Professional Conduct and Guidelines govern lawyers; they do not regulate paralegals.
- If a paralegal's activities violate the Rules of Professional Conduct, the paralegal's employer is at fault. The lawyer employer is responsible for the paralegal's direction and ethical guidance. The supervisory measures that the lawyer applies should take account of the fact that paralegals are not subject to professional discipline.
- At the beginning of all professional communications with others, the paralegal shall disclose that he or she is a paralegal. The lawyer shall instruct the paralegal to make this disclosure. If the lawyer is present, the lawyer should introduce the paralegal and identify him/her as a paralegal.

- A paralegal cannot answer a docket call of an attorney. Missouri Bar Ass'n, *Informal Opinion 1* (7/9/82)
- It would be an improper splitting of a fee with a paralegal if an attorney agrees not to pay a paralegal unless an entire particular fee is collected. Missouri Bar Ass'n, *Informal Opinion 20* (6/16/78).
- An attorney who hires a nurse to review medical records can be named on the attorney's letterhead if it is clear she is not an attorney such as by calling her a legal assistant. Missouri Bar Ass'n, *Informal Advisory Opinion 970159* (www.mobar .org/mobarforms/opinionResult.aspx).
- An attorney can hire a disbarred attorney as a paralegal. Missouri Bar Ass'n, *Informal Advisory Opinion 960228* (www .mobar.org/mobarforms/opinionResult.aspx).
- An attorney can have a paralegal sign the attorney's name to correspondence and pleadings after the attorney has reviewed, approved the content, and supervised the production of the document. The paralegal should indicate that the paralegal signed attorney's name to the document. One method of indicating this fact is for the paralegal to initial the signature. Missouri Bar Ass'n, *Informal Advisory Opinion 950158* (www .mobar.org/mobarforms/opinionResult.aspx).
- To what extent is an attorney disqualified from handling cases against attorneys in a firm which previously employed the attorney's paralegal? ANSWER: Attorney would not be required to withdraw from or decline cases adverse to clients of the paralegal's former firm as long as (1) the paralegal is screened from participation in those cases and (2) the paralegal does not reveal any confidential information from the former employment to any person in the attorney's firm. These measures apply to all situations in the former firm, regardless of whether the paralegal had any involvement in those cases. Missouri Bar Ass'n, *Informal Advisory Opinion 930097* (www.mobar.org/mobar-forms/opinionResult.aspx).

DEFINING THE PRACTICE OF LAW IN MISSOURI

§ 484.010 (*Vernon's Annotated Statutes*): 1. The "practice of the law" is hereby defined to be and is the appearance as an advocate in a representative capacity or the drawing of papers, pleadings or documents or the performance of any act in such capacity in connection with proceeding spending or prospective before any court of record, commissioner, referee or any body, board, committee or commission constituted by law or having authority to settle controversies.

2. The "law business" is hereby defined to be and is the advising or counseling for a valuable consideration of any person, firm, association, or corporation as to any secular law or the drawing or the procuring of or assisting in the drawing for a valuable consideration of any paper, document or instrument affecting or relating to secular rights or the doing of any act for a valuable consideration in a representative capacity, obtaining or tending to obtain or securing or tending to secure for any person, firm, association or corporation any property or property rights whatsoever.

MISSOURI ETHICS AND PRACTICE RULES ON THE INTERNET

- www.law.cornell.edu/ethics/missouri.html
- www.courts.mo.gov/page.asp?id=707
- www.mobar.org/2d377f21–9993–4fa6-a60c-e6350b37bed9.aspx

PARALEGALS (AND OTHER NONATTORNEYS) IN MISSOURI STATE AND FEDERAL COURTS

- *Winsor v. Terex-Telelect-Inc.*, 43 S.W.3d 460 (Missouri Court of Appeals, 2001) (default judgments entered after a recently hired paralegal fails to enter a case into the office database; default judgment set aside, however, when court rules the error was negligent, not reckless).
- *Logan v. Hyatt Legal Plans, Inc.*, 874 S.W.2d 548 (Missouri Court of Appeals, 1994) (paralegal works for a law firm that represents the wife in a divorce action; paralegal has an affair with the husband of this client(!); paralegal is charged with disclosing confidential strategy information to her lover).
- *Missouri v. Jenkins*, 491 U.S. 274, 109 S. Ct. 2463, 105 L.Ed. 2d 229 (U.S. Supreme Court, 1989) (award of paralegal fees; see discussion of this case in Chapter 1).
- *In re Kroh Brothers . . .* , 105 Bankruptcy Reporter 515, 529 (U.S. Bankruptcy Court, W.D. Missouri, 1989) (in a request for attorney fees, the attorney fails to explain why some of the tasks performed by attorneys "were not performed by a paralegal").
- *Carter v. Kansas City Southern Ry. Co.*, 2005 WL 1000078 (U.S. District Court, W.D. Missouri, 2005) (The Court will disallow the billing entries where a paralegal records time for performing secretarial duties such as copying documents, making telephone calls, filing pleadings, and downloading pleadings. Organizing documents, however, is appropriate paralegal work.)

- *Johnson v. Barnhart*, 2004 WL 213183 (U.S. District Court, W.D. Missouri, 2004) (Purely clerical or secretarial tasks should not be billed at a lawyer or paralegal rate, regardless of who performs them. It is appropriate to distinguish between legal work, in the strict sense, and clerical work, and other work which can often be accomplished by nonlawyers but which a lawyer may do because he has no other help available. Such nonlegal work may command a lesser rate. Its dollar value is not enhanced just because a lawyer does it.)

DOING LEGAL RESEARCH IN MISSOURI LAW

Statutes: www.moga.mo.gov/statutesearch
Cases: www.courts.mo.gov
Court Rules: www.llrx.com/courtrules-gen/state-Missouri .html
General: law.wustl.edu/Library/index.asp?id=1655

FINDING EMPLOYMENT IN MISSOURI

- legal.jobs.net/Missouri.htm
- jobs.careerbuilder.com/al.ic/Missouri_Legal.htm
- www.indeed.com/q-Paralegal-l-Missouri-jobs.html
- stlouis.craigslist.org/lgl

MONTANA

DEFINING LEGAL ASSISTANTS/ PARALEGALS IN MONTANA

"Paralegal" or "legal assistant" means a person qualified through education, training, or work experience to perform substantive legal work that requires knowledge of legal concepts and that is customarily but not exclusively performed by a lawyer and who may be retained or employed by one or more lawyers, law offices, governmental agencies, or other entities or who may be authorized by administrative, statutory, or court authority to perform this work. Montana Code Annotated, § 37–60–101 (12).

ETHICAL RULES AND GUIDELINES IN MONTANA

- For a discussion of the state's ethical Rule 5.3 ("Responsibilities Regarding Nonlawyer Assistants") in the *Montana Rules of Professional Conduct*, see the end of Section C in chapter 5. For the text of 5.3 in Montana, see also www.montanaodc.org.
- An attorney must not split a fee with a nonattorney. State Bar of Montana, *Opinion (1)* (9/13/85).
- It is unethical for a law firm to pay "runners" to recommend the law firm to injured railroad workers. State Bar of Montana, *Opinion 930927* (1994) (19 Montana Lawyer 15 (1/1994)).
- Paralegals employed by law firms cannot appear on behalf of creditors at section 341 hearings in bankruptcy proceedings to question and examine debtors. The appearance would constitute an unauthorized practice of law. State Bar of Montana, *Ethics Opinion 871008*.
- Attorneys are responsible for the work product of their paralegal employees. There is no need to establish a bureaucracy to provide additional regulation on who can be a paralegal and how they can be used. *In the Matter of the Proposed Adoption of Rules Relating to Paralegals and Legal Assistants*, No. 94–577 (Supreme Court of Montana, 7/17/95).

DEFINING THE PRACTICE OF LAW IN MONTANA

- *Pulse v. North American Land Title Co. of Montana*, 707 P.2d 1105 (Supreme Court of Montana, 1985): What constitutes the practice of law is not easily defined. "The line between what is and what is not the practice of law cannot be drawn with precision. Lawyers should be the first to recognize that between the two there is a region wherein much of what lawyers do every day in their practice may also be done by others without wrongful invasion of the lawyer's field." (citing *Cowern v. Nelson*, 290 N.W. 795 (Minnesota, 1940)) While there is a sizeable minority of cases which hold that the drafting or filling in of blanks in printed forms of instruments dealing with land may not constitute the unauthorized practice of law, the majority of cases take the contrary view. We agree with the majority.

- *Montana Supreme Court Com'n on Unauthorized Practice of Law v. O'Neil*, 147 P.3d 200 (Supreme Court of Montana, 2006): A person who makes it his business to act and who does act for and by the warrant of others in legal formalities, negotiations or proceedings, practices law; and when his acts consist in advising clients touching legal matters pending or to be brought before a court of record, or in preparing pleadings or proceedings for use in a court of record, or in appearing before a court of record, either directly or by a partner or proxy, he is practicing law in a court of record.

- § 37–61–201 (*Montana Code Annotated*): Who is considered to be practicing law. Any person who shall hold himself out or advertise as an attorney or counselor at law or who shall appear in any court of record or before a judicial body, referee, commissioner, or other officer appointed to determine any question of law or fact by a court or who shall engage in the business and duties and perform such acts, matters, and things as are usually done or performed by an attorney at law in the practice of his profession for the purposes of parts 1 through 3 of this chapter shall be deemed practicing law.

IMPORTANT MONTANA MALPRACTICE LAW ON PARALEGALS

§ 27–2–206 (*Montana Code Annotated*): Actions for legal malpractice. An action against an attorney licensed to practice law in Montana or a paralegal assistant or a legal intern employed by an attorney based upon the person's alleged professional negligent act or for error or omission in the person's practice must be commenced within 3 years after the plaintiff discovers or through the use of reasonable diligence should have discovered the act, error, or omission, whichever occurs last, but in no case may the action be commenced after 10 years from the date of the act, error, or omission.

MONTANA ETHICS AND PRACTICE RULES ON THE INTERNET

- www.law.cornell.edu/ethics/montana.html
- www.montanabar.org/ethics/index.html

PARALEGALS (AND OTHER NONATTORNEYS) IN MONTANA STATE AND FEDERAL COURTS

- *Sparks v. Johnson*, 826 P.2d 928 (Supreme Court of Montana, 1992) (nonattorneys cannot practice in the justice's court on a recurring basis even though § 25–31–601 of the *Montana Code* says "any person" may act as an attorney in this court; the statute is a "one-time only" grant of a privilege of lay representation).
- *State ex rel. Montana Dept. of Transportation v. Slack*, 29 P.3d 503 (Supreme Court of Montana, 2001 (award of paralegal fees; allegation of duplicative billing).
- *In re Sirefco, Inc.*, 144 Bankruptcy Reporter 495, 497 (U.S. Bankruptcy Court, Montana, 1992) (paralegal fees

disallowed; the paralegal's work in this case was duplicative and not beneficial; the attorney failed to establish that the paralegal's work "was not merely secretarial in nature").

- *Montana Land and Mineral Owners Ass'n, Inc. v. Devon Energy Corp.*, 2006 WL 1876859 (U.S. District Court, 2006) (plaintiffs waived the work-product privilege regarding the preparation of the paralegals' summary; therefore, a deposition of the paralegals can be made concerning the preparation).

DOING LEGAL RESEARCH IN MONTANA LAW

Statutes: data.opi.mt.gov/bills/mca_toc/index.htm
Cases: courts.mt.gov/library/mt_law.asp#judicial
Court Rules: www.llrx.com/courtrules-gen/state-Montana .html
General: www.megalaw.com/mt/mt.php

FINDING EMPLOYMENT IN MONTANA

- montanabar.legalstaff.com
- www.indeed.com/q-Paralegal-l-Montana-jobs.html
- montana.craigslist.org/lgl

NEBRASKA

ETHICAL RULES AND GUIDELINES IN NEBRASKA

- For a discussion of the state's ethical Rule 5.3 ("Responsibilities Regarding Nonlawyer Assistants") in the *Nebraska Rules of Professional Conduct*, see the end of Section C in chapter 5. For the text of 5.3 in Nebraska, see also www.supremecourt. ne.gov/rules.
- Paralegals can be listed on law firm letterhead if their nonattorney status is clear. Nebraska State Bar Ass'n, *Opinion 88–2*.
- Several attorneys who are not partners, associates, or otherwise affiliated with each other share office space and share nonattorney personnel. They represent clients who are opposite each other in cases. This is not improper if the clients are aware of and consent to the arrangement and if steps are taken to ensure confidentiality—such as preventing common access to case files and preventing the nonattorneys from working both sides on a case. Nebraska State Bar Ass'n, *Opinion 89–2*.
- Hiring someone who has worked for an opposing law firm in matters related to a particular case automatically disqualifies the hiring firm from the case. A Chinese Wall or cone of silence erected around an attorney, law clerk, paralegal, secretary or other ancillary staff member is insufficient to prevent disqualification due to a conflict of interest and appearance of impropriety. Nebraska State Bar Ass'n, *Opinion 94–4*.
- A suspended attorney may be employed as a paralegal if the employment is at a place and in such a manner as to not give the appearance of practicing law. A suspended attorney may not be employed as a paralegal at an office where he or she previously shared office space or practiced law. Nebraska State Bar Ass'n, *Opinion 96–1*. Affirmed in *Opinion 06–6*.
- (d) A lawyer shall not knowingly allow a support person to participate or assist in the representation of a current client in the same or a substantially related matter in which another lawyer or firm with which the support person formerly was associated had previously represented a client: (1) whose interests are materially adverse to the current client; and (2) about whom the support person has acquired confidential information that is material to the matter, unless the former client gives informed consent, confirmed in writing.

(e) If a support person, who has worked on a matter, is personally prohibited from working on a particular matter under Rule 1.9(d), the lawyer or firm with which that person is presently associated will not be prohibited from representing the current client in that matter if:
(1) the former client gives informed consent, confirmed in writing, or
(2) the support person is screened from any personal participation in the matter to avoid communication to others in the firm of confidential information that both the support person and the firm have a legal duty to protect.
(f) For purposes of Rules 1.9(d) and (e), a support person shall mean any person, other than a lawyer, who is associated with a lawyer or a law firm and shall include but is not necessarily limited to the following: law clerks, paralegals, legal assistants, secretaries, messengers and other support personnel employed by the law firm. *Nebraska Rules of Professional Conduct*, Rule 1.9.

DEFINING THE PRACTICE OF LAW IN NEBRASKA

- *Nebraska . . . v. Butterfield*, 111 N.W.2d 543 545 (Supreme Court of Nebraska, 1961): The Supreme Court of this state has the inherent power to define and regulate the practice of law in this state. . . . While an all-embracing definition of the term "practicing law" would involve great difficulty, it is generally defined as the giving of advice or rendition of any sort of service by a person, firm, or corporation when the giving of such advice or rendition of such service requires the use of any degree of legal knowledge or skill . . . . In an ever-changing economic and social order, the "practice of law" must necessarily change, making it practically impossible to formulate an enduring definition . . . . In determining what constitutes the practice of law it is the character of the act and not the place where the act is performed that is the controlling factor . . . . Whether or not a fee is charged is not a decisive factor in determining if one has engaged in the practice of law.

  Rule 5 (*West's Nebraska Court Rules and Procedure*): Admission of Attorneys.

  (3) For purposes of this rule, "practice of law" means: . . .

  (b) Employment as a lawyer for a corporation, partnership, trust, individual, or other entity with the primary duties of:

  (i) Furnishing legal counsel, drafting documents and pleadings, and interpreting and giving advice with respect to the law, or

  (ii) Preparing cases for presentation to or trying before courts, executive departments, or administrative bureaus or agencies; . . .

- *State ex rel. Johnson v. Childe*, 295 N.W. 381 (Nebraska Supreme Court, 1941): A layman may prepare simple, elementary documents of a routine character and may also advise persons as to matters of business, although minor legal questions are incidentally involved, without engaging in prohibited "practice of law" where the legal training, knowledge and skill required are not beyond range of average man.

NEBRASKA ETHICS AND PRACTICE RULES ON THE INTERNET

- www.law.cornell.edu/ethics/nebraska.html
- www.nebar.com/ethics/index.htm
- www.nebar.com/ethics/ne_code.htm
- www.supremecourt.ne.gov/rules/pdf/rulesprof conduct-34.pdf

PARALEGALS (AND OTHER NONATTORNEYS) IN NEBRASKA STATE AND FEDERAL COURTS

- *State ex rel. Counsel for Discipline of Nebraska Supreme Court v. Huston*, 631 N.W.2d 913 (Nebraska Supreme Court, 2001) (charges attorney claimed for a legal assistant were excessive, given that much of the itemized work was more secretarial in nature).
- *Rockwell v. Talbott, Adams & Moore*, 2006 WL 436041 (U.S. District Court, Nebraska, 2006) (I also find that there was not a proper delegation of work from the attorney level to the legal assistant level, resulting in Mr. Cox doing work that arguably should have been performed in the first instance by a legal assistant. For example, drafts of the written discovery and summaries of the Defendant's discovery responses could have been prepared by legal assistants for the attorney's review. It is reasonable for a client to expect that work will be allocated within a law firm based on the level of expertise required of the task in order to provide efficiency and economy in the rendering of quality legal services.)
- *State ex rel. Creighton University v. Hickman*, 512 N.W.2d 374 (Nebraska Supreme Court, 1994) (attorney works on a case and is disbarred; he then goes to work as a legal assistant to do discovery work for the opposing attorney on the same case; the new employer is disqualified from continuing on the case).
- *Nebraska v. Garvey*, 457 N.W.2d 297 (Nebraska Supreme Court, 1990) (suspended attorney ordered to perform fifty hours of pro bono paralegal work).

DOING LEGAL RESEARCH IN NEBRASKA LAW

Statutes: www.unicam.state.ne.us
Cases: www.supremecourt.ne.gov/opinions
Court Rules: www.llrx.com/courtrules-gen/state-Nebraska.html
General: www.washlaw.edu/uslaw/states/Nebraska

FINDING EMPLOYMENT IN NEBRASKA

- nebar.legalstaff.com
- www.indeed.com/q-Paralegal-l-Nebraska-jobs.html
- www.simplyhired.com/job-search/l-Nebraska/o-232000/t-Paralegal
- lincoln.craigslist.org/lgl

NEVADA

DEFINING LEGAL ASSISTANTS/ PARALEGALS IN NEVADA

State Bar of Nevada, Legal Assistants Division: Definition. A legal assistant (also known as a paralegal) is a person, qualified through education, training or work experience, who is employed or retained by a lawyer, law office, governmental agency or other entity in a capacity or function which involves the performance, under the ultimate direction and supervision of an attorney, of specifically delegated substantive legal work, which work, for the most part, requires sufficient knowledge of legal concepts that, absent such an assistant, the attorney would perform the task. *ByLaws of the Legal Assistants Division of the State Bar of Nevada*, § 3 (www.nvbar.org/PDF/LegalAsst_ByLaws.pdf)

ETHICAL RULES AND GUIDELINES IN NEVADA

- For a discussion of the state's ethical Rule 5.3 ("Responsibilities Regarding Nonlawyer Assistants") in the *Nevada Rules of Professional Conduct*, see the end of Section C in chapter 5. For the text of 5.3 in Nevada, see also www.leg.state.nv.us/CourtRules/RPC.html.
- A practicing lawyer can operate a collateral business through which he places temporary secretarial and clerical help in other law offices so long as (a) he does not place temporary help in offices with which he has matters pending; (b) the employees clearly understand they must preserve client confidences and avoid working on matters they have worked on for the lawyer or in other law offices; and (c) the lawyers who use the temporary secretarial service are told that the owner/operator of the service is himself an active lawyer. State Bar of Nevada, *Formal Opinion No. 6* (9/24/87).
- The business card of an out-of-state attorney working in Nevada should state that he is a "legal assistant" or otherwise shows the nature of his employment. State Bar of Nevada, *Opinion No. 3* (3/19/75).
- Code of Ethics and professional Responsibility of the Legal Assistants Division of the State Bar of Nevada (www.nvbar.org/PDF/LegalAsst_Ethics.pdf).
- Legal Assistants Pledge of Professionalism (State Bar of Nevada) (www.nvbar.org/PDF/LegalAsst_Pledge.pdf).

DEFINING THE PRACTICE OF LAW IN NEVADA

Rule 51.5 (*Supreme Court Rules*): Admission to practice.
2. Practice of law. For purposes of this rule, the term "practice of law" shall mean: . . .
(b) practice as an attorney for an individual, a corporation, partnership, trust, or other entity, with the primary duties of furnishing legal counsel, researching legal issues, drafting legal documents, pleadings, and memoranda, interpreting and giving advice regarding the law, or preparing, trying or presenting cases before courts, departments of government or administrative agencies . . . .

NEVADA ETHICS AND PRACTICE RULES ON THE INTERNET

- www.law.cornell.edu/ethics/nevada.html
- www.nvbar.org/Ethics/e2k.htm
- www.nvbar.org/Ethics/Ethics_Opinions.htm

PARALEGALS (AND OTHER NONATTORNEYS) IN NEVADA STATE AND FEDERAL COURTS

- *Leibowitz v. Eighth Judicial District . . .* , 78 P.3d 515 (Supreme Court of Nevada, 2003) (Screening of a nonlawyer employee may allow a hiring law firm to avoid imputed attorney disqualification based on the employee's acquisition, in the former employment, of confidences of the adversary of the hiring law firm's client. If the nonlawyer employee hired by a law firm acquired, during the employee's former employment, confidences of an adversary of the hiring law firm's client, the hiring law firm must, at a minimum: (1) caution the employee not to disclose any information relating to the representation of the adversary; (2) instruct the employee not to work on any matter on which she worked during the prior employment or regarding which she has information relating to the former employer's representation; and (3) take reasonable steps to ensure that the employee does not work in connection with matters on which she worked during the prior employment, absent the adversary's consent, i.e., unconditional waiver after consultation.) (Overruling in part *Ciaffone v. Eighth Judicial District* . . . , 945 P.2d 950 (Supreme Court of Nevada, 1997).

- See also *Brown v. Eighth Judicial District Court ex rel. County of Clark*, 14 P.3d 1266 (Supreme Court of Nevada 2000) (disqualification not warranted when legal secretary switches firms).

- *In re Ginji*, 117 Bankruptcy Reporter 983, 993 (U.S. Bankruptcy Court, Nevada, 1990) (award of paralegal fees; work that "was done by an attorney which should have been done by a paralegal . . . shall be billed at a lower rate").

- *Trustees of Const. Industry and Laborers Health and Welfare Trust v. Redland Ins. Co.*, 460 F.3d 1253 (U.S. Court of Appeals, 9th Circuit (Nevada), 2006) (If the attorney's hourly rate already incorporates the cost of work performed by nonattorneys, then courts should not compensate for these costs as an additional "reasonable attorney's fee." The key is the billing custom in the relevant market. Thus, fees for work performed by nonattorneys such as paralegals may be billed separately, at market rates, if this is the prevailing practice in a given community.)

- *Recio v. Clark County School Dist.*, 2006 WL 3149363 (U.S. District Court, Nevada, 2006) (counsel seeks an award of paralegal fees for the work of Cheryl Jung but fails to offer evidence that Jung is qualified through education, training, or work experience to perform substantive legal work as a paralegal).

- *Greenwell v. Paralegal Center*, 836 P.2d 70 (Supreme Court of Nevada, 1992) (injunction granted against a typing service for the unauthorized practice of law, but the court orders the state bar to investigate the alleged unavailability of legal services for low- and middle-income Nevadans).

- *Pioneer Title v. State Bar*, 326 P.2d 408 (Supreme Court of Nevada, 1958) (some simple legal services may be so necessary that they could properly be provided by nonattorneys if they would otherwise be unavailable).

DOING LEGAL RESEARCH IN NEVADA LAW

Statutes: www.leg.state.nv.us/law1.cfm
Cases: www.nvsupremecourt.us
Court Rules: www.leg.state.nv.us/CourtRules
General: www.co.clark.nv.us/law_library/nv_research.htm

FINDING EMPLOYMENT IN NEVADA

- www.nvbar.org/careercenter.htm
- www.indeed.com/q-Litigation-Paralegal-l-Nevada-jobs.html
- www.simplyhired.com/job-search/l-Nevada/o-232000/t-Paralegal
- careers.findlaw.com
- lasvegas.craigslist.org/lgl

NEW HAMPSHIRE

DEFINING LEGAL ASSISTANTS/ PARALEGALS IN NEW HAMPSHIRE

[T]he term "legal assistant" shall mean a person not admitted to the practice of law in New Hampshire who is an employee of or an assistant to an active member of the New Hampshire Bar . . . and who, under the control and supervision of an active member

of the New Hampshire Bar, renders services related to but not constituting the practice of law. *Rules of The Supreme Court of the State of New Hampshire*, Rule 35(C) (www.courts.state.nh.us/rules/scr/scr-35.htm).

ETHICAL RULES AND GUIDELINES IN NEW HAMPSHIRE

- For a discussion of the state's ethical Rule 5.3 ("Responsibilities Regarding Nonlawyer Assistants") in the *New Hampshire Rules of Professional Conduct*, see the end of Section C in chapter 5. For the text of 5.3 in New Hampshire, see also www.courts.state.nh.us/rules/index.htm.

- Rule 35 (*New Hampshire Supreme Court Rules*) (www.courts. state.nh.us/rules/scr/scr-35.htm). *Rule 1:* Paralegals must not give legal advice, but they can, with adequate attorney supervision, provide information concerning legal matters. *Rule 2:* An attorney may not permit a legal assistant to represent a client in judicial or administrative proceedings unless authorized by statute, court rule or decision, administrative rule or regulation, or customary practice. *Rule 3:* A paralegal shall not be delegated any task that requires the exercise of professional legal judgment. The attorney must supervise the paralegal. *Rule 4:* An attorney must take care that the legal assistant does not reveal information relating to representation of a client or use such information to the disadvantage of the client. *Rule 5:* An attorney shall not form a partnership with a paralegal if any part of the partnership consists of the practice of law. *Rule 6:* An attorney shall not share fees with a paralegal but can include the paralegal in a retirement plan based on a profit-sharing arrangement. *Rule 7:* A paralegal's name may not be included on the letterhead of an attorney. A paralegal can have a business card that prints the name of the law firm where he or she works, if the card indicates the paralegal's nonattorney capacity and the firm does not use the paralegal to solicit business for the firm improperly. *Rule 8:* When dealing with clients, attorneys, or the public, the paralegal must disclose at the outset that he or she is not an attorney. *Rule 9:* An attorney must exercise care to prevent a legal assistant from engaging in conduct that would involve the attorney unethical conduct.

- A law firm cannot list legal assistants on its letterhead. New Hampshire Bar Ass'n, *Ethics Opinion 1982–3/20* (3/17/83).

- Paralegals must avoid communications that involve the offering of legal advice, which is the exclusive function of the attorney. New Hampshire Bar Ass'n, *Successful Law Practice with Paralegals* (1992). See also New Hampshire Bar Ass'n, *Guidelines for the Utilization of the Services of Legal Assistants* (1977).

- Without the prior written approval of the court, no person who is not a lawyer may represent a person other than himself or be listed on the notice of appeal or other appeal document, or on the brief, or sit at counsel table in the courtroom or present oral argument. *Rules Of The Supreme Court of the State of New Hampshire*, Rule 33(2).

- An ethics article written by of the New Hampshire Bar Ethics Committee on hiring a disbarred or suspended attorney as a paralegal urges the Supreme Court and the Professional Conduct Committee to establish guidelines and rules to assist practitioners in determining whether to employ suspended or disbarred attorneys and, if so, under what restrictions. NHBA Ethics Committee, *Disbarred or Suspended Attorneys: Resources or Pariahs* (3/9/92) (www.nhbar.org/pdfs/PEA3–92.pdf).

DEFINING THE PRACTICE OF LAW IN NEW HAMPSHIRE

- *New Hampshire v. Settle*, 480 A.2d 6, 8 (Supreme Court of New Hampshire, 1984): The only statutory definition of the unauthorized practice of law is provided in RSA 311:7 which states: "No person shall be permitted commonly to practice as an attorney in court unless he has been admitted by the court. . . ." The defendant argues that unless an individual is actually practicing in court, his conduct is not proscribed by the statute. We cannot read RSA 311:7 to limit the unauthorized practice of law to those instances in which an individual has physically appeared in the courtroom to represent a litigant. At the very least, this provision also encompasses the filing of documents in the court system. . . . There is no "single factor to determine whether someone is engaged in the unauthorized practice of law … [Rather, such a] determination must be made on a case-by-case basis."

- *Kamasinski v. McLaughlin*, 2003 WL 367745 (Superior Court of New Hampshire, 2003): For the purposes of this case, the Court defines the practice of law to include (but not be limited to) the following: 1. Giving advice or counsel to others as to their legal rights or the legal rights or responsibilities of others for fees or other consideration. 2. Selection, drafting, or completion of legal documents or agreements which affect the legal rights of an entity or person(s). 3. Representation of another entity or person(s) in a court, or in a formal administrative adjudicative proceeding or other formal dispute resolution process or in an administrative adjudicative proceeding in which legal pleadings are filed or a record is established as the basis for judicial review. 4. Negotiation of legal rights or responsibilities on behalf of another entity or person(s). HB 1420, Chapter 218:1, Laws of 2002, Task Force on the Definition of the Practice of Law.

- Ethical Consideration 3–5 of the former *Code of Professional Responsibility*: It is neither necessary nor desirable to attempt the formulation of a single, specific definition of what constitutes the practice of law. Functionally, the practice of law relates to the rendition of services for others that call for the professional judgment of a lawyer. The essence of the professional judgment of a lawyer is his educated ability to relate the general body and philosophy of law to a specific legal problem of a client. . . .

NEW HAMPSHIRE ETHICS AND PRACTICE RULES ON THE INTERNET

- www.law.cornell.edu/ethics/nh.html
- www.law.cornell.edu/ethics/nh/code/NH_CODE.HTM
- www.nhbar.org/legal-links/ethics-opinions-practical-ethics-articles.asp

PARALEGALS (AND OTHER NONATTORNEYS) IN NEW HAMPSHIRE STATE AND FEDERAL COURTS

- *Tocci's Case*, 663 A.2d 88 (Supreme Court of New Hampshire, 1995) (§ 311.1 of the New Hampshire Revised Statutes says, "A party in any cause or proceeding may appear, plead, prosecute or defend in his or her proper person, that is, pro se, or may be represented by any citizen of good character." This section allows a nonlawyer to appear in an individual case; it does not allow persons "otherwise unable to practice law to act commonly, entering repeated appearances before the courts of this State").

- (See also New Hampshire Supreme Court Rule 33(2), which implies that a nonattorney with court approval "may

represent a person other than himself or be listed on the notice of appeal or other appeal document, or on the brief, or sit at counsel table in the courtroom or present oral argument." (www.courts.state.nh.us/rules/scr/scr-33.htm).

- *Kalled's Case*, 607 A.2d 613 (Supreme Court of New Hampshire, 1992) (excessive billing by an attorney such as charging the client for 1,489 hours of paralegal time at $60 per hour).

- *Van Dorn Retail Management, Inc. v. Jim's Oxford Shop, Inc.*, 874 F. Supp. 476, 490 (U.S. District Court, New Hampshire, 1994) (paralegal fees reduced; "attorneys and paralegals duplicated their efforts"; paralegals "performed clerical functions").

DOING LEGAL RESEARCH IN NEW HAMPSHIRE LAW

Statutes: www.gencourt.state.nh.us/ie
Cases: www.courts.state.nh.us
Court Rules: www.courts.state.nh.us/rules/index.htm
General: www.romingerlegal.com/state/newhampshire.html

FINDING EMPLOYMENT IN NEW HAMPSHIRE

- careers.findlaw.com
- www.indeed.com/q-Paralegal-l-New-Hampshire-jobs.html
- www.simplyhired.com/job-search/l-New-Hampshire/o-232000/t-Paralegal
- nh.craigslist.org/lgl

NEW JERSEY

DEFINING LEGAL ASSISTANTS/ PARALEGALS IN NEW JERSEY

[A paralegal is] a person qualified through education, training or work experience; is employed or retained by a lawyer, law office, government agency, or other entity; works under the ultimate direction and supervision of an attorney; performs specifically delegated legal work, which, for the most part, requires a sufficient knowledge of legal concepts; and performs such duties that, absent such an assistant, the attorney would perform such tasks. *In re Opinion No. 24*, 607 A.2d 962 (Supreme Court of New Jersey, 1992) (citing the definition of the American Bar Association).

ETHICAL RULES AND GUIDELINES IN NEW JERSEY

- For a discussion of the state's ethical Rule 5.3 ("Responsibilities Regarding Nonlawyer Assistants") in the *New Jersey Rules of Professional Conduct*, see the end of Section C in chapter 5. For the text of 5.3 in New Jersey, see also www.courts.state.nh.us/rules/pcon/index.htm.

- New Jersey has added an additional subsection to Rule 5.3 of the *Model Rules of Professional Conduct* that is not is the ABA *Model Rules*. The N.J. addition is (c)(3): attorneys must make a "reasonable investigation of circumstances that would disclose past instances of conduct by the nonlawyer" that are "incompatible with the professional obligations of an attorney, which evidence a propensity for such conduct."

- It is not the unauthorized practice of law for a nonattorney broker to conduct residential real estate closings and settlements without attorneys as long as the broker notifies the buyer and seller of the risk of not having attorney representation and of the conflicting interest that brokers and title companies have. *In re Opinion No. 26 of Committee on Unauthorized Practice of Law*, 1995 WL 121535.

■ It is unethical for attorneys to hire a paralegal to screen calls of prospective clients to determine whether the case involves "good liability and damages." The paralegal would discuss the claims of the callers and make a determination of whether to refer the case to an attorney. This is the unauthorized practice of law. New Jersey Supreme Court Advisory Committee on Professional Ethics, *Opinion 645* (10/4/90) (126 New Jersey Law Journal 894) (1990 WL 441602). In agreement: *Opinion 6* (10/4/90) of the New Jersey Supreme Court Advisory Committee on Attorney Advertising.

■ A paralegal can have a business card as long as the name of the employing law firm is also printed on it. New Jersey Supreme Court Advisory Committee on Professional Ethics, *Opinion 647* (1990) (126 New Jersey Law Journal 1525) (1990 WL 441612). See also the following opinions that allow nonattorney employees, e.g., office managers, to have business cards: *Opinion 471*, (2/12/81), 107 New Jersey Law Journal 127, 1981 WL 89073; *Opinion 553* (1/24/85), 115 New Jersey Law Journal 96, 1985 WL 150698.

■ The names of paralegals may be printed on attorney letterhead and in advertisements. "[T]he respect accorded paralegals and the work they perform has increased immeasurably over the last 10 to 15 years." New Jersey Supreme Court Committee on Attorney Advertising, *Opinion 16* (1/24/94) (136 New Jersey Law Journal 375) (1994 WL 45949). This opinion superseded *Opinion 296* (1975). Compare *Opinion 330* (6/3/76), 99 New Jersey Law Journal 473.

■ Nonattorney employees of the country welfare agency may represent litigants before the Office of Administrative Law. New Jersey Supreme Court Advisory Committee on Professional Ethics, *Opinion 580* (2/27/86).

■ Paralegals can sign law firm correspondence concerning routine tasks such as gathering factual information and documents. They should not sign correspondence to clients, adverse attorneys, or tribunals. Minor exceptions are allowed such as "a purely routine request to a court clerk for a docket sheet." New Jersey Supreme Court Advisory Committee on Professional Ethics, *Opinion 611* (2/23/88) (121 New Jersey Law Journal 301) (1988 WL 356368).

■ A paralegal switches jobs between law firms that opposed each other in litigation. The paralegal worked on the litigation while at the former firm. The new employer is not disqualified if a Chinese Wall is built around the paralegal and she would work for an attorney who has no involvement in the litigation. Also, her office would be located in another end of the building. New Jersey Supreme Court Advisory Committee on Professional Ethics, *Opinion 665* (8/3/92) (131 New Jersey Law Journal 1074) (1992 WL 465626), modifying the prohibition announced in *Opinion 546* (11/8/84) (114 New Jersey Law Journal 496) (1984 WL 140946). See also *Opinion 633* (11/2/89) (a law firm litigating tobacco cases can hire a nonattorney who had been involved in tobacco litigation at another firm if the nonattorney had no substantial responsibility in the tobacco litigation at the other firm, obtained no confidential information concerning the litigation, and is screened from such litigation at the present firm).

DEFINING THE PRACTICE OF LAW IN NEW JERSEY

■ *In re Opinion No. 24 of the Committee on the Unauthorized Practice of Law*, 607 A.2d 962, 966 (Supreme Court of New Jersey, 1992): No satisfactory, all-inclusive definition of what constitutes the practice of law has ever been devised. None will be attempted here. That has been left, and wisely so, to the courts when parties present them with concrete factual situations. . . . "What is now considered the practice of law is something which may be described more readily than defined." . . . Essentially, the Court decides what constitutes the practice of law on a case-by-case basis. . . . The practice of law is not subject to precise definition. It is not confined to litigation but often encompasses "legal activities in many non-litigious fields which entail specialized knowledge and ability." Therefore, the line between permissible business and professional activities and the unauthorized practice of law is often blurred. . . . There is no question that paralegals' work constitutes the practice of law. N.J.S.A. 2A:170–78 and 79 deem unauthorized the practice of law by a nonlawyer and make such practice a disorderly-persons offense. However, N.J.S.A. 2A:170–81 (f) excepts paralegals from being penalized for engaging in tasks that constitute legal practice if their supervising attorney assumes direct responsibility for the work that the paralegals perform. N.J.S.A. 2A:170–81(f) states: Any person or corporation furnishing to any person lawfully engaged in the practice of law such information or such clerical assistance in and about his professional work as, except for the provisions of this article, may be lawful, but the lawyer receiving such information or service shall at all times maintain full professional and direct responsibility to his client for the information and service so rendered. Consequently, paralegals who are supervised by attorneys do not engage in the unauthorized practice of law.

SPECIAL RULES AN PARALEGAL REPRESENTATION IN NEW JERSEY

■ New Jersey Administrative Code, title 1, 1:1–5.4 Representation by non-lawyers: [T]he following non-lawyers may apply for permission to represent a party at a contested case hearing: . . . 4. Legal service paralegals or assistants.

■ New Jersey Court Rules, Rule 1–21–1(f) Appearances Before Office of Administrative Law and Administrative Agencies. Subject to such limitations and procedural rules as may be established by the Office of Administrative Law, an appearance by a non-attorney in a contested case before the Office of Administrative Law or an administrative agency may be permitted, on application, in any of the following circumstances: (1) where required by federal statute or regulation; . . . (4) to assist in providing representation to an indigent as part of a Legal Services program if the non-attorney is a paralegal or legal assistant employed by that program; . . . (7) to assist an individual who is not represented by an attorney provided (i) the presentation appears likely to be enhanced by such assistance, (ii) the individual certifies that he or she lacks the means to retain an attorney and that representation is not available through a Legal Services program and (iii) the conduct of the proceeding by the Office of Administrative Law will not be impaired by such assistance.

NEW JERSEY ETHICS AND PRACTICE RULES ON THE INTERNET

- www.law.cornell.edu/ethics/nj.html
- lawlibrary.rutgers.edu/ethics/search.html

PARALEGALS (AND OTHER NONATTORNEYS) IN NEW JERSEY STATE AND FEDERAL COURTS

- *In re Opinion No. 24 of the Committee on the Unauthorized Practice of Law*, 607 A.2d 962 (Supreme Court of New Jersey, 1992) (see chapter 5) (attorneys may delegate tasks to paralegals whether the paralegal is employed by the attorney or is an independent paralegal who is retained by the attorney as long as the attorney maintains a direct relationship with his or her clients, supervises the paralegal's work, and is responsible for the paralegal's work product). This opinion overruled *Advisory Opinion 24* (1990) of the New Jersey Unauthorized Practice of Law Committee, which said that attorneys cannot hire paralegals as independent contractors because of the difficulty of providing them with needed day-to-day supervision and the danger of conflict-of-interest because the paralegals work for different attorneys.
- *Infante v. Gottesman*, 558 A.2d 1338 (Superior Court of New Jersey, 1989) (it is unethical for an attorney to form a partnership and split fees with a paralegal/investigation service).
- *Argila v. Argila*, 607 A.2d 675, 679 (Superior Court of New Jersey, 1992) (the application for paralegal fees failed to provide the qualifications of the paralegals and data on the prevailing market rate for paralegals).
- *Deptford Tp. School Dist. v. H.B.*, 2006 WL 3779820 (U.S. District Court, New Jersey, 2006) ("Mr. Epstein recorded 1.2 hours to review three certificates of service and file return of service with this Court. This task could have (and should have) been performed by a paralegal or capable legal assistant, or, if actually done by Mr. Epstein personally, these should have been billed at a much lower rate or absorbed as routine office overhead").
- *Microsoft Corp. v. United Computer Resources of New Jersey*, 216 F. Supp. 2d 383 (U.S. District Court, New Jersey 2002) ("54 hours in paralegal time spent preparing for an eight-hour hearing is excessive. Accordingly, the paralegal's time will be reduced").
- *Buccilli v. Timby, Brown, Timby*, 660 A.2d 1261 (Superior Court of New Jersey, 1995) (New Jersey paralegal who worked for a Pennsylvania law firm claims she was fired because she told the firm she was subjected to sexual harassment, she intended to file a workers' compensation claim, and she objected to the lack of attorney supervision of her work and being asked to forge her attorney's name to court documents).
- *United States v. Barber*, 808 F. Supp. 361 (U.S. District Court, New Jersey, 1992) (disbarred attorney acts as paralegal).

DOING LEGAL RESEARCH IN NEW JERSEY LAW

Statutes: www.njleg.state.nj.us
Cases: lawlibrary.rutgers.edu/search.shtml
Court Rules: njlawnet.com/njcourtrules
General: www.njstatelib.org/Research_Guides/Law/index.php

FINDING EMPLOYMENT IN NEW JERSEY

- njsba.legalstaff.com/Common/HomePage.aspx?abbr=NJSBA
- www.njparalegal.com/pwelcome.htm
- www.indeed.com/q-Paralegal-l-New-Jersey-jobs.html
- newjersey.craigslist.org/lgl
- careers.findlaw.com

NEW MEXICO

DEFINING LEGAL ASSISTANTS/PARALEGALS IN NEW MEXICO

A. a "paralegal" is a person who: (1) contracts with or is employed by an attorney, law firm, corporation, governmental agency or other entity; (2) performs substantive legal work under the supervision of a licensed attorney who assumes professional responsibility for the final work product; and (3) meets one or more of the education, training or work experience qualifications set forth in Rule 20–115 NMRA of these rules; and

B. "substantive legal work" is work that requires knowledge of legal concepts and is customarily, but not exclusively, performed by a lawyer. Examples of substantive legal work performed by a paralegal include: case planning, development and management; legal research and analysis; interviewing clients; fact gathering and retrieving information; drafting legal documents; collecting, compiling, and utilizing technical information to make an independent decision and recommendation to the supervising attorney; and representing clients before a state or federal administrative agency if that representation is authorized by law. Substantive legal work performed by a paralegal for a licensed attorney shall not constitute the unauthorized practice of law. *Rules Governing Paralegal Services*, Rule 20–102, New Mexico Rules Annotated. (www.nmbar.org/Template.cfm?Section=Paralegal_Division).

ETHICAL RULES AND GUIDELINES IN NEW MEXICO

- For a discussion of the state's ethical Rule 5.3 [Rule 16–503] ("Responsibilities Regarding Nonlawyer Assistants") in the *New Mexico Rules of Professional Conduct*, see the end of Section C in chapter 5. For the text of 5.3 [Rule 16–503] in New Mexico, see also www.law.cornell.edu/ethics/nm/code/NM_CODE.htm.
- *Rules Governing Paralegal Services*, New Mexico Rules Annotated (excerpts)
  - **20–101.** The employment of paralegals is a particularly significant means by which lawyers can render legal services more economically, in greater volume and with maximum efficiency while maintaining the quality of legal services.
  - **20–213.** A paralegal shall not provide legal advice; represent a client in court except to the extent authorized by law; select, explain, draft, or recommend the use of any legal document to or for any person other than the attorney who supervises the paralegal, unless the supervising attorney so directs; engage in conduct that constitutes the unauthorized practice of law; establish fees; perform any services for a consumer except as performed under the supervision of the attorney unless allowed statute or other law.
  - **20–104.** A lawyer will require the paralegal for whose work the lawyer is responsible to disclose to all persons with whom the paralegal communicates that the paralegal is not a lawyer. (Commentary: Common sense would indicate that a routine disclosure be made at the beginning of any conversation.)
  - **20–105.** A lawyer has an affirmative obligation to ensure that the paralegal for whose work the lawyer is responsible preserves the confidences and secrets of a client.
  - **20–106.** A lawyer will maintain active personal communication with the client. (Commentary: This rule does not preclude a paralegal from meeting with or talking to the client, nor does it mandate regular and frequent meetings between the lawyer and client.)

- **20–107.** A paralegal may not act as an advocate on behalf of the client and cannot appear in court or any other tribunal, either in person or on record, as a representative of or advocate for the client, except to the extent authorized by law.

- **20–108.** A lawyer is responsible to ensure that no personal, social or business interest or relationship of the paralegal impinges upon, or appears to impinge upon, the services rendered to the client. (Commentary: If a lawyer accepts a matter in which the paralegal may have a conflict of interest, the lawyer will exclude that paralegal from participation in any services performed in connection with that matter. Furthermore, the lawyer must specifically inform the client that a nonlawyer employee has a conflict of interest which, was it the lawyer's conflict, would prevent further representation of the client in connection with the matter.

- **20–109.** The lawyer will not permit, encourage or influence the paralegal for whose work the lawyer is responsible to recommend that the lawyer or the lawyer's firm be retained by any person or entity, nor shall the lawyer condone such activity on the part of a paralegal.

- **20–110.** A lawyer is responsible to ensure that a paralegal is competent to perform the work which the lawyer delegates to the paralegal. (Commentary: The paralegal has a duty to inform the lawyer of any assignment which the assistant regards as being beyond his capability.

- **20–111.** A lawyer will not form a partnership or other entity with a paralegal for the purpose of practicing law. (Commentary: A lawyer will not share fees with a paralegal. The compensation of a paralegal may not include a percentage of profits, fees received generally or fees received specifically from a client who came to the lawyer or the firm by reason of acquaintance or other association with the paralegal. But paralegals can be included in a retirement or profit-sharing arrangement plan, since such inclusion does not aid or encourage laymen to practice law.)

- **20–112.** The paralegal is directly accountable to the lawyer. The lawyer maintains ultimate responsibility for and has an ongoing duty to actively supervise the paralegal's work performance, conduct and product.

- **20–113.** The letterhead of a lawyer or law firm may not include the name of a paralegal. However, a lawyer or law firm may permit its name to appear on the business card of a paralegal, provided the paralegal's capacity is clearly indicated. (Commentary: A lawyer may permit a paralegal to sign correspondence on his letterhead or on the letterhead of a law firm, as long as the nonlawyer status of the paralegal is clearly disclosed by a title accompanying the signature, such as "paralegal". The business card of a paralegal may contain the name, address and telephone number of the paralegal's employer. However, the card must on its face be clearly intended to identify the paralegal and not the lawyer or law firm.)

- **20–114.** A lawyer has an affirmative obligation to ensure that a legal assistant, paralegal or other non-lawyer support staff for whose work the lawyer is responsible does not engage in any activities which, if engaged in by the lawyer, would constitute a violation of the Rules of Professional Conduct.

- **20–115.** A paralegal shall meet specified educational, training or work experience qualifications. (www.nmbar.org/Template.cfm?Section=Paralegal_Division).

■ Attorneys must tell clients how much services to be rendered by office nonattorneys will cost. Advisory Opinions Committee of the State Bar of New Mexico, *Opinion 1990–4* (6/9/90).

■ The word "Associates" in a law firm's name cannot refer to or include paralegal, legal assistants, or other nonattorney employees. Advisory Opinions Committee of the State Bar of New Mexico, *Opinion 2006–1* (4/3/06).

DEFINING THE PRACTICE OF LAW IN NEW MEXICO

■ *State ex rel. Norvell v. Credit Bureau of Albuquerque, Inc.*, 514 P.2d 40 (Supreme Court of New Mexico, 1973): [I]ndicia of the practice of law, insofar as court proceedings are concerned, include the following: (1) representation of parties before judicial or administrative bodies, (2) preparation of pleadings and other papers incident to actions and special proceedings, (3) management of such action and proceeding, and non-court related activities such as (4) giving legal advice and counsel, (5) rendering a service that requires the use of legal knowledge or skill, (6) preparing instruments and contracts by which legal rights are secured.

NEW MEXICO ETHICS AND PRACTICE RULES ON THE INTERNET

- www.law.cornell.edu/ethics/nm.html
- chrome.law.cornell.edu/ethics/nm/code/index.htm
- www.nmbar.org (click "Attorney Services", then "Ethics Advisory Opinions")
- www.nmbar.org/Template.cfm?Section=Opinion_Summaries

PARALEGALS (AND OTHER NONATTORNEYS) IN NEW MEXICO STATE AND FEDERAL COURTS

■ *In re Houston*, 985 P.2d 752 (New Mexico Supreme Court, 1999) (having a legal assistant conduct all meetings with the clients, during which the clients' objectives and the means for pursuing them are discussed and decided, raises serious questions of unauthorized practice; the attorney needs instruction on the proper division of duties between lawyers and legal assistants and the ethical limits of the functions of a legal assistant).

■ *In the Matter of Martinez*, 754 P.2d 842 (New Mexico Supreme Court, 1988) (attorney suspended for failing to supervise a paralegal to ensure that the conduct of the paralegal comported with the ethical obligations of the attorney).

■ *In the Matter of Rawson*, 833 P.2d 235 (New Mexico Supreme Court, 1992) (disbarred attorney can act as paralegal).

■ *Aragon v. Westside Jeep/Eagle*, 876 P.2d 235 (New Mexico Supreme Court, 1994) (law firm failed to file a notice of appeal and the appeal was dismissed; the firm alleges that the failure to file was caused by a "clerical difficulty" of its paralegal who had a heavy workload and was busy training a new employee when the notice of appeal should have been filed).

■ *Sanchez v. Matta*, 2005 WL 2313621 (U.S. District Court, New Mexico, 2005) (courts may award expenses for law clerk and paralegal services, if such services are not "already reflected in the normal area billing rate").

DOING LEGAL RESEARCH IN NEW MEXICO LAW

Statutes: legis.state.nm.us/lcs
Cases: www.supremecourt.nm.org
Court Rules: www.llrx.com/courtrules-gen/state-New-Mexico.html
General: www.supremecourtlawlibrary.org

FINDING EMPLOYMENT IN NEW MEXICO

- nmbar.legalstaff.com
- www.indeed.com/q-Litigation-Paralegal-l-New-Mexico-jobs.html
- careers.findlaw.com
- albuquerque.craigslist.org/lgl

NEW YORK

DEFINING LEGAL ASSISTANTS/ PARALEGALS IN NEW YORK

A legal assistant/paralegal is a person who is qualified through education, training or work experience to be employed or retained by a lawyer, law office, governmental agency, or other entity in a capacity or function that involves the performance, under the ultimate direction and supervision of, and/or accountability to, an attorney, of substantive legal work, that requires a sufficient knowledge of legal concepts such that, absent such legal assistant/paralegal, the attorney would perform the task. The terms "legal assistant" and "paralegal" are synonymous and are not to be confused with numerous other legal titles which have proliferated with the public and within the legal community. New York State Bar Association, *Guidelines for the Utilization by Lawyers of the Services of Legal Assistants* (1997) (see Web site below.)

ETHICAL RULES AND GUIDELINES IN NEW YORK

- New York State Bar Association, *Guidelines for the Utilization by Lawyers of the Services of Legal Assistants* (1997). (www.nysba.org/Content/NavigationMenu/Attorney_Resources/Practice_Management/Paralegal_Information/Paralegal-guidelines.pdf). *Guideline I:* An attorney can permit a paralegal to perform services in the representation of a client if the attorney retains a direct relationship with the client, supervises the paralegal, and is fully responsible for the paralegal. *Guideline II:* An attorney must not assist a paralegal in engaging in the unauthorized practice of law. *Guideline III:* A paralegal may perform certain functions otherwise prohibited only to the extent authorized by law. An example would be a law that allows nonlawyer advocacy of clients at particular administrative agencies. *Guideline IV:* An attorney must take reasonable measures to ensure that all client confidences are preserved by paralegals and take appropriate measures to avoid conflicts of interest arising from their employment. *Guideline V:* An attorney shall not form a partnership with a paralegal if any part of the firm's activity consists of the practice of law, nor shall an attorney share legal fees with a paralegal. *Guideline VI:* An attorney shall require that a paralegal, when dealing with a client, disclose at the outset that the paralegal is not an attorney. The attorney shall also require such disclosure at the outset when the paralegal is dealing with a court, an administrative agency, attorneys, or the public if there is any reason for their believing that the paralegal is an attorney or associated with an attorney. *Guideline VII:* An attorney should promote the professional development of the paralegal. Examples include providing opportunities for continuing legal education, pro bono projects, and participation in professional associations.

- When a law firm hires a paralegal who has previously worked at another law firm, the law firm must adequately supervise the conduct of the paralegal. Supervisory measures may include i) instructing the paralegal not to disclose protected information acquired at the former law firm and ii) instructing lawyers not to exploit such information if proffered. In some circumstances, it is advisable that the law firm inquire whether the paralegal acquired confidential information from the former law firm about a current representation of the new firm or conduct a more comprehensive conflict check based on the paralegal's prior work. The results of such an inquiry will help determine whether the new firm should take further steps, such as seeking the opposing party's consent and/or screening the paralegal. New York State Bar Ass'n, *Opinion 774 (3/23/04).*

- A judge should not preside in cases in which members of a law firm which employs the judge's spouse in a paralegal/clerical position, appear before the judge, but the disqualification is subject to remittal of disqualification. New York Advisory Committee on Judicial Ethics, *Opinion 99–87 (6/18/99)* (1999 WL 33721217).

- A part-time town judge who is employed as a paralegal by a law firm must recuse himself/herself in cases in which the law firm appears, but such cases may be heard by the other town judge. New York Advisory Committee on Judicial Ethics, *Opinion 94–108 (11/15/94)* (1994 WL 907359).

- Paralegal names *can* be printed on a firm's letterhead if their nonattorney status is clear. New York State Bar Ass'n, *Ethics Opinion 500 (12/6/78)* (1978 WL 14163). This opinion overturns *Opinion 261* (1972). A paralegal may sign letters on a lawyer's letterhead so long as the paralegal is clearly designated as a nonlawyer. New York State Bar Ass'n, *Opinion 255 (6/26/72).*

- The titles *paralegal* and *senior paralegal* are acceptable, but the following titles are unacceptable because they are ambiguous: *paralegal coordinator, legal associate, public benefits advocate, legal advocate, family law advocate, housing law advocate, disability benefits advocate,* and *public benefits specialist.* The public might be misled about the non-attorney status of the people with these titles. New York State Bar Ass'n, *Ethics Opinion 640* (1992) (1992 WL 450730).

- An attorney may include on letterhead and other materials the identification of a nonlegal employee as a "Certified Legal Assistant," provided that term is accompanied by the statement that the certification is afforded by the National Association of Legal Assistants (NALA), and provided further that the attorney has satisfied himself or herself that NALA is a bona fide organization that provides such certification to all who meet objective and consistently applied standards relevant to the work of legal assistants. New York State Bar Ass'n, *Opinion 695 (8/25/97).*

- A lawyer may allow a paralegal to use a signature stamp to execute escrow checks from a client trust account so long as the lawyer supervises the delegated work closely and exercises complete professional responsibility for the acts of the paralegal. New York State Bar Ass'n, *Opinion 693 (8/22/97).*

- An attorney can use a legal research service that uses nonlawyers as long as the lawyer reviews the work of the service and the use of the service does not diminish the effective representation of the client. New York State Bar Ass'n, *Opinion 721 (9/27/99).*

- A nonlawyer should not independently advise a client of his or her rights or duties. New York State Bar Ass'n, *Opinion 44 (1/26/67).*

- New York statutes allow nonlawyers to be licensed to represent claimants before the workers' compensation agency (McKinney's Workers' Compensation Law § 24-a). A lawyer can employ such a representative to appear on behalf of the lawyer's client in a workers' compensation proceeding in which the lawyer has entered an appearance. New York State Bar Ass'n, *Opinion 446 (12/3/76).*

- An attorney may not accept referrals from an accounting firm in return for an agreement to share contingent fees with the accounting firm on a personal injury matter. New York State Bar Ass'n, *Opinion 727* (2/4/00) (2000 WL 567964).

- There are circumstances in which an attorney can send his or her paralegal to attend a real estate closing alone. The attorney must determine that the closing calls for "merely ministerial" as opposed to discretionary duties, must be sure the background of the paralegal makes him or her suitable to attend, and must have a plan to cope with the unforeseen such as being available by telephone to the paralegal. "[F]rom an ethical standpoint, the lawyer who assigns a non-lawyer to work on a client's matter had better be right about the suitability of that task for delegation, and the suitability of that employee for the task at hand." New York State Bar Ass'n, *Opinion 677* (12/12/95) (1995 WL 870964).

- A paralegal cannot conduct a deposition or supervise the execution of a will. New York State Bar Ass'n, *Ethics Opinion 304* (1973) and *Ethics Opinion 343*.

- Nonlawyers may be compensated based on a profit sharing arrangement but may not be paid a percentage of profits or fees attributable to particular client matters referred by the employee. New York State Bar Ass'n, *Opinion 733* (10/5/00), *Opinion 282* (1/25/73).

- Corporate legal department lawyers and paralegals have been asked to participate in the corporation's "compliance with law" program. The program, influenced by the Federal Sentencing Guidelines, requires all employees "to report all instances of unlawful or otherwise unethical behavior by any employee." Employees may satisfy this obligation by speaking with personnel department representatives, management personnel, corporate officers or department heads, or with "any member of the Corporate Legal Department." In addition, and as an alternative reporting device, lawyers and legal assistants will staff and answer a "help line" telephone in the corporate legal department, taking reports from employees. The fruits of these calls will be passed on to the corporation's compliance officer for further investigation and such other responses as may be appropriate. Held to be ethical with qualifications. New York State Bar Ass'n, *Opinion 650* (6/30/93).

- A lawyer who continues to represent a client in a transaction in which the counter-party has chosen to be represented by a non-lawyer is not thereby aiding the unauthorized practice of law even if the representation by the non-lawyer *is* the unauthorized practice of law. New York State Bar Ass'n, *Opinion 809* (2/12/07).

- An attorney can give credit or recognition to a nonattorney for work performed in the preparation of a brief as long as his or her nonattorney status is clear. New York State Bar Ass'n, *Ethics Opinion 299*.

- An attorney cannot allow a nonattorney to engage in settlement negotiations or to appear at a pretrial conference. Bar Ass'n of Nassau County, *Opinion 86–40* (9/12/89).

- A nonattorney can attend a real estate closing to perform ministerial functions involving only formalities. His or her nonattorney status must be disclosed at the closing. Bar Ass'n of Nassau County, *Opinion 86–43* (10/21/86); reaffirmed in *Opinion 90–13* (3/18/90).

- As attorney cannot divide a fee with a paralegal who brings clients to the attorney. Bar Ass'n of Nassau County, *Opinion 87–37* (10/1/87).

- Nonattorneys cannot be referred to as *associates* of an attorney. Bar Ass'n of Nassau County, *Opinion 88–34* (9/29/88).

- Nonattorneys can be listed on attorney letterhead if such employees are clearly described and identified as nonattorneys. Bar Ass'n of Nassau County, *Opinion 91–32* (1991) (accountants); *Opinion 87–14* (1987) (paralegals).

- An attorney may not represent a defendant in a criminal case when the complainant in the case is an investigator whom the attorney used in an unrelated case. There would be an appearance of impropriety in such a representation. Bar Ass'n of Nassau County, *Opinion 89–1* (1/18/89).

- A New York lawyer may ethically outsource legal support services overseas to a non-lawyer, if the New York lawyer (a) rigorously supervises the non-lawyer, so as to avoid aiding the non-lawyer in the unauthorized practice of law and to ensure that the non-lawyer's work contributes to the lawyer's competent representation of the client; (b) preserves the client's confidences and secrets when outsourcing; (c) avoids conflicts of interest when outsourcing; (d) bills for outsourcing appropriately; and (e) when necessary, obtains advance client consent to outsourcing. Ass'n of the Bar of the City of New York, *Opinion 2006–3* (8/2006).

- An attorney cannot form a partnership with a nonattorney to practice law. An attorney who shares an office with a nonattorney must avoid misleading the public into believing the nonattorney is an attorney. Ass'n of the Bar of the City of New York, *Opinion 1987–1* (2/23/87).

- A law firm may issue an announcement that it has hired a law student or other nonattorney provided the announcement makes clear the fact that the person is not an attorney and is working in a nonattorney capacity. Ass'n of the Bar of the City of New York, *Opinion 1996–2* (2/26/96).

- It is improper for a law firm to send out an announcement listing a non-lawyer assistant as "associated" with the firm because this implies the person is a lawyer. Ass'n of the Bar of the City of New York, *Opinion 454* (1938).

- Attorneys must effectively supervise their nonattorney employees, refrain from aiding or encouraging them to engage in the unauthorized practice of law, and be sure that they maintain client confidences and that the public is not misled by their nonattorney status. Ass'n of the Bar of the City of New York, *Opinion 1995–11* (7/6/95) (1995 WL 607778). This opinion modifies *Opinion 884* (1974).

- It is improper for lawyer or law firm to employ disbarred or suspended attorney in any capacity related to practice of law. Ass'n of the Bar of the City of New York, *Opinion 1998–1* (12/21/98).

- Paralegals can be listed on the letterhead of a law firm and on a business card that prints the name of the law firm (without printing the name of the supervising attorney) as long as their nonattorney status is indicated. New York County Lawyers' Ass'n, *Opinion 673* (12/23/89).

- A lawyer may not assign a legal assistant tasks that involve the exercise of professional judgment. A lawyer may not hire in any capacity a disbarred or suspended lawyer. New York County Lawyers' Ass'n, *Opinion 666* (10/29/85).

DEFINING THE PRACTICE OF LAW IN NEW YORK

- *New York Code of Professional Responsibility*, Ethical Consideration 3–5: It is neither necessary nor desirable to attempt the formulation of a single, specific definition of what constitutes the practice of law. Functionally, the practice of law relates to the rendition of services for others that call for the professional judgment of a lawyer. The essence of the professional judgment of the lawyer is the educated ability to relate the general body and philosophy of law to a specific legal problem of a client.

- *El Gemayel v. Seaman*, 533 N.E.2d 245, 248, 536 N.Y.S.2d 406, 409 (Court of Appeals of New York, 1988): The "practice" of law reserved to duly licensed New York attorneys includes the rendering of legal advice as well as appearing in court and holding oneself out to be a lawyer. . . . Additionally, such advice or services must be rendered to particular clients. This is the essential of legal practice—the representation and the advising of a particular person in a particular situation.

- § 118.1 (*McKinney's New York Rules of Court*): Registration of attorneys.
  (g) For purposes of this section, the "practice of law" shall mean the giving of legal advice or counsel to, or providing legal representation for, [a] particular body or individual in a particular situation in either the public or private sector in the State of New York or elsewhere [;] it shall include the appearance as an attorney before any court or administrative agency.

NEW YORK ETHICS AND PRACTICE RULES ON THE INTERNET

- www.law.cornell.edu/ethics/ny.html
- www.nysba.org (click "Publications" then "Ethics Opinions")
- www.nycbar.org/Publications/reports/reports_ethics.php
- www.nycla.org/index.cfm?section=News_AND_Publications&page=Ethics_Opinions
- www.nassaubar.org/ethic_opinions.cfm

PARALEGALS (AND OTHER NONATTORNEYS) IN NEW YORK STATE AND FEDERAL COURTS

- *In the Matter of Feldman*, 785 N.Y.S.2d 600 (Supreme Court, Appellate Division, 3d Dept., 2004 (Laid-off paralegal is not required to accept a job as a legal secretary to qualify for unemployment compensation. "While both the paralegal position and the legal secretary position were characterized as legal support staff, the paralegal duties are more extensive and required different skills than that of a legal secretary.")

- *Fine v. Facet Aerospace Products Co.*, 133 Federal Rules Decisions 439 (U.S. District Court, S.D. New York, 1990) (handwritten notes made by a paralegal on a document in the course of discovery in another case are protected from disclosure under the work product doctrine).

- *Glover Bottled Gas Corp. v. Circle M. Beverage Barn*, 514 N.Y.S.2d 440 (Supreme Court, Appellate Division, 2d Dept., 1987) (attorney is disqualified after hiring a paralegal who worked on specific litigation while previously employed by the opposing counsel in the litigation).

- *In the Matter of Lowell*, 784 N.Y.S.2d 69 (Supreme Court, Appellate Division, 1st Dept., 2004) (Attorney acted unethically by failing to create and maintain a Chinese wall separating a paralegal, who had formerly worked for law firm that represented the opposing party in a matrimonial action, from any association with the matrimonial matter while in attorney's office, by requiring the paralegal to work on the case, and by questioning her about the adversary's litigation strategies.)

- *Mulhern v. Calder*, 763 N.Y.S.2d 741 (Supreme Court, Albany County, 2003) (Law firm's efforts to construct a Chinese wall around a secretary who had assisted the opponent's attorney on the case before being hired by the firm were sufficient to prevent the firm's disqualification. Neither existing ethical rules nor case law requires automatic disqualification of law firms simply because they hire nonlawyers who have had access to confidences of their opponents.)

- *NYC Medical & Neurodiagnostic, P.C.*, 784 N.Y.S.2d 840 (Civil Court, Kings County, 2004) (A clerk employed by the law firm in its mailroom will not cause the law firm to be disqualified from representing the plaintiff, simply because the clerk's testimony is necessary in establishing the elements of plaintiff's prima facie case. The disqualification rules governing lawyers do not apply to "non-lawyers" employees of law firm.)

- *M.K.B v. Eggleston*, 414 F. Supp. 2d 469 (U.S. District Court, S.D. New York, 2006) (paralegals and interns of law firm that currently represented plaintiffs were not barred by advocate-witness rule from testifying on behalf of plaintiffs in civil rights action).

- *First Deposit Nat'l Bank v. Moreno*, 606 N.Y.S.2d 938 (City Court of the City of New York, New York County, 1993) (a claim for paralegal fees must itemize what was done and how much time was spent by attorneys and by others; "paralegals often competently perform certain services equivalent to those done by attorneys, while generally charging their time at a lesser rate than attorneys, thus benefitting those who pay the fees").

- *United States v. Hooper*, 43 F.3d 26 (U.S. Court of Appeals, 2d Circuit, 1994) (a paralegal's mistake on the deadline for filing a criminal appeal is not "excusable neglect" justifying permission to file the appeal late; the paralegal thought she had thirty days to file rather than ten).

- *In the Matter of Saltz*, 536 N.Y.S.2d 126 (Supreme Court, Appellate Division, 2d Dept, 1988) (attorney disciplined for lying when he claimed that his paralegal "doctored" divorce papers).

- *Sussman v. Grado*, 746 N.Y.S.2d 548 (District Court, Nassau County, 2002) ("Regardless of her intentions to help the plaintiff, this independent paralegal operated without the supervision of an attorney. She tried to create a legal document without the required knowledge, skill or training. As a result the plaintiff may have lost the ability to execute against two bank accounts.")

- *Paralegal Institute, Inc. v. American Bar Ass'n*, 475 F. Supp. 1123 (U.S. District Court, S.D. New York, 1979) (court dismisses paralegal school's antitrust charges against the American Bar Association).

DOING LEGAL RESEARCH IN NEW YORK LAW

Statutes: public.leginfo.state.ny.us/menugetf.cgi?COMMONQUERY=LAWS
Cases: www.law.cornell.edu/nyctap
Court Rules: www.courts.state.ny.us/rules
General: www.aallnet.org/chapter/llagny/ny.html

FINDING EMPLOYMENT IN NEW YORK

- www.nbocellistaffing.com/aboutus.asp
- hotjobs.yahoo.com/job-search-l-New_York-NY-c-Legal
- www.filcro.com/page14.html
- careers.findlaw.com
- www.nbocellistaffing.com/aboutus.asp
- newyork.craigslist.org/lgl

NORTH CAROLINA

DEFINING LEGAL ASSISTANTS/PARALEGALS IN NORTH CAROLINA

A legal assistant (or paralegal) is a person, qualified through education, training or work experience, who is employed or retained by a lawyer, law office, corporation, governmental agency, or other entity, and who performs specifically delegated substantive legal work for which a lawyer is responsible. *Guidelines for Use of Non-Lawyers in Rendering Legal Services*, North Carolina State Bar (1986, revised 1998).

CERTIFICATION OF PARALEGALS IN NORTH CAROLINA

- www.nccertifiedparalegal.gov
- legalassistantsdivision.ncbar.org/Committees/Profession alism+Committee/default.aspx
- See Exhibit 4.8 in chapter 4 for an overview of certification in North Carolina.

ETHICAL RULES AND GUIDELINES IN NORTH CAROLINA

- For a discussion of the state's ethical Rule 5.3 ("Responsibilities Regarding Nonlawyer Assistants") in the *North Carolina Rules of Professional Conduct*, see the end of Section C in chapter 5. For the text of 5.3 in North Carolina, see also www.ncbar.com/rules/rpcsearch.asp.
- *Guidelines for Use of Non-Lawyers in Rendering Legal Services*, North Carolina State Bar (1986, revised 1998). *Guideline 1:* A lawyer shall not permit an assistant to engage in the practice of law. A lawyer may, however, allow an assistant to perform legally-related tasks, provided the lawyer and the assistant comply with these guidelines. *Guideline 2:* A lawyer shall not permit an assistant to appear on behalf of a client in a deposition, in court or before any agency or board, in person or on the record, unless permitted by the North Carolina General Statutes and a rule of a particular court, agency or board. *Guideline 3:* A lawyer shall require that an assistant disclose that he or she is not a lawyer when necessary to avoid misrepresentation. This is so even if the assistant is authorized to represent a client under Guideline 2. Common sense suggests a routine disclosure at the outset of a conference or any type of communication. The lawyer has an obligation to ensure that his or her assistant does not communicate directly with a party known to be represented by an attorney, without that attorney's consent. *Guideline 4:* A partner in a law firm shall make reasonable efforts to ensure that the firm has in effect measures giving reasonable assurance that the assistant's conduct is compatible with the professional obligations of the lawyer. See Rule 5.3(a). Lawyers with management responsibility for the firm must familiarize legal assistants with all relevant provisions of the Rules of Professional Conduct, particularly the obligation to maintain the confidentiality of information received incident to the representation of clients. A lawyer should ensure that a non-lawyer is properly educated or trained to perform any delegated task. When the assistant is not working as an employee of the lawyer, but instead contracts independently to perform legally-related tasks, the lawyer is still responsible for the assistant's work product and ethical conduct. Special care must be taken by the lawyer to make sure that the assistant performs both competently and ethically before entrusting services to an independent assistant. A lawyer who discovers that a non-lawyer has misappropriated money from the attorney's trust account must inform the State Bar. *Guideline 5:* A lawyer having direct supervisory authority over an assistant shall make reasonable efforts to ensure that the assistant's conduct is compatible with the professional obligations of the

lawyer. See Rule 5.3(c). *Guideline 6:* A lawyer shall maintain an active, direct, and personal relationship with the client, supervise the assistant's performance of duties, and remain fully responsible for the work performed. An assistant should inform the responsible lawyer of all significant actions and services performed by the assistant. Only by thorough supervision of the assistant can the lawyer ensure that the assistant is neither engaging in the unauthorized practice of law nor involving the lawyer in any violation of the lawyer's professional responsibilities. *Guideline 7:* A lawyer shall ensure that no interest or relationship of the assistant impinges upon the services rendered to the client. If the interests of a legal assistant might materially limit or otherwise adversely affect the lawyer's representation of a prospective or current client, the lawyer must decline or discontinue the representation. If a lawyer accepts a matter in which the assistant has a conflict of interest that does not affect or limit the lawyer's representation of the client, the lawyer should totally screen the assistant from participation in the case. In addition, the lawyer should inform the client that a non-lawyer employee has a conflict of interest which, were it the lawyer's conflict, might prevent further representation of the client in connection with the matter. The nature of the conflict should be disclosed. *Guideline 8:* A lawyer may charge a client for legal work performed by a legal assistant but shall not form a partnership or other business entity with an assistant for the practice of law. A lawyer cannot share fees with a non-lawyer. Compensation of an assistant may not include a percentage of the fees received by the lawyer, nor should the assistant receive any remuneration, directly or indirectly, for referring matters of a legal nature to the lawyer. *Guideline 9:* A lawyer's letterhead or a business card may include the name of a non-lawyer assistant if the assistant's capacity is clearly indicated and the document is otherwise neither false nor misleading. An assistant may also sign correspondence on a lawyer's or a law firm's letterhead, subject, however, to the same requirements. *Guideline 10:* A lawyer may use a non-lawyer, non-employee freelance legal assistant if the lawyer adequately supervises the non-lawyer's work and inquires into the freelance assistant's potential conflicts of interest. The lawyer should disclose to the client the use of a freelance assistant, the name of the freelance assistant and how the freelance assistant's services will be charged to the client, if the client inquires.

- A paralegal switches jobs. She now works for an attorney whose client opposes a party represented by the paralegal's former employer who says the paralegal worked on the case while there. The former employer seeks the disqualification of the current employer on the case. The request is denied. The imputed disqualification rules in Rule 5.11 do not apply to nonlawyers. But the current employer "must take extreme care" to ensure the paralegal is "totally screened" from the case even if her involvement in the case at the prior employment was negligible. North Carolina State Bar, *RPC 176* (7/21/94) (1994 WL 899356). In agreement: *RPC 74* (10/20/89) (1989 WL 550603).
- An attorney may not pay a paralegal a percentage of fees as a bonus. A bonus for productivity can be given, but not as a percentage of fees. North Carolina State Bar, *RPC 147* (1/15/93) (1992 WL 753129).
- The compensation of a nonlawyer law firm employee who represents Social Security disability claimants before the Social Security Administration may be based upon the income generated by such representation. Nonlawyers are allowed to earn fees in

Social Security agency cases. North Carolina State Bar, *Formal Ethics Opinion 6*, (10/21/05)(2005 WL 3964318).

- Legal representation of a borrower requires the presence of the lawyer at the closing of a residential real estate refinancing. A nonlawyer may oversee the execution of documents outside the presence of the lawyer provided the lawyer adequately supervises the nonlawyer and is present at the closing conference to complete the transaction. North Carolina State Bar, *Formal Ethics Opinion 4*, (10/19/01) (2001 WL 1949444) "The lawyer must be physically present at the closing conference and may not be present through a surrogate such as a paralegal." *Formal Ethics Opinion 8*, (10/19/01) (2001 WL 1949448). See also *Formal Ethics Opinion 13* (7/21/00) (2000 WL 33300697).

- With proper supervision, a real estate lawyer can engage a "free-lance" paralegal as an independent contractor to perform title searches for real estate closings. The lawyer must also check for conflicts of interest. North Carolina State Bar, *RPC 216* (7/17/97) (1997 WL 331712).

- If warranted by exigent circumstances, a lawyer may allow a paralegal to sign his or her name to court documents so long as it does not violate any law and the lawyer provides the appropriate level of supervision. North Carolina State Bar, 2006 *Formal Ethics Opinion 13* (10/20/06) (www.ncbar.com/ethics).

- A legal assistant can communicate and negotiate with a claims adjuster if directly supervised by an attorney. However, "[u]nder no circumstances should the legal assistant be permitted to exercise independent legal judgment regarding the value of the case, the advisability of making or accepting any offer of settlement or any other related matter." North Carolina State Bar, *RPC 70* (10/20/89).

- An attorney can represent a client in an action to abate a nuisance even though his paralegal may be called as a witness against the opponent. North Carolina State Bar, *Revised RPC 213* (10/20/95) (1995 WL 853891).

- An attorney may not permit his paralegal to examine or represent a witness at a deposition. North Carolina State Bar, *RPC 183* (10/21/94) (1994 WL 901318).

- A lawyer or law firm shall not employ a disbarred or suspended lawyer as a law clerk or legal assistant if that individual was associated with such lawyer or law firm at any time on or after the date of the acts which resulted in disbarment or suspension through and including the effective date of disbarment or suspension. *Revised Rules of Professional Conduct*, Rule 5.5(e); See also *Proposed Formal Ethics Opinion 7*, (4/16/98)(1998 WL 609812).

DEFINING THE PRACTICE OF LAW IN NORTH CAROLINA

§ 84–2.1 (General Statutes of North Carolina): The phrase "practice law" as used in this chapter is defined to be performing any legal service for any other person, firm or corporation, with or without compensation, specifically including the preparation or aiding in the preparation of deeds, mortgages, wills, trust instruments, inventories, accounts or reports of guardians, trustees, administrators or executors, or preparing or aiding in the preparation of any petitions or orders in any probate or court proceeding; abstracting or passing upon titles, the preparation and filing of petitions for use in any court, including administrative tribunals and other judicial or quasi-judicial bodies, or assisting by advice, counsel, or otherwise in any legal work; and to advise or give opinion upon the legal rights of any person, firm or corporation: Provided, that the above reference to particular acts which are specifically included within the definition of the phrase "practice law" shall

not be construed to limit the foregoing general definition of the term, but shall be construed to include the foregoing particular acts, as well as all other acts within the general definition.

NORTH CAROLINA ETHICS AND PRACTICE RULES ON THE INTERNET

- www.ncbar.com (click "Ethics")
- www.law.cornell.edu/ethics/nc.html
- www.ncbar.com/rules/rpcsearch.asp
- www.law.cornell.edu/ethics/nc/code/NC_CODE.HTM

PARALEGALS (AND OTHER NONATTORNEYS) IN NORTH CAROLINA STATE AND FEDERAL COURTS

- *North Carolina v. Cummings*, 389 S.E.2d 66, 74 (Supreme Court of North Carolina, 1990) (paralegal allowed to testify about hearsay statement of victim made during intake interview).

- *Lea Co. v. North Carolina Board of Transportation*, 374 S.E.2d 868 (Supreme Court of North Carolina, 1989) (paralegal fees denied; the paralegal work in this case was largely clerical in nature and therefore part of ordinary office overhead to be subsumed in the hourly attorney rate).

- *Cunningham v. Riley*, 611 S.E.2d 423 (Court of Appeals of North Carolina, 2005) (The trial court did not err by denying a successful plaintiff costs for legal assistants and administrative support staff. These are not listed as recoverable expenses under N.C.G.S. 7A 305(d) and there is no logical reason to find that these costs are recoverable when attorney fees are not generally recoverable.)

- *Hyatt v. Barnhart*, 315 F.3d 239 (U.S. Court of Appeals, 4th Circuit, North Carolina, 2002) (Paralegal expenses are separately recoverable only as part of a prevailing party's award for attorney's fees and expenses, and even then only to the extent that the paralegal performs work traditionally performed by an attorney. Otherwise, paralegal expenses are separately unrecoverable overhead expenses.)

- *In re Thomas*, 2004 WL 2296550 (U.S. Bankruptcy Court, M.D., North Carolina, 2004) (bankruptcy petition preparers are prohibited from providing paralegal services).

- *In re Inquiry Concerning a Judge*, 614 S.E.2d 529 Supreme Court of North Carolina, 2005) (censure recommended for a judge who sexually harassed a paralegal).

DOING LEGAL RESEARCH IN NORTH CAROLINA LAW

Statutes: www.ncga.state.nc.us
Cases: www.findlaw.com/11stategov/nc/courts.html
Court Rules: www.nccourts.org/Courts/CRS/Policies/LocalRules
General: library.law.unc.edu/research/nc_legal_databases.html

FINDING EMPLOYMENT IN NORTH CAROLINA

- www.ncparalegal.org/mc/page.do?sitePageId=35034&orgId=ncpa
- www.simplyhired.com/job-search/l-North-Carolina/o-232000/t-Paralegal
- www.indeed.com/q-Litigation-Paralegal-l-North-Carolina-jobs.html
- careers.findlaw.com
- www.grahamjobs.com

NORTH DAKOTA

DEFINING LEGAL ASSISTANTS/ PARALEGALS IN NORTH DAKOTA

"Legal Assistant" (or paralegal) means a person who assists lawyers in the delivery of legal services, and who through formal education, training, or experience, has knowledge and expertise regarding the legal system and substantive and procedural law which qualifies the person to do work of a legal nature under the direct supervision of a licensed lawyer. *North Dakota Rules of Professional Conduct*, Rule 1.0(h).

ETHICAL RULES AND GUIDELINES IN NORTH DAKOTA

- For a discussion of the state's ethical Rule 5.3 ("Responsibilities Regarding Nonlawyer Assistants") in the *North Dakota Rules of Professional Conduct*, see the end of Section C in chapter 5. For the text of 5.3 in North Dakota, see also www.court.state.nd.us/rules/conduct/contents.htm.

- A lawyer may charge for work performed by a legal assistant. A lawyer may not split legal fees with a legal assistant or pay a legal assistant for the referral of legal business. A lawyer may compensate a legal assistant based on the quantity and quality of the legal assistant's work and value of that work to a law practice. The legal assistant's compensation may not be contingent, by advance agreement, upon the outcome of a case or upon the profitability of the lawyer's practice. Rule 1.5(f) & (g), *North Dakota Rules of Professional Conduct*. (www.court.state.nd.us/rules/conduct/frameset.htm).

- In cases involving fixed fees or contingent fees, the total fees are agreed upon in advance and there should be no separate charge for legal assistant services. In matters charged on the basis of "fee for service" or "charge by the hour", a lawyer may include separate charges for work performed by legal assistants or otherwise include legal assistant hours in calculating the amount of fees to be charged. It may be appropriate to value such services at "market rates" rather than "actual costs" to the lawyer. The lawyer should disclose to the client, either at the outset of the representation or at the point during the representation when the lawyer determines a legal assistant should be used, that the lawyer proposes to use a legal assistant and obtain the client's agreement to any separate charges for legal assistant services. A lawyer may not split fees with a legal assistant, whether characterized as splitting of contingent fees, "forwarding" fees or other sharing of legal fees. There is no general prohibition against a lawyer recognizing the contribution of the legal assistant with a discretionary bonus. Likewise, a lawyer is not prohibited from compensating a legal assistant who aids materially in a practice with compensation greater than that generally paid to legal assistants in the geographic area working in less lucrative law practices. *North Dakota Rules of Professional Conduct*, Comment to Rule 1.5 Rule 1.0(h).

- With respect to a nonlawyer employed or retained by or associated with a lawyer, the lawyer shall make reasonable efforts to put into effect measures giving reasonable assurance that the nonlawyer's conduct is compatible with the professional obligations of the lawyer. A lawyer may not delegate to a legal assistant: (i) responsibility for establishing an attorney-client relationship; (ii) responsibility for establishing the amount of a fee to be charged for a legal service; (iii) responsibility for a legal opinion rendered to a client; or (iv) responsibility for

the work product. The lawyer shall make reasonable efforts to ensure that clients, courts, and other lawyers are aware that a legal assistant is not licensed to practice law. Rule 5.3, *North Dakota Rules of Professional Conduct*. (www.court.state.nd.us/rules/conduct/frameset.htm). The key to appropriate delegation is proper supervision, which includes adequate instruction when assigning projects, monitoring of the project, and review of the project. Comment to Rule 5.3.

- A lawyer may identify a legal assistant on the lawyer's letterhead and on business cards identifying the lawyer's firm, provided the legal assistant's status is clearly identified. Rule 7.5 (e), *North Dakota Rules of Professional Conduct*. (www.court.state.nd.us/rules/conduct/frameset.htm).

DEFINING THE PRACTICE OF LAW IN NORTH DAKOTA

- *Ranta v. McCarney*, 391 N.W.2d 161, 162, 163 (Supreme Court of North Dakota, 1986): Practice of law under modern conditions consists in no small part of work performed outside of any court and having no immediate relation to proceedings in court. It embraces conveyancing, the giving of legal advice on a large variety of subjects, and the preparation and execution of legal instruments covering an extensive field of business and trust relations and other affairs. Although these transactions may have no direct connection with court proceedings, they are always subject to become involved in litigation. They require in many aspects a high degree of legal skill, a wide experience with men and affairs, and great capacity for adaptation to difficult and complex situations. These "customary functions of an attorney or counsellor at law" . . . bear an intimate relation to the administration of justice by the courts. No valid distinction . . . can be drawn between that part which involves appearance in court and that part which involves advice and drafting of instruments in his office. The work of the office lawyer is the ground work for future possible contests in courts. It has profound effect on the whole scheme of the administration of justice. It is performed with that possibility in mind, and otherwise would hardly be needed . . . . It is of importance to the welfare of the public that these manifold customary functions be performed by persons possessed of adequate learning and skill, of sound moral character, and acting at all times under the heavy trust obligation to clients which rests upon all attorneys. The underlying reasons which prevent corporations, associations and individuals other than members of the bar from appearing before the courts apply with equal force to the performance of these customary functions of attorneys and counsellors at law outside of courts. . . . If compensation is exacted either directly or indirectly, "all advice to clients, and all action taken for them in matters connected with the law," constitute practicing law.

NORTH DAKOTA ETHICS AND PRACTICE RULES ON THE INTERNET

- www.law.cornell.edu/ethics/nd.html
- www.court.state.nd.us/rules/conduct/frameset.htm

PARALEGALS (AND OTHER NONATTORNEYS) IN NORTH DAKOTA STATE AND FEDERAL COURTS

- *In the Matter of Nassif*, 547 N.W.2d 541 (Supreme Court of North Dakota, 1996) (attorney disciplined for allowing untrained "paralegals" to recruit and advise clients, negotiate fees, and perform unsupervised legal work for clients).

- *In re Disciplinary Action against Hellerud*, 714 N.W.2d 38 (Supreme Court of North Dakota, 2006) (attorney inappropriately charged his legal assistant's time at a rate of $275 per hour without disclosure to his client).
- *State v. Niska*, 380 N.W.2d 646 (Supreme Court of North Dakota, 1986) (nonattorney drafts pleadings and advises another on court actions in violation of § 27–11–01, practicing law without a license).
- *In the Matter of Johnson*, 481 N.W.2d 225 (Supreme Court of North Dakota, 1992) (disbarred attorney is not allowed to practice as a paralegal).
- *Nat'l Farmers Union . . . v. Souris River Telephone . . .*, 75 F.3d 1268 (U.S. Court of Appeals, 8th Circuit, 1996) (award of paralegal fees).
- *Gassler v. Rayl*, 862 F.2d 706 (U.S. Court of Appeals, 8th Circuit, 1988) (inmate paralegal assistance).

DOING LEGAL RESEARCH IN NORTH DAKOTA LAW

Statutes: www.legis.nd.gov
Cases: www.court.state.nd.us/search/opinions.asp
Court Rules: www.court.state.nd.us/rules/ndroc/frameset.htm
General: www.court.state.nd.us/research

FINDING EMPLOYMENT IN NORTH DAKOTA

- sband.legalstaff.com/Common/HomePage.aspx?abbr=SBAND
- www.indeed.com/q-Paralegal-l-North-Dakota-jobs.html
- careers.findlaw.com
- nd.craigslist.org/lgl

OHIO

DEFINING LEGAL ASSISTANTS/ PARALEGALS IN OHIO

- A paralegal is a person, qualified by education, training or work experience who is employed or retained by a lawyer, law office, corporation, governmental agency or other entity and who performs substantive legal work for which a lawyer is responsible. Ohio Bar Association (www.ohiobar.org/join/?articleid=273).
- A person qualified through education in legal studies that is employed by a lawyer or government entity to perform substantial legal work. Ohio Common Pleas Court of Greene County, Domestic Relations Division (www.co.greene.oh.us/DRC/forms/DRC_Local_Rules_of_Court.pdf).

CERTIFICATION OF PARALEGALS IN OHIO

- www.ohiobar.org/pub/?articleid=785
- downloads.ohiobar.org/pub/PCS.pdf
- www.lawcrossing.com/article/index.php?id=1786

ETHICAL RULES AND GUIDELINES IN OHIO

- For a discussion of the state's ethical Rule 5.3 ("Responsibilities Regarding Nonlawyer Assistants") in the *Ohio Rules of Professional Conduct*, see the end of Section C in chapter 5. For the text of 5.3 in Ohio, see also www.sconet.state.oh.us/Atty-Svcs/ProfConduct.

- It is improper for an insurance defense attorney to abide by an insurance company's litigation management guidelines (e.g., on when to delegate tasks to a paralegal) in the representation of an insured when the guidelines directly interfere with the professional judgment of the attorney. Board of Commissioners on Grievances and Discipline, *Opinion 2000–3* (6/1/00) (2000 WL 1005223).
- A legal assistant can sign law firm correspondence on law firm stationery as long as his or her nonattorney status is clearly indicated. Board of Commissioners on Grievances and Discipline *Opinion 89–11* (4/14/89) (1989 WL 535016).
- Nonattorneys *cannot* be listed on law firm letterhead. They can, however, have business cards as long as their nonattorney status is clear. Board of Commissioners on Grievances and Discipline, *Opinion 89–16* (6/16/89) (1989 WL 535021).
- The words "Group" or "Law Group" should not be used in a law firm name to refer to paralegals or other non-attorney personnel. Board of Commissioners on Grievances and Discipline, *Opinion 2006–2* (2/10/06) (2006 WL 2000104).
- A paralegal should not be referred to as an associate. Commissioners on Grievances and Discipline, *Opinion 1995–1* (2/3/95).
- It is unethical for an attorney to allow a paralegal to take a deposition or represent a deponent at a deposition. Board of Commissioners on Grievances and Discipline, *Opinion 2002–4* (6/14/02) (2002 WL 1426124).
- Child support enforcement caseworkers do not engage in the unauthorized practice of law when they interview parents seeking child support enforcement and prepare paternity complaints. Board of Commissioners on Grievances and Discipline, *Opinion 1990–10* (6/15/90)
- It is unethical for an attorney to split a contingency fee with a nonattorney investigator. Board of Commissioners on Grievances and Discipline, *Opinion 1994–8* (6/17/94).
- Attorneys in separate practices can share nonattorney staff if they maintain office procedures that preserve client confidentiality. Board of Commissioners on Grievances and Discipline, *Opinion 1991–9* (4/12/91).
- A retired or inactive attorney may not perform the duties of a paralegal, since such attorneys "may not render any legal service for an attorney" in active status. Board of Commissioners on Grievances and Discipline, *Opinion 92–4* (2/14/92) (1992 WL 739414). But a suspended or disbarred attorney can act as a paralegal. *Opinion 90–06* (4/20/90) (1990 WL 640501).
- Law firm letterhead can print the names and titles of nonattorney employees as long as their nonattorney status is clear and they are listed separately from the attorneys. Columbus Bar Ass'n, *Opinion (6)* (11/17/88).
- Law firm letterhead can list the names and titles of nonattorney employees, and the latter can also have their own business card as long as their nonattorney status is made clear. Cleveland Bar Ass'n, *Opinion 89–1* (2/25/89).

DEFINING THE PRACTICE OF LAW IN OHIO

- *Cleveland Bar Assn. v. Pearlman*, 832 N.E.2d 1193 (Supreme Court of Ohio, 2005): The unauthorized practice of law is the rendering of legal services for another by any person not admitted to practice in Ohio. The term "rendering of legal services" has been defined further: "The practice of law is not limited to the conduct of cases in court. It embraces the preparation of pleadings and other papers incident to actions and special proceedings and the management of such actions and proceedings on behalf of clients before judges and courts, and in addition conveyancing, the preparation of legal instruments of all kinds, and in general all advice to clients and all action taken for them in matters connected with the law." *Land Title Abstract & Trust Co. v. Dworken*, 193 N.E. 650 (Supreme Court of Ohio 1934).

OHIO ETHICS AND PRACTICE RULES ON THE INTERNET

- www.law.cornell.edu/ethics/ohio.html
- www.sconet.state.oh.us/BOC/default.asp
- www.sconet.state.oh.us/Atty-Svcs/ProfConduct/rules

PARALEGALS (AND OTHER NONATTORNEYS) IN OHIO STATE AND FEDERAL COURTS

- Paralegal fees are compensable as an element of attorney fees. *Specht v. Finnegan*, 149 Ohio App.3d 201 (Court of Appeals of Ohio, 2002).

- It is beyond dispute that a reasonable attorney's fee includes compensation for the work of paralegals. Counsel contends that reimbursement for paralegal time must be limited to the amount actually paid to the paralegals. This is incorrect. Paralegal time, like attorney time, is measured in comparison to the market rate, if the prevailing practice in the area is to bill paralegal time separately at market rates. *Cleveland Area Bd. of Realtors v. City of Euclid*, 965 F. Supp. 1017, 1019 (U.S. District Court, N.D. Ohio, 1997).

- The court deducts 10 percent of counsel's reported hours for his performance of tasks that could have been performed by a paralegal (including the making of numerous telephone calls and arranging schedules). *Alexander v. Local 496, Laborers' Intern. Union of North America*, 2000 WL 1751297 (U.S. District Court, N.D. Ohio, 2000).

- To avoid discipline, an attorney induced a former legal assistant to execute a false affidavit claiming that her law office had prepared a client's file for retrieval. *Cincinnati Bar Assn. v. Statzer*, 101 Ohio St.3d 14 (Supreme Court of Ohio, 2003).

- The attorney's failure to adequately supervise his legal assistant, which resulted in client files being lost or destroyed, violated the disciplinary rule barring attorneys from engaging in actions that adversely reflect on the lawyer's fitness to practice law. *Lorain Cty. Bar Assn. v. Noll*, 105 Ohio St.3d 6 (Supreme Court of Ohio, 2004).

- An attorney's secretary once worked for the attorney representing an opposing party on a current case. "In ruling on a motion to disqualify a lawyer based on that lawyer's employment of a nonattorney once employed by the lawyer representing an opposing party, a court must use the following analysis: (1) Is there a substantial relationship between the matter at issue and the matter of the nonattorney employee's former firm's representation? (2) Did the moving party present credible evidence that the nonattorney employee was exposed to confidential information in his or her former employment relating to the matter at issue? (3) If such evidence was presented, did the challenged attorney rebut the resulting presumption of disclosure with evidence either that (a) the employee had no contact with or knowledge of the related matter or (b) the new law firm erected and followed adequate and timely screens to rebut the evidence presented in prong (2) so as to avoid disqualification?" *Green v. Toledo Hosp.*, 94 Ohio St.3d 480 (Supreme Court of Ohio, 2002).

- Legal assistant's conduct in preparing legal documents for the attorney's clients without the assistance or oversight of the attorney, and filing those documents before they had been reviewed and approved by the attorney constituted the unauthorized practice of law. R.C. § 4705.01; Government of the Bar Rule VII(2)(A). Although laypersons may assist lawyers in preparing legal papers to be filed in court and managing pending claims, those activities must be carefully supervised and approved by a licensed practitioner to avoid unauthorized practice of law. *Columbus Bar Assn. v. Thomas*, 846 N.E.2d 31 (Supreme Court of Ohio, 2006).

- In light of the informal setting of workers' compensation proceedings, nonattorneys can help someone file or respond to a claim at an agency hearing, but they cannot examine and cross-examine witnesses, give legal interpretations of laws or testimony, give legal advice to workers or employers, provide stand-alone representation at a hearing by charging a fee specifically associated with such hearing representation without providing other services. Nonattorneys who appear and practice in a representative capacity before the Industrial Commission and Bureau of Workers' Compensation within these restrictions are not engaged in the unauthorized practice of law. *Cleveland Bar Assn. v. CompManagement, Inc.*, 818 N.E.2d 1181 (Supreme Court of Ohio, 2004).

DOING LEGAL RESEARCH IN OHIO LAW

Statutes: codes.ohio.gov
Cases: www.megalaw.com/oh/ohcases.php
Court Rules: www.sconet.state.oh.us/Rules
General: www.uakron.edu/law/library/olrlinks.php

FINDING EMPLOYMENT IN OHIO

- ohiobar.legalstaff.com
- jobs.careerbuilder.com/al.ic/Ohio_Legal.htm
- www.indeed.com/q-Litigation-Paralegal-l-Ohio-jobs.html
- careers.findlaw.com
- cleveland.craigslist.org/lgl

OKLAHOMA

DEFINING LEGAL ASSISTANTS/ PARALEGALS IN OKLAHOMA

A legal assistant or paralegal is a person qualified by education, training, or work experience who is employed or retained by a lawyer, law office, corporation, governmental agency, or other entity who performs specifically delegated substantive legal work for which a lawyer is responsible, and absent such assistant, the lawyer would perform the task. Oklahoma Bar Association, *Minimum Qualification Standards for Legal Assistants/Paralegals* (2000). (www.okbar.org/members/committees/lasa.htm).

ETHICAL RULES AND GUIDELINES IN OKLAHOMA

- For a discussion of the state's ethical Rule 5.3 ("Responsibilities Regarding Nonlawyer Assistants") in the *Oklahoma Rules of Professional Conduct*, see the end of Section C in chapter 5. For the text of 5.3 in Oklahoma, see also www.okbar.org/ethics/ORPC07.pdf.

- Education and experience requirements for a qualified paralegal: www.okbar.org/members/committees/lasa.htm.

- A licensed supervising attorney may delegate to non-lawyers clerical assignments such as researching case law, finding and interviewing witnesses, examining court records, and delivering papers or messages. However, a licensed supervising attorney must not delegate to a non-lawyer, including a disbarred or suspended lawyer, tasks such as providing legal advice to clients, preparing legal documents for clients, or conducting court proceedings. Oklahoma Bar Ass'n, *Ethics Opinion 319* (12/13/02).

- Delegation of tasks that may require professional judgment to secretaries or any other nonlawyer employee is unethical. Oklahoma Bar Ass'n, *Ethics Opinion 260* (3/19/71).

- Lawyers must preserve client confidences. This duty outlasts the lawyer's employment, and extends as well to his or her employees." Oklahoma Bar Ass'n, *Ethics Opinion 238* (3/17/66).

DEFINING THE PRACTICE OF LAW IN OKLAHOMA

Edwards v. Hert, 504 P.2d 407, 416, 417 (Supreme Court of Oklahoma, 1972): [P]ractice of law: the rendition of services requiring the knowledge and the application of legal principles and technique to serve the interests of another with his consent . . . . [A] service which otherwise would be a form of the practice of law does not lose that character merely because it is rendered gratuitously . . . ."[I]t is not a prerequisite that a fee should be paid before the relation of attorney and client may exist" . . . . [A]n unlicensed practitioner's performance of legal service is not sanctified by his failure to require pay. . . .It has been urged upon us that acts which properly are part of the lawyer's work also may form an integral part of the legitimate activity of another calling, and that, for performance of these acts by an unlicensed person, incidental to such an independent vocation, penalties should not be inflicted upon the theory that thereby he practices law. To a certain extent, this contention is sound. "There is authority for the proposition that the drafting of documents, when merely incidental to the work of a distinct occupation, is not the practice of law, although the documents have legal consequences.". . . If the practitioner of the "distinct occupation" goes beyond the determination of legal questions for the purpose of performing his special service, and, instead, advises his patron as to the course to be taken to secure a desired legal status, he is engaged in the practice of law. The title searcher is exempt if he performs his task "without giving opinion or advice as to the legal effect of what is found." . . . The work of the accountant is exempt only if it is "dissociated from legal advice." One who, in the exercise of a commission to draw a conveyance, selects language designed to create a certain effect is practicing law . . . . So is one who draws estate plans, involving legal analysis . . . . A layman who draws a will for another necessarily is practicing law. . . . So is one who draws legal instruments or contracts . . . . A layman who evaluates a claim, and undertakes to settle it, based upon applicable legal principles, is practicing law . . . . A bank which furnishes "legal information or legal advice with respect to investments, taxation, stocks, bonds, notes or other securities or property" is involved in "a considerable practice of law," despite the argument that this is an incident to the investment trade.

OKLAHOMA ETHICS AND PRACTICE RULES ON THE INTERNET

- www.law.cornell.edu/ethics/oklahoma.html
- www.law.cornell.edu/ethics/ok/code/OK_CODE.HTM
- www.okbar.org/ethics/default.htm

PARALEGALS (AND OTHER NONATTORNEYS) IN OKLAHOMA STATE AND FEDERAL COURTS

- *Taylor v. Chubb Group of Insurance Companies*, 874 P.2d 806, 809 (Supreme Court of Oklahoma, 1994) (award of paralegal fees is for substantive legal work, not for copying documents or for performing other secretarial tasks; a party must "prove that the charges made for nonattorney's time covered work that a lawyer would have had to perform but for the performance of such services by a legal assistant" at a lower total charge than a lawyer would have charged; a legal assistant may interview clients; draft pleadings and other documents; carry out conventional and computer legal research; research public documents; prepare discovery requests and responses; schedule depositions and prepare notices and subpoenas; summarize depositions and other discovery responses; coordinate and manage document production; locate and interview witnesses; organize pleadings, trial exhibits and other documents; prepare witness and exhibit lists; prepare trial notebooks; prepare for attendance of witnesses at trial; and assist lawyers at trials).

- *Hayes v. Central States Orthopedic Specialists*, 51 P.3d 562 (Supreme Court of Oklahoma, 2002) (The trial court erred when it found that Oklahoma law requires a firm to be disqualified when it hires a nonlawyer employee who had acquired confidential information while working on litigation for the firm's opponent's firm, although the firm has set up a "Chinese wall" screening device to insure that the nonlawyer employee did not reveal confidences and would be screened from exposure to the litigation.)

- *Jones v. Eagle-North Hills Shopping Centre*, 478 F. Supp. 2d 1321 (U.S. District Court, E.D. Oklahoma, 2007) (Counsel's legal assistant aptly "fell on the sword" for her employer, claiming that she made a typographical error when entering the deadline in their calendar program. It is this court's view, however, that the buck stops with counsel, not his loyal employees.)

- *State ex rel. Oklahoma Bar Ass'n v. Simank*, 19 P.3d 860 (Supreme Court of Oklahoma, 2001) (failure to supervise a nonattorney employee).

- *Brown v. Ford*, 905 P.2d 223 (Supreme Court of Oklahoma, 1995) (paralegal alleges sexual harassment by attorney at work).

DOING LEGAL RESEARCH IN OKLAHOMA LAW

Statutes: www.oscn.net/applications/oscn/index. asp?ftdb=STOKST&level=1
Cases: www.oscn.net/applications/oscn/start.asp
Court Rules: www.llrx.com/courtrules-gen/ state-Oklahoma.html
General: www.okbar.org/research/links1.htm

FINDING EMPLOYMENT IN OKLAHOMA

- www.indeed.com/q-Litigation-Paralegal-l-Oklahoma-jobs.html
- www.simplyhired.com/job-search/l-Oklahoma/ o-232000/t-Paralegal
- careers.findlaw.com
- tulsa.craigslist.org/lgl

OREGON

ETHICAL RULES AND GUIDELINES IN OREGON

- For a discussion of the state's ethical Rule 5.3 ("Responsibilities Regarding Nonlawyer Assistants") in the *Oregon Rules of*

Professional Conduct, see the end of Section C in chapter 5. For the text of 5.3 in Oregon, see also www.osbar.org/_docs/rulesregs/orpc.pdf.

- Nonlawyer personnel can be listed, together with the positions they hold, on a lawyer's letterhead (e.g., John Doe, Legal Assistant) so long as the information is not misleading. Oregon State Bar, *Formal Opinion 2005–65* (8/05) (2005 WL 5679654). See also *Formal Opinion 1991–65* (7/91).

- Two law firms can employ the same nonlawyer on a part-time basis if they take reasonable care to make sure that the nonlawyer does not work on or acquire information relating to the representation of a client with respect to any matter on which the two firms' clients are adverse. Oregon State Bar, *Formal Opinion 2005–44* (8/05) (2005 WL 5679632). See also *Formal Opinion 1991–44* (7/91).

- A lawyer may comply with the insurance company guidelines that certain tasks be delegated to a paralegal if, in the lawyer's independent professional judgment, the particular task is appropriate for performance by a paralegal in the particular case. Oregon State Bar, *Formal Opinion 2002–166* (1/02) (2002 WL 32062455).

- It is unethical for an attorney to let his legal assistant draft pleadings that the attorney would sign but not review prior to filing. Oregon State Bar Ass'n, *Formal Opinion 1991–20* (7/91) (1991 WL 279161).

- Nonattorneys in an estate-planning service are engaged in the unauthorized practice of law when they give legal advice to clients in connection with the service, even if an attorney reviews and executes the documents involved. Oregon State Bar, *Opinion 523* (3/89).

- Nonattorney employees can have their own business cards that contain the name of their attorney-employer. Oregon State Bar, *Opinion 295* (7/75).

- A paralegal can write and sign letters on attorney letterhead. Oregon State Bar, *Opinion 349* (6/77) and *Opinion 295* (7/75).

- A paralegal cannot take (i.e., conduct) depositions. Oregon State Bar, *Opinion 449* (7/80).

- A well-trained legal assistant can do almost anything an attorney can do. However, a legal assistant cannot accept a case, set a fee, give legal advice, or represent a client in judicial proceedings. The Legal Assistants (Joint) Committee of the Oregon State Bar, *The Lawyer and the Legal Assistant* (1988).

- A law firm can hire a suspended or disbarred lawyer as a legal assistant so long as they do not give legal advice or share in legal fees. Oregon State Bar, *Formal Opinion 2005–24* (8/05) (2005 WL 5679610). See also *Formal Opinion 1991–24* (7/1991) (1991 WL 279165).

DEFINING THE PRACTICE OF LAW IN OREGON

- *Taub v. Weber*, 366 F.3d 966 (U.S. Court of Appeals, 9th Circuit, 2004) Thus, in Oregon, at a minimum "the 'practice of law' means the exercise of professional judgment in applying legal principles to address another person's individualized needs through analysis, advice, or other assistance." See also Oregon State Bar, *Formal Opinion Number 2005–101*.

- *Oregon State Bar v. Security Escrows, Inc.*, 377 P.2d 334, 337 (Supreme Court of Oregon, 1962): Documents creating legal rights abound in the business community. The preparation of some of these documents is the principal occupation of some lawyers. The preparation of business documents also occupies part of the time of accountants, automobile salesmen, insurance agents, and many others. The practice of law manifestly includes the drafting of many documents which create legal rights. It does not follow, however, that the drafting of all such documents is always the practice of law. The problem, as is frequently the case, is largely one of drawing a recognizable line. Here the line must be drawn between those services which laymen ought not to undertake and those services which laymen can perform without harm to the public.

- Rule 9.700 (Oregon State Bar, *Rules of the Unlawful Practice of Law Committee*): The practice of law includes, but is not limited to, any of the following: . . . appearing, personally or otherwise, on behalf of another in any judicial or administrative proceeding; 3) providing advice or service to another on any matter involving the application of legal principles to rights, duties, obligations or liabilities.

OREGON ETHICS AND PRACTICE RULES ON THE INTERNET

- www.law.cornell.edu/ethics/oregon.html
- www.law.cornell.edu/ethics/or/code
- www.osbar.org/ethics/ethicsops.html

PARALEGALS (AND OTHER NONATTORNEYS) IN OREGON STATE AND FEDERAL COURTS

- *Confederated Tribes of Siletz Indians of Oregon v. Weyerhaeuser Co.*, 2003 WL 23715982 (U.S. District Court, Oregon, 2003) (A significant portion of Kelly's time involved discovery matters: reviewing and organizing documents received from Weyerhaeuser and others, or preparing documents and interrogatory responses for submission to Weyerhaeuser. That is classic paralegal work. Kelly also helped locate and interview witnesses, research and summarize the relevant facts, sift through a mountain of documents, and prepare demonstrative exhibits. Again, this is within the realm of paralegal tasks, particularly in a complex case.)

- *Mendoza v. SAIF*, 859 P.2d 582 (Court of Appeals of Oregon, 1993) (an attorney does not establish "good cause" for failure to file a request for a hearing by arguing that he told his legal assistant twice to file it but she failed to do so).

- *Oregon State Bar v. Taub*, 78 P.3d 114 (Court of Appeals of Oregon, 2003) (For purposes of determining whether an unauthorized person has engaged in the practice of law, the application of legal principles to individual circumstances occurs, for example, when a paralegal gives advice to clients that is specific to the individual client or when a nonlawyer recommends particular legal forms tailored to the recipient's particular problems.)

- *In re Conduct of Morin*, 878 P.2d 393 (Supreme Court of Oregon, 1994) (it is not the unauthorized practice of law for paralegals to give seminars on living trusts and answer general questions about living trust packages; it is the unauthorized practice of law for the paralegal to advise clients or potential clients on legal matters specific to them or to help them select among the legal forms available).

- *Robins v. Scholastic Book Fairs*, 928 F. Supp. 1027 (U.S. District Court, Oregon, 1996) (paralegal fees reduced; 210 hours spent by paralegals were excessive in a straightforward case).

- *In the Matter of Griffith*, 913 P.2d 695 (Supreme Court of Oregon, 1995) (disbarred attorney acts as paralegal at his old law firm).

DOING LEGAL RESEARCH IN OREGON LAW

Statutes: landru.leg.state.or.us/ors
Cases: www.publications.ojd.state.or.us
Court Rules: www.llrx.com/courtrules-gen/state-Oregon
.html
General: lawlib.lclark.edu/research/oregonlaw.php

FINDING EMPLOYMENT IN OREGON

- osbar.legalstaff.com
- careers.findlaw.com
- www.theassociatesinc.com
- www.indeed.com/q-Litigation-Paralegal-l-Oregon-jobs
  .html
- portland.craigslist.org/lgl
- eastoregon.craigslist.org/lgl

PENNSYLVANIA

ETHICAL RULES AND GUIDELINES IN PENNSYLVANIA

- For a discussion of the state's ethical Rule 5.3 ("Responsibilities Regarding Nonlawyer Assistants") in the *Pennsylvania Rules of Professional Conduct*, see the end of Section C in chapter 5. For the text of 5.3 in Pennsylvania, see also www.padisciplinaryboard.org/attorneys.php.

- Pennsylvania Bar Ass'n, *Ethical Considerations in the Use of Nonlawyer Assistants*, Formal Opinion Number 98–75 (12/4/98) (1998 WL 988168). A nonlawyer assistant who arrives with a disqualifying conflict of interest may be employed if she is screened and the client is notified. A nonlawyer assistant cannot appear before a court or an administrative tribunal unless such appearance is authorized by statute, court rule or administrative regulation. This includes even routine matters such as seeking a postponement. A nonlawyer assistant cannot conduct a deposition even with predetermined approval by the lawyer. Attendance at a real estate settlement in the capacity of representing either the seller or the purchaser by anyone other than a lawyer constitutes the unauthorized practice of law. Lawyers and their nonlawyer assistants should make certain that clients and other persons dealing with them are aware that the nonlawyer assistant is not a lawyer and cannot give legal advice. Nonlawyers may not sign engagement letters, set fees, or solicit legal business for the lawyer or law firm. However, the name of a nonlawyer assistant may appear on the lawyer's or law firm letterhead if her status is properly revealed. Nonlawyer assistants may sign letters on firm stationery, again, if they are properly identified, and the letters do not contain legal advice. They may also have business cards with the name of the firm on it if they are properly identified and the information on the card conforms to the ethical rule on advertising. A lawyer may not share particular fees with a nonlawyer. It would be proper to compensate a nonlawyer on the basis of a fixed salary plus a percentage of the firm's net profits. The fees and expenses of legal assistants may be billed to a client who has consented to the arrangement. A suspended or disbarred lawyer may be engaged as a nonlawyer assistant.

- See also Pennsylvania Bar Ass'n, *Ethical Considerations in the Employment of legal Assistants* (Formal Opinion 1975–1) (4/9/75) (1975 WL 37366).

- It would be unethical for a law firm to give a nonattorney employee a day off for referring a new client to the office. Rule 7.2(c) of the *Rules of Professional Conduct* provides that an attorney shall not give "anything of value" to a person for recommending the lawyer's services. Pennsylvania Bar Ass'n, *Informal Opinion 2005–81* (6/28/05) (2005 WL 2291089). See also *Informal Opinion 2006–41* (5/4/06), which prohibits giving a percentage of fees to a nonattorney for client referrals.

- A husband (H) has several conversations with Attorney B at a law firm about possible legal problems. Nothing formal comes of these conversations. Later, Attorney A at the firm represents the wife of H in a divorce action. Attorney B has since left the firm and now represents H in the divorce. Attorney A has inquired about any ethical problems in continuing to represent the wife. The response states that a conflict of interest "would exist if a paralegal or secretary at your firm worked with Attorney B on H's case and in so doing gained material information adverse to H. In that circumstance, the knowledge of the secretary or paralegal will be imputed to you and would create a conflict of interest for your firm." Pennsylvania Bar Ass'n, *Informal Opinion 2000–36* (5/16/00) (2000 WL 1616461).

- A law firm, in an effort to educate itself in the event a particular case was re-tried, proposed to have a paralegal telephone jurors, post-trial. The paralegals conducting the post-trial interviews would follow a script and, in the event any reluctance was encountered by any juror, the conversation would be terminated. This would be ethical. Pennsylvania Bar Ass'n, *Informal Opinion 2001–78* (10/18/01) (2001 WL 34404901) (agreeing with *Informal Opinion 91–52* (4/3/91)).

- An attorney cannot hire an accountant on a contingent fee basis. This would be sharing a fee with a nonattorney. "If this arrangement was allowed, one could then have the paralegal or secretary be hired with similar type of arrangements and you could, obviously, see the problems that would create." Pennsylvania Bar Ass'n, *Informal Opinion 93–164* (10/17/93) (1993 WL 851259).

- It is permissible to place the name of a paralegal or legal assistant on the firm's letterhead so long as the non-lawyer is clearly identified to be a paralegal or legal assistant. Pennsylvania Bar Ass'n, *Informal Opinion 85–145*. The same is true of a properly identified employee who is a private investigator. *Informal Opinion 90–54* (4/23/90) (1990 WL 709607).

- A paralegal cannot conduct any aspect of a deposition. Pennsylvania Bar Ass'n, *Informal Opinion 91–137* (10/18/91) (1991 WL 78708).

- Suspended attorneys can work in a law office so long as they perform no legal or paralegal work or law related activities. They can perform administrative tasks. Licensed attorneys within the firm would be responsible to ensure that they did no legal, paralegal, or law related work. Pennsylvania Bar Ass'n, *Opinion 2007–3* (3/07) (2007 WL 1793144). See also *Opinion 2005–10* (7/05). Under Rule 217(j)(3) of the *Pennsylvania Disciplinary Rules of Enforcement*, "A formerly admitted attorney may have direct communication with a client . . . only if the communication is limited to ministerial matters such as scheduling, billing, updates, confirmation of receipt or sending of correspondence and messages. The formerly admitted attorney shall clearly indicate in any such communication that he or she is a legal assistant and identify the supervising attorney." (42 Pa.C.S.A.).

- Philadelphia Bar Ass'n, Professional Responsibility Committee, *Professional Responsibility for Nonlawyers* (1989). *Guideline 1:* Consider all work of the office confidential, even public knowledge about a client. Do not discuss the business of your office or your firm's clients with any outsider unless you have specific authorization from an attorney. It is illegal and unethical to disclose or to use any information about a company that might be of significance to the securities market in financial transactions such as the purchase or sale of stocks, bonds or other security. *Guideline 2:* A paralegal may not sign papers to be filed in court, ask questions at a deposition, or handle court appearances. A client with whom the paralegal has developed rapport will often ask the paralegal questions such as, "What do you think my chances of recovery are?" Such questions seek advice and the paralegal should refer them to an attorney. *Guideline 3:* If an attorney allows a nonattorney to sign letters on law firm stationery, a descriptive title such as *legal assistant* should be used to clearly indicate the nonattorney's position. *Guideline 4:* If you interview a witness who does not have his or her own attorney, explain who you are and who your office represents. You cannot give the witness any advice except to secure his or her own attorney. If the opposing party has an attorney, you cannot talk with that party without his or her attorney's permission. You might also need this permission to talk to any employees of the opposing party. *Guideline 5:* A paralegal must be truthful when dealing with others on behalf of a client. *Guideline 6:* If the law firm has possession of a client's money or other property, it must be kept completely separate from the attorney's or law firm's money or property, and a proper accounting must be maintained.

- A law firm can pay non-lawyer employee collectors a bonus if the gross amount collected as a result of their efforts exceeds a predetermined figure provided that the bonus is not tied to or contingent on the payment of a fee from a particular case or specific class of cases relating to a particular client or debtor. But the lawyer may not pay his non-law partnership for the services of the non-law partnership's collectors based upon the gross amount of money collected by the non-law partnership each month. Such an arrangement unethically shares fees with non-lawyers. Philadelphia Bar Ass'n, *Opinion 2001–7 (7/01)* (2001 WL 914187).

- Nonattorneys are authorized to represent clients at Social Security agency hearings and to collect fees for such representation. A law firm can have its nonattorney employee represent Social Security clients at these hearings. The salary of the nonattorney, however, cannot be directly related to the fees derived from his cases. Philadelphia Bar Ass'n, *Guidance Opinion 98–1 (2/98)* (1998 WL 63080).

- Paralegals can draft demand letters as long as an attorney has reviewed the work product for accuracy and completeness and the paralegal has identified his/herself as a paralegal. Philadelphia Bar Ass'n, *Guidance Opinion 90–5 (4/90)* (1990 WL 303921).

- The paralegal title can be used on law firm letterhead to identify a nonattorney employee. Philadelphia Bar Ass'n, *Guidance Opinion 87–18 (6/25/87)* (1987 WL 109743).

CERTIFICATION OF PARALEGALS IN PENNSYLVANIA

- keystoneparalegals.org
- keystoneparalegals.org/certification.html

DEFINING THE PRACTICE OF LAW IN PENNSYLVANIA

- *Harkness v. Unemployment Compensation Board of Review*, 920 A.2d 162 (Supreme Court of Pennsylvania, 2007): [O]ur Court set forth three broad categories of activities that may constitute the practice of law: (1) the instruction and advising of clients in regard to the law so that they may pursue their affairs and be informed as to their rights and obligations; (2) the preparation of documents for clients requiring familiarity with legal principles beyond the ken of ordinary laypersons; and (3) the appearance on behalf of clients before public tribunals in order that the attorney may assist the deciding official in the proper interpretation and enforcement of the law. More recently, our Court expressed that the practice of law is implicated by the holding out of oneself to the public as competent to exercise legal judgment and the implication that he or she has the technical competence to analyze legal problems and the requisite character qualifications to act in a representative capacity. Thus, the character of the actions taken by the individual in question is a significant factor in the determination of what constitutes the practice of law.

- § 2524, title 42 (*Pennsylvania Consolidated Statutes Annotated*): [A]ny person, including, but not limited to, a paralegal or legal assistant, who within this Commonwealth shall practice law, or who shall hold himself out to the public as being entitled to practice law, or use or advertise the title of lawyer, attorney at law, attorney and counselor at law, counselor, or the equivalent in any language, in such a manner as to convey the impression that he is a practitioner of the law of any jurisdiction, without being an attorney at law or a corporation complying with 15 Pa.C.S. Ch. 29 (relating to professional corporations), commits a misdemeanor of the third degree upon a first violation. A second or subsequent violation of this subsection constitutes a misdemeanor of the first degree.

PENNSYLVANIA ETHICS AND PRACTICE RULES ON THE INTERNET

- www.law.cornell.edu/ethics/pennsylvania.html
- www.law.cornell.edu/ethics/pa/narr
- www.philadelphiabar.org/page/EthicsOpinions

PARALEGALS (AND OTHER NONATTORNEYS) IN PENNSYLVANIA STATE AND FEDERAL COURTS

- *Brown v. Hammond*, 810 F. Supp. 644 (U.S. District Court, E.D. Pennsylvania, 1993) (paralegal dismissed for disclosing illegal billing practices) (see text of case in chapter 5).

- *Anderson v. Boothe*, 1986 WL 6737, (U.S. District Court, E.D. Pennsylvania, 1986) (judge awards $244,490 in fees for services performed by paralegals).

- *In re Busy Beaver Building Centers*, 19 F.3d 833 (U.S. Court of Appeals, 3d Circuit, 1994) (award of paralegal fees in bankruptcy case; extensive discussion of the role of the litigation paralegal as opposed to a legal secretary; amicus brief filed by the National Federation of Paralegal Associations; trial court disallowed compensation for those services performed by paralegals that it considered "purely clerical functions" and therefore part of an attorney's overhead for which there can be no separate payment; on appeal this decision was reversed; page 838: "if the court were to disallow paralegal assistance on such matters, the paralegal profession would suffer a major setback, and attorneys would instead perform those services but at greater expense" to the client; the standard on what paralegal services are compensable will be whether such services are compensable in nonbankruptcy cases: whether nonbankruptcy attorneys typically charge and collect from their clients fees for the kind of services in question, and the rates charged and collected therefor; the case was sent back to the lower court to apply this standard).

- *Harkness v. Unemployment Compensation Board of Review*, 920 A.2d 162 (Supreme Court of Pennsylvania, 2007) (A Pennsylvania statute allows claimants to be represented by nonattorneys at hearings of the Unemployment Compensation Board of Review (43 P.S. § 862). Nonattorneys can also represent the employer without engaging in the practice of law.)

- *German v. UCBR*, 489 A.2d 308 (Commonwealth Court of Pennsylvania, 1985) (Hearsay and best evidence rule objections were waived for the purposes of an appeal to the Commonwealth Court because the paralegal representing the claimant at the referee hearing failed to object.)

- *Baldauf v. UCBR*, 854 A.2d 689 Commonwealth Court of Pennsylvania, 2004) (Paralegal is fired for searching for a job during work hours (theft of company time) and is denied unemployment compensation.)

DOING LEGAL RESEARCH IN PENNSYLVANIA LAW

Statutes: www.legis.state.pa.us/cfdocs/legis/LI/PUBLIC/cons_index.cfm
Cases: www.jenkinslaw.org/researchlinks/index.php?rl=128
Court Rules: www.llrx.com/courtrules-gen/state-Pennsylvania.html
General: www.pennsylvanialegalresearch.com

FINDING EMPLOYMENT IN PENNSYLVANIA

- pabar.legalstaff.com
- careers.findlaw.com
- www.indeed.com/q-Paralegal-l-Pennsylvania-jobs.html
- www.simplyhired.com/job-search/l-Pennsylvania/o-232000/t-Paralegal
- philadelphia.craigslist.org/lgl

RHODE ISLAND

DEFINING LEGAL ASSISTANTS/ PARALEGALS IN RHODE ISLAND

A legal assistant is one who under the supervision of a lawyer, shall apply knowledge of law and legal procedures in rendering direct assistance to lawyers, clients and courts; design, develop and modify procedures, technique, services and processes; prepare and interpret legal documents; detail procedures for practicing in certain fields of law; research, select, assess, compile and use information from the law library and other references; and analyze and handle procedural problems that involve independent decisions. More specifically, a legal assistant is one who engages in the functions set forth in Guideline 2. Rhode Island Supreme Court, *Provisional Order No 18* (www.courts.state.ri.us/supreme/pdf-files/Rules_Of_Professional_Conduct.pdf).

ETHICAL RULES AND GUIDELINES IN RHODE ISLAND

- For a discussion of the state's ethical Rule 5.3 ("Responsibilities Regarding Nonlawyer Assistants") in the *Rhode Island Rules of Professional Conduct*, see the end of Section C in chapter 5. For the text of 5.3 in Rhode Island, see also www.courts.ri.gov/supreme/pdf-files/Rules_Of_Professional_Conduct.pdf.

- *Guidelines on the Use of Legal Assistants* (Rhode Island Supreme Court, *Provisional Order No 18* (see Web site above)): *Guideline 1*: A lawyer shall not permit a legal assistant to engage in the unauthorized practice of law. The lawyer shares in the ultimate accountability for a violation of this guideline. The legal assistant remains individually accountable for engaging in the unauthorized practice of law. *Guideline 2*: A legal assistant may perform the following functions, together with other related duties, to assist lawyers in their representation of clients: attend client conferences; correspond with and obtain information from clients; draft legal documents; assist at closing and similar meetings between parties and lawyers; witness execution of documents; prepare transmittal letters; maintain estate/guardianship trust accounts; transfer securities and other assets; assist in the day-to-day administration of trusts and estates; index and organize documents; conduct research; check citations in briefs and memoranda; draft interrogatories and answers thereto, deposition notices and requests for production; prepare summaries of depositions and trial transcripts; interview witnesses; obtain records from doctors, hospitals, police departments, other agencies and institutions; and obtain information from courts. Legal documents, including, but not limited to, contracts, deeds, leases, mortgages, wills, trusts, probate forms, pleadings, pension plans and tax returns, shall be reviewed by a lawyer before being submitted to a client or another party. A legal assistant may represent clients before administrative agencies or courts where such representation is permitted by statute or agency or court rules. *Guideline 3*: A lawyer shall instruct the legal assistant regarding the confidential nature of the attorney/client relationship, and shall direct the legal assistant to refrain from disclosing any confidential information obtained from a client or in connection with representation of a client. *Guideline 4*: A lawyer shall direct a legal assistant to disclose that he or she is not a lawyer at the outset in contacts with clients, courts, administrative agencies, attorneys, or when acting in a professional capacity, the public. *Guideline 5*: A lawyer may permit a legal assistant to sign correspondence relating to the legal assistant's work, provided the legal assistant's non-lawyer status is clear and the contents of the letter do not constitute legal advice. Correspondence containing substantive instructions or legal advice to a client shall be signed by an attorney. *Guideline 6*: Except where permitted by statute, or court rule or decision, a lawyer shall not permit a legal assistant to appear in court as a legal advocate on behalf of a client. Nothing in this Guideline shall be construed to bar or limit a legal assistant's right or obligation to appear in any forum as a witness on behalf of a client. *Guideline 7*: A lawyer may permit a legal assistant to use a business card, with the employer's name indicated, provided the card is approved by the employer and the legal assistant's nonlawyer status is clearly indicated. *Guideline 8*: A lawyer shall not form a partnership with a legal assistant if any part of the partnership's activity involves the practice of law. *Guideline 9*: Compensation of legal assistants shall not be in the manner of sharing legal fees, nor shall the legal assistant receive any remuneration for referring legal matters to a lawyer. *Guideline 10*: A lawyer shall not use or employ as a legal assistant any attorney who has been suspended or disbarred pursuant to an order of this Court, or an attorney who has resigned in this or any other jurisdiction for reasons related to a breach of ethical conduct.

- A law firm's letterhead must place the title *legal assistant* after the name of an attorney who is licensed in another state but who is ineligible to sit for the Rhode Island bar examination because he was graduated from an unaccredited law school.

Ethics Advisory Panel of the Rhode Island Supreme Court, *Opinion 93–28* (5/12/93). See also *Opinion 92–6* (1992), where the term *legal assistant* is preferred over *paralegal* for non-attorney employees.

■ An attorney may not hire a suspended or disbarred attorney as a paralegal. Ethics Advisory Panel of the Rhode Island Supreme Court, *Opinion 90–12* (2/27/90); *Opinion 91–64* (9/19/91).

DEFINING THE PRACTICE OF LAW IN RHODE ISLAND

■ § 11–27–2 (*Rhode Island Statutes*): The term "practice law" as used in this chapter shall be deemed to mean the doing of any act for another person usually done by attorneys at law in the course of their profession, and, without limiting the generality of the foregoing, shall be deemed to include the following: (1) The appearance or acting as the attorney, solicitor, or representative of another person before any court, referee, master, auditor, division, department, commission, board, judicial person, or body authorized or constituted by law to determine any question of law or fact or to exercise any judicial power, or the preparation of pleadings or other legal papers incident to any action or other proceeding of any kind before or to be brought before the court or other body; (2) The giving or tendering to another person for a consideration, direct or indirect, of any advice or counsel pertaining to a law question or a court action or judicial proceeding brought or to be brought; (3) The undertaking or acting as a representative or on behalf of another person to commence, settle, compromise, adjust, or dispose of any civil or criminal case or cause of action; (4) The preparation or drafting for another person of a will, codicil, corporation organization, amendment, or qualification papers, or any instrument which requires legal knowledge and capacity and is usually prepared by attorneys at law.

RHODE ISLAND ETHICS AND PRACTICE RULES ON THE INTERNET

● www.law.cornell.edu/ethics/ri.html
● www.law.cornell.edu/ethics/ri/code
● www.courts.state.ri.us/supreme/ethics/ethicsadvisorypanelopinions.htm

PARALEGALS (AND OTHER NONATTORNEYS) IN RHODE ISLAND STATE AND FEDERAL COURTS

■ *Schroff, Inc. v. Taylor-Peterson*, 732 A.2d 719 (Supreme Court of Rhode Island, 1999) (award of paralegal fees; utilizing services of paralegals should result in reducing, rather than enhancing, attorney fees).

■ *Donovan v. Bowling*, 706 A.2d 937 (Supreme Court of Rhode Island, 1998) (paralegal can be called as a witness to give testimony on possible prior inconsistent statements by a witness).

■ *In re Almacs*, 178 Bankruptcy Reporter 598 (U.S. Bankruptcy Court, Rhode Island, 1995) (some of the paralegal charges are for tasks that are clerical in nature and should be treated as overhead rather than as separate paralegal fees).

■ *Unauthorized Practice of Law Committee v. State, Dept. of Workers' Compensation*, 543 A.2d 662 (Supreme Court of Rhode Island, 1988) (The statute authorizing employee assistants to assist injured employees in informal hearings before the Department of Workers' Compensation did

not violate the Supreme Court's exclusive power under Constitution to regulate practice of law. Gen.Laws 1956, §§ 28–33–1.1(i)(1)(C), 42–94–1 to 42–94–18.)

DOING LEGAL RESEARCH IN RHODE ISLAND LAW

Statutes: www.rilin.state.ri.us/Statutes/Statutes.html
Cases: www.findlaw.com/11stategov/ri/laws.html
Court Rules: www.llrx.com/courtrules-gen/state-Rhode-Island.html
General: www.alphalegal.com/ri/legalres.htm

FINDING EMPLOYMENT IN RHODE ISLAND

● ribar.legalstaff.com
● careers.findlaw.com
● www.indeed.com/q-Paralegal-l-Rhode-Island-jobs.html
● providence.craigslist.org/lgl

SOUTH CAROLINA

ETHICAL RULES AND GUIDELINES IN SOUTH CAROLINA

■ For a discussion of the state's ethical Rule 5.3 ("Responsibilities Regarding Nonlawyer Assistants") in the *South Carolina Rules of Professional Conduct*, see the end of Section C in chapter 5. For the text of 5.3 in South Carolina, see also www.judicial.state.sc.us/courtReg/newrules/NewRules.cfm.

■ South Carolina Bar, *Guidelines for the Utilization by Lawyers of the Services of Legal Assistants* (12/11/81). *Guideline I:* An attorney shall not permit his or her legal assistant to engage in the unauthorized practice of law. *Guideline II:* A legal assistant may perform certain functions otherwise prohibited when and to the extent permitted by court or administrative agency. *Guideline III:* A legal assistant can perform services for the lawyer if (a) the client understands that the legal assistant is not an attorney, (b) the attorney supervises the legal assistant, and (c) the attorney is fully responsible for what the legal assistant does or fails to do. *Guideline IV:* The attorney must instruct the legal assistant to preserve the confidences and secrets of a client and shall exercise care that the legal assistant does so. *Guideline V:* An attorney shall not form a partnership with a legal assistant if any part of the partnership consists of the practice of law. Nor shall an attorney share, on a proportionate basis, legal fees with a legal assistant. The legal assistant, however, can be included in a retirement plan even though based in whole or in part on a profit-sharing arrangement. A legal assistant shall not be paid, directly or indirectly for referring legal matters to an attorney. *Guideline VI:* The letterhead of an attorney may not include the name of a legal assistant, but a legal assistant can have a business card that prints the name of his or her attorney as long as the legal assistant's capacity or status is clearly indicated. A legal assistant can sign letters on an attorney's letterhead as long as the legal assistant's signature is followed by an appropriate designation (e.g., "legal assistant") so that it is clear the signer is not an attorney. *Guideline VII:* An attorney shall require a legal assistant, when dealing with a client, to disclose at the outset that he or she is not an attorney. This disclosure is also required when the paralegal is dealing with a court, administrative agency, attorney, or the public if there is any reason for their believing the legal assistant is an attorney or is associated with an attorney. This guideline applies even in administrative agencies where the legal assistant is allowed to represent clients. *Guideline VIII:* Except as otherwise provided by law, any grievances or complaints of the use of legal assistants by attorneys shall be referred for action to the Board of Commissioners on Grievances and Discipline.

- A compensation system in which a paralegal receives a bonus based on the charges billed to a client is a profit-sharing arrangement and expressly permitted under Rule 5.4(a)(3). A law firm, however, may run afoul of fee-splitting rules if the bonus is based on a percentage of a particular fee earned. South Carolina Bar, *Ethics Advisory Opinion 97–02* (3/1997).
- A paralegal, under the supervision and at the direction of the responsible attorney, can interview clients alone in order to gather information, but cannot alone assist clients in the execution of the documents. South Carolina Bar, *Opinion 02–12* (4/20/02) (2002 WL 2069864).
- A lawyer may employ the services of an independent paralegal assistance service provided the lawyer adequately supervises the work of the paralegals and remains responsible for their work product. In billing for the paralegal organization's services, the lawyer should comply with his fiduciary duty to disclose to his clients the basis of his fee and expenses. South Carolina Bar, *Ethics Advisory Opinion 96–13* (1996).
- A lawyer may not bill a client for paralegal services rendered by an individual who is not performing paralegal services. The issuance of paralegal certificates to a lawyer's staff does not transform all of the duties of those individuals into paralegal services. South Carolina Bar, *Ethics Advisory Opinion 94–37* (1/1995).
- A nonattorney switching jobs raises the possibility of disqualification of her new employer because of a conflict of interest. South Carolina Bar, *Ethics Advisory Opinion 93–29* (10/1993).
- A nonlawyer who works full time for a prosecutor can work part-time for a lawyer if she is strictly screened from any criminal matters and maintains confidentiality. South Carolina Bar, *Opinion 07–02* (4/20/07)(2007 WL 2069864).
- A lawyer who represents a client in a matter adverse to a corporate party may hire as a paralegal a former employee of the corporate party, at least when the paralegal had no decision making role while employed by the corporation, possesses no protected information, and is not likely to be called as a witness in the litigation. South Carolina Bar, *Opinion 91–12* (5/91)(1991 WL 787742).
- A full-time paralegal in a "Legal Services" office can also hold a position as a part-time magistrate within the same county. Any conflict with Legal Services cases could be avoided by the disqualification of the magistrate. South Carolina Bar, *Ethics Advisory Opinion 88–12* (1988) (1988 WL 582713).
- A lawyer who is disbarred, suspended, or transferred due to incapacity to inactive status shall not be employed by a member of the South Carolina Bar as a paralegal, as an investigator, or in any other capacity connected with the law. Appellate Court Rule 413, Lawyer Disciplinary Enforcement Rule 34.
- *In re Chastain*, 587 S.E.2d 115 (Supreme Court of South Carolina, 2003). Note, however, that a law firm can hire a convicted felon as an in-house investigator if properly supervised. South Carolina Bar, *Ethics Advisory Opinion 92–26* (9/92).
- As long as the business card is not false or misleading, a legal assistant may have a business card with the name of the law firm placed on the card. South Carolina Bar, *Ethics Advisory Opinion 90–23* (10/90) (1990 WL 709803). (This opinion supersedes Opinion 88–06.)
- An attorney can hire nonattorneys to fill in preprinted real estate forms and do title searches as long as they are supervised by the attorney and the attorney maintains direct contact with clients. South Carolina Bar, *Opinion 88–2* (6/1988). On title searches, see also *Opinion 78–26* (10/1978).
- It is the unauthorized practice of law for a nonattorney to have an ownership interest, along with an attorney, in a corporation that drafts and provides real estate documents if the nonattorney controls any of the legal services provided. South Carolina Bar, *Opinion 84–3* (9/1985).

DEFINING THE PRACTICE OF LAW IN SOUTH CAROLINA

The South Carolina Medical Malpractice Joint Underwriting Association v. Froelich, 377 S.E.2d 306, 307 (Supreme Court of South Carolina, 1989): Conduct constituting the practice of law includes a wide range of activities. It is too obvious for discussion that the practice of law is not limited to the conduct of cases in courts. According to the generally understood definition of the practice of law in this country, it embraces the preparation of pleadings and other papers incident to actions and special proceedings and the management of such actions and proceedings on behalf of clients before judges and courts, and in addition conveyancing, the preparation of legal instruments of all kinds, and in general all advice to clients and all action taken for them in matters connected with the law.

SOUTH CAROLINA ETHICS AND PRACTICE RULES ON THE INTERNET

- www.law.cornell.edu/ethics/sc.html
- www.law.cornell.edu/ethics/sc/code
- www.judicial.state.sc.us//adv_opinion/index.cfm

PARALEGALS (AND OTHER NONATTORNEYS) IN SOUTH CAROLINA STATE AND FEDERAL COURTS

- *In re Matthews*, 639 S.E.2d 45 (Supreme Court of South Carolina, 2006) (the attorney delegated the responsibility of reconciling his trust accounts to a nonlawyer assistant without providing proper training or supervision; as a result, significant errors were made).
- *In re Ingalls*, 633 S.E.2d 512 (Supreme Court of South Carolina, 2006) (attorney disciplined for allowing nonattorneys to conduct real estate closings without an attorney being present).
- *Lucas v. Guyton*, 901 F. Supp. 1047, 1059 (U.S. District Court, South Carolina, 1995) (the "court observed Ms. Pope to be a diligent and very able paralegal who assisted in many respects during the trial including reading the depositions of Plaintiff's death row witnesses, taking notes throughout the proceeding and, on numerous occasions, conferring with counsel during his presentation of the case").
- *In re Unauthorized Practice of Law Rules Proposed by the South Carolina Bar*, 422 S.E. 2d 123 (Supreme Court of South Carolina, 1992) (a business can be represented by a nonattorney employee in civil magistrate's court proceedings; a South Carolina state agency may authorize nonattorneys to appear and represent clients before the agency; an arresting police officer—a nonattorney—may prosecute traffic offenses in magistrate's court and in municipal court).

- *In re Easler*, 272 S.E.2d 32, 32–33 (Supreme Court of South Carolina, 1980) (the activities of a paralegal do not constitute the practice of law as long as they are limited to work of a preparatory nature).
- *South Carolina v. Robinson*, 468 S.E.2d 290 (Supreme Court of South Carolina, 1996) (injunction against paralegal who advertises in Yellow Pages—"If your civil rights have been violated, call me"—as a paralegal and represents clients in court; § 40–5–80 of the *South Carolina Code Annotated* allows a nonattorney to represent another in court if the permission of the court is first obtained—"with leave of the court"—but the paralegal in this case did not always obtain this permission).
- *In the Matter of Jenkins*, 468 S.E.2d 869 (Supreme Court of South Carolina, 1996) (attorney disciplined for asking her paralegal to notarize a forged signature).

DOING LEGAL RESEARCH IN SOUTH CAROLINA LAW

Statutes: www.scstatehouse.net
Cases: www.judicial.state.sc.us/opinions/index.cfm
Court Rules: www.llrx.com/courtrules-gen/
state-South-Carolina.html
General: www.ll.georgetown.edu/states/southcarolina.cfm

FINDING EMPLOYMENT IN SOUTH CAROLINA

- careers.findlaw.com
- www.indeed.com/q-Litigation-Paralegal-l-South-Carolina-jobs.html
- charleston.craigslist.org/lgl

SOUTH DAKOTA

DEFINING LEGAL ASSISTANTS/ PARALEGALS IN SOUTH DAKOTA

Legal assistants (also known as paralegals) are a distinguishable group of persons who assist licensed attorneys in the delivery of legal services. Through formal education, training, and experience, legal assistants have knowledge and expertise regarding the legal system, substantive and procedural law, the ethical considerations of the legal profession, and the Rules of Professional Conduct as stated in chapter 16–18, which qualify them to do work of a legal nature under the employment and direct supervision of a licensed attorney. This rule shall apply to all unlicensed persons employed by a licensed attorney who are represented to the public or clients as possessing training or education which qualifies them to assist in the handling of legal matters or document preparation for the client. *South Dakota Codified Laws*, § 16–18–34.

ETHICAL RULES AND GUIDELINES IN SOUTH DAKOTA

- For a discussion of the state's ethical Rule 5.3 ("Responsibilities Regarding Nonlawyer Assistants") in the *South Dakota Rules of Professional Conduct*, see the end of Section C in chapter 5. For the text of 5.3 in South Dakota, see also www.sdbar.org/Rules/Rules/PC_Rules.htm.
- Any person employed by a licensed attorney as a legal assistant must meet minimum qualifications of formal training or in-house training as a legal assistant. *South Dakota Codified Laws*, § 16–18–34.1.

  (1) A legal assistant can assist in all aspects of the attorney's representation of a client, provided that:

(a) The status of the legal assistant is disclosed at the outset of any professional relationship with a client, other attorneys, courts or administrative agencies, or members of the general public;

(b) The attorney establishes the attorney–client relationship, is available to the client, and maintains control of all client matters;

(c) The attorney reviews the legal assistant's work product and supervises performance of the duties assigned;

(d) The attorney remains responsible for the services performed by the legal assistant to the same extent as though such services had been furnished entirely by the attorney and such actions were those of the attorney;

(e) The services performed by the legal assistant supplement, merge with and become part of the attorney's work product;

(f) The services performed by the legal assistant do not require the exercise of unsupervised legal judgment; this provision does not prohibit a legal assistant appearing and representing a client at an administrative hearing provided that the agency or board having jurisdiction does not have a rule forbidding persons other than licensed attorneys to do so and providing that the other rules pertaining to the utilization of legal assistants are met; and

(g) The attorney instructs the legal assistant concerning standards of client confidentiality.

- A legal assistant may not establish the attorney-client relationship, set legal fees, give legal advice or represent a client in court; nor encourage, engage in, or contribute to any act which would constitute the unauthorized practice of law.
  (2) A legal assistant may author and sign correspondence on the attorney's letterhead, provided the legal assistant's status is indicated and the correspondence does not contain legal opinions or give legal advice.
  (3) An attorney may identify a legal assistant by name and title on the attorney's letterhead and on business cards identifying the attorney's firm. *South Dakota Codified Laws*, § 16–18–34.2.

- The proper use of assistants who are not licensed attorneys significantly increases the ability of attorneys to provide quality professional services to the public at reasonable cost. An attorney cannot, however, delegate his or her ethical proscriptions by claiming that the violation was that of an employee. Thus, in order to secure compliance with the Rules of Professional Conduct:

  (1) An attorney shall ascertain the assistant's abilities, limitations, and training, and must limit the assistant's duties and responsibilities to those that can be competently performed in view of those abilities, limitations, and training.

  (2) An attorney shall educate and train assistants with respect to the ethical standards which apply to the attorney.

  (3) An attorney is responsible for monitoring and supervising the work of assistants in order to assure that the services rendered by the assistant are performed competently and in a professional manner.

  (4) An attorney is responsible for assuring that the assistant does not engage in the unauthorized practice of law.

  (5) An attorney is responsible for the improper behavior or activities of assistants and must take appropriate action to prevent recurrence of improper behavior or activities.

  (6) Assistants who deal directly with an attorney's clients must be identified to those clients as nonlawyers, and the attorney is responsible for obtaining the understanding of

the clients with respect to the rule of and the limitations which apply to those assistants.

(7) A legal assistant should understand the Rules of Professional Conduct and these rules in order to avoid any action which would involve the attorney in a violation of chapter 16–18, or give the appearance of professional impropriety.

(8) An attorney takes reasonable measures to insure that all client confidences are preserved by a legal assistant.

(9) An attorney takes reasonable measures to prevent conflicts of interest resulting from a legal assistant's other employment or interest insofar as such other employment or interest would present a conflict of interest if it were that of the attorney.

(10) An attorney may include a charge for the work performed by a legal assistant in setting a charge for legal services.

(11) An attorney may not split legal fees with a legal assistant nor pay a legal assistant for the referral of legal business. An attorney may compensate a legal assistant based on the quantity and quality of the legal assistant's work and the value of that work to a law practice, but the legal assistant's compensation may not be, by advance agreement, contingent upon the profitability of the attorney's practice. *South Dakota Codified Laws*, § 16–18–34.3.

■ The following persons shall not serve as a legal assistant in the State of South Dakota except upon application to and approval of the Supreme Court: (1) Any person convicted of a felony; (2) Any person disbarred or suspended from the practice of law; (3) Any person placed on disability inactive status; (4) Any person placed on temporary suspension from the practice of law. *South Dakota Codified Laws*, § 16–18–34.4.

■ It is unethical for an attorney to give 5% of the fees collected from clients referred by a nonattorney. State Bar of South Dakota, *Opinion 94–12*.

■ A law firm can list paralegals on their letterhead (referring to graduates of law school who have not yet passed the bar exam). State Bar of South Dakota, *Opinion 90–10 (9/22/90)*.

DEFINING THE PRACTICE OF LAW IN SOUTH DAKOTA

Persche v. Jones, 387 N.W.2d 32, 36 (Supreme Court of South Dakota, 1986): Practicing law "is not limited to conducting litigation, but includes giving legal advice and counsel, and rendering services that require the use of legal knowledge or skill and the preparing of instruments and contracts by which legal rights are secured, whether or not the matter is pending in a court."

SOUTH DAKOTA ETHICS AND PRACTICE RULES ON THE INTERNET

- www.law.cornell.edu/ethics/sd.html
- www.sdbar.org/Ethics/ethics.shtm

PARALEGALS (AND OTHER NONATTORNEYS) IN SOUTH DAKOTA STATE AND FEDERAL COURTS

■ *Mock v. South Dakota Bd. of Regents*, 296 F. Supp. 2d 1061 (U.S. District Court, South Dakota, 2003) (Court comments on work of paralegal during the trial: "The Court observed Ms. Ford during the trial in this case and noted that she provided exceptional assistance to both Ms. Chanti and Mr. Jensen during their examinations of witnesses.")

■ *Nienaber v. Citibank*, 2007 WL 2003761 (U.S. District Court, South Dakota, 2007) ($125 per hour for paralegals approved as reasonable).

■ *In re Discipline of Mines*, 612 N.W.2d 619 (Supreme Court of South Dakota, 2000) (disbarment of attorney warranted due in part to improper use of legal assistant and improper billing).

■ *In re Yankton College*, 101 Bankruptcy Reporter 151, 159 (U.S. Bankruptcy Court, South Dakota, 1989) ("Paraprofessional Billing": if paralegal work is to be compensated, the qualifications of the paralegal should be established to justify the charge; "[s]imply classifying a secretary as a paralegal for billing purposes does not justify compensating secretary time" which should be part of overhead).

DOING LEGAL RESEARCH IN SOUTH DAKOTA LAW

Statutes: legis.state.sd.us/statutes
Cases: www.findlaw.com/11stategov/sd/index.html
Court Rules: www.llrx.com/courtrules-gen/state-South-Dakota.html
General: www.lawguru.com/search/states/southdakota.html

FINDING EMPLOYMENT IN SOUTH DAKOTA

- careers.findlaw.com
- www.indeed.com/q-Paralegal-l-South-Dakota-jobs.html
- www.simplyhired.com/job-search/o-232000/t-Paralegal
- sd.craigslist.org/lgl

TENNESSEE

ETHICAL RULES AND GUIDELINES IN TENNESSEE

■ For a discussion of the state's ethical Rule 5.3 ("Responsibilities Regarding Nonlawyer Assistants") in the *Tennessee Rules of Professional Conduct*, see the end of Section C in chapter 5. For the text of 5.3 in Tennessee, see also www.tba.org/ethics2002.html.

■ If appropriate screening devices are in place and Client "A" consents, an entire law firm need not be disqualified from representing Client "A" simply because a "tainted" attorney in the firm once worked at another firm that represented Client "B" in a case adverse to Client "A." Furthermore, "the disqualification rules and screening procedures are applicable to lawyer, law clerk, paralegal, and legal secretary." Board of Professional Responsibility of the Supreme Court of Tennessee, *Formal Ethics Opinion 89-F-118 (3/10/89)*. See also *Clinard v. Blackwood* below.

■ It is the unauthorized practice of law for an attorney to allow his or her paralegal to appear at a section 341 meeting of creditors in bankruptcy cases to ask questions of debtors unless a court expressly authorizes it. Board of Professional Responsibility of the Supreme Court of Tennessee, *Advisory Ethics Opinion 92-A-473(a) (5/12/92)*, confirming *Opinion 92-A-475 (1/1991)*. See *In re Kincaid* below, which *does* authorize it.

■ It is the unauthorized practice of law for an attorney to allow his or her paralegal to appear in court at docket calls on behalf of the attorney to schedule cases. Board of Professional Responsibility of the Supreme Court of Tennessee, *Formal Ethics Opinion 85-F-94 (5/6/85)*.

■ A suspended attorney should not act as a paralegal. Board of Professional Responsibility of the Supreme Court of Tennessee, *Ethics Opinion 83-F-50 (8/12/83)*.

- It is the unauthorized practice of law for an unsupervised independent paralegal to provide the public with the service of filling out legal documents such as bankruptcy petitions, uncontested divorce petitions, wills, and premarital agreements for a fee. Attorney General of Tennessee, *Opinion 92–01* (1/9/92).

DEFINING THE PRACTICE OF LAW IN TENNESSEE

- § 23-3-101 (*Tennessee Code Annotated*): (1) "Law business" means the advising or counseling for a valuable consideration of any person as to any secular law, or the drawing or the procuring of or assisting in the drawing for a valuable consideration of any paper, document or instrument affecting or relating to secular rights, or the doing of any act for a valuable consideration in a representative capacity, obtaining or tending to secure for any person any property or property rights whatsoever, or the soliciting of clients directly or indirectly to provide such services . . . (3) "Practice of law" means the appearance as an advocate in a representative capacity or the drawing of papers, pleadings or documents or the performance of any act in such capacity in connection with proceedings pending or prospective before any court, commissioner, referee or any body, board, committee or commission constituted by law or having authority to settle controversies, or the soliciting of clients directly or indirectly to provide such services.
- Rule 9, § 20.2(e) (*Rules of the Supreme Court of Tennessee*): The term, "the practice of law" shall be defined as any service rendered involving legal knowledge or legal advice, whether of representation, counsel or advocacy, in or out of court, rendered in respect to the rights, duties, regulations, liabilities or business relations of one requiring the services. It shall encompass all public and private positions in which the attorney may be called upon to examine the law or pass upon the legal effect of any act, document or law.

TENNESSEE ETHICS AND PRACTICE RULES ON THE INTERNET

- www.law.cornell.edu/ethics/tennessee.html
- www.tba.org/ethics2002.html
- www.tsc.state.tn.us

PARALEGALS (AND OTHER NONATTORNEYS) IN TENNESSEE STATE AND FEDERAL COURTS

- *Clinard v. Blackwood*, 46 S.W. 3d 177 (Supreme Court of Tennessee, 2001) (A conflict of interest created by switching jobs by attorneys, law clerks, paralegals, and legal secretaries does not lead to disqualification if appropriate screening procedures are followed.)
- *In re Kincaid*, 146 Bankruptcy Reporter 387 (U.S. Bankruptcy Court, W.D. Tennessee, 1992) (a nonattorney regularly employed by a corporate-creditor could appear on behalf of the employer at a creditors' meeting in a bankruptcy case and question debtors without engaging in unauthorized practice of law).
- *Alexander v. Inman*, 903 S.W.2d 686, 704 (Court of Appeals of Tennessee, 1995) (the request to the court for an award of fees for paralegal services explained the services they provided in such general terms "that no finder of fact would be able to determine whether they were required or reasonable").
- *Hall v. City of Clarksville*, 2006 WL 2038004 (U.S. District Court, M.D., Tennessee, 2006) (Defendant objects to eighteen paralegal time entries, for a total of 51.55 hours, for work such as making copies, preparing and disassembling witness and trial notebooks, gathering exhibits and burning CD-ROMs for trial, and copying exhibits. The court agrees that some reduction for clerical tasks is warranted. Because some of the time entries involved work ordinarily performed by a paralegal, however, the court will reduce the challenged 51.55 hours by 15 hours. The court will award paralegal compensation for 165.65 hours at $75 per hour for a total of $12,423.75.)
- *Keisling v. Keisling*, 196 S.W.3d 703 (Court of Appeals of Tennessee, 2005) (The guardian *ad litem* may be an attorney or a specially trained nonlawyer such as the court-appointed special advocates (CASA). The role of the guardian *ad litem*, whether attorney or nonattorney, should be the same—to protect the child's interest and to gather and present facts for the court's consideration.)

DOING LEGAL RESEARCH IN TENNESSEE LAW

Statutes: www.legislature.state.tn.us
Cases: www.tsc.state.tn.us/geninfo/Courts/AppellateCourts.htm
Court Rules: www.tsc.state.tn.us
General: www.law.utk.edu/library/research.htm

FINDING EMPLOYMENT IN TENNESSEE

- legal.jobs.net/Tennessee.htm
- careers.findlaw.com
- jobs.careerbuilder.com/al.ic/Tennessee_Legal.htm
- www.kingeryandassociates.com
- memphis.craigslist.org/lgl

TEXAS

DEFINING LEGAL ASSISTANTS/ PARALEGALS IN TEXAS

A paralegal is a person, qualified through various combinations of education, training, or work experience, who is employed or engaged by a lawyer, law office, governmental agency, or other entity in a capacity or function which involves the performance, under the ultimate direction and supervision of a licensed attorney, of specifically delegated substantive legal work, which work, for the most part, requires a sufficient knowledge of legal principles and procedures that, absent such a person, an attorney would be required to perform the task. State Bar of Texas, *Paralegal Standards* (txpd.org).

ETHICAL RULES AND GUIDELINES IN TEXAS

- For a discussion of the state's ethical Rule 5.3 [5.03] ("Responsibilities Regarding Nonlawyer Assistants") in the *Texas Disciplinary Rules of Professional Conduct*, see the end of Section C in chapter 5. For the text of 5.3 [5.03] in Texas, see also www.txethics.org/reference_rules.asp?view=conduct.
- State Bar of Texas, *Paralegal Standards* (2005) (txpd.org): *A*. Attorneys should promote paralegal continuing legal education, certification, and bar division membership. If a person does not have formal paralegal education, it is suggested that they have at least four years of performing "substantive legal work" to be considered a paralegal. *B*. "Substantive legal work" includes, but is not limited to, the following: conducting client interviews and maintaining general contact with the client; locating and interviewing witnesses; conducting investigations and statistical and documentary research;

drafting documents, correspondence, and pleadings; summarizing depositions, interrogatories, and testimony; and attending executions of wills, real estate closings, depositions, court or administrative hearings, and trials with an attorney. "Substantive legal work" does not include clerical or administrative work. Accordingly, a court may refuse to provide recovery of paralegal time for such non-substantive work. *C. Consideration of Ethical Obligations.* 1. *Attorney.* The employing attorney has the responsibility for ensuring that the conduct of the paralegal performing the services is compatible with the professional obligations of the attorney. It also remains the obligation of the employing or supervising attorney to fully inform a client as to whether a paralegal will work on the legal matter, what the paralegal's fee will be, and whether the client will be billed for any non-substantive work performed by the paralegal. 2. *Paralegal.* A paralegal is prohibited from engaging in the practice of law, providing legal advice, signing pleadings, negotiating settlement agreements, soliciting legal business on behalf of an attorney, setting a legal fee, accepting a case, or advertising or contracting with members of the general public for the performance of legal functions (www.texasbar.com/paralegalstandards).

- State Bar of Texas, *General Guidelines for the Utilization of the Services of Legal Assistants by Attorneys* (January 22, 1993). *Guideline I:* An attorney should ensure that a legal assistant does not give legal advice or otherwise engage in the unauthorized practice of law. *Guideline II:* The attorney must take reasonable measures to ensure that the legal assistant's conduct is consistent with the Texas rules of ethics. *Guideline III:* An attorney may, with the client's consent, perform supervised functions authorized by law and ethics. *Guideline IV:* When dealing with others, the status of the legal assistant must be disclosed at the outset. *Guideline V:* The attorney must not assign functions to a legal assistant that require the exercise of independent professional legal judgment. The attorney must maintain a direct relationship with the client. The attorney is responsible for the actions taken and not taken by a legal assistant. *Guideline VI:* An attorney may not delegate to a legal assistant responsibility for establishing the attorney-client relationship, setting fees, or giving legal advice to a client. *Guideline VII:* An attorney must instruct the legal assistant to preserve the sanctity of all confidences and secrets and take reasonable measures to ensure that this is done. *Guideline VIII:* The attorney should take reasonable measures to prevent conflicts of interest resulting from a legal assistant's other employment or interests. *Guideline IX:* An attorney can charge and bill for a legal assistant's time but may not share legal fees with a legal assistant. *Guideline X:* An attorney may not split legal fees with a legal assistant nor pay a legal assistant for the referral of legal business. A legal assistant's compensation cannot be contingent, by advance agreement, upon the profitability of the attorney's practice. *Guideline XI:* The legal assistant can have a business card that names the firm as long as the status of the legal assistant is included on the card. The attorney must take reasonable measures to ensure that the card is not used in a deceptive way for unethical solicitation. See also State Bar of Texas, Paralegal Division, *Code of Ethics for Legal Assistants* (Texas Center for Legal Ethics and Professionalism) at *www.txethics.org/reference_ethics.asp*. See also State Bar of Texas, Paralegal Division, *Canons of Ethics and Professional Responsibility* (txpd.org/page.asp?p=Ethics%20Brochure).

- Law firm letterhead can print the name of legal assistants and can indicate that they have been certified (with a notation that they are legal assistants and are not licensed to practice law). State Bar of Texas, *Opinion 436* (6/20/86), which overrules *Opinion 390* (4/78).

- A legal assistant can write a letter on the law firm's letterhead as long as he or she signs as a legal assistant. The letter should not contain legal advice, judgment, strategy, or settlement negotiations. Such letters should be signed by an attorney. State Bar of Texas, *Opinion 381* (3/1975).

- A legal assistant may have a business card with the law firm's name appearing on it provided the status of the legal assistant is clearly disclosed. State Bar of Texas, *Opinion 403* (1982) (www.txethics.org/reference_opinions.asp?opinionnum=403).

- The name of an employee can be printed on an outdoor sign of a law firm as long as the nonattorney status of the employee is clear on the sign. Professional Ethics Committee of the State Bar of Texas, *Opinion 437* (6/20/86). See, however, *Opinion 426* (9/85) that an outdoor sign of a law firm cannot include the name of an investigator who is an independent contractor.

- It is unethical for attorneys to take a case in which they know or believe that they may have to call their nonattorney employee as an expert witness. State Bar of Texas, *Opinion 516* (6/2/95).

- A legal assistant switches sides between law firms who are opposing each other on a case. The new employer is not disqualified if he takes steps to ensure there will be no breach of confidentiality by the legal assistant. State Bar of Texas, *Opinion 472* (6/20/91).

- A lawyer cannot agree with an insurance company to restrictions (e.g., when a paralegal should draft a document) that interfere with the lawyer's independent professional judgment in rendering legal services to the insured/client. State Bar of Texas, *Opinion 533* (9/2000) (www.txethics.org/reference_opinions.asp?opinionnum=533).

- Ethical problems of supervision and professional judgment exist when a legal assistant (employed by a collection agency) sits in a lawyer's office making collection calls to debtors. Supreme Court of Texas, Ethics Committee, *Opinion 401* (1/82).

- When an attorney fails to supervise his paralegal, the attorney is responsible for the malpractice of the paralegal, such as the theft of client funds by the paralegal. "In the future, you should establish greater controls over your paralegals." Dallas Bar Ass'n, *Opinion 1989–5*.

DEFINING THE PRACTICE OF LAW IN TEXAS

- § 81.101 (*Vernon's Texas Statutes and Codes Annotated*): (a) In this chapter the "practice of law" means the preparation of a pleading or other document incident to an action or special proceeding or the management of the action or proceeding on behalf of a client before a judge in court as well as a service rendered out of court, including the giving of advice or the rendering of any service requiring the use of legal skill or knowledge, such as preparing a will, contract, or other instrument, the legal effect of which under the facts and conclusions involved must be carefully determined.

- (c) In this chapter, the "practice of law" does not include the design, creation, publication, distribution, display, or sale, including publication, distribution, display, or sale by means of an Internet web site, of written materials, books, forms, computer software, or similar products if the products clearly and conspicuously state that the products are not a substitute for the advice of an attorney.

TEXAS ETHICS AND PRACTICE RULES ON THE INTERNET

- www.law.cornell.edu/ethics/texas.html
- www.law.cornell.edu/ethics/tx/code
- www.txethics.org/reference_opinions.asp

PARALEGALS (AND OTHER NONATTORNEYS) IN TEXAS STATE AND FEDERAL COURTS

- *In re Mitcham*, 133 S.W.3d 274 (Supreme Court of Texas, 2004) (For purposes of determining whether attorney disqualification is warranted, for legal assistants, there is an irrebuttable presumption that they gain confidential information only on cases on which they work, and a rebuttable presumption that they share that information with a new employer; the presumption is rebutted not by denials of disclosure, but by prophylactic measures assuring that the legal assistants do not work on matters related to their prior employment.)

- *In re TXU U.S. Holdings*, 110 S.W.3d 62 (Court of Appeals of Texas, 2002) (Unlike the irrebuttable presumption that exists for a disqualified attorney, a rebuttable presumption exists that a nonlawyer has shared the confidences of a former client with his new employer, for purposes of determining disqualification based on future representation that is adverse to former client; presumption may be rebutted only by establishing that sufficient precautions have been taken to guard against any disclosure of confidences.)

- *In re Bell Helicopter Textron*, 87 S.W.3d 139 (Court of Appeals of Texas, 2002) (Screening legal support staff that worked for counsel that represented an opposing party requires that the newly hired nonlawyer must be cautioned not to disclose any information relating to the representation of a client of the former employer, the nonlawyer must be instructed not to work on any matter on which she worked during the prior employment, or regarding which she has information relating to the former employer's representation, and the new firm should take other reasonable steps to ensure that the nonlawyer does not work in connection with matters on which she worked during the prior employment, absent client consent after consultation.)

- *Phoenix Founders, Inc. v. Marshall*, 887 S.W.2d 831, 834 (Supreme Court of Texas, 1994) (there is a rebuttable presumption that a nonattorney who switches sides in ongoing litigation, after having gained confidential information at the first firm, will share the information with members of the new firm; but the presumption may be rebutted to avoid disqualification upon a showing of sufficient precautions, e.g., building a Chinese Wall, to guard against any disclosure of confidences). See also *In re American Home Products Corp.*, 985 S.W.2d 68 (Supreme Court of Texas, 1998).

- *All Seasons Window . . . v. Red Dot Corp.*, 181 S.W.3d 490 (Court of Appeals of Texas, 2005) (An award of attorney fees may include a legal assistant's time to the extent that the work performed has traditionally been done by any attorney. To recover such fees, the evidence must establish: (1) the qualifications of the legal assistant to perform substantive legal work; (2) that the legal assistant performed substantive legal work under the direction and supervision of an attorney; (3) the nature of the legal work performed; (4) the legal assistant's hourly rate; and (5) the number of hours expended by the legal assistant.)

- *Shaw v. Palmer*, 197 S.W.2d 854 (Court of Appeals of Texas, 2006) (paralegal fails to prove the existence of a contract

to accept a lower salary in exchange for bonuses based on increases in the firm's profits).

- *State Bar of Texas v. Faubion*, 821 S.W.2d 203 (Court of Appeals of Texas, 1991) (it was unethical for an attorney to pay a paralegal/investigator up to one-third of the fees generated from particular cases on which the paralegal worked; a bonus is proper if it is not based on a percentage of the law firm's profits or on a percentage of particular legal fees).

- *In re Witts*, 180 Bankruptcy Reporter 171, 173 (U.S. Bankruptcy Court, E.D. Texas, 1995) (attorney cannot recover paralegal rates for such clerical tasks as organizing files, proofreading and revising documents, faxing and copying).

- *Jones v. Krown*, 218 S.W.3d 746 (Court of Appeals of Texas, 2007) (a will prepared by an attorney is void when it gives assets to a paralegal employed as an in-office independent contractor in the office of the attorney; to reach this result, the court applied Probate Code, § 58b).

- *Cunningham v. Columbia/St. David's Healthcare Sys.* 185 S.W. 3d 7 (Court of Appeals of Texas, 2005) (because lawyers are responsible for the actions of the legal assistants that they supervise, the procedural mistakes made by a legal assistant are imputed to the supervising attorney).

- *Welch v. McLean*, 191 S.W.3d 147 (Court of Appeals of Texas, 2005) (a party tries to strike a paralegal as a juror in a malpractice case; he said he did not take paralegals on juries due to the "grave risk that they will get into the jury room and start telling folks about legal matters, of what the meaning of legal things is").

- *Teague v. Dretke*, 384 F. Supp. 2d 999 (U.S. District Court, N.D. Texas, 2005) (In many prison disciplinary proceedings, a non-lawyer advocate, known as "substitute counsel" is appointed to assist the inmate in presenting his defense.)

- *Petroleos Mexicanos v. Crawford Enterprises, Inc.*, 826 F.2d 392 (U.S. Court of Appeals, 5th Circuit, 1987) (court appoints paralegal as a special master to monitor a company's discovery compliance).

- *Rea v. Cofer*, 879 S.W.2d 224 (Court of Appeals of Texas, 1994) (former client sues attorney and paralegal for legal malpractice).

DOING LEGAL RESEARCH IN TEXAS LAW

Statutes: tlo2.tlc.state.tx.us/statutes/statutes.html
Cases: www.state.tx.us/category.jsp?categoryId=6.3
Court Rules: www.llrx.com/courtrules-gen/state-Texas .html
General: tarlton.law.utexas.edu/vlibrary/online/internet

FINDING EMPLOYMENT IN TEXAS

- texasbar.legalstaff.com
- careers.findlaw.com
- jobs.careerbuilder.com/al.ic/Texas_Legal.htm
- www.simplyhired.com/job-search/l-Texas/o-232000/ t-Paralegal
- dallas.craigslist.org/lgl

UTAH

DEFINING LEGAL ASSISTANTS/ PARALEGALS IN UTAH

A paralegal is a person, qualified through education, training or work experience who is employed or retained by a lawyer, law office, governmental agency or other entity in a capacity or function which involves the performance, under the ultimate direction and supervision of an attorney, of specifically delegated substantive legal work, which work for the most part, requires a sufficient knowledge of legal concepts that, absent the [paralegal] the attorney would perform the task. Supreme Court of Utah, *In re Petition Creation of a Legal Assistant Division of the Utah State Bar* (3/26/96) (www.utahbar .org/sections/paralegals/assets/order_petition_division.pdf).

ETHICAL RULES AND GUIDELINES IN UTAH

- For a discussion of the state's ethical Rule 5.3 ("Responsibilities Regarding Nonlawyer Assistants") in the *Utah Rules of Professional Conduct*, see the end of Section C in chapter 5. For the text of 5.3 in Utah, see also www.law.cornell.edu/ ethics/ut/code/UT_CODE.HTM.

- Utah State Bar, Paralegal Division, *Guidelines for the Utilization of Paralegals* (www.utahbar.org/sections/paralegals/canons_of_ ethics.html):

  A. - Paralegals shall:
  (1) Disclose their status as paralegals at the outset of any professional relationship with a client, other attorneys, a court or administrative agency or personnel thereof, or members of the general public;
  (2) Preserve the confidences and secrets of all clients; and
  (3) Understand the Rules of Professional Conduct, as amended, and these guidelines in order to avoid any action which would involve the attorney in violation of the Rules, or give the appearance of professional impropriety.

  B. - Paralegals may perform services for an attorney in the representation of a client, provided:
  (1) The services performed by the paralegal do not require the exercise of independent professional legal judgment;
  (2) The attorney maintains a direct relationship with the client and maintains control of all client matters;
  (3) The attorney supervises the paralegal;
  (4) The attorney remains professionally responsible for all work on behalf of the client, including any actions taken or not taken by the paralegal in connection therewith; and
  (5) The services performed supplement, merge with and become the attorney's work product.

  C. - In the supervision of paralegals, attorneys shall:
  (1) Design work assignments that correspond to the paralegal's abilities, knowledge, training and experience;
  (2) Educate and train the paralegal with respect to professional responsibility, local rules and practices, and firm policies;
  (3) Monitor the work and professional conduct of the paralegal to ensure that the work is substantively correct and timely performed;
  (4) Provide continuing education for the paralegal in substantive matters through courses, institutes, workshops, seminars and in-house training; and
  (5) Encourage and support membership and active participation in professional organizations.

  D. - Except as otherwise provided by statute, court rule or decision, administrative rule or regulation, or the attorney's Rules of Professional Conduct; and within the preceding parameters and proscriptions, a paralegal may perform any function delegated by an attorney, including but not limited to the following:
  (1) Conduct client interviews and maintain general contact with the client after the establishment of the attorney-client relationship, so long as the client is aware of the status and function of the paralegal, and the client contact is under the supervision of the attorney;
  (2) Locate and interview witnesses, so long as the witnesses are aware of the status and function of the paralegal;
  (3) Conduct investigations and statistical and documentary research for review by the attorney;
  (4) Draft legal documents for review by the attorney;
  (5) Draft correspondence and pleadings for review by and signature of the attorney;
  (6) Summarize depositions, interrogatories and testimony for review by the attorney;
  (7) Attend executions of wills, real estate closings, depositions, court or administrative hearings and trials with the attorney;
  (8) Author and sign letters provided the paralegal's status is clearly indicated and the correspondence does not contain independent legal opinions or legal advice; and
  (9) Conduct legal research for review by the attorney.

  E. A lawyer may not split fees with a paralegal nor pay the paralegal for the referral of legal business. A lawyer may compensate a paralegal based on the quality of the paralegal's work and the value of that work to the law practice. A lawyer may not compensate a paralegal based solely upon a quota of revenues generated for the firm by a paralegal's work on a specific case or a group of cases within a certain prescribed time period, although a paralegal may participate in a firm's profit sharing plan.

- Utah State Bar, Paralegal Division, *Canons of Ethics* (www .utahbar.org/sections/paralegals/canons_of_ethics.html).

- A lawyer can use nonlawyer paraprofessionals to provide representation of clients in hearings before a government agency (Social Security Administration) that authorizes nonlawyer representation. Utah State Bar, *Opinion 03–03* (6/23/03) (2003 WL 21488086).

- Utah lawyers may hire outside paralegals on an independent-contractor basis, provided the paralegal does not control the lawyer's professional judgment. In addition, if the amounts paid for services are not tied to specific cases, Utah lawyers or law firms may share fees with nonlawyer employees in a compensation plan. Utah State Bar, *Opinion 02–07* (9/13/02) (2002 WL 31079593). See also *Opinion 139* (1/27/94).

- An attorney can employ a paralegal who owns an interest in a collection agency the attorney represents as a client so long as there is no sham arrangement in which the paralegal would nominally own an interest in a collection agency that is in reality owned by the attorney. Utah State Bar, *Opinion 96–10* (12/6/96).

- A lawyer who negotiates or otherwise communicates with an opposing party's legal assistant representative on substantive matters affecting the rights of parties to a particular matter is not assisting in the unauthorized practice of law if that representative is supervised by a lawyer. Utah State Bar, *Opinion 99–02* (4/30/99).

- A lawyer may not use the word "associate" in its name if there are no associated attorneys in the firm even if it "employs one or more associated nonattorneys such as paralegals or investigators." Utah State Bar, *Opinion 138* (1/27/94).

- A nonattorney may be listed on the letterhead of an attorney as long as the nonattorney's status is clear. Utah State Bar, *Opinion 131* (5/20/93).

DEFINING THE PRACTICE OF LAW IN UTAH

- Rule 14–802 (*Supreme Court Rules of Professional Practice*):
  (a) The "practice of law" is the representation of the interests of another person by informing, counseling, advising,

assisting, advocating for or drafting documents for that person through application of the law and associated legal principles to that person's facts and circumstances.

(c) Whether or not it constitutes the practice of law, the following activity by a non-lawyer, who is not otherwise claiming to be a lawyer or to be able to practice law, is permitted:

(c) (1) Making legal forms available to the general public, whether by sale or otherwise, or publishing legal self-help information by print or electronic media.

(c) (2) Providing general legal information, opinions or recommendations about possible legal rights, remedies, defenses, procedures, options or strategies, but not specific advice related to another person's facts or circumstances.

(c) (3) Providing clerical assistance to another to complete a form provided by a court for protection from harassment or domestic violence or abuse when no fee is charged to do so.

(c) (4) When expressly permitted by the court after having found it clearly to be in the best interests of the child or ward, assisting one's minor child or ward in a juvenile court proceeding.

(c) (5) Representing a natural person in small claims court without compensation and upon the express approval of the court or representing a legal entity as an employee representative in small claims court . . . .

(c) (8) Acting as a representative before administrative tribunals or agencies as authorized by tribunal or agency rule or practice.

UTAH ETHICS AND PRACTICE RULES ON THE INTERNET

- www.law.cornell.edu/ethics/utah.html
- www.utcourts.gov/resources/rules
- www.utahbar.org/rules_ops_pols

PARALEGALS (AND OTHER NONATTORNEYS) IN UTAH STATE AND FEDERAL COURTS

- *Barnard v. Utah State Bar*, 857 P.2d 917 (Supreme Court of Utah, 1993) (attorney charged with unauthorized practice of law for using paralegals to help clients file their own divorces).
- *Utah v. Long*, 844 P.2d 381 (Court of Appeals of Utah, 1992) (attorney disciplined for failing to supervise his legal assistant who gave a client incorrect legal advice).
- *Anderson v. Secretary of Health and Human Services*, 80 F.3d 1500 (U.S. Court of Appeals, 10th Circuit, 1996) (paralegal costs denied where no documentation—other than the statement of the lead attorney—was submitted on what the paralegal did).
- *Baldwin v. Burton*, 850 P.2d 1188, 1200 (Supreme Court of Utah, 1993) ("allowing recovery for legal assistant fees promotes lawyer efficiency and decreases client litigation costs").
- *Gold Standard, Inc. v. American Barrick Resources Corp.*, 805 P.2d 164, 169 (Supreme Court of Utah, 1990) (a nonattorney's work in preparation for litigation is protected by the attorney work-product rule).

DOING LEGAL RESEARCH IN UTAH LAW

Statutes: www.le.state.ut.us/~code/code.htm
Cases: www.utcourts.gov/opinions
Court Rules: www.utcourts.gov/resources/rules
General: www.megalaw.com/ut/ut.php

FINDING EMPLOYMENT IN UTAH

- www.indeed.com/q-Litigation-Paralegal-l-Utah-jobs.html
- careers.findlaw.com
- jobs.careerbuilder.com/al.ic/Utah_Legal.htm
- saltlakecity.craigslist.org/lgl

VERMONT

DEFINING LEGAL ASSISTANTS/ PARALEGALS IN VERMONT

A paralegal/legal assistant is a person qualified through education, training or work experience to perform substantive legal work that requires knowledge of legal concepts and is customarily, but not exclusively, performed by a lawyer. This person may be retained or employed by a lawyer, law office, governmental agency, or other entity or may be authorized by administrative, statutory or court authority to perform this work. Vermont Bar Association, *Constitution* (www.vtbar.org/Upload%20Files/attachments/Constitution.pdf).

ETHICAL RULES AND GUIDELINES IN VERMONT

- For a discussion of the state's ethical Rule 5.3 ("Responsibilities Regarding Nonlawyer Assistants") in the *Vermont Rules of Professional Conduct*, see the end of Section C in chapter 5. For the text of 5.3 in Vermont, see also www.vermontjudiciary.org/PRB1.htm.
- A paralegal may not sign court pleadings with an attorney's name and the paralegal's initials after the attorney's name. Vermont Bar Ass'n, *Opinion 01–5* (2001).
- A supervising attorney may permit a paralegal to conduct a loan closing on behalf of a lender client where the client consents, the paralegal's role is ministerial in nature, and the attorney is available for questions, at least by telephone. Vermont Bar Ass'n, *Opinion 99–3* (1999).
- Law Firm A may employ a paralegal who formerly was employed by Law Firm B, despite the fact that the two firms are engaged in litigation against each other in a matter in which the paralegal participated for Law Firm B. However, Law Firm A must now screen the paralegal from involvement in the pending litigation and any matter in which the interests of Law Firm B's client are adverse to those of any client of Law Firm A. Further, Law Firm A must ensure that no information relating to the representation of the client of Law Firm B is revealed by the paralegal to any person in Law Firm A. Vermont Bar Ass'n, *Opinion 97–9* (1997).
- A law firm cannot continue to represent a defendant in a civil case after hiring a nonattorney employee who had previously performed extensive work on the same case while employed by the law firm representing the plaintiff. Vermont Bar Ass'n, *Opinion 85–8* (1985). For other disqualification cases involving paralegals, see also *Opinion 79–28* (1979), *Opinion 89–4* (1989), *Opinion 87–15* (1987), and *Opinion 78–2* (1978).
- Law firms must supervise the independent paralegals they use to prevent breaches of confidentiality and must check the systems used by the paralegal to prevent conflict of interest. Once employed, the hiring firm must develop methods for effectively screening the independent paralegal from information concerning other clients. Vermont Bar Ass'n, *Opinion 2002–02*.
- The letterhead of a law firm may list certain non-lawyer employees such as paralegals and law clerks wherever the inclusion of such names would not be deceptive and might

reasonably be expected to supply information relevant to the selection of counsel. Vermont Bar Ass'n, *Opinion 79–13*.

- In a conversation with a nonattorney employee, if a prospective client threatens to kill someone, the employee who believes the threat can warn the potential victim. Vermont Bar Ass'n, *Opinion 86–3*.

DEFINING THE PRACTICE OF LAW IN VERMONT

- *In re Welch*, 185 A.2d 458, 459 (Supreme Court of Vermont, 1962): In general, one is deemed to be practicing law whenever he furnishes to another advice or service under circumstances which imply the possession and use of legal knowledge and skill. The practice of law includes "all advice to clients, and all actions taken for them in matters connected with the law." . . . Practice of law includes the giving of legal advice and counsel, and the preparation of legal instruments and contracts [by] which legal rights are secured. . . . Where the rendering of services for another involves the use of legal knowledge or skill on his behalf—where legal advice is required and is availed of or rendered in connection with such services—these services necessarily constitute or include the practice of law. . . . We cannot over-emphasize the necessity of legal training in the proper drafting of legal documents and advice relating thereto. The absence of such training may result in legal instruments faulty in form and contents, and also lead to a failure of purpose, litigation, and expense.

- *In re Conner*, 917 A.2d 442 (Supreme Court of Vermont, 2006): [T]he essence of the practicing lawyer's function is the exercise of professional judgment, bringing to bear all of the lawyer's education, experience, and skill to resolve a specific legal problem for a particular client or case in controversy.

VERMONT ETHICS AND PRACTICE RULES ON THE INTERNET

- www.law.cornell.edu/ethics/vermont.html
- www.vermontjudiciary.org/Committes/prbrules/rpc.aspx
- www.libraries.vermont.gov/prb/pcb1.html

PARALEGALS (AND OTHER NONATTORNEYS) IN VERMONT STATE AND FEDERAL COURTS

- *In re Fibermark, Inc.*, 349 Bankruptcy Reporter 385 (U.S. Bankruptcy Court, Vermont, 2006) (A paralegal or other paraprofessional is eligible to be compensated from a bankruptcy estate, subject to the same scrutiny as that of a professional in the case. 11 U.S.C.A. § 330(a)(1)(A).)

- *In re S.T.N. Enterprises, Inc.*, 70 Bankruptcy Reporter 823 (U.S. Bankruptcy Court, Vermont, 1987) (court will reduce an attorney's rate of compensation for performing tasks that could have been performed by a paralegal at a lower rate).

- *McSweeney v. McSweeney*, 618 A.2d 1332 (Supreme Court of Vermont, 1992) (it is not the unauthorized practice of law for nonattorney employees of the Office of Child Support to prepare and file complaints and motions in child support cases before a magistrate [4 V.S.A. § 464,] but they cannot handle URESA cases involving interstate support issues before a magistrate).

- *Hohman v. Hogan*, 458 F. Supp. 669 (U.S. District Court, Vermont, 1978) (paralegal assistance to inmates).

- *Berry v. Schweiker*, 675 F.2d 464 (U.S. Court of Appeals, 2d Circuit, 1982) (paralegal represents client at disability benefits hearing).

DOING LEGAL RESEARCH IN VERMONT LAW

Statutes: www.leg.state.vt.us/statutes/statutes2.htm
Cases: www.vermontjudiciary.org/Resources/docs/Opinions.htm
Court Rules: www.llrx.com/courtrules-gen/state-Vermont.html
General: www.megalaw.com/vt/vt.php

FINDING EMPLOYMENT IN VERMONT

- careers.findlaw.com
- www.indeed.com/q-Paralegal-l-Vermont-jobs.html
- jobs.careerbuilder.com/al.ic/Vermont_Legal.htm
- burlington.craigslist.org/lgl

VIRGINIA

DEFINING LEGAL ASSISTANTS/ PARALEGALS IN VIRGINIA

Although there are several formal definitions of a legal assistant, in general, a legal assistant in a specially trained individual who performs substantive legal work that requires a knowledge of legal concepts. Legal Assistants either work under the supervision of an attorney, who assumes responsibility for the final work product, or work in areas where lay individuals are explicitly authorized by statute or regulation to assume certain law-related responsibilities. (The term "legal assistant" is used interchangeably with the term "paralegal.") Recommended by the Virginia State Bar, Standing Committee on the Unauthorized Practice of Law (3/8/95) (www.geocities.com/rala1982/guidelines.html).

ETHICAL RULES AND GUIDELINES IN VIRGINIA

- For a discussion of the state's ethical Rule 5.3 ("Responsibilities Regarding Nonlawyer Assistants") in the *Virginia Rules of Professional Conduct*, see the end of Section C in chapter 5. For the text of 5.3 in Virginia, see also www.vsb.org/docs/rules-pc_2006–07pg.pdf.

- A nonlawyer employee working under the direct supervision of a Virginia attorney may participate in gathering information from a client during an initial interview (a client intake), provided that this involves nothing more than the gathering of factual data and the nonlawyer renders no legal advice. In contrast, a nonlawyer employee may not determine the validity of the client's legal claim, as that determination appears to directly involve the application of legal principles to facts, purposes, or desires and is therefore considered the practice of law. The nonlawyer employee may transmit the attorney/client fee agreement to the client and obtain the client's signature on the document. While a nonlawyer employee is permitted to answer straightforward, factual questions regarding the fee agreement, such answers must not include any advice as to the legal ramifications of the contract provisions. Concerning settlement negotiations, a nonlawyer employee may transmit information and documents between the attorney and the client. For example, the employee could share with the client the latest settlement offer. However, it would not be permissible for the employee to evaluate the offer or to recommend to the client whether or not to accept an offer. In contrast, it would be permissible for the nonlawyer to communicate with the client the lawyer's evaluation or recommendation. Unauthorized Practice of Law Committee of the Virginia State Bar, *Opinion 191* (9/29/98).

- The paralegal, of course, cannot provide advice or service directly to the client or members of the general public, as that would clearly constitute the unauthorized practice of law. Unauthorized Practice of Law Committee, *Opinion 129* (2/22/89).

- A paralegal shall not communicate with clients, outside attorneys, or the public without disclosing his or her nonattorney status. *Code of Professional Responsibility*, DR 3–104(E).

- An attorney is not required to withdraw from a case as long as a nonattorney employee does not disclose confidential information learned while she worked for an opposing attorney. Standing Committee on Legal Ethics of the Virginia State Bar, *Opinion 745* (1985).

- An attorney represents a client in a case in which the attorney's former nonattorney employee will testify against this client. The attorney is not disqualified from representing this client as long as the client is informed of this situation and still wants the attorney to represent him. Standing Committee on Legal Ethics of the Virginia State Bar, *Opinion 891* (4/1/87).

- A law firm can print the names of nonattorney employees on its letterhead as long as their nonattorney status is clear. These employees can participate in a profit-sharing plan of the firm as part of a compensation or retirement program. Standing Committee on Legal Ethics of the Virginia State Bar, *Opinion 762* (1/29/86). See also *Opinion 970* (9/30/87) (attorney may list name and title of firm's chief investigator as long as listing includes affirmative statement that investigator is not licensed to practice law).

- An attorney must not split fees with nonattorneys, but they can be paid a bonus that is based on profit-sharing. Standing Committee on Legal Ethics of the Virginia State Bar, *Opinion 806* (6/25/86).

- A law firm engaged in collection work can pay its nonattorney employee a percentage of profits from the collections received plus a salary. Standing Committee on Legal Ethics of the Virginia State Bar, *Opinion 885* (3/11/87).

- It is unethical for a nonattorney employee of a law firm to contact prospective collections clients in order to suggest that they hire the law firm for their collections work. Standing Committee on Legal Ethics of the Virginia State Bar, *Opinion 1290* (10/25/89).

- A "real estate paralegal company" can provide assistance to an attorney in closing real estate loans that have been referred to this company by the closing attorney. This is not the unauthorized practice of law as long as designated procedures are followed. Unauthorized Practice of Law Committee, *Opinion 147* (4/19/91).

- It is not the unauthorized practice of law for a non-attorney to give a judicial officer information (present facts) that concerns the weight of the evidence in bail cases. Unauthorized Practice of Law Committee, *Opinion 186* (9/7/95).

- It is not the unauthorized practice of law for a paralegal to appear in court to collect monies resulting from a garnishment as long as this appearance involves only a ministerial or clerical act. Unauthorized Practice of Law Committee, *Opinion 72* (12/12/84).

- Under both the IDEA and Rehabilitation Act, the states and localities must comply with federal law and regulations requiring due process hearings for parents having disputes with local school boards. 34 C.F.R. §300.58 permits the aggrieved parents in IDEA hearings to be represented by counsel or a lay advocate, provided the lay advocate is a person having special knowledge or training concerning the problems of children with disabilities. No certification or training program is administered to test or evaluate the competency or knowledge of a lay advocate. See Virginia's IDEA statute (§ 22.1–214C) Unauthorized Practice of Law Committee, *Opinion 187* (2/15/96).

- A lawyer employing a lawyer as a legal assistant when that lawyer's license is suspended or revoked for professional misconduct shall not represent any client represented by the disciplined lawyer or by any lawyer with whom the disciplined lawyer practiced on or after the date of the acts that resulted in suspension or revocation. Rule 5.5, *Rules of Professional Conduct*, *Virginia Rules of Court*.

- A paralegal cannot work for a suspended attorney because the paralegal would not have attorney supervision. Unauthorized Practice of Law Committee, *Opinion 137* (1/8/90).

- A paralegal's name can be printed on the door of the paralegal's private office as long as it does not create the impression that the paralegal is an attorney. Unauthorized Practice of Law Committee, *Opinion 225* (5/21/73) and *Opinion 326* (6/19/79).

- A private law firm employs a paralegal whose husband is an attorney who represents the government in cases against clients of the law firm. The law firm can continue to employ this paralegal, but it must tell its clients and the court of the relationship between the paralegal and the government attorney. Unauthorized Practice of Law Committee, *Opinion 358* (3/10/80).

- An attorney can instruct his paralegal to call a prospective defendant to ask if it manufactures a particular product. This does not violate the rule against contacting the other side, since there is no litigation under way. The call is part of proper investigation. Unauthorized Practice of Law Committee, *Opinion 1190* (1/4/89). See also *Opinion 1504* (12/14/92) (paralegal can contact opponent to obtain information under Virginia Freedom of Information Act) and *Opinion 1639* (4/24/95) (OK for paralegal to contact the other side to provide information as a courtesy).

- A non-lawyer inmate of a correctional facility cannot represent a fellow inmate by way of in-court oral argument and out-of-court settlement negotiations in pending civil litigation. Unauthorized Practice of Law Committee, *Opinion 48* (12/1/83).

DEFINING THE PRACTICE OF LAW IN VIRGINIA

Virginia Rules of Court, Rules of the Supreme Court of Virginia:
Part 6. Section I. Unauthorized Practice Rules and Considerations. [O]ne is deemed to be practicing law whenever—

(1) One undertakes for compensation, direct or indirect, to advise another, not his regular employer, in any matter involving the application of legal principles to facts or purposes or desires.

(2) One, other than as a regular employee acting for his employer, undertakes, with or without compensation, to prepare for another legal instruments of any character, other than notices or contracts incident to the regular course of conducting a licensed business.

(3) One undertakes, with or without compensation, to represent the interest of another before any tribunal—judicial, administrative, or executive—otherwise than in the presentation of facts, figures, or factual conclusions, as distinguished from legal conclusions, by an employee regularly and bona fide employed on a salary basis, or by one specially employed as an expert in respect to such facts and figures when such representation by such employee or expert does not involve the examination of witnesses or preparation of pleadings.

VIRGINIA ETHICS AND PRACTICE RULES ON THE INTERNET

- www.law.cornell.edu/ethics/virginia.html
- www.vsb.org/site/regulation
- www.vsb.org/site/regulation/ethics-opinions
- www.vsb.org/profguides/opinions.html

PARALEGALS (AND OTHER NONATTORNEYS) IN VIRGINIA STATE AND FEDERAL COURTS

- *J.P. v. County School Bd. of Hanover County*, 2007 WL 840090 (U.S. District Court, E.D. Virginia, 2007) ($105 per hour for paralegal services comports with rates approved in other cases for paralegal fees in the Richmond area and reflects the skill and experience of these professionals).
- *In re Hall*, 296 Bankruptcy Reporter 707 (U.S. Bankruptcy Court, E.D. Virginia, 2002) ($90 per hour is an excessive rate for paralegal time. Based on the court's general familiarity with prevailing rates in Alexandria, Virginia (derived from reviewing fee applications in other cases), the court determines that $75 per hour is currently the general market rate for paralegal time, and the court will allow compensation at that rate.)
- *County School Bd of York County v. A.L.*, 2007 WL 756586 (U.S. District Court, E.D. Virginia, 2007) (It is appropriate to distinguish between legal work, in the strict sense, and investigation, clerical work, compilation of facts and statistics, and other work that can often be accomplished by nonlawyers but that a lawyer may do because he or she has no other help available. Such nonlegal work may command a lesser rate. Its dollar value is not enhanced just because a lawyer does it.)
- *In re Bryant*, 346 Bankruptcy Reporter 406 (U.S. Bankruptcy Court, E.D. Virginia, 2006) (the Court denies the time requested for a paralegal's services for lack of contemporaneous time records on the tasks performed).
- *U.S. v. Smallwood*, 365 F. Supp. 2d 689 (U.S. District Court, E.D. Virginia, 2005) (Of course, most assistants . . . cannot themselves be held accountable for unethical behavior unless it also amounts to criminal conduct. Nonetheless, the fact that corrective measures cannot usually be implemented directly against these assistants does not mean that their conduct is beyond regulation. In certain circumstances, as here, it may be possible to sanction such assistants and investigators by reducing their compensation.)
- *Mullins v. Va. Lutheran Homes, Inc.*, 44 Va. Cir. 156, 1997 WL 1070493 (Circuit Court of Virginia, 1997) ("It may markedly aid the lawyer to have his paralegal assistant present. However, in my view, neither the client nor, in this case, the opposing party, should have to expect to pay an additional sum, over and above the lawyer's hourly fee, for this aid.")
- *Musselman v. Willoughby Corp.*, 337 S.E.2d 724 (Supreme Court of Virginia, 1985) (paralegal negligence asserted in legal malpractice case brought by client against attorney).
- *Tanksley v. Garrett*, 175 Bankruptcy Reporter 434 (U.S. Bankruptcy Court, W.D. Virginia, 1994) (U. S. Trustee seeks to enjoin a law firm from allowing a paralegal to represent clients at Section 341 bankruptcy hearing).

DOING LEGAL RESEARCH IN VIRGINIA LAW

Statutes: leg1.state.va.us/000/src.htm
Cases: www.courts.state.va.us/opin.htm

Court Rules: www.llrx.com/courtrules-gen/state-Virginia.html
General: www.law.virginia.edu/main/virginia+research

FINDING EMPLOYMENT IN VIRGINIA

- careers.findlaw.com
- www.bizport.biz/staffing
- www.indeed.com/q-Paralegal-l-Virginia-jobs.html
- jobs.careerbuilder.com/al.ic/Virginia_Legal.htm
- www.simplyhired.com/job-search/l-Virginia/o-232000/t-Paralegal
- washingtondc.craigslist.org/nva/lgl

WASHINGTON STATE

DEFINING LEGAL ASSISTANTS/ PARALEGALS IN WASHINGTON STATE

A legal assistant is a person, qualified through education, training, or work experience, who is employed or retained by a lawyer, law office, governmental agency, or other entity in a capacity or function which involves a performance, under the ultimate direction and supervision of an attorney, of specifically delegated substantive legal work, which work, for the most part, requires a sufficient knowledge of legal concepts that, absent such assistant, the attorney would perform the task. *Absher Construction Co. v. Kent School District*, 917 P.2d 1086, 1088 (Court of Appeals of Washington State, 1995) (approving the definition of the American Bar Association).

ETHICAL RULES AND GUIDELINES IN WASHINGTON STATE

- For a discussion of the state's ethical Rule 5.3 ("Responsibilities Regarding Nonlawyer Assistants") in the *Washington State Rules of Professional Conduct*, see the end of Section C in chapter 5. For the text of 5.3 in Washington State, see also www.law.cornell.edu/ethics/wa/code/WA_CODE.HTM.
- The titles "paralegal" or "legal assistant" can be used to designate employees on their business cards and on attorney stationery so long as it is clear they are not attorneys. Washington State Bar Ass'n, *Informal Opinion 1065* (1987).
- There would not be a general conflict of interest between the attorneys who employed paralegals volunteering at a clinic and all clinic clients. A conflict of interest could exist between an attorney and a party with an adverse interest to the clinic client served by the paralegal regularly employed by that attorney. There would not be a conflict of interest for that attorney that would prevent him or her from providing legal services to clinic clients served by other staff provided that there are adequate screening mechanisms in place at the clinic to insure that the paralegal does not have access to information from or about other clients served by the clinic. Washington State Bar Ass'n, *Informal Opinion 1861* (1999).
- An attorney cannot share fees with nonattorneys who are authorized to represent claimants before the Social Security Administration. Washington State Bar Ass'n, *Informal Opinion 1348* (1990).
- Serious ethical problems exist (e.g., sharing fees with a nonattorney) in a proposed arrangement with a paralegal company whereby the attorney would be referred clients by a financial planner to whom they had been referred by the paralegal company. Washington State Bar Ass'n, *Informal Opinion 1135* (1990).

- Serious ethical problems exist (e.g., aiding the unauthorized practice of law) if an attorney hires a paralegal to operate a law office on the attorney's behalf, and under his supervision, in a nearby town. The paralegal would place advertisements with his photograph in publications aimed at persons of his ethnicity. Washington State Bar Ass'n, *Informal Opinion 1816* (1998).

- An attorney cannot let a collection agency use his name on court documents unless the attorney provides legal assistance on each particular case. Rubber-stamping legal papers of nonattorneys is unethical. Washington State Bar Ass'n, *Opinion 18* (1952) and *Opinion 76* (1960).

- An attorney can enter into a contract with an independent paralegal whereby the paralegal will receive a $250 flat fee for an initial file review and conference with the attorney. Compensation would be hourly after this initial review. (The client would be billed for these payments, even in contingency cases.) This flat-fee arrangement is not improper fee splitting with a nonlawyer. Washington State Bar Ass'n, *Informal Opinion 1774* (1997).

- A suspended lawyer is not allowed to serve as a paralegal, clerk or assistant in law related matters. Washington State Bar Ass'n, *Informal Opinion 1772* (1997). See also *Informal Opinion 2003* (2002) and *Formal Opinion 184* (1990).

DEFINING THE PRACTICE OF LAW IN WASHINGTON STATE

- Rule 24 (*West's Washington Court Rules*): Part I, General Rules (GR).

  (a) General Definition. The practice of law is the application of legal principles and judgment with regard to the circumstances or objectives of another entity or person(s) which require the knowledge and skill of a person trained in the law. This includes but is not limited to:

  (1) Giving advice or counsel to others as to their legal rights or the legal rights or responsibilities of others for fees or other consideration.

  (2) Selection, drafting, or completion of legal documents or agreements which affect the legal rights of an entity or person(s).

  (3) Representation of another entity or person(s) in a court, or in a formal administrative adjudicative proceeding or other formal dispute resolution process or in an administrative adjudicative proceeding in which legal pleadings are filed or a record is established as the basis for judicial review.

  (4) Negotiation of legal rights or responsibilities on behalf of another entity or person(s).

  (b) Exceptions and Exclusions. Whether or not they constitute the practice of law, the following are permitted:

  (1) Practicing law authorized by a limited license to practice pursuant to Admission to Practice Rules 8 (special admission for: a particular purpose or action; indigent representation; educational purposes; emeritus membership; house counsel), 9 (legal interns), 12 (limited practice for closing officers), or 14 (limited practice for foreign law consultants). . . .

  (3) Acting as a lay representative authorized by administrative agencies or tribunals.

  (6) Providing assistance to another to complete a form provided by a court for protection under RCW chapters 10.14 (harassment) or 26.50 (domestic violence prevention) when no fee is charged to do so. . . .

  (c) Nonlawyer Assistants. Nothing in this rule shall affect the ability of nonlawyer assistants to act under the supervision of a lawyer in compliance with Rule 5.3 of the Rules of Professional Conduct.

  (d) General Information. Nothing in this rule shall affect the ability of a person or entity to provide information of a general nature about the law and legal procedures to members of the public.

For the guidelines of the Supreme Court of Washington on limited licensing, see Exhibit 4.4 in chapter 4.

WASHINGTON STATE ETHICS AND PRACTICE RULES ON THE INTERNET

- www.law.cornell.edu/ethics/washington.html
- www.wsba.org/lawyers/rules
- www.wsba.org/lawyers/ethics/formalopinions

PARALEGALS (AND OTHER NONATTORNEYS) IN WASHINGTON STATE AND FEDERAL COURTS

- *Trainer v. Kitsap County*, 107 Wash. App. 1035, 2001 WL 873826 (Court of Appeals of Washington, 2001) (relevant criteria for determining whether legal assistant services should be compensated: (1) the services performed by the nonlawyer personnel must be legal in nature; (2) the performance of these services must be supervised by an attorney; (3) the qualifications of the person performing the services must be specified in the request for fees in sufficient detail to demonstrate that the person is qualified by virtue of education, training, or work experience to perform substantive legal work; (4) the nature of the services performed must be specified in the request for fees in order to allow the reviewing court to determine that the services performed were legal rather than clerical; (5) as with attorney time, the amount of time expended must be set forth and must be reasonable; and (6) the amount charged must reflect reasonable community standards for charges by that category of personnel (citing *Absher Construction v. Kent School District*, 917 P. 2d 1086 (Court of Appeals of Washington, 1995)).

- *Tumelson Family Ltd. Partnership v. World Financial News Network*, 2005 WL 2293588 (U.S. District Court, W.D. Washington, 2005) (Despite counsel's statement that they have endeavored to remove "clerical" work that their paralegals performed from their fee request, they have not gone far enough. Their invoices still include numerous entries for unquestionably clerical work (e.g., preparing copies, finalizing copies, scanning documents, creating compact discs). Even more entries describe time that might constitute legal services, and might be clerical (e.g., preparing exhibits, working on exhibits, making phone calls, reviewing transcripts). Some describe work that is probably legal (legal research, drafting pleadings). For the substantial majority of the paralegal time, the Tumelsons do not prove that the time is recoverable under the standards set forth in *Absher*. The court must therefore make a substantial deduction for paralegal time.)

- *Tegman v. Accident & Medical Investigations, Inc.*, 30 P.3d 8, 11 (Court of Appeals of Washington, 2001) (paralegals charged with unauthorized practice of law and negligence; "[w]hen a paralegal performs legal services with knowledge that there is no supervising attorney responsible for the case, the paralegal will be held to an attorney's standard of care"; "[n]onattorneys who attempt to practice law will be held to the same standards of competence demanded of attorneys and will be liable for negligence if these standards are not met").

- *Richards v. Jain*, 168 F. Supp. 2d 1195, 1200 (U.S. District Court, W.D. Washington, 2001) (law firm is disqualified when its paralegal viewed privileged documents of the opponent. The supervising attorney failed to take reasonable steps to ensure that its nonlawyer employees complied with ethical rules. Paralegals are not held to a lower standard of ethical behavior than attorneys. "[N]onlawyers and lawyers are bound by the same ethical duties").

■ *In the Matter of Gillingham*, 896 P.2d 656 (Supreme Court of Washington, 1995) (discipline of attorney for failure to supervise paralegal).

DOING LEGAL RESEARCH IN WASHINGTON STATE LAW

Statutes: apps.leg.wa.gov/rcw/default.aspx
Cases: www.courts.wa.gov/opinions
Court Rules: www.courts.wa.gov/court_rules
General: lib.law.washington.edu/research/research.html

FINDING EMPLOYMENT IN WASHINGTON STATE

* www.wsba.org/jobs/special.htm
* careers.findlaw.com
* www.acteva.com/booking.cfm?bevaID=44362
* www.indeed.com/jobs?q=paralegal&l=seattle

WEST VIRGINIA

DEFINING LEGAL ASSISTANTS/ PARALEGALS IN WEST VIRGINIA

A legal assistant is a person, qualified through education, training or work experience, who is employed or retained by a lawyer, law office, governmental agency, or other entity, in a capacity or function which involves the performance, under the ultimate direction and supervision of an attorney, of delegated substantive legal work, which work, for the most part, requires a sufficient knowledge of legal concepts that, absent such assistance, the attorney would perform the task. West Virginia State Bar (7/16/99) (www .wvbar.org/BARINFO/lawyer/2000/feb00/legalassistants.htm).

ETHICAL RULES AND GUIDELINES IN WEST VIRGINIA

■ For a discussion of the state's ethical Rule 5.3 ("Responsibilities Regarding Nonlawyer Assistants") in the *West Virginia Rules of Professional Conduct*, see the end of Section C in chapter 5. For the text of 5.3 in West Virginia, see also www.wvbar.org/ BARINFO/rulesprofconduct.

■ Anything delegated to a nonattorney must lose its separate identity and be merged in the service of the attorney. When communicating with persons outside the office, a paralegal "must disclose his status as such." Nonattorneys can sign letters on law firm stationery as long as their nonattorney status is clearly indicated. *Legal Ethics Inquiry* 76–7 (3 W.Va. State Bar Journal (Spring 1977)).

■ A corporation can be represented by a nonattorney in Magistrates Court. "Any party to a civil action in a magistrate court may appear and conduct such action in person, by agent or by attorney . . . . [T]he appearance by an agent shall not constitute the unauthorized practice of law . . . ." (*W. Va. Code* § 50–4–4a). West Virginia State Bar Committee on Unlawful Practice, *Advisory Opinion 93–001*.

DEFINING THE PRACTICE OF LAW IN WEST VIRGINIA

Court Rules, *Michie's West Virginia Code Annotated* 535 (1996). "Practice of Law Definitions": In general, one is deemed to be practicing law whenever he or it furnishes another advice or service under circumstances which imply the possession or use of legal knowledge and skill. More specifically but without purporting to formulate a precise and completely comprehensive definition of the practice of law or to prescribe limits to the scope of that activity, one is deemed to be practicing law whenever (1) one undertakes, with or without compensation and whether or not in connection with another activity, to advise another in any matter involving the application of legal principles to facts, purposes or desires; (2) one undertakes, with or without compensation and whether or not in connection with another activity, to prepare for another legal instruments of any character; or (3) one undertakes, with or without compensation and whether or not in connection with another activity, to represent the interest of another before any judicial tribunal or officer, or to represent the interest of another before any executive or administrative tribunal, agency or officer otherwise than in the presentation of facts, figures or factual conclusions as distinguished from legal conclusions in respect to such facts and figures. Nothing in this paragraph shall be deemed to prohibit a lay person from appearing as agent before a justice of the peace or to prohibit a bona fide full-time lay employee from performing legal services for his regular employer (other than in connection with representation of his employer before any judicial, executive or administrative tribunal, agency or officer) in matters relating solely to the internal affairs of such employer, as distinguished from such services rendered to or for others. Quoted in *Lawyer Disciplinary Bd. v. Allen*, 479 S.E. 2d 317, 333 (Supreme Court of Appeals of West Virginia, 1996).

WEST VIRGINIA ETHICS AND PRACTICE RULES ON THE INTERNET

* www.law.cornell.edu/ethics/wv.html
* www.wvbar.org/barinfo/rulesprofconduct
* www.wvbar.org/BARINFO/ODC/LEIs/chrono_index.htm
* www.wvbar.org/barinfo/ODC/LEIs/leoindex.htm

PARALEGALS (AND OTHER NONATTORNEYS) IN WEST VIRGINIA STATE AND FEDERAL COURTS

■ *State ex rel. Youngblood v. Sanders*, 575 S.E.2d 864 (Supreme Court of West Virginia, 2002) (A generalized discussion between the first codefendant's wife and the attorney's paralegal did not establish that the wife communicated confidential information so as to disqualify the attorney from representing the second codefendant, based on a conflict of interest, after the first codefendant decided not to hire attorney.)

■ *Office of Disciplinary Counsel v. Battistelli*, 465 S.E.2d 644 (Supreme Court of Appeals of West Virginia, 1995) (suspended attorney can work as a paralegal but must have no contact with clients).

■ *Stacy v. B.O. Stroud*, 845 F. Supp. 1135, 1145 (U.S. District Court, S.D. West Virginia, 1993) (award of attorney fees; "Delegating appropriate tasks to paralegals reduces the overall costs of . . . litigation").

■ *In re Heck's, Inc.*, 112 Bankruptcy Reporter 775 (U.S. Bankruptcy Court, S.D. West Virginia, 1990) (objections filed to claims for paralegal fees).

DOING LEGAL RESEARCH IN WEST VIRGINIA LAW

Statutes: www.legis.state.wv.us/WVCODE/ masterfrm3Banner.cfm

Cases: www.state.wv.us/wvsca/opinions.htm
Court Rules: www.llrx.com/courtrules-gen/state-West-Virginia.html
General: www.romingerlegal.com/state/westvirginia.html

FINDING EMPLOYMENT IN WEST VIRGINIA

- wvbar.legalstaff.com
- careers.findlaw.com
- www.indeed.com/q-Paralegal-l-West-Virginia-jobs.html
- wv.craigslist.org/lgl

WISCONSIN

DEFINING LEGAL ASSISTANTS/PARALEGALS IN WISCONSIN

"Paralegal" means an individual qualified through education and training, employed or retained to perform substantive legal work and supervised by an attorney licensed to practice law in this state, requiring a sufficient knowledge of legal concepts that, absent the paralegal, the attorney would perform the work. State Bar of Wisconsin, Paralegal Practice Task Force, *Final Report* (2004) (in the search box of www.wisbar.org, type "paralegal task force").

ETHICAL RULES AND GUIDELINES IN WISCONSIN

- For a discussion of the state's ethical Rule 5.3 [20:5.3] ("Responsibilities Regarding Nonlawyer Assistants") in the *Wisconsin Rules of Professional Conduct for Attorneys*, see the end of Section C in chapter 5. For the text of 5.3 [20:5.3] in Wisconsin, see also www.legis.state.wi.us/rsb/scr/5200.pdf.

- Wisconsin State Bar, Paralegal Task Force, *Proposed Ethics Rules for Paralegals*. (in the search box of www.wisbar.org, type "ethics rules for paralegals").

- A paralegal can attend a real estate closing on behalf of a client without a supervising attorney being present if the paralegal is trained and the client consents, but the paralegal cannot give legal advice or legal opinions at the closing. Wisconsin State Bar, *Opinion E-95–3* (7/1998).

- An attorney whose license to practice law is suspended or revoked or who is suspended from the practice of law may not engage in the practice of law or in any law work activity customarily done by paralegals. Rule 22.26(f)(2).

- Law firm letterhead can include the names of paralegals as long as their nonattorney status is made clear. State Bar of Wisconsin, *Opinion E-85–6* (10/1985). See also *Opinion E-83–3* allowing announcements of nonattorneys joining a firm (reversing *Opinion E-80–15*).

- The office of the district attorney and the office of a circuit judge can share the services of a paralegal as long as the paralegal is supervised so as to maintain the confidentiality of each office. State Bar of Wisconsin, *Opinion E-86–13* (9/24/86).

- A paralegal can have a business card containing the law firm's name but cannot be listed on the law firm's letterhead. State Bar of Wisconsin, *Opinion E-75–22*. (Note: *Opinion E-85–6* changes the letterhead portion of *E-75–22*.)

- A paralegal can be listed on law firm letterhead. State Bar of Wisconsin, *Opinion E-85–6*.

- A paralegal who is a licensed real estate broker cannot appear at a real estate closing. "If a paralegal from the attorney's office appears at the closing, it will *seem* that he is there in a legal capacity." State Bar of Wisconsin, *Opinion E-80–2*.

- A law firm can hire a litigation paralegal who will also provide court reporting services to other attorneys. State Bar of Wisconsin, *Opinion E-86–19* (12/12/86).

DEFINING THE PRACTICE OF LAW IN WISCONSIN

§ 757.30 (*Wisconsin Statutes Annotated*): (2) Every person who appears as agent, representative or attorney, for or on behalf of any other person, or any firm, partnership, association or corporation in any action or proceeding in or before any court of record, court commissioner, or judicial tribunal of the United States, or of any state, or who otherwise, in or out of court, for compensation or pecuniary reward gives professional legal advice not incidental to his or her usual or ordinary business, or renders any legal service for any other person, or any firm, partnership, association or corporation, shall be deemed to be practicing law within the meaning of this section.

WISCONSIN ETHICS AND PRACTICE RULES ON THE INTERNET

- www.law.cornell.edu/ethics/wisconsin.html
- www.law.cornell.edu/ethics/wi/code/WI_CODE.HTM
- www.wisbar.org/AM/Template.cfm?Section=wisconsin_ethics_opinions

PARALEGALS (AND OTHER NONATTORNEYS) IN WISCONSIN STATE AND FEDERAL COURTS

- *In re Disciplinary Proceedings Against Compton*, 744 N.W.2d 78 (Supreme Court of Wisconsin, 2008) (Attorney's conduct in submitting bills to the office of the State Public Defender for work he alleged that he had performed, but was in fact performed by paralegal, violated the professional rules that prohibited a lawyer from engaging in conduct involving dishonesty, fraud, deceit or misrepresentation and required a lawyer to make reasonable efforts to ensure that his nonlawyer assistant's conduct was compatible with the professional obligations of the lawyer.)

- *In re Disciplinary Proceedings Against Robinson*, 700 N.W.2d 757 (Supreme Court of Wisconsin, 2005) (Attorney's act in instructing legal assistant to notarize a signature indicating that the signer of the deed was present when in fact he was not violated professional rule making an attorney responsible for conduct of nonlawyer assistants. SCR 20:5.3(c)(1).)

- *Austin v. CUNA Mutual Insurance Society*, 240 Federal Rules Decisions 420 (U.S. District Court, W.D., Wisconsin, 2006) (paralegals (called "law specialists") sue for failure to pay overtime compensation).

- *Abbott v. Marker*, 722 N.W.2d 162 (Court of Appeals of Wisconsin, 2006) (Nonlawyer's alleged agreement with attorney to refer potential clients in exchange for a percentage of the attorney fees violated public policy and statutes providing that it is illegal for a party to solicit retainers or agreements from another party for an attorney and illegal for an attorney to split legal fees with nonattorneys and, thus, was unenforceable.)

- *In the Matter of Hinnawi*, 549 N.W.2d 245 (Supreme Court of Wisconsin, 1996) (a suspended or disbarred attorney may not work as a paralegal; SCR 22.26).

- *In re Webster*, 120 Bankruptcy Reporter 111 (U.S. Bankruptcy Court, E.D. Wisconsin, 1990) (injunction against nonattorney for engaging in unauthorized practice of law in providing bankruptcy services).

- *Alexander v. City of Milwaukee*, 2006 WL 277114 (U.S. District Court, E.D., Wisconsin, 2006) ("I am well aware that counsel is more comfortable attending a deposition when the paralegal is at his or her side. However, when the deposition being taken is that of your own clients, generally speaking there is little need for the attendance of a paralegal. On the other hand, because of the voluminous material involved in this case, I will allow compensation for the paralegal's attendance at the deposition of the Defendants and others identified with the defense.")

- *Hutchison v. Amateur Electronic Supply*, 42 F.3d 1037, 1048 (U.S. Court of Appeals, 7th Circuit, 1994) (fee award reduced for "failure to utilize paralegals").

- *EEOC v. Accurate Mechanical Contractors, Inc.*, 863 F. Supp. 828 (U.S. District Court, E.D. Wisconsin, 1994) (paralegal fees are limited to work performed by paralegals that would otherwise be performed by an attorney).

- *Purdy v. Security Savings . . .*, 727 F. Supp. 1266, 1270 (U.S. District Court, E. D. Wisconsin, 1989) (it is "clearly excessive" to claim six and a half hours of paralegal time to cite check a document with only forty citations in it).

DOING LEGAL RESEARCH IN WISCONSIN LAW

Statutes: www.legis.state.wi.us/rsb/stats.html
Cases: www.wicourts.gov/opinions/supreme.htm
Court Rules: www.llrx.com/courtrules-gen/state-Wisconsin.html
General: www.aallnet.org/chapter/llaw/paliguide/index.htm

FINDING EMPLOYMENT IN WISCONSIN

- wisbar.legalstaff.com
- careers.findlaw.com
- www.midwestparalegal.com
- www.indeed.com/q-Paralegal-l-Wisconsin-jobs.html
- www.simplyhired.com/job-search/l-Wisconsin/o-232000/t-Paralegal
- jobs.careerbuilder.com/al.ic/Wisconsin_Legal.htm

WYOMING

ETHICAL RULES AND GUIDELINES IN WYOMING

- For a discussion of the state's ethical Rule 5.3 ("Responsibilities Regarding Nonlawyer Assistants") in the *Wyoming Rules of Professional Conduct of Attorneys at Law*, see the end of Section C in chapter 5. For the text of 5.3 in Wyoming, see also courts.state.wy.us/CourtRules.aspx.

- The rule of imputed disqualification in Rule 1.10 "does not prohibit representation by others in the law firm where the person prohibited from involvement in a matter is a nonlawyer, such as a paralegal or legal secretary." *Wyoming Rules of Professional Conduct for Attorneys-at-Law.*

- It is professional misconduct for a lawyer to (g) knowingly employ any person in the practice of law who has been dis-

barred or is under suspension from the practice of law in any position or capacity as a paralegal. Rule 8.4. *Wyoming Court Rules*. Rules of Professional Conduct for Attorneys.

DEFINING THE PRACTICE OF LAW IN WYOMING

Rule 11 (*Wyoming Rules of Court*): (a)(1) "Practice of law" means advising others and taking action for them in matters connected with law. It includes preparation of legal instruments and acting or proceeding for another before judges, courts, tribunals, commissioners, boards or other governmental agencies.

WYOMING ETHICS AND PRACTICE RULES ON THE INTERNET

- www.secure.law.cornell.edu/ethics/wyoming.html
- www.courts.state.wy.us/CourtRules.aspx
- www.law.cornell.edu/ethics/wyoming.html

PARALEGALS (AND OTHER NONATTORNEYS) IN WYOMING STATE AND FEDERAL COURTS

- *Skinner v. Uphoff*, 324 F. Supp. 2d 1278 (U.S. District Court, Wyoming, 2004) (if paralegal services are not reflected in the attorney's fee, the court may award them separately as part of the fee for legal services).

- *Board of Professional Responsibility, Wyoming State Bar v. Fulton*, 133 P.3d 514 (Supreme Court of Wyoming, 2006) (Respondent violated Rule of Professional Conduct 1.5(a) by including paralegal time for legal services that should be generally covered by the contingency percentage.)

- *Brooks v. Zebre*, 792 P.2d 196, 220 (Supreme Court of Wyoming, 1990) (a "lawyer who approaches a represented third party without going through counsel should be severely punished. And this is so though the lawyer uses a law representative or paralegal to do his dirty work").

- *Mendicino v. Whitchurch*, 565 P.2d 460, 478 (Supreme Court of Wyoming, 1977) (a suspended attorney shall not participate in the practice of law as an attorney or paralegal).

- *Van Riper v. Wyoming*, 882 P.2d 230 (Supreme Court of Wyoming, 1994) (felony defendant with paralegal training defends himself).

DOING LEGAL RESEARCH IN WYOMING LAW

Statutes: legisweb.state.wy.us
Cases: courts.state.wy.us
Court Rules: courts.state.wy.us/CourtRules.aspx
General: www.romingerlegal.com/state/wyoming.html

FINDING EMPLOYMENT IN WYOMING

- careers.findlaw.com
- www.simplyhired.com/job-search/l-Wyoming/o-232000/t-Paralegal
- www.hg.org/legal_jobs_wyoming.asp
- wyoming.craigslist.org/lgl

Ethical Codes of NALA, NFPA, and NALS

As indicated in chapter 4, the major national paralegal associations have ethical codes. (See Exhibit 5.4 in chapter 5.) Here are excerpts from these codes.

NALA CODE OF ETHICS AND PROFESSIONAL RESPONSIBILITY

NATIONAL ASSOCIATION OF LEGAL ASSISTANTS (www.nala.org/code.htm)

Each NALA member agrees to follow the canons of the NALA Code of Ethics and Professional Responsibility. Violations of the Code may result in cancellation of membership. First adopted by the NALA membership in May of 1975, the Code of Ethics and Professional Responsibility is the foundation of ethical practices of paralegals in the legal community.

A paralegal must adhere strictly to the accepted standards of legal ethics and to the general principles of proper conduct. The performance of the duties of the paralegal shall be governed by specific canons as defined herein so that justice will be served and goals of the profession attained. . . .

The canons of ethics set forth hereafter are adopted by the National Association of Legal Assistants, Inc., as a general guide intended to aid paralegals and attorneys. The enumeration of these rules does not mean there are not others of equal importance although not specifically mentioned. Court rules, agency rules and statutes must be taken into consideration when interpreting the canons.

Definition: Legal assistants, also known as paralegals, are a distinguishable group of persons who assist attorneys in the delivery of legal services. Through formal education, training and experience, legal assistants have knowledge and expertise regarding the legal system and substantive and procedural law which qualify them to do work of a legal nature under the supervision of an attorney. In 2001, NALA members adopted the ABA definition of a legal assistant/paralegal, as follows: A legal assistant or paralegal is a person qualified by education, training or work experience who is employed or retained by a lawyer, law office, corporation, governmental agency or other entity who performs specifically delegated substantive legal work for which a lawyer is responsible. (Adopted by the ABA in 1997)

Canon 1. A paralegal must not perform any of the duties that attorneys only may perform nor take any actions that attorneys may not take.

Canon 2. A paralegal may perform any task which is properly delegated and supervised by an attorney, as long as the attorney is ultimately responsible to the client, maintains a direct relationship with the client, and assumes professional responsibility for the work product.

Canon 3. A paralegal must not: (a) engage in, encourage, or contribute to any act which could constitute the unauthorized practice of law; and (b) establish attorney-client relationships, set fees, give legal opinions or advice or represent a client before a court or agency unless so authorized by that court or agency; and (c) engage in conduct or take any action which would assist or involve the attorney in a violation of professional ethics or give the appearance of professional impropriety.

Canon 4. A paralegal must use discretion and professional judgment commensurate with knowledge and experience but must not render independent legal judgment in place of an attorney. The services of an attorney are essential in the public interest whenever such legal judgment is required.

Canon 5. A paralegal must disclose his or her status as a paralegal at the outset of any professional relationship with a client, attorney, a court or administrative agency or personnel thereof, or a member of the general public. A paralegal must act prudently in determining the extent to which a client may be assisted without the presence of an attorney.

Canon 6. A paralegal must strive to maintain integrity and a high degree of competency through education and training with respect to professional responsibility, local rules and practice, and through continuing education in substantive areas of law to better assist the legal profession in fulfilling its duty to provide legal service.

Canon 7. A paralegal must protect the confidences of a client and must not violate any rule or statute now in effect or hereafter enacted controlling the doctrine of privileged communications between a client and an attorney.

Canon 8. A paralegal must disclose to his or her employer or prospective employer any pre-existing client or personal relationship that may conflict with the interests of the employer or prospective employer and/or their clients.

Canon 9. A paralegal must do all other things incidental, necessary, or expedient for the attainment of the ethics and responsibilities as defined by statute or rule of court.

Canon 10. A paralegal's conduct is guided by bar associations' codes of professional responsibility and rules of professional conduct.

NFPA MODEL CODE OF ETHICS AND PROFESSIONAL RESPONSIBILITY

NATIONAL FEDERATION OF PARALEGAL ASSOCIATIONS (www.paralegals.org)

1.1. A paralegal shall achieve and maintain a high level of competence.

EC 1.1(a) A paralegal shall achieve competency through education, training, and work experience.

EC 1.1(b) A paralegal shall aspire to participate in a minimum of twelve (12) hours of continuing legal education, to include at least one (1) hour of ethics education, every two (2) years in order to remain current on developments in the law.

EC 1.1(c) A paralegal shall perform all assignments promptly and efficiently.

1.2. A paralegal shall maintain a high level of personal and professional integrity.

EC 1.2(a) A paralegal shall not engage in any ex parte communications involving the courts or any other adjudicatory body in an attempt to exert undue influence or to obtain advantage or the benefit of only one party.

EC 1.2(b) A paralegal shall not communicate, or cause another to communicate, with a party the paralegal knows to be represented by a lawyer in a pending matter without the prior consent of the lawyer representing such other party.

EC 1.2(c) A paralegal shall ensure that all timekeeping and billing records prepared by the paralegal are thorough, accurate, honest, and complete.

EC 1.2(d) A paralegal shall not knowingly engage in fraudulent billing practices. Such practices may include, but are not limited to: inflation of hours billed to a client or employer; misrepresentation of the nature of tasks performed; and/or submission of fraudulent expense and disbursement documentation.

EC 1.2(e) A paralegal shall be scrupulous, thorough and honest in the identification and maintenance of all funds, securities, and other assets of a client and shall provide accurate accounting as appropriate.

EC 1.2(f) A paralegal shall advise the proper authority of non-confidential knowledge of any dishonest or fraudulent acts by any person pertaining to the handling of the funds, securities or other assets of a client. The authority to whom the report is made shall depend on the nature and circumstances of the possible misconduct, (e.g., ethics committees of law firms, corporations and/or paralegal associations, local or state bar associations, local prosecutors, administrative agencies, etc.). Failure to report such knowledge is in itself misconduct and shall be treated as such under these rules.

1.3. A paralegal shall maintain a high standard of professional conduct.

EC-1.3(a) A paralegal shall refrain from engaging in any conduct that offends the dignity and decorum of proceedings before a court or other adjudicatory body and shall be respectful of all rules and procedures.

EC-1.3(b) A paralegal shall avoid impropriety and the appearance of impropriety and shall not engage in any conduct that would adversely affect his/her fitness to practice. Such conduct may include, but is not limited to: violence, dishonesty, interference with the administration of justice, and/or abuse of a professional position or public office.

EC-1.3(c) Should a paralegal's fitness to practice be compromised by physical or mental illness, causing that paralegal to commit an act that is in direct violation of the Model Code/Model Rules and/or the rules and/or laws governing the jurisdiction in which the paralegal practices, that paralegal may be protected from sanction upon review of the nature and circumstances of that illness.

EC-1.3(d) A paralegal shall advise the proper authority of non-confidential knowledge of any action of another legal professional that clearly demonstrates fraud, deceit, dishonesty, or misrepresentation. The authority to whom the report is made shall depend on the nature and circumstances of the possible misconduct, (e.g., ethics committees of law firms, corporations and/or paralegal associations, local or state bar associations, local prosecutors, administrative agencies, etc.). Failure to report such knowledge is in itself misconduct and shall be treated as such under these rules.

EC-1.3(e) A paralegal shall not knowingly assist any individual with the commission of an act that is in direct violation of the Model Code/Model Rules and/or the rules and/or laws governing the jurisdiction in which the paralegal practices.

EC-1.3(f) If a paralegal possesses knowledge of future criminal activity, that knowledge must be reported to the appropriate authority immediately.

1.4. A paralegal shall serve the public interest by contributing to the improvement of the legal system and delivery of quality legal services, including pro bono publico services.

EC-1.4(a) A paralegal shall be sensitive to the legal needs of the public and shall promote the development and implementation of programs that address those needs.

EC-1.4(b) A paralegal shall support efforts to improve the legal system and access thereto and shall assist in making changes.

EC-1.4(c) A paralegal shall support and participate in the delivery of Pro Bono Publico services directed toward implementing and improving access to justice, the law, the legal system or the paralegal and legal professions.

EC-1.4(d) A paralegal should aspire annually to contribute twenty-four (24) hours of Pro Bono Publico services under the supervision of an attorney or as authorized by administrative, statutory or court authority to: persons of limited means; or charitable, religious, civic, community, governmental and educational organizations in matters that are designed primarily to address the legal needs of persons with limited means; or individuals, groups or organizations seeking to secure or protect civil rights, civil liberties or public rights. The twenty-four (24) hours of Pro Bono Publico services contributed annually by a paralegal may consist of such services as detailed in this EC-1.4(d), and/or administrative matters designed to develop and implement the attainment of this aspiration as detailed above in EC-1.4(a) B (c), or any combination of the two.

1.5. A paralegal shall preserve all confidential information provided by the client or acquired from other sources before, during, and after the course of the professional relationship.

EC-1.5(a) A paralegal shall be aware of and abide by all legal authority governing confidential information in the jurisdiction in which the paralegal practices.

EC-1.5(b) A paralegal shall not use confidential information to the disadvantage of the client.

EC-1.5(c) A paralegal shall not use confidential information to the advantage of the paralegal or of a third person.

EC-1.5(d) A paralegal may reveal confidential information only after full disclosure and with the client's written consent; or, when required by law or court order; or, when necessary to prevent the client from committing an act that could result in death or serious bodily harm.

EC-1.5(e) A paralegal shall keep those individuals responsible for the legal representation of a client fully informed of any confidential information the paralegal may have pertaining to that client.

EC-1.5(f) A paralegal shall not engage in any indiscreet communications concerning clients.

1.6. A paralegal shall avoid conflicts of interest and shall disclose any possible conflict to the employer or client, as well as to the prospective employers or clients.

EC-1.6(a) A paralegal shall act within the bounds of the law, solely for the benefit of the client, and shall be free of compromising influences and loyalties. Neither the paralegal's personal or business interest, nor those of other clients or third persons, should compromise the paralegal's professional judgment and loyalty to the client.

EC-1.6(b) A paralegal shall avoid conflicts of interest that may arise from previous assignments, whether for a present or past employer or client.

EC-1.6(c) A paralegal shall avoid conflicts of interest that may arise from family relationships and from personal and business interests.

EC-1.6(d) In order to be able to determine whether an actual or potential conflict of interest exists a paralegal shall create and maintain an effective recordkeeping system that identifies clients, matters, and parties with which the paralegal has worked.

EC-1.6(e) A paralegal shall reveal sufficient non-confidential information about a client or former client to reasonably ascertain if an actual or potential conflict of interest exists.

EC-1.6(f) A paralegal shall not participate in or conduct work on any matter where a conflict of interest has been identified.

EC-1.6(g) In matters where a conflict of interest has been identified and the client consents to continued representation, a paralegal shall comply fully with the implementation and maintenance of an Ethical Wall.

1.7. A paralegal's title shall be fully disclosed.

EC-1.7(a) A paralegal's title shall clearly indicate the individual's status and shall be disclosed in all business and professional communications to avoid misunderstandings and misconceptions about the paralegal's role and responsibilities.

EC-1.7(b) A paralegal's title shall be included if the paralegal's name appears on business cards, letterhead, brochures, directories, and advertisements.

EC-1.7(c) A paralegal shall not use letterhead, business cards or other promotional materials to create a fraudulent impression of his/her status or ability to practice in the jurisdiction in which the paralegal practices.

EC-1.7(d) A paralegal shall not practice under color of any record, diploma, or certificate that has been illegally or fraudulently obtained or issued or which is misrepresentative in any way.

EC-1.7(e) A paralegal shall not participate in the creation, issuance, or dissemination of fraudulent records, diplomas, or certificates.

1.8. A paralegal shall not engage in the unauthorized practice of law.

EC-1.8(a) A paralegal shall comply with the applicable legal authority governing the unauthorized practice of law in the jurisdiction in which the paralegal practices.

NALS CODE OF ETHICS

NALS THE ASSOCIATION FOR LEGAL PROFESSIONALS (www.nals.org/aboutnals/Code)

Members of NALS are bound by the objectives of this association and the standards of conduct required of the legal profession. Every member shall:

- Encourage respect for the law and the administration of justice;
- Observe rules governing privileged communications and confidential information;
- Promote and exemplify high standards of loyalty, cooperation, and courtesy;
- Perform all duties of the profession with integrity and competence; and
- Pursue a high order of professional attainment.

Integrity and high standards of conduct are fundamental to the success of our professional association. This Code is promulgated by the NALS and accepted by its members to accomplish these ends.

Canon 1. Members of this association shall maintain a high degree of competency and integrity through continuing education to better assist the legal profession in fulfilling its duty to provide quality legal services to the public.

Canon 2. Members of this association shall maintain a high standard of ethical conduct and shall contribute to the integrity of the association and the legal profession.

Canon 3. Members of this association shall avoid a conflict of interest pertaining to a client matter.

Canon 4. Members of this association shall preserve and protect the confidences and privileged communications of a client.

Canon 5. Members of this association shall exercise care in using independent professional judgment and in determining the extent to which a client may be assisted without the presence of a lawyer and shall not act in matters involving professional legal judgment.

Canon 6. Members of this association shall not solicit legal business on behalf of a lawyer.

Canon 7. Members of this association, unless permitted by law, shall not perform paralegal functions except under the direct supervision of a lawyer and shall not advertise or contract with members of the general public for the performance of paralegal functions.

Canon 8. Members of this association, unless permitted by law, shall not perform any of the duties restricted to lawyers or do things which lawyers themselves may not do and shall assist in preventing the unauthorized practice of law.

Canon 9. Members of this association not licensed to practice law shall not engage in the practice of law as defined by statutes or court decisions.

Canon 10. Members of this association shall do all other things incidental, necessary, or expedient to enhance professional responsibility and participation in the administration of justice and public service in cooperation with the legal profession.

California Legislation

One of the most dramatic events in the last decade has been the enactment of a law in California on who can be called a paralegal or legal assistant. The law also created the position of legal document assistant (LDA), an independent contractor who sells services to the public without attorney supervision. The law governing the LDA also applies to the unlawful detainer assistant (UDA), a position created earlier in the state. These developments are described in detail in chapter 4. Given the importance of these developments, the text of the new California law is reprinted here from *West's Annotated California Business & Professions Code*.

Note that Section 6407 of the law requires identification cards of legal document assistants to insert the following statements:

> "This person is not a lawyer."
> "The county clerk has not evaluated this person's knowledge, experience, or services."

For an example of an identification card that complies with this requirement, see Exhibit 4.5 in chapter 4.

§ 6450. PARALEGAL; DEFINED; PROHIBITIONS; CERTIFICATIONS

(a) "Paralegal" means a person who holds himself or herself out to be a paralegal, who is qualified by education, training, or work experience, and who either contracts with or is employed by an attorney, law firm, corporation, governmental agency, or other entity, and who performs substantial legal work under the direction and supervision of an active member of the State Bar of California, as defined in Section 6060, or an attorney practicing law in the federal courts of this state, that has been specifically delegated by the attorney to him or her. Tasks performed by a paralegal may include, but are not limited to, case planning, development, and management; legal research; interviewing clients; fact gathering and retrieving information; drafting and analyzing legal documents; collecting, compiling, and utilizing technical information to make an independent decision and recommendation to the supervising attorney; and representing clients before a state or federal administrative agency if that representation is permitted by statute, court rule, or administrative rule or regulation.

(b) Notwithstanding subdivision (a), a paralegal shall not do any of the following:

(1) Provide legal advice.

(2) Represent a client in court.

(3) Select, explain, draft, or recommend the use of any legal document to or for any person other than the attorney who directs and supervises the paralegal.

(4) Act as a runner or capper, as defined in Sections 6151 and 6152.

(5) Engage in conduct that constitutes the unlawful practice of law.

(6) Contract with, or be employed by, a natural person other than an attorney to perform paralegal services.

(7) In connection with providing paralegal services, induce a person to make an investment, purchase a financial product or service, or enter a transaction from which income or profit, or both, purportedly may be derived.

(8) Establish the fees to charge a client for the services the paralegal performs, which shall be established by the attorney who supervises the paralegal's work. This paragraph does not apply to fees charged by a paralegal in a contract to provide paralegal services to an attorney, law firm, corporation, governmental agency, or other entity as provided in subdivision (a).

(c) A paralegal shall possess at least one of the following:

(1) A certificate of completion of a paralegal program approved by the American Bar Association.

(2) A certificate of completion of a paralegal program at, or a degree from, a postsecondary institution that requires the successful completion of a minimum of 24 semester, or equivalent, units in law-related courses and that has been accredited by a national or regional accrediting organization or approved by the Bureau for Private Postsecondary and Vocational Education.

(3) A baccalaureate degree or an advanced degree in any subject, a minimum of one year of law-related experience under the supervision of an attorney who has been an active member of the State Bar of California for at least the preceding three years or who has practiced in the federal courts of this state for at least the preceding three years, and a written declaration from this attorney stating that the person is qualified to perform paralegal tasks.

(4) A high school diploma or general equivalency diploma, a minimum of three years of law-related experience under the supervision of an attorney who has been an active member of the State Bar of California for at least the preceding three years or who has practiced in the federal courts of this state for at least the preceding three years, and a written declaration from this attorney stating that the person is qualified to perform

paralegal tasks. This experience and training shall be completed no later than December 31, 2003.

(d) Every two years, commencing January 1, 2007, any person that is working as a paralegal shall be required to certify completion of four hours of mandatory continuing legal education in legal ethics and four hours of mandatory continuing legal education in either general law or in an area of specialized law. All continuing legal education courses shall meet the requirements of Section 6070. Certification of these continuing education requirements shall be made with the paralegal's supervising attorney. The paralegal shall be responsible for keeping a record of the paralegal's certifications.

(e) A paralegal does not include a nonlawyer who provides legal services directly to members of the public, or a legal document assistant or unlawful detainer assistant as defined in Section 6400, unless the person is a person described in subdivision (a)....

§ 6451. PARALEGAL; UNLAWFUL PRACTICES; SERVICES FOR CONSUMERS

It is unlawful for a paralegal to perform any services for a consumer except as performed under the direction and supervision of the attorney, law firm, corporation, government agency, or other entity that employs or contracts with the paralegal. Nothing in this chapter shall prohibit a paralegal who is employed by an attorney, law firm, governmental agency, or other entity from providing services to a consumer served by one of these entities if those services are specifically allowed by statute, case law, court rule, or federal or state administrative rule or regulation. "Consumer" means a natural person, firm, association, organization, partnership, business trust, corporation, or public entity.

§ 6452. PARALEGAL; UNLAWFUL PRACTICES; PERSONS IDENTIFYING THEMSELVES AS PARALEGALS

(a) It is unlawful for a person to identify himself or herself as a paralegal on any advertisement, letterhead, business card or sign, or elsewhere unless he or she has met the qualifications of subdivision (c) of Section 6450 and performs all services under the direction and supervision of an attorney who is an active member of the State Bar of California or an attorney practicing law in the federal courts of this state who is responsible for all of the services performed by the paralegal. The business card of a paralegal shall include the name of the law firm where he or she is employed or a statement that he or she is employed by or contracting with a licensed attorney.

(b) An attorney who uses the services of a paralegal is liable for any harm caused as the result of the paralegal's negligence, misconduct, or violation of this chapter.

§ 6453. DUTY OF PARALEGAL; CONFIDENTIALITY

A paralegal is subject to the same duty as an attorney specified in subdivision (e) of Section 6068 to maintain inviolate the confidentiality, and at every peril to himself for herself to preserve the attorney-client privilege, of a consumer for whom the paralegal has provided any of the services described in subdivision (a) of Section 6450.

§ 6454. DEFINITIONS

The terms "paralegal," "legal assistant," "attorney assistant," "freelance paralegal," "independent paralegal," and "contract paralegal" are synonymous for purposes of this chapter.

§ 6455. INJURED CONSUMERS; FILING OF COMPLAINTS; VIOLATIONS AND PUNISHMENT

(a) Any consumer injured by a violation of this chapter may file a complaint and seek redress in any municipal or superior court for injunctive relief, restitution, and damages. Attorney's fees shall be awarded in this action to the prevailing plaintiff.

(b) Any person who violates the provisions of Section 6451 or 6452 is guilty of an infraction for the first violation, which is punishable upon conviction by a fine of up to two thousand five hundred dollars ($2,500) as to each consumer with respect to whom a violation occurs, and is guilty of a misdemeanor for the second and each subsequent violation, which is punishable upon conviction by a fine of two thousand five hundred dollars ($2,500) as to each consumer with respect to whom a violation occurs, or imprisonment in a county jail for not more than one year, or by both that fine and imprisonment. Any person convicted of a violation of this section shall be ordered by the court to pay restitution to the victim pursuant to Section 1202.4 of the Penal Code.

§ 6456. EXEMPTIONS FROM CHAPTER

An individual employed by the state as a paralegal, legal assistant, legal analyst, or similar title, is exempt from the provisions of this chapter.

§ 6400. DEFINITIONS

(a) "Unlawful detainer assistant" means any individual who for compensation renders assistance or advice in the prosecution or defense of an unlawful detainer claim or action, including any bankruptcy petition that may affect the unlawful detainer claim or action.

(b) "Unlawful detainer claim" means a proceeding, filing, or action affecting rights or liabilities of any person that arises under Chapter 4 (commencing with Section 1159) of Title 3 of Part 3 of the Code of Civil Procedure and that contemplates an adjudication by a court.

(c) "Legal document assistant" means:

(1) Any person who is not exempted under Section 6401 and who provides, or assists in providing, or offers to provide, or offers to assist in providing, for compensation, any self-help service to a member of the public who is representing himself or herself in a legal matter, or who holds himself or herself out as someone who offers that service or has that authority. This paragraph shall not apply to any individual whose assistance consists merely of secretarial or receptionist services.

(2) A corporation, partnership, association, or other entity that employs or contracts with any person not exempted under Section 6401 who, as part of his or her responsibilities, provides, or assists in providing, or offers to provide, or offers to assist in providing, for compensation, any self-help service to a member of the public who is representing himself or herself in a legal matter or holds himself or herself out as someone who offers that service or has that authority. This paragraph shall not apply to an individual whose assistance consists merely of secretarial or receptionist services.

(d) "Self-help service" means all of the following:

(1) Completing legal documents in a ministerial manner, selected by a person who is representing himself or herself in a legal matter, by typing or otherwise completing the documents at the person's specific direction.

(2) Providing general published factual information that has been written or approved by an attorney, pertaining to legal procedures, rights, or obligations to a person who is representing himself or herself in a legal matter, to assist the person in representing himself or herself. This service in and of itself, shall not require registration as a legal document assistant.

(3) Making published legal documents available to a person who is representing himself or herself in a legal matter.

(4) Filing and serving legal forms and documents at the specific direction of a person who is representing himself or herself in a legal matter.

(e) "Compensation" means money, property, or anything else of value.

(f) A legal document assistant, including any legal document assistant employed by a partnership or corporation, shall not provide any self-help service for compensation after January 1, 2000, unless the legal document assistant is registered in the county in which his or her principal place of business is located and in any other county in which he or she performs acts for which registration is required.

(g) A legal document assistant shall not provide any kind of advice, explanation, opinion, or recommendation to a consumer about possible legal rights, remedies, defenses, options, selection of forms, or strategies. A legal document assistant shall complete documents only in the manner prescribed by paragraph (1) of subdivision (d).

§ 6401. CHAPTER APPLICATION EXCEPTIONS

This chapter does not apply to any person engaged in any of the following occupations, provided that the person does not also perform the duties of a legal document assistant in addition to those occupations:

(a) Any government employee who is acting in the course of his or her employment.

(b) A member of the State Bar of California, or his or her employee, paralegal, or agent, or an independent contractor while acting on behalf of a member of the State Bar.

(c) Any employee of a nonprofit, tax-exempt corporation who either assists clients free of charge or is supervised by a member of the State Bar of California who has malpractice insurance.

(d) A licensed real estate broker or licensed real estate salesperson, as defined in Chapter 3 (commencing with Section 10130) of Part 1 of Division 4, who acts pursuant to subdivision (b) of Section 10131 on an unlawful detainer claim as defined in subdivision (b) of Section 6400, and who is a party to the unlawful detainer action.

(e) An immigration consultant, as defined in Chapter 19.5 (commencing with Section 22441) of Division 8.

(f) A person registered as a process server under Chapter 16 (commencing with Section 22350) or a person registered as a professional photocopier under Chapter 20 (commencing with Section 22450) of Division 8.

(g) A person who provides services relative to the preparation of security instruments or conveyance documents as an integral part of the provision of title or escrow service.

(h) A person who provides services that are regulated by federal law.

(i) A person who is employed by, and provides services to, a supervised financial institution, holding company, subsidiary or affiliate.

§ 6401.5. PRACTICE OF LAW BY NON-LAWYERS

This chapter does not sanction, authorize, or encourage the practice of law by nonlawyers. Registration under this chapter, or an exemption from registration, does not immunize any person from prosecution or liability pursuant to Section 6125, 6126, 6126.5, or 6127.

§ 6401.6. LEGAL DOCUMENT ASSISTANT; LIMITATION ON SERVICE; SERVICES OF ATTORNEY

A legal document assistant may not provide service to a client who requires assistance that exceeds the definition of self-help service in subdivision (d) of Section 6400, and shall inform the client that the client requires the services of an attorney.

§ 6402. REGISTRATION REQUIREMENT; REGISTRATION OF DISBARRED AND SUSPENDED LAWYERS PROHIBITED

A legal document assistant or unlawful detainer assistant shall be registered pursuant to this chapter by the county clerk in the county in which his or her principal place of business is located (deemed primary registration), and in any other county in which he or she performs acts for which registration is required (deemed secondary registration).

Any registration in a county, other than the county of the person's place of business, shall state the person's principal place of business and provide proof that the registrant has satisfied the bonding requirement of Section 6405. No person who has been disbarred or suspended from the practice of law pursuant to Article 6 (commencing with Section 6100) of Chapter 4 may, during the period of any disbarment or suspension, register as a legal document assistant or unlawful detainer assistant. The Department of Consumer Affairs shall develop the application required to be completed by a person for purposes of registration as a legal document assistant. The application shall specify the types of proof that the applicant shall provide to the county clerk in order to demonstrate the qualifications and requirements of Section 6402.1.

§ 6407. REGISTER; IDENTIFICATION CARDS

(a) The county clerk shall maintain a register of legal document assistants, and a register of unlawful detainer assistants, assign a unique number to each legal document assistant, or unlawful detainer assistant, and issue an identification card to each one. Additional cards for employees of legal document assistants or unlawful detainer assistants shall be issued upon the payment of ten dollars ($10) for each card. Upon renewal of registration, the same number shall be assigned, provided there is no lapse in the period of registration.

(b) The identification card shall be a card 3 1/2 by 2 1/4 inches, and shall contain at the top, the title "Legal Document Assistant" or "Unlawful Detainer Assistant," as appropriate, followed by the registrant's name, address, registration number, date of expiration, and county of registration. It shall also contain a photograph of the registrant in the lower left corner. The front of the card, above the title, shall also contain the following statement in 12-point boldface type: "This person is not a lawyer." The front of the card, at the bottom, shall also contain the following statement in 12-point boldface type: "The county clerk has not evaluated this person's knowledge, experience, or services."

§ 6408.5(A). ADVERTISEMENTS AND SOLICITATION; REQUIRED DISCLAIMERS

All advertisements or solicitations published, distributed, or broadcast offering legal document assistant or unlawful detainer assistant services shall include the following statement: "I am not an attorney. I can only provide self help services at your specific direction." This subdivision does not apply to classified or "yellow pages" listings in a telephone or business directory of three lines or less that state only the name, address, and telephone number of the legal document assistant or unlawful detainer assistant. . . .

§ 6402.1. REGISTRATION ELIGIBILITY

To be eligible to apply for registration under this chapter as a legal document assistant, the applicant shall possess at least one of the following:

(a) A high school diploma or general equivalency diploma, and either a minimum of two years of law-related experience under the supervision of a licensed attorney, or a minimum of two years experience, prior to January 1, 1999, providing self-help service.

(b) A baccalaureate degree in any field and either a minimum of one year of law-related experience under the supervision of a licensed attorney, or a minimum of one year of experience, prior to January 1, 1999, providing self-help service.

(c) A certificate of completion from a paralegal program that is institutionally accredited but not approved by the American Bar Association, that requires successful completion of a minimum of 24 semester units, or the equivalent, in legal specialization courses.

(d) A certificate of completion from a paralegal program approved by the American Bar Association.

§ 6410. WRITTEN CONTRACTS REQUIRED; CONTENTS; RESCINDING AND VOIDING

(a) Every legal document assistant or unlawful detainer assistant who enters into a contract or agreement with a client to provide services shall, prior to providing any services, provide the client with a written contract, the contents of which shall be prescribed by regulations adopted by the Department of Consumer Affairs.

(b) The written contract shall include provisions relating to the following:

(1) The services to be performed.

(2) The costs of the services to be performed.

(3) There shall be printed on the face of the contract in 12-point boldface type a statement that the legal document assistant or unlawful detainer assistant is not an attorney and may not perform the legal services that an attorney performs.

(4) The contract shall contain a statement in 12-point boldface type that the county clerk has not evaluated or approved the registrant's knowledge or experience, or the quality of the registrant's services.

(5) The contract shall contain a statement in 12-point boldface type that the consumer may obtain information regarding free or low-cost representation through a local bar association or legal aid foundation and that the consumer may contact local law enforcement, a district attorney, or a legal aid foundation if the consumer believes that he or she has been a victim of fraud, the unauthorized practice of law, or any other injury.

(6) The contract shall contain a statement in 12-point boldface type that a legal document assistant or unlawful detainer assistant is not permitted to engage in the practice of law, including providing any kind of advice, explanation, opinion, or recommendation to a consumer about possible legal rights, remedies, defenses, options, selection of forms, or strategies.

(c) The provisions of the written contract shall be stated both in English and in any other language comprehended by the client and principally used in any oral sales presentation or negotiation leading to execution of the contract. The legal document assistant or the unlawful detainer assistant shall be responsible for translating the contract into the language principally used in any oral sales presentation or negotiation leading to the execution of the contract.

(d) Failure of a legal document assistant or unlawful detainer assistant to comply with subdivisions (a), (b), and (c) shall make the contract or agreement for services voidable at the option of the client. Upon the voiding of the contract, the legal document assistant or unlawful detainer assistant shall immediately return in full any fees paid by the client.

(e) In addition to any other right to rescind, the client shall have the right to rescind the contract within 24 hours of the signing of the contract. The client may cancel the contract by giving the legal document assistant or the unlawful detainer assistant any written statement to the effect that the contract is canceled. If the client gives notice of cancellation by mail addressed to the legal document assistant or unlawful detainer assistant, with first-class postage prepaid, cancellation is effective upon the date indicated on the postmark. Upon the voiding or rescinding of the contract or agreement for services, the legal document assistant or unlawful detainer assistant shall immediately return to the client any fees paid by the client, except fees for services that were actually, necessarily, and reasonably performed on the client's behalf by the legal document assistant or unlawful detainer assistant with the client's knowing and express written consent. The requirements of this subdivision shall be conspicuously set forth in the written contract.

Paralegal
Business Cards

Most paralegals have their own business cards. As indicated in chapter 5 and in appendix E, it is ethical for an attorney to allow a paralegal employee to have a business card that also prints the name of the employer. Here are several examples of such cards in use today:

BURR & FORMAN LLP

MICHAEL CARL IVEY, CLA
CERTIFIED LEGAL ASSISTANT

3100 SOUTHTRUST TOWER
420 NORTH 20TH STREET, BIRMINGHAM, AL 35203
DIRECT: (205) 458-5380   MAIN: (205) 251-3000
FACSIMILE: (205) 458-5100   INTERNET: MIVEY@BURR.COM

BIRMINGHAM • HUNTSVILLE • ATLANTA

Deborah Baer McKinney, RP
PACE Registered Paralegal

Cors & Bassett, LLC
ATTORNEYS AT LAW

537 East Pete Rose Way
Suite 400
Cincinnati, Ohio 45202-3502
telephone (513) **852-8218**
facsimile (513) **852-8222**
dbm@corsbassett.com

BYH | BENJAMIN, YOCUM & HEATHER, LLC
ATTORNEYS AT LAW

JOSÉ PEDRO SANTOS
SENIOR PARALEGAL

312 ELM STREET
SUITE 1850
CINCINNATI, OHIO 45202-2763

TELEPHONE: (513) 721-5672
FAX: (513) 562-4388
WEB SITE: byhlaw.com
E-MAIL: jpsantos@byhlaw.com

Pamela R. Horn
Senior Paralegal
Board Certified Legal Assistant
Civil Trial Law · Texas Bd. of Legal Specialization

prodigy™

Prodigy Communications L.P.
6500 River Place Blvd., Bldg. III, Austin, TX 78730-1111
Tel 512-527-1161 Fax 512-527-1199
Email phom@corp.prodigy.com

CELIA C. ELWELL, RP
PACE Registered Paralegal
Legal Assistant II

The City of
OKLAHOMA CITY

OFFICE OF THE MUNICIPAL COUNSELOR
200 N. WALKER, SUITE 400
OKLAHOMA CITY, OK 73102
405/297-2695
FAX 405/297-2118 •297-3851
email: celia.elwell@ci.okc.ok.us

---

corvette@qnis.net

Robin J. Schumacher, LDA
Document Preparation & Filing
Registration # X20011000000 Exp. 01-31-03

(559) 442-4969
Fax (559) 264-5010
3045 W. Lincoln Ave.
Fresno, CA 93706

Bonded and Licensed
Bankruptcy, Divorce,
Child Support, Wills,
Trusts & Misc.

ELECTRONIC BUSINESS CARD

The following card of Christina Koch is printed at the bottom of all of the e-mail messages she sends out. ACP stands for advanced certified paralegal, the certification of the National Association of Legal Assistants (see Exhibit 4.7 in chapter 4); AAJ is the American Association of Justice (formerly called the Association of Trial Lawyers of America), which allows affiliate membership for paralegals (www.atla.org/Networking/Tier3/ParalegalAffiliates.aspx).

	Representing Injured Plaintiffs For Over 50 Years
Christina L. Koch, ACP *Advanced Certified Paralegal/AAJ Paralegal Affiliate* clkoch@inserra.com	**INSERRA & KELLEY** 6790 Grover Street, Suite 200 Omaha, NE 68106-3612 tel: 402-391-4000 fax: 402-391-4039 mobile: 402-980-0789

State Resources

ABBREVIATIONS

AG: attorney general
BA: bar associations in the state (see also appendix C)
CP: consumer protection
CS: court system of the state

GO: governor's office
LF: law firms in the state
LL: law library of the state (or alternative)
LR: legal research sources on state law
MV: motor vehicle laws of the state
PR: public records search in the state

SF: state forms, e.g., summons, will, or probate
SL: state legislature
SS: secretary of state (or equivalent office)
WC: workers' compensation in the state

ALABAMA

AG: www.ago.state.al.us
BA: www.findlaw.com/11stategov/al/associations.html
CP: www.ago.state.al.us/consumer.cfm
CS: www.judicial.state.al.us
www.findlaw.com/11stategov/al/courts.html
GO: www.governor.state.al.us
LF: www.attorneylocate.com/scripts/city.asp?city_statecode=AL
www.directory.findlaw.com/lawyer/servlet/
SCityFirm?state=AL
LL: www.alalinc.net/library
LR: www.law.cornell.edu/states/alabama.html
www.findlaw.com/11stategov/al/index.html
MV: www.ador.state.al.us/motorvehicle/index.html
PR: www.publicrecordfinder.com/states/alabama.html
publicrecords.onlinesearches.com/Alabama.htm
SF: www.alllaw.com/state_resources/alabama/forms
forms.lp.findlaw.com/states/al.html
SL: www.legislature.state.al.us
SS: www.sos.state.al.us
WC: dir.alabama.gov/wc

ALASKA

AG: www.law.state.ak.us
BA: www.findlaw.com/11stategov/ak/associations.html
CP: www.law.state.ak.us/department/civil/consumer/cpindex.html
CS: www.state.ak.us/courts
GO: www.gov.state.ak.us
LF: www.attorneylocate.com/scripts/city.asp?city_statecode=AK
www.directory.findlaw.com/lawyer/servlet/
SCityFirm?state=AK
LL: www.state.ak.us/courts/library.htm
www.state.ak.us/courts/libhrs.htm
LR: www.findlaw.com/11stategov/ak/index.html
www.loc.gov/law/guide/us-ak.html
MV: www.state.ak.us/dmv

PR: www.publicrecordfinder.com/states/alaska.html
www.searchsystems.net/list.php?nid=14
SF: www.alllaw.com/state_resources/alaska/forms
forms.lp.findlaw.com/states/ak.html
SL: www.legis.state.ak.us
SS: www.gov.state.ak.us/ltgov
www.commerce.state.ak.us/occ/home.htm
WC: www.labor.state.ak.us/wc/wc.htm

ARIZONA

AG: www.ag.state.az.us
BA: www.findlaw.com/11stategov/az/associations.html
CP: www.azag.gov/consumer
CS: www.supreme.state.az.us/nav2/sitemap.htm
www.ncsconline.org/D_KIS/info_court_web_sites.html
GO: www.governor.state.az.us
LF: www.attorneylocate.com/scripts/city.asp?city_statecode=AZ
www.directory.findlaw.com/lawyer/servlet/
SCityFirm?state=AZ
LL: www.lib.az.us
LR: www.findlaw.com/11stategov/az/index.html
www.loc.gov/law/guide/us-az.html
MV: www.azdot.gov/mvd
PR: publicrecords.onlinesearches.com/Arizona.htm
SF: www.alllaw.com/state_resources/arizona/forms
forms.lp.findlaw.com/states/az.html
SL: www.azleg.gov
SS: www.azsos.gov
WC: www.ica.state.az.us

ARKANSAS

AG: www.ag.state.ar.us
BA: www.findlaw.com/11stategov/ar/associations.html
CP: www.ag.state.ar.us/consumers_tips.html
CS: www.courts.state.ar.us
www.findlaw.com/11stategov/ar/courts.html

GO: www.state.ar.us/governor
LF: www.attorneylocate.com/scripts/city.asp?city_statecode=AR
     courts.state.ar.us/attorneys/attorney_search.cfm
LR: www.findlaw.com/11stategov/ar/index.html
     www.loc.gov/law/guide/us-ar.html
MV: www.arkansas.gov/dfa/motor_vehicle/mv_index.html
PR: www.publicrecordfinder.com/states/arkansas.html
     www.searchsystems.net/list.php?nid=16
SF: www.alllaw.com/state_resources/arkansas/forms
     forms.lp.findlaw.com/states/ar.html
SL: www.arkleg.state.ar.us
SS: www.sosweb.state.ar.us
WC: www.awcc.state.ar.us

CALIFORNIA

AG: www.caag.state.ca.us
BA: california.lp.findlaw.com/ca03_associations/cabar.html
CP: www.caag.state.ca.us/consumers
CS: www.courtinfo.ca.gov
GO: www.governor.ca.gov
LF: www.attorneylocate.com/scripts/city.asp?city_statecode=CA
     www.directory.findlaw.com/lawyer/servlet/
     SCityFirm?state=CA
LL: www.publiclawlibrary.org
LR: california.lp.findlaw.com
     www.loc.gov/law/guide/us-ca.html
MV: www.dmv.ca.gov
PR: http://www.publicrecordfinder.com/states/california.html
SF: www.alllaw.com/state_resources/california/forms
     forms.lp.findlaw.com/states/ca.html
SL: www.leginfo.ca.gov
SS: www.ss.ca.gov
WC: www.dir.ca.gov/DWC/dwc_home_page.htm

COLORADO

AG: www.ago.state.co.us/index.cfm
BA: www.findlaw.com/11stategov/co/associations.html
CP: www.ago.state.co.us/consumer_protection.
     cfm?MenuPage=True
CS: www.courts.state.co.us
GO: www.state.co.us
LF: www.attorneylocate.com
     www.directory.findlaw.com/lawyer/servlet/
     SCityFirm?state=CO
LL: www.attorneylocate.com/scripts/city.asp?city_statecode=CO
LR: www.loc.gov/law/guide/us-co.html
     www.findlaw.com/11stategov/co/index.html
MV: www.revenue.state.co.us/mv_dir/home.asp
PR: www.searchsystems.net/list.php?nid=18
SF: www.alllaw.com/state_resources/colorado/forms
     forms.lp.findlaw.com/states/co.html
SL: www.leg.state.co.us
SS: www.sos.state.co.us
WC: www.coworkforce.com/DWC

CONNECTICUT

AG: www.cslib.org/attygenl
BA: www.findlaw.com/11stategov/ct/associations.html
CP: www.ct.gov/ag/cwp/browse.asp?a=2066&agNav=|422771
CS: www.jud.state.ct.us
GO: www.state.ct.us/governor
LF: www.attorneylocate.com/scripts/city.asp?city_statecode=CT
     www.directory.findlaw.com/lawyer/servlet/
     SCityFirm?state=CT

LL: www.jud.state.ct.us/LawLib
LR: www.loc.gov/law/guide/us-ct.html
     www.jud.state.ct.us/lawlib/state.htm
     www.findlaw.com/11stategov/ct/index.html
MV: www.dmvct.org
PR: www.searchsystems.net/list.php?nid=19
SF: www.alllaw.com/state_resources/connecticut/forms
     forms.lp.findlaw.com/states/ct.html
SL: www.cga.ct.gov
SS: www.sots.state.ct.us
WC: wcc.state.ct.us

DELAWARE

AG: attorneygeneral.delaware.gov
BA: www.findlaw.com/11stategov/de/associations.html
CP: attorneygeneral.delaware.gov/consumers/protection/safe-
     guarding.shtml
CS: courts.state.de.us
GO: www.state.de.us/governor/index.htm
LF: www.directory.findlaw.com/lawyer/servlet/
     SCityFirm?state=DE
     www.attorneylocate.com/scripts/city.asp?city_statecode=DE
LR: www.findlaw.com/11stategov/de/index.html
     www.loc.gov/law/guide/us-de.html
MV: www.delaware.gov/yahoo/DMV
PR: www.publicrecordfinder.com/states/delaware.html
SF: www.alllaw.com/state_resources/delaware/forms
     forms.lp.findlaw.com/states/de.html
SL: www.legis.state.de.us/Legislature.nsf/?Opendatabase
SS: sos.delaware.gov
WC: www.delawareworks.com/industrialaffairs/services/
     workerscomp.shtml

DISTRICT OF COLUMBIA

AG: http://occ.dc.gov/occ/site/default.asp
BA: www.findlaw.com/11stategov/dc/associations.html
CP: occ.dc.gov/occ/cwp/view,a,1223,q,531576,occNav,%7C3168
     8%7C,.asp
CS: www.dcsc.gov
GO: dc.gov/mayor/index.shtm
LF: www.attorneylocate.com/scripts/city.asp?city_statecode=DC
     www.directory.findlaw.com/lawyer/servlet/
     SCityFirm?state=DC
LL: www.ll.georgetown.edu/states/dc.cfm
LR: www.findlaw.com/11stategov/dc/index.html
     www.loc.gov/law/guide/us-dc.html
MV: www.dmv.washingtondc.gov
PR: www.os.dc.gov/os/cwp/view,a,1207,q,522721.asp
SF: forms.lp.findlaw.com/states/dc.html
SS: www.knowx.com/districtofcolumbia/districtofcolumbia-
     corporate-records.jsp
SL: www.dccouncil.washington.dc.us
WC: does.dc.gov/does/cwp/view,a,1232,q,537428.asp

FLORIDA

AG: myfloridalegal.com
BA: www.findlaw.com/11stategov/fl/associations.html
CP: myfloridalegal.com/consumer
CS: www.flcourts.org
GO: http://www.flgov.com
LF: www.attorneylocate.com/scripts/city.asp?city_statecode=FL
     www.directory.findlaw.com/lawyer/servlet/
     SCityFirm?state=FL
LL: library.flcourts.org

LR: www.findlaw.com/11stategov/fl/index.html
www.loc.gov/law/guide/us-fl.html
MV: www.hsmv.state.fl.us
PR: www.publicrecordfinder.com/states/florida.html
SF: www.alllaw.com/state_resources/florida/forms
forms.lp.findlaw.com/states/fl.html
SL: www.leg.state.fl.us
SS: www.dos.state.fl.us
WC: www.fldfs.com/wc

GEORGIA

AG: www.ganet.org/ago
BA: www.findlaw.com/11stategov/ga/associations.html
CP: www.ganet.org/ago/consumer_info.html
CS: www.georgiacourts.org
GO: gov.state.ga.us
LF: www.attorneylocate.com/scripts/city.asp?city_statecode=GA
www.directory.findlaw.com/lawyer/servlet/
SCityFirm?state=GA
LL: gsll.georgia.gov
LR: www.findlaw.com/11stategov/ga/index.html
www.loc.gov/law/guide/us-ga.html
MV: www4.co.honolulu.hi.us/mvrreg
PR: www.publicrecordfinder.com/states/georgia.html
SF: www.alllaw.com/state_resources/georgia/forms
forms.lp.findlaw.com/states/ga.html
SL: www2.state.ga.us/Legis
SS: www.sos.state.ga.us
WC: sbwc.georgia.gov/02/sbwc/home/0,2235,11394008,00.html

HAWAII

AG: www.hawaii.gov/ag
BA: www.findlaw.com/11stategov/hi/associations.html
CP: www.hawaii.gov/dcca/areas/ocp
CS: www.courts.state.hi.us
GO: gov.state.hi.us
LF: www.attorneylocate.com/scripts/city.asp?city_statecode=HI
www.directory.findlaw.com/lawyer/servlet/
SCityFirm?state=HI
LL: www.courts.state.hi.us (click "Law Library" under "Services")
LR: www.findlaw.com/11stategov/hi/index.html
www.loc.gov/law/guide/us-hi.html
MV: www.hawaii.gov/dot
PR: www.publicrecordfinder.com/states/hawaii.html
SF: www.alllaw.com/state_resources/hawaii/forms
forms.lp.findlaw.com/states/hi.html
SL: www.capitol.hawaii.gov
SS: www.knowx.com/hawaii/hawaii-corporate-records.jsp
WC: http://www.hawaii.gov/labor/workcomp2.shtml

IDAHO

AG: www2.state.id.us/ag
BA: www.findlaw.com/11stategov/id/associations.html
CP: www2.state.id.us/ag/consumer/index.htm
CS: www.isc.idaho.gov
GO: www2.state.id.us/gov
LF: www.attorneylocate.com/scripts/city.asp?city_statecode=ID
www.directory.findlaw.com/lawyer/servlet/SCityFirm?state=ID
LL: www.isll.idaho.gov
LR: www.findlaw.com/11stategov/id/index.html
www.loc.gov/law/guide/us-id.html
MV: itd.idaho.gov/DMV
PR: www.publicrecordfinder.com/states/idaho.html
SF: www.alllaw.com/state_resources/idaho/forms

forms.lp.findlaw.com/states/id.html
SL: http://www.legislature.idaho.gov
SS: www.idsos.state.id.us
WC: www.iic.idaho.gov

ILLINOIS

AG: www.ag.state.il.us
BA: www.findlaw.com/11stategov/il/associations.html
CP: www.ag.state.il.us/consumers/index.html
CS: www.state.il.us/court
GO: www100.state.il.us/gov
LF: www.attorneylocate.com/scripts/city.asp?city_statecode=IL
www.directory.findlaw.com/lawyer/servlet/
SCityFirm?state=IL
LL: www.law.siu.edu/lawlib
LR: www.findlaw.com/11stategov/il/index.html
www.loc.gov/law/guide/us-il.html
MV: www.cyberdriveillinois.com
PR: www.publicrecordfinder.com/states/illinois.html
SF: www.alllaw.com/state_resources/illinois/forms
forms.lp.findlaw.com/states/il.html
SL: www.ilga.gov
SS: www.sos.state.il.us
WC: www.state.il.us/agency/iic

INDIANA

AG: www.in.gov/attorneygeneral
BA: www.findlaw.com/11stategov/in/associations.html
CP: www.in.gov/attorneygeneral/consumer
CS: www.ai.org/judiciary
GO: www.state.in.us/gov
LF: www.attorneylocate.com/scripts/city.asp?city_statecode=IN
www.directory.findlaw.com/lawyer/servlet/
SCityFirm?state=IN
LL: www.in.gov/judiciary/library
LR: www.findlaw.com/11stategov/in/index.html
www.loc.gov/law/guide/us-in.html
MV: www.in.gov/bmv
PR: www.publicrecordfinder.com/states/indiana.html
SF: www.alllaw.com/state_resources/indiana/forms
forms.lp.findlaw.com/states/in.html
SL: www.state.in.us/legislative
SS: www.state.in.us/sos
WC: www.in.gov/workcomp

IOWA

AG: www.state.ia.us/government/ag
BA: www.findlaw.com/11stategov/ia/associations.html
CP: www.state.ia.us/government/ag/protecting_consumers
CS: www.judicial.state.ia.us
GO: www.state.ia.us/governor
LF: www.attorneylocate.com/scripts/city.asp?city_statecode=IA
www.directory.findlaw.com/lawyer/servlet/
SCityFirm?state=IA
LL: www.statelibraryofiowa.org/services/law-library
LR: www.findlaw.com/11stategov/ia/index.html
www.loc.gov/law/guide/us-ia.html
MV: www.dot.state.ia.us/sitemap.htm
PR: www.publicrecordfinder.com/states/iowa.html
SF: www.alllaw.com/state_resources/iowa/forms
forms.lp.findlaw.com/states/ia.html
SL: www.legis.state.ia.us
SS: www.sos.state.ia.us
WC: www.iowaworkforce.org/wc

KANSAS

AG: www.ksag.org/home
BA: www.findlaw.com/11stategov/ks/associations.html
CP: www.ksag.org/content/page/id/39
CS: www.kscourts.org
GO: www.governor.ks.gov
LF: www.attorneylocate.com/scripts/city.asp?city_statecode=KS
www.directory.findlaw.com/lawyer/servlet/
SCityFirm?state=KS
LL: www.kscourts.org/ctlib
LR: www.findlaw.com/11stategov/ks/index.html
www.loc.gov/law/guide/us-ks.html
MV: http://www.ksrevenue.org/vehicle.htm
PR: www.publicrecordfinder.com/states/kansas.html
SF: www.alllaw.com/state_resources/kansas/forms
www.megalaw.com/forms/ks/ksforms.php
SL: www.kslegislature.org
SS: www.kssos.org
WC: www.dol.ks.gov/WC/HTML/wc_ALL.html

KENTUCKY

AG: ag.ky.gov
BA: www.findlaw.com/11stategov/ky/associations.html
CP: ag.ky.gov/helping.htm
CS: www.kycourts.net
GO: governor.ky.gov
LF: www.attorneylocate.com/scripts/city.asp?city_statecode=KY
www.directory.findlaw.com/lawyer/servlet/
SCityFirm?state=KY
LL: www.uky.edu/Law/library
LR: www.findlaw.com/11stategov/ky/index.html
www.loc.gov/law/guide/us-ky.html
MV: www.kytc.state.ky.us/DrLic/home.htm
PR: www.publicrecordfinder.com/states/kentucky.html
SF: www.alllaw.com/state_resources/kentucky/forms
forms.lp.findlaw.com/states/ky.html
SL: www.lrc.state.ky.us/home.htm
SS: http://www.sos.ky.gov
WC: labor.ky.gov/dwc

LOUISIANA

AG: www.ag.state.la.us
BA: www.findlaw.com/11stategov/la/associations.html
CP: www.ag.state.la.us/ConsumerProtection.aspx
CS: www.lasc.org
GO: www.gov.state.la.us
LF: www.attorneylocate.com/scripts/city.asp?city_statecode=LA
www.directory.findlaw.com/lawyer/servlet/
SCityFirm?state=LA
LL: www.lasc.org/law_library/library_information.asp
LR: www.findlaw.com/11stategov/la/index.html
www.loc.gov/law/guide/us-la.html
MV: omv.dps.state.la.us
PR: www.publicrecordfinder.com/states/louisiana.html
SF: www.alllaw.com/state_resources/louisiana/forms
forms.lp.findlaw.com/states/la.html
SL: www.legis.state.la.us
SS: www.sec.state.la.us
WC: www.laworks.net

MAINE

AG: www.maine.gov/ag
BA: www.findlaw.com/11stategov/me/associations.html
CP: www.maine.gov/ag/index.php?r=clg
CS: www.courts.state.me.us
GO: www.state.me.us/governor
LF: www.attorneylocate.com/scripts/city.asp?city_statecode=ME
www.directory.findlaw.com/lawyer/servlet/
SCityFirm?state=ME
LL: www.state.me.us/legis/lawlib/homepage.htm
LR: www.findlaw.com/11stategov/me/index.html
www.loc.gov/law/guide/us-me.html
MV: www.state.me.us/sos/bmv
PR: www.publicrecordfinder.com/states/maine.html
SF: www.alllaw.com/state_resources/maine/forms
SL: janus.state.me.us/legis
SS: www.state.me.us/sos
WC: www.state.me.us/wcb

MARYLAND

AG: www.oag.state.md.us
BA: www.findlaw.com/11stategov/md/associations.html
CP: www.oag.state.md.us/Consumer/index.htm
CS: www.courts.state.md.us
GO: www.gov.state.md.us
LF: www.attorneylocate.com/scripts/city.asp?city_statecode=MD
www.directory.findlaw.com/lawyer/servlet/
SCityFirm?state=MD
LL: www.lawlib.state.md.us
LR: www.findlaw.com/11stategov/md/index.html
www.loc.gov/law/guide/us-md.html
MV: www.mva.state.md.us
PR: www.publicrecordfinder.com/states/maryland.html
SF: www.oag.state.md.us/publications.htm
www.alllaw.com/state_resources/maryland/forms
SL: www.mlis.state.md.us
SS: www.sos.state.md.us
WC: www.wcc.state.md.us

MASSACHUSETTS

AG: www.ago.state.ma.us
BA: www.findlaw.com/11stategov/ma/associations.html
CP: www.ago.state.ma.us/sp.cfm?pageid=2373
CS: http://www.mass.gov/courts
GO: www.state.ma.us/gov
LF: www.attorneylocate.com/scripts/city.asp?city_statecode=MA
www.directory.findlaw.com/lawyer/servlet/
SCityFirm?state=MA
LL: www.aallnet.org/chapter/llne
LR: www.findlaw.com/11stategov/ma/index.html
www.loc.gov/law/guide/us-ma.html
MV: www.state.ma.us/rmv
PR: www.publicrecordfinder.com/states/massachusetts.html
SF: www.alllaw.com/state_resources/massachusetts/forms
forms.lp.findlaw.com/states/ma.html
SL: www.state.ma.us/legis
SS: www.state.ma.us/sec
WC: www.state.ma.us/dia

MICHIGAN

AG: www.michigan.gov/ag
BA: www.findlaw.com/11stategov/mi/associations.html
CP: www.michigan.gov/ag/0,1607,7–164–17337—-,00.html
CS: courts.michigan.gov
GO: www.michigan.gov/gov
LF: www.attorneylocate.com/scripts/city.asp?city_statecode=MI
www.directory.findlaw.com/lawyer/servlet/
SCityFirm?state=MI

LL: www.michigan.gov/hal/0,1607,7–160–17449_18639——,00.html
LR: www.findlaw.com/11stategov/mi/index.html
     www.loc.gov/law/guide/us-mi.html
MV: www.michigan.gov/sos
PR: www.publicrecordfinder.com/states/michigan.html
SF: www.alllaw.com/state_resources/michigan/forms
     forms.lp.findlaw.com/states/mi.html
SL: www.michiganlegislature.org
SS: www.michigan.gov/sos
WC: www.michigan.gov/wca

MINNESOTA

AG: www.ag.state.mn.us
BA: www.findlaw.com/11stategov/mn/associations.html
CP: www.ag.state.mn.us/Consumer/Complaint.asp
CS: www.courts.state.mn.us
GO: www.governor.state.mn.us
LF: www.attorneylocate.com/scripts/city.asp?city_statecode=MN
     www.directory.findlaw.com/lawyer/servlet/
     SCityFirm?state=MN
LL: www.lawlibrary.state.mn.us
LR: www.findlaw.com/11stategov/mn/index.html
     www.loc.gov/law/guide/us-mn.html
MV: www.dps.state.mn.us/dvs
PR: www.publicrecordfinder.com/states/minnesota.html
SF: www.lawlibrary.state.mn.us/forms.html
     www.alllaw.com/state_resources/minnesota/forms
SL: www.leg.state.mn.us
SS: www.sos.state.mn.us
WC: www.doli.state.mn.us/workcomp.html

MISSISSIPPI

AG: www.ago.state.ms.us
BA: www.findlaw.com/11stategov/ms/associations.html
CP: www.ago.state.ms.us/divisions/consumer
CS: www.mississippi.gov/ms_sub_sub_template.jsp?Category_
     ID=13
GO: www.governor.state.ms.us
LF: www.attorneylocate.com/scripts/city.asp?city_statecode=MS
     www.directory.findlaw.com/lawyer/servlet/
     SCityFirm?state=MS
LL: www.mssc.state.ms.us/library/default.asp
LR: www.findlaw.com/11stategov/ms/index.html
     www.loc.gov/law/guide/us-ms.html
MV: www.ms.gov/hp/drivers/license/Main.do
PR: www.publicrecordfinder.com/states/mississippi.html
SF: www.alllaw.com/state_resources/mississippi/forms
SL: www.ls.state.ms.us
SS: www.sos.state.ms.us
WC: www.mwcc.state.ms.us

MISSOURI

AG: ago.mo.gov
BA: www.findlaw.com/11stategov/mo/associations.html
CP: ago.mo.gov/Consumer-Protection.htm
CS: www.courts.mo.gov
GO: gov.missouri.gov
LF: www.attorneylocate.com/scripts/city.asp?city_statecode=MO
     www.directory.findlaw.com/lawyer/servlet/
     SCityFirm?state=MO
LL: www.law.missouri.edu/library
LR: www.findlaw.com/11stategov/mo/index.html
     www.loc.gov/law/guide/us-mo.html
MV: dor.mo.gov/mvdl

PR: www.publicrecordfinder.com/states/missouri.html
SF: www.alllaw.com/state_resources/missouri/forms
SL: www.moga.state.mo.us
     www.megalaw.com/forms/mo/moforms.php
SS: www.sos.mo.gov
WC: www.dolir.mo.gov/wc

MONTANA

AG: www.doj.mt.gov
BA: www.findlaw.com/11stategov/mt/associations.html
CP: www.doj.mt.gov/consumer
CS: www.montanacourts.org
GO: governor.mt.gov
LF: www.attorneylocate.com/scripts/city.asp?city_statecode=MT
     www.directory.findlaw.com/lawyer/servlet/
     SCityFirm?state=MT
LL: courts.mt.gov/library
LR: www.findlaw.com/11stategov/mt/index.html
     www.loc.gov/law/guide/us-mt.html
MV: www.doj.mt.gov/driving
PR: www.publicrecordfinder.com/states/montana.html
SF: www.alllaw.com/state_resources/montana/forms
     forms.lp.findlaw.com/states/mt.html
SL: www.leg.state.mt.us
SS: www.sos.state.mt.us
WC: wcc.dli.mt.gov

NEBRASKA

AG: www.ago.state.ne.us
BA: www.findlaw.com/11stategov/ne/associations.html
CP: www.ago.state.ne.us
CS: court.nol.org
GO: http://www.gov.state.ne.us
LF: www.attorneylocate.com/scripts/city.asp?city_statecode=NE
     www.directory.findlaw.com/lawyer/servlet/
     SCityFirm?state=NE
LL: www.supremecourt.ne.gov/state-library/index.shtml?sub15
LR: www.findlaw.com/11stategov/ne/index.html
     www.loc.gov/law/guide/us-ne.html
MV: www.dmv.state.ne.us
PR: www.publicrecordfinder.com/states/nebraska.html
SF: www.alllaw.com/state_resources/nebraska/forms
     forms.lp.findlaw.com/states/ne.html
SL: nebraskalegislature.gov
SS: www.sos.state.ne.us
WC: www.wcc.ne.gov

NEVADA

AG: www.ag.state.nv.us
BA: www.findlaw.com/11stategov/nv/associations.html
CP: www.ag.state.nv.us/org/bcp/bcp.htm
CS: www.nvsupremecourt.us
GO: www.gov.state.nv.us
LF: www.attorneylocate.com/scripts/city.asp?city_statecode=NV
     www.directory.findlaw.com/lawyer/servlet/
     SCityFirm?state=NV
LL: lawlibrary.nvsupremecourt.us
LR: www.findlaw.com/11stategov/nv/index.html
     www.loc.gov/law/guide/us-nv.html
MV: nevadadmv.state.nv.us/nvreg.htm
PR: www.publicrecordfinder.com/states/nevada.html
SF: www.clan.lib.nv.us/polpac/nsc/forms.html
     www.alllaw.com/state_resources/nevada/forms
SL: www.leg.state.nv.us

SS: www.sos.state.nv.us
WC: www.dirweb.state.nv.us

NEW HAMPSHIRE

AG: www.state.nh.us/nhdoj
BA: www.findlaw.com/11stategov/nh/associations.html
CP: doj.nh.gov/consumer
CS: www.courts.state.nh.us
GO: www.state.nh.us/governor
LF: www.attorneylocate.com/scripts/city.asp?city_statecode=NH
      www.directory.findlaw.com/lawyer/servlet/
      SCityFirm?state=NH
LL: www.courts.state.nh.us/lawlibrary
LR: www.findlaw.com/11stategov/nh/index.html
      www.loc.gov/law/guide/us-nh.html
MV: www.nh.gov/safety/divisions/dmv
PR: www.publicrecordfinder.com/states/new_hampshire.html
SF: www.alllaw.com/state_resources/new_hampshire/forms
      forms.lp.findlaw.com/states/nh.html
SL: www.gencourt.state.nh.us/ns
SS: www.sos.nh.gov
WC: labor.state.nh.us

NEW JERSEY

AG: www.state.nj.us/lps
BA: www.findlaw.com/11stategov/nj/associations.html
CP: www.nj.gov/oag/ca/columns.htm
CS: www.judiciary.state.nj.us
GO: www.state.nj.us/governor
LF: www.attorneylocate.com/scripts/city.asp?
      city_statecode=NJ
      www.directory.findlaw.com/lawyer/servlet/
      SCityFirm?state=NJ
LL: www.njlawnet.com/lawlibs.html
LR: www.findlaw.com/11stategov/nj/index.html
      www.loc.gov/law/guide/us-nj.html
MV: www.state.nj.us/mvc
PR: www.publicrecordfinder.com/states/new_jersey.html
SF: www.alllaw.com/state_resources/new_jersey/forms
      forms.lp.findlaw.com/states/nj.html
SL: www.njleg.state.nj.us
SS: www.state.nj.us/state
WC: www.nj.gov/labor/wc/wcindex.html

NEW MEXICO

AG: www.ago.state.nm.us
BA: www.findlaw.com/11stategov/nm/associations.html
CP: www.ago.state.nm.us/protectcons/protectcons.htm
CS: www.nmcourts.com
GO: www.governor.state.nm.us
LF: www.attorneylocate.com/scripts/city.asp?city_
      statecode=NM
      www.directory.findlaw.com/lawyer/servlet/
      SCityFirm?state=NM
LL: www.fscll.org
LR: www.findlaw.com/11stategov/nm/index.html
      www.loc.gov/law/guide/us-nm.html
MV: www.state.nm.us/tax/mvd/mvd_home.htm
PR: www.publicrecordfinder.com/states/new_mexico.html
SF: www.alllaw.com/state_resources/new_mexico/forms
      forms.lp.findlaw.com/states/nm.html
SL: www.legis.state.nm.us
SS: www.sos.state.nm.us
WC: www.state.nm.us/wca

NEW YORK

AG: www.oag.state.ny.us
BA: www.findlaw.com/11stategov/ny/associations.html
CP: www.oag.state.ny.us/consumer/consumer_issues.html
CS: www.courts.state.ny.us
GO: www.state.ny.us/governor
LF: www.attorneylocate.com/scripts/city.asp?city_statecode=NY
      www.directory.findlaw.com/lawyer/servlet/
      SCityFirm?state=NY
LL: www.nycourts.gov/lawlibraries/courtlawlibraries.shtml
LR: www.findlaw.com/11stategov/ny/index.html
      www.loc.gov/law/guide/us-ny.html
MV: www.nydmv.state.ny.us
PR: www.publicrecordfinder.com/states/new_york.html
SF: www.alllaw.com/state_resources/new_york/forms
      forms.lp.findlaw.com/states/ny.html
SL: www.assembly.state.ny.us
      www.senate.state.ny.us
SS: www.dos.state.ny.us
WC: www.wcb.state.ny.us

NORTH CAROLINA

AG: www.ncdoj.com
BA: www.findlaw.com/11stategov/nc/associations.html
CP: www.ncdoj.com/consumerprotection/cp_about.jsp
CS: www.nccourts.org
GO: www.governor.state.nc.us
LF: www.attorneylocate.com/scripts/city.asp?city_statecode=NC
      www.directory.findlaw.com/lawyer/servlet/
      SCityFirm?state=NC
LL: www.aoc.state.nc.us/www/public/html/sc_library.htm
LR: www.findlaw.com/11stategov/nc/index.html
      www.loc.gov/law/guide/us-nc.html
MV: www.dmv.dot.state.nc.us
PR: www.publicrecordfinder.com/states/north_carolina.html
SF: www.alllaw.com/state_resources/north_carolina/forms
      forms.lp.findlaw.com/states/nc.html
SL: www.ncga.state.nc.us
SS: www.secstate.state.nc.us
WC: www.comp.state.nc.us

NORTH DAKOTA

AG: www.ag.state.nd.us
BA: www.findlaw.com/11stategov/nd/associations.html
CP: www.ag.state.nd.us/CPAT/CPAT.htm
CS: www.court.state.nd.us/court/courts.htm
GO: www.governor.state.nd.us
LF: www.attorneylocate.com/scripts/city.asp?city_statecode=ND
      www.directory.findlaw.com/lawyer/servlet/
      SCityFirm?state=ND
LL: http://www.court.state.nd.us/lawlib/www6.htm
LR: www.findlaw.com/11stategov/nd/index.html
      www.loc.gov/law/guide/us-nd.html
MV: www.dot.nd.gov
PR: www.publicrecordfinder.com/states/north_dakota.html
SF: www.alllaw.com/state_resources/north_dakota/forms
      forms.lp.findlaw.com/states/nd.html
SL: www.legis.nd.gov
SS: www.nd.gov/sos
WC: www.workforcesafety.com

OHIO

AG: www.ag.state.oh.us
BA: www.findlaw.com/11stategov/oh/associations.html

CP: www.ag.state.oh.us/citizen/consumer
CS: www.sconet.state.oh.us/Web_Sites/courts
GO: www.state.oh.us/gov
LF: www.attorneylocate.com/scripts/city.asp?
city_statecode=OH
www.directory.findlaw.com/lawyer/servlet/
SCityFirm?state=OH
LL: www.sconet.state.oh.us/lawlibrary
LR: www.findlaw.com/11stategov/oh/index.html
www.loc.gov/law/guide/us-oh.html
MV: http://www.bmv.ohio.gov/bmv.asp
PR: www.publicrecordfinder.com/states/ohio.html
SF: www.alllaw.com/state_resources/ohio/forms
www.uslegalforms.com/Ohio.htm
SL: www.legislature.state.oh.us
SS: www.state.oh.us/sos
WC: www.ohiobwc.com

OKLAHOMA

AG: www.oag.state.ok.us
BA: www.findlaw.com/11stategov/ok/associations.html
CP: www.oag.state.ok.us/oagweb.nsf/Consumer!OpenPage
CS: www.ok.gov/3167/3512/3168/3174
GO: www.governor.state.ok.us
LF: www.attorneylocate.com/scripts/city.asp?city_statecode=OK
www.directory.findlaw.com/lawyer/servlet/
SCityFirm?state=OK
LL: www.odl.state.ok.us/lawinfo
LR: www.findlaw.com/11stategov/ok/index.html
www.loc.gov/law/guide/us-ok.html
MV: www.dps.state.ok.us/dls
PR: www.publicrecordfinder.com/states/oklahoma.html
SF: www.alllaw.com/state_resources/oklahoma/forms
forms.lp.findlaw.com/states/ok.html
SL: www.lsb.state.ok.us
SS: www.sos.state.ok.us
WC: www.oklaosf.state.ok.us/~okdol/workcomp/index.htm

OREGON

AG: www.doj.state.or.us
BA: www.findlaw.com/11stategov/or/associations.html
CP: www.doj.state.or.us/finfraud
CS: www.ojd.state.or.us
GO: www.governor.state.or.us
LF: www.attorneylocate.com/scripts/city.asp?city_statecode=OR
www.directory.findlaw.com/lawyer/servlet/
SCityFirm?state=OR
LL: www.ojd.state.or.us/library
LR: www.findlaw.com/11stategov/or/index.html
www.loc.gov/law/guide/us-or.html
MV: www.oregon.gov/ODOT/DMV
PR: www.publicrecordfinder.com/states/oregon.html
SF: www.alllaw.com/state_resources/oregon/forms
www.stevensness.com
SL: www.leg.state.or.us
SS: www.sos.state.or.us
WC: www.cbs.state.or.us/wcd

PENNSYLVANIA

AG: www.attorneygeneral.gov
BA: www.findlaw.com/11stategov/pa/associations.html
CP: www.attorneygeneral.gov/complaints.aspx?id=451
CS: www.courts.state.pa.us
GO: www.governor.state.pa.us

LF: www.attorneylocate.com/scripts/city.asp?city_statecode=PA
www.directory.findlaw.com/lawyer/servlet/
SCityFirm?state=PA
LL: www.law.upenn.edu/bll
LR: www.findlaw.com/11stategov/pa/index.html
www.loc.gov/law/guide/us-pa.html
MV: www.dmv.state.pa.us
PR: www.publicrecordfinder.com/states/pennsylvania.html
SF: www.alllaw.com/state_resources/pennsylvania/forms
forms.lp.findlaw.com/states/pa.html
SL: www.legis.state.pa.us
SS: www.dos.state.pa.us
WC: www.dli.state.pa.us/landi/cwp/browse.asp?A=198

RHODE ISLAND

AG: www.riag.state.ri.us
BA: www.findlaw.com/11stategov/ri/associations.html
CP: www.riag.state.ri.us/civil/unit.php?name=consumer
CS: www.courts.state.ri.us
GO: www.governor.state.ri.us
LF: www.attorneylocate.com/scripts/city.asp?city_statecode=RI
www.directory.findlaw.com/lawyer/servlet/
SCityFirm?state=RI
LL: www.courts.state.ri.us/library/defaultlibrary.htm
LR: www.findlaw.com/11stategov/ri/index.html
www.loc.gov/law/guide/us-ri.html
MV: www.dmv.state.ri.us
PR: www.publicrecordfinder.com/states/rhode_island.html
SF: www.alllaw.com/state_resources/rhode_island/forms
forms.lp.findlaw.com/states/ri.html
SL: www.rilin.state.ri.us
SS: www.state.ri.us
WC: www.dlt.ri.gov/wc

SOUTH CAROLINA

AG: www.scattorneygeneral.org
BA: www.findlaw.com/11stategov/sc/associations.html
CP: www.scconsumer.gov
CS: www.judicial.state.sc.us
GO: www.scgovernor.com
LF: www.attorneylocate.com/scripts/city.asp?city_statecode=SC
www.directory.findlaw.com/lawyer/servlet/
SCityFirm?state=SC
LL: www.law.sc.edu/library
LR: www.findlaw.com/11stategov/sc/index.html
www.loc.gov/law/guide/us-sc.html
MV: www.scdmvonline.com/DMVNew/default.aspx
PR: www.publicrecordfinder.com/states/south_carolina.html
SF: www.alllaw.com/state_resources/south_carolina/forms
SL: www.scstatehouse.net
SS: www.scsos.com
WC: www.wcc.state.sc.us

SOUTH DAKOTA

AG: www.state.sd.us/attorney
BA: www.findlaw.com/11stategov/sd/associations.html
CP: www.state.sd.us/attorney/office/divisions/consumer
CS: www.sdjudicial.com
GO: www.state.sd.us/governor
LF: www.attorneylocate.com/scripts/city.asp?
city_statecode=SD
www.directory.findlaw.com/lawyer/servlet/
SCityFirm?state=SD
LL: www.usd.edu/lawlib

LR: www.findlaw.com/11stategov/sd/index.html
     www.loc.gov/law/guide/us-sd.html
MV: www.state.sd.us/drr2/motorvehicle
PR: www.publicrecordfinder.com/states/south_dakota.html
SF: www.alllaw.com/state_resources/south_dakota/forms
     www.findlegalforms.com/xcart/customer/sitemap.
     php?state=SD
SL: legis.state.sd.us
SS: www.sdsos.gov
WC: www.state.sd.us/dol/dlm/dlm-home.htm

TENNESSEE

AG: www.attorneygeneral.state.tn.us
BA: www.findlaw.com/11stategov/tn/associations.html
CP: www.attorneygeneral.state.tn.us/cpro/cpro.htm
CS: www.tsc.state.tn.us
GO: www.state.tn.us/governor
LF: www.attorneylocate.com/scripts/city.asp?city_statecode=TN
     www.directory.findlaw.com/lawyer/servlet/
     SCityFirm?state=TN
LL: www.tsc.state.tn.us/GENINFO/library/Libraries.htm
LR: www.findlaw.com/11stategov/tn/index.html
     www.loc.gov/law/guide/us-tn.html
MV: www.state.tn.us/safety
PR: www.publicrecordfinder.com/states/tennessee.html
SF: www.alllaw.com/state_resources/tennessee/forms
     forms.lp.findlaw.com/states/tn.html
SL: www.legislature.state.tn.us
SS: www.state.tn.us/sos
WC: www.state.tn.us/labor-wfd/wcomp.html

TEXAS

AG: www.oag.state.tx.us
BA: www.findlaw.com/11stategov/tx/associations.html
CP: www.oag.state.tx.us/consumer/consumer.shtml
CS: www.courts.state.tx.us
GO: www.governor.state.tx.us
LF: www.attorneylocate.com/scripts/city.asp?city_statecode=TX
     www.directory.findlaw.com/lawyer/servlet/
     SCityFirm?state=TX
LL: www.sll.state.tx.us
LR: www.findlaw.com/11stategov/tx/index.html
     www.loc.gov/law/guide/us-tx.html
     suefaw.home.texas.net/texas.html
MV: www.dot.state.tx.us
PR: www.publicrecordfinder.com/states/texas.html
SF: www.alllaw.com/state_resources/texas/forms
     forms.lp.findlaw.com/states/tx.html
SL: www.capitol.state.tx.us
SS: www.sos.state.tx.us
WC: www.tdi.state.tx.us/wc/indexwc.html

UTAH

AG: www.attygen.state.ut.us
BA: www.findlaw.com/11stategov/ut/associations.html
CP: www.attygen.state.ut.us/consumerassistance.html
CS: www.utcourts.gov
GO: www.governor.state.ut.us
LF: www.attorneylocate.com/scripts/city.asp?city_statecode=UT
     www.directory.findlaw.com/lawyer/servlet/
     SCityFirm?state=UT
LL: http://www.utcourts.gov/lawlibrary
LR: www.findlaw.com/11stategov/ut/index.html
     www.loc.gov/law/guide/us-ut.html

MV: dmv.utah.gov
PR: www.publicrecordfinder.com/states/utah.html
SF: www.alllaw.com/state_resources/utah/forms
     forms.lp.findlaw.com/states/ut.html
SL: www.le.state.ut.us
SS: www.mycorporation.com/secretary-state/utah.html
WC: laborcommission.utah.gov/indacc/indacc.htm

VERMONT

AG: www.state.vt.us/atg
BA: www.findlaw.com/11stategov/vt/associations.html
CP: www.atg.state.vt.us/display.php?smod=8
CS: www.vermontjudiciary.org
GO: www.vermont.gov/governor
LF: www.attorneylocate.com/scripts/city.asp?city_statecode=VT
     www.directory.findlaw.com/lawyer/servlet/
     SCityFirm?state=VT
LL: www.vermontlaw.edu/library/index.cfm
LR: www.findlaw.com/11stategov/vt/index.html
     www.loc.gov/law/guide/us-vt.html
MV: www.aot.state.vt.us/dmv/dmvhp.htm
PR: www.publicrecordfinder.com/states/vermont.html
SF: www.vermontjudiciary.org/attorneys
SL: www.leg.state.vt.us
SS: www.sec.state.vt.us
WC: www.labor.vermont.gov

VIRGINIA

AG: www.oag.state.va.us
BA: www.findlaw.com/11stategov/va/associations.html
CP: www.oag.state.va.us/CONSUMER
CS: www.courts.state.va.us
GO: www.governor.virginia.gov
LF: www.attorneylocate.com/scripts/city.asp?city_statecode=VA
     www.directory.findlaw.com/lawyer/servlet/
     SCityFirm?state=VA
LL: www.courts.state.va.us/library/library.htm
LR: www.loc.gov/law/guide/us-va.html
     www.findlaw.com/11stategov/va/index.html
MV: www.dmv.state.va.us
PR: www.publicrecordfinder.com/states/virginia.html
SF: www.alllaw.com/state_resources/virginia/forms
     forms.lp.findlaw.com/states/va.html
SL: legis.state.va.us
SS: www.soc.vipnet.org
WC: www.vwc.state.va.us

WASHINGTON

AG: www.atg.wa.gov
BA: www.findlaw.com/11stategov/wa/associations.html
CP: www.atg.wa.gov/SafeguardingConsumers/default.aspx
CS: www.courts.wa.gov
GO: www.governor.wa.gov
LF: www.directory.findlaw.com/lawyer/servlet/
     SCityFirm?state=WA
     www.attorneylocate.com/scripts/city.asp?city_statecode=WA
LL: www.courts.wa.gov/library
LR: www.loc.gov/law/guide/us-wa.html
     www.findlaw.com/11stategov/wa/index.html
MV: www.wa.gov/dol
PR: www.publicrecordfinder.com/states/washington.html
SF: www.alllaw.com/state_resources/washington/forms
     forms.lp.findlaw.com/states/wa.html
SL: http://www.leg.wa.gov/legislature

SS: www.secstate.wa.gov
WC: www.lni.wa.gov/ClaimsIns/default.asp

WEST VIRGINIA

AG: www.wvago.gov
BA: www.findlaw.com/11stategov/wv/associations.html
CP: www.wvago.gov/consumers.cfm
CS: www.state.wv.us/wvsca/wvsystem.htm
GO: www.wvgov.org
LF: www.directory.findlaw.com/lawyer/servlet/
      SCityFirm?state=WV
      www.attorneylocate.com/scripts/city.asp?city_statecode=WV
LL: www.state.wv.us/wvsca/library/menu.htm
LR: www.loc.gov/law/guide/us-wv.html
      www.findlaw.com/11stategov/wv/index.html
MV: www.wvdot.com/6_motorists/dmv/6G_DMV.HTM
PR: www.50states.com/publicrecords/westvirginia.htm
SF: www.alllaw.com/state_resources/west_virginia/forms
      forms.lp.findlaw.com/states/wv.html
SL: www.legis.state.wv.us
SS: www.wvsos.com
WC: www.state.wv.us/bep/WC

WISCONSIN

AG: www.doj.state.wi.us
BA: www.findlaw.com/11stategov/wi/associations.html
CP: www.doj.state.wi.us/dls/ConsProt/newcp.asp
CS: www.courts.state.wi.us
GO: www.wisgov.state.wi.us
LF: www.attorneylocate.com/scripts/city.asp?city_statecode=WI
      www.directory.findlaw.com/lawyer/servlet/
      SCityFirm?state=WI

LL: www.wsll.state.wi.us
LR: www.loc.gov/law/guide/us-wi.html
      www.findlaw.com/11stategov/wi/index.html
MV: www.dot.wisconsin.gov/drivers
PR: www.publicrecordfinder.com/states/wisconsin.html
SF: www.alllaw.com/state_resources/wisconsin/forms
      forms.lp.findlaw.com/states/wi.html
      www.wisbar.org/AM/Template.cfm?Section=Forms2
SL: www.legis.state.wi.us
SS: www.sos.state.wi.us
WC: www.dwd.state.wi.us/wc/default.htm

WYOMING

AG: attorneygeneral.state.wy.us
BA: www.romingerlegal.com/statebars/wyoming.html
      www.findlaw.com/11stategov/wy/associations.html
CP: attorneygeneral.state.wy.us/consumer.htm
CS: www.courts.state.wy.us
GO: governor.wy.gov/governor_home.asp
LF: www.directory.findlaw.com/lawyer/servlet/
      SCityFirm?state=WY
      www.attorneylocate.com/scripts/city.asp?city_statecode=WY
LL: courts.state.wy.us/LawLibrary
LR: www.loc.gov/law/guide/us-wy.html
      www.findlaw.com/11stategov/wy/index.html
MV: www.dot.state.wy.us
PR: www.50states.com/publicrecords/wyoming.htm
SF: www.alllaw.com/state_resources/wyoming/forms
      www.megalaw.com/forms/wy/wyforms.php
SL: legisweb.state.wy.us
SS: soswy.state.wy.us
WC: wydoe.state.wy.us/doe.asp?ID=9

Starting a Freelance Paralegal Business

INTRODUCTION

Sometime during their career, most paralegals wonder what it would be like to own their own business and be their own boss as a freelance paralegal.

There are two major kinds of businesses that paralegals have formed:

1. A business that offers legal and law-related services directly to the public without attorney supervision. The service providers are independent contractors who are sometimes called *freelance paralegals, independent paralegals, or legal technicians*. (In California, however, they have titles such as *legal document assistant* because only individuals who work under attorney supervision can be called paralegals or legal assistants. In Arizona, they must use the title *legal document preparer*. See chapter 4.)
2. A business that offers services to attorneys. The service providers are independent contractors who are sometimes called *freelance paralegals, independent paralegals, or contract paralegals*. They perform their services under attorney supervision even though they are not employees of attorneys.

Our focus in this appendix is primarily on the freelance paralegal who offers services to attorneys, although much of what is said will apply as well to the first category of business. (See also chapter 4 for a discussion of the legal issues involved when nonattorneys sell services directly to the public.)

Running your own business is a major undertaking. Veteran freelance paralegals frequently comment on the time commitment that they must make. "You need to understand that you'll never work harder than when you own your own business."[1] If you become successful, nine-to-five work days will probably be rare. "There are no 'normal' work hours," reports a freelance paralegal in California who once had an attorney client show up on Sunday, December 24, 2000, "with paperwork that had to be prepared before the rules changed on January 1, 2001."[2] Another freelancer cautions that you need to subscribe to the "old adage that you work 80 hours a week just so you don't have to work 40 hours a week for someone else."[3]

Yet the rewards of success in this endeavor can be substantial. In an article called *Following My Dream*, a freelance paralegal exclaimed, upon receiving her first check as a freelance paralegal, "I thought I had died and gone to entrepreneurial paralegal heaven."[4]

SHOULD I DO IT?

Is owning a freelance business a realistic option for you? Should you do it? Not many paralegals are in business as freelance paralegals. Surveys show that they constitute between 1 and 2 percent of paralegals in the state,[5] although the percentage who have tried to start such a business without success is higher. The two most important questions you need to ask yourself when deciding whether to start your own freelance business are as follows: Do you have the expertise that attorneys want? Can you survive without a steady cash flow during your first year in business?

Expertise

Attorneys expect you to be an expert in what they are asking you to do. They will take the time to tell you what they want done; *they will almost never take the time to explain to you how to do it*. You are expected to know. Consequently, the vast majority of successful freelance paralegals do not go into business until they have had years of experience, primarily as traditional paralegals employed by attorneys. Here are some examples of tasks commonly performed by freelance paralegals that you will need to know how to do *before* anyone is likely to hire you to perform them:

- Digest the transcript of depositions or other litigation documents
- Collect and digest medical records
- Prepare the 706 federal estate tax return and other applicable federal and estate returns
- Prepare all the documents needed to probate an estate
- Prepare trial exhibits
- Incorporate a business
- Conduct an asset search and other public record searches
- Conduct a due-diligence search
- Compile a chain of title to real property
- Prepare and file trademark and patent applications

Whether you are able to perform any of these tasks will, of course, depend on what specialties you developed while you were an employed paralegal. There are some freelance assignments that do not require great skill. For example:

- Bates stamp litigation documents
- Encode litigation documents in a computer database
- Complete service of process
- File pleadings in court

Yet these assignments usually pay the least, and there may not be enough of them to keep a full-time business running. You need to be able to offer *specialized* skills. If the tasks to be done did not require such skills, the attorney would not need a competent paralegal. A temporary secretary would be sufficient for most of them.

Cash Flow

If you need the security of a steady flow of income every week or month, it is too soon to start your freelance business. You need to have a cash reserve that will keep you in minimum survival mode until you find out whether your business will work. How long will it take to find this out? Although circumstances will differ from person to person, as a rule of thumb, you should have enough savings to sustain your personal life and your new business for six months to a year.

The cash flow problem is not simply due to the fact that it will take time to develop attorney clients for your business. Payment delays also cause cash flow headaches. A freelance paralegal may not be paid immediately upon completing an assignment. Law firms have their own cash flow problems. An attorney might take the position that the freelance paralegal will be paid when the attorney is paid. In some cases, the attorney must wait months for payment. This, of course, can place great strains on the finances of a paralegal's business. (On one of the paralegal listservs discussed later, a freelance paralegal sent out the following call for help: "As a freelance paralegal, I find it very difficult to receive payment in a timely manner from attorneys. My terms are net/15; however, some payments are not received for 30–60 days after the due date. Anyone have any collection tips?") You need to know at the outset whether you may have to wait an extended period to be paid. If a special payment arrangement cannot be established with the attorney on such a case (e.g., a monthly payment schedule), you may have to decline the work. Many freelance paralegals require monthly payment in the agreement they sign with their attorney clients. (See the discussion of agreements below.) This, however, does not always eliminate the cash flow problem.

BEGIN MODESTLY

Given these economic realities, you are strongly advised to begin modestly. Do not give up your day job too soon. Consider starting on a part-time basis. Find out if your current employer would have any objections to your taking some freelance cases from other law firms in the evening, on the weekend, or during your vacation. Your employer needs to know if you are working on freelance cases because of the conflict of interest issues to be discussed later.

Keep your overhead low. Work out of your home if possible. The expenses of renting an office and paying a new set of utility bills can be substantial. At a minimum, you will need:

- A phone line dedicated to your business
- An answering machine
- E-mail communication
- A Web site that describes your services
- A computer, word processing software such as Word, and a printer
- A basic accounting program such as Quicken
- A fax machine
- Business cards
- A flyer or brochure that lists your services

If you need a copier, start by purchasing one of the smaller ones without the expensive bells and whistles. Find out if your Internet service provider will allow you to set up a Web site at little or no additional charge. Many freelance paralegals, however, say their Internet site is not very useful for generating business, although they like to have it in order to project a professional image.

Do not hire employees at the outset. You will have enough to do in getting your business off the ground and in sorting out the myriad of problems that you have probably never faced before. Even if you have enough work to justify bringing on help, it would be unwise to do so until you feel confident that the business is running smoothly. Obtaining good help is not always easy. You will have to supervise anyone who joins your staff. Too often the time required to train and monitor a new person outweighs the benefit that person provides as an assistant. Hence you need to choose carefully. Consider these options when you are ready for help:

- Contact area paralegal schools to find out if they would be interested in having any of their students intern at your office. If you are unable to pay an intern, ask the school if an unpaid internship is possible.
- If you can pay someone, consider offering part-time employment at the outset. This will give you an opportunity to assess the person's competence and the extent to which your personalities match. Terminating a full-time employee can be a wrenching experience.

LEGALITIES

You need to know the rules and regulations that govern businesses in your state. In Google or another search engine, run a search that contains the phrase "starting a small business" plus the name of your state. Examples:

"starting a small business" California
"starting a small business" Pennsylvania

In addition, consult the information available from the Small Business Administration (*www.sba.gov*), Counselors to America's Small Business (*www.score.org*), and your local chamber of commerce. Organizations such as these can often send you a packet or kit on starting a new business or can tell you where you can obtain one, often at no cost. The organizations can also give you guidance on writing a business plan. Specialty groups in the area (e.g., professional women's groups, minority rights associations) may also be able to give you leads to available assistance for new businesses.

If you are starting out on your own, you will probably operate your business as a sole proprietorship, the simplest kind of business entity. In a sole proprietorship, one person owns all of the assets of the business and assumes all of its debts or liabilities. As a sole proprietor, you cannot separate your business debts from your personal debts. If you default on your business debts, your creditors can reach your personal assets (e.g., a car). Similarly, your business assets (e.g., a computer) can be reached to satisfy your personal debts. Other business formats exist such as the corporation, partnership, and limited liability company. Although you should find out what the requirements, advantages, and disadvantages are for these other formats in your state, the simpler sole-proprietorship format will usually be sufficient to start a modest, one-person freelance business.

If you operate as a sole proprietorship and conduct a business under a name that does not include your surname, you may need to register your assumed or fictitious name with the state.[6]

One of your first steps should be to go to the phone book and look up the names and numbers of the agencies in your state, county, and city that have jurisdiction over businesses. They might be called the Department of Economic Development, Bureau of Licenses, Secretary of State, etc. You want to obtain information on starting a business. For example:

- Do you need a business license from the local or state government? From both?
- As a business, what reporting requirements do you have?
- Can you operate your business out of your home? Are there any zoning restrictions on such businesses?

Almost all governments have agencies that provide literature on the legal requirements for operating a business. The literature may also give you suggestions on the different kinds of business formats you can choose. Most of these agencies have Internet sites that provide the same information.

Also contact the tax departments of the federal, state, and local governments. You want to know what kind of tax returns you will have to file for your business. Don't wait until the end of the year (or until April) to find out. As a sole proprietorship, for example, you will probably report your income on Schedule C of your federal return. As a self-employed individual, you must make estimated tax payments every three months. Substantial social security taxes will have to be paid on your self-employment income. You may also have to pay personal property taxes on your business property. Obtain all the necessary forms and instructions well before filing time. Hiring a tax accountant to do your returns can be expensive. Even if you eventually use an accountant or other tax preparer, the best way to work intelligently with him or her is to know how to do the returns yourself.

The Internal Revenue Service (IRS) has pamphlets on tax obligations and record keeping for small businesses. They are also available on its Internet site (*www.irs.gov*). Find out if your state and local tax authorities have similar material available on the Internet and/or that can be snail-mailed to you.

One of the tax issues faced by attorneys is whether they are trying to avoid paying employment taxes by using freelance paralegals who are not really independent contractors. The IRS may consider you to be an employee even if you have your own business license, have a home office, and are not on anyone's payroll. The test is not what your title is. The more control the attorney has over the "manner and means" of the work assigned to you, the greater the likelihood that the IRS will treat you as an employee. The IRS uses 20 factors to decide whether someone is an employee as opposed to an independent contractor. For more on this issue, type *independent contractor* in the search feature at *www.irs.gov*. Also call the IRS 800 number (see the federal government pages in your local phone book) and ask for publications on independent contractors such as Publication 15-A.

INSURANCE

Ask every attorney for whom you work whether you are covered by the firm's malpractice liability insurance policy. These policies usually cover independent contractors the attorney hires such as freelance paralegals, but you should check. Because these policies often provide such coverage, not many freelance paralegals have purchased their own policy.

If you work out of your home, you may have a homeowners policy that covers fire, theft, and liability arising out of the property. Although such insurance will not cover malpractice liability, you need to know to what extent it does cover your business. For example, if any of your business equipment is stolen, is it covered? Do you need to tell your insurance carrier what equipment you have? How is portable equipment covered, e.g., a laptop computer that you take with you wherever you go? Does the policy cover the lawsuit that is brought against you because your dog bites the crosstown delivery person who comes to your home to deliver a deposition you will be digesting?

MARKETING

How do you market yourself? Where do you find attorney clients who will hire you? The most important initial source of clients will be the network of attorneys that you developed while you worked as a traditional paralegal. When you decide to leave your current employment, one of the first questions you should ask your employer is:

After I leave, would you be interested in having me do some work for you on a freelance basis?

Many attorneys will see the advantages of such an arrangement. It lowers their overhead costs such as paying full-time salaries and benefits. They also avoid paying employment taxes (unless, as indicated, the IRS concludes that the freelancer is really still an employee). Furthermore, under a freelance arrangement, the attorneys are able to continue to work with someone who has proven his or her competence—you. Once this new arrangement proves to be successful, the attorney will often help you find additional attorney clients in the area's legal community. As mentioned earlier, you should explore the possibility of taking some freelance assignments from other law firms on your own time with the knowledge and cooperation of your employer. You want to try to line up as many attorney clients as possible before you quit your current job.

Find out if your state or local bar association allows paralegals to become associate or affiliate members. If so, join. Even if such membership is not allowed, you may be able to attend continuing legal education (CLE) sessions of the bar in the areas of your specialty. You want to meet as many attorneys as possible who might be interested in the kind of services you offer. Don't be shy. Walk up to attorneys at these sessions, introduce yourself, and hand them your card or a flyer that lists your services. Extensive networking at such functions is a must.

Some paralegals place brief ads in the magazine or newsletter that the bar association sends to all its members. The cost of such an ad, however, may be prohibitive. Furthermore, ads may not be as effective a marketing tool as the networking you do on your own and the referrals obtained from the attorneys with whom you have worked.

When you meet with new attorneys who want to know more about your services, be prepared to show them (1) samples of the kind of work you can do, e.g., the first page of a deposition digest, and (2) a list of references. Have a portfolio of samples readily available. If any of your writing samples come from a real client document, be sure that actual names and other identifying information are blocked out to preserve confidentiality. The list of references should consist primarily of your present and prior attorney clients who have told you that you can list them as references.

Develop a network among fellow freelance paralegals in the state. They can be a source of mutual referrals. A freelance paralegal may be willing to refer an attorney client to you because of a busy schedule, a conflict of interest, or a lack of expertise in the work sought by the client. You, of course, must be willing to make similar referrals. Where can you meet other freelance paralegals? Find out if there are any Web sites in your state. In Google or another search engine, run a search that contains the phrase "freelance paralegal" and the name of your state. Examples:

"freelance paralegal" Massachusetts
"freelance paralegal" New Mexico

Also check if there is a freelance section of your paralegal association. If one does not exist, organize one. Whenever you are in the company of paralegals, ask them if they know of any freelance paralegals in the area. With persistence, you'll soon know the names of most of them. Some may be reluctant to talk with you because you might be viewed as a competitive threat. If, however, your willingness to share what you know becomes clear, many fellow freelance paralegals will be receptive to the idea of helping to create a mutual support network.

Some paralegal associations have placement services that allow freelance members to list their availability for hire. Find out if your association has such a service. Also, join paralegal listservs. Freelance paralegals are often members of such listservs. You can direct questions to them. For example, on one listserv, someone could post the following question: "I'm trying to start a freelance business and want to write a promotional brochure to give out to attorneys. Have any of you had any luck with such brochures? I'd appreciate any suggestions." As a result of this e-mail message, scores of responses might materialize from all over the country. You will also occasionally see messages posted such as the following: "Anyone know a good freelancer in Springfield who can track down some real property records for us at the county courthouse? If so, please contact me ASAP." A number of paralegal listservs exist. For example, check the e-mail lists sponsored by *Legal Assistant Today* (www.legalassistanttoday.com). Other options include searching for "freelance paralegal" at the following sites:

- www.groups.yahoo.com
- www.groups.google.com

FEES

How much should you charge attorneys for your services? Experienced paralegals determine their fees primarily on the basis of the complexity of the task and their own experience. Most bill by the hour, although a flat fee may be charged for some tasks, particularly those that can be completed within a predictable amount of time, e.g., filing papers in court. You need to find out what the market will bear. What is the competition charging? Do any of the freelance paralegals in your area have billing rate sheets that you can examine? Freelancers sometimes send fliers to attorneys advertising their services. Ask your attorney contacts if they have any in their files that you could examine. Some freelance paralegals charge two-thirds of the hourly rate that attorneys charge their clients for the time of their traditional paralegals.[7] Others try to charge one-half of the attorney's hourly rate.

Out-of-pocket expenses are usually paid in addition to hourly or flat fees. For example, if a freelance paralegal is asked to use an overnight shipping service or to take a cab to file a pleading in court, the costs of doing so should be separately charged to the attorney. Long-distance calls are also normal cost items. This needs to be made clear in the freelancer's agreement with the attorney.

The agreement that both the freelance paralegal and the attorney sign should state:

- The tasks to be performed
- Due dates
- Fees and costs to be paid
- Time of payment

In your networking contacts with fellow freelance paralegals, find out if any standard service contracts are in use. If they are, you should consider adapting them to your own needs.

ETHICS

A freelance paralegal has the same ethical responsibilities as a traditional paralegal. Phrased another way, attorneys have the same ethical responsibilities working with freelance paralegals as they do working with their salaried paralegal employees.

The ethical duty of supervision is particularly important. An attorney must supervise the paralegal—traditional or freelance. This is not always easy, particularly in a busy office. Some attorneys do an inadequate job of supervising the paralegal employees they work with in the office every day. Supervising freelance paralegals who may work at their own office or at home can be an even greater challenge. At one time, New Jersey considered making it unethical for attorneys to use freelance paralegals because of the great difficulty of supervising them from a distance. Although the New Jersey Supreme Court eventually rejected this extreme position, the court did caution attorneys that extra care was needed to fulfill their duty of supervising paralegals who do not work in the same office.[8]

Busy attorneys who have great confidence in the ability of freelance paralegals are likely to give them minimal supervision. Of course, you can't control the conduct of the attorneys who hire you. Yet, to protect yourself, you need to reinforce the importance of supervision whenever you can. Some freelance paralegals insert a clause in their agreement for hire stating that the attorney will provide adequate supervision on all assignments. (Such a clause is not legally significant; the attorney has the supervision duty even in the absence of such a clause. Yet the clause helps get across the message that you consider such supervision to be critical.) Ask for feedback as often as possible. "Have you looked at the deposition digest I prepared?" "What did you think of the complaint I drafted for you?" "I want to keep improving my skills, so I hope you'll let me know how it could have been better." Focusing on your need for feedback will probably be more productive than pointing out the attorney's ethical duty to supervise you.

Be careful about the unauthorized practice of law (UPL). Friends, relatives, clients, and strangers *regularly* ask freelance paralegals for legal advice or other help that only an attorney can provide. You may find it awkward to refuse their requests, particularly if you are an expert in the area of their need. Yet you must refuse. Your integrity and professionalism are on the line. If you have a list of attorneys that you feel comfortable recommending, have their phone numbers readily available to give out. If you do not have such a list, memorize the phone number of the local bar association's lawyer referral service so that you can give it to the large number of people who will be asking you questions that should be directed to attorneys.

Disclose your status. Busy freelance paralegals often have contact with many people. You may think that someone you meet for the first or second time already knows you are not an attorney. Avoid making this assumption. Let everyone know that you are not an attorney. A clear communication might be as follows: "I am a paralegal. I am not an attorney, but I work under the supervision of one."

Preserve client confidentiality. Treat everything you learn about an attorney's client the same way you would treat personal information about yourself that you do not want anyone to know. If you travel from office to office, be scrupulous about not letting strangers see your files, including the names of the parties on the front cover of any of the files. Carelessness in this area not only is an ethical violation but also can lead to a waiver of the attorney-client privilege. What a paralegal learns about a client may be covered by the attorney-client privilege. If, however, the information protected by the privilege is disclosed or inadvertently revealed, the privilege may be lost.

Avoid conflicts of interest. Freelance paralegals who work for more than one attorney run the risk of creating a disqualifying conflict of interest. Attorney X, for example, may hire you for a project on a client's case without knowing that you now work or once worked on the case of Attorney Y's client whose interests are adverse to Attorney X's client. To avoid a conflict of interest:

- Keep a *Career Client List* of parties and attorneys involved in all your present and prior paralegal work; for every case on which you have worked, the list should contain the names of the parties and attorneys for both sides, what you did on the case, and the dates of your involvement.
- Before you take a new assignment, ask for the names of the parties on both sides and all of their attorneys.
- Be ready to refuse to take the assignment if you once worked in opposition to the party you are now being asked to help or if you once worked for the party on the other side, even if it was on a different case.
- Allow the attorney hiring you to see your list of parties and attorneys so that he or she can make an informed decision on whether hiring you might create a conflict of interest.

For an example of a Career Client List that you can use, see Exhibit 5.8 in chapter 5.

Also let the attorney know of any personal connection you might have to the case, e.g., your brother works or once worked for the opponent of a current client or you recently bought stock in the company of a client. Let the attorney decide whether these personal facts raise conflicts issues.

KEEPING CURRENT

You need to maintain your expertise. The main vehicle for doing so is continuing legal education (CLE). Often, CLE sessions will discuss the latest cases, statutes, and regulations that you need to know about in your specialty. In the middle of an assignment, a freelance paralegal never wants to have to say, "I didn't know the law changed on that." To maintain your expertise:

- Attend CLE sponsored by paralegal associations.
- Attend CLE sponsored by bar associations.
- Join the specialty section of your paralegal association; if one does not exist in your area of expertise, organize one.
- Take advanced courses offered by area paralegal schools.
- Read (and consider subscribing to) specialty magazines and other periodicals in your area of expertise.

RESOURCES

Articles and Books

- Katrina Bakke, *Freelance/Contract Paralegals: How Can They Help?* (At the Washington State bar site (www.wsba.org), type "freelance" in the search box.)
- Cathy Heath, *Paralegal Services: How to Manage Your Own Firm* (Rimrock, 2000)
- Dorothy Secol, *Starting and Managing Your Own Business: A Freelancing Guide for Paralegals* (Aspen, 1997)
- Victoria Ring, *How to Start a Bankruptcy Forms Processing Service* 2d ed. (Graphico, 2004) (www.bankruptcybook.net)
- Miscellaneous Articles on Freelancing (www.paralegalgateway.com/tempwork.html)

HELPFUL WEB SITES ON FREELANCE PARALEGALS

American Freelance Paralegal Association
www.freelanceparalegal.org

National Association of Freelance Legal Professionals
freelancelegalprofessionals.blogspot.com

Counselors to America's Small Business
www.score.org

Independent Contractor Resource
www.guru.com

Entrepreneur
entrepreneur.com

Internal Revenue Service
www.irs.gov

National Association for the Self-Employed
www.nase.org

Colorado Freelance Paralegal Network
www.paralegalsfreelance.com

Freelancers on the Internet
www.paralegalserv.com (see Exhibit 2.2 in chapter 2)
www.paralegalpartners.com
www.google.com (search for "paralegal services" and "freelance paralegal")

Virtual Assistants
www.abanet.org/lpm/lpt/articles/mgt04062.shtml
virtualassistants.com
www.ivaa.org

Legal Document Assistants
www.calda.org
www.aldap.com
www.naldp.org
www.azaip.com
en.wikipedia.org/wiki/legal_document_assistant

ENDNOTES

1. Cathy Heath, *Paralegal Services: How to Manage Your Own Firm*, vii (Rimrock, 2000) (www.rimrockpublishing.com).
2. *They Do It Their Way*, 15 National Paralegal Reporter 32 (April/May 2001).
3. Chere Estrin, *When to Say "No (Thank You)" to Your Dream Job*, Recap 12 (California Alliance of Paralegal Associations, Spring 1999).
4. Lee Davis, *Following My Dream*, 25 National Paralegal Reporter 5 (April/May 2001).
5. See, for example, the *2000 Michigan Legal Assistant Survey* (www2.oakland.edu/contin-ed/legalassistant/2000survey.htm).
6. Mary Willard, *Is It Time to Freelance?*, 28 Facts & Findings 18, 20 (National Association of Legal Assistants, May 2001).
7. Mary Uriko, *Freelancing 101*, 18 Legal Assistant Today 83, 84 (September/October 2000).
8. See *In re Opinion No. 26 of Committee on Unauthorized Practice of Law*, 654 A.2d 1344 (N.J. 1995), and *In re Opinion 24 on Unauthorized Practice of Law*, 607 A.2d 962 (N.J. 1992).

"Paralegal Day"

In many states, governors and mayors have issued proclamations that set aside a particular day or week to honor paralegals. Here are two examples:

GOVERNOR ARNOLD SCHWARZENEGGER

June 24, 2005

California Alliance of Paralegal Associations

On behalf of all Californians, I am pleased to extend warm greetings as you celebrate California Paralegal Day.

In our judicial system, paralegals play an important role in fulfilling crucial research and administrative duties. They serve as liaisons between lawyers and their clients, and perform essential functions in many legal proceedings such as bankruptcy, foreclosures, estate planning, and business and family law.

I commend you for your efforts to acknowledge and celebrate paralegals' contributions to the legal profession in California. I offer my congratulations to the CAPA for your support and recognition of these distinguished professionals.

Please accept my best wishes for every future success.

Sincerely,

Arnold Schwarzenegger

STATE CAPITOL • SACRAMENTO, CALIFORNIA 95814 • (916) 445-2841

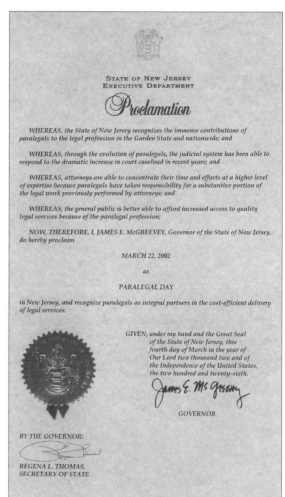

Source: www.sbparalegals.org/pdf/hpsc78.pdf

News Stories, War Stories, and Parting Shots

LEGAL ASSISTANT ELECTED PROBATE JUDGE

In November 1987, Arleen G. Keegan, a legal assistant, was elected probate judge in the town of Litchfield, Connecticut. A law degree is not required to be a probate judge in Connecticut. Judge Keegan handles a wide variety of cases. In one case, for example, family members argued that their mother was incompetent when she prepared her will. "It was a tough decision because I had to get in the middle of a situation with family members pulling against a close friend of the decedent." "I get to deal with a lot of people, and I find people totally intriguing." Howard, *A Legal Assistant Is Elected Probate Judge*, 5 Legal Assistant Today 32 (March/April 1988).

Probate Judge (and former legal assistant) Arleen Keegan, at the courthouse in Litchfield, Connecticut.

PARALEGAL ARGUES BEFORE THE FLORIDA SUPREME COURT

Karen McLead is a prominent paralegal in Florida. When the Florida Supreme Court considered proposals to amend ethical rules governing attorneys and paralegals, Karen was invited to express her opinion of the proposals before the full bench of the Supreme Court. The proposed amendments placed limitations on who could be called a paralegal in Florida. Karen opposed the amendments because they were unduly restrictive. See photos of Karen on page 824. The court adopted the amendments. See Florida in appendix E.

PARALEGAL APPOINTED CHAIRMAN OF BAR ASSOCIATION COMMITTEE

The Colorado Bar Association has appointed Joanna Hughbanks "to serve as chairman of the Legal Assistants Committee of the Colorado Bar Association." Ms. Hughbanks is an independent paralegal in Denver. She is believed to be the first nonattorney to chair a standing committee of a bar association. Letter from Christopher R. Brauchi, President of the Colorado Bar Association, to Joanna Hughbanks, June 27, 1989. As more and more bar associations allow paralegals to become associate or affiliate members (see chapter 4), leadership roles for paralegals on bar committees are becoming increasingly common. A recent dramatic example is paralegal Karen McLead, who served in the sensitive and high-profile position of chair of the Florida Bar's Unlicensed Practice of Law Committee between 1998 and 2000. Mary Micheletti, *Karen McLead Serving with Distinction*, 17 Legal Assistant Today 52 (September/October 1999).

PARALEGAL APPOINTED BANKRUPTCY TRUSTEE

A Fort Worth paralegal, Twalla Dupriest, was appointed by the Bankruptcy Court as trustee for the estate of T. Cullen Davis, who was one of the wealthiest men in the United States. Twalla was responsible for gathering all of Davis's assets for the purpose of repaying creditors and presided at the meetings of creditors. *Paralegal Appointed Trustee to Cullen Davis Estate*, Newsletter (Dallas Ass'n of Legal Assistants, September 1987).

NEW YORK PARALEGALS ON 9/11

Oliver Gierke, a Wall Street paralegal, remembers talking with a secretary when they both noticed paper flying around outside, some of it burned. Kristan Exner was in her law firm on the fiftieth floor of the North Tower when the planes struck. As she walked down the stairs to safety, she "passed countless firefighters climbing toward the fire." She remembers one fireman in particular about her age (twenty-two) pausing to rest. He looked terrified. "Of all the memories I have, that one stands out the most." R. Hughes, *Five Years Later*, 24 Legal Assistant Today 66, 67 (September/October 2006).

PARALEGAL RUNS FOR THE LEGISLATURE

Rosemary Mulligan, an Illinois paralegal, ran for a seat in the Illinois House of Representatives in 1990 against an incumbent. The election was held in a district in a suburb of Chicago. The vote was so close that it was declared a tie. By law, such elections are

Paralegal Karen McLead argues before the Supreme Court of Florida in opposition to proposed amendments that would restrict who can be called a paralegal in Florida.

decided by lottery—a toss of the coin. Although the paralegal won the toss, a court later declared her opponent the victor after reviewing some disputed ballots. *Toss of Coin to Decide Race in Illinois*, New York Times, July 18, 1990, at A12. In 1992, Ms. Mulligan ran again, and this time she won outright. Prior to her election she was a paralegal with a specialty in municipal land development and family law (*www.repmulligan.org/biography.html*).

PARALEGAL CHARGED WITH INSIDER TRADING

A twenty-four-year-old paralegal was charged with insider trading by the Securities and Exchange Commission. The complaint against the paralegal alleged that she had access to confidential information pertaining to the proposed merger of a client of the firm where she worked. She "tipped" her friends by giving them confidential information. The friends then used this information to earn $823,471 through the purchase of 65,020 shares. A civil complaint sought damages of $3.29 million. The paralegal was fired by the law firm. *Securities and Exchange Commission v. Hurton*, 43 S.E.C. Docket 1422, 1989 WL 991581 (May 16, 1989).

A $90,000,000 MISTAKE!

A paralegal for Prudential Insurance Company inadvertently left off the last three zeros on a mortgage used to secure a $92,885,000 loan made by Prudential to a company that is now bankrupt. As a result of the mistake, Prudential was left with only a $92,885 lien. Prudential's attorneys have asked the U.S. Bankruptcy Court in New York City to ignore the mistake—and restore the zeros. *17 At Issue* (San Francisco Legal Assistants Ass'n, Dec. 1990).

PARALEGAL CONVICTED

Mershan Shaddy was an independent paralegal in San Diego. He charged clients $180 to handle uncontested divorces, plus $50 if property had to be divided, and $30 for each child. He was arrested after an undercover investigator posed as a divorce client and secretly recorded him giving legal advice in violation of the California law against the unauthorized practice of law. He was convicted and sentenced to forty-five days in jail. *Paralegal's Role in Legal System Stirs a Debate*, San Diego Union, March 29, 1990, at B-1.

BILLIONAIRE PARALEGAL PREFERS PRISON TO FILLING OUT TIME SHEETS

Michael Milken, the billionaire "junk bond king," went to prison for illegal activities stemming from his Wall Street career. While still under the jurisdiction of federal prison and parole authorities,

Milken worked as a "paralegal" in a law firm. He did not enjoy the experience. Comparing prison to the law firm, he told reporters that he would rather have other people keep track of his time than to have to "fill out those . . . time sheets every day." *News across the Country*, KLAS Action (Kansas Legal Assistants Society, December/January 1994).

DID THE PARALEGAL WORK 43 HOURS ON JANUARY 10?

Hotel magnate Leona Helmsley (infamous for her wealth and her comment that "only little people pay taxes") sued a New York law firm for $35 million because she claimed they submitted fraudulent bills for fees and expenses. Among the allegedly fraudulent items cited in the suit was a bill for forty-three hours of work charged by a paralegal for one day—January 10. Andrew Blum, *The Empress Strikes Back*, The National Law Journal, July 11, 1994, at A6.

DON'T BE PHOTOGRAPHED IN THAT T-SHIRT

An insurance company challenged a bill for attorney and paralegal time submitted by the Los Angeles law firm of Latham & Watkins. During a court proceeding on the dispute, the company embarrassed the firm by introducing into evidence a photograph of the paralegal working on the case while wearing a T-shirt that read "Born to Bill." *Take Note of This*, California Paralegal 9 (January/March 1992).

LAW FIRM SUES ITS FORMER PARALEGAL

Richard Trotter once worked as a paralegal for a Denver law firm. He wrote a book called *A Toothless Paper Tiger* about his experiences at the law firm. The book alleged that the firm improperly authorized him and other paralegals at the firm to perform the work of attorneys. The law firm sought an injunction to prevent the release of the book. Hicks, *Law Firm Fights Book by Former Employee*, National Law Journal, August 6, 1990, at 39.

PARALEGAL ORDERED TO PAY $925,000 IN ATTORNEY FEES

Los Angeles Superior Court Judge Arnold Gold dismissed the sexual harassment lawsuit brought by a paralegal, Elizabeth Saret-Cook, against her former law firm employer, Gilbert, Kelly, Crowley & Jannett. She alleged that she had been harassed after getting pregnant with the child of an attorney at the firm, Clifford Woosley. Calling her suit "frivolous" and "completely without merit," the judge ordered the paralegal to pay $925,000 in attorney fees to the law firm and to Woosley. This decision was affirmed on appeal. *Saret-Cook v. Gilbert, Kelly, Crowley & Jennett*, 88 Cal. Rptr. 2d 732 (Cal. App. 2d Dist. 1999). According to court documents, the law firm had earlier offered to settle the suit for $400,000, but Saret-Cook refused the offer. Rebecca Liss, *Paralegal Ordered to Pay Fees in Harassment Case*, Los Angeles Daily Journal, September 27, 1996, at 2.

HE'S NOT AN ATTORNEY?

"Brian T. Valery is our hero. He figured out a way to save $100K on a legal education—namely, by not getting one." While a paralegal at a New York City law firm, Valery told his superiors that he was going to night law school at Fordham. When he announced that he had graduated and passed the bar, no one had any reason to doubt him. The truth (that he never attended law school and never took the bar exam) was not discovered until two years later—while Valery was litigating a case in Connecticut! "This story simply proves," said a reporter for the *Washington Post*, "you often don't really need a law degree to provide decent legal services to a client." His legal career in ruins, Valery now faces perjury charges. (www.abovethelaw.com/2006/11/lawyer_paralegal_of_the_day_br_1.php) (www.law.com/jsp/article.jsp?id=1163757925037).

LAW FIRM SETTLES SUIT BROUGHT BY PARALEGALS

A class action was brought by paralegals and clerical workers who claimed that the Oakland firm where they worked failed to pay them overtime compensation. The case was eventually settled for $170,000, which was distributed among the paralegals and clerical workers. Ziegler, *Firm Settles Suit on Overtime for Paralegals*, San Francisco Banner Daily Journal, January 25, 1989.

"WILL THE LEGAL ASSISTANT PLEASE TELL THE COURT THE FACTS OF THE CASE?"

At a paralegal association meeting in Houston, Judge Lynn Hughes, a federal district court judge, drew a "big laugh" concerning an incident in her courtroom. During a hearing, she watched a "Big Gun" senior partner constantly turn to his associate for information on the facts of the case. This associate, in turn, would ask his legal assistant for this information. Finally, Judge Hughes asked the legal assistant to stand up and tell the court the facts of the case! *National News . . . Houston Legal Assistants Association*, 21 Outlook 5 (Illinois Paralegal Ass'n, Spring 1991).

"THEN YOU SHOULD HAVE USED A PARALEGAL!"

At oral argument before the U.S. Supreme Court in a case on paralegal fees, an attorney was interrupted by Justice Thurgood Marshall during the attorney's description of the custom of billing in New Orleans. In the following fascinating excerpt from the transcript of the oral argument, a clearly irritated Justice Marshall suggested that the attorney was unprepared because he did not have a paralegal working with him on the case:

JUSTICE MARSHALL:	Is all that in the record?
ATTORNEY:	I'm sorry . . .
JUSTICE MARSHALL:	Is that in the record?
ATTORNEY:	I'm not . . .
JUSTICE MARSHALL:	What you've just said, that the custom of billing and all in New Orleans, is that in the record?
ATTORNEY:	I think it is Justice Marshall.
JUSTICE MARSHALL:	You think? Didn't you try the case?
ATTORNEY:	I tried the case, but whether or not that particular item is in the record, it is certainly in the briefs, but . . .
JUSTICE MARSHALL:	Then you should have used a paralegal!

Official Transcript Proceedings before the Supreme Court of the United States, Arthur J. Blanchard, Petitioner v. James Bergerson, et al., Case 87–1485, at 25 (November 28, 1988).

THE PERFECT RECIPE

"To one paralegal, add a pound of variety, eight ounces of flexibility, four ounces of creativity, and a healthy sense of humor. The result? One cost-effective, efficient litigation paralegal." Vore, *A Litigation Recipe*, On Point (Nat'l Capital Area Paralegal Ass'n, November 1990).

PARALEGAL TRAPPED

A paralegal, on his way to an assignment on another floor, became trapped in an elevator just after getting on. Fellow employees gathered around the elevator door. The time-conscious paralegal called out from inside the elevator, "Is this billable or nonbillable time?" *A Lighter Note*, MALA Advance 15 (Summer 1989).

SUSPENSE NOVEL ABOUT A PARALEGAL BY A PARALEGAL

E. P. Dalton has published *Housebreaker*, a novel by David Linzee, who has worked as a litigation paralegal. It is about Megan Lofting. "Megan used to be a probate paralegal at a Connecticut law firm. She used to try hard never to do something wrong. But then she was unjustly fired. Now a big-time criminal is offering her a chance to make a fortune, and to strike back at the client who got her fired, and the lawyer—once her lover—who let it happen." *The First Suspense Novel Ever about a Paralegal . . . by a Former Paralegal*, 4 Viewpoint 10 (Massachusetts Paralegal Ass'n, July/August 1987).

THE COST OF WHAT?

Recently, a paralegal was given an unusual assignment by her supervising attorney. She was asked to determine how much it would cost to purchase a penguin! *How Much Does a Penguin Cost?* SJPA Reporter 3 (South Jersey Paralegal Ass'n September 1990).

PARALEGAL WATCHES EXORCISM

Kevin McKinley is a paralegal at a West Palm Beach law firm that represented a defendant in a murder case. While working on the case, Kevin found an urn in the room of the defendant where the latter allegedly practiced voodoo and black magic. The family of the defendant was concerned that if the urn was opened in the courtroom, the spirit within it would harm those attending the trial. Hence an exorcism was performed to remove the defendant's control over this spirit. Kevin's assignment was to be a witness at this exorcism. *Columbus Dispatch* (January 6, 1991).

THE PARALEGAL FLORAL STRATEGY

A litigation legal assistant was given the task of serving a subpoena on a defendant who was unlikely to open the door. She came up with a creative approach. On her way to the defendant's house, she stopped at a flower shop and picked up a plant. Upon her arrival, she rang the doorbell. The defendant looked out, saw a person with flowers, opened the door, and was presented with a plant . . . and a subpoena! Anderson, *In the Line of Duty*, MALA Advance 17 (Minnesota Ass'n of Legal Assistants, Spring 1991).

WANTED: ADVENTUROUS PARALEGAL 107 POUNDS OR UNDER

The following want ad appeared in the classified section of a San Francisco legal newspaper. "ADVENTUROUS PARALEGAL. Travel in pvt. aircraft around the country up to 3 wks/mo. investigating franchise cases. Duties incl: client interviews, lgl research & witness invest. Your weight max: 107 lbs. (flight requirement)." *Daily Journal Classifieds*, The Daily Journal, May 17, 1993, at 18.

URBAN LEGEND: A PARALEGAL'S SUSHI MEMO

In 2003, a paralegal made the front page of the *New York Times*. The story was about a memo that the paralegal had written about sushi restaurants in the Manhattan area of the law firm. The memo was three pages long, and replete with exhibits and footnotes. Is this what happens, the *Times* story suggested, when you ask a simple question ("Where's a good place for sushi?") to someone in the legal community? The memo soon became an urban legend as news of the memo spread around the world. Some believed that it was a parody or joke, but sources at the law firm (the venerable Paul, Weiss, Rifkind, Wharton & Garrison) insisted that it was genuine. They were quick to add, however, that the paralegal's time in drafting the memo was not billed to any clients (en.wikipedia.org/wiki/Sushi_memo).

WANTED: PARALEGAL WITH MINIMUM OF 203 YEARS OF EXPERIENCE

A paralegal placement agency is seeking a person "w/at least 203 yrs exp in paralegal field." The ad was either a typo or the first step in getting recognition in the next edition of the Guinness record book. *Employment Registry*, Reporter, 11 (Los Angeles Paralegal Ass'n, June 1993).

BUMPER STICKER AWARD

The Alaska Association of Legal Assistants had a bumper sticker contest. The top three winners were as follows:

> PARALEGALS KNOW THEIR MOTIONS

> PARALEGALS GET ON YOUR CASE

> PARALEGALS KNOW BRIEFS

Reprinted with permission of the Alaska Association of Paralegals.

PARALEGAL
Go Ahead, Try to do it Without Me

PARALEGAL
The Real Power of Attorney

For Counsel: Products and Gifts for Lawyers (www.forcounsel.com). Reprinted with permission of Now and Zen Productions, Inc.

"WHAT IT IS THAT I DO"

A. Pergola, Newsletter, Rocky Mountain Paralegal Association (June 1980). Reprinted with permission of Anna M. Pergola.

THE WORLD OF ATTORNEYS

- "I served with General Washington in the legislature of Virginia before the revolution, and during it, with Dr. Franklin in Congress. If the present Congress errs in too much talking, how could it do otherwise in a body to which the people send 150 lawyers, whose trade it is to question everything, yield nothing & talk by the hour?" *Autobiography 1743–1790*, Thomas Jefferson.

- If a man were to give another man an orange, he would say, simply, "Have an orange." But if the transaction were entrusted to an attorney, he would say: "I hereby give, grant, bargain and sell to you, all my right, title and interest in, of, and to said orange, together with all its rind, skin, juice, pulp, and pips, and all rights and advantages therein, with full power to bite, cut, and otherwise eat of the same, or give the same away, with or without the rind, skin, juice, pulp, and pips, anything hereinbefore or hereinafter, or in any other deed or deeds, instrument or instruments, of whatever kind or nature whatsoever to the contrary in any wise notwithstanding." Hirsch, *Pittsburgh Legal Journal*.

- A document recently filed in the U.S. Bankruptcy Court in Tennessee contained the following language: "Debtors hereby amend the Amendment to Second Amended and Restated Disclosure Statement, Third Amended and Restated Plan of Reorganization, and Amendment to Third Amended and Restated Plan of Organization as follows. Wherever the name 'Mortgage Company' appears in the Amendment to Second Amended and Restated Disclosure Statement, Third Amended and Restated Plan of Reorganization and Amendment to Third Amended and Restated Plan of Organization, the name 'Bank' shall be inserted in lieu thereof." *The Reporter* 15 (Delaware Paralegal Ass'n, May/June 1991).

- Question: How many lawyers does it take to change a light bulb? Answer. Three senior partners to contemplate the history of light; two junior partners to check for conflicts of interest; ten associates to do the research on the antitrust implications of using a particular brand, on the cost-benefits of electric lighting versus candle light, on the health aspects of incandescent versus fluorescent bulb lighting, on the electric components that make light bulbs work, etc. And, of course, a paralegal to screw the bulb into the socket! *On the Lighter Side*, Par Spectives 5 (Paralegal Ass'n of Rochester, May 1990).

MURPHY'S LAWS FOR PARALEGALS

1. The day you wear comfortable, ugly old shoes is the day you are called into the managing partner's office or have to meet with an important client.
2. The day you wear attractive, stylish pumps that pinch your toes, bite your instep, and chafe your heels is the day that you have to serve papers at Nick Tahou's in an unpaved part of the county.
3. The night when you have a date, theater tickets, or fifteen dinner guests due at 7:30 is the night you are asked to stay late.
4. The day your car is in the garage and you carpooled is the day that you receive a fifteen-hour project that has to be done before you go home.
5. Your mother, your spouse, your significant other, or your bookie always call when the boss is standing in your office.
6. Clients who work near you never have to sign anything. The number of documents that need to be signed by a client increases in proportion to the number of miles between their home or office and your office.

7. Whatever you lost is what everyone must have immediately.
8. Whatever can't be found was last in the possession of a paralegal.
9. Whatever needs to be hand delivered or picked up is always beyond the messenger's responsibility.
10. The day you have liverwurst and onion for lunch is the day that you have to attend an unscheduled meeting with an important client or attorney.
11. The volume of Carmody-Wait 2nd that you require to prepare a motion is always missing from the library.
12. Nobody ever asks you about subjects with which you are familiar. If you are an expert on the mating habits of mosquitoes, you will be asked to digest a deposition or prepare research about the malfunction of the farabus and ullie pin connection in Yugoslavian lawnmowers.

Celeste E. Ciaccia, Murphy's Laws for Paralegals, 9 Newsletter 12 (Dallas Ass'n of Legal Assistants, September 1985).

A SUIT TO COMPENSATE A TREE

In one of the oddest court opinions ever written, a three-judge panel in Michigan affirmed a lower court decision that denied relief for damage caused by the defendant's Chevrolet to the plaintiff's tree. The opinion is *Fisher v. Lowe*, 333 N.W.2d 67 (Mich. Ct. App. 1983). Here is the opinion:

> We thought that we would never see
> A suit to compensate a tree.
> A suit whose claim in tort is prest
> Upon a mangled tree's behest;
> A tree whose battered trunk was prest
> Against a Chevy's crumpled crest;
> A tree that faces each new day
> With bark and limb in disarray;
> A tree that may forever bear
> A lasting need for tender care.
> Flora lovers though we three,
> We must uphold the court's decree.
> Affirmed.

AND FINALLY:
Truth in Advertising

The remnants of the once proud firms of
DAZZLE & DROWN
and
BETTEROFF, SOMEWHERE & ELSE
are pleased to announce the merger
of what is left of their practices. They will
continue under the name of
BETTEROFF & DROWN

The firm will continue to specialize
in whatever it takes to survive.

DREAMS BEE & DASHED

A Professional Corporation

is pleased to announce
the relocation of its office to

Grant Avenue Safeway FoodMart

1001 Grant Avenue
Collegial, AZ
Telephone (393) 422-9987

The Firm will continue to seek subtenants for
its penthouse suite in the Palace Tower

HAPPY & BLIND

is pleased to announce that

Truman R. Rightwig

formerly a partner for 27 years before being let go by

Shining, Star & Nomore

has joined the firm as a Contract Attorney

Mr. Rightwig will continue to specialize in litigating
Nixon's 1971 Price Control Act

The Law Firm of
HURTING & SMARTING
is pleased to announce
the terminations of

Harvey Notgood, Partner
Constance Reminder, Partner
Cynthia Snorz, Partner
Frederick Grating, Associate
Mildred Muddle, Associate
Eric Tomorrow, Paralegal
Janet Time, Secretary
Raymont Rabbit, Messenger

as part of its strategic plan to
fit the size of the firm to its
level of business.

GARGLE,
MUMBLE & NUMB
Attorneys at Law

is pleased to announce
the cessation of its
recruiting program and
the decrease in its
first year associate starting
salary to $32,000

Applicants can
take it or leave it.

Jim Cowan, Truth in Advertising, 10 ALA Newsletter 30(Association of Legal Administrators, August/September 1991) (Reprinted with permission)

Glossary

A

A. (1) Annotated. (2) Atlantic Reporter.

A.2d *See* Atlantic 2d.

AAfPE American Association for Paralegal Education (www.aafpe.org).

ABA American Bar Association (www.abanet.org).

abstract A summary or abridgment. An overview. *See also* digest.

abuse of process A tort consisting of (1) the use of a civil or criminal process, (2) for a purpose for which the process is not designed, (3) resulting in actual damage.

accounts receivable A list of who owes money to the office, how much, how long the debt has been due, etc.

accreditation The process by which an authoritative organization (usually nongovernmental) evaluates and recognizes an institution or a program of study as meeting specified qualifications or standards.

ACP Advanced Certified Paralegal. *See* specialty certification.

acquit To declare that the accused is innocent of the crime.

act *See* statute.

active voice The grammatical verb form in which the subject or thing performing or causing the action is the main focus.

ad damnum clause A clause stating the damages claimed.

add-on question A question that is added to the end of another related question, both stated in one sentence.

adjourn To halt the proceedings temporarily.

adjudicate To hear and resolve a legal matter judicially. To judge. The noun is *adjudication*; the adjective is *adjudicative*. *See also* quasi-adjudication.

adjudicative body A court or other tribunal with authority to resolve a legal dispute.

ad litem For the purposes of this litigation.

administrative agency A governmental body, other than a court or legislature, that carries out (i.e., administers or executes) the statutes of the legislature, the executive orders of the chief executive, and its own regulations.

administrative code A collection of administrative regulations organized by subject matter rather than chronologically or by date.

administrative decision An administrative agency's resolution of a controversy (following a hearing) involving the application of the regulations, statutes, or executive orders that govern the agency. Sometimes called an *administrative ruling*.

administrative hearing A proceeding at an administrative agency presided over by a hearing officer (e.g., an administrative law judge) to resolve a controversy.

administrative law judge (ALJ) A government officer who presides over a hearing at an administrative agency. Also called *hearing examiner*.

Administrative Procedure Act (APA) The statute that governs procedures before federal administrative agencies. Many states have their own APA for procedures before state administrative agencies.

administrative regulation A law written by an administrative agency designed to explain or carry out the statutes, executive orders, or other regulations that govern the agency. Also called *administrative rule*.

administrative ruling *See* administrative decision.

admiralty law An area of the law that covers accidents and injuries on navigable waters. Also called *maritime law*.

admissible Allowed into court to determine its truth or believability.

admission (1) An assertion of the truth of a fact. (2) An official acknowledgment of someone's right to practice law.

admonition A milder form of private reprimand. Also called a *private warning* or *private reproval*. *See also* reprimand.

ADR *See* alternative dispute resolution.

Advanced Certified Paralegal (ACP) *See* specialty certification.

advance session law service *See* legislative service.

advance sheet A pamphlet that comes out before (in advance of) a later volume.

adversarial Involving conflict or adversaries. *See also* hearing.

adversary hearing A hearing at which all parties to a dispute are present before the judge or presiding officer to argue their positions.

adversary system A method of resolving a legal dispute whereby the parties (alone or through their advocates) argue their conflicting claims before a neutral decision maker.

adverse interest A goal or claim of one person that is different from or opposed to the goal or claim of another.

adverse judgment A judgment or decision against you.

advertising Calling the attention of the public to a service or product for sale. (Advertising on the Internet is sometimes called *netvertising*.)

advisement *See* take under advisement.

advocacy The process by which you attempt to influence the behavior of others, often according to predetermined goals.

affidavit A written or printed statement of facts made by a person (called the *affiant*) before a person with authority to administer the oath.

affirm To agree with or uphold the lower court judgment.

affirmative defense A defense raising new facts that will defeat the plaintiff's claim even if the plaintiff's fact allegations are proven.

aged accounts receivable report A report showing all cases that have outstanding balances due and how long these balances are past due. (Also called *firm utilization report.*)

agency practitioner An individual authorized to practice before an administrative agency. This individual often does not have to be an attorney.

ALA Association of Legal Administrators (www.alanet.org).

allegation A claimed fact. A fact that a party will try to prove at trial.

alphabetical filing system A method of storing client files in alphabetical order by the client's surname or organization name.

A.L.R., A.L.R.2d, A.L.R.3d, A.L.R.4th, A.L.R.5th, A.L.R.6th, A.L.R. Fed., A.L.R. Fed. 2d *See* American Law Reports.

A.L.R. Bluebook of Supplemental Decisions A set of books that allows you to update the annotations in *A.L.R. 1st.*

alternate An extra juror who will take the place of a regular juror if one becomes incapacitated during the trial.

alternative dispute resolution (ADR) A method or procedure for resolving a legal dispute without litigating it in a court or administrative agency.

ALWD Citation Manual A guidebook on citation form. It is the major competitor to the *Bluebook.*

ambulance chasing Approaching accident victims (or others with potential legal claims) to encourage them to hire a particular attorney. If the attorney uses someone else to do the soliciting, the latter is called a *runner.* If this other person uses deception or fraud in the solicitation, he or she is sometimes called a *capper* or a *steerer. See also* court runner.

American Digest System Three digests of West Group that give summaries of every state and federal court that publishes its opinions: *Century Digest* covers opinions prior to 1897; *Decennial Digest* covers opinions during ten-year periods; and *General Digest* covers opinions since the last *Decennial Digest.*

American Jurisprudence 2d (Am. Jur. 2d). *See* legal encyclopedia.

American Law Reports (A.L.R., A.L.R.2d, A.L.R.3d, A.L.R.4th, A.L.R.5th, A.L.R.6th, A.L.R. Fed., A.L.R. Fed. 2d) A reporter that prints selected opinions and extensive annotations based on issues in the opinions. See also *annotated reporter* and *annotation.*

American rule The winning party cannot recover attorney fees and costs of litigation from the losing party unless (1) a statute authorizes such payment, (2) a contract between the parties provides for such payment, or (3) the court finds that the losing party acted in bad faith in the litigation. *See also* English rule.

amicus curiae brief ("friend of the court" brief) An appellate brief submitted by a nonparty who obtains court permission to file the brief with its views on the case.

Am. Jur. 2d *See* legal encyclopedia.

analogous (1) Sufficiently similar to justify a similar outcome or result. (2) Sufficiently similar to lend support. (3) On point; germane. Involving the same or similar issues; involving facts and rules that are similar to those now under consideration.

analogy A comparison of similarities and differences.

ann. Annotated.

annotate To provide notes or commentary. A text is annotated if such notes and commentary are provided along with the text.

annotated bibliography A bibliography that briefly states why you included each entry in the bibliography.

annotated reporter A set of books that contains the full text of court opinions plus notes or commentary on them called *annotations.*

annotated statutory code A collection of statutes organized by subject matter rather than by date, along with research references such as historical notes and summaries of court opinions that have interpreted the statutes.

annotation (1) A note or commentary that summarizes or provides explanation. (2) A research paper in American Law Reports.

answer (1) The first pleading of the defendant that responds to the plaintiff's claims. (2) To assume someone else's liability.

anticontact rule An advocate should not contact an opposing party without permission of the latter's attorney; if the party is unrepresented, the advocate must not convey the impression that the advocate is disinterested.

antitrust law The law governing unlawful restraints of trade, price fixing, and monopolies.

APA *See* Administrative Procedure Act.

appeal Asking a higher tribunal to review or reconsider the decision of an inferior tribunal.

appeal as a matter of right The appeal of a case that an appellate court must hear; it has no discretion on whether to take the appeal.

appearance Formally coming before a tribunal as a party or as a representative of a party.

appellant The party bringing an appeal because of alleged errors made by a lower tribunal. Sometimes called *petitioner.*

appellate brief A document submitted (filed) by a party to an appellate court (and served on an opposing party) in which arguments are presented on why the appellate court should affirm (approve), reverse, or otherwise modify what a lower court has done.

appellate jurisdiction The power of an appellate court to review and correct the decisions of a lower tribunal.

appellee The party against whom an appeal is brought. Also called the *respondent.*

application Connecting facts to a rule of law in order to determine whether the rule applies to the facts.

applications software A computer program that performs specific tasks directly for the consumer or end user.

approval The recognition that comes from accreditation, certification, licensure, registration, or other form of acknowledgment.

arbitration A method of alternate dispute resolution (ADR) in which the parties avoid litigation by submitting their dispute to a neutral third person (the arbitrator) who renders a decision resolving the dispute.

arraignment A court proceeding in which the defendant is formally charged with a crime and enters a plea. Arrangements are then made for the next proceeding.

arrest To take someone into custody to answer a criminal charge.

Article III court *See* constitutional court.

assigned counsel An attorney (usually in private practice) appointed by the court to represent an indigent person in a criminal or civil case. If the attorney is a government employee handling criminal cases, he or she is often called a *public defender.*

associate An attorney employee of a partnership who hopes eventually to be promoted to partner. *See also* law clerk (1).

at common law All the case law and statutory law in England and in the American colonies before the Revolution. The phrase also sometimes means judge-made law that existed before it was changed by statute. *See also* common law.

Atlantic Digest A regional digest of West Group that gives summaries of opinions in the Atlantic Reporter.

Atlantic Reporter 2d (A.2d) A regional reporter of West Group that prints state court opinions of nine states and Washington, D.C. (Conn., Del., D.C., Me., Md., N.H., N.J., Pa., R.I., and Vt.). A.2d is the second series of this reporter. The first series is *Atlantic Reporter* (A.).

attentive listening Taking affirmative, ongoing steps to let an interviewee know that you have heard what he or she has said and that you consider the meeting with him or her to be important.

attestation clause A clause stating that you saw (witnessed) someone sign a document or perform other tasks related to the validity of the document.

attorney attestation A signed statement by an attorney that a paralegal applying for membership in an association meets one or more of the criteria of the association.

attorney-client privilege A client and an attorney can refuse to disclose any communication between them if the purpose of the communication was to facilitate the provision of legal services to the client.

attorney general The chief attorney for the government. *See also* opinion of the attorney general.

attorney in fact One authorized to act in place of or for another, often in a business transaction.

attorney of record The attorney noted in court files as the attorney representing a particular party.

attorney work product *See* work product rule.

at-will employee An employee who can quit or be terminated at any time and for any reason. An employee with no union or other contractual protection.

authentication Evidence that a writing or other physical item is genuine and that it is what it purports to be.

authority Any source that a court could rely on in reaching its decision.

Auto-Cite An online citator of LexisNexis that tells you whether an opinion you

are checking is still good law. *See also* citator.

B

backspace The key that allows you to delete the character to the left of the cursor.

backup A copy of your data stored in a different location for safekeeping.

bail (1) Money or other property deposited with the court as security to ensure that the defendant will reappear at designated times. Failure to appear forfeits the security. (2) Release of the defendant upon posting this security.

bailiff A court employee who keeps order in the courtroom and renders general administrative assistance to the judge.

bankruptcy petition preparer (BPP) A nonattorney who is authorized to charge fees for preparing (without attorney supervision) a bankruptcy petition or any other bankruptcy document that a debtor will file in a federal court.

bar Prevent or stop.

bar code A sequence of numbers and vertical lines of different shapes that can be read by an optical scanner.

barratry The crime of stirring up quarrels or litigation; persistently instigating lawsuits, often groundless ones. The illegal solicitation of clients.

barrister A lawyer in England who represents clients in the higher courts.

Bates stamp A desk tool used to place a sequential number on a page. After using the stamp on a page, it automatically advances to the next number, ready to stamp the next page.

below (1) Pertaining to a lower court in the judicial system. (2) Later in the document.

bench conference A discussion between the judge and the attorneys held at the judge's bench so that the jury cannot hear what is being said. Also called a *sidebar conference*.

bench trial A trial without a jury. Also called a *nonjury trial*.

best evidence rule To prove the contents of a private writing, the original writing should be produced unless it is unavailable.

beyond a reasonable doubt Not having any doubt that would cause prudent persons to hesitate before acting in matters of importance to themselves.

bias Prejudice for or against something or someone. An inclination or tendency to think or to act in a certain way. A danger of prejudgment.

bicameral Having two houses in the legislature. If there is only one house, it is *unicameral*.

bill A proposed statute.

billable hours quota A minimum number of hours expected from a timekeeper on client matters that can be charged (billed) to clients per week, month, year, or other time period.

billable tasks Those tasks requiring time that can be charged to a client.

black letter law A statement of a fundamental or basic principle of law.

blended hourly rate A single hourly rate based on a blend or mix of the rates normally charged by different individuals, e.g., a partner, a senior associate, a junior associate, and sometimes a paralegal. *See also* fee.

blind ad A want ad that does not give the name and address of the prospective employer. The contact is made through a third party, e.g., a newspaper.

block A group of characters, e.g., a word, a sentence, a paragraph. Block movement is a feature of a word processor that allows the user to define a block of text and then do something with that block, e.g., move it or delete it.

block billing Grouping multiple tasks under a single time charge rather than describing each task separately and assigning the actual time associated with each task. The timekeeper enters the total time spent working on a case without itemizing the time spent on specific tasks for the case.

blog A journal or diary available on the World Wide Web (called *blawg* if the topic is legal).

blue and white book A source for parallel cites of the opinions in a single state.

bluebook (also spelled *blue book*) (1) *The Bluebook: A Uniform System of Citation*, the a guidebook on citation form. (2) The *National Reporter Blue Book*, a source for parallel cites in all states. (3) The *A.L.R. Bluebook of Supplemental Decisions*, a set of books that allows you to update the annotations in A.L.R.1st. (4) A directory of government offices and employees.

bluebook it Cite an authority according to the rules in *The Bluebook: A Uniform System of Citation*.

BNA Bureau of National Affairs (www .bna.com). *See* United States Law Week.

board of appeals The unit within an administrative agency to which a party can appeal a decision of the agency.

boilerplate Standard language that is commonly used in a certain kind of document. Standard verbiage.

boldface Heavier or darker than normal type.

bona fide Good faith.

bond An obligation to perform an act (e.g., pay a sum of money) upon the occurrence or nonoccurrence of a designated condition.

bonus A payment beyond one's regular salary, usually as a reward or recognition. *See also* incentive billing.

booking Entering charges against someone on a police register.

bookmarking Inserting the address of a favorite Internet site on a list in your browser so that you can easily return to the site in the future.

Boolean search A search that allows words to be specifically included or excluded through operatives such as AND, OR, and NOT.

booting up Turning on or restarting the computer and loading the operating system.

bound over Held or transferred for further court proceedings.

boutique law firm A firm that specializes in one area of the law.

breach of contract A cause of action in which a party seeks a court remedy for the alleged failure of a party to perform the term(s) of an enforceable contract.

brief A summary of the main or essential parts of a court opinion. *See also* appellate brief *and* trial brief.

brief bank A collection of appellate briefs and related documents drafted in prior cases that might be used as models and adapted for current cases.

broadband A service that provides high-speed data communication.

browser *See* Web browser.

budget performance report A report that compares a firm's actual income and expenditures with budgeted or projected income and expenditures.

"bugs" Manufacturing or design errors that exist in products such as computer hardware or software glitches.

bulletin An ongoing (e.g., monthly) publication that prints documents of administrative agencies chronologically (e.g., *Internal Revenue Bulletin*). Also called *register*, *gazette*, and *journal*.

bundled legal services All tasks needed to represent a client; all-inclusive legal services. *See also* unbundled legal services.

burden of proof The responsibility of proving a fact at trial.

Bureau of National Affairs (BNA) *See* United States Law Week.

business entry An out-of-court statement found in business records made in the regular course of business by someone whose duty is to make such entries. (An exception to the hearsay rule.)

byte The storage equivalent of one space or character of the alphabet typed into a computer.

C

calendar *See* docket.

California Reporter 2d (Cal. Rptr. 2d) An unofficial reporter of West Group that publishes opinions of California state courts.

CALR *See* computer-assisted legal research.

Cal. Rptr. 2d *See* California Reporter 2d.

cap *See* fee cap.

capital partner *See* equity partner.

capped fee An hourly rate leading to a final bill that will not exceed a predetermined amount. *See also* fee.

capper *See* ambulance chasing *and* runner.

caption The heading or introductory part of a pleading, court opinion, memo, or other document that identifies what it is, the names of the parties, the court involved, etc.

caption of memorandum The beginning of a memorandum containing its title or name.

career client list A confidential list of every client and matter you worked on in any law office from the beginning of your legal career to the present time that can be used to help determine whether any of your future work might create a conflict of interest.

CARTWHEEL A technique designed to help you think of a large variety of words and phrases to check in indexes, tables of contents, and online search engines.

CAS California Advanced Specialist, a person who has passed the California Advanced Specialty Examination.

case (1) A court's written explanation of how it applied the law to the facts to resolve a legal dispute. Also called *opinion*. (2) A pending matter on a court calendar. (3) A client matter handled by a law office.

casebook A law-school textbook containing numerous edited court opinions and related materials assembled for a course.

case clerk An assistant to a paralegal; an entry-level paralegal.

case evaluation *See* neutral evaluation.

case-in-chief The presentation of evidence by one side, not including the evidence it introduces to counter the other side.

case management Application software used to help a law office maintain control over its appointments and deadlines.

case note A relatively brief commentary on a recent court opinion.

case reports *See* reporter.

case synopsis *See* syllabus.

cause A legally sufficient reason to do something. Sometimes referred to as *just cause* or *good cause*.

cause of action A legally acceptable reason for suing. Facts that give a party the right to judicial relief.

CD–ROM (compact disk read-only memory) A compact disk that stores data in a digital format.

central processing unit (CPU) The part of the computer that controls all of its parts.

Century Digest *See* American Digest System.

cert. *See* writ of certiorari.

certificated Having met the qualifications for certification from a school or training program. Some prefer *certificated* to *certified* when the certification comes from schools or training programs.

certificate of service *See* proof of service.

certification The process by which a nongovernmental organization grants recognition to a person who has met the qualifications set by that organization.

certified Having complied with or met the qualifications for certification.

certified legal assistant *See* CLA.

certified paralegal (CP) *See* CLA.

certiorari *See* writ of certiorari.

CFLA Certified Florida Legal Assistant. To earn this title, a paralegal must first pass the CLA (Certified Legal Assistant) exam of NALA and then pass a special exam on Florida law.

C.F.R. *See* Code of Federal Regulations.

challenge for cause A request from a party to a judge that a prospective juror not be allowed to become a member of this jury because of specified causes or reasons. *See also* peremptory challenge.

champerty Promoting someone else's litigation, often by helping to finance the litigation in exchange for a share in the recovery.

character A letter, number, or symbol. Character enhancement includes underlining, boldfacing, subscripting, and superscripting.

charge *See* jury instructions.

charter The fundamental law of a municipality or other local unit of government authorizing it to perform designated governmental functions.

checks and balances An allocation of governmental powers whereby one branch of government can block, check, or review what another branch wants to do (or has done) in order to maintain a balance of power among the legislative, executive, and judicial branches.

Chinese wall Steps taken to prevent a tainted employee (e.g., attorney or paralegal) from having any contact with the case of a particular client in the office because the employee has created a conflict of interest between that client and someone else. A Chinese wall is also called an *ethical wall* and a *cone of silence*. A tainted employee is also called a *contaminated* employee. Once the Chinese wall is set up around the tainted employee, the latter is referred to as a *quarantined employee*.

chronological digest A summary of a deposition transcript that presents the events described in the deponent's answers in their chronological order.

chronological question A question designed to encourage the interviewee to describe what happened in the order in which events occurred—by date, step by step.

chronological résumé A résumé that presents biographical data on education and experience in a chronological sequence starting with the present and working backward.

churning Providing services beyond what the circumstances warrant for the primary purpose of generating fees and commissions.

circumlocution The use of more words than are needed to express something.

circumstantial evidence Evidence of one fact from which another fact (not personally observed or known) can be inferred. Also called *indirect evidence*.

CIS *See* Congressional Information Service.

citation; cite (1) A reference to any legal authority printed on paper or stored in a computer database that will allow you to locate the authority. As a verb, to *cite* something means to give its location (e.g., volume number or Web address) where you can read it. It is the paper or online "address" where you can read something. (2) An order to appear in court to answer a charge. (3) An official notice of a violation.

citator A book, CD–ROM, or online service containing lists of citations that can (1) help you assess the current validity of an opinion, statute, or other item; and (2) give you leads to additional relevant materials.

cite *See* citation.

cite checking Examining citations in a document to assess whether the format of the citation is correct, whether a parallel cite is needed, whether quoted material is accurately quoted, and whether the law cited is still valid.

cited material The case, statute, regulation, or other document that you are shepardizing.

citing material The case, article, or annotation that mentions, treats, or discusses whatever you are shepardizing, i.e., that mentions, treats, or discusses the cited material.

civil Pertaining to a private right or matter. Noncriminal; nonmilitary.

civil cover sheet A cover sheet filed in federal court along with the complaint indicating the names and addresses of the parties and their attorneys, the kind of action being filed, etc.

civil dispute A legal controversy in which (1) one private person or entity (e.g., a business) sues another, (2) a private person or entity sues the government, or (3) the government sues a private person or entity for a matter other than the commission of a crime.

civil law (1) The law governing civil disputes. Any law other than criminal law. *See also* civil dispute. (2) *See* civil law system.

civil law system The legal system of many Western European countries (other than England) that places a greater emphasis on statutory or code law than do countries (such as England and the United States) whose common law system places a greater emphasis on case law.

civil service Nonmilitary government employment, often obtained through merit and competitive exams.

C.J.S. *See* legal encyclopedia.

CLA or CP The certification credential bestowed by the National Association of Legal Assistants. CLA: (Certified Legal Assistant); CP: (Certified Paralegal) (www.nala.org).

claim preclusion *See* res judicata.

claims-made policy Insurance that covers only claims actually filed (i.e., made) during the period in which the policy is in effect.

CLE *See* continuing legal education.

CLE materials Books, video, or materials in other formats for use in continuing legal education. *See also* continuing legal education.

clerk The court employee who assists judges with record keeping and other administrative duties. *See also* law clerk.

CLI *See* Current Law Index.

client security fund A fund (often run by a bar association or foundation) used to compensate victims of designated kinds of attorney misconduct.

client trust account A bank account controlled by an attorney that contains client funds that may not be used for office operating expenses or for any personal purpose of the attorney.

clinical education A training program in which students work on real cases under attorney supervision.

closed-ended question A narrowly structured question that usually can be answered in one or two words, often *yes* or *no*. Also called a *directed question*.

closed file The file of a client whose case is no longer active in the firm. Also called a *dead file* or a *retired file*.

closing The meeting in which a transaction is finalized. Also called *settlement*.

closing argument The final statements by opposing trial attorneys to the jury (or to the trial judge if there is no jury) summarizing the evidence and requesting a favorable decision. Also called *final argument*, *summation*, and *summing up*.

code (1) Any set of rules that regulates conduct. (2) A collection of laws or rules organized by subject matter regardless of when they were enacted.

codefendant One of two or more defendants sued in the same civil case or prosecuted in the same criminal case.

Code of Federal Regulations (C.F.R.) A publication containing many current federal administrative regulations organized by subject matter. *See also* Federal Register.

codified cite The citation to a statute (or other enacted law) that has been printed in a code and, therefore, is organized by subject matter.

codify To arrange laws or rules by subject matter regardless of when they were enacted.

combination question A question that has more than one part.

commingling Mixing what should be kept separate, e.g., depositing client funds in a single account with general law firm funds or with an attorney's personal funds.

committee print A compilation of information prepared by committee staff members on a bill, consisting of comparative analysis of related bills, statistics, studies, reports, etc.

committee report A summary of a bill and a statement of the reasons for and against its enactment by the legislature.

common law (1) Court opinions, all of case law. (2) The legal system of England and of those countries such as the United States whose legal system is based on England's. (3) The case law and statutory law in England and in the American colonies before the American Revolution. (4) Judge-made law in the absence of controlling statutory law or other higher law. *See also* at common law *and* enacted law.

common representation *See* multiple representation.

competent (1) Using the knowledge and skill that are reasonably necessary to represent a particular client. (2) Allowed (having the legal capacity) to give testimony because the person understands the obligation to tell the truth, has the ability to communicate, and has knowledge of the topic of his or her testimony. The noun is *competency*.

competency *See* competent (2).

complaint (1) A plaintiff's first pleading, stating a cause of action against the defendant. Also called *petition*. (2) A formal criminal charge.

computer-assisted legal research (CALR) Performing legal research in computer databases.

concurrent jurisdiction The power of a court to hear a particular kind of case, along with other courts that could also hear it.

concurring opinion An opinion written by less than a majority of the judges on the court that agrees with the result reached by the majority but not with all of its reasoning.

cone of silence *See* Chinese wall.

conference committee A temporary committee consisting of members of both chambers of the legislature that seeks to reach a compromise on two versions of the same bill each chamber passed.

confidential That which should not be revealed; pertaining to information that others do not have a right to receive.

confirmatory letter A letter that verifies or confirms that something important has been done or said.

conflict of interest Divided loyalty that actually or potentially harms someone who is owed undivided loyalty.

conflict of laws Differences in the laws of two coequal legal systems (e.g., two states) involved in a legal dispute. The choice of which law to apply in such disputes.

conflicts check A determination of whether a conflict of interest exists that might disqualify a law office from representing a client or from continuing the representation. *See also* conflicts specialist.

conflicts specialist A law firm employee, often a paralegal, who helps the firm determine whether a conflict of interest exists between prospective clients and current or former clients. Also called a *conflicts analyst* or *conflicts technician*.

confrontation Being present when others give evidence against you and having the opportunity to question them.

Cong. Rec. *See* Congressional Record.

Congressional Information Service (CIS) A major publisher of materials on the legislative history of the statutes of Congress.

Congressional Record (Cong. Rec.) The official record of the proceedings and debates of the U.S. Congress.

connectors Characters, words, or symbols used to show the relationship between the words and phrases in a database query.

consent (1) To agree; to waive a right. (2) Voluntary agreement or permission, express or implied.

consideration A bargained-for promise, act, or forbearance. Something of value exchanged between the parties.

consolidated litigation More than one lawsuit being resolved in the same litigation.

constitution The fundamental law that creates the branches of government, allocates power among them, and defines some basic rights of individuals.

constitutional court A court created within the constitution. (At the federal level, they are called Article III courts because they are created within Article III of the U.S. Constitution.)

construction Interpretation (the verb is *construe*).

contaminated Pertaining to an employee who brings a conflict of interest to the office. *See also* Chinese wall.

contemporaneous Existing or occurring in the same period of time; pertaining to records that are prepared on events as the events are occurring or shortly thereafter.

contest To challenge; to raise a defense against a claim.

contingency case A case in which clients pay attorney and paralegal fees only if they win through litigation or settlement.

contingent fee A fee that is paid only if the case is successfully resolved by litigation or settlement. (The fee is also referred to as a contingency.) A defense contingent fee (also called a *negative contingency*) is a fee for the defendant's attorney that is dependent on the outcome of the case.

continuance The adjournment or postponement of a proceeding until a later date.

continuing legal education (CLE) Training in the law (usually short term) that a person receives after completing his or her formal legal training.

contract attorney An attorney hired to work for a relatively short period of time, usually on specific cases or projects. Also called a *project attorney*.

contract paralegal A self-employed paralegal who often works for several different attorneys on a freelance basis. *See also* freelance paralegal.

control character A coded character that does not print but is part of the command sequence in a word processor.

controlling authority *See* mandatory authority.

convention *See* treaty.

copyright (©) The exclusive right for a fixed number of years to print, copy, sell, or perform original works. 17 U.S.C. § 101.

corporate counsel An in-house attorney, often the chief attorney, of a corporation. Sometimes called *general counsel*.

corporate legal department A law office within a corporation containing salaried attorneys (called *in-house attorneys*) who advise and represent the corporation. Also called a *law department*.

corroborative question A question designed to verify (corroborate) facts by seeking information beyond what is provided by the interviewee.

counterclaim A claim by one side in a case (usually the defendant) that is filed in response to a claim asserted by an opponent (usually the plaintiff).

court (1) A tribunal in our legal system for the resolution of legal disputes. (2) The judge.

court costs Charges or fees imposed by the court directly related to litigation in that court.

court of appeals *See* U.S. Court of Appeals.

court of final resort The highest court within a judicial system.

court of first instance A trial court; a court with original jurisdiction.

court rules *See* rules of court.

cover letter A letter that tells the recipient what physical items are being sent in the envelope or package. Also called *transmittal letter* or *enclosure letter*.

cover sheet *See* civil cover sheet.

CP Certified paralegal. *See* CLA.

credibility The extent to which something is believable.

credible Believable.

criminal dispute A legal controversy in which the government alleges the commission of a crime.

cross-claim A claim brought by one defendant against another defendant or by one plaintiff against another plaintiff in the same action. Also called a *cross-action*.

cross-examination Questioning of a witness at a hearing by an opponent after the other side has conducted a direct examination of that witness.

cumulative That which repeats earlier material and consolidates it with new material into one place or unit. A cumulative supplement, for example, contains new supplemental material and repeats earlier supplemental material.

cure To correct or overcome; to remove a legal defect or error.

Current Law Index (CLI) A comprehensive index to legal periodical literature. An online version of CLI is called LegalTrac. (On Westlaw and LexisNexis, it is called Legal Resource Index.)

cursor The marker or pointer on the screen that indicates where the next letter or other character will be displayed on the screen.

D

daily time sheet A paper form on which timekeepers record how much time they spend on particular client matters.

damages An award of money paid by the wrongdoer to compensate the person who has been harmed.

data Information that can be used by a computer.

database management Application software that allows you to organize, search, retrieve, and sort information or data.

Decennial Digest See American Digest System.

decision See administrative decision *and* opinion.

declarant A person who makes a declaration or statement.

declaratory judgment A binding judgment that declares rights, status, or other legal relationships without ordering anything to be done.

declination A formal rejection.

deep pocket (1) An individual, a business, or another organization with resources to pay a potential judgment. (2) Sufficient assets for this purpose. The opposite of *shallow pocket*.

default judgment A judgment against a party for failure to file a required pleading or otherwise respond to an opponent's claim.

defense (1) An allegation of fact (or a legal theory) offered to offset or defeat a claim or demand. (2) The defendant and his or her attorney.

defense contingent fee A fee received by the defendant's attorney that is dependent on the outcome of the case. Also called a *negative contingency*.

demand letter An advocacy letter that asks the recipient to take or refrain from specific action affecting the client.

demurrer See failure to state a cause of action.

de novo Anew; starting over.

deponent See deposition.

depose Ask questions of a witness in a deposition.

deposition A method of discovery by which parties and their prospective witnesses are questioned outside the courtroom before trial. A pretrial question-and-answer session to help parties prepare for trial. The person questioned is called the *deponent*.

depository library See federal depository library.

depo summarizer An employee whose main job is digesting (summarizing) discovery documents, particularly depositions.

derogation A partial repealing or abolishing of a law, as by a subsequent act that limits its scope or force.

deskbook A one- or two-volume collection of the rules of court for one or more courts, often within the same judicial system.

detainer Withholding possession of land or goods from another. See also unlawful detainer assistant.

dictum (1) A statement or observation made by a judge in an opinion that is not essential to resolve the issues before the court; comments that go beyond the facts before the court. Also called *obiter dictum*. (2) An authoritative, formal statement or announcement.

digest An organized summary or abridgment. A set of volumes that contain brief summaries (sometimes called *abstracts* or *squibs*) of court opinions, arranged by topic and by court or jurisdiction.

digesting Summarizing transcripts and documents, often in preparation for litigation.

dilatory Causing delay, usually without merit or justification.

directed question See closed-ended question.

directed verdict A judge's decision not to allow the jury to deliberate because only one verdict is reasonable. Called a *judgment as a matter of law* (see this phrase) in federal court and in some state courts.

direct evidence Evidence (based on personal knowledge or observation) that tends to establish a fact (or to disprove a fact) without the need for an inference. Also called *positive evidence*.

direct examination The first questioning of a witness by the party who has called the witness. Also called *examination in chief*.

directory A search tool in which you select from a list of broad subject categories and then keep clicking through subcategories of that subject until you find what you want.

disbarment The revocation or termination of the right to practice law as punishment for unethical conduct.

disbursements Out-of-pocket expenses.

Disciplinary Rule (DR) See Model Code of Professional Responsibility.

discount adjustment A write-down (decrease) in the bill.

discounted hourly fee An hourly or fixed fee that is reduced because of the volume of business the client gives the office. See also fee.

discoverable Pertaining to information or other materials an opponent can obtain through deposition, interrogatories, or other discovery device.

discovery Compulsory pretrial disclosure of information related to litigation by one party to another party. Discovery can also be used in postjudgment enforcement proceedings. See also deposition, interrogatories, *and* request for admission.

discretion The power to choose among various courses of conduct based solely on one's reasoned judgment or preference.

discretionary statute A statute that permits something to be done but does not require or mandate it.

disengagement See letter of disengagement.

disinterested Not working for one side or the other in a controversy; not deriving benefit if one side of a dispute wins or loses; objective.

disposition A court's final order reached as a result of its holding(s).

disqualification See imputed disqualification.

dissent A judge's vote against the result reached by the judges in the majority (or plurality) on a case.

dissenting opinion An opinion that disagrees with the result and the reasoning used by the majority or plurality opinion.

district court See U.S. District Court.

diversity of citizenship The disputing parties are citizens of different states and the amount in controversy exceeds $75,000. This diversity gives jurisdiction to a U.S. District Court.

divided loyalty See conflict of interest.

docket (1) A court's list of its pending cases. Also called *calendar*. (2) A record containing brief notations on the proceedings that have occurred in a court case.

docket number A consecutive number assigned to a case by the court and used on all documents filed with the court during the litigation of that case.

document clerk An individual whose main responsibility is to organize, file, code, or digest litigation or other client documents.

document preparer A person who assists someone in the preparation of forms and documents using information provided by a self-represented person.

double billing Fraudulently charging a client twice for the same service.

download To move data from a remote computer (e.g., a central computer or Web site) to your computer. Data is uploaded when you transfer it from your computer to the remote computer.

DR Disciplinary Rule. *See* Model Code of Professional Responsibility.

draft (1) To write. (She drafted a memorandum.) (2) A document in one of its preliminary stages. (I was asked to proofread a draft of a contract before it was printed.) (3) *See* draft bill.

draft bill A billing memorandum prepared by a law office on a particular client case stating expenses, costs, time spent, and billing rates of attorneys and paralegals working on the case.

draw A partner's advance against profits or net income.

due diligence Reasonable efforts to find and verify factual information needed to carry out an obligation, to avoid harming someone, or to make an important decision, e.g., to determine the true market value of a potential investment.

duty of loyalty The obligation to protect the interests of a client without having a similar obligation to anyone else that would present an actual or potential conflict.

DWI Descriptive Word Index, an index to the digests of West Group.

E

EC Ethical Consideration. *See* Model Code of Professional Responsibility.

e-CFR *See* electronic Code of Federal Regulations.

EDD *See* electronic data discovery.

e-discovery *See* electronic data discovery.

edition A version of a text that is usually a revision of an earlier version.

EEOC *See* Equal Employment Opportunity Commission.

e-evidence Evidence generated by or stored in a computer such as e-mail messages, online spreadsheets, Web pages, and database records.

e-filing Electronic filing in court of pleadings and other documents.

ejusdem generis Where general words follow a list of particular words, the general words will be interpreted as applying only to things of the same class or category as the particular words in the list.

electronic Code of Federal Regulations (e-CFR) An unofficial, online update of the Code of Federal Regula-

tions (CFR) published by the Office of the Federal Register.

electronic citation A citation to online material.

electronic data discovery (EDD) The discovery of data found in e-mails, databases, and other digital formats. Also called *e-discovery.*

element A portion of a rule that is a precondition of the applicability of the entire rule. *See also* element in contention.

element in contention The portion of a rule about which the parties cannot agree. The disagreement may be over the definition of the element, whether the facts fit within the element, or both.

e-mail A message sent electronically.

employment at will *See* at-will employee.

enabling statute The statute that allows (enables) an administrative agency to carry out specified delegated powers.

enacted law Any law that is not created within litigation. Law written by a deliberative body such as a legislature or constitutional convention after it is proposed and often debated and amended.

en banc By the entire court.

enclosure letter *See* cover letter.

encrypted Converted into a code that renders the data incomprehensible until they are reconverted to a readable format by an authorized recipient.

encyclopedia *See* legal encyclopedia.

endnote A numbered citation or explanatory text that is printed at the end of a document or chapter. If printed at the bottom of the page, the citation or text is a footnote.

engagement letter A letter that identifies the scope of services to be provided by a professional and the payments to be made for such services.

English rule The losing side in litigation must pay the winner's attorney fees and costs.

engrossed bill The version of a bill passed by one of the chambers of the legislature after incorporating amendments or other changes.

enrolled agent An attorney or nonattorney who is authorized to represent taxpayers before the Internal Revenue Service (www.naea.org).

enrolled bill A bill that is ready to be sent to the chief executive after both chambers of the legislature have passed it.

enrollment *See* registration.

entry-level certification Certification acquired by meeting eligibility requirements that do *not* include work experience.

Equal Employment Opportunity Commission (EEOC) The federal agency that investigates employment

discrimination that violates federal law (www.eeoc.gov).

equity Justice administered according to fairness in a particular case, as contrasted with strictly formalized rules once followed by common law courts.

equity partner A full owner-partner of a law firm. Also called a *capital partner.*

errata page A list of corrections to a transcript or document.

estate (1) All of the assets and liabilities of a decedent after he or she dies. (2) An interest in real or personal property. (3) The extent and nature of one's interest in real or personal property. (4) All of the property of whatever kind owned by a person. (5) Land.

et al. And others.

Ethical Consideration (EC) *See* Model Code of Professional Responsibility.

ethical wall *See* Chinese wall.

ethics Rules that embody standards of behavior to which members of an organization are expected to conform.

et seq. And following.

evidence Anything that could be offered to prove or disprove an alleged fact (e.g., testimony, documents, and fingerprints). A separate determination must be made on whether a particular item of evidence is relevant or irrelevant, admissible or inadmissible.

evidence log An ongoing record that provides identification and other data about documents and other tangible objects that might eventually be introduced into evidence.

examination Questioning, asking questions of.

examination in chief *See* direct examination.

exclusive jurisdiction The power of a court to hear a particular kind of case, to the exclusion of other courts.

excused the jury Asked the jury to leave the courtroom.

execution (1) Signing and doing whatever else is needed to finalize a document and make it legal. (2) Carrying out or performing some act to its completion, e.g., the process of carrying into effect the decisions in a judgment. (3) A command or writ to a court officer (e.g., sheriff) to seize and sell the property of the losing litigant in order to satisfy the judgment debt. Also called *general execution* and *writ of execution.* (4) Implementing a death sentence.

executive agreement An agreement between the United States and another country that does not require the approval of the Senate.

executive branch The branch of government with primary responsibility for carrying out, executing, or administering the laws.

executive department agency An administrative agency that exists within the executive branch of government, often at the cabinet level.

executive order A law issued by the chief executive pursuant to specific statutory authority or to the executive's inherent authority to direct the operation of governmental agencies.

exempt employee An employee who is not entitled to overtime compensation under the Fair Labor Standards Act because the employee is a professional, administrative, or executive employee.

exhaust administrative remedies To go through all dispute-solving avenues that are available in an administrative agency before asking a court to review what the agency did.

exhibit A document, chart, or other object offered or introduced into evidence.

ex parte With only one side present; involving one party only. An ex parte order is a court order requested by one party and issued without notice to the other party. *See also* hearing.

ex parte communication A communication with the court in the absence of the attorney for the other side.

ex parte hearing A hearing at which only one party is present. A court order issued at such a hearing is an ex parte order.

expense slip A form used by an office to indicate that an expense has been incurred for which a client may or may not be billed.

expert witness A person qualified by scientific, technical, or other specialized knowledge or experience to give an expert opinion relevant to a fact in dispute.

ex rel. (*ex relatione*) Upon relation or information. A suit ex rel. is brought by the government in the name of the real party in interest (called the *realtor*).

external/advocacy memorandum of law A memorandum that analyzes the law in order to convince someone outside your office to take or to refrain from certain action. *See also* memorandum of law *and* office memorandum of law.

external hard drive *See* hard drive.

extranet The part of an intranet to which selected outsiders have been given access. *See also* intranet.

F

F.3d *See* Federal Reporter.

fact (1) An actual event; a real occurrence. Anything that is alleged to exist or that can be shown to exist, e.g., an incident, a relationship, an intention, an opinion, or an emotion. (2) An event or state of mind that can lead to (but that is separate from) its legal consequences.

fact issue *See* legal issue.

factor One of the circumstances or considerations that will be weighted in making a decision, no one of which is conclusive.

fact particularization (FP) A fact-gathering technique to generate a large list of factual questions (who, what, where, how, when, and why) that will help you obtain a specific and comprehensive picture of all available facts that are relevant to a legal issue.

fact pleading A statement of every ultimate fact. A fact is ultimate if it is essential to establish an element of a cause of action.

failure to state a cause of action Failure of a party to allege enough facts that, if proved, would entitle the party to judicial relief. Sometimes called a *demurrer* or a *failure to state a claim upon which relief can be granted*.

Fair Labor Standards Act (FLSA) The federal statute that regulates conditions of employment such as when overtime compensation must be paid. *See also* exempt employee (www.dol.gov/esa/whd/flsa).

F. App'x. *See* Federal Appendix.

Federal Appendix (F. App'x.) A West Group reporter that prints unpublished opinions of some U.S. Courts of Appeals. *See also* opinion (1).

federal depository library A public or private library that receives free federal government publications (e.g., the statutes of Congress) to which it must allow access by the general public without cost. (In some states there is a comparable program for state government publications.)

federalism The division of powers between the federal government and the state governments.

Federal Practice Digest A West Group digest of federal court opinions organized by the key number system.

federal questions Issues that arise from or are based on the federal constitution, federal statutes, federal administrative regulations, or other federal laws.

Federal Register (Fed. Reg.) A daily publication of the federal government that prints proposed federal regulations, notices of agency hearings, executive orders, and related information about federal agencies. *See also* Code of Federal Regulations.

Federal Reporter The West Group reporter currently containing opinions of the U.S. Courts of Appeals. Now in its third series (F.3d).

Federal Rules Decisions (F.R.D.) The West Group reporter that prints opinions of some U.S. District Courts on procedural issues and related materials (e.g., speeches).

Federal Rules of Civil Procedure (FRCP) The technical rules governing the manner in which civil cases are brought in and progress through the U.S. District Courts, which are the main federal trial courts (www.law.cornell.edu/rules/frcp).

Federal Supplement The West Group reporter currently containing opinions of the U.S. District Courts. Now in its second series (F. Supp. 2d).

Fed. Reg. *See* Federal Register.

fee The amount charged for services rendered. An *hourly rate fee* is based on the number of hours worked. A *blended hourly rate* is a single hourly rate based on a blend or mix of rates normally charged by different individuals, e.g., a partner, an associate, and sometimes a paralegal. A *fixed fee* is a flat fee for the service regardless of the amount of time needed to complete it. A *capped fee* is an hourly rate leading to a total bill that will not exceed a predetermined amount. An *hourly plus fixed fee* is an hourly rate charged until the nature and scope of the legal problem are identified, at which time a fixed fee is charged for services provided thereafter. *See also* contingent fee, fee splitting, incentive billing, task-based billing, *and* value billing.

fee cap A maximum amount or maximum percentage that can be charged as a fee in particular kinds of cases.

fee sharing *See* fee splitting.

fee shifting The process of forcing one party to pay another's attorney fees and costs in litigation.

fee splitting A single client bill covering the fees of two or more attorneys who are not in the same firm. Also called *fee sharing*.

felony Any crime punishable by death or imprisonment for a term exceeding a year; a crime more serious than a misdemeanor.

fiduciary One whose duty is to act in the interests of another with a high standard of care. Someone in whom another has a right to place great trust and to expect great loyalty.

field A portion of a document in Westlaw that can be separately searched.

file To deliver a document to a court officer so that it can become part of the official collection of documents in a case. To deliver a document to a government agency.

final argument *See* closing argument.

final resort *See* court of final resort.

firewall Security hardware or software that limits access to your computer when you are on a network by attempting to filter out viruses and other unauthorized or potentially dangerous material.

first impression New; that which has come before the court for the first time.

first instance, court of A trial court; a court with original jurisdiction.

fixed fee A flat fee for services, regardless of the amount of time needed to complete the task. *See also* fee.

flash drive *See* USB flash drive.

flextime A system that allows employees some control over aspects of their work schedule such as the times that they arrive at and leave from work during the day.

FLSA *See* Fair Labor Standards Act.

FOIA *See* Freedom of Information Act.

font The design or style of printed letters of the alphabet, punctuation marks, or other characters.

footer The same text that is printed at the bottom of every page.

forensic (1) Pertaining to the use of scientific techniques to discover and examine evidence. (2) Belonging to or suitable in courts of law. (3) Concerning argumentation. (4) Forensics (ballistics or firearms evidence).

format In word processing, the layout of the page when printed, e.g., the number of lines and margin settings.

form book A collection of sample or model forms, often with practical guidance on how to use them. Also called a *practice manual*.

forum The court where the case is to be tried.

forwarding fee A fee received by one attorney from another to whom the first attorney referred a client. Also called a *referral fee*.

FRCP Federal Rules of Civil Procedure (www.law.cornell.edu/rules/frcp)

F.R.D. *See* Federal Rules Decisions.

Freedom of Information Act (FOIA) A statute that gives citizens access to certain information in the possession of the government (www.usdoj.gov/oip).

freelance paralegal An independent contractor who sells his or her paralegal services to, and works under the supervision of, one or more attorneys. *See also* independent paralegal.

friendly divorce A divorce proceeding in which the parties have no significant disputes between them.

frivolous position A position taken on behalf of a client that the attorney can-not support by a good-faith argument based on existing law or on the need for a change in existing law.

F. Supp. 2d *See* Federal Supplement.

FTC Federal Trade Commission (www.ftc.gov).

full faith and credit One state must recognize and enforce valid public acts of other states, e.g., a valid court judgment. U.S. Constitution, art IV, § 1.

full-text search A search of every word in every document in a database.

functional résumé A résumé that clusters skills and experience together regardless of when they were developed or occurred.

G

gazette *See* bulletin.

general counsel The chief attorney in a corporate law department. Also called *corporate counsel*.

General Digest *See* American Digest System.

general jurisdiction The power of a court to hear any kind of civil or criminal case, with certain exceptions.

general practitioner A professional who handles any kind of case.

general schedule (GS) The pay scale system used in the federal government.

generic citation *See* public domain citation.

geographic jurisdiction The area of the state or country over which a court has power to render decisions.

gigabyte One billion bytes (approximately).

global In word processing, an instruction that will be carried out throughout the document.

GlobalCite An online citator of Loislaw (www.loislaw.com). *See also* citator.

go bare To engage in an occupation or profession without malpractice (liability) insurance.

GOD The Great Overtime Debate. *See also* exempt employee.

government In a criminal case, *government* refers to the prosecutor.

government corporation A government-owned entity that is a mixture of a business corporation and a government agency created to serve a predominantly business function in the public interest.

grammar checker A computer software program that identifies possible grammatical errors in a document with suggested corrections.

grand jury A jury of inquiry (not a trial jury) that receives accusations in criminal cases, hears the evidence of the prosecutor, and issues indictments when satisfied that a trial should be held.

ground A reason that is legally sufficient to obtain a remedy or other result.

group legal services *See* prepaid legal services.

groupware Software that allows computers on a network to work together.

GS *See* general schedule.

guideline (1) Suggested conduct that will help an applicant obtain accreditation, certification, licensure, registration, or approval. (2) A statement of policy or procedure, often with options on carrying it out.

H

HALT Help Abolish Legal Tyranny, an organization that seeks to reform the legal profession, primarily by eliminating the monopoly of attorneys over the practice of law (www.halt.org).

harassment *See* hostile environment harassment *and* quid pro quo harassment.

hard copy A paper copy of what has been prepared on a computer. Also called a *printout*. A "soft" form of text is what exists on disk or on a computer screen.

hard disk A rigid magnetic disk that stores data. *See also* hard drive.

hardware The physical equipment of a computer system.

header The same text that is printed at the top of every page.

headhunter Someone who tries to locate people to work in a particular office.

headnote A short-paragraph summary of a portion of a court opinion (usually covering a single legal issue) printed before the opinion begins.

hearing (1) A proceeding designed to resolve issues of fact or law. Usually, an impartial officer presides, evidence is presented, etc. The hearing is ex parte if only one party is present; it is adversarial if both parties are present. (2) A meeting of a legislative committee to consider proposed legislation or other legislative matters. (3) A meeting in which one is allowed to argue a position. (4) A proceeding convened to resolve a dispute during which parties in the dispute can present their case.

hearing examiner One who presides over an administrative hearing.

hearing memorandum A memorandum of law submitted to a hearing officer.

hearsay An out-of-court statement offered to prove the truth of the matter asserted in the statement.

historical note Information on the legislative history of a statute printed after the text of the statute.

holding A court's answer to one of the legal issues in the case. Also called a *ruling*.

hornbook A legal treatise that summarizes an area of the law often covered within a single law school course, designed primarily for the law school student.

hostile environment harassment Unwelcome sexual advances, requests for sexual favors, and other verbal or physical conduct of a sexual nature when this conduct explicitly or implicitly and unreasonably interferes with an individual's work performance or creates an intimidating, hostile, or offensive work environment.

hourly plus fixed fee An hourly rate charged until the nature and scope of the legal problem are known, at which time fixed fees are charged for services provided thereafter. *See also* fee.

hypertext A method of displaying and linking information found in different locations on the same site or on different sites of the World Wide Web.

hypothetical Not actual or real but presented for purposes of discussion or analysis; based on an assumed set of facts; based on a hypothesis.

hypothetical question A question in which the interviewee is asked to respond to a set of assumed facts provided by the interviewer.

I

icon A picture or graphic that is "clicked" on with a mouse in order to execute it.

id. The same as the immediately preceding cited authority.

identity theft Knowingly using a means of identification of another person with the intent to commit any unlawful activity.

Ill. Dec. *See* Illinois Decisions.

Illinois Decisions (Ill. Dec.) A reporter of West Group that publishes opinions of Illinois state courts.

ILP *See* Index to Legal Periodicals and Books.

imaging The process by which a scanner digitizes text or images. Also called *document imaging*.

impaired attorney An attorney with a drug or alcohol problem.

impaneled Selected and sworn in (referring to a jury) (also spelled *empaneled*).

impeach To *challenge*; to attack the credibility of.

imputed disqualification All attorneys in the same firm are ineligible to represent a client because one of the attorneys or other employees in the firm has a conflict of interest with that client. Also called *vicarious disqualification*.

incentive billing A fee that is increased if a designated target is met; an increased fee for achieving an exceptional result. Also called a *performance bonus*.

income partner *See* nonequity partner.

independent contractor One who operates his or her own business and contracts to do work for others who do not control many of the administrative details of how the work is performed.

independent paralegal An independent contractor (1) who sells his or her paralegal services to, and works under the supervision of, one or more attorneys; or (2) who sells his or her paralegal services directly to the public without attorney supervision. Also called *freelance paralegal* and *legal technician*. In some states, however, the *paralegal* and *legal assistant* titles are limited to those who work under attorney supervision.

independent regulatory agency An administrative agency that regulates an aspect of society. It often exists outside the executive department of government.

Index to Legal Periodicals and Books (ILP) A comprehensive general index to legal periodical literature. Available in paper volumes, in CD-ROM, and online.

indictment A formal document issued by a grand jury accusing the defendant of a crime. *See also* grand jury.

indigent A person who is without funds to hire a private attorney. Impoverished.

indirect evidence *See* circumstantial evidence.

inference A deduction or conclusion reached from facts.

inferior court (1) A trial court of limited or special jurisdiction. (2) Any court that is subordinate to the court of final resort.

information A document accusing the defendant of a crime (used in states without a grand jury).

informational interview An interview whose primary purpose is to gain a better understanding of an area of law or kind of employment.

informational letter A letter that provides or seeks information.

information and belief Good-faith belief as to the truth of an allegation, not based on firsthand knowledge.

informed consent Agreement to let something happen after obtaining a reasonable explanation of the benefits and risks involved.

infra Below; mentioned or referred to later in the document.

in issue In dispute or question.

initial appearance The first criminal court appearance by the accused during which the court (1) informs him or her of the charges, (2) makes a decision on bail, and (3) determines the date of the next court proceeding.

initiative The electorate's power to propose and directly enact a statute or change in the constitution or to force the legislature to vote on the proposal.

injunction An equitable remedy that orders a person or organization to do or to refrain from doing something.

in personam jurisdiction *See* personal jurisdiction.

in propria persona (in pro per) In one's own proper person. *See also* pro se.

inquisitorial system A method of resolving a legal dispute in some civil law countries in which the judge has a more active role in questioning the witnesses and in conducting the trial than in an adversary system.

In re In the matter of.

in rem jurisdiction The court's power over a particular thing or status ("res") located within the territory over which the court has authority.

insert mode When new text is typed in a line that already has text, the line opens to receive the new text. Nothing is erased or overtyped.

insider trading Improperly using material, nonpublic information to trade in the shares of a company.

instructions *See* jury instructions.

instrument A formal written document that gives expression to or embodies a legal act or agreement, e.g., a contract or mortgage.

insurance defense Representing insurance companies on claims brought against them or their policy holders.

intake memo A memorandum that summarizes the facts given by a client during the initial client interview.

intangible evidence *See* tangible evidence.

integrated bar association A state bar association to which an attorney must belong in order to practice law in the state. Also called a *mandatory* or *unified bar association*.

integrated package Software that contains more than one application (e.g., word processing, spreadsheet calculations, and database management) in a single program.

intellectual property law The law governing patents, copyrights, trademarks, and trade names.

interfiling Inserting new or revised pages anywhere they belong in an existing text such as a looseleaf volume.

interlocutory appeal An appeal of a trial court ruling before the trial court reaches its final judgment.

intermediate appellate court A court with appellate jurisdiction to which parties can appeal before they appeal to the highest court in the judicial system.

intern *See* legal intern.

internal hard drive A disk drive that contains the hard disk. If this drive is located inside the CPU, it is called an *internal hard drive*. If it sits outside the CPU, it is called an *external hard drive*.

internal memorandum of law *See* office memorandum of law.

international law The legal principles and laws governing relations between nations. Also called *law of nations* and *public international law*.

International Paralegal Management Association An association of paralegal managers (www.paralegalmanagement. org). Formerly called Legal Assistant Managers Association.

Internet A worldwide electronic network of networks on which millions of computer users can share information.

Internet service provider (ISP) A company that provides access to the Internet, usually for a monthly fee.

Interest on Lawyers' Trust Accounts *See* IOLTA.

interoffice memorandum of law *See* office memorandum.

interrogatories A method of discovery consisting of written questions about a lawsuit submitted by one party to another to help the sender prepare for trial.

interstate compact An agreement between two or more states governing a problem of mutual concern.

interviewee The person being interviewed.

intra-agency appeal An appeal within an administrative agency, before the case is appealed to a court.

intranet A private network of computers within a particular firm, company, or other organization, established so that the computers can share information online, often using features similar to those of the World Wide Web.

introduce evidence To place evidence formally before a court or other tribunal so that it will become part of the record for consideration by the judge, jury, or other decision maker.

investigation *See* legal investigation.

invisible Web The part of the Internet that is not found by traditional search engines.

IOLTA program (Interest on Lawyers' Trust Accounts) A program that helps fund legal services for the poor with funds that attorneys are required to turn over from interest earned in client trust accounts containing client funds.

IRAC An acronym that stands for the components of legal analysis: issue (I), rule (R), application of the rule to the facts (A), and conclusion (C). IRAC provides a structure for legal analysis.

irrebuttable Conclusive; evidence to the contrary is inadmissible. An irrebuttable presumption is an inference that cannot be overcome; it is nonrebuttable.

ISP *See* Internet service provider.

issue (1) A question to be resolved. *See also* legal issue. (2) A single copy of a periodical pamphlet.

issue of fact; issue of law *See* legal issue.

issues on appeal The claimed errors committed by a lower court.

J

jailhouse lawyer An incarcerated paralegal, usually self-taught, who has a limited right to provide other inmates with legal services if the institution does not provide adequate alternatives to such services. Also called a *writ writer*.

jargon Technical language; language that does not have an everyday meaning.

job bank A service that lists available jobs, sometimes available only to members of an organization.

joint and several liability Legally responsible together and individually. Each wrongdoer is individually responsible for the entire judgment; the plaintiff can choose to collect from one wrongdoer or from all of them until the judgment is satisfied.

journal *See* bulletin *and* law review.

judgment The final conclusion of a court that resolves a legal dispute or that specifies what further proceedings are needed to resolve it.

judgment as a matter of law A judgment on an issue in a federal jury trial (and in some state jury trials) that is ordered by the judge against a party because there is no legally sufficient evidentiary basis for a reasonable jury to find for that party on that issue. A judgment as a matter of law may be rendered before or after the verdict. In some state courts, this judgment is called a *directed verdict* if it is rendered before the jury reaches a verdict and is called a *judgment notwithstanding the verdict* if it is rendered after the jury reaches a verdict.

judgment creditor The person to whom a court-awarded money judgment (damages) is owed.

judgment debtor The person ordered by a court to pay a money judgment (damages).

judgment notwithstanding the verdict (JNOV or judgment n.o.v.) A judgment by the trial judge that is contrary to the verdict reached by the jury because the verdict was not reasonable, in effect, overruling the jury. Called a *judgment as a matter of law* (see this phrase) in federal court and in some state courts.

judgment on the merits A judgment, rendered after evidentiary inquiry and argument, determining which party is in the right, as opposed to a judgment based solely on a technical point or procedural error.

judicial branch The branch of government with primary responsibility for interpreting laws by resolving disputes that arise under them.

judicial notice A court's acceptance of a well-known fact without requiring proof of that fact.

judicial review The power of a court to determine the constitutionality of a statute or other law, including the power to refuse to enforce it if the court concludes that it violates the constitution.

jump cite *See* pinpoint cite.

jurisdiction (1) The power of a court to decide a matter in dispute. (2) The geographic area over which a particular court system or other government unit has authority. (3) The scope of power or authority that a person or entity can exercise. *See also* personal jurisdiction, in rem jurisdiction, quasi in rem jurisdiction, *and* subject matter jurisdiction.

jury instructions A statement of the guidelines and law given to the jury by the judge for use in deciding the issues of fact in its verdict. Also called the *charge*.

jury panel *See* panel.

jury trial A trial in which a group of citizens resolve the issues or questions of fact.

justification In word processing, a feature for making lines of text even at the margins.

K

k (1) A measure of capacity in a computer system. (2) *See* k number.

KeyCite An online citator of Westlaw (www.westlaw.com). *See also* citator.

key fact A critical fact; a fact that is essential or very important to the decision (holding) reached by the court.

key number A general topic and a number for one of its subtopics. Key numbers are used by West Group to organize millions of cases by topic in its digests.

key word search A search through a list of specified words that functions like an index to a database.

kilobyte One thousand bytes (approximately).

KM *See* knowledge management.

knowledge management (KM) A system of linking into the knowledge base of a law office embodied in the documents generated by all of the cases it has handled so that it can better meet the needs of current and prospective clients. KM is a productivity tool for capturing and reusing knowledge.

k number A number in Westlaw that corresponds to the general key topics in the bound digest volumes of West Group.

L

LAMA Legal Assistant Management Association. *See* International Paralegal Management Association.

landmen Paralegals who work in the area of oil and gas law. Also called *land technicians*.

laser printer A printer that uses a laser beam of light to reproduce images.

lateral hire Anyone hired from another law office.

law clerk (1) An attorney's employee who is in law school studying to become an attorney or who has graduated from law school and is waiting to pass the bar examination. If law clerks work only in the summer, they are sometimes called *summer associates*. (2) One who provides research and writing assistance to a judge. (3) A nonattorney who is a "trained professional doing independent legal work" in Ontario, Canada.

law department The legal department of a corporation.

law directory A list of attorneys.

law journal *See* law review.

law review A legal periodical published by a law school. Sometimes called a *law journal*.

LCP Louisiana Certified Paralegal, a person who has passed the Louisiana Certified Paralegal Exam.

LDA *See* legal document assistant.

leading question A question that suggests an answer within the question.

L. Ed. 2d *See* United States Supreme Court Reports, Lawyers' Edition 2d.

legal administrator An individual, usually a nonattorney, who has responsibility for the day-to-day administration of a law office.

legal advice The application of laws or legal principles to the facts of a particular person's legal problem. *See also* professional judgment.

legal analysis The application of one or more rules to the facts of a client's case in order to answer a legal question that will help (1) keep a legal dispute from arising, (2) resolve a legal dispute that has arisen, or (3) prevent a legal dispute from becoming worse.

legal assistant A title that is usually synonymous with *paralegal* (see this word), although recently some individuals and organizations have argued that the *legal assistant* title has become more associated with secretarial tasks.

legal assistant clerk A person who assists a paralegal or legal assistant in clerical tasks such as document numbering, alphabetizing, filing, and any other task that does not require substantive knowledge of litigation or of a particular transaction.

legal assistant division A bar association division that allows paralegals to join. An example is the Paralegal Division of the State Bar of Texas.

legal bias *See* bias.

legal dictionary An alphabetical list of legal words and phrases that are defined.

legal document assistant (LDA) A nonattorney in California who is authorized to charge fees for providing "self-help" service (without attorney supervision) to anyone representing himself or herself in a legal matter.

legal encyclopedia An alphabetical summary of every important legal topic. The major national legal encyclopedias are published by West Group: *Corpus Juris Secundum* (C.J.S.), available in volumes; and *American Jurisprudence 2d* (Am. Jur. 2d), available in volumes and online on Westlaw and LexisNexis. In addition, several single-state legal encyclopedias exist, e.g., *California Jurisprudence*.

legal executive A trained and certified employee of a solicitor in England; the equivalent of an American paralegal but with more training and credentials.

legal insurance *See* prepaid legal services.

legal intern A student in a law office seeking practical experience.

legal investigation The process of gathering additional facts and verifying presently known facts in order to advise a client on how to solve or avoid a legal problem.

legal issue A question of law; a question of what the law is, or what the law means, or how the law applies to a set of facts. Also called *issue of law*. If the dispute is over the existence or nonexistence of the alleged facts, it is referred to as a *question of fact*, a *factual issue*, or an *issue of fact*.

legalman A nonattorney in the U.S. Navy who assists attorneys in the practice of law.

legal newsletter A special interest legal periodical (published daily, weekly, etc.) covering practical suggestions and current developments in a particular area of the law.

legal newspaper A newspaper (published daily, weekly, etc.) devoted primarily to legal news.

legal periodical A pamphlet on legal topics that is issued at regular intervals.

The major examples are law reviews and bar journals.

Legal Resource Index (LRI) *See* Current Law Index.

legal technician A self-employed paralegal who works for several different attorneys, or a self-employed paralegal who works directly for the public. Sometimes called an *independent paralegal* or a *freelance paralegal*.

legal thesaurus A volume of word alternatives for legal terms.

LegalTrac *See* Current Law Index.

legal treatise A book written by a private individual (or by a public individual writing as a private citizen) that provides an overview, summary, or commentary on a legal topic.

legislation (1) The process of making statutory law. (2) A statute (*see* this term).

legislative branch The branch of government with primary responsibility for making or enacting the law.

legislative court A court created by the legislature. (At the federal level, they are called *Article I courts* because Article I of the U.S. Constitution gives Congress the authority to create special courts.)

legislative history Hearings, debates, amendments, committee reports, and all other events that occur in the legislature before a bill is enacted into a statute.

legislative intent The design or purpose of the legislature in passing (enacting) a particular statute.

legislative service A publication that prints recently enacted session laws. Also called *session law service* or *advance session law service*. In addition, the service may print bills, which are proposed statutes.

letterhead The top part of stationery, which identifies the name and address of the office (often with the names of owners and selected employees).

letter of disengagement A letter sent to a client formally notifying him or her that the law office will no longer be representing the client.

letter of nonengagement A letter sent to a prospective client that explicitly states that the law office will not be representing him or her.

leveraging Making profit from the income-generating work of others.

LexisNexis A fee-based system of computer-assisted legal research owned by Elsevier.

liable Legally responsible.

licensure The process by which an agency of government grants permission to persons meeting specified qualifications to engage in an occupation and often to use a particular title.

limine *See* motion in limine.

limited jurisdiction The power of a court to hear only certain kinds of cases. Also called *special jurisdiction.*

limited liability Restricted liability; liability that can be satisfied out of business assets, not out of personal assets.

limited liability entity A company or partnership whose owners are taxed like a partnership and have the limited liability of a corporation.

limited licensure The process by which an agency of government grants permission to persons meeting specified qualifications to engage in designated activities that are now customarily (but not always exclusively) performed by another license holder. Also called *specialty licensure.*

limited practice officer (LPO) A nonattorney in Washington State who has the authority to select and prepare approved legal documents for designated property transactions.

LINUX An open-source operating system. *See also* open-source software *and* operating system.

lis pendens A pending suit.

listserv A program that manages computer mailing lists automatically, including the receipt and distribution of messages from and to members of the list.

litigation (1) The formal process of resolving a legal dispute through the courts. (2) A lawsuit.

litigation status The procedural category of a party during any stage of litigation, e.g., plaintiff, defendant, or appellant.

litigation support Application software used to help a law office store, retrieve, and track facts and documents that pertain to a lawsuit.

litigious Inclined to resolve disputes through litigation; quarrelsome.

local area network (LAN) A multiuser system linking computers that are in close proximity to each other so that they can share data and resources.

lodestar A method of calculating an award of attorney fees authorized by statute. The number of reasonable hours spent on the case is multiplied by a reasonable hourly rate. Other factors might also be considered above the lodestar in setting the fee, e.g., the quality of representation, any delay in receiving payment, and the risk at the outset of the litigation that the prevailing attorney will receive no fee.

Loislaw A fee-based legal research service (www.loislaw.com).

looseleaf service A lawbook with a binding (often three ringed) that allows easy insertion and removal of pages for updating.

LPO *See* limited practice officer.

lurking Reading online messages of others without sending any of your own.

M

macro An automated way to insert frequently used text or to perform other repetitive functions.

magistrate A judicial officer having some but not all the powers of a judge.

majority opinion The opinion whose result and reasoning are supported by at least half plus one of the judges on the court.

malicious prosecution A tort with the following elements: (1) To initiate or procure the initiation of civil or criminal legal proceedings; (2) without probable cause; (3) with malice or an improper purpose; and (4) the proceedings terminate in favor of the person against whom the proceedings were brought.

malpractice Professional misconduct or wrongdoing such as an ethical violation, crime, negligence, battery, or other tort.

managing partner The partner of a law firm who has day-to-day responsibility for management of the firm.

mandate The order of the court.

mandatory authority Any authority that a court must rely on in reaching its decision. Also called *controlling authority.*

mandatory bar association *See* integrated bar association.

mandatory statute A statute that requires something to be done.

marital communications privilege A husband and a wife can refuse to disclose communications between them during the marriage.

maritime law *See* admiralty law.

market rate The prevailing rate in the area.

Martindale-Hubbell Law Directory A national directory of attorneys (www.martindale.com).

matter of law *See* judgment as a matter of law.

matter of right *See* appeal as a matter of right.

MDP *See* multidisciplinary practice.

med-arb A method of alternative dispute resolution (ADR) in which the parties first try mediation, and if it does not work, they try arbitration.

mediation A method of alternate dispute resolution (ADR) in which the parties avoid litigation by submitting their dispute to a neutral third person (the mediator) who helps the parties resolve their dispute; he or she does not render a decision resolving it for them.

medium-neutral citation *See* public domain citation.

megabyte One million bytes (approximately).

memorandum of law A written explanation of how the law might apply to the facts of a client's case.

memorandum of points and authorities A document submitted to a trial court that makes arguments with supporting authorities for something a party wishes to do, e.g., have a motion granted.

memorandum opinion (mem.) The decision of a court with few or no supporting reasons, often because it follows established principles. Also called *memorandum decision.*

memory The internal storage capacity of a computer.

menu In word-processing and other programs, a list of commands or prompts on the display screen.

merits *See* on the merits.

metadata Data about data. Data about a computer document that are hidden within the document itself, e.g., earlier versions of the document.

metasearch A search for terms in more than one search engine simultaneously.

microform Images or photographs that have been reduced in size. Microforms include microfilms, which store material on reels or cassettes, and ultrafiche, which store material that has been reduced by a factor of 100 or more on a single sheet of film.

minimum-fee schedule A bar association list of the lowest fees an attorney can charge for specific kinds of legal services.

minitrial *See* summary jury trial.

misdemeanor A crime, not as serious as a felony, punishable by fine or by detention in an institution other than a prison or penitentiary.

mitigate To reduce or minimize the severity of impact. To render less painful.

mock trial *See* summary jury trial.

model act *See* uniform laws.

Model Code of Professional Responsibility An earlier edition of the ethical rules governing attorneys recommended by the American Bar Association. The *Model Code* consisted of Ethical Considerations (ECs), which represented the objectives toward which each attorney should strive, and Disciplinary Rules (DRs), which were mandatory statements of the minimum conduct below which no attorney could fall without being subject to discipline (www.law.cornell.edu/ethics/aba/mcpr/MCPR.HTM).

Model Guidelines for the Utilization of Paralegal Services Ethical guidelines recommended by the American

Bar Association for the ethical use of paralegals by attorneys (www.abanet.org/legalservices/paralegals/downloads/modelguidelines.pdf).

model jury instructions *See* pattern jury instructions.

Model Rule 5.3 The rule in the ABA *Model Rules of Professional Conduct* governing the responsibility of different categories of attorneys for the misconduct of paralegals and other nonattorney assistants in a law firm.

Model Rules of Professional Conduct The current set of ethical rules governing attorneys recommended by the American Bar Association (www.abanet.org/cpr/mrpc/mrpc_toc.html). These rules revised the ABA's earlier rules found in the Model Code of Professional Responsibility.

modem A communications device that allows computers at different locations to use telephone lines to exchange data.

monitor A display screen; a TV-like device used to display what is typed at the keyboard and the response of the computer.

monitoring legislation Finding current information on the status of a proposed statute in the legislature.

motion An application or request made to a court or other decision-making body seeking to obtain a favorable action or ruling. The person making the motion is the *movant*. The verb is *move*.

motion for a judgment as a matter of law *See* judgment as a matter of law.

motion for a new trial A request that the judge set aside the judgment and order a new trial on the basis that the trial was improper or unfair due to specified prejudicial errors that occurred.

motion for summary judgment *See* summary judgment.

motion in limine A request for a ruling on the admissibility of evidence prior to or during trial but before the evidence has been offered.

motion to dismiss A request, usually made before the trial begins, that the judge dismiss the case because of lack of jurisdiction, insufficiency of the pleadings, or the reaching of a settlement.

mouse A handheld input device that moves the cursor by rolling, clicking, and dragging motions.

movant *See* motion.

move *See* motion.

move into evidence To request that the items be formally declared admissible.

multidisciplinary practice (MDP) A partnership consisting of attorneys and nonlegal professionals that offers legal and nonlegal services.

multiple-choice question A question that asks the interviewee to choose among two or more options stated in the question.

multiple representation Representing more than one side in a legal matter or controversy. Also called *common representation*.

multitasking Having the capacity to run several large programs simultaneously.

N

NALA National Association of Legal Assistants (www.nala.org).

NALS the Association for Legal Professionals An association consisting of legal secretaries, legal assistants, and paralegals (www.nals.org). The association was once called the National Association of Legal Secretaries.

National Paralegal Reporter A periodical of the National Federation of Paralegal Associations.

National Reporter Blue Book A source for parallel cites.

National Reporter System The reporters of the West Group that cover the opinions of state courts (e.g., the seven regional reporters such as A.2d) and federal courts (e.g., S. Ct., F.3d). The reporters use key numbers to classify the issues in the opinions.

natural language Plain English as spoken or written every day as opposed to language that is specially designed for computer communication.

N.E.2d *See* North Eastern Reporter 2d.

negative contingency *See* contingent fee.

negligence Harm caused by the failure to use reasonable care.

negotiated plea *See* plea bargaining.

neighborhood justice center (NJC) A government or private center where disputes can be resolved by mediation or another method of alternative dispute resolution (ADR).

neighborhood legal service office A law office that serves the legal needs of the poor, often publicly funded.

netvertising *See* advertising.

network A group of computers that are linked or connected together by telephone lines, fiber-optic cables, satellites, or other systems.

networking Establishing contacts with people who might become personal or professional resources.

neutral evaluation A method of alternative dispute resolution (ADR) in which both sides hire an experienced attorney or an expert in the area involved in the dispute who will listen to an abbreviated version of the evidence and arguments of each side and offer an evaluation in the hope that this will stimulate more serious settlement discussions. Sometimes called *case evaluation*.

new file worksheet A form used by some law firms that is the source document for the creation of all necessary accounting records that are needed when a law firm begins working on a new client case or matter. Also called a *new matter sheet* or *new business sheet*.

newspaper *See* legal newspaper.

new trial *See* motion for a new trial.

New York Supplement 2d (N.Y.S.2d) A reporter of West Group that publishes court opinions of state courts in New York.

NFPA National Federation of Paralegal Associations (www.paralegals.org).

NJC *See* neighborhood justice center.

NLRB National Labor Relations Board (www.nlrb.gov).

nolle prosequi A statement by the prosecutor that he or she is unwilling to prosecute the case.

nominalization A noun formed from a verb or adjective.

nominative reporter A reporter volume that is identified by the name of the person responsible for compiling and printing the opinions in the volume.

nonadversarial Pertaining to a conflict resolution proceeding in which all opposing parties to the conflict or dispute are not present. *See also* adversary hearing.

nonauthority (1) Any primary or secondary authority that is not on point because it is not relevant and does not cover the facts of the client's problem. (2) An invalid primary authority such as an unconstitutional statute. (3) Materials that are solely finding aids (e.g., digests) or validating tools (e.g., citators).

nonbillable time Time spent on tasks for which clients cannot be asked to pay.

nonengagement *See* letter of nonengagement.

nonequity partner A special category of partner who does not own the firm in the sense of an equity or capital partner. Also called an *income partner*.

nonexempt employee An employee who must be paid overtime compensation.

North Eastern Reporter 2d (N.E.2d) A regional reporter of West Group that prints state court opinions of five states (Ill., Ind., Mass., N.Y., and Ohio). N.E.2d is the second series of this reporter. The first series is North Eastern Reporter (N.E.).

North Western Digest A regional digest of West Group that gives summaries of opinions in the North Western Reporter.

North Western Reporter 2d (N.W.2d) A regional reporter of West Group that prints state court opinions of seven states (Iowa, Mich., Minn., Neb., N.D., S.D., and Wis.). N.W.2d is the second series of this reporter. The first series is North Western Reporter (N.W.).

notary public A person who witnesses (i.e., attests to the authenticity of) signatures, administers oaths, and performs related tasks. In Europe, a notary often has more extensive authority.

notes of decisions Summaries of opinions that have interpreted a statute, usually printed beneath the text of the statute in annotated codes.

notice Information about a fact; knowledge of something.

notice of appeal Notice given to a court (through filing) and to the opposing party (through service) of an intention to appeal.

notice of appearance A formal notification to a court by an attorney that he or she is representing a party in the litigation.

notice pleading A short and plain statement of the claim showing that the pleader is entitled to relief.

nov *See* judgment notwithstanding the verdict.

numerical filing system A method of storing client files by numbers or letter-number combinations.

nutshell A legal treatise (written in pamphlet form) that summarizes a topic that is covered in a law school course.

N.W.2d *See* North Western Reporter 2d.

N.Y.S.2d *See* New York Supplement, 2d.

O

oath A sworn statement that what you say is true.

obiter dictum *See* dictum.

objection A formal challenge usually directed at the evidence that the other side is trying to pursue or introduce.

objectivity The state of being dispassionate; the absence of a bias. *See also* bias.

occurrence policy Insurance that covers all occurrences (e.g., a negligent error or omission) during the period the policy is in effect, even if the claim is not actually filed until after the policy expires.

occurrence witness Someone who actually observed an event.

OCR Optical character recognition. Software that allows scanned documents to be edited as regular text.

of counsel An attorney who is semiretired or has some other special status in the law firm.

office memorandum of law A memorandum that objectively analyzes the law;

the memo is written for your supervisor or for other individual(s) in your office. Also called an *interoffice memorandum of law*. *See also* external/advocacy memorandum of law *and* memorandum of law.

office politics The interaction among coworkers who do not always have the same goals, expectations, abilities, or timetables for performing the work of the office.

office sharing Attorneys who are sole practitioners share the use and overhead costs of an office.

official reporter *See* reporter (1).

official statutory code *See* statutory code.

offprint reporter *See* special edition state reporter.

OJT On-the-job training.

on all fours Exactly the same, or almost so; being a very close precedent.

online (1) Connected to another computer or computer network, often through the Internet. (2) Residing on a computer and available for use; activated and ready for use on a computer.

on point Raising or covering the same issue as the one before you. Relevant to the issues of a research problem. *See also* analogous.

on the merits Pertaining to a court decision that is based on the facts and on the substance of the claim, rather than on a procedural ground. *See also* judgment on the merits.

on the record Noted or recorded in an official record of the proceeding.

open-ended question A broad, unstructured question that rarely can be answered in one or two words.

opening statement An attorney's statement to the jury made before presenting evidence that summarizes the case he or she intends to try to establish during the trial.

open-source software Software whose source code is freely available to the public for use and modification. An example is LINUX.

operating system The software that tells the computer how to operate. It is the master or central software program that the hardware and all other software depend on to function.

opinion (1) A court's written explanation of how it applied the law to the facts to resolve a legal dispute. Also called a *case*. Opinions are printed in volumes called reporters. *See also* concurring opinion, dissenting opinion, majority opinion, *and* plurality opinion. (2) An unpublished opinion (also called *unpublished case*) is an opinion designated by the court as not for official publication even though you may be able to read

it online or in special reporters. (3) An inference from a fact. (4) A belief or conclusion expressing a value judgment that is not objectively verifiable.

opinion letter A letter to a client explaining the application of the law and providing legal advice based on that explanation.

opinion of the attorney general Formal legal advice given by the chief law officer of the government to another government official or agency.

optical character recognition *See* OCR.

oral argument A spoken presentation to the court on a legal issue, e.g., telling an appellate court why the rulings of a lower tribunal were valid or were in error.

order An official command by a court requiring, allowing, or forbidding some act to be done.

ordinance A law passed by the local legislative branch of government (e.g., city council) that declares, commands, or prohibits something. (Same as a statute, but at the local level of government.) *See also* statute.

original jurisdiction The power of a court to be the first to hear a case before it is reviewed by another court.

outside counsel An attorney used by a company who is not an employee of the company.

outsourcing Paying an outside company or service to perform tasks usually performed by one's own employees.

outstanding Still unresolved; still unpaid.

overhead The operating expenses of a business (e.g., office rent, furniture, insurance, and clerical staff) for which customers or clients are not charged a separate fee.

overreaching Taking unfair advantage of another's naïveté or other vulnerability, especially by deceptive means.

override To supersede or change a result. To approve a bill over the veto of the chief executive.

overrule (1) To decide against or deny. (2) To reject or cancel an earlier opinion as precedent by rendering an opposite decision on the same question of law in a different litigation. To *reverse* means to overturn a holding on appeal in the same litigation.

overview question An open-ended question that asks for a summary of an event or condition.

P

P.3d *See* Pacific Reporter 3d.

PACER *See* Public Access to Court Electronic Records.

PACE Registered Paralegal *See* RP.

Pacific Digest A regional digest of West Group that gives summaries of opinions in the Pacific Reporter

Pacific Reporter 3d (P.3d) A regional reporter of West Group that prints state court opinions of fifteen states (Alaska, Ariz., Cal., Colo., Haw., Idaho, Kan., Mont., Nev., N.M., Okla., Or., Utah, Wash., and Wyo.). P.3d is the third series of this reporter. The second series is Pacific Reporter 2d (P.2d). The first series is Pacific Reporter (P.).

padding Adding something without justification; adding unnecessary material in order to make something larger.

page 52 debate A debate on whether there should be limited licensing for paralegals (based on a recommendation in favor of such licensing on page 52 of a report of an American Bar Association commission).

page/line digest A summary of a deposition transcript that indicates the pages and lines of the deponent's answers in the order in which the questions were asked.

panel (1) A group of judges, usually three, who decide a case in a court with a larger number of judges. (2) A list of individuals summoned for jury duty; from this list, juries for particular trials are selected. (3) A group of attorneys available in a group legal services plan. (4) Members of a commission.

paralegal A person with legal skills who works under the supervision of an attorney or who is otherwise authorized to use those skills; this person performs tasks that do not require all the skills of an attorney and that most secretaries are not trained to perform. See also *legal assistant* and *traditional paralegal*.

Paralegal Advanced Certification Exam (PACE) The credential bestowed by the National Federation of Paralegal Associations for meeting its criteria such as passing a national certification exam for experienced paralegals.

paralegal code Rules and guidelines covering ethical issues involving paralegals.

paralegal fee A fee that an attorney can collect for the nonclerical work of his or her paralegal on a client case.

paralegal manager A person who helps recruit, train, and supervise all paralegals in a law office. Also known as a *legal assistant manager*.

paralegal specialist The major civil service job classification for paralegals who work for the federal government and for some state governments.

parallel cite An additional citation where you can find the same written material in the library or online.

parallelism Using a consistent (i.e., parallel) grammatical structure when phrasing logically related ideas in a list.

parol evidence Evidence of an oral statement.

parol evidence rule Prior or contemporaneous oral statements cannot be introduced to alter or contradict the terms of a written document if the parties intended the written document to be a complete statement of the agreement.

partnership A voluntary association of two or more persons to place their resources in a jointly owned business or enterprise, with a proportional sharing of profits and losses. Partners make the ultimate decisions on how the business or enterprise (e.g., law firm) should be managed.

passive voice The grammatical verb form in which the object of the action is the main focus. The emphasis is on what is being done rather than on who or what is performing or causing the action.

patch A software update that provides additional features and corrections to previous versions of the software.

pattern jury instructions Suggested instructions to a jury that can be adapted to specific trials. Also called *model jury instructions*.

PDA (personal digital assistant) A handheld multifunction digital organizer.

PDF (portable document format) A file format consisting of an electronic image of a document that preserves the features or elements of the document (e.g., its line spacing, photographs, and font size) that existed before it was converted into a digital document.

pecuniary Relating to money. (A pecuniary interest is a financial interest.)

people The state or government as a party.

percentage fee A fee that is a percentage of the amount involved in the transaction or award.

per curiam opinion (an opinion "by the court" as a whole) A court opinion, usually a short one, that does not name the judge who wrote it.

peremptory challenge A request from a party to a judge asking that a prospective juror not be allowed to become a member of this jury without stating a reason for the request. See also *challenge for cause*.

performance bonus See incentive billing.

performance review An analysis of the extent to which a person or program has met designated objectives. Also called *performance appraisal*.

personal digital assistant See PDA.

personal jurisdiction A court's power over a person to adjudicate his or her personal rights. Also called *in personam jurisdiction*. More limited kinds of

jurisdiction include the court's power over a person's interest in specific property (quasi in rem jurisdiction) or over the property itself (in rem jurisdiction).

personal liability Liability that can be satisfied out of an individual's personal assets. See also limited liability.

personal recognizance Pretrial release of a defendant in a criminal case without posting a bond, based solely on a promise to appear. Also called *release on own recognizance* (ROR).

persuasive authority Any authority a court relies on in reaching its decision that it is not required to rely on.

petition (1) A formal request or motion. (2) A complaint.

petitioner One who presents a petition or complaint to a tribunal. See also appellant.

phishing The fraudulent attempt to obtain personal information by tricking the recipient of an e-mail message into believing that the sender seeking the information is legitimate.

physical evidence That which can be seen or touched. Also called *tangible evidence*.

PI cases Personal injury (tort) cases.

pinpoint cite A reference to material on a specific page number within a document (e.g., a court opinion or legal periodical article) as opposed to the page number on which the document begins. Also called a *jump cite*. In some court opinions, the pinpoint reference is to a specific paragraph number in the opinion.

pirated software Software that has been placed ("loaded") in a computer that is not authorized by the terms of the purchase or lease of the software.

plagiarism Using another's original ideas or expressions as one's own.

plaintiff The person who initiates a civil action in court.

plea bargaining Negotiations whereby an accused pleads guilty to a lesser included offense or to one of multiple charges in exchange for the prosecution's agreement to support a dismissal of some charges or a lighter sentence. Also called a *negotiated plea*.

plead To file a pleading, enter a plea, or argue a case in court.

pleading Formal litigation documents filed by parties that state or respond to the claims and defenses they have against each other. The main pleadings are the complaint and answer.

PL number Public law number.

PLS Professional legal secretary.

plurality opinion The controlling opinion that is joined by the largest number of judges on the bench short of a majority.

pocket part A pamphlet inserted into a small pocket built into the inside back (and occasionally front) cover of a hardcover volume. The pamphlet contains text that supplements or updates the material in the hardcover volume.

pocket veto The chief executive's "silent" rejection of a bill by not acting on it within 10 days of receiving it if the legislature adjourns during this period.

podcast An Internet audio file that the public can download and listen to through a browser or on audio devices such as iPods and MP3 players. Also called an *audioblog*.

point A measure of the size of printed letters of the alphabet, punctuation marks, or other characters. (One point is approximately 1/72 of an inch tall.)

point heading A conclusion that a party wants a court to accept on one of the issues in the case.

points and authorities memorandum A memorandum of law submitted to a judge or hearing officer. Sometimes called a *trial memorandum*.

poll (1) To ask each member of a body (e.g., a jury) that has just voted to state how he or she individually voted. (2) To seek a sampling of opinions.

popular name A phrase or short title identifying a particular statute.

portable document format *See* PDF.

positive evidence *See* direct evidence.

postoccurrence witness Someone who did not observe an event but who can give a firsthand account of what happened after the event.

power of attorney (1) A document that authorizes another to act as one's agent or attorney in fact. (2) The authority itself.

PP (professional paralegal) The certification credential bestowed by NALS the Association for Legal Professionals.

practice of law Using legal skills to assist a specific person in resolving his or her specific legal problem.

praecipe A formal request to the court (usually made through the court clerk) that something be done.

prayer for relief The request for damages or other form of judicial relief.

precedent A prior decision covering a similar issue that can be used as a standard or guide in a later case.

preempt Displace or take precedence over. The noun is *preemption*. Under the Supremacy Clause of the U.S. Constitution, federal laws take precedence over (preempt) state laws when Congress (1) expressly mandates the preemption, (2) regulates an area so pervasively that

an intent to preempt the entire field may be inferred, or (3) enacts a law that directly conflicts with state law.

preliminary hearing A pretrial criminal proceeding to determine if probable cause exists that the accused has committed a crime. Also called *probable cause hearing*.

preliminary print An advance sheet for *United States Reports*.

premium adjustment A write-up (increase) of a bill.

preoccurrence witness Someone who did not observe an event but who can give a firsthand account of what happened before the event.

prepaid legal services A plan by which a person pays premiums to cover future legal services. Also called *legal plan* and *group legal services*.

preponderance of the evidence The burden of proof that is met when the evidence establishes that it is more likely than not that the facts are as alleged. Also called *fair preponderance of evidence*.

presentation graphics Application software used to combine text with charts, graphs, video, clip art, and sound in order to communicate data more effectively.

presumption An assumption or inference that a certain fact is true once another fact is established.

pretrial conference A meeting of the attorneys and the judge (or magistrate) before the trial to attempt to narrow the issues, to secure stipulations, and to make a final effort to settle the case without a trial. Also called a *trial management conference*.

prima facie (1) On the face of it, at first sight. (2) Sufficient.

prima facie case A case, as presented, that will prevail unless contradicted and overcome by contrary evidence.

primary authority Any *law* that a court could rely on in reaching its decision.

print preview In word processing, a feature that enables you to view a representation on the screen of how the document will look when printed.

private judging A method of alternative dispute resolution (ADR) consisting of arbitration or mediation in which the arbitrator or mediator is a retired judge. Sometimes called *rent-a-judge*.

private law A statute that applies to specifically named individuals or groups and has little or no permanence or general interest.

private law firm A law firm that generates its income from the fees of individual clients.

private reprimand *See* reprimand.

private sector Offices in which operating funds come from client fees or the corporate treasury. *See also* public sector.

privilege (1) A special legal benefit, right, immunity, or protection. (2) A defense that authorizes conduct that would otherwise be wrongful.

privilege against self-incrimination A criminal defendant cannot be forced to testify. The right not to answer incriminating questions by the government that could directly or indirectly connect you to the commission of a crime.

privileged Protected by a privilege, e.g., does not have to be disclosed.

privilege log A list of information or documents claimed to be covered by privilege and, therefore, protected from disclosure in discovery or during trial.

probable cause A reasonable belief that a specific crime has been committed and that the accused committed the crime.

probable cause hearing *See* preliminary hearing.

probate (1) The procedure to establish the validity of a will and to oversee the administration of the estate. (2) To establish the validity of a will.

probation (1) Supervised punishment in the community in lieu of incarceration. (2) Allowing an attorney to continue to practice, but under specified conditions, e.g., submitting to periodic audits or making restitution to a client.

pro bono Concerning or involving legal services that are provided for the public good (*pro bono publico*) without fee or compensation. Sometimes also applied to services given at a reduced rate. Shortened to pro bono.

procedural due process Procedural protections that are required before the government can take away or refuse to grant liberty or a public benefit.

procedural law The rules that govern the mechanics of resolving a dispute in court or in an administrative agency, e.g., a rule on the time by which a party must respond to a complaint.

process The means (e.g., a summons, writ, or other court order) used by the court to acquire or exercise its power or jurisdiction over a person. *See also* service of process.

process server Someone with the authority to serve or deliver process.

professional corporation (P.C.) A corporation consisting of persons performing services that require a professional license, e.g., attorneys.

professional judgment Relating or applying the general body and philosophy of law to a specific legal problem.

When communicated to a client, the result is known as *legal advice*.

professional paralegal *See* PP.

project attorney *See* contract attorney.

project billing *See* task-based billing.

proof Enough evidence to establish the truth or falsity of a fact.

proof of service Evidence that a summons or other process has been served on a party in an action. Also called *certificate of service* and *return of service*.

pro per *See* pro se.

proposed findings and rulings Recommended conclusions presented to someone else in the administrative agency who will make the final decision.

pro se (on one's own behalf) Appearing for or representing oneself. Also called *in propria persona* and *pro per*.

prosecution (1) Bringing and processing criminal proceedings against someone. (2) The attorney representing the government in a criminal case, also called the *prosecutor*. (3) Bringing and processing civil proceedings against someone.

prospective Governing future events; effective (having an effective date) in the future.

Public Access to Court Electronic Records (PACER) An electronic public access service that allows subscribers to obtain case and docket information from federal courts via the Internet (pacer.psc.uscourts.gov).

public benefits Government benefits.

public defender An attorney (usually a government employee) appointed by a court and paid by the government to represent an indigent defendant in a criminal case.

public domain Work product or other property that is not protected by copyright or patent. A status that allows access by anyone without fee.

public domain citation A citation that is medium neutral (meaning that it can be read in a paper volume or online) and vendor neutral (meaning that it does not contain volume, page, or other identifying information created by particular vendors such as a commercial publisher). Also called *generic citation*.

public law A statute that applies to the general public or to a segment of the public and has permanence or general interest.

public policy Principles inherent in customs and societal values that are embodied in a law.

public reprimand *See* reprimand.

public sector Offices in which operating funds come from charity or the government. *See also* private sector.

Q

qualify To present evidence of a person's education and experience sufficient to convince the court that the witness has expertise in a particular area.

quarantined Isolated. *See also* Chinese wall.

quarantined employee *See* Chinese wall.

quasi-adjudication An administrative decision written by an administrative agency that has some characteristics of an opinion written by a court.

quasi-independent regulatory agency An administrative agency that has characteristics of an executive department agency and an independent regulatory agency.

quasi in rem jurisdiction A court's power over a person, but restricted to his or her specific interest in property within the territory over which the court has authority.

quasi-judicial proceeding A proceeding within an administrative agency that seeks to resolve a dispute in a manner that is similar to a court (i.e., judicial) proceeding to resolve a dispute.

quasi-legislation An administrative regulation enacted by an administrative agency that has some characteristics of the legislation (statutes) enacted by the legislature.

query A question that is used to try to find something in a computer database.

question of law/question of fact *See* legal issue.

questions presented A statement of the legal issues in an appellate brief that a party wants the appellate court to resolve. Also called *issues presented*.

quid pro quo harassment Unwelcome sexual advances, requests for sexual favors, and other verbal or physical conduct of a sexual nature when this conduct explicitly or implicitly is made a condition of employment decisions such as hiring or promotion.

R

rainmaker An attorney who brings fee-generating cases into the office due to his or her extensive contacts and/or reputation as a skilled attorney.

RAM *See* random access memory.

random access memory (RAM) Memory that stores temporary data that are erased (unless properly saved) whenever the computer's power is turned off.

ratify (1) To adopt or confirm a prior act or transaction, making one bound by it. (2) To give formal approval.

re Concerning; in the matter of.

read-only Able to read data on a device but not to alter, remove, or add to the data.

read-only memory (ROM) Memory that stores data that cannot be altered, removed, or added to. The data can be read only.

read/write Able to read data on a device and write or insert additional data into it.

realization rate The hourly rate that a law office actually collects from the billable hours submitted by an attorney or paralegal.

really simply syndication (RSS) A method of notifying subscribers of new content (e.g., news stories and product updates) on an Internet site by syndicating (feeding) notice of the new content to subscribers.

real-time Occurring now; happening as you are watching; able to respond immediately.

reasonable doubt Such doubt as would cause prudent persons to hesitate before acting in matters of importance to themselves.

reasonable fee A fee that is not excessive in light of the amount of time and labor involved, the complexity of the case, the experience and reputation of the attorney, the customary fee charged in the locality for the same kind of case, etc.

reasoning An explanation of why the court resolved a legal issue the way it did—why it reached the particular holding for that issue.

rebut To refute or oppose.

rebuttable Not conclusive; evidence to the contrary is admissible.

rebuttable presumption An inference of fact that can be overcome (rebutted) by sufficient contrary evidence.

receivables Accounts due and payable.

record (1) The official collection of all the trial pleadings, exhibits, orders, and word-for-word testimony given during the trial. (2) To make an official note of; to enter in a document. (3) The facts that have been inscribed or stored. (4) A collection of data fields that constitute a single unit, e.g., an employee record.

recordable DVD drive A drive that allows data to be recorded on DVD disks.

record information manager Someone in charge of files in a large office.

recross-examination Another cross-examination of a witness after redirect examination.

redact To edit or prepare a document for publication or release, often by deleting, altering, or blocking out text that you do not want disclosed.

redirect examination Another direct examination of a witness after he or she was cross-examined.

referendum The electorate's power to give final approval to an existing provision of the constitution or statute of the legislature.

referral fee *See* forwarding fee.

regional digest A West Group digest that summarizes court opinions that are printed in full in its corresponding regional reporter.

regional reporter A West Group reporter that contains state court opinions of states within a region of the country. West Group has divided the country into seven regions.

register A regularly published collection of regulations and other documents of administrative agencies and the chief executive. *See also* bulletin.

registered agent A nonattorney authorized to practice before the U.S. Patent and Trademark Office.

registered paralegal *See* RP.

registration The process by which individuals or institutions list their names on a roster kept by an agency of government or by a nongovernmental organization. Also called *enrollment*.

regulation Any governmental or nongovernmental method of controlling conduct. *See also* administrative regulation.

rehearing A second hearing by a court to reconsider the decision it made after an earlier hearing.

release on own recognizance (ROR) *See* personal recognizance.

relevant (1) Logically tending to establish or disprove a fact. Pertinent. Relevant evidence is evidence having any tendency to make the existence of a fact more probable or less probable than it would be without the evidence. (2) Contributing to the resolution of a problem or issue. The noun is *relevancy*.

rem *See* in rem jurisdiction *and* quasi in rem jurisdiction.

remand To send back a case to a lower tribunal with instructions from a higher tribunal (e.g., an appellate court) on how to proceed.

rent-a-judge *See* private judging.

reply A plaintiff's response to the defendant's counterclaim, plea, or answer.

reply brief (1) An appellate brief of the appellant that responds to the appellate brief of the appellee. (2) Any appellate brief that responds to an opponent's appellate brief.

reported Printed in a reporter.

reporter (1) A volume (or set of volumes) of court opinions. Also called *case reports*. An official reporter is printed under the authority of the government, often by a government printing office. An unofficial reporter is printed by a commercial publishing company without special authority from the

government. (2) The person in charge of reporting the decisions of a court. (3) The person who takes down and transcribes proceedings.

reprimand An official declaration that an attorney's conduct was unethical. The declaration does not affect the attorney's right to practice law. A private reprimand is not disclosed to the public; a public reprimand is.

reproval A disapproval or rebuke. *See also* admonition.

request for admission (RFA) A method of discovery in which one party asks another to admit the truth of any matter that pertains to a statement or opinion of fact or the application of law to fact.

res A thing or a status. *See* in rem jurisdiction.

res gestae exceptions Exceptions to the hearsay rule that consist of statements or utterances closely connected to or concurrent with an occurrence.

res judicata ("a thing adjudicated") A final judgment on the merits will preclude the same parties from later relitigating the same claim and any other claim based on the same facts or transaction that could have been raised in the first suit but was not. Also called *claim preclusion*.

respondeat superior Let the master (boss) answer. An employer is responsible (liable) for the wrongs committed by an employee within the scope of employment.

respondent *See* appellee.

Restatement Any treatise of the American Law Institute (e.g., Restatement of Torts 2d) that states the law and indicates changes in the law that the institute would like to see implemented.

rest one's case To announce formally that you have concluded the presentation of evidence.

retainer (1) An amount of money (or other property) paid by a client as a deposit or advance against future fees, costs, and expenses of providing services. (2) The act of hiring or engaging the services of someone, usually a professional. (The verb is *retain*.)

retroactive Applying to facts that arise before as well as after the effective date. *See also* prospective.

retroactive negotiated fee A client bill that is finalized after the services are rendered.

return of service *See* proof of service.

reverse *See* overrule.

review The power of a court to examine the correctness of what a lower tribunal has done. Short for *judicial review*.

RFA *See* request for admission.

right justified Every line of a paragraph on the right margin is aligned (except for the last line if it ends before the margin).

roadmap paragraph An overview or thesis paragraph at the beginning of a memorandum of law that tells the reader what issues will be covered and briefly states the conclusions that will be reached.

ROM *See* read-only memory.

root expander An exclamation mark (!) that stands for one or more characters added to the root of a term you are searching in a Westlaw database or LexisNexis library.

ROR *See* personal recognizance.

RP or PACE registered paralegal The certification credentials bestowed by the National Federation of Paralegal Associations: RP (registered paralegal), PACE (Paralegal Advanced Certification Examination).

RSS *See* really simple syndication.

rule *See* administrative regulation and rules of court.

rule-making function Writing administrative regulations.

rule of three A general guideline used by some law firms to identify budget expectations from hiring paralegals: gross revenue generated through paralegal billing should equal three times a paralegal's salary.

rule on witnesses A rule that requires certain witnesses to be removed from the courtroom until it is time for their individual testimony so that they will not be able to hear each other's testimony.

rules of court The procedural laws that govern the mechanics of litigation (practice and procedure) before a particular court. Also called *court rules*.

ruling *See* administrative decision.

run To cause a program to (1) be loaded into the computer from a disk drive and (2) begin to perform its task.

runner (1) One who solicits business, especially accident cases. (2) An employee who delivers and files papers.

S

S. *See* Southern Reporter.

sanction (1) Penalty or punishment imposed for unacceptable conduct. (2) Permission or approval.

satisfy To comply with a legal obligation.

save To cause a program or data in the computer memory to be moved to or stored on a diskette or hard drive.

scanner An input device that converts text and images into an electronic or digital format that a computer can recognize.

scienter 1. Intent to deceive or mislead. 2. Knowingly done.

Scope Note The summary of coverage of a topic within a West Group digest.

scope of employment That which is foreseeably done by an employee for an employer under the latter's specific or general control.

scrivener A professional copyist; a document preparer.

scrolling In word-processing and other programs, moving a line of text onto or off the screen.

S. Ct. *See* Supreme Court Reporter.

search engine A search tool that will find sites on the Internet that contain terms that you enter on any subject.

secondary authority Any *nonlaw* (e.g., a legal periodical article) that a court could rely on in reaching its decision. Writings that describe or explain, but do not constitute, the law.

second chair A seat at the counsel's table in the courtroom used by an assistant to the trial attorney during the trial.

segment A portion of a document in LexisNexis that can be separately searched.

senior associate An attorney who has been passed over for partner status but who remains at the firm.

sequester (1) To separate or isolate a jury or witness. (2) To seize or take and hold funds or other property. Sometimes called *sequestrate*.

series A succession of numbered volumes in a set of books that will eventually use a new numbering order for volumes added to the set. The added volumes will not constitute a new edition.

server A computer program that provides resources or services to other computers.

service company A business that sells particular services, usually to other businesses.

service of process A formal delivery of notice to a defendant that a suit has been initiated to which he or she must respond. *Process* is the means used by the court to acquire or exercise its power or jurisdiction over a person.

session (1) A continuous sitting of a legislature or court. (2) Any time in the day during which such a body sits.

session law cite The citation to a statute that has not been printed in a code and therefore is organized chronologically.

session laws The uncodified statutes of the legislature printed chronologically rather than by subject matter. Sometimes called *statutes at large*. Uncodified means *not* printed in a code. If the session law is a public law, it will eventually be printed in a code. *See also* codify.

set for trial To schedule a date when the trial is to begin.

settlement (1) An agreement resolving a dispute without full litigation. (2) Payment or satisfactory adjustment of an account. (3) Distributing the assets and paying the debts of an estate. (4) The meeting in which a transaction is finalized. Also called *closing*.

settlement work-up A summary of the major facts in the case presented in a manner designed to encourage the other side (or its liability insurance company) to settle the case. Also called a *settlement brochure*.

sexual harassment *See* hostile environment harassment *and* quid pro quo harassment.

shadow jurors Persons hired by one side to observe a trial as members of the general audience (gallery) and, as the trial progresses, to give feedback to a jury consultant hired by the attorney of one of the parties, who will use the feedback to assess strategy for the remainder of the trial.

shallow pocket An actual or potential defendant without resources to pay a potential judgment. *See also* deep pocket.

shareware Software that users receive without cost but are expected to purchase if they want to keep it after trying it out.

Shepard's Citations A major citator that is available online, in CD-ROM, and in paper formats. *See also* citator *and* shepardize.

Shepard's Code of Federal Regulations Citations A citator that allows you to shepardize federal regulations in the C.F.R. *See also* citator *and* shepardize.

Shepard's Federal Citations A citator that allows you to shepardize federal statutes. *See also* citator *and* shepardize.

Shepard's United States Citations A citator that allows you to shepardize opinions of the U.S. Supreme Court. *See also* citator *and* shepardize.

shepardize To use *Shepard's Citations* (in book form, on CD–ROM, or online) to obtain validation and other data on whatever you are shepardizing. *See also* citator.

short form citation An abbreviated citation format of an authority for which you have provided a complete citation elsewhere in what you are writing.

sidebar conference *See* bench conference.

situs Location.

skiptracing Efforts to locate persons (e.g., debtors) or assets.

slip law A single act passed by the legislature and printed in a single pamphlet.

slip opinion The first printing of a single court opinion.

So. 2d *See* Southern Reporter 2d.

software A computer program that tells or instructs the hardware what to do.

sole practitioner An attorney who practices alone. There are no partners or associates in the office.

sole proprietorship A form of business that does not have a separate legal identity apart from the one person who owns all assets and assumes all debts and liabilities.

solicitation (1) An appeal or request for clients or business. (2) An attempt to obtain something by persuasion or application.

solicitor (1) One who solicits. (2) A lawyer in England who handles day-to-day legal problems of clients with only limited rights to represent clients in certain lower courts. *See also* barrister. (3) The title given to some government attorneys, e.g., the solicitor general of the United States argues cases before the U.S. Supreme Court on behalf of the federal government.

source code The programming language of software.

South Eastern Digest A regional digest of West Group that gives summaries of opinions in the South Eastern Reporter.

South Eastern Reporter 2d (S.E.2d) A regional reporter of West Group that prints state court opinions of five states (Ga., N.C., S.C., Va., and W.Va.). S.E.2d is the second series of this reporter. The first series is South Eastern Reporter (S.E.).

Southern Reporter 2d (So. 2d) A regional reporter of West Group that prints state court opinions of four states (Ala., Fla., La., and Miss.). So. 2d is the second series of this reporter. The first series is Southern Reporter (So.).

South Western Reporter 3d (S.W.3d) A regional reporter of West Group that prints state court opinions of five states (Ark., Ky., Mo., Tenn., and Tex.). S.W.3d is the third series of this reporter. The second series is South Western Reporter 2d (S.W.2d). The first series is South Western Reporter (S.W.).

spam Unsolicited e-mail messages, often consisting of commercial advertising; unsolicited junk mail.

special damages Actual and provable economic losses, e.g., lost wages.

special edition state reporter A reporter that prints the court opinions of one state with the same features (e.g., key numbers) that they have in the regional reporter that covers that state. Also called *offprint reporter*.

special interest group An organization that serves a particular group or cause.

special jurisdiction *See* limited jurisdiction.

specialty certification Recognition of competency in a particular area of law.

The National Association of Legal Assistants, for example, has a specialty certification program to recognize a person as an ACP (Advanced Certified Paralegal). A paralegal must be (or eventually become) a Certified Legal Assistant (CLA) or Certified Paralegal (CP) and then take special online courses and test modules.

specific performance An equitable remedy that orders the performance of a contract according to the precise terms agreed upon by the parties.

speech recognition The ability of a computer to receive information (data) by talking into a microphone.

spell checker The identification of possible spelling errors in a computer-generated document with suggested corrections.

spoliation Intentionally destroying, altering, or concealing evidence.

spreadsheet Application software that automatically performs calculations on numbers and values that you enter.

squibs *See* digest.

staff attorney A full-time attorney employee who has no expectation of becoming a full partner. Sometimes called a *second-tier attorney*.

staffing agency An employment agency that places temporary workers, often directly paying the workers and handling all of the financial aspects of the placement.

stand-alone computer A computer that is not connected to a network.

standard of proof A statement of how convincing a version of a fact must be before the trier of facts (usually the jury) can accept it as true.

stare decisis ("stand by things decided") Courts should decide similar cases in the same way unless there is good reason for the court to do otherwise. In resolving an issue before it, a court should be reluctant to reject precedent—a prior opinion covering a similar issue.

star paging A special notation (e.g., an asterisk and an inverted T) that is placed next to text in a book or online database that will tell you on what page that same text can also be found in another book or edition.

Stat. *See* United States Statutes at Large.

statement of principles Guidelines that try to identify the activities of specified law-related occupations that do not constitute the unauthorized practice of law.

statement of the case The portion of an appellate brief that summarizes the procedural history of the case to date and presents the essential facts of the dispute. It may also state the appellate court's subject matter jurisdiction.

state questions Issues that arise from or are based on the state constitution, state statutes, state administrative regulations, state common law, or other state laws.

stating a cause of action Including facts in a pleading that, if proved at trial, would entitle the party to judicial relief (assuming the other party does not plead and prove any defenses that would defeat the effort).

status letter A letter telling a client what has happened in the case thus far and what next steps are expected.

status line A message line that states the current position of the cursor and provides other formatting information.

statute A law passed by the state or federal legislature that declares, commands, or prohibits something. Also called *act* and *legislation*. (*Statute*, *act*, and *legislation* are sometimes used in a broader sense to include laws passed by any legislature, which would include ordinances passed by a city council.)

statute at large *See* session laws.

statute in derogation of the common law A statute that changes the common law.

statute of limitations A law stating that civil or criminal actions are barred if not brought within a specified period of time.

statutory code A collection of statutes organized by subject matter rather than by date. An *official* statutory code is one published by the government or by a private company with special permission or authority from the government. An *unofficial* statutory code is one published by a private company without special permission or authority from the government.

statutory fee case A case applying a special statute that gives a judge authority to order the losing party to pay the winning party's attorney and paralegal fees.

stay The suspension of a judgment or proceeding.

steerer *See* ambulance chasing *and* runner.

stipulation An agreement between opposing parties about a particular matter. The verb is *stipulate*.

STOP A writing technique alerting you to the need for a counteranalysis: after writing a Sentence, Think carefully about whether the Other side would take a Position that is different from the one you took in the sentence.

stop words Common words (e.g., *a*, *an*, *the*) that some search engines do not recognize as part of the search query.

strike from the record To remove the testimony or evidence from the written record or transcript of the trial.

sua sponte Voluntarily; of its own will.

subject matter jurisdiction The court's power to resolve a particular kind or category of dispute.

subpoena A command to appear at a certain time and place.

subpoena ad testificandum A command to appear at a certain time and place to give testimony.

subpoenaed (1) Commanded to appear in a court, agency, or other tribunal. (2) Ordered to turn over or produce something.

subpoena duces tecum A command that a witness appear at a certain time and place and bring specified things such as documents or records.

subscript A number (or other character) that is printed below the usual text baseline.

subscription A signature; the act of signing one's name.

substantive law Nonprocedural laws that define or govern rights and duties.

substantive legal work Nonclerical tasks that require legal experience or training; tasks that justify an award of paralegal fees.

substituted service Service by an authorized method (e.g., by mail) other than personal service. Also called *constructive service*.

summation *See* closing argument.

summary Quick, expedited, without going through a full adversary hearing.

summary judgment A judgment of the court that is rendered without a full trial because of the absence of conflict on any of the material facts.

summary jury trial A method of alternative dispute resolution (ADR) in which the parties present their evidence and arguments to an advisory jury, which renders a nonbinding verdict. Also called *mock trial* or *minitrial*.

summer associate *See* law clerk.

summing up *See* closing argument.

summons (1) A notice directing the defendant to appear in court and answer the plaintiff's complaint or face a default judgment. (2) A notice directing a witness or juror to appear in court.

superior court Usually a trial court.

superscript A number (or other character) that is printed above the usual text baseline.

superseded Outdated and replaced.

supplemented Added to.

suppression Preventing evidence from being admissible.

supra Above; mentioned earlier in the document.

Supremacy Clause The clause in the U.S. Constitution (art. VI, cl. 2) that has been interpreted to mean that when valid federal law conflicts with state law, federal law controls.

supreme court The highest court in a judicial system. (In New York, however, the supreme court is a lower court.)

Supreme Court Reporter (S. Ct.) An unofficial reporter of West Group that prints opinions of the U.S. Supreme Court.

surrogate court A special court with subject matter jurisdiction over wills, probate, guardianships, etc.

suspension The removal of an attorney from the practice of law for a specified minimum period, after which the attorney can apply for reinstatement.

sustain (1) To uphold or agree with. (2) To support or encourage. (3) To endure or withstand.

S.W.2d *See* South Western Reporter 3d.

syllabus A brief summary or outline. For court opinions, it is also called a *case synopsis* and is printed before the opinion begins. It is usually a summary of the entire opinion.

T

table A word-processing feature that allows the creation of a table of information using rows and columns.

table of authorities (TOA) A list of primary authority (e.g., cases and statutes) and secondary authority (e.g., legal periodical articles and legal treatises) that a writer has cited in an appellate brief or other document. The list includes page numbers where each authority is cited in the document.

table of cases An alphabetical list of all the opinions printed or referred to in the volume, and where they are found in the volume.

table of statutes A list of all the statutes printed or referred to in the volume, and where they are found in the volume.

tainted Having or causing a conflict of interest; contaminated. *See also* Chinese wall.

tainted paralegal A paralegal who brings a conflict of interest to a law office because of the paralegal's prior work at another law office.

take under advisement To delay ruling on the motion until another time.

TANF Temporary Assistance for Needy Families, a federal welfare program.

tangible evidence Evidence that can be seen or touched; evidence that has a physical form. *Intangible evidence* is evidence without physical form such as a right that a person has. Such rights, however, are usually embodied or evidenced by something physical, e.g., a written contract.

task-based billing Charging a specific amount for each legal task performed. Also called *unit billing* or *project billing*. *See also* fee.

task padding Inflating a client's bill by charging for tasks that were not performed.

template A set of formulas created to perform a designated task.

term of art A word or phrase that has a special or technical meaning.

terms and connectors Relationships between terms in a search query that specify documents that should be included in or excluded from the search.

testator One who has died leaving a valid will.

test case Litigation brought to try to create a new legal principle or right.

testimony Evidence given by a witness under oath.

thesaurus A volume of word alternatives.

The Bluebook *See* bluebook.

third chair *See* second chair.

third-party complaint A defendant's complaint against someone who is not now a party on the basis that the latter may be liable for all or part of what the plaintiff might recover from the defendant.

tickler A system designed to provide reminders of important dates.

timekeeping Recording time spent on a client matter for purposes of billing and productivity assessment.

timeline A chronological presentation of significant events, often organized as a straight-line diagram.

timely Within the time set by contract or law.

time padding Inflating a client's bill by charging for time that was not spent.

tool bar A list of shortcuts (usually represented by icons) that can quickly execute commonly used functions.

topical digest A summary of a deposition transcript organized by specific topics covered in the answers of the deponent.

topic and key number *See* key number.

tort A civil wrong (other than a breach of contract) that causes injury or other damage for which our legal system deems it just to provide a remedy such as compensation.

trace a key number To find out what case law, if any, is digested (summarized) under a particular key number in different digests of West Group.

traditional paralegal A paralegal who is an employee of an attorney.

transactional paralegal One who provides paralegal services for an attorney who represents clients in transactions such as entering contracts, incorporating a business, closing a real estate sale, or planning an estate.

transcribed *See* transcript.

transcript A word-for-word account. A written copy of oral testimony. *Transcribed* means taken down in a word-for-word account.

transmittal letter *See* cover letter.

treatise *See* legal treatise.

treaty A formal agreement between two or more nations. Also called a *convention*. *See also* executive agreement.

trial book *See* trial brief (1).

trial brief (1) An attorney's personal notes on how to conduct a trial. Also called *trial manual* and *trial book*. (2) An attorney's presentation to a trial court of the legal issues and positions of his or her client. Also called *trial memorandum*.

trial de novo A new trial as if a prior one had not taken place.

trial management conference *See* pretrial conference.

trial manual *See* trial brief (1).

trial memorandum *See* points and authorities memorandum *and* trial brief.

trial notebook A collection of documents, arguments, and strategies that an attorney plans to use during a trial.

truncated passive A form of passive voice in which the doer or subject of the action is not mentioned. *See also* active voice *and* passive voice.

typeover mode When new text is typed in a line that already has text, the old text is erased or overtyped with each keystroke. *See also* insert mode.

U

UDA *See* unlawful detainer assistant.

ultrafiche *See* microform.

unauthorized practice of law (UPL) Conduct by a person who does not have a license to practice law or other special authorization needed for that conduct.

unbundled legal services Discrete task representation. *See also* bundled legal services.

uncodified Organized chronologically by date of enactment rather than by subject matter.

uncontested Unchallenged; without opposition.

unemployment compensation Temporary income from the government to persons who have lost their jobs (for reasons other than misconduct) and are looking for work.

unicameral Having one house in the legislature. *See also* bicameral.

unified bar association *See* integrated bar association.

uniform laws Laws proposed to state legislatures in areas where uniformity is deemed appropriate. Each state can adopt, modify, or reject the proposals (www.nccusl.org). Sometimes called *model acts.*

uniform resource locator (URL) The address of a resource (or any page) on the Internet.

unit billing *See* task-based billing.

United States Code (U.S.C.) The official statutory code containing the statutes of Congress published by the government.

United States Code Annotated (U.S.C.A.) An unofficial annotated statutory code containing the statutes of Congress published by West Group.

United States Code Congressional and Administrative News (U.S.C.C.A.N.) A West Group publication that prints recent public laws of Congress, committee reports of congressional committees, executive orders of the president, etc.

United States Code Service (U.S.C.S.) An unofficial annotated statutory code containing the statutes of Congress published by LexisNexis.

U.S. Court of Appeals The main intermediate appellate court in the federal court system.

U.S. District Court The main trial court in the federal judicial system.

United States Law Week (U.S.L.W.) An unofficial looseleaf service that prints opinions of the U.S. Supreme Court. The publisher is the Bureau of National Affairs (BNA).

United States Reports (U.S.) The official reporter for opinions of the U.S. Supreme Court.

United States Statutes at Large (Stat.) The session laws of Congress consisting of every public and private law, all printed chronologically.

United States Supreme Court The court of final resort in the federal judicial system (www.supremecourtus.gov).

United States Supreme Court Digest A West Group digest of U.S. Supreme Court opinions organized by the key number system.

United States Supreme Court Reports, Lawyers' Edition 2d (L. Ed. 2d) An unofficial reporter that prints opinions of the U.S. Supreme Court. The publisher is LexisNexis.

universal character An asterisk (*) that stands for one character within a term you are searching in a Westlaw database or LexisNexis library.

unlawful detainer assistant (UDA) A nonattorney in California who is authorized to charge fees for providing assistance or advice (without attorney supervision) to landlords or tenants in actions for the possession of land.

unofficial reporter A volume (or set of volumes) of court opinions printed by a commercial publishing company without special authority from the government. *See also* reporter (1).

unofficial statutory code *See* statutory code.

unpublished case; unpublished opinion *See* opinion.

UPL *See* unauthorized practice of law.

upload *See* download.

URL *See* uniform resource locator.

U.S. (1) The federal government. (2) United States. (3) United States Reports.

USB flash drive A portable memory drive that is inserted into and taken out of the computer's USB port. Also called *jump drive, pen drive, key drive, USB key,* and *USB stick.*

U.S.C. *See* United States Code.

U.S.C.A. *See* United States Code Annotated.

U.S.C.C.A.N. *See* United States Code Congressional and Administrative News.

U.S.C.S. *See* United States Code Service.

V

vacate (1) To cancel or set aside. (2) To surrender possession.

validation research Using citators and other legal materials to check the current validity of every primary authority (case, statute, etc.) you intend to rely on in the memorandum of law, appellate brief, or other document you are helping to prepare.

value billing A method of charging for legal services based on factors such as the complexity of the case or the results achieved rather than solely on the number of hours spent on the client's case.

valuing the bill Determining whether there should be a write-down or a write-up of a bill to be sent to the client. *See also* write down *and* write up.

vendor-neutral citation A citation that does not refer to the reporters of any particular publishing vendors. *See also* public domain citation.

venire A jury panel. *See also* panel (2).

venue The proper county or geographical area in which a court with jurisdiction may hear a case. The place of the trial.

verdict The final conclusion of the jury.

verification An affidavit stating that a party has read the pleading (e.g., a com-

plaint) and swears that it is true to the best of his or her knowledge.

veto A rejection by the chief executive of a bill passed by the legislature.

vicarious disqualification *See* imputed disqualification.

vicarious liability Liability imposed on one party for the conduct of another, based solely upon the status of the relationship between the two (e.g., employer and employee).

videoconference A meeting that occurs in more than one location between individuals who can hear and see each other on computer screens.

virtual Existing in a computer-generated environment.

virus A program that can reproduce itself and damage or destroy data on computers.

voir dire ("to speak the truth") A preliminary examination of prospective jurors for the purpose of selecting persons qualified to sit on a jury.

volume discount *See* discounted hourly fee *and* fee.

W

Wage and Hour Division The unit within the U.S. Department of Labor that administers the Fair Labor Standards Act, which governs overtime compensation and related matters. *See also* exempt employee *and* Fair Labor Standards Act.

waiver The express or implied relinquishment of a right or privilege. Examples of an implied relinquishment include the failure to claim it at the proper time or acting in a manner that is inconsistent with its existence. The verb is *waive.*

warrant An order from a judicial officer authorizing an act, e.g., the arrest of an individual or the search of property.

Web browser A program that allows you to read pages on the World Wide Web.

West Group A major legal publisher of reporters and codes. Its online service is Westlaw.

Westlaw A fee-based system of computer-assisted legal research owned by West Group.

wide area network (WAN) A multiuser system linking computers over a large geographical area so that they can share data and resources.

wildcard A special character (e.g., *, !, ?) that can be used to represent one or more characters in a search query.

word processor Application software that allows you to enter and edit data in order to create and revise documents.

word wrap A word is automatically moved to the next line if it goes past the right margin.

work product rule Notes, working papers, memoranda, or similar things prepared by or for an attorney in anticipation of litigation are not discoverable by an opponent, absent a showing of substantial need. They are protected by privilege.

WIP Work in progress. A list of tasks on which you are currently working.

World Wide Web A system of sites on the Internet that can be accessed through hypertext links.

wrap-up question A question asked at the end of the interview (or at the end of a separate topic within the interview) in which the interviewee is asked if there is anything he or she thinks has been left out or inadequately covered.

write down Deduct an amount from the bill. Also called a *discount adjustment*.

write up Add an amount to the bill. Also called a *premium adjustment*.

writ of certiorari (cert.) An order (or writ) by a higher court that a lower court send up the record of a case because the higher court has decided to use its discretion to review that case.

writ writer *See* jailhouse lawyer.

WYSIWYG What You See (on the screen) Is What You Get (when the screen is printed).

Index